Major English Writers of the
EIGHTEENTH CENTURY

Major English

Edited by

Writers of the

EIGHTEENTH

CENTURY

Harold E. Pagliaro

Swarthmore College

THE FREE PRESS, New York
COLLIER-MACMILLAN LIMITED, London

Front cover, *left to right:*
JOHN DRYDEN, JOSEPH ADDISON, OLIVER GOLDSMITH,
ALEXANDER POPE

Spine:
SAMUEL JOHNSON

Back cover, *top:*
RICHARD STEELE

Below, left to right:
THOMAS OTWAY, JONATHAN SWIFT, WILLIAM CONGREVE,
THOMAS GRAY

To
Judith

Preface

THIS FIRST VOLUME of a two-part anthology attempts to provide a representative selection of English neoclassical poetry, drama, and non-critical prose, by offering a sampling of the works of Dryden, Swift, Pope, and Johnson, as well as a handful of the works of other eighteenth-century authors somewhat below these four in reputation. Though all of Johnson's *Rasselas* is here printed, it would not, of course, be accurate to say that the eighteenth-century novel has been represented as a genre. The consideration of space made necessary the omission of *Gulliver's Travels*, but Swift's *A Tale of a Tub* was saved entire. With the exceptions of *The Hind and the Panther* and *The Dunciad* (each represented by an entire part), individual essays from collections of eighteenth-century periodical literature, and *Lives of the Poets*, of which the *Life of Gray* appears, the works in this anthology are complete.

The second volume, now in progress, will contain critical prose by eighteenth-century hands (along with some verse), treating ideas, themes or works in the first. This principle of division between the two volumes has been suspended once or twice, when it seemed that the usefulness of the first might be impaired by its consistent application; accordingly, Pope's *An Essay on Criticism* appears here, rather than in the second part, while Collins's "Ode on the Poetical Character" will be printed in the companion volume. Having time and again reconsidered my choices for the present volume, I am convinced that with equal plausibility I might have selected other works (and other authors) to represent the age. Yet I am fairly well persuaded from the experience of several of my colleagues in the field and from my own efforts in the classroom that the selection is reasonable, if not uniquely representative.

The copy texts on which the present edition is based are identified at the end of the headnote preceding each selection. They are most often the basis of the best modern editions. For Pope's poetry, I have used Warburton's text. It is with few exceptions sound. I decided that to use other copy texts would have required either many silent corrections, or an elaborate record (inappropriate here) of variant readings. My aim throughout the anthology has been to provide a good classroom text. Unless I have otherwise noted, the spelling of the copy text has been kept; but I have sometimes altered punctuation slightly, although never, I trust, in such a way as to change meaning or (in the case of verse) meter. At the end of each work appears the date of its first publication.

Biographical sketches of authors have been kept to a minimum. It seemed best to avoid the perhaps misleading impression that might result from a brief attempt at characterization. The headnotes, on the other hand, pointing as they do to a more confined subject than the whole man, are slightly more ambitious. They try to offer such historical information as may make the work they introduce accessible, or to provide a critical clue that may serve as a point of departure in discussing the piece or in writing or thinking about it. Occasionally, a cue title appears in the biographies or the headnotes (e.g., Boswell, *Life*, II, p. 150); readers will find the full citation in the appropriate bibliography.

Notes for the works vary enormously in density. Universal in its terminology, *Rasselas* is almost without annotation, while such topical or otherwise difficult pieces as *The Way of the World* and *A Tale of a Tub* have rather full notes. When I felt my task was to supply an elementary level of information not generally available in standard editions (or anywhere else, very often), as in *A Tale of a Tub*, for example, my notes are patterned accordingly. But when I judged the kind of note supplied by well-known editions was appropriate to my purposes, I began by consulting such editions. In annotating *The Way of the World*, for instance, I was often guided to difficulties in the text by the editions of Nettleton and Case and of Herbert Davis; and though not limited by their suggestions, I was sometimes speeded by their example. For this help, I am grateful to them. In a very few instances, editors offered what seemed to me useful information that I could not verify independently, and accordingly, I cited the editors themselves as my sources; the names of their editions appear either in the appropriate author's bibliography or in the general bibliography, under item IX, Eighteenth-Century Anthologies, at the back of the book, where they may readily be identified.

The very brief bibliographies for each author differ in length roughly in proportion to the amount of the author's work offered in the anthology; needless to say, other factors (such as the difficulty of the material and the availability of modern critical studies and editions) played an important part in my choices. I trust that, as curtailed as they are, these lists may prove useful in acquainting students with the kind of scholarship available to them if they wish to explore the literature independently. It seems reasonable to suppose these titles will provide a rich beginning for any such undertaking, though I am keenly aware that my suggestions might have been different from what they are in many cases. With perhaps one or two exceptions, titles are arranged in the following order: (1) bibliography; (2) standard editions of the whole canon or of principal works; (3) editions of works here anthologized; (4) editions of other works; (5) biography; (6) critical studies—books; (7) critical studies—collections of essays; (8) individual articles. In items 3 to 5, works appear in the order of publication; in items 6 to 8, entries are alphabetical, according to the author's last name. Only the longer of these bibliographies contain works in all the categories listed here.

About the general bibliography, I have rather more serious reservations than I have about the aforementioned lists. It seemed to me at first that any attempt to produce such a bibliography—brief as it would have to be—must inevitably fail, because no rationale of selection was possible. How could so vast a field as eighteenth-century English literature be represented by one hundred or so titles, no matter how they were chosen? Eventually, I decided I could not hope to avoid serious omissions; nor could I, it seemed equally clear, leave out a general bibliography altogether. I could only try to include some of the titles in one way or another important to eighteenth-century studies, and it was on this quite general principle that I proceeded.

A few abbreviations occur with varying frequency throughout the notes and bibliographies. Here they are, with the titles they stand for:

CBEL   *Cambridge Bibliography of English Literature*
JEGP   *Journal of English and Germanic Philology*
OED   *Oxford English Dictionary*
PMLA   *Publications of the Modern Language Association of America*

RES   *Review of English Studies*
SEL   *Studies in English Literature, 1500–1900*
SP   *Studies in Philology*

For invaluable help in procuring Restoration and eighteenth-century texts, I wish to thank the staff of Special Collections of the Columbia University Library; Miss Dorothy Mason of the Folger Shakespeare Library; Mr. Lyman W. Riley, Bibliographer, and Dr. Neda M. Westlake, Librarian of Rare Books, University of Pennsylvania Library; Miss Ellen Shaffer, Librarian of Rare Books, The Free Library, Philadelphia; and Professor James F. Govan, Librarian, and the staff of Swarthmore College Library. To my friend Professor Daniel B. Dodson, my gratitude for his patience in receiving and satisfying several of my requests for help in locating texts. For his useful comments on principles for selecting works to be anthologized, I am grateful to Professor A. Walton Litz. I am happy to repay with thanks a special debt to my friend Professor Louis T. Milic, who at the outset made several helpful suggestions about the table of contents and who has since commented on the entire manuscript. His numerous criticisms have been very useful to me. Two of my former students, Nicoletta Grimoldi and David Schaps, were kind enough to corroborate my translation of Swift's Latin tags in *A Tale of a Tub*, and in three cases to improve them; I am grateful for their eager assistance. For her willingness to take on the task of typing large sections of the manuscript, and for her patience in its execution, I wish to thank Miss Marjorie Webb of the Registrar's Office, Swarthmore College.

I acknowledge the kindness of The Clarendon Press, Oxford, for permission to reprint "Verses on the Death of Dr. Swift," *The Poems of Jonathan Swift*, 3 vols., ed. Harold Williams, second edition, 1958, pp. 553–572.

HAROLD E. PAGLIARO
Swarthmore, Pennsylvania

Contents

Joseph Addison 1672–1719
Richard Steele 1672–1729

Alexander Pope 1688–1744

Samuel Johnson 1709–1784

Thomas Gray 1716–1771

Oliver Goldsmith 1730?–1774

Major English Writers of the
EIGHTEENTH CENTURY

John Dryden

1631-1700

Dryden was born at Aldwinkle All Saints, Northamptonshire, where his maternal grandfather, according to tradition, was rector. Little in fact is known of Dryden's early life. He was educated at Westminster and Trinity College, Cambridge, where he took a B.A. in 1654. Only months later Dryden's father died and left him a small estate.

Dryden went up to London, where he may have been employed by his cousin, Sir Gilbert Pickering, who held a minor post in Cromwell's government. Dryden's very first verses had been written on the death of his schoolmate Lord Hastings; in 1659 he wrote his first considerable poem, *Heroique Stanzas*, on Cromwell's death. Not long after, he did what the poets of the nation did; he composed lines to celebrate the return of Charles in *Astrea Redux* (1660) and in *To His Sacred Majesty* (1661). It is possible that Dryden did some hack-work for the bookseller Herringman, through whom, it has been conjectured, he became acquainted with Sir Robert Howard, son of the Earl of Berkshire. Howard became both Dryden's collaborator (together they wrote *The Indian Queen*, produced in 1664 with great success) and his brother-in-law (Dryden married Elizabeth Howard in 1663).

Dryden's first produced play, *The Wild Gallant* (performed at the King's Theatre, 1663), was a failure, being overshadowed by a rival at Duke's. His second, *The Rival Ladies* (1664), enjoyed a better fate. A sequel to the work co-authored with Howard, *The Indian Emperor*, was produced in 1665, with a repetition of the first success.

Plague closed the theaters in 1665–1666, and Dryden retired to the country where he wrote *Annus Mirabilis*, as well as *An Essay of Dramatick Poesy*, his first venture into literary criticism and now one

3

of his best-known works. Although during his lifetime Dryden produced important compositions in almost all the literary forms then in use, he continued to write critical pieces as well, in the prefaces to his plays and elsewhere, until the preface to the *Fables* (1700), his last work, which is quoted as often as *An Essay*. After the opening of the theaters, Dryden began a long succession of plays. *Secret Love*, produced in 1667, starred Nell Gwyn, the famous Restoration actress later to be mistress to Charles II. *Sir Martin Mar-all* (1667) followed, along with an adaptation of Shakespeare's *Tempest*. Dryden at this time contracted with the King's Company to produce three plays a year, and while he did not live up to the letter of his agreement, by any standards he must be considered a productive playwright.

In 1670, Dryden was appointed Laureate and Historiographer Royal, posts that more indicate the general regard in which he was held at court than any monetary increase in his fortunes.

It was at about this time and over the next several years that he produced many of his best-known heroic plays: *Tyrannick Love* (1669); *The Conquest of Granada*, in two parts (1670); and *Aureng-Zebe* (1675), his last rhymed heroic play. (See the headnote to the drama.) His last play for the King's Company, *All for Love* (1677), is Dryden's version of the material of Shakespeare's *Antony and Cleopatra*. After his departure (and Nathaniel Lee's), the Company suffered an even greater decline than that which may have caused Dryden's defection, and to save itself it merged with its rival. His later plays are generally regarded as being of less significance than the earlier ones.

As Dryden's interest in the stage waned, he began to emerge as a verse satirist of great force. In 1682, he produced three brilliant satires, the politically aimed *Absalom and Achitophel* and *The Medal*, and *Mac Flecknoe*, for the most part a literary satire that reduced the playwright Thomas Shadwell, long Dryden's impersonal opponent in critical controversy. Also in 1682, he celebrated his Anglican faith in the poem *Religio Laici*; five years later (1687) he wrote *The Hind and the Panther* to mark his conversion to Roman Catholicism in the months following James's accession in 1685. When Protestant William and Mary succeeded to the throne in 1688, however, Dryden's Catholicism cost him all of his pensions (which had been infrequently paid despite his associations with the monarchs Charles and James), and he had to rely on the income from his writings alone. In the last years of his life, he brought out a translation of Vergil (1697) and his *Fables*, adaptations from Homer, Ovid, Chaucer, and Boccaccio (1700). Six weeks after the publication of the *Fables*, on May 1, Dryden died. He was buried in Westminster Abbey.

John Dryden—Selective Bibliography

Hugh Macdonald, *John Dryden: A Bibliography of Early Editions and Drydeniana*, Oxford, Clarendon Press, 1939.

Samuel Holt Monk, *John Dryden: A List of Critical Studies Published from 1895–1950*, Minneapolis, U. of Minnesota Press, 1950. See also *CBEL*, II, pp. 262 f.

The elaborate critical edition of Dryden's works planned by The University of California Press, originally under the editorship of E. N. Hooker and H. T. Swedenberg, has had great difficulty in making progress, largely because of the death of Edward Niles Hooker in 1957. So far three volumes have appeared. Vol. I: *Poems, 1649–1680*, eds. Hooker and Swedenberg; V. A. Dearing, textual editor; and F. M. Carey et al., associate editors, Berkeley and Los Angeles, U. of California Press, 1956; Vol. VIII: *Plays: The Wild Gallant, The Rival Ladies, The Indian Queen*, eds. J. H. Smith, D. Macmillan, and Dearing, 1962; Vol. IX: *Plays: The Indian Emperour, Secret Love, Sir Martin Mar-all*, eds. John Loftis and Dearing, 1966.

Sir Walter Scott, ed., *The Works of John Dryden*, 18 vols., London, 1808; revised and enlarged by George Saintsbury, ed., 18 vols., Edinburgh, for William Patterson by T. and A. Constable, 1882–1893; very inadequate, the only complete edition.

James Kinsley, ed., *The Poems of John Dryden*, 4 vols., Oxford, Clarendon Press, 1958; superb edition, invaluable to students of Dryden's poetry.

George R. Noyes, ed., *The Poetical Works of Dryden*, Boston, Houghton Mifflin, 1909; new edition, revised and enlarged, 1950.

William B. Gardner, ed., *The Prologues and Epilogues of John Dryden*, New York, for U. of Texas by Columbia U. P., 1951.

Montague Summers, ed., *Dryden. The Dramatic Works*, 6 vols., London, Nonesuch Press, 1931–1932.

Charles E. Ward, ed., *The Letters of John Dryden, with Letters Addressed to Him*. Durham, N.C., Duke U. P., 1942.

James M. Osborn, *John Dryden: Some Biographical Facts and Problems*, New York, Columbia U. P., 1940; rev. ed., Gainesville, U. of Florida Press, 1965.

Charles E. Ward, *The Life of John Dryden*, Chapel Hill, U. of North Carolina Press, 1961.

Louis I. Bredvold, *The Intellectual Milieu of John Dryden*, Ann Arbor, U. of Michigan Press, 1934; Ann Arbor Paperback, 1956.

T. S. Eliot, *Homage to John Dryden: Three Essays on the Poetry of the Seventeenth Century*, London, L. & V. Woolf, 1924.

———, *John Dryden. The Poet, the Dramatist, the Critic*, New York, T. & Elsa Holliday, 1932.

Arthur W. Hoffman, *John Dryden's Imagery*, Gainesville, U. of Florida Press, 1962.

Arthur C. Kirsch, *Dryden's Heroic Drama*, Princeton U. P., 1965.

Bernard N. Schilling, *Dryden and the Conservative Myth: A Reading of "Absalom and Achitophel,"* New Haven, Yale U. P., 1961.

Mark Van Doren, *The Poetry of John Dryden*, New York, Harcourt, Brace and Howe, 1920; rev. ed., *John Dryden, A Study of His Poetry*, Bloomington, Indiana U. P., 1946.

H. T. Swedenberg, *Essential Articles for the Study of John Dryden*, Hamden, Conn., Archon Books, 1966.

Thomas H. Fujimura, "Dryden's *Religio Laici:* An Anglican Poem," *PMLA*, LXXVI (1961), 205–217.

Victor M. Hamm, "Dryden's *Religio Laici* and Roman Catholic Apologetics," *PMLA*, LXXX (1965), 190–198.

Otto Reinert, "Passion and Pity in *All for Love:* A Reconsideration," *The Hidden Sense and Other Essays*, by Maren-Sofie Røstvig and others, Oslo, Universitetsforlaget, 1963, pp. 159–195.

Headnote to
ABSALOM and ACHITOPHEL

Although Charles II "scattered his Maker's image through the land," he was without a legitimate heir, whose anticipated succession would have smoothed the waters of his father's troubled reign, particularly during its closing years. In 1678, about seven years before Charles died, a certain Titus Oates, a disgruntled failure of a man—once sent down from Cambridge, and after his conversion to Rome, twice expelled from Catholic colleges in which he sought to train for the priesthood—contrived to appear before the Privy Council, to which he swore persuasively that a Popish plot threatened the life of the King, the government, and English Protestantism itself. These desperate allegations probably would not have found attentive ears had it not been for the political and closely related religious temper of the moment. First, Charles had for some time waited out the will of his countrymen (who had beheaded his father and who only belatedly called him to the throne) in the court of the Catholic Louis XIV, a fact that in the minds of many associated the English King with the inimical court of France. In addition, Charles's brother, James, Duke of York, heir to the kingdom in the absence of the King's legitimate issue, was an avowed Roman Catholic. In these circumstances, socially engaged Englishmen for the most part divided themselves along political-religious lines. Accordingly, some became part of the newly emerging Tory faction, often landed royalists, among whom were not only Catholics but Protestants more or less willing to pay the price of James's Catholicism to ensure stability in the succession. Others became Whigs, frequently wealthy London commoners, who so preferred a non-Catholic succession that they were willing to bypass James in favor of the Protestant Duke of Monmouth, Charles's illegitimate son. Despite these difficulties all might have quieted down, except that after Titus Oates delivered his hot charge to an already kindled nation, it was discovered that Edward Coleman, the Duchess of York's secretary, had been exchanging letters with Louis XIV's Jesuit confessor, discussing possible means of securing England to the Roman Church. Though probably unrelated to the charges made by Oates, this and other rash acts by Catholics kept the pot boiling dangerously.

Anthony Ashley Cooper, first Earl of Shaftesbury, an unscrupulously ambitious man, sought to make political capital of this unrest.

Having helped shape the group that was to become the Whig Party, he attempted to have passed a law excluding the Catholic James from the succession; he also urged the Duke of Monmouth to rebel against his father. These and other maneuvers by the restless politician may have contributed to the shift in public sentiment in favor of Charles, who though he loved Monmouth very much, did not want to violate the laws of succession. In this moderately congenial climate of public opinion, the Crown arrested Shaftesbury on a charge of high treason; Dryden's *Absalom and Achitophel,* probably written at the King's suggestion, comments on this general situation, by extending the often observed analogy between Charles and the Biblical David, an analogy based on II Samuel 13–16. There, King David's handsome son Absalom is by degrees estranged from his father, against whose authority he rebels as he gains the affection of the people by traveling among them and acting the part of their judge and protector. He is specifically encouraged in the crucial stages of his rebellion by the minister Achitophel, who recommends David's deposition. The King, slow to anger, says to his generals as he sends them against his son, " 'Deal gently for my sake with the young man, even with Absalom.' And all the people heard when the king gave all the captains charge concerning Absalom." Despite this temperate command, Absalom is slain, and so the King's triumph is destroyed by the father's loss.

Dryden could of course rely on the late seventeenth-century reader's detailed knowledge of the Old Testament narrative; he could also rely on the reader's predisposition to accept as sound the poem's implicit correlation of religion, politics, and family life. Indeed, one of the work's dominant metaphors, developed gradually from the beginning to the end of the piece, intimates that Charles, the father and the king, is also somehow God, or at least strongly suggestive of Him, an association that seems blasphemous only if one fails to recall the theory of the king's divine right and of his power as God's representative on earth. In the various forms of this metaphor, Charles's paternal concern shifts back and forth from children, to subjects, to mankind (the chosen people) itself. But whatever offices he may perform, he is bountiful, loving, temperate, merciful, and strong—yet uneasy because the free-willed beings of his making (children, subjects, men) confuse liberty with license and so threaten the order of all three (interdependent) realms with chaos. While David-Charles-God hopes his children will avoid the repetition of Adam's sin—the violation of just limits, within whose bounds are grace and responsible liberty—Achitophel-Shaftesbury-Satan tempts Absalom-Monmouth, the son, to emulate Christ the Saviour, a presumptuous effort ironically treated by the poet.

Absalom and Achitophel ends with a speech by David, one which reveals his God-like qualities and heralds a new age. Such a resolution of the action, less dramatic and less definitive than the Biblical one, may on the face of it seem dictated by Dryden's social purpose in writing the composition—to calm the English people. And in one sense such a critical judgment may be sound. But the conclusion to the poem reveals itself to be not only socially but also structurally appropriate, when one considers the earlier movements of the work. These, for the most part, may be divided into two groups—those of chaos and those of order. In the first, one observes unrestrained energy, restless discontent, latent violence, and unfulfilled ambition, qualities revealed in the poem in the form of the threat of mob rule, the characters of David's enemies, the temptation scenes, and (comically treated to mitigate its irresponsible side) the King's promiscuity. These bold elements dominate the entire poem until David's speech. But the reader may also observe the forces of order (though they are at first much less dramatically presented) in the satiric voice of the speaker himself, and then tentatively in Absalom's remnant of filial sense for David, later in the belated characterizations of David's loyal followers, and finally of course in the long, stately, moderating, highly structured speech of the King, who has himself altered his presence from the beginning of the poem, where he is treated as a promiscuous lover, to the end, where his pronouncements are literally punctuated by heavenly thunder. In short, the voices of chaos dominating the early poem gradually give way until they are balanced by the voices of order ultimately gathered into the unifying voice of David-Charles-God.

Listed below are the chief names from the Old Testament narrative on which Dryden drew, with their Restoration correlatives. They are offered in one place so that the reader may early grasp the poem's analogy through a comprehensive knowledge of the terms it employs.

AARON'S RACE—The priesthood generally.

ABBETHDIN—A judge.

ABSALOM—Duke of Monmouth, Charles's illegitimate son.

ACHITOPHEL — Anthony Ashley Cooper, 1st Earl of Shaftesbury, leader of the anti-court faction.

ADRIEL—Earl of Mulgrave, Dryden's patron.

AGAG—Variously identified as a Justice Scraggs, impartial judge at trials growing out of Oates's charges; Sir Edmund Berry Godfrey, a London magistrate found dead in 1678; Lord Stafford, jailed

(1678) and condemned (1680) on evidence by Oates.

AMIEL—Edward Seymour, Speaker of the House of Commons.

AMNON — Someone (unidentified) whose murder Monmouth is said to have ordered.

ANNABEL—Anne Scott, Monmouth's wife.

THE ARK—The national religion.

BALAAM—Probably Theophilus Hastings, 7th Earl of Huntington, who shifted allegiance from Monmouth to York.

BARZILLAI—Duke of Ormond, loyal friend and counsellor to Charles.

BATHSHEBA—Duchess of Portsmouth, Charles's mistress.

CALEB—Perhaps Lord Grey, who winked at an affair between his wife and Monmouth.

CHOSEN PEOPLE—Protestants.

CORAH—Titus Oates.

DAVID—Charles.

EGYPT—France.

EGYPTIAN RITES—Roman Catholic practices satirized by means of their comparison with the pagan.

GATH—Brussels, where Charles lived just before his restoration.

HEBREW PRIESTS — The Anglican clergy.

HEBRON—Scotland, where Charles had first been crowned.

HUSHAI—Lawrence Hyde, First Lord of the Treasury, and later Earl of Rochester (1682).

ISHBOSHETH — Cromwell's son Richard.

ISRAEL—England.

ISRAELITES—The English.

ISSACHAR — Thomas Thynne, a squire who supported Monmouth on his tour through Western England.

JEBUSITES—Catholics.

JERUSALEM—London.

JEWISH RABBINS — The Anglican clergy.

JEWS—The English.

JONAS—Sir William Jones, who prosecuted members of the Popish Plot, and who later opposed the Court as an exclusionist.

JORDAN'S SAND—The coast of Dover, Charles's landing place for his restoration.

JOTHAM—George Savile, Lord Halifax, who, though sympathetic to Shaftesbury's views generally, opposed him in the attempt to exclude the Duke of York from the succession.

JUDGE'S DAYS—The period of the interregnum, when England had no king.

LEVITES—Presbyterians.

MICHAL—Catherine, Charles's barren queen.

NADAB—William, Lord Howard of Escrick, who was said to rail against the King.

NILE—Seine.

PHARAOH—Louis XIV of France.

RECHABITE—One who for religious reasons does not drink.

SAGAN OF JERUSALEM—The Bishop of London.

SANHEDRIN—Parliament.

SAUL—Cromwell.

SHIMEI—Slingsby Bethel, Whig Sheriff of London, anti-royalist.

SION—England.

SOLYMAEAN ROUT—The London mob (Solyma is a name for Jerusalem).

TYRUS—Holland.

ZADOC—Archbishop of Canterbury.

ZIMRI—George Villiers, Duke of Buckingham, who with Shaftesbury led the Whigs.

TEXT. *Absalom and Achitophel. A Poem* (London, 1681).

Absalom and Achitophel

a poem

*Si Propiùs stes Te Capiet Magis**

To the Reader

'*Tis not my intention to make an Apology for my* Poem: *Some will think it needs no Excuse; and others will receive none. The Design, I am sure, is honest: but he who draws his Pen for one Party, must expect to make Enemies of the other. For* Wit *and* Fool *are Consequents of* Whig *and* Tory: *And every man is a Knave or an Ass to the contrary side. There's a Treasury of Merits in the* Phanatick Church, *as well as in the* Papist; *and a Pennyworth to be had of Saintship, Honesty, and Poetry, for the Leud, the Factious, and the Blockheads: But the longest Chapter in* Deuteronomy *has not Curses enow for an Anti-*Bromingham.[1] *My Comfort is, their manifest Prejudice to my Cause will render their Judgment of less Authority against me. Yet if a* Poem *have a Genius, it will force its own reception in the World. For there's a sweet-* 10 *ness in good Verse, which Tickles even while it Hurts: And no man can be heartily angry with him who pleases him against his will. The Commendation of Adversaries is the greatest Triumph of a Writer, because it never comes unless Extorted. But I can be satisfied on more easy termes: If I happen to please the more Moderate sort, I shall be sure of an honest Party; and, in all probability, of the best Judges; for the least Concern'd are commonly the least Corrupt: And, I confess, I have laid in for those, by rebating the* Satyre *(where Justice woud allow it) from carrying too sharp an Edge. They who can Criticize so weakly as to imagine I have done my Worst may be Convinc'd, at their own Cost, that I can write Severely with more ease than I can Gently. I have but laught at some men's Follies, when I coud have declaim'd against their Vices;* 20 *and other men's Vertues I have commended, as freely as I have tax'd their Crimes. And now, if you are a Malitious* Reader, *I expect you should return upon me, that I affect to be thought more Impartial than I am. But, if men are not to be judg'd by their Professions, God forgive you* Commonwealth's-men *for professing so plausibly for the Government. You cannot be so Unconscionable as to charge me for not Subscribing of my Name; for that woud reflect too grosly upon your own Party, who never dare, though they have the advantage of a Jury to secure them. If you like not my* Poem, *the fault may, possibly, be in my Writing: (though 'tis hard for an Authour to judge against himself); but, more probably, 'tis in your Morals, which cannot bear the truth of it. The Violent, on both sides, will condemn the Character of* Absalom, *as either* 30 *too favourably or too hardly drawn. But they are not the Violent whom I desire to please. The fault, on the right hand, is to Extenuate, Palliate and Indulge; and, to confess freely, I have endeavour'd to commit it. Besides the respect which I owe his Birth,*

---

* *Si Propiùs Stes Te Capiet Magis:* The full sentence from Horace, *Ars Poetica*, ll. 361–362, translates, "A poem is like a picture [Ut pictura poesis]: one strikes your fancy more, the closer you stand; another, the farther away."

[1] *Anti-Bromingham:* A Tory.

I have a greater for his Heroique Vertues; and David *himself coud not be more tender of the Young-man's Life than I woud be of his Reputation. But since the most excellent Natures are always the most easy; and, as being such, are the soonest perverted by ill Counsels, especially when baited with Fame and Glory; 'tis no more a wonder that he withstood not the temptations of* Achitophel, *than it was for* Adam *not to have resisted the two Devils, the Serpent and the Woman. The conclusion of the Story I purposely forbore to prosecute, because I coud not obtain from my self to shew* Absalom *Unfortunate. The Frame of it was cut out but for a Picture to the Wast; and if the Draught be so far true, 'tis as much as I design'd.*

Were I the Inventour, who am only the Historian, I shoud certainly conclude the   10 *Piece with the Reconcilement of* Absalom *to* David. *And who knows but this may come to pass? Things were not brought to an Extremity where I left the Story: There seems yet to be room left for a Composure; hereafter, there may only be for pity. I have not so much as an uncharitable Wish against* Achitophel, *but am content to be Accus'd of a good natur'd Errour, and to hope with* Origen[2] *that the Devil himself may at last be sav'd. For which reason, in this* Poem, *he is neither brought to set his House in order, nor to dispose of his Person afterwards as he in Wisedom shall think fit. God is infinitely merciful; and his Vicegerent is only not so, because he is not Infinite.*

The true end of Satyre *is the amendment of Vices by correction. And he who writes Honestly is no more an Enemy to the Offendour than the Physician to the Patient when*   20 *he prescribes harsh Remedies to an inveterate Disease: for those are only in order to prevent the* Chyrurgeon's *work of an* Ense rescindendum,[3] *which I wish not to my very Enemies. To conclude all, If the Body Politique have any Analogy to the Natural, in my weak judgment, an* Act *of* Oblivion *were as necessary in a Hot, Distemper'd State, as an* Opiate *woud be in a Raging Fever.*

IN pious times, e'r Priest-craft did begin,
Before *Polygamy* was made a sin;
When man on many multiply'd his kind,
E'r one to one was cursedly confind:
When Nature prompted, and no law deny'd   5
Promiscuous use of Concubine and Bride;
Then *Israel's* Monarch after Heaven's own heart,
His vigorous warmth did variously impart
To Wives and Slaves: And, wide as his Command,
Scatter'd his Maker's Image through the Land.   10
Michal, of Royal blood, the Crown did wear,
A Soyl ungratefull to the Tiller's care:
Not so the rest; for several Mothers bore
To Godlike *David,* several Sons before.
But since like slaves his bed they did ascend,   15
No True Succession could their seed attend.

---

[2] *Origen:* A Church Father of the third century thought to believe that God would put a term to the sinner's punishment after death.

[3] *Ense Rescindendum:* The knife must cut away.

Of all this Numerous Progeny was none
So Beautifull, so brave as *Absolon:*
Whether, inspir'd with some diviner Lust,
His Father got him with a greater Gust;   20
Or that his Conscious destiny made way
By manly beauty to Imperiall sway.
Early in Foreign fields he won Renown,
With Kings and States ally'd to *Israel's* Crown:
In Peace the thoughts of War he coud remove,   25
And seem'd as he were only born for love.
What e'r he did was done with so much ease,
In him alone 'twas Natural to please.
His motions all accompanied with grace,
And *Paradise* was open'd in his face.   30
With secret Joy indulgent *David* view'd
His Youthfull Image in his Son renew'd:
To all his wishes Nothing he deny'd,
And made the Charming *Annabel* his Bride.
What faults he had (for who from faults is free?)   35
His Father coud not, or he woud not see.
Some warm excesses, which the Law forbore,
Were constru'd Youth that purg'd by boyling o'r:
And *Amnon's* Murther, by a specious Name,
Was call'd a Just Revenge for injur'd Fame.   40
Thus Prais'd, and Lov'd, the Noble Youth remain'd,
While *David*, undisturb'd, in *Sion* raign'd.
But Life can never be sincerely blest:
Heaven punishes the bad, and proves the best.
The *Jews*, a Headstrong, Moody, Murmuring race,   45
As ever try'd th'extent and stretch of grace;
God's pamper'd people, whom, debauch'd with ease,
No King could govern, nor no God could please;
(Gods they had tri'd of every shape and size
That God-smiths could produce, or Priests devise.)   50
These *Adam*-wits, too fortunately free,
Began to dream they wanted libertie;
And when no rule, no president was found,
Of men, by Laws less circumscrib'd and bound,
They led their wild desires to Woods and Caves,   55
And thought that all but Savages were Slaves.
They who, when *Saul* was dead, without a blow,
Made foolish *Isbosheth* the Crown forgo;
Who banisht *David* did from *Hebron* bring,
And, with a Generall Shout, proclaim'd him King: 60
Those very *Jewes*, who, at their very best,
Their Humour more than Loyalty exprest,
Now wondred why so long they had obey'd

An Idoll Monarch which their hands had made:
Thought they might ruine him they could create,   65
Or melt him to that Golden Calf, a State.
But these were randome bolts: No form'd Design,
Nor Interest made the Factious Croud to joyn:
The sober part of *Israel*, free from stain,
Well knew the value of a peacefull raign: 70
And, looking backward with a wise afright,
Saw Seames of wounds, dishonest to the sight;
In contemplation of whose ugly Scars,
They Curst the memory of Civil Wars.
The moderate sort of Men, thus qualifi'd,   75
Inclin'd the Ballance to the better side:
And *David's* mildness manag'd it so well,
The Bad found no occasion to Rebell.
But, when to Sin our byast Nature leans,
The carefull Devil is still at hand with means;   80
And providently Pimps for ill desires;
The Good old Cause reviv'd, a Plot requires.
Plots, true or false, are necessary things,
To raise up Common-wealths, and ruin Kings.

   Th' inhabitants of old *Jerusalem*   85
Were *Jebusites:* the Town so call'd from them;
And their's the Native right——
But when the chosen people grew more strong,
The rightfull cause at length become the wrong:
And every loss the men of *Jebus* bore,   90
They still were thought God's enemies the more.
Thus, worn and weaken'd, well or ill content,
Submit they must to *David's* Government:
Impoverisht and depriv'd of all Command,
Their Taxes doubled as they lost their Land,   95
And what was harder yet to flesh and blood,
Their Gods disgrac'd, and burnt like common wood.
This set the Heathen Priesthood in a flame;
For Priests of all Religions are the same:
Of whatsoe'r descent their Godhead be,   100
Stock, Stone, or other homely pedigree,
In his defence his Servants are as bold
As if he had been born of beaten gold.
The *Jewish Rabbins* thô their Enemies,
In this conclude them honest men and wise: 105
For 'twas their duty, all the Learned think,

66. *Golden Calf:* A golden idol set up
by Aaron, Exodus 32; see also I Kings
12:28–29.

T'espouse his Cause by whom they eat and drink.
From hence began that Plot, the Nation's Curse,
Bad in it self, but represented worse.
Rais'd in extremes, and in extremes decry'd;   110
With Oaths affirm'd, with dying Vows deny'd.
Not weigh'd, or winnow'd by the Multitude;
But swallow'd in the Mass, unchew'd and Crude.
Some Truth there was, but dash'd and brew'd with Lyes;
To please the Fools, and puzzle all the Wise.   115
Succeeding times did equal folly call,
Believing nothing, or believing all,
Th' *Egyptian* Rites the *Jebusites* imbrac'd;
Where Gods were recommended by their Tast.
Such savory Deities must needs be good,   120
And serv'd at once for Worship and for Food.
By force they could not Introduce these Gods;
For Ten to One, in former days was odds.
So Fraud was us'd (the Sacrificers trade);
Fools are more hard to Conquer than Perswade.   125
Their busie Teachers mingled with the *Jews*;
And rak'd, for Converts, even the Court and Stews:
Which *Hebrew* Priests the more unkindly took,
Because the Fleece accompanies the Flock.
Some thought they God's Anointed meant to Slay   130
By Guns, invented since full many a day:
Our Authour swears it not; but who can know
How far the Devil and *Jebusites* may go?
This Plot, which fail'd for want of common Sense,
Had yet a deep and dangerous Consequence: 135
For as when raging Fevers boyl the Blood,
The standing Lake soon floats into a Flood,
And every hostile Humour, which before
Slept quiet in its Channels, bubbles o'r:
So several Factions from this first Ferment,   140
Work up to Foam, and threat the Government.
Some by their Friends, more by themselves thought wise,
Oppos'd the Power to which they could not rise.
Some had in Courts been Great, and thrown from thence,
Like Feinds were harden'd in Impenitence.   145
Some by their Monarch's fatal mercy grown,
From Pardon'd Rebels, Kinsmen to the Throne,
Were rais'd in Power and publick Office high:
Strong Bands, if Bands ungratefull men could tye.

---

138. *Every . . . Humour:* According to
Medieval and Renaissance physiology, the
four humours or fluids—blood, phlegm,
yellow bile, and black bile—determined a
person's health and temperament.

Of these the false *Achitophel* was first: 150
A Name to all succeeding Ages Curst.
For close Designs, and crooked Counsell fit;
Sagacious, Bold, and Turbulent of wit:
Restless, unfixt in Principle and Place;
In Power unpleas'd, impatient of Disgrace.   155
A fiery Soul, which working out its way,
Fretted the Pigmy Body to decay:
And o'r inform'd the Tenement of Clay.
A daring Pilot in extremity;
Pleas'd with the Danger, when the Waves went high   160
He sought the Storms; but for a Calm unfit,
Would Steer too nigh the Sands, to boast his Wit.
Great Wits are sure to Madness near ally'd,
And thin Partitions do their Bounds divide:
Else why should he, with Wealth and Honour blest,   165
Refuse his Age the needful hours of Rest?
Punish a Body which he coud not please;
Bankrupt of Life, yet Prodigal of Ease?
And all to leave what with his Toyl he won,
To that unfeather'd, two Leg'd thing, a Son: 170
Got, while his Soul did hudled Notions try;
And born a shapeless Lump, like Anarchy.
In Friendship False, Implacable in Hate:
Resolv'd to Ruine or to Rule the State.
To Compass this the Triple Bond he broke;   175
The Pillars of the publick Safety shook:
And fitted *Israel* for a Foreign Yoke.
Then, seiz'd with Fear, yet still affecting Fame,
Assum'd a Patriott's All-attoning Name.
So easie still it proves in Factious Times,   180
With publick Zeal to cancel private Crimes:
How safe is Treason, and how sacred ill,
Where none can sin against the People's Will:
Where Crouds can wink, and no offence be known,
Since in another's guilt they find their own.   185
Yet, Fame deserv'd, no Enemy can grudge;
The Statesman we abhor, but praise the Judge.

156–158. Dryden has frequently been scored for his triplets—by Swift and Johnson among others—on the grounds that they are marks of slovenly workmanship. Van Doren, in his study of Dryden's poetry, while acknowledging the justice of this charge in some instances, argues persuasively (pp. 77 f.) that the poet also uses the triplet to advantage; for example, he observes, "The third line of a triplet in Dryden frequently represents a lowering of the voice to the level of parenthesis or innuendo. . . ."

170. *Unfeather'd, two Leg'd thing:* Plato is supposed to have defined man as a "two-legged unfeathered animal."

175. *Triple Bond:* England, Sweden, and Holland were allied against France. Actually Charles in 1670 arranged a secret treaty with France, so that Dryden's simple charge against Shaftesbury is misleading.

In *Israel's* Courts ne'r sat an *Abbethdin*
With more discerning Eyes, or Hands more clean:
Unbrib'd unsought, the Wretched to redress;   190
Swift of Dispatch, and easie of Access.
Oh, had he been content to serve the Crown,
With vertues only proper to the Gown;
Or, had the rankness of the Soyl been freed
From Cockle, that opprest the Noble seed: 195
David, for him his tunefull Harp had strung,
And Heaven had wanted one Immortal song,
But wilde Ambition loves to slide, not stand;
And Fortune's Ice prefers to Vertue's Land:
Achitophel, grown weary to possess   200
A lawfull Fame, and lazy Happiness;
Disdain'd the Golden fruit to gather free,
And lent the Croud his Arm to shake the Tree.
Now, manifest of Crimes, contriv'd long since,
He stood at bold Defiance with his Prince: 205
Held up the Buckler of the People's Cause
Against the Crown, and sculk'd behind the Laws.
The wish'd occasion of the Plot he takes,
Some Circumstances finds, but more he makes.
By buzzing Emissaries, fills the ears   210
Of listning Crowds with Jealosies and Fears
Of Arbitrary Counsels brought to light,
And proves the King himself a *Jebusite*:
Weak Arguments! which yet he knew fulwell
Were strong with People easie to Rebell.   215
For govern'd by the *Moon*, the giddy *Jews*
Tread the same track when she the Prime renews:
And once in twenty Years, their Scribes Record,
By natural Instinct they change their Lord.
Achitophel still wants a Chief, and none   220
Was found so fit as Warlike *Absolon*:
Not that he wish'd his Greatness to create
(For Polititians neither love nor hate)
But, for he knew his Title not allow'd,
Would keep him still depending on the Crowd: 225
That Kingly power, thus ebbing out, might be
Drawn to the dregs of a Democracy.
Him he attempts, with studied Arts to please,
And sheds his Venome, in such words as these.

180–191. These lines do not appear in   195. *Cockle:* A kind of weed.
the first London edition of 1681, on which
the present text is based, but they were
added in the second edition.

"Auspicious Prince! at whose Nativity   230
Some Royal Planet rul'd the Southern sky;
Thy longing Countrie's Darling and Desire;
Their cloudy Pillar, and their guardian Fire:
Their second *Moses*, whose extended Wand
Shuts up the Seas, and shews the promis'd Land: 235
Whose dawning Day, in every distant age,
Has exercis'd the Sacred Prophet's rage:
The People's Prayer, the glad Deviner's Theam,
The Young-men's Vision, and the Old men's Dream!
Thee, *Saviour*, Thee, the Nation's Vows confess;   240
And, never satisfi'd with seeing, bless;
Swift, unbespoken Pomps, thy steps proclaim,
And stammerring Babes are taught to lisp thy Name.
How long wilt thou the general Joy detain;
Starve, and defraud the People of thy Reign?   245
Content ingloriously to pass thy days
Like one of Vertue's Fools that feeds on Praise;
Till thy fresh Glories, which now shine so bright,
Grow Stale and Tarnish with our daily sight.
Believe me, Royal Youth, thy Fruit must be,   250
Or gather'd Ripe, or rot upon the Tree.
Heav'n has to all allotted, soon or late,
Some lucky Revolution of their Fate:
Whose Motions, if we watch and guide with Skill,
(For humane Good depends on humane Will)   255
Our Fortune rolls, as from a smooth Descent,
And from the first Impression, takes the Bent:
But, if unseiz'd, she glides away like wind;
And leaves repenting Folly far behind.
Now, now she meets you with a glorious prize,   260
And spreads her Locks before her as she flies.
Had thus Old *David*, from whose Loyns you spring,
Not dar'd, when Fortune call'd him, to be King,
At *Gath* an Exile he might still remain,
And heavens Anointing Oyle had been in vain.   265
Let his successfull Youth your hopes engage,
But shun th' example of Declining Age:
Behold him setting in his Western Skies,
The Shadows lengthning as the Vapours rise.
He is not now, as when on *Jordan's* Sand   ⎫   270
The Joyfull People throng'd to see him Land,   ⎬
Cov'ring the *Beach*, and blackning all the *Strand*: ⎭
But, like the Prince of Angels from his height,
Comes tumbling downward with diminish'd light;

235. *Shuts up the Seas:* Some later texts
give Divides the Sea.

Betray'd by one poor Plot to publick Scorn   275
(Our only blessing since his Curst Return),
Those heaps of People which one Sheaf did bind,
Blown off and scatter'd by a puff of Wind.
What strength can he to your Designs oppose,
Naked of Friends, and round beset with Foes?   280
If *Pharaoh's* doubtfull Succour he shoud use,
A Foreign Aid woud more Incense the *Jews*:
Proud *Egypt* woud dissembled Friendship bring;
Foment the War, but not support the King:
Nor woud the Royal Party e'r unite   285
With *Pharoah's* Arms t'assist the *Jebusite*;
Or if they shoud, their Interest soon woud break,
And with such odious Aid make *David* weak.
All sorts of men by my successfull Arts,
Abhorring Kings, estrange their alter'd Hearts   290
From *David's* Rule: And 'tis the general Cry,
Religion, Common-wealth, and Liberty.
If you as Champion of the publique Good,
Add to their Arms a Chief of Royal Blood;
What may not *Israel* hope, and what Applause   295
Might such a General gain by such a Cause?
Not barren Praise alone, that Gaudy Flower,
Fair only to the sight, but solid Power:
And Nobler is a limited Command,
Giv'n by the Love of all your Native Land,   300
Than a Successive Title, Long, and Dark,
Drawn from the Mouldy Rolls of *Noah's* Ark."

What cannot Praise effect in Mighty Minds,
When Flattery Sooths, and when Ambition Blinds!
Desire of Power, on Earth a Vitious Weed,   305
Yet, sprung from High, is of Cælestial Seed:
In God 'tis Glory: And when men Aspire,
'Tis but a Spark too much of Heavenly Fire.
Th' Ambitious Youth, too Covetous of Fame,
Too full of Angell's Metal in his Frame,   310
Unwarily was led from Vertue's ways,
Made Drunk with Honour, and Debauch'd with Praise.
Half loath, and half consenting to the Ill
(For Loyal Blood within him struled still)
He thus reply'd——"And what Pretence have I   315
To take up Arms for Publick Liberty?
My Father Governs with unquestion'd Right;
The Faith's Defender, and Mankind's Delight:

314. *Loyal Blood:* Some later texts give
Royal Blood.

Good, Gracious, Just, observant of the Laws;
And Heav'n by Wonders has Espous'd his Cause.   320
Whom has he Wrong'd in all his Peaceful Reign?
Who sues for Justice to his Throne in Vain?
What Millions has he Pardon'd of his Foes,
Whom Just Revenge did to his Wrath expose?
Mild, Easy, Humble, Studious of our Good;   325
Enclin'd to Mercy, and averse from Blood.
If Mildness Ill with Stubborn *Israel* Suite,
His Crime is God's beloved Attribute.
What could he gain, his People to Betray,
Or change his Right for Arbitrary Sway?   330
Let Haughty *Pharaoh* Curse with such a Reign,
His Fruitfull *Nile*, and Yoak a Servile Train.
If *David's* Rule *Jerusalem* Displease,
The *Dog-star* heats their Brains to this Disease.
Why then shoud I, Encouraging the Bad,   335
Turn Rebell, and run Popularly Mad?
Were he a Tyrant, who by Lawless Might,
Opprest the *Jews* and Rais'd the *Jebusite*,
Well might I Mourn; but Nature's Holy Bands
Woud Curb my Spirits, and Restrain my Hands: 340
The People might assert their Liberty;
But what was Right in them were Crime in me.
His Favour leaves me nothing to require,
Prevents my Wishes, and outruns Desire.
What more can I expect while *David* lives,   345
All but his Kingly Diadem he gives;
And that": But there he Paus'd; then Sighing, said,
"Is Justly Destin'd for a Worthier Head.
For when my Father from his Toyls shall Rest,
And late Augment the Number of the Blest: 350
His Lawfull Issue shall the Throne ascend,
Or the *Collateral* Line where that shall end.
His Brother, though Opprest with Vulgar Spight,
Yet Dauntless and Secure of Native Right,
Of every Royal Vertue stands possest;   355
Still Dear to all the Bravest, and the Best.
His Courage Foes, his Friends his Truth Proclaim;
His Loyalty the King, the World his Fame.
His Mercy even th'Offending Crowd will find,
For sure he comes of a Forgiving Kind.   360
Why shoud I then Repine at Heaven's Decree;
Which gives me no Pretence to Royalty?
Yet oh that Fate Propitiously Enclind,
Had rais'd my Birth, or had debas'd my Mind;
To my large Soul not all her Treasure lent,   365

And then Betray'd it to a mean Descent.
I find, I find my mounting Spirits Bold,
And *David's* Part disdains my Mother's Mold.
Why am I Scanted by a Niggard Birth,
My Soul Disclaims the Kindred of her Earth: 370
And made for Empire, Whispers me within;
'Desire of Greatness is a Godlike Sin.' "

    Him Staggering so when Hell's dire Agent found,
While fainting Vertue scarce maintain'd her Ground,
He pours fresh Forces in, and thus Replies: 375
    "Th' Eternal God, Supreamly Good and Wise,
Imparts not these Prodigous Gifts in vain;
What Wonders are Reserv'd to bless your Reign?
Against your will your Arguments have shown,
Such Vertue's only given to guide a Throne.   380
Not that your Father's Mildness I condemn;
But Manly Force becomes the Diadem.
'Tis true, he grants the People all they crave;
And more perhaps than Subjects ought to have:
For Lavish grants suppose a Monarch tame,   385
And more his Goodness than his Wit proclaim.
But when shoud People strive their Bonds to break,
If not when Kings are Negligent or Weak?
Let him give on till he can give no more,
The Thrifty Sanhedrin shall keep him poor: 390
And every Sheckle which he can receive,
Shall cost a Limb of his Prerogative.
To ply him with new Plots shall be my care,
Or plunge him deep in some Expensive War;
Which when his Treasure can no more Supply,   395
He must, with the Remains of Kingship, buy.
His faithful Friends, our Jealousies and Fears,
Call *Jebusites*, and *Pharaoh's* Pentioners:
Whom when our Fury from his Aid has torn,
He shall be Naked left to publick Scorn.   400
The next Successor, whom I fear and hate,
My Arts have made Obnoxious to the State;
Turn'd all his Vertues to his Overthrow,
And gain'd our Elders to pronounce a Foe.
His Right, for Sums of necessary Gold,   405
Shall first be Pawn'd, and afterwards be Sold:
Till time shall Ever-wanting *David* draw,
To pass your doubtfull Title into Law:
If not, the People have a Right Supreme
To make their Kings; for Kings are made for them.   410
All Empire is no more than Pow'r in Trust,

Which when resum'd, can be no longer Just.
Succession, for the general Good design'd,
In its own wrong a Nation cannot bind:
If altering that, the People can relieve,   415
Better one Suffer, than a Million grieve.
The *Jews* well know their power: e'r *Saul* they Chose,
God was their King, and God they durst Depose.
Urge now your Piety, your Filial Name,
A Father's Right, and fear of future Fame;   420
The publick Good, that Universal Call,
To which even Heav'n Submitted, answers all.
Nor let his Love Enchant your generous Mind;
'Tis Nature's trick to Propagate her Kind.
Our fond Begetters, who woud never dye,   425
Love but themselves in their Posterity.
Or let his Kindness by th' Effects be try'd,
Or let him lay his vain Pretence aside.
God said he lov'd your Father; coud he bring
A better Proof, than to Anoint him King?   430
It surely shew'd he lov'd the Shepherd well,
Who gave so fair a Flock as *Israel*.
Woud *David* have you thought his Darling Son?
What means he then, to Alienate the Crown?
The name of Godly he may blush to bear: 435
'Tis after God's own heart to Cheat his Heir.
He to his Brother gives Supreme Command;
To you a Legacy of Barren Land:
Perhaps th' old Harp, on which he thrums his Layes:
Or some dull *Hebrew* Ballad in your Praise.   440
Then the next Heir, a Prince, Severe and Wise,
Already looks on you with Jealous Eyes;
Sees through the thin Disguises of your Arts,
And markes your Progress in the People's Hearts.
Though now his mighty Soul its Grief contains;   445
He meditates Revenge who least Complains.
And like a Lyon, Slumbring in the way,
Or Sleep-dissembling, while he waits his Prey,
His fearless Foes within his Distance draws,
Constrains his Roaring, and Contracts his Paws;   450
Till at the last, his time for Fury found,
He shoots with suddain Vengeance from the Ground:
The Prostrate Vulgar, passes o'r, and Spares;
But with a Lordly Rage, his Hunters teares.
Your Case no tame Expedients will afford;   455
Resolve on Death, or Conquest by the Sword,

416. *A Million grieve:* Some later texts
give a Nation grieve.

Which for no less a Stake than Life, you Draw;
And Self-defence is Nature's Eldest Law.
Leave the warm People no Considering time;
For then Rebellion may be thought a Crime.   460
Prevail your self of what Occasion gives,
But try your Title while your Father lives:
And that your Arms may have a fair Pretence,
Proclaim you take them in the King's Defence:
Whose Sacred Life each minute woud Expose   465
To Plots from seeming Friends and secret Foes.
And who can sound the depth of *David's* Soul?
Perhaps his fear, his kindness may Controul.
He fears his Brother, though he loves his Son,
For plighted Vows too late to be undone.   470
If so, by Force he wishes to be gain'd,
Like women's Leachery, to seem Constrain'd:
Doubt not, but when he most affects the Frown,
Commit a pleasing Rape upon the Crown.
Secure his Person to secure your Cause;   475
They who possess the Prince, possess the Laws."

　　He said, And this Advice above the rest,
With *Absalom's* Mild nature suited best;
Unblam'd of Life (Ambition set aside),
Not stain'd with Cruelty, nor puft with Pride;   480
How happy had be been, if Destiny
Had higher plac'd his Birth, or not so high?
His Kingly Vertues might have claim'd a Throne,
And blest all other Countries but his own:
But charming Greatness, since so few refuse,   485
'Tis Juster to Lament him than Accuse.
Strong were his hopes a Rival to remove,
With blandishments to gain the publick Love;
To Head the Faction while their Zeal was hot,
And Popularly prosecute the Plot.   490
To farther this, *Achitophel* Unites
The Malecontents of all the *Israelites*;
Whose differing Parties he could wisely Joyn,
For several Ends, to serve the same Design.
The Best, and of the Princes some were such,   495
Who thought the power of Monarchy too much:
Mistaken Men, and Patriots in their Hearts;
Not Wicked, but Seduc'd by Impious Arts.
By these the Springs of Property were bent,
And wound so high, they Crack'd the Government.   500
The next for Interest sought t' embroil the State,
To sell their Duty at a dearer rate;

And make their *Jewish* Markets of the Throne,
Pretending publick Good, to serve their own.
Others thought Kings an useless heavy Load,   505
Who Cost too much, and did too little Good.
These were for laying Honest *David* by,
On Principles of pure good Husbandry.
With them Joyn'd all th' Haranguers of the Throng,
That thought to get Preferment by the Tongue.   510
Who follow next, a double Danger bring,
Not only hating *David*, but the King;
The *Solymæan* Rout, well Verst of old
In Godly Faction, and in Treason bold;
Cowring and Quaking at a Conqueror's Sword,   515
But Lofty to a Lawfull Prince Restor'd;
Saw with Disdain an *Ethnick* Plot begun,
And Scorn'd by *Jebusites* to be Out-done.
Hot *Levites* Headed these; who pul'd before
From th' *Ark*, which in the Judge's days they bore,   520
Resum'd their Cant, and with a Zealous Cry,
Pursu'd their old belov'd Theocracy.
Where Sanhedrin and Priest inslav'd the Nation,
And justifi'd their Spoils by Inspiration;
For who so fit for Reign as *Aaron's* Race,   525
If once Dominion they could found in Grace?
These led the Pack; tho not of surest scent,
Yet deepest mouth'd against the Government.
A numerous Host of dreaming Saints succeed,
Of the true old Enthusiastick breed: 530
'Gainst Form and Order they their Power employ,
Nothing to Build and all things to Destroy.
But far more numerous was the herd of such,
Who think too little, and who talk too much.
These, out of meer instinct, they knew not why,   535
Ador'd their fathers' God and Property:
And, by the same blind benefit of Fate,
The Devil and the Jebusite did hate:
Born to be sav'd, even in their own despight;
Because they could not help believing right.   540
Such were the tools; but a whole Hydra more
Remains, of sprouting heads too long to score.
Some of their Chiefs were Princes of the Land:
In the first Rank of these did *Zimri* stand:
A man so various, that he seem'd to be   545
Not one, but all Mankind's Epitome.
Stiff in Opinions, always in the wrong;
Was every thing by starts, and nothing long:
But, in the course of one revolving Moon,

Was Chymist, Fidler, States-Man, and Buffoon: 550
Then all for Women, Painting, Rhiming, Drinking,
Besides ten thousand freaks that dy'd in thinking.
Blest Madman, who coud every hour employ,
With something New to wish, or to enjoy!
Rayling and praising were his usual Theams; 555
And both (to shew his Judgment) in Extreams:
So over Violent, or over Civil,
That every man, with him, was God or Devil.
In squandring Wealth was his peculiar Art:
Nothing went unrewarded but Desert. 560
Begger'd by Fools, whom still he found too late:
He had his Jest, and they had his Estate.
He laught himself from Court, then sought Relief
By forming Parties, but coud ne're be Chief:
For, spight of him, the weight of Business fell 565
On *Absalom* and wise *Achitophel*:
Thus, wicked but in will, of means bereft,
He left not Faction, but of that was left.

Titles and Names 'twere tedious to Reherse
Of Lords, below the Dignity of Verse. 570
Wits, warriors, Common-wealthsmen were the best:
Kind Husbands and meer Nobles all the rest.
And therefore in the name of Dulness, be
The well hung *Balaam* and cold *Caleb* free.
And Canting *Nadab* let Oblivion damn, 575
Who made new porridge for the Paschal Lamb.
Let Friendship's holy band some Names assure:
Some their own Worth, and some let Scorn secure.
Nor shall the Rascall Rabble here have Place,
Whom Kings no Titles gave, and God no Grace: 580
Not Bull-fac'd-*Jonas*, who could Statutes draw
To mean Rebellion, and make Treason Law.
But he, tho bad, is follow'd by a worse,
The wretch, who Heaven's Annointed dar'd to Curse.
Shimei, whose early Youth did Promise bring 585
Of Zeal to God and Hatred to his King;
Did wisely from Expensive Sins refrain,
And never broke the Sabbath, but for Gain:
Nor ever was he known an Oath to vent,

576. *Porridge:* Dissenters used the term to refer to Anglican services, because they thought them a hodgepodge. *Paschal Lamb:* The Animal slain for the Passover meal; later, Jesus Christ; finally, by association the reenactment of the Last Supper, Holy Communion. Line 576 gains meaning if one knows that Lord Howard (Nadab), imprisoned in the Tower, is supposed to have taken Holy Communion, following the Book of Common Prayer, but using hot ale and roasted apple pulp in place of wine.

Or Curse unless against the Government.   590
Thus, heaping Wealth, by the most ready way
Among the Jews, which was to Cheat and Pray;
The City, to reward his pious Hate
Against his Master, chose him Magistrate:
His Hand a Vare of Justice did uphold;   595
His Neck was loaded with a Chain of Gold.
During his Office, Treason was no Crime.
The Sons of *Belial* had a glorious Time:
For *Shimei*, though not prodigal of pelf,
Yet lov'd his wicked Neighbour as himself: 600
When two or three were gather'd to declaim
Against the Monarch of *Jerusalem*,
Shimei was always in the midst of them.
And if they Curst the King when he was by,
Woud rather Curse than break good Company.   605
If any durst his Factious Friends accuse,
He pact a Jury of dissenting Jews:
Whose fellow-feeling, in the godly Cause,
Would free the suffring Saint from Humane Laws.
For Laws are only made to Punish those,   610
Who serve the King, and to protect his Foes.
If any leisure time he had from Power
(Because 'tis Sin to misimploy an hour),
His business was, by Writing, to Persuade,
That Kings were Useless, and a Clog to Trade: 615
And that his noble Stile he might refine,
No *Rechabite* more shund the fumes of Wine.
Chast were his Cellars, and his Shrieval Board
The Grossness of a City Feast abhor'd:
His Cooks, with long disuse, their Trade forgot;   620
Cool was his Kitchen, tho his Brains were hot.
Such frugal Vertue Malice may accuse,
But sure 'twas necessary to the Jews:
For Towns once burnt, such Magistrates require
As dare not tempt God's Providence by fire.   625
With Spiritual food he fed his Servants well,
But free from flesh that made the Jews Rebel:
And *Moses's* Laws he held in more account,
For forty days of Fasting in the Mount.
To speak the rest, who better are forgot,   630
Would tyre a well breath'd Witness of the Plot:
Yet, *Corah*, thou shalt from Oblivion pass;
Erect thy self thou Monumental Brass:

595. *Vare:* Wand or rod.
598. *Belial:* The name of a devil.
618. *Shrieval Board:* Sheriff's dining table. Slingsby Bethel (Shimei), Whig Sheriff of London, was so abstemious as to be mean.

High as the Serpent of thy mettall made,
While Nations stand secure beneath thy shade.   635
What tho his Birth were base, yet Comets rise
From Earthy Vapours ere they shine in Skies.
Prodigious Actions may as well be done
By Weaver's issue, as by Prince's Son.
This Arch-Attestor for the Publick Good   640
By that one Deed Enobles all his Bloud.
Who ever ask'd the Witnesses' high race,
Whose Oath with Martyrdom did *Stephen* grace?
Ours was a *Levite*, and as times went then,
His Tribe were Godalmighty's Gentlemen.   645
Sunk were his Eyes, his Voyce was harsh and loud,
Sure signs he neither Cholerick was, nor Proud:
His long Chin prov'd his Wit; his Saintlike Grace,
A Church Vermilion, and a *Moses's* Face,
His Memory, miraculously great,   650
Could Plots, exceeding man's belief, repeat;
Which therefore cannot be accounted Lies,
For humane Wit could never such devise.
Some future Truths are mingled in his Book;
But where the witness faild, the Prophet Spoke: 655
Some things like Visionary flights appear;
The Spirit caught him up, the Lord knows where:
And gave him his *Rabinical* degree
Unknown to Foreign University.
His Judgment yet his Memory did excel;   660
Which peic'd his wondrous Evidence so well:
And suited to the temper of the times,
Then groaning under Jebusitick Crimes.
Let *Israel's* foes suspect his heav'nly call,
And rashly judge his wit Apocryphal;   665
Our Laws for such affronts have forfeits made:
He takes his life, who takes away his trade.
Were I my self in witness *Corah's* place,
The wretch who did me such a dire disgrace,
Should whet my memory, though once forgot,   670
To make him an Appendix of my Plot.
His Zeal to heav'n made him his Prince despise,
And load his person with indignities:
But Zeal peculiar priviledg affords;
Indulging latitude to deed and words.   675
And *Corah* might for *Agag's* murther call,

---

634. *Serpent of thy mettall:* See Num.
21:6–9 for the brass serpent set up by
Moses at God's command so that those
bitten by His fiery serpents might live.

642–643. *Witnesses' high race . . .
Stephen grace:* See Acts 6:9–15 for the
narrative of false witnesses against Stephen.

In terms as course as *Samuel* us'd to *Saul*.
What others in his Evidence did Joyn
(The best that could be had for love or coyn),
In *Corah's* own predicament will fall: 680
For *witness* is a Common Name to all.

Surrounded thus with Freinds of every sort,
Deluded *Absalom* forsakes the Court:
Impatient of high hopes, urg'd with renown,
And Fir'd with near possession of a Crown;   685
Th' admiring Croud are dazled with surprize,
And on his goodly person feed their eyes:
Dissembling Joy, he sets himself to show,
On each side bowing popularly low:
His looks, his gestures, and his words he frames,   690
And with familiar ease repeats their Names.
Thus form'd by Nature, furnish'd out with Arts,
He glides unfelt into their secret hearts:
Then with a kind compassionating look,
And sighs, bespeaking pity ere he spoak: 695
Few words he said, but easy those and fit:
More slow than Hybla drops, and far more sweet.

"I mourn, my Countrymen, your lost Estate;
Tho far unable to prevent your fate:
Behold a Banisht man, for your dear cause   700
Expos'd a prey to Arbitrary laws!
Yet oh! that I alone cou'd be undone,
Cut off from Empire, and no more a Son!
Now all your Liberties a spoil are made;
Ægypt and *Tyrus* intercept your Trade,   705
And *Jebusites* your Sacred Rites invade.
My Father, whom with reverence yet I name,
Charm'd into Ease, is careless of his Fame:
And brib'd with petty summs of Forreign Gold,
Is grown in *Bathsheba's* Embraces old: 710
Exalts his Enemies, his Freinds destroys:
And all his pow'r against himself employs.
He gives, and let him give my right away:
But why should he his own, and yours betray?
He only, he can make the Nation bleed,   715
And he alone from my revenge is freed.
Take then my tears" (with that he wip'd his Eyes),

677. *Samuel us'd to Saul:* See I Samuel 15, where Samuel rebukes Saul for disobeying the words of the Lord.
688. *Dissembling Joy:* Some later texts give His joy conceal'd.

697. *Hybla:* A town in Sicily celebrated for its bees; hence Hybla means honey.

"'Tis all the Aid my present power supplies:
No Court Informer can these Arms accuse,
These Arms may Sons against their Fathers use,   720
And, tis my wish, the next Successor's Reign
May make no other *Israelite* complain."

Youth, Beauty, Graceful Action, seldom fail:
But Common Interest always will prevail:
And pity never Ceases to be shown   725
To him, who makes the people's wrongs his own.
The Croud (that still believes their Kings oppress)
With lifted hands their young *Messiah* bless:
Who now begins his Progress to ordain
With Chariots, Horsemen, and a numerous train: 730
From East to West his Glories he displaies:
And, like the Sun, the promis'd land survays.
Fame runs before him, as the morning Star;
And shouts of Joy salute him from afar:
Each house receives him as a Guardian God,   735
And Consecrates the Place of his aboad:
But hospitable treats did most Commend
Wise *Issachar*, his wealthy western friend.
This moving Court, that caught the people's Eyes,
And seem'd but Pomp, did other ends disguise: 740
Achitophel had form'd it, with intent
To sound the depth, and fathom where it went:
The People's hearts, distinguish Friends from Foes,
And try their strength, before they came to blows:
Yet all was colour'd with a smooth pretence   745
Of specious love, and duty to their Prince.
Religion and Redress of Grievances,
Two names that always cheat and always please,
Are often urg'd; and good King *David's* life
Indanger'd by a Brother and a Wife.   750
Thus in a Pageant Show a Plot is made;
And Peace it self is War in Masquerade.
Oh foolish *Israel!* never warn'd by ill,
Still the same baite, and circumvented still!
Did ever men forsake their present ease,   755
In midst of health Imagine a desease;
Take pains Contingent mischiefs to foresee,
Make Heirs for Monarks, and for God decree?
What shall we think! can People give away,
Both for themselves and Sons, their Native sway?   760
Then they are left Defensless to the Sword
Of each unbounded Arbitrary Lord:
And Laws are vain by which we Right enjoy,

If Kings unquestiond can those laws destroy.
Yet, if the Crowd be Judge of fit and Just,   765
And Kings are onely Officers in trust,
Then this resuming Cov'nant was declar'd
When Kings were made, or is for ever bar'd:
If those who gave the Scepter coud not tye
By their own deed their own Posterity,   770
How then coud *Adam* bind his future Race?
How coud his forfeit on mankind take place?
Or how coud heavenly Justice damn us all,
Who nere consented to our Father's fall?
Then Kings are slaves to those whom they Command,   775
And Tenants to their People's pleasure stand.
That Pow'r, which is for Property allowd,
Is mischeivously seated in the Crowd:
For who can be secure of private Right,
If Sovereign sway, may be dissolv'd by might?   780
Nor is the People's Judgment always true:
The most may err as grosly as the few.
And faultless Kings run down, by Common Cry,
For Vice, Oppression, and for Tyranny.
What Standard is there in a fickle rout,   785
Which, flowing to the mark, runs faster out?
Nor only Crowds, but Sanhedrins may be
Infected with this publick Lunacy:
And Share the madness of Rebellious times,
To Murther Monarchs for Imagin'd crimes.   790
If they may Give and Take when e'r they please,
Not Kings alone (the Godhead's Images)
But Government it self at length must fall
To Nature's state, where all have Right to all.
Yet, grant our Lords the People Kings can make,   795
What Prudent men a setled Throne woud shake?
For whatsoe'r their Sufferings were before,
That Change they Covet makes them suffer more.
All other Errors but disturb a State;
But Innovation is the Blow of Fate.   800
If ancient Fabricks nod and threat to fall,
To Patch the Flaws and Buttress up the Wall,
Thus far 'tis Duty; but here fix the Mark:
For all beyond it is to touch our Ark.
To change Foundations, cast the Frame anew,   805
Is work for Rebels who base Ends pursue:
At once Divine and Humane Laws controul,
And mend the Parts by ruine of the Whole.
The Tampering World is subject to this Curse,
To Physick their Disease into a worse.   810

Now what Relief can Righteous *David* bring?
How Fatall 'tis to be too good a King!
Friends he has few, so high the Madness grows;
Who dare be such, must be the People's Foes:
Yet some there were, ev'n in the worst of days;   815
Some let me name, and Naming is to praise.

In this short File *Barzillai* first appears;
Barzillai crown'd with Honour and with Years:
Long since, the rising Rebells he withstood
In Regions Waste, beyond the *Jordan's* Flood: 820
Unfortunately Brave to buoy the State;
But sinking underneath his Master's Fate:
In Exile with his Godlike Prince he Mourn'd;
For him he Suffer'd, and with him Return'd.
The Court he practis'd, not the Courtier's art: 825
Large was his Wealth, but larger was his Heart,
Which well the Noblest Objects knew to choose,
The Fighting Warriour, and Recording Muse.
His Bed coud once a Fruitfull Issue boast:
Now more than half a Father's Name is lost.   830
His Eldest Hope, with every Grace adorn'd,
By me (so Heav'n will have it) always Mourn'd,
And always honour'd, snatcht in Manhood's prime
By unequal Fates, and Providence's crime:
Yet not before the Goal of Honour won,   835
All parts fulfill'd of Subject and of Son;
Swift was the Race, but short the Time to run.
Oh Narrow Circle, but of Pow'r Divine,
Scanted in Space, but perfect in thy Line!
By Sea, by Land, thy Matchless Worth was known;   840
Arms thy Delight, and War was all thy Own:
Thy force, Infus'd, the fainting *Tyrians* prop'd:
And Haughty *Pharaoh* found his Fortune stop'd.
Oh Ancient Honour, Oh Unconquer'd Hand,
Whom Foes unpunish'd never coud withstand!   845
But *Israel* was unworthy of thy Birth;
Short is the date of all Immoderate Worth.
It looks as Heaven our Ruine had design'd,
And durst not trust thy Fortune and they Mind.
Now, free from Earth, thy disencumbred Soul   850
Mounts up and leaves behind the Clouds and Starry Pole:
From thence thy kindred legions mayst thou bring
To aid the guardian Angel of thy King.
Here stop my Muse, here cease thy painfull flight;

846–847. *Birth*/*Worth*: Some later texts
give Name/Fame as the rhyme.

No Pinions can pursue Immortal height: 855
Tell good *Barzillai* thou canst sing no more,
And tell thy Soul she should have fled before;
Or fled she with his life, and left this Verse
To hang on her departed Patron's Herse?
Now take thy steepy flight from heaven, and see   ' 860
If thou canst find on earth another *He*;
Another he would be too hard to find,
See then whom thou canst see not far behind.
Zadock the Priest, whom, shunning Power and Place,
His lowly mind advanc'd to *David's* Grace: 865
With him the *Sagan* of *Jerusalem*,
Of hospitable Soul and noble Stem;
Him of the Western dome, whose weighty sense
Flows in fit words and heavenly eloquence.
The Prophets' Sons by such example led,   870
To Learning and to Loyalty were bred:
For *Colleges* on bounteous Kings depend,
And never Rebell was to Arts a friend.
To these succeed the Pillars of the Laws,
Who best cou'd plead and best can judge a Cause.   875
Next them a train of Loyal Peers ascend:
Sharp judging *Adriel* the Muses' friend,
Himself a Muse—In Sanhedrin's debate
True to his Prince, but not a Slave of State,
Whom *David's* love with Honours did adorn,   880
That from his disobedient Son were torn.
Jotham of ready wit and pregnant thought,
Indew'd by nature, and by learning taught
To move Assemblies, who but onely try'd
The worse awhile, then chose the better side;   885
Nor chose alone, but turn'd the balance too;
So much the weight of one brave man can doe.
Hushai the friend of *David* in distress,
In publick storms of manly stedfastness;
By foreign treaties he inform'd his Youth;   890
And join'd experience to his native truth.
His frugal care supply'd the wanting Throne,
Frugal for that, but bounteous of his own:
'Tis easy conduct when Exchequers flow,
But hard the task to manage well the low: 895
For Soveraign power is too deprest or high,
When Kings are forc'd to sell, or Crowds to buy.
Indulge one labour more my weary Muse,
For *Amiel*; who can *Amiel's* praise refuse?

868. *Him of the Western dome:* John
Dolben, Dean of Westminster, a royalist,
who was wounded at Marston Moor and
York.

Of ancient race by birth, but nobler yet   900
In his own worth, and without Title great:
The Sanhedrin long time as chief he rul'd,
Their Reason guided and their Passion coold;
So dexterous was he in the Crown's defence,
So form'd to speak a Loyal Nation's Sense,   905
That as their band was *Israel's* Tribes in small,
So fit was he to represent them all.
Now rasher Charioteers the Seat ascend,
Whose loose Carriers his steady Skill commend:
They, like th'unequal Ruler of the Day,   910
Misguide the Seasons and mistake the Way;
While he withdrawn at their mad Labour smiles,
And safe enjoys the Sabbath of his Toyls.

   These were the chief, a small but faithful Band
Of Worthies, in the Breach who dar'd to stand   } 915
And tempt th'united Fury of the Land.
With grief they view'd such powerful Engines bent,
To batter down the lawful Government.
A numerous Faction with pretended frights,
In Sanhedrins to plume the Regal Rights.   920
The true Successour from the Court remov'd.
The Plot, by hireling Witnesses, improved.
These Ills they saw, and as their Duty bound,
They shew'd the King the danger of the Wound:
That no Concessions from the Throne woud please,   925
But Lenitives fomented the Disease:
That *Absalom*, ambitious of the Crown,
Was made the Lure to draw the People down;
That false *Achitophel's* pernitious Hate
Had turn'd the Plot to Ruine Church and State: 930
The Councill violent, the Rabble worse
That *Shimei* taught *Jerusalem* to Curse.

   With all these loads of Injuries opprest,
And long revolving in his carefull Breast
Th' event of things, at last his patience tir'd,   935
Thus from his Royal Throne by Heav'n inspir'd,
The God-like *David* spoke: with awfull fear
His Train their Maker in their Master hear.

   "Thus long have I, by native mercy sway'd,
My wrongs dissembl'd, my revenge delay'd: 940
So willing to forgive th' Offending Age,
So much the Father did the King asswage.
But now so far my Clemency they slight,
Th' Offenders question my Forgiving Right.

That one was made for many, they contend: 945
But 'tis to Rule, for that's a Monarch's End.
They call my tenderness of Blood, my Fear,
Though Manly tempers can the longest bear.
Yet, since they will divert my Native course,
'Tis time to shew I am not Good by Force.   950
Those heap'd Affronts that haughty Subjects bring,
Are burthens for a Camel, not a King:
Kings are the publick Pillars of the State,
Born to sustain and prop the Nation's weight:
If my Young *Samson* will pretend a Call   955
To shake the Column, let him share the Fall:
But oh that yet he would repent and live!
How easie 'tis for parents to forgive!
With how few Tears a Pardon might be won
From Nature, pleading for a Darling Son!   960
Poor pitied Youth, by my Paternal care,
Rais'd up to all the Height his Frame coud bear:
Had God ordain'd his fate for Empire born,
He woud have given his Soul another turn:
Gull'd with a Patriot's name, whose Modern sense   965
Is one that would by Law destroy his Prince:
The People's Brave, the Politician's Tool;
Never was Patriot yet, but was a Fool.
Whence comes it that Religion and the Laws
Should more be *Absalom's* than *David's* Cause?   970
His old Instructor, e're he lost his Place,
Was never thought indu'd with so much Grace.
Good Heav'ns, how Faction can a Patriot Paint!
My Rebel ever proves my People's Saint:
Would *They* impose an Heir upon the Throne?   975
Let Sanhedrins be taught to give their Own.
A King's at least a part of Government,
And mine as requisite as their Consent:
Without my Leave a future King to choose,
Infers a Right the Present to Depose: 980
True, they Petition me t' approve their Choise,
But *Esau's* Hands suite ill with *Jacob's* Voice.
My Pious Subjects for my Safety pray,
Which to Secure they take my Power away.
From Plots and Treasons Heaven preserve my years,   985
But Save me most from my Petitioners.
Unsatiate as the barren Womb or Grave;
God cannot Grant so much as they can Crave.

957–960. These lines do not appear in
the first London edition.
    966. *Destroy his Prince:* Some later
texts give supplant his Prince.
    982. *Esau's Hands . . . Jacob's Voice:* See

Genesis 27, where Jacob pretends to be his
brother Esau in order to receive his blind
father's blessing, intended for the elder
child.

What then is left but with a Jealous Eye
To guard the Small remains of Royalty?   990
The Law shall still direct my peacefull Sway,
And the same Law teach Rebels to Obey:
Votes shall no more Establish'd Pow'r controul,
Such Votes as make a Part exceed the Whole:
No groundless Clamours shall my Friends remove,   995
Nor Crowds have power to Punish e're they Prove:
For Gods and Godlike Kings their Care express,
Still to Defend their Servants in distress.
Oh that my Power to Saving were confin'd:
Why am I forc'd, like Heaven, against my mind,   } 1000
To make Examples of another Kind?
Must I at length the Sword of Justice draw?
Oh curst Effects of necessary Law!
How ill my Fear they by my Mercy scan,
Beware the Fury of a Patient Man.   1005
Law they require, let Law then shew her Face;
They coud not be content to look on Grace,
Her hinder parts, but with a daring Eye
To tempt the terror of her Front, and Dye.
By their own arts 'tis Righteously decreed,   1010
Those dire Artificers of Death shall bleed.
Against themselves their Witnesses will Swear,
Till Viper-like their Mother Plot they tear:
And suck for Nutriment that bloody gore
Which was their Principle of Life before.   1015
Their *Belial* with their *Belzebub* will fight;
Thus on my Foes, my Foes shall do me Right:
Nor doubt th' event: for Factious crowds engage
In their first Onset, all their Brutal Rage;
Then, let 'em take an unresisted Course,   1020
Retire, and Traverse, and Delude their Force:
But when they stand all Breathless, urge the fight,
And rise upon 'em with redoubled might:
For Lawfull Pow'r is still Superior found;
When long driven back, at length it stands the ground."   1025

He said. Th' Almighty, nodding, gave Consent;
And Peals of Thunder shook the Firmament.
Henceforth a Series of new time began,
They mighty Years in long Procession ran:
Once more the Godlike *David* was Restor'd,   1030
And willing Nations knew their Lawfull Lord.

(1681)

1016. *Belial, Belzebub:* The names of
devils.

MAC FLECKNOE

Shaftesbury used the doubt and terror attending the Popish Plot (the period 1678–1680) to secure his own political ends. First, he took advantage of the occasion to do away with personal enemies and to try to exclude James from the succession, in favor of Monmouth. Later, in 1680, in extreme opposition to Charles, he attempted to bring James to trial for religious nonconformity (recusancy); and he actually brought armed followers to the Parliament at Oxford (1681). For these and other actions against the crown he was sent to the Tower, accused of high treason, in July, 1681; but a Whig grand jury rejected the charge. Upon his release, Shaftesbury's followers struck a medal in his honor, a commemorative tribute for which Dryden satirized him in *The Medal* (March, 1682).

Though this poem has the advantage over *Absalom and Achitophel* that it concentrates on a single character, it is a less effective satire than the earlier piece. Nevertheless it provoked a reply, *The Medal of John Bayes*, probably by Thomas Shadwell, once Dryden's very close friend but by this time a spiteful enemy. No one knows the reason for this change. It is true that they argued in print for about ten years over the quality of Ben Jonson's wit and other critical matters, but nothing approaching animosity appears in this intermittent dialogue. Perhaps the literary disagreement took a personal turn that at first was given only private expression. Whatever the circumstances, it was late in their relationship (1678) that a copy of *Mac Flecknoe*, Dryden's brilliant satire upon Shadwell as a literary dunce, began to circulate, without known provocation; and in 1682, shortly after the appearance of *The Medal of John Bayes*, *Mac Flecknoe* was published.

Richard Flecknoe (c. 1600–1678), Shadwell's literary sire in the poem, was in real life a Catholic priest, who after traveling in America, Europe, and Asia became a dramatist, chiefly of religious subjects, and a versifier in London. Andrew Marvel satirized him playfully in "Flecknoe, an English Priest at Rome," and he was generally regarded, it seems, as an object of ridicule by the wits of the day. By the time Dryden chose him to be father of the Prince of Dullness, he had come to represent the would-be poet of indifferent abilities. It must be observed that the logic of the poem requires that his talents in dullness, though great, should not be uniquely so, because he, like Christ's predecessor John the Baptist, "was sent before but to prepare the way" for the consummation of the ideal he heralded. Flecknoe, accordingly, is only the prophet-precursor of the true son of unrelieved darkness and stupidity—Mac Flecknoe, his son.

This distorted Biblical allusion, though strong and clear, is absorbed into a larger structural scheme. The more dominant idea includes the predictable, orderly, and appropriate succession to the throne, presaging not only a continuance of the excellent dullness of the previous reign, but its increase—a matter Dryden plays with in dozens of biting inventions. The poet's ironic skirmishers (deployed along a simple line of measured loss for the old monarch and extravagant hope for the new) need no auxiliary force to succeed. Nevertheless their effort is indeed reinforced by the social context that provided the occasion for the poem in the first place. For in support, behind the individual thrusts of Dryden's satire, is the general contrast between the rough and uncertain succession of Charles and the smooth and secure one of Flecknoe. It is a perverted universe that thwarts the first while it graciously sponsors the second, a fact to which Pope must have been sensitive or he would not have done as he did—appropriate the idea for his much more serious satire upon dullness, *The Dunciad.*

TEXT. *Miscellany Poems. . . . By the most Eminent Hands* (London, 1684).

Mac Flecknoe

ALL humane things are subject to decay,
And, when Fate summons, Monarchs must obey:
This *Fleckno* found, who, like *Augustus*, young
Was call'd to Empire, and had govern'd long:
In Prose and Verse, was own'd, without dispute   5
Through all the Realms of *Nonsense*, absolute,
This aged Prince now flourishing in Peace,
And blest with issue of a large increase,
Worn out with business, did at length debate
To settle the succession of the State: 10
And pond'ring which of all his Sons was fit

3. *Augustus:* Nephew of Julius Caesar, who at the age of thirty-six became the first Roman Emperor. He ruled from 27 B.C. to A.D. 14, and he chose his own successor.

To Reign, and wage immortal War with Wit;
Cry'd, 'tis resolv'd; for Nature pleads that He
Should onely rule, who most resembles me:
Sh—— alone my perfect image bears,   15
Mature in dullness from his tender years.
Sh—— alone, of all my Sons, is he
Who stands confirm'd in full stupidity.
The rest to some faint meaning make pretence,
But *Sh*—— never deviates into sense.   20
Some Beams of Wit on other souls may fall,
Strike through and make a lucid intervall;
But *Sh*——'s genuine night admits no ray,
His rising Fogs prevail upon the Day:
Besides his goodly Fabrick fills the eye,   25
And seems design'd for thoughtless Majesty:
Thoughtless as Monarch Oakes, that shade the plain,
And, spread in solemn state, supinely reign.
Heywood and *Shirley* were but Types of thee,
Thou last great Prophet of Tautology: 30
Even I, a dunce of more renown than they,
Was sent before but to prepare thy way;
And coursly clad in *Norwich* Drugget came
To teach the Nations in thy greater name.
My warbling Lute, the Lute I whilom strung   35
When to King *John* of *Portugal* I sung,
Was but the prelude to that glorious day,
When thou on silver *Thames* did'st cut thy way,
With well tim'd Oars before the Royal Barge,
Swell'd with the Pride of thy Celestial charge;   40
And big with Hymn, Commander of an Host,
The like was ne'er in *Epsom* Blankets tost.
Methinks I see the new *Arion* Sail,
The Lute still trembling underneath thy nail.
At thy well sharpned thumb from Shore to Shore   45

25. *Goodly Fabrick:* Shadwell was a large, fat man.

29. *Heywood and Shirley:* Thomas Heywood (1574?–1641) and James Shirley (1596–1666), who along with Thomas Dekker (1570?–1632) are used by Dryden at several places in the poem to represent poor dramatists succeeded by a worse, Flecknoe-Shadwell; elsewhere, John Fletcher (1579–1625) and Ben Jonson (1572–1637), as well as the Restoration playwrights Sir Charles Sedley (1639?–1701) and George Etherege (1634?–1691?), to represent good dramatists.

33. *Norwich Drugget:* Coarse cloth of wool or mixed stuff—wool and cotton or linen.

36. *To King John of Portugal I sung:* Flecknoe visited Portugal during his extensive travels, which took him over a period of ten years from the Levant to Brazil. His *A Relation of Ten Years' Travels in Europe, Asia, Affrique, and America* provides the best information about his activities.

42. *In Epsom Blankets tost:* In Shadwell's *The Virtuoso* (1676) Sir Samuel Hearty is tossed in a blanket.

43. *Arion:* A semi-legendary Greek poet-musician, placed by tradition in the seventh century B.C. With his music he charmed even the dolphins who swam about his ship.

The Treble squeaks for fear, the Bases roar:
Echoes from *Pissing Ally*, *Sh*—— call,
And *Sh*—— they resound from *A*—— *Hall*.
About thy boat the little Fishes throng,
As at the Morning Toast, that Floats along.   50
Sometimes as Prince of thy Harmonious band
Thou weild'st thy Papers in thy threshing hand.
St. *Andre's* feet ne'er kept more equal time,
Not ev'n the feet of thy own *Psyche's* rhime:
Though they in number as in sense excell;   55
So just, so like tautology they fell,
That, pale with envy, *Singleton* forswore
The Lute and Sword which he in Triumph bore,
And vow'd he ne'er would act *Villerius* more.
Here stopt the good old *Syre*, and wept for joy   60
In silent raptures of the hopefull boy.
All arguments, but most his Plays, perswade,
That for anointed dullness he was made.
    Close to the Walls which fair *Augusta* bind
(The fair *Augusta* much to fears inclin'd)   65
An ancient fabrick, rais'd t' inform the sight,
There stood of yore, and *Barbican* it hight:
A watch Tower once; but now, so Fate ordains,
Of all the Pile an empty name remains.
From its old Ruins Brothel houses rise,   70
Scenes of lewd loves, and of polluted joys.
Where their vast Courts the Mother Strumpets keep
And, undisturb'd by Watch, in silence sleep.
Near these a Nursery erects its head,
Where Queens are form'd, and future Heroes bred;   75
Where unfledg'd Actors learn to laugh and cry,
Where infant Punks their tender Voices try,
And little *Maximins* the Gods defy.
Great *Fletcher* never treads in Buskings here,
Nor greater *Johnson* dares in Socks appear.   80

---

47. *Pissing Ally:* More than one short
street in London was so named.
    48. *A*—— *Hall:* The first edition, 1682,
gives Aston Hall. No such place has been
identified. Dryden may have been pun-
ning in the spirit of the preceding line and
the two that follow. See Pope's note on
The Dunciad, II, 75.
    53. *St. Andre's feet:* St. Andre was a
dancing teacher of the day.
    54. *Psyche's rhime:* Shadwell wrote a
play named *Psyche*.
    57. *Singleton:* An operatic performer
who played Valerius (Villerius, l. 59) in a
play by William Davenant.

64. *Augusta:* London.
    74. *A Nursery:* One of several schools
for young actors founded after the Restoration.
    77. *Punks:* Harlots.
    78. *Maximins:* Maximin is the over-
drawn tyrant in Dryden's *Tyrannick Love*,
a heroic play.
    79–80. *Fletcher . . . Buskings/Johnson . . .
Socks:* Fletcher (n. l. 29) wears the tragic
boot (buskin), but he is not to be associated
with the poor tragedy here described; and
so for Jonson (n. l. 29) and comedy (socks).

But gentle *Simkin* just reception finds
Amidst this Monument of vanisht minds:
Pure Clinches, the suburbian Muse affords;
And *Panton* waging harmless War with words.
Here *Fleckno*, as a place to Fame well known,   85
Ambitiously design'd his *Sh*——'s Throne.
For ancient *Decker* prophesi'd long since,
That in this Pile should Reign a mighty Prince,
Born for a scourge of Wit, and flayle of Sense:
To whom true dulness should some *Psyches* owe,   90
But Worlds of *Misers* from his pen should flow;
Humorists and Hypocrites it should produce,
Whole *Raymond* families, and Tribes of *Bruce*.
Now Empress *Fame* had publisht the renown,
Of *Sh*——'s Coronation through the Town.   95
Rows'd by report of Fame, the Nations meet,
From near *Bun Hill*, and distant *Watling-street*.
No *Persian* Carpets spread th' Imperial way,
But scatter'd Limbs of mangled Poets lay:
From dusty shops neglected Authors come,   100
Martyrs of Pies, and Reliques of the Bum.
Much *Heywood*, *Shirly*, *Ogleby* there lay,
But loads of *Sh*—— almost choakt the way.
Bilk't *Stationers* for Yeomen stood prepar'd,
And *H*—— was Captain of the Guard.   105
The hoary Prince in Majesty appear'd,
High on a Throne of his own Labours rear'd.
At his right hand our young *Ascanius* sat
Rome's other hope, and pillar of the State.
His Brows thick fogs, instead of glories, grace,   110
And lambent dullness plaid arround his face.
As *Hannibal* did to the Altars come,

---

81. *Simkin:* A low-comedy part associated with drolls—brief farces or burlesques.
83. *Clinches:* Puns.
84. *Panton:* Another character of low-comedy; perhaps he was a punster.
87. *Decker:* Dekker. See n. l. 29.
90–93. *Psyches:* Here begins a series of references to Shadwell's plays and two characters in them. The plays are *Psyche*, *The Miser*, *The Humorists*, and *The Hypocrite*; Raymond is a wit in *The Humorists* and Bruce a similar character in *The Virtuoso*, another of Shadwell's plays.
101. *Martyrs of Pies, and . . . Bum:* Dryden reviews two of the uses to which the paper from the books of neglected authors may be put. Kinsley (p. 1918) quotes this passage from *Essay of Dramatic Poesy:* ". . . they have bought more Editions of

his works then would serve to lay under all their Pies at the Lord Mayor's *Christmas*." The Bum means the posteriors.
102. *Heywood, Shirly, Ogleby:* For the first two see n. l. 29. John Ogilby (1600–1676) prolific translator, printer, publisher, and cartographer, founded the Dublin Theatre.
104. *Stationers:* Stationers were booksellers, often publishing booksellers.
105. *H*——: Herringman. Henry Herringman was Dryden's publisher and the publisher of Shadwell's plays until 1678.
108. *Ascanius:* The son of Aeneas, founder of Rome.
112 f. *Hannibal:* The shift in identification of Flecknoe-Shadwell from (1) founder of Rome (Aeneas–Ascanius) and —because the son is seated at the father's

Sworn by his *Syre* a mortal Foe to *Rome*;
So *Sh*—— swore, nor should his Vow bee vain,
That he till Death true dullness would maintain;   115
And in his father's Right, and Realms defence,
Ne'er to have peace with Wit, nor truce with Sense.
The King himself the sacred Unction made,
As King by Office, and as Priest by Trade:
In his sinister hand, instead of Ball,   120
He plac'd a mighty Mug of potent Ale;
Love's Kingdom to his right he did convey,
At once his Sceptre and his rule of Sway;
Whose righteous Lore the Prince had practis'd young,
And from whose Loyns recorded *Psyche* sprung.   125
His Temples last with Poppies were o'erspread,
That nodding seem'd to consecrate his head:
Just at that point of time, if Fame not lye,
On his left hand twelve reverend *Owls* did fly.
So *Romulus*, 'tis sung, by *Tyber's Brook*,   130
Presage of Sway from twice six Vultures took.
Th' admiring throng loud acclamations make,
And Omens of his future Empire take.
The *Syre* then shook the honours of his head,
And from his brows damps of oblivion shed   135
Full on the filial dullness: long he stood,
Repelling from his Breast the raging God;
At length burst out in this prophetick mood:
    Heavens bless my Son, from *Ireland* let him reign
To farr *Barbadoes* on the Western main;   140
Of his Dominion may no end be known,
And greater than his Father's be his Throne.
Beyond loves Kingdom let him stretch his Pen;
He paus'd, and all the people cry'd *Amen*.
Then thus, continu'd he, my Son advance   145
Still in new Impudence, new Ignorance.
Success let others teach, learn thou from me
Pangs without birth, and fruitless Industry.

---

right hand—God–Christ to (2) altar-
supplicating foes of Rome (Hamilcar–
Hannibal) to (3) repudiators of the symbols of authority (ball and sceptre–mug
of ale) compresses the entire range of
elements underlying Dryden's irony and
stresses the downward movement of
values from hope and glories (ll. 109–110)
to dullness and death (l. 115).
    119. *Priest by Trade:* Flecknoe was a
Catholic priest.
    122. *Love's Kingdom:* A play by Fleck-
noe.

125. *Psyche:* See n. ll. 90–93.
    129. *Owls:* The flights of birds were
taken as omens in classical times. Owls are
birds of ostensible wisdom only.
    130–131. *Romulus/Vultures:* Romulus
and Remus, twin sons of Rhea, princess
royal of Rome, and Mars, placed themselves on one of the hills of Rome, the
Palatine, to await a sign as to which of
them should be king. Remus first saw
six vultures; then Romulus saw twelve.
They fought after the inconclusive omen,
and Romulus slew Remus.

Let *Virtuosos* in five years be Writ;
Yet not one thought accuse thy toyl of wit.   150
Let gentle *George* in triumph tread the Stage,
Make *Dorimant* betray, and *Loveit* rage;
Let *Cully, Cockwood, Fopling,* charm the Pit,
And in their folly shew the Writers wit.
Yet still thy fools shall stand in thy defence,   155
And justifie their Author's want of sense.
Let 'em be all by thy own model made
Of dullness, and desire no foreign aid:
That they to future ages may be known,
Not Copies drawn, but Issue of thy own.   160
Nay let thy men of wit too be the same,
All full of thee, and differing but in name;
But let no alien *S—dl—y* interpose
To lard with wit thy hungry *Epsom* prose.
And when false flowers of *Rhetorick* thou would'st cull,   165
Trust Nature, do not labour to be dull;
But write thy best, and top; and in each line,
Sir *Formal's* oratory will be thine.
Sir *Formal*, though unsought, attends thy quill,
And does thy *Northern Dedications* fill.   170
Nor let false friends seduce thy mind to fame,
By arrogating *Johnson's* Hostile name.
Let Father *Fleckno* fire thy mind with praise,
And Uncle *Ogleby* thy envy raise.
Thou art my blood, where *Johnson* has no part;   175
What share have we in Nature or in Art?
Where did his wit on learning fix a brand,
And rail at Arts he did not understand?
Where made he love in Prince *Nicander's* vein,
Or swept the dust in *Psyche's* humble strain?   180
Where sold he Bargains, Whip stitch, kiss my Arse,
Promis'd a Play and dwindled to a Farce?
When did his Muse from *Fletcher* scenes purloin,
As thou whole *Eth'ridg* dost transfuse to thine?

---

149. *Virtuosos:* See n. ll. 90–93. Dryden had elsewhere expressed the view that Shadwell was slow at composition.

151. *Gentle George:* George Etherege. See n. l. 29.

152–153. *Dorimant, Loveit/Cully, Cockwood, Fopling:* Characters in Etherege's plays.

163. *S—dl—y:* Sedley. See n. l. 29.

164. *Epsom:* Sedley wrote a prologue for *Epsom-Wells*, one of Shadwell's plays.

168. *Sir Fomal:* A character in Shadwell's *The Virtuoso;* he is known for his extravagant rhetoric.

170. *Northern Dedications:* Several of Shadwell's plays were dedicated to the Duke or Duchess of Newcastle, whose estate was in the north.

179–180. *Nicander/Psyche:* In Shadwell's *Psyche,* the character Nicander courts Psyche.

181. *Sold he Bargains, Whip stitch:* To sell bargains here means to answer indecently and flippantly in conversation. Whip-stitch means with a sudden shift or movement.

183–184. *Fletcher/Eth'ridg:* See n. l. 29.

But so tranfus'd as Oyl on Waters flow,   185
His always floats above, thine sinks below.
This is thy Province, this thy wondrous way,
New Humours to invent for each new Play:
This is that boasted Byas of thy mind,
By which one way, to dullness, 'tis inclin'd.   190
Which makes thy writings lean on one side still,
And in all changes that way bends thy will.
Nor let thy mountain belly make pretence
Of likeness; thine's a tympany of sense.
A Tun of Man in thy Large bulk is writ,   195
But sure thou'rt but a Kilderkin of wit.
Like mine thy gentle numbers feebly creep,
Thy Tragick Muse gives smiles, thy Comick sleep.
With whate'er gall thou sett'st thy self to write,
Thy inoffensive Satyrs never bite.   200
In thy fellonious heart, though Venom lies,
It does but touch thy *Irish* pen, and dyes.
Thy Genius calls thee not to purchase fame
In keen Iambicks, but mild Anagram:
Leave writing Plays, and chuse for thy command   205
Some peacefull Province in Acrostick Land.
There thou maist wings display and Altars raise,
And torture one poor word Ten thousand ways.
Or if thou would'st thy diff'rent talants suit,
Set thy own Songs, and sing them to thy lute.   210
He said, but his last words were scarcely heard,
For *Bruce* and *Longvil* had a *Trap* prepar'd,
And down they sent the yet declaiming Bard.
Sinking he left his Drugget robe behind,
Born upwards by a subterranean wind.   215
The Mantle fell to the young Prophet's part,
With double portion of his Father's Art.

(1682)

195–196. *Tun/Kilderkin:* A tun is a large cask or barrel, used often for storing wine or beer; a kilderkin is a similar vessel, smaller in size.

212. *Bruce . . . Longvil . . . Trap:* Bruce and Longvil in Shadwell's *The Virtuoso* get rid of Sir Formal (see n. l. 168) through a trap door.

Headnote to
RELIGIO LAICI

The occasion for Dryden's *Religio Laici* was the translation by his young friend Henry Dickinson of *Histoire Critique du Vieux Testament* (1678), a rationalistic treatment of the Bible by the French scholar Richard Simon. Father Simon's learned book upset may people, because it treated the Old Testament as a literary product and insisted that no religious principles could be inferred from texts as unreliably transmitted as the scriptures had been. It was Simon's position that in such circumstances ecclesiastical authority alone could ensure religious stability.

Dryden's poem argues directly against this view by opposing the Catholic claim of infallibility as a basis for faith; it also takes the opportunity to reject sources of religious principle proposed by the deists— reason and the universality of truth, both thought by them to operate quite outside any church. It must be added that Dryden's poem is equally opposed to nonconformists, who are presumed to seek, individually, scriptural support for their prejudices. While Dryden probably longed for an infallible church, in *Religio Laici* he pronounces himself a Church of England man, led by the general light of reason and the social sense that the world needs order.

Though in 1682 Dryden could find no consolation in the point of view of Rome, he changed his mind about the authority of the Catholic Church a few years later. But this shift to Catholicism had been gradual—the steady development of a fideistic attitude, signs of which may be seen in earlier works—rather than a swift and expedient change prompted by the accession of the Catholic James II in 1685. One does well to recall that the deposition of the monarch in 1688, in favor of the Protestant William and Mary, made no difference religiously to Dryden (he remained a Catholic to his death), though it cost him a world of court preference.

The quest for order (and perhaps for personal security as well) that underlies so many of the speaker's views in *Absalom and Achitophel* is no less present in *Religio Laici*, where despite the specifically religious nature of the subject, secular matters are treated; the clear implication in both poems is that the concerns of the spirit are inescapably related to those of this world. But whereas the form and structure of *Absalom and Achitophel* encourage a literary as well as an historical appraisal of the piece, the abstractly speculative and pedagogic language of *Religio Laici* may give the modern reader and critic pause. As if anticipating such a response, Dryden himself (in his preface to the poem) comments on the form of the work and on the Horatian tradition from which it derives:

> It remains that I acquaint the Reader, that the Verses were written for an ingenious young Gentleman my Friend; upon his Translation of *The Critical History of the Old Testament*, compos'd by the learned Father Simon: The Verses therefore are address'd to the Translatour of that Work, and the style of them is, what it ought to be, Epistolary.
>
> If any one be so lamentable a Critique as to require the Smoothness, the Numbers and the Turn of Heroick Poetry in this Poem; I must tell him, that if he has not read Horace, I have studied him, and hope the style of his Epistles is not ill imitated here. The Expressions of a Poem, design'd purely for Instruction, ought to be Plain and Natural, and yet Majestick: for here the Poet is presum'd to be a kind of Law-giver, and those three qualities which I have nam'd are proper to the Legislative style. The Florid, Elevated and Figurative way is for the Passions; for Love and Hatred, Fear and Anger, are begotten in the Soul by shewing their Objects out of their true proportion; either greater than the Life, or less; but Instruction is to be given by shewing them what they naturally are. A Man is to be cheated into Passion, but to be reason'd into Truth.

TEXT. *Religio Laici or a Layman's Faith. A Poem* (London, 1682).

Religio Laici
Or, A Layman's Faith

DIM as the borrow'd beams of Moon and Stars
To *lonely, weary, wandering* Travellers,
Is *Reason* to the *Soul*: And as on high
Those rowling Fires *discover* but the Sky,
Not light us *here*, So *Reason's* glimmering Ray   5
Was lent, not to *assure* our *doubtfull* way,
But *guide* us upward to a *better Day*.
And as those nightly Tapers disappear
When Day's bright Lord ascends our Hemisphere,
So pale grows *Reason* at *Religions* sight,   10
So *dyes*, and so *dissolves* in *Supernatural Light*.

Some few, whose Lamp shone brighter, have been led
From Cause to Cause, to *Nature's* secret head;
And found that *one first principle* must be:
But *what*, or *who*, that *UNIVERSAL HE*;   15
Whether some *Soul* incompassing this Ball
Unmade, unmov'd, yet *making, moving All*;
Or various *Atoms* interfering Dance
Leapt into *Form* (the Noble work of *Chance*);
Or this great *All* was from *Eternity*;   20
Not ev'n the *Stagirite* himself could see;
And *Epicurus Guess'd* as well as He:
As *blindly grop'd* they for a *future State*;

Opinions of the several Sects of Philosophers concerning the Summum Bonum.

As *rashly Judg'd* of *Providnce* and *Fate*:
But least of all could their Endeavours find   25
What most concern'd the good of Humane kind:
For *Happiness* was never to be found;
But vanish'd from 'em, like Enchanted ground.
One thought *Content* the Good to be enjoy'd;
This, every little *Accident* destroy'd: 30
The *wiser Madmen* did for *Vertue* toyl:
A Thorny, or at best a barren Soil:
In *Pleasure* some their glutton Souls would steep;
But found their Line too short, the Well too deep;
And leaky Vessels which no *Bliss* cou'd keep   35
Thus, *anxious Thoughts* in *endless Circles* roul,
Without a *Centre* where to fix the *Soul*:
In this wilde Maze their vain Endeavours end.
How can the *less* the *Greater* comprehend?
Or *finite Reason* reach *Infinity*?   40
For what cou'd *Fathom GOD* were *more* than *He*.

The *Deist* thinks he stands on firmer ground;   *Systeme of Deisme.*
Cries ἔυρεκα! the mighty Secret's found:
God is that *Spring of Good*; *Supreme*, and *Best*;
We, made to *serve*, and in that Service *blest*;   45
If so, some *Rules* of Worship must be given,
Distributed alike to all by Heaven:
Else *God* were *partial*, and to *some* deny'd
The Means his Justice shou'd for *all* provide.
This *general Worship* is to *PRAISE* and *PRAY*:   50
One part to *borrow* Blessings, one to *pay*:
And when frail Nature slides into *Offence*,

---

21. *Stagirite:* Aristotle.
22. *Epicurus:* Greek philosopher (c. 341–270 B.C.) who held that the universe results from the collision (Dryden's "interfering Dance," l. 18) and fusion of atoms

43. ἔυρεκα: The form is actually εὕρηκα; that is, *eureka*, "I have found [it]," said to be the cry of Archimedes when he discovered a means of determining the purity of gold.

The *Sacrifice* for *Crimes* is *Penitence.*
Yet since th' Effects of Providence we find
Are variously dispens'd to Humane kind;   55
That *Vice Triumphs,* and *Vertue suffers* here
(A Brand that Sovereign Justice cannot bear),
Our Reason prompts us to a *future* State:
The *last Appeal* from *Fortune* and from *Fate*:
Where God's all-righteous ways will be declar'd;   60
The *Bad* meet *Punishment,* the *Good, Reward.*

   Thus Man by his own strength to Heaven wou'd soar,
And wou'd not be Oblig'd to God for more.
Vain, wretched Creature, how art thou misled   *Of Re-*   65
To think thy Wit these God-like Notions bred !   *veal'd*
These Truths are not the product of thy Mind,   *Religion.*
But dropt from Heaven, and of a Nobler kind.
Reveal'd Religion first inform'd thy Sight,
And *Reason* saw not, till *Faith* sprung the Light.
Hence all thy *Natural Worship* takes the *Source*:   70
'Tis *Revelation* what thou think'st *Discourse.*
Else, how com'st *Thou* to see these truths so clear,
Which so obscure to *Heathens* did appear?
Not *Plato* these, nor *Aristotle* found:
Nor He whose Wisedom *Oracles* renown'd.   *Socrates.*   75
Hast thou a Wit so deep, or so sublime,
Or canst thou lower dive, or higher climb?
Canst *Thou,* by *Reason,* more of *God-head* know
Than *Plutarch, Seneca,* or *Cicero*?
Those *Gyant Wits,* in happyer Ages born,   80
(When *Arms,* and *Arts* did *Greece* and *Rome* adorn)
Knew no such *Systeme:* no such Piles cou'd raise
Of *Natural Worship,* built on *Pray'r* and *Praise,*
To One sole GOD.
Nor did Remorse, to Expiate Sin, prescribe: 85
But slew their fellow Creatures for a Bribe:
The guiltless *Victim* groan'd for their Offence;
And *Cruelty,* and *Blood* was *Penitence.*
If *Sheep* and *Oxen* cou'd Attone for Men
Ah ! at how cheap a rate the *Rich* might Sin !   90
And great Oppressours might Heaven's Wrath beguile
By offering his own Creatures for a Spoil !

   Dar'st thou, poor Worm, offend *Infinity*?
And must the Terms of Peace be given by *Thee*?
Then *Thou* art *Justice* in the *last Appeal*;   95
Thy easie God instructs Thee to *rebell*:
And like a King remote and weak, must take
What Satisfaction *Thou* art pleas'd to make.

But if there be a *Pow'r* too *Just* and *strong*
To wink at *Crimes* and bear unpunish'd *Wrong*;   100
Look humbly upward, see his Will disclose
The *Forfeit* first, and then the *Fine* impose:
A *Mulct thy* Poverty cou'd never pay
Had not *Eternal Wisedom* found the way:
And with Cœlestial Wealth supply'd thy Store: 105
His Justice makes the *Fine*, his *Mercy* quits the *Score*.
See God descending in thy Humane Frame;
Th' *offended*, suff'ring in th' *Offender's* Name:
All thy Misdeeds to him imputed see,
And all his Righteousness devolv'd on thee.   110

    For granting we have Sin'd, and that th'offence
Of *Man* is made against *Omnipotence*,
Some Price, that bears *proportion*, must be paid,
And *Infinite* with *Infinite* be weigh'd.
See then the *Deist lost: Remorse* for *Vice*,   115
Not paid, or *paid, inadequate* in price:
What farther means can *Reason* now direct,
Or what Relief from *humane Wit* expect?
That shews us *sick*; and sadly are we sure
Still to be *Sick*, till *Heav'n* reveal the *Cure*:   120
If then *Heaven's Will* must needs be understood,
(Which must, if we want *Cure*, and *Heaven* be *Good*),
Let all Records of *Will reveal'd* be shown;
With *Scripture*, all in equal ballance thrown,
And *our one Sacred Book* will be *That one*.   125

    Proof needs not here, for whether we compare
That Impious, Idle, Superstitious Ware
Of *Rites, Lustrations, Offerings* (which before,
In various Ages, various Countries bore)
With *Christian Faith* and *Vertues*, we shall find   130
None answ'ring the great ends of humane kind
But *This one Rule of Life: That* shews us best
How *God* may be *appeas'd*, and *Mortals* blest.
Whether from length of *Time* its worth we draw,
The *World* is scarce more *Ancient* than the *Law*:   135
Heav'ns early Care prescrib'd for every Age;
First, in the *Soul*, and after, in the *Page*.
Or, whether more abstractedly we look,
Or on the *Writers*, or the *written Book*,
Whence, but from *Heav'n*, cou'd men unskill'd in Arts,   140
In several Ages born, in several parts,

Weave such *agreeing Truths*? or *how*, or *why*
Shou'd *all* conspire to cheat us with a *Lye*?
Unask'd their *Pains*, *ungratefull* their *Advice*,
Starving their *Gain*, and *Martyrdom* their *Price*.   145

    If on the Book it self we cast our view,
Concurrent Heathens prove the Story *True*:
The *Doctrine*, *Miracles*; which must convince,
For *Heav'n* in *Them* appeals to *humane Sense*:
And though they *prove* not, they *Confirm* the Cause,   150
When what is *Taught* agrees with *Nature's Laws*.

    Then for the *Style; Majestick* and *Divine*,
It speaks no less than God in every Line:
Commanding words; whose *Force* is still the same
As the first *Fiat* that produc'd our Frame.   155
All Faiths *beside*, or did by *Arms* ascend,
Or *Sense* indulg'd has made *Mankind* their *Friend*:
This *onely* Doctrine does our *Lusts* oppose:
Unfed by Nature's Soil, in which it grows;
Cross to our *Interests*, curbing Sense, and Sin;   160
Oppress'd without, and undermin'd within,
It thrives through pain; its own Tormentours tires;
And with a stubborn patience still aspires.
To what can *Reason* such *Effects* assign
Transcending *Nature*, but to *Laws Divine*?   165
Which in that Sacred Volume are contain'd;
Sufficient, clear, and for that use ordain'd.

    But stay: the *Deist* here will urge anew,   *Objection*
No *Supernatural Worship* can be *True*:   *of the*
Because a *general Law* is that alone   *Deist.*
Which must to *all*, and every *where* be known: 170
A Style so large as not *this* Book can claim
Nor ought that bears *reveal'd* Religions *Name*.
'Tis said the sound of a *Messiah's Birth*
Is gone through all the habitable Earth: 175
But still that Text must be confin'd alone
To what was *Then* inhabited and known:
And what Provision cou'd from *thence* accrue
To *Indian* Souls, and Worlds discover'd *New*?
In other parts it helps, that Ages past,   180
The Scriptures there were *known*, and were *imbrac'd*,
Till Sin spread once again the Shades of Night:
What's that to these who never *saw* the Light?

The Ob-jection answer'd.   Of all Objections this indeed is chief
                  To startle Reason, stagger frail Belief: 185
                  We grant, 'tis true, that Heav'n from humane Sense
                  Has hid the secret paths of *Providence*:
                  But *boundless Wisedom, boundless Mercy*, may
                  Find ev'n for those *be-wildred* Souls, a *way*:
                  If from his *Nature Foes* may Pity claim,   190
                  Much more may *Strangers* who ne'er heard his *Name.*
                  And though *no Name* be for *Salvation* known,
                  But that of his *Eternal Sons* alone;
                  Who knows how far transcending Goodness can
                  Extend the *Merits* of *that Son* to *Man?*   195
                  Who knows what *Reasons* may his *Mercy* lead;
                  Or *Ignorance invincible* may plead?
                  Not onely *Charity* bids hope the *best*,
                  But *more* the great Apostle has exprest:
                  That if the Gentiles (whom no Law inspir'd),   200
                  By Nature did what was by *Law requir'd*;
                  They, who the written Rule had never known,
                  Were to themselves both Rule and Law alone:
                  To Nature's plain indictment they shall plead;
                  And, by their Conscience, be condemn'd or freed.   205
                  Most righteous Doom! because a *Rule reveal'd*
                  Is *none* to *Those* from whom it was *conceal'd.*
                  Then those who follow'd *Reason's* Dictates right;
                  Liv'd up, and lifted high their *Natural Light*;
                  With *Socrates* may see their Maker's Face,   210
                  While Thousand *Rubrick-Martyrs* want a place.

                  Nor does it baulk my *Charity* to find
                  Th' *Egyptian* Bishop of another mind:
                  For though his *Creed Eternal Truth* contains,
                  'Tis hard for *Man* to doom to *endless pains*   215
                  All who believ'd not all his Zeal requir'd;
                  Unless he first cou'd prove he was inspir'd.
                  Then let us either think he meant to say
                  This Faith, where *publish'd,* was the onely way;
                  Or else conclude that, *Arius* to confute,   220
                  The good Old Man, too eager in dispute,
                  Flew high; and as his *Christian* Fury rose,
                  Damn'd all for *Hereticks* who durst *oppose.*

206. *Doom:* The word means judgment and had in Dryden's day not yet acquired the connotation of unhappy destiny.

211. *Rubrick-Martyrs:* The martyrs included in the calendar of saints.

213. *Egyptian Bishop:* Athanasius (c. 296–373), a Christian leader, the steady opponent of Arius (see Dryden's l. 220), who had maintained that Christ was not the eternal son of God.

*Digres-
sion to
the
Trans-
latour of
Father
Simon's
Critical
History of
the Old
Testa-
ment.*

Thus far my Charity this path has try'd
(A much unskilfull, but well meaning guide);   225
Yet what they are, ev'n these crude thoughts were bred
By reading that, which better thou hast read.
Thy Matchless Author's work, which thou, my Friend,
By well translating better dost commend:
Those youthfull hours which, of thy Equals most   230
In *Toys* have *squander'd*, or in *Vice* have *lost*;
Those hours hast thou to Nobler use employ'd;
And the severe Delights of Truth enjoy'd.
Witness this weighty Book, in which appears
The crabbed Toil of many thoughtfull years,   235
Spent by thy Authour, in the Sifting Care
Of *Rabbins*' old Sophisticated Ware
From Gold Divine; which he who well can sort
May afterwards make *Algebra* a Sport.
A Treasure, which if *Country-Curates* buy,   240
They *Junius* and *Tremellius* may defy:
Save pains in various readings, and Translations,
And without *Hebrew* make most learn'd quotations.
A Work so full with various Learning fraught,
So nicely pondred, yet so strongly wrought,   245
As Nature's height and Art's last hand requir'd:
As much as Man cou'd compass, uninspir'd.
Where we may see what *Errours* have been made
Both in the *Copier's* and *Translater's Trade*:
How *Jewish*, *Popish* Interests have prevail'd,   250
And where *Infallibility* has *fail'd*.

For some, who have his secret meaning ghes'd,
Have found our Authour not too *much* a *Priest*:
For *Fashion-sake* he seems to have recourse
To *Pope*, and *Councils*, and *Tradition's* force: 255
But he that *old* Traditions cou'd subdue,
Cou'd not but find the weakness of the *New*:
If *Scripture*, though deriv'd from *heav'nly birth*,
Has been but carelesly preserv'd on *Earth*;
If *God's own People*, who of *God* before   260
Knew what we know, and had been promis'd more,
In fuller Terms, of Heaven's assisting Care,
And who did neither *Time* nor *Study* spare
To keep this Book *untainted*, *unperplext*;
Let in gross *Errours* to corrupt the *Text*:   265
Omitted *paragraphs*, embroyl'd the *Sense*;
With vain *Traditions* stopt the gaping Fence,

241. *Junius and Tremellius:* Franz   Emanuel Tremellius (1510–1580) trans-
Junius (1545–1602), who together with   lated the Bible into Latin.

Which every common hand pull'd up with ease:
What Safety from such *brushwood-helps* as these?
If *written words* from time are not secur'd,   270
How can we think have *oral Sounds* endur'd?
Which *thus* transmitted, if *one* Mouth has fail'd,
Immortal Lyes on *Ages* are intail'd:
And that some such have been is prov'd too plain;
If we consider *Interest*, *Church*, and *Gain*.   275

"Oh, but," says one, "*Tradition* set aside,   *Of the*
Where can we hope for an *unerring Guid*?   *Infalli-*
                                                       bility of
For since th' *original* Scripture has been lost,   *Tradi-*
All Copies *disagreeing*, *maim'd* the *most*,   *tion, in*
                                                       General.
Or *Christian Faith* can have no *certain* ground,   280
Or *Truth* in *Church Tradition* must be found."

Such an *Omniscient* Church we wish indeed;
'Twere worth *Both* *Testaments*, and cast in the *Creed*:
But if *this Mother* be a *Guid* so sure,
As can all *doubts resolve*, all *truth secure*,   285
Then her *Infallibility*, as well
Where Copies are *corrupt*, or *lame*, can tell;
Restore *lost Canon* with as little pains,
As *truly explicate* what still *remains*:
Which yet no *Council* dare *pretend* to doe;   ⎫   290
Unless like *Esdras* they cou'd *write* it new: ⎬
Strange Confidence, still to *interpret* true,   ⎭
Yet not be sure that all they have explain'd,
Is in the blest *Original* contain'd.
More Safe, and much more modest 'tis to say   295
God wou'd not leave Mankind without a way:
And that the *Scriptures*, though not *every where*
Free from Corruption, or intire, or clear,
Are uncorrupt, sufficient, clear, intire,
In *all* things which our needfull *Faith* require.   300
If *others* in the *same Glass better* see
'Tis for *Themselves* they look, but not for *me*:
For *MY* Salvation must its Doom receive
Not from what *OTHERS* but what *I* believe.

Must *all Tradition* then be set aside?   *Objec-*   305
This to affirm were Ignorance, or Pride.   *tion in*
                                                    behalf of
Are there not many points, some needfull sure   *Tradi-*
To saving Faith, that Scripture leaves obscure?   *tion;*
Which every Sect will wrest a several way   *urg'd by*
                                                    Father
(For what *one* Sect Interprets, *all* Sects *may*); *Simon.*   310

291. *Esdras:* In II Esdras 14 (The Apo-   Ezra) shall write "all that has happened in
crypha) Moses agrees that Esdras (or   the world since the beginning."

We hold, and say we prove from Scripture plain, ⎫
That *Christ* is *GOD*; the bold *Socinian*   ⎬
From the *same* Scripture urges he's but *MAN*. ⎭
Now what Appeal can end th' important Suit;
Both parts *talk* loudly, but the *Rule* is *mute*?   315

   Shall I speak plain, and in a Nation free
Assume an honest *Layman's Liberty*?
I think (according to my little Skill,
To my own Mother-Church submitting still)
That many have been sav'd, and many may,   320
Who never heard this Question brought in play.
Th' *unletter'd* Christian, who believes in *gross*,
Plods on to *Heaven*, and ne'er is at a loss:
For the *Streight-gate* wou'd be made *streighter* yet,
Were *none* admitted there but men of *Wit*.   325
The few, by Nature form'd, with Learning fraught,
Born to instruct, as others to be taught,
Must Study well the Sacred Page, and see
Which Doctrine, this, or that, does best agree
With the whole Tenour of the Work Divine: 330
And plainlyest points to Heaven's reveal'd Design:
Which Exposition flows from *genuine Sense*;
And which is *forc'd* by *Wit* and *Eloquence*.
Not that Tradition's parts are useless here:
When general, old, disinteress'd and clear: 335
That Ancient Fathers thus expound the Page,
Gives *Truth* the reverend Majesty of *Age*:
Confirms its force, by biding every *Test*;
For best *Authority's* next *Rules* are *best*.
And still the nearer to the Spring we go,   340
More limpid, more unsoyl'd the Waters flow.
Thus, *first Traditions* were a proof alone;
Cou'd we be *certain* such they *were*, so *known*:
But since some Flaws in long descent may be,
They make not *Truth* but *Probability*.   345
Even *Arius* and *Pelagius* durst provoke
To what the *Centuries preceding* spoke.
Such difference is there in an oft-told Tale:
But Truth by its own Sinews will prevail.

312. *Socinian:* The Italian theologian Faustus Socinius (Sozzini), a rationalist, who denied the Trinity and the divinity of Christ.

339. *Authority's:* Kinsley, p. 1937, rejects the emendation to Authorities (offered by Scott and others) and suggests this reading: "The rules of the best authority (the Fathers), being nearest (next) in time from the original texts."

346. *Arius and Pelagius durst provoke:* Both Arius (see n. l. 213 above) and Pelagius were heretics; even so, Dryden says, they may provoke—call upon—the traditions of earlier times.

Tradition *written* therefore more commends   350
Authority, than what from *Voice* descends:
And this, as perfect as its kind can be,
Rouls down to us the Sacred History:
Which, from the *Universal Church receiv'd*,
Is *try'd*, and *after*, for its *self* believ'd.   355

*The Sec-
ond Ob-
jection.*   The partial *Papists* wou'd infer from hence
                Their Church, in last resort, shou'd Judge the *Sense*,
*Answer
to the
Objection.*   But first they wou'd assume, with wondrous Art,
                Themselves to be the *whole*, who are but *part*
                Of that vast Frame, the Church; yet grant they were   360
The handers down, can they from thence infer
A right t' interpret? or wou'd they alone
Who brought the Present, claim it for their own?
The *Book's* a *Common Largess* to *Mankind*;
Not more for *them* than *every* Man design'd: 365
The *welcome News* is in the *Letter* found;
The *Carrier's* not Commission'd to *expound*.
It *speaks* it *Self*, and what it does contain,
In all things *needfull* to be *known*, is *plain*.

In times o'ergrown with Rust and Ignorance,   370
A gainfull Trade their Clergy did advance:
When want of Learning kept the *Laymen* low,
And none but *Priests* were *Authoriz'd* to *know*:
When what small Knowledge was, in them did dwell;
And he a *God* who cou'd but *Reade* or *Spell*;   375
Then *Mother Church* did mightily prevail:
She parcel'd out the Bible by *retail*:
But still *expounded* what She *sold* or *gave*;
To keep it in *her Power* to *Damn* and *Save*:
Scripture was *scarce*, and as the Market went,   380
Poor *Laymen* took *Salvation* on *Content*;
As needy men take Money, good or bad:
God's Word they had not, but the *Priest's* they had.
Yet, whate'er *false Conveyances* they made,
The *Lawyer* still was *certain* to be paid.   385
In those dark times they learn'd their knack so well,
That by long use they grew *Infallible*:
At last, a knowing Age began t'enquire
If *they* the Book, or *That* did *them* inspire:
And making narrower search they found, thô late,   390
That what they thought the *Priest's*, was *Their* Estate:
Taught by the *Will produc'd* (the written Word)
How long they had been *cheated* on *Record*.
Then every man who saw the Title fair,

Claim'd a Child's part, and put in for a Share: 395
Consulted Soberly his private good;
And sav'd himself as cheap as e'er he cou'd.

    'Tis true, my Friend (and far be Flattery hence)
This good had full as bad a Consequence:
The Book thus put in every vulgar hand,   400
Which each presum'd he best cou'd understand,
The *Common Rule* was made the *common Prey*;
And at the mercy of the *Rabble* lay.
The tender Page with horney Fists was gaul'd;
And he was gifted most that loudest baul'd: 405
The *Spirit* gave the *Doctoral Degree*:
And every member of a *Company*
Was of *his Trade*, and of the *Bible free*.
Plain *Truths* enough for needfull *use* they found;
But men wou'd still be itching to *expound*:   410
Each was ambitious of th' obscurest place,
No measure ta'n from *Knowledge*, all from GRACE.
Study and *Pains* were now no more their Care;
Texts were explain'd by *Fasting*, and by *Prayer*:
This was the Fruit the *private Spirit* brought;   415
Occasion'd by *great Zeal*, and *little Thought*.
While Crouds unlearn'd, with rude Devotion warm,
About the Sacred Viands buz and swarm,
The *Fly-blown Text* creates a *crawling Brood*;
And turns to *Maggots* what was meant for *Food*.   420
A Thousand daily Sects rise up, and dye;
A Thousand more the perish'd Race supply:
So all we make of Heaven's discover'd Will
Is not to have it, or to use it ill.
The Danger's much the same; on several Shelves,   425
If *others* wreck *us*, or *we* wreck our *selves*.

    What then remains, but, waving each Extreme,
The Tides of Ignorance, and Pride to stem?
Neither so rich a Treasure to forgo;
Nor proudly seek beyond our pow'r to know;   430
Faith is not built on disquisitions vain;
The things we *must* believe are *few* and *plain*:
But since men *will* believe more than they *need*;
And every man will make *himself* a Creed:
In doubtfull questions 'tis the safest way   435
To learn what unsuspected Ancients say:
For 'tis not likely *we* shou'd higher Soar
In search of Heav'n than *all the Church before*:
Nor can we be deceiv'd, unless we see

The *Scripture*, and the *Fathers disagree*.   440
If after all, they stand suspected still
(For no man's Faith depends upon his Will),
'Tis some Relief, that points not clearly known,
Without much hazard may be let alone:
And after hearing what our Church can say,   445
If still our Reason runs another way,
That private Reason 'tis more Just to curb,
Than by Disputes the publick Peace disturb.
For points obscure are of small use to learn:
But *Common quiet* is *Mankind's concern*.   450

   Thus have I made my own Opinions clear:
Yet neither Praise expect, nor Censure fear:
And this unpolish'd, rugged Verse I chose,
As fittest for Discourse, and nearest Prose:
For while from *Sacred Truth* I do not swerve,   455
Tom Sternhold's or *Tom Sha——ll's Rhimes* will serve.

   (1682)

456. *Tom Sternhold's or Tom Sha——ll's:* Thomas Sternhold (1500–1549), joint author of the English version of Psalms; Thomas Shadwell (c. 1642–1692), English dramatist, ridiculed by Dryden in *Mac Flecknoe*.

TO THE MEMORY OF
MR. OLDHAM

A few critics have called *To the Memory of Mr. Oldham* Dryden's most nearly perfect poem. Others further qualify their praise by saying it is the best of its kind among his works. Probably all would agree that in this elegy for his friend John Oldham, a poet who died at the early age of thirty, Dryden transforms personal feelings into poetry. He does this in part by universalizing them with references to the remote Nisus, a youth, who with Euryalus, a boy, ran a footrace in the funeral games for Anchises (*Aeneid* V, 373–441) and to Marcellus, the nephew of the emperor Augustus, dead at twenty (*Aeneid* VI, 1188–1366). This fusion of the particular and the general is again accomplished in Dryden's continuous agricultural image, developed in liness 11 through 21; that is, all the world's individual lives are part of a larger cycle of seasonal birth and death. Moreover, a different form of the same idea is reinforced throughout the poem by the narrator's two responses to Oldham, whom he first mourns much as he might a son (ll. 1–4) and therefore as a finite creature of the moment, forever lost to him; but whom he also respects as a fellow poet (ll. 4–8, 15–18, 24) and therefore as a being in a way exempt from time and (through his works) always available. The closing couplet epitomizes this double view.

TEXT. *Remains of Mr. John Oldham in Verse and Prose* (London, 1684).

To the Memory of
Mr. Oldham

FAREWEL, too little and too lately known,
Whom I began to think and call my own;
For sure our Souls were near ally'd; and thine
Cast in the same Poetick mould with mine.
One common Note on either Lyre did strike,   5

And Knaves and Fools we both abhorr'd alike:
To the same Goal did both our Studies drive,
The last set out the soonest did arrive.
Thus *Nisus* fell upon the slippery place,
While his young Friend perform'd and won the Race.   10
O early ripe! to thy abundant store
What could advancing Age have added more?
It might (what Nature never gives the young)
Have taught the numbers of thy native Tongue.
But Satyr needs not those, and Wit will shine   15
Through the harsh cadence of a rugged line.
A noble Error, and but seldom made,
When Poets are by too much force betray'd.
Thy generous fruits, though gather'd ere their prime
Still shew'd a quickness; and maturing time   20
But mellows what we write to the dull sweets of Rime.
Once more, hail and farewel; farewel thou young,
But ah too short, *Marcellus* of our Tongue;
Thy Brows with Ivy, and with Laurels bound;
But Fate and gloomy Night encompass thee around.   25

(1684)

Headnote to
THE HIND AND
THE PANTHER

Upon the death of Charles in February, 1685, his Catholic brother ascended the throne as James II of England. By January of the following year at the latest, Dryden had become a Roman Catholic. Louis I. Bredvold, in *The Intellectual Milieu of John Dryden*, demonstrates that *Religio Laici* in many ways anticipated Dryden's need for the "impregnable fortification" of Catholicism to which he retreated only a few years after writing that poem. According to Bredvold's well-grounded argument, *The Hind and the Panther* presents in verse the religious culmination of the poet's growing skepticism, anti-rationalism, and acceptance of authority, not his obeisance to the religion of the king. (See the headnote to *Religio Laici* in the present edition.)

The poem may also be thought of as an example of theological polemics presented in the time-honored form of animal fable. Though Charles Montagu, Earl of Halifax, and Matthew Prior proved the ease with which Dryden's basic allegory can be ridiculed (*The Hind and the Panther Transvers'd to the Story of the Country Mouse and the City Mouse*, 1687), it remains a fact that one who recognizes the convention of fable quickly accepts Dryden's talking animals. It would be futile to deny, however, that Dryden's allegory, in which the milk-white hind stands for the Catholic Church, the panther for the Church of England, and the bear for the Protestant independents, is now sometimes neglected. But this neglect cannot be ascribed to the poet's use of a convention that violates the literal truth—many well-regarded works like France's *Penguin Island* and Orwell's *Animal Farm* do so in similar ways. It probably results from the fact that the reader has to prepare himself to make the subject matter of the poem accessible. The political and religious tension (personal and public) that marked late seventeenth-century England is remote from the twentieth-century reader. Nevertheless, this difficulty can be met.

Other reasons for the present qualified acceptance of this poem, traditionally regarded as central to an understanding of Dryden's thought, are not hard to come by. Indeed, one may reasonably suggest limits to the value of the work as literature, however important it may be as a document in the history of ideas. Obviously the poem has the energy of abundance (its 2600-odd lines make it about twice as long as

Pope's *Essay on Man*), but it offers few signs of the vitality that shapes and controls art. In fact, most of the poem's structure derives immediately from the genre of which it is an example, rather than from more internal principles—those that seem to grow out of a work's individuality. Doubtless Dryden's ingenuity was taxed as he sought the means of stating intricate points of religious argument metered in rhyme; on the other hand his art seems too often sacrificed to his polemical need.

But the poem has strikingly good qualities, despite its inordinate length and looseness of structure. Perhaps its chief virtue is clear argument, particularly in the Second Part, where far from requiring much historical information, the reader may actually infer a great deal about the religious temper of Dryden's England. Moreover, in this section of the poem, the use of animal debate as a vehicle for theoretical argument sustains the illusion that abstract matters are being made concrete and therefore accessible. Quite different from this central section are Part I, which presents the animals and reviews the history and the problems of the institutions each represents, and Part III, which is chiefly concerned with showing the dangers of extremism in both Anglican and Catholic Churches, largely by means of analogical narratives, related by the Panther and the Hind. It seems just to say that neither of these sections achieves the integration of form and content approached by the Second Part, presented here.

At the conclusion of Part I, the Lyon (King James), "with an awfull roar," encourages the timid Hind to approach the watering place with her young, assuring her that she will not be bothered by fierce beasts. This allegorical reference to the King's Declaration of Indulgence of April, 1687 (issued to both Catholics and Dissenters and making religious choice a matter of individual conscience) sets the stage for the debate between the Hind and the Panther in Part II, for after the others have left the pool, these two walk towards the Hind's "lowly roof," exchanging views as they go.

TEXT. *The Hind and the Panther. A Poem* (London, 1687).

The Hind and the Panther

a poem

IN THREE PARTS

Antiquam exquirite matrem.
Et vera, incessu, patuit Dea.
—VIRG.*

To the Reader

 The Nation is in too high a Ferment for me to expect either fair War, or even so much as fair Quarter from a Reader of the opposite Party. All Men are engag'd either on this side or that: and tho' Conscience is the common Word, *which is given by both, yet if a Writer fall among Enemies, and cannot give the Marks of* Their *Conscience, he is knock'd down before the Reasons of his own are heard. A* Preface, *therefore, which is but a bespeaking of Favour, is altogether useless. What I desire the* Reader *should know concerning me, he will find in the Body of the Poem; if he have but the patience to peruse it. Only this Advertisement let him take before hand, which relates to the Merits of the Cause. No general Characters of Parties (call 'em either Sects or Churches) can be so fully and exactly drawn as to Comprehend all the several Members* 10 *of 'em; at least all such as are receiv'd under that Denomination. For example, there are some of the Church by Law Establish'd, who envy not Liberty of Conscience to Dissenters; as being well satisfied that, according to their own Principles, they ought not to persecute them. Yet these, by reason of their fewness, I could not distinguish from the Numbers of the rest with whom they are Embodied in one common Name: On the other side there are many of our Sects, and more indeed then I could reasonably have hop'd, who have withdrawn themselves from the Communion of the* Panther; *and embrac'd this Gracious Indulgence of His Majesty in point of Toleration. But neither to the one nor the other of these is this Satyr any way intended: 'tis aim'd only at the refractory and disobedient on either side. For those who are come over to the Royal* 20 *Party are consequently suppos'd to be out of Gunshot. Our Physicians have observ'd, that in Process of Time, some Diseases have abated of their Virulence, and have in a manner worn out their Malignity, so as to be no longer Mortal: and why may not I suppose the same concerning some of those who have formerly been Enemies to Kingly Government, As well as Catholick Religion? I hope they have now another Notion of both, as having found, by Comfortable Experience, that the Doctrine of Persecution is far from being an Article of our Faith.*

---

 * *Antiquam exquirite matrem:* Aeneid III, 96. Seek your ancient mother. *Et vera, incessu, patuit Dea:* Aeneid I, 405. The goddess is known by her stately movement.

61

'Tis not for any Private Man to Censure the Proceedings of a Foreign Prince:[1] *but, without suspicion of Flattery, I may praise our own, who has taken contrary Measures, and those more suitable to the Spirit of Christianity. Some of the Dissenters in their Addresses to His Majesty have said* That he has restor'd God to his Empire over Conscience: *I Confess I dare not stretch the Figure to so great a boldness: but I may safely say, that Conscience is the Royalty and Prerogative of every Private man. He is absolute in his own Breast, and accountable to no Earthly Power, for that which passes only betwixt God and Him. Those who are driven into the Fold are, generally speaking, rather made Hypocrites then Converts.*

This Indulgence being granted to all the Sects, it ought in reason to be expected, 10 *that they should both receive it, and receive it thankfully. For at this time of day to refuse the Benefit, and adhere to those whom they have esteem'd their Persecutors, what is it else, but publickly to own that they suffer'd not before for Conscience sake; but only out of Pride and Obstinacy to separate from a Church for those Impositions, which they now judge may be lawfully obey'd? After they have so long contended for their Classical Ordination (not to speak of Rites and Ceremonies) will they at length submit to an Episcopal? if they can go so far out of Complaisance to their old Enemies, methinks a little reason should perswade 'em to take another step, and see whether that wou'd lead 'em.*

Of the receiving this Toleration thankfully, I shall say no more, than that they 20 *ought, and I doubt not they will consider from what hands they receiv'd it. 'Tis not from a* Cyrus, *a Heathen Prince, and a Foreigner, but from a Christian King, their Native Sovereign; who expects a Return in* Specie *from them; that the Kindness which He has Graciously shown them may be retaliated on those of his own perswasion.*

As for the Poem in general, I will only thus far satisfie the Reader: That it was neither impos'd on me, nor so much as the Subject given me by any man. It was written during the last Winter and the beginning of this Spring; though with long interruptions of ill health, and other hindrances. About a Fortnight before I had finish'd it, His Majesties Declaration for Liberty of Conscience came abroad: which, if I had so soon expected, I might have spar'd my self the labour of writing many things which are 30 *contain'd in the third part of it. But I was alwayes in some hope, that the Church of* England *might have been perswaded to have taken off the* Penal Lawes *and the* Test, *which was one Design of the Poem when I propos'd to my self the writing of it.*

'Tis evident that some part of it was only occasional, & not first intended. I mean that defence of my self, to which every honest man is bound, when he is injuriously attacqu'd in Print: and I refer my self to the judgment of those who have read the An-swer to the Defence of the late King's Papers, and that of the Dutchess[2] *(in which*

---

[1] *Proceedings of a Foreign Prince:* In October, 1685, Louis XIV revoked the Edict of Nantes (1598), which had guaranteed certain religious rights to the Huguenots; as a result these French Protestants migrated to England, where they were well received.

[2] *"Answer to the Defence of the late King's Papers," and that of the "Dutchess":* Three papers, two supposed to be by Charles II and the third by Anne Hyde, Duchess of York, deceased first wife of James, were ordered printed by the King in 1686; they were defenses of Catholicism. The Dean of St. Paul's, Stillingfleet, wrote *An Answer* to the third of these, in which the Duchess explained her conversion to Catholicism. Then the Roman Catholics produced *A Defense of the Papers. . .* , part of which Dryden wrote. Finally, Stillingfleet replied with *A Vindication of the Answer to some Late Papers . . .* , which Dryden here refers to as the *Answer to the Defence. . . .*

last I was concerned) *how charitably I have been represented there. I am now inform'd both of the Author and Supervisers of his Pamphlet: and will reply when I think he can affront me: for I am of* Socrates's *Opinion that all Creatures cannot. In the mean time let him consider, whether he deserv'd not a more severe reprehension then I gave him formerly; for using so little respect to the Memory of those whom he pretended to answer: and, at his leisure look out for some Original Treatise of Humility, written by any Protestant in English* (*I believe I may say in any other Tongue*); *for the magnified Piece of* Duncomb *on that Subject, which either be must mean or none, and with which another of his Fellows has upbraided me, was Translated from the Spanish of* Rodriguez:[3] *tho' with the Omission of the* 17th, *the* 24th, *the* 25th, *and the last Chapter,* 10 *which will be found in comparing of the Books.*

He would have insinuated to the World that Her late Highness died not a Roman Catholick: He declares himself to be now satisfied to the contrary; in which he has giv'n up the Cause: for matter of Fact was the Principal Debate betwixt us. In the mean time he would dispute the Motives of her Change: how prepostrously let all men judge, when he seem'd to deny the Subject of the Controversy, the Change it self. And because I would not take up this ridiculous Challenge, he tells the World I cannot argue: but he may as well infer that a Catholick can not fast, because he will not take up the Cudgels against Mrs. James,[4] *to confute the Protestant Religion.*

I have but one word more to say concerning the Poem as such, and abstracting from 20 *the Matters either Religious or Civil which are handled in it. The first part, consisting most in general Characters and Narration, I have endeavour'd to raise, and give it the Majestick Turn of Heroick Poesie. The second, being Matter of Dispute, and chiefly concerning Church Authority, I was oblig'd to make as plain and perspicuous as possibly I cou'd: yet not wholly neglecting the Numbers, though I had not frequent occasions for the Magnificence of Verse. The third, which has more of the Nature of Domestick Conversation, is, or ought to be more free and familiar than the two former.*

There are in it two Episodes, *or* Fables, *which are interwoven with the main Design; so that they are properly parts of it, though they are also distinct Stories of themselves. In both of these I have made use of the Common Places of* Satyr, *whether true or false,* 30 *which are urg'd by the Members of the one Church against the other. At which I hope no* Reader *of either Party will be scandaliz'd; because they are not of my Invention: but as old, to my knowledge, as the Times of* Boccace *and* Chawcer *on the one side, and as those of the Reformation on the other.*

[3] *Duncomb ... Translated ... Spanish ... Rodriguez:* In his part of the *Defense,* Dryden charged that Protestants knew nothing about humility and indeed had no books on the subject. Stillingfleet claimed that such a book had appeared shortly before, referring probably to such a work by a certain William Allen. Dryden's reference to this "piece of Duncomb" as a translation from the Spanish seems to be his literal or metaphoric rejection of the Dean's claim.

[4] *Mrs. James:* Kinsley, p. 1970, says "Elinor James, widow of a London printer, was the author of Mrs. James's *Vindication of the Church of England* (1687) and a religious eccentric."

The Hind and the Panther

The Second Part

DAME, said the *Panther*, times are mended well
Since late among the *Philistines* you fell;
The toils were pitch'd, a spacious tract of ground
With expert hunts-men was encompass'd round;
Th' Enclosure narrow'd; the sagacious pow'r   5
Of hounds and death, drew nearer ev'ry hour.
'Tis true, the younger *Lyon* scap'd the snare,
But all your priestly calves lay strugling there;
As sacrifices on their Altars laid;
While you their carefull mother wisely fled,   10
Not trusting destiny to save your head.
For what e'er promises you have apply'd
To your unfailing church, the surer side
Is four fair leggs in danger to provide.
And what e'er tales of *Peter's* chair you tell,   15
Yet, saving reverence of the miracle,
The better luck was yours to 'scape so well.

   As I remember, said the sober *Hind*,
Those toils were for your own dear self design'd,
As well as me; and, with the self same throw,   20
To catch the quarry, and the vermin too
(Forgive the sland'rous tongues that call'd you so).
How e'er you take it now, the common cry
Then ran you down for your rank loyalty;
Besides, in Popery they thought you nurst   25
(As evil tongues will ever speak the worst),
Because some forms, and ceremonies some
You kept, and stood in the main question dumb.
Dumb you were born indeed, but thinking long
The *Test* it seems at last has loos'd your tongue.   30
And, to explain what your forefathers meant,
By real presence in the sacrament
(After long fencing push'd, against a wall),
Your *salvo* comes, that he's not there at all:
There chang'd your faith, and what may change may fall.   35

2. *Philistines:* All those who, like Titus Oates (see the headnote to *Absalom and Achitophel*), sought the reduction of the Roman Catholic Church in England.

7. *Younger Lyon:* The reference is to James when he was Duke of York.

30. *The Test:* In 1673, Parliament passed a bill to exclude from military and civil office anyone who would not take the oath of allegiance and supremacy, or who would not receive communion in the Anglican Church, or who would not renounce belief in transubstantiation. Directed against Catholics, it affected all non-Anglicans. In 1678, the bill was extended to Parliament, which it had not earlier included.

34. *Salvo:* A quibbling excuse.

Who can believe what varies every day,
Nor ever was, nor will be at a stay?

    Tortures may force the tongue untruths to tell,
And I ne'er own'd my self infallible,
Reply'd the *Panther*; grant such Presence were,   40
Yet in your sense I never own'd it there.
A real *vertue* we by faith receive,
And that we in the sacrament believe.

    Then said the *Hind*, as you the matter state
Not onely *Jesuits* can equivocate;   45
For *real*, as you now the word expound,
From solid substance dwindles to a sound.
Methinks an *Æsop's* fable you repeat;
You know who took the shadow for the meat:
Your churches substance thus you change at will,   50
And yet retain your former figure still.
I freely grant you spoke to save your life,
For then you lay beneath the butcher's knife.
Long time you fought, redoubl'd batt'ry bore,
But, after all, against your self you swore;   55
Your former self, for ev'ry hour your form
Is chop'd and chang'd, like winds before a storm.
Thus fear and int'rest will prevail with some,
For all have not the gift of martyrdome.

    The *Panther* grin'd at this, and thus reply'd;   60
That men may err was never yet deny'd.
But, if that common principle be true,
The Cannon, Dame, is level'd full at you.
But, shunning long disputes, I fain wou'd see
That wond'rous wight infallibility.   65
Is he from heav'n this mighty champion come,
Or lodg'd below in subterranean *Rome*?
First, seat him somewhere, and derive his race,
Or else conclude that nothing has no place.

    Suppose (though I disown it) said the *Hind*,   70
The certain mansion were not yet assign'd,
The doubtfull residence no proof can bring
Against the plain existence of the thing.
Because *Philosophers* may disagree,
If sight b'emission or reception be,   75
Shall it be thence inferr'd, I do not see?

67. *Subterranean Rome*: Double enten-   p. 1975, n. 67) and to the reputed clandes-
dre referring to the catacombs (cf. Kinsley,   tine maneuvering of the Roman Church.

But you require an answer positive,
Which yet, when I demand, you dare not give,
For fallacies in Universals live.
I then affirm that this unfailing guide   80
In Pope and gen'ral councils must reside;
Both lawfull, both combin'd, what one decrees
By numerous votes, the other ratifies:
On this undoubted sense the church relies.
'Tis true, some Doctours in a scantier space,   85
I mean in each apart contract the place.
Some, who to greater length extend the line,
The churches after acceptation join.
This last circumference appears too wide,
The church diffus'd is by the council ty'd;   90
As members by their representatives
Oblig'd to laws which Prince and Senate gives:
Thus some contract, and some enlarge the space;
In Pope and council who denies the place,
Assisted from above with God's unfailing grace?   95
Those Canons all the needfull points contain;
Their sense so obvious, and their words so plain,
That no disputes about the doubtfull Text
Have, hitherto, the lab'ring world perplex'd:
If any shou'd in after times appear,   100
New Councils must be call'd, to make the meaning clear.
Because in them the pow'r supreme resides;
And all the promises are to the guides.
This may be taught with sound and safe defence:
But mark how sandy is your own pretence,   105
Who setting Councils, Pope, and Church aside,
Are ev'ry man his own presuming guide.
The sacred books, you say, are full and plain,
And ev'ry needfull point of truth contain:
All who can read, Interpreters may be: 110
Thus though your sev'ral churches disagree,
Yet ev'ry Saint has to himself alone
The secret of this Philosophick stone.
These principles your jarring sects unite,
When diff'ring Doctours and disciples fight.   115
Though *Luther, Zuinglius, Calvin*, holy chiefs,
Have made a battel Royal of beliefs;
Or like wild horses sev'ral ways have whirl'd

---

85. *Doctours in a scantier space:* The discussion here and following speculates about attempts to fix the locus of Church power.
    116. *Luther, Zuinglius, Calvin:* Martin Luther (1483–1546), Huldreich Zwingli (1484–1531), and John Calvin (1509–1564), three of the most influential Protestants of the Reformation.

The tortur'd Text about the christian World;
Each *Jehu* lashing on with furious force,   120
That *Turk* or *Jew* cou'd not have us'd it worse.
No matter what dissention leaders make
Where ev'ry private man may save a stake,
Rul'd by the Scripture and his own advice
Each has a blind by-path to Paradise;   125
Where driving in a circle slow or fast,
Opposing sects are sure to meet at last.
A wondrous charity you have in store
For all reform'd to pass the narrow door:
So much, that *Mahomet* had scarcely more.   130
For he, kind Prophet, was for damning none,
But *Christ* and *Moyses* were to save their own:
Himself was to secure his chosen race,
Though reason good for *Turks* to take the place,
And he allow'd to be the better man   135
In virtue of his holier *Alcoran*.

    True, said the *Panther*, I shall ne'er deny
My breth'ren may be sav'd as well as I:
Though *Huguenots* contemn our ordination,
Succession, ministerial vocation,   140
And *Luther*, more mistaking what he read,
Misjoins the sacred Body with the Bread;
Yet, *Lady*, still remember I maintain,
The Word in needfull points is onely plain.

    Needless or needfull I not now contend,   145
For still you have a loop-hole for a friend
(Rejoyn'd the Matron) but the rule you lay
Has led whole flocks, and leads them still astray
In weighty points, and full damnation's way.
For did not *Arius* first, *Socinus* now,   150
The Son's eternal god-head disavow;
And did not these by Gospel Texts alone
Condemn our doctrine, and maintain their own?
Have not all hereticks the same pretence
To plead the Scriptures in their own defence?   155

120. *Jehu:* The son of Nimshi, who in II Kings 9:20 is said to drive furiously.

136. *Alcoran:* Koran, the sacred book of Islam, supposed to have been revealed by God to Mohammed.

139. *Huguenots:* French Protestants; members of the Reformed or Calvinist Communion.

141–142. *Luther . . . misjoins:* In 1529, Luther, at the conference at Marburg, maintained his views as to the Real Presence in the Eucharist. This belief in Con-substantiation—the actual substantial presence of Christ with the bread and wine of Communion—is to be distinguished from Transubstantiation—the change of bread and wine to the body and blood of Christ, but without a change in their appearance.

150. *Arius, Socinus:* See n. ll. 312, 346 in *Religio Laici*.

How did the *Nicene* council then decide
That strong debate, was it by Scripture try'd?
No, sure to those the Rebel would not yield,
Squadrons of Texts he marshal'd in the field;
That was but civil war, an equal set,   160
Where Piles with piles, and eagles Eagles met.
With Texts point-blank and plain he fac'd the Foe:
And did not *Sathan* tempt our Saviour so?
The good old Bishops took a simpler way,
Each ask'd but what he heard his Father say,   165
Or how he was instructed in his youth,
And by traditions force upheld the truth.

The *Panther* smil'd at this, and when, said she,
Were those first Councils disallow'd by me?
Or where did I at sure tradition strike,   170
Provided still it were Apostolick?

Friend, said the *Hind*, you quit your former ground,
Where all your Faith you did on Scripture found;
Now 'tis tradition join'd with holy writ,
But thus your memory betrays your wit.   175

No, said the *Panther*, for in that I view,
When your tradition's forg'd, and when 'tis true.
I set 'em by the rule, and as they square
Or deviate from undoubted doctrine there
This Oral fiction, that old Faith declare.   180

(*Hind*.) The Council steer'd it seems a diff'rent course;
They try'd the Scripture by tradition's force;
But you tradition by the Scripture try;
Pursu'd, by Sects, from this to that you fly,
Nor dare on one foundation to rely.   185
The word is then depos'd, and in this view,
You rule the Scripture, not the Scripture you.
Thus said the *Dame*, and smiling, thus pursu'd,
I see tradition then is disallow'd,
When not evinc'd by Scripture to be true,   190
And Scripture, as interpreted by you.
But here you tread upon unfaithfull ground;

156. *Nicene council:* A general Council convened by Constantine in Nice in Asia Minor in 325 as a countermeasure to the Arian heresy, which maintained that Christ, though endowed with divine power, was not as God.
161. *Piles . . . Eagles:* Piles were Roman javelins; and Eagles were the standards of the Roman legions.
163. *Sathan tempt our Saviour:* See Matt. 4:1–11, Mark 1:12–13, Luke 4:1–13, where Jesus is tempted by the devil or Satan.

Unless, you cou'd infallibly expound;
Which you reject as odious Popery,
And throw that doctrine back with scorn on me.   195
Suppose we on things traditive divide,
And both appeal to Scripture to decide;
By various texts we both uphold our claim,
Nay, often ground our titles on the same:
After long labour lost, and times expence,   200
Both grant the words, and quarrel for the sense.
Thus all disputes for ever must depend;
For no dumb rule can controversies end.
Thus when you said tradition must be try'd
By Sacred Writ, whose sense your selves decide,   205
You said no more, but that your selves must be
The judges of the Scripture sense, not we.
Against our church tradition you declare
And yet your Clerks wou'd sit in *Moyses* chair:
At least 'tis prov'd against your argument,   210
The rule is far from plain, where all dissent.

   If not by Scriptures how can we be sure
(Reply'd the *Panther*) what tradition's pure?
For you may palm upon us new for old,
All, as they say, that glitters is not gold.   215

   How but by following her, reply'd the Dame,
To whom deriv'd from sire to son they came;
Where ev'ry age do's on another move,
And trusts no farther than the next above;
Where all the rounds like *Jacob's* ladder rise,   220
The lowest hid in earth, the topmost in the skyes.

   Sternly the salvage did her answer mark,
Her glowing eye' balls glitt'ring in the dark,
And said but this, since lucre was your trade,
Succeeding times such dreadfull gaps have made   225
'Tis dangerous climbing: to your sons and you
I leave the ladder, and its omen too.

   (*Hind.*) The *Panther's* breath was ever fam'd for sweet,
But from the *Wolfe* such wishes oft I meet:
You learn'd this language from the blatant beast,   230
Or rather did not speak, but were possess'd.

---

220. *Jacob's ladder:* See Gen. 28:12, where Jacob dreams of a ladder that is set up on the earth and reaches heaven.
229. *Wolfe:* Presbyterian.

230. *Blatant beast:* In *The Faerie Queene*, Spenser's beast of calumny, with a thousand tongues.

As for your answer 'tis but barely urg'd;
You must evince tradition to be forg'd;
Produce plain proofs; unblemish'd authours use
As ancient as those ages they accuse;   235
Till when 'tis not sufficient to defame:
An old possession stands, till Elder quitts the claim.
Then for our int'rest which is nam'd alone
To load with envy, we retort your own.
For when traditions in your faces fly,   240
Resolving not to yield, you must decry:
As when the cause goes hard, the guilty man
Excepts, and thins his jury all he can;
So when you stand of other aid bereft,
You to the twelve Apostles would be left.   245
Your friend the *Wolfe* did with more craft provide
To set those toys traditions quite aside:
And *Fathers* too, unless when reason spent
He cites 'em but sometimes for ornament.
But, Madam *Panther*, you, though more sincere,   250
Are not so wise as your Adulterer:
The private spirit is a better blind
Than all the dodging tricks your authours find.
For they, who left the Scripture to the crowd,
Each for his own peculiar judge allow'd;   } 255
The way to please 'em was to make 'em proud.
Thus with full sails they ran upon the shelf;
Who cou'd suspect a couzenage from himself?
On his own reason safer 'tis to stand,
Than be deceiv'd and damn'd at second hand.   260
But you who *Fathers* and traditions take,
And garble some, and some you quite forsake,
Pretending church auctority to fix,
And yet some grains of private spirit mix,
Are like a *Mule* made up of diff'ring seed,   265
And that's the reason why you never breed;
At least not propagate your kind abroad,
For home-dissenters are by statutes aw'd.
And yet they grow upon you ev'ry day,   ⎫
While you (to speak the best) are at a stay;   ⎬ 270
For sects that are extremes, abhor a middle way.   ⎭
Like tricks of state, to stop a raging flood,   ⎫
Or mollify a mad-brain'd Senate's mood: ⎬
Of all expedients never one was good.   ⎭ 275
Well may they argue (nor can you deny)
If we must fix on church auctority,
Best on the best, the fountain, not the flood,

248. *Fathers:* The Fathers of the Church.

That must be better still, if this be good.
Shall she command, who has herself rebell'd?
Is *Antichrist* by *Antichrist* expell'd?   280
Did we a lawfull tyranny displace,
To set aloft a bastard of the race?
Why all these wars to win the Book, if we
Must not interpret for our selves, but she?
Either be wholly slaves or wholly free.   285
For *purging* fires traditions must not fight;
But they must prove Episcopacy's right:
Thus those led horses are from service freed;
You never mount 'em but in time of need.
Like mercenary's, hir'd for home defence,   290
They will not serve against their native Prince.
Against domestick foes of *Hierarchy*
These are drawn forth, to make fanaticks fly,
But when they see their countrey-men at hand,
Marching against 'em under church-command,   295
Straight they forsake their colours, and disband.

    Thus she, nor cou'd the *Panther* well enlarge
With weak defence against so strong a charge;
But said, for what did *Christ* his Word provide,
If still his church must want a living guide?   300
And if all saving doctrines are not there,
Or sacred Pen-men cou'd not make 'em clear,
From after ages we should hope in vain
For truths, which men inspir'd, cou'd not explain.

    Before the Word was written, said the *Hind*,   305
Our Saviour preach'd his Faith to humane kind;
From his Apostles the first age receiv'd
Eternal truth, and what they taught, believ'd.
Thus by tradition faith was planted first;
Succeeding flocks succeeding Pastours nurs'd.   310
This was the way our wise Redeemer chose
(Who sure could all things for the best dispose)
To fence his fold from their encroaching foes.
He cou'd have writ himself, but well foresaw
Th' event wou'd be like that of *Moyses* law;   315
Some difference wou'd arise, some doubts remain,
Like those, which yet the jarring *Jews* maintain.

286. *Purging fires:* Purgatory.
287. *Episcopacy's right:* The Hind
derides the Anglican view that Church
traditions cannot be used to support the

Catholic idea of purgatory by pointing
out that the Anglican Church (Episcopacy) must appeal to the same source—
traditions—for its own authority.

No written laws can be so plain, so pure,
But wit may gloss, and malice may obscure,
Not those indited by his first command,   320
A Prophet grav'd the text, an Angel held his hand.
Thus faith was e'er the written word appear'd,
And men believ'd, not what they read, but heard.
But since th' Apostles cou'd not be confin'd,
To these, or those, but severally design'd   325
Their large commission round the world to blow;
To spread their faith they spread their labours too.
Yet still their absent flock their pains did share,
They hearken'd still, for love produces care.
And as mistakes arose, or discords fell,   330
Or bold seducers taught 'em to rebell,
As charity grew cold, or faction hot,
Or long neglect, their lessons had forgot,
For all their wants they wisely did provide,
And preaching by Epistles was supply'd: 335
So great Physicians cannot all attend,
But some they visit, and to some they send.
Yet all those letters were not writ to all;
Nor first intended, but occasional:
Their absent sermons; nor if they contain   340
All needfull doctrines, are those doctrines plain.
Clearness by frequent preaching must be wrought,
They writ but seldome, but they daily taught.
And what one Saint has said of holy *Paul*,
He darkly writ, is true apply'd to all.   345
For this obscurity could heav'n provide
More prudently than by a living guide,   ⎫
As doubts arose, the difference to decide?   ⎬
A guide was therefore needfull, therefore made,   ⎭
And, if appointed, sure to be obey'd.   350
Thus, with due rev'rence, to th' Apostles writ,
By which my sons are taught, to which, submit;
I think, those truths their sacred works contain,
The church alone can certainly explain,
That following ages, leaning on the past,   355
May rest upon the Primitive at last.
Nor wou'd I thence the word no rule infer,
But none without the church interpreter.
Because, as I have urg'd before, 'tis mute,
And is it self the subject of dispute.   360

345. *He darkly writ:* II Pet. 3:16: "As
also in all [Paul's] epistles, speaking in
them of these things; in which are
some things hard to be understood. . . ."
356. *Primitive:* Original.

But what th' Apostles their successours taught,
They to the next, from them to us is brought,
Th' undoubted sense which is in scripture sought.
From hence the church is arm'd, when errours rise,
To stop their entrance, and prevent surprise;   365
And safe entrench'd within, her foes without defies.
By these all festring sores her councils heal,
Which time or has disclos'd, or shall reveal,
For discord cannot end without a last appeal.
Nor can a council national decide   370
But with subordination to her Guide
(I wish the cause were on that issue try'd);
Much less the scripture; for suppose debate
Betwixt pretenders to a fair estate,
Bequeath'd by some Legator's last intent   375
(Such is our dying Saviour's Testament):
The will is prov'd, is open'd, and is read;
The doubtfull heirs their diff'ring titles plead:
All vouch the words their int'rest to maintain,
And each pretends by those his cause is plain.   380
Shall then the testament award the right?
No, that's the *Hungary* for which they fight;
The field of battel, subject of debate,
The thing contended for, the fair estate.
The sense is intricate, 'tis onely clear   385
What vowels and what consonants are there.
Therefore 'tis plain, its meaning must be try'd
Before some judge appointed to decide.

Suppose (the fair Apostate said) I grant
The faithfull flock some living guide should want,   390
Your arguments an endless chase persue:
Produce this vaunted Leader to our view,
This mighty *Moyses* of the chosen crew.

The Dame, who saw her fainting foe retir'd,
With force renew'd, to victory aspir'd   395
(And looking upward to her kindred sky,
As once our Saviour own'd his Deity,
Pronounc'd his words—*she whom ye seek am I*).
Nor less amaz'd this voice the *Panther* heard,
Than were those *Jews* to hear a god declar'd.   400
Then thus the matron modestly renew'd;

---

382. *The Hungary for which they fight:*
The Mohammedan (Turks) and the
Christian (Austrians) armies contended for
Hungary for several hundred years.
401. *Modestly:* The first edition gives
modesty.

Let all your prophets and their sects be view'd,
And see to which of 'em your selves think fit
The conduct of your conscience to submit:
Each Proselyte wou'd vote his Doctor best,   405
With absolute exclusion to the rest:
Thus wou'd your *Polish* Diet disagree,
And end as it began in Anarchy:
Your self the fairest for election stand,
Because you seem crown-gen'ral of the land;   410
But soon against your superstitious lawn
Some Presbyterian Sabre wou'd be drawn;
In your establish'd laws of sov'raignty
The rest some fundamental flaw wou'd see,
And call Rebellion gospel-liberty.   415
To church-decrees your articles require
Submission modify'd, if not entire;
Homage deny'd, to censures you proceed;
But when *Curtana* will not doe the deed,
You lay that pointless clergy-weapon by,   420
And to the laws, your sword of justice, fly.
Now this your sects the more unkindly take
(Those prying varlets hit the blots you make)
Because some ancient friends of yours declare
Your onely rule of faith the Scriptures are,   425
Interpreted by men of judgment sound,
Which ev'ry sect will for themselves expound:
Nor think less rev'rence to their doctours due
For sound interpretation, than to you.
If then, by able heads, are understood   430
Your brother prophets, who reform'd abroad,
Those able heads expound a wiser way,
That their own sheep their shepherd shou'd obey.
But if you mean your selves are onely sound,
That doctrine turns the reformation round,   435
And all the rest are false reformers found.
Because in sundry points you stand alone,
Not in communion join'd with any one;
And therefore must be all the church, or none.
Then, till you have agreed whose judge is best,   440
Against this forc'd submission they protest:
While *sound* and *sound* a diff'rent sense explains,

---

407. *Polish Diet:* Early in the fifteenth century, the Polish gentry forced King Alexander to acknowledge the power of the Sejm, or diet, any member of which could dissolve it and even annul its earlier decisions. This *librum veto* was used with particular recklessness in Dryden's day.

419. *Curtana:* A blunted sword.
423. *Hit the blots:* A blot in Back-gammon is an exposed piece; hence to hit the blots means to take such pieces, or more generally, to move against weak points in any adversary's defense.

Both play at hard-head till they break their brains:
And from their chairs each others force defy,
While unregarded thunders vainly fly.   445
I pass the rest, because your church alone
Of all usurpers best cou'd fill the throne.
But neither you, nor any sect beside
For this high office can be qualify'd,
With necessary gifts requir'd in such a guide.   450
For that which must direct the whole, must be
Bound in one bond of faith and unity:
But all your sev'ral churches disagree.
The *Consubstantiating* church and Priest
Refuse communion to the *Calvinist*;   455
The *French* reform'd, from preaching you restrain,
Because you judge their ordination vain;
And so they judge of yours, but Donors must ordain.
In short, in doctrine, or in discipline,
Not one reform'd can with another join;   460
But all from each, as from damnation fly;
No union, they pretend, but in *Non-Popery*,
Nor shou'd their members in a synod meet;
Cou'd any church presume to mount the seat
Above the rest; their discords to decide;   465
None wou'd obey, but each wou'd be the guide:
And face to face dissentions wou'd encrease;
For onely distance now preserves the peace.
All in their turns accusers, and accus'd:
Babel was never half so much confus'd.   470
What one can plead, the rest can plead as well;
For amongst equals lies no last appeal,
And all confess themselves are fallible.
Now since you grant some necessary guide,
All who can err are justly laid aside: 475
Because a trust so sacred to confer
Shows want of such a sure interpreter:
And how can he be needfull who can err?
Then, granting that unerring guide we want,
That such there is you stand oblig'd to grant: 480
Our Saviour else were wanting to supply
Our needs, and obviate that necessity.
It then remains that church can onely be
The guide, which owns unfailing certainty;
Or else you slip your hold, and change your side,   485
Relapsing from a necessary guide.

---

454. *Consubstantiating church:* Luther-
ans. See n. ll. 141–142 above.
456. *French reform'd:* Huguenot ministers, who unless reordained could not conduct the Anglican service.

But this annex'd condition of the crown,
Immunity from errours, you disown.
Here then you shrink, and lay your weak pretensions down.
For petty royalties you raise debate;   490
But this unfailing universal state
You shun; nor dare succeed to such a glorious weight.
And for that cause those promises detest
With which our Saviour did his Church invest:
But strive t'evade, and fear to find 'em true,   495
As conscious they were never meant to you:
All which the mother church asserts her own,
And with unrivall'd claim ascends the throne.
So when of old th' Almighty father sate
In Council, to redeem our ruin'd state,   500
Millions of millions at a distance round,
Silent the sacred Consistory crown'd,
To hear what mercy mixt with justice cou'd propound.
All prompt with eager pity, to fulfill
The full extent of their Creatour's will: 505
But when the stern conditions were declar'd,
A mournfull whisper through the host was heard,
And the whole hierarchy with heads hung down
Submissively declin'd the pondrous proffer'd crown.
Then, not till then, th' eternal Son from high   510
Rose in the strength of all the Deity;
Stood forth t' accept the terms, and underwent
A weight which all the frame of heav'n had bent,
Nor he Himself cou'd bear, but as omnipotent.
Now, to remove the least remaining doubt,   515
That ev'n the blear-ey'd sects may find her out,
Behold what heav'nly rays adorn her brows,
What from his Wardrobe her belov'd allows
To deck the wedding-day of his unspotted spouse.
Behold what marks of majesty she brings;   520
Richer than ancient heirs of Eastern kings:
Her right hand holds the sceptre and the keys,
To shew whom she commands, and who obeys:
With these to bind, or set the sinner free,
With that t' assert spiritual Royalty.   525

Marks of
the Cath-
olick   One in herself not rent by schism, but sound,
Church   Entire, one solid shining Diamond,
from the   Not sparkles shatter'd into sects like you,
Nicene
Creed.   One is the church, and must be to be true:

518. *From his Wardrobe:* See Rev. 21:2:   Heaven, prepared as a bride adorned for
"And I John saw the holy city, new   her husband."
Jerusalem, coming down from God out of

One central principle of unity.   530
As undivided, so from errours free,
As one in faith, so one in sanctity.
Thus she, and none but she, th' insulting rage
Of Hereticks oppos'd from age to age:
Still when the Gyant-brood invades her throne   535
She stoops from heav'n, and meets 'em half way down,
And with paternal thunder vindicates her crown.
But like *Ægyptian* Sorcerers you stand,
And vainly lift aloft your magick wand,
To sweep away the swarms of vermin from the land;   540
You cou'd like them, with like infernal force
Produce the plague, but not arrest the course.
But when the boils and botches, with disgrace
And publick scandal sat upon the face,
Themselves attack'd, the *Magi* strove no more,   545
They saw God's finger, and their fate deplore;
Themselves they cou'd not cure of the dishonest sore.

  Thus one, thus pure, behold her largely spread
Like the fair ocean from her mother bed;
From East to West triumphantly she rides,   550
All shoars are water'd by her wealthy Tides.

  The Golspel's-sound diffus'd from Pole to Pole,
Where winds can carry, and where waves can roll.
The self same doctrine of the Sacred page
Convey'd to ev'ry clime in ev'ry age.   555

  Here let my sorrow give my satyr place,
To raise new blushes on my *British* race;
Our sayling ships like common shoars we use,
And through our distant colonies diffuse
The draughts of Dungeons, and the stench of stews.   560
Whom, when their home-bred honesty is lost,
We disembogue on some far *Indian* coast:
Thieves, Pandars, Palliards, sins of ev'ry sort,
Those are the manufactures we export;
And these the Missionaires our zeal has made: 565
For, with my countrey's pardon be it said,
Religion is the least of all our trade.

---

535. *Gyant-brood:* In Ovid, *Metamor-
phoses,* I, 151 f., Giants attack Heaven's
throne, and they are repulsed.
  538. *Ægyptian Sorcerers:* The ineffectual magicians who in Exodus 8, 9 try to
rival Moses and Aaron.
  563. *Palliards:* Vagabonds, thence
lechers.

Yet some improve their traffick more than we,
For they on gain, their onely God, rely:
And set a publick price on piety   570
Industrious of the needle and the chart,
They run full sail to their *Japponian* Mart:
Prevention fear, and prodigal of fame
Sell all of Christian to the very name;
Nor leave enough of that, to hide their naked shame.   575

Thus, of three marks which in the Creed we view,
Not one of all can be apply'd to you:
Much less the fourth; in vain alas you seek
Th' ambitious title of Apostolick:
God-like descent! 'tis well your bloud can be   580
Prov'd noble, in the third or fourth degree:
For all of ancient that you had before
(I mean what is not borrow'd from our store)
Was Errour fulminated o'er and o'er.
Old Heresies condemn'd in ages past,   585
By care and time recover'd from the blast.

'Tis said with ease, but never can be prov'd,
The church her old foundations has remov'd,
And built new doctrines, on unstable sands:
Judge that ye winds and rains; you prov'd her, yet she stands.   590
Those ancient doctrines charg'd on her for new,
Shew when, and how, and from what hands they grew.
We claim no pow'r when Heresies grow bold
To coin new faith, but still declare the old.
How else cou'd that obscene disease be purg'd   595
When controverted texts are vainly urg'd?
To prove tradition new, there's somewhat more
Requir'd, than saying, 'twas not us'd before.
Those monumental arms are never stirr'd
Till Schism or Heresie call down *Goliah's* sword.   600

Thus, what you call corruptions, are in truth,
The first plantations of the gospel's youth,

572. *Japponian Mart:* Japanese Market. Dutch merchants enjoyed exclusive trading privileges in Japan, even during the seventeenth-century persecution of Christians, because they did not involve themselves in religious matters.

576. *Creed:* The reference here is to the Nicene Creed, not to the Apostle's Creed. The "marks" the Hind says the Anglican Church may not claim are the attributes of the true Church given in the Nicene Creed, where the Church is said to be one, holy, Catholic, and apostolic. (The Anglican version of the Creed still omits "one," the result of a textual error by Archbishop Cranmer.)

600. *Goliah's sword:* See I Sam. 21:8–10, where David asks the priest Ahimelech for a weapon and receives the sword of Goliath the Philistine, whom he had slain.

Old standard faith: but cast your eyes again
And view those errours which new sects maintain
Or which of old disturb'd the churches peacefull reign,   605
And we can point each period of the time,
When they began, and who begot the crime;
Can calculate how long th' eclipse endur'd,
Who interpos'd, what digits were obscur'd:
Of all which are already pass'd away,   610
We know the rise, the progress and decay.

   Despair at our foundations then to strike
Till you can prove your faith Apostolick;
A limpid stream drawn from the native source;
Succession lawfull in a lineal course.   615
Prove any church oppos'd to this our head,
So one, so pure, so unconfin'dly spread,
Under one chief of the spiritual state,
The members all combin'd, and all subordinate.
Shew such a seamless coat, from schism so free,   620
In no communion join'd with heresie:
If such a one you find, let truth prevail:
Till when your weights will in the balance fail:
A church unprincipl'd kicks up the scale.

   But if you cannot think (nor sure you can   625
Suppose in God what were unjust in man)
That he, the fountain of eternal grace,
Should suffer falshood for so long a space
To banish truth, and to usurp her place:
That nine successive ages should be lost   630
And preach damnation at their proper cost;
That all your erring ancestours should dye,
Drown'd in th' Abyss of deep Idolatry;
If piety forbid such thoughts to rise,
Awake and open your unwilling eyes: 635
God has left nothing for each age undone
From this to that wherein he sent his Son:
Then think but well of him, and half your work is done.

   See how his church adorn'd with ev'ry grace
With open arms, a kind forgiving face,   640
Stands ready to prevent her long lost sons embrace.
Not more did *Joseph* o'er his brethren weep,
Nor less himself cou'd from discovery keep,
When in the croud of suppliants they were seen,

609. *Digits:* The diameter of the sun or moon is calibrated into twelve digits for measuring the magnitude of an eclipse.

630. *Nine successive ages:* Other editions give seav'n, not nine.

And in their crew his best beloved *Benjamin*.   645
That pious *Joseph* in the church behold,   *The re-*
To feed your famine, and refuse your gold;   *nuncia-*
                                                         tion of
The *Joseph* you exil'd, the *Joseph* whom you sold.   *the Bene-*
                                                         dictines
                                                         to the
Thus, while with heav'nly charity she spoke,   *Abby*
A streaming blaze the silent shadows broke: *Lands.*   650
Shot from the skyes a chearfull azure light;
The birds obscene to forests wing'd their flight,
And gaping graves receiv'd the wandring guilty spright.

Such were the pleasing triumphs of the sky
For *James* his late nocturnal victory: 655
The pledge of his Almighty patron's love,
The fire-works which his angel made above.
Poëta   I saw my self the lambent easie light
loquitur.   Guild the brown horrour and dispell the night;
The messenger with speed the tidings bore,   660
News which three lab'ring nations did restore,
But heav'ns own *Nuncius* was arriv'd before.

By this, the *Hind* had reach'd her lonely cell;
And vapours rose, and dews unwholsome fell.
When she, by frequent observation wise,   665
As one who long on heav'n had fix'd her eyes,
Discern'd a change of weather in the skyes.
The Western borders were with crimson spread,
The moon descending look'd all flaming red,
She thought good manners bound her to invite   670
The stranger Dame to be her guest that night.
'Tis true, course dyet and a short repast
(She said) were weak inducements to the tast
Of one so nicely bred, and so unus'd to fast.
But what plain fare her cottage cou'd afford,   675
A hearty welcome at a homely board
Was freely hers; and, to supply the rest,
An honest meaning and an open breast.
Last, with content of mind, the poor man's Wealth;
A grace-cup to their common Patron's health.   680
This she desir'd her to accept and stay,
For fear she might be wilder'd in her way,
Because she wanted an unerring guide;

646. *That pious Joseph:* The Benedic-
tines of Dryden's gloss were like Joseph
(Genesis 37–50) "exil'd" and "sold" (l.
648) during the Reformation; and like
Joseph they forgave their "brothers" by
legally renouncing their abbey lands so
that the new owners could rest easy.

655. *James his . . . victory:* Kinsley, p.
1979, follows Scott in suggesting that
" 'James his late nocturnal victory' is the
defeat of Monmouth in the night engagements at Sedgmoor on 6 July 1685."
662. *Nuncius:* Messenger.

And then the dew-drops on her silken hide
Her tender constitution did declare,   685
Too Lady-like a long fatigue to bear,
And rough inclemencies of raw nocturnal air.
But most she fear'd that travelling so late,
Some evil minded beasts might lye in wait;
And without witness wreak their hidden hate.   690

    The *Panther*, though she lent a list'ning ear,
Had more of *Lyon* in her than to fear:
Yet wisely weighing, since she had to deal
With many foes, their numbers might prevail,
Return'd her all the thanks she cou'd afford;   695
And took her friendly hostess at her word.
Who ent'ring first her lowly roof (a shed
With hoary moss and winding Ivy spread,
Honest enough to hide an humble Hermit's head)
Thus graciously bespoke her welcome guest: 700
So might these walls, with your fair presence blest
Become your dwelling-place of everlasting rest,
Not for a night, or quick revolving year,
Welcome an owner, not a sojourner.
This peacefull Seat my poverty secures,   705
War seldom enters but where wealth allures;
Nor yet despise it, for this poor aboad
Has oft receiv'd, and yet receives a god;
A god victorious of the Stygian race
Here laid his sacred limbs, and sanctified the place. 710
This mean retreat did mighty *Pan* contain;
Be emulous of him, and pomp disdain,
And dare not to debase your soul to gain.

    The silent stranger stood amaz'd to see
Contempt of wealth, and wilfull poverty: 715
And, though ill habits are not soon controll'd,
A while suspended her desire of gold.
But civily drew in her sharpn'd paws,
Not violating hospitable laws,
And pacify'd her tail, and lick'd her frothy jaws.   720

    The *Hind* did first her country Cates provide;
Then couch'd her self securely by her side.

(1687)

709. *A god . . . Stygian race:* Alcides, nephew of Pluto, overcame Cerberus, the three-headed dog guarding the entrance to the underworld. Kinsley p. 1979, points out that Dryden here draws "a fanciful parallel" between this victory of Alcides and that of Christ's Harrowing of Hell, which includes His forcing Hell's gates.

Headnote to
A SONG FOR ST. CECILIA'S DAY and
ALEXANDER'S FEAST

Beginning in 1683, the feast of St. Cecilia, patroness of music, was celebrated with a concert on November 22. Twice, once in 1687 and again in 1697, Dryden was asked to write odes for the occasion by its sponsors, a London musical society. As was the practice, both were set to music, the first "A Song for St. Cecilia's Day" by the Italian composer Giovanni Draghi and the second and longer ode, "Alexander's Feast," by Jeremiah Clarke. Later, in the eighteenth century, Handel composed a score for each, and it is with his music that they are now most often associated.

The second ode bears the subtitle "The Power of Music," which might have been given to the first one as well, for in both poems music is shown to have a mighty range of influence, the extent of which is indicated by its power both to form the created world and its creatures, and to control and destroy them as well. In "A Song for St. Cecilia's Day" unwieldy chaos, at the dawn of time, yields to the harmonies of "the tuneful voice . . . from high" (l. 6); and in "Alexander's Feast" the will of the emblematic man of action, Alexander the Great, yields to the "trembling notes" of the master musician "Timotheus, plac'd on high" (l. 20). From their elevated positions, God and Timotheus shape the universe and man. But God as musician and the musician as god are not only makers, but destroyers as well, with limitless powers of manipulation. Accordingly, the world's last hour will be heralded by a sounding trumpet, and "Music will untune the sky" ("A Song," l. 63); and in the second ode, Timotheus, having drawn Alexander through several disparate moods (in which the conqueror is shown to experience the victor's pride, then his guilt, and later a lover's overpowering desire) finally moves the young king to burn the Persian city of Persepolis.

It seems obvious that the references to destruction that end (or nearly end) each ode are best regarded as metaphors expressing the scope of musical power rather than its nature. They are in fact the means of completing the image that dominates the structure of both poems. In these odes music is not a destroyer merely; nor is it just a maker. It is the power in which the beginnings and endings of all being and action find their source.

Structurally, the ode was of great interest to seventeenth- and eighteenth-century poets, many of whom understood the form, derived from the odes of Pindar (522–433 B.C.), but few of whom wrote true Pindarics. Most classical scholars agree that the typical Pindaric ode is composed of three identical parts, each of which is subdivided into a strophe, an antistrophe, and an epode. In this scheme, the poet is free to fix the length and metrical pattern of the first strophe, presumably so that it is appropriate to his treatment of the subject; the first antistrophe must duplicate the strophe in form, but the epode is not restricted by what precedes it. Having determined for himself (within the assigned limits) the shape of the first third of the ode, the poet repeats the pattern twice.

It was not only Pindar's structure but the religious tone, and the content of his odes as well, that offered difficulty to would-be imitators. The Greek poet was commissioned to celebrate athletic victories at the early Olympic (and other such) games. In fulfilling his obligation, he used a set of well-known conventions, beginning often with an invocation and including praises of the victor (or of the victor's owner in the case of chariot racing), of the place of his victory, and of such members of his family as he might designate. Pindar would also integrate into his work mythological allusions shaped for the occasion, to which a prayer and a moral were often added. All this he accomplished by means of a daring freedom of metaphors made apt by the entire context in which they occurred.

Dryden, like most neoclassical poets—exceptions are Congreve and Gray—does not follow the structure of the typical Pindaric. Nevertheless his two odes for St. Cecilia's Day are about the right length; that is, the shorter one is not so short as *Olympia 4* and the longer is exceeded in length by *Pythia 4*. And like Pindar's, both originate and repeat metrical patterns that convey a sense of freedom and of order and, at the same time, a sense that freedom and order alike grow out of the poet's treatment of his subject. Of course Dryden does not concern himself with athletic victories; but like Pindar's, his odes are commissioned, they praise a triumph in heroic terms tempered by sacred references, they employ myths (Christian and classical), and, as has been suggested, their two most daring metaphors are explained only when the reader has considered them in relation to their context.

TEXTS. *A Song for St. Cecilia's Day, 1687* (London, 1687).
    Alexander's Feast; or the Power of Musique. An Ode, In Honour of St. Cecilia's Day (London, 1697).

A Song for St. Cecilia's Day, 1687*

1

FROM Harmony, from Heav'nly Harmony
    This Universal Frame began.
  When Nature underneath a heap
    Of jarring Atoms lay,
  And cou'd not heave her Head,   5
The tuneful Voice was heard from high,
    Arise ye more than dead.
Then cold, and hot, and moist, and dry,
In order to their stations leap,
    And Musick's Pow'r obey.   10
From Harmony, from Heav'nly Harmony
  This Universal Frame began:
    From Harmony to Harmony
Through all the compass of the Notes it ran,
The Diapason closing full in Man.   15

2

What Passion cannot Musick raise and quell!
    When *Jubal* struck the corded Shell,
    His list'ning Brethren stood around
    And wond'ring, on their Faces fell
    To worship that Celestial Sound.   20
Less than a God they thought there cou'd not dwell
    Within the hollow of that Shell
    That spoke so sweetly and so well.
What Passion cannot Musick raise and quell!

---

* *St. Cecilia:* Cecilia, a noble Roman, who with her husband suffered martyrdom for her Christian beliefs (c. 176) under Marcus Aurelius, is said to have praised God with vocal and instrumental music. In Renaissance times she was particularly associated with the organ.

8. *Then cold, and hot, and moist, and dry:* These are references to the attributes of the elements in ancient philosophy—earth (cold and dry), water (cold and moist), air (hot and moist), fire (hot and dry)—elements making up the entire Creation.

15. *Diapason:* Here, a harmony somehow including all notes and tones.

17. *Jubal:* See Gen. 4:21, where Jubal is called "the father of all such as handle the harp and organ."

3

The Trumpets loud Clangor   25
   Excites us to Arms
With shrill Notes of Anger
And mortal Alarms.
The double double double beat
   Of the thundring Drum   30
Cries, heark the Foes come;
Charge, Charge, 'tis too late to retreat.

4

The soft complaining Flute
In dying Notes discovers
The Woes of hopeless Lovers,   35
Whose Dirge is whisper'd by the warbling Lute.

5

Sharp Violins proclaim
Their jealous Pangs, and Desperation,
Fury, frantick Indignation,
Depth of Pains, and height of Passion,   40
   For the fair, disdainful Dame.

6

But oh! what Art can teach
   What, human Voice can reach
The sacred Organs praise?
Notes inspiring holy Love,   45
Notes that wing their Heav'nly ways
   To mend the Choires above.

7

Orpheus cou'd lead the savage race;
And Trees unrooted left their place;
   Sequacious of the Lyre: 50
But bright *CECILIA* rais'd the wonder high'r;
When to her Organ, vocal Breath was giv'n
An Angel heard, and straight appear'd
   Mistaking Earth for Heav'n.

48. *Orpheus:* The legendary Thracian
poet who could tame wild beasts with his
music.

Grand Chorus

As from the pow'r of Sacred Lays   55
   The Spheres began to move.
And sung the great Creator's praise
   To all the bless'd above;
So when the last and dreadful hour
This crumbling Pageant shall devour,   60
The Trumpet *shall be heard on high,*
The Dead shall live, the Living die,
And Musick *shall untune the Sky.*

   (1687)

Alexander's Feast
Or, The Power of Musique

AN ODE IN HONOUR OF
ST. CECILIA'S DAY

I

'TWAS at the Royal Feast, for *Persia* won,
    By *Philip's* Warlike Son:
Aloft in awful State
The God-like Heroe sate
      On his Imperial Throne: 5
   His valiant Peers were plac'd around;
Their Brows with Roses and with Myrtles bound.
   (So shou'd Desert in Arms be Crown'd.)
The Lovely *Thais* by his side,
Sate like a blooming *Eastern* Bride   10
In Flow'r of Youth and Beauty's Pride.
    Happy, happy, happy Pair!
    None but the Brave
    None but the Brave
    None but the Brave deserves the Fair.   15

Chorus

   Happy, happy, happy Pair!
   None but the Brave
   None but the Brave
   None but the Brave deserves the Fair.

II

Timotheus plac'd on high   20
   Amid the tuneful Quire,
  With flying Fingers touch'd the Lyre:
The trembling Notes ascend the Sky,
    And Heav'nly Joys inspire.

2. *Philip's Warlike Son:* Alexander the Great.
9. *Thais:* A Greek courtesan, who is supposed to have induced Alexander to burn Persepolis. Dryden uses only that portion of the tradition which makes Alexander her lover. It is Timotheus (l. 20), poet and musican of Miletus, who moves Alexander to burn the city.
20. *Timotheus:* See n. l. 9.

The Song began from *Jove*,   25
Who left his blissful Seats above
(Such is the Pow'r of mighty Love).
A Dragon's fiery Form bely'd the God:
Sublime on Radiant Spires He rode,
    When He to fair *Olympia* press'd: 30
    And while He sought her snowy Breast:
Then, round her slender Waste he curl'd,
And stamp'd an Image of himself, a Sov'raign of the World.
The list'ning Crowd admire the lofty Sound,
A present Deity, they shout around: 35
A present Deity the vaulted Roofs rebound.
      With ravish'd Ears
      The Monarch hears,
      Assumes the God,
      Affects to nod,   40
   And seems to shake the Spheres.

Chorus

With ravish'd Ears
The Monarch hears,
Assumes the God,
Affects to Nod,   45
And seems to shake the Spheres.

III

The Praise of *Bacchus* then, the sweet Musician sung;
    Of *Bacchus* ever Fair, and ever Young:
      The jolly God in Triumph comes;
      Sound the Trumpets; beat the Drums;   50
        Flush'd with a purple Grace
        He shews his honest Face,
Now give the Hautboys breath; He comes, He comes.
      Bacchus ever Fair and Young,
        Drinking Joys did first ordain: 55
      Bacchus Blessings are a Treasure;
      Drinking is the Soldiers Pleasure;
        Rich the Treasure,
        Sweet the Pleasure;
      Sweet is Pleasure after Pain.   60

30. *Olympia:* Olympias, Alexander's
mother.

Chorus

Bacchus Blessings are a Treasure,
Drinking is the Soldier's Pleasure;
Rich the Treasure,
Sweet the Pleasure;
Sweet is Pleasure after Pain.   65

IV

Sooth'd with the Sound the King grew vain;
Fought all his Battails o'er again;
And thrice He routed all his Foes; and thrice He slew the slain.
The Master saw the Madness rise;
His glowing Cheeks, his ardent Eyes;   70
And while He Heav'n and Earth defy'd,
Chang'd his hand, and check'd his Pride.
He chose a Mournful Muse
Soft Pity to infuse:
He sung *Darius* Great and Good,   75
By too severe a Fate,
Fallen, fallen, fallen, fallen,
Fallen from his high Estate
And weltring in his Blood:
Deserted at his utmost Need,   80
By those his former Bounty fed:
On the bare Earth expos'd He lyes,
With not a Friend to close his Eyes.

With down-cast Looks the joyless Victor sate,
Revolveing in his alter'd Soul   85
The various Turns of Chance below;
And, now and then, a Sigh he stole;
And Tears began to flow.

Chorus

Revolveing in his alter'd Soul
The various Turns of Chance below;   90
And, now and then, a Sigh he stole;
And Tears began to flow.

V

The Mighty Master smil'd to see
That Love was in the next Degree:

75. *Darius:* Darius III, King of Persia,
overthrown by Alexander.

'Twas but a Kindred-Sound to move;   95
For Pity melts the Mind to Love.
    Softly sweet, in *Lydian* Measures,
    Soon He sooth'd his Soul to Pleasures.
    War, he sung, is Toil and Trouble;
    Honour but an empty Bubble.   100
      Never ending, still beginning,
    Fighting still, and still destroying,
      If the World be worth thy Winning,
    Think, O think, it worth Enjoying.
      Lovely *Thais* sits beside thee,   105
      Take the Good the Gods provide thee.

The Many rend the Skies, with loud Applause;
So Love was Crown'd, but Musique won the Cause.
    The Prince, unable to conceal his Pain,
      Gaz'd on the Fair   110
      Who caus'd his Care,
    And sigh'd and look'd, sigh'd and look'd,
    Sigh'd and look'd, and sigh'd again:
At length, with Love and Wine at once oppress'd,
The vanquish'd Victor sunk upon her Breast.   115

Chorus

The Prince, unable to conceal his Pain,
    Gaz'd on the Fair
    Who caus'd his Care,
    And sigh'd and look'd, sigh'd and look'd,
    Sigh'd and look'd, and sigh'd again: 120
At length, with Love and Wine at once oppress'd,
The vanquish'd Victor sunk upon her Breast.

VI

Now strike the Golden Lyre again:
A lowder yet, and yet a lowder Strain.
Break his Bands of Sleep asunder,   125
And rouze him, like a rattling Peal of Thunder.
    Hark, hark, the horrid Sound
    Has rais'd up his Head,
    As awak'd from the Dead,
    And amaz'd, he stares around.   130

97. *Lydian Measures:* In ancient Greek
music, a mode of a soft and effeminate
character.

Revenge, Revenge, *Timotheus* cries,
　　　　See the Furies arise!
　　　　See the Snakes that they rear,
　　　　How they hiss in their Hair,
　　And the Sparkles that flash from their Eyes!　　　135
　　　　Behold a ghastly Band,
　　　　Each a Torch in his Hand!
Those are *Grecian* Ghosts, that in Battail were slayn,
　　　　　　And unbury'd remain
　　　　　　Inglorious on the Plain.　　　140
　　　　Give the Vengeance due
　　　　To the Valiant Crew.
Behold how they toss their Torches on high,
　　　How they point to the *Persian* Abodes,
And glitt'ring Temples of their Hostile Gods!　　　145
The Princes applaud, with a furious Joy;
And the King seyz'd a Flambeau, with Zeal to destroy;
　　　　Thais led the Way,
　　　　To light him to his Prey,
And, like another *Hellen*, fir'd another *Troy*.　　　150

Chorus

And the King seyz'd a Flambeau, with Zeal to destroy;
　　　Thais *led the Way,*
　　　To light him to his Prey,
And, like another Hellen, *fir'd another* Troy.

VII

　　　Thus, long ago　　　155
　'Ere heaving Bellows learn'd to blow,
　　While Organs yet were mute;
　Timotheus, to his breathing Flute,
　　　And sounding Lyre,
Cou'd swell the Soul to rage, or kindle soft Desire.　　　160
　At last Divine *Cecilia* came,
　Inventress of the Vocal Frame;
The sweet Enthusiast, from her Sacred Store,
　　Enlarg'd the former narrow Bounds,
　　And added Length to solemn Sounds,　　　165
With Nature's Mother-Wit, and Arts unknown before.
　Let old *Timotheus* yield the Prize,
　　Or both divide the Crown;

132. *Furies:* Avengers of crimes against　　winged women, often with snakes in their
the ties of kinship; they are represented as　　hair.

He rais'd a Mortal to the Skies;
She drew an Angel down.   170

Grand Chorus

At last, Divine Cecilia came,
Inventress of the Vocal Frame;
The sweet Enthusiast, from her Sacred Store,
Enlarg'd the former narrow Bounds,
And added Length to solemn Sounds,   175
With Nature's Mother-Wit, and Arts unknown before.
Let old Timotheus yield the Prize,
Or both divide the Crown;
He rais'd a Mortal to the Skies;
She drew an Angel down.   180

(1697)

170. *She drew an Angel down:* See
ll. 53–54 of "A Song for St. Cecilia's Day."

PROLOGUES, EPILOGUES,
and SONGS
from Dryden's Plays

Though the dramatists of Dryden's day regularly made use of prologues and epilogues, they did not always write their own, nor were these pieces often an integral part of the plays they preceded or followed. Indeed, the chief reason for the prologue was to warm the audience, which might otherwise respond with such emphatic criticism as to ruin not only a single performance of a play but its general reputation as well. Theatrical success has always been a precarious matter. It has never been more so than during the Restoration and the eighteenth century. As a result of the doubtful issue, playwrights called upon friends to support their productions, sometimes with cheers, and sometimes with prologues, epilogues, or both. For example, in 1713, Pope wrote the prologue to Addison's *Cato* (cheers being incidentally provided by representatives of both political parties, Whigs and Tories, who wanted to be associated with the noble Roman, hero of the play). Much later, in 1758, Dr. Johnson suspended his good judgment to cheer his friend Dodsley's *Cleone*, the play with "more blood than brains"; and another friend, the minor poet William Shenstone, contributed the epilogue.

Under such circumstances, it is not surprising that prologues and epilogues became independent literary forms, fulfilling the demands of the occasion for which they were written. They had to be brief, clear, and lively; in addition they were generally casual in tone, though certain in rhyme and meter. As a result of Dryden's success with the form, other dramatists often asked him to write prologues and epilogues for their plays, and as his reputation grew, he was able to command a sizable fee for such assignments—often the equivalent of a quarter or a third of the playwright's entire profits.

The following selections from Dryden's own dramatic works include two prologues (one of these is in two parts), one epilogue, and several songs. The first prologue to *Secret Love* (it makes sense to speak of two distinct prologues here) is not really typical because of its brevity and its use of triplets; the second, on the other hand, which treats not the play it precedes but the nature of prologues and the audiences to whom they are addressed, in twenty or so witty couplets, is indeed representative, as is the topical prologue to *Marriage a-la-Mode*, which follows.

TEXTS. *Secret Love, or The Maiden-Queen* (London, 1668).
       Marriage a-la-Mode. A Comedy (London, 1673).
       The Conquest of Granada by the Spaniards: In Two Parts (London, 1672).
       Amphitryon; or, The Two Socia's. A Comedy (London, 1690).

Prologue and Song from Secret Love

Prologue

I

HE who writ this, not without pains and thought
From *French* and *English* Theaters has brought
Th' exactest Rules by which a Play is wrought.

II

The Unities of Action, Place, and Time;
The Scenes unbroken; and a mingled chime   5
Of *Johnson's* humour, with *Corneille's* rhyme.

III

But while dead colours he with care did lay,
He fears his Wit, or Plot he did not weigh,
Which are the living Beauties of a Play.

4. *Unities of Action, Place, and Time:* See the headnote on drama.
6. *Johnson's humour . . . Corneille's rhyme:* Ben Jonson's comedies often made use of humours; that is, of characters not psychologically rounded, but dominated by a ruling passion or tendency or humor. The name of the French dramatist Corneille is here pronounced as if spelled Cornélly.

IV

Plays are like Towns, which howe're fortifi'd   10
By Engineers, have still some weaker side
By the o'reseen Defendant unespy'd.

V

And with that Art you make approaches now;
Such skilful fury in Assaults you show,
That every Poet without shame may bow.   15

VI

Ours therefore humbly would attend your doom,
If Souldier-like, he may have termes to come
With flying colours, and with beat of Drum.

[*The Prologue goes out, and stayes while a Tune is play'd, after which
he returnes again.*

Second Prologue

I HAD forgot one half I do protest,
And now am sent again to speak the rest.
He bowes to every great and noble Wit,
But to the little Hectors of the Pit
Our Poet's sturdy, and will not submit.   5
He'll be before-hand with 'em, and not stay
To see each peevish Critick stab his Play:
Each Puny Censor, who his skill to boast,
Is cheaply witty on the Poet's cost.
No Critick's verdict, should, of right, stand good,   10
They are excepted all as men of blood:
And the same Law should shield him from their fury
Which has excluded Butchers from a Jury.
You'd all be Wits—
But writing's tedious, and that way may fail;   15
The most compendious method is to rail:
Which you so like, you think your selves ill us'd
When in smart Prologues you are not abus'd.
A civil Prologue is approv'd by no man;
You hate it as you do a Civil woman: 20
Your Fancy's pall'd, and liberally you pay
To have it quicken'd, e're you see a Play.
Just as old Sinners worn from their delight,

Give money to be whip'd to appetite.
But what a Pox keep I so much ado   25
To save our Poet? he is one of you;
A Brother Judgment, and as I hear say,
A cursed Critick as e're damn'd a Play.
Good salvage Gentlemen your own kind spare,
He is, like you, a very Wolf, or Bear;   30
Yet think not he'll your ancient rights invade,
Or stop the course of your free damning trade:
For he (he vows) at no friends Play can sit
But he must needs find fault to shew his Wit:
Then, for his sake, ne're stint your own delight,   35
Throw boldly, for he sets to all that write;
With such he ventures on an even lay,
For they bring ready money into Play.
Those who write not, and yet all Writers nick,
Are Bankrupt Gamesters, for they damn on Tick.   40

Song

I FEED a flame within which so torments me
That it both pains my heart, and yet contents me:
'Tis such a pleasing smart, and I so love it,
That I had rather die, then once remove it.

Yet he for whom I grieve shall never know it,   5
My tongue does not betray, nor my eyes show it:
Not a sigh nor a tear my pain discloses,
But they fall silently like dew on Roses.

Thus to prevent my love from being cruel,
My heart's the sacrifice as 'tis the fuel: 10
And while I suffer this to give him quiet,
My faith rewards my love, though he deny it.

On his eyes will I gaze, and there delight me;
While I conceal my love, no frown can fright me:
To be more happy I dare not aspire;   15
Nor can I fall more low, mounting no higher.

(1668)

25. *What a Pox:* A curse, similar in force to "what the devil."
29. *Salvage:* Savage.
37. *Even lay:* A gambling term, as are throw and set in the preceding line.

40. *On Tick:* On credit. Those who criticize without ever having written have not earned the right to do so.

Song from
The Conquest of Granada

1

BENEATH a Myrtle shade
Which Love for none but happy Lovers made,
I slept, and straight my Love before me brought
Phillis the object of my waking thought;
Undress'd she came my flames to meet,   5
While Love strow'd flow'rs beneath her feet;
Flow'rs, which so press'd by her, became more sweet.

2

From the bright Visions head
A careless vail of Lawn was loosely spread:
From her white temples fell her shaded hair,   10
Like cloudy sunshine not too brown nor fair:
Her hands, her lips did love inspire;
Her every grace my heart did fire:
But most her eyes which languish'd with desire.

3

Ah, Charming fair, said I,   15
How long can you my bliss and yours deny?
By Nature and by love this lonely shade
Was for revenge of suffring Lovers made:
Silence and shades with love agree:
Both shelter you and favour me;   20
You cannot blush because I cannot see.

4

No, let me dye, she said,
Rather than loose the spotless name of Maid:
Faintly me thought she spoke, for all the while
She bid me not believe her, with a smile.   25

22. *No, let me dye:* To die had a double
meaning, the second of which was to have
a sexual consummation.

Then dye, said I, she still deny'd:
And, is it thus, thus, thus she cry'd
You use a harmless Maid, and so she dy'd!

5

I wak'd, and straight I knew
I lov'd so well it made my dream prove true: 30
Fancy, the kinder Mistress of the two,
Fancy had done what *Phillis* wou'd not do!
Ah, Cruel Nymph, cease your disdain,
While I can dream you scorn in vain;
Asleep or waking you must ease my pain.   35

(1672)

Prologue, Epilogue and Songs from Marriage a-la-Mode

Prologue

LORD, how reform'd and quiet we are grown,
Since all our Braves and all our Wits are gone:
Fop-corner now is free from Civil War:
White-Wig and Vizard make no longer jar.
France, and the Fleet, have swept the Town so clear,   5
That we can Act in peace, and you can hear.
'Twas a sad sight, before they march'd from home,
To see our Warriours, in Red Wastecoats, come,
With hair tuck'd up, into our Tireing-room.
But 'twas more sad to hear their last Adieu,   10
The Women sob'd, and swore they would be true;
And so they were, as long as e're they cou'd:
But powerful *Guinnee* cannot be withstood,
And they were made of Play house flesh and bloud.
Fate did their Friends for double use ordain,   15
In Wars abroad, they grinning Honour gain,
And Mistresses, for all that stay, maintain.
Now they are gone, 'tis dead Vacation here,
For neither Friends nor Enemies appear.
Poor pensive Punk now peeps ere Plays begin,   20
Sees the bare Bench, and dares not venture in:
But manages her last Half-crown with care,
And trudges to the *Mall*, on foot, for Air.
Our City Friends so far will hardly come,

---

2. *All our Braves and . . . Wits are gone:* They had gone to war, declared against Holland in March, 1672. France (l. 5) was England's ally.

3. *Fop-corner:* A section of the pit taken over by dandies.

4. *White-Wig and Vizard:* White-Wigs are the men and Vizards (masks worn by women at the plays, hence) prostitutes or other females engaged in dickering or flirtation.

9. *Tireing-room:* Dressing room (attiring-room).

13. *Powerful Guinnee:* A gold coin, hence the incentive of money.

20. *Punk:* Prostitute.

22. *Her last Half-crown:* "A half-crown was the price of admission to the pit, and a whore's charge." Kinsley, p. 1855.

23. *Mall:* A tree-bordered walk in St. James's Park.

They can take up with Pleasures nearer home;   25
And see gay Shows, and gawdy Scenes elsewhere:
For we presume they seldom come to hear.
But they have now ta'n up a glorious Trade,
And cutting *Moorcraft*, struts in Masquerade.
There's all our hope, for we shall show to day,   30
A Masquing Ball, to recommend our Play:
Nay, to endear 'em more, and let 'em see,
We scorn to come behind in Courtesie,
We'll follow the new Mode which they begin,
And treat 'em with a Room, and Couch within: 35
For that's one way, how e're the Play fall short,
T' oblige the Town, the City, and the Court.

Epilogue

THUS have my Spouse and I inform'd the Nation,
And led you all the way to Reformation.
Not with dull Morals, gravely writ, like those,
Which men of easie Phlegme, with care compose—
Your Poets of stiff words, and limber sense,   5
Born on the confines of indifference.
But by examples drawn, I dare to say,
From most of you, who hear, and see the Play.
There are more *Rhodophils* in this Theatre,
More *Palamedes*, and some few Wives, I fear.   10
But yet too far our Poet would not run,
Though 'twas well offer'd, there was nothing done.
He would not quite the Woman's frailty bare,
But stript 'em to the waste, and left 'em there.
And the men's faults are less severely shown,   15
For he considers that himself is one.
Some stabbing Wits, to bloudy Satyr bent,
Would treat both Sexes with less complement:
Would lay the Scene at home, of Husbands tell,
For Wenches, taking up their Wives i'th' *Mell*,   20

25. *Pleasures nearer home:* This is a reference to a rival theater in Dorset Garden.

29. *Cutting Moorcraft:* Swaggering Moorcraft, a usurer who becomes a gallant in Fletcher's play *The Scornful Lady*.

32–37. These lines have been variously explained. Certain entertainments in the form of masquerades, popular around 1672, are supposed to have featured the retiring-room and the couch. Kinsley suggests (p. 1856) that Dryden here refers to "tiring-room facilities" at the rival theater, Dorset Gardens.

4. *Men of easie Phlegme:* Phlegmatic men.

9–10. *Rhodophils/Palamedes:* These are the chief male characters in *Marriage a-la-Mode*. The action involves a double intrigue—between Palamede and Doralice (Rhodophil's wife) and between Rhodophil and Melantha (Palamede's fiancée)—an intrigue that does not come off (l. 28). In fact all agree to end the attempted exchanges of mates.

And a brisk bout which each of them did want,
Made by mistake of Mistris and Gallant.
Our modest Authour, thought it was enough
To cut you off a Sample of the stuff:
He spar'd my shame, which you, I'm sure, would not,   25
For you were all for driving on the Plot:
You sigh'd when I came in to break the sport,
And set your teeth when each design fell short.
To Wives, and Servants all good wishes lend,
But the poor Cuckold seldom finds a friend.   30
Since therefore Court and Town will take no pity,
I humbly cast my self upon the City.

Songs

I

1

WHY should a foolish Marriage Vow
   Which long ago was made,
Oblige us to each other now
   When Passion is decay'd?
We lov'd, and we lov'd, as long as we cou'd,   5
   Till our love was lov'd out in us both:
But our Marriage is dead, when the Pleasure is fled:
   'Twas Pleasure first made it an Oath.

2

If I have Pleasures for a Friend,
   And farther love in store,   10
What wrong has he whose joys did end,
   And who cou'd give no more?

'Tis a madness that he
Should be jealous of me,
Or that I shou'd bar him of another: 15
For all we can gain,
Is to give our selves pain,
When neither can hinder the other.

II

Song

1

WHIL'ST *Alexis* lay prest
In her Arms he lov'd best,

With his hands round her neck,
And his head on her breast,
He found the fierce pleasure too hasty to stay,   5
And his soul in the tempest just flying away.

                                2

When *Cælia* saw this,
With a sigh, and a kiss,
She cry'd, Oh my dear, I am robb'd of my bliss;
'Tis unkind to your Love, and unfaithfully done,   10
To leave me behind you, and die all alone.

                                3

The Youth, though in haste,
And breathing his last,
In pity dy'd slowly, while she dy'd more fast;
Till at length she cry'd, Now, my dear, now let us go,   15
Now, die, my *Alexis*, and I will die too.

                                4

Thus intranc'd they did lie,
Till *Alexis* did try
To recover new breath, that again he might die:
Then often they di'd; but the more they did so,   20
The Nymph di'd more quick, and the Shepherd more slow.

    (1673)

    11. *Die all alone:* See n. 22 to Song
from *The Conquest of Granada*, above.

Mercury's Song to Phaedra from Amphitryon

I

FAIR *Iris* I love, and hourly I dye,
But not for a Lip, nor a languishing Eye:
She's fickle and false, and there we agree;
For I am as false, and as fickle as she:
We neither believe what either can say;   5
And, neither believing, we neither betray.

II

'Tis civil to swear, and say things of course;
We mean not the taking for better for worse.
When present, we love; when absent, agree:
I think not of *Iris*, nor *Iris* of me: 10
The Legend of Love no Couple can find
So easie to part, or so equally join'd.

(1690)

Headnote to
RESTORATION AND EIGHTEENTH-CENTURY DRAMA

In the summer of 1660, Charles II, only recently crowned, issued two patents for theatrical productions to his friends Sir William Davenant and Thomas Killigrew. Ultimately, this franchise gave them an effective monopoly of the theater in London, though various forms of dramatic entertainment offered intermittent competition. Of the two companies of actors formed by these royally sponsored producers, Killigrew's became known as the King's players, and after some years, in 1674, settled in the new Theatre Royal in Drury Lane. Davenant's group, which enjoyed the patronage of the Duke of York, had been earlier (1671) housed, also in a new theater, in Dorset Garden. The two were generally competitors for London audiences; but despite the monopoly they enjoyed, it was necessary for them to join forces more than once in order to ensure the survival of the King's Company, which had experienced a wide range of difficulties, from the loss by fire of one of its older theaters to dissensions among the actors. When the student who knows the period only slightly learns that theaters (forbidden by the Commonwealth government to produce plays from 1642 to 1660) reopened at the Restoration with many innovations, and with the royal patent to protect them, he is likely to be surprised that financial difficulties should have beset them. New playhouses were better designed and more comfortable than older ones; they made a much greater use of scenery, props, and machinery to increase the scope and variety of the spectacle; they introduced women to act the parts of female characters, replacing the boy actors who had played these parts and adding another element of pleasure (men of the age assure us) to the theater; and their programs were more full than they had been, with singing and dancing between the acts and a generally increased use of musical accompaniment. Nevertheless, the Restoration drama, in many ways vital and successful, did not enjoy the popularity the English stage had known in 1600. Part of the reason for this curtailed appeal is to be discovered in the Puritans' effectively expressed distrust of the drama; another (perhaps related) cause may be found in the subject matter and forms of the plays themselves. The most important of these were musical drama (which requires a more specialized

105

commentary than can be offered here), heroic drama in rimed couplets, and the comedy of manners.

The heroic play attempted to offer in dramatic form certain of the features of epic. Accordingly, its characters were high-born men and women occupied with matters of state, which for the most part were settled by force of arms; unlike persons in most epic literature, however, those in heroic drama were often consumed by love. Presumably as a result of the serious treatment of this double concern—love and valor—their language tends to be dignified and elevated, though more often it is only falsely elevated, and sometimes bombastic and downright ridiculous. Dryden's essay *Of Heroic Plays*, prefixed to his *The Conquest of Granada* (1672), besides explaining the virtues of the genre and its epical affinities, points out the debt it owes to the Elizabethan tradition and to the tradition of "Corneille and some French Poets." Later, in his preface to *All for Love* (1678) and *The Spanish Friar* (1681), Dryden was to withdraw his approval of the type; nevertheless, he is generally regarded as the leading playwright of the heroic drama and its chief critical exponent as well. It is Roger Boyle, Earl of Orrery, however, who is thought to be its actual originator. His play *The History of Henry the Fifth* was produced in London on August 13, 1664. Though *The Indian Queen* by Dryden and his brother-in-law, Sir Robert Howard, was presented earlier, on January 25, 1663/4, Orrery's play was written first, and in fact it had been acted in Dublin in 1662. For the decade beginning with these plays, it was Dryden who dominated the heroic drama. In 1665, he brought on a sequel to his first success—*The Indian Emperor*—and in 1669, *Tyrannick Love*. A kind of culmination of the form occurs in Dryden's two-part *Conquest of Granada* (1670, 1671), in which for ten acts the hero Almanzor, a Moorish general preternaturally gifted in military skill, declaims with as much authority as he campaigns. At the same time, in 1671, George Villiers, Duke of Buckingham, with the help of several collaborators, presented *The Rehearsal*, a burlesque of heroic drama and particularly an attack on Dryden, the character Bayes in the play. The chief device of Buckingham's satire is to have friends of the dramatist (Bayes) attend a rehearsal at which both he and his play are made ridiculous. Despite the enormous success of *The Rehearsal*, heroic drama continued to thrive. In fact it was 1675 before Dryden produced his last rimed heroic play, *Aureng-Zebe*.

Heroic drama extended its vitality in a less direct way as well, by influencing the blank-verse tragedy of the period. Tragedians working in this form—who, besides Dryden, are best represented by Nathaniel Lee (c. 1649–1692), Thomas Otway (1652–1685), and Thomas Southerne (1660–1746)—also drew in varying degrees upon the Elizabethan "tragedy of blood" and upon the French neoclassicism based on Aristotle and Seneca and exemplified in the plays of Racine. To be sure, Dryden and some lesser blank-verse tragedians were at times responsive to the neoclassical restrictions imposed by the unities of action, time, and place; but Lee, Otway, and Southerne generally were not. Such divisions of view were common among playwrights and critics, and so it is important to have some sense for what was at stake. The idea that all the parts of a play should contribute to the development of a single theme—unity of action—seemed to many a reasonable theory, but most acknowledged that successful dramatists had in some degree violated the principle. Still, it was the most seriously regarded of these neoclassical unities. The unity of time—derived from one slight reference in Aristotle's *Poetics* (1449b)—required the action of a play to take place within a period of twenty-four hours (presumably to help facilitate the all-important unity of action); and the unity of place —derived from the unity of time, but without Aristotelian authority— required the action to be confined to a space no larger than that which the characters can cover within the allotted twenty-four hours. If Racine had succeeded within the limits of these and other rules—all of which focus the dramatist's attention on his characters and their proper limits, and require his unvarying concern with human feelings and states of mind—it was also true that another successful French playwright, Corneille, and England's greatest dramatist, Shakespeare, had been careless of them. Most Englishmen, like Dryden in *An Essay of Dramatic Poesy*, while fascinated with the "rules," ultimately questioned or rejected their rigid use. Sometimes, the critical speculations of the age, while ostensibly rejecting the three unities, revealed a genuine concern for unity of action, though no simple or clear definition was forthcoming. At other times a playwright would offer a play according to the rules of French neoclassicism—Rymer's *Edgar* (1678) and Addison's *Cato* (1713), for example—but generally such a venture would gather compliments for its "correctness" or receive party acceptance for its political allegory, real or fancied. And sometimes, though these plays were popular—Congreve's *Mourning Bride* (1697)— they were so obviously without tragic force that they soon lost favor. An exception among these tragedies is Dryden's *All for Love* (1677). Though it conforms to neoclassical patterns and draws upon the same material Shakespeare used to better advantage in his *Antony and Cleo-patra*, it is a dignified and moving play, whose characters are well drawn and wedded to the action.

Between 1675 and 1682, Nathaniel Lee, who unlike Dryden (poet, critic, comedian, heroic dramatist, neoclassical tragedian, translator) concentrated exclusively on tragedy, worked to bring together the force and language of Elizabethan and French tragedy and heroic romance. The combination may in part account for his scenes of extraordinarily tender love and those which attempt sublimity but too often achieve only rant and anxious gesture. In the next generation, Nicholas Rowe (1674–1718), in such tragedies as his *Jane Shore* (1714) was to make better use of the Shakespearean manner. But Lee's plays were popular and effective, both for their power and their near sentimentality. Otway, in his most successful pieces, *The Orphan* (1680) and *Venice Preserv'd* (1682), continues the quasi-sentimental strain of Lee; indeed, his plays effected a kind of pathos—awakening tender and pitying feelings in his audience and moving them to tears—a pathos soon to reveal itself, in a similar form, in the comedy of the period. His power to move his audience so did not prevent his dignified treatment of political matters, but his reputation relies most, Dr. Johnson thought, on his ability to understand human nature by understanding his own feelings. And this interest in private feelings, often expressed as domestic pathos, outweighs his other concerns. The tendency in Otway to repudiate French neoclassicism and the heroics of French romance is more marked in the plays of Southerne, who returns to the loose structure, mixed comic and tragic modes, and high passion that often characterized the Elizabethan stage. But he too contributes to the current of intense pathos that began to pervade the tragedy and, only slightly later, the comedy of the age. In fact, with few exceptions in the period 1660–1800, tragedy is either dependent upon remote traditions for whatever shaping force it has, or it draws upon domestic relationships and treats them with an inescapable pathos that gradually displaces the larger (national or cultural) problems of more representative tragedy. This reduction in the scope of tragic subject is epitomized in George Lillo's *The London Merchant* (1731). By turning frankly to the middle class for its subject matter—the "hero" is a London apprentice—this straightforward play caught the imagination of generations of Londoners and of Europeans as well. Lillo drew on an Elizabethan ballad for his story; his use of this old material provided the opportunity for a dramatic excursion congenial both to him and to his audience, but he inspired almost no followers among the dramatists of England. His instinct for the vitality of middle-class material for the most part had results among his audiences only. More long-term effects of his work are to be found in the English melodrama of the early nineteenth century, which owed a debt indirectly to Lillo, by way of French and German drama.

The best comedies of the period, examples of the comedy of manners, were witty, satirical, urbane. They were also often indecent, with few, if any, of the socially constructive elements that have usually characterized comedy, however ribald. Their heroes and heroines—cynical, selfish and overwhelmingly proud of their aplomb—derided the standards of behavior at least nominally accepted by ordinary mortals. Inevitably, most men would feel uncomfortable in such an environment, bright and superficially textured as it was. The world of these plays has been said to appeal to aristocrats but not to the middle class—a view that seems only partly true, even though middle-class persons are sometimes the object of its humor. It is more likely a world that appeals to relatively few men of any class, because it is (right or wrong) morally bankrupt and seriously limited in its interests. Its characters, who often seem emotionally if not sexually independent of each other, and its high style probably found a readier acceptance (as art, not "life") among aristocrats, though it seems doubtful that one's social origins could account entirely for the preference.

Whatever the reason for the circumscribed interest in the comedy of manners—the form of the drama that the Restoration bequeathed to generations of later playwrights—it had a spectacular yet limited success during two brief periods of the last quarter of the seventeenth century. The first, which ran from 1668 to 1676, saw the production of such plays as Sir George Etherege's *She Would If She Could* (1667/8) and *The Man of Mode* (1676) and William Wycherly's *The Plain Dealer* (1676); the second, which began in 1691 and lasted until 1700, may be represented by such plays as Sir John Vanbrugh's *The Relapse* (1696), George Farquhar's *Love and a Bottle* (1698), and William Congreve's *The Way of the World* (1700). This last—Congreve's masterpiece and the best example of the genre, many have thought—was not a popular success. No one knows just why. Literary historians point out as possible yet doubtful causes both the attempts to reform the morality of the stage and the philosophically inspired shift in taste, away from witty dramatic satire and toward reformed comedy, which finally became downright sentimental. Jeremy Collier's *A Short View of the Immorality and Profaneness of the English Stage* (1698) doubtless made its mark, but plays it specifically condemned continued to do well. Nevertheless, it seems likely that Collier's censures not only expressed but also nourished a moral view congenial to many of his countrymen. Similarly, it is hard to say how much the eighteenth century's benevolist view of man (Shaftesbury's, for example), mostly a reaction in one form or another against earlier mechanistic theories of human endeavor (like Hobbes's), is expressed through the new sentimental comedy and how much that view in fact shaped these plays. It must also be observed that many works stressing the new sensitivity—Shaftesbury's *Characteristics* (1711) —did not appear until well after the first examples of the new drama had been produced.

In 1696, even before Congreve's brilliant comedy of manners *The Way of the World*, Colley Cibber produced *Love's Last Shift*, a play in which an unfaithful husband, Loveless, is swiftly converted to fidelity by his wife, who to move him masquerades as a prostitute. Though it cannot accurately be called the very first sentimental comedy, it was the first such play to have a notable success. Besides, its importance was increased as time passed, because Cibber dominated the English theater until mid-century. *The Careless Husband* (1704), also Cibber's, provides another rapidly changed husband, altered by nothing more than an ordinary act of kindness. These last-minute conversions of the husband to benevolence are of course preceded by four acts of his outrageous behavior. Cibber was no reformer; he sensed the temper of the times, and he wrote accordingly. It was Sir Richard Steele who was chiefly responsible for offering London audiences ". . . Comedy which might be no improper Entertainment in a Christian Commonwealth," as he puts it. From his earliest play, *The Funeral: or Grief a-la-Mode* (1701), one may observe that at least some of his characters are consistently more human and more reputable than those in most earlier Restoration comedy. Bourgeois attitudes, sentimentally and piously mixed with genteel virtues, dominate his dramatic works. For example, the unabashedly middle-class play *The Conscious Lovers* (1722) presents a young man and woman whose love is so "conscious" (their awareness of each other's feelings so shared) that they have never felt the need to discuss it; further, the hero is loyal not only to love, but to his father's authority as well; finally, he idealizes his fiancée out of all proportion to reality. One can hardly resist a glow of human warmth at all this unrelieved goodness. And Fielding (himself a powerful writer of comedy and farce), in *Joseph Andrews* (the end of Bk. III, ch. XI), satirizes the play by having the good but literal-minded Parson Adams praise it: " 'I never heard of any plays fit for a Christian to read but *Cato* [a neoclassical tragedy by Addison] and *The Conscious Lovers*; and I must own, in the latter there are some things almost solemn enough for a sermon.' " It is indeed true that Steele had finally eliminated a good deal of the vitality of comedy for the sake of the new sensibility. Fun is still in evidence, but without the force and relish of energy one expects in comedy. Until the end of the century, in one form or another, sentimentalism was to continue to be a feature of English drama, with few exceptions.

In 1773, Oliver Goldsmith in the essay *A Comparison Between Laughing and Sentimental Comedy* offered his objections to the turn comedy had taken. He gets to the heart of the matter by asking whether "human distress" or "human absurdity" is more likely to entertain. Elsewhere in the piece he speculates that mankind's distress may be a popular subject because it is a novelty in comedy and because it flatters every man into believing himself more warm-hearted than he is. Goldsmith finally censures these plays for their lack of *vis comica;* and he charges audiences with being so fastidious as to threaten all humor on the stage. These opinions were published just before the production of Goldsmith's unsentimental *She Stoops to Conquer* (1773), a play that inspired laughter on the first night and has continued to do so ever since. Certain of its features are implausible. A gentleman's mansion, however informally run, cannot long be mistaken for a country inn, nor is an intelligent and well-educated young man likely to mistake a lady for a barmaid. One need not look far for similar demands on credulity. But the almost farcical quality of the piece saves it from censure for such violations of common sense, and audiences seem always to respond with pleasure to the energetic movements of its early defined and consistently (though oddly) behaved characters. Along with Goldsmith, Richard Brinsley Sheridan is often thought (not quite accurately) to be the late eighteenth-century playwright who saved the stage from sentimentality. Among the seven or so pieces he wrote for the stage—including a comic opera, *The Duenna* (1775)—there are five plays. Two of these, *The Rivals* (1775) and *The School for Scandal* (1777), are high comedies on which his reputation chiefly rests. They have all the wit of dialogue and urbanity of manner of the most elegant Restoration comedy. But they are purged of the indecencies that marked the earlier plays. Both Goldsmith and Sheridan made contributions to the repertoire of English drama; neither of them stopped the flow of sentimental drama, however. They simply stole attention from it briefly, but it reidentified itself (like Lillo's tragedy) in melodrama or in the drama of "humanitarian purpose."

TEXTS. *All for Love: or, The World Well Lost* ([London], 1678).
      Venice Preserv'd, or, A Plot Discover'd (London, 1696).
      The Way of the World (London, 1700).
      She Stoops to Conquer; or, The Mistakes of a Night, 5th ed. (London, 1773).

All for Love
Or, The World Well Lost

From the Preface

The death of *Anthony* and *Cleopatra*, is a Subject which has been treated by the greatest Wits of our Nation, after *Shakespeare*; and by all so variously, that their example has given me the confidence to try my self in this Bowe of *Ulysses* amongst the Crowd of Sutors; and, withal, to take my own measures, in aiming at the Mark. I doubt not but the same Motive has prevailed with all of us in this attempt; I mean the excellency of the Moral: for the chief persons represented, were famous patterns of unlawful love; and their end accordingly was unfortunate. All reasonable men have long since concluded, That the Heroe of the Poem, ought not to be a character of perfect Virtue, for, then, he could not, without injustice, be made unhappy; nor yet altogether wicked, because he 10 could not then be pitied: I have therefore steer'd the middle course; and have drawn the character of *Anthony* as favourably as *Plutarch, Appian,* and *Dion Cassius* wou'd give me leave: the like I have observ'd in *Cleopatra*. That which is wanting to work up the pity to a greater heighth, was not afforded me by the story: for the crimes of love which they both committed, were not occasion'd by any necessity, or fatal ignorance, but were wholly voluntary; since our passions are, or ought to be, within our power. The Fabrick of the Play is regular enough, as to the inferior parts of it; and the Unities of Time, Place and Action, more exactly observ'd, than, perhaps, the English Theater requires. Particularly, the Action is so much one, that it is the only of the kind without Episode, or 20 Underplot; every Scene in the Tragedy conducing to the main design, and every Act concluding with a turn of it. The greatest errour in the contrivance seems to be in the person of *Octavia*: For, though I might use the priviledge of a Poet, to introduce her into *Alexandria*, yet I had not enough consider'd, that the compassion she mov'd to her self and children, was destructive to that which I reserv'd for *Anthony* and *Cleopatra*; whose mutual love being founded upon vice, must lessen the favour of the Audience to them, when Virtue and Innocence were oppress'd by it. And, though I justified *Anthony* in some measure, by making *Octavia's* departure, to proceed wholly from her self; yet the force of the first Machine* still remain'd; and the dividing of pity, like the cutting of a 30 River into many Channels, abated the strength of the natural stream. But this is an Objection which none of my Critiques have urg'd against me; and therefore I might have let it pass, if I could have resolv'd to have been partial to my self. The faults my Enemies have found, are rather cavils concerning little, and not essential Decencies; which a Master of the Ceremonies may decide betwixt us. The *French* Poets, I confess, are strict Observers of these Punctilios: They would not, for example, have suffer'd *Cleopatra* and *Octavia* to have met; or if they had

* *Machine:* Dramatic device.

met, there must only have pass'd betwixt them some cold civilities, but no eagerness of repartée, for fear of offending against the greatness of their Characters,
and the modesty of their Sex. This Objection I foresaw, and at the same time
contemn'd: for I judg'd it both natural and probable, that *Octavia*, proud of
her new-gain'd Conquest, would search out *Cleopatra* to triumph over her;
and that *Cleopatra*, thus attacqu'd, was not of a spirit to shun the encounter:
and 'tis not unlikely, that two exasperated Rivals should use such Satyre as
I have put into their mouths; for after all, though the one were a *Roman*, and
the other a Queen, they were both Women. 'Tis true, some actions, though
natural, are not fit to be represented; and broad obscenities in words, ought in   10
good manners to be avoided: expressions therefore are a modest cloathing of
our thoughts, as Breeches and Petticoats are of our bodies. If I have kept my
self within the bounds of modesty, all beyond it is but nicety and affectation;
which is no more but modesty deprav'd into a vice: they betray themselves who
are too quick of apprehension in such cases, and leave all reasonable men to
imagine worse of them, than of the Poet. . . .

Prologue

WHAT Flocks of Critiques hover here to day,
As Vultures wait on Armies for their Prey,
All gaping for the Carcass of a Play!
With Croaking Notes they bode some dire event;
And follow dying Poets by the scent.   5
Ours gives himself for gone; y'have watch'd your time!
He fights this day unarm'd; without his Rhyme.
And brings a Tale which often has been told;
As sad as Dido's; and almost as old.
His Heroe, whom you Wits his Bully call,   10
Bates of his mettle; and scarce rants at all:
He's somewhat lewd; but a well-meaning mind;
Weeps much; fights little; but is wond'rous kind.
In short, a Pattern, and Companion fit,
For all the keeping Tonyes of the Pit.   15
I cou'd name more; A Wife, and Mistress too;
Both (to be plain) too good for most of you:
The Wife well-natur'd, and the Mistress true.
    Now, Poets, if your fame has been his care;
Allow him all the candour you can spare.   20
A brave Man scorns to quarrel once a day;
Like Hectors, in at every petty fray.
Let those find fault whose Wit's so very small,
They've need to show that they can think at all:
Errours like Straws upon the surface flow;   25
He who would search for Pearls must dive below.
Fops may have leave to level all they can;
As Pigmies wou'd be glad to lopp a Man.
Half-Wits are Fleas; so little and so light;
We scarce cou'd know they live, but that they bite.   30
But, as the Rich, when tir'd with daily Feasts,
For change, become their next poor Tenants Ghests;
Drink hearty Draughts of Ale, from plain brown Bowls,
And snatch the homely Rasher from the Coals:
So you, retiring from much better Cheer,   35
For once, may venture to do penance here.
And since that plenteous Autumn now is past,
Whose Grapes and Peaches have Indulg'd your taste,

---

7. *Without his Rhyme:* Dryden had regularly used rhyme in his heroic drama; *Aureng-Zebe,* 1675, was the last such play in which he used rhymed couplets, though his adaptation of *Paradise Lost, The State of Innocence,* 1677, never performed, was a rhymed opera.

11. *Scarce rants:* Antony reduces (bates) the bombastic language of earlier heroic drama.

15. *Tonyes:* A Tony was a foolish person.

22. *Hectors:* Bullies or street-brawlers.

> Take in good part from our poor Poets boord,
> Such rivell'd Fruits as Winter can afford.   40

Persons Represented

Marc Anthony
Ventidius, his General
Dollabella, his Friend
Alexas, the Queen's Eunuch
Serapion, Priest of Isis
Another Priest
Servants to Anthony

Cleopatra, Queen of Egypt
Octavia, Anthony's Wife
Charmion ⎫
Iras   ⎬ Cleopatra's Maids
Anthony's two little Daughters

SCENE, Alexandria

Act I

SCENE, The Temple of Isis

[Enter Serapion, Myris, Priests of Isis.

   Serap. Portents, and Prodigies, are grown so frequent,
That they have lost their Name. Our fruitful Nile
Flow'd ere the wonted Season, with a Torrent
So unexpected, and so wondrous fierce,
That the wild Deluge overtook the haste   5
Ev'n of the Hinds that watch'd it: Men and Beasts
Were born above the tops of Trees, that grew
On th' utmost Margin of the Water-mark.
Then, with so swift an Ebb, the Floud drove backward,
It slipt from underneath the Scaly Herd: 10
Here monstrous Phocæ panted on the Shore;
Forsaken Dolphins there, with their broad tails,
Lay lashing the departing Waves: Hard by 'em,
Sea-Horses floundring in the slimy mud,
Toss'd up their heads, and dash'd the ooze about 'em.   15
          [Enter Alexas behind them.
   Myr. Avert these Omens, Heav'n.
   Serap. Last night, between the hours of Twelve and One,

---

40. Rivell'd: Dried and wrinkled.   11. Phocæ: Seals.

In a lone Isle o'th' Temple while I walk'd,
A Whirl-wind rose, that, with a violent blast,
Shook all the *Dome:* the Doors around me clapt,   20
The Iron Wicket, that defends the Vault,
Where the long Race of *Ptolomies* is lay'd,
Burst open, and disclos'd the mighty dead.
From out each Monument, in order plac'd,
An Armed Ghost start up: the Boy-King last   25
Rear'd his inglorious head. A peal of groans
Then follow'd, and a lamentable voice
Cry'd, *Ægypt* is no more. My blood ran back,
My shaking knees against each other knock'd;
On the cold pavement down I fell intranc'd,   30
And so unfinish'd left the horrid Scene.
    Alex. [*showing himself*]. And, Dream'd you this? or, Did invent
     the Story?
To frighten our *Ægyptian* Boys withal,
And train 'em up betimes in fear of Priesthood?
    Serap. My Lord, I saw you not,   35
Nor meant my words should reach your ears; but what
I utter'd was most true.
    Alex. A foolish Dream,
Bred from the fumes of indigested Feasts,
And holy Luxury.
    Serap. I know my duty:
This goes no farther.
    Alex. 'Tis not fit it should.   40
Nor would the times now bear it, were it true.
All Southern, from yon hills, the *Roman* Camp
Hangs o'er us black and threatning, like a Storm
Just breaking on our heads.
    Serap. Our faint *Ægyptians* pray for *Antony*;   45
But in their Servile hearts they own *Octavius*.
    Myr. Why then does *Antony* dream out his hours,
And tempts not Fortune for a noble Day,
Which might redeem, what *Actium* lost?
    Alex. He thinks 'tis past recovery.
    Serap. Yet the Foe   50
Seems not to press the Siege.
    Alex. O, there's the wonder.
Mæcenas and *Agrippa*, who can most
With *Cæsar*, are his Foes. His Wife *Octavia*,

---

25. *Start up:* Sprang up. *Boy-King:*
Ptolemy, XIV Dionysus, Cleopatra's
brother (and her nominal husband), who
had perished during Caesar's campaign,
48–47 B.C.

49. *Actium:* The ancient town in
Acarnania, Greece, where Octavius defeated Antony in a naval battle, 31 B.C.
52. *Who can most:* Who has most
power.

Driv'n from his House, solicits her revenge;
And *Dolabella*, who was once his Friend,   55
Upon some private grudge, now seeks his ruine:
Yet still War seems on either side to sleep.
    Serap. 'Tis strange that *Antony*, for some dayes past,
Has not beheld the face of *Cleopatra*;
But here, in *Isis* Temple, lives retir'd,   60
And makes his heart a prey to black despair.
    Alex. 'Tis true; and we much fear he hopes by absence
To cure his mind of Love.
    Serap. If he be vanquish'd,
Or make his peace, *Ægypt* is doom'd to be
A *Roman* Province; and our plenteous Harvests   65
Must then redeem the scarceness of their Soil.
While *Antony* stood firm, our *Alexandria*
Rival'd proud *Rome* (Dominion's other Seat)
And Fortune striding, like a vast *Colossus*,
Cou'd fix an equal foot of Empire here.   70
    Alex. Had I my wish, these Tyrants of all Nature
Who Lord it o'er Mankind, should perish, perish,
Each by the other's Sword; but, since our will
Is lamely follow'd by our pow'r, we must
Depend on one; with him to rise or fall.   75
    Serap. How stands the Queen affected?
    Alex. O, she dotes,
She dotes, *Serapion*, on this vanquish'd Man,
And winds her self about his mighty ruins,
Whom would she yet forsake, yet yield him up,
This hunted prey, to his pursuers' hands,   80
She might preserve us all; but 'tis in vain——
This changes my designs, this blasts my Counsels,
And makes me use all means to keep him here,
Whom I could wish divided from her Arms
Far as the Earth's deep Center. Well, you know   85
The state of things; no more of your ill Omens,
And black Prognosticks; labour to confirm
The people's hearts.
    [*Enter* Ventidius, *talking aside with a Gentleman of* Antony's.
    Serap. These *Romans* will o'rehear us.
But, Who's that Stranger? By his Warlike port,
His fierce demeanor, and erected look,   90
He's of no vulgar note.
    Alex. O 'tis *Ventidius*,
Our Emp'ror's great Lieutenant in the East,
Who first show'd *Rome* that *Parthia* could be conquer'd.
When *Antony* return'd from *Syria* last,
He left this Man to guard the *Roman* Frontiers.   95

Serap. You seem to know him well.
　Alex. Too well. I saw him in *Cilicia* first,
When *Cleopatra* there met *Antony*:
A mortal foe he was to us, and *Ægypt*.
But, let me witness to the worth I hate,　　　　　　100
A braver Roman never drew a Sword.
Firm to his Prince; but, as a friend, not slave.
He ne'r was of his pleasures; but presides
O're all his cooler hours and morning counsels:
In short, the plainness, fierceness, rugged virtue　　　105
Of an old true-stampt Roman lives in him.
His coming bodes I know not what of ill
To our affairs. Withdraw, to mark him better;
And I'll acquaint you why I sought you here,
And what's our present work.
　　Ventidius. Not see him, say you?　　　　　　110
　　[*They withdraw to a corner of the Stage; and* Ventidius,
　　　with the other, comes forwards to the front].
I say, I must, and will.
　　Gent. He has commanded,
On pain of death, none should approach his presence.
　　Ven. I bring him news will raise his drooping Spirits,
Give him new life.
　　Gent. He sees not *Cleopatra*.
　　Ven. Would he had never seen her.　　　　　　115
　　Gent. He eats not, drinks not, sleeps not, has no use
Of any thing, but thought; or, if he talks,
'Tis to himself, and then 'tis perfect raving:
Then he defies the World, and bids it pass;
Sometimes he gnawes his Lip, and Curses loud　　　120
The Boy *Octavius*; then he draws his mouth
Into a scornful smile, and cries, Take all,
The World's not worth my care.
　　Ven. Just, just his nature.
Virtue's his path; but sometimes 'tis too narrow
For his vast Soul; and then he starts out wide,　　　125
And bounds into a Vice that bears him far
From his first course, and plunges him in ills:
But, when his danger makes him find his fault,
Quick to observe, and full of sharp remorse,
He censures eagerly his own misdeeds,　　　　　　130
Judging himself with malice to himself,
And not forgiving what as Man he did,
Because his other parts are more than Man.
He must not thus be lost.　　[Alexas *and the* Priests *come forward.*
　　Alex. You have your full Instructions, now advance;　　135
Proclaim your Orders loudly.

Serap. *Romans*, *Ægyptians*, hear the Queen's Command.
Thus *Cleopatra* bids, Let Labor cease,
To Pomp and Triumphs give this happy day,
That gave the World a Lord: 'tis *Antony's*.　　　　140
Live, *Antony*; and *Cleopatra* live.
Be this the general voice sent up to Heav'n,
And every publick place repeat this eccho.
　　Ven. [*aside*]. Fine Pageantry!
　　Serap. Set out before your doors
The Images of all your sleeping Fathers,　　　　145
With Laurels crown'd; with Laurels wreath your posts,
And strow with Flow'rs the Pavement; Let the Priests
Do present Sacrifice; pour out the Wine,
And call the Gods to joyn with you in gladness.
　　Ven. Curse on the tongue that bids this general joy.　　　　150
Can they be friends of *Antony*, who Revel
When *Antony's* in danger? Hide, for shame,
You *Romans*, your Great grandsires' Images,
For fear their Souls should animate their Marbles,
To blush at their degenerate Progeny.　　　　155
　　Alex. A love which knows no bounds to *Antony*,
Would mark the Day with honors; when all Heaven
Labor'd for him, when each propitious Star
Stood wakeful in his Orb, to watch that hour,
And shed his better influence. Her own Birth-day　　　　160
Our Queen neglected, like a vulgar Fate,
That pass'd obscurely by.
　　Ven. Would it had slept,
Divided far from his; till some remote
And future Age had call'd it out, to ruin
Some other Prince, not him.
　　Alex. Your Emperor,　　　　165
Tho grown unkind, would be more gentle, than
T'upbraid my Queen, for loving him too well.
　　Ven. Does the mute Sacrifice upbraid the Priest?
He knows him not his Executioner.
O, she has deck'd his ruin with her love,　　　　170
Led him in golden bands to gaudy slaughter,
And made perdition pleasing: She has left him
The blank of what he was;
I tell thee, Eunuch, she has quite unman'd him:
Can any Roman see, and know him now,　　　　175
Thus alter'd from the Lord of half Mankind,
Unbent, unsinew'd, made a Woman's Toy,
Shrunk from the vast extent of all his honors,
And crampt within a corner of the World?
O, *Antony!*　　　　180

Thou bravest Soldier, and thou best of Friends!
Bounteous as Nature; next to Nature's God!
Could'st thou but make new Worlds, so wouldst thou give
   'em,
As bounty were thy being. Rough in Battel,
As the first *Romans*, when they went to War;   185
Yet, after Victory, more pitiful,
Than all their Praying Virgins left at home!
   Alex. Would you could add to those more shining Virtues,
His truth to her who loves him.
   Ven. Would I could not.
But, Wherefore waste I precious hours with thee?   190
Thou art her darling mischief, her chief Engin,
Antony's other Fate. Go, tell thy Queen,
Ventidius is arriv'd, to end her Charms.
Let your *Ægyptian* Timbrels play alone;
Nor mix Effeminate Sounds with *Roman* Trumpets.   195
You dare not fight for *Antony*; go Pray,
And keep your Cowards'-Holy-day in Temples.
                       [*Exeunt* Alex., Serap.

        [. . . *Enter a second Gentleman of* M. Antony.
   2. Gent. The Emperor approaches, and commands,
On pain of Death, that none presume to stay.
   1. Gent. I dare not disobey him.   [*Going out with the other.*
   Vent. Well, I dare.   200
But, I'll observe him first unseen, and find
Which way his humour drives: the rest I'll venture.
             [*Withdraws.*
     [*Enter* Antony, *walking with a disurb'd Motion before he
     speaks.*
   Antony. They tell me, 'tis my Birth-day, and I'll keep it
With double pomp of sadness.
'Tis what the day deserves, which gave me breath.   205
Why was I rais'd the Meteor of the World,
Hung in the Skies, and blazing as I travel'd,
Till all my fires were spent; and then cast downward
To be trod out by *Cæsar*?
   Ven. [*aside*]. On my Soul,
'Tis mournful, wondrous mournful!
   Ant. Count thy gains.   210
Now, *Antony*, Wouldst thou be born for this?
Glutton of Fortune, thy devouring youth
Has starv'd thy wanting Age.
   Ven. How sorrow shakes him!   [*Aside.*

---

   *Stage direction after 197: . . . Enter a
second Gentleman:* The original stage direc-   tion reads, "Re-enter the Gentleman of
M. Antony."

So, now the Tempest tears him up by th' Roots,
And on the ground extends the noble ruin.   215
   Ant. [having thrown himself down].
Lye there, thou shadow of an Emperor;
The place thou pressest on thy Mother Earth
Is all thy Empire now: now it contains thee;
Some few dayes hence, and then twill be too large,
When thou'rt contracted in thy narrow Urn,   220
Shrunk to a few cold Ashes; then *Octavia*
(For *Cleopatra* will not live to see it),
Octavia then will have thee all her own,
And bear thee in her Widow'd hand to *Cæsar*;
Cæsar will weep, the Crocodile will weep,   225
To see his Rival of the Universe
Lye still and peaceful there. I'll think no more on't.
Give me some Musick; look that it be sad:
I'll sooth my Melancholy, till I swell,
And burst my self with sighing———   *[Soft Musick.* 230
'Tis somewhat to my humor. Stay, I fancy
I'm now turn'd wild, a Commoner of Nature;
Of all forsaken, and forsaking all;
Live in a shady Forrest's *Sylvan* Scene,
Stretch'd at my length beneath some blasted Oke;   235
I lean my head upon the Mossy Bark,
And look just of a piece, as I grew from it:
My uncomb'd Locks, matted like mistletoe,
Hang o're my hoary Face; a murm'ring Brook
Runs at my foot.
   Ven. Methinks I fancy   240
My self there too.
   Ant. The Herd come jumping by me,
And fearless, quench their thirst, while I look on,
And take me for their fellow-Citizen.
More of this Image, more; it lulls my thoughts.
        [Soft Musick again.
   Ven. I must disturb him; I can hold no longer.   245
        [Stands before him.
   Ant. [starting up]. Art thou *Ventidius?*
   Ven. Are you *Antony?*
I'm liker what I was, than you to him
I left you last.
   Ant. I'm angry.
   Vent. So am I.
   Ant. I would be private: leave me.
   Ven. Sir, I love you,

238. *Mistletoe:* The copy text gives
Misleto.

And therefore will not leave you.
    Ant. Will not leave me?   250
Where have you learnt that Answer? Who am I?
    Ven. My Emperor; the Man I love next Heaven:
If I said more, I think 'twere scarce a Sin;
Y'are all that's good, and good-like.
    Ant. All that's wretched.
You will not leave me then?
    Ven. 'Twas too presuming   255
To say I would not; but I dare not leave you:
And, 'tis unkind in you to chide me hence
So soon, when I so far have come to see you.
    Ant. Now thou hast seen me, art thou satisfy'd?
For, if a Friend, thou hast beheld enough;   260
And, if a Foe, too much.
    Ven. [*weeping*]. Look, Emperor, this is no common Dew,
I have not wept this Forty year; but now
My Mother comes afresh into my eyes;
I cannot help her softness.   265
    Ant. By Heav'n, he weeps, poor good old Man, he weeps!
The big round drops course one another down
The furrows of his cheeks. Stop 'em, *Ventidius*,
Or I shall blush to death: they set my shame,
That caus'd 'em, full before me.
    Ven. I'll do my best.   270
    Ant. Sure there's contagion in the tears of Friends:
See, I have caught it too. Believe me, 'tis not
For my own griefs, but thine——Nay, Father.
    Ven. Emperor.
    Ant. Emperor! Why, that's the stile of Victory,
The Conqu'ring Soldier, red with unfelt wounds,   275
Salutes his General so: but never more
Shall that sound reach my ears.
    Ven. I warrant you.
    Ant. Actium, Actium! Oh—
    Ven. It sits too near you.
    Ant. Here, here it lies; a lump of Lead by day,
And, in my short distracted nightly slumbers,   280
The Hag that rides my Dreams——
    Ven. Out with it; give it vent.
    Ant. Urge not my shame.
I lost a Battel.
    Ven. So has *Julius* done.
    Ant. Thou favour'st me, and speak'st not half thou think'st;
For *Julius* fought it out, and lost it fairly: 285
But *Antony*——

262. *Dew:* The copy text gives Deaw.

Ven. Nay, stop not.
    Ant. Antony
(Well, thou wilt have it) like a coward, fled,
Fled while his Soldiers fought; fled first, *Ventidius.*
Thou long'st to curse me, and I give thee leave.
I know thou cam'st prepar'd to rail.
    Ven. I did.   290
        Ant. I'll help thee—I have been a Man, *Ventidius,*
    Ven. Yes, and a brave one; but——
        Ant. I know they meaning.
But, I have lost my Reason, have disgrac'd
The name of Soldier, with inglorious ease.
In the full Vintage of my flowing honors,   295
Sate still, and saw it prest by other hands.
Fortune came smiling to my youth, and woo'd it,
And purple greatness met my ripen'd years.
When first I came to Empire, I was born
On Tides of People, crouding to my Triumphs;   300
The wish of Nations; and the willing World
Receiv'd me as its pledge of future peace;
I was so great, so happy, so belov'd,
Fate could not ruine me; till I took pains
And work'd against my Fortune, chid her from me,   305
And turn'd her loose; yet still she came again.
My careless dayes, and my luxurious nights,
At length have weary'd her, and now she's gone,
Gone, gone, divorc'd for ever. Help me, Soldier,
To curse this Mad-man, this industrious Fool,   310
Who labour'd to be wretched: pr'ythee curse me.
    Ven. No.
    Ant. Why?
    Ven. You are too sensible already
Of what y'have done, too conscious of your failings,
And like a Scorpion, whipt by others first
To fury, sting your self in mad revenge.   315
I would bring Balm, and pour it in your wounds,
Cure your distemper'd mind, and heal your fortunes.
    Ant. I know thou would'st.
    Ven. I will.
    Ant. Ha, ha, ha, ha.
    Ven. You laugh.
    Ant. I do, to see officious love
Give Cordials to the dead.
    Ven. You would be lost then?   320
    Ant. I am.
    Ven. I say, you are not. Try your fortune.
    Ant. I have, to th'utmost. Dost thou think me desperate,

Without just cause? No, when I found all lost
Beyond repair, I hid me from the World,
And learnt to scorn it here; which now I do   325
So heartily, I think it is not worth
The cost of keeping.
    Ven. *Cæsar* thinks not so:
He'll thank you for the gift he could not take.
You would be kill'd, like *Tully*, would you? do,
Hold out your Throat to *Cæsar*, and dye tamely.   330
    Ant. No, I can kill my self; and so resolve.
    Ven. I can dy with you too, when time shall serve;
But Fortune calls upon us now to live,
To fight, to Conquer.
    Ant. Sure thou Dream'st, *Ventidius.*
    Ven. No; 'tis you Dream; you sleep away your hours   335
In desperate sloth, miscall'd *Phylosophy.*
Up, up, for Honor's sake; twelve Legions wait you,
And long to call you Chief: by painful journeys,
I led 'em, patient, both of heat and hunger,
Down from the *Parthian* Marches, to the *Nile.*   340
'Twill do you good to see their Sun-burnt faces,
Their skar'd cheeks, and chopt hands; there's virtue in 'em,
They'l sell those mangled limbs at dearer rates
Than yon trim Bands can buy.
    Ant. Where left you them?
    Ven. I said, in lower *Syria.*
    Ant. Bring 'em hither;   345
There may be life in these.
    Ven. They will not come.
    Ant. Why did'st thou mock my hopes with promis'd aids
To double my despair? They'r mutinous.
    Ven. Most firm and loyal.
    Ant. Yet they will not march
To succor me. Oh trifler!
    Ven. They petition   350
You would make hast to head 'em.
    Ant. I'm besieg'd.
    Ven. There's but one way shut up: How came I hither?
    Ant. I will not stir.
    Ven. They would perhaps desire
A better reason.

---

329. *Tully:* Marcus Tullius Cicero (106–43 B.C.) was overtaken by Antony's men as he prepared to leave Italy. Instead of resisting, he offered himself to the sword and was killed on the spot, after which his head and hands were displayed on the *rostra*.

340. *Parthian Marches:* Parthian borderlands.

342. *Chopt:* Dried and cracked, chapped.

Ant. I have never us'd
My Soldiers to demand a reason of   355
My actions. Why did they refuse to March?
   Ven. They said they would not fight for *Cleopatra.*
   Ant. What was't they said?
   Ven. They said, they would not fight for *Cleopatra.*
Why should they fight indeed, to make her Conquer,   360
And make you more a Slave? to gain you Kingdoms,
Which, for a kiss, at your next midnight Feast,
You'll sell to her? then she new names her Jewels,
And calls this Diamond such or such a Tax,
Each Pendant in her ear shall be a Province.   365
   Ant. Ventidius, I allow your Tongue free licence
On all my other faults; but, on your life,
No word of *Cleopatra*: She deserves
More World's than I can lose.
   Ven. Behold, you Pow'rs,
To whom you have intrusted Humankind;   370
See *Europe, Africk, Asia* put in ballance,
And all weigh'd down by one light worthless Woman!
I think the gods are *Antony's,* and give
Like Prodigals, this neather World away,
To none but wastful hands.
   Ant. You grow presumptuous.   375
   Ven. I take the priviledge of plain love to speak.
   Ant. Plain love! plain arrogance, plain insolence:
Thy Men are Cowards; thou, an envious Traitor;
Who, under seeming honesty, hast vented
The burden of thy rank o'reflowing Gall.   380
O that thou wert my equal; great in Arms
As the first *Cæsar* was, that I might kill thee
Without a Stain to Honor!
   Ven. You may kill me;
You have done more already, call'd me Traitor.
   Ant. Art thou not one?
   Ven. For showing you your self,   385
Which none else durst have done; but had I been
That name, which I disdain to speak again,
I needed not have sought your abject fortunes,
Come to partake your fate, to dye with you.
What hindred me t' have led my Conqu'ring Eagles   390
To fill *Octavius's* Bands? I cou'd have been
A Traitor then, a glorious happy Traitor,
And not have been so call'd.
   Ant. Forgive me, Soldier:
I've been too passionate.

354. *Us'd:* Accustomed.

Ven. You thought me false;
Thought my old age betray'd you: kill me, Sir;   395
Pray kill me; yet you need not, your unkindness
Has left your Sword no work.
    Ant. I did not think so;
I said it in my rage: pr'ythee forgive me:
Why did'st thou tempt my anger, by discovery
Of what I would not hear?
    Ven. No Prince but you,   400
Could merit that sincerity I us'd,
Nor durst another Man have ventur'd it;
But you, ere Love misled your wand'ring eyes,
Were sure the chief and best of Human Race,
Fram'd in the very pride and boast of Nature,   405
So perfect, that the gods who form'd you wonder'd
At their own skill, and cry'd, A lucky hit
Has mended our design. Their envy hindred,
Else you had been immortal, and a pattern,
When Heav'n would work for ostentation sake,   410
To copy out again.
    Ant. But *Cleopatra*———
Go on; for I can bear it now.
    Ven. No more.
    Ant. Thou dar'st not trust my Passion; but thou may'st:
Thou only lov'st; the rest have flatter'd me.
    Ven. Heav'n's blessing on your heart, for that kind word.   415
May I believe you love me? speak again.
    Ant. Indeed I do. Speak this, and this, and this.
                                 [*Hugging him.*
Thy praises were unjust; but, I'll deserve 'em,
And yet mend all. Do with me what thou wilt;
Lead me to victory, thou know'st the way.   420
    Ven. And, Will you leave this———
    Ant. Pr'ythee do not curse her,
And I will leave her; though, Heav'n knows, I love
Beyond Life, Conquest, Empires; all, but Honor:
But I will leave her.
    Ven. That's my Royal Master.
And, Shall we fight?
    Ant. I warrant thee, old Soldier,   425
Thou shalt behold me once again in Iron,
And at the head of our old Troops, that beat
The *Parthians*, cry alloud, Come follow me.
    Ven. O now I hear my Emperor! in that word
Octavius fell. Gods, let me see that day,   430
And, if I have ten years behind, take all;
I'll thank you for th' exchange.

Ant. Oh *Cleopatra!*

Ven. Again?

Ant. I've done: in that last sigh, she went.
Cæsar shall know what 'tis to force a Lover,
From all he holds most dear.

    Ven. Methinks you breath   435
Another Soul: Your looks are more Divine;
You speak a Heroe, and you move a God.

    Ant. O, thou hast fir'd me; my Soul's up in Arms,
And Man's each part about me: once again,
That noble eagerness of fight has seiz'd me;   440
That eagerness, with which I darted upward
To *Cassius's* Camp: In vain the steepy Hill,
Oppos'd my way; in vain a War of Speares
Sung round my head; and planted all my shield:
I won the Trenches, while my formost Men   445
Lagg'd on the Plain below.

    Ven. Ye Gods, ye Gods,
For such another hour.

    Ant. Come on, My Soldier!
Our hearts and armes are still the same: I long
Once more to meet our foes; that Thou and I,
Like Time and Death, marching before our Troops,   450
May taste fate to e'm; Mowe e'm out a passage,
And, entring where the foremost Squadrons yield,
Begin the noble Harvest of the Field.   [*Exeunt.*

Act II

[*Cleopatra, Iras,* and *Alexas.*

Cleo. What shall I do, or whither shall I turn?
Ventidius has o'rcome, and he will go.

    Alex. He goes to fight for you.

    Cleo. Then he wou'd see me, ere he went to fight:
Flatter me not: if once he goes, he's lost: 5
And all my hopes destroy'd.

    Alex. Does this weak passion
Become a Mighty Queen?

    Cleo. I am no Queen;
Is this to be a Queen, to be besieg'd
By yon insulting *Roman*; and to wait
Each hour the Victor's Chain? These ills are small;   10
For *Antony* is lost, and I can mourn
For nothing else but him. Now come, *Octavius,*
I have no more to lose; prepare thy Bands;

446. *Lagg'd:* The copy text gives
Lag'd.

I'm fit to be a Captive: *Antony*
Has taught my mind the fortune of a Slave.   15
   Iras. Call Reason to assist you.
   Cleo. I have none.
And none would have: my Love's a noble madness,
Which shows the cause deserv'd it. Moderate sorrow
Fits vulgar Love; and for a vulgar Man:
But I have lov'd with such transcendent passion,   20
I soard, at first, quite out of Reason's view,
And now am lost above it——No, I'm proud
'Tis thus: would *Antony* could see me now;
Think you he would not sigh? though he must leave me,
Sure he would sigh; for he is noble-natur'd,   25
And bears a tender heart: I know him well.
Ah, no, I know him not; I knew him once,
But now 'tis past.
   Iras. Let it be past with you:
Forget him, Madam.
   Cleo. Never, never, *Iras.*
He once was mine; and once, though now 'tis gone,   30
Leaves a faint Image of possession still.
   Alex. Think him unconstant, cruel, and ungrateful.
   Cleo. I cannot: if I could, those thoughts were vain;
Faithless, ungrateful, cruel, though he be,
I still must love him.   [*Enter* Charmion.
Now, What news my *Charmion*?   35
Will he be kind? and, Will he not forsake me?
Am I to live, or dye? nay, Do I live?
Or am I dead? for, when he gave his answer,
Fate took the word, and then I liv'd, or dy'd.
   Char. I found him, Madam——
   Cleo. A long Speech preparing?   40
If thou bring'st comfort, hast, and give it me;
For never was more need.
   Iras. I know he loves you.
   Cleo. Had he been kind, her eyes had told me so,
Before her tongue could speak it: now she studies,
To soften what he said; but give me death,   45
Just as he sent it, *Charmion*, undisguis'd,
And in the words he spoke.
   Char. I found him then
Incompass'd round, I think, with Iron Statues,
So mute, so motionless his Soldiers stood,
While awfully he cast his eyes about,   50
And ev'ry Leader's hopes or fears survey'd:
Methought he look'd resolv'd, and yet not pleas'd.
When he beheld me strugling in the croud,

He blush'd, and bade, make way.

   Alex. There's comfort yet.

   Char. Ventidius fixt his eyes upon my passage,   55
Severely, as he meant to frown me back,
And sullenly gave place: I told my message,
Just as you gave it, broken and disorder'd;
I numbred in it all your sighs and tears,
And while I mov'd your pitiful request,   60
That you but only beg'd a last farewel,
He fetch'd an inward groan, and ev'ry time
I nam'd you, sigh'd, as if his heart were breaking,
But shun'd my eyes, and guiltily look'd down;
He seem'd not now that awful *Antony*   65
Who shook an Arm'd Assembly with his Nod,
But making show as he would rub his eyes,
Disguis'd and blotted out a falling tear.

   Cleop. Did he then weep? and, Was I worth a tear?
If what thou hast to say be not as pleasing,   70
Tell me no more, but let me dye contented.

   Char. He bid me say, He knew himself so well,
He could deny you nothing, if he saw you;
And therefore———

   Cleop. Thou would'st say, he wou'd not see me?

   Charm. And therefore beg'd you not to use a power,   75
Which he could ill resist; yet he should ever
Respect you as he ought.

   Cleo. Is that a word
For *Antony* to use to *Cleopatra*?
Oh that faint word, Respect! how I disdain it!
Disdain my self, for loving after it!   80
He should have kept that word for cold *Octavia.*
Respect is for a Wife: Am I that thing,
That dull insipid lump, without desires,
And without pow'r to give 'em?

   Alex. You misjudge;
You see through Love, and that deludes your sight: 85
As, what is strait, seems crooked through the Water;
But I, who bear my reason undisturb'd,
Can see this *Antony,* this dreaded Man,
A fearful slave, who fain would run away,
And shuns his Master's eyes: if you pursue him,   90
My life on't, he still drags a chain along,
That needs must clog his flight.

   Cleo. Could I believe thee!———

   Alex. By ev'ry circumstance I know he Loves.
True, he's hard prest, by Intrest and by Honor;
Yet he but doubts, and parlyes, and casts out   95

Many a long look for succor.

   Cleo. He sends word,
He fears to see my face.

   Alex. And would you more?
He shows his weakness who declines the Combat;
And you must urge your fortune. Could he speak
More plainly? To my ears, the Message sounds   100
Come to my rescue, *Cleopatra*, come;
Come, free me from *Ventidius*; from my Tyrant:
See me, and give me a pretence to leave him.
I hear his Trumpets. This way he must pass.
Please you, retire a while; I'll work him first,   105
That he may bend more easie.

   Cleo. You shall rule me;
But all, I fear, in vain.   [*Exit with* Char. *and* Iras.

   Alex. I fear so too;
Though I conceal'd my thoughts, to make her bold:
But, 'tis our utmost means, and Fate befriend it.   [*Withdraws.*
     [*Enter* Lictors *with Fasces; one bearing the Eagle: then*
     Enter Antony *with* Ventidius, *follow'd by other Com-*
     manders.

   Ant. Octavius is the Minion of blind Chance,   110
But holds from Virtue nothing.

   Ven. Has he courage?

   Ant. But just enough to season him from Coward.
O, 'tis the coldest youth upon a Charge,
The most deliberate fighter! if he ventures
(As in *Illyria* once they say he did   115
To storm a Town) 'tis when he cannot chuse,
When all the World have fixt their eyes upon him;
And then he lives on that for seven years after,
But, at a close revenge he never fails.

   Ven. I heard, you challeng'd him.

   Ant. I did, *Ventidius.*   120
What think'st thou was his answer? 'twas so tame,——
He said he had more wayes than one to dye;
I had not.

   Ven. Poor!

   Ant. He has more wayes than one;
But he would chuse 'em all before that one.

   Ven. He first would chuse an Ague, or a Fever: 125

   Ant. No: it must be an Ague, not a Fever;
He has not warmth enough to dye by that.

   Ven. Or old Age, and a Bed.

   Ant. Aye, there's his choice.

128. *Aye, there's his choice:* The copy
text gives I, there's his choice.

He would live, like a Lamp, to the last wink,
And crawl upon the utmost verge of life: 130
O *Hercules*! Why should a Man like this,
Who dares not trust his fate for one great action,
Be all the care of Heav'n? Why should he Lord it
O're Fourscore thousand Men, of whom, each one
Is braver than himself?
　　Ven. You conquer'd for him: 135
Philippi knows it; there you shar'd with him
That Empire, which your Sword made all your own.
　　Ant. Fool that I was, upon my Eagle's Wings
I bore this Wren, till I was tir'd with soaring,
And now he mounts above me.   140
Good Heav'ns, Is this, is this the Man who braves me?
Who bids my age make way: drives me before him,
To the World's ridge, and sweeps me off like rubbish?
　　Ven. Sir, we lose time; the Troops are mounted all.
　　Ant. Then give the word to March: 145
I long to leave this Prison of a Town,
To joyn thy Legions; and, in open Field,
Once more to show my face. Lead, my Deliverer.
　　　　　　　　　　　　[*Enter* Alex.
　　Alex. Great Emperor,
In mighty Arms renown'd above Mankind,   150
But, in soft pity to th' opprest, a God:
This message sends the mournful *Cleopatra*
To her departing Lord.
　　Ven. Smooth Sycophant!
　　Alex. A thousand wishes, and ten thousand Prayers,
Millions of blessings wait you to the Wars,   155
Millions of sighs and tears she sends you too,
And would have sent
As many dear embraces to your Arms,
As many parting kisses to your Lips;
But those, she fears, have weary'd you already.   160
　　Ven. [*aside*]. False Crocodyle!
　　Alex. And yet she begs not now, you would not leave her,
That were a wish too mighty for her hopes,
Too presuming for her low Fortune, and your ebbing love,
That were a wish for her more prosp'rous dayes,   165
Her blooming beauty, and your growing kindness.
　　Ant. [*aside*]. Well, I must Man it out: What would the
　　　　Queen?
　　Alex. First, to these noble Warriors, who attend,

136. *Philippi:* The town in Macedonia
where Brutus and Cassius were defeated
by Antony and Octavius in 42 B.C.

Your daring courage in the Chase of Fame
(Too daring, and too dang'rous for her quiet)   170
She humbly recommends all she holds dear,
All her own cares and fears, the care of you.
    Ven. Yes, witness *Actium*.
    Ant. Let him speak, *Ventidius*.
    Alex. You, when his matchless valor bears him forward,   175
With ardor too Heroick, on his foes
Fall down, as she would do, before his feet;
Lye in his way, and stop the paths of Death;
Tell him, this God is not invulnerable,
That absent *Cleopatra* bleeds in him;   180
And, that you may remember her Petition,
She begs you wear these Trifles, as a pawn,
Which, at your wisht return, she will redeem.
            [*Gives Jewels to the Commanders.*
With all the Wealth of *Ægypt*:
This, to the great *Ventidius* she presents,   185
Whom she can never count her Enemy,
Because he loves her Lord.
    Ven. Tell her I'll none on't;
I'm not asham'd of honest Poverty:
Not all the Diamonds of the East can bribe
Ventidius from his faith. I hope to see   190
These, and the rest of all her sparkling store,
Where they shall more deservingly be plac'd.
    Ant. And who must wear 'em then?
    Ven. The wrong'd *Octavia*.
    Ant. You might have spar'd that word.
    Ven. And he that Bribe.
    Ant. But have I no remembrance?
    Alex. Yes, a dear one: 195
Your slave, the Queen——
    Ant. My Mistress.
    Alex. Then your Mistress,
Your Mistress would, she sayes, have sent her Soul,
But that you had long since; she humbly begs
This Ruby bracelet, set with bleeding hearts
(The emblems of her own), may bind your Arme.   200
            [*Presenting a Bracelet.*
    Ven. Now, my best Lord, in Honor's name, I ask you,
For Manhood's sake, and for your own dear safety,
Touch not these poyson'd gifts,
Infected by the sender, touch 'em not,
Miriads of blewest Plagues lye underneath 'em,   205
And more than Aconite has dipt the Silk.
    Ant. Nay, now you grow too Cynical, *Ventidius*.

A Lady's favors may be worn with honor.
What, to refuse her Bracelet! On my Soul,
When I lye pensive in my Tent alone,   210
'Twill pass the wakeful hours of Winter nights,
To tell these pretty Beads upon my arm,
To count for every one a soft embrace,
A melting kiss at such and such a time;
And now and then the fury of her love.   215
When—— And what harm's in this?
   Alex. None, none my Lord,
But what's to her, that now 'tis past for ever.
   Ant. [*going to tye it*]. We Soldiers are so aukward——
     help me tye it.
   Alex. In faith, my Lord, we Courtiers too are aukward
In these affairs: so are all Men indeed;   220
Ev'n I, who am not one. But shall I speak?
   Ant. Yes, freely.
   Alex. Then, my Lord, fair hands alone
Are fit to tye it; she, who sent it, can.
   Ven. Hell, Death; this Eunuch Pandar ruins you.
You will not see her?
       [Alexas *whispers an Attendant, who goes out.*
   Ant. But to take my leave.   225
   Ven. Then I have wash'd an Æthiope. Y'are undone;
Y'are in the Toils; y'are taken; y'are destroy'd:
Her eyes do *Cæsar's* work.
   Ant. You fear too soon.
I'm constant to my self: I know my strength;
And yet she shall not think me Barbarous, neither.   230
Born in the depths of *Africk*: I'm a Roman,
Bred to the Rules of soft humanity.
A guest, and kindly us'd, should bid farewel.
   Ven. You do not know
How weak you are to her, how much an Infant;   235
You are not proof against a smile, or glance;
A sigh will quite disarm you.
   Ant. See, she comes!
Now you shall find your error. Gods, I thank you:
I form'd the danger greater than it was,
And, now 'tis near, 'tis lessen'd.
   Ven. Mark the end yet.   240
       [*Enter* Cleopatra, Charmion *and* Iras.
   Ant. Well, Madam, we are met.
   Cleo. Is this a Meeting?
Then, we must part?
   Ant. We must.
   Cleo. Who sayes we must?

Ant. Our own hard fates.
Cleo. We make those Fates our selves.
Ant. Yes, we have made 'em; we have lov'd each other
Into our mutual ruin.   245
    Cleo. The Gods have seen my Joys with envious eyes;
I have no friends in Heav'n; and all the World
(As 'twere the bus'ness of Mankind to part us)
Is arm'd against my Love: ev'n you your self
Joyn with the rest; you, you are arm'd against me.   250
    Ant. I will be justify'd in all I do
To late Posterity, and therefore hear me.
If I mix a lye
With any truth, reproach me freely with it;
Else, favor me with silence.
    Cleo. You command me,   255
And I am dumb:
    Ven. I like this well: he shows Authority.
    Ant. That I derive my ruin
From you alone——
    Cleo. O Heav'ns! I ruin you!
    Ant. You promis'd me your silence, and you break it   260
Ere I have scarce begun.
    Cleo. Well, I obey you.
    Ant. When I beheld you first, it was in *Ægypt*,
Ere *Cæsar* saw your Eyes; you gave me love,
And were too young to know it; that I setled
Your Father in his Throne, was for your sake;   265
I left th' acknowledgment for time to ripen.
Cæsar stept in, and with a greedy hand
Pluck'd the green fruit, ere the first blush of red,
Yet cleaving to the bough. He was my Lord,
And was, beside, too great for me to rival,   270
But, I deserv'd you first, though he enjoy'd you.
When, after, I beheld you in *Cilicia*,
An Enemy to *Rome*, I pardon'd you.
    Cleo. I clear'd my self——
    Ant. Again you break your Promise.
I lov'd you still, and took your weak excuses,   275
Took you into my bosome, stain'd by *Cæsar*,
And not half mine: I went to *Ægypt* with you
And hid me from the bus'ness of the World,
Shut out enquiring Nations from my sight,
To give whole years to you.   280
    Ven. Yes, to your shame be't spoken.   [*aside.*
    Ant. How I lov'd
Witness ye Dayes and Nights, and all your hours,
That Danc'd away with Down upon your Feet,

As all your bus'ness were to count my passion.
One day past by, and nothing saw but Love; 285
Another came, and still 'twas only Love:
The Suns were weary'd out with looking on,
And I untyr'd with loving.
I saw you ev'ry day, and all the day;
And ev'ry day was still but as the first: 290
So eager was I still to see you more.
Ven. 'Tis all too true.
Ant. Fulvia, my Wife, grew jealous,
As she indeed had reason; rais'd a War
In *Italy,* to call me back.
Ven. But yet
You went not.
Ant. While within your arms I lay, 295
The World fell mouldring from my hands each hour,
And left me scarce a grasp (I thank your love for't).
Ven. Well push'd : that last was home.
Cleop. Yet may I speak?
Ant. If I have urg'd a falshood, yes; else, not.
Your silence says I have not. *Fulvia* dy'd 300
(Pardon, you gods, with my unkindness dy'd).
To set the World at Peace, I took *Octavia,*
This Cesar's Sister; in her pride of youth
And flow'r of Beauty did I wed that Lady,
Whom blushing I must praise, because I left her. 305
You call'd; my Love obey'd the fatal summons:
This rais'd the Roman Arms; the Cause was yours.
I would have fought by Land, where I was stronger;
You hindred it: yet, when I fought at Sea,
Forsook me fighting; and (Oh stain to Honor! 310
Oh lasting shame!) I knew not that I fled;
But fled to follow you.
Ven. What haste she made to hoist her purple Sails!
And, to appear magnificent in flight,
Drew half our strength away.
Ant. All this you caus'd. 315
And, Would you multiply more ruins on me?
This honest Man, my best, my only friend,
Has gather'd up the Shipwrack of my Fortunes;
Twelve Legions I have left, my last recruits,
And you have watch'd the news, and bring your eyes 320
To seize them too. If you have ought to answer,
Now speak, you have free leave.
Alex. [*aside*]. She stands confounded:
Despair is in her eyes.
Ven. Now lay a Sigh i'th way, to stop his passage:

Prepare a Tear, and bid it for his Legions;   325
'Tis like they shall be sold.
    Cleo. How shall I plead my cause, when you, my Judge
Already have condemn'd me? Shall I bring
The Love you bore me for my Advocate?
That now is turn'd against me, that destroys me;   330
For, love once past, is, at the best, forgotten;
But oftner sours to hate: 'twill please my Lord
To ruine me, and therefore I'll be guilty.
But, could I once have thought it would have pleas'd you,
That you would pry, with narrow searching eyes   335
Into my faults, severe to my destruction,
And watching all advantages with care,
That serve to make me wretched? Speak, my Lord,
For I end here. Though I deserve this usage,
Was it like you to give it?
    Ant. O you wrong me,   340
To think I sought this parting, or desir'd
To accuse you more than what will clear my self,
And justifie this breach.
    Cleo. Thus low I thank you.
And, since my innocence will not offend,
I shall not blush to own it.
    Ven. After this   345
I think she'll blush at nothing.
    Cleo. You seem griev'd
(And therein you are kind) that *Cæsar* first
Enjoy'd my love, though you deserv'd it better:
I grieve for that, my Lord, much more than you;
For, had I first been yours, it would have sav'd   350
My second choice: I never had been his,
And ne'r had been but yours. But *Cæsar* first,
You say, possess'd my love. Not so, my Lord:
He first possess'd my Person; you my Love:
Cæsar lov'd me; but I lov'd *Antony*.   355
If I endur'd him after, 'twas because
I judg'd it due to the first name of Men;
And, half constrain'd, I gave, as to a Tyrant,
What he would take by force.
    Ven. O Syren! Syren!
Yet grant that all the love she boasts were true,   360
Has she not ruin'd you? I still urge that,
The fatal consequence.
    Cleo. The consequence indeed,
For I dare challenge him, my greatest foe,
To say it was design'd: 'tis true, I lov'd you,
And kept you far from an uneasie Wife   365

(Such *Fulvia* was).
Yes, but he'll say, you left *Octavia* for me——
And, Can you blame me to receive that love,
Which quitted such desert, for worthless me?
How often have I wish'd some other *Cæsar*,   370
Great as the first, and as the second young,
Would court my Love to be refus'd for you!
    Ven. Words, words; but *Actium*, Sir, remember *Actium*.
    Cleo. Ev'n there, I dare his malice. True, I Counsel'd
To fight at Sea; but, I betray'd you not.   375
I fled; but not to the Enemy. 'Twas fear;
Would I had been a Man, not to have fear'd,
For none would then have envy'd me your friendship,
Who envy me your Love.
    Ant. We're both unhappy:
If nothing else, yet our ill fortune parts us,   380
Speak; Would you have me perish, by my stay?
    Cleo. If as a friend you ask my Judgment, go;
If as a Lover, stay. If you must perish:
'Tis a hard word; but stay.
    Ven. See now th' effects of her so boasted love!   385
She strives to drag you down to ruine with her:
But, could she scape without you, oh how soon
Would she let go her hold, and haste to shore,
And never look behind!
    Cleo. Then judge my love by this.
                    [*Giving* Antony *a Writing.*
Could I have born   390
A life or death, a happiness or woe
From yours divided, this had giv'n me means.
    Ant. By *Hercules*, the Writing of *Octavius*!
I know it well; 'tis that Proscribing hand,
Young as it was, that led the way to mine,   395
And left me but the second place in Murder.
See, see, *Ventidius*! here he offers *Ægypt*,
And joyns all *Syria* to it, as a present,
So, in requital, she forsake my fortunes,
And joyn her Arms with his.
    Cleo. And yet you leave me!   400
You leave me, *Anthony;* and, yet I love you.
Indeed I do: I have refus'd a Kingdom,
That's a Trifle:
For I could part with life; with any thing,
But onely you. O let me dye but with you!   405
Is that a hard request?
    Ant. Next living with you,
'Tis all that Heav'n can give.

Alex. [*aside*]. He melts; We conquer.

Cleo. No: you shall go: your Int'rest calls you hence;
Yes; your dear interest pulls too strong for these
Weak Armes to hold you here.   [*Takes his hand.*
Go; leave me, Soldier   410
(For you're no more a Lover); leave me dying:
Push me all pale and panting from your bosome,
And, when your March begins, let one run after
Breathless almost for Joy; and cry, she's dead:
The Souldiers shout; you then perhaps may sigh,   415
And muster all your *Roman* Gravity;
Ventidius chides; and strait your Brow cleares up.
As I had never been.

Ant. Gods, 'tis too much; too much for Man to bear!

Cleo. What is't for me then,
A weak forsaken Woman? and a Lover?   420
Here let me breathe my last: envy me not
This minute in your Armes: I'll dye apace:
As fast as ere I can; and end your trouble.

Ant. Dye! Rather let me perish: looss'nd Nature
Leap from its hinges. Sink the props of Heav'n,   425
And fall the Skyes to crush the neather World.
My Eyes, my Soul; my all!   [*Embraces her.*

Ven. And what's this Toy
In ballance with your fortune, Honor, Fame?

Ant. What is't, *Ventidius*? it out-weighs 'em all;
Why, we have more than conquer'd *Cæsar* now: 430
My Queen's not only Innocent, but Loves me.
This, this is she who drags me down to ruin!
But, could she scape without me, with what haste
Would she let slip her hold, and make to shore,
And never look behind!   435
Down on thy knees, Blasphemer as thou art,
And ask forgiveness of wrong'd Innocence.

Ven. I'll rather dye, than take it. Will you go?

Ant. Go! Whither? go from all that's excellent!
Faith, Honor, Virtue, all good things forbid,   440
That I should go from her, who sets my love
Above the price of Kingdoms. Give, you Gods,
Give to your Boy, your *Cæsar*,
This Rattle of a Globe to play withal,
This Gu-gau World, and put him cheaply off: 445
I'll not be pleas'd with less than *Cleopatra*.

Cleo. She['s] wholly yours. My heart's so full of joy,
That I shall do some wild extravagance
Of Love, in publick; and the foolish World,
Which knows not tenderness, will think me Mad.   450

Ven. O Women! Women! Women! all the gods
Have not such pow'r of doing good to Man,
As you of doing harm.   [*Exit.*
    Ant. Our Men are Arm'd.
Unbar the Gate that looks to *Cæsar's* Camp;
I would revenge the Treachery he meant me: 455
And long security makes Conquest easie.
I'm eager to return before I go;
For, all the pleasures I have known, beat thick
On my remembrance: how I long for night!
That both the sweets of mutual love may try,   460
And once Triumph o're *Cæsar* we dye.   [*Exeunt.*

Act III

[*At one door, Enter* Cleopatra, Charmion, Iras, *and*
Alexas, *a Train of Ægyptians: at the other,* Antony *and*
Romans. *The entrance on both sides is prepar'd by Musick;
the Trumpets first sounding on* Antony's *part: then answer'd
by Timbrels, &c. on* Cleopatra's. Charmion *and* Iras *hold
a Laurel Wreath betwixt them. A Dance of Ægyptians.
After the Ceremony,* Cleopatra *Crowns* Antony.]

    Ant. I thought how those white arms would fold me in,
And strain me close, and melt me into love;
So pleas'd with that sweet Image, I sprung forwards,
And added all my strength to every blow;
    Cleo. Come to me, come, my Soldier, to my Arms;   5
You've been too long away from my embraces;
But, when I have you fast, and all my own,
With broken murmurs, and with amorous sighs,
I'll say, you were unkind, and punish you,
And mark you red with many an eager kiss.   10
    Ant. My Brighter *Venus!*
    Cleo. O my greater *Mars!*
    Ant. Thou joinst us well, my Love!
Suppose me come from the *Phlegræan* Plains,
Where gasping Gyants lay, cleft by my Sword:
And Mountain tops par'd off each other blow,   15
To bury those I slew: receive me, goddess:
Let *Cæsar* spread his subtile Nets, like Vulcan;
In thy embraces I would be beheld
By Heav'n and Earth at once:

13. *Phlegræan Plains:* The Greek name
for sections of Campania, Terra di Lavoro,
roughly extending from Rome into
southern Italy, west of Naples, a place
rich in mythology; there giants were
fabled to be buried, according to Strabo,
Diodorus Siculus, and other classical
commentators.

And make their envy what they meant their sport.   20
Let those who took us blush; I would love on
With awful State, regardless of their frowns,
As their superior god.
There's no satiety of Love, in thee;
Enjoy'd, thou still art new; perpetual Spring   25
Is in thy armes; the ripen'd fruit but falls,
And blossoms rise to fill its empty place;
And I grow rich by giving.
                  [*Enter* Ventidius, *and stands apart.*
    Alex. O, now the danger's past, your General comes.
He joyns not in your joys, nor minds your Triumphs;   30
But, with contracted brows, looks frowning on,
As envying your Success.
    Ant. Now, on my Soul, he loves me; truely loves me;
He never flatter'd me in any vice,
But awes me with his virtue: ev'n this minute   35
Methinks he has a right of chiding me.
Lead to the Temple: I'll avoid his presence;
It checks too strong upon me.   [*Exeunt the rest.*
    [*As* Antony *is going,* Ventidius *pulls him by the Robe.*
    Ven. Emperor.
    Ant. [*looking back*]. 'Tis the old argument; I pry'thee spare me.
    Ven. But this one hearing, Emperor.
    Ant. Let go   40
My Robe; or, by my Father *Hercules*————
    Ven. By *Hercules* his Father, that's yet greater,
I bring you somewhat you would wish to know.
    Ant. Thou see'st we are observ'd; attend me here,
And I'll return.   [*Exit.*   45
    Ven. I'm waining in his favor, yet I love him;
I love this Man, who runs to meet his ruine;
And, sure the gods, like me, are fond of him:
His Virtues lye so mingled with his Crimes,
As would confound their choice to punish one,   50
And not reward the other.   [*Enter* Antony.
    Ant. We can conquer.
You see, without your aid.
We have dislodg'd their Troops,
They look on us at distance, and, like Curs
Scap'd from the Lions paws, they bay far off,   55
And lick their wounds, and faintly threaten War.
Five thousand *Romans* with their faces upward,
Lye breathless on the Plain.
    Ven. 'Tis well: and he

41. *My Father Hercules:* Plutarch cites
the tradition that the Antonys were descended from Hercules by one of the
god's sons, Anton.

Who lost 'em, could have spar'd Ten thousand more.
Yet if, by this advantage, you could gain   60
An easier Peace, while *Cæsar* doubts the Chance
Of Arms!——
    Ant. O think not on't, *Ventidius*;
The Boy pursues my ruin, he'll no peace:
His malice is considerate in advantage;
O, he's the coolest Murderer; so stanch,   65
He kills, and keeps his temper.
    Ven. Have you no friend
In all his Army, who has power to move him?
Mæcenas or *Agrippa* might do much.
    Ant. They're both too deep in *Cæsar's* interests.
We'll work it out by dint of Sword, or perish.   70
    Ven. Fain I would find some other.
    Ant. Thank thy love.
Some four or five such Victories as this,
Will save thy farther pains.
    Ven. Expect no more; *Cæsar* is on his Guard:
I know, Sir, you have conquer'd against odds;   75
But still you draw Supplies from one poor Town,
And of *Ægyptians:* he has all the World,
And, at his back, Nations come pouring in,
To fill the gaps you make. Pray think again.
    Ant. Why dost thou drive me from my self, to search   80
For Forreign aids? to hunt my memory,
And range all o'er a waste and barren place
To find a Friend? The wretched have no Friends——
Yet I had one, the bravest youth of *Rome*,
Whom *Cæsar* loves beyond the love of Women;   85
He could resolve his mind, as Fire does Wax;
From that hard rugged Image, melt him down,
And mould him in what softer form he pleas'd.
    Ven. Him would I see; that man of all the world:
Just such a one we want.
    Ant. He lov'd me too;   90
I was his Soul; he liv'd not but in me:
We were so clos'd within each others brests,
The rivets were not found that join'd us first.
That does not reach us yet: we were so mixt,
As meeting streams, both to our selves were lost;   95
We were one mass; we could not give or take,
But from the same; for he was I, I he.
    Ven. [*aside*]. He moves as I would wish him.
    Ant. After this,
I need not tell his name: 'twas *Dollabella*.

75. *Odds:* The copy text gives ods.

Ven. He's now in *Cæsar's* Camp.

  Ant. No matter where,   100
Since he's no longer mine. He took unkindly
That I forbade him *Cleopatra's* sight;
Because I fear'd he lov'd her: he confest
He had a warmth, which, for my sake, he stifled;
For 'twere impossible that two, so one,   105
Should not have lov'd the same. When he departed,
He took no leave; and that confirm'd my thoughts.

  Ven. It argues that he lov'd you more than her,
Else he had staid; but he perceiv'd you jealous,
And would not grieve his friend: I know he loves you.   110

  Ant. I should have seen him then ere now.

  Ven. Perhaps
He has thus long been lab'ring for your peace.

  Ant. Would he were here.

  Ven. Would you believe he lov'd you?
I read your answer in your eyes; you would.
Not to conceal it longer, he has sent   115
A Messenger from *Cæsar's* Camp, with Letters.

  Ant. Let him appear.

  Ven. I'll bring him instantly.   [*Exit* Ventidius;
    [*Re-enters immediately with* Dollabella.

  Ant. 'Tis he himself, himself, by holy Friendship!
      [*Runs to embrace him.*
Art thou return'd at last, my better half?
Come, give me all my self.
Let me not live,   120
If the young Bridegroom, longing for his night,
Was ever half so fond.

  Dolla. I must be silent; for my Soul is busie
About a nobler work: she's new come home,
Like a long-absent man, and wanders o'er   125
Each room, a stranger to her own, to look
If all be safe.

  Ant. Thou hast what's left of me.
For I am now so sunk from what I was,
Thou find'st me at my lowest water-mark.
The Rivers that ran in, and rais'd my fortunes,   130
Are all dry'd up, or take another course:
What I have left is from my native Spring;
I've still a heart that swells, in scorn of fate,
And lifts me to my banks.

  Dolla. Still you are Lord of all the World to me.   135

  Ant. Why, then I yet am so; for thou art all.
If I had any joy when thou wert absent,
I grudg'd it to my self; methought I robb'd

Thee of thy part. But, Oh my *Dollabella!*
Thou hast beheld me other than I am.   140
Hast thou not seen my morning Chambers fill'd
With Scepter'd Slaves, who waited to salute me:
With Eastern Monarchs, who forgot the Sun,
To worship my uprising? Menial Kings
Ran coursing up and down my Palace-yard,   145
Stood silent in my presence, watch'd my eyes,
And, at my least command, all started out
Like Racers to the Goal.
    Dolla. Slaves to your fortune:
    Ant. Fortune is *Cæsar's* now; and what am I?
    Ven. What you have made your self; I will not flatter.   150
    Ant. Is this friendly done?
    Dolls. Yes, when his end is so, I must join with him;
Indeed I must, and yet you must not chide:
Why am I else your friend?
    Ant. Take heed, young man,
How thou upbraid'st my love: the Queen has eyes,   155
And thou too hast a Soul. Canst thou remember
When, swell'd with hatred, thou beheld'st her first
As accessary to thy Brother's death?
    Dolla. Spare my remembrance; 'twas a guilty day,
And still the blush hangs here.
    Ant. To clear her self,   160
For sending him no aid, she came from *Egypt.*
Her Gally down the Silver *Cydnos* row'd,
The Tackling Silk, the Streamers wav'd with Gold,
The gentle Winds were lodg'd in Purple sails:
Her Nymphs, like *Nereids*, round her Couch, were plac'd;   165
Where she, another Sea-born *Venus*, lay.
    Dolla. No more: I would not hear it.
    Ant. O, you must!
She lay, and leant her cheek upon her hand,
And cast a look so languishingly sweet,
As if, secure of all beholders' hearts,   170
Neglecting she could take 'em: Boys, like *Cupids*,
Stood fanning, with their painted wings, the winds
That plaid about her face: but if she smil'd,
A darting glory seem'd to blaze abroad:
That men's desiring eyes were never weary'd;   175
But hung upon the object: to soft Flutes
The Silver Oars kept time; and while they plaid,
The hearing gave new pleasure to the sight;
And both to thought: 'twas Heav'n, or somewhat more;
For she so charm'd all hearts, that gazing crowds   180
Stood panting on the shore, and wanted breath

To give their welcome voice.
Then, *Dollabella*, where was then thy Soul?
Was not thy fury quite disarm'd with wonder?
Didst thou not shrink behind me from those eyes,   185
And whisper in my ear, Oh tell her not
That I accus'd her of my Brother's death?
    Dolla. And should my weakness be a plea for yours?
Mine was an age when love might be excus'd,
When kindly warmth, and when my springing youth   190
Made it a debt to Nature. Yours———
    Ven. Speak boldly.
Yours, he would say, in your declining age,
When no more heat was left but what you forc'd,
When all the sap was needful for the Trunk,
When it went down, then you constrain'd the course,   195
And robb'd from Nature, to supply desire;
In you (I would not use so harsh a word)
But 'tis plain dotage.
    Ant. Ha!
    Dolla. 'Twas urg'd too home.
But yet the loss was private that I made;
'Twas but my self I lost: I lost no Legions;   200
I had no World to lose, no people's love.
    Ant. This from a friend?
    Dolla. Yes, *Anthony*, a true one;
A friend so tender, that each word I speak
Stabs my own heart, before it reach your ear.
O, judge me not less kind because I chide: 205
To *Cæsar* I excuse you.
    Ant. O ye Gods!
Have I then liv'd to be excus'd to *Cæsar*?
    Dolla. As to your equal.
    Ant. Well, he's but my equal:
While I wear this, he never shall be more.
    Dolla. I bring Conditions from him.
    Ant. Are they Noble?   210
Methinks thou shouldst not bring 'em else; yet he
Is full of deep dissembling; knows no Honour,
Divided from his Int'rest. Fate mistook him;
For Nature meant him for an Usurer;
He's fit indeed to buy, not conquer Kingdoms.   215
    Ven. Then, granting this,
What pow'r was theirs who wrought so hard a temper
To honourable Terms!
    Ant. It was my *Dollabella*, or some God.
    Dolla. Nor I; nor yet *Mæcenas*, nor *Agrippa:*   220
They were your Enemies; and I a Friend

Too weak alone; yet 'twas a *Roman's* deed.
 Ant. 'Twas like a *Roman* done: show me that man
Who has preserv'd my life, my love, my honour;
Let me but see his face.
 Ven. That task is mine,   225
And, Heav'n, thou know'st how pleasing. [*Exit Vent.*
 Dolla. You'll remember
To whom you stand oblig'd?
 Ant. When I forget it,
Be thou unkind, and that's my greatest curse.
My Queen shall thank him too.
 Dolla. I fear she will not.
 Ant. But she shall do't: the Queen, my *Dollabella!* 230
Hast thou not still some grudgings of thy Fever?
 Dolla. I would not see her lost.
 Ant. When I forsake her,
Leave me, my better Stars; for she has truth
Beyond her beauty. *Cæsar* tempted her,
At no less price than Kingdoms, to betray me; 235
But she resisted all: and yet thou chid'st me
For loving her too well. Could I do so?
 Dolla. Yes, there's my reason.
    [*Re-enter* Ventidius, *with* Octavia, *leading* Antony's *two*
       little Daughters.
 Ant. Where?————*Octavia* there ! [*Starting back.*
 Ven. What, is she poyson to you? a Disease?
Look on her, view her well; and those she brings: 240
Are they all strangers to your eyes? has Nature
No secret call, no whisper they are yours?
 Dolla. For shame, my Lord, if not for love, receive 'em
With kinder eyes. If you confess a man,
Meet 'em, embrace 'em, bid 'em welcome to you. 245
Your arms should open, ev'n without your knowledge,
To clasp 'em in; your feet should turn to wings,
To bear you to 'em; and your eyes dart out,
And aim a kiss ere you could reach the lips.
 Ant. I stood amaz'd to think how they came hither. 250
 Vent. I sent for 'em, I brought 'em in, unknown
To *Cleopatra's* Guards.
 Dolla. Yet are you cold?
 Octav. Thus long I have attended for my welcome,
Which, as a stranger, sure I might expect.
Who am I?
 Ant. *Cæsar's* Sister.
 Octav. That's unkind !   255
Had I been nothing more than *Cæsar's* Sister,

244. *Confess:* Admit you are.

Know, I had still remain'd in *Cæsar's* Camp;
But your *Octavia*, your much injur'd Wife,
Tho' banish'd from your Bed, driv'n from your House,
In spight of *Cæsar's* Sister, still is yours.   260
'Tis true, I have a heart disdains your coldness,
And prompts me not to seek what you should offer;
But a Wife's Virtue still surmounts that pride:
I come to claim you as my own; to show
My duty first, to ask, nay beg, your kindness: 265
Your hand, my Lord; 'tis mine, and I will have it.
                    [*Taking his hand.*
    Ven. Do, take it; thou deserv'st it.
    Dolla. On my Soul,
And so she does: she's neither too submissive,
Nor yet too haughty; but so just a mean,
Shows, as it ought, a Wife and *Roman* too.   270
    Ant. I fear, *Octavia*, you have begg'd my life.
    Octav. Begg'd it, my Lord?
    Ant. Yes, begg'd it, my Ambassadress,
Poorly and basely begg'd it of your Brother.
    Octav. Poorly and basely I could never beg;
Nor could my Brother grant.   275
    Ant. Shall I, who, to my kneeling Slave, could say,
Rise up, and be a King; shall I fall down
And cry, Forgive me, *Cæsar*? shall I set
A Man, my Equal, in the place of *Jove*,
As he could give me being? No; that word,   280
Forgive, would choke me up,
And die upon my tongue.
    Dolla. You shall not need it.
    Ant. I will not need it. Come, you've all betray'd me:
My Friend too! To receive some vile conditions.
My Wife has bought me, with her prayers and tears;   285
And now I must become her branded Slave:
In every peevish mood she will upbraid
The life she gave: if I but look awry,
She cries, I'll tell my Brother.
    Octav. My hard fortune
Subjects me still to your unkind mistakes.   290
But the Conditions I have brought are such
You need not blush to take: I love your Honour,
Because 'tis mine; it never shall be said
Octavia's Husband was her Brother's Slave.
Sir, you are free; free, ev'n from her you loath;   295
For, tho' my Brother bargains for your love,
Makes me the price and cement of your peace,

280. *As:* As though.

I have a Soul like yours; I cannot take
Your love as alms, nor beg what I deserve.
I'll tell my Brother we are reconcil'd;   300
He shall draw back his Troops, and you shall march
To rule the East: I may be dropt at *Athens*;
No matter where, I never will complain,
But only keep the barren Name of Wife,
And rid you of the trouble.   305
  Ven. Was ever such a strife of sullen Honour!
Both scorn to be oblig'd.
  Dolla. O, she has toucht him in the tender'st part;
See how he reddens with despight and shame
To be out-done in Generosity!   310
  Ven. See how he winks! how he dries up a tear,
That fain would fall!
  Ant. *Octavia*, I have heard you, and must praise
The greatness of your Soul;
But cannot yield to what you have propos'd: 315
For I can ne'er be conquer'd but by love;
And you do all for duty. You would free me,
And would be dropt at *Athens*; was't not so?
  Octav. It was, my Lord.
  Ant. Then I must be oblig'd
To one who loves me not, who, to her self,   320
May call me thankless and ungrateful Man:
I'll not endure it, no.
  Ven. I'm glad it pinches there.
  Octav. Would you triumph o'er poor *Octavia's* Virtue?
That pride was all I had to bear me up;   325
That you might think you ow'd me for your life,
And ow'd it to my duty, not my love.
I have been injur'd, and my haughty Soul
Could brook but ill the Man who slights my Bed.
  Ant. Therefore you love me not.
  Octav. Therefore, my Lord,   330
I should not love you.
  Ant. Therefore you wou'd leave me?
  Octav. And therefore I should leave you————if I could.
  Dolla. Her Soul's too great, after such injuries,
To say she loves; and yet she lets you see it.
Her modesty and silence plead her cause.   335
  Ant. O, *Dollabella*, which way shall I turn?
I find a secret yielding in my Soul;
But *Cleopatra*, who would die with me,
Must she be left? Pity pleads for *Octavia*;
But does it not plead more for *Cleopatra*?   340
  Ven. Justice and Pity both plead for *Octavia*;

For *Cleopatra*, neither.
One would be ruin'd with you; but she first
Had ruin'd you: the other, you have ruin'd,
And yet she would preserve you.   345
In every thing their merits are unequal.
    Ant. O, my distracted Soul!
    Octav. Sweet Heav'n compose it.
Come, come, my Lord, if I can pardon you,
Methinks you should accept it. Look on these;
Are they not yours? Or stand they thus neglected   350
As they are mine? Go to him, Children, go;
Kneel to him, take him by the hand, speak to him;
For you may speak, and he may own you too,
Without a blush; and so he cannot all
His Children: go, I say, and pull him to me,   355
And pull him to your selves, from that bad Woman.
You, *Agrippina*, hang upon his arms;
And you, *Antonia*, clasp about his waste:
If he will shake you off, if he will dash you
Against the Pavement, you must bear it, Children;   360
For you are mine, and I was born to suffer.
          [*Here the Children go to him,* &c.
    Ven. Was ever sight so moving! Emperor!
    Dolla. Friend!
    Octav. Husband!
    Both Childr. Father!
    Ant. I am vanquish'd: take me,
Octavia; take me, Children; share me all.   [*Embracing them.*
I've been a thriftless Debtor to your loves,   365
And run out much, in riot, from your stock;
But all shall be amended.
    Octav. O blest hour!
    Dolla. O happy change!
    Ven. My joy stops at my tongue;
But it has found two chanels here for one,
And bubbles out above.   370
    Ant. [*to Octav.*]. This is thy Triumph; lead me where thou
      wilt;
Ev'n to thy Brother's Camp.
    Octav. All there are yours.
               [*Enter* Alexas *hastily.*
    Alex. The Queen, my Mistress, Sir, and yours———
    Ant. 'Tis past. *Octavia*, you shall stay this night;
    To morrow,
Cæsar and we are one.   375
      [*Ex. leading* Octavia, Dol. *and the Children follow.*

366. *In riot:* In extravagant waste.

Ven. There's news for you: run,
My officious Eunuch,
Be sure to be the first; haste foreward:
Haste, my dear Eunuch, haste.   [*Exit.*
     Alex. This downright fighting Fool, this thick-scull'd Hero,
This blunt unthinking Instrument of death,   380
With plain dull Virtue, has out-gone my Wit:
Pleasure forsook my early'st Infancy,
The luxury of others robb'd my Cradle,
And ravish'd thence the promise of a Man:
Cast out from Nature, disinherited   385
Of what her meanest Children claim by kind;
Yet, greatness kept me from contempt: that's gone.
Had *Cleopatra* follow'd my advice,
Then he had been betray'd, who now forsakes.
She dies for love; but she has known its joys: 390
Gods, is this just, that I, who knows no joys,
Must die, because she loves?
                    [*Enter Cleopatra, Charmion, Iras, Train.*
Oh, Madam, I have seen what blasts my eyes!
Octavia's here!
     Cleop. Peace with that Raven's note.
I know it too; and now am in   395
The pangs of death.
     Alex. You are no more a Queen;
Egypt is lost.
     Cleop. What tell'st thou me of *Egypt*?
My Life, my Soul is lost! *Octavia* has him!
O fatal name to *Cleopatra's* love!
My kisses, my embraces now are hers;   400
While I—— But thou hast seen my Rival; speak;
Does she deserve this blessing? Is she fair,
Bright as a Goddess? and is all perfection
Confin'd to her? It is. Poor I was made
Of that course matter which, when she was finish'd,   405
The Gods threw by, for rubbish.
     Alex. She's indeed a very Miracle.
     Cleop. Death to my hopes, a Miracle!
     Alex. [*bowing*]. A Miracle;
I mean of Goodness; for in Beauty, Madam,
You make all wonders cease.
     Cleop. I was too rash: 410
Take this in part of recompence. But, Oh,   [*Giving a Ring.*
I fear thou flatter'st me.
     Char. She comes! she's here!
     Iras. Flie, Madam, *Cæsar's* Sister!
     Cleop. Were she the Sister of the Thund'rer *Jove*,

And bore her Brother's Lightning in her eyes,   415
Thus would I face my Rival.
   [*Meets* Octav. *with* Ventid., Octav. *bears up to her.*
   Their Trains come up on either side.
   Octav. I need not ask if you are *Cleopatra,*
Your haughty carriage——
   Cleop. Shows I am a Queen:
Nor need I ask you who you are.
   Octav. A *Roman*:
A name that makes, and can unmake a Queen.   420
   Cleop. Your Lord, the Man who serves me, is a *Roman.*
   Octav. He was a *Roman*, till he lost that name
To be a Slave in *Egypt*; but I come
To free him thence.
   Cleop. Peace, peace, my Lover's *Juno.*
When he grew weary of that Houshold-Clog,   425
He chose my easier bonds.
   Octav. I wonder not
Your bonds are easie; you have long been practis'd
In that lascivious art: he's not the first
For whom you spread your snares: let *Cæsar* witness.
   Cleop. I lov'd not *Cæsar*; 'twas but gratitude   430
I paid his love: the worst your malice can,
Is but to say the greatest of Mankind
Has been my Slave. The next, but far above him,
In my esteem, is he whom Law calls yours,
But whom his love made mine.
   Oct. [*coming up close to her*]. I would view nearer   435
That face, which has so long usurp'd my right,
To find th'inevitable charms, that catch
Mankind so sure, that ruin'd my dear Lord.
   Cleop. O, you do well to search; for had you known
But half these charms, you had not lost his heart.   440
   Octav. Far be their knowledge from a *Roman* Lady,
Far from a modest Wife. Shame of our Sex,
Dost thou not blush, to own those black endearments
That make sin pleasing?
   Cleop. You may blush, who want 'em.
If bounteous Nature, if indulgent Heav'n   445
Have giv'n me charms to please the bravest Man,
Should I not thank 'em? should I be asham'd,
And not be proud? I am, that he has lov'd me;
And, when I love not him, Heav'n change this Face
For one like that.
   Octav. Thou lov'st him not so well.   450
   Cleop. I love him better, and deserve him more.
   Octav. You do not: cannot: you have been his ruine.

Who made him cheap at *Rome*, but *Cleopatra*?
Who made him scorn'd abroad, but *Cleopatra*?
At *Actium*, who betray'd him? *Cleopatra*.   455
Who made his Children Orphans? and poor me
A wretched Widow? only *Cleopatra*?
    Cleop. Yet she who loves him best is *Cleopatra*.
If you have suffer'd, I have suffer'd more.
You bear the specious Title of a Wife,   460
To guild your Cause, and draw the pitying World
To favour it: the World contemns poor me;
For I have lost my Honour, lost my Fame,
And stain'd the glory of my Royal House,
And all to bear the branded Name of Mistress.   465
There wants but life, and that too I would lose
For him I love.
    Octav. Be't so then; take thy wish.   [*Exit with her train.*
    Cleop. And 'tis my wish,
Now he is lost for whom alone I liv'd.
My sight grows dim, and every object dances,   470
And swims before me, in the maze of death.
My spirits, while they were oppos'd, kept up;
They could not sink beneath a Rival's scorn:
But now she's gone they faint.
    Alex. Mine have had leisure
To recollect their strength, and furnish counsel,   475
To ruine her; who else must ruine you.
    Cleop. Vain Promiser!
Lead me, my *Charmion*; nay, your hand too, *Iras*:
My grief has weight enough to sink you both.
Conduct me to some solitary Chamber,
And draw the Curtains round;   480
Then leave me to my self, to take alone
My fill of grief:
    There I till death will his unkindness weep:
    As harmless Infants moan themselves asleep.   [*Exeunt.*

Act IV

[*Antony, Dollabella.*

    Dolla. Why would you shift it from your self on me?
Can you not tell her you must part?
    Ant. I cannot.
I could pull out an eye, and bid it go,
And t'other should not weep. Oh, *Dollabella*,

Stage direction after 467: Exit with her
train: The copy text gives *Exit cum suis.*

How many deaths are in this word *Depart!*   5
I dare not trust my tongue to tell her so:
One look of hers, would thaw me into tears
And I should melt till I were lost agen.
　Dolla. Then let *Ventidius*;
He's rough by nature.
　Ant. Oh, he'll speak too harshly;   10
He'll kill her with the news: Thou, only thou.
　Dolla. Nature has cast me in so soft a mould,
That but to hear a story feign'd for pleasure
Of some sad Lover's death, moistens my eyes,
And robs me of my Manhood.—I should speak   15
So faintly; with such fear to grieve her heart,
She'd not believe it earnest.
　Ant. Therefore; therefore
Thou only, thou art fit: think thy self me,
And when thou speak'st (but let it first be long)
Take off the edge from every sharper sound,   20
And let our parting be as gently made
As other Loves begin: wilt thou do this?
　Dolla. What you have said, so sinks into my Soul,
That, if I must speak, I shall speak just so.
　Ant. I leave you then to your sad task: Farewel.   25
I sent her word to meet you.　[*Goes to the door, and comes back.*
I forgot;
Let her be told, I'll make her peace with mine:
Her Crown and Dignity shall be preserv'd,
If I have pow'r with *Cæsar.*——O, be sure
To think on that.
　Dolla. Fear not, I will remember.   30
　　　　[*Antony goes again to the door, and comes back.*
　Ant. And tell her, too, how much I was constrain'd;
I did not this, but with extreamest force:
Desire her not to hate my memory,
For I still cherish hers;——insist on that.
　Dolla. Trust me, I'll not forget it.
　Ant. Then that's all.　　[*Goes out, and returns again.*   35
Wilt thou forgive my fondness this once more?
Tell her, tho' we shall never meet again,
If I should hear she took another Love,
The news would break my heart.—Now I must go;
For every time I have return'd, I feel   40
My Soul more tender; and my next command
Would be to bid her stay, and ruine both.　　[*Exit.*
　Dolla. Men are but Children of a larger growth,
Our appetites as apt to change as theirs,
And full as craving too, and full as vain;   45

And yet the Soul, shut up in her dark room,
Viewing so clear abroad, at home sees nothing;
But, like a Mole in Earth, busie and blind,
Works all her folly up, and casts it outward
To the World's open view: thus I discover'd,   50
And blam'd the love of ruin'd *Antony*;
Yet wish that I were he, to be so ruin'd.
                [*Enter* Ventidius *above.*
    Ven. Alone? and talking to himself? concern'd too?
Perhaps my ghess is right; he lov'd her once,
And may pursue it still.
    Dolla. O Friendship! Friendship!   55
Ill canst thou answer this; and Reason, worse:
Unfaithful in th' attempt; hopeless to win;
And, if I win, undone: meer madness all.
And yet th' occasion's fair. What injury,
To him, to wear the Robe which the throws by?   60
    Ven. None, none at all. This happens as I wish,
To ruine her yet more with *Antony*.
        [*Enter* Cleopatra, *talking with* Alexas, Charmion, Iras *on
        the other side.*
    Dolla. She comes! What charms have sorrow on that face!
Sorrow seems pleas'd to dwell with so much sweetness;
Yet, now and then, a melancholy smile   65
Breaks loose, like Lightning, in a Winter's night,
And shows a moment's day.
    Ven. If she should love him too! Her Eunuch there!
That *Porc'pisce* bodes ill weather. Draw, draw nearer,
Sweet Devil, that I may hear.
    Alex. Believe me; try   70
        [*Dollabella goes over to* Charmion *and* Iras; *seems to talk
        with them.*
To make him jealous; jealousie is like
A polisht Glass held to the lips when life's in doubt:
If there be breath, 'twill catch the damp and show it.
    Cleop. I grant you jealousie's a proof of love,
But 'tis a weak and unavailing Med'cine;   75
It puts out the disease, and makes it show,
But has no pow'r to cure.
    Alex. 'Tis your last remedy, and strongest too:
And then this *Dollabella*; who so fit
To practice on? He's handsom, valiant, young,   80
And looks as he were laid for Nature's bait
To catch weak Women's eyes.
He stands already more than half suspected
Of loving you: the least kind word, or glance,

69. *Porc'pisce: Porcus piscis* (porpoise).   76. *Puts out:* Distresses, aggravates.

You give this Youth, will kindle him with love: 85
Then, like a burning Vessel set adrift,
You'll send him down amain before the wind,
To fire the heart of jealous *Antony.*
    Cleop. Can I do this? Ah no; my love's so true,
That I can neither hide it where it is,   90
Nor show it where it is not. Nature meant me
A Wife, a silly harmless houshold Dove,
Fond without art, and kind without deceit;
But Fortune, that has made a Mistress of me,
Hast thrust me out to the wide World, unfurnish'd   95
Of falshood to be happy.
    Alex. Force your self.
Th' event will be, your Lover will return
Doubly desirous to possess the good
Which once he fear'd to lose.
    Cleop. I must attempt it;
But Oh with what regret!   100
        [*Exit Alex. She comes up to Dolabella.*
    Ven. So, now the Scene draws near: they're in my reach.
    Cleop. [*to Dol.*]. Discoursing with my Women! Might not I
Share in your entertainment?
    Char. You have been
The Subject of it, Madam.
    Cleop. How; and how?
    Iras. Such praises of your beauty!
    Cleop. Meer Poetry.   105
Your *Roman* Wits, your *Gallus* and *Tibullus,*
Have taught you this from *Citheris* and *Delia.*
    Dolla. Those *Roman* Wits have never been in *Egypt,*
Citheris and *Delia* else had been unsung:
I, who have seen——had I been born a Poet,   110
Should chuse a nobler name.
    Cleop. You flatter me.
But, 'tis your Nation's vice: all of your Country
Are flatterers, and all false. Your Friend's like you.
I'm sure he sent you not to speak these words.
    Dolla. No, Madam; yet he sent me——
    Cleop. Well, he sent you——   115
    Della. Of a less pleasing errand.
    Cleop. How less pleasing?
Less to your self, or me?
    Dolla. Madam, to both;

106. *Gallus and Tibullus:* Gaius Cornelius Gallus (69–26 B.C.) was a soldier, poet, and, under Augustus (Octavius Caesar), first prefect of Egypt; in four books of elegiacs he celebrated his love for an actress, Citheris. Albius Tibullus (c. 60–19 B.C.) was a poet; one of his two books of verse was known as *Delia,* the name of the woman it praised.

For you must mourn, and I must grieve to cause it.
 Cleop. You, *Charmion*, and your Fellow, stand at distance.
[*Aside*]. Hold up, my Spirits. Well, now your mournful
  matter;   120
For I'm prepar'd, perhaps can ghess it too.
 Dolla. I wish you would; for 'tis a thankless office
To tell ill news: and *I*, of all your Sex,
Most fear displeasing you.
 Cleop. Of all your Sex,
I soonest could forgive you, if you should.   125
 Ven. Most delicate advances! Woman! Woman!
Dear damn'd, inconstant Sex!
 Cleop. In the first place,
I am to be forsaken; is't not so?
 Dolla. I wish I could not answer to that question.
 Cleop. Then pass it o'er, because it troubles you: 130
I should have been more griev'd another time.
Next, I'm to lose my Kingdom.——Farewel, *Egypt.*
Yet, is there any more?
 Dolla. Madam, I fear
Your too deep sense of grief has turn'd your reason.
 Cleop. No, no, I'm not run mad; I can bear Fortune: 135
And Love may be expell'd by other Love,
As Poysons are by Poysons.
 Dolla. You o'erjoy me, Madam,
To find your griefs so moderately born.
You've heard the worst; all are not false, like him. 140
 Cleop. No; Heav'n forbid they should.
 Dolla. Some men are constant.
 Cleop. And constancy deserves reward, that's certain.
 Dolla. Deserves it not; but give it leave to hope.
 Ven. I'll swear thou hast my leave. I have enough:
But how to manage this! Well, I'll consider.   [*Exit.* 145
 Dolla. I came prepar'd,
To tell you heavy news; news, which I thought,
Would fright the blood from your pale cheeks to hear:
But you have met it with a cheerfulness
That makes my task more easie; and my tongue, 150
Which on another's message was employ'd,
Would gladly speak its own.
 Cleop. Hold, *Dollabella.*
First tell me, were you chosen by my Lord?
Or sought you this employment?
 Dolla. He pick'd me out; and, as his bosom-friend, 155
He charg'd me with his words.
 Cleop. The message then
I know was tender, and each accent smooth,

To mollifie that rugged word *Depart*.
    Dolla. Oh, you mistake: he chose the harshest words,
With fiery eyes, and with contracted brows,   160
He coyn'd his face in the severest stamp:
And fury, shook his Fabrick like an Earthquake;
He heav'd for vent, and burst like bellowing *Ætna*,
In sounds scarce humane, "Hence, away for ever:
Let her begone, the blot of my renown,   165
And bane of all my hopes:
        [*All the time of this speech,* Cleop. *seems more and more*
        concern'd, till she sinks quite down.
Let her be driv'n as far as men can think
From Man's commerce: She'll poyson to the Center."
    Cleop. Oh, I can bear no more!
    Dolla. Help, help: Oh Wretch! Oh cursed, cursed Wretch! 170
What have I done?
    Char. Help, chafe her Temples, *Iras.*
    Iras. Bend, bend her forward quickly.
    Char. Heav'n be prais'd,
She comes again.
    Cleop. Oh, let him not approach me.
Why have you brought me back to this loath'd Being,
Th' abode of Falshood, violated Vows,   175
And injur'd Love? For pity, let me go;
For, if there be a place of long repose,
I'm sure I want it. My disdainful Lord
Can never break that quiet; nor awake
The sleeping Soul, with hollowing in my Tomb   180
Such words as fright her hence. Unkind, unkind.
    Dolla. [*kneeling*]. Believe me, 'tis against my self I speak,
That sure deserves belief; I injur'd him:
My Friend ne'er spoke those words. Oh, had you seen
How often he came back, and every time   185
With something more obliging and more kind,
To add to what he said; what dear Farewels;
How almost vanquisht by his love he parted,
And lean'd to what unwillingly he left:
I, Traitor as I was, for love of you   190
(But what can you not do, who made me false!)
I forg'd that lye; for whose forgiveness kneels
This self-accus'd, self-punish'd Criminal.
    Cleop. With how much ease believe we what we wish!
Rise, *Dollabella*; if you have been guilty,   195
I have contributed, and too much love
Has made me guilty too.
Th' advance of kindness which I made, was feign'd,
To call back fleeting love by jealousie;

But 'twould not last. Oh, rather let me lose   200
Than so ignobly trifle with his heart.

    Dolla. I find your breast fenc'd round from humane reach,
Transparent as a Rock of solid Crystal;
Seen through, but never pierc'd. My Friend, my Friend!
What endless treasure hast thou thrown away,   205
And scatter'd, like an Infant, in the Ocean,
Vain sums of Wealth which none can gather thence.

    Cleop. Could you not beg
An hour's admittance to his private ear?
Like one who wanders through long barren Wilds,   210
And yet foreknows no hospitable Inn
Is near to succour hunger,
Eats his fill, before his painful march:
So would I feed a while my famish'd eyes
Before we part; for I have far to go,   215
If death be far, and never must return.

                [Ventidius, *with* Octavia, *behind.*

    Ven. From hence you may discover———Oh, sweet, sweet!
Would you indeed? the pretty hand in earnest? [*Takes her hand.*

    Dolla. I will, for this reward.——Draw it not back,
'Tis all I e'er will beg.   220

    Ven. They turn upon us.

    Octav. What quick eyes has guilt!

    Ven. Seem not to have observ'd 'em, and go on.

                [*They enter.*

    Dolla. Saw you the Emperor, *Ventidius?*

    Ven. No.
I sought him; but I heard that he was private,
None with him, but *Hipparchus* his Freedman.   225

    Dolla. Know you his bus'ness?

    Ven. Giving him Instructions,
And Letters, to his Brother *Cæsar.*

    Dolla. Well,
He must be found.   [*Exeunt* Dol. *and* Cleop.

    Octav. Most glorious impudence!

    Ven. She look'd methought
As she would say, Take your old man, *Octavia;*   230
Thank you, I'm better here.
Well, but what use
Make we of this discovery?

    Octav. Let it die.

    Ven. I pity *Dollabella;* but she's dangerous:
Her eyes have pow'r beyond *Thessalian* Charms
To draw the Moon from Heav'n; for Eloquence,   235
The Sea-green Syrens taught her voice their flatt'ry;
And, while she speaks, Night steals upon the Day,

Unmark'd of those that hear: Then she's so charming,
Age buds at sight of her, and swells to youth:
The holy Priests gaze on her when she smiles;   240
And with heav'd hands forgetting gravity,
They bless her wanton eyes: Even I who hate her,
With a malignant joy behold such beauty;
And, while I curse, desire it. *Anthony*
Must needs have some remains of passion still,   245
Which may ferment into a worse relapse,
If now not fully cur'd. I know, this minute,
With *Cæsar* he's endeavouring her peace.
  Octav. You have prevail'd: but for a farther purpose
           [Walks off.
I'll prove how he will relish this discovery.   250
What, make a Strumpet's peace! it swells my heart:
It must not, sha' not be.
  Ven. His Guards appear.
Let me begin, and you shall second me.
         [Enter Antony.
  Ant. Octavia, I was looking you, my love:
What, are your Letters ready? I have giv'n   255
My last Instructions.
  Octav. Mine, my Lord, are written.
  Ant. Ventidius!   *[Drawing him aside.*
  Ven. My Lord?
  Ant. A word in private.
When saw you *Dollabella*?
  Ven. Now, my Lord,
He parted hence; and *Cleopatra* with him.
  Ant. Speak softly. 'Twas by my command he went,   260
To bear my last farewel.
  Ven. [aloud]. It look'd indeed
Like your farewel.
  Ant. More softly.———My farewel?
What secret meaning have you in those words
Of my Farewel? He did it by my Order.
  Ven. [aloud]. Then he obey'd your Order. I suppose   265
You bid him do it with all gentleness,
All kindness, and all———love.
  Ant. How she mourn'd,
The poor forsaken Creature!
  Ven. She took it as she ought; she bore your parting
As she did *Cæsar's,* as she would another's,   270
Were a new Love to come.
  Ant. [aloud]. Thou dost belye her;
Most basely, and maliciously belye her.
  Ven. I thought not to displease you; I have done.

Octav. [*coming up*]. You seem disturb'd, my Lord.

Ant. A very trifle.

Retire, my Love.

Ven. It was indeed a trifle.   275

He sent————.

  Ant. [*angrily*]. No more. Look how thou disobey'st me;

Thy life shall answer it.

  Octav. Then 'tis no trifle.

  Ven. [*to Octav.*]. 'Tis less; a very nothing: you too saw it,

As well as I, and therefore 'tis no secret.

  Ant. She saw it!

  Ven. Yes: she saw young *Dollabella*————   280

  Ant. Young *Dollabella!*

  Ven. Young, I think him young,

And handsom too; and so do others think him.

But what of that? He went by your command,

Indeed 'tis probable, with some kind message;

For she receiv'd it graciously; she smil'd: 285

And then he grew familiar with her hand,

Squeez'd it, and worry'd it with ravenous kisses;

She blush'd, and sigh'd, and smil'd, and blush'd again;

At last she took occasion to talk softly,

And brought her cheek up close, and lean'd on his: 290

At which, he whisper'd kisses back on hers;

And then she cry'd aloud, that constancy

Should be rewarded.

  Octav. This I saw and heard.

  Ant. What Woman was it, whom you heard and saw

So playful with my Friend!

Not *Cleopatra?*   295

  Ven. Ev'n she, my Lord!

  Ant. My *Cleopatra?*

  Ven. Your *Cleopatra;*

Dollabella's Cleopatra:

Every Man's *Cleopatra.*

  Ant. Thou ly'st.

  Ven. I do not lye, my Lord.   300

Is this so strange? Should Mistresses be left,

And not provide against a time of change?

You know she's not much us'd to lonely nights.

  Ant. I'll think no more on't.

I know 'tis false, and see the plot betwixt you.   305

You needed not have gone this way, *Octavia.*

What harms it you that *Cleopatra's* just?

She's mine no more. I see; and I forgive:

Urge it no farther, Love.

  Octav. Are you concern'd

That she's found false?

Ant. I should be, were it so;   310
For, tho 'tis past, I would not that the World
Should tax my former choice: That I lov'd one
Of so light note; but I forgive you both.

Ven. What has my age deserv'd, that you should think
I would abuse your ears with perjury?   315
If Heav'n be true, she's false.

Ant. Tho Heav'n and Earth
Should witness it, I'll not believe her tainted.

Ven. I'll bring you then a Witness
From Hell to prove her so. Nay, go not back;
           [*Seeing* Alexas *just ent'ring, and starting back.*
For stay you must and shall.

Alex. What means my Lord?   320

Ven. To make you do what most you hate; speak truth.
You are of *Cleopatra's* private Counsel,
Of her Bed-Counsel, her lascivious hours;
Are conscious of each nightly change she makes,
And watch her, as *Chaldeans* do the Moon,   325
Can tell what Signs she passes through, what day.

Alex. My Noble Lord.

Ven. My most Illustrious Pandar,
No fine set Speech, no Cadence, no turn'd Periods,
But a plain home-spun Truth, is what I ask:
I did, my self, o'erhear your Queen make love   330
To *Dollabella.* Speak; for I will know,
By your confession, what more past betwixt 'em;
How near the bus'ness draws to your employment;
And when the happy hour.

Ant. Speak truth, *Alexas*, whether it offend   335
Or please *Ventidius*, care not: justifie
Thy injur'd Queen from malice: dare his worst.

Oct. [*aside*]. See, how he gives him courage! how he fears
To find her false! and shuts his eyes to truth,
Willing to be misled!   340

Alex. As far as love may plead for Woman's frailty,
Urg'd by desert and greatness of the Lover;
So far (Divine *Octavia!*) may my Queen
Stand ev'n excus'd to you, for loving him,
Who is your Lord: so far, from brave *Ventidius*,   345
May her past actions hope a fair report.

Ant. 'Tis well, and truly spoken: mark, *Ventidius.*

Alex. To you, most Noble Emperor, her strong passion
Stands not excus'd, but wholly justifi'd.
Her Beauty's charms alone, without her Crown,   350
From *Ind* and *Meroe* drew the distant Vows

Of sighing Kings; and at her feet were laid
The Scepters of the Earth, expos'd on heaps,
To choose where she would Reign:
She thought a *Roman* only could deserve her;   355
And, of all *Romans*, only *Antony*.
And, to be less than Wife to you, disdain'd
Their lawful passion.
    Ant. 'Tis but truth.
    Alex. And yet, tho love, and your unmatch'd desert,
Have drawn her from the due regard of Honor,   360
At last, Heav'n open'd her unwilling eyes
To see the wrongs she offer'd fair *Octavia*,
Whose holy Bed she lawlessly usurpt,
The sad effects of this improsperous War,
Confirm'd those pious thoughts.
    Ven. [*aside*]. O, wheel you there?   365
Observe him now; the Man begins to mend,
And talk substantial reason. Fear not, Eunuch,
The Emperor has giv'n thee leave to speak.
    Alex. Else had I never dar'd t' offend his ears
With what the last necessity has urg'd   370
On my forsaken Mistress; yet I must not
Presume to say her heart is wholly alter'd.
    Ant. No, dare not for thy life, I charge thee dare not,
Pronounce that fatal word.
    Octav. [*aside*]. Must I bear this? good Heav'n, afford me
        patience.   375
    Ven. On, sweet Eunuch; my dear half man, proceed.
    Alex. Yet *Dollabella*
Has lov'd her long, he, next my God-like Lord,
Deserves her best; and should she meet his passion,
Rejected, as she is, by him she lov'd———   380
    Ant. Hence, from my sight; for I can bear no more:
Let Furies drag thee quick to Hell; let all
The longer damn'd have rest; each torturing hand
Do thou employ, till *Cleopatra* comes,
Then joyn thou too, and help to torture her.   385
           [*Exit* Alexas, *thrust out by* Antony.
    Octav. 'Tis not well,
Indeed, my Lord, 'tis much unkind to me,
To show this passion, this extream concernment
For an abandon'd, faithless Prostitute.
    Ant. Octavia, leave me: I am much disorder'd.   390
Leave me, I say.
    Octav. My Lord?
    Ant. I bid you leave me.
    Ven. Obey him, Madam: best withdraw a while,

And see how this will work.

    Octav. Wherein have I offended you, my Lord,
That I am bid to leave you? Am I false,   395
Or infamous? Am I a *Cleopatra*?
Were I she,
Base as she is, you would not bid me leave you;
But hang upon my neck, take slight excuses,
And fawn upon my falshood.

    Ant. 'Tis too much,   400
Too much, *Octavia;* I am prest with sorrows
Too heavy to be born; and you add more:
I would retire, and recollect what's left
Of Man within, to aid me.

    Octav. You would mourn
In private, for your Love, who has betray'd you;   405
You did but half return to me: your kindness
Linger'd behind with her. I hear, my Lord,
You make Conditions for her,
And would include her Treaty. Wondrous proofs
Of love to me!

    Ant. Are you my Friend, *Ventidius*?   410
Or are you turn'd a *Dollabella* too,
And let this Fury loose?

    Ven. Oh, be advis'd,
Sweet Madam, and retire.

    Octav. Yes, I will go; but never to return.
You shall no more be haunted with this Fury.   415
My Lord, my Lord, love will not always last,
When urg'd with long unkindness, and disdain;
Take her again whom you prefer to me;
She stays but to be call'd. Poor cozen'd Man!
Let a feign'd parting give her back your heart,   420
Which a feign'd love first got; for injur'd me,
Tho' my just sense of wrongs forbid my stay,
My duty shall be yours.
To the dear pledges of our former love,
My tenderness and care shall be transferr'd,   425
And they shall cheer, by turns, my Widow'd Nights:
So, take my last farewel; for I despair
To have you whole, and scorn to take you half.   [*Exit.*

    Ven. I combat Heav'n, which blasts my best designs:
My last attempt must be to win her back;   430
But Oh, I fear in vain.   [*Exit.*

    Ant. Why was I fram'd with this plain honest heart,
Which knows not to disguise its griefs and weakness,
But bears its workings outward to the World?
I should have kept the mighty anguish in,   435

And forc'd a smile at *Cleopatra's* falshood:
Octavia had believ'd it, and had staid;
But I am made a shallow-forded Stream,
Seen to the bottom: all my clearness scorn'd,
And all my faults expos'd!————See, where he comes,   440
            [*Enter* Dollabella.
Who has prophan'd the Sacred Name of Friend,
And worn it into vileness!
With how secure a brow, and specious form
He guilds the secret Villain! Sure that face
Was meant for honesty; but Heav'n mis-match'd it,   445
And furnish'd Treason out with Nature's pomp,
To make its work more easie.
    Dolla. O, my Friend!
    Ant. Well, *Dollabella*, you perform'd my message?
    Dolla. I did, unwillingly.
    Ant. Unwillingly?
Was it so hard for you to bear our parting?   450
You should have wisht it.
    Dolla. Why?
    Ant. Because you love me.
And she receiv'd my message, with as true,
With as unfeign'd a sorrow, as you brought it?
    Dolla. She loves you, ev'n to madness.
    Ant. Oh, I know it.
You, *Dollabella*, do not better know   455
How much she loves me. And should I
Forsake this Beauty? This all-perfect Creature?
    Dolla. I could not, were she mine.
    Ant. And yet you first
Perswaded me: how come you alter'd since?
    Dolla. I said at first I was not fit to go;   460
I could not hear her sighs, and see her tears,
But pity must prevail: and so, perhaps,
It may again with you; for I have promis'd
That she should take her last farewel: and, see,
She comes to claim my word.
               [*Enter* Cleopatra.
    Ant. False *Dollabella*!   465
    Dolla. What's false, my Lord?
    Ant. Why, *Dollabella's* false,
And *Cleopatra's* false; both false and faithless.
Draw near, you well-join'd wickedness, you Serpents,
Whom I have, in my kindly bosom, warm'd
Till I am stung to death.
    Dolla. My Lord, have I   470
Deserv'd to be thus us'd?

Cleop. Can Heav'n prepare
A newer Torment? Can it find a Curse
Beyond our separation?
　　Ant. Yes, if Fate
Be just, much greater: Heav'n should be ingenious
In punishing such crimes. The rowling Stone,　　　　　　475
And gnawing Vulture, were slight pains, invented
When *Jove* was young, and no examples known
Of mighty ills; but you have ripen'd sin
To such a monstrous growth, 'twill pose the Gods
To find a equal Torture. Two, two such,　　　　　　480
Oh there's no farther name, two such————to me,
To me, who lock'd my Soul within your breasts,
Had no desires, no joys, no life, but you;
When half the Globe was mine, I gave it you
In Dowry with my heart; I had no use,　　　　　　485
No fruit of all, but you: a Friend and Mistress
Was what the World could give. Oh, *Cleopatra!*
Oh, *Dollabella!* how could you betray
This tender heart, which with an Infant-fondness
Lay lull'd betwixt your bosoms, and there slept　　　　　490
Secure of injur'd Faith?
　　Dolla. If she has wrong'd you,
Heav'n, Hell, and You revenge it.
　　Ant. If she wrong'd me,
Thou wouldst evade thy part of guilt; but swear
Thou lov'st not her.
　　Dolla. Not so as I love you.
　　Ant. Not so! Swear, swear, I say, thou dost not love her.　495
　　Dolla. No more than Friendship will allow.
　　Ant. No more?
Friendship allows thee nothing: thou art perjur'd.————
And yet thou didst not swear thou lov'dst her not;
But not so much, no more. Oh trifling Hypocrite,
Who dar'st not own to her thou dost not love,　　　　　500
Nor own to me thou dost! *Ventidius* heard it;
Octavia saw it.
　　Cleop. They are enemies.
　　Ant. Alexas is not so: he, he confest it;
He, who, next Hell, best knew it, he avow'd it.
[*To Dol.*]. Why do I seek a proof beyond your self?　　505
You whom I sent to bear my last Farewel,
Return'd to plead her stay.

---

475. *The rowling Stone:* The stone
which Sisyphus, in Hades, had to roll
uphill continuously; when he neared the
top, it would tumble down again, and he
would have to begin his task anew.

476. *Gnawing Vulture:* Zeus (Jove)
condemned Prometheus to be bound to
Mt. Caucasus and to have a vulture consume his liver every day.

Dolla. What shall I answer?
If to have lov'd be guilt, then I have sinn'd;
But if to have repented of that love
Can wash away my crime, I have repented.   510
Yet, if I have offended past forgiveness,
Let not her suffer: she is innocent.
    Cleop. Ah, what will not a Woman do who loves!
What means will she refuse, to keep that heart
Where all her joys are plac'd! 'Twas I encourag'd,   515
'Twas I blew up the fire that scorch'd his Soul,
To make you jealous; and by that regain you.
But all in vain; I could not counterfeit:
In spight of all the damms, my love broke o'er,
And drown'd my heart again: Fate took th' occasion;   520
And thus one minute's feigning has destroy'd
My whole life's truth.
    Ant. Thin Cobweb Arts of Falshood;
Seen, and broke through at first.
    Dolla. Forgive your Mistress.
    Cleop. Forgive your Friend.
    Ant. You have convinc'd your selves;
You plead each other's Cause: What Witness have you,   525
That you but meant to raise my jealousie?
    Cleop. Our selves, and Heav'n.
    Ant. Guilt witnesses for guilt. Hence, Love and Friendship;
You have no longer place in humane breasts,
These two have driv'n you out: avoid my sight;   530
I would not kill the Man whom I lov'd;
And cannot hurt the Woman; but avoid me,
I do not know how long I can be tame;
For, if I stay one minute more to think
How I am wrong'd, my Justice and Revenge   535
Will cry so loud within me, that my pity
Will not be heard for either.
    Dolla. Heav'n has but
Our sorrow for our sins; and then delights
To pardon erring Man: sweet Mercy seems
Its darling Attribute, which limits Justice;   540
As if there were degrees in Infinite;
And Infinite would rather want perfection
Than punish to extent.
    Ant. I can forgive
A Foe; but not a Mistress, and a Friend:
Treason is there in its most horrid shape,   545
Where trust is greatest: and the Soul resign'd
Is stabb'd by its own Guards: I'll hear no more;

524. *Convinc'd:* Convicted.

Hence from my sight, for ever.
    Cleop. How? for ever!
I cannot go one moment from your sight,
And must I go for ever?   550
My joys, my only joys are center'd here:
What place have I to go to? my own Kingdom?
That I have lost for you: or to the *Romans*?
They hate me for your sake: or must I wander
The wide World o'er, a helpless, banish'd Woman,   555
Banish'd for love of you; banish'd from you;
Aye, there's the Banishment! Oh hear me; hear me,
With strictest Justice: for I beg no favour:
And if I have offended you, then kill me,
But do not banish me.
    Ant. I must not hear you.   560
I have a Fool within me takes your part;
But Honour stops my ears.
    Cleop. For pity hear me!
Wou'd you cast off a Slave who follow'd you,
Who crouch'd beneath your Spurn?——He has no pity!
See, if he gives one tear to my departure;   565
One look, one kind farewel: Oh Iron heart!
Let all the Gods look down, and judge betwixt us,
If he did ever love!
    Anth. No more: *Alexas!*
    Dolla. A perjur'd Villain!
    Anth. [*to Cleop.*]. Your *Alexas*; yours.
    Cleop. O 'twas his plot: his ruinous design   570
T' ingage you in my love by jealousie.
Hear him; confront him with me; let him speak.
    Anth. I have; I have.
    Cleop. And if he clear me not——
    Ant. Your Creature! one who hangs upon your smiles!
Watches your eye to say or to unsay   575
Whate'er you please! I am not to be mov'd.
    Cleop. Then must we part? Farewel, my cruel Lord,
Th' appearance is against me; and I go
Unjustifi'd, for ever from your sight.
How I have lov'd, you know; how yet I love,   580
My only confort is, I know my self:
I love you more, ev'n now you are unkind,
Than when you lov'd me most; so well, so truly,
I'll never strive against it; but die pleas'd
To think you once were mine.   585
    Ant. Good Heav'n, they weep at parting.

557. *Aye, there's the Banishment:* The
copy text gives I, there's the Banishment.

Must I weep too? that calls 'em innocent.
I must not weep; and yet I must, to think
That I must not forgive.———
Live; but live wretched, 'tis but just you shou'd,   590
Who made me so: Live from each other's sight:
Let me not hear you meet: Set all the Earth,
And all the Seas, betwixt your sunder'd Loves:
View nothing common but the Sun and Skys:
Now, all take several ways;   595
    And each your own sad fate with mine deplore;
    That you were false, and I could trust no more.
        [*Exeunt severally.*

Act V

[*Cleopatra. Charmion, Iras.*

  Char. Be juster, Heav'n: such virtue punish'd thus,
Will make us think that Chance rules all above,
And shuffles, with a random hand, the Lots
Which Man is forc'd to draw.
  Cleop. I cou'd tear out these eyes, that gain'd his heart,   5
And had not pow'r to keep it. O the curse
Of doting on, ev'n when I find it Dotage!
Bear witness, Gods, you heard him bid me go;
You whom he mock'd with imprecating Vows
Of promis'd Faith.——I'll die, I will not bear it.   10
    [*She pulls out her Dagger, and they hold her.*
You may hold me.——
But I can keep my breath; I can die inward,
And choak this Love.
        [*Enter Alexas.*
  Iras. Help, O *Alexas*, help!
The Queen grows desperate, her Soul struggles in her,
With all the Agonies of Love and Rage,   15
And strives to force its passage.
  Cleop. Let me go.
Art thou there, Traitor——
O, for a little breath, to vent my rage!
Give, give me way, and let me loose upon him.
  Alex. Yes, I deserve it, for my ill-tim'd truth.   20
Was it for me to prop
The Ruins of a falling Majesty?
To place my self beneath the mighty flaw,
Thus to be crush'd, and pounded into Atomes,
By its o'erwhelming weight? 'Tis too presuming   25
For Subjects, to preserve that wilful pow'r

Which courts its own destruction.
 Cleop. I wou'd reason
More calmly with you. Did not you o'er-rule,
And force my plain, direct, and open love
Into these crooked paths of jealousie?   30
Now, what's th' event? *Octavia* is remov'd;
But *Cleopatra's* banish'd. Thou, thou, Villain,
Has push'd my Boat, to open Sea; to prove,
At my sad cost, if thou canst steer it back.
It cannot be; I'm lost too far; I'm ruin'd: 35
Hence, thou Impostor, Traitor, Monster, Devil.———
I can no more: thou, and my griefs, have sunk
Me down so low, that I want voice to curse thee.
 Alex. Suppose some shipwrack'd Seaman near the shore,
Dropping and faint, with climbing up the Cliff,   40
If, from above, some charitable hand
Pull him to safety, hazarding himself
To draw the other's weight; wou'd he look back
And curse him for his pains? The case is yours;
But one step more, and you have gain'd the heighth.   45
 Cleop. Sunk, never more to rise.
 Alex. Octavia's gone, and *Dollabella* banish'd.
Believe me, Madam, *Antony* is yours.
His heart was never lost; but started off
To Jealousie, Love's last retreat and covert: 50
Where it lies hid in Shades, watchful in silence,
And list'ning for the sound that calls it back,
Some other, any man ('tis so advanc'd)
May perfect this unfinish'd work, which I
(Unhappy only to my self) have left   55
So easie to his hand.
 Cleop. Look well thou do't; else———
 Alex. Else, what your silence threatens.——*Antony*
Is mounted up the *Pharos*; from whose Turret,
He stands surveying our *Egyptian* Gallies,
Engag'd with *Cæsar's* Fleet: now Death, or Conquest.   60
If the first happen, Fate acquits my promise:
If we o'ercome, the Conqueror is yours.
       [*A distant Shout within.*
 Char. Have comfort, Madam: did you mark that Shout?
       [*Second Shout nearer.*
 Iras. Hark; they redouble it.
 Alex. 'Tis from the Port.
The loudness shows it near: good news, kind Heavens.   65
 Cleop. Osiris make it so.
       [*Enter* Serapion.
 Serap. Where, where's the Queen?

Alex. How frightfully the holy Coward stares!
As if not yet recover'd of th' assault,
When all his Gods, and what's more dear to him,
His Offerings were at stake.
    Serap. O horror, horror!   70
Egypt has been; our latest hour is come:
The Queen of Nations from her ancient seat,
Is sunk for ever in the dark Abyss:
Time has unrowl'd her Glories to the last,
And now clos'd up the Volume.
    Cleop. Be more plain: 75
Say, whence thou cam'st (though Fate is in thy face,
Which from thy haggard eyes looks wildly out,
And threatens ere thou speak'st).
    Serap. I came from *Pharos*;
From viewing (share me and imagine it)
Our Lands last hope, your Navy.——
    Cleop. Vanquish'd?
    Serap. No.   80
They fought not.
    Cleop. Then they fled.
    Serap. Nor that. I saw,
With *Antony*, your well-appointed Fleet
Row out; and thrice he wav'd his hand on high,
And thrice with cheerful cries they shouted back:
'Twas then, false Fortune, like a fawning Strumpet,   85
About to leave the Bankrupt Prodigal,
With a dissembled smile wou'd kiss at parting,
And flatter to the last; the well-tim'd Oars
Now dipt from every bank, now smoothly run
To meet the Foe; and soon indeed they met,   90
But not as Foes. In few, we saw their Caps
On either side thrown up; th' *Egyptian* Gallies
(Receiv'd like Friends) past through, and fell behind
The *Roman* rear: and now, they all come forward,
And ride within the Port.
    Cleop. Enough, *Serapion*:   95
I've heard my doom. This needed not, you Gods:
When I lost *Antony*, your work was done;
'Tis but superfluous malice. Where's my Lord?
How bears he this last blow?
    Serap. His fury cannot be express'd by words: 100
Thrice he attempted headlong to have faln
Full on his foes, and aim'd at *Cæsar's* Galley:
With-held, he raves on you; cries, He's betray'd.
Should he now find you.——
    Alex. Shun him, seek your safety,

Till you can clear your innocence.
    Cleop. I'll stay.   105
    Alex. You must not, haste you to your Monument,
While I make speed to *Cæsar*.
    Cleop. Cæsar! No,
I have no business with him.
    Alex. I can work him
To spare your life, and let this madman perish.
    Cleop. Base fawning Wretch! wouldst thou betray him
        too?   110
Hence from my sight, I will not hear a Traytor;
'Twas thy design brought all this ruine on us;
Serapion, thou art honest; counsel me:
But haste, each moment's precious.
    Serap. Retire; you must not yet see *Antony*.   115
He who began this mischief,
'Tis just he tempt the danger: let him clear you;
And, since he offer'd you his servile tongue,
To gain a poor precarious life from *Cæsar*,
Let him expose that fawning eloquence,   120
And speak to *Antony*.
    Alex. O Heavens! I dare not,
I meet my certain death.
    Cleop. Slave, thou deserv'st it.
Not that I fear my Lord, will I avoid him;
I know him noble: when he banish'd me,
And thought me false, he scorn'd to take my life;   125
But I'll be justifi'd, and then die with him.
    Alex. O pity me, and let me follow you.
    Cleop. To death, if thou stir hence. Speak, if thou canst,
Now for thy life, which basely thou wou'dst save;
While mine I prize at this. Come, good *Serapion*.   130
           [*Exeunt Cleop. Serap. Char. Iras.*
    Alex. O that I less cou'd fear to lose this being,
Which, like a Snow-ball, in my coward hand,
The more 'tis grasp'd, the faster melts away.
Poor Reason! what a wretched aid art thou!
For still, in spight of thee,   135
These two long Lovers, Soul and Body, dread
Their final separation. Let me think:
What can I say, to save my self from death?
No matter what becomes of *Cleopatra*.
    Ant. [*within*]. Which way? where?
    Ven. [*within*]. This leads to th' Monument.   140
    Alex. Ah me! I hear him; yet I'm unprepar'd:
My gift of lying's gone;
And this Court-Devil, which I so oft have rais'd,

Forsakes me at my need. I dare not stay;
Yet cannot far go hence.   [*Exit.*   145
     [*Enter* Antony *and* Ventidius.
 Ant. O happy *Cæsar!* Thou hast men to lead:
Think not 'tis thou hast conquer'd *Antony*;
But *Rome* has conquer'd *Egypt.* I'm betray'd.
 Ven. Curse on this treach'rous Train!
Their Soil and Heav'n infect 'em all with baseness: 150
And their young Souls come tainted to the World
With the first breath they draw.
 Ant. Th' original Villain sure no God created;
He was a Bastard of the Sun, by *Nile,*
Ap'd into Man; with all his Mother's Mud   155
Crusted about his Soul.
 Ven. The Nation is
One Universal Traitor; and their Queen
The very Spirit and Extract of 'em all.
 Ant. Is there yet left
A possibility of aid from Valor?   160
Is there one God unsworn to my Destruction?
The least unmortgag'd hope? for, if there be,
Methinks I cannot fall beneath the Fate
Of such a Boy as *Cæsar.*
The World's one half is yet in *Antony*;   165
And, from each limb of it that's hew'd away,
The Soul comes back to me.
 Ven. There yet remain
Three Legions in the Town: The last assault
Lopt off the rest: if death be your design,
As I must wish it now, these are sufficient   170
To make a heap about us of dead Foes,
An honest Pile for burial.
 Ant. They're enough.
We'll not divide our Stars; but side by side
Fight emulous: and with malicious eyes
Survey each other's acts: so every death   175
Thou givest, I'll take on me, as a just debt,
And pay thee in a Soul.
 Ven. Now you shall see I love you. Not a word
Of chiding more. By my few hours of life,
I am so pleas'd with this brave *Roman* Fate,   180
That I wou'd not be *Cæsar,* to out-live you.
When we put off this flesh, and mount together,
I shall be shown to all th' Etherial crowd;
Lo, this is he who dy'd with *Antony.*
 Ant. Who knows but we may pierce through all their
  Troops,   185

And reach my Veterans yet? 'Tis worth the tempting,
T' o'er-leap this Gulph of Fate,
And leave our wond'ring Destinies behind.
                              [*Enter* Alexas, *trembling.*
  Ven. See, see, that Villain;
See *Cleopatra* stampt upon that face,   190
With all her cunning, all her arts of falshood!
How she looks out through those dissembling eyes!
How he has set his count'nance for deceit;
And promises a lye, before he speaks!
Let me dispatch him first.   [*Drawing.*
  Alex. O, spare me, spare me.   195
  Ant. Hold; he's not worth your killing. On thy life
(Which thou mayst keep, because I scorn to take it)
No syllable to justifie thy Queen;
Save thy base tongue its office.
  Alex. Sir, she's gone,
Where she shall never be molested more   200
By Love, or you.
  Ant. Fled to her *Dollabella!*
Die, Traitor, I revoke my promise, die.   [*Going to kill him.*
  Alex. O hold, she is not fled.
  Ant. She is: my eyes
Are open to her falshood; my whole life
Has been a golden dream, of Love and Friendship.   205
But, now I wake, I'm like a Merchant, rows'd
From soft repose, to see his Vessel sinking,
And all his Wealth cast o'er. Ingrateful Woman!
Who follow'd me, but as the Swallow Summer,
Hatching her young ones in my kindly Beams,   210
Singing her flatt'ries to my morning wake;
But, now my Winter comes, she spreads her wings,
And seeks the Spring of *Cæsar.*
  Alex. Think not so:
Her Fortunes have, in all things, mixt with yours.
Had she betray'd her Naval force to *Rome,*   215
How easily might she have gone to *Cæsar,*
Secure by such a bribe!
  Ven. She sent it first,
To be more welcome after.
  Ant. 'Tis too plain;
Else wou'd she have appear'd, to clear her self.
  Alex. Too fatally she has; she could not bear   220
To be accus'd by you; but shut her self
Within her Monument: look'd down, and sigh'd;
While, from her unchang'd face, the silent tears
Dropt, as they had not leave, but stole their parting.

Some undistinguish'd words she inly murmur'd;   225
At last, she rais'd her eyes; and, with such looks
As dying *Lucrece* cast,——
 Ant. My heart forebodes.——
 Ven. All for the best: go on.
 Alex. She snatch'd her Ponyard,
And, ere we cou'd prevent the fatal blow,
Plung'd it within her breast: then turn'd to me,   230
Go, bear my Lord (said she) my last Farewel;
And ask him if he yet suspect my Faith.
More she was saying, but death rush'd betwixt.
She half pronounc'd your Name with her last breath,
And bury'd half within her.
 Ven. Heav'n be prais'd.   235
 Ant. Then art thou innocent, my poor dear Love?
And art thou dead?
O those two words! their sound shou'd be divided:
Hadst thou been false, and dy'd; or hadst thou liv'd,
And hadst been true——But Innocence and Death!   240
This shows not well above. Then what am I,
The Murderer of this Truth, this Innocence!
Thoughts cannot form themselves in words so horrid
As can express my guilt!
 Ven. Is't come to this? The Gods have been too gracious: 245
And thus you thank 'em for't.
 Ant. [*to Alex.*]. Why stay'st thou here?
Is it for thee to spy upon my Soul,
And see its inward mourning? Get thee hence;
Thou art not worthy to behold, what now
Becomes a *Roman* Emperor to perform.   250
 Alex. [*aside*]. He loves her still:
His grief betrays it. Good! The joy to find
She's yet alive, compleats the reconcilement.
I've sav'd my self, and her. But, Oh! the *Romans!*
Fate comes too fast upon my Wit,   255
Hunts me too hard, and meets me at each double.   [*Exit.*
 Ven. Wou'd she had dy'd a little sooner tho,
Before *Octavia* went; you might have treated:
Now 'twill look tame, and wou'd not be receiv'd.
Come, rouze your self, and let's die warm together.   260
 Ant. I will not fight: there's no more work for War.
The bus'ness of my angry hours is done.
 Ven. Cæsar is at your Gates.
 Ant. Why, let him enter;
He's welcom now.
 Ven. What Lethargy has crept into your Soul?   265
 Ant. 'Tis but a scorn of life, and just desire

To free my self from bondage.
    Ven. Do it bravely.
    Ant. I will; but not by fighting. O, *Ventidius!*
What shou'd I fight for now? My Queen is dead.
I was but great for her; my Pow'r, my Empire,   270
Were but my Merchandise to buy her love;
And conquer'd Kings, my Factors. Now she's dead,
Let *Cæsar* take the World,———
An Empty Circle, since the Jewel's gone
Which made it worth my strife: my being's nauseous;   275
For all the bribes of life are gone away.
    Ven. Wou'd you be taken?
    Ant. Yes, I wou'd be taken;
But, as a *Roman* ought, dead, my *Ventidius*:
For I'll convey my Soul from *Cæsar's* reach,
And lay down life my self. 'Tis time the World   280
Shou'd have a Lord, and know whom to obey.
We two have kept its homage in suspence,
And bent the Globe on whose each side we trod,
Till it was dinted inwards: Let him walk
Alone upon 't; I'm weary of my part.   285
My Torch is out; and the World stands before me
Like a black Desart, at th' approach of night:
I'll lay me down, and stray no farther on.
    Ven. I cou'd be griev'd,
But that I'll not out-live you: choose your death;   290
For, I have seen him in such various shapes,
I care not which I take: I'm only troubled
The life I bear, is worn to such a rag,
'Tis scarce worth giving. I cou'd wish indeed
We threw it from us with a better grace;   295
That, like two Lyons taken in the Toils,
We might at least thrust out our paws, and wound
The Hunters that inclose us.
    Ant. I have thought on't.
Ventidius, you must live.
    Ven. I must not, Sir.
    Ant. Wilt thou not live, to speak some good of me?   300
To stand by my fair Fame, and guard th'approaches
From the ill Tongues of Men?
    Ven. Who shall guard mine,
For living after you?
    Ant. Say, I command it.
    Ven. If we die well, our deaths will speak themselves,
And need no living witness.
    Ant. Thou hast lov'd me,   305
And fain I wou'd reward thee: I must die;

Kill me, and take the merit of my death
To make thee Friends with *Cæsar*.
  Ven. Thank your kindness.
You said I lov'd you; and, in recompence,
You bid me turn a Traitor: did I think   310
You wou'd have us'd me thus? that I shou'd die
With a hard thought of you?
  Ant. Forgive me, *Roman.*
Since I have heard of *Cleopatra's* death,
My reason bears no rule upon my tongue,
But lets my thoughts break all at random out: 315
I've thought better; do not deny me twice.
  Ven. By Heav'n, I will not.
Let it not be t' out-live you.
  Ant. Kill me first,
And then die thou: for 'tis but just thou serve
Thy Friend, before thy self.
  Ven. Give me your hand.   320
We soon shall meet again. Now, Farewel, Emperor!
          [*Embrace.*
Methinks that word's too cold to be my last:
Since Death sweeps all distinctions, Farewel, Friend.
That's all.———
I will not make a bus'ness of a trifle: 325
And yet I cannot look on you, and kill you;
Pray turn your face.
  Ant. I do: strike home be sure.
  Ven. Home, as my Sword will reach. [*Kills himself.*
  Ant. O, thou mistak'st;
That wound was none of thine: give it me back:
Thou robb'st me of my death.   330
  Ven. I do indeed;
But, think 'tis the first time I e'er deceiv'd you;
If that may plead my pardon. And you, Gods,
Forgive me, if you will; for I die perjur'd,
Rather than kill my Friend.   [*Dies.*
  Ant. Farewel. Ever my Leader, ev'n in death! 335
My Queen and thou have got the start of me,
And I'm the lag of Honour.——Gone so soon?
Is death no more? He us'd him carelessly,
With a familiar kindness: ere he knock'd,
Ran to the door, and took him in his arms,   340
As who shou'd say, Y'are welcome at all hours,
A Friend need give no warning. Books had spoil'd him;
For all the Learn'd are Cowards by profession.
'Tis not worth
My farther thought; for death, for ought I know, 345

Is but to think no more. Here's to be satisfi'd.
       [Falls on his Sword.
I've mist my heart. O unperforming hand!
Thou never cou'dst have err'd in a worse time.
My Fortune jades me to the last; and death,
Like a great Man, takes state, and makes me wait   350
For my admittance.――――   *[Trampling within.*
Some perhaps from *Cæsar*:
If he shou'd find me living, and suspect
That I plaid booty with my life! I'll mend
My work, ere they can reach me.   *[Rises upon his knees.*
       [Enter Cleopatra, Charmion, Iras.
 Cleop. Where is my Lord? where is he?
 Char. There he lies,   355
And dead *Ventidius* by him.
 Cleop. My fears were Prophets; I am come too late.
O that accurs'd *Alexas!*   *[Runs to him.*
 Ant. Art thou living?
Or am I dead before I knew? and thou
The first kind Ghost that meets me?
 Cleop. Help me seat him.   360
Send quickly, send for help. *[They place him in a Chair.*
 Ant. I am answer'd.
We live both. Sit thee down, my *Cleopatra*:
I'll make the most I can of life, to stay
A moment more with thee.
 Cleop. How is it with you?
 Ant. 'Tis as with a man   365
Removing in a hurry; all pack'd up,
But one dear Jewel that his haste forgot;
And he, for that, returns upon the spur:
So I come back, for thee.
 Cleop. Too long, you Heav'ns, you have been cruel to me; 370
Now show your mended Faith, and give me back
His fleeting life.
 Ant. It will not be, my Love.
I keep my Soul by force.
Say but thou art not false.
 Cleop. 'Tis now too late
To say I'm true: I'll prove it, and die with you.   375
Unknown to me, *Alexas* feign'd my death:
Which, when I knew, I hasted, to prevent
This fatal consequence. My Fleet betray'd
Both you and me.
 Ant. And *Dollabella.*――――
 Cleop. Scarce esteem'd before he lov'd; but hated now.   380
 Ant. Enough; my life's not long enough for more.

Thou sayst thou wilt come after: I believe thee;
For I can now believe whate'er thou sayst,
That we may part more kindly.
    Cleop. I will come:
Doubt not, my life, I'll come, and quickly too: 385
Cæsar shall triumph o'er no part of thee.
    Ant. But grieve not, while thou stay'st,
My last disastrous times:
Think we have had a clear and glorious day;
And Heav'n did kindly to delay the storm   390
Just till our close of ev'ning. Ten years' love,
And not a moment lost, but all improv'd
To th' utmost joys: What Ages have we liv'd?
And now to die each other's; and, so dying,
While hand in hand we walk in Groves below,   395
Whole Troops of Lovers Ghosts shall flock about us,
And all the Train be ours.
    Cleop. Your words are like the Notes of dying Swans,
Too sweet to last. Were there so many hours
For your unkindness, and not one for love?   400
    Ant. No, not a minute.——This one kiss——more worth
Than all I leave to *Cæsar*.   [*Dies.*
    Cleop. O, tell me so again,
And take ten thousand kisses, for that word.
My Lord, my Lord: speak, if you yet have being;   405
Sigh to me, if you cannot speak; or cast
One look: Do any thing that shows you live.
    Iras. He's gone too far, to hear you;
And this you see, a lump of sensless Clay,
The leavings of a Soul.
    Char. Remember, Madam,   410
He charg'd you not to grieve.
    Cleop. And I'll obey him.
I have not lov'd a *Roman* not to know
What should become his Wife; his Wife, my *Charmion*;
For 'tis to that high Title I aspire,
And now I'll not die less. Let dull *Octavia*   415
Survive, to mourn him dead; my Nobler Fate
Shall knit our Spousals with a tie too strong
For *Roman* Laws to break.
    Iras. Will you then die?
    Cleop. Why shou'dst thou make that question?
    Iras. *Cæsar* is merciful.
    Cleop. Let him be so   420
To those that want his mercy: my poor Lord
Made no such Cov'nant with him, to spare me
When he was dead. Yield me to *Cæsar's* pride?

What, to be led in triumph through the Streets,
A spectacle to base *Plebeian* eyes;   425
While some dejected Friend of *Antony's*,
Close in a corner, shakes his head, and mutters
A secret curse on her who ruin'd him?
I'll none of that.
    Char. Whatever you resolve,
I'll follow ev'n to death.
     Iras. I only fear'd   430
For you; but more shou'd fear to live without you.
    Cleop. Why, now 'tis as it shou'd be. Quick, my Friends,
Dispatch; ere this, the Town's in *Cæsar's* hands:
My Lord looks down concern'd, and fears my stay,
Lest I shou'd be surpriz'd;   435
Keep him not waiting for his love too long.
You, *Charmion*, bring my Crown and richest Jewels,
With 'em, the Wreath of Victory I made
(Vain Augury !) for him who now lies dead;
You, *Iras*, bring the cure of all our ills.   440
    Iras. The Aspicks, Madam?
    Cleop. Must I bid you twice?   [*Exeunt* Char. *and* Iras.
'Tis sweet to die, when they wou'd force life on me,
To rush into the dark aboad of death,
And seize him first; if he be like my Love,
He is not frightful sure.   445
We're now alone, in secresie and silence;
And is not this like Lovers? I may kiss
These pale, cold lips; *Octavia* does not see me;
And, Oh ! 'tis better far to have him thus,
Than see him in her arms.——O welcome, welcome.   450
             [*Enter* Charmion, Iras.
    Char. What must be done?
    Cleop. Short Ceremony, Friends;
But yet it must be decent. First, this Laurel
Shall crown my Hero's Head: he fell not basely,
Nor left his Shield behind him. Only thou
Cou'dst triumph o'er thy self; and thou alone   455
Wert worthy so to triumph.
    Char. To what end
These Ensigns of your Pomp and Royalty?
    Cleop. Dull, that thou art ! why, 'tis to meet my Love;
As when I saw him first, on *Cydnos* bank,
All sparkling, like a Goddess; so adorn'd,   460
I'll find him once again: my second Spousals
Shall match my first, in Glory. Haste, haste, both,
And dress the Bride of *Antony*.
    Char. 'Tis done.

Cleop. Now seat me by my Lord. I claim this place;
For I must conquer *Cæsar* too, like him,   465
And win my share o'th' World. Hail, you dear Relicks
Of my Immortal Love!
O let no Impious hand remove you hence;
But rest for ever here: let *Egypt* give
His death that peace, which it deny'd his life.   470
Reach me the Casket.
    Iras. Underneath the fruit the Aspick lies.
    Cleop. [*putting aside the leaves*]. Welcom, thou kind Deceiver!
Thou best of Thieves; who, with an easie key,
Dost open life, and, unperceiv'd by us,
Ev'n steal us from our selves: discharging so   475
Death's dreadful office, better than himself,
Touching our limbs so gently into slumber,
That Death stands by, deceiv'd by his own Image,
And thinks himself but Sleep.
    Serap. [*within*]. The Queen, where is she?
The Town is yielded; *Cæsar*'s at the Gates.   480
    Cleop. He comes too late t' invade the Rights of Death.
Haste, bare my Arm, and rouze the Serpent's fury.
        [*Holds out her Arm, and draws it back.*
Coward Flesh——
Would'st thou conspire with *Cæsar*, to betray me,
As thou wert none of mine? I'll force thee to't,   485
And not be sent by him,
But bring my self my Soul to *Antony*.
        [*Turns aside, and then shows her Arm bloody.*
Take hence; the work is done.
    Serap. [*within*]. Break ope the door,
And guard the Traitor well.
    Char. The next is ours.
    Iras. Now, *Charmion*, to be worthy   490
Of our great Queen and Mistress.   [*They apply the Aspicks.*
    Cleop. Already, Death, I feel thee in my Veins;
I go with such a will to find my Lord,
That we shall quickly meet.
A heavy numness creeps through every limb,   495
And now 'tis at my head: my eye-lids fall,
And my dear Love is vanish'd in a mist.
Where shall I find him, where? O turn me to him,
And lay me on his breast.——*Cæsar*, thy worst;
Now part us, if thou canst.   500
        [*Dies.* Iras *sinks down at her feet, and dies;* Charmion *stands
        behind her Chair, as dressing her head.*
        [*Enter* Serapion, *two Priests,* Alexas *bound, Egyptians.*
    2 Priests. Behold, *Serapion*, what havock Death has made!

Serap. 'Twas what I fear'd.
Charmion, is this well done?
    Char. Yes, 'tis well done, and like a Queen, the last
Of her great Race: I follow her.   [*Sinks down; Dies.*
    Alexas. 'Tis true,
She has done well: much better thus to die,   505
Than live to make a Holy-day in *Rome.*
    Serap. See, see how the Lovers sit in State together,
As they were giving Laws to half Mankind.
Th' impression of a smile left in her face,
Shows she dy'd pleas'd with him for whom she liv'd,   510
And went to charm him in another World.
Cæsar's just ent'ring; grief has now no leisure.
Secure that Villain, as our pledge of safety
To grace th'Imperial Triumph. Sleep, blest Pair,
Secure from humane chance, long Ages out,   515
While all the Storms of Fate fly o'er your Tomb;
    And Fame, to late Posterity, shall tell,
    No Lovers liv'd so great, or dy'd so well.

Epilogue

POETS, *like Disputants, when Reasons fail,*
Have one sure Refuge left; and that's to rail.
Fop, Coxcomb, Fool, are thunder'd through the Pit;
And this is all their Equipage of Wit.
We wonder how the Devil this diff'rence grows,   5
Betwixt our Fools in Verse, and yours in Prose:
For, 'Faith, the quarrel rightly understood,
'Tis Civil War *with their own Flesh and Blood.*
The thread-bare Author hates the gawdy Coat;
And swears at the Guilt Coach, but swears a foot: 10
For 'tis observ'd of every Scribling Man,
He grows a Fop as fast as e'er he can;
Prunes up, and asks his Oracle the Glass,
If Pink or Purple best become his face.
For our poor Wretch, he neither rails nor prays;   15
Nor likes your Wit just as you like his Plays;
He has not yet so much of Mr. Bays.
He does his best; and, if he cannot please,
Wou'd quietly sue out his Writ of Ease.
Yet, if he might his own Grand Jury call,   20
By the Fair Sex he begs to stand or fall.
Let Cæsar's *Pow'r the Men's ambition move,*

---

17. *Mr. Bays:* A character (Dryden) in Buckingham's *The Rehearsal.* See the headnote on drama.

19. *Writ of Ease:* "A certificate of discharge from employment." *OED.*

But grace *You* him who lost the *World* for *Love.*
Yet if some antiquated *Lady* say,
The last *Age* is not *Copy'd* in his *Play;*   25
Heav'n help the *Man* who for that face must drudge,
Which only has the wrinkles of a *Judge.*
Let not the *Young* and *Beauteous* join with those;
For shou'd you raise such numerous *Hosts* of *Foes,*
Young Wits and *Sparks* he to his aid must call;   30
'Tis more than one *Man's* work to please you all.

(1678)

Thomas Otway

1652-1685

O tway was born at Trotton, Sussex, on March 3, 1652, the son of a curate. He was educated at Winchester and Christ Church, Oxford, but left before taking a degree to pursue a career on the stage. His acting an utter failure, Otway turned to the writing of plays. His first work, the tragedy *Alcibiades*, was accepted in 1675 by Thomas Betterton, actor and partner in the management of Dorset Garden; the production starred the beautiful Mrs. Elizabeth Barry in her first role, after which she acted the chief characters in Otway's plays.

He wrote *Don Carlos* in 1676; the following year, he adapted two works from the French, Molière's *The Cheats of Scapin* (*Fourberies de Scapin*) and Racine's *Titus and Berenice* (*Bérénice*). His *Friendship in Fashion* (1678), a coarse though amusing comedy, was popular when it first appeared, but a later production, in 1749, long after the playwright's death, was rejected by the audience for its indecencies.

An unsatisfied passion for Mrs. Barry (mistress to the Earl of Rochester) prompted Otway to seek a commission with a regiment in Holland; he returned to England the following year, in 1679.

Sixteen-eighty saw the production at Dorset Garden of *The Orphan*, one of the two works considered to be his tragic masterpieces. *The History and Fall of Caius Marius* was produced in the same year; in 1681, a comedy, *The Soldier's Fortune;* and in 1682, the second of his two great tragedies, *Venice Preserv'd.*

Otway died in abject poverty in 1685. A work published posthumously, *Heroick Friendship*, has been attributed to him, but its authorship is uncertain.

Thomas Otway—Selective Bibliography

Otway Bibliography: *CBEL*, II, pp. 413 f.

J. C. Ghosh, ed., *The Works of Thomas Otway*, 2 vols., Oxford, Clarendon Press, 1932.

Roswell Gray Ham, *Otway and Lee: Biography from a Baroque Age*, New Haven, Yale U. P., 1931.

Aline Mackenzie Taylor, *Next to Shakespeare: Otway's Venice Preserv'd and The Orphan and Their History on the London Stage*, Durham, N.C., Duke U. P., 1950.

David R. Hauser, "Otway Preserved: Theme and Form in *Venice Preserv'd*," *SP*, LV (1958), 481–493.

William H. McBurney, "Otway's Tragic Muse Debauched: Sensuality in *Venice Preserv'd*," *JEGP*, LVIII (1959), 380–399.

Venice Preserv'd
Or, A Plot Discover'd

Epistle Dedicatory

To Her Grace the Dutchess of Portsmouth[1]

MADAM,

Were it possible for me to let the World know how entirely your Graces Goodness has devoted a poor man to your service; were there words enough in speech to express the mighty sense I have of your great bounty towards me; surely I should write and talk of it for ever: But your Grace has given me so large a Theam, and laid so very vast a foundation, that Imagination wants stock to build upon it. I am as one dumb when I would speak of it, and when I strive to write, I want a scale of thought sufficient to comprehend the height of it. Forgive me then, Madam, if (as a poor Peasant once made a Present of an Apple to an Emperour) I bring this small Tribute, the humble growth of my little Garden, and lay it at your feet. Believe it is paid you with the utmost gratitude, believe that so long as I have thought to remember, how very much I owe 10 *your generous Nature, I will ever have a heart that shall be grateful for it too: Your Grace, next Heaven, deserves it amply from me; That gave me life, but on a hard condition, till your extended favour taught me to prize the gift, and took the heavy burthen it was clogg'd with from me: I mean hard Fortune: When I had enemies, that with malicious power kept back and shaded me from those Royal Beams, whose warmth is all I have, or hope to live by; Your noble pity and compassion found me, where I was far cast backward from my blessing, down in the rear of Fortune; call'd me up, plac'd me in the shine, and I have felt its comfort. You have in that restor'd me to my native Right, for a steady Faith, and Loyalty to my Prince, was all the Inheritance my Father left me, and however hardly my ill Fortune deal with me, 'tis what I prize* 20 *so well that I ne'r pawn'd it yet, and hope I ne'r shall part with it. Nature and Fortune were certainly in league when you were born, and as the first took care to give you beauty enough to enslave the hearts of all the World, so the other resolv'd to do its merit Justice, that none but a Monarch, fit to rule that World, should e'er possess it, and in it he had an Empire. The Young Prince[2] you have given him, by his blooming Vertues, early declares the mighty stock he came from; and as you have taken all the pious care of a dear Mother and a prudent Guardian to give him a noble and generous education; may it succeed according to his merits and your wishes: May he grow up to be a Bulwark to his illustrious Father, and a Patron to his Loyal Subjects, with Wisdom and Learning to assist him, whenever call'd to his Councils, to defend his* 30 *Right against the encroachments of Republicans in his Senates, to cherish such men as*

---

[1] *Dutchess of Portsmouth:* Louise de Kéroualle (1649–1743), mistress of Charles II, tried without much success to influence him in favor of the French alliance. The King ennobled her (1673) and her son, making him Duke of Richmond.

[2] *Young Prince:* Otway's reference is of course metaphoric. Though legitimized, the Duke of Richmond (see n. 1, above) was not a prince.

shall be able to vindicate the Royal Cause, that good and fit servants to the Crown, may never be lost for want of a Protectour. May He have courage and conduct, fit to fight his Battels abroad, and terrifie his Rebells at home; and that all these may be yet more sure, may He never, during the Spring-time of his years, when those growing Vertues ought with care to be cherish'd, in order to their ripening; may he never meet with vitious Natures, or the tongues of faithless, sordid, insipid flatterers, to blast 'em: To conclude; may He be as great as the hand of Fortune (with his Honour) shall be able to make him: And may your Grace, who are so good a Mistress, and so noble a Patroness, never meet with a less gratefull Servant, than,

Madam,

Your Graces entirely
Devoted Creature,
Thomas Otway.

Personae Dramatis

Duke of *Venice*
Priuli, Father to *Belvidera*, a Senatour
Antonio, A fine Speaker in the Senate
Jaffeir
Pierre
Renault ⎫
Bedamar ⎪
Spinosa ⎪
Theodore ⎪
Eliot ⎪
Revillido ⎬ Conspiratours
Durand ⎪
Mezzana ⎪
Brainveil ⎪
Ternon ⎪
Brabe ⎭
Belvidera
Aquilina
Two Women, Attendants on *Belvidera*
Two Women, Servants to *Aquilina*
The Council of Ten
Officer
Guards
Friar
Executioner and Rable

Prologue

IN these distracted times, when each man dreads
The bloudy stratagems of busie heads;
When we have fear'd three years we know not what, ⎫
Till Witnesses begin to die o' th' rot, ⎪
What made our Poet meddle with a Plot? ⎬ 5
Was't that he fansy'd, for the very sake
And name of Plot, his trifling Play might take?
For there's not in't one Inch-board Evidence, ⎫
But 'tis, he says, to reason plain and sense, ⎬ 10
And that he thinks a plausible defence. ⎭
Were Truth by Sense and Reason to be try'd,
Sure all our Swearers might be laid aside:
No, of such Tools our Author has no need,

3. *Fear'd three years:* Though Titus Oates began to arouse these fears in 1678 (see the headnote to *Absalom and Achitophel*) four years before the appearance of *Venice Preserv'd,* he did not publish his *True Narrative of the Horrid Plot . . . against . . . his Sacred Majesty . . .* until 1679.

8. *Inch-board:* To swear through an inch-board is to swear firmly.

To make his Plot, or make his Play succeed;
He, of black Bills, has no prodigious Tales,   15
Or Spanish Pilgrims cast a-shore in Wales;
Here's not one murther'd Magistrate at least,
Kept rank like Ven'son for a City feast,
Grown four days stiff, the better to prepare
And fit his plyant limbs to ride in Chair.   20
Yet here's an Army rais'd, though under ground,
But no man seen, nor one Commission found;
Here is a Traitour too, that's very old,
Turbulent, subtle, mischievous and bold,
Bloudy, revengeful, and to crown his part,   25
Loves fumbling with a Wench, with all his heart;
Till after having many changes pass'd,
In spight of Age (thanks Heaven) is hang'd at last:
Next is a Senatour that keeps a Whore,
In Venice none a higher office bore;   30
To lewdness every night the Letcher ran,
Shew me, all London, such another man,
Match him at Mother Creswold's if you can.
Oh Poland, Poland! had it been thy lot,
T' have heard in time of this Venetian Plot,   35
Thou surely chosen hadst one King from thence,
And honour'd them as thou hast England since.

Act I Scene I

[*Enter* Priuli *and* Jaffeir.

Priu. No more! I'll hear no more; begone and leave.
Jaff. Not hear me! by my sufferings but you shall!
My Lord, my Lord; I'm not that abject wretch
You think me: Patience! where's the distance throws
Me back so far, but I may boldly speak   5
In right, though proud oppression will not hear me!
    Priu. Have you not wrong'd me?
    Jaff.   Could my Nature e'er
Have brook'd Injustice or the doing wrongs,
I need not now thus low have bent my self,

---

14. *Make:* The text of 1696, source of the present text, gives may, not make.
15. *Black Bills:* Halberds, long-handled axes, sometimes with points for thrusting.
16. *Spanish Pilgrims:* A mischievous euphemism for disguised Irish soldiers, who were, according to rumor, to be landed in Wales by the Jesuits.
20. *To ride in Chair:* The reference is to the disposition of the murdered body of Sir Edmund Berry Godfrey (1622–1678), whose death was central to Oates's allegations.
23. *A Traitour:* The character Renault in the play.
33. *Mother Creswold's:* A well-known house of pleasure in London.
34. *Poland:* The Tories accused Shaftesbury of aspiring to the Polish throne during a period of political upheaval in 1675.

To gain a Hearing from a Cruel father!   10
Wrong'd you?
    Priu.   Yes! wrong'd me, in the nicest point:
The Honour of my House; you have done me wrong;
You may remember (For I now will speak,
And urge its baseness): When you first came home
From Travel, with such hopes, as made you lookt on   15
By all men's Eyes, a Youth of expectation;
Pleas'd with your growing Virtue, I receiv'd you;
Courted, and sought to raise you to your Merits:
My House, my Table, nay my Fortune too,
My very self, was yours; you might have us'd me   20
To your best service; like an open friend,
I treated, trusted you, and thought you mine;
When in requital of my best Endeavours,
You treacherously practis'd to undo me,
Seduc'd the weakness of my Age's Darling,   25
My only Child, and stole her from my bosome:
Oh *Belvidera!*
    Jaff.   'Tis to me you owe her,
Childless you had been else, and in the Grave,
Your name Extinct, nor no more *Priuli* heard of.
You may remember, scarce five years are past,   30
Since in your Brigandine you sail'd to see
The *Adriatick* wedded by our Duke,
And I was with you: Your unskilful Pilot
Dash't us upon a Rock; when to your Boat
You made for safety; entred first your self;   35
The affrighted *Belvidera* following next,
As she stood trembling on the Vessel-side,
Was by a Wave washt off into the Deep,
When instantly I plung'd into the Sea,
And buffeting the Billows to her rescue,   40
Redeem'd her Life with half the loss of mine;
Like a rich Conquest in one hand I bore her,
And with the other dasht the sawcy Waves,
That throng'd and prest to rob me of my prize:
I brought her, gave her to your despairing Arms: 45
Indeed you thank't me; but a nobler gratitude
Rose in her soul: for from that hour she lov'd me,
Till for her Life she paid me with her self.
    Priu. You stole her from me, like a Theif you stole her,
At dead of night; that cursed hour you chose   50
To rifle me of all my Heart held dear.
May all your Joys in her prove false like mine;

32. *Adriatick wedded by our Duke:* The   Adriatic; that is, he ritually celebrated his
Doge of Venice each year married the   city's wedding to the sea.

A steril Fortune, and a barren Bed,
Attend you both: Continual discord make
Your Days and Nights bitter and grievous: Still   55
May the hard hand of a vexatious Need
Oppress, and grind you; till at last you find
The Curse of Disobedience all your Portion.
    Jaff. Half of your Curse you have bestow'd in vain,
Heav'n has already crown'd our faithful Loves   60
With a young Boy, sweet as his mother's Beauty:
May he live to prove more Gentle than his Grandsire,
And happier than his Father!
    Priu.   Rather live
To bait thee for his bread, and din your ears
With hungry Cries: Whilst his unhappy Mother   65
Sits down and weeps in bitterness of want.
    Jaff. You talk as if it would please you.
    Priu.   'Twould by Heav'n.
Once she was dear indeed; the Drops that fell
From my sad heart, when she forgot her Duty,
The fountain of my Life was not so precious: 70
But she is gone, and if I am a man
I will forget her.
    Jaff. Would I were in my Grave.
    Priu.   And she too with thee:
For, living here, you're but my curs'd Remembrancers
I once was happy.   75
    Jaff. You use me thus, because you know my soul
Is fond of *Belvidera*: You perceive
My Life feeds on her, therefore thus you treat me;
Oh! could my Soul ever have known satiety:
Were I that Theif, the doer of such wrongs   80
As you upbraid me with, what hinders me,
But I might send her back to you with Contumely,
And court my fortune where she wou'd be kinder!
    Priu. You dare not do't.——
    Jaff.   Indeed, my Lord, I dare not.
My heart that awes me is too much my Master: 85
Three years are past since first our Vows were plighted,
During which time, the World must bear me witness,
I have treated *Belvidera* like your Daughter,
The Daughter of a Senator of *Venice*;
Distinction, Place, Attendance and Observance,   90
Due to her Birth, she always has commanded;
Out of my little Fortune I have done this;
Because (though hopeless e're to win your Nature)
The World might see, I lov'd her for her self,
Not as the Heiress of the great *Priuli.*——   95

Priu. No more!

Jaff.   Yes! all, and then adieu for ever.
There's not a Wretch that lives on common Charity
But's happier than me: for I have known
The Luscious Sweets of Plenty; every night
Have slept with soft content about my head,   100
And never waked but to a joyful morning,
Yet now must fall like a full Ear of Corn,
Whose blossom scap'd, yet's withered in the ripening.

Priu. Home and be humble, study to retrench;
Discharge the lazy Vermin of thy Hall,   105
Those Pageants of thy Folly,
Reduce the glittering Trappings of thy Wife
To humble Weeds, fit for thy little state;
Then to some suburb Cottage both retire;
Drudge, to feed loathsome life: Get Brats, and Starve——   110
Home, home, I say.——   [*Exit* Priuli.

Jaff.   Yes, if my heart would let me——
This proud, this swelling heart: Home I would go,
But that my Dores are hateful to my eyes,
Fill'd and damm'd up with gaping Creditors,
Watchful as Fowlers when their Game will spring;   115
I have now not 50 Ducats in the World,
Yet still I am in love, and pleas'd with Ruin.
Oh *Belvidera*! oh she's my Wife——
And we will bear our wayward Fate together,
But ne'er know Comfort more.

         [*Enter* Pierre.

Pierr.   My Friend good morrow!   120
How fares the honest Partner of my Heart?
What, melancholy! not a word to spare me?

Jaff. I'm thinking, *Pierre*, how that damn'd starving
         Quality
Call'd Honesty, got footing in the World.

Pierr. Why, pow'rful Villainy first set it up,   125
For its own ease and safety: Honest men
Are the soft easy Cushions on which Knaves
Repose and fatten: Were all mankind Villains,
They'd starve each other; Lawyers wou'd want practice,
Cut-Throats Rewards: Each man would kill his Brother   130
Himself, none would be paid or hang'd for Murder:
Honesty was a Cheat invented first
To bind the Hands of bold deserving Rogues,
That Fools and Cowards might sit safe in Power,
And lord it uncontroul'd above their Betters.   135

Jaff. Then Honesty is but a Notion.

Pierr.   Nothing else,

Like wit, much talkt of, not to be defin'd:
He that pretends to most too, has least share in't;
'Tis a ragged Virtue: Honesty! no more on't.
    Jaff. Sure thou art Honest?
    Pierr.   So indeed men think me,   140
But they're mistaken *Jaffeir*: I am a Rogue
As well as they;
A fine gay bold fac'd Villain, as thou seest me;
'Tis true, I pay my debts when they'r contracted;
I steal from no man; would not cut a Throat   145
To gain admission to a great man's purse,
Or a Whore's bed; I'd not betray my Friend,
To get his Place or Fortune: I scorn to flatter
A Blown-up Fool above me, or Crush the wretch beneath me,
Yet, *Jaffeir*, for all this, I am a Villain!   150
    Jaff. A Villain——
    Pierr.   Yes a most notorious Villain:
To see the suffrings of my fellow Creatures,
And own my self a Man: To see our Senators
Cheat the deluded people with a shew
Of Liberty, which yet they ne'er must taste of;   155
They say, by them our hands are free from Fetters,
Yet whom they please they lay in basest bonds;
Bring whom they please to Infamy and Sorrow;
Drive us like Wracks down the rough Tide of Power,
Whilst no hold's left to save us from Destruction;   160
All that bear this are Villains; and I one,
Not to rouse up at the great Call of Nature,
And check the Growth of these Domestick spoilers,
That make us slaves and tell us 'tis our Charter.
    Jaff. Oh *Aquilina!* Friend, to lose such Beauty,   165
The Dearest Purchase of thy noble Labours;
She was thy Right by Conquest, as by Love.
    Pierr. Oh *Jaffeir!* I'd so fixt my heart upon her,
That wheresoe'er I fram'd a Scheme of Life
For time to come, she was my only Joy   170
With which I wisht to sweeten future Cares;
I fancy'd pleasures, none but one that loves
And dotes as I did can Imagine like 'em:
When in the Extremity of all these Hopes,
In the most Charming hour of Expectation,   175
Then when our Eager Wishes soar the highest,
Ready to stoop and grasp the lovely Game,
A Haggard Owl, a Worthless Kite of Prey,
With his foul Wings sayl'd in and spoyl'd my Quarry.
    Jaff. I know the Wretch, and scorn him as thou hat'st him.   180
    Pierr. Curse on the Common Good that's so protected,

Where every slave that heaps up wealth enough
To do much Wrong, becomes a Lord of Right:
I, who believ'd no Ill could e'er come near me,
Found in the Embraces of my *Aquilina*   185
A Wretched old but itching Senator;
A wealthy Fool, that had bought out my Title,
A Rogue, that uses Beauty like a Lambskin,
Barely to keep him warm: That filthy Cuckoo too
Was in my absence crept into my Nest,   190
And spoyling all my Brood of noble Pleasure.
     Jaff. Didst thou not chace him thence?
     Pierr.   I did, and drove
The rank old bearded *Hirco* stinking home:
The matter was complain'd of in the Senate,
I summon'd to appear, and censur'd basely,   195
For violating something they call *priviledge*——
This was the Recompence of my service:
Would I'd been rather beaten by a Coward!
A Souldier's Mistress *Jaffeir's* his Religion,
When that's profan'd, all other Tyes are broken,   200
That even dissolves all former bonds of service,
And from that hour I think my self as free
To be the Foe as e'er the Friend of *Venice*——
Nay, Dear Revenge, when e'er thou call'st I am ready.
     Jaff. I think no safety can be here for Virtue,   205
And grieve my friend as much as thou to live
In such a wretched State as this of *Venice*;
Where all agree to spoil the Publick Good,
And Villains fatten with the brave man's Labours.
     Pierr. We have neither safety, Unity, nor Peace,   210
For the foundation's lost of Common Good;
Justice is lame as well as blind amongst us;
The Laws (corrupted to their ends that make 'em)
Serve but for Instruments of some new Tyranny,
That every day starts up to enslave us deeper: 215
Now could this glorious Cause but find out friends
To do it right! Oh *Jaffeir!* then might'st thou
Not wear these seals of Woe upon thy Face,
The proud *Priuli* should be taught humanity,
And learn to value such a son as thou art.   220
I dare not speak! But my heart bleeds this moment!
     Jaff. Curst be the Cause, though I thy friend be part on't:
Let me partake the troubles of thy bosom,
For I am us'd to misery, and perhaps

---

193. *Hirco:* Lecher; hircus means he-goat.

199. *A Souldier's Mistress . . .:* This line may be read A soldier's mistress, Jaffeir, is a soldier's religion.

May find a way to sweeten't to thy spirit.   225
Pierr. Too soon it will reach thy knowledge——
Jaff.   Then from thee
Let it proceed. There's Virtue in thy Friendship
Would make the saddest Tale of sorrow pleasing,
Strengthen my Constancy, and welcome Ruin.
Pierr. Then thou art ruin'd!
Jaff.   That I long since knew,   230
I and ill Fortune have been long Acquaintance.
Pierr. I past this very moment by thy doors,
And found them guarded by a Troop of Villains;
The sons of publick Rapine were destroying:
They told me, by the sentence of the Law   235
They had Commission to seize all thy Fortune,
Nay more, *Priuli's* cruel hand hath sign'd it.
Here stood a Ruffian with a horrid face
Lording it o'er a pile of massy Plate,
Tumbled into a heap for publick sale: 240
There was another making villainous jests
At thy undoing; he had ta'en possession
Of all thy antient most domestick Ornaments,
Rich hangings, intermixt and wrought with gold;
The very bed, which on thy Wedding-night   245
Receiv'd thee to the Arms of *Belvidera,*
The scene of all thy Joys, was violated
By the course hands of filthy Dungeon Villains,
And thrown amongst the common Lumber.
Jaff. Now thanks Heav'n——   250
Pierr. Thank Heav'n! for what?
Jaff.   That I am not worth a Ducat.
Pierr. Curse thy dull Stars and the worse Fate of *Venice,*
Where Brothers, Friends, and Fathers, all are false;
Where there's no trust, no truth; where Innocence
Stoop's under vile Oppression; and Vice lords it: 255
Hadst thou but seen, as I did, how at last
Thy Beauteous *Belvidera,* like a Wretch
That's doom'd to Banishment, came weeping forth,
Shining through Tears, like *April* Sun's in showers
That labour to o'ercome the Cloud that loads 'em, 260
Whilst two young Virgins, on whose Arms she lean'd,
Kindly lookt up, and at her Grief grew sad,
As if they catcht the Sorrows that fell from her:
Even the lewd Rabble that were gather'd round
To see the sight, stood mute when they beheld her; 265
Govern'd their roaring throats and grumbled pity:
I cou'd have hugg'd the greazy Rogues: They pleas'd me.
Jaff. I thank thee for this story from my soul,

Since now I know the worst that can befall me:
Ah *Pierre!* I have a Heart, that could have born   270
The roughest Wrong my Fortune could have done me:
But when I think what *Belvidera* feels,
The bitterness her tender spirit tasts of,
I own my self a Coward: Bear my weakness,
If throwing thus my Arms about thy Neck,   275
I play the Boy, and blubber in thy bosome.
Oh! I shall drown thee with my Sorrows!
 Pierr.   Burn!
First burn, and Level *Venice* to thy Ruin!
What starve like Beggar's Brats in frosty weather,
Under a Hedge, and whine our selves to Death!   280
Thou, or thy Cause, shall never want assistance,
Whilst I have Blood or Fortune fit to serve thee;
Command my heart: Thou art every way its master.
 Jaff. No: there's a secret Pride in bravely dying.
 Pierr. Rats die in Holes and Corners, Dogs run mad;   285
Man knows a braver Remedy for sorrow:
Revenge! the Attribute of Gods, they stampt it
With their great Image on our Natures; die!
Consider well the Cause that calls upon thee:
And if thou art base enough, dye then: Remember   290
Thy *Belvidera* suffers: *Belvidera!*
Dye——Damn first——what be decently interr'd
In a Church-yard, and mingle thy brave dust
With stinking Rogues that rot in dirty winding sheets,
Surfeit-slain Fools, the common Dung o'th Soyl!   295
 Jaff. Oh!
 Pierr.   Well said, out with't, Swear a little——
 Jaff.   Swear!
By Sea and Air! by Earth, by Heaven and Hell,
I will revenge my *Belvidera's* Tears!
Heark thee my Friend—*Priuli*—is—a Senator!
 Pierr. A Dog!
 Jaff.   Agreed.
 Pierr.   Shoot him.
 Jaff.   With all my heart.   300
No more: Where shall we meet at Night?
 Pierr.   I'll tell thee;
On the *Ryalto* every Night at Twelve
I take my Evening's walk of Meditation,
There we two will meet, and talk of precious
Mischief——   305
 Jaff. Farewel.
 Pierr.   At Twelve.
 Jaff.   At any hour, my plagues

Will keep me waking.   [*Ex.* Pierr.
Tell me why, good Heav'n,
Thou mad'st me what I am, with all the Spirit,
Aspiring thoughts and Elegant desires   310
That fill the happiest Man? Ah! rather why
Did'st thou not form me sordid as my Fate,
Base minded, dull, and fit to carry Burdens?
Why have I sence to know the Curse that's on me?
Is this just dealing, Nature? *Belvidera!*   315
                    [*Enter* Belvidera.
Poor *Belvidera!*
    Belv.   Lead me, lead me my Virgins!
To that kind Voice. My Lord, my Love, my Refuge!
Happy my Eyes, when they behold thy Face:
My heavy heart will leave its doleful beating
At sight of thee, and bound with sprightful joys.   320
Oh smile, as when our Loves were in their Spring,
And cheer my fainting Soul.
    Jaff.   As when our Loves
Were in their Spring? has then my Fortune chang'd?
Art thou not *Belvidera,* still the same,
Kind, good, and tender, as my Arms first found thee?   325
If thou art alter'd, where shall I have harbour?
Where ease my loaded Heart? Oh! where complain?
    Belv. Does this appear like Change, or Love decaying?
When thus I throw my self into thy bosom,
With all the resolution of a strong Truth: 330
Beat's not my heart, as 'twou'd alarm thine
To a new Charge of bliss? I joy more in thee,
Than did thy Mother when she hugg'd thee first,
And bless'd the Gods for all her Travel past.
    Jaff. Can there in Woman be such glorious Faith?   335
Sure all ill stories of thy Sex are false;
Oh Woman! lovely Woman! Nature made thee
To temper Man: We had been Brutes without you;
Angels are Painted fair, to look like you;
There's in you all that we believe of Heav'n,   340
Amazing Brightness, Purity and Truth,
Eternal Joy, and everlasting Love.
    Belv. If Love be Treasure, we'll be wondrous rich:
I have so much, my heart will surely break with't;
Vow's cannot express it, when I wou'd declare   345
How great's my Joy, I am dumb with the big thought;
I swell, and sigh, and labour with my longing.
Oh lead me to some Desart wide and wild,
Barren as our Misfortunes, where my Soul
May have its vent: Where I may tell aloud   350

To the high Heavens, and every list'ning Planet,
With what a boundless stock my bosom's fraught;
Where I may throw my eager Arms about thee,
Give loose to Love with kisses, kindling Joy,
And let off all the Fires that's in my Heart.   355
 Jaff. Oh *Belvidera!* double I am a Beggar,
Undone by Fortune, and in debt to thee;
Want! worldly Want! that hungry meager Fiend
Is at my heels, and chaces me in view;
Can'st thou bear Cold and Hunger? Can these Limbs,   360
Fram'd for the tender Offices of Love,
Endure the bitter Gripes of smarting Poverty?
When banisht by our miseries abroad
(As suddenly we shall be) to seek out
(In some far Climate where our Names are strangers)   365
For charitable succour; wilt thou then,
When in a Bed of straw we shrink together,
And the bleak winds shall whistle round our heads;
Wilt thou then talk thus to me? Wilt thou then
Hush my Cares thus, and shelter me with Love?   370
 Belv. Oh I will love thee, even in Madness love thee:
Tho my distracted Senses should forsake me,
I'd find some intervals, when my poor heart
Should swage it self and be let loose to thine.
Though the bare Earth be all our Resting-place,   375
Its Root's our food, some Clift our Habitation,
I'll make this Arm a Pillow for thy Head;
As thou sighing ly'st, and swell'd with sorrow,
Creep to thy Bosom, pour the balm of Love
Into thy Soul, and kiss thee to thy Rest;   380
Then praise our God, and watch thee 'till the Morning.
 Jaff. Hear this you Heav'ns, and wonder how you
   made her!
Reign, reign ye Monarchs that divide the World,
Busy Rebellion ne'er will let you know
Tranquility and Happiness like mine;   385
Like gawdy Ships, th' obsequious Billows fall
And rise again, to lift you in your Pride;
They wait but for a storm and then devour you:
I, in my private Bark, already wreck'd,
Like a poor Merchant driven on unknown Land,   390
That had by chance packt up his choicest Treasure
In one dear Casket, and sav'd only that:
 Since I must wander further on the shore,
 Thus hug my little, but my precious store;
 Resolv'd to scorn, and trust my Fate no more.   [*Exeunt.* 395

Act II

[*Enter* Pierre *and* Aquilina.]

Aquil. By all thy Wrongs, thou art dearer to my Arms
Than all the Wealth of *Venice*: Prithee stay,
And let us love to night.
    Pierr.   No: There's Fool,
There's Fool about thee: When a Woman sells
Her Flesh to Fools, her Beauty's lost to me;   5
They leave a Taint, a sully where th'ave past;
There's such a baneful Quality about 'em,
Even spoyls Complexions with their own Nauseousness;
They infect all they touch; I cannot think
Of tasting any thing a Fool has pall'd.   10
    Aquil. I loath and scorn that Fool thou mean'st, as much
Or more than thou can'st; But the Beast has Gold
That makes him necessary: Power too,
To qualifie my Character, and poise me
Equal with peevish Virtue, that beholds   15
My Liberty with Envy: In their Hearts
Are loose as I am; But an ugly Power
Sits in their Faces, and frights Pleasures from 'em.
    Pierr. Much good may't do you, Madam, with your Senator.
    Aquil. My Senator! why can'st thou think that Wretch   20
E're fill'd thy *Aquilina's* Arms with Pleasure?
Think'st thou, because I sometimes give him leave
To foyle himself at what he is unfit for;
Because I force my self to endure and suffer him,
Think'st thou I love him? No, by all the Joys   25
Thou ever gav'st me, his Presence is my Pennance;
The worst thing an old Man can be's a Lover,
A meer *Memento Mori* to poor woman.
I never lay by his decrepit side,
But all that night I ponder'd on my Grave.   30
    Pierr. Would he were well sent thither.
    Aquil.   That's my wish too:
For then, my *Pierre*, I might have cause with pleasure
To play the Hypocrite: Oh! how I could weep
Over the dying Dotard, and kiss him too,
In hopes to smother him quite; then, when the time   35
Was come to pay my Sorrows at his Funeral,
For he has already made me Heir to Treasures,
Would make me out-act a real Widow's whining:
How could I frame my face to fit my mourning!

4. *There's Fool about thee:* The defiling
quality of the fool Antonio clings to you.

10. *Pall'd:* Made disgusting.

23. *To foyle:* To thrust.

With wringing hands attend him to his Grave,   40
Fall swooning on his Hearse: Take mad possession,
Even of the Dismal Vault, where he lay bury'd,
There like the *Ephesian* Matron dwell, till Thou,
My lovely Soldier, comest to my Deliverance;
Then throwing up my Veil, with open Arms   45
And laughing Eyes, run to new dawning Joy.
    Pierr. No more! I have Friends to meet me here to Night,
And must be private. As you prize my Friendship,
Keep up your Coxcomb: Let him not pry nor listen,
Nor fisk about the House as I have seen him,   50
Like a tame mumping Squirrel with a Bell on;
Currs will be abroad to bite him, if you do.
    Aquil. What Friends to meet? may I not be of your Council?
    Pierr. How! a Woman ask Questions out of Bed?
Go to your Senator, ask him what passes   55
Amongst his Brethren, he'll hide nothing from you;
But pump not me for Politicks. No more!
Give order that whoever in my name
Comes here, receive Admittance: so good night.
    Aquil. Must we ne're meet again! Embrace no more!   60
Is Love so soon and utterly forgotten!
    Pierr. As you hence-forward treat your Fool, I'll think on't.
    Aquil. Curst be all Fools, and doubly curst my self,
The worst of Fools—I die if he forsakes me;
And now to keep him, Heav'n or Hell instruct me.   [*Exeunt.*   65

SCENE *The Ryalto*
[*Enter* Jaffeir.

    Jaff. I am here, and thus, the Shades of Night around me,
I look as if all Hell were in my Heart,
And I in Hell. Nay, surely 'tis so with me;——
For every step I tread, methinks some Fiend
Knocks at my Breast, and bids it not be quiet: 70
I've heard, how desperate Wretches, like my self,
Have wander'd out at this dead time of Night
To meet the Foe of Mankind in his walk:
Sure I am so Curst, that, tho' of Heav'n forsaken,
No Minister of Darkness cares to Tempt me.   75
Hell! Hell! why sleepest thou?
[*Enter* Pierre.

43. *The Ephesian Matron:* The *Satyricon* of Petronius, Ch. XI. A soldier assigned to keep several crucified thieves from being buried by friends, meets, and by degrees, seduces an inconsolable widow who is just placing her husband in his tomb.

49. *Keep up your Coxcomb:* Control your coxcomb (Antonio).
50. *Fisk:* Frisk.
51. *Mumping:* Moving the jaws as if chewing.

Pierr. Sure I have stay'd too long:
The Clock has struck, and I may lose my Proselyte.
Speak, who goes there?
    Jaff.   A Dog, that comes to howl
At yonder Moon: What's he that asks the Question?   80
    Pierr. A Friend to Dogs, for they are honest Creatures,
And ne're betray their Masters; never Fawn
On any that they love not: Well met, Friend:
Jaffeir!
    Jaff. The same. Oh *Pierre*! Thou art come in season,
I was just going to Pray.
    Pierr.   Ah that's Mechanick,   85
Priests make a Trade on't, and yet starve by it too:
No Praying, it spoils Business, and time's precious;
Where's *Belvidera*?
    Jaff.   For a Day or two
I've lodg'd her privately, 'till I see farther
What Fortune will do with me. Prithee, Friend,   90
If thou would'st have me fit to hear good Council,
Speak not of *Belvidera*——
    Pierr.   Speak not of her.
    Jaff. Oh no!
    Pierr.   Nor name her. May be I wish her well.
    Jaff. Who well?
    Pierr.   Thy Wife, thy lovely *Belvidera*,
I hope a man may wish his Friend's Wife well,   95
And no harm done!
    Jaff.   Y'are merry *Pierre!*
    Pierr.   I am so:
Thou shalt smile too, and *Belvidera* smile;
We'll all rejoyce, here's something to buy Pins,
Marriage is Chargeable.
    Jaff.   I but half wisht
To see the Devil, and he's here already.   100
Well!
What must this buy, Rebellion, Murder, Treason?
Tell me which way I must be damn'd for this.
    Pierr. When last we parted, we had no qualms like these,
But entertain'd each other's thoughts like Men,   105
Whose Souls were well acquainted. Is the World
Reform'd since our last meeting? What new miracles
Have happen'd? Has *Priuli's* heart relented?
Can he be honest?
    Jaff.   Kind Heav'n! let heavy Curses
Gall his old Age; Cramps, Aches, rack his Bones;   110
And bitterest disquiet wring his Heart;

99. *Chargeable:* Expensive.

Oh let him live 'till Life become his burden!
Let him groan under't long, linger an Age
In the worst Agonies and Pangs of Death,
And find its ease, but late.
    Pierr.   Nay, could'st thou not   115
As well, my Friend, have stretcht the Curse to all
The Senate round, as to one single Villain?
    Jaff. But Curses stick not: Could I kill with Cursing,
By Heav'n I know not thirty Heads in *Venice*
Should not be blasted; Senators should rot   120
Like Dogs on Dunghills; but their Wives and Daughters
Dye of their own diseases. Oh for a Curse
To kill with!
    Pierr.   Daggers, Daggers, are much better!
    Jaff. Ha!
    Pierr.   Daggers.
    Jaff.   But where are they?
    Pierr.   Oh, a Thousand
May be dispos'd in honest hands in *Venice*.   125
    Jaff. Thou talk'st in Clouds.
    Pierr.   But yet a Heart half wrong'd
As thine has been, would find the meaning, *Jaffeir.*
    Jaff. A thousand Daggers, all in honest hands;
And have not I a Friend will stick one here?
    Pierr. Yes, if I thought thou wert not to be cherisht   130
To a nobler purpose, I'd be that Friend.
But thou hast better Friends, Friends, whom thy Wrongs
Have made thy Friends; Friends, worthy to be call'd so;
I'll trust thee with a secret: There are Spirits
This hour at work. But as thou art a Man,   135
Whom I have pickt and chosen from the World,
Swear, that thou wilt be true to what I utter,
And when I have told thee, that which only Gods
And Men like Gods are privy to, then swear,
No Chance or Change shall wrest it from thy Bosom.   140
    Jaff. When thou would'st bind me, is there need of Oaths?
(Green-sickness Girls lose Maiden-heads with such Counters)
For thou art so near my heart, that thou may'st see
Its bottom, sound its strength, and firmness to thee:
A Coward, Fool, or Villian, in my face?   145
If I seem none of these, I dare believe
Thou would'st not use me in a little Cause,
For I am fit for Honour's toughest task;
Nor ever yet found fooling was my Province;
And for a villainous inglorious enterprize,   150
I know thy heart so well, I dare lay mine
Before thee, set it to what Point thou wilt.

Pierr. Nay, It's a Cause thou wilt be fond of *Jaffeir.*
For it is founded on the noblest Basis,
Our Liberties, our natural Inheritance;   155
There's no Religion, no Hypocrisie in't;
We'll do the Business, and ne'er fast and pray for't:
Openly act a deed, the World shall gaze
With wonder at, and envy when it is done.
   Jaff. For Liberty!
   Pierr.   For Liberty my Friend: 160
Thou shalt be freed from base *Priuli's* Tyranny,
And thy sequestred Fortunes heal'd again.
I shall be freed from opprobrious Wrongs,
That press me now, and bend my Spirit downward:
All *Venice* free, and every growing Merit   165
Succeed to its just Right: Fools shall be pull'd
From Wisdoms Seat; those baleful unclean Birds,
Those Lazy-Owls, who (perch'd near Fortune's Top)
Sit only watchful with their heavy Wings
To cuff down new fledg'd Virtues, that would rise   170
To nobler heights, and make the Grove harmonious.
   Jaff. What can I do?
   Pierr.   Cans't thou not kill a Senator?
   Jaff. Were there one wise or honest, I could kill him
For herding with that nest of Fools and Knaves;
By all my Wrongs, thou talk'st as if revenge   175
Were to be had, and the brave Story warms me.
   Pierr. Swear then!
   Jaff.   I do, by all those glittering Stars,
And yond great Ruling Planet of the Night!
By all good Pow'rs above, and ill below!
By Love and Friendship, dearer than my Life!   180
No Pow'r or Death shall make me false to thee.
   Pierr. Here we embrace, and I'll unlock my Heart.
A Councel's held hard by, where the destruction
Of this great Empire's hatching: There I'll lead thee!
But be a Man, for thou art to mix with Men   185
Fit to disturb the Peace of all the World,
And rule it when it's wildest——
   Jaff.   I give thee thanks
For this kind warning: Yes, I will be a Man,
And charge thee, *Pierre,* when e'er thou see'st my fears
Betray me less, to rip this Heart of mine   190
Out of my Breast, and shew it for a Coward's.
Come let's begone, for from this hour I chase
All little thoughts, all tender humane Follies
Out of my bosom: Vengeance shall have room:
Revenge!

Pierr. And Liberty!

Jaff.   Revenge! Revenge——   [*Exeunt.*   195

The Scene *changes to* Aquilina's *house, the Greek Curtezan.*

[*Enter* Renault.

Renault. Why was my choice Ambition, the worst ground
A Wretch can build on? it's indeed at distance
A good Prospect, tempting to the View,
The Height delights us, and the Mountain Top
Looks beautiful, because it's nigh to Heav'n,   200
But we ne're think how sandy's the Foundation,
What Storm will batter, and what Tempest shake us!
Who's there?

[*Enter* Spinosa.

Spino.   *Renault,* good morrow! for by this time
I think the Scale of Night has turn'd the ballance,
And weighs up Morning: Has the Clock struck Twelve?   205

Rena. Yes, Clocks will go as they are set: But Man,
Irregular Man's ne'er constant, never certain:
I've spent at least three precious hours of darkness
In waiting dull attendance; 'tis the Curse
Of diligent Virtue to be mixt like mine,   210
With giddy Tempers, Souls but half resolv'd.

Spino. Hell seize that Soul amongst us, it can frighten.

Rena. What's then the cause that I am here alone?
Why are we not together?

[*Enter* Eliot.

O Sir, welcome!   215
You are an *Englishman*: When Treason's hatching
One might have thought you'd not have been behind-hand.
In what Whore's lap have you been lolling?
Give but an *Englishman* his Whore and ease,
Beef and a Sea-coal fire, he's yours for ever.   220

Eliot. Frenchman, you are sawcy.

Rena.   How!

[*Enter* Bedamore *the Embassador,* Theodore, Brainveil,
Durand, Brabe, Revellido, Mezzana, Ternon, Retrosi,
Conspirators.

Bedam.   At difference, fye.
Is this a time for quarrels? Thieves and Rogues
Fall out and brawl: Should Men of your high calling,
Men separated by the Choice of Providence,
From the gross heap of Mankind, and set here   225
In this great assembly as in one great Jewel,
T'adorn the bravest purpose it er'e smil'd on;
Should you like Boys wrangle for trifles?

220. *Sea-coal:* Mineral coal cast up by
the sea.

Rena.   Boys!
Beda. Renault, thy Hand!
Rena.   I thought I'd given my Heart
Long since to every Man that mingles here;   230
But grieve to find it trusted with such Tempers,
That can't forgive my froward Age its weakness.
    Beda. Eliot, thou once had'st Vertue, I have seen
Thy stubborn Temper bend with godlike Goodness,
Not half thus courted: 'Tis thy Nation's Glory,   235
To hugg the Foe that offers brave Alliance.
Once more embrace, my Friends—we'll all embrace——
United thus, we are the mighty Engin
Must twist this rooted Empire from its Basis!
Totters it not already?
    Eliot.   Would it were tumbling.   240
    Beda. Nay it shall down: This Night we Seal its ruine.
                 [*Enter* Pierre.
Oh *Pierre!* thou art welcome!
Come to my breast, for by its hopes thou look'st
Lovelily dreadful, and the Fate of *Venice*
Seems on thy Sword already. Oh my *Mars!*   245
The Poets that first feign'd a God of War
Sure prophecy'd of thee.
    Pierr.   Friends! was not *Brutus*
(I mean that *Brutus,* who in open Senate
Stabb'd the first *Cæsar* that usurp'd the World)
A Gallant Man?
    Rena.   Yes, and *Cateline* too;   250
Tho story wrong his Fame: for he conspir'd
To prop the reeling Glory of his Country:
His Cause was good.
    Beda.   And ours as much above it,
As *Renault* thou art Superior to *Cethegus,*
Or *Pierre* to *Cassius.*
    Pierr.   Then to what we aim at   255
When do we start? or must we talk for ever?
    Beda. No *Pierre,* the Deed's near Birth: Fate seems to
      have set
The Business up and given it to our care:
I hope there's not a heart nor hand amongst us
But is firm and ready.   260
    All. All! We'll die with *Bedamore.*
    Beda.   Oh Men,

---

250. *Cateline:* Catiline, a dissolute and impoverished Roman patrician who by revolutionary means sought power during Cicero's consulship, 63 B.C.

254. *Cethegus:* One of Catiline's followers.

Matchless, as will your Glory be hereafter.
The Game is for a Matchless Prize, if won;
If lost, disgraceful Ruine.
  Rena.   What can lose it?
The publick Stock's a Beggar; one *Venetian*   265
Trusts not another: Look into their Stores
Of general safety; Empty Magazines,
A tatter'd Fleet, a murmuring unpaid Army,
Bankrupt Nobility, a harrast Commonalty,
A Factious, giddy, and divided Senate,   270
Is all the strength of *Venice*: Let's destroy it;
Let's fill their Magazines with Arms to awe them,
Man out their Fleet, and make their Trade maintain it;
Let loose the murmuring Army on their Masters,
To pay themselves with plunder; Lop their Nobles 275
To the base Roots, whence most of 'em first sprung;
Enslave the Rout, whom smarting will make humble,
Turn out their droning Senate, and possess
That Seat of Empire which our Souls were fram'd for.
  Pierr. Ten thousand men are Armed at your Nod, 280
Commanded all by Leaders fit to guide
A Battle for the freedom of the World;
This wretched State has starv'd them in its service,
And by your bounty quicken'd, they're resolv'd
To serve your Glory, and revenge their own!   285
Th' have all their different Quarters in this City,
Watch for th' Alarm, and grumble 'tis so tardy,
  Beda. I doubt not Friend, but thy unweary'd diligence
Has still kept waking, and it shall have ease;
After this Night it is resolv'd we meet   290
No more, 'till *Venice* own us for her Lords.
  Pierr. How lovely the *Adriatique* Whore,
Drest in her Flames, will shine! devouring Flames!
Such as shall burn her to the watery bottom
And hiss in her Foundation.
  Beda.   Now if any   295
Amongst us that owns this glorious Cause,
Have friends or Interest, he'd wish to save,
Let it be told, the general Doom is Seal'd;
But I'de forgo the Hopes of a World's Empire,
Rather than wound the Bowels of my Friend.   300
  Pierr. I must confess you there have toucht my weakness,
I have a Friend; hear it, such a Friend!
My heart was ne'er shut to him: Nay, I'l tell you,
He knows the very Business of this Hour;
But he rejoyces in the Cause, and loves it,   305
W' have chang'd a Vow to live and die together,

And He's at hand to ratify it here.
   Rena. How! all betray'd?
   Pierr.   No—I've dealt nobly with you;
I've brought my All into the publick Stock;
I had but one Friend, and him I'll share amongst you!   310
Receive and Cherish him: Or if, when seen
And searcht, you find him worthless, as my Tongue
Has lodg'd this Secret in his faithful Breast,
To ease your fears I wear a Dagger here
Shall rip it out again, and give you rest.   315
Come forth, thou only Good I e'er could boast of.
               [*Enter* Jaffeir *with a Dagger.*
   Beda. His Presence bears the show of Manly Vertue.
   Jaff. I know you'll wonder all, that thus uncall'd,
I dare approach this place of fatal Councels;
But I am amongst you, and by Heav'n it glads me,   320
To see so many Vertues thus united,
To restore Justice and dethrown Oppression.
Command this Sword, if you would have it quiet,
Into this Brest; but if you think it worthy
To cut the Throats of reverend Rogues in Robes,   325
Send me into the curs'd assembl'd Senate;
It shrinks not, tho I meet a Father there;
Would you behold this City Flaming? Here's
A hand shall bear a lighted Torch at noon
To the Arsenal, and set its Gates on fire   330
   Rena. You talk this well, Sir.
   Jaff.   Nay—by Heav'n I'll do this.
Come, come, I read distrust in all your faces,
You fear me a Villain, and indeed it's odd
To hear a stranger talk thus at first meeting,
Of matters, that have been so well debated;   335
But I come ripe with Wrongs as you with Councels;
I hate this Senate, am a Foe to *Venice*;
A Friend to none, but Men resolv'd like me,
To push on Mischief: Oh did you but know me,
I need not talk thus!
   Beda.   *Pierre!* I must embrace him,   340
My heart beats to this Man as if it knew him.
   Rena. I never lov'd these huggers:
   Jaff.   Still I see
The cause delights me not. Your Friends survey me,
As I were dangerous—but I come Arm'd
Against all doubts, and to your trust will give   345
A Pledge, worth more than all the World can pay for.
My *Belvidera!* Ho! my *Belvidera!*
   Beda. What wonder next?

Jaff.   Let me entreat you,
As I have henceforth hopes to call ye friends,
That all but the Ambassador, this   350
Grave Guide of Councels, with my friend that owns me,
Withdraw a while to spare a Woman's blushes.
                    [*Ex. all but* Beda. Rena. Jaff. Pierr.
    Beda. Pierre, whither will this Ceremony lead us?
    Jaff. My *Belvidera! Belvidera!*
                    [*Enter* Belvidera.
    Belv.   Who?
Who calls so lowd at this late peaceful hour?   355
That Voice was wont to come in gentler whispers,
And fill my Ears with the soft breath of Love:
Thou hourly Image of my Thoughts, where art thou?
    Jaff. Indeed 'tis late.
    Belv.   Oh! I have slept, and dreamt,
And dreamt again: Where hast thou been thou Loyterer?   360
Tho my Eyes clos'd, my Arms have still been open'd;
Stretcht every way betwixt my broken slumbers,
To search if thou wert come to crown my Rest;
There's no repose without thee: Oh the day
Too soon will break, and wake us to our sorrow;   365
Come, come to bed, and bid thy Cares good Night.
    Jaff. Oh *Belvidera!* we must change the Scene
In which the past Delights of Life were tasted:
The poor sleep little, we must learn to watch
Our labours late, and early every Morning,   370
Mid'st winter Frosts, th[i]n clad and fed with sparing,
Rise to our toils, and drudge away the day.
    Belv. Alas! where am I! whither is't you lead me!
Methinks I read distraction in your face,
Something less gentle than the Fate you tell me: 375
You shake and tremble too! your blood runs cold!
Heavens guard my Love, and bless his heart with Patience.
    Jaff. That I have Patience, let our Fate bear witness,
Who has ordain'd it so, that thou and I
(Thou the divinest Good man e'er possest,   380
And I the wretched'st of the Race of Man)
This very hour, without one tear, must part.
    Belv. Part! must we part? Oh! am I then forsaken?
Will my Love cast me off? have my misfortunes
Offended him so highly, that he'll leave me?   385
Why drag you from me? whither are you going?
My Dear! my Life! my Love!
    Jaff.   Oh Friends!
    Belv.   Speak to me.
    Jaff. Take her from my heart,

She'll gain such hold else, I shall ne'er get loose.
I charge thee take her, but with tender'st care,   390
Relieve her Troubles and asswage her sorrows.
   Rena. Rise, Madam! and Command amongst your
     Servants!
   Jaff. To you, Sirs, and your Honours, I bequeath her,
And with her this, when I prove unworthy——
                 [*Gives a dagger.*
You know the rest:—Then strike it to her heart;   395
And tell her, he, who three whole happy years
Lay in her Arms, and each kind Night repeated
The passionate Vows of still encreasing Love,
Sent that Reward for all her Truth and Sufferings.
   Belv. Nay, take my Life, since he has sold it cheaply;   400
Or send me to some distant Clime your slave,
But let it be far off, least my complainings
Should reach his guilty Ears, and shake his peace.
   Jaff. No *Belvidera*, I've contriv'd thy honour;
Trust to my Faith, and be but Fortune kind   405
To me, as I'll preserve that faith unbroken,
When next we meet, I'll lift thee to a height,
Shall gather all the gazing World about thee,
To wonder what strange Virtue plac'd thee there.
But if we ner'e meet more——
   Belv.   Oh thou unkind one,   410
Never meet more! have I deserv'd this from you?
Look on me, tell me, tell me, speak thou dear deceiver,
Why am I separated from thy Love?
If I am false, accuse me; but if true,
Don't, prithee don't in poverty forsake me.   415
But pitty the sad heart, that's torn with parting.
Yet hear me! yet recal me——   [*Ex. Rena. Beda. and Belv.*
   Jaff.   Oh my Eyes!
Look not that way, but turn your selves awhile
Into my heart, and be wean'd all together.
My Friend, where art thou?
   Pierr.   Here, my Honour's Brother.   420
   Jaff. Is *Belvidera* gone?
   Pierr.   *Renault* has lead her
Back to her own Apartment: but, by Heav'n!
Thou must not see her more till our work's over.
   Jaff. No:
   Pierr.   Not for your life.
   Jaff.   Oh *Pierre*, wert thou but she,
How I could pull thee down into my heart,   425
Gaze on thee till my Eye-strings crackt with Love,
Till all my sinews with its fire extended,

Fixt me upon the Rack of ardent longing;
Then swelling, sighing, raging to be blest,
Come like a panting Turtle to thy Breast,   430
On thy soft Bosom, hovering, bill and play,
Confess the cause why last I fled away;
    Own 'twas a fault, but swear to give it o'er,
    And never follow false Ambition more.   [*Ex.* Ambo.

Act III

[Enter Aquilina *and her* Maid.

Aquil. Tell him I am gone to bed: Tell him I am not at
home; tell him I've better Company with me,
or any thing; tell him in short I will not see him, the
eternal troublesome vexatious Fool: He's worse Company
than an ignorant Physician—I'll not be disturb'd at these   5
unseasonable hours.

Maid. But Madam! He's here already, just enter'd the
doors.

Aquil. Turn him out agen, you unnecessary, useless,
giddy-brain'd Ass! if he will not begone, set the house a   10
fire and burn us both: I had rather meet a Toad in my
dish than that old hideous Animal in my Chamber to
Night.

[Enter Antonio.

Anto. Nacky, Nacky, Nacky—how dost do *Nacky?*
Hurry durry. I am come little *Nacky*; past eleven a Clock,   15
a late hour; time in all Conscience to go to bed *Nacky*—
Nacky did I say? Ay *Nacky; Aquilina, lina, lina, quilina,
quilina, quilina, Aquilina, Naquilina, Naquilina, Acky,
Acky, Nacky, Nacky,* Queen *Nacky*—come let's to bed—
you Fubbs, you Pugg you—you little Puss—Purree   20
Tuzzey—I am a Senator.

Aquil. You are a Fool, I am sure.

Anto. May be so too sweet-heart. Never the worse
Senator for all that. Come *Nacky, Nacky,* lets have a
Game at Rump, *Nacky.*   25

Aquil. You would do well Signior to be troublesome here
no longer, but leave me to my self, be sober and go home, Sir.

Anto. Home *Madona!*

Aquil. Ay home, Sir. Who am I?

Anto. Madona, as I take it you are my—you are—thou   30
art my little *Nicky Nacky*—that's all!

Stage direction after 13: Enter Antonio: who was Anthony Ashley Cooper, aged
The use of the name Antonio is probably 61 in 1782 (see l. 40, below).
a way of satirizing the Earl of Shaftesbury,

Aquil. I find you are resolv'd to be troublesome, and so
to make short of the matter in few words, I hate you,
detest you, loath you, I am weary of you, sick of you—
hang you, you are an Old, Silly, Impertinent, Impotent,   35
Sollicitous Coxcomb, Crazy in your head, and lazy in your
Body, love to be medling with every thing, and if you had
not Money, you are good for nothing.

Anto. Good for nothing! Hurry durry, I'l try that presently. Sixty one years Old, and good for nothing; that's   40
brave. [*To the Maid*]. Come come come Mistress fiddle-
faddle, turn you out for a season; go turn out I say, it is
our will and pleasure to be private some moments—out,
out when you are bid to—[*Puts her out and locks the door.*]
Good for nothing you say?   45

Aquil. Why what are you good for?

Anto. In the first place, Madam, I am Old, and consequently very wise, very wise, *Madona*, d'e mark that? in
the second place take notice, if you please, that I am a
Senator, and when I think fit can make Speeches *Madona*.   50
Hurry durry, I can make a Speech in the Senate-house
now and then—wou'd make your hair stand on end,
Madona.

Aquil. What care I for your Speeches in the Senate-
house? if you wou'd be silent here, I should thank you.   55

Anto. Why, I can make Speeches to thee too, my lovely
Madona: for Example——
My cruel fair one,
[*Takes out a Purse of Gold, and at every pawse shakes it.*
Since it is my Fate, that you should with
Your Servant angry prove; tho late at Night——   60
I hope 'tis not too late with this to gain
reception for my Love——
there's for thee my little *Nicky Nacky*—take it, here take
it—I say take it, or I'll throw it at your head—how now,
rebel!   65

Aquil. Truly, my Illustrious Senator, I must confess
your Honour is at present most profoundly eloquent
indeed.

Anto. Very well: Come, now let's sit down and think
upon't a little—come sit I say—sit down by me a little my   70
Nicky Nacky, hah—[*Sits down*]. Hurry durry—good for
nothing—

Aquil. No Sir, if you please I can know my distance and
stand.

Anto. Stand: How? *Nacky* up and I down! Nay then   75
let me exclaim with the Poet:
  Shew me a Case more pitiful who can,

A standing Woman, and a falling Man.
Hurry durry—not sit down—*see this ye Gods*—You won't
sit down?   80
 Aquil. No Sir.
 Anto. Then look you now, suppose me a Bull, a *Basan-*
Bull, the Bull of Bulls, or any Bull. Thus up I get and
with my brows thus bent—I broo, I say I broo, I broo,
I broo. You won't sit down will you?—I broo—   85
  [*Bellows like a Bull, and drives her about.*
 Aquil. Well, Sir, I must endure this. [*She sits down*].
Now your honour has been a Bull, pray what Beast will
your Worship please to be next?
 Anto. Now I'll be a Senator agen, and thy Lover little
Nicky Nacky! [*He sits by her*]. Ah toad, toad, toad, toad!   90
spit in my Face a little, *Nacky*—spit in my Face prithee,
spit in my Face, never so little: spit but a little bit—spit,
spit, spit, spit when you are bid I say; do, prithee spit—
now, now, now, spit: what you won't spit, will you? Then
I'll be a Dog.   95
 Aquil. A Dog my Lord?
 Anto. Ay a Dog—and I'll give thee this t'other purse to
let me be a Dog—and to use me like a Dog a little. Hurry
durry—I will—here 'tis.——   [*Gives the Purse.*
 Aquil. Well, with all my heart. But let me beseech your   100
Dogship to play your trick's over as fast as you can, that
you may come to stinking the sooner, and be turn'd out of
doors as you deserve.
 Anto. Ay, ay—no matter for that—that [*He gets under
the Table*]. shan't move me—Now, bough waugh waugh,   105
bough waugh——   [*Barks like a Dog.*
 Aquil. Hold, hold, hold Sir, I beseech you: what is't you
do? If Curs bite, they must be kickt, Sir. Do you see,
kickt thus.
 Anto. Ay with all my heart: do kick, kick on, now I am   110
under the Table, kick agen—kick harder—harder yet,
bough waugh waugh, waugh, bough—'odd, I'll have a
snap at thy shins—bough waugh wough, waugh, bough—
'odd she kicks bravely.——
 Aquil. Nay then I'l go another way to work with you: 115
and I think here's an Instrument fit for the purpose. [*Fetches
a Whip and Bell*]. What bite your Mistress, sirrah! out,
out of doors, you Dog, to kennel and be hang'd—bite your
Mistress by the Legs, you rogue?—— [*She Whips him.*
 Anto. Nay prithee *Nacky*, now thou art too loving: 120

82–83. *Basan-Bull*: Ps. 22:12: ". . .
strong bulls of Bashan have beset me
round."

Hurry durry, 'odd I'll be a Dog no longer.

Aquil. Nay none of your fawning and grinning: But be
gone, or here's the discipline: What bite your Mistress by
the Legs you mungril? out of doors—hout hout, to kennel
sirra! go.   125

Anto. This is very barbarous usage *Nacky*, very barbarous: look you, I will not go—I will not stir from the door,
that I resolve—hurry durry, what shut me out?

[*She Whips him out.*

Aquil. Ay, and if you come here any more to night I'll
have my Foot-men lug you, you Curr: What bite your   130
poor Mistress *Nacky*, sirrah!

[*Enter* Maid.

Maid. Heav'ns Madam! Whats the matter?

[*He howls at the door like a Dog.*

Aquil. Call my Foot-men hither presently.

[*Enter two Foot-men.*

Maid. They are here already Madam, the house is all
alarm'd with a strange noise, that no body knows what to   135
make of.

Aquil. Go all of you and turn that troublesome Beast in
the next room out of my house—If I ever see him within
these walls again, without my leave for his Admittance,
you sneaking Rogues—I'll have you poison'd all, poison'd,   140
like Rats: every Corner of the house shall stink of one of
you: Go, and learn hereafter to know my pleasure. So
now for my *Pierre:*

> *Thus when Godlike Lover was displeas'd;*
> *We Sacrifice our Fool and he's appeas'd.*   [*Exeunt.*   145

SCENE *The Second*

[*Enter* Belvidera.

Belvid. I'm Sacrific'd! I am sold! betray'd to shame!
Inevitable Ruin has inclos'd me!
No sooner was I to my bed repair'd,
To weigh, and (weeping) ponder my condition,
But the old hoary Wretch, to whose false Care   5
My Peace and Honour was intrusted, came
(Like *Tarquin*) ghastly with infernal Lust.
Oh thou *Roman Lucrece!*
Thou could'st find friends to vindicate thy Wrong;
I never had but one, and he's prov'd false;   10
He that should guard my Virtue, has betray'd it;

7. *Like Tarquin:* Sextus, son of Tar-
quinus Superbus, tyrant of Rome, violated Lucrece, who told her husband of the
outrage and took her own life. This incident inspired a revolution in which the
Tarquins (perhaps Etruscan masters) were
expelled from Rome.

Left me! undone me! Oh that I could hate him!
Where shall I go! Oh whither whither wander?
                    [*Enter* Jaffeir.
    Jaff. Can *Belvidera* want a resting place
When these poor Arms are open to receive her?   15
Oh 'tis in vain to struggle with Desires
Strong as my Love to thee; for every moment
I am from thy sight, the Heart within my Bosom
Moans like a tender Infant in its Cradle
Whose Nurse had left it: Come, and with the Songs   20
Of gentle Love perswade it to its peace.
    Belvid. I fear the stubborn Wanderer will not own me,
'Tis grown a Rebel to be rul'd no longer,
Scorns the Indulgent Bosom that first lull'd it,
And like a Disobedient Child disdains   25
The soft Authority of *Belvidera.*
    Jaff. There was a time——
    Belv.   Yes, yes, there was a time,
When *Belvidera's* tears, her cries, and sorrows,
Were not despis'd; when if she chanc'd to sigh,
Or look but sad;—there was indeed a time   30
When *Jaffeir* would have ta'en her in his Arms,
Eas'd her declining Head upon his Breast,
And never left her 'till he found the Cause.
But let her now weep Seas,
Cry, 'till she rend the Earth; sigh 'till she burst   35
Her heart asunder; still he bears it all;
Deaf as the Wind, and as the Rocks unshaken.
    Jaff. Have I been deaf? am I that Rock unmov'd,
Against whose root, Tears beat and sighes are sent
In vain? have I beheld thy Sorrows calmly?   40
Witness against me Heav'ns, have I done this?
Then bear me in a Whirlwind back agen,
And let that angry dear one ne'er forgive me!
Oh thou too rashly censur'st of my Love!
Could'st thou but think how I have spent this night,   45
Dark and alone, no pillow to my Head,
Rest in my Eyes, nor quiet in my Heart,
Thou would'st not *Belvidera,* sure thou would'st not
Talk to me thus, but like a pitying Angel
Spreading thy wings come settle on my breast,   50
And hatch warm comfort there e'er sorrows freeze it.
    Belv. Why, then poor Mourner, in what baleful Corner
Hast thou been talking with that Witch the Night?
On what cold stone hast thou been stretcht along,
Gathering the grumbling Winds about thy Head,   55
To mix with theirs the Accents of thy Woes?

Oh now I find the Cause my Love forsakes me!
I am no longer fit to bear a share
In his Concernments: My weak female Virtue
Must not be trusted; 'Tis too frail and tender.   60
    Jaff. Oh *Porcia! Porcia!* What a Soul was thine?
    Belv. That *Porcia* was a Woman, and when *Brutus*,
Big with the fate of *Rome* (Heav'n guard thy safety!)
Conceal'd from her the Labours of his Mind,
She let him see, her Blood was great as his,   65
Flow'd from a Spring as noble, and a Heart
Fit to partake his Troubles, as his Love:
Fetch, fetch that Dagger back, the dreadful dower
Thou gav'st last night in parting with me; strike it
Here to my heart; and as the Blood flows from it,   70
Judge if it run not pure as *Cato's* Daughter's.
    Jaff. Thou art too good, and I indeed unworthy,
Unworthy so much Virtue: Teach me how
I may deserve such matchless Love as thine,
And see with what attention I'll obey thee.   75
    Belv. Do not despise me: that's the All I ask.
    Jaff. Despise thee! Hear me——
    Belv.   Oh thy charming Tongue
Is but too well acquainted with my weakness,
Knows, let it name but Love, my melting heart
Dissolves within my Breast; 'till with clos'd Eyes   80
I reel into thy Arms, and all's forgotten.
    Jaff. What shall I do?
    Belv.   Tell me! be just, and tell me
Why dwells that busy Cloud upon thy face?
Why am I made a stranger? why that sigh,
And I not know the Cause? Why when the World   85
Is wrapt in Rest, why chooses then my Love
To wander up and down in horrid darkness,
Loathing his bed, and these desiring Arms?
Why are these Eyes Blood shot, with tedious watching?
Why starts he now? and looks as if he wisht   90
His Fate were finisht? Tell me, ease my fears;
Least when we next time meet, I want the power
To search into the sickness of thy Mind,
But talk as wildly then as thou look'st now.
    Jaff. Oh *Belvidera!*   95
    Belv. Why was I last night deliver'd to a Villain?
    Jaff. Hah, a Villain!
    Belv. Yes! to a Villain! Why at such an hour

---

61. *Porcia:* Daughter of Cato of Utica
and wife of Marcus Brutus. She was a
strong supporter of the republican cause,
and to show how worthy she was to participate in her husband's plans, she wounded
herself.

Meets that assembly all made up of Wretches
That look as Hell had drawn 'em into League?   100
Why, I in this hand, and in that a Dagger,
Was I deliver'd with such dreadful Ceremonies?
"To you, Sirs, and to your Honour I bequeath her,
And with her this: When e'er I prove unworthy,
You know the rest, then strike it to her Heart."   105
Oh! why's that *rest* conceal'd from me? must I
Be made the hostage of a hellish Trust?
For such I know I am; that's all my value!
But by the Love and Loyalty I owe thee,
I'l free thee from the Bondage of these Slaves;   110
Strait to the Senate, tell 'em all I know,
All that I think, all that my fears inform me!
   Jaff. Is this the *Roman* Virtue! this the Blood
That boast[s] its purity with *Cato's* Daughter!
Would she have e'er betray'd her *Brutus*?
   Belv.   No: 115
For *Brutus* trusted her: Wer't thou so kind,
What would not *Belvidera* suffer for thee?
   Jaff. I shall undo my self, and tell thee all.
   Belv. Look not upon me as I am, a Woman,
But as a Bone, thy Wife, thy Friend; who long   120
Has had admission to thy heart, and there
Study'd the Virtues of thy gallant Nature;
Thy Constancy, thy Courage and thy Truth,
Have been my daily lesson: I have learnt them,
Am bold as thou, can suffer or despise   125
The worst of Fates for thee; and with thee share them.
   Jaff. Oh you divinest Powers! look down and hear
My Prayers! instruct me to reward this Virtue!
Yet think a little, e'er thou tempt me further:
Think I have a Tale to tell, will shake thy Nature,   130
Melt all this boasted Constancy thou talk'st of
Into vile tears and despicable sorrows:
Then if thou shoud'st betray me!
   Belv.   Shall I swear?
   Jaff. No: do not swear: I would not violate
Thy tender Nature with so rude a Bond: 135
But as thou hop'st to see me live my days,
And love thee long, lock this within thy Breast;
I've bound my self by all the strictest Sacraments,
Divine and humane——

120. *As a Bone:* Gen. 2:23: "And Adam
said, This is now bone of my bones, and
flesh of my flesh. . . ."

Belv.   Speak!——
Jaff.   To kill thy Father——
Belv. My Father!
Jaff.   Nay the Throats of the whole Senate   140
Shall bleed, my *Belvidera*: He amongst us
That spares his Father, Brother, or his Friend,
Is Damn'd: How rich and beauteous will the face
Of Ruin look, when these wide streets run blood;
I and the glorious Partners of my Fortune   145
Shouting, and striding o'er the prostrate Dead;
Still to new waste; whilst thou, far off in safety
Smiling, shalt see the wonders of our daring;
And when night comes, with Praise and Love receive me.
    Belv. Oh!
Jaff.   Have a care, and shrink not even in thought!   150
For if thou do'st——
    Belv.   I know it, thou wilt kill me,
Do, strike thy Sword into this bosom: Lay me
Dead on the Earth, and then thou wilt be safe:
Murder my Father! tho his Cruel Nature
Has persecuted me to my undoing,   155
Driven me to basest wants; Can I behold him
With smiles of Vengeance, butcher'd in his Age?
The sacred Fountain of my life destroy'd?
And canst thou shed the blood that gave me being?
Nay, be a Traitor too, and sell thy Country?   160
Can thy great Heart descend so vilely low,
Mix with hired Slaves, Bravoes, and Common stabbers,
Nose-slitters, Ally-lurking Villians! joyn
With such a Crew, and take a Ruffian's Wages,
To cut the Throats of Wretches as they sleep?   165
    Jaff. Thou wrong'st me, *Belvidera!* I've engag'd
With Men of Souls: fit to reform the ills
Of all Mankind: There's not a Heart amongst them,
But's as stout as Death, yet honest as the Nature
Of Man first made, e'er Fraud and Vice were fashions.   170
    Belv. What's he, to whose curst hands last night thou
        gav'st me?
Was that well done? Oh! I could tell a story
Would rowse thy Lyon Heart out of its Den,
And make it rage with terrifying fury.
    Jaff. Speak on I charge thee!
    Belv.   Oh my Love! if e'er   175
Thy *Belvidera's* Peace deserv'd thy Care,
Remove me from this place: Last night, last night!
    Jaff. Distract me not, but give me all the Truth.
    Belv. No sooner wer't thou gone, and I alone,

Left in the pow'r of that old Son of Mischief;   180
No sooner was I lain on my sad Bed,
But that vile Wretch approacht me; loose, unbutton'd,
Ready for violation: Then my Heart
Throbb'd with its fears: Oh how I wept and sigh'd,
And shrunk and trembled; wish'd in vain for him   185
That should protect me. Thou alas! wert gone!
 Jaff. Patience, sweet Heav'n! 'till I make vengeance sure.
 Belv. He drew the hideous Dagger forth thou gav'st him,
And with upbraiding smiles he said, *behold it;*
This is the pledge of a false Husband's love: 190
And in my Arms then prest, and wou'd have clasp'd me;
But with my Cries I scar'd his Coward heart,
'Till he withdrew, and mutter'd vows to Hell.
These are thy Friends! with these thy Life, thy Honour,
Thy Love, all's stak't, and all will go to ruine.   195
 Jaff. No more: I charge thee keep this secret close;
Clear up thy sorrows, look as if thy wrongs
Were all forgot, and treat him like a Friend,
As no complaint were made. No more, retire,
Retire my Life, and doubt not of my Honour;   200
I'll heal its failings, and deserve thy Love.
 Belv. Oh should I part with thee, I fear thou wilt
In Anger leave me, and return no more.
 Jaff. Return no more! I would not live without thee
Another Night to purchase the Creation.   205
 Belv. When shall we meet again?
 Jaff.   Anon at Twelve!
I'll steal my self to thy expecting Arms,
Come like a Travell'd Dove and bring thee Peace.
 Belv. Indeed!
 Jaff. By all our loves!
 Belv.   'Tis hard to part:
But sure no falshood e'er lookt so fairly.   210
Farewell—Remember Twelve.   [*Ex.* Belvid.
 Jaff.   Let Heav'n forget me
When I remember not thy Truth, thy Love.
How curst is my Condition, toss'd and justl'd,
From every Corner; Fortune's Common Fool,
The jest of Rogues, an Instrumental Ass   215
For Villains to lay loads of Shame upon,
And drive about just for their ease and scorn.
       [*Enter* Pierre.
 Pierr. Jaffeir!
 Jaff. Who calls!
 Pierr.   A Friend, that could have wisht
T'have found thee otherwise imploy'd: what, hunt

A Wife on the dull foil! sure a stanch Husband   220
Of all Hounds is the dullest? wilt thou never,
Never be wean'd from Caudles and Confections?
What feminine Tale hast thou been listening to,
Of unayr'd shirts; Catharrs and Tooth Ach got
By thin-sol'd shooes? Damnation! that a Fellow   225
Chosen to be a Sharer in the Destruction
Of a whole People, should sneak thus in Corners
To ease his fulsom Lusts, and Fool his Mind.
    Jaff. May not a Man then trifle out an hour
With a kind Woman and not wrong his calling?   230
    Pierr. Not in a Cause like ours.
    Jaff.   Then Friend our Cause
Is in a damn'd condition: for I'l tell thee,
That Canker-worm call'd *Letchery* has toucht it,
'Tis tainted vilely: would'st thou think it, *Renault*
(That mortify'd old wither'd Winter Rogue)   235
Loves simple Fornication like a Priest,
I found him out for watering at my Wife:
He visited her last night like a kind Guardian:
Faith she has some Temptations, that's the truth on't.
    Pierr. He durst not wrong his Trust!
    Jaff.   'Twas something late tho   240
To take the freedome of a Ladies Chamber.
    Pierr. Was she in bed?
    Jaff.   Yes faith in Virgin sheets
White as her bosom, *Pierre*, disht neatly up,
Might tempt a weaker appetite to taste.
Oh how the old Fox stunk I warrant thee   245
When the rank fit was on him.
    Pierr.   Patience guide me!
He us'd no violence?
    Jaff.   No, no! out on't, violence!
Play'd with her neck; brusht her with his Gray-beard,
Struggl'd and towz'd, tickl'd her 'till she squeak'd a little
May be, or so—but not a jot of violence——   250
    Pierr. Damn him.
    Jaff.   Ay, so say I: but hush, no more on't;
All hitherto is well, and I believe
My self no Monster yet: Tho no Man knows
What Fate he's born to: sure 'tis near the hour
We all should meet for our concluding Orders: 255
Will the Ambassador be here in person?

---

220. *Foil:* "The track of a hunted animal." OED.
222. *Caudles:* A warm drink given to sick people.

253. *Monster:* Cuckold.

Pierr. No: he has sent Commission to that Villain, *Renault*,
To give the Executing Charge;
I'd have thee be a Man if possible
And keep thy temper; for a brave Revenge   260
Ne'er comes too late.
  Jaff.   Fear not, I am cool as Patience:
Had he compleated my dishonour, rather
Then hazard the Success our hopes are ripe for,
I'd bear it all with mortifying Vertue.
  Pierr. He's yonder coming this way through the Hall;   265
His thoughts seem full.
  Jaff.   Prithee retire, and leave me
With him alone: I'll put him to some tryal,
See how his rotten part will bear the touching.
  Pierr. Be careful then.   [*Ex.* Pierre.
  Jaff.   Nay never doubt, but trust me.
What be a Devil! take a Damning Oath   270
For shedding native blood! can there be a sin
In merciful repentance? Oh this Villain.
      [*Enter* Renault.
  Renault. Perverse! and peevish! what a slave is Man!
To let his itching flesh thus get the better of him!
Dispatch the Tool her Husband—that were well.   275
Who's there?
  Jaff. A Man.
  Rena.   My Friend, my near Ally!
The hostage of your faith, my beauteous Charge,
Is very well.
  Jaff. Sir, are you sure of that?
Stands she in perfect health? beats her pulse even?
Neither too hot nor cold?
  Rena.   What means that question?   280
  Jaff. Oh, Women have fantastick Constitutions,
Inconstant as their Wishes, always wavering,
And ne'er fixt; was it not boldly done
Even at first sight to trust the Thing I lov'd
(A tempting Treasure too!) with Youth so fierce   285
And vigorous as thine? but thou art honest.
  Rena. Who dares accuse me?
  Jaff.   Curst be him that doubts
Thy virtue, I have try'd it, and declare,
Were I to choose a Guardian of my Honour
I'd put it into thy keeping: for I know thee.   290
  Rena. Know me!
  Jaff.   Ay know thee: There's no falshood in thee.
Thou look'st just as thou art: Let us embrace.
Now would'st thou cut my Throat or I cut thine?

Rena. You dare not do't.

Jaff.   You lye Sir.

Rena.   How!

Jaff.   No more.

'Tis a base World, and must reform, that's all.   295

    [*Enter* Spinosa, Theodore, Eliot, Revellido, Durand,
    Brainveil, *and the rest of the Conspirators.*

Rena. Spinosa! Theodore!

Spin.   The same.

Rena.   You are welcome!

Spin. You are trembling, Sir.

Rena.   'Tis a cold Night indeed, I am Aged,

Full of decay and natural infirmities;

    [Pierre *re-enters.*

We shall be warm, my Friend, I hope to morrow.

Pierr. 'Twas not well done, thou shou'd'st have stroakt him   300

And not have gall'd him.

Jaff.   Damn him, let him chew on't.

Heav'n! where am I? beset with cursed Fiends,

That wait to Damn me: What a Devil's man,

When he forgets his nature—hush my heart.

Rena. My Friends, 'tis late: are we assembled all?   305

Where's *Theodore?*

Theo.   At hand.

Rena.   Spinosa.

Spin.   Here.

Rena. Brainveil.

Brain.   I am ready.

Rena.   *Durand* and *Brabe.*

Dur.   Command us,

We are both prepar'd!

Rena.   *Mezzana, Revellido,*

Ternon, Retrosi; Oh you are Men I find

Fit to behold your Fate, and meet her Summons;   310

To morrow's rising Sun must see you all

Deckt in your honours! are the Souldiers ready?

Omn. All, all.

Rena. You, *Durand*, with your thousand must possess

St. *Marks*; You, Captain, know your charge already;   315

'Tis to secure the Ducal Palace: you

Brabe with a hundred more must gain the *Secque.*

With the like number *Brainveil* to the *Procuralle.*

Be all this done with the least tumult possible,

'Till in each place you post sufficient guards: 320

---

317. *The Secque:* The mint. A Sequin
was a Venetian gold coin.
318. *Procuralle:* Procuratía. The official
dwelling place of the procurators of Venice,
in St. Mark's.

Then sheath your Swords in every breast you meet.
Jaff. Oh reverend Cruelty: Damn'd bloody Villain!
Rena. During this Execution, *Durand*, you
Must in the mid'st keep your Battalia fast,
And *Theodore* be sure to plant the Canon   325
That may Command the streets; whilst *Revellido*,
Mezzana, *Ternon* and *Retrosi* Guard you.
(This done!) we'll give the General Alarm,
Apply Petards, and force the Ars'nal Gates;
Then fire the City round in several places,   330
Or with our Canon (if it dare resist)
Batter't to Ruin. But above all I charge you,
Shed blood enough, spare neither Sex nor Age,
Name nor Condition; if there live a Senator
After to morrow, tho the dullest Rogue   335
That e'er said nothing, we have lost our ends;
If possible, let's kill the very Name
Of Senator, and bury it in blood.
Jaff. Merciless, horrid slave!—Ay, blood enough!
Shed blood enough, old *Renault*: how thou charm'st me!   340
Rena. But one thing more, and then farewell till Fate
Join us again, or separate us ever:
First, let's embrace, Heav'n knows who next shall thus
Wing ye together: But let's all remember
We wear no common Cause upon our Swords,   345
Let each Man think that on his single Virtue
Depends the Good and Fame of all the rest;
Eternal Honour or perpetual Infamy.
Let's remember, through what dreadful hazards
Propitious Fortune hitherto has led us,   350
How often on the brink of some discovery
Have we stood tottering, and yet still kept our ground
So well, the busiest searchers ne'er could follow
Those subtle Tracks which puzzled all suspicion:
You droop Sir.
Jaff.   No: with a most profound attention   355
I've h[e]ard it all, and wonder at thy vertue.
Rena. Though there be yet few hours' twixt them and Ruin,
Are not the Senate lull'd in full security,
Quiet and satisfy'd, as Fools are always!
Never did so profound repose forerun   360
Calamity so great: Nay our good Fortune
Has blinded the most piercing of Mankind:
Strengthen'd the fearfull'st, charm'd the most suspectful,

329. *Apply Petards:* Petards were small
military devices for blowing in a gate or a
door, or for breaching a wall.

Confounded the most subtle: for we live,
We live my Friends, and quickly shall our Life   365
Prove fatal to these Tyrants: Let's consider
That we destroy Oppression, Avarice,
A People nurst up equally with Vices
And loathsome Lusts, which Nature most abhors,
And such as without shame she cannot suffer.   370
    Jaff. Oh *Belvidera*, take me to thy Arms
And shew me where's my Peace, for I've lost it.   [*Ex.* Jaff.
    Rena. Without the least remorse then let's resolve
With Fire and Sword t'exterminate these Tyrants;
And when we shall behold those curst Tribunals,   375
Stain'd by the Tears and sufferings of the Innocent,
Burning with flames rather from Heav'n than ours,
The raging furious and unpitying Souldier
Pulling his reeking Dagger from the bosoms
Of gasping Wretches; Death in every Quarter,   380
With all that sad disorder can produce,
To make a Spectacle of horror: Then,
Then let's call to mind, my dearest Friends,
That there's nothing pure upon the Earth,
That the most valu'd things have most allays,   385
And that in change of all those vile Enormities,
Under whose weight this wretched Country labours,
The Means are only in our hands to Crown them.
    Pierr. And may those Powers above that are propitious
To gallant minds record this Cause, and bless it.   390
    Rena. Thus happy, thus secure of all we wish for,
Should there my Friends be found amongst us one
False to this glorious Enterprize, what Fate,
What Vengeance were enough for such a Villian?
    Eliot. Death here without repentance, Hell hereafter.   395
    Rena. Let that be my lot if as here I stand
Lifted by Fate amongst her darling Sons,
Tho I had one only Brother, dear by all
The strictest ties of Nature; tho one hour
Had given us birth, one Fortune fed our wants,   400
One only love, and that but of each other,
Still fill'd our minds: Could I have such a Friend
Joyn'd in this Cause, and had but ground to fear
Meant foul play; may this right hand drop from me,
If I'd not hazard all my future peace,   405
And stab him to the heart before you: who
Would do less? Would'st not thou *Pierre* the same?
    Pierr. You have singled me, Sir, out for this hard question,
As if 'twere started only for my sake!

385. *Allays:* Alien elements.

Am I the thing you fear? Here, here's my bosom,   410
Search it with all your Swords! am I a Traytor?
Rena. No: but I fear your late commended Friend
Is little less: Come Sirs, 'tis now no time
To trifle with our safety. Where's this *Jaffeir*?
Spin. He left the room just now in strange disorder.   415
Rena. Nay, there is danger in him: I observ'd him,
During the time I took for Explanation,
He was transported from most deep attention
To a confusion which he could not smother.
His looks grew full of sadness and surprize,   420
All which betray'd a wavering Spirit in him,
That labour'd with reluctancy and sorrow;
What's requisite for safety must be done
With speedy Execution: he remains
Yet in our power: I for my own part wear   425
A Dagger.
Pierr. Well.
Rena.   And I could wish it——
Pierr.   Where?
Rena. Bury'd in his heart.
Pierr.   Away! w'are yet all friends;
No more of this, 'twill Breed ill blood amongst us.
Spin. Let us all draw our Swords, and search the house,
Pull him from the dark hole where he sits brooding   430
O'er his cold fears, and each man kill his share of him.
Pierr. Who talks of killing? who's he'll shed the blood
That's dear to me? is't you? or you? or you Sir?
What not one speak? how you stand gaping all
On your grave Oracle, your wooden God there;   435
Yet not a word: Then Sir I'll tell you a secret:
Suspicion's but at best a Coward's Virtue!   [*To Rena.*
Rena. A Coward——   [*Handles his Sword.*
Pierr.   Put, put up thy Sword, old Man,
Thy hand shakes at it; come let's heal this breach,
I am too hot: we yet may live Friends.   440
Spin. 'Till we are safe, our Friendship cannot be so.
Pierr. Again: who's that?
Spin.   'Twas I.
Theo.   And I.
Revell.   And I.
Eliot. And all.
Rena. Who are on my side?
Spin.   Every honest Sword:
Let's die like men and not be sold like Slaves.   445
Pierr. One such word more, by Heav'n I'll to the Senate
And hang ye all, like Dogs in Clusters.

Why peep your Coward Swords half out their shells?
Why do you not all brandish them like mine?
You fear to die, and yet dare talk of Killing?   450
    Rena. Go to the Senate and betray us, hasten,
Secure thy wretched life, we fear to die
Less than thou dar'st be honest.
    Pierr.   That's rank falshood,
Fear'st not thou death? fy, there's a knavish itch
In that salt blood, an utter foe to smarting.   455
Had *Jaffeir's* Wife prov'd kind, he had still been true.
Foh—how that stinks?
Thou dy! thou kill my Friend! or thou, or thou,
Or thou, with that lean wither'd wretched Face!
Away! disperse all to your several Charges,   460
And meet to morrow where your honour calls you,
I'll bring that man, whose blood you so much thirst for,
And you shall see him venture for you fairly——
Hence, hence, I say.   [*Ex.* Renault *angrily.*
    Spin.   I fear we have been to blame,
And done too much.   465
    Theo. 'Twas too far urg'd against the man you lov'd.
    Revell. Here, take our Swords and crush 'em with your
       feet.
    Spin. Forgive us, gallant Friend.
    Pierr.   Nay, now y' have found
The way to melt and cast me as you will:
I'll fetch this Friend and give him to your mercy: 470
Nay he shall dye if you will take him from me,
For your repose I'll quit my heart's Jewel;
But would not have him torn away by Villains
And spitefull villany.
    Spin.   No; may you both
For ever live and fill the world with fame!   475
    Pierr. Now you are to[o] kind. Whence rose all this discord?
Oh what a dangerous precipice have we scap'd!
How near a fall was all we had long been building!
What an eternal blot had stain'd our glories,
If one the bravest and the best of men   480
Had fallen a Sacrifice to rash suspicion,
Butcher'd by those whose Cause he came to cherish:
Oh could you know him all as I have known him,
How good he is, how just, how true, how brave,
You wou'd not leave this place till you had seen him;   485
Humbled your selves before him, kiss'd his feet,

466. *'Twas too far urg'd:* The copy text
gives 'Twas too much far urg'd, and so
offers an unidiomatic line that does not
scan. The probable error may result from
the transposition of "too much" from the
line above.

And gain'd remission for the worst of follies;
   Come but to morrow all your doubts shall end,
   And to your Loves me better recommend,
   That I've preserv'd your Fame, and sav'd my Friend.

                                      [Exeunt omnes.

Act IV

[Enter Jaffeir *and* Belvidera.

Jaff. Where dost thou lead me? Every step I move,
Methinks I tread upon some mangled Limb
Of a rack'd Friend: Oh my dear charming ruine!
Where are we wandring?
   Belv.   To eternal Honour;
To doe a deed shall Chronicle thy name,   5
Among the glorious Legends of those few
That have sav'd sinking Nations: thy Renown
Shall be the future Song of all the Virgins,
Who by thy piety have been preserv'd
From horrid violation: Every Street   10
Shall be adorn'd with Statues to thy honour,
And at thy feet this great Inscription written,
   Remember him that prop'd the fall of Venice.
   Jaff. Rather, Remember him, who after all
The sacred Bonds of Oaths and holier Friendship,   15
In fond compassion to a Woman's tears
Forgot his Manhood, Vertue, Truth and Honour,
To sacrifice the Bosom that reliev'd him.
Why wilt thou damn me?
   Belv.   Oh inconstant man!
How will you promise? how will you deceive?   20
Do, return back, re-place me in my Bondage,
Tell all thy Friends how dangerously thou lov'st me;
And let thy Dagger do its bloody office.
Oh that kind Dagger, *Jaffeir,* how 'twill look
Stuck through my heart, drench'd in my blood to th' hilts!   25
Whilst these poor dying eyes shall with their tears
No more torment thee, then thou wilt be free:
Or if thou think'st it nobler, Let me live
Till I am a Victim to the hateful lust
Of that Infernal Devil, that old Fiend   30
That's Damn'd himself and wou'd undo Mankind:
Last night, my Love!
   Jaff.   Name, name it not again.
It shews a beastly Image to my fancy,
Will wake me into madness. Oh the Villain!

That durst approach such purity as thine   35
On terms so vile: Destruction, swift destruction
Fall on my Coward-head, and make my Name
The common scorn of Fools if I forgive him;
If I forgive him, if I not revenge
With utmost rage, and most unstaying fury,   40
Thy suffering thou dear darling of my life, Love.
    Belv. Delay no longer then, but to the Senate;
And tell the dismal'st story e'er utter'd,
Tell 'em what bloodshed, rapines, desolations,
Have been prepar'd, how near's the fatal hour!   45
Save thy poor Country, save the Reverend bloud
Of all its Nobles, which to morrow's Dawn
Must else see shed: Save the poor tender lives
Of all those little Infants which the Swords
Of murtherers are whetting for this moment;   50
Think thou already heard'st their dying screams,
Think that thou seest their sad distracted Mothers
Kneeling before thy feet, and begging pity
With torn dishevel'd hair and streaming eyes,
Their naked mangled breasts besmeard with blood,   55
And even the Milk with which their fondled Babes
Softly they hush'd, dropping in anguish from 'em.
Think thou seest this, and then consult thy heart.
    Jaff. Oh!
    Belv.   Think too, If thou lose this present minute,
What miseries the next day brings upon thee.   60
Imagine all the horrours of that night,
Murther and Rapine, Waste and Desolation,
Confusedly ranging. Think what then may prove
My Lot! the Ravisher may then come safe,
And midst the terrour of the publick ruine   65
Do a damn'd deed; perhaps to lay a Train
May catch thy life; then where will be revenge,
The dear revenge that's due to such a wrong?
    Jaff. By all Heaven's powers, Prophetick truth dwells in
        thee,
For every word thou speak'st strikes through my heart   70
Like a new light, and shows it how't has wander'd;
Just what th'hast made me, take me, *Belvidera*,
And lead me to the place where I'm to say
This bitter Lesson, where I must betray
My truth, my vertue, constancy and friends: 75
Must I betray my friend? Ah take me quickly,
Secure me well before that thought's renew'd;
If I relapse once more, all's lost for ever.
    Belv. Hast thou a friend more dear than *Belvidera*?

Jaff. No, th'art my Soul it self; wealth, friendship,
  honour,   80
All present joys, and earnest of all future,
Are summ'd in thee: methinks when in thy arms
Thus leaning on thy breast, one minute's more
Than a long thousand years of vulgar hours.
Why was such happiness not given me pure?   85
Why dash'd with cruel wrongs, and bitter wantings?
Come, lead me forward now like a tame Lamb
To Sacrifice: thus in his fatal Garlands,
Deck'd fine and pleas'd, The wanton skips and plays,
 Trots by the enticing flattering Priestess' side,   90
 And much transported with his little pride,
 Forgets his dear Companions of the plain,
 Till by Her, bound, Hee's on the Altar layn;
 Yet then too hardly bleats, such pleasure's in the pain.
    [*Enter* Officer *and* 6 Guards.
 Offic. Stand: who goes there?   95
 Belv. Friends.
 Jaff. Friends, *Belvidera!* hide me from my Friends,
By Heaven I'd rather see the face of Hell,
Than meet the man I love.
 Offic.   But what friends are you?
 Belv. Friends to the Senate and the State of *Venice.*   100
 Offic. My orders are to seize on all I find
At this late hour, and bring 'em to the Council,
Who now are sitting.
 Jaff.   Sir, you shall be obey'd.
Hold, Brutes, stand off, none of your paws upon me.
Now the Lot's cast, and Fate do what thou wilt.   105
       [*Exeunt guarded.*

SCENE, *The Senate-house, Where appear sitting, the Duke of* Venice,
  Priuli, Antonio, *And Eight other Senators.*

 Duke. Antony, Priuli, Senators of *Venice,*
Speak; why are we assembled here this night?
What have you to inform us of, concerns
The State of *Venice,* honour, or its safety?
 Priu. Could words express the story I have to tell you, 110
Fathers, these tears were useless, these sad tears
That fall from my old eyes; but there is cause
We all should weep; tear off these purple Robes,
And wrap our selves in Sack-cloth, sitting down
On the sad Earth, and cry aloud to Heaven.   115
Heaven knows if yet there be an hour to come
E'er *Venice* be no more!
 All Senators.   How!

Priu.   Nay we stand
Upon the Very brink of gaping ruine,
Within this City's form'd a dark Conspiracy,
To massacre us all, our Wives and Children,   120
Kindred and Friends, our Palaces and Temples
To lay in Ashes: nay the hour too, fixt;
The Swords, for ought I know, drawn even this moment,
And the wild Waste begun: from unknown hands
I had this warning: but if we are men   125
Let's not be tamely butcher'd, but do something
That may inform the world in after Ages,
Our Virtue was not ruin'd though we were.
    [*A noise without*]. Room, room, make room for some
        Prisoners——
    2 Senat. Let's raise the City.
                    [*Enter* Officer *and* Guard.
    Priu.   Speak there, what disturbance?   130
    Offic. Two Prisoners have the Guard seiz'd in the Streets,
Who say they come to inform [t]his Reverend Senate
About the present danger.
                    [*Enter* Jaffeir *and* Belvidera *guarded.*
    All.   Give 'em entrance——
Well, who are you?
    Jaff.   A Villain.
    Anto.   Short and pithy.
The man speaks well.
    Jaff.   Would every man that hears me   135
Would deal so honestly, and own his title.
    Duke. 'Tis rumour'd that a Plot has been contriv'd
Against this State; that you have a share in't too.
If you are a Villain, to redeem your honour,
Unfold the truth and be restor'd with Mercy.   140
    Jaff. Think not that I to save my life come hither,
I know its value better; but in pity
To all those wretches whose unhappy dooms
Are fix'd and seal'd. You see me here before you,
The sworn and Covenanted foe of *Venice*.   145
But use me as my dealings may deserve
And I may prove a friend.
    Duke.   The Slave Capitulates,
Give him the Tortures.
    Jaff.   That you dare not do,
Your fears won't let you, nor the longing Itch
To hear a story which you dread the truth of: 150
Truth which the fear of smart shall ne'er get from me.
Cowards are scar'd with threatnings. Boys are whipt
Into confessions: but a Steady mind

Acts of its self, ne'er asks the body Counsell.
Give him the Tortures! Name but such a thing   155
Again; by Heaven I'll shut these lips for ever,
Not all your Racks, your Engines or your Wheels
Shall force a groan away——that you may guess at.
    Anto. A bloudy minded fellow I'll warrant;
A damn'd bloudy minded fellow.   160
    Duke. Name your Conditions.
    Jaff.   For my self full pardon,
Besides the lives of two and twenty friends
                [*Delivers a list.*
Whose names are here inroll'd: Nay, let their Crimes
Be ne'er so monstrous, I must have the Oaths
And sacred promise of this Reverend Council,   165
That in a full Assembly of the Senate
The thing I ask be ratifi'd. Swear this,
And I'll unfold the secrets of your danger.
    All. We'll swear.
    Duke.   Propose the Oath.
    Jaff.   By all the hopes
Ye have of Peace and Happiness hereafter,   170
Swear.
    All. We all swear.
    Jaff.   To grant me what I've ask'd,
Ye swear.
    All.   We swear.
    Jaff.   And as ye keep the Oath,
May you and your posterity be blest
Or curst for ever.
    All.   Else be curst for ever.
    Jaff. Then here's the list, and with't the full disclose   175
Of all that threatens you.   [*Delivers another paper.*
Now Fate thou hast caught me.
    Anto. Why what a dreadfull Catalogue of Cut-throats is
here! I'll warrant you not one of these fellows but has a
face like a Lion. I dare not so much as read their names   180
over.
    Duke. Give orders that all diligent search be made
To seize these men, their characters are publick,
The paper intimates their Rendevouz
To be at the house of a fam'd Grecian Curtezan   185
Call'd *Aquilina;* see that place secur'd.
    Anto. What my Nicky Nacky, Hurry Durry, Nicky
Nacky in the Plot!——I'll make a Speech. Most noble
Senators,
What headlong apprehension drives you on,   190
Right noble, wise and truly solid Senators,

To violate the Laws and right of Nations?
The Lady is a Lady of renown.
'Tis true, she holds a house of fair Reception,
And though I say't my self, as many more   195
Can say as well as I——
    2 Senat.   My Lord, long Speeches
Are frivolous here, when dangers are so near us;
Well all well know your Interest in that Lady,
The world talks loud on't.
    Anto.   Verily I have done,
I say no more.
    Duke.   But since he has declar'd   200
Himself concern'd, Pray, Captain, take great caution
To treat the fair one as becomes her Character,
And let her Bed-chamber be search'd with decency.
You, *Jaffeir*, must with patience bear till morning,
To be our Prisoner.
    Jaff.   Would the Chains of death   205
Had bound me fast e'er I had known this minute!
I've done a deed will make my Story hereafter
Quoted in competition with all ill ones:
The History of my wickedness shall run
Down through the low traditions of the vulgar,   210
And Boys be taught to tell the tale of *Jaffeir*.
    Duke. Captain, withdraw your Prisoner.
    Jaff.   Sir, if possible,
Lead me where my own thoughts themselves may lose me,
Where I may doze out what I've left of life,
Forget my self and this day's guilt and falshood.   215
Cruel remembrance how shall I appease thee!   [*Ex. guarded.*
    [*Noise without*]. More Traitors; room, room, make room
        there.
    Duke. How's this, Guards?
Where are our Guards? shut up the Gates, the Treason's
Already at our Doors.
                [*Enter* Officer.
    Offic.   My Lords, more Traitors: 220
Seiz'd in the very act of Consultation;
Furnish'd with Arms and Instruments of mischief.
Bring in the prisoners.
        [*Enter* Pierre, Renault, Theodore, Elliot, Revillido *and*
        other Conspirators, *in fetters, guarded.*
    Pierr.   You, my Lords and Fathers
(As you are pleas'd to call your selves) of *Venice*;
If you sit here to guide the course of Justice,   225
Why these disgracefull chains upon the limbs
That have so often labour'd in your service?

Are these the wreaths of triumphs ye bestow
On those that bring you Conquests home and Honours?
    Duke. Go on, you shall be heard, Sir.   230
    Anto. And be hang'd too, I hope.
    Pierr. Are these the Trophies I've deserv'd for fighting
Your Battels with confederated Powers,
When winds and Seas conspir'd to overthrow you,
And brought the Fleets of *Spain* to your own Harbours?   235
When you, great Duke, shrunk trembling in your Palace,
And saw your Wife, th'Adriatick, plough'd
Like a lew'd Whore by bolder Prows than yours,
Stept not I forth, and taught your loose Venetians
The task of honour and the way to greatness,   240
Rais'd you from your capitulating fears
To stipulate the terms of su'd for peace,
And this my recompence? If I am a Traitor,
Produce my charge; or shew the wretch that's base enough
And brave enough to tell me I am a Traitor.   245
    Duke. Know you one *Jaffeir*?   [*All the conspirators murmur.*
    Pierr.   Yes, and know his Vertue.
His Justice, Truth, his general Worth, and Sufferings
From a hard father taught me first to love him.
    Duke. See him brought forth.   [*Enter* Jaffeir *guarded.*
    Pierr.   My friend too bound? nay then
Our Fate has conquer'd us, and we must fall.   250
Why droops the man whose welfare's so much mine
They're but one thing? these Reverend Tyrants, *Jaffeir*,
Call us all Traitors, art thou one, my Brother?
    Jaff. To thee I am the falsest, veryest slave
That e'er betray'd a generous trusting friend,   255
And gave up honour to be sure of ruine.
All our fair hopes which morning was to have crown'd
Has this curst tongue o'erthrown.
    Pierr.   So, then all's over:
Venice has lost her freedom; I my life;
No more, farewell.
    Duke.   Say; will you make confession   260
Of your vile deeds and trust the Senate's mercy?
    Pierr. Curst be your Senate: Curst your Constitution:
The Curse of growing factions and division
Still vex your Councils, shake your publick safety,
And make the Robes of Government, you wear,   265
Hatefull to you, as these base Chains to me.
    Duke. Pardon or death?
    Pierr.   Death, honourable death.
    Renault. Death's the best thing we ask or you can give.
    All Conspir. No shamefull bonds, but honourable death.

Duke. Break up the Council: Captain, guard your
    prisoners.   270
Jaffeir, y'are free, but these must wait for judgment.
               [*Ex. all the Senators* 〈 *and* Belv. 〉
    Pierr. Come, where's my Dungeon? lead me to my straw:
It will not be the first time I've lodg'd hard
To do your Senate service.
    Jaff.   Hold one moment.
    Pierr. Who's he disputes the Judgment of the Senate?   275
Presumptuous Rebel——on——   [*Strikes* Jaff.
    Jaff.   By Heaven you stir not.
I must be heard, I must have leave to speak:
Thou hast disgrac'd me, *Peirre,* by a vile blow:
Had not a dagger done thee nobler justice?
But use me as thou wilt, thou canst not wrong me,   280
For I am fallen beneath the basest injuries;
Yet look upon me with an eye of mercy,
With pity and with charity behold me;
Shut not thy heart against a friend's repentance,
But as there dwells a God-like nature in thee,   285
Listen with mildness to my supplications.
    Pierr. What whining Monk art thou? what holy cheat
That wou'dst encroach upon my credulous ears
And cant'st thus vilely? hence. I know thee not.
Dissemble and be nasty: leave me, Hippocrite.   290
    Jaff. Not know me, *Peirre?*
    Pierr.   No, know thee not: what art thou?
    Jaff. Jaffeir, thy friend, thy once lov'd, valu'd friend,
Though now deservedly scorn'd, and us'd most hardly.
    Pierr. Thou *Jaffeir!* Thou my once lov'd, valu'd friend!
By Heavens thou ly'st; the man so call'd, my friend,   295
Was generous, honest, faithfull, just and valiant,
Noble in mind, and in his person lovely,
Dear to my eyes and tender to my heart:
But thou a wretched, base, false, worthless Coward,
Poor even in Soul, and loathsome in thy aspect,   300
All eyes must shun thee, and all hearts detest thee.
Prithee avoid, nor longer cling thus round me,
Like something banefull, that my nature's chill'd at.
    Jaff. I have not wrong'd thee, by these tears I have not.
But still am honest, true, and hope too, valiant;   305
My mind still full of thee: therefore still noble.
Let not thy eyes then shun me, nor thy heart
Detest me utterly: Oh look upon me,
Look back and see my sad sincere submission!
How my heart swells, as even 'twould burst my bosom;   310
Fond of its Gaol, and labouring to be at thee!

What shall I do? what say to make thee hear me?

   Pierr. Hast thou not wrong'd me? dar'st thou call thy self
Jaffeir, that once lov'd, valued friend of mine,
And swear thou hast not wrong'd me? whence these chains?   315
Whence the vile death, which I may meet this moment?
Whence this dishonour, but from thee, thou false one?

   Jaff. All's true, yet grant one thing, and I've done asking.

   Pierr. What's that?

   Jaff.   To take thy life on such conditions
The Council have propos'd: Thou and thy friends   320
May yet live long, and to be better treated.

   Pierr. Life! ask my life! confess! record my self
A villain for the privilege to breath,
And carry up and down this cursed City
A discontented and repining spirit,   325
Burthensome to it self, a few years longer,
To lose, it may be, at last in a lewd quarrel
For some new friend, treacherous and false as thou art!
No, this vile world and I have long been jangling,
And cannot part on better terms than now,   330
When onely men like thee are fit to live in't.

   Jaff. By all that's just——

   Pierr.   Swear by some other powers,
For thou hast broke that sacred Oath too lately.

   Jaff. Then by that hell I merit, I'll not leave thee,
Till to thy self at least, thou'rt reconcil'd,   335
However thy resentments deal with me.

   Pierr. Not leave me!

   Jaff.   No, thou shalt not force me from thee.
Use me reproachfully, and like a slave,
Tread on me, buffet me, heap wrongs on wrongs
On my poor head; I'll bear it all with patience,   340
Shall weary out thy most unfriendly cruelty,
Lie at thy feet and kiss 'em though they spurn me,
Till, wounded by my sufferings, thou relent,
And raise me to thy arms with dear forgiveness.

   Pierr. Art thou not——

   Jaff.   What?

   Pierr.   A Traitor?

   Jaff.   Yes.

   Pierr.   A Villain?   345

   Jaff. Granted.

   Pierr.   A Coward, a most scandalous Coward,
Spiritless, void of honour, one who has sold
Thy everlasting Fame, for shameless life?

   Jaff. All, all, and more, much more: my faults are
     Numberless.

Pierr. And wouldst thou have me live on terms like thine?   350
Base as thou art false?
  Jaff.   No, 'tis to me that's granted.
The safety of thy life was all I aim'd at,
In recompence for faith, and trust so broken.
  Pierr. I scorn it more because preserv'd by thee.
And as when first my foolish heart took pity   355
On thy misfortunes, sought thee in thy miseries,
Reliev'd thy wants, and rais'd thee from thy State
Of wretchedness in which thy fate had plung'd thee,
To rank thee in my list of noble friends;
All I receiv'd in surety for thy truth,   360
Were unregarded oaths; and this, this dagger,
Given with a worthless pledge, thou since hast stoln:
So I restore it back to thee again,
Swearing by all those powers which thou hast violated,
Never from this curs'd hour to hold communion,   365
Friendship or interst with thee, though our years
Were to exceed those limited the world.
Take it—farewell—for now I owe thee nothing.
  Jaff. Say thou wilt live then.
  Pierr.   For my life, dispose it
Just as thou wilt, because tis what I'em tir'd with.   370
  Jaff. Oh, *Pierre!*
  Pierr.   No more.
  Jaff.·   My eyes won't lose the sight of thee,
But languish after thine, and ake with gazing.
  Pierr. Leave me——Nay, then thus, thus, I throw thee
    from me.
And curses, great as is thy falsehood, catch thee.   ⟨ *Ex.* ⟩
  Jaff. Amen.   375
He's gone, my father, friend, preserver,
And here's the portion he has left me.   [*Holds the dagger up.*
This dagger, well remembred, with this dagger
I gave a solemn vow of dire importance,
Parted with this and *Belvidera* together;   380
Have a care, Mem'ry, drive that thought no farther;
No, I'll esteem it as a friend's last legacy,
Treasure it up in this wretched bosom,
Where it may grow acquainted with my heart,
That when they meet, they start not from each other;   385
So; now for thinking: A blow, call'd Traitor, Villain,
Coward, dishonourable coward, fogh!
Oh for a long sound sleep, and so forget it!
Down, busie Devil.——
      [*Enter* Belvidera.
 Belv.   Whither shall I fly?

Where hide me and my miseries together? 390
Where's now the Roman Constancy I boasted?
Sunk into trembling fears and desperation!
Not daring now to look up to that dear face
Which us'd to smile even on my faults, but down
Bending these miserable eyes to earth, 395
Must move in penance, and implore much Mercy.
    Jaff. Mercy! kind Heaven has surely endless stores
Hoarded for thee of blessings yet untasted;
Let wretches loaded hard with guilt as I am,
Bow [with] the weight and groan beneath the burthen, 400
Creep with a remnant of that strength th' have left,
Before the footstool of that Heaven th' have injur'd.
Oh *Belvidera!* I'm the wretchedst creature
E'er crawl'd on earth; now if thou hast Vertue, help me,
Take me into thy Arms, and speak the words of peace 405
To my divided Soul, that wars within me,
And raises every Sense to my confusion;
By Heav'n I am tottering on the very brink
Of Peace; and thou art all the hold I've left.
    Belv. Alas! I know thy sorrows are most mighty; 410
I know th' hast cause to mourn; to mourn, my *Jaffeir,*
With endless cries, and never ceasing wailings;
Th' hast lost——
    Jaff.   Oh I have lost what can't be counted;
My friend too, *Belvidera,* that dear friend,
Who, next to thee, was all my health rejoyc'd in, 415
Has us'd me like a slave; shamefully us'd me;
'Twould break thy pitying heart to hear the story.
What shall I do? resentment, indignation,
Love, pity, fear, and mem'ry how I've wrong'd him,
Distract my quiet with the very thought on't, 420
And tear my heart to pieces in my bosome.
    Belv. What has he done?
    Jaff.   Thou'dst hate me, should I tell thee.
    Belv. Why?
    Jaff.   Oh he has us'd me—yet by Heaven I bear it——
He has us'd me, *Belvidera,*—but first swear
That when I've told thee, thou'lt not loath me utterly, 425
Though vilest blots and stains appear upon me;
But still at least with charitable goodness,
Be near me in the pangs of my affliction,
Not scorn me, *Belvidera,* as he has done.
    Belv. Have I then e'er been false that now I am doubted? 430
Speak, what's the cause I am grown into distrust,
Why thought unfit to hear my Love's complaining?
    Jaff. Oh!

Belv.   Tell me.

Jaff.   Bear my failings, for they are many,
Oh my dear Angel! in that friend I've lost
All my Soul's peace; for every thought of him   435
Strikes my Sense hard, and deads it in my brains;
Wouldst thou believe it——
    Belv.   Speak.
    Jaff.   Before we parted,
E'er yet his Guards had led him to his prison,
Full of severest sorrows for his suff'rings,
With eyes o'rflowing and a bleeding heart,   440
Humbling my self almost beneath my nature,
As at his feet I kneel'd, and su'd for mercy,
Forgetting all our friendship, all the dearness,
In which w' have liv'd so many years together,
With a reproachful hand, he dash'd a blow,   445
He struck me, *Belvidera*, by Heaven, he struck me,
Buffeted, call'd me Traitor, Villain, Coward;
Am I a Coward? am I a Villain? tell me:
Th'art the best Judge, and mad'st me, if I am so.
Damnation; Coward!
    Belv.   Oh! forgive him, *Jaffeir.*   450
And if his sufferings wound thy heart already,
What will they do to morrow?
    Jaff.   Hah!
    Belv.   To morrow,
When thou shalt see him stretch'd in all the Agonies
Of a tormenting and a shameful death,
His bleeding bowels, and his broken limbs,   455
Insulted o'er by a vile butchering villain;
What will thy heart do then? Oh sure 'twill stream
Like my eyes now.
    Jaff.   What means thy dreadfull story?
Death, and to morrow? broken limbs and bowels?
Insulted o'er by a vile butchering Villain?   460
By all my fears I shall start out to madness,
Whith barely guessing, if the truth's hid longer.
    Belv. The faithless Senators, 'tis they've decre'd it:
They say according to our friend's request,
They shall have death, and not ignoble bondage: 465
Declare their promis'd mercy all as forfeited;
False to their oaths, and deaf to intercession;
Warrants are pass'd for publick death to morrow.
    Jaff. Death! doom'd to die! condemn'd unheard! un-
        pleaded!
    Belv. Nay, cruell'st racks and torments are preparing,   470
To force confessions from their dying pangs;

Oh do not look so terribly upon me,
How your lips shake, and all your face disorder'd!
What means my Love?

Jaff. Leave me, I charge thee leave me—strong temptations   475
Wake in my heart.

Belv.   For what?

Jaff.   No more, but leave me.

Belv. Why?

Jaff.   Oh! by Heaven I love thee with that fondness
I would not have thee stay a moment longer,
Near these curst hands: are they not cold upon thee?
        [*Pulls the dagger half out of his bosom and puts it back
        agen.*

Belv. No, everlasting comfort's in thy arms.   480
To lean thus on thy breast is softer ease
Than downy pillows deck'd with leaves of roses.

Jaff. Alas thou thinkest not of the thorns 'tis fill'd with,
Fly e'er they gall thee: there's a lurking serpent
Ready to leap and sting thee to thy heart: 485
Art thou not terrifi'd?

Belv.   No.

Jaff.   Call to mind
What thou hast done, and whither thou hast brought me.

Belv. Hah!

Jaff.   Where's my friend? my friend, thou smiling
        mischief?
Nay, shrink not, now 'tis too late, thou shouldst have fled
When thy Guilt first had cause, for dire revenge   490
Is up and raging for my friend. He groans,
Hark how he groans, his screams are in my ears
Already; see, th' have fixt him on the wheel,
And now they tear him——Murther! perjur'd Senate!
Murther—Oh!—hark thee, Traitress, thou hast done this;   495
Thanks to thy tears and false perswading love.
        [*Fumbling for his Dagger.*
How her eyes speak! Oh thou bewitching creature!
Madness cannot hurt thee: Come, thou little trembler,
Creep, even into my heart, and there lie safe;
'Tis thy own Cittadel——hah——yet stand off,   500
Heaven must have Justice, and my broken vows
Will sink me else beneath its reaching mercy;
I'll wink and then 'tis done——
        [*Draws the dagger, offers to stab her.*

Belv. What means the Lord
Of me, my life and love, what's in thy bosom,

---

484. *Gall:* The copy text gives call;
other editions give gall.

Thou graspst at so? nay, why am I thus treated?   505
What wilt thou doe? Ah, do not kill me, *Jaffeir*,
Pity these panting breasts, and trembling limbs,
That us'd to clasp thee when thy looks were milder,
That yet hang heavy on my unpurg'd Soul,
And plunge it not into eternal darkness.   510
   Jaff. No, *Belvidera*, when we parted last
I gave this dagger with thee as in trust
To be thy portion, If I e'er prov'd false.
On such condition was my truth believ'd:
But now 'tis forfeited and must be paid for.   515
           [*Offers to stab her again.*
  Belv. Oh, mercy!   [*Kneeling.*
  Jaff.   Nay, no strugling.
  Belv.   Now then kill me
     [*Leaps upon his neck and kisses him.*
While thus I cling about thy cruel neck,
Kiss thy revengefull lips and die in joys
Greater than any I can guess hereafter.
  Jaff. I am, I am a Coward; witness't, Heaven,   520
Witness it, Earth, and every being Witness;
'Tis but one blow yet: by immortal Love,
I cannot longer bear a thought to harm thee,
    [*He throws away the dagger and embraces her.*
The Seal of providence is sure upon thee.
And thou wert born for yet unheard of wonders: 525
Oh thou wert either born to save or damn me!
By all the power that's given thee o'er my soul,
By thy resistless tears and conquering smiles,
By the victorious love that still waits on thee;
Fly to thy cruel Father: save my friend,   530
Or all our future Quiet's lost for ever:
Fall at his feet, cling round his reverend knees;
Speak to him with thy Eyes, and with thy tears
Melt the hard heart, and wake dead nature in him;
Crush him in th'Arms, and torture him with thy softness: 535
   Nor, till thy Prayers are granted, set him free,
   But conquer him, as thou hast vanquish'd me.   [*Ex. ambo.*

Act V

[*Enter Priuli solus.*

  Priu. Why, cruel Heaven, have my unhappy days
Been lengthen'd to this sad one? Oh! dishonour
And deathless infamy is fallen upon me.
Was it my fault? Am I a traitor? No.
But then, my only child, my daughter, wedded;   5

There my best bloud runs foul, and a disease
Incurable has seiz'd upon my memory,
To make it rot and stink to after ages.
Curst be the fatal minute when I got her;
Or wou'd that I'd been any thing but man,   10
And rais'd an issue which wou'd ne'r have wrong'd me.
The miserablest Creatures (man excepted)
Are not the less esteem'd, though their posterity
Degenerate from the vertues of their fathers;
The vilest Beasts are happy in their offsprings,   15
While only man gets Traitours, Whores and Villains,
Curst be the names, and some swift blow from Fate
Lay his head deep, where mine may be forgotten.
          [*Enter* Belvidera *in a long mourning Veil.*
    Belv. He's there, my father, my inhumane father,
That, for three years, has left an only child   20
Expos'd to all the outrages of Fate.
And cruel ruin——oh !——
    Priu.   What child of sorrow
Art thou that com'st thus wrapt in weeds of sadness,
And mov'st as if thy steps were towards a grave?
    Belv. A wretch, who from the very top of happiness   25
Am fallen into the lowest depths of misery,
And want your pitying hand to raise me up again.
    Priu. Indeed thou talk'st as thou hadst tasted sorrows;
Would I could help thee.
    Belv.   'Tis greatly in your power,
The world too, speaks you charitable, and I,   30
Who ne'er ask'd alms before, in that dear hope
Am come a begging to you, Sir.
    Priu.   For what?
    Belv. Oh, well regard me, is this voice a strange one?
Consider too, when beggars once pretend
A case like mine, no little will content 'em.   35
    Priu. What wouldst thou beg for?
    Belv.   Pity and forgiveness;
          [*Throws up her Veil.*
By the kind tender names of child and father,
Hear my complaints and take me to your love.
    Priu. My daughter?
    Belv.   Yes, your daughter, by a mother
Vertuous and noble, faithfull to your honour,   40
Obedient to your will, kind to your wishes,
Dear to your arms; by all the joys she gave you,
When in her blooming years she was your treasure,
Look kindly on me; in my face behold
The lineaments of hers y'have kiss'd so often,   45

Pleading the cause of your poor cast-off Child.
    Priu. Thou art my daughter.
    Belv.   Yes——And y'have oft told me
With smiles of love and chaste paternal kisses,
I'd much resemblance of my mother.
    Priu.   Oh!
Hadst thou inherited her matchless vertues   50
I'd been too bless'd.
    Belv.   Nay, do not call to memory
My disobedience, but let pity enter
Into your heart, and quite deface the impression;
For could you think how mine's perplext, what sadness,
Fears and despairs distract the peace within me,   55
Oh, you wou'd take me in your dear, dear Arms,
Hover with strong compassion o'er your young one,
To shelter me with a protecting wing,
From the black gather'd storm, that's just, just breaking.
    Priu. Don't talk thus.
    Belv.   Yes, I must, and you must hear too.   60
I have a husband.
    Priu.   Damn him.
    Belv.   Oh, do not curse him!
He would not speak so hard a word towards you
On any terms, how e'er he deal with me.
    Priu. Hah! what means my child?
    Belv.   Oh there's but this short moment
'Twixt me and Fate, yet send me not with curses   65
Down to my grave, afford me one kind blessing
Before we part: just take me in your arms
And recommend me with a prayer to Heaven,
That I may dye in peace; and when I'm dead——
    Priu. How my Soul's catcht?
    Belv.   Lay me, I beg you, lay me   70
By the dear ashes of my tender mother.
She would have pitied me, had fate yet spared her.
    Priu. By Heaven, my aking heart forebodes much mischief.
Tell me thy story, for I'm still thy father.
    Belv. No, I'm contented.
    Priu.   Speak.
    Belv.   No matter.
    Priu.   Tell me.   75
By yon blest Heaven, my heart runs o'r with fondness.
    Belv. Oh!
    Priu.   Utter't.
    Belv.   Oh my husband, my dear husband
Carries a dagger in his once kind bosome
To pierce the heart of your poor *Belvidera.*

Priu. Kill thee?

Belv.   Yes, kill me; when he pass'd his faith   80
And covenant against your State and Senate,
He gave me up as hostage for his truth,
With me a dagger and a dire commission,
When e'er he fail'd, to plunge it through this bosome;
I learnt the danger, chose the hour of love   85
T'attempt his heart, and bring it back to honour;
Great love prevail'd and bless'd me with success,
He came, confest, betray'd his dearest friends
For promis'd mercy; now they're doom'd to suffer,
Gall'd with remembrance of what then was sworn,   90
If they are lost, he vows t'appease the Gods
With this poor life, and make my blood th' attonement.

Priu. Heavens!

Belv. Think you saw what pass'd at our last parting;
Think you beheld him like a raging lion,   95
Pacing the earth and tearing up his steps,
Fate in his eyes, and roaring with the pain
Of burning fury; think you saw his one hand
Fix't on my throat, while the extended other
Grasp'd a keen threatning dagger; oh 'twas thus   100
We last embrac'd, when, trembling with revenge,
He dragg'd me to the ground, and at my bosome
Presented horrid death, cried out, my friends,
Where are my friends? swore, wept, rag'd, threaten'd, lov'd,
For he yet lov'd, and that dear love preserv'd me,   105
To this last tryal of a father's pity.
I fear not death, but cannot bear a thought
That that dear hand should do th' unfriendly office;
If I was ever then your care, now hear me;
Fly to the Senate, save the promis'd lives   110
Of his dear friends, e'er mine be made the sacrifice.

Priu. Oh, my heart's comfort!

Belv.   Will you not, my father?
Weep not but answer me.

Priu.   By Heaven, I will.
Not one of 'em but what shall be immortal.
Canst thou forgive me all my follies past?   115
I'll henceforth be indeed a father; never,
Never more thus expose, but cherish thee,
Dear as the vital warmth that feeds my life,
Dear as these eyes that weep in fondness o'er thee.
Peace to thy heart. Farewel.

Belv.   Go, and remember,   120
'Tis *Belvidera's* life her father pleads for.   [*Ex. severally.*
                    [*Enter* Antonio.

[*Anto.*] Hum, hum, hah, Seignior *Priuli*, my Lord *Priuli*,
my Lord, my Lord, my Lord: Now, we Lords love to call
one another by our Titles. My Lord, my Lord, my Lord
——Pox on him, I am a Lord as well as he, And so let him   125
fiddle—I'll warrant him he's gone to the Senate-house, and
I'll be there too, soon enough for somebody. Odd—here's
a tickling speech about the Plot, I'll prove there's a Plot
with a Vengeance—would I had it without book; let me
see—   130
    Most Reverend Senatours,
That there is a Plot, surely by this time, no man that hath
eyes or understanding in his head will presume to doubt,
'tis as plain as the light in the Cowcumber—no—hold there
—Cowcumber does not come in yet—'tis as plain as the   135
light in the Sun, or as the man in the Moon, even at noon
day; It is indeed a Pumpkin-Plot, which, just as it was
mellow, we have gathered, and now we have gathered it,
prepar'd and dress'd it, shall we throw it like a pickled
Cowcumber out at the window? no: that it is not onely a   140
bloody, horrid, execrable, damnable and audacious Plot,
but it is, as I may so say, a sawcy Plot: and we all know,
most Reverend Fathers, that what is sawce for a Goose is
sawce for a Gander: Therefore, I say, as those blood-
thirsty Ganders of the conspiracy would have destroyed   145
us Geese of the Senate, let us make haste to destroy them;
so I humbly move for hanging—hah, hurry durry—I think
this will do, tho' I was something out, at first, about the
Sun and the Cowcumber.
                [*Enter* Aquilina.
    Aquil. Good morrow, Senatour.   150
    Anto. Nacky, my dear Nacky, morrow, Nacky, odd I am
very brisk, very merry, very pert, very jovial—haaaaa—
kiss me, Nacky; how dost thou do, my little Tory rory
Strumpet, kiss me, I say, hussy, kiss me.
    Aquil. Kiss me, Nacky! hang you, Sir Coxcomb, hang   155
you, Sir.
    Anto. Hayty tayty, is it so indeed, with all my heart,
faith—*Hey then up go we*, faith—*hey then up go we*, dum
dum derum dump.   [*Sings.*
    Aquil. Seignior.   160
    Anto. Madona.
    Aquil. Do you intend to die in your bed?——
    Anto. About threescore years hence; much may be done,
my dear.
    Aquil. You'll be hang'd, Seignior.   165
    Anto. Hang'd, sweet heart! prithee be quiet, hang'd
quoth-a, that's a merry conceit, with all my heart; why

thou jok'st, Nacky, thou art given to joking, I'll swear;
well, I protest, Nacky, nay, 1 must protest, and will protest
that I love joking dearly, man. And I love thee for joking,   170
and I'll kiss thee for joking, and towse thee for joking, and
odd, I have a devilish mind to take thee aside about that
business for joking too, odd I have, and *Hey then up go we,*
dum dum derum dump.   [*Sings.*
Aquil. See you this, Sir?   [*Draws a dagger.*   175
Anto. O Laud, a dagger! Oh Laud! it is naturally my
aversion, I cannot endure the sight on't, hide it, for
Heaven's sake, I cannot look that way till it be gone—hide
it, hide it, oh, oh, hide it!
Auil. Yes, in your heart, I'll hide it.   180
Anto. My heart! what, hide a dagger in my heart's
blood!
Aquil. Yes, in thy heart, thy throat, thou pamper'd
     Devil;
Thou hast help'd to spoil my peace, and I'll have vengeance
On thy curst life, for all the bloody Senate,   185
The perjur'd faithless Senate: Where's my Lord,
My happiness, my love, my God, my Hero,
Doom'd by thy accursed tongue, amongst the rest,
T' a shamefull wrack? By all the rage that's in me
I'll be whole years in murthering thee.   190
Anto. Why, Nacky, Wherefore so passionate? what have
I done? what's the matter, my dear Nacky? am not I thy
Love, thy Happiness, thy Lord, thy Hero, thy Senator, and
every thing in the World, Nacky?
Aquil. Thou! thinkst thou, thou art fit to meet my joys;   195
To bear the eager clasps of my embraces?
Give me my *Pierre,* or——
Anto. Why, he's to be hang'd, little Nacky, Trust up for
Treason, and so forth, Child.
Aquil. Thou ly'st, stop down thy throat that hellish
     sentence,   200
Or 'tis thy last: swear that my Love shall live,
Or thou art dead.
Anto.   Ah h h h.
Aquil.   Swear to recal his doom,
Swear at my feet, and tremble at my fury.
Anto. I do; now if she would but kick a little bit, one
kick now Ah h h h.   205
Aquil. Swear, or——
Anto. I do, by these dear fragrant foots and little toes,
sweet as, e e e e my Nacky Nacky Nacky.
Aquil. How!
Anto. Nothing but untie thy shoe-string a little faith   210

and troth, that's all, that's all, as I hope to live, Nacky,
that's all.

Aquil. Nay, then——

Anto.　　Hold, hold, thy Love, thy Lord, thy Hero
Shall be preserv'd and safe.

Aquil.　　　　　　　Or may this Poniard
Rust in thy heart.

Anto.　　With all my soul.

Aquil.　　　　　　　Farewell——[*Ex.* Aquil.　215

Anto. Adieu. Why what a bloody-minded, inveterate,
termagant Strumpet have I been plagu'd with! oh h h yet
more! nay then I die, I die—I am dead already.

　　　　　　[*Stretches himself out.*
　　　　　　[*Enter* Jaffeir.

Jaff. Final destruction seize on all the world:
Bend down, ye Heavens, and shutting round this earth,　220
Crush the Vile Globe into its first confusion;
Scorch it, with Elemental flames, to one curst Cindar,
And all us little creepers in't, call'd men,
Burn, burn to nothing: but let *Venice* burn
Hotter than all the rest: Here kindle Hell　　225
Ne'er to extinguish, and let souls hereafter
Groan here, in all those pains which mine feels now.

　　　　　　[*Enter* Belvidera.

Belv. My Life——　　　　　[*Meeting him.*
Jaff.　　　My Plague——　　[*Turning from her.*
Belv.　　　　　　Nay then I see my ruine,
If I must die!

Jaff.　　No, Death's this day too busie,
Thy Father's ill timed Mercy came too late,　　230
I thank thee for thy labours tho' and him too,
But all my poor betray'd unhappy friends
Have Summons to prepare for Fate's black hour;
And yet I live.

Belv.　　Then be the next my doom.
I see thou hast pass'd my sentence in thy heart,　235
And I'll no longer weep or plead against it,
But with the humblest, most obedient patience
Meet thy dear hands, and kiss 'em when they wound me;
Indeed I am willing, but I beg thee do it
With some remorse, and where thou giv'st the blow,　240
View me with eyes of a relenting love,
And shew me pity, for 'twill sweeten Justice.

Jaff. Shew pity to thee?

Belv.　　　　　Yes, and when thy hands,
Charg'd with my fate, come trembling to the deed,
As thou hast done a thousand thousand dear times,　245

To this poor breast, when kinder rage has brought thee,
When out sting'd hearts have leap'd to meet each other,
And melting kisses seal'd our lips together,
When joys have left me gasping in thy arms,
So let my death come now, and I'll not shrink from't.   250
    Jaff. Nay, *Belvidera*, do not fear my cruelty,
Nor let the thoughts of death perplex thy fancy,
But answer me to what I shall demand,
With a firm temper and unshaken spirit.
    Belv. I will when I've done weeping——
    Jaff.   Fie, no more on't——   255
How long is't since the miserable day
We wedded first——
    Belv.   Oh h h.
    Jaff.   Nay, keep in thy tears,
Lest they unman me too.
    Belv.   Heaven knows I cannot;
The words you utter sound so very sadly,
These streams will follow——
    Jaff.   Come, I'll kiss 'em dry then.   260
    Belv. But, was't a miserable day?
    Jaff.   A curs'd one.
    Belv. I thought it otherwise, and you've oft sworn,
In the transporting hours of warmest love
When sure you spoke the truth, you've sworn you bless'd it.
    Jaff. Twas a rash oath.
    Belv.   Then why am I not curs'd too?   265
    Jaff. No, *Belvidera*; by th' eternal truth,
I doat with too much fondness.
    Belv.   Still so kind?
Still then do you love me?
    Jaff.   Nature, in her workings,
Inclines not with more ardour to Creation,
Than I doe now towards thee; man ne'er was bless'd,   270
Since the first pair first met, as I have been.
    Belv. Then sure you will not curse me.
    Jaff.   No, I'll bless thee.
I came on purpose, *Belvidera*, to bless thee.
'Tis now, I think, three years w'have liv'd together.
    Belv. And may no fatal minute ever part us,   275
Till, reverend grown, for age and love, we go
Down to one Grave, as our last bed, together,
There sleep in peace till an eternal morning.
    Jaff. When will that be?   *[Sighing.*
    Belv.   I hope long Ages hence.
    Jaff. Have I not hitherto (I beg thee tell me   280
Thy very fear) us'd thee with tender'st love?

Did e'er my Soul rise up in wrath against thee?
Did [I] e'er frown when *Belvidera* smil'd,
Or, by the least unfriendly word, betray
A bating passion? have I ever wrong'd thee?   285
   Belv. No.
   Jaff.   Has my heart, or have my eyes e'er wandred
To any other woman?
   Belv.   Never, never——
I were the worst of false one[s] should I accuse thee.
I own I've been too happy, bless'd above
My Sex's Charter.
   Jaff.   Did I not say I came   290
To bless thee?
   Belv. Yes.
   Jaff.   Then hear me, bounteous Heaven,
Pour down your blessings on this beauteous head,
Where everlasting sweets are always springing.
With a continual giving hand, let peace,
Honour and safety always hover round her,   295
Feed her with plenty, let her eyes ne'er see
A sight of sorrow, nor her heart know mourning,
Crown all her days with joy, her nights with rest,
Harmless as her own thoughts, and prop her vertue,
To bear the loss of one that too much lov'd,   300
And comfort her with patience in our parting.
   Belv. How, parting, parting!
   Jaff.   Yes, for ever parting,
I have sworn, *Belvidera*; by yo[n] Heaven,
That best can tell how much I lose to leave thee,
We part this hour for ever.
   Belv.   Oh, call back   305
Your cruel blessings, stay with me and curse me!
   Jaff. No. 'Tis resolv'd.
   Belv.   Then hear me too, just Heaven,
Pour down your curses on this wretched head
With never-ceasing Vengeance, let despair,
Danger or infamy, nay all surround me;   310
Starve me with wantings, let my eyes ne'er see
A sight of comfort, nor my heart know peace,
But dash my days with sorrow, nights with horrours
Wild as my own thoughts now, and let loose fury
To make me mad enough for what I lose,   315
If I must lose him; If I must! I will not.
Oh turn and hear me!
   Jaff.   Now hold, heart, or never.
   Belv. By all the tender days we have liv'd together,
By all our charming nights, and joys that crown'd 'em,

Pity my sad condition, speak, but speak.   320
   Jaff. Oh h h.
   Belv. By these arms that now cling round thy neck,
By this dear kiss and by ten thousand more,
By these poor streaming eyes——
   Jaff.   Murther! unhold me:
By th'immortal destiny that doom'd me   [*Draws his Dagger.*
To this curs'd minute, I'll not live one longer.   325
Resolve to let me go or see me fall——
   Belv. Hold, Sir, be patient.   [*Passing-bell towles.*
   Jaff.   Hark, the dismal Bell
Towls out for death, I must attend its call too,
For my poor friend, my dying *Pierre* expects me,
He sent a message to require I'd see him   330
Before he dy'd, and take his last forgiveness.
Farewel for ever.
              [*Going out looks back at her.*
   Belv.   Leave thy dagger with me.
Bequeath me something—Not one kiss at parting?
Oh my poor heart, when wilt thou break?
   Jaff.   Yet stay,
We have a Child, as yet a tender Infant.   335
Be a kind mother to him when I am gone,
Breed him in vertue and the paths of Honour,
But let him never know his father's story;
I charge thee guard him from the wrongs my Fate
May do his future fortune or his name.   340
Now——nearer yet—   [*Approaching each other.*
Oh that my arms were rivetted
Thus round thee ever! But my friends, my oath!
This and no more.   [*Kisses her.*
   Belv.   Another, sure another,
For that poor little one you've ta'n care of,   345
I'll giv't him truly.
   Jaff.   So, now farewel.
   Belv.   For ever?
   Jaff. Heaven knows for ever; all good Angels guard thee.
                          ⟨ *Ex.* ⟩
   Belv. All ill ones sure had charge of me this moment.
Curst be my days, and doubly curst my nights,
Which I must now mourn out in widow'd tears;   350
Blasted be every herb and fruit and tree,
Curst be the rain that falls upon the earth,
And may the general Curse reach man and beast;
Oh give me daggers, fire or water,
How I could bleed, how burn, how drown the waves   355
Huzzing and booming round my sinking head,

Till I descended to the peacefull bottom!
Oh there's all quiet, here all rage and fury,
The Air's too thin, and pierces my weak brain,
I long for thick substantial sleep: Hell, Hell,   360
Burst from the Centre, rage and roar aloud,
If thou art half so hot, so mad as I am.
     [*Enter* Priuli *and* Servants.
Who's there?
  Priu. Run, seize and bring her safely home,
      [*They seize her.*
Guard her as you would life: Alas poor creature!
  Belv. What? to my husband then conduct me quickly,   365
Are all things ready? shall we dye most gloriously?
Say not a word of this to my old father,
Murmuring streams, soft shades, and springing flowers,
Lutes, Laurells, Seas of Milk, and ships of Amber. [*Ex.*
  [*Scene opening discovers a Scaffold and a Wheel prepar'd*
   for the executing of Pierre, *then enter Officers,* Pierre *and*
   Guards, a Friar, executioner and a great Rabble.
  Offic. Room room there——stand all by, make room for
  the prisoner.   370
  Pierr. My friend not come yet?
  Father.   Why are you so obstinate?
  Pierr. Why you so troublesome, that a poor wretch
Cannot dye in peace?
But you, like Ravens will be croaking round him——
  Fath. Yet, Heaven——
  Pierr.   I tell thee Heaven and I are friends,   375
I ne'er broke Peace with't yet, by cruel murthers,
Rapine, or perjury, or vile deceiving,
But liv'd in moral Justice towards all men,
Nor am a foe to the most strong believers:
How e'er my own short-sighted Faith confine me.   380
  Fath. But an all-seeing Judge——
  Pierr.   You say my conscience
Must be mine accuser: I have search'd that Conscience,
And find no records there of crimes that scare me.
  Fath. 'Tis strange you should want faith.
  Pierr.   You want to lead
My Reason blindfold, like a hamper'd Lion,   385
Check'd of its nobler vigour; then, when baited
Down to obedient tameness, make it couch,
And shew strange tricks which you call signs of Faith.
So silly Souls are gull'd and you get money.
Away, no more: Captain, I would hereafter   390
This fellow write no lyes of my conversion,
Because he has crept upon my troubled hours.

[*Enter* Jaffeir.

Jaff. Hold: Eyes, be dry;
Heart, strengthen me to bear
This hideous sight, and humble me to take   395
The last forgiveness of a dying friend,
Betray'd by my vile falshood, to his ruine.
Oh *Pierre!*
    Pierr. Yet nearer.
    Jaff.   Crawling on my knees,
And prostrate on the earth, let me approach thee:
How shall I look up to thy injur'd face,   400
That always us'd to smile, with friendship, on me?
It darts an air of so much manly virtue,
That I, methinks, look little in thy sight,
And stripes are fitter for me than embraces.
    Pierr. Dear to my Arms, though thou hast undone my
        fame,   405
I cannot forget to love thee: prithee *Jaffeir,*
Forgive that filthy blow my passion dealt thee;
I am now preparing for the land of peace,
And fain would have the charitable wishes
Of all good men, like thee, to bless my journy.   410
    Jaff. Good! I am the vilest creature, worse then e'er
Suffer'd the shamefull Fate thou art going to tast of.
Why was I sent for to be us'd thus kindly?
Call, call me villain, as I am, describe
The foul complexion of my hatefull deeds,   415
Lead me to the Rack, and stretch me in thy stead,
I've crimes enough to give it its full load,
And do it credit: Thou wilt but spoil the use on't,
And honest men hereafter bear its figure
About 'em, as a charm from treacherous friendship.   420
    Offic. The time grows short, your friends are dead already.
    Jaff. Dead!
    Pierr. Yes, dead, *Jaffeir,* they've all dy'd like men too,
Worthy their Character.
    Jaff.   And what must I do?
    Pierr. Oh, *Jaffeir!*
    Jaff.   Speak aloud thy burthen'd Soul,   425
And tell thy troubles to thy tortur'd friend.
    Pierr. Friend! Could'st thou yet be a Friend, a generous
        friend,
I might hope Comfort from thy noble sorrows.
Heav'n knows I want a Friend.
    Jaff.   And I a kind one,
That would not thus scorn my repenting Vertue,   430
Or think, when he is to dye, my thoughts are idle.

Pierr. No! live, I charge thee, *Jaffeir.*

Jaff.   Yes, I will live,
But it shall be to see thy fall reveng'd
At such a rate, as *Venice* long shall groan for.

    Pierr. Wilt thou?

Jaff.   I will, by Heav'n.

    Pierr.   Then still thou'rt noble,   435
And I forgive thee, oh—yet—shall I trust thee?

    Jaff. No: I've been false already.

    Pierr.   Dost thou love me?

    Jaff. Rip up my heart, and satisfie thy doubtings.

    Pierr. Curse on this weakness.   [*He weeps.*

    Jaff.   Tears! Amazement! Tears!
I never saw thee melted thus before;   440
And know there's something lab'ring in thy bosom
That must have vent: Though I'm a Villain, tell me.

    Pierr. Seest thou that Engine?   [*Pointing to the Wheel.*

    Jaff. Why?

    Pierr. Is't fit a Souldier, who has liv'd with Honour,   445
Fought Nation's Quarrels, and been Crown'd with Conquest,
Be expos'd a common Carcass on a Wheel?

    Jaff. Hah!

    Pierr.   Speak! is't fitting?

    Jaff.   Fitting?

    Pierr.   Yes, Is't fitting?

    Jaff. What's to be done?

    Pierr.   I'd have thee undertake
Something that's Noble, to preserve my Memory   450
From the disgrace that's ready to attaint it.

    Offic. The day grows late, Sir.

    Pierr.   I'll make haste! oh *Jaffeir*,
Though thou'st betray'd me, do me some way Justice.

    Jaff. No more of that: Thy wishes shall be satisfi'd,
I have a Wife, and she shall bleed, my Child too   455
Yield up his little Throat, and all t'appease thee—
            [*Going away Pier. holds him.*

    Pierr. No——this——no more!   [*He whispers* Jaffeir.

    Jaff.   Hah! is't then so?

    Pierr.   Most certainly.

    Jaff. I'll do't.

    Pierr.   Remember.

    Offic.   Sir.

    Pierr.   Come, now I'm ready.
Captain, you should be a Gentleman of honour,
        [*He and* Jaffeir *ascend the Scaffold.*
Keep off the Rabble, that I may have room   460
To entertain my Fate, and dy with Decency.

Come! [*Takes off his Gown. Executioner prepares to bind him.*
  Fath. Son!
  Pierr.   Hence, Tempter.
  Offic.   Stand off, Priest.
  Pierr.   I thank you, Sir.
You'll think on't.   [*To* Jaffeir.
  Jaff.   'Twon't grow stale before to morrow.
  Pierr. Now, *Jaffeir!* now I am going. Now;—
                  [*Executioner having bound him.*
  Jaff.   Have at thee,
Thou honest heart, then——here——   [*Stabs him.* 465
And this is well too.   [*Then stabs himself.*
  Fath. Damnable Deed!
  Pierr.   Now thou hast indeed been faithful.
This was done Nobly——We have deceiv'd the Senate.
  Jaff. Bravely.
  Pierr.   Ha ha ha——oh oh——   [*Dies.*
  Jaff.   Now, you curs'd Rulers,
Thus of the blood y'have shed I make Libation,   470
And sprinkl't mingling: May it rest upon you,
And all your Race: Be henceforth Peace a stranger
Within your Walls; let Plagues and Famine waste
Your Generations—oh poor *Belvidera!*
Sir, I have a Wife, bear this in safety to her,   475
A Token that with my dying breath I blest her,
And the dear little Infant left behind me.
I am sick——I'm quiet——   [*Jaff. dyes.*
  Offic.   Bear this news to the Senate,
And guard their Bodies till there's farther order:
Heav'n grant I dye so well—   [*Scene shuts upon them.* 480
     [*Soft Musick. Enter* Belvidera *distracted, led by two of her*
     Women, Priuli *and Servants.*
  Priu. Strengthen her heart with Patience, pitying Heav'n.
  Belv. Come come come come come. Nay, come to bed!
Prithee my Love. The Winds! hark how they whistle!
And the Rain beats: oh how the weather shrinks me!
You are angry now, who cares? pish, no indeed.   485
Choose then, I say you shall not go, you shall not;
Whip your ill nature; get you gone then! oh,
             [Jaffeir's *Ghost rises.*
Are you return'd? See, Father, here he's come agen,
Am I to blame to love him! oh thou dear one.
             [*Ghost sinks.*
Why do you fly me? are you angry still then?   490
Jaffeir! where art thou? Father, why do you do thus?
Stand off, don't hide him from me. He's here somewhere.
Stand off I say! what gone? remember't, Tyrant!

I may revenge my self for this trick one day.
                    [*Enter Officer and others.*
I'll do't—I'll do't. *Renault's* a nasty fellow.   495
Hang him, hang him, hang him.
   Priu.   News, what news? [*Offic. whispers* Priuli.
   Offic.   Most sad, Sir.
Jaffeir upon the Scaffold, to prevent
A shamefull death, stab'd *Pierre*, and next himself:
Both fell together.
   Priu.   Daughter.
   Belv.   Hah, look there!
     [*The Ghosts of* Jaff. *and* Pierr. *rise together both bloody.*
My Husband bloody, and his friend too! Murther!   500
Who has done this? speak to me thou sad Vision,
                [*Ghosts sink.*
On these poor trembling Knees I beg it. Vanisht——
Here they went down; Oh I'll dig, dig the Den up.
You shan't delude me thus. Hoa, *Jaffeir, Jaffeir,*
Peep up and give me but a look. I have him!   505
I've got him, Father: Oh now how I'll smuggle him!
My Love! my Dear! my Blessing! help me, help me!
They have hold on me, and drag me to the bottom.
Nay—now they pull so hard——farewel—   [*She dyes.*
   Maid.   She's dead.
Breathless and dead.
   Priu.   Then guard me from the sight on't: 510
Lead me into some place that's fit for mourning;
Where the free Air, Light and the chearful Sun
May never enter: Hang it round with Black;
Set up one Taper that may last a day
As long as I've to live: And there all leave me.   515
      Sparing no Tears when you this Tale relate,
      But bid all Cruel Fathers dread my Fate.
              [*Ex. omnes. Curtain falls.*

Epilogue

THE Text is done, and now for Application,
And when that's ended pass your Approbation.
Though the Conspiracy's prevented here,
Methinks I see another hatching there;
And there's a certain Faction fain would sway,   5
If they had strength enough, and damn this Play;
But this the Author bad me boldly say:
If any take his plainness in ill part,
He's glad on't from the bottom of his heart;
Poets in honour of the Truth shou'd write,   10

With the same Spirit brave men for it fight;
And though against him causeless hatreds rise,
And daily where he goes of late, he spies
The scowles of sullen and revengeful eyes;
'Tis what he knows with much contempt to bear, 15
And serves a cause too good to let him fear:
He fears no poison from an incens'd Drabb,
No Ruffian's five-foot-sword, nor Rascal's stab;
Nor any other snares of mischief laid,
Not a Rose-alley Cudgel-Ambuscade 20
From any private cause where malice reigns,
Or general Pique all Block-heads have to brains:
Nothing shall daunt his Pen when Truth does call,
No not the *Picture-mangler at Guild-hall.
The Rebel-Tribe, of which that Vermin's one, 25
Have now set forward and their course begun;
And while that Prince's figure they deface,
   As they before had massacred his Name,
Durst their base fears but look him in the face,
   They'd use his Person as they've us'd his Fame; 30
A face, in which such lineaments they read
Of that great Martyr's, whose rich bloud they shed,
That their rebellious hate they still retain,
And in his Son would murther Him again:
With indignation then, let each brave heart 35
Rouse and unite to take his injur'd part;
Till Royal Love and Goodness call him home,
And Songs of Triumph meet him as he come;
Till Heaven his Honour and our Peace restore,
And Villains never wrong his Vertue more. 40

(1682)

* *The Rascal that cut the Duke of York's Picture.*

---

20. *Rose-alley Cudgel-Ambuscade:* On December 18, 1679, Dryden was set upon by three men in Rose Alley and severely beaten, possibly for a satire he was thought to have written against John Wilmot, Earl of Rochester, the *Essay upon Satire*, actually by Mulgrave.

32. *Great Martyr's:* Charles I, beheaded January 30, 1649, was the martyr.

37. *Call him home:* The Duke of York was in Scotland, where he had been since October, 1680; he returned in March, 1682, a month or less after the play opened.

William Congreve

1670-1729

Congreve was born near Leeds in 1670. His family moved to Ireland when he was a boy, and it was there he was educated, at Kilkenny Grammar School and Trinity College, Dublin, where Swift was a fellow-student. Upon his return to London, Congreve entered the Middle Temple.

Congreve's first work, a novel called *Incognita, or Love and Duty Reconciled*, published in 1692, became quite popular. The following year he had a spectacular success with his first play, *The Old Bachelor*, produced with the help (and the praise) of Dryden. In November of the same year followed *The Double Dealer*, but it failed to attain the popularity of the former work. *Love for Love* was produced in 1695; in 1697, Congreve's only tragedy, *The Mourning Bride*, appeared; it was quite successful at the time, although now it is chiefly remembered as the source of two homilies, "Music hath charms to soothe the savage breast," and "Heaven has no rage like love to hatred turned."

In 1698, Congreve, along with Dryden, Vanbrugh, and other Restoration dramatists, was attacked by Jeremy Collier in his "A Short View of . . . the English Stage." Congreve replied to the attack ("Amendments of Mr. Collier's False and Imperfect Citations") but without notable success.

Although Congreve was under contract to Lincoln's Inn Theatre to produce a play a year, he was to write but one more work, *The Way of the World* (1700), generally considered the finest comedy of the Restoration. The play was poorly received; he lived for almost three decades after its appearance, yet produced nothing more.

Congreve was well liked, it seems; he had many friends, among them the actress Mrs. Ann Bracegirdle (who starred in all the major roles for women in his plays) and Henrietta, Duchess of Marlborough (to whom he left the bulk of his estate). In his later years, Congreve was sought out by Voltaire during the Frenchman's visit to England.

His support of the Whig party brought the author a few minor official posts, which enabled him to live comfortably until his death on January 19, 1729, following a coach accident. He was buried in Westminster Abbey.

William Congreve—Selective Bibliography

Congreve Bibliography: *CBEL*, II, pp. 414 f.

F. W. Bateson, ed., *The Works of Congreve: Comedies, Incognita, Poems*, London, Peter Davies, 1930.

Montague Summers, ed., *The Complete Works of William Congreve*, 4 vols., London, Nonesuch Press, 1923.

Herbert Davis, ed., *William Congreve, Complete Plays*, Chicago, U. of Chicago Press, 1967.

Kathleen Lynch, ed., *The Way of the World*, Lincoln, U. of Nebraska Press, 1965.

Bonamy Dobrée, ed., *Comedies, by William Congreve*, London, H. Milford; New York, Oxford U. P., 1925.

John C. Hodges, ed., *William Congreve: Letters and Documents*, New York, Harcourt, Brace, and World, 1964.

———, *William Congreve the Man*, New York, Modern Language Association, 1941; reprinted, N.Y., Kraus, 1966.

Emmett L. Avery, *Congreve's Plays on the Eighteenth-Century Stage*, New York, Modern Language Association, 1951.

Norman N. Holland, *The First Modern Comedies; The Significance of Etherege, Wycherly, and Congreve*, Cambridge, Mass., Harvard U. P., 1959.

Kathleen Lynch, *A Congreve Gallery* [Essays on William Congreve and his friends], Cambridge, Mass., Harvard U. P., 1951.

The Way of the World

Dedication

To the Right Honourable Ralph, Earl of Mountague,[1] *&c.*

My LORD,

Whether the World will arraign me of Vanity, or not, that I have presum'd to Dedicate this Comedy to your Lordship, I am yet in doubt: Tho' it may be it is some degree of Vanity even to doubt of it. One who has at any time had the Honour of your Lordship's Conversation, cannot be suppos'd to think very meanly of that which he would prefer to your Perusal: Yet it were to incur the Imputation of too much Sufficiency, to pretend to such a Merit as might abide the Test of your Lordship's Censure.

Whatever Value may be wanting to this Play while yet it is mine, will be sufficiently made up to it, when it is once become your Lordship's; and it is my Security, that I cannot have overrated it more by my Dedication, than your Lordship will dignifie it by your Patronage.

That it succeeded on the Stage, was almost beyond my Expectation;[2] for but little of it was prepar'd for that general Taste which seems now to be predominant in the Pallats of our Audience.

Those Characters which are meant to be ridiculous in most of our Comedies, are of Fools so gross, that in my humble Opinion, they should rather disturb than divert the well-natur'd and reflecting part of an Audience; they are rather Objects of Charity than Contempt; and instead of moving our Mirth, they ought very often to excite our Compassion.

This Reflection mov'd me to design some Characters, which should appear ridiculous not so much thro' a natural Folly (which is incorrigible, and therefore not proper for the Stage) as thro' an affected Wit; a Wit, which at the same time that it is affected, is also false. As there is some Difficulty in the formation of a Character of this Nature, so there is some Hazard which attends the progress of its Success, upon the Stage: For many come to a play so overcharg'd with Criticism, that they very often let fly their Censure, when through their rashness they have mistaken their Aim. This I had occasion lately to observe: For this Play had been Acted two or three Days, before some of these hasty Judges cou'd find the leisure to distinguish betwixt the Character of a *Witwoud*[3] and a *Truewit.*

I must beg your Lordship's Pardon for this Digression from the true Course of this Epistle; but that it may not seem altogether impertinent, I beg, that I may plead the occasion of it, in part of that Excuse of which I stand in need, for recommending this Comedy to your Protection. It is only by the Countenance

---

[1] *Mountague:* Ralph, First Duke of Montagu (c. 1638–1709), was an English diplomat. An earl in 1700, when Congreve wrote, he was raised to a dukedom in 1705.

[2] *Beyond my Expectation:* When first acted, the play was not well received.

[3] *Witwoud:* A character in the play, who, as his name suggests, strains to be witty.

of your Lordship, and the *Few* so qualified, that such who write with Care and Pains can hope to be distinguish'd: For the Prostituted Name of *Poet* promiscuously levels all that bear it.

Terence,[4] the most correct Writer in the World, had a *Scipio* and a *Lelius* if not to assist him, at least to support him in his Reputation: And notwithstanding his extraordinary Merit, it may be, their Countenance was not more than necessary.

The Purity of his Stile, the Delicacy of his Turns, and the Justness of his Characters, were all of them Beauties, which the greater part of his Audience were incapable of Tasting: Some of the coursest Strokes of *Plautus*,[5] so severely censured by *Horace*, were more likely to affect the Multitude; such, who come with expectation to Laugh out the last Act of a Play, and are better entertained with two or three unseasonable Jests, than with the artful Solution of the *Fable*.

As *Terence* excell'd in his Performances, so had he great Advantages to encourage his Undertakings; for he built most on the Foundations of *Menander*:[6] His Plots were generally modell'd, and his Characters ready drawn to his Hand. He, copied *Menander*; and *Menander* had no less Light in the Formation of his Characters, from the Observations of *Theophrastus*,[7] of whom he was a Disciple; and *Theophrastus* it is known was not only the Disciple, but the immediate Successor of *Aristotle*, the first and greatest Judge of Poetry. These were great Models to design by; and the further Advantage which *Terence* possess'd, towards giving his Plays the due Ornaments of Purity of Stile, and Justness of Manners, was not less considerable, from the freedom of Conversation, which was permitted him with *Lelius* and *Scipio*, two of the greatest and most polite Men of his Age. And indeed, the Privilege of such a Conversation, is the only certain Means of attaining to the Perfection of Dialogue.

If it has hapned in any part of this Comedy, that I have gain'd a Turn of Stile, or Expression more Correct, or at least more Corrigible than in those which I have formerly written, I must, with equal Pride and Gratitude, ascribe it to the Honour of your Lordship's admitting me into your Conversation, and that of a Society where every-body else was so well worthy of you, in your Retirement last Summer from the Town: For it was immediately after, that this Comedy was written. If I have fail'd in my Performance, it is only to be regretted, where there were so many, not inferiour either to a *Scipio* or a *Lelius*, that there should be one wanting equal to the Capacity of a *Terence*.

If I am not mistaken, Poetry is almost the only Art, which has not yet laid claim to your Lordship's Patronage. Architecture, and Painting, to the great Honour of our Country, have flourish'd under your Influence and Protection.

---

[4] *Terence:* Publius Terentius Afer (195 or 185–159 B.C.), the second of the great Roman comedians whose works survive (the other being Plautus). A slave, probably of African origin, he was educated and freed by his master and soon befriended by the powerful Scipio and by Laelius.

[5] *Plautus:* Titus Maccus (c. 254–184 B.C.), a Roman playwright whose comedies, coarser than Terence's, had a more popular appeal.

[6] *Menander:* Menandros (c. 342–292 B.C.), was a Greek writer of New Comedy, on which the Roman comedians drew heavily.

[7] *Theophrastus:* Theophrastos (c. 371–c. 287 B.C.) was a Greek author on a wide range of subjects, including *Characters*, in which he describes various types of men. He was Aristotle's student and Menander's teacher.

In the mean time, Poetry, the eldest Sister of all Arts, and Parent of most, seems to have resign'd her Birth-right, by having neglected to pay her Duty to your Lordship; and by permitting others of a later Extraction, to prepossess that Place in your Esteem, to which none can pretend a better Title. Poetry, in its Nature, is sacred to the Good and Great; the relation between them is reciprocal, and they are ever propitious to it. It is the Privilege of Poetry to address to them, and it is their Prerogative alone to give it Protection.

This receiv'd Maxim, is a general Apology for all Writers who Consecrate their Labours to great Men: But I could wish at this time, that this Address were exempted from the common pretence of all Dedications; and that as I can distinguish your Lordship even among the most Deserving, so this Offering might become remarkable by some particular Instance of Respect, which should assure your Lordship, that I am, with all due Sense of your extream Worthiness and Humanity,

My LORD,

Your Lordship's most obedient
and most oblig'd humble Servant,
Will. Congreve.

Prologue

Spoken by Mr. Betterton[1]

OF those few Fools, who with ill Stars are curs'd,
Sure scribbling Fools, call'd Poets, fare the worst.
For they're a sort of Fools which Fortune makes,
And after she has made 'em Fools, forsakes.
With Nature's Oafs 'tis quite a diff'rent Case,   5
For Fortune favours all her Idiot-Race:
In her own Nest the Cuckow-Eggs we find,
O'er which she broods to hatch the Changling-Kind.
No Portion for her own she has to spare,
So much she doats on her adopted Care.   10
    Poets are Bubbles,[2] by the Town drawn in,
Suffer'd at first some trifling Stakes to win:
But what unequal Hazards do they run!
Each time they write, they-venture all they've won:
The 'Squire that's butter'd[3] still, is sure to be undone.   15
This Author, heretofore, has found your Favour,
But pleads no Merit from his past Behaviour.
To build on that might prove a vain Presumption,
Should Grants to Poets made, admit Resumption:
And in Parnassus he must lose his Seat,   20
If that be found a forfeited Estate.
    He owns, with Toil, he wrought the following Scenes,
But if they're naught ne're spare him for his Pains:
Damn him the more; have no Commiseration
For Dulness on mature Deliberation.   25
He swears he'll not resent one hiss'd-off Scene,
Nor, like those peevish Wits, his Play maintain,
Who, to assert their Sense, your Taste arraign.
Some Plot we think he has, and some new Thought;
Some Humour too, no Farce; but that's a Fault.   30
Satire, he thinks, you ought not to expect,
For so Reform'd a Town, who dares Correct?
To please, this time, has been his sole Pretence,
He'll not instruct least it should give Offence.
Should he by chance a Knave or Fool expose,   35
That hurts none here, sure here are none of those.
In short, our Play, shall (with your leave to shew it)

---

[1] Mr. Betterton: Thomas Betterton (c. 1635–1710), English actor, adapter of dramas, and theater manager. He played Fainall.

[2] Bubbles: Gulls or dupes.

[3] The 'Squire that's butter'd: To be buttered is to have the stakes raised against one at every throw or at every game. The application of the slang gambling term here seems to be that the poet, to succeed, must outdo himself with every new work (his public raises the stakes; he is buttered), so he eventually fails (loses the game).

Give you one Instance of a Passive Poet.
Who to your Judgments yields all Resignation;
So Save or Damn, after your own Discretion.   40

Personae Dramatis

MEN.
Fainall, In Love with Mrs. Marwood.
Mirabell, In Love with Mrs. Millamant.
Witwoud, } Followers of Mrs. Millamant.
Petulant, }
Sir Wilfull Witwoud, Half Brother to *Witwoud,* and Nephew to *Lady Wishfort.*
Waitwell, Servant to *Mirabell.*

WOMEN.
Lady Wishfort, Enemy to *Mirabell,* for having falsely pretended Love to her.
Mrs. Millamant, A fine Lady, Niece to *Lady Wishfort,* and loves *Mirabell.*
Mrs. Marwood, Friend to Mr. *Fainall,* and likes *Mirabell.*
Mrs. Fainall, Daughter to *Lady Wishfort,* and Wife to *Fainall,* formerly Friend
    to *Mirabell.*
Foible, Woman to *Lady Wishfort.*
Mincing, Woman to *Mrs. Millamant.*

Dancers, Footmen, *and* Attendants.

SCENE, *London*
The Time equal to that of the Presentation

Act I Scene I

A Chocolate-House
[Mirabell *and* Fainall, *Rising from Cards.* Betty *waiting.*

Mira. You are a fortunate Man, Mr. *Fainall.*
Fain. Have we done?
Mira. What you please. I'll play on to entertain you.
Fain. No, I'll give you your Revenge another time, when you are not so
indifferent; you are thinking of something else now, and play too negligently;
the Coldness of a losing Gamester lessens the Pleasure of the Winner. I'd no
more play with Man that slighted his ill Fortune, than I'd make Love to a
Woman who undervalu'd the Loss of her Reputation.
Mira. You have a Taste extreamly delicate, and are for refining on your
Pleasures.   10
Fain. Prithee, why so reserv'd? Something has put you out of Humour.
Mira. Not at all: I happen to be grave to day; and you are gay; that's all.

Fain. Confess, *Millamant* and you quarrell'd last Night, after I left you; my fair Cousin has some Humours that wou'd tempt the Patience of a Stoick. What, some Coxcomb came in, and was well receiv'd by her, while you were by.

Mira. *Witwoud* and *Petulant*; and what was worse, her Aunt, your Wife's Mother, my evil Genius; or to sum up all in her own Name, my old *Lady Wishfort* came in.————

Fain. O there it is then———— She has a lasting Passion for you, and with Reason.————What, then my Wife was there?

Mira. Yes, and *Mrs. Marwood*, and three or four more, whom I never saw 10 before; seeing me, they all put on their grave Faces, whisper'd one another; then complain'd aloud of the Vapours, and after fell into a profound Silence.

Fain. They had a mind to be rid of you.

Mira. For which Reason I resolv'd not to stir. At last the good old Lady broke thro' her painful Taciturnity, with an Invective against long Visits. I would not have understood her, but *Millamant* joining in the Argument, I rose, and with a constrain'd Smile told her, I thought nothing was so easie as to know when a Visit began to be troublesome; she redned and I withdrew, without expecting[1] her Reply.

Fain. You were to blame to resent what she spoke only in Compliance 20 with her Aunt.

Mira. She is more Mistress of her self, than to be under the necessity of such a resignation.

Fain. What? tho' half her Fortune depends upon her marrying with my Lady's Approbation?

Mira. I was then in such a Humour, that I shou'd have been better pleas'd if she had been less discreet.

Fain. Now I remember, I wonder not they were weary of you; last Night was one of their Cabal-Nights; they have 'em three times a Week, and meet by turns, at one another's Apartments, where they come together like the 30 Coroner's Inquest, to sit upon the murder'd Reputations of the Week. You and I are excluded; and it was once propos'd that all the Male Sex shou'd be excepted; but somebody mov'd that to avoid Scandal there might be one Man of the Community; upon which motion *Witwoud* and *Petulant* were enroll'd Members.

Mira. And who may have been the Foundress of this Sect? My *Lady Wishfort*, I warrant, who publishes her Detestation of Mankind; and full of the Vigour of Fifty five, declares for a Friend and *Ratafia*;[2] and let Posterity shift for it self, she'll breed no more.

Fain. The discovery of your sham Addresses to her to conceal your Love 40 to her Niece, has provok'd this Separation: Had you dissembl'd better, Things might have continu'd in the state of Nature.

Mira. I did as much as Man cou'd, with any reasonable Conscience; I proceeded to the very last Act of Flattery with her, and was guilty of a Song in her Commendation. Nay, I got a Friend to put her into a Lampoon, and com-

---

[1] *Expecting:* Waiting for.
[2] *Ratafia:* A liquer flavored with   fruit or fruit kernels.

pliment her with the Imputation of an Affair with a young Fellow, which I carry'd so far, that I told her the malicious Town took notice that she was grown fat of a suddain; and when she lay in of a Dropsie, persuaded her she was reported to be in Labour. The Devil's in't, if an old Woman is to be flatter'd further, unless a Man shou'd endeavour downright personally to debauch her; and that my Virtue forbad me. But for the Discovery of this Amour, I am indebted to your Friend, or your Wife's Friend, *Mrs. Marwood*.

Fain. What shou'd provoke her to be your Enemy, unless she has made you Advances, which you have slighted? Women do not easily forgive Omissions of that Nature. 10

Mira. She was always civil to me, 'till of late; I confess I am not one of those Coxcombs who are apt to interpret a Woman's good Manners to her Prejudice; and think that she who does not refuse 'em every thing, can refuse 'em nothing.

Fain. You are a galant Man, *Mirabell*; and tho' you may have Cruelty enough, not to satisfy a Lady's longing; you have too much Generosity, not to be tender of her Honour. Yet you speak with an Indifference which seems to be affected; and confesses you are conscious of a Negligence.

Mira. You pursue the Argument with a distrust that seems to be unaffected, and confesses you are conscious of a Concern for which the Lady is more indebted to you, than is your Wife. 20

Fain. Fie, fie, Friend, if you grow Censorious I must leave you;——I'll look upon the Gamesters in the next Room.

Mira. Who are they?

Fain. Petulant and *Witwoud*,——Bring me some Chocolate. [*Exit.*

Mira. Betty, what says your Clock?

Bet. Turn'd of the last Canonical Hour,[3] Sir. [*Exit.*

Mira. How pertinently the Jade answers me! Ha? almost one a Clock! [*Looking on his Watch.*] O, y'are come——

[*Enter a Servant.*

Well; is the grand Affair over? You have been something tedious.

Serv. Sir, there's such Coupling at *Pancras*,[4] that they stand behind one 30 another, as 'twere in a Country Dance. Ours was the last Couple to lead up; and no hopes appearing of dispatch, besides, the Parson growing hoarse, we were afraid his Lungs wou'd have fail'd before it came to our turn; so we drove round to *Duke's Place*; and there they were riveted in a trice.

Mira. So, so, you are sure they are Married.

Serv. Married and Bedded, Sir: I am Witness.

Mira. Have you the Certificate?

Serv. Here it is, Sir.

Mira. Has the Taylor brought *Waitwell's* Cloaths home, and the new Liveries? 40

Serv. Yes, Sir.

---

[3] *Turn'd of the last Canonical Hour:* At the date of the play, Canonical Hours, during which various church services, like marriage, might be performed, were from 8:00 A.M. to 12 noon. Turn'd here means past.

[4] *At Pancras:* Both St. Pancras Church and St. James's (Duke's Place, mentioned below) were places where marriages could be performed expeditiously, upon payment of a fee.

Mira. That's well. Do you go home again, d'ee hear, and adjourn the Consummation till farther Order; bid *Waitwell* shake his Ears, and Dame *Partlet*[5] rustle up her Feathers, and meet me at One a Clock by *Rosamond's* Pond;[6] that I may see her before she returns to her Lady: And as you tender[7] your Ears be secret.   [*Exit Servant.*

[*Re-Enter* Fainall.

Fain. Joy of your Success, *Mirabell*; you look pleas'd.

Mira. Ay; I have been engag'd in a Matter of some sort of Mirth, which is not yet ripe for discovery. I am glad this is not a Cabal-night. I wonder, *Fainall*, that you who are Married, and of Consequence should be discreet, will suffer your Wife to be of such a Party.   10

Fain. Faith, I am not Jealous. Besides, most who are engag'd are Women and Relations; and for the Men, they are of a Kind too Contemptible to give Scandal.

Mira. I am of another Opinion. The greater the Coxcomb, always the more the Scandal: For a Woman who is not a Fool, can have but one Reason for associating with a Man that is.

Fain. Are you jealous as often as you see *Witwoud* entertain'd by *Millamant*?

Mira. Of her Understanding I am, if not of her Person.

Fain. You do her wrong; for to give her her Due, she has Wit.

Mira. She has Beauty enough to make any Man think so; and Complaisance enough not to contradict him who shall tell her so.   20

Fain. For a passionate Lover, methinks you are a Man somewhat too discerning in the Failings of your Mistress.

Mira. And for a discerning Man, somewhat too passionate a Lover; for I like her with all her Faults; nay like her for her Faults. Her Follies are so natural, or so artful, that they become her; and those Affectations which in another Woman wou'd be odious, serve but to make her more agreeable. I'll tell thee, *Fainall*, she once us'd me with that Insolence, that in Revenge I took her to pieces; sifted her, and separated her Failings; I study'd 'em, and got 'em by rote. The Catalogue was so large, that I was not without hopes, one one Day or other to hate her heartily: To which end I so us'd my self to think   30 of 'em, that at length, contrary to my Design and Expectation, they gave me ev'ry Hour less and less disturbance; 'till in a few Days it became habitual to me, to remember 'em without being displeas'd. They are now grown as familiar to me as my own Frailties; and in all probability in a little time longer I shall like 'em as well.

Fain. Marry her, marry her; be half as well acquainted with her Charms, as you are with her Defects, and my Life on't, you are your own Man again.

Mira. Say you so?

Fain. [Ay], [Ay], I have Experience: I have a Wife, and so forth.   40

[*Enter Messenger.*

Mess. Is one Squire *Witwoud* here?

Betty. Yes; What's your Business?

---

[5] *Partlet:* Pertelote, wife and sister of the rooster Chauntecleer in the tale of the cock and the fox, the basis of Chaucer's *Nun's Priest's Tale.*

[6] *Rosamond's Pond:* A pond in St. James's Park, where lovers met.

[7] *Tender:* Value.

Mess. I have a Letter for him, from his Brother *Sir Wilfull*, which I am charg'd to deliver into his own Hands.

Betty. He's in the next Room, Friend——that way. [*Exit Mess.*

Mira. What, is the Chief of that noble Family in Town, *Sir Wilfull Witwoud?*

Fain. He is expected to Day. Do you know him?

Mira. I have seen him; he promises to be an extraordinary Person; I think you have the Honour to be related to him.

Fain. Yes; he is half Brother to this *Witwoud* by a former Wife, who was Sister to my *Lady Wishfort*, my Wife's Mother. If you marry *Millamant*, you 10
must call Cousins too.

Mira. I had rather be his Relation than his Acquaintance.

Fain. He comes to Town in order to Equip himself for Travel.

Mira. For Travel? Why the Man that I mean is above Forty.[8]

Fain. No matter for that; 'tis for the Honour of *England*, that all *Europe* shoud know we have Blockheads of all Ages.

Mira. I wonder there is not an Act of Parliament to save the Credit of the Nation, and prohibit the Exportation of Fools.

Fain. By no means, 'tis better as 'tis; 'tis better to trade with a little Loss, than to be quite eaten up with being overstock'd. 20

Mira. Pray, are the Follies of this Knight-errant, and those of the Squire his Brother, any thing related?

Fain. Not at all; *Witwoud* grows by the Knight, like a Medlar grafted on a Crab.[9] One will melt in your Mouth, and t'other set your Teeth on edge; one is all Pulp, and the other all Core.

Mira. So one will be rotten before he be ripe, and the other will be rotten without ever being ripe at all.

Fain. Sir Wilful is an odd mixture of Bashfulness and Obstinacy.—But when he's drunk, he's as loving as the Monster in the Tempest,[10] and much after the same manner. To give t'other his due, he has something of good 30
Nature, and does not always want Wit.

Mira. Not always; but as often as his Memory fails him, and his common-place of Comparisons. He is a Fool with a good Memory, and some few Scraps of other Folks' Wit. He is one whose Conversation can never be approv'd, yet it is now and then to be endur'd. He has indeed one good Quality, he is not Exceptious; for he so passionately affects the Reputation of understanding Raillery, that he will construe an Affront into a Jest; and call downright Rudeness and ill Language, Satyr and Fire.

Fain. If you have a mind to finish his Picture, you have an opportunity to do it at full length. Behold the Original. 40
[*Enter* Witwoud.

---

[8] *Above Forty:* English gentleman often went abroad (making the grand tour of Europe) right after college.

[9] *Medlar . . . on a Crab:* Medlar is a tree (very much like a crabapple) whose fruit is not edible until the early stages of decay; crab here of course means crab-apple. See *As You Like It*, III, ii, where Rosalind teases Touchstone with a play on medlar.

[10] *Monster in the Tempest:* Caliban, in Shakespeare's play.

Wit. Afford me your Compassion, my Dears; pity me, *Fainall*; *Mirabell*, pity me.

Mira. I do from my Soul.

Fain. Why, what's the Matter?

Wit. No Letters for me, *Betty*?

Betty. Did not the Messenger bring you one but now, Sir?

Wit. Ay, but no other?

Betty. No, Sir.

Wit. That's hard, that's very hard;——A Messenger, a Mule, a Beast of Burden, he has brought me a Letter from the Fool my Brother, as heavy as a 10 Panegyrick in a Funeral Sermon, or a Copy of Commendatory Verses from one Poet to another. And what's worse, 'tis as sure a forerunner of the Author, as an Epistle Dedicatory.

Mira. A Fool, and your Brother, *Witwoud!*

Wit. Ay, ay, my half Brother. My half Brother he is, no nearer upon Honour.

Mira. Then 'tis possible he may be but half a Fool.

Wit. Good, good, *Mirabell, le Drôle!*[11] Good, good; hang him, don't let's talk of him:——*Fainall*, how does your Lady? Gad, I say any thing in the World to get this Fellow out of my Head. I beg Pardon that I shou'd ask a Man 20 of Pleasure, and the Town, a Question at once so Foreign and Domestick. But I Talk like an old Maid at a Marriage; I don't know what I say: But she's the best Woman in the World.

Fain. 'Tis well you don't know what you say, or else your Commendation wou'd go near to make me either Vain or Jealous.

Wit. No Man in Town lives well with a Wife but *Fainall*. Your Judgment, *Mirabell*?

Mira. You had better step and ask his Wife, if you wou'd be credibly inform'd.

Wit. Mirabell. 30

Mira. Ay.

Wit. My Dear, I ask ten thousand Pardons;——Gad I have forgot what I was going to say to you.

Mira. I thank you heartily, heartily.

Wit. No, but prithee excuse me,——my Memory is such a Memory.

Mira. Have a care of such Apologies, *Witwoud*;——for I never knew a Fool but he affected to complain, either of the Spleen or his Memory.

Fain. What have you done with *Petulant*?

Wit. He's reckoning his Mony,——my Mony it was—— I have no Luck To-day. 40

Fain. You may allow him to win of you at Play;——for you are sure to be too hard for him at Repartee: Since you monopolize the Wit that is between you, the Fortune must be his of Course.

Mira. I don't find that *Petulant* confesses the Superiority of Wit to be your Talent, *Witwoud*.

Wit. Come, come, you are malicious now, and wou'd breed Debates——

---

[11] *Le Drôle:* Clever rascal.

Petulant's my Friend, and a very honest Fellow, and a very pretty Fellow, and has a smattering——Faith and Troth a pretty deal of an odd sort of a small Wit: Nay, I'll do him Justice. I'm his Friend, I won't wrong him neither.—— And if he had but any Judgment in the World,——he wou'd not be altogether contemptible. Come, come, don't detract from the Merits of my Friend.

Fain. You don't take your Friend to be overnicely bred.

Wit. No, no, hang him, the Rogue has no Manners at all, that I must own ——No more breeding than a Bum-baily,[12] that I grant you—— 'Tis pity; the Fellow has Fire and Life.

Mira. What, Courage? 10

Wit. Hum, faith I don't know as to that,——I can't say as to that.—— Yes, faith, in a Controversie, he'll contradict any body.

Mira. Tho' 'twere a Man whom he fear'd, or a Woman whom he lov'd.

Wit. Well, well, he does not always think before he speaks;——We have all our Failings: You're too hard upon him, you are, Faith. Let me excuse him,—— I can defend most of his Faults, except one or two: One he has, that's the Truth on't; if he were my Brother, I could not acquit him—That indeed I cou'd wish were otherwise.

Mira. Ay marry, what's that, *Witwoud*?

Wit. O pardon me——Expose the Infirmities of my Friend.—No, my Dear, 20 excuse me there.

Fain. What, I warrant he's unsincere, or 'tis some such Trifle.

Wit. No, no, what if he be? 'Tis no matter for that, his Wit will excuse that: A Wit shou'd no more be sincere, than a Woman constant; one argues a decay of parts, as t'other of Beauty.

Mira. May be you think him too positive?

Wit. No, no, his being positive is an Incentive to Argument, and keeps up Conversation.

Fain. Too Illiterate.

Wit. That? that's his Happiness.——His want of Learning gives him the 30 more opportunities to shew his natural Parts.

Mira. He wants Words.

Wit. Ay: But I like him for that now; for his want of Words gives me the pleasure very often to explain his Meaning.

Fain. He's Impudent.

Wit. No, that's not it.

Mira. Vain.

Wit. No.

Mira. What, he speaks unseasonable Truths sometimes, because he has not Wit enough to invent an Evasion. 40

Wit. Truths! Ha, ha, ha! No, no; since you will have it,—I mean, he never speaks Truth at all,——that's all. He will lie like a Chambermaid, or a Woman of Quality's Porter. Now that is a Fault.

[*Enter Coachman.*

Coach. Is Master *Petulant* here, Mistress?

---

[12] *Bum-baily:* Bumbailiff, a bailiff or usually one who makes arrests.
sheriff's officer of the meanest kind,

Betty. Yes.

Coach. Three Gentlewomen in the Coach wou'd speak with him.

Fain. O brave *Petulant!* Three!

Betty. I'll tell him.

Coach. You must bring two Dishes of Chocolate and a Glass of Cinnamon-water.   ⟨ *Exeunt* Betty *and Coachman.* ⟩

Wit. That shou'd be for two fasting Strumpets, and a Bawd troubl'd with Wind. Now you may know what the three are.

Mira. You are very free with your Friend's Acquaintance.

Wit. Ay, ay, Friendship without Freedom is as dull as Love without Enjoyment, or Wine without Toasting; but to tell you a Secret, these are Trulls whom he allows Coach-hire, and something more by the Week, to call on him once a Day at publick Places.

Mira. How!

Wit. You shall see he won't go to 'em, because there's no more Company here to take notice of him—— Why this is nothing to what he us'd to do:—— Before he found out this Way, I have known him call for himelf——

Fain. Call for himself! What dost thou mean?

Wit. Mean, why he wou'd slip you out of this Chocolate-house, just when you had been talking to him——As soon as your Back was turn'd—Whip he was gone;—Then trip to his Lodging, clap on a Hood and Scarf, and a Mask, slap into a Hackney-Coach, and drive hither to the Door again in a trice; where he wou'd send in for himself, that [is] I mean, call for himself, wait for himself, nay and what's more, not finding himself, sometimes leave a Letter for himself.

Mira. I confess this is something extraordinary——I believe he waits for himself now, he is so long a coming: O I ask his Pardon.

[*Enter* Petulant ⟨ *and* Betty ⟩.

Betty. Sir, the Coach stays.   ⟨ *Exit.* ⟩

Pet. Well, well; I come;——'Sbud,[13] a Man had as good be a profess'd Midwife, as a profest Whoremaster, at this rate; to be knock'd up and rais'd at all Hours, and in all Places. Pox on 'em, I won't come—— D'ee hear, tell 'em I won't come——Let 'em snivel and cry their Hearts out.

Fain. You are very cruel, *Petulant.*

Pet. All's one, let it pass—— I have a Humour to be cruel.

Mira. I hope they are not Persons of Condition that you use at this rate.

Pet. Condition, Condition's a dry'd Fig, if I am not in Humour—— By this Hand, if they were your a—a—your What-dee-call-'ems themselves, they must wait or rub off,[14] if I want Appetite.

Mira. What-dee-call-'ems! What are they, *Witwoud?*

Wit. Empresses, my Dear—— By your What-dee-call-'ems he means Sultana Queens.

Pet. Ay, *Roxolanas.*[15]

Mira. Cry you Mercy.

---

[13] *'Sbud:* A euphemistic shortening of God's bodikins—God's dear body.
[14] *Rub off:* Leave me.
[15] *Roxolanas:* In D'Avenant's play

The Siege of Rhodes, Roxolana is first concubine, then wife of Solyman the Magnificent.

Fain. Witwoud says they are——

Pet. What does he say th'are?

Wit. I; fine Ladies I say.

Pet. Pass on, *Witwoud*——Hearkee, by this Light his Relations——Two Coheiresses his Cousins, and an old Aunt, who loves Catterwauling better than a Conventicle.[16]

Wit. Ha, ha, ha, I had a Mind to see how the Rogue wou'd come off— Ha, ha, ha; Gad I can't be angry with him, if he had said they were my Mother and my Sisters.

Mira. No.   10

Wit. No; the Rogue's Wit and Readiness of Invention charm me, dear *Petulant.*   〈 *Re-enter* Betty. 〉

Betty. They are gone, Sir, in great Anger.

Pet. Enough, let 'em trundle. Anger helps Complexion, saves Paint.

Fain. This Continence is all dissembled; this is in order to have something to brag of the next time he makes Court to *Millamant*, and swear he has abandon'd the whole Sex for her Sake.

Mira. Have you not left off your impudent Pretensions there yet? I shall cut your Throat, some time or other, *Petulant*, about that Business.

Pet. Ay, ay, let that pass——There are other Throats to be cut.——   20

Mira. Meaning mine, Sir?

Pet. Not I—I mean no Body—I know nothing——But there are Uncles and Nephews in the World——And they may be Rivals——What then? All's one for that——

Mira. How! Hearkee, *Petulant*, come hither—Explain, or I shall call your Interpreter.

Pet. Explain; I know nothing——Why you have an Uncle, have you not, lately come to Town, and lodges by my *Lady Wishfort's?*

Mira. True.

Pet. Why that's enough—You and he are not Friends, and if he shou'd   30
marry and have a Child, you may be disinherited ha?

Mira. Where hast thou stumbled upon all this Truth?

Pet. All's one for that; why then say I know something.

Mira. Come, thou art an honest Fellow, *Petulant*, and shalt make Love to my Mistress, thou sha't, Faith. What hast thou heard of my Uncle?

Pet. I, nothing I. If Throats are to be cut, let Swords clash; snug's the Word, I shrug and am silent.

Mira. O Raillery, Raillery. Come, I know thou art in the Women's Secrets —— What, you're a Cabalist; I know you staid at *Millamant's* last Night, after I went. Was there any Mention made of my Uncle, or me? Tell me. If thou   40
hadst but good-Nature equal to thy Wit. *Petulant, Tony Witwoud*, who is now thy Competitor in Fame, wou'd shew as dim by thee as a dead Whiting's Eye by a Pearl of Orient; he wou'd no more be seen by thee,[17] than *Mercury* is by the Sun. Come, I'm sure thou wo't tell me.

---

[16] *Catterwauling . . . Conventicle:* Cater-
wauling is the noise (and by extension the
play) proper to cats at mating time; a
conventicle is a kind of fundamentalist
church meeting.

[17] *Be seen by thee:* His presence would
not be observed.

Pet. If I do, will you grant me common Sense then, for the future?

Mira. Faith I'll do what I can for thee, and I'll pray that Heav'n may grant it thee in the mean time.

Pet. Well, harkee.   ⟨ *They speak in dumb-show.* ⟩

Fain. Petulant and you both will find *Mirabell* as warm a Rival as a Lover.

Wit. Pshaw, pshaw, that she laughs at *Petulant* is plain.—And for my part —— But that is almost a Fashion to admire her, I shou'd—Hearkee—— To tell you a Secret, but let it go no further—Between Friends, I shall never break my Heart for her.

Fain. How!

Wit. She's handsome; but she's a sort of an uncertain Woman.

Fain. I thought you had dy'd for her.

Wit. Umh—No——

Fain. She has Wit.

Wit. 'Tis what she will hardly allow any Body else.——Now, Demme, I shou'd hate that, if she were as handsome as *Cleopatra. Mirabell* is not so sure of her as he thinks for.

Fain. Why do you think so?

Wit. We staid pretty late there last Night; and heard something of an Uncle to *Mirabell*, who is lately come to Town,—and is between him and the best Part of his Estate; *Mirabell* and he are at some distance, as my *Lady Wishfort* has been told; and you know she hates *Mirabell* worse than a Quaker hates a Parrot, or than a Fishmonger hates a hard Frost. Whether this Uncle has seen *Mrs. Millamant* or not, I cannot say; but there were Items of such a Treaty being in Embrio; and if it shou'd come to Life, poor *Mirabell* wou'd be in some sort unfortunately fobb'd[18] i'faith.

Fain. 'Tis impossible *Millamant* shou'd hearken to it.

Wit. Faith, my Dear, I can't tell; she's a Woman, and a kind of a Humorist.

Mira. ⟨ *In a separate conversation with* Petulant. ⟩ And this is the Sum of what you cou'd collect last Night.

Pet. The Quintessence. May be *Witwoud* knows more, he stay'd longer. —— Besides, they never mind him; they say any thing before him.

Mira. I thought you had been the greatest Favourite.

Pet. Ay, *teste a teste*,[19] but not in publick, because I make Remarks.

Mira. You do?

Pet. Ay, ay; pox, I'm malicious, Man. Now he's soft, you know; they are not in awe of him——The Fellow's well bred; he's what you call a—— What-dee-call-'em, a fine Gentleman! But he's silly withal.

Mira. I thank you, I know as much as my Curiosity requires. *Fainall*, are you for the *Mall*?[20]

Fain. Ay, I'll take a turn before Dinner.

Wit. Ay, we'll all walk in the Park; the Ladies talk'd of being there.

Mira. I thought you were oblig'd to watch for your Brother *Sir Wilfull's* Arrival.

---

[18] *Fobb'd:* Duped.
[19] *Teste a teste: Tête à tête.*
[20] *The Mall:* A walk in St. James's Park.

Wit. No, no; he comes to his Aunt's, my *Lady Wishfort:* pox on him, I shall be troubled with him too; what shall I do with the Fool?

Pet. Beg him for his Estate, that I may beg you afterwards; and so have but one Trouble with you both.

Wit. O rare *Petulant*; thou art as quick as Fire in a frosty Morning; thou shalt to the *Mall* with us, and we'll be very severe.

Pet. Enough, I'm in a Humour to be severe.

Mira. Are you? Pray then walk by your selves.—— Let not us be accessary to your putting the Ladies out of Countenance with your senseless Ribaldry, which you roar out aloud as often as they pass by you; and when you have made a handsome Woman blush, then you think you have been severe.

Pet. What, what? Then let 'em either shew their Innocence by not understanding what they hear, or else shew their Discretion by not hearing what they wou'd not be thought to understand.

Mira. But hast not thou then Sense enough to know that thou ought'st to be most asham'd thy Self, when thou hast put another out of Countenance?

Pet. Not I, by this Hand—— I always take blushing either for a Sign of Guilt, or ill Breeding.

Mira. I confess you ought to think so. You are in the right, that you may plead the error of your Judgment in defence of your Practice.

> *Where Modesty's ill Manners, 'tis but fit*
> *That Impudence and Malice pass for Wit.*   [*Exeunt.*

Act II Scene I

[*Enter* Mrs. Fainall *and* Mrs. Marwood.

Mrs. Fain. Ay, ay, dear *Marwood*, if we will be happy, we must find the means in our selves, and among our selves. Men are ever in Extreams; either doating, or averse. While they are Lovers, if they have Fire and Sense, their Jealousies are insupportable: And when they cease to Love (we ought to think at least) they loath; they look upon us with Horror and Distate; they meet us like the Ghosts of what we were, and as from such, fly from us.

Mrs. Mar. True, 'tis an unhappy Circumstance of Life, that Love shou'd ever die before us; and that the Man so often shou'd out-live the Lover. But say what you will, 'tis better to be left, than never to have been lov'd. To pass our Youth in dull Indifference, to refuse the Sweets of Life because they once must leave us, is as preposterous, as to wish to have been born Old, because we one Day must be Old. For my part, my Youth may wear and waste, but it shall never rust in my Possession.

Mrs. Fain. Then it seems you dissemble an Aversion to Mankind, only in compliance to my Mother's Humour.

Mrs. Mar. Certainly. To be free; I have no Taste of those insipid dry Discourses, with which our Sex of force must entertain themselves, apart from Men. We may affect Endearments to each other, profess eternal Friendships, and seem to doat like Lovers; but 'tis not in our Natures long to persevere.

Love will resume his Empire in our Breasts, and every Heart, or soon or late, receive and readmit him as its lawful Tyrant.

Mrs. Fain. Bless me, how have I been deceiv'd! Why you profess a Libertine.

Mrs. Mar. You see my Friendship by my Freedom. Come, be as sincere, acknowledge that your Sentiments agree with mine.

Mrs. Fain. Never.

Mrs. Mar. You hate Mankind?

Mrs. Fain. Heartily, Inveterately.

Mrs. Mar. Your Husband? 10

Mrs. Fain. Most transcendently; ay, tho' I say it, meritoriously.

Mrs. Mar. Give me your Hand upon it.

Mrs. Fain. There.

Mrs. Mar. I join with you; what I have said has been to try you.

Mrs. Fain. Is it possible? Dost thou hate those Vipers Men?

Mrs. Mar. I have done hating 'em, and am now come to despise 'em; the next thing I have to do, is eternally to forget 'em.

Mrs. Fain. There spoke the Spirit of an *Amazon*, a *Penthesilea*.[1]

Mrs. Mar. And yet I am thinking sometimes to carry my Aversion further.

Mrs. Fain. How? 20

Mrs. Mar. Faith by Marrying; if I cou'd but find one that lov'd me very well, and would be thoroughly sensible of ill usage, I think I should do my self the violence of undergoing the Ceremony.

Mrs. Fain. You would not make him a Cuckold?

Mrs. Mar. No; but I'd make him believe I did, and that's as bad.

Mrs. Fain. Why had not you as good do it?

Mrs. Mar. O if he shou'd ever discover it, he wou'd then know the worst, and be out of his Pain; but I wou'd have him ever to continue upon the Rack of Fear and Jealousy.

Mrs. Fain. Ingenious Mischief! Wou'd thou wert married to *Mirabell*. 30

Mrs. Mar. Wou'd I were.

Mrs. Fain. You change Colour.

Mrs. Mar. Because I hate him.

Mrs. Fain. So do I; but I can hear him nam'd. But what Reason have you to hate him in particular?

Mrs. Mar. I never lov'd him; he is, and always was insufferably proud.

Mrs. Fain. By the Reason you give for your Aversion, one wou'd think it dissembled; for you have laid a Fault to his Charge, of which his Enemies must acquit him.

Mrs. Mar. O then it seems you are one of his favourable Enemies. Methinks 40 you look a little pale, and now you flush again.

Mrs. Fain. Do I? I think I am a little sick o' the suddain.

Mrs. Mar. What ails you?

Mrs. Fain. My Husband. Don't you see him? He turn'd short upon me unawares, and has almost overcome me.

[*Enter* Fainall *and* Mirabell.

---

[1] *Penthesilea:* An Amazon queen killed by Achilles at Troy.

Mrs. Mar. Ha, ha, ha; he comes opportunely for you.

Mrs. Fain. For you, for he has brought *Mirabell* with him.

Fain. My Dear.

Mrs. Fain. My Soul.

Fain. You don't look well to Day, Child.

Mrs. Fain. D'ee think so?

Mira. He is the only Man that do's, Madam.

Mrs. Fain. The only Man that wou'd tell me so at least; and the only Man from whom I could hear it without Mortification.

Fain. O my Dear I am satisfy'd of your Tenderness; I know you cannot   10
resent any thing from me; especially what is an effect of my Concern.

Mrs. Fain. Mr. *Mirabell*, my Mother interrupted you in a pleasant Relation last Night; I wou'd fain hear it out.

Mira. The Persons concern'd in that Affair, have yet a tollerable Reputation.
——I am afraid Mr. *Fainall* will be censorious.

Mrs. Fain. He has a Humour more prevailing than his Curiosity, and will willingly dispence with the hearing of one scandalous Story, to avoid giving an occasion to make another by being seen to walk with his Wife. This way, Mr. *Mirabell*, and I dare promise you will oblige us both.

[*Exeunt* Mrs. Fainall *and* Mirabell.

Fain. Excellent Creature! Well, sure if I shou'd live to be rid of my Wife,   20
I shou'd be a miserable Man.

Mrs. Mar. Ay!

Fain. For having only that one Hope, the accomplishment of it, of Consequence must put an end to all my hopes; and what a Wretch is he who must survive his hopes! Nothing remains when that Day comes, but to sit down and weep like *Alexander*, when he wanted other Worlds to conquer.

Mrs. Mar. Will you not follow 'em?

Fain. Faith, I think not.

Mrs. Mar. Pray let us; I have a Reason.

Fain. You are not Jealous?   30

Mrs. Mar. Of whom?

Fain. Of *Mirabell.*

Mrs. Mar. If I am, is it inconsistent with my Love to you that I am tender of your Honour?

Fain. You wou'd intimate then, as if they were a *fellow-feeling* between my Wife and him.

Mrs. Mar. I think she do's not hate him to that degree she wou'd be thought.

Fain. But he, I fear, is too Insensible.

Mrs. Mar. It may be you are deceiv'd.   40

Fain. It may be so. I do not now begin to apprehend it.

Mrs. Mar. What?

Fain. That I have been deceiv'd, Madam, and you are false.

Mrs. Mar. That I am false! What mean you?

Fain. To let you know I see through all your little Arts——Come, you both love him; and both have equally dissembl'd your Aversion. Your mutual Jealousies of one another have made you clash 'till you have both struck Fire.

I have seen the warm Confession red'ning on your Cheeks, and sparkling from your Eyes.

Mrs. Mar. You do me wrong.

Fain. I do not——'Twas for my ease to oversee and wilfully neglect the gross advances made him by my Wife; that by permitting her to be engag'd, I might continue unsuspected in my Pleasures; and take you oftner to my Arms in full Security. But cou'd you think, because the nodding Husband wou'd not wake, that e'er the watchful Lover slept?

Mrs. Mar. And wherewithal can you reproach me?

Fain. With Infidelity, with loving another, with Love of *Mirabell*.   1

Mrs. Mar. 'Tis false. I challenge you to shew an Instance that can confirm your groundless Accusation. I hate him.

Fain. And wherefore do you hate him? He is insensible, and your Resentment follows his Neglect. An Instance! The Injuries you have done him are a proof: Your interposing in his Love. What cause had you to make Discoveries of his pretended Passion? To undeceive the credulous Aunt, and be the officious Obstacle of his Match with *Millamant*?

Mrs. Mar. My Obligations to my Lady urg'd me: I had profess'd a Friendship to her; and cou'd not see her easie Nature so abus'd by that Dissembler.

Fain. What, was it Conscience then? Profess'd a Friendship! O the pious   2
Friendships of the Female Sex!

Mrs. Mar. More tender, more sincere, and more enduring, than all the vain and empty Vows of Men, whether professing Love to us, or mutual Faith to one another.

Fain. Ha, ha, ha; you are my Wife's Friend too.

Mrs. Mar. Shame and Ingratitude! Do you reproach me? You, you upbraid me! Have I been false to her, thro' strict Fidelity to you, and sacrific'd my Friendship to keep my Love inviolate? And have you the Baseness to charge me with the Guilt, unmindful of the Merit! To you it shou'd be meritorious, that I have been vicious: And do you reflect that Guilt upon me, which   3
shou'd lie buried in your Bosom?

Fain. You misinterpret my Reproof. I meant but to remind you of the slight Account you once cou'd make of strictest Ties, when set in Competition with your Love to me.

Mrs. Mar. 'Tis false, you urg'd it with deliberate Malice—— 'Twas spoke in scorn, and I never will forgive it.

Fain. Your Guilt, not your Resentment, begets your Rage. If yet you lov'd, you cou'd forgive a Jealousy: But you are stung to find you are discover'd.

Mrs. Mar. It shall be all discover'd. You too shall be discover'd; be sure you   4
shall. I can but be expos'd——If I do it my self I shall prevent[2] your Baseness.

Fain. Why, what will you do?

Mrs. Mar. Disclose it to your Wife; own what has past between us.

Fain. Frenzy!

Mrs. Mar. By all my Wrongs I'll do't——I'll publish to the World the

---

[2] *Discover'd . . . prevent:* Discovered   is to anticipate.
here probably means revealed; to prevent

Injuries you have done me, both in my Fame and Fortune: With both I trusted you, you Bankrupt in Honour, as indigent of Wealth.

Fain. Your Fame I have preserv'd. Your Fortune has been bestow'd as the prodigality of your Love would have it, in Pleasures which we both have shar'd. Yet, had not you been false, I had e'er this repaid it.—— 'Tis true;—— had you permitted *Mirabell* with *Millamant* to have stoll'n their Marriage, my Lady had been incens'd beyond all means of reconcilement: *Millamant* had forfeited the Moiety of her Fortune; which then wou'd have descended to my Wife;—— And wherefore did I marry, but to make lawful Prize of a rich Widow's Wealth, and squander it on Love and you? 10

Mrs. Mar. Deceit and frivolous Pretence.

Fain. Death, am I not married? What's pretence? Am I not Imprison'd, Fetter'd? Have I not a Wife? Nay a Wife that was a Widow, a young Widow, a handsom Widow; and wou'd be again a Widow, but that I have a Heart of Proof, and something of a Constitution to bustle thro' the ways of Wedlock and this World. Will you yet be reconcil'd to Truth and me?

Mrs. Mar. Impossible. Truth and you are inconsistent——I hate you, and shall for ever.

Fain. For loving you?

Mrs. Mar. I loath the name of Love after such Usage; and next to the Guilt 20 with which you wou'd asperse me, I scorn you most. Farewell.

Fain. Nay, we must not part thus.

Mrs. Mar. Let me go.

Fain. Come, I'm sorry.

Mrs. Mar. I care not——Let me go——Break my Hands, do——I'd leave 'em to get loose.

Fain. I would not hurt you for the World. Have I no other Hold to keep you here?

Mrs. Mar. Well, I have deserv'd it all.

Fain. You know I love you. 30

Mrs. Mar. Poor dissembling! O that—— Well, it is not yet——

Fain. What? What is it not? What is it not yet? It is not yet too late——

Mrs. Mar. No, it is not yet too late——I have that Comfort.

Fain. It is, to love another.

Mrs. Mar. But not to loath, detest, abhor Mankind, my self and the whole treacherous World.

Fain. Nay, this is Extravagance——Come, I ask your Pardon—No Tears ——I was to blame; I cou'd not love you and be easie in my Doubts—— Pray forbear——I believe you; I'm convinc'd I've done you wrong; and any way, ev'ry way will make amends;——I'll hate my Wife yet more, 40 Damn her, I'll part with her, rob her of all she's worth, and we'll retire somewhere, any where, to another World, I'll marry thee——Be pacify'd——'Sdeath they come; hide your Face, your Tears——You have a Mask; wear it a moment. This way, this way, be persuaded. [*Exeunt.*

[*Enter* Mirabell *and* Mrs. Fainall.

Mrs. Fain. They are here yet.

Mira. They are turning into the other Walk.

Mrs. Fain. While I only hated my Husband, I cou'd bear to see him; but since I have despis'd him, he's too offensive.

Mira. O you shou'd Hate with Prudence.

Mrs. Fain. Yes, for I have Lov'd with Indiscretion.

Mira. You shou'd have just so much disgust for your Husband, as may be sufficient to make you relish your Lover.

Mrs. Fain. You have been the Cause that I have lov'd without Bounds, and wou'd you set Limits to that Aversion, of which you have been the occasion? Why did you make me marry this Man?

Mira. Why do we daily commit disagreeable and dangerous Actions? To save that Idol Reputation. If the familiarities of our Loves had produc'd that Consequence, of which you were apprehensive, Where cou'd you have fix'd a Father's Name with Credit, but on a Husband? I knew *Fainall* to be a Man lavish of his Morals, an interested and professing Friend, a false and a designing Lover; yet one whose Wit and outward fair Behaviour, have gain'd a Reputation with the Town, enough to make that Woman stand excus'd, who has suffer'd her self to be won by his Addresses. A better Man ought not to have been sacrific'd to the Occasion; a worse had not answer'd to the Purpose. When you are weary of him, you know your Remedy.

Mrs. Fain. I ought to stand in some degree of Credit with you, *Mirabell.*

Mira. In Justice to you, I have made you privy to my whole Design, and put it in your Pow'r to ruin or advance my Fortune.

Mrs. Fain. Whom have you instructed to represent your pretended Uncle?

Mira. Waitwell, my Servant.

Mrs. Fain. He is an humble Servant to *Foible,* my Mother's Woman, and may win her to your Interest.

Mira. Care is taken for that——She is won and worn by this time. They were married this Morning.

Mrs. Fain. Who?

Mira. Waitwell and *Foible.* I wou'd not tempt my Servant to betray me by trusting him too far. If your Mother, in hopes to ruin me, shou'd consent to marry my pretended Uncle, he might, like *Mosca* in the *Fox,*[3] stand upon Terms; so I made him sure beforehand.

Mrs. Fain. So, if my poor Mother is caught in a Contract you will discover the Imposture betimes; and release her by producing a Certificate of her Gallant's former Marriage.

Mira. Yes, upon Condition that she consent to my Marriage with her Niece, and surrender the Moiety of her Fortune in her Possession.

Mrs. Fain. She talk'd last Night of endeavouring at a Match between *Millamant* and your Uncle.

Mira. That was by *Foible's* Direction, and my Instruction, that she might seem to carry it more privately.

Mrs. Fain. Well, I have an Opinion of your Success; for I believe my Lady will do any thing to get an Husband; and when she has this, which you have provided for her, I suppose she will submit to any thing to get rid of him.

---

[3] *Mosca in the Fox:* In Ben Jonson's *Volpone* (fox), Mosca stands upon terms (makes demands of, blackmails) his master, V, xii.

Mira. Yes, I think the good Lady wou'd marry any Thing that resembl'd a Man, though 'twere no more than what a Butler could pinch out of a Napkin.

Mrs. Fain. Female Frailty! We must all come to it, if we live to be Old, and feel the craving of a false Appetite when the true is decay'd.

Mira. An old Woman's Appetite is deprav'd like that of a Girl—'tis the Green Sickness of a second Childhood; and like the faint Offer of a latter Spring, serves but to usher in the Fall; and withers in an affected Bloom.

Mrs. Fain. Here's your Mistress.

[*Enter* Mrs. Millamant, Witwoud, Mincing.

Mira. Here she comes I'faith full Sail, with her Fan spread and Streamers out, and a shoal of Fools for Tenders—— Ha, no, I cry her Mercy.　　10

Mrs. Fain. I see but one poor empty Sculler; and he tows her Woman after him.

Mira. You seem to be unattended, Madam,——You us'd to have the *Beaumond* Throng after you; and a Flock of gay fine Perrukes hovering round you.

Wit. Like Moths about a Candle——I had like to have lost my Comparison for want of Breath.

Milla. O I have deny'd my self Airs to Day. I have walk'd as fast through the Crowd——

Wit. As a Favourite in disgrace; and with as few Followers.

Milla. Dear Mr. *Witwoud*, truce with your Similitudes: For I am as sick　20 of 'em——

Wit. As a Phisician of a good Air——I cannot help it, Madam, tho' 'tis against my self.

Milla. Yet again! *Mincing*, stand between me and his Wit.

Wit. Do, Mrs. *Mincing*, like a Skreen before a great Fire. I confess I do blaze to Day, I am too bright.

Mrs. Fain. But, dear *Millamant*, why were you so long?

Milla. Long? Lord, have I not made violent haste? I have ask'd every living Thing I met for you; I have enquir'd after you, as after a new Fashion.

Wit. Madam, Truce with your Similitudes——No, you met her Husband,　30 and did not ask him for her.

Mira. By your leave *Witwoud*, that were like enquiring after an old Fashion, to ask a Husband for his Wife.

Wit. Hum, a hit, a hit, a palpable hit, I confess it.

Mrs. Fain. You were dress'd before I came abroad.

Milla. Ay, that's true——O but then I had——*Mincing*, what had I? Why was I so long?

Minc. O Mem, your Laship staid to peruse a Pecquet of Letters.

Milla. O ay, Letters—I had Letters—I am persecuted with Letters—I hate Letters—No Body knows how to write Letters; and yet one has 'em, one does　40 not know why——They serve one to pin up one's Hair.

Wit. Is that the way? Pray, Madam, do you pin up your Hair with all your Letters; I find I must keep Copies.

Milla. Only with those in Verse, Mr. *Witwoud*. I never pin up my Hair with Prose. I think I try'd once, *Mincing*.

Minc. O Mem, I shall never forget it.

Milla. Ay, poor *Mincing* tift[4] and tift all the Morning.

Min. 'Till I had the Cremp in my Fingers, I'll vow, Mem. And all to no purpose. But when your Laship pins it up with Poetry, it sits so pleasant the next Day as any Thing, and is so pure and so crips.[5]

Wit. Indeed, so crips?

Minc. You're such a Critick, Mr. *Witwoud.*

Milla. *Mirabell,* Did you take Exceptions last Night? O ay, and went away——Now I think on't I'm angry?——No, now I think on't I'm pleas'd——For I believe I gave you some Pain.

Mira. Does that please you?

Milla. Infinitely; I love to give Pain.

Mira. You wou'd affect a Cruelty which is not in your Nature; your true Vanity is in the power of pleasing.

Milla. O I ask your Pardon for that——One's Cruelty is one's Power, and when one parts with one's Cruelty, one parts with one's Power; and when one has parted with that, I fancy one's Old and Ugly.

Mira. Ay, ay, suffer your Cruelty to ruin the object of your Power, to destroy your Lover—And then how vain, how lost a Thing you'll be? Nay, 'tis true: You are no longer handsome when you've lost your Lover; your Beauty dies upon the Instant: For Beauty is the Lover's Gift; 'tis he bestows your Charms—— Your Glass is all a Cheat. The Ugly and the Old, whom the Looking-glass mortifies, yet after Commendation can be flatter'd by it, and discover Beauties in it: For that reflects our Praises, rather than your Face.

Milla. O the Vanity of these Men! *Fainall,* d'ee hear him? If they did not commend us, we were not handsome? Now you must know they could not commend one, if one was not handsome. Beauty the Lover's Gift——Lord, what is a Lover, that it can give? Why one makes Lovers as fast as one pleases, and they live as long as one pleases, and they die as soon as one pleases: And then if one pleases one makes more.

Wit. Very pretty. Why you make no more of making of Lovers, Madam, than of making so many Card-matches.[6]

Milla. One no more owes one's Beauty to a Lover, than one's Wit to an Eccho: They can but reflect what we look and say; vain empty Things if we are silent or unseen, and want a being.

Nina. Yet, to those two vain empty Things, you owe two the greatest Pleasures of your Life.

Milla. How so?

Mira. To your Lover you owe the Pleasure of hearing your selves prais'd; and to an Eccho the pleasure of hearing your selves talk.

Wit. But I know a Lady that loves talking so incessantly, she wont' give an Eccho fair play; she has that everlasting Rotation of Tongue, that an Eccho must wait till she dies, before it can catch her last Words.

Milla. O Fiction; *Fainall,* let us leave these Men.

Mira. Draw off *Witwoud.*   [*Aside to* Mrs. Fainall.

Mrs. Fain. Immediately; I have a Word or two for Mr. *Witwoud.*

---

[4] *Tift:* To put in order, to dress.
[5] *Crips:* Crisp.

[6] *Card-matches:* "Pieces of card dipped in melted sulphur." OED.

Mira. I wou'd beg a little private Audience too——

[*Exit* Witwoud *and* Mrs. Fainall.

You had the Tyranny to deny me last Night; tho' you knew I came to impart a Secret to you that concern'd my Love.

Milla. You saw I was engag'd.

Mira. Unkind. You had the leisure to entertain a Herd of Fools; Things who visit you from their excessive Idleness; bestowing on your easiness that time, which is the incumbrance of their Lives. How can you find Delight in such Society? It is impossible they shou'd admire you, they are not capable: Or if they were, it shou'd be to you as a Mortification; for sure to please a Fool is some degree of Folly. 10

Milla. I please my self——Besides, sometimes to converse with Fools is for my Health.

Mira. Your Health! Is there a worse Disease than the Conversation of Fools?

Milla. Yes, the Vapours;[7] Fools are Physick for it, next to *Assa-fœtida.*

Mira. You are not in a Course of Fools?[8]

Milla. Mirabell, if you persist in this offensive Freedom—— You'll displease me—— I think I must resolve after all, not to have you—— We shan't agree.

Mira. Not in our Physick it may be.

Milla. And yet our Distemper in all likelihood will be the same; for we 20 shall be sick of one another. I shan't endure to be reprimanded, nor instructed; 'tis so dull to act always by Advice, and so tedious to be told of one's Faults—— I can't bear it. Well, I won't have you *Mirabell*——I'm resolv'd——I think—— You may go—Ha, ha, ha. What wou'd you give, that you cou'd help loving me?

Mira. I wou'd give something that you did not know I cou'd not help it.

Milla. Come, don't look grave then. Well, what do you say to me?

Mira. I say that a Man may as soon make a Friend by his Wit, or a Fortune by his Honesty, as win a Woman with plain Dealing and Sincerity.

Milla. Sententious *Mirabell!* Prithee don't look with that violent and in- 30 flexible wise Face, like *Solomon* at the dividing of the Child in an old Tapestry-hanging.

Mira. You are merry, Madam, but I would perswade you for a Moment to be serious.

Milla. What, with that Face? No, if you keep your Countenance, 'tis impossible I shou'd hold mine. Well, after all there is something very moving in a love-sick Face. Ha, ha, ha—Well I won't laugh, don't be peevish—— Heigho! Now I'll be melancholly, as melancholly as a Watch-light.[9] Well, *Mirabell,* if ever you will win me [woo] me now—— Nay, if you are so tedious, fare you well;——I see they are walking away. 40

Mira. Can you not find in the variety of your Disposition one Moment——

---

[7] *Vapours:* Fantastic ideas or boasts, or the illness of one who suffers delusions involving such ideas. Asofoetida (*Assa-foetida*) was used medically as an anti-spasmodic.

[8] *Course of Fools:* In a course of physic one takes medicines; the turn here suggests fools are the prescribed medicine.

[9] *Watch-light:* A light used by a watchman.

Milla. To hear you tell me *Foible's* married, and your Plot like to speed——No.

Mira. But how you came to know it——

Milla. Without the help of the Devil, you can't imagine; unless she should tell me her self. Which of the two it may have been, I will leave you to consider; and when you have done thinking of that, think of me.   [*Exit.*

Mira. I have something more——Gone——Think of you! To Think of a Whirlwind, tho' 'twere in a Whirlwind, were a Case of more steady Contemplation; a very tranquillity of Mind and Mansion. A Fellow that lives in a Windmill, has not a more whimsical Dwelling than the Heart of a Man that is lodg'd in a Woman. There is no Point of the Compass to which they cannot turn, and by which they are not turn'd; and by one as well as another; for Motion not Method is their Occupation. To know this, and yet continue to be in Love, is to be made wise from the Dictates of Reason, and yet persevere to play the Fool by the force of Instinct.——O here come my Pair of Turtles,[10]——What, billing so sweetly! Is not *Valentine's* Day over with you yet?

[*Enter* Waitwell *and* Foible.

Sirrah, *Waitwell*, why sure you think you were married for your own Recreation, and not for my Conveniency.

Wait. Your Pardon, Sir. With Submission, we have indeed been solacing in lawful Delights; but still with an Eye to Business, Sir. I have instructed her as well as I cou'd. If she can take your Directions as readily as my Instructions, Sir, your Affairs are in a prosperous way.

Mira. Give you Joy, Mrs. *Foible.*

Foib. O las, Sir, I'm so asham'd——I'm afraid my Lady has been in a thousand Inquietudes for me. But I protest, Sir, I made as much haste as I could.

Wait. That she did indeed, Sir. It was my Fault that she did not make more.

Mira. That I believe.

Foib. But I told my Lady as you instructed me, Sir. That I had a prospect of seeing Sir *Rowland,* your Uncle; and that I wou'd put her Ladyship's Picture in my Pocket to shew him; which I'll be sure to say has made him so enamour'd of her Beauty, that he burns with Impatience to lie at her Ladyship's Feet and worship the Original.

Mira. Excellent *Foible!* Matrimony has made you eloquent in Love.

Wait. I think she has profited, Sir. I think so.

Foib. You have seen Madam *Millamant,* Sir?

Mira. Yes.

Foib. I told her, Sir, because I did not know that you might find an Opportunity; she had so much Company last Night.

Mira. Your Diligence will merit more—in the mean time——

[*Gives Mony.*

Foib. O dear Sir, your humble Servant.

Wait. Spouse.

Mira. Stand off, Sir, not a Penny——Go on and prosper, *Foible*——The Lease shall be made good and the Farm stock'd, if we succeed.

Foib. I don't question your Generosity, Sir: And you need not doubt of

[10] *Turtles:* Turtle-doves.

Success. If you have no more Commands, Sir, I'll be gone; I'm sure my Lady
is at her Toilet, and can't dress 'till I come.——O dear, I'm sure that [*Looking
out.*] was *Mrs. Marwood* that went by in a Mask; if she has seen me with you I'm
sure she'll tell my Lady. I'll make haste home and prevent[11] her. Your Servant,
Sir. B'w'y *Waitwell*.

 Wait. Sir *Rowland*, if you please. The Jade's so pert upon her Preferment she
forgets her self.

 Mira. Come, Sir, will you endeavour to forget your self——And transform
into Sir *Rowland*.

 Wait. Why, Sir, it will be impossible I shou'd remember my self—— 10
Marry'd, Knighted and attended all in one Day! 'Tis enough to make any
Man forget himself. The Difficulty will be how to recover my Acquaintance
and Familiarity with my former self; and fall from my Transformation to a
Reformation into *Waitwell*. Nay, I shan't be quite the same *Waitwell* neither——
for now I remember me, I'm married, and can't be my own Man again.

  Ay there's my Grief; that's the sad Change of Life;
  To lose my Title, and yet keep my Wife.   [*Exeunt.*

Act III Scene I

A Room in Lady Wishfort's *House*

[Lady Wishfort *at her Toilet*, Peg *waiting.*

 Lady. Merciful,[1] no News of *Foible* yet?

 Peg. No, Madam.

 Lady. I have no more patience—If I have not fretted my self 'till I am pale 20
again, there's no Veracity in me. Fetch me the Red——the Red, do you hear,
Sweetheart? An errant Ash colour, as I'm a Person. Look you how this Wench
stirs! Why dost thou not fetch me a little Red? Did'st thou not hear me,
Mopus?[2]

 Peg. The red *Ratafia* does your Ladyship mean, or the Cherry Brandy?

 Lady. Ratafia, Fool. No, Fool. Not the *Ratafia*, Fool—Grant me Patience!
I mean the *Spanish* Paper,[3] Idiot, Complexion, Darling. Paint, Paint, Paint,
dost thou understand that, Changeling, dangling thy Hands like Bobbins
before thee? Why dost thou not stir, Puppet? thou wooden Thing upon Wires.

 Peg. Lord, Madam, your Ladyship is so impatient——I cannot come at 30
the Paint, Madam; Mrs. *Foible* has lock'd it up, and carry'd the Key with her.

 Lady. A Pox take you both——Fetch me the Cherry-Brandy then.

                [*Exit Peg.*
I'm as pale and as faint, I look like Mrs. Qualmsick the Curate's Wife, that's
always breeding——Wench, come, come, Wench, what art thou doing,
Sipping? Tasting? Save thee, dost thou not know the Bottle?

    [*Enter* Peg *with a Bottle and* China-Cup.

 Peg. Madam, I was looking for a Cup.

---

[11] *Prevent:* Anticipate.
[1] *Merciful:* Merciful God.
[2] *Mopus:* A mope, a dull person.

[3] *Spanish Paper:* Rouge-filled paper for
coloring lips and cheeks.

Lady. A Cup, save thee, and what a Cup hast thou brought! Dost thou take me for a *Fairy*, to drink out of an *Acorn*? Why didst thou not bring thy Thimble? Hast thou ne'er a Brass-Thimble clinking in thy Pocket with a bit of Nutmeg?[4] I warrant thee. Come, fill, fill.——So—again. [*One knocks.*] See who that is——Set down the Bottle first. Here, here, under the Table—— What, wou'dst thou go with the Bottle in thy Hand like a Tapster. As I'm a Person, this Wench has liv'd in an Inn upon the Road, before she came to me, like *Maritornes* the *Asturian* in *Don Quixote*.[5] No *Foible* yet?

Peg. No Madam, *Mrs. Marwood.*

Lady. O *Marwood*, let her come in. Come in, good *Marwood*.   1●

[*Enter* Mrs. Marwood.

Mrs. Mar. I'm surpriz'd to find your Ladyship in *dishabilie* at this time of day.

Lady. *Foible's* a lost Thing; has been abroad since Morning, and never heard of since.

Mrs. Mar. I saw her but now, as I came mask'd through the Park, in Conference with *Mirabell.*

Lady. With *Mirabell!* You call my Blood into my Face, with mentioning that Traytor. She durst not have the Confidence. I sent her to Negotiate an Affair in which if I'm detected I'm undone. If that wheadling Villain has wrought upon *Foible* to detect me, I'm ruin'd. Oh my dear Friend, I'm a   2● Wretch of Wretches if I'm detected.

Mrs. Mar. O Madam, you cannot suspect Mrs. *Foible's* Integrity.

Lady. O, he carries Poyson in his Tongue that wou'd corrupt Integrity it self. If she has given him an Opportunity, she has as good as put her Integrity into his Hands. Ah dear *Marwood*, what's Integrity to an Opportunity?— Hark! I hear her——Go you Thing and send her in. [*Ex.* Peg.] Dear Friend, retire into my Closet, that I may examine her with more freedom——You'll pardon me, dear Friend, I can make bold with you——There are Books over the Chimney——*Quarles* and *Pryn*,[6] and the *Short View of the Stage*,[7] with *Bunyan's* Works[8] to entertain you——   [*Exit* Marwood.   3●

[*Enter* Foible.

O *Foible*, where hast thou been? what hast thou been doing?

Foib. Madam, I have seen the Party.

Lady. But what hast thou done?

Foib. Nay, 'tis your Ladyship has done, and are to do; I have only promis'd. But a Man so enamour'd——so transported! Well, if worshipping of Pictures be a Sin—Poor Sir *Rowland*, I say.

Lady. The Miniature has been counted like—— But hast thou not betray'd

---

[4] *Brass-Thimble . . . Nutmeg:* These items are identified as good-luck charms by Nettleton and Case, p. 325.

[5] *Maritornes the Asturian in Don Quixote:* See Part I, Bk. III, Ch. ii for a description of the Asturian wench, one of the ugliest females in literature.

[6] *Quarles and Pryn:* Francis Quarles (1592–1644) was a religious versifier; William Prynne (1600–1699), a Puritan writer, found fault with the stage in *Histrio-mastix*, 1632.

[7] *Short View of the Stage:* A book by Jeremy Collier (1650–1726), a clergyman, attacking the stage and its playwrights, including Congreve.

[8] *Bunyan's Works:* John Bunyan (1622–1688) is best known for his Christian works *Grace Abounding* (1666) and *Pilgrim's Progress* (1678).

me, *Foible*? Hast thou not detected me to that faithless *Mirabell*?——What hadst thou to do with him in the Park? Answer me, has he got nothing out of thee?

Foib. So, the Devil has been beforehand with me; what shall I say?—— Alas, Madam, cou'd I help it, if I met that confident Thing? Was I in Fault? If you had heard how he us'd me, and all upon your Ladyship's Account, I'm sure you wou'd not suspect my Fidelity. Nay, if that had been the worst I cou'd have born: But he had a Fling at your Ladyship too; and then I cou'd not hold: But I'faith I gave him his own.

Lady. Me? What did the filthy Fellow say?   10

Foib. O Madam; 'tis a shame to say what he said——With his Taunts and his Fleers,[9] tossing up his Nose. Humh (says he) what, you are a hatching some Plot (says he), you are so early abroad, or Catering (says he), ferreting for some disbanded Officer, I warrant——Half Pay is but thin Subsistance (says he)—Well, what Pension does your Lady propose? Let me see (says he), what, she must come down pretty deep now, she's superannuated (says he), and——

Lady. Ods my Life, I'll have him, I'll have him murder'd. I'll have him poyson'd. Where does he eat? I'll marry a Drawer to have him poyson'd in his Wine. I'll send for *Robin* from Locket's[10]—Immediately.

Foib. Poyson him? Poysoning's too good for him. Starve him, Madam,   20
starve him; marry Sir *Rowland*, and get him disinherited. O you wou'd bless your self, to hear what he said.

Lady. A Villain, superannuated!

Foib. Humh (says he), I hear you are laying Designs against me too (says he), and *Mrs. Millament* is to marry my Uncle (he does not suspect a Word of your Ladyship); but (says he) I'll fit you for that, I warrant you (says he) I'll hamper you for that (says he), you and your old Frippery[11] too (says he), I'll handle you.——

Lady. Audacious Villain! handle me, wou'd he durst——Frippery? old Frippery! Was there ever such a foul-mouth'd Fellow? I'll be married to   30
Morrow, I'll be contracted to Night.

Foib. The sooner the better, Madam.

Lady. Will Sir *Rowland* be here, say'st thou? when, *Foible*?

Foib. Incontinently, Madam. No new Sheriff's Wife expects the Return of her Husband after Knighthood, with that Impatience in which Sir *Rowland* burns for the dear hour of kissing your Ladyship's Hands after Dinner.

Lady. Frippery? Superannuated Frippery! I'll Frippery the Villain; I'll reduce him to Frippery and Rags: A Tatterdemalion——I hope to see him hung with Tatters, like a Long-Lane Penthouse,[12] or a Gibbet-thief. A slander-mouth'd Railer: I warrant the Spendthrift Prodigal's in Debt as much as the   40
Million Lottery,[13] or the whole Court upon a Birth Day.[14] I'll spoil his Credit

[9] *Fleers:* Mocking looks or speeches.

[10] *Robin from Locket's:* Robin is to be the Drawer (of liquor) mentioned just above; he will poison the wine. Locket's was a well-known tavern.

[11] *Frippery:* Cheap and ostentatious clothing.

[12] *Penthouse:* An appendage to a building, in this case a stall in which old clothes were sold.

[13] *Million Lottery:* A national lottery of 1694.

[14] *Court upon a Birth Day:* Members of the court were required by custom to appear in new (and very expensive) clothing on the king's birthday.

with his Taylor. Yes, he shall have my Niece with her Fortune, he shall.

Foib. He! I hope to see him lodge in *Ludgate*[15] first, and angle into *Black Friers* for Brass Farthings, with an old Mitten.

Lady. Ay dear *Foible*; thank thee for that, dear *Foible*. He has put me out of all patience. I shall never recompose my Features, to receive Sir *Rowland* with any Oeconomy of Face. This Wretch has fretted me that I am absolutely decay'd. Look, *Foible*.

Foib. Your Ladyship has frown'd a little too rashly, indeed, Madam. There are some Cracks discernible in the white Vernish.

Lady. Let me see the Glass——Cracks, say'st thou? Why I am arrantly   10
flea'd——I look like an old peel'd Wall. Thou must repair me, *Foible*, before Sir *Rowland* comes; or I shall never keep up to my Picture.

Foib. I warrant you, Madam; a little Art once made your Picture like you; and now a little of the same Art must make you like your Picture. Your Picture must sit for you, Madam.

Lady. But art thou sure Sir *Rowland* will not fail to come? Or will a not fail when he does come? Will he be Importunate, *Foible*, and push? For if he shou'd not be importunate——I shall never break Decorums——I shall die with Confusion, if I am forc'd to advance—Oh no, I can never advance—I shall swoon if he should expect advances. No, I hope Sir *Rowland* is better bred,   20
than to put a Lady to the necessity of breaking her Forms; I won't be too coy neither.——I won't give him despair——But a little Disdain is not amiss; a little Scorn is alluring.

Foib. A little Scorn becomes your Ladyship.

Lady. Yes, but Tenderness becomes me best——A sort of a dyingness ——You see that Picture has a sort of a——Ha *Foible*? A Swimminess in the Eyes—Yes, I'll look so—My Niece affects it; but she wants Features. Is Sir *Rowland* handsome? Let my Toilet be remov'd—I'll dress above. I'll receive Sir *Rowland* here. Is he handsome? Don't answer me. I won't know: I'll be sur-priz'd. I'll be taken by Surprize.   30

Foib. By Storm, Madam. Sir *Rowland's* a brisk Man.

Lady. Is he? O then he'll importune, if he's a brisk Man. I shall save De-corums if Sir *Rowland* importunes. I have a mortal Terror at the Apprehension of offending against Decorums. Nothing but Importunity can surmount Decorums. O I'm glad he's a brisk Man. Let my Things be remov'd, good *Foible*.   [*Exit.*

[*Enter* Mrs. Fainall.

Mrs. Fain. O *Foible*, I have been in a Fright, least I shou'd come too late. That Devil *Marwood* saw you in the Park with *Mirabell*, and I'm afraid will dis-cover it to my Lady.

Foib. Discover what, Madam?   40

Mrs. Fain. Nay, nay, put not on that strange Face; I am privy to the whole Design, and know that *Waitwell* to whom thou wert this Morning Married, is to personate *Mirabell's* Uncle, and as such, winning my Lady, to involve her

---

[15] *Ludgate:* Presumably debtors im-prisoned in The Fleet (in Ludgate), in the district of Blackfriars, which extended down to the Thames, would beg by hold-ing out their mittens.

in those Difficulties from which *Mirabell* only must release her, by his making his Conditions to have my Cousin and her Fortune left to her own disposal.

Foib. O dear Madam, I beg your Pardon. It was not my Confidence in your Ladyship that was deficient; but I thought the former good Correspondence between your Ladyship and Mr. *Mirabell*, might have hinder'd his communicating this Secret.

Mrs. Fain. Dear *Foible*, forget that.

Foib. O dear Madam, Mr. *Mirabell* is such a sweet winning Gentleman—— But your Ladyship is the Pattern of Generosity.——Sweet Lady, to be so good! Mr. *Mirabell* cannot chuse but be grateful. I find your Ladyship has his Heart   10 still. Now, Madam, I can safely tell your Ladyship our success; *Mrs. Marwood* had told my Lady; but I warrant I manag'd my self. I turn'd it all for the better. I told my Lady that Mr. *Mirabell* rail'd at her; I laid horrid Things to his Charge, I'll vow; and my Lady is so incens'd, that she'll be contracted to Sir *Rowland* to Night, she says;——I warrant I work'd her up, that he may have her for asking for, as they say of a *Welch* Maidenhead.

Mrs. Fain. O rare *Foible*!

Foib. Madam, I beg your Ladyship to acquaint Mr. *Mirabell* of his Success. I wou'd be seen as little as possible to speak to him——besides, I believe Madam *Marwood* watches me.——She has a Month's Mind;[16] but I know   20 Mr. *Mirabell* can't abide her.——   [*Enter Footman.* *John*——remove my Lady's Toilet. Madam, your Servant. My Lady is so impatient, I fear she'll come for me, if I stay.

Mrs. Fain. I'll go with you up the back Stairs, lest I shou'd meet her,
                                    [*Exeunt.*
                    [*Enter* Mrs. Marwood.

Mrs. Mar. Indeed, Mrs. Engine,[17] is it thus with you? Are you become a go-between of this Importance? Yes, I shall watch you. Why this Wench is the *Pass-par-toute*, a very Master-Key to every Bodie's strong Box. My Friend *Fainall*, have you carry'd it so swimmingly? I thought there was something in it; but it seems it's over with you. Your loathing is not from a want of Appetite then, but from a Surfeit. Else you could never be so cool to fall   30 from a Principal to be an Assistant; to procure for him! A Pattern of Generosity, that I confess. Well, Mr. *Fainall*, you have met with your Match.—— O Man, Man! Woman, Woman! The Devil's an Ass: If I were a Painter, I would draw him like an Idiot, a Driveler with Bib and Bells. Man shou'd have his Head and Horns, and Woman the rest of him. Poor simple Fiend! Madam *Marwood* has a Month's Mind, but he can't abide her——'Twere better for him you had not been his Confessor in that Affair; without you could have kept his Counsel closer. I shall not prove another Pattern of Generosity; and stalk for him, till he takes his Stand to aim at a Fortune;——he has not oblig'd me to that with those Excesses of himself; and now I'll have none of   40 him. Here comes the good Lady, panting ripe; with a Heart full of Hope, and a Head full of Care, like any Chymist upon the Day of Projection.[18]

---

[16] *A Month's Mind:* A Requiem Mass said on the thirtieth day after a person's death or burial, and by extension, any very strong inclination.

[17] *Mrs. Engine:* Mrs. Ingenuity.

[18] *Day of Projection:* The day on which the alchemist would change base metal into silver or gold.

[*Enter* Lady Wishfort.]

Lady. O Dear *Marwood*, what shall I say for this rude forgetfulness———
But my dear Friend is all Goodness.

Mrs. Mar. No Apologies, dear Madam, I have been very well entertain'd.

Lady. As I'm a Person, I am in a very Chaos to think I shou'd so forget my
self———But I have such an Olio[19] of Affairs, really I know not what to do———
[*Calls.*]———Foible———I expect my Nephew *Sir Wilfull* every Moment too:———
Why *Foible*———He means to Travel for Improvement.

Mrs. Mar. Methinks *Sir Wilfull* shou'd rather think of Marrying than Travelling at his Years. I hear he is turn'd of Forty.

Lady. O he's in less Danger of being spoil'd by his Travels———I am against   10
my Nephew's marrying too young. It will be time enough when he comes
back, and has acquir'd Discretion to choose for himself.

Mrs. Mar. Methinks *Mrs. Millamant* and he wou'd make a very fit Match.
He may Travel afterwards. 'Tis a Thing very usual with young Gentlemen.

Lady. I promise you I have thought on't———And since 'tis your Judgment,
I'll think on't again. I assure you I will; I value your Judgment extreamly. On
my Word I'll propose it.

[*Enter* Foible.]

Lady. Come, come, *Foible*———I had forgot my Nephew will be here before
Dinner———I must make haste.

Foib. Mr. *Witwoud* and Mr. *Petulant* are come to dine with your Ladyship.   20

Lady. O Dear, I can't appear 'till I am dress'd. Dear *Marwood*, shall I be
free with you again, and beg you to entertain 'em. I'll make all imaginable haste.
Dear Friend, excuse me.   [*Exit* Lady *and* Foible.]

[*Enter* Mrs. Millamant *and* Mincing.]

Milla. Sure never any thing was so Unbred as that odious Man.———
Marwood, your Servant.

Mrs. Mar. You have a Colour; what's the matter?

Milla. That horrid Fellow *Petulant* has provok'd me into a Flame———I
have broke my Fan———*Mincing*, lend me yours; is not all the Powder out of
my Hair?

Mrs. Mar. No. What has he done?   30

Milla. Nay, he has done nothing; he has only talk'd—Nay, he has said
nothing neither; but he has contradicted ev'ry Thing that has been said. For
my part, I thought *Witwoud* and he wou'd have quarrell'd.

Minc. I vow, Mem, I thought once they wou'd have fit.

Milla. Well, 'tis a lamentable thing I swear, that one has not the liberty of
choosing one's Acquaintance as one does one's Clothes.

Mrs. Mar. If we had that liberty, we shou'd be as weary of one Set of
Acquaintance, tho' never so good, as we are of one Suit, tho' never so fine.
A Fool and a *Doily* Stuff[20] wou'd now and then find Days of Grace, and be
worn for variety.   40

Milla. I could consent to wear 'em, if they wou'd wear alike; but Fools never
wear out———they are such *Drap-duberry*[21] Things! without one cou'd give
'em to one's Chamber-maid after a Day or two.

[19] *Olio:* Mixture, variety.
[20] *Doily Stuff:* A cheap woolen fabric
for summer wear.

[21] *Drap-duberry:* A fairly heavy woolen
cloth from Berry, France.

Mrs. Mar. 'Twere better so indeed. Or what think you of the Playhouse? A fine gay glossy Fool shou'd be given there, like a new masking Habit, after the Masquerade is over, and we have done with the Disguise. For a Fool's Visit is always a Disguise; and never admitted by a Woman of Wit, but to blind her Affair with a Lover of Sense. If you wou'd but appear barefac'd now, and own *Mirabell*; you might as easily put off *Petulant* and *Witwoud*, as your Hood and Scarf. And indeed 'tis time, for the Town has found it: The Secret is grown too big for the Pretence. 'Tis like Mrs. *Primly's* great Belly; she may lace it down before, but it burnishes[22] on her Hips. Indeed, *Millament*, you can no more conceal it, than my Lady *Strammel*[23] can her Face, that goodly Face, which in Defiance of her Rhenish-wine Tea,[24] will not be comprehended in a Mask.

Milla. I'll take my Death, *Marwood*, you are more Censorious than a decay'd Beauty, or a discarded Toast; *Mincing*, tell the Men they may come up. My Aunt is not dressing; their Folly is less provoking than your Malice. The Town has found it! [*Exit* Mincing.] What has it found? That *Mirabell* loves me is no more a Secret than it is a Secret that you discover'd it to my Aunt, or than the Reason why you discover'd it is a Secret.

Mrs. Mar. You are nettl'd.

Milla. You'r mistaken. Ridiculous!

Mrs. Mar. Indeed, my Dear, you'll tear another Fan, if you don't mitigate those violent Airs.

Milla. O silly! Ha, ha, ha. I cou'd laugh immoderately. Poor *Mirabell*! His Constancy to me has quite destroy'd his Complaisance for all the World beside. I swear, I never enjoin'd it him, to be so coy——If I had the Vanity to think he wou'd obey me, I wou'd command him to shew more Gallantry ——'Tis hardly well bred to be so particular on one hand, and so insensible on the other. But I despair to prevail, and so let him follow his own way. Ha, ha, ha. Pardon me, dear Creature, I must laugh, ha, ha, ha. Tho' I grant you 'tis a little barbarous, ha, ha, ha.

Mrs. Mar. What pity 'tis so much fine Raillery, and deliver'd with so significant Gesture, shou'd be so unhappily directed to miscarry.

Milla. [Heh?] Dear Creature, I ask your Pardon——I swear I did not mind you.

Mrs. Mar. Mr. *Mirabell* and you both may think it a Thing impossible, when I shall tell him, by telling you——

Milla. O dear, what? for it is the same thing, if I hear it——Ha, ha, ha.

Mrs. Mar. That I detest him, hate him, Madam.

Milla. O Madam, why so do I——And yet the Creature loves me, ha, ha, ha. How can one forbear laughing to think of it——I am a Sibyl if I am not amaz'd to think what he can see in me. I'll take my Death, I think you are handsomer——and within a Year or two as young——If you cou'd but stay for me, I shou'd overtake you——But that cannot be.——Well, that Thought makes me Melancholly.——Now I'll be sad.

[22] *It burnishes:* Though she ties it down in front, it will protrude at the hips.

[23] *Lady Strammel:* Nettleton and Case, p. 328, give "Ill-favored person."

[24] *Rhenish-wine Tea:* Summers, III, p. 215, says, "Rhenish wine was . . . taken to reduce corpulence and correct a high color." Davis, p. 433, notes, "Perhaps thin tea, the color of hock."

Mrs .Mar. Your merry Note may be chang'd sooner than you think.

Milla. D'ee say so? Then I'm resolv'd I'll have a Song to keep up my Spirits.

[*Enter* Mincing.

Minc. The Gentlemen stay but to Comb, Madam; and will wait on you.

Milla. Desire Mrs.————that is in the next Room to sing the Song I wou'd have learnt Yesterday. You shall hear it, Madam————Not that there's any great matter in it————But 'tis agreeable to my Humour.

Song

[*Set by* Mr. John Eccles,[25] *and Sung by* Mrs. Hodgson.

I

Love's but the Frailty of the Mind,
When 'tis not with Ambition join'd;
A sickly Flame, which, if not fed, expires,
And feeding, wastes in Self-consuming Fires.   10

II

'Tis not to wound a wanton Boy,
Or am'rous Youth, that gives the Joy;
But 'tis the Glory to have pierc'd a Swain,
For whom inferior Beauties sigh'd in vain.

III

Then I alone the Conquest prize,
When I insult a Rival's Eyes:
If there's Delight in Love, 'tis when I see
That Heart, which others bleed for, bleed for me.

[*Enter* Petulant, Witwoud.

Milla. Is your Animosity compos'd, Gentlemen?

Wit. Raillery, Raillery, Madam; we have no Animosity—We hit off a little   20
Wit now and then, but no Animosity—The falling-out of Wits is like the falling-out of Lovers————We agree in the main, like Treble and Base. Ha, *Petulant?*

Pet. Ay, in the main————But when I have a Humour to contradict————

Wit. Ay, when he has a Humour to contradict, then I contradict too. What, I know my Cue. Then we contradict one another like two Battledores: For Contradictions beget one another like *Jews.*

Pet. If he says Black's Black—if I have a Humour to say 'tis Blue————Let that pass————All's one for that. If I have a Humour to prove it, it must be granted.   30

---

[25] *John Eccles:* Eccles or Eagles (1668– 1735) was a famous composer for the theater. He is supposed to have written other music for *The Way of the World* as well as this.

Wit. Not positively must——But it may——It may.

Pet. Yes, it positively must, upon Proof positive.

Wit. Ay, upon Proof positive it must; but upon Proof presumptive it only may. That's a Logical Distinction now, Madam.

Mrs. Mar. I perceive your Debates are of Importance, and very learnedly handl'd.

Pet. Importance is one Thing, and Learning's another; but a Debate's a Debate, that I assert.

Wit. *Petulant's* an Enemy to Learning; he relies altogether on his Parts.

Pet. No, I'm no Enemy to Learning; it hurts not me.   10

Mrs. Mar. That's a Sign indeed it's no Enemy to you.

Pet. No, no, it's no Enemy to any Body, but them that have it.

Milla. Well, an illiterate Man's my Aversion: I wonder at the Impudence of any illiterate Man, to offer to make Love.

Wit. That, I confess, I wonder at too.

Milla. Ah! to marry an Ignorant? that can hardly Read or Write.

Pet. Why shou'd a Man be any further from being marry'd tho' he can't Read, than he is from being Hang'd. The Ordinary's paid for setting the *Psalm*,[26] and the Parish-Priest for reading the Ceremony. And for the rest which is to follow in both Cases, a Man may do it without Book——So all's one for that.   20

Milla. D'ee hear the Creature? Lord, here's Company; I'll be gone.

[*Exeunt* Millamant *and* Mincing.

Wit. In the Name of *Bartlemew* and his Fair[27] what have we here?

Mrs. Mar. 'Tis your Brother, I fancy. Don't you know him?

Wit. Not I——Yes, I think it is he——I've almost forgot him; I have not seen him since the Revolution.[28]

[*Enter* Sir Wilfull Witwoud *in a Country Riding Habit; and Servant to* Lady Wishfort.

Serv. Sir, my Lady's dressing. Here's Company; if you please to walk in, in the mean time.

Sir Wil. Dressing! What, 'tis but Morning here I warrant with you in *London;* we shou'd count it towards Afternoon in our Parts, down in *Shropshire* ——Why then belike my Aunt han't din'd yet——Ha, Friend?   30

Serv. Your Aunt, Sir?

Sir Wil. My Aunt, Sir; yes my Aunt, Sir, and your Lady, Sir; your Lady is my Aunt, Sir—— Why, what, dost thou not know me, Friend? Why then send Somebody here that does. How long hast thou liv'd with thy Lady, Fellow, ha?

Serv. A Week, Sir; longer than any Body in the House, except my Lady's Woman.

Sir Wil. Why then belike thou dost not know thy Lady, if thou seest her, ha, Friend?

---

[26] *Ordinary's paid . . . Psalm:* The ordinary (chaplain of Newgate Prison) went along with prisoners who were to be executed, and he read them a psalm.

[27] *Bartlemew . . . Fair:* Bartholomew Fair was held annually, on August 24, from 1133 to 1855, in West Smithfield.

[28] *The Revolution:* In 1688, Catholic James was dethroned to make way for Protestant William and Mary—The Glorious Revolution; it was bloodless.

Serv. Why truly, Sir, I cannot safely swear to her Face in a Morning, before she is dress'd. 'Tis like I may give a shrewd Guess at her by this time.

Sir Wil. Well, prithee try what thou canst do; if thou canst not guess, enquire her out, dost hear, Fellow? And tell her, her Nephew, *Sir Willfull Witwoud*, is in the House.

Serv. I shall, Sir.

Sir Wil. Hold ye, hear me, Friend; a Word with you in your Ear; prithee who are these Gallants?

Serv. Really, Sir, I can't tell; here come so many here, 'tis hard to know 'em all.   [*Exit Servant.* 10

Sir Wil. Oons[29] this Fellow knows less than a Starling; I don't think a'knows his own Name.

Mrs. Mar. Mr. *Witwoud*, your Brother is not behindhand in forgetfulness ——I fancy he has forgot you too.

Wit. I hope so—— The Devil take him that remembers first, I say.

Sir Wil. Save you, Gentlemen and Lady.

Mrs. Mar. For shame, Mr. *Witwoud*; why won't you speak to him?—— And you, Sir.

Wit. Petulant, speak.

Pet. And you, Sir.   20

Sir Wil. No Offence, I hope.   [*Salutes* Marwood ⟨ i.e., kisses her ⟩.

Mrs. Mar. No, sure, Sir.

Wit. This is a vile Dog, I see that already. No Offence! Ha, ha, ha, to him; to him, *Petulant,* smoke him.[30]

Pet. It seems as if you had come a Journey, Sir; hem, hem.

[*Surveying him round.*

Sir Wil. Very likely, Sir, that it may seem so.

Pet. No Offence, I hope, Sir.

Wit. Smoke the Boots, the Boots; *Petulant,* the Boots; Ha, ha, ha.

Sir Wil. May be not, Sir; thereafter as 'tis meant, Sir.

Pet. Sir, I presume upon the Information of your Boots.   30

Sir Wil. Why, 'tis like you may, Sir: If you are not satisfy'd with the Information of my Boots, Sir, if you will step to the Stable, you may enquire further of my Horse, Sir.

Pet. Your Horse, Sir! Your Horse is an Ass, Sir!

Sir Wil. Do you speak by way of Offence, Sir?

Mrs. Mar. The Gentleman's merry, that's all, Sir——S'life, we shall have a Quarrel betwixt an Horse and an Ass, before they find one another out. You must not take any thing amiss from your Friends, Sir. You are among your Friends here, tho' it may be you don't know it——If I am not mistaken, you are *Sir Wilfull Witwoud*.   40

Sir Wil. Right, Lady; I am *Sir Wilfull Witwoud*, so I write my self; no Offence to any Body, I hope; and Nephew to the *Lady Wishfort* of this Mansion.

Mrs. Mar. Don't you know this Gentleman, Sir?

---

[29] *Oons:* Like 'Swounds, a form of God's wounds.

[30] *Smoke him:* Chaff him (with words).

Smoke could also mean observe, "take in," as it does just following its occurrence here.

Sir Wil. Hum! What, sure 'tis not——Yea by'r Lady, but 'tis——'Sheart I know not whether 'tis or no——Yea, but 'tis, by the *Rekin*.[31] Brother *Anthony!* What, *Tony*, i'faith! What, dost thou not know me? By'r Lady nor I thee, thou art so Becravated, and so Beperriwig'd——'Sheart why do'st not speak? Art thou o'erjoy'd?

Wit. Odso Brother, is it you? Your Servant, Brother.

Sir Wil. Your Servant! Why yours, Sir. Your Servant again——'Sheart, and your Friend and Servant to that——And a—(*puff*) and a flap Dragon[32] for your Service, Sir: And a Hare's Foot, and a Hare's Scut[33] for your Service, Sir; an you be so cold and so courtly!

Wit. No Offence, I hope, Brother.

Sir Wil. 'Sheart, Sir, but there is, and much Offence——A Pox, is this your Inns o' Court Breeding,[34] not to know your Friends and your Relations, your Elders, and your Betters?

Wit. Why, Brother *Wilfull* of *Salop*,[35] you may be as short as a *Shrew[s]bury* Cake,[36] if you please. But I tell you 'tis not modish to know Relations in Town. You think you're in the Country, where great lubberly Brothers slabber and kiss one another when they meet, like a Call of Serjeants[37]——'Tis not the Fashion here; 'tis not indeed, dear Brother.

Sir Wil. The Fashion's a Fool; and you're a Fop, dear Brother. 'Sheart, I've suspected this——By'r Lady I conjectur'd you were a Fop, since you began to change the Stile of your Letters, and write in a scrap of Paper gilt round the Edges, no bigger than a *Subpæna*. I might expect this when you left off, Honour'd Brother; and hoping you are in good Health, and so forth—To begin with a Rat me,[38] Knight, I'm so sick of a last Night's Debauch—O'ds Heart, and then tell a familiar Tale of a Cock and a Bull, and a Whore and a Bottle, and so conclude——You cou'd write News before you were out of your Time, when you liv'd with honest *Pumple Nose* the Attorney of *Furnival's* Inn—You cou'd intreat to be remember'd then to your Friends round the *Rekin*. We could have Gazetts then, and *Dawks's* Letter,[39] and the Weekly Bill,[40] 'till of late Days.

Pet. 'Slife, *Witwoud*, were you ever an Attorney's Clerk? Of the Family of the *Furnivals*. Ha, ha, ha!

Wit. Ay, ay, but that was but for a while. Not long, not long; pshaw, I was not in my own Power then. An Orphan, and this Fellow was my Guardian; ay, ay, I was glad to consent to that Man to come to *London*. He had the disposal of me then, If I had not agreed to that, I might have been bound Prentice

---

[31] *Rekin:* Wrekin, a small mountain in Shropshire and its chief landmark.

[32] *Flap Dragon:* Flap-dragon is a game in which raisins are caught out of burning brandy and extinguished in the player's mouth. The term was also slang for gonorrhea or syphilis.

[33] *Scut:* A short, erect tail.

[34] *Inns o' Court Breeding:* The Inns of Court were four legal societies which trained and admitted young men to the bar.

[35] *Salop:* Shropshire; it occurs usually in the form of the adjective Salopian.

[36] *Shrew[s]bury Cake:* A flat, round, crisp biscuit-like cake.

[37] *A Call of Serjeants:* A group of lawyers of high rank—sergeant-at-law—and of equal seniority in that rank.

[38] *Rat me:* Rot me: God rot me, drat me.

[39] *Dawks's Letter:* A newsletter of the day, printed up in the form of a hand-written letter.

[40] *Weekly Bill:* A list of deaths, usually published by the parish.

to a Felt-maker in *Shrewsbury*; this Fellow would have bound me to a Maker of Felts.

Sir Wil. 'Sheart, and better than to be bound to a Maker of Fops; where, I suppose, you have serv'd your Time; and now you may set up for your self.

Mrs. Mar. You intend to Travel, Sir, as I'm inform'd.

Sir Wil. Belike I may, Madam. I may chance to sail upon the salt Seas, if my Mind hold.

Pet. And the Wind serve.

Sir Wil. Serve or not serve, I shan't ask License of you, Sir; nor the Weather-Cock your Companion. I direct my Discourse to the Lady, Sir; 'Tis like my   10
Aunt may have told you, Madam——— Yes, I have settl'd my Concerns, I may say now, and am minded to see Foreign Parts. If an how that the Peace holds,[41] whereby that is, Taxes abate.

Mrs. Mar. I thought you had designed for *France* at all Adventures.

Sir Wil. I can't tell that; 'tis like I may, and 'tis like I may not. I am some-what dainty in making a Resolution,——because when I make it I keep it. I don't stand shill I, shall I, then; if I say't, I'll do't: But I have Thoughts to tarry a small matter in Town, to learn some what of your *Lingo* first, before I cross the Seas. I'd gladly have a spice of your *French* as they say, whereby to hold Discourse in Foreign Countries.   20

Mrs. Mar. Here's an Academy in Town for that use.

Sir Wil. There is? 'Tis like there may.

Mrs. Mar. No doubt you will return very much improv'd.

Wit. Yes, refin'd like a *Dutch* Skipper from a Whale-fishing.[42]

[*Enter* Lady Wishfort *and* Fainall.

Lady. Nephew, you are welcome.

Sir Wil. Aunt, your Servant.

Fain. Sir *Wilfull*, your most faithful Servant.

Sir Wil. Cousin *Fainall*, give me your Hand.

Lady. Cousin *Witwoud*, your Servant; Mr. *Petulant*, your Servant——— Nephew, you are welcome again. Will you drink any Thing after your   30
Journey, Nephew, before you eat? Dinner's almost ready.

Sir Wil. I'm very well I thank you, Aunt——However, I thank you for your courteous Offer. 'Sheart I was afraid you wou'd have been in the fashion too, and have remember'd to have forgot your Relations. Here's your Cousin *Tony*, belike, I mayn't call him Brother for fear of Offence.

Lady. O he's a Rallier, Nephew—My Cousin's a Wit: And your great Wits always rally their best Friends to chuse. When you have been abroad, Nephew, you'll understand Raillery better.

[*Fain. and* Mrs. Marwood *talk apart.*

Sir Wil. Why then let him hold his Tongue in the mean time; and rail when that day comes.

[*Enter* Mincing.

Minc. Mem, I come to acquaint your Laship that Dinner is impatient.

---

[41] *Peace holds:* The Peace of Ryswick, which in 1697 ended the War of the Grand Alliance; taxes for the war had been high.

[42] *Like . . . Whale-fishing:* Odorous.

Sir Wil. Impatient? Why then belike it won't stay 'till I pull off my Boots. Sweet-heart, can you help me to a pair of Slippers?——My Man's with his Horses, I warrant.

Lady. Fie, fie, Nephew, you wou'd not pull off your Boots here——Go down into the Hall——Dinner shall stay for you——My Nephew's a little unbred, you'll pardon him, Madam,——Gentlemen, will you walk? *Marwood?*

Mrs. Mar. I'll follow you, Madam,—Before Sir *Wilfull* is ready.

[*Manent* Mrs. Marwood *and* Fainall.

Fain. Why then *Foible's* a Bawd, an Errant, Rank, Match-making Bawd. And I it seems am a Husband, a Rank-Husband; and my Wife a very Errant, Rank-Wife,—all in the Way of the *World*. 'Sdeath to be an Anticipated Cuck- 10 old, a Cuckold in Embrio? Sure I was born with budding Antlers like a young Satyre, or a Citizen's Child[43] 'Sdeath to be Out-witted, to be Out-jilted—Out-Matrimony'd,—If I had kept my Speed like a Stag, 'twere somewhat—but to crawl after, with my Horns like a Snail, and be out-stripp'd by my Wife— 'tis scurvy Wedlock.

Mrs. Mar. Then shake it off; you have often wish'd for an Opportunity to part;—and now you have it. But first prevent their Plot,——the half of *Milla-mant's* Fortune is too considerable to be parted with, to a Foe, to *Mirabell.*

Fain. Dam him, that had been mine——had you not made that fond Discovery—— That had been forfeited, had they been Married. My Wife 20 had added Lustre to my Horns, by that Encrease of Fortune; I cou'd have worn 'em tipt with Gold, tho' my forehead had been furnish'd like a Deputy-Lieutenant's Hall.[44]

Mrs. Mar. They may prove a Cap of Maintenance[45] to you still, if you can away with your Wife. And she's no worse than when you had her—— I dare swear she had given up her Game, before she was Marry'd.

Fain. Hum! That may be——She might throw up her Cards; but Ile be hang'd if she did not put Pam[46] in her Pocket.

Mrs. Mar. You Married her to keep you; and if you can contrive to have her keep you better than you expected; why should you not keep her longer 30 than you intended?

Fain. The Means, the Means.

Mrs. Mar. Discover to my Lady your Wife's Conduct; threaten to part with her——My Lady loves her, and will come to any Composition to save her reputation. Take the Opportunity of breaking it, just upon the discovery of this imposture. My Lady will be enraged beyond bounds, and Sacrifice Niece, and Fortune, and all at that Conjuncture. And let me alone to keep her warm; if she shou'd Flag in her part, I will not fail to prompt her.

Fain. Faith, this has an appearance.

Mrs. Mar. I'm sorry I hinted to my Lady to endeavour a match between 40 *Millamant* and Sir *Wilful*; that may be an Obstacle.

[43] *Citizen's Child:* Middle-class wives were supposed to be the prey of aristocratic lovers; it was said that antlers (horns) grew from the cuckold's head (and, it seems, from the head of his wife's illegitimate child).

[44] *Deputy-Lieutenant's Hall:* Presumably with many antlers on its walls.

[45] *Cap of Maintenance:* A cap borne before the sovereign of England at a coronation; also before some mayors.

[46] *Pam:* The Jack of clubs, highest trump card in five-card Loo.

Fain. O for that matter leave me to manage him; I'll disable him for that, he will drink like a *Dane*: After Dinner, I'll set his Hand in.[47]

Mrs. Mar. Well, how do you stand affected towards your Lady?

Fain. Why faith I'm thinking of it.——Let me see——I am married already; so that's over——My Wife has plaid the Jade with me——Well, that's over too——I never lov'd her, or if I had, why that wou'd have been over too by this time——Jealous of her I cannot be, for I am certain; so there's an end of Jealousie. Weary of her, I am and shall be——No, there's no end of that; No, no, that were too much to hope. Thus far concerning my repose. Now for my Reputation,——As to my own, I married not for it; so that's out of the Question.——And as to my Part in my Wife's——Why she had parted with hers before; so bringing none to me, she can take none from me; 'tis against all rule of Play, that I should lose to one, who has not wherewithal to stake.

Mrs. Mar. Besides you forget, Marriage is honourable.

Fain. Hum! Faith and that's well thought on; Marriage is honourable, as you say; and if so, wherefore should Cuckoldom be a Discredit, being deriv'd from so honourable a root?

Mrs. Mar. Nay I know not; if the Root be honourable, why not the Branches?

Fain. So, so, why this point's clear.—Well how do we proceed?

Mrs. Mar. I will contrive a Letter which shall be deliver'd to my Lady at the time when that Rascal who is to act Sir *Rowland* is with her. It shall come as from an unknown hand——for the less I appear to know of the truth, the better I can play the Incendiary. Besides, I would not have *Foible* provok'd if I could help it,——because you know she knows some Passages——Nay I expect all will come out——But let the Mine be sprung first and then I care not if I am discover'd.

Fain. If the worst come to the worst,——I'll turn my Wife to Grass——I have already a deed of Settlement of the best part of her Estate; which I wheadl'd out of her; and that you shall partake at least.

Mrs. Mar. I hope you are convinc'd that I hate *Mirabell*; Now you'll be no more Jealous.

Fain. Jealous, no,——by this Kiss——let Husbands be Jealous; but let the Lover still believe: Or if he doubt, let it be only to endear his pleasure, and prepare the Joy that follows, when he proves his Mistress true. But let Husband's Doubts convert to endless Jealousie; or if they have Belief, let it Corrupt to Superstition, and blind Credulity. I am single, and will herd no more with 'em. True, I wear the Badge; but I'll disown the Order. And since I take my leave of 'em, I care not if I leave 'em a common Motto to their common Crest.

> All Husbands must, or Pain, or Shame, endure;
> The Wise too jealous are, Fools too secure.   [*Exeunt.*

---

[47] *Set his Hand in:* Get him going.

Act IV Scene I

SCENE *continues*

[*Enter* Lady Wishfort *and* Foible.

Lady. Is Sir *Rowland* coming say'st thou, *Foible*? and are things in Order?

Foib. Yes, Madam. I have put Wax-Lights in the Sconces: and plac'd the Footmen in a Row in the Hall, in their best Liveries, with the Coachman and Postilion to fill up the Equipage.

Lady. Have you pullvill'd[1] the Coach-man and Postilion, that they may not stink of the Stable, when Sir *Rowland* comes by?

Foib. Yes, Madam.

Lady. And are the Dancers and the Musick ready, that he may be entertain'd in all Points with Correspondence to his Passion?

Foib. All is ready, Madam.   10

Lady. And——well——and how do I look, *Foible*?

Foib. Most killing well, Madam.

Lady. Well, and how shall I receive him? In what Figure shall I give his Heart the first Impression? There is a great deal in the first Impression. Shall I sit?—— No, I won't sit——I'll walk——ay I'll walk from the door upon his entrance; and then turn full upon him——No, that will be too sudden. I'll lie——ay, I'll lie down——I'll receive him in my little dressing Room; there's a Couch—— Yes, yes, I'll give the first Impression on a Couch——I won't lie neither, but loll and lean upon one Elbow; with one Foot a little dangling off, Jogging in a thoughtful way——Yes——and then as soon as he appears, start, ay, start and   20 be surpriz'd, and rise to meet him in a pretty disorder——Yes——O, nothing is more alluring than a Levee from a Couch in some Confusion——It shews the Foot to advantage, and furnishes with Blushes, and recomposing Airs beyond Comparison. Hark! There's a Coach.

Foib. 'Tis he, Madam.

Lady. O dear, has my Nephew made his Addresses to *Millamant*? I order'd him.

Foib. Sir *Wilfull* is set in to Drinking, *Madam*, in the Parlour.

Lady. Ods my Life, I'll send him to her. Call her down, *Foible*; being her hither. I'll send him as I go——When they are together, then come to me,   30 *Foible*, that I may not be too long alone with Sir *Rowland*.   [*Exit.*

[*Enter* Mrs. Millamant *and* Mrs. Fainall.

Foib. Madam, I stay'd here, to tell your Ladyship that Mr. *Mirabell* has waited this half Hour for an Opportunity to talk with you. Tho' my Lady's Orders were to leave you and Sir *Wilfull* together. Shall I tell Mr. *Mirabell* that you are at leisure?

Milla. No——What wou'd the dear Man have? I am thoughtful, and wou'd amuse my self,——bid him come another time.

> There never yet was Woman made,
>   Nor shall, but to be curs'd.[2]   [*Repeating and walking about.*

That's hard!   40

---

[1] *Pullvill'd:* Pulvil is a cosmetic or perfumed powder.

[2] *. . . but to be curs'd:* First lines of a poem by Sir John Suckling.

Mrs. Fain. You are very fond of Sir *John Suckling* to day, *Millamant*, and the Poets.

Milla. He? Ay, and filthy Verses——So I am.

Foib. Sir Wilfull is coming, Madam. Shall I send Mr. *Mirabell* away?

Milla. Ay, if you please, *Foible*, send him away,——Or send him hither, ——just as you will, dear *Foible.*——I think I'll see him——Shall I? Ay, let the Wretch come.

Thyrsis, a Youth of the Inspir'd Train.[3] [*Repeating.*

Dear *Fainall*, Entertain *Sir Wilfull*——Thou hast Philosophy to undergo a Fool, thou art Married and hast Patience——I would confer with my own Thoughts.

Mrs. Fain. I am oblig'd to you, that you would make me your Proxy in this Affair; but I have business of my own.

[*Enter* Sir Wilfull.

O *Sir Wilfull*; you are come at the Critical Instant. There's your Mistress up to the Ears in Love and Contemplation; pursue your Point, now or never.

Sir Wil. [*This while* Milla. *walks about Repeating to her self.*] Yes; my Aunt will have it so,——I would gladly have been encourag'd with a Bottle or two, because I'm somewhat wary at first, before I am acquainted;——But I hope, after a time, I shall break my mind——that is upon further acquaintance ——So for the present, Cousin, I'll take my leave——If so be you'll be so kind to make my Excuse, I'll return to my Company——

Mrs. Fain. O fie, *Sir Wilfull!* What, you must not be Daunted.

Sir Wil. Daunted, no, that's not it, it is not so much for that——for if so be that I set on't, I'll do't. But only for the present, 'tis sufficient 'till further acquaintance, that's all——your Servant.

Mrs. Fain. Nay, I'll swear you shall never lose so favourable an opportunity, if I can help it. I'll leave you together, and lock the Door. [*Exit.*

Sir Wil. Nay, nay Cozen,—I have forgot my Gloves,——What d'ee do? 'Sheart a'has lock'd the Door indeed; I think——Nay, Cozen *Fainall*, open the Door——Pshaw, what a Vixon Trick is this?——Nay, now a'has seen me too——Cozen, I made bold to pass thro' as it were——I think this Door's inchanted——

Milla. [*Repeating.*]

I prithee spare me, gentle Boy,
Press me no more for that slight Toy.[4]

Sir Wil. Anan? Cozen, your Servant.

Milla.——*That foolish Trifle of a Heart—Sir Wilfull?*

Sir Wil. Yes——your Servant. No Offence I hope, Cozen.

Milla. [*Repeating.*]

I swear it will not do its Part,
Tho' thou dost thine, employ'st thy Power and Art.

Natural, easie *Suckling!*

---

[3] . . . *the Inspir'd Train:* First lines of Edmund Waller's *The Story of Phoebus and Daphne, Applied.*

[4] . . . *that slight Toy:* These two lines, together with the next three lines of verse Millamant speaks, make up the first stanza of a Suckling poem; it has no title.

Sir Wil. Anan?⁵ *Suckling?* No such Suckling neither, Cozen, nor Stripling: I thank Heav'n, I'm no Minor.

Milla. Ah Rustick, ruder than *Gothick.*⁶

Sir Wil. Well, well, I shall understand your *Lingo* one of these Days, Cozen; in the mean while I must answer in plain *English.*

Milla. Have you any business with me, *Sir Wilfull?*

Sir Wil. Not at present, Cozen,——Yes, I made bold to see, to come and know if that how you were dispos'd to fetch a walk this Evening, if so be that I might not be troublesome, I would have sought a walk⁷ with you.

Milla. A Walk? What then?   10

Sir Wil. Nay, nothing——Only for the walk's sake, that's all——

Milla. I nauseate Walking; 'tis a Country diversion; I loathe the Country and every thing that relates to it.

Sir Wil. Indeed! Hah! Look ye, look ye, you do? Nay, 'tis like you may ——Here are choice of Pastimes here in Town, as Plays and the like; that must be confess'd indeed——

Milla. Ah *l'etourdie!*⁸ I hate the Town too.

Sir Wil. Dear Heart, that's much——Hah? that you should hate 'em both? Hah! 'tis like you may; there are some can't relish the Town, and others can't away with the Country,——'tis like you may be one of those, Cozen.   20

Milla. Ha, ha, ha. Yes, 'tis like I may.——You have nothing further to say to me?

Sir Wil. Not at present, Cozen.——'Tis like when I have an Opportunity to be more private,——I may break my mind in some measure——I conjecture you partly guess——However that's as time shall try,——But spare to speak and spare to speed, as they say.

Milla. If it is of no great Importance, *Sir Wilfull,* you will oblige me to leave me: I have just now a little business.——

Sir Wil. Enough, enough, Cozen: Yes, yes, all a case——When you're dispos'd, when you're dispos'd. Now's as well as another time; and another   30 time as well as now. All's one for that,——Yes, yes, if your Concerns call you, there's no hast; it will keep cold as they say——Cozen, your Servant.——I think this door's lock'd.

Milla. You may go this way, Sir.

Sir Wil. Your Servant, then with your leave I'll return to my Company.
[Exit.

Milla. Ay, ay; ha, ha, ha.
Like Phœbus sung the no less am'rous Boy.⁹
[Enter Mirabell.

Mira.—*Like* Daphne *she, as Lovely and as Coy.*

Do you lock your self up from me, to make my search more Curious?¹⁰ Or is this pretty Artifice Contriv'd, to Signify that here the Chace must end, and   40 my pursuit be Crown'd, for you can fly no further?——

---

⁵ *Anan:* "Beg your pardon! Sir! Eh?" OED.

⁶ *Gothick:* Barbarous, rude, in bad taste.

⁷ *Sought a walk:* the copy text gives *fought,* not *sought.*

⁸ *Ah l'étourdie:* Ah, the giddy-headed people.

⁹ . . . *am'rous Boy:* The third line of Waller's poem, n. 3.

¹⁰ *Curious:* Difficult.

Milla. Vanity! No——I'll fly and be follow'd to the last Moment, tho' I am upon the very Verge of Matrimony, I expect you shou'd solicit me as much as if I were wavering at the grate of a Monastery, with one foot over the threshold. I'll be solicited to the very last, nay and afterwards.

Mira. What, after the last?

Milla. O, I should think I was poor and had nothing to bestow, if I were reduc'd to an Inglorious ease; and freed from the Agreeable fatigues of solicitation.

Mira. But do not you know, that when Favours are conferr'd upon Instant and tedious Solicitation, that they diminish in their value, and that both the   1(
Giver loses the grace, and the Receiver lessens his Pleasure?

Milla. It may be in Things of common Application; but never sure in Love. O, I hate a Lover that can dare to think he draws a moment's air, Independent on the Bounty of his Mistress. There is not so Impudent a thing in Nature, as the sawcy look of an assured man, Confident of Success. The Pedantick arrogance of a very Husband, has not so Pragmatical[11] an Air. Ah! I'll never marry, unless I am first made sure of my will and pleasure.

Mira. Wou'd you have 'em both before Marriage? Or will you be contented with the first now, and stay for the other 'till after grace?[12]

Milla. Ah! don't be Impertinent——My dear Liberty, shall I leave thee?   2(
my faithful Solitude, my darling Contemplation, must I bid you then Adieu? Ay-h adieu——My morning thoughts, agreeable wakings, indolent slumbers, all ye *douceurs*,[13] ye *Someils du Matin*,[14] *adieu.*——I can't do't, 'tis more than impossible——Positively, *Mirabell*, I'll lie a-bed in a morning as long as I please.

Mira. Then I'll get up in a morning as early as I please.

Milla. Ah? Idle Creature, get up when you will——And d'ee hear, I won't be call'd names after I'm Married; positively I won't be call'd Names.

Mira. Names!

Milla. Ay, as Wife, Spouse, My dear, Joy, Jewel, Love, Sweet-heart, and the rest of that Nauseous Cant, in which Men and their Wives are so fulsomly   3(
familiar,—I shall never bear that——Good *Mirabell*, don't let us be familiar or fond, nor kiss before folks, like my Lady *Fadler*[15] and Sir *Francis*: Nor goe to *Hide-Park* together the first *Sunday* in a New Chariot, to provoke Eyes and Whispers; And then never be seen there together again; as if we were proud of one another the first Week, and asham'd of one another for ever After. Let us never Visit together, nor go to a Play together; But let us be very strange[16] and well-bred: Let us be as strange as if we had been married a great while; and as well-bred as if we were not marri'd at all.

Mira. Have you any more Conditions to offer? Hitherto your demands are pretty reasonable.   4(

Milla. Trifles,——As Liberty to pay and receive visits to and from whom I please; to write and receive Letters, without Interrogatories or wry Faces on your part; to wear what I please; and choose Conversation with regard only

---

[11] *Pragmatical:* Self-important.
[12] *Grace:* The prayer with which the marriage ceremony is ended.
[13] *Douceurs:* Relaxing pleasures.

[14] *Someils du Matin:* Morning slumbers.
[15] *Lady Fadler:* Nettleton and Case, p. 335, give Lady Fondler.
[16] *Strange:* Distant.

to my own taste; to have no obligation upon me to converse with Wits that I don't like, because they are your acquaintance; or to be intimate with Fools, because they may be your Relations. Come to Dinner when I please; dine in my dressing-room when I'm out of humour, without giving a reason. To have my Closet[17] Inviolate; to be sole Empress of my Tea-Table, which you must never presume to approach without first asking leave. And, lastly, where ever I am, you shall always knock at the door before you come in. These Articles subscrib'd, If I continue to endure you a little longer, I may by degrees dwindle into a Wife.

Mira. Your Bill of Fare is something advanc'd in this latter account. Well,   10
have I Liberty to offer Conditions——That when you are dwindled into a Wife, I may not be beyond Measure enlarg'd into a Husband.

Milla. You have free leave; propose your utmost, speak and spare not.

Mira. I thank you. *I[m]primis* then, I Covenant that your acquaintance be general; that you admit no sworn Confident, or Intimate of your own Sex; No she friend to skreen her affairs under your Countenance, and tempt you to make trial of a mutual Secresie. No Decoy-duck to wheadle you a *fop-scrambling*[18] to the Play in a Mask——then bring you home in a pretended fright, when you think you shall be found out——And rail at me for missing the Play, and disappointing the Frolick which you had to pick me up and prove   20
my Constancy.

Milla. Detestable *Imprimis!* I go to the Play in a Mask!

Mira. *Item,* I Article[19] that you continue to like your own Face, as long as I shall: And while it passes Current with me, that you endeavour not to new Coin it. To which end, together with all Vizards for the day, I prohibit all Masks for the Night, made of oil'd-skins, and I know not what——Hog's Bones, Hare's Gall, Pig Water, and the marrow of a roasted Cat. In short, I forbid all Commerce with the Gentlewoman in *what-de-call-it* Court.[20] *Item,* I shut my doors against all Bauds with Baskets, and penny-worths of *Muslin, China, Fans, Atlases*[21] &c.——*Item,* when you shall be Breeding——   30

Milla. Ah! name it not.

Mira. Which may be presum'd with a blessing on our endeavours——

Milla. Odious endeavours!

Mira. I denounce against all strait Laceing, squeezing for a Shape, 'till you mold my boy's head like a Sugar-loaf; and instead of a Man-child, make me Father to a Crooked-billet. Lastly, to the Dominion of the *Tea Table* I submit.
——But with *proviso,* that you exceed not in your province; but restrain your self to Native and Simple *Tea Table* drinks, as *Tea, Chocolate,* and *Coffee.* As likewise to Genuine and Authoriz'd *Tea Table* Talk——such as mending of Fashions, spoiling Reputations, railing at absent Friends, and so forth——but   40
that on no account you encroach upon the men's prerogative, and presume to to drink healths, or toast fellows; for prevention of which I banish all *Foreign Forces,* all *Auxiliaries* to the *Tea Table,* as *Orange-Brandy,* all *Anniseed, Cinamon,*

---

[17] *Closet:* A small room.
[18] *Fop-scrambling:* Chasing after fops.
[19] *I Article:* I require.
[20] *Gentlewoman . . . Court:* Nettleton

and Case, p. 335, suggest ". . . a seller of cosmetics well-known in her day."
[21] *Atlases:* "Satins flowered with gold or silver." *OED.*

Citron and *Barbado's Waters*, together with *Ratafia*, and the most noble Spirit of *Clary*.[22]———But for *Couslip-Wine*, *Poppy-Water*, and all *Dormitives*, those I allow.———These *Proviso's* admitted, in other things I may prove a tractable and complying Husband.

Milla. O horrid *Proviso's!* filthy strong-Waters! I toast fellows! Odious Men! I hate your odious Proviso's.

Mira. Then we're agreed. Shall I kiss your hand upon the Contract? And here comes one to be a witness to the Sealing of the Deed.

[*Enter* Mrs. Fainall.

Milla. Fainall, what shall I do? Shall I have him? I think I must have him.

Mrs. Fain. Ay, ay, take him, take him, what shou'd you do?   10

Milla. Well then———I'll take my death I'm in a horrid fright——— *Fainall*, I shall never say it———Well———I think———I'll endure you.

Mrs. Fain. Fy, fy, have him, have him, and tell him so in plain terms: For I am sure you have a mind to him.

Milla. Are you? I think I have———and the horrid Man looks as if he thought so too———Well, you ridiculous thing you, I'll have you———I won't be kiss'd, nor I won't be thank'd———here, kiss my hand tho'——— So, hold your tongue now, don't say a word.

Mrs. Fain. Mirabell, there's a Necessity for your obedience;———You have neither time to talk nor stay. My Mother is coming; and in my Conscience   20 if she shou'd see you, wou'd fall into fits, and may be not recover time enough to return to Sir *Rowland*, who, as *Foible* tells me, is in a fair way to succeed. Therefore spare your Extacies for another occasion, and slip down the back stairs, where *Foible* waits to consult you.

Milla. Ay, go, go. In the mean time I suppose you have said something to please me.

Mira. I am all Obedience.   [*Exit* Mira.

Mrs. Fain. Yonder Sir *Wilfull's* drunk, and so noisy that my Mother has been forc'd to leave Sir *Rowland* to appease him; but he answers her only with Singing and Drinking———What they may have done by this time I know   30 not; but *Petulant* and he were upon quarrelling as I came by.

Milla. Well, if *Mirabell* shou'd not make a good Husband, I am a lost thing; ———for I find I love him violently.

Mrs Fain. So it seems; for you mind not what's said to you.———If you doubt him, you had best take up with Sir *Wilfull*.

Milla. How can you name that super-annuated Lubber? Foh!

[*Enter* Witwoud *from drinking*.

Mrs. Fain. So, is the Fray made up, that you have left 'em?

Wit. Left 'em? I cou'd stay no longer———I have laugh'd like ten Christnings———I am tipsy with laughing———If I had staid any longer I shou'd have burst,—I must have been let out and piec'd in the sides like an unsiz'd Camlet[23]   40

---

[22] *Clary:* Clary was a mild beverage, including wine and honey; clary-water, that "most noble spirit," was a strong cordial.

[23] *Camlet:* Originally camlet was a costly eastern fabric made of wool and silk; the turn here derives from the practice of attempting to approximate the qualities of camlet by cheap means.

—Yes, yes, the fray is compos'd; my Lady came in like a *Noli prosequi,*[24] and stopp'd the proceedings.

Milla. What was the dispute?

Wit. That's the Jest; there was no dispute. They cou'd neither of 'em speak for rage, and so fell a sputt'ring at one another like two roasting Apples.

[*Enter* Petulant *drunk.*

Now, *Petulant,* all's over, all's well. Gad my head begins to whim it about[25] ———Why dost thou not speak? Thou art both as drunk and as mute as a Fish.

Pet. Look you, Mrs. *Millamant*——if you can love me, dear Nymph— say it—and that's the Conclusion——Pass on, or pass off,——that's all.

Wit. Thou hast utter'd *Volumes, Folios,* in less than *Decimo Sexto,*[26] my Dear   10 *Lacedemonian.*[27] Sirrah, *Petulant,* thou art an Epitomizer of words.

Pet. Witwoud———You are an annihilator of sense.

Wit. Thou art a retailer of Phrases; and dost deal in Remnants of Remnants, like a Maker of Pincushions—thou art in truth (Metaphorically speaking) a speaker of short-hand.

Pet. Thou art (without a figure) Just one half of an Ass, and *Baldwin*[28] yon- der, thy half Brother, is the rest.——A *gemini*[29] of Asses split wou'd make just four of you.

Wit. Thou dost bite, my dear Mustard-seed; kiss me for that.

Pet. Stand off———I'll kiss no more Males——I have kiss'd your *twin*   20 yonder in a humour of reconciliation, 'till he (*hiccup*) rises upon my stomach like a Radish.

Milla. Eh! filthy Creature———What was the quarrel?

Pet. There was no quarrel———There might have been a quarrel.

Wit. If there had been words enow between 'em to have express'd provo- cation, they had gone together by the Ears like a pair of Castanets.

Pet. You were the Quarrel.

Milla. Me!

Pet. If I have a humour to quarrel, I can make less matters conclude pre- mises.———If you are not handsom, what then; if I have a humour to prove   30 it? If I shall have my Reward, say so; if not, fight for your Face that next time your self——I'll go sleep.

Wit. Do, rap thy self up like a *Wood-louse,* and dream Revenge—And hear me, if thou canst learn to write by to-morrow Morning, Pen me a Challenge— I'll carry it for thee.

Pet. Carry your Mistress's *Monkey a Spider*——go flea Dogs, and read Romances———I'll go to bed to my Maid.   [*Exit.*

Mrs. Fain. He's horridly drunk——— How came you all in this pickle?

Wit. A plot, a plot, to get rid of the Knight,———Your Husband's Advice; but he sneak'd off.   40

[*Enter* Lady, *and* Sir Wilfull *drunk.*

---

[24] *Noli prosequi: Nolle prosequi,* in law an entry denoting that the prosecutor will proceed no farther.

[25] *Whim it about:* Toss and spin.

[26] *Decimo Sexto:* A very small volume.

[27] *Lacedemonian:* Spartan; Spartans were known for their very few words.

[28] *Baldwin:* The name of an ass in beast epic.

[29] *Gemini:* A couple.

Lady. Out upon't, out upon't, at years of Discretion, and Comport your self at this Rantipole[30] rate.

Sir Wil. No Offence, Aunt.

Lady. Offence? As I'm a Person, I'm asham'd of you—Fogh! how you stink of Wine! D'ye think my Niece will ever endure such a *Borachio!*[31] you're an absolute *Borachio.*

Sir Wil. Borachio!

Lady. At a time when you shou'd commence an Amour, and put your best foot foremost————

Sir Wil. 'Sheart, an you grutch me your Liquor, make a Bill————Give   10
me more drink, and take my Purse.

[*Sings.*]   *Pry'thee fill me the Glass*
                          'Till it laugh in my Face,
                   With Ale that is Potent and Mellow;
                       He that Whines for a Lass
                           Is an Ignorant Ass,
                   For a Bumper *has not its Fellow.*

But if you wou'd have me Marry my Cosen,—Say the Word, and I'll do't
————*Wilfull* will do't, that's the Word————*Wilfull* will do't, that's my
Crest————my Motto I have forgot.   20

Lady. My Nephew's a little overtaken, Cosen————but 'tis with drinking your
Health————O' my Word you are oblig'd to him.

Sir Wil. In vino veritas,[32] Aunt:————If I drunk your Health To-day, Cosen
————I am a *Borachio.* But if you have a mind to be Marry'd, say the Word,
and send for the Piper; *Wilfull* will do't. If not, dust it away,[33] and let's
have t'other round————*Tony,* Ods heart where's *Tony?*————*Tony's* an honest
fellow; but he spits after a Bumper, and that's a Fault.

[*Sings.*]   *We'll drink and we'll never have done, Boys,*
                   Put the glass then around with the Sun, Boys,
                   Let Apollo's *Example invite us;*   30
                       For he's drunk ev'ry Night,
                       And that makes him so bright,
                   That he's able next Morning to light us.

The Sun's a good Pimple,[34] an honest Soaker; he has a Cellar at your *Antipodes.*[35] If I travel, Aunt, I touch at your *Antipodes*————Your *Antipodes* are a good
rascally sort of topsy turvy Fellows— If I had a Bumper, I'd stand upon my
Head and drink a Health to 'em————A Match or no Match, Cosen, with the hard
Name————Aunt, *Wilfull* will do't. If she has her Maidenhead, let her look to't;
if she has not, let her keep her own Counsel in the mean time, and cry out at
the Nine Month's End.   40

Milla. Your Pardon, Madam, I can stay no longer————Sir *Wilfull* grows
very powerful. Egh! how he smells! I shall be overcome if I stay. Come,
Cosen.   [*Exit* Milla. *and* Mrs. Fain.

---

[30] *Rantipole:* Reckless.
[31] *Borachio:* Boracho, Spanish for a leather bag for wine; a drunkard.
[32] *In vino veritas:* There is truth in wine; that is, one who drinks tells the truth.

[33] *Dust it away:* Drink it down.
[34] *A good Pimple:* A good fellow.
[35] *Antipodes:* The parts of the globe (or the people) located directly opposite to one.

Lady. Smells! he would poison a Tallow-chandler and his Family. Beastly Creature, I know not what to do with him——Travel quoth-a; ay, travel, travel, get thee gone, get thee but far enough, to the *Saracens*, or the *Tartars*, or the *Turks*—for thou art not fit to live in a Christian Commonwealth, thou beastly Pagan.

Sir Wil. *Turks*, no; no *Turks*, Aunt: Your *Turks* are Infidels, and believe not in the Grape. Your *Mahometan*, your *Mussulman* is a dry Stinkard—No Offence, Aunt. My Map says that your *Turk* is not so honest a Man as your Christian——I cannot find by the Map that your *Mufti*[36] is Orthodox—Whereby it is a plain Case, that Orthodox is a hard Word, Aunt, and (*hiccup*)   10
Greek for Claret.

[*Sings.*] 　　　To drink is a Christian Diversion,
　　　　　　　Unknown to the Turk or the Persian:
　　　　　　　　Let Mahometan Fools
　　　　　　　　Live by Heathenish Rules,
　　　　　　　And be damn'd over Tea-cups and Coffee.
　　　　　　　　But let British Lads sing,
　　　　　　　　Crown a Health to the King,
　　　　　　　And a Fig for your Sultan and Sophy.[37]

Ah, *Tony!* 　　　　　　　　　[*Enter* Foible *and whispers* Lady.   20

Lady. Sir *Rowland* impatient? Good lack! what shall I do with this beastly Tumbril?[38]——Go lie down and sleep, you Sot——Or as I'm a person, I'll have you bastinado'd with Broom-sticks. Call up the Wenches.

　　　　　　　　　　　　　　　　　　　　[*Exit* Foib.

Sir Wil. Ahey! Wenches, where are the Wenches?

Lady. Dear Cosen *Witwoud*, get him away, and you will bind me to you inviolably. I have an Affair of moment that invades me with some precipitation—You will oblige me to all Futurity.

Wit. Come, Knight—Pox on him, I don't know what to say to him—Will you go to a Cock-match?

Sir Wil. With a Wench, *Tony*? Is she a shake-bag,[39] Sirrah? Let me bite   30
your Cheek for that.

Wit. Horrible! he has a Breath like a Bagpipe——Ay, ay, come, will you March, my *Salopian*?[40]

Sir Wil. Lead on, little *Tony*—I'll follow thee, my *Anthony*, My *Tantony*. Sirrah, thou shalt be my *Tantony*, and I'll be thy *Pig*.[41]

—*And a Fig for your* Sultan *and* Sophy.　　[*Exit singing with* Witwoud.

Lady. This will never do. It will never make a Match:
—At least before he has been abroad.

　　　　　[*Enter* Waitwell *disguis'd as for Sir* Rowland.

Lady. Dear Sir *Rowland*, I am Confounded with Confusion at the Retrospection of my own rudeness,—I have more pardons to ask than the *Pope*   40

---

[36] *Mufti:* A Mohammedan advisor in religious law.
[37] *Sophy:* A western title for one of the Persian Safavi dynasty.
[38] *Tumbril:* A cart or wagon.

[39] *Shake-bag:* A large fighting cock.
[40] *Salopian:* A native of Shropshire; see III, n. 35.
[41] *Tantony:* Anthony, patron saint of swineherds.

distributes in the Year of *Jubilee*.[42] But I hope where there is likely to be so near an alliance,—we may unbend the severity of *Decorum*—and dispense with a little Ceremony.

Wait. My Impatience, Madam, is the effect of my transport;—and 'till I have the possession of your adoreable Person, I am tantaliz'd on a rack; and do but hang, Madam, on the tenter of Expectation.

Lady. You have Excess of gallantry, Sir *Rowland*; and press things to a Conclusion with a most prevailing Vehemence.—But a day or two for Decency of Marriage.——

Wait. For Decency of Funeral, Madam. The Delay will break my Heart ——or, if that shou'd fail, I shall be Poyson'd. My Nephew will get an inkling of my Designs, and Poison me,—and I wou'd willingly starve him before I die—I wou'd gladly go out of the World with that Satisfaction.—— That wou'd be some Comfort to me, If I cou'd but live so long as to be reveng'd on that Unnatural *Viper*.

Lady. Is he so Unnatural, say you? Truely I wou'd Contribute much both to the saving of your Life, and the accomplishment of your revenge—— Not that I respect[43] my self; tho' he has been a perfidious wretch to me.

Wait. Perfidious to you !

Lady. O Sir *Rowland*, the hours that he has dy'd away at my Feet, the Tears that he has shed, the Oaths that he has sworn, the Palpitations that he has felt, the Trances and the Tremblings, the Ardors and the Ecstacies, the Kneelings and the Risings, the Heart-heavings and the Hand-Gripings, the Pangs and the Pathetick Regards of his protesting Eyes ! Oh no memory can Register.

Wait. What, my Rival ! Is the Rebell my Rival? a'dies.

Lady. No, don't kill him at once, Sir *Rowland*, starve him gradually inch by inch.

Wait. I'll do't. In three weeks he shall be bare-foot; in a month out at knees with begging an *Alms*——He shall starve upward and upward 'till he has nothing living but his head, and then go out in a stink like a Candle's end upon a Saveall.[44]

Lady. Well, Sir *Rowland*, you have the way,——You are no Novice in the Labyrinth of Love——You have the Clue——But as I am a Person, Sir *Rowland*, you must not attribute my yielding to any sinister appetite, or indigestion of Widowhood; nor Impute my Complacency to any Lethargy of Continence—— I hope you do not think me prone to any Iteration of Nuptials.——

Wait. Far be it from me——

Lady. If you do, I protest I must recede——or think that I have made a prostitution of decorums; but in the Vehemence of Compassion, and to save the Life of a Person of so much Importance——

Wait. I esteem it so——

Lady. Or else you wrong my Condescension——

Wait. I do not, I do not——

---

[42] *Year of Jubilee:* A year of official indulgence, in which slaves were freed or sinners forgiven, proclaimed every fifty (or twenty-five) years.

[43] *Respect:* Regard.

[44] *Saveall:* A candle stand with a short spur for holding the candle until it burned to the end.

Lady. Indeed you do.

Wait. I do not, fair Shrine of Vertue.

Lady. If you think the least scruple of Carnality was an Ingredient——

Wait. Dear Madam, no. You are all *Camphire*[45] and *Frankincense*, all *Chastity* and *Odour.*

Lady. Or that——

[*Enter* Foible.

Foib. Madam, the Dancers are ready, and there's one with a Letter, who must deliver it into your own hands.

Lady. Sir *Rowland*, will you give me leave? Think favourably, Judge Candidly, and conclude you have found a Person who would suffer racks in   10
honour's cause, dear Sir *Rowland*, and will wait on you Incessantly.

[*Exit.*

Wait. Fie, fie——What a Slavery have I undergone? Spouse, hast thou any *Cordial?* I want *Spirits.*

Foib. What a washy Rogue art thou, to pant thus for a Quarter of an hour's lying and swearing to a fine Lady?

Wait. O, she is the *Antidote* to desire. Spouse, thou wilt fare the worse for't
——I shall have no appetite to iteration of Nuptials——this eight and forty Hours——By this Hand I'd rather be a *Chairman* in the *Dogdays*——than act Sir *Rowland* 'till this time To morrow.

[*Enter* Lady *with a Letter.*

Lady. Call in the Dancers;——Sir *Rowland*, we'll sit, if you please, and see   20
the Entertainment.   [*Dance.*

Now, with your permission, Sir *Rowland*, I will peruse my Letter——I would open it in your presence, because I would not make you Uneasie. If it should make you Uneasie, I would burn it——speak if it do's——but you may see the Superscription is like a Woman's Hand.

Foib. By Heav'n! *Mrs. Marwood's,* I know it,——my Heart akes—get it from her——   [*To him.*

Wait. A Woman's Hand? No, Madam, that's no Woman's Hand, I see that already. That's some body whose throat must be cut.

Lady. Nay, Sir *Rowland*, since you give me a proof of your Passion by your   30
Jealousie, I promise you I'll make a return, by a frank Communication——
You shall see it——we'll open it together——look you here.

[*Reads.*]——*Madam, though unknown to you* [Look you there, 'tis from no body that I know.]——*I have that honour for your Character, that I think my self oblig'd to let you know you are abus'd. He who pretends to be Sir* Rowland *is a cheat and a Rascal*——

Oh Heavens! what's this?

Foib. Unfortunate, all's ruin'd.

Wait. How, how, let me see, let me see——[*Reading.*] *A Rascal and disguis'd and subborn'd for that Imposture,*——O villany! O villany!——*by the Contrivance*   40
of——

Lady. I shall faint, I shall die, oh!

[45] *Camphire:* Nettleton and Case, p. 339, say, "Used during this period as an   antaphrodisiac."

Foib. Say 'tis your Nephew's Hand.——Quickly, his plot, swear, swear it.—— [*To him.*

Wait. Here's a Villain! *Madam,* don't you perceive it, don't you see it?

Lady. Too well, too well. I have seen too much.

Wait. I told you at first I knew the hand——A Woman's hand? The Rascal writes a sort of a large hand; your *Roman* Hand——I saw there was a throat to be cut presently. If he were my Son, as he is my Nephew, I'd Pistoll him——

Foib. O Treachery! But are you sure, Sir *Rowland,* it is his writing?

Wait. Sure! Am I here? do I live? do I love this Pearl of *India?* I have twenty   10
Letters in my Pocket from him, in the same Character.

Lady. How!

Foib. O what Luck it is, Sir *Rowland,* that you were present at this Juncture! This was the business that brought Mr. *Mirabell* disguis'd to *Madam Millamant* this Afternoon. I thought something was contriving, when he stole by me and would have hid his Face.

Lady. How, how!——I heard the Villain was in the house indeed; and now I remember, my Niece went away abruptly, when *Sir Wilfull* was to have made his addresses.

Foib. Then, then Madam, Mr. *Mirabell* waited for her in her Chamber; but   20
I would not tell your Ladyship to discompose you when you were to receive Sir *Rowland.*

Wait. Enough, his date is short.

Foib. No, good Sir *Rowland,* don't incurr the Law.

Wait. Law! I care not for Law. I can but die, and 'tis in a good cause—— My Lady shall be satisfy'd of my Truth and Innocence, tho' it cost me my life.

Lady. No, dear Sir *Rowland,* don't fight, if you should be kill'd I must never shew my face; or hang'd,——O consider my Reputation, Sir *Rowland.*—— No you shan't fight,——I'll go in and Examine my Niece; I'll make her Confess. I conjure you, Sir *Rowland,* by all your Love not to fight.   30

Wait. I am charm'd, Madam, I obey. But some proof you must let me give you; I'll go for a black box, which Contains the Writings of my whole Estate, and deliver that into your hands.

Lady. Ay dear Sir *Rowland,* that will be some Comfort, bring the Blackbox.

Wait. And may I presume to bring a Contract to be sign'd this Night? May I hope so farr?

Lady. Bring what you will; but come alive, pray come alive. O this is a happy discovery.

Wait. Dead or alive I'll come——and married we will be in spite of treach-   40
ery; Ay and get an Heir that shall defeat the last remaining glimpse of hope in my abandon'd *Nephew.* Come, my Buxom Widdow.

<blockquote>

Ere long you shall substantial Proof receive
That I'm an arrant Knight——
</blockquote>

Foib.   Or arrant Knave. [*Exeunt.*

Act V Scene I

SCENE *continues*

Lady Wishfort, *and* Foible.

Lady. Out of my House, out of my House, thou *Viper*, thou *Serpent*, that I have foster'd; thou bosom traitress, that I rais'd from nothing———Begon, begon, begon, go, go.———That I took from Washing of old Gause and Weaving of dead Hair,[1] with a bleak blew Nose, over a Chafeing-dish of starv'd Embers, and Dining behind a Traver's Rag, in a Shop no bigger than a Bird-cage,———go, go, starve again, do, do.

Foib. Dear *Madam*, I'll beg Pardon on my knees.

Lady. Away, out, out, go set up for your self again———do, drive a Trade, do, with your three-penny-worth of small Ware, flaunting upon a Packthread, under a Brandy-seller's Bulk,[2] or against a dead Wall by a Ballad-monger. 10 Go, hang out an old *Frisoneer-gorget*,[3] with a yard of Yellow *Colberteen*[4] again; do; an old gnaw'd *Mask*, two rowes of *Pins*, and a *Child's Fiddle*; A *Glass Necklace* with the Beads broken, and a *Quilted Night-cap* with one Ear. Go, go, drive a trade,———These were your *Commodities*, you treacherous Trull, this was the *Merchandize* you dealt in, when I took you into my House, plac'd you next my self, and made you Governante[5] of my whole Family. You have forgot this, have you, now you have feather'd your Nest?

Foib. No, no, dear Madam. Do but hear me, have but a Moment's patience ———I'll Confess all. Mr. *Mirabell* seduc'd me; I am not the first that he has wheadl'd with his dissembling Tongue; Your Ladyship's own Wisdom has 20 been deluded by him, then how should I, a poor Ignorant, defend my self? O *Madam*, if you knew but what he promis'd me, and how he assur'd me your Ladyship should come to no damage———Or else the Wealth of the *Indies* should not have brib'd me to conspire against so Good, so Sweet, so kind a Lady as you have been to me.

Lady. No damage? What to Betray me, to Marry me to a Cast-serving-Man; to make me a receptacle, an Hospital for a decay'd Pimp? No damage? O thou frontless[6] Impudence, more than a big-Belly'd Actress.

Foib. Pray do but hear me, *Madam*; he could not marry your Ladyship, *Madam*———No indeed his Marriage was to have been void in Law; for he was 30 marry'd to me first, to secure your Ladyship. He could not have bedded your Ladyship; for if he had consummated with your Ladyship, he must have run the risque of the Law, and been put upon his *Clergy*[7]———Yes indeed, I enquir'd of the Law in that case before I would meddle or make.

Lady. What, then I have been your Property, have I? I have been convenient to you, it seems,—while you were catering for *Mirabell*; I have been broaker

---

[1] . . . *dead Hair:* Weaving hair into wigs.

[2] *Bulk:* A projection from the front of a shop; a stall.

[3] *Frisoneer-gorget:* A collar or wimple made of wool.

[4] *Colberteen:* An inexpensive lace.

[5] *Governante: Gouvernante,* a housekeeper.

[6] *Frontless:* Unblushing.

[7] *Upon his Clergy:* Benefit of his clergy (or upon his clergy) was the exemption of clergymen (later anyone who could read) from trial by secular courts. Finally it became a way of avoiding the death penalty for all but the worst capital crimes.

for you? What, have you made a passive Bawd of me?——this Exceeds all precedent; I am brought to fine uses, to become a botcher[8] of second-hand Marriages between *Abigails* and *Andrews*.[9] I'll couple you. Yes, I'll baste you together, you and your *Philander*.[10] I'll *Duke's-Place* you,[11] as I'm a Person. Your Turtle is in Custody already: You shall Coo in the same Cage, if there be Constable or Warrant in the Parish.   [*Exit.*

Foib. O that ever I was Born, O that I was ever Married,——a Bride, ay I shall be a *Bridewell*-Bride.[12] Oh !
                    [*Enter* Mrs. Fainall.

Mrs. Fain. Poor *Foible*, what's the matter?

Foib. O Madam, my Lady's gone for a Constable; I shall be had to a Justice, and put to *Bridewell* to beat Hemp; poor *Waitwell's* gone to Prison already.

Mrs. Fain. Have a good Heart, *Foible*; *Mirabell's* gone to give security for him. This is all *Marwood's* and my Husband's doing.

Foib. Yes, yes; I know it, Madam; she was in my Lady's Closet, and over-heard all that you said to me before Dinner. She sent the Letter to my Lady; and that missing Effect, Mr. *Fainall* laid this Plot to arrest *Waitwell*, when he pretended to go for the Papers; and in the mean time Mrs. *Marwood* declar'd all to my Lady.

Mrs. Fain. Was there no mention made of me in the Letter?——My Mother do's not suspect my being in the Confederacy? I fancy *Marwood* has not told her, tho' she has told my husband.

Foib. Yes, Madam; but my Lady did not see that part: We stifled the Letter before she read so far. Has that mischievous Devil told Mr. *Fainall* of your Ladyship then?

Mrs. Fain. Ay, all's out, my affair with *Mirabell*, every thing discover'd, This is the last day of our liveing together, that's my Comfort.

Foib. Indeed Madam, and so 'tis a Comfort if you knew all——he has been even with your Ladyship; which I cou'd have told you long enough since, but I love to keep Peace and Quietness by my good Will: I had rather bring friends together, than set 'em at distance. But Mrs. *Marwood* and He are nearer related than ever their Parents thought for.

Mrs. Fain. Say'st thou so, *Foible*? Canst thou prove this?

Foib. I can take my Oath of it, Madam, so can Mrs. *Mincing*; we have had many a fair Word from *Madam Marwood*, to conceal something that passed in our Chamber one Evening when you were at *Hide-Park*;——and we were thought to have gone a Walking: But we went up unawares,——tho' we were sworn to secresie too; *Madam Marwood* took a Book and swore us upon it: But it was but a Book of Verses and Poems,——So long as it was not a Bible-Oath, we may break it with a safe Conscience.

Mrs. Fain. This Discovery is the most opportune thing I cou'd wish. Now *Mincing*?
                    [*Enter* Mincing.

Minc. My Lady wou'd speak with Mrs. *Foible, Mem.* Mr. *Mirabell* is with

---

[8] *A botcher:* A mender, a patcher.
[9] *Abigails and Andrews:* Generic names for waiting women and valets.
[10] *Philander:* Lover.
[11] *Duke's-Place you:* See I, n. 4.
[12] *Bridewell:* An old prison in London, between Fleet Street and the Thames.

her; he has set your Spouse at liberty, Mrs. *Foible*, and wou'd have you hide your
self in my Lady's Closet, 'till my old Lady's anger is abated. O, my old Lady is
in a perilous passion, at something Mr. *Fainall* has said; he swears, and my old
Lady cry's. There's a fearful Hurricane I vow. He says *Mem*, how that he'll
have my Lady's Fortune made over to him, or he'll be divorc'd.

Mrs. Fain. Do's your Lady or *Mirabell* know that?

Minc. Yes *Mem*, they have sent me to see if *Sir Wilfull* be sober, and to
bring him to them. My Lady is resolved to have him I think, rather than lose
such a vast Summ as six thousand Pound. O, come Mrs. *Foible*, I hear my old
Lady.   10

Mrs. Fain. *Foible*, you must tell *Mincing*, that she must prepare to vouch
when I call her.

Foib. Yes, yes, Madam.

Minc. O yes *Mem*, I'll vouch any thing for your Ladyship's service, be what
it will.   [*Exeunt* Minc. *and* Foib.

[*Enter* Lady *and* Marwood.

Lady. O my dear Friend, how can I Enumerate the benefits that I have
receiv'd from your goodness? To you I owe the timely discovery of the false
vows of *Mirabell*; to you I owe the Detection of the Impostor Sir *Rowland*.
And now you are become an Intercessor with my Son-in-law, to save the
Honour of my House, and compound for the Frailtys of my Daughter. Well   20
Friend, You are enough to reconcile me to the bad World, or else I would
retire to Desarts and Solitudes; and feed harmless Sheep by *Groves* and *purling
Streams*. Dear *Marwood*, let us leave the World, and retire by our selves and be
Shepherdesses.

Mrs. Mar. Let us first dispatch the affair in hand, *Madam*. We shall have
Leisure to think of Retirement afterwards. Here is one who is concerned in the
treaty.

Lady. O Daughter, Daughter, is it possible thou should'st be my Child,
Bone of my Bone, and Flesh of my Flesh, and as I may say, another Me, and
yet transgress the most minute Particle of severe Vertue? Is it possible you should   30
lean aside to Iniquity, who have been cast in the direct Mold of Vertue? I have
not only been a Mold but a Pattern for you, and a Model for you, after you
were brought into the World.

Mrs. Fain. I don't understand your Ladyship.

Lady. Not understand? Why have you not been Naught?[13] Have you not
been Sophisticated?[14] Not understand? Here I am ruin'd to Compound for
Caprices and your *Cuckoldoms*. I must pawn my *Plate* and my *Jewels*, and ruine
my *Niece*, and all little enough——

Mrs. Fain. I am wrong'd and abus'd, and so are you. 'Tis a false accusation,
as false as *Hell*, as false as your Friend there, ay or your Friend's Friend, my false   40
Husband.

Mrs. Mar. My Friend, *Mrs. Fainall*? Your Husband my Friend, what do
you mean?

Mrs. Fain. I know what I mean, *Madam*, and so do you; and so shall the
World at a time Convenient.

---

[13] *Naught:* Wicked.   [14] *Sophisticated:* Debased.

Mrs. Mar. I am sorry to see you so passionate, Madam. More Temper[15] would look more like Innocence. But I have done. I am sorry my Zeal to serve your Ladyship and Family, should admit of Misconstruction, or make me liable to affronts. You will pardon me, *Madam*, if I meddle no more with an affair, in which I am not Personally concern'd.

Lady. O dear Friend, I am so asham'd that you should meet with such re-turns;——You ought to ask Pardon on your Knees, Ungratefull Creature; she deserves more from you, than all your life can accomplish——O don't leave me destitute in this Perplexity;——No, stick to me, my good Genius.

Mrs. Fain. I tell you, *Madam*, you're abus'd——Stick to you? ay, like a   10
Leach, to suck your best Blood——she'll drop off when she's full. *Madam*, you shan't pawn a Bodkin, nor part with a *Brass Counter*, in Composition for me. I defie 'em all. Let 'em prove their aspersions: I know my own Innocence, and dare stand a tryall.   [*Exit.*

Lady. Why, if she should be Innocent, if she should be wrong'd after all, ha? I don't know what to think,——and I promise you, her Education has been unexceptionable——I may say it; for I chiefly made it my own Care to Initiate her very Infancy in the Rudiments of Vertue, and to Impress upon her tender Years a Young *Odium* and *Aversion* to the very sight of Men,——ay Friend, she would ha' shriek'd If she had but seen a Man, 'till she was in her   20
Teens. As I'm a Person 'tis true——She was never suffer'd to play with a Male-Child, tho' but in Coats; Nay her very Babies[16] were of the *Feminine Gender*,——O, she never look'd a Man in the Face but her own Father, or the Chaplain, and him we made a shift to put upon her for a Woman, by the help of his long Garments, and his sleek Face; 'till she was going in her Fifteen.

Mrs. Mar. 'Twas much she should be deceiv'd so long.

Lady. I warrant you, or she would never have born to have been Cate-chiz'd by him; and have heard his long lectures against Singing and Dancing, and such Debaucheries; and going to filthy *Plays*; and Profane *Musick-meetings*, where the Leud Trebles squeek nothing but Bawdy, and the Bases roar *Blas-*   30
phemy. O, she would have swoon'd at the sight or name of an obscene Play-book—and can I think after all this, that my Daughter can be Naught? What, a Whore? And thought it excommunication to set her foot within the door of a Play-house. O dear friend, I can't believe it, no, no; as she says, let him prove it, let him prove it.

Mrs. Mar. Prove it, Madam? What, and have your name prostituted in a publick Court; yours and your Daughter's reputation worry'd at the Barr by a pack of Bawling Lawyers? To be usher'd in with an *O Yez* of Scandal; and have your Case open'd by an old fumbling Leacher in a Quoif[17] like a Man Midwife, to bring your Daughter's Infamy to light; to be a Theme for legal   40
Punsters, and Quiblers by the Statute; and become a Jest, against a Rule of Court, where there is no Precedent for a Jest in any record; not even in *Dooms-day-Book*: To discompose the gravity of the Bench, and provoke Naughty In-terrogatories in more Naughty Law *Latin*; while the good Judge, tickl'd with the

---

15 *Temper:* Control.
16 *Babies:* Dolls or puppets.

17 *Quoif:* Coif, a white cap worn by a serjeant-at-law.

proceeding, simpers under a Gray beard, and figes off and on his Cushion as if he had swallow'd *Cantharides*,[18] or sat upon *Cow-Itch*.[19]

Lady. O, 'tis very hard!

Mrs. Mar. And then to have my Young Revellers of the *Temple* take Notes, like Prentices at a *Conventicle;* and after talk it over again in Commons, or before Drawers in an *Eating-House*.

Lady. Worse and worse.

Mrs. Mar. Nay this is nothing; if it would end here 'twere well. But it must after this be consign'd by the Short-hand Writers to the publick Press; and from thence be transferr'd to the hands nay into the Throats and Lungs of   10 Hawkers, with Voices more licentious than the loud *Flounderman's*, or the *Woman* that crys *Grey-pease*. And this you must hear 'till you are stunn'd; nay you must hear nothing else for some days.

Lady. O, 'tis Insupportable. No, no, dear Friend, make it up, make it up; ay, ay, I'll Compound. I'll give up all, my self and my all, my *Niece* and her all ——any thing, every thing for Composition.

Mrs. Mar. Nay, *Madam*, I advise nothing, I only lay before you, as a Friend, the Inconveniences which perhaps you have Overseen. Here comes Mr. *Fainall*; if he will be satisfy'd to huddle up all in Silence, I shall be glad. You must think I would rather Congratulate than Condole with you.   20

[*Enter* Fainall.

Lady. Ay, ay, I do not doubt it, dear *Marwood*: No, no, I do not doubt it.

Fain. Well, *Madam*; I have suffer'd my self to be overcome by the Importunity of this Lady your Friend; and am content you shall enjoy your own proper Estate during Life; on condition you oblige your self never to Marry, under such Penalty as I think convenient.

Lady. Never to Marry?

Fain. No more Sir *Rowlands*,——the next Imposture may not be so timely detected.

Mrs. Mar. That condition, I dare answer, my Lady will consent to, without difficulty; she has already but too much experienc'd the perfidiousness of Men.   30 Besides, Madam, when we retire to our pastoral Solitude we shall bid adieu to all other Thoughts.

Lady. Ay, that's true; but in Case of Necessity; as of Health, or some such Emergency——

Fain. O, if you are prescrib'd Marriage, you shall be consider'd: I will only reserve to my self the Power to chuse for you. If your Physick be wholsom, it matters not who is your Apothecary. Next, my Wife shall settle on me the remainder of her Fortune, not made over already; and for her Maintenance depend entirely on my Discretion.

Lady. This is most inhumanly savage; exceeding the Barbarity of a *Musco-*   40 *vite* Husband.

Fain. I learn'd it from his *Czarish* Majestie's Retinue,[20] in a Winter Even-

---

[18] *Cantharides:* Spanish Fly, an aphrodisiac.

[19] *Cow-Itch:* The stinging fibers of the pod of the tropical plant cowage or cowhage.

[20] *Czarish Majestie's Retinue:* Czar Peter the Great had been to England during his tour of Europe, 1697–1698.

ing's Conference over Brandy and Pepper, amongst other secrets of Matrimony and Policy, as they are at present practis'd in the *Northern* Hemisphere. But this must be agreed unto, and that positively. Lastly, I will be endow'd, in right of my Wife, with that six thousand Pound, which is the Moiety of *Mrs. Millamant's* Fortune in your Possession; and which she had forfeited (as will appear by the last Will and Testament of your deceas'd Husband, Sir *Jonathan Wishfort*) by her Disobedience in Contracting her self against your Consent or Knowledge; and by refusing the offer'd Match with *Sir Wilfull Witwoud*, which you, like a careful Aunt, had provided for her.

Lady. My Nephew was *non Compos*,[21] and could not make his Addresses.   10

Fain. I come to make Demands——I'll hear no objections.

Lady. You will grant me time to Consider?

Fain. Yes, while the Instrument is drawing, to which you must set your Hand 'till more sufficient Deeds can be perfected: which I will take care shall be done with all possible speed. In the mean while I will go for the said Instrument, and 'till my Return you may Ballance this Matter in your own Discretion.   [*Exit* Fain.

Lady. This Insolence is beyond all Precedent, all Parallel; must I be subject to this merciless Villain?

Mrs. Mar. 'Tis severe indeed, Madam, that you shou'd smart for your   20 Daughter's wantonness.

Lady. 'Twas against my Consent that she Married this Barbarian, but she wou'd have him tho' her Year was not out.[22]——Ah! her first Husband my Son *Languish*, wou'd not have carry'd it thus,[23] Well, that was my Choice, this is hers; she is match'd now with a Witness[24]——I shall be mad, Dear Friend, is there no Comfort for me? Must I live to be confiscated at this Rebelrate?——Here come two more of my *Egyptian* Plagues too.[25]

[*Enter* Millamant *and* Sir Wilfull.

Sir Wil. Aunt, your Servant.

Lady. Out *Caterpillar*, call not me Aunt; I know thee not.

Sir Wil. I confess I have been a little in disguise,[26] as they say,——'Sheart!   30 and I'm sorry for't. What wou'd you have? I hope I committed no Offence, Aunt——and if I did I am willing to make satisfaction; and what can a man say fairer? If I have broke any thing I'll pay for't, an it cost a Pound. And so let that content for what's past, and make no more words. For what's to come, to pleasure you I'm willing to marry my Cozen. So pray let's all be Friends; she and I are agreed upon the matter before a Witness.

Lady. How's this, dear Niece? Have I any comfort? Can this be true?

Milla. I am content to be a Sacrifice to your repose, Madam; and to Convince you that I had no hand in the Plot, as you were misinform'd, I have laid my Commands on *Mirabell* to come in Person, and be a Witness that I give my   40 hand to this flower of *Knighthood*; and for the Contract that pass'd between

[21] . . . *non Compos:* Not in control of his mind.
[22] *Her Year was not out:* Her year of mourning as a widow.
[23] *Carry'd it thus:* Behaved in such a way.

[24] *With a Witness:* And no mistake!
[25] *Egyptian Plagues too:* In Exodus 3–12, Moses and Aaron are the Lord's instruments for bringing ten plagues to Pharaoh.
[26] *A little in disguise:* Drunk.

Mirabell and me, I have oblig'd him to make a Resignation of it in your Lady-ship's presence;——He is without, and waits your leave for admittance.

Lady. Well, I'll swear I am something reviv'd at this Testimony of your Obedience; but I cannot admit that Traytor;——I fear I cannot fortifie my self to support his appearance. He is as terrible to me as a *Gorgon*; if I see him I fear I shall turn to Stone, petrify Incessantly.

Milla. If you disoblige him he may resent your refusal, and insist upon the contract still. Then 'tis the last time he will be offensive to you.

Lady. Are you sure it will be the last time?——If I were sure of that—— shall I never see him again?　　　　　　　　　　　　　　　　10

Milla. Sir Wilfull, you and he are to Travel together, are you not?

Sir Wil. 'Sheart the Gentleman's a civil Gentleman, Aunt, let him come in; why we are sworn Brothers and fellow-Travellers.——We are to be *Pylades* and *Orestes,*[27] he and I——He is to be my Interpreter in foreign Parts. He has been Over-seas once already; and with *proviso* that I Marry my Cozen will cross 'em once again, only to bear me Company.——'Sheart, I'll call him in,——an I set on't once, he shall come in; and see who'll hinder him.　　[*Exit.*

Mrs. Mar. This is precious Fooling, if it wou'd pass; but I'll know the bottom of it.

Lady. O dear *Marwood,* you are not going?　　　　　　　　　20

Mar. Not far, Madam; I'll return immediately.　　　　[*Exit.*

[*Re-enter* Sir Wilfull *and* Mirabell.

Sir Wil. Look up, Man, I'll stand by you, 'sbud an she do frown, she can't kill you;——besides——Hearkee she dare not frown desperately, because her face is none of her own; 'Sheart, and she shou'd her forehead wou'd wrinkle like the Coat of a Cream-cheese; but mum for that, fellow-Traveller.

Mira. If a deep sense of the many Injuries I have offer'd to so good a Lady, with a sincere remorse, and a hearty Contrition, can but obtain the least glance of Compassion, I am too Happy,——Ah Madam, there was a time——but let it be forgotten—I confess I have deservedly forfeited the high Place I once held, of sighing at your Feet; nay kill me not, by turning from me in disdain　30 ——I come not to plead for favour;——Nay not for Pardon; I am a Suppliant only for pity——I am going where I never shall behold you more——

Sir Wil. How, fellow-Traveller!——You shall go by your self then.

Mira. Let me be pitied first, and afterwards forgotten.——I ask no more.

Sir Wil. By'r Lady a very reasonable request, and will cost you nothing, Aunt,—Come, come, Forgive and Forget, Aunt; why you must an you are a Christian.

Mira. Consider, Madam, in reality, you cou'd not receive much prejudice; it was an Innocent device; tho' I confess it had a Face of guiltiness,——it was at most an Artifice which Love Contriv'd——And errours which Love pro-　40 duces have ever been accounted *Venial.* At least think it is Punishment enough, that I have lost what in my heart I hold most dear, that to your cruel Indigna-tion I have offer'd up this Beauty, and with her my Peace and Quiet; nay all my Hopes of future Comfort.

---

[27] *Pylades and Orestes:* In *The Libation Bearers* and *The Eumenides* of Aeschylus, Pylades loyally accompanies his friend Orestes through great difficulties.

Sir Wil. An he do's not move me, wou'd I might never be *O' the Quorum.*[28]
——An it were not as good a deed as to drink, to give her to him again,
——I wou'd I might never take Shipping——Aunt, if you don't forgive
quickly, I shall melt, I can tell you that. My contract went no farther than a
little Mouth-Glew,[29] and that's hardly dry;——One doleful Sigh more from
my fellow-Traveller, and 'tis dissolv'd.

Lady. Well, *Nephew,* upon your account——Ah, he has a false Insinuating
Tongue——Well, Sir, I will stifle my just resentment at my *Nephew's* Request.
——I will endeavour what I can to forget,——but on *proviso* that you resign the
Contract with my Niece Immediately.   10

Mira. It is in Writing, and with Papers of Concern; but I have sent my
Servant for it, and will deliver it to you, with all acknowledgments for your
transcendent goodness.

Lady. Oh, he has *Witchcraft* in his Eyes and Tongue;——When I did not
see him I cou'd have brib'd a Villain to his Assassination; but his appearance
rakes the *Embers* which have so long layn smother'd in my Breast——[*apart.*

[*Enter* Fainall *and* Mrs. Marwood.

Fain. Your date of deliberation, *Madam,* is expir'd. Here is the Instrument;
are you prepar'd to sign?

Lady. If I were prepar'd, I am not Impower'd. My Niece exerts a lawful
claim, having Match'd her self by my direction to *Sir Wilfull.*   20

Fain. That sham is too gross to pass on me——tho' 'tis impos'd on you,
Madam.

Milla. Sir, I have given my consent.

Mira. And, Sir, I have resign'd my pretensions.

Sir Wil. And, Sir, I assert my right; and will maintain it in defiance of you,
Sir, and of your Instrument. S'heart an you talk of an Instrument, Sir, I have
an old *Fox*[30] by my Thigh shall hack your Instrument of *Ram Vellam*[31] to shreds,
Sir. It shall not be sufficient for a *Mittimus*[32] or a Taylor's Measure; therefore
withdraw your Instrument, Sir, or by'r Lady I shall draw mine.

Lady. Hold, *Nephew,* hold.   30

Milla. Good *Sir Wilfull,* respite your valour.

Fain. Indeed? Are you provided of your Guard, with your single Beef-
eater there? But I'm prepared for you; and insist upon my first proposal.
You shall submit your own Estate to my management, and absolutely make
over my Wife's to my sole use; as pursuant to the Purport and Tenor of this
other Covenant——I suppose, Madam, your Consent is not requisite in this
Case; nor, Mr. *Mirabell,* your resignation; nor, *Sir Wilfull,* your right.——You
may draw your Fox if you please, Sir, and make a *Bear-garden* flourish somewhere else: For here it will not avail. This, my *Lady Wishfort,* must be subscrib'd, or your Darling Daughter's turn'd a-drift, like a Leaky hulk, to sink   40
or swim, as she and the Current of this Lewd Town can agree.

---

[28] *O' the Quorum:* Those justices of the
peace whose presence was necessary to
constitute a bench of magistrates.
[29] . . . *Mouth-Glew:* His commitment
was only spoken, not written.
[30] *An old Fox:* A kind of sword.

[31] . . . *Ram Vellam:* Parchment, on
which a legal document is inscribed.
[32] *Mittimus:* A warrant directing a
prison warden to hold the person sent to
him and specified in the order.

Lady. Is there no means, no Remedy to stop my ruine? Ungrateful Wretch! dost thou not owe thy being, thy subsistence, to my Daughter's Fortune?

Fain. I'll answer you when I have the rest of it in my possession.

Mira. But that you wou'd not accept of a Remedy from my hands—— I own I have not deserv'd you shou'd owe any Obligation to me; or else perhaps I cou'd advise——

Lady. O what? what? to save me and my Child from Ruine, from Want. I'll forgive all that's past; Nay, I'll consent to any thing to come, to be deliver'd from this Tyranny.

Mira. Ay *Madam*; but that is too late, my reward is intercepted. You have dispos'd of her, who only cou'd have made me a Compensation for all my Services;——But be it as it may, I am resolv'd I'll serve you; you shall not be wrong'd in this *Savage* manner.

Lady. How! Dear Mr. *Mirabell*, can you be so generous at last! But it is not possible. Hearkee, I'll break my *Nephew's* Match; you shall have my *Niece* yet, and all her fortune, if you can but save me from this imminent danger.

Mira. Will you? I take you at your word. I ask no more. I must have leave for two Criminals to appear.

Lady. Ay, ay, any Body, any body.

Mira. *Foible* is one, and a Penitent.

[*Enter* Mrs. Fainall, Foible, *and* Mincing.

Mrs. Mar. O my shame! These Corrupt things are brought hither to expose me.   [*To* Fain.

[Mira. *and* Lady *go to* Mrs. Fain. *and* Foib.

Fain. If it must all come out, why let 'em know it; 'tis but the *way of the World.* That shall not urge me to relinquish or abate one tittle of my Terms; no, I will insist the more.

Foib. Yes indeed, *Madam*, I'll take my Bible-oath of it.

Minc. And so will I, *Mem.*

Lady. O *Marwood, Marwood*, art thou false? My Friend deceive me! Hast thou been a wicked accomplice with that profligate Man?

Mrs. Mar. Have you so much Ingratitude and Injustice, to give credit against your Friend to the Aspersions of two such Mercenary Truls?

Minc. Mercenary, *Mem*? I scorn your words. 'Tis true we found you and Mr. *Fainall* in the Blew garret; by the same token, you swore us to Secresie upon *Messalina's* Poems.[33] Mercenary? No, if we wou'd have been Mercenary, we shou'd have held our Tongues; you wou'd have brib'd us sufficiently.

Fain. Go, you are an Insignificant thing.——Well, what are you the better for this! Is this Mr. *Mirabell's* Expedient? I'll be put off no longer——You, thing, that was a Wife, shall smart for this. I will not leave thee wherewithal to hide thy Shame: Your Body shall be Naked as your Reputation.

Mrs. Fain. I despise you, and defie your Malice——You have aspers'd me wrongfully——I have prov'd your falshood——Go you and your treacherous —I will not name it, but starve together——perish.

---

[33] *Messalina's Poems: Miscellany Poems* was a common title given to collections of verse. According to Dobrée and other editors, Mincing has probably confused the name with Messalina, a Roman matron with a reputation for profligacy.

Fain. Not while you are worth a Groat, indeed my dear. *Madam,* I'll be fool'd no longer.

Lady. Ah Mr. *Mirabell,* this is small comfort, the detection of this affair.

Mira. O in good time——Your leave for the other Offender and Penitent to appear, Madam.

[*Enter* Waitwell *with a Box of Writings.*

Lady. O Sir *Rowland*——Well, Rascal.

Wait. What your Ladyship pleases.——I have brought the Black-box at last, *Madam.*

Mira. Give it me. *Madam,* you remember your promise.

Lady. Ay, dear Sir.   10

Mira. Where are the Gentlemen?

Wait. At hand, Sir, rubbing their Eyes,—just risen from Sleep.

Fain. S'death what's this to me? I'll not wait your private concerns.

[*Enter* Petulant, Witwoud.

Pet. How now? what's the matter? who's hand's out?

Wit. Hey day? what are you all got together, like Players at the end of the last Act?

Mira. You may remember, Gentlemen, I once requested your hands as Witnesses to a certain Parchment.

Wit. Ay I do, my hand I remember——*Petulant* set his Mark.

Mira. You wrong him, his name is fairly written, as shall appear——You   20 do not remember, Gentlemen, any thing of what that Parchment contained
——   [*Undoing the Box.*

Wit. No.

Pet. Not I. I writ, I read nothing.

Mira. Very well, now you shall know—*Madam,* your Promise.

Lady. Ay, ay, Sir, upon my Honour.

Mira. Mr. *Fainall,* it is now Time that you shou'd know, that your Lady, while she was at her own disposal, and before you had by your Insinuations wheedl'd her out of a pretended Settlement of the greatest part of her for-tune——

Fain. Sir! pretended!   30

Mira. Yes, Sir. I say that this Lady while a Widdow, having it seems receiv'd some Cautions respecting your Inconstancy and Tyranny of temper, which from her own partial Opinion and fondness of you she cou'd never have sus-pected—she did, I say, by the wholsom advice of Friends and of Sages learned in the Laws of this Land, deliver this same as her Act and Deed to me in trust, and to the uses within mention'd. You may read if you please—[*Holding out the Parchment.*] tho' perhaps what is written on the back may serve your occasions.

Fain. Very likely, Sir. What's here? Damnation?

[*Reads.*] *A Deed of Conveyance of the whole Estate real of* Arabella Languish, *Widdow, in* Trust *to* Edward Mirabell.   40
Confusion!

Mira. Even so, Sir, 'tis *the way of the World,* Sir; of the Widdows of the World. I suppose this Deed may bear an elder Date than what you have obtain'd from your Lady.

Fain. Perfidious Fiend! then thus I'll be revenge'd.——

[*Offers to run at Mrs. Fain.*

Sir Wil. Hold, Sir, now you may make your *Bear-Garden* flourish somewhere else, Sir.

Fain. Mirabell, you shall hear of this, Sir, be sure you shall,——Let me pass, *Oafe.* [*Exit.*

Mrs. Fain. Madam, you seem to stifle your Resentment: You had better give it Vent.

Mrs. Mar. Yes, it shall have Vent——and to your Confusion, or I'll perish in the Attempt. [*Exit.*

Lady. O Daughter, Daughter, 'tis plain thou hast inherited thy Mother's 10 prudence.

Mrs. Fain. Thank Mr. *Mirabell,* a Cautious Friend, to whose advice all is owing.

Lady. Well, Mr. *Mirabell,* you have kept your promise—and I must perform mine.——First I pardon for your sake Sir *Rowland* there and *Foible*—— The next thing is to break the Matter to my Nephew—and how to do that——

Mira. For that, Madam, give your self no trouble,—let me have your Consent——Sir *Wilfull* is my Friend; he has had compassion upon Lovers, and generously engag'd a Volunteer in this Action, for our Service; and now designs to prosecute his Travells. 20

Sir Wil. 'Sheart, Aunt, I have no mind to marry. My Cousin's a Fine Lady, and the Gentleman loves her, and she loves him, and they deserve one another; my resolution is to see Foreign Parts——I have set on't——and when I'm set on't, I must do't. And if these two Gentlemen wou'd Travel too, I think they may be spar'd.

Pet. For my part, I say little—I think things are best off or on.[34]

Wit. I Gad I understand nothing of the matter,—I'm in a maze yet, like a *Dog* in a *Dancing-School.*

Lady. Well, Sir, take her, and with her all the Joy I can give you.

Milla. Why does not the man take me? Wou'd you have me give my 30 self to you over again?

Mira. Ay, and over and over again; [*Kisses her Hand.*] for I wou'd have you as often as possibly I can. Well, heav'n grant I love you not too well, that's all my fear.

Sir Wil. 'Sheart you'll have time enough to toy after you're married; or if you will toy now, let us have a Dance in the mean time; that we who are not Lovers may have some other employment, besides looking on.

Mira. With all my Heart, dear Sir *Willfull,* What shall we do for Musick?

Foib. O Sir, Some that were provided for Sir *Rowland's* Entertainment are yet within Call. 40

A DANCE

Lady. As I am a Person I can hold out no longer;—I have wasted my spirits so to day already, that I am ready to sink under the fatigue; and I cannot but have some fears upon me yet, that my Son *Fainall* will pursue some desperate Course.

[34] *Off or on:* This way or that.

Mira. Madam, disquiet not your self on that account; to my knowledge his Circumstances are such, he must of force comply. For my part I will Contribute all that in me lies to a Reunion: In the mean time, *Madam,* [*To Mrs. Fain.*] let me before these Witnesses restore to you this deed of trust; it may be a means, well manag'd, to make you live Easily together.

> *From hence let those be warn'd, who mean to wed;*
> *Lest mutual falshood stain the Bridal-Bed:*
> *For each deceiver to his cost may find,*
> *That marriage frauds too oft are paid in kind.*

[Exeunt Omnes.

Epilogue

Spoken by Mrs. Bracegirdle[1]

AFTER *our* Epilogue *this Crowd dismisses,*
I'm thinking how this Play'll be pull'd to Pieces.
But pray consider, ere you doom its fall,
How hard a thing 'twould be, to please you all.
There are some Criticks so with Spleen diseas'd,   5
They scarcely come inclining to be Pleas'd:
And sure he must have more than mortal Skill,
Who pleases any one against his Will.
Then, all bad Poets we are sure are Foes,
And how their Numbers swell'd, the Town well knows: 10
In shoals, I've mark'd 'em judging in the Pit;
Tho' theyre on no pretence for Judgment fit,
But that they have been Damn'd for want of wit.
Since when, they by their own offences taught,
Set up for Spys on Plays, and finding Fault.   15
Others there are whose Malice we'd prevent;
Such, who watch Plays, with scurrilous intent
To mark out who by Characters *are meant.*
And tho' no perfect likeness they can Trace;
Yet each pretends to know the Copy'd *Face.*   20
These, with false Glosses feed their own Ill-nature,
And turn to Libel, what was meant a Satire.
May such malicious Fops this Fortune find,
To think themselves alone the Fools design'd:
If any are so arrogantly Vain,   25
To think they singly can support a Scene,
And furnish Fool enough to entertain.

---

[1] *Mrs. Bracegirdle:* Anne Bracegirdle (c. 1663–1748); the actress was renowned for her beauty (and her virtue) no less than for her performances in the plays of Congreve.

For well the Learn'd and the Judicious know,
That Satire *scorns to stoop so meanly low,*
As any one abstracted Fop *to shew,*   30
For, as when Painters form a matchless Face,
They from each Fair one *catch some different Grace;*
And shining Features in one Portrait blend,
To which no single Beauty must pretend:
So Poets oft, do in one Piece expose   35
Whole Belles Assemblées² *of* Cocquetts *and* Beaux.

(1700)

² *Belles Assemblées:* Fashionable gather-
ings.

Jonathan Swift

1667-1745

Swift was born November 30, 1667, in Dublin (of English parents) some months after the death of his father. He was educated at Kilkenny Grammar School, where Congreve was a contemporary, and at Trinity College, Dublin, where he took a B.A. in 1686. In 1692, he received the M.A. at Oxford. Some time before this, Swift began his employment as secretary to Sir William Temple, the noted diplomatist, who resided at Moor Park, Surrey, in whose household he was to remain, with one fairly long interruption, until Sir William's death in 1699. There, Swift made the acquaintance of Esther Johnson, "Stella," of the famous *Journal to Stella*. It was while he was with Temple that Swift wrote the *Battel of the Books*, partly in defense of his employer, though the work was not published until 1704. The piece was in fact closely related to the greater *A Tale of a Tub*, with which it appeared, and to *The Mechanical Operation of the Spirit*. At one point, Swift grew restless at Moor Park, and apparently having decided to try another career, he was ordained in Dublin in 1694, after which he was preferred (assigned) to the vicarage of Kilroot, near Belfast. But in 1696 he returned to Temple's employ and resigned the living (appointment). After Temple died, Swift was in uncertain waters. He accepted a position as chaplain and secretary to Lord Berkeley, who was then going to Ireland as Lord Justice; and he was also helped with several small livings in the Irish Church, the chief of these being the vicarage of Laracor.

Between 1699 and 1710, Swift's reputation as a political and religious essayist grew considerably, among Londoners especially. He joined the circle of Whigs led by Addison, a gesture that seems reasonable enough when one considers Swift's Whig birth and education, including his years with Temple. But it did not take into account his uncompromising loyalty to the Church of England, which led him ultimately to reject the Whigs, though not until he had experienced a good deal of uneasiness about the choice open to him. In 1710, Swift went over to the Tories, who under Robert Harley, Lord Oxford, and Henry St. John, Lord Bolingbroke, were to bring an end to the Whig-supported War of the Spanish Succession (1701–1713) and who were to remain in power until Queen Anne's death in 1714. While employed by the Oxford-Bolingbroke ministry, whose avowed moderate conservatism he (naïvely) did not doubt, Swift wrote the *Examiner*, a Tory journal, until June 14, 1711, and numerous political essays, including *The Conduct of the Allies* (1711) and *History of the Four Last Years of the Queen*, written in 1712–1713, but not published until 1758. (It was during this period too that he joined Pope, Arbuthnot, and others in the Scriblerus Club, which satirized dullness in various literary works.) As a reward for his political services, Swift was named Dean of St. Patrick's in Dublin. He probably had hoped for an appointment in England, perhaps as Dean of St. Paul's, but he was never to receive such preferment.

With the death of Queen Anne on August 1, 1714, the Tories lost power, and Swift returned to Dublin with a considerable sense of defeat, but not "nearly lost to despair," as some of his earlier biographers have asserted. Nevertheless he experienced at least one complicated private difficulty quite apart from his political and social disappointments. He was followed to Ireland by Esther (Vanessa) Vanomrigh, whose family he had come to know during his residence in England. Apparently Vanessa conceived an uncontrollable passion for the Dean —a passion that ended in misfortune for her. After having attempted for years to thrust herself between Swift and Stella (Esther Johnson), who had corresponded steadily with each other during his absence from Ireland, Vanessa was at last rebuffed, and turning finally against Swift it seems, she died in 1723. Swift's relationship with Stella was at this time (as it was throughout his life) ambiguous. Although it has been suggested that they were secretly married, no real evidence supports this view. Obviously they were very close to each other, but no one knows the nature of their relationship.

About 1720, Swift began the series of pamphlets that established his reputation as an Irish patriot. In that year, he brought out *Proposal for the Universal Use of Irish Manufacture*; in 1724–1725, the *Drapier's Letters*.

Swift returned to England briefly in 1726, to publish his most famous work, *Gulliver's Travels*, and again in the summer of 1727, to arrange for the publication of *Miscellanies in Prose and Verse*, written with Pope.

Less than a year later, on January 28, 1728, Swift's long friendship with Stella was terminated by her death. Despite his loss, however, Swift remained active, composing a variety of pieces, including *A Modest Proposal*, 1729, and some of his best verse during his later years. It was not until late in his life, in 1742, that he was found incompetent. On October 19, 1745 he died, having lived his last years in senility. He was interred in St. Patrick's next to Stella.

Jonathan Swift—Selective Bibliography

Louis A. Landa and James E. Tobin, eds., *Jonathan Swift, A List of Critical Studies Published from 1895 to 1945*, New York, Cosmopolitan Science & Art Service Co., 1945.

James J. Stathis, *A Bibliography of Swift Studies, 1945–1965*, Nashville, Tenn., Vanderbilt U. P., 1967. See also *CBEL*, II, pp. 581 f.

Herbert Davis, ed., *The Prose Works of Jonathan Swift*, 14 vols., Oxford, B. Blackwell for the Shakespeare Head Press, 1939–1968. No modern edition of the complete works exists, that edited by Sir Walter Scott, 19 vols., Edinburgh, A. Constable, having appeared in 1814. But various individual editions of all the works are available.

Harold Williams, ed., *The Poems of Jonathan Swift*, 3 vols., Oxford, Clarendon Press, 1937; revised 1958.

A. C. Guthkelch and D. Nichol Smith, eds., *"A Tale of a Tub," To Which Is Added "The Battle of the Books" and "The Mechanical Operation of the Spirit" by Jonathan Swift*, Oxford, Clarendon Press, 1920; 2nd ed., 1958.

Harold Williams, ed., *The Correspondence of Jonathan Swift*, 5 vols., Oxford, Clarendon Press, 1963–1965.

———, *Journal to Stella*, 2 vols., Oxford, Clarendon Press, 1948.

———, *Gulliver's Travels*, London, First Edition Club, 1926.

Irvin Ehrenpreis, *Swift: The Man, His Works, and the Age* (of 3 vols. planned, 2 have appeared): I, *Mr. Swift and His Contemporaries;* II, *Dr. Swift*, Cambridge, Mass., Harvard U. P., 1962, 1967.

John M. Bullit, *Jonathan Swift and the Anatomy of Satire*, Cambridge, Mass., Harvard U. P., 1953.

Arthur E. Case, *Four Essays on "Gulliver's Travels,"* Princeton [N.J.] U. P., 1945.

Herbert Davis, *The Satire of Jonathan Swift*, New York, Macmillan, 1947.

Philip Harth, *Swift and Anglican Rationalism: The Religious Background of "A Tale of a Tub,"* Chicago, U. of Chicago Press, 1961.

Maurice Johnson, *The Sin of Wit: Jonathan Swift as a Poet*, Syracuse [N.Y.] U. P., 1950.

Louis T. Milic, *A Quantitative Approach to the Style of Jonathan Swift*, The Hague and Paris, Mouton & Co., 1967.

Ronald Paulson, *Theme and Structure in Swift's "Tale of a Tub,"* New Haven, Yale U. P., 1960.

Martin Price, *Swift's Rhetorical Art*, New Haven, Yale U. P., 1953; Hamden Conn., Archon Books, 1963.

Ricardo Quintana, *The Mind and Art of Jonathan Swift*, New York and London, Oxford U. P., 1936; revised 1954.

————, *Swift: An Introduction*, London and New York, Oxford U. P., 1955.

Edward W. Rosenheim, Jr., *Swift and the Satirist's Art*, Chicago, U. of Chicago Press, 1963.

Miriam K. Starkman, *Swift's Satire on Learning in "A Tale of a Tub,"* Princeton [N.J.] U.P., 1950.

Kathleen Williams, *Jonathan Swift and the Age of Compromise*, Lawrence, U. of Kansas Press, 1958.

Herbert Davis, *Jonathan Swift, Essays on His Satires and Other Studies*, New York, Oxford U. P., 1964.

Ernest Lee Tuveson, *Swift: A Collection of Critical Essays*, Englewood Cliffs, N.J., Prentice-Hall, 1964.

Barry Alepian, "The Ironic Intention of Swift's Verses on his Own Death," *RES*, new ser., XIV (1963), 249–256.

Headnote to
A TALE OF A TUB and
THE BATTEL OF
THE BOOKS

In 1704, Swift had published anonymously a volume containing three
very closely related satires—*A Tale of a Tub, The Battel of the Books,*
and *The Mechanical Operation of the Spirit.* Indeed, it is possible that he
considered the three to be parts of the same work. Though scholars
vary in fixing the degree to which the three are interdependent, most
acknowledge the controlling theme in all of them to be the ridicule
of new ideas that were regarded by many of Swift's contemporaries
as a measure of progress over older notions. Specifically, *The Tale*
derides certain abuses in religious practice—abuses that represent
departures from uncorrupted Christianity; it also satirizes modern
learning for its corruptions. *The Battel* scores the upstart presumption
of modern authors who confuse irresponsible new-fangledness with
excellence, because they assume mere change to be progress. *The
Mechanical Operation* ridicules religious zealots, both members of
nonconformist congregations and their ranting preachers.

At one fairly superficial level, these satires (*The Battel* particularly)
may be thought of as Swift's contribution to the quarrel of the ancients
and moderns, as it is usually called, a quarrel that had taken shape and
assumed vast proportions in France throughout the previous century.
Although very complicated, the opposing views can be represented,
rather simply, in just a few sentences. Those who espoused the cause of
the ancients thought classical man—probably closer to an hypothesized
pristine condition than modern man, and somehow closer to nature
and to God—had accomplished works, not to be surpassed, in all significant fields of endeavor—philosophy, history, the arts. They further
maintained that mankind at best could not improve, and that probably
he grew worse and worse with succeeding ages. It follows of course
that the moderns, who generally believed mankind profits significantly
from the lessons of the past, or that the generations of men in some
way improve with time's passage, would find the ancients pessimistic,
or ignorant about the recent strides forward in the sciences and in
scholarly techniques, or sentimentally attached to bygone days.

There were many reasons for Swift to have been drawn into the quarrel, the most important of them growing out of his own deep convictions—moral, artistic, intellectual, religious, social, and political convictions. The list is so long as to seem almost ludicrous. And though obviously Swift's mind was capable of very subtle discriminations, it is probably true that he would not have catalogued his beliefs if asked about them, because he seems to have thought of them as unified into a single attitude. This important personal reason apart, Swift entered the quarrel in order to take the side of his employer, Sir William Temple, who had himself joined the ranks of the ancients in 1690, with his essay *Upon the Ancient and Modern Learning*. There, Temple tried to explode the modern view that one could prove historically the superiority of modern over ancient civilization. Unfortunately, in making his case he cited Aesop's *Fables* and the *Epistles* of Phalaris to demonstrate the greatness of ancient prose; and though he survived an attack by William Wotton fairly well—*Reflections upon Ancient and Modern Learning* (1694)—he was demolished by the great philologist Richard Bentley, who in a *Dissertation* appended to a later edition of Wotton's *Reflections* (1697), demonstrated that both the *Fables* and the *Epistles* were not classical works.

Swift's stake in the quarrel was probably different from Temple's. It is less likely that he approved whole-heartedly the views of the ancients than that he disputed the claims of the moderns, which seemed to him presumptuous. Classical authors had indeed written well; but their works continued to please not because they were venerable, but because they were excellent. Upstarts who assumed they surpassed the old masters simply because they had more of the race's experience to draw upon were guilty of a foolish and dangerous error. Incompetent classical authors must have written; probably little of their work had survived for the reason that it had not withstood the test of time. By Swift's day, the relatively few surviving classics had been dignified by the measured approval of generations of readers. On the other hand, modern authors without any qualification other than their modernity seemed to litter the world, making it difficult to see the truth. At the same time, their excessive self-assurance and false sense of purpose ("enthusiasm") deluded many of their gullible contemporaries. Swift's problem was to tear away this covering of optimism to reveal what lay beneath.

In order to accomplish his purpose, he chose the indirect means of satire. Generally the narrator in any literary work identifies himself to his reader fairly quickly. If the narrator does not directly offer his credentials as, say, clergyman, philosopher, or physician, he at least exposes himself sufficiently to qualify as the story-teller one can trust to tell the truth, after which his reader relaxes, assured that he need only read and agree in order to understand. The satirist makes a different demand. He requires the reader to infer the character behind the voice of the narrator, so that what the voice says may be appraised accordingly, rather than accepted at face value. As soon as the reader learns the peculiar point of view of the narrator, he makes the necessary adjustment and reads on with understanding. The voice may exaggerate; for example: "Unless, the vile, disease-ridden slums are cleared from all our cities immediately, I assure you this nation will cease to be, within the next generation." Or it may use simple irony: "The wide expanse of our slums, charmingly punctuated with filth and disease-ridden children as it is, makes it an excellent place through which to conduct a leisurely tour of one's guests from out of town." In either case, the reader works to accommodate himself to the distortion of the truth, and reads along, perpetually encountering the narrator's skewed vision and perpetually correcting it. In the process, the reader's scrutiny of matters only casually observed by him before is intensified because of the permeation of his own workaday view by the satirist's distortion. Still, it is possible to adjust to such a steady demand and in fact to anticipate the narrator's peculiarities of vision after a time. In such cases, the satire loses much of its power, a possibility Swift avoided by a wide variety of means.

In *A Tale of a Tub* and *The Battel of the Books* Swift never permits his reader to rest easy in the knowledge that he has once and for all identified the character of the narrator, chiefly by introducing new narrators in successive sections of the work. In this way, he keeps one hypersensitive to the necessity of appraising statements at every turn. And just to make certain of keeping his reader awake always, Swift sometimes engineers a sudden shift of perspective in the character of one of his narrators, as he does, for example, in the Tale's *Preface*. But instead of throwing the work aside because it has failed in consistency, the reader accepts the new terms, prepared as he has been by its unpredictable climate to expect the perverse changes in weather. Having had the world of the work only doubtfully identified to him, the reader can hardly complain that the author has violated an implicit contract between them. Bewildered, perhaps, yet ultimately flattered that perpetual judgment is required of him, the reader proceeds, awake and ready.

The structure of *A Tale of a Tub* is very carefully controlled to reinforce meaning in the satire. With the inclusion of "An Apology For the, &c." to the fifth edition, 1710 (the text here presented), the various parts of the work number seventeen. These may be divided conveniently into three categories—prefatory apparatus and conclusion (seven parts), religious allegory (five parts), and digressions (five parts). The prefatory apparatus and conclusion of course frame the work, and the religious allegory and digressions with one exception alternate in filling the middle of the satire.

Generally, the prefatory material satirizes the learning and books of the moderns, which often included great lists of works projected by authors or publishers; lengthy dedications, explanations, apologies, introductions, prefaces—in effect, any means of filling the book short of getting down to writing it; and the loose structure (non-method) associated with the moderns, particularly the hacks of Grub Street. Digressions, in the central section of the work, satirize abuses in modern learning and modern writing in a variety of ways. And the allegorical sections satirize abuses in religion: Martin (Church of England), Jack (Dissenting Protestantism), and Peter (Roman Catholicism), three brothers who are left a very clear will by their father, a will intended to preserve the pristine quality of their cloaks (emblems of religious practice), at first distort and later ignore its simple requirements. Ultimately, Peter becomes a proud organizer of grand projects; Jack becomes zealous to the point of madness; and Martin, after some doubtful practices that have left many readers dissatisfied with him, comes round again to an even course.

Finally, the three parts are unified thematically and structurally, in ways that can be suggested here only briefly. Irrational confidence in personal views, having no basis in objective fact, over and over marks the attitude and behavior of moderns, just as it does (in both the digressions and prefatory material) the abusive religious practices of Peter and Jack. Moreover the impression given by the very long list of the prefatory items is very much like the impression given by the very obtrusive digressions of the later sections of the work—both seem at one level to be irrelevant to the "actual" subject of the book, the story of Martin, Jack, and Peter. One brings the whole amazing structure around full circle, simply by observing that similar content makes the religious episodes in some sense like the digressions, which after all are like the prefatory items.

The Battel of the Books is structurally much less complicated than the

Tale, though by no means simple. Unlike the *Tale*, it employs not five or six narrators besides characters (Martin, Jack, and Peter), but three—Bookseller, Author, and Historian, the last of whom assures the reader of his impartiality as he offers his account of the battle between ancient and modern books at the royal library, St. James's. It soon becomes obvious from his choice of words and tone, however, that the historian, far from being neutral, favors the ancients. Nevertheless, in other sections this partiality, which might have weakened the satire, is rendered impossible of expression by Swift's choice of genre—mock epic fragment—a choice that in some degree determines the techniques of language employed in the piece. (See the headnote to *The Rape of the Lock* for a discussion of mock epic.) After an introductory section, during which the battle lines are drawn, Swift introduces the allegory of the bee, a clear-thinking, productive ancient, in close harmony with nature; the spider, an ingenious, mathematically disposed militarist who regards himself (infallible sign of a modern) the center of the world's activity; and Aesop who reidentifies himself as an ancient (Bentley notwithstanding) and explains the allegory. The Greek personification of criticism and fault-finding, Momus, next appears, prepared to assist her modern son Wotton, also Temple's enemy, of course. The remainder of the work is devoted, like much epic, to episodes of battle between principal ancients and moderns, culminating in the burlesque encounter that pairs Bentley and Wotton against Temple and Boyle (Charles Boyle, Fourth Earl of Orrery, 1621–1679), editor of the spurious *Epistles of Phalaris*, which had indirectly precipitated Temple's involvement in the quarrel of ancients and moderns. The "fragment" breaks off appropriately with an epic simile, which informs the reader that Bentley and Wotton have been impaled like a brace of trussed woodcocks on Boyle's spear. Swift of course knew that the woodcock, like Momus, is nocturnal (in Hesiod, a male child of primeval night); and of course he knew what every hunter knows— the point had become proverbial in England—the woodcock is easily taken in a snare or net, despite his nocturnal habits, his marshy dwelling place, and his tricky flight.

Every serious student of *A Tale of a Tub* (and *The Battel of the Books*) should consult the Guthkelch–Nichol Smith edition of the *Tale*, Miriam Kosh Starkman's *Swift's Satire on Learning in A Tale of a Tub*, and Ronald Paulson's *Theme and Structure in Swift's Tale of a Tub*. Any documentation that would be more than generally valuable to a new reader of the work would have to include much more material than it is possible to offer here. In reluctant acknowledgment of this fact, the present edition has kept annotation to a useful minimum.

TEXT. *A Tale of a Tub*, 5th ed., With the author's apology and explanatory notes. By W. W—tt—n, B.D. and others (London, 1710).

A Tale of a Tub

WRITTEN FOR THE UNIVERSAL IMPROVEMENT OF MANKIND

Treatises wrote by the same Author, most of them mentioned in the following Discourses; which will be speedily published.

A Character of the present Set of Wits *in this Island.*
A Panegyrical Essay upon the Number THREE.
A Dissertation upon the principal Productions of Grub-street.
Lectures upon a Dissection of Human Nature.
A Panegyrick upon the World.
An Analytical Discourse upon Zeal, Histori-theo-physi-logically *considered.*
A general History of Ears.
A modest Defence of the Proceedings of the Rabble *in all Ages.*
A Description of the Kingdom of Absurdities.
A Voyage into England, *by a Person of Quality in* Terra Australis incognita, *translated from the Original.*
A Critical Essay upon the Art of Canting, *Philosophically, Physically, and Musically considered.*

An Apology for the, &c.

If good and ill Nature equally operated upon Mankind, I might have saved my self the Trouble of this Apology; for it is manifest by the Reception the following Discourse hath met with, that those who approve it, are a great Majority among the Men of Tast; yet there have been two or three Treatises written expresly against it, besides many others that have flirted at it occasionally, without one Syllable having been ever published in its Defence, or even Quotation to its Advantage, that I can remember, except by the Polite Author of a late Discourse between a Deist and a Socinian.

Therefore, since the Book seems calculated to live at least as long as our Language, and our Tast admit no great Alterations, I am content to convey some Apology along with it. 10

The greatest Part of that Book was finished above thirteen Years since, 1696. which is eight Years before it was published. The Author was then young, his Invention at the Height, and his Reading fresh in his Head. By the Assistance of some Thinking, and much Conversation, he had endeavour'd to Strip himself of as many real Prejudices as he could; I say real ones, because under the Notion of Prejudices, he knew to what dangerous Heights some Men have proceeded. Thus prepared, he thought the numerous and gross Corruptions in Religion and Learning might furnish Matter for a Satyr, that would be useful and diverting: He resolved to proceed in a manner, that should be altogether new, the World having been already too long nauseated with endless Repetitions upon every Subject. The Abuses in Religion he proposed to set forth in the 20 *Allegory of the Coats, and the three Brothers, which was to make up the Body of the Discourse. Those in Learning he chose to introduce by way of Digressions. He was*

331

then a young Gentleman much in the World, and wrote to the Tast of those who were like himself; therefore in order to allure them, he gave a Liberty to his Pen, which might not suit with maturer Years, or graver Characters, and which he could have easily corrected with a very few Blots, had he been Master of his Papers for a Year or two before their Publication.

Not that he would have governed his Judgment by the ill-placed Cavils of the Sour, the Envious, the Stupid, and the Tastless, which he mentions with disdain. He acknowledges there are several youthful Sallies, which from the Grave and the Wise may deserve a Rebuke. But he desires to be answerable no farther than he is guilty, and that his Faults may not be multiply'd by the ignorant, the unnatural, and uncharitable 10 *Applications of those who have neither Candor to suppose good Meanings, nor Palate to distinguish true Ones. After which, he will forfeit his Life, if any one Opinion can be fairly deduced from that Book, which is contrary to Religion or Morality.*

Why should any Clergyman of our Church be angry to see the Follies of Fanaticism and Superstition exposed, tho' in the most ridiculous Manner? since that is perhaps the most probable way to cure them, or at least to hinder them from further spreading. Besides, tho' it was not intended for their Perusal; it raillies nothing but what they preach against. It contains nothing to provoke them by the least Scurillity upon their Persons or their Functions. It Celebrates the Church of England as the most perfect of all others in Discipline and Doctrine, it advances no Opinion they reject, nor condemns 20 *any they receive. If the Clergy's Resentments lay upon their Hands, in my humble Opinion, they might have found more proper Objects to employ them on:* Nondum tibi defuit Hostis;[1] *I mean those heavy, illiterate Scriblers, prostitute in their Reputations, vicious in their Lives, and ruin'd in their Fortunes, who to the shame of good Sense as well as Piety, are greedily read, meerly upon the Strength of bold, false, impious Assertions, mixt with unmannerly Reflections upon the Priesthood, and openly intended against all Religion; in short, full of such Principles as are kindly received, because they are levell'd to remove those Terrors that Religion tells Men will be the Consequence of immoral Lives. Nothing like which is to be met with in this Discourse, tho' some of them are pleased so freely to censure it. And I wish, there* 30 *were no other Instance of what I have too frequently observed, that many of that Reverend Body are not always very nice in distinguishing between their Enemies and their Friends.*

Had the Author's Intentions met with a more candid Interpretation from some whom out of Respect he forbears to name, he might have been encouraged to an Examination of Books written by some of those Authors above-described, whose Errors, Ignorance, Dullness and Villany, he thinks he could have detected and exposed in such a Manner, that the Persons who are most conceived to be infected by them, would soon lay them aside and be ashamed: But he has now given over those Thoughts, since the weightiest Men in the weightiest Stations are pleased to think it a more dangerous Point to laugh 40 *at those Corruptions in Religion, which they themselves must disapprove, than to endeavour pulling up those very Foundations, wherein all Christians have agreed.*

He thinks it no fair Proceeding, that any Person should offer determinately to fix a name upon the Author of this Discourse, who hath all along concealed himself from

---

[1] *Nondum tibi defuit Hostis:* So far [Rome] has never been without a foreign enemy.

most of his nearest Friends: Yet several have gone a farther Step, and pro-
nounced another Book to have been the Work of the same Hand with this;
which the Author directly affirms to be a thorough mistake; he having yet
never so much as read that Discourse, a plain Instance how little Truth, there often is
in general Surmises, or in Conjectures drawn from a Similitude of Style, or way of
thinking.

Had the Author writ a Book to expose the Abuses in Law, or in Physick, he believes
the Learned Professors in either Faculty, would have been so far from resenting it, as
to have given him Thanks for his Pains, especially if he had made an honourable
Reservation for the true Practice of either Science: But Religion they tell us ought not   10
to be ridiculed, and they tell us Truth, yet surely the Corruptions in it may; for we are
taught by the tritest Maxim in the World, that Religion being the best of Things, its
Corruptions are likely to be the worst.

There is one Thing which the judicious Reader cannot but have observed, that
some of those Passages in this Discourse, which appear most liable to Objection are
what they call Parodies, where the Author personates the Style and Manner of other
Writers, whom he has a mind to expose. I shall produce one Instance, it is in the 51st
Page.[3] Dryden, L'Estrange, *and some others I shall not name, are here levelled at,*
who having spent their Lives in Faction, and Apostacies, and all manner of Vice, pre-
tended to be Sufferers for Loyalty and Religion. So Dryden *tells us in one of his*   20
Prefaces of his Merits and Suffering, thanks God that he possesses his Soul in
Patience: *In other Places he talks at the same Rate, and* L'Estrange *often uses the like*
Style, and I believe the Reader may find more Persons to give that Passage an Applica-
tion: But this is enough to direct those who may have over-look'd the Authors
Intention.

There are three or four other Passages which prejudiced or ignorant Readers have
drawn by great Force to hint at ill Meanings; as if they glanced at some Tenets in
Religion, in answer to all which, the Author solemnly protests he is entirely Innocent,
and never had it once in his Thoughts that any thing he said would in the least be
capable of such Interpretations, which he will engage to deduce full as fairly from the   30
most innocent Book in the World. And it will be obvious to every Reader, that this
was not any part of his Scheme or Design, the Abuses he notes being such as all Church
of England *Men agree in, nor was it proper for his Subject to meddle with other*
Points, than such as have been perpetually controverted since the Reformation.

To instance only in that Passage about the three wooden Machines mentioned in the
Introduction: In the Original Manuscript there was a description of a Fourth, which
those who had the Papers in their Power, blotted out, as having something in it of Satyr,
that I suppose they thought was too particular, and therefore they were forced to change
it to the Number Three, *from whence some have endeavour'd to squeeze out a dangerous*
Meaning that was never thought on. And indeed the Conceit was half spoiled by chan-   40
ging the Numbers; that of Four *being much more Cabalistick, and therefore better*
exposing the pretended Virtue of Numbers, a Superstition there intended to be ridicul'd.

Another Thing to be observed is, that there generally runs an Irony through the
Thread of the whole Book, which the Men of Tast will observe and distinguish, and

---

[2] *Letter of Enthusiasm: A Letter con-*   1711.
cerning Enthusiasm to My Lord . . . , is a   [3] *51st Page:* Page 359 in this edition.
section of Shaftesbury's *Characteristics,*

which will render some Objections that have been made, very weak and insignificant.

This Apology being chiefly intended for the Satisfaction of future Readers, it may be thought unnecessary to take any notice of such Treatises as have been writ against this ensuing Discourse, which are already sunk into waste Paper and Oblivion; after the usual Fate of common Answerers to Books, which are allowed to have any Merit: They are indeed like Annuals that grow about a young Tree, and seem to vye with it for a Summer, but fall and die with the Leaves in Autumn, and are never heard of any more. When Dr. Eachard writ his Book about the Contempt of the Clergy,[4] numbers of those Answerers immediately started up, whose Memory if he had not kept alive by his Replies, it would now be utterly unknown that he were ever answered 10 *at all. There is indeed an Exception, when any great Genius thinks it worth his while to expose a foolish Piece; so we still read Marvel's Answer to Parker[5] with Pleasure, tho' the Book it answers be sunk along ago; so the Earl of Orrery's Remarks[6] will be read with Delight, when the Dissertation he exposes will neither be sought nor found; but these are no Enterprises for common Hands, nor to be hoped for above once or twice in an Age. Men would be more cautious of losing their Time in such an Undertaking, if they did but consider, that to answer a Book effectually, requires more Pains and Skill, more Wit, Learning, and Judgment than were employ'd in the Writing it. And the Author assures those Gentlemen who have given themselves that Trouble with him, that his Discourse is the Product of the Study, the Observation, and the* 20 *Invention of several Years, that he often blotted out much more than he left, and if his Papers had not been a long time out of his Possession, they must have still undergone more severe Corrections; and do they think such a Building is to be battered with Dirt-Pellets however envenom'd the Mouths may be that discharge them. He hath seen the Productions but of two Answerers, One of which first appear'd as from an unknown hand, but since avowed by a Person, who upon some Occasions hath discover'd no ill Vein of Humor. 'Tis a Pity any Occasions should put him under a necessity of being so hasty in his Productions, which otherwise might often be entertaining. But there were other Reasons obvious enough for his Miscarriage in this; he writ against the Conviction of his Talent, and enter'd upon one of the wrongest Attempts* 30 *in Nature, to turn into ridicule by a Weeks Labour, a Work which had cost so much time, and met with so much Success in ridiculing others, the manner how he has handled his Subject, I have now forgot, having just look'd it over when it first came out, as others did, meerly for the sake of the Title.*

The other Answer is from a Person of a graver Character,[7] and is made up of half Invective, and half Annotation. In the latter of which he hath generally succeeded well enough. And the Project at that time was not amiss, to draw in Readers to his Pamphlet, several having appear'd desirous that there might be some Explication of the more diffi-

---

[4] *Dr. Eachard . . . Clergy:* John Eachard (1636?–1697) was the author of *The Grounds and Occasions of the Contempt of the Clergy . . . Enquired into.*

[5] *Marvel's Answer to Parker:* Andrew Marvell (1621–1678) answered Samuel Parker's attack on nonconformity in *The Rehearsal Transpros'd*, 1672–1673.

[6] *Orrery's Remarks:* The Fourth Earl of Orrery, Charles Boyle, had edited the *Epistles of Phalaris*. See the headnote to *Tale of a Tub.*

[7] *Person of a graver Character:* William Wotton is that person. He had directed his *Reflections upon Ancient and Modern Learning* against Temple, and to it he had added *Observations upon the Tale of a Tub* in 1705, when the third edition of his work appeared. Though Wotton's notes were largely hostile to Swift, many were truly informative, and Swift either permitted or engineered their addition to the fifth edition of the *Tale*, in 1710.

cult Passages. Neither can he be altogether blamed for offering at the Invective Part, because it is agreed on all hands that the Author had given him sufficient Provocation. The great Objection is against his manner of treating it, very unsuitable to one of his Function. It was determined by a fair Majority, that this Answer had in a way not to be pardon'd, drawn his Pen against a certain great Man then alive,[8] *and universally reverenced for every good Quality that could possibly enter into the Composition of the most accomplish'd Person; it was observed, how he was pleased and affected to have that noble Writer call'd his Adversary, and it was a Point of Satyr well directed, for I have been told, Sir W.T. was sufficiently mortify'd at the Term. All the Men of Wit and Politeness were immediately up in Arms, through Indignation, which prevailed over* 10 *their Contempt, by the Consequences they apprehended from such an Example, and it grew to be Porsenna's Case; Idem trecenti juravimus.*[9] *In short, things were ripe for a general Insurrection, till my Lord* Orrery *had a little laid the Spirit, and settled the Ferment. But his Lordship being principally engaged with another Antagonist,*[10] *it was thought necessary in order to quiet the Minds of Men, that this Opposer should receive a Reprimand, which partly occasioned that Discourse of the Battle of the Books, and the Author was farther at the Pains to insert one or two Remarks on him in the Body of the Book.*

This Answerer has been pleased to find Fault with about a dozen Passages, which the Author will not be at the Trouble of defending, farther than by assuring the Reader, 20 *that for the greater Part the Reflecter is entirely mistaken, and forces Interpretations which never once entered into the Writer's Head, nor will he is sure into that of any Reader of Tast and Candor; he allows two or three at most there produced to have been deliver'd unwarily, for which he desires to plead the Excuse offered already, of his Youth, and Franckness of Speech, and his Papers being out of his Power at the Time they were published.*

But this Answerer insists, and says, what he chiefly dislikes, is the Design; *what that was I have already told, and I believe there is not a Person in* England *who can understand that Book, that ever imagined it to have been any thing else, but to expose the Abuses and Corruptions in Learning and Religion.* 30

But it would be good to know what Design *this Reflecter was serving, when he concludes his Pamphlet with a Caution to Readers, to beware of thinking the Authors Wit was entirely his own, surely this must have had some Allay of Personal Animosity, at least mixt with the Design of serving the Publick by so useful a Discovery; and it indeed touches the Author in a very tender Point, who insists upon it, that through the whole Book he has not borrowed one single Hint from any Writer in the World; and he thought, of all Criticisms, that would never have been one, He conceived it was never disputed to be an Original, whatever Faults it might have. However this Answerer produces three Instances to prove this Author's Wit is not his own in many Places. The first is, that the Names of* Peter, Martin *and* Jack *are borrowed from* 40 *a Letter of the late Duke of* Buckingham. *Whatever Wit is contained in those three Names, the Author is content to give it up, and desires his Readers will substract as*

---

[8] *Great Man then alive:* Sir William Temple, who had died in 1699. See the headnote to *Tale of a Tub.*

[9] *Idem trecenti juravimus:* Three hundred of us have sworn to try the same thing [an attack]. Porsenna, Etruscan king attempting to recapture a newly freed Rome, was told by a Roman captive, who, as he made the threat, held his hand in a fire to demonstrate his courage and that of his 300 countrymen.

[10] *Another Antagonist:* Bentley.

much as they placed upon that Account; at the same time protesting solemnly that he never once heard of that Letter, except in this Passage of the Answerer: So that the Names were not borrowed as he affirms, tho' they should happen to be the same which however is odd enough, and what he hardly believes; that of Jack, *being not quite so obvious as the other two.* The second Instance to shew the Author's Wit is not his own, *is* Peter's Banter *(as he calls it in his* Alsatia *Phrase) upon Transubstantiation, which is taken from the same Duke's Conference with an* Irish *Priest, where a Cork is turned into a Horse. This the Author confesses to have seen, about ten Years after his Book was writ, and a Year or two after it was published. Nay, the Answerer over-throws this himself; for he allows the Tale was writ in 1697; and I think that Pamphlet was not printed in many Years after. It was necessary, that Corruption should have some Allegory as well as the rest; and the Author invented the properest he could, without enquiring what other People had writ, and the commonest Reader will find, there is not the least Resemblance between the two Stories. The third Instance is in these Words:* I have been assured, that the Battle in St. *James's* Library, is *mutatis mutandis,* taken out of a *French* Book, entituled, *Combat des livres, if* I misremember not. *In which Passage there are two Clauses observable:* I have been assured; *and, if* I misremember not. *I desire first to know, whether if that Conjecture proves an utter falshood, those two Clauses will be a sufficient Excuse for this worthy Critick. The Matter is a Trifle; but, would he venture to pronounce at this Rate upon one of greater Moment? I know nothing more contemptible in a Writer than the Character of a Plagiary; which he here fixes at a venture, and this, not for a Passage, but a whole Discourse, taken out from another Book only* mutatis mutandis. *The Author is as much in the dark about this as the Answerer; and will imitate him by an Affirmation at Random; that if there be a word of Truth in this Reflection, he is a paultry, imitating Pedant, and the Answerer is a Person of Wit, Manners and Truth. He takes his Bold-ness, from never having seen any such Treatise in his Life nor heard of it before; and he is sure it is impossible for two Writers of different Times and Countries to agree in their Thoughts after such a Manner, that two continued Discourses shall be the same only* mutatis mutandis. *Neither will he insist upon the mistake of the Title, but let the Answerer and his Friend[11] produce any Book they please, he defies them to shew one single Particular, where the judicious Reader will affirm he has been obliged for the smallest Hint; giving only Allowance for the accidental encountring of a single Thought, which he knows may sometimes happen; tho' he has never yet found it in that Discourse, nor has heard it objected by any body else.*

So that if ever any design was unfortunately executed, it must be that of this Answerer, who when he would have it observed that the Author's Wit is not his own, is able to produce but three Instances, two of them meer Trifles, and all three manifestly false. If this be the way these Gentlemen deal with the World in those Criticisms, where we have not Leisure to defeat them, their Readers had need be cautious how they rely upon their Credit; and whether this Proceeding can be reconciled to Humanity or Truth, let those who think it worth their while, determine.

It is agreed, this Answerer would have succeeded much better, if he had stuck wholly to his Business as a Commentator upon the Tale of a Tub, *wherein it cannot be deny'd that he hath been of some Service to the Publick, and has given very fair Conjectures towards clearing up some difficult Passages; but, it is the frequent Error of those Men*

---

[11] *Friend:* Bentley.

(otherwise very commendable for their Labors) to make *Excursions beyond their Talent and their Office,* by pretending to point out the *Beauties* and the *Faults;* which is no part of their *Trade,* which they always fail in, which the *World* never expected from them, nor gave them any thanks for endeavouring at. *The Part of* Min-ellius, *or* Farnaby[12] *would have fallen in with his Genius, and might have been serviceable to many Readers who cannot enter into the abstruser Parts of that Discourse; but* Optat ephippia bos piger.[13] *The dull, unwieldy, ill-shaped Ox would needs put on the Furniture of a Horse, not considering he was born to Labour, to plow the Ground for the Sake of superior Beings, and that he has neither the Shape, Mettle nor Speed of that nobler Animal he would affect to personate.*

It is another *Pattern* of this *Answerer's* fair dealing, to give us *Hints* that the *Author* is dead, and yet to lay the *Suspicion* upon somebody, *I* know not who, in the *Country;* to which can be only returned, that he is absolutely mistaken in all his *Conjectures;* and surely *Conjectures* are at best too light a *Pretence* to allow a *Man* to assign a *Name* in *Publick.* He condemns a *Book,* and consequently the *Author,* of whom he is utterly ignorant, yet at the same time fixes in *Print,* what he thinks a disadvantageous *Character* upon those who never deserved it. A *Man* who receives a *Buffet* in the *Dark* may be allowed to be vexed; but it is an odd kind of *Revenge* to go to *Cuffs* in broad day with the first he meets with, and lay the last *Nights Injury* at his *Door.* And thus much for this discreet, candid, pious, and ingenious *Answerer.*

How the *Author* came to be without his *Papers,* is a *Story* not proper to be told, and of very little use, being a private *Fact* of which the *Reader* would believe as little or as much as he thought good. He had however a blotted *Copy* by him, which he intended to have writ over, with many *Alterations,* and this the *Publishers* were well aware of, having put it into the *Booksellers Preface,* that they apprehended a surreptitious *Copy,* which was to be altered, *&c. This* though not regarded by *Readers,* was a real *Truth,* only the surreptitious *Copy* was rather that which was printed, and they made all hast they could, which indeed was needless; the *Author* not being at all prepared; but he has been told, the *Bookseller* was in much *Pain,* having given a good *Sum* of *Money* for the *Copy.*

In the *Authors Original Copy* there were not so many *Chasms* as appear in the *Book;* and why some of them were left he knows not; had the *Publication* been trusted to him, he should have made several *Corrections* of *Passages* against which nothing hath been ever objected. He should likewise have altered a few of those that seem with any *Reason* to be excepted against, but to deal freely, the greatest *Number* he should have left untouch'd, as never suspecting it possible any wrong *Interpretations* could be made of them.

The *Author* observes, at the *End* of the *Book* there is a *Discourse* called A Fragment; which he more wondered to see in *Print* than all the rest. Having been a most imperfect *Sketch* with the *Addition* of a few loose *Hints,* which he once lent a *Gentleman* who had designed a *Discourse* of somewhat the same *Subject;* he never thought of it afterwards, and it was a sufficient *Surprize* to see it pieced up together, wholly out of the *Method* and *Scheme* he had intended, for it was the *Ground-work* of a much larger *Discourse,* and he was sorry to observe the *Materials* so foolishly employ'd.

[12] *Min-ellius, or Farnaby:* Scholars of the previous century.
[13] *Optat ephippia bos piger:* Horace, *Epistles,* I, xiv, 43: *Optat ephippia bos,* *piger optat arare caballus:* The ox longs for the horse's life; the horse, when bored, longs to plow.

There is one farther Objection made by those who have answered this Book, as well as by some others, that Peter *is frequently made to repeat Oaths and Curses. Every Reader observes it was necessary to know that* Peter *did Swear and Curse. The Oaths are not printed out, but only supposed, and the Idea of an Oath is not immoral, like the Idea of a Prophane or Immodest Speech. A Man may laugh at the Popish Folly of cursing People to Hell, and imagine them swearing, without any crime; but lewd Words, or dangerous Opinions though printed by halves, fill the Readers Mind with ill Idea's; and of these the Author cannot be accused. For the judicious Reader will find that the severest Stroaks of Satyr in his Book are levelled against the modern Custom of Employing Wit upon those Topicks, of which there is a remarkable Instance* 1(*in the* 153d. *Page,*[14] *as well as in several others, tho' perhaps once or twice exprest in too free a manner, excusable only for the Reasons already alledged. Some Overtures have been made by a third Hand to the Bookseller for the Author's altering those Passages which he thought might require it. But it seems the Bookseller will not hear of any such Thing, being apprehensive it might spoil the Sale of the Book.*

The Author cannot conclude this Apology, without making this one Reflection; that, as Wit is the noblest and most useful Gift of humane Nature, so Humor is the most agreeable, and where these two enter far into the Composition of any Work, they will render it always acceptable to the World. Now, the great Part of those who have no Share or Tast of either, but by their Pride, Pedantry and Ill Manners, lay themselves 2(*bare to the Lashes of Both, think the Blow is weak, because they are insensible, and where Wit hath any mixture of Raillery; 'Tis but calling it* Banter, *and the work is done. This Polite Word of theirs was first borrowed from the Bullies in* White-Fryars,[15] *then fell among the Footmen, and at Last retired to the Pedants, by whom it is applied as properly to the Productions of Wit, as if I should apply it to* Sir Isaac Newton's *Mathematicks, but, if this* Bantring *as they call it, be so despisable a Thing, whence comes it to pass they have such a perpetual Itch towards it themselves? To instance only in the Answerer already mentioned; it is grievous to see him in some of his Writings at every turn going out of his way to be waggish, to tell us of a* Cow *that prickt up her Tail, and in his answer to this Discourse, he says it is all a Farce and a Ladle:* 3(*With other Passages equally shining. One may say of these* impedimenta Literarum, *that Wit ows them a Shame; and they cannot take wiser Counsel than to keep out of harms way, or at least not to come till they are sure they are called.*

To conclude; with those Allowances above-required, this Book should be read, after which the Author conceives, few things will remain which may not be excused in a young Writer. He wrote only to the Men of Wit and Tast, and he thinks he is not mistaken in his Accounts, when he says they have been all of his side, enough to give him the vanity of telling his Name, wherein the World with all its wise Conjectures, is yet very much in the dark, which Circumstance is no disagreeable Amusement either to the Publick or himself. 4

The Author is informed, that the Bookseller has prevailed on several Gentlemen, to write some explanatory Notes,[16] *for the goodness of which he is not to answer, having*

[14] *153d. Page:* Page 392 in the present edition.

[15] *White-Fryars:* A place offering sanctuary, between Fleet Street and the Thames.

[16] *Explanatory Notes:* If the notes—those in the margin as well as those at the bottom of the page—are not by Swift, he let pass the chance to change or to delete them before the fifth edition, 1710. Marginal notes had appeared in earlier editions, footnotes first in 1710. (Numbered notes in this edition are of course the present editor's.)

never seen any of them, nor intends it, till they appear in Print, when it is not unlikely he may have the Pleasure to find twenty Meanings, which never enter'd into his Imagination.
June 3, 1709.

Postscript

Since the writing of this which was about a Year ago; a Prostitute Bookseller[17] hath publish'd a foolish Paper, under the Name of Notes on the Tale *of a* Tub, *with some Account of the Author, and with an Insolence which I suppose is punishable by Law, hath presumed to assign certain Names. It will be enough for the Author to assure the World, that the Writer of that Paper is utterly wrong in all his Conjectures upon that Affair. The Author farther asserts that the whole Work is entirely of one Hand, which every Reader of Judgment will easily discover. The Gentleman who gave the Copy to the Bookseller, being a Friend of the Author, and using no other Liberties besides that of expunging certain Passages where now the Chasms appear under th[e] Name of* Desiderata. *But if any Person will prove his Claim to three Lines in the whole Book, let him step forth and tell his Name and Titles, upon which the Bookseller shall have Orders to prefix them to the next Edition, and the Claimant shall from henceforward be acknowledged the undisputed Author.*

To the Right Honourable, John, Lord Sommers[18]

My LORD,

THO' the Author has written a large Dedication, yet That being address'd to a Prince, whom I am never likely to have the Honor of being known to; A Person, besides, as far as I can observe, not at all regarded, or thought on by any of our present Writers; And, being wholly free from that Slavery, which Booksellers usually lie under, to the Caprices of Authors; I think it a wise Piece of Presumption, to inscribe these Papers to your Lordship, and to implore your Lordship's Protection of them. God and your Lordship know their Faults, and their Merits; for as to my own Particular, I am altogether a Stranger to the Matter; And, tho' every Body else should be equally ignorant, I do not fear the Sale of the Book, at all the worse, upon that Score. Your Lordship's Name on the Front, in Capital Letters, will at any time get off one Edition: Neither would I desire any other Help, to grow an Alderman, than a Patent for the sole Priviledge of Dedicating to your Lordship.

I should now, in right of a Dedicator, give your Lordship a List of your own Virtues, and at the same time, be very unwilling to offend your Modesty; But, chiefly, I should celebrate your Liberality towards Men of great Parts and small Fortunes, and give you broad Hints, that I mean my self. And, I was just going on in the usual Method, to peruse a hundred or two of Dedications, and transcribe an Abstract, to be applied to your Lordship; But, I was diverted by a

10

20

30

---

[17] *Prostitute Bookseller:* Edmund Curll, who had published earlier in 1710, *A Complete Key to the Tale of a Tub.*
[18] *Lord Sommers:* John, First Baron Somers (1651–1716) after the Revolution of 1688 rose step by step to become Chancellor in 1697. He was William's most trusted minister and a great patron of the arts.

certain Accident. For, upon the Covers of these Papers, I casually observed written in large Letters, the two following Words, *DETUR DIGNISSIMO*;[19] which, for ought I knew, might contain some important Meaning. But, it unluckily fell out, that none of the Authors I employ, understood *Latin* (tho' I have them often in pay, to translate out of that Language); I was therefore compelled to have recourse to the Curate of our Parish, who Englished it thus, *Let it be given to the Worthiest*; And his Comment was, that the Author meant, his Work should be dedicated to the sublimest Genius of the Age, for Wit, Learning, Judgment, Eloquence and Wisdom. I call'd at a Poet's Chamber (who works for my Shop) in an Alley hard by, shewed him the Translation, and desired his Opinion, who it was that the Author could mean; He told me, after some Consideration, that Vanity was a Thing he abhor'd; but by the Description, he thought Himself to be the Person aimed at; And, at the same time, he very kindly offer'd his own Assistance *gratis*, towards penning a Dedication to Himself. I desire him, however, to give a second Guess; Why then, said he, It must be I, or my Lord *Sommers*. From thence I went to several other Wits of my Acquaintance, with no small Hazard and Weariness to my Person, from a prodigious Number of dark, winding Stairs; But found them all in the same Story, both of your Lordship and themselves. Now, your Lordship is to understand, that this Proceeding was not of my own Invention; For, I have somewhere heard, it is a Maxim, that those, to whom every Body allows the second Place, have an undoubted Title to the First.

THIS infallibly convinced me, that your Lordship was the Person intended by the Author. But, being very unacquainted in the Style and Form of Dedications, I employ'd those Wits aforesaid, to furnish me with Hints and Materials, towards a Panegyrick upon your Lordship's Virtues.

IN two Days, they brought me ten Sheets of Paper, fill'd up on every Side. They swore to me, that they had ransack'd whatever could be found in the Characters of *Socrates, Aristides, Epaminondas, Cato, Tully, Atticus*, and other hard Names, which I cannot now recollect. However, I have Reason to believe, they imposed upon my Ignorance, because, when I came to read over their Collections, there was not a Syllable there, but what I and every body else knew as well as themselves: Therefore, I grievously suspect a Cheat; and, that these Authors of mine, stole and transcribed every Word, from the universal Report of Mankind. So that I look upon my self, as fifty Shillings out of Pocket, to no manner of Purpose.

IF, by altering the Title, I could make the same Materials serve for another Dedication (as my Betters have done) it would help to make up my Loss: But, I have made several Persons, dip here and there in those Papers, and before they read three Lines, they have all assured me, plainly, that they cannot possibly be applied to any Person besides your Lordship.

I expected, indeed, to have heard of you[r] Lordship's Bravery, at the Head of an Army; Of your undaunted Courage, in mounting a Breach, or scaling a Wall; Or, to have had your Pedigree trac'd in a Lineal Descent from the House of *Austria*; Or, of your wonderful Talent at Dress and Dancing; Or,

---

[19] *Detur Dignissimo:* Let it be given to the most worthy, as Swift explains a few   lines down.

your Profound Knowledge in *Algebra*, *Metaphysicks*, and the Oriental Tongues. But to ply the World with an old beaten Story of your Wit, and Eloquence, and Learning, and Wisdom, and Justice, and Politeness, and Candor, and Evenness of Temper in all Scenes of Life; Of that great Discernment in Discovering, and Readiness in Favouring deserving Men; with forty other common Topicks: I confess, I have neither Conscience, nor Countenance to do it. Because, there is no Virtue, either of a Publick or Private Life, which some Circumstances of your own, have not often produced upon the Stage of the World; And those few, which for want of Occasions to exert them, might otherwise have pass'd unseen or unobserved by your *Friends*, your *Enemies* have at length brought to   10
Light.[20]

'TIS true, I should be very loth, the Bright Example of your Lordship's Virtues should be lost to After-Ages, both for their sake and your own; but chiefly, because they will be so very necessary to adorn the History of a *late Reign*,[21] And That is another Reason, why I would forbear to make a Recital of them here; Because, I have been told by Wise Men, that as Dedications have run for some Years past, a good Historian will not be apt to have Recourse thither, in search of Characters.

THERE is one Point, wherein I think we Dedicators would do well to change our Measures; I mean, instead of running on so far, upon the Praise of   20
our Patron's *Liberality*, to spend a Word or two, in admiring their *Patience*. I can put no greater Compliment on your Lordship's, than by giving you so ample an Occasion to exercise it at present. Tho', perhaps, I shall not be apt to reckon much Merit to your Lordship upon that Score, who having been formerly used to tedious Harangues, and sometimes to as little Purpose, will be the readier to pardon this, especially, when it is offered by one, who is with all Respect and Veneration,

My LORD,

Your Lordship's most Obedient,
and most Faithful Servant,
The Bookseller.

The Bookseller to the Reader

It is now Six Years since these Papers came first to my Hand, which seems to have been about a Twelvemonth after they were writ: For, the Author tells us in his Pre-face to the first Treatise, that he hath calculated it for the Year 1697, and in several   30 Passages of that Discourse, as well as the second,[22] it appears, they were written about that Time.

As to the Author, I can give no manner of Satisfaction; However, I am credibly in-formed that this Publication is without his Knowledge; for he concludes the Copy is lost, having lent it to a Person, since dead, and being never in Possession of it after:

[20] *Enemies . . . brought to Light:* Often attacked and threatened with censure by Commons, Somers, in 1701, was im-peached by that House, but Lords dis-missed the charges.
[21] *A late Reign:* William's.
[22] *The second: The Battel of the Books.*

So that, whether the Work received his last Hand, or, whether he intended to fill up the defective Places, is like to remain a Secret.

If I should go about to tell the Reader, by what Accident, I became Master of these Papers, it would, in this unbelieving Age, pass for little more than the Cant, or Jargon of the Trade. I, therefore, gladly spare both him and my self so unnecessary a Trouble. There yet remains a difficult Question, why I publish'd them no sooner. I forbore upon two Accounts: First, because I thought I had better Work upon my Hands; and Secondly, because, I was not without some Hope of hearing from the Author, and receiving his Directions. But, I have been lately alarm'd with Intelligence of a surreptitious Copy, which a certain great Wit had new polish'd and refin'd, or as our present 1 Writers express themselves, fitted to the Humor of the Age; *as they have already done, with great Felicity, to* Don Quixot, Boccalini, la Bruyere *and other Authors.*[23] *However, I thought it fairer Dealing, to offer the whole Work in its Naturals. If any Gentleman will please to furnish me with a Key, in order to explain the more difficult Parts, I shall very gratefully acknowledge the Favour, and print it by it self.*

The Epistle Dedicatory

To His Royal Highness, Prince Posterity

SIR,

I here present *Your Highness* with the Fruits of a very few leisure Hours, stollen from the short Intervals of a World of Business, and of an Employment quite alien from such Amusements as this: The poor Production of that Refuse of Time which has lain heavy upon my Hands, during a long Prorogation of Parliament, a great Dearth of Forein News, and a tedious Fit of rainy Weather: 2 For which, and other Reasons, it cannot chuse extreamly to deserve such a Patronage as that of *Your Highness*, whose numberless Virtues in so few Years, make the World look upon You as the future Example to all Princes: For altho' *Your Highness* is hardly got clear of Infancy, yet has the universal learned World already resolv'd upon appealing to Your future Dictates with the lowest and most resigned Submission: Fate having decreed You sole Arbiter of the Productions of human Wit, in this polite and most accomplish'd Age. Methinks, the Number of Appellants were enough to shock and startle any Judge of a Genius less unlimited than Yours: But in order to prevent such glorious Tryals, the *Person* (it seems) to whose Care the Education of *Your Highness* is 3 committed, has resolved (as I am told) to keep you in almost an universal Ignorance of our Studies, which it is Your inherent Birth-right to inspect.

IT is amazing to me, that this *Person* should have Assurance in the face of

The Citation out of Irenæus *in the Title-Page, which seems to be all* Gibberish, *is a Form of Initiation used antiently by the* Marcosian Hereticks. W. Wotton.

It is the usual Style of decry'd Writers to appeal to Posterity, *who is here represented as a Prince in Nonage, and* Time *as his Governor, and the Author begins in a way very frequent with him, by personating other Writers, who sometimes offer such Reasons and Excuses for publishing their Works as they ought chiefly to conceal and be asham'd of.*

[23] . . . *and other Authors:* The works of many foreign writers had been loosely translated in what was perhaps irresponsibly thought by the translators to be an English equivalent to the spirit of the original.

the Sun, to go about persuading *Your Highness*, that our Age is almost wholly illiterate, and has hardly produc'd one Writer upon any Subject. I know very well, that when *Your Highness* shall come to riper Years, and have gone through the Learning of Antiquity, you will be too curious to neglect inquiring into the Authors of the very age before You: And to think that this *Insolent*, in the Account he is preparing for Your View, designs to reduce them to a Number so insignificant as I am asham'd to mention; it moves my Zeal and my Spleen for the Honor and Interest of our vast flourishing Body, as well as of my self, for whom I know by long Experience, he has profess'd, and still continues a peculiar Malice.   10

'TIS not unlikely, that when *Your Highness* will one day peruse what I am now writing, You may be ready to expostulate with Your *Governour* upon the Credit of what I here affirm, and command Him to shew You some of our Productions. To which he will answer (for I am well informed of his Designs), by asking *Your Highness*, where they are? and what is become of them? and pretend it a Demonstration that there never were any, because they are not then to be found: Not to be found! Who has mislaid them? Are they sunk in the Abyss of Things? 'Tis certain, that in their own Nature they were *light* enough to swim upon the Surface for all Eternity. Therefore the Fault is in Him, who tied Weights so heavy to their Heels, as to depress them to the Center. Is their very   20 Essence destroyed? Who has annihilated them? Were they drowned by *Purges* or martyred by *Pipes*? Who administred them to the Posteriors of———? But that it may no longer be a Doubt with *Your Highness*, who is to be the Author of this universal Ruin; I beseech You to observe that large and terrible *Scythe* which your *Governour* affects to bear continually about him. Be pleased to re-mark the Length and Strength, the Sharpness and Hardness of his *Nails* and *Teeth*: Consider his baneful abominable *Breath*, Enemy to Life and Matter, infectious and corrupting: And then reflect whether it be possible for any mortal Ink and Paper of this Generation to make a suitable Resistance. Oh, that *Your Highness* would one day resolve to disarm this Usurping *Maitre du   30 *Palais*,[24] of his furious Engins, and bring Your Empire †*hors de Page*.

IT were endless to recount the several Methods of Tyranny and Destruction, which Your *Governour* is pleased to practise upon this Occasion. His inveterate Malice is such to the Writings of our Age, that of several Thousands produced yearly from this renowned City, before the next Revolution of the Sun, there is not one to be heard of: Unhappy Infants, many of them barbarously destroyed, before they have so much as learnt their *Mother-Tongue* to beg for Pity. Some he stifles in their Cradles, others he frights into Convulsions, whereof they sud-denly die; Some he flays alive, others he tears Limb from Limb. Great Num-bers are offered to *Moloch*,[25] and the rest tainted by his Breath, die of a languish-   40 ing Consumption.

BUT the Concern I have most at Heart, is for our Corporation of *Poets*,

---

* *Comptroller.*   † *Out of Guardianship.*

---

[24] *Maitre du Palais:* Correctly *maire du palais*, chief steward of the royal household, a designation perhaps clearer than comp-troller.

[25] *Moloch:* A Canaanitish god of fire to whom children were sacrificed.

from whom I am preparing a Petition to *Your Highness*, to be subscribed with the Names of one hundred thirty six of the first Rate, but whose immortal Productions are never likely to reach your Eyes, tho' each of them is now an humble and an earnest Appellant for the Laurel,[26] and has large comely Volumes ready to shew for a Support to his Pretensions. The *never-dying* Works of these illustrious Persons, Your *Governour*, Sir, has devoted to unavoidable Death, and *Your Highness* is to be made believe, that our Age has never arrived at the Honor to produce one single Poet.

WE confess *Immortality* to be a great and powerful Goddess, but in vain we offer up to her our Devotions and our Sacrifices, if *Your Highness's Governour*, who has usurped the *Priesthood*, must by an unparallel'd Ambition and Avarice, wholly intercept and devour them.

TO affirm that our Age is altogether Unlearned, and devoid of Writers in any kind, seems to be an Assertion so bold and so false, that I have been sometime thinking, the contrary may almost be proved by uncontroulable Demonstration. 'Tis true indeed, that altho' their Numbers be vast, and their Productions numerous in proportion, yet are they hurryed so hastily off the Scene, that they escape our Memory, and delude our Sight. When I first thought of this Address, I had prepared a copious List of *Titles* to present *Your Highness* as an undisputed Argument for what I affirm. The Originals were posted fresh upon all Gates and Corners of Streets; but returning in a very few Hours to take a Review, they were all torn down, and fresh ones in their Places: I enquired after them among Readers and Booksellers, but I enquired in vain, the *Memorial of them was lost among Men, their Place was no more to be found:* and I was laughed to scorn, for a *Clown* and a *Pedant*, without all Taste and Refinement, little versed in the Course of *present* Affairs, and that knew nothing of what had pass'd in the best Companies of Court and Town. So that I can only avow in general to *Your Highness*, that we do abound in Learning and Wit; but to fix upon Particulars, is a Task too slippery for my slender Abilities. If I should venture in a windy Day, to affirm to *Your Highness*, that there is a large Cloud near the *Horizon* in the Form of a *Bear*, another in the *Zenith* with the Head of an *Ass*, a third to the Westward with Claws like a *Dragon*; and *Your Highness* should in a few Minutes think fit to examine the Truth, 'tis certain, they would all be changed in Figure and Position, new ones would arise, and all we could agree upon would be, that Clouds there were, but that I was grosly mistaken in the *Zoography* and *Topography* of them.

BUT Your *Governour*, perhaps, may still insist, and put the Question: What is then become of those immense Bales of Paper, which must needs have been employ'd in such Numbers of Books? Can these also be wholly annihilate, and so of a sudden as I pretend? What shall I say in return of so invidious an Objection? It ill befits the Distance between *Your Highness* and me, to send You for ocular Conviction to a *Jakes*,[27] or an *Oven*; to the Windows of a *Bawdy-house*, or to a sordid *Lanthorn*.[28] Books, like Men their Authors, have no more than one Way of coming into the World, but there are ten Thousand to go out of it, and return no more.

---

[26] *For the Laurel:* For the appointment to the post of Poet-Laureate, which lapsed when the sovereign died.

[27] *A Jakes:* A privy.
[28] *Lanthorn:* Lantern, a transparent case.

I profess to *Your Highness*, in the Integrity of my Heart, that what I am going to say is literally true this Minute I am writing: What Revolutions may happen before it shall be ready for your Perusal, I can by no means warrant: However I beg You to accept it as a Specimen of our Learning, our Politeness and our Wit. I do therefore affirm upon the Word of a sincere Man, that there is now actually in being, a certain Poet called *John Dryden*, whose Translation of *Virgil* was lately printed in a large Folio,[29] well bound, and if diligent search were made, for ought I know, is yet to be seen. There is another call'd *Nahum Tate*,[30] who is ready to make Oath that he has caused many Rheams of Verse to be published, whereof both himself and his Bookseller (if lawfully required)   10 can still produce authentick Copies, and therefore wonders why the World is pleased to make such a Secret of it. There is a Third, known by the Name of *Tom Durfey*,[31] a Poet of a vast Comprehension, an universal Genius, and most profound Learning. There are also one Mr. *Rymer*, and one Mr. *Dennis*,[32] most profound Criticks. There is a Person styl'd Dr. *B—tl-y*, who has written near a thousand Pages of immense Erudition, *giving a full and true Account* of a certain *Squable* of wonderful Importance between himself and a Bookseller: He is a Writer of infinite Wit and Humour; no Man raillyes with a better Grace, and in more sprightly Turns. Farther, I avow to *Your Highness*, that with these Eyes I have beheld the Person of *William W—tt-n*, B. D. who has written a good   20 sizeable Volume against a *Friend of Your Governor* (from whom, alas! he must therefore look for little Favour) in a most gentlemanly Style, adorned with utmost Politeness and Civility; replete with Discoveries equally valuable for their Novelty and Use: and embellish'd with *Traits* of Wit so poignant and so apposite, that he is a worthy Yokemate to his foremention'd *Friend*.

WHY should I go upon farther Particulars, which might fill a Volume with the just Elogies of my cotemporary Brethren? I shall bequeath this Piece of Justice to a larger Work: wherein I intend to write a Character of the present Set of *Wits* in our Nation: Their Persons I shall describe particularly, and at Length, their Genius and Understandings in *Mignature*.   30

IN the mean time, I do here make bold to present *Your Highness* with a faithful Abstract drawn from the Universal Body of all Arts and Sciences, intended wholly for your Service and Instruction? Nor do I doubt in the least, but *Your Highness* will peruse it as carefully, and make as considerable Improvements, as *other* young *Princes* have already done by the many Volumes of late Years written for a Help to their Studies.

THAT *Your Highness* may advance in Wisdom and Virtue, as well as Years, and at last out-shine all Your Royal Ancestors, shall be the daily Prayer of,

SIR,

Decemb.   *Your Highness's*

1697.   *Most devoted*, &c.

---

[29] *A large Folio: The Works of Virgil* translated by Dryden appeared in 1697.

[30] *Nahum Tate:* Tate (1652–1715) was an Irish poet and dramatist who became Poet-Laureate in 1692, succeeding Shadwell. He was reappointed by Queen Anne in 1702.

[31] *Tom Durfey:* Durfey (1653–1723),
Restoration dramatist and song-writer.

[32] *One Mr. Rymer, and one Mr. Dennis:* Thomas Rymer (1641–1713) was a rigid neoclassical critic and an historian; John Dennis (1657–1734) was a solid critic rather too harshly treated by contemporaries.

The Preface

THE Wits of the present Age being so very numerous and penetrating, it seems, the Grandees of *Church* and *State* begin to fall under horrible Apprehensions, lest these Gentlemen, during the intervals of a long Peace, should find leisure to pick Holes in the weak sides of Religion and Government. To prevent which, there has been much Thought employ'd of late upon certain Projects for taking off the Force, and Edge of those formidable Enquirers, from canvasing and reasoning upon such delicate Points. They have at length fixed upon one, which will require some Time as well as Cost, to perfect. Mean while the Danger hourly increasing, by new Levies of Wits all appointed (as there is Reason to fear) with Pen, Ink, and Paper which may at an hours Warning be   10 drawn out into Pamphlets, and other Offensive Weapons, ready for immediate Execution: It was judged of absolute necessity, that some present Expedient be thought on, till the main Design can be brought to Maturity. To this End, at a Grand Committee, some Days ago, this important Discovery was made by a certain curious and refined Observer; That Sea-men have a Custom when they meet a *Whale*, to fling him out an empty *Tub*, by way of Amusement, to divert him from laying violent Hands upon the Ship. This Parable was immediately mythologiz'd: The *Whale* was interpreted to be *Hob's Leviathan*,[33] which tosses and plays with all other Schemes of Religion and Government, whereof a great many are hollow, and dry, and empty, and noisy, and wooden, and given to   20 Rotation. This is the *Leviathan* from whence the terrible Wits of our Age are said to borrow their Weapons. The *Ship* in danger, is easily understood to be its old Antitype the *Commonwealth*. But, how to analyze the *Tub*, was a Matter of difficulty; when after long Enquiry and Debate, the literal Meaning was preserved: And it was decreed, that in order to prevent these *Leviathans* from tossing and sporting with the *Commonwealth* (which of it self is too apt to *fluctuate*), they should be diverted from that Game by a *Tale of a Tub*. And my Genius being conceived to lye not unhappily that way, I had the Honor done me to be engaged in the Performance.

THIS is the sole Design in publishing the following Treatise, which I hope   30 will serve for an *Interim* of some Months to employ those unquiet Spirits, till the perfecting of that great Work: into the Secret of which, it is reasonable the courteous Reader should have some little Light.

IT is intended that a large Academy be erected, capable of containing nine thousand seven hundred forty and three Persons;[34] which by modest Computation is reckoned to be pretty near the current Number of Wits in this Island. These are to be disposed into the several Schools of this Academy, and there pursue those Studies to which their Genius most inclines them. The Undertaker himself will publish his Proposals with all convenient speed, to which I shall refer the curious Reader for a more particular Account, mentioning at pre-   4

---

[33] *Hob's Leviathan:* Thomas Hobbes (1588–1679), English philosopher, in 1651 published *The Leviathan, or the Matter, Form and Power of a Commonwealth, Ecclesiastical and Civil,* in which he maintains that man is not a social being but a purely selfish one.

[34] *Nine thousand . . . Persons:* It has been suggested that Swift here refers to the number of parishes in England, to each of which a clergyman was appointed at a salary (or living) that varied enormously from parish to parish.

sent only a few of the Principal Schools. There is first, a large *Pederastick* School, with *French* and *Italian* Masters. There is also, the *Spelling* School, *a very spacious Building:* the School of *Looking Glasses:* The School of *Swearing:* the School of *Criticks:* the School of *Salivation:* The School of *Hobby-Horses:* The School of *Poetry:* *The School of *Tops:* The School of *Spleen:* The School of *Gaming:* with many others too tedious to recount. No Person to be admitted Member into any of these Schools, without an Attestation under two sufficient Persons Hands, certifying him to be a *Wit*.

BUT, to return. I am sufficiently instructed in the Principal Duty of a Preface, if my Genius were capable of arriving at it. Thrice have I forced my Imagination to make the *Tour* of my Invention, and thrice it has returned empty; the latter having been wholly drained by the following Treatise. Not so, my more successful Brethren the *Moderns,* who will by no means let slip a Preface or Dedication, without some notable distinguishing Stroke, to surprize the Reader at the Entry, and kindle a Wonderful Expectation of what is to ensue. Such was that of a most ingenious Poet, who solliciting his Brain for something new, compared himself to the *Hangman,* and his Patron to the *Patient:* This was †*Insigne, recens, indictum ore alio.* When I went thro' That necessary and noble ‡Course of Study, I had the happiness to observe many such egregious Touches. which I shall not injure the Authors by transplanting: Because I have remarked, that nothing is so very tender as a *Modern* Piece of Wit, and which is apt to suffer so much in the Carriage. Some things are extreamly witty *to day,* or *fasting,* or *in this place,* or *at eight a clock,* or *over a Bottle,* or *spoke by Mr.* What d'y'call'm, or *in a Summer's Morning:* Any of which, by the smallest Transposal or Misapplication, is utterly annihilate. Thus, *Wit* has its Walks and Purlieus, out of which it may not stray the breadth of an Hair, upon peril of being lost. The *Moderns* have artfully fixed this *Mercury,*[35] and reduced it to the Circumstances of Time, Place and Person. Such a Jest there is, that will not pass out of *Covent-Garden;*[36] and such a one, that is no where intelligible but at *Hide-Park* Corner.[37] Now, tho' it sometimes tenderly affects me to consider, that all the towardly Passages I shall deliver in the following Treatise, will grow quite out of date and relish with the first shifting of the present Scene: yet I must need subscribe to the Justice of this Proceeding: because, I cannot imagine why we should be at Expence to furnish Wit for succeeding Ages, when the former have made no sort of Provision for ours; wherein I speak the Sentiment of the very newest, and consequently the most Orthodox Refiners,[38] as well as my own. However, being extreamly

† *Hor.*
‡ *Reading Prefaces,* &c.

---

* *This I think the Author should have omitted, it being of the very same Nature with the* School of Hobby-Horses, *if one may venture to censure one who is so severe a Censurer of others, perhaps with too little Distinction.*

† *Something extraordinary, new and never hit upon before.*

---

[35] *Mercury:* To reduce mercury in alchemy is to combine it with another substance to produce a solid.

[36] *Covent-Garden:* Before the erection of the Covent-Garden Theatre in 1732, the location was most frequently mentioned in seventeenth- and early eighteenth-

century literature as a center of dissipation.

[37] *Hide-Park:* In Swift's day Hyde Park, in West London, was a place where races were held and where at least one famous duel took place.

[38] *Orthodox Refiners:* Moderns. (See the headnote.)

sollicitous, that every accomplished Person who has got into the Taste of Wit, calculated for this present Month of *August*, 1697, should descend to the very *bottom* of all the *Sublime* throughout this Treatise; I hold fit to lay down this general Maxim. Whatever Reader desires to have a thorow Comprehension of an Author's Thoughts, cannot take a better Method, than by putting himself into the Circumstances and Postures of Life, that the Writer was in, upon every important Passage as it flow'd from his Pen; For this will introduce a Parity and strict Correspondence of Idea's between the Reader and the Author. Now, to assist the diligent Reader in so delicate an Affair, as far as brevity will permit, I have recollected, that the shrewdest Pieces of this Treatise, were conceived   10
in Bed, in a Garret: At other times (for a Reason best known to my self) I thought fit to sharpen my Invention with Hunger; and in general, the whole Work was begun, continued, and ended, under a long Course of Physick, and a great want of Money. Now, I do affirm, it will be absolutely impossible for the candid Peruser to go along with me in a great many bright Passages, unless upon the several Difficulties emergent, he will please to capacitate and prepare himself by these Directions. And this I lay down as my principal *Postulatum.*

BECAUSE I have profess'd to be a most devoted Servant of all *Modern* Forms: I apprehend some curious *Wit* may object against me, for proceeding thus far in a Preface, without declaiming, according to the Custom, against the   20
Multitude of Writers whereof the whole Multitude of Writers most reasonably complains. I am just come from perusing some hundreds of Prefaces, wherein the Authors do at the very beginning address the gentle Reader concerning this enormous Grievance. Of these I have preserved a few Examples, and shall set them down as near as my Memory has been able to retain them.

One begins thus;
For a Man to set up for a Writer, when the Press swarms with, &c.

Another;
The Tax upon Paper does not lessen the Number of Scriblers, who daily pester, &c.   30

Another;
When every little Would-be-wit takes Pen in hand, 'tis in vain to enter the Lists, &c.

Another;
To observe what Trash the Press swarms with, &c.

Another;
SIR, *It is meerly in Obedience to your Commands that I venture into the Publick; for who upon a less Consideration would be of a Party with such a Rabble of Scriblers,* &c.

NOW, I have two Words in my own Defence, against this Objection.   40
First: I am far from granting the Number of Writers, a Nuisance to our Nation, having strenuously maintained the contrary in several Parts of the following Discourse. Secondly: I do not well understand the Justice of this Proceeding, because I observe many of these polite Prefaces, to be not only from the same

Hand, but from those who are most voluminous in their several Productions. Upon which I shall tell the Reader a short Tale.

A Mountebank in Leicester-Fields, *had drawn a huge Assembly about him. Among the rest, a fat unweildy Fellow, half stifled in the Press, would be every fit crying out, Lord! what a filthy Crowd is here? Pray, good People, give way a little, Bless me! what a Devil has rak'd this Rabble together: Z——ds, what squeezing is this! Honest Friend, remove your Elbow. At last, a* Weaver *that stood next him could hold no longer: A Plague confound you* (said he) *for an over-grown Sloven; and who (in the Devil's Name) I wonder, helps to make up the Crowd half so much as yourself? Don't you consider (with a Pox) that you take up more room with that Carkass than any five here? Is not the Place as free for us as for you? Bring your own Guts to a reasonable Compass (and be d——n'd) and then I'll engage we shall have room enough for us all.*

THERE are certain common Privileges of a Writer, the Benefit whereof, I hope, there will be no Reason to doubt; Particularly, that where I am not understood, it shall be concluded, that something very useful and profound is couch'd and underneath, And again, that whatever word or Sentence is Printed in a different Character, shall be judged to contain something extraordinary either of *Wit* or *Sublime.*

AS for the Liberty I have thought fit to take of praising my self, upon some Occasions or none; I am sure it will need no Excuse, if a Multitude of great Examples be allowed sufficient Authority: For it is here to be noted, that *Praise* was originally a Pension paid by the World: but the *Moderns* finding the Trouble and Charge too great in collecting it, have lately bought out the *Fee-Simple*;[39] since which time, the Right of Presentation is wholly in our selves. For this Reason it is, that when an Author makes his own Elogy, he uses a certain form to declare and insist upon his Title, which is commonly in these or the like words, *I speak without Vanity*; which I think plainly shews it to be a Matter of Right and Justice. Now, I do here once for all declare, that in every Encounter of this Nature, thro' the following Treatise, the Form aforesaid is imply'd; which I mention, to save the Trouble of repeating it on so many Occasions.

'TIS a great Ease to my Conscience that I have writ so elaborate and useful a Discourse without one grain of Satyr intermixt; which is the sole point wherein I have taken leave to dissent from the famous Originals of our Age and Country. I have observ'd some Satyrists to use the Publick much at the Rate that Pedants do a naughty Boy ready Hors'd for Discipline: First expostulate the Case, then plead the Necessity of the Rod, from great Provocations, and conclude every Period with a Lash. Now, if I know any thing of Mankind, these Gentlemen might very well spare their Reproof and Correction: For there is not through all Nature, another so callous and insensible a Member as the *World's Posteriors* whether you apply to it the *Toe* or the *Birch*. Besides, most of our late Satyrists seem to lye under a sort of Mistake, that because Nettles have the Prerogative to Sting, therefore all *other Weeds* must do so too. I make not

---

[39] *Fee-Simple:* An ownership or title to land, without restriction.

this Comparison out of the least Design to detract from these worthy Writers: For it is well known among *Mythologists*, that *Weeds* have the Preeminence over all other Vegetables; and therefore the first *Monarch* of this Island, whose Taste and Judgment were so acute and refined, did very wisely root out the *Roses* from the Collar of the *Order*,[40] and plant the *Thistles* in their stead as the nobler Flower of the two. For which Reason it is conjectured by profounder Antiquaries, that the Satyrical Itch, so prevalent in this part of our Island, was first brought among us from beyond the *Tweed*.[41] Here may it long flourish and abound; May it survive and neglect the Scorn of the World, with as much Ease and Contempt as the World is insensible to the Lashes of it. May their own 10 Dullness, or that of their Party, be no Discouragement for the Authors to proceed; but let them remember, it is with *Wits* as with *Razors*, which are never so apt to *cut* those they are employ'd on, as when they have *lost their Edge*. Besides, those whose Teeth are too rotten to bite, are best of all others, qualified to revenge that Defect with their Breath.

I am not like other Men, to envy or undervalue the Talents I cannot reach; for which Reason I must needs bear a true Honour to this large eminent Sect of our *British* Writers. And I hope, this little Panegyrick will not be offensive to their Ears, since it has the Advantage of being only designed for themselves. Indeed, Nature her self has taken order, that Fame and Honour should be 20 purchased at a better Pennyworth by Satyr, than by any other Productions of the Brain; the World being soonest provoked to *Praise* by *Lashes*, as Men are to *Love*, There is a Problem in an ancient Author, why Dedications, and other Bundles of Flattery run all upon stale musty Topicks, without the smallest Tincture of any thing New; not only to the torment and nauseating of the *Christian* Reader, but (if not suddenly prevented) to the universal spreading of that pestilent Disease, the Lethargy, in this Island: whereas, there is very little Satyr which has not something in it untouch'd before, The Defects of the former are usually imputed to the want of Invention among those who are Dealers in that kind: But, I think, with a great deal of Injustice; the Solution being 30 easy and natural. For, the Materials of Panegyrick being very few in Number, have been long since exhausted: For, as Health is but one Thing, and has been always the same, whereas Diseases are by thousands, besides new and daily Additions; So, all the Virtues that have been ever in Mankind, are to be counted upon a few Fingers, but his Follies and Vices are innumerable, and Time adds hourly to the Heap. Now, the utmost a poor Poet can do, is to get by heart a List of the Cardinal Virtues, and deal them with his utmost Liberality to his Hero or his Patron: He may ring the Changes as far as it will go, and vary his Phrase till he has talk'd round; but the Reader quickly finds, it is all *Pork,[42] with a little variety of Sawce: For there is no inventing Terms of Art   * *Plutarch.*   40 beyond our Idea's; and when Idea's are exhausted, Terms of Art must be so too.

BUT, tho' the Matter for Panegyrick were as fruitful as the Topicks of

[40] *Collar of the Order:* James II, in 1687, established (perhaps reestablished) the Order of the Thistle, which did not, contrary to Swift's teasing assertion, affect the roses in the collar of the Order of the Garter.

[41] *Beyond the Tweed:* In Scotland.

[42] *All Pork:* All the same thing. See Plutarch's *Life of Titus Quintius Flaminius,* XVII.

Satyr, yet would it not be hard to find out a sufficient Reason, why the latter will be always better received than the first. For, this being bestowed only upon one or a few Persons at a time, is sure to raise Envy, and consequently ill words from the rest, who have no share in the Blessing: But Satyr being levelled at all, is never resented for an offence by any, since every individual Person makes bold to understand it of others, and very wisely removes his particular Part of the Burthen upon the shoulders of the World, which are broad enough, and able to bear it. To this purpose, I have sometimes reflected upon the Difference between *Athens* and *England*, with respect to the Point before us. In the *Attick* *Commonwealth, it was the Privilege and Birth-right of every Citizen and Poet, to rail aloud and in publick, or to expose upon the Stage by Name, any Person they pleased, tho' of the greatest Figure, whether a *Creon*, an *Hyperbolus*, an *Alcibiades*, or a *Demosthenes*:[43] But on the other side the least reflecting word let fall against the *People* in general, was immediately caught up, and revenged upon the Authors, however considerable for their Quality or their Merits. Whereas, in *England* it is just the Reverse of all this. Here, you may securely display your utmost *Rhetorick* against Mankind, in the Face of the World; tell them, *"That all are gone astray; That there is none that doth good, no not one; That we live in the very Dregs of Time; That Knavery and Atheism are Epidemick as the Pox; That Honesty is fled with Astræa"*;[44] with any other Common places *equally* new and eloquent, which are furnished by the †*Splendida bilis.* And when you have done, the whole Audience, far from being offended, shall return you thanks as a Deliverer of precious and useful Truths. Nay farther; It is but to venture your Lungs and you may preach in *Convent-Garden*[45] against Foppery and Fornication, and *something else*: Against Pride, and Dissimulation, and Bribery, at *White Hall*: You may expose Rapins and Injustice in the *Inns* of *Court* Chappel: And in a *City* Pulpit be as fierce as you please, against Avarice, Hypocrisie and Extortion. 'Tis but a *Ball* bandied to and fro, and every Man carries a *Racket* about Him to strike it from himself among the rest of the Company. But on the other side, whoever should mistake the Nature of things so far, as to drop but a single Hint in publick, How *such a one*, starved half the Fleet, and half-poison'd the rest: How *such a one*, from a true Principle of *Love* and *Honour*, pays no Debts but for *Wenches* and *Play*: How *such a one* has got a Clap and runs out of his Estate: ‡How *Paris* bribed by *Juno* and *Venus*, loath to offend either Party, slept out the whole Cause on the Bench: Or, how *such an Orator* makes long Speeches in the Senate with much Thought, little Sense, and to no Purpose; whoever, I say, should venture to be thus particular, must expect to be imprisoned for *Scanda-*

* *Vid. Xenoph.*

† *Hor.*

---

† *Spleen.*
‡ Juno and Venus *are Money and a Mistress, very powerful Bribes to a Judge, if Scandal says true. I remember such Reflexions were cast about that time, but I cannot fix the Person intended here.*

---

[43] *Or a Demosthenes:* The *Clouds* of Aristophanes illustrates Swift's claim. The demagogue (prominent during the Peloponnesian war) is Cleon, not Creon.
[44] *Fled with Astræa:* Astrea was identified with Dike, or justice. Apparently this section was inspired by Psalm 14.
[45] *Convent-Garden:* The original name for Covent Garden. See n. 36.

lum Magnatum: to have *Challenges* sent him; to be sued for *Defamation*; and to be *brought before the Bar of the House.*

BUT I forget that I am expatiating on a Subject, wherein I have no concern, having neither a Talent nor an Inclination for Satyr? On the other side, I am so entirely satisfied with the whole present Procedure of human Things, that I have been for some Years preparing Materials towards *A Panegyrick upon the World*,[46] to which I intended to add a Second Part, entituled, *A Modest Defence of the Proceedings of the Rabble in all Ages.* Both these I had Thoughts to publish by way of Appendix[47] to the following Treatise? but finding my Common-Place-Book fill much slower than I had reason to expect, I have chosen to defer them to another Occasion. Besides, I have been unhappily prevented in that Design, by a certain Domestick Misfortune, in the Particulars whereof, tho' it would be very seasonable, and much in the *Modern* way, to inform the *gentle Reader*, and would also be of great Assistance towards extending this Preface into the Size now in Vogue, which by Rule ought to be *large* in proportion as the subsequent Volume is *small?* Yet I shall now dismiss our impatient Reader from any farther Attendance at the *Porch;* and having duly prepared his Mind by a preliminary Discourse, shall gladly introduce him to the sublime Mysteries that ensue.

A Tale of a Tub, &c.

Sect. I. The Introduction

WHOEVER hath an Ambition to be heard in a Crowd, must press, and squeeze, and thrust, and climb with indefatigable Pains, till he has exalted himself to a certain Degree of Altitude above them. Now, in all Assemblies, tho' you wedge them ever so close, we may observe this peculiar Property; that, over their Heads there is Room enough; but how to reach it, is the difficult Point; It being as hard to get quit of *Number* as of *Hell;*

> **———Evadere ad auras,*
> *Hoc opus, hic labor est.*

TO this End, the Philosopher's Way in all Ages has been by erecting certain *Edifices in the Air;* But, whatever Practice and Reputation these kind of Structures have formerly possessed, or may still continue in, not excepting even that of *Socrates*, when he was suspended in a Basket to help Contemplation,[48] I think, with due Submission, they seem to labour under two Inconveniences. *First,* That the Foundations being laid too high, they have been often out of *Sight,* and ever out of *Hearing. Secondly,* That the Materials, being very transitory,

---

* But to return, and view the cheerful Skies;
In this the Task and mighty Labour lies.

---

[46] *A Panegyrick upon the World:* See *Treatises wrote by the same Author,* above.

[47] *Appendix:* See the headnote: Bentley's *Dissertation* was appended to the second edition of Wotton's *Reflections,* 1697.

[48] *To help Contemplation:* The *Clouds* of Aristophanes, ll. 220 ff.

have suffer'd much from Inclemencies of Air, especially in these North-West Regions.

THEREFORE, towards the just Performance of this great Work, there remain but three Methods that I can think on; Whereof the Wisdom of our Ancestors being highly sensible, has, to encourage all aspiring Adventurers, thought fit to erect three wooden Machines, for the Use of those Orators who desire to talk much without Interruption. These are, the *Pulpit*, the *Ladder*, and the *Stage-Itinerant*. For, as to the *Bar*, tho' it be compounded of the same Matter, and designed for the same Use, it cannot however be well allowed the Honor of a fourth, by reason of its level or inferior Situation, exposing it to perpetual   10
Interruption from Collaterals. Neither can the *Bench* it self, tho raised to a proper Eminency, put in a better Claim, whatever its Advocates insist on. For if they please to look into the original Design of its Erection, and the Circumstances or Adjuncts subservient to that Design, they will soon acknowledge the present Practice exactly correspondent to the Primitive Institution, and both to answer the Etymology of the Name, which in the *Phœnician* Tongue is a Word of great Signification, importing, if literally interpreted, *The Place of Sleep*; but in common Acceptation, *A Seat well bolster'd and cushion'd, for the Repose of old and gouty Limbs: Senes ut in otia tuta recedant.* Fortune being indebted to them this Part of Retaliation, that, as formerly, they have long *Talkt*, whilst   20
others *Slept*, so now they may *Sleep* as long whilst others *Talk*.

BUT if no other Argument could occur to exclude the *Bench* and the *Bar* from the List of Oratorial Machines, it were sufficient, that the Admission of them would overthrow a Number which I was resolved to establish, whatever Argument it might cost me; in imitation of that prudent Method observed by many other Philosophers and great Clerks, whose chief Art in Division has been, to grow fond of some proper mystical Number, which their Imaginations have rendred Sacred, to a Degree, that they force common Reason to find room for it in every part of Nature; reducing, including, and adjusting every *Genus* and *Species* within that Compass, by coupling some against their Wills, and   30
banishing others at any Rate. Now among all the rest, the profound Number THREE is that which hath most employ'd my sublimest Speculations, nor ever without wonderful Delight.[49] There is now in the Press (and will be publish'd next Term), a Panegyrical Essay of mine upon this Number, wherein I have by most convincing Proofs, not only reduced the *Senses* and the *Elements* under its Banner, but brought over several Deserters from its two great Rivals SEVEN and NINE.[50]

NOW, the first of these Oratorial Machines in Place as well as Dignity, is the *Pulpit*. Of *Pulpits* there are in this Island several sorts; but I esteem only That   40
made of Timber from the *Sylva Caledonia*,[51] which agrees very well with our Climate. If it be upon its Decay, 'tis the better, both for Conveyance of Sound, and for other Reasons to be mentioned by and by. The Degree of Perfection

---

[49] *Wonderful Delight:* For Swift's earlier reference to the number three see *Treatises wrote by the same Author,* above.

[50] *Seven and Nine:* According to one view, ages that were multiples of 7 years (7, 14, 21, etc.) were climacterics (important times of physical or spiritual change); the grand climacteric was held to be 7×9 years.

[51] *Sylva Caledonia:* Scottish wood. This is a satiric thrust at Scottish Protestantism, Presbyterianism.

in Shape and Size, I take to consist, in being extreamly narrow, with little Ornament, and best of all without a Cover (for by antient Rule, it ought to be the only uncover'd *Vessel* in every Assembly where it is rightfully used); by which means, from its near Resemblance to a Pillory, it will ever have a mighty Influence on human Ears.

OF *Ladders*[52] I need say nothing: 'Tis observed by Foreigners themselves, to the Honor of our Country, that we excel all Nations in our Practice and Understanding of this Machine. The ascending Orators do not only oblige their Audience in the agreeable Delivery, but the whole World in their *early* Publication of these Speeches; which I look upon as the choicest Treasury of our   10 *British* Eloquence, and whereof I am informed, that worthy Citizen and Bookseller, Mr. *John Dunton*, hath made a faithful and a painful Collection, which he shortly designs to publish in Twelve Volumes in Folio, illustrated with Copper-Plates. A Work highly useful and curious, and altogether worthy of such a Hand.

THE last Engine of Orators, is the **Stage Itinerant*, erected with much Sagacity, †*sub Jove pluvio, in triviis & quadriviis*. It is the great Seminary of the two former, and its Orators are sometime preferred to the One, and sometimes to the Other, in proportion to their Deservings, there being a strict and perpetual Intercourse between all three.   20

FROM this accurate Deduction it is manifest, that for obtaining Attention in Publick, there is of necessity required a *superiour Position of Place*. But, altho' this Point be generally granted, yet the Cause is little agreed in; and it seems to me, that very few Philosophers have fallen into a true, natural Solution of this *Phænomenon*. The deepest Account, and the most fairly digested of any I have yet met with, is this, That Air being a heavy Body, and therefore (according to the System of ‡*Epicurus*) continually descending, must   ‡ *Lucret: Lib. 2,* needs be more so, when loaden and press'd down by Words; which are also Bodies of much Weight and Gravity, as it is manifest from those deep *Impressions* they make and leave upon us; and therefore must be delivered from   30 a due Altitude, or else they will neither carry a good Aim, nor fall down with a sufficient Force.

> §*Corpoream quoque enim vocem constare fatendum est,*
> *Et sonitum, quoniam possunt impellere Sensus.* Lucr. *Lib.4.*

AND I am the readier to favour this Conjecture, from a common Observation; that in the several Assemblies of these Orators, Nature it self hath instructed the Hearers, to stand with their Mouths open, and erected parallel to the Horizon, so as they may be intersected by a perpenducular Line from the

---

* *Is the* Mountebank's Stage, *whose Orators the Author determines either to the* Gallows *or a* Conventicle.

† *In the open Air, and in Streets where the greatest Resort is.*

§ *'Tis certain then, that* Voice *that thus can wound*
  Is all Material; *Body every* Sound.

---

[52] *Of Ladders:* Swift probably refers to the fact that criminals about to be executed traditionally made speeches.

Zenith to the Center of the Earth. In which Position, if the Audience be well compact, every one carries home a Share, and little or nothing is lost.

I confess, there is something yet more refined in the Contrivance and Structure of our Modern Theatres. For, First; the Pit is sunk below the Stage with due regard to the institution above-deduced; that whatever *weighty* Matter shall be delivered thence (whether it be *Lead* or *Gold*) may fall plum into the Jaws of certain *Criticks* (as I think they are called) which stand ready open to devour them. Then, the Boxes are built round, and raised to a Level with the Scene, in deference to the Ladies, because, That large Portion of Wit laid out in raising Pruriences and Protuberances, is observ'd to run much upon a Line, and ever in   10 a Circle. The whining Passions and little starved Conceits, are gently wafted up by their own extreme Levity, to the middle Region, and there fix and are frozen by the frigid Understandings of the Inhabitants. Bombastry and Buffoonry, by Nature lofty and light, soar highest of all, and would be lost in the Roof, if the prudent Architect had not with much Foresight contrived for them a fourth Place, called *the Twelve-Peny Gallery*, and there planted a suitable Colony, who greedily intercept them in their Passage.

NOW this Physico-logical Scheme of Oratorial Receptacles or Machines, contains a great Mystery, being a Type, a Sign, an Emblem, a Shadow, a Symbol, bearing Analogy to the spacious Commonwealth of Writers, and to those   20 Methods by which they must exalt themselves to a certain Eminency above the inferiour World. By the *Pulpit* are adumbrated the Writings of our *Modern Saints* in *Great Britain*, as they have spiritualized and refined them from the Dross and Grossness of *Sense* and *Human Reason*, The Matter, as we have said, is of rotten Wood, and that upon two Considerations; Because it is the Quality of rotten Wood to give *Light* in the Dark: And secondly, Because its Cavities are full of Worms: which is a *Type with a Pair of Handles, having a Respect to the two principal Qualifications of the Orator, and the two different Fates attending upon his Works.

THE *Ladder* is an adequate Symbol of *Faction* and of *Poetry*, to both of which   30 so noble a Number of Authors are indebted for their Fame. †Of *Faction*, because[53] *   *   *   *   *   *   *   *   *   *   *   *   *
*   *   *   *   *   *   *   *   *   *   *   *
*   *   *   *   *   *   *   *   *   *   *   *   *Hiatus in MS.*
*   *   *   *   *   *   *   *   *   *   *   *

*   *   *   Of *Poetry*, because its Orators do *perorare*[54] with a Song; and because climbing up by slow Degrees, Fate is sure to turn them off before they can reach within many Steps of the Top: And because it is a Preferment attained by transferring of Propriety, and a confounding of *Meum* and *Tuum*.

* *The Two Principal Qualifications of a Phanatick Preacher are, his Inward Light, and his Head full of Maggots, and the Two different Fates of his Writings are, to be burnt or Worm eaten.*

† *Here is pretended a Defect in the Manuscript, and this is very frequent with our Author, either when he thinks he cannot say any thing worth Reading, or when he has no mind to enter on the Subject, or when it is a Matter of little Moment, or perhaps to amuse his Reader (whereof he is frequently very fond) or lastly, with some Satyrical Intention.*

[53] *Of Faction, because. . . . :* Here, of course, begins a pretended defect in the manuscript, as the note in the text indicates.   [54] *Perorare:* Finish up.

UNDER the *Stage-Itinerant* are couched those Productions designed for the Pleasure and Delight of Mortal Man; such as, *Six-peny-worth of Wit*, Westminster *Drolleries*, *Delightful Tales*, *Compleat Jesters*, and the like, by which the Writers of and for GRUB-STREET, have in these latter Ages so nobly triumph'd over *Time*; have clipt his Wings, pared his Nails, filed his Teeth, turn'd back his Hour-Glass, blunted his Scythe, and drawn the Hob-Nails out of his Shoes. It is under this Classis, I have presumed to list my present Treatise, being just come from having the Honor conferred upon me, to be adopted a Member of that Illustrious Fraternity.

NOW, I am not unaware, how the Productions of the *Grub-street* Brotherhood, have of late Years fallen under many Prejudices, nor how it has been the perpetual Employment of two *Junior* start-up Societies, to ridicule them and their Authors, as unworthy their established Post in the Commonwealth of Wit and Learning. Their own Consciences will easily inform them, whom I mean; Nor has the World been so negligent a Looker on, as not to observe the continual Efforts made by the Societies of *Gresham*[55] and of *Will's* to edify a Name and Reputation upon the Ruin of OURS. And this is yet a more feeling Grief to Us upon the Regards of Tenderness as well as of Justice, when we reflect on their Proceedings, not only as unjust, but as ungrateful, undutiful, and unnatural. For, how can it be forgot by the World or themselves (to say nothing of our own Records, which are full and clear in the Point), that they both are Seminaries, not only of our *Planting*, but our *Watering* too? I am informed, Our two *Rivals* have lately made an Offer to enter into the Lists with united Forces, and Challenge us to a Comparison of Books, both as to *Weight* and *Number*. In Return to which (with Licence from our *President*), I humbly offer two Answers: First, We say, the proposal is like that which *Archimedes* made upon a †*smaller* Affair, including an impossibility in the Practice; For, where can they find Scales of *Capacity* enough for the first, or an Arithmetician of *Capacity* enough for the Second. †*Viz. About moving the Earth.* Secondly, We are ready to accept the Challenge, but with this Condition, that a third indifferent Person be assigned, to whose impartial Judgment it shall be left to decide, which Society each Book, Treatise or Pamphlet do most properly belong to. This Point, God knows, is very far from being fixed at present; For, We are ready to produce a Catalogue of some Thousands, which in all common Justice ought to be entitled to Our Fraternity, but by the revolted and new-fangled Writers, most perfidiously ascribed to the others. Upon all which, we think it very unbecoming our Prudence, that the Determination should be remitted to the Authors themselves; when our Adversaries by Briguing[56] and Caballing, have caused so universal a Defection from us, that

---

* Will's Coffee-House, *was formerly the Place where the Poets usually met, which tho it be yet fresh in memory, yet in some Years may be forgot, and want this Explanation.*

---

[55] *Societies of Gresham:* The Royal Society, whose activities began about 1660, met in Gresham College, in London, until 1710.

[56] *Briguing:* Briguer in French means to intrigue or to canvas for. The word in Swift's day was in regular use in English.

the greatest Part of our Society hath already deserted to them, and our nearest Friends begin to stand aloof, as if they were half-ashamed to own Us.

THIS is the utmost I am authorized to say upon so ungrateful and melancholy a Subject; because We are extreme unwilling to inflame a Controversy, whose Continuance may be so fatal to the Interests of Us All, desiring much rather that Things be amicably composed; and We shall so far advance on our Side, as to be ready to receive the two *Prodigals* with open Arms, *Virtuoso* whenever they shall think fit to return from their *Husks* and their *Experi-* *Harlots*; which I think from the *present Course of their Studies they *ments,* *and* most properly may be said to be engaged in; and like an indulgent *Modern* 10 Parent, continue to them our Affection and our Blessing. *Comedies.*

BUT the greatest Maim given to that general Reception, which the Writings of our Society have formerly received (next to the transitory State of all sublunary Things), hath been a superficial Vein among many Readers of the present Age, who will by no means be persuaded to inspect beyond the Surface and the Rind of Things; whereas, *Wisdom* is a *Fox*, who after long hunting, will at last cost you the Pains to dig out: 'Tis a *Cheese*, which by how much the richer, has the thicker, the homelier, and the courser Coat; and whereof to a judicious Pate, the *Maggots* are the best. 'Tis a *Sack-Posset*, wherein the deeper you go, you will find it the sweeter. *Wisdom* is a *Hen*, whose *Cackling* 20 we must value and consider, because it is attended with an *Egg*; But then, lastly, 'tis a *Nut*, which unless you chuse with Judgment, may cost you a Tooth, and pay you with nothing but a *Worm*. In consequence of these momentous Truths, the *Grubæan* Sages[57] have always chosen to convey their Precepts and their Arts, shut up within the Vehicles of Types and Fables, which having been perhaps more careful and curious in adorning, than was altogether necessary, it has fared with these Vehicles after the usual Fate of Coaches over-finely painted and gilt; that the transitory Gazers have so dazzled their Eyes, and fill'd their Imaginations with the outward Lustre, as neither to regard or consider, the Person or the Parts of the Owner within. A Misfortune we undergo with 30 somewhat less Reluctancy, because it has been common to us with *Pythagoras*, *Æsop*, *Socrates*, and other of our Predecessors.

HOWEVER, that neither the World nor our selves may any longer suffer by such misunderstandings, I have been prevailed on, after much importunity from my Friends, to travel in a compleat and laborious Dissertation upon the prime Productions of our Society, which besides their beautiful Externals for the Gratification of superficial Readers, have darkly and deeply couched under them, the most finished and refined Systems of all Sciences and Arts; as I do not doubt to lay open by Untwisting or Unwinding, and either to draw up by Exantlation,[58] or display by Incision. 40

THIS great Work was entred upon some Years ago, by one of our most eminent Members: He began with the History of †*Reynard* the *Fox*, but neither

† *The Author seems here to be mistaken, for I have seen a Latin Edition of* Reynard *the* Fox, *above an hundred Years old, which I take to be the Original; for the rest it has been thought by many People to contain some Satyrical Design in it.*

---

[57] *Grubæan Sages:* Sages of Grub-street, the locus of hack writers.

[58] *Exantlation:* "To draw out as from a well." *OED.*

lived to publish his Essay, nor to proceed farther in so useful an Attempt which is very much to be lamented, because the Discovery he made, and communicated with his Friends, is now universally received; nor, do I think, any of the Learned will dispute, that famous Treatise to be a compleat Body of Civil Knowledge, and the *Revelation*, or rather the *Apocalyps* of all State-*Arcana*. But the Progress I have made is much greater, having already finished my Annotations upon several Dozens; From some of which, I shall impart a few Hints to the candid Reader, as far as will be necessary to the Conclusion at which I aim.

THE first Piece I have handled is that of *Tom Thumb*, whose Author was a *Pythagorean* Philosopher. This dark Treatise contains the whole Scheme of the *Metampsycosis*,[59] deducing the Progress of the Soul thro' all her Stages.

THE next is Dr. *Faustus*, penn'd by *Artephius*, an Author *bonæ notæ*, and an *Adeptus*; He published it in the *nine hundred eighty fourth Year of his Age; this Writer proceeds wholly by *Reincrudation*,[60] or in the *via humida*:[61] And the Marriage between *Faustus* and *Helen*, does most conspicuously dilucidate the fermenting of the *Male* and *Female Dragon*.

> * *He lived a thousand.*

WHITTINGTON *and his Cat*, is the Work of that Mysterious *Rabbi*, *Jehuda Hannasi*,[62] containing a Defence of the *Gemara* of the *Jerusalem Misna*, and its just preference to that of *Babylon*, contrary to the vulgar Opinion.

THE *Hind and Panther*.[63] This is the Master-piece of a famous Writer †now living, intended for a compleat Abstract of sixteen thousand Schoolmen from *Scotus* to *Bellarmin*.

> † Viz *in the Year* 1698.

TOMMY POTTS.[64] Another Piece supposed by the same Hand, by way of Supplement to the former.

THE *Wise Men of* Goatham, *cum Appendice*.[65] This is a Treatise of immense Erudition, being the great Original and Fountain of those Arguments, bandied about both in *France* and *England*, for a just Defence of the *Moderns'* Learning and Wit, against the Presumption, the Pride, and the Ignorance of the *Antients*. This unknown Author hath so exhausted the Subject, that a penetrating Reader will easily discover, whatever hath been written since upon that Dispute, to be little more than Repetition. ‡An Abstract of this Treatise hath been lately published by a *worthy Member* of our Society.

THESE Notices may serve to give the Learned Reader an Idea as well as a Taste of what the whole Work is likely to produce: wherein I have now altogether circumscribed my Thoughts and my Studies; and if I can bring it to a

‡ *This I suppose to be understood of Mr.* W–tt–ns *Discourse of Antient and Modern Learning.*

---

[59] *Metampsycosis:* Metempsychosis. Passage of the soul of a human or an animal at death into a new body.

[60] *Reincrudation:* In alchemy, the reduction of a metal.

[61] *Via humida:* The humid path; humid here is related to humour, a fluid of the body. Male and Female Dragon are terms for sulphur and mercury, in alchemy.

[62] *Jehuda Hannasi:* A distinguished member of a group of Jewish scholars who during the first two centuries A.D.

recorded unwritten law.

[63] *The Hind and Panther:* Part II of Dryden's poem appears in the present volume.

[64] *Tommy Potts:* A character in a Scottish ballad "The Lovers Quarrel." He wins the hand of fair Rosamund, daughter of Lord Arundel.

[65] *The Wise Men . . . Appendice:* Swift refers here to Wotton's *Reflections*, second edition, with Bentley's *Dissertation* as an appendix: 1697.

Perfection before I die, shall reckon I have well employ'd the *poor Remains of an unfortunate Life. This indeed is more than I can justly expect from a Quill worn to the Pith in the Service of the State, in *Pro's* and *Con's* upon *Popish Plots*, and †*Meal-Tubs*, and *Exclusion Bills*, and *Passive Obedience*, and *Addresses of Lives and Fortunes*; and *Prerogative*, and *Property*, and *Liberty of Conscience*, and *Letters to a Friend:* From an Understanding and a Conscience, thread-bare and ragged with perpetual turning; From a Head broken in a hundred places, by the Malignants of the opposite Factions, and from a Body spent with Poxes ill cured, by trusting to Bawds and Surgeons, who (as it afterwards appeared) were profess'd Enemies to Me and the Government, and revenged their Party's Quarrel upon my Nose and Shins. Fourscore and eleven Pamphlets have I written under three Reigns, and for the Service of six and thirty Factions. But finding the State has no farther Occasion for Me and my Ink, I retire willingly to draw it out into Speculations more becoming a Philosopher, having, to my unspeakable Comfort, passed a long Life, with a Conscience void of Offence.

BUT to return. I am assured from the Reader's Candor, that the brief Specimen I have given, will easily clear all the rest of our Society's Productions from an Aspersion grown, as it is manifest, out of Envy and Ignorance: That they are of little farther Use or Value to Mankind, beyond the common Entertainments of their Wit and their Style: For these I am sure have never yet been disputed by our keenest Adversaries: In both which, as well as the more profound and mystical Part, I have throughout this Treatise closely followed the most applauded Originals. And to render all compleat, I have with much Thought and Application of Mind, so ordered, that the chief Title prefixed to it (I mean, That under which I design it shall pass in the common Conversations of Court and Town) is modelled exactly after the Manner peculiar to *Our* Society. ‡*The Title Page in the Original was so torn, that it was not possible to recover several Titles which the Author here speaks of.*

I confess to have been somewhat liberal in the Business of ‡Titles, having observed the Humor of multiplying them, to bear great Vogue among certain Writers, whom I exceedingly Reverence. And indeed, it seems not unreasonable, that Books, the Children of the Brain, should have the Honor to be Christned with variety of Names, as well as other Infants of Quality. Our famous *Dryden* has ventured to proceed a Point farther, endeavouring to introduce also a Multiplicity of §*God-fathers*;[66] which is an Improvement of much more Advantage, upon a very obvious Account. 'Tis a Pity this admirable Invention has not been better cultivated, so as to grow by this time into general Imitation, when such an Authority serves it for a Precedent. Nor §*See Virgil translated, &c.*

---

* *Here the Author seems to personate L'estrange, Dryden, and some others, who after having past their Lives in Vices, Faction and Falshood, have the Impudence to talk of Merit and Innocence and Sufferings.*

† *In King* Charles *the* II. *Time, there was an Account of a* Presbyterian *Plot, found in a Tub, which then made much Noise.*

---

[66] *Multiplicity of God-fathers:* It is Dryden's *Virgil* to which Swift's note refers. There, besides using a great deal of prefatory apparatus of other sorts, Dryden dedicates the translation to three patrons.

has my Endeavours been wanting to second so useful an Example: But it seems, there is an unhappy Expence usually annexed to the Calling of a God-Father, which was clearly out of my Head, as it is very reasonable to believe. Where the Pinch lay, I cannot certainly affirm; but having employ'd a World of Thoughts and Pains, to split my Treatise into forty Sections, and having entreated forty Lords of my Acquaintance, that they would do me the Honor to stand, they all made it a Matter of Conscience, and sent me their Excuses.

Section II.

ONCE upon a Time, there was a Man who had Three *Sons by one Wife, and all at a Birth, neither could the Mid-Wife tell certainly which was the Eldest. Their Father died while they were young, and upon his Death-Bed,   10 calling the Lads to him, spoke thus,

SONS; *because I have purchased no Estate, nor was born to any, I have long considered of some good Legacies to bequeath You; And at last, with much Care as well as Expence, have provided each of you (here they are) a new †Coat. Now, you are to understand, that these Coats have two Virtues contained in them: One is, that with good wearing, they will last you fresh and sound as long as you live: The other is, that they will grow in the same proportion with your Bodies, lengthning and widening of themselves, so as to be always fit. Here, let me see them on you before I die. So, very well, Pray Children, wear them clean, and brush them often. You will find in my ‡Will (here it is) full Instructions in every particular concerning the Wearing and   20 Management of your Coats; wherein you must be very exact, to avoid the Penalties I have appointed for every Transgression or Neglect, upon which your future Fortunes will entirely depend. I have also commanded in my Will, that you should live together in one House like Brethren and Friends, for then you will be sure to thrive, and not otherwise.*

HERE the Story says, this good Father died, and the three Sons went all together to seek their Fortunes.

I shall not trouble you with recounting what Adventures they met for the first seven Years,[67] any farther than by taking notice, that they carefully observed their Father's Will, and kept their Coats in very good Order; That they   30 travelled thro' several Countries, encountred a reasonable Quantity of Gyants, and slew certain Dragons.

BEING now arrived at the proper Age for producing themselves, they came up to Town, and fell in love with the Ladies, but especially three, who

---

* *By these three Sons,* Peter, Martyn *and* Jack; *Popery, the* Church *of* England, *and our* Protestant *Dissenters are designed.* W. Wotton.
† *By his Coats which he gave his Sons, the Garments of the* Israelites. W. Wotton.
An Error (with Submission) of the learned Commentator; for by the Coats are meant the Doctrine and Faith of Christianity, by the Wisdom of the Divine Founder fitted to all Times, Places and Circumstances. Lambin.[68]
‡ *The New Testament.*

---

[67] *First seven Years:* The first significant period of time, following which one would expect some change.

[68] *Lambin:* Denis Lambin (1520–1572) was a great French classical scholar. Swift has him contradict Wotton's notes for the fun of it.

about that time were in chief Reputation: The *Dutchess *d' Argent, Madame de Grands Titres,* and the Countess *d' Orgueil.* On their first Appearance, our three Adventurers met with a very bad Reception; and soon with great Sagacity guessing out the Reason, they quickly began to improve in the good Qualities of the Town: They Writ, and Raillyed, and Rhymed, and Sung, and Said, and said Nothing; They Drank, and Fought, and Whor'd, and Slept, and Swore, and took Snuff: They went to new Plays on the first Night, haunted the *Chocolate*-Houses, beat the Watch, lay on Bulks,[69] and got Claps:[70] They bilkt Hackney-Coachmen, ran in Debt with Shop-keepers, and lay with their Wives: They kill'd Bayliffs, kick'd Fidlers down Stairs, eat at *Locket's*,[71] loytered   10 at *Will's*:[72] They talk'd of the Drawing-Room and never came there, Dined with Lords they never saw; Whisper'd a Dutchess, and spoke never a Word; exposed the Scrawls of their Laundress for Billetdoux of Quality: came ever just from Court and were never seen in it; attended the Levee *sub dio*; Got a list of Peers by heart in one Company, and with great Familiarity retailed them in another. Above all, they constantly attended those Committees of Senators who are silent in the *House,* and loud in the *Coffee-House,* where they nightly adjourn to chew the Cud of Politicks, and are encompass'd with a Ring of Disciples, who lye in wait to catch up their Droppings. The three Brothers had acquired forty other Qualifications of the like Stamp, too tedious to recount,   20 and by consequence, were justly reckoned the most accomplish'd Persons in the Town: But all would not suffice, and the Ladies aforesaid continued still inflexible: To clear up which Difficulty, I must with the Reader's good Leave and Patience, have recourse to some Points of Weight, which the Authors of that Age have not sufficiently illustrated.

FOR, *about this Time it happened a Sect arose, whose Tenents[73] obtained and spread very far, especially in the *Grand Monde,* and among every Body of good Fashion. They worshipped a sort of †*Idol,* who, as their Doctrine delivered, did daily create Men, by a kind of Manufactory Operation. This ‡*Idol* they placed in the highest Parts of the House, on an Altar erected about three Foot: 30 He was shewn in the Posture of a *Persian* Emperor, sitting on a *Superficies,*[74] with his Legs interwoven under him. This God had a *Goose*[75] for his Ensign; whence it is, that some Learned Men pretend to deduce his Original from *Jupiter Capitolinus.*[76] At his left Hand, beneath the Altar, *Hell* seemed to open,

---

* *Their Mistresses are the* Dutchess d'Argent, Madamoiselle de Grands Titres, *and the* Countess d'Orgueil, *i.e.* Covetousness, Ambition *and* Pride, *which were the three great Vices that the ancient Fathers inveighed against as the first Corruptions of Christianity.* W. Wotton.
† *This is an Occasional Satyr upon Dress and Fashion, in order to introduce what follows.*
‡ *By this* Idol *is meant a Taylor.*

---

[69] *Bulks:* A bulk was a stall projecting from the front of a shop.
[70] *Claps:* Gonorrhoea.
[71] *Locket's:* A fashionable eating-house, at Charing Cross.
[72] *Will's:* A well known coffee-house, Dryden's favorite.
[73] *Tenents:* Tenets.
[74] *Superficies:* Here, simply a flat surface.
[75] *Goose:* "A tailor's smoothing-iron." OED.
[76] *Jupiter Capitolinus:* Jupiter of the Capitol, chief Roman god, whose hill was saved from the Gauls by the cries of (thereafter sacred) geese that awakened Roman soldiers.

and catch at the Animals the *Idol* was creating; to prevent which, certain of his Priests hourly flung in Pieces of the uninformed Mass, or Substance, and sometimes whole Limbs already enlivened, which that horrid Gulph insatiably swallowed, terrible to behold. The *Goose* was also held a subaltern Divinity, or *Deus minorum Gentium*; before whose Shrine was sacrificed that Creature, whose hourly Food is humane Gore, and who is in so great Renown abroad, for being the Delight and Favourite of the **Ægyptian Cercopithecus.* Millions of these Animals were cruelly slaughtered every Day, to appease the Hunger of that consuming Deity. The chief *Idol* was also worshipped as the Inventor of the *Yard* and the *Needle*, whether as the God of Seamen, or on Account of certain   1C
other mystical Attributes, hath not been sufficiently cleared.

THE Worshippers of this Deity had also a System of their Belief, which seemed to turn upon the following Fundamental. They held the Universe to be a large *Suit of Cloaths*, which *invests* every Thing: That the Earth is *invested* by the Air; The Air is *invested* by the Stars; and the Stars are *invested* by the *Primum Mobile*. Look on this Globe of Earth, you will find it to be a very compleat and fashionable *Dress*. What is that which some call *Land*, but a fine Coat faced with Green? or the Sea, but a Wastcoat of Water-Tabby?[77] Proceed to the particular Works of the Creation, you will find how curious *Journey-man* Na-   2C
ture hath been, to trim up the *vegetable* Beaux: Observe how sparkish a Perewig adorns the Head of a *Beech*, and what a fine Doublet of white Satin is worn by the *Birch*. To conclude from all, what is Man himself but a †*Micro-Coat*, or rather a compleat Suit of Cloaths with all its Trimmings? As to his Body, there can be no dispute; but examine even the Acquirements of his Mind, you will find them all contribute in their Order, towards furnishing out an exact Dress: To instance no more; Is not Religion a *Cloak*, Honesty a *Pair of Shoes*, worn out in the Dirt, Self-love a *Surtout*, Vanity a *Shirt*, and Conscience a *Pair of Breeches*, which, tho' a Cover for Lewdness as well as Nastiness, is easily slipt down for the Service of both.

THESE *Postulata*[78] being admitted, it will follow in due Course of Reason-   3C
ing, that those Beings which the World calls improperly *Suits of Cloaths*, are in Reality the most refined Species of Animals, or to proceed higher, that they are Rational Creatures, or Men. For, is it not manifest, that They live, and move, and talk, and perform all other Offices of Human Life? Are not Beauty, and Wit, and Mien, and Breeding, their inseparable Proprieties? In short, we see nothing but them, hear nothing but them. Is it not they who walk the Streets, fill up *Parliament——Coffee—, Play—. Bawdy-Houses*. 'Tis true indeed, that these Animals, which are vulgarly called *Suits of Cloaths*, or *Dresses*, do according to certain Compositions receive different Appellations. If one of them be trimm'd up with a Gold Chain, and a red Gown, and a white Rod, and a great Horse,   4C
it is called a *Lord-Mayor*; If certain Ermins and Furs be placed in a certain Posi-

* *The Ægyptians worship'd a Monkey, which Animal is very fond of eating Lice, styled here Creatures that feed on Human Gore.*
† *Alluding to the Word* Microcosm, *or a little World, as Man hath been called by Philosophers.*

---

[77] *Water-Tabby:* A kind of silk.   [78] *Postulata:* Claims.

tion, we stile them a *Judge*, and so, an apt Conjunction of Lawn and black Sattin, we intitle a *Bishop*.

OTHERS of these Professors though agreeing in the main System, were yet more refined upon certain Branches of it; and held that Man was an Animal compounded of two *Dresses*, the *Natural* and the *Celestial Suit*, which were the Body and the Soul: That the Soul was the outward, and the Body the inward Cloathing; that the latter was *ex traduce*;[79] but the former of daily Creation and Circumfusion, This last they proved by *Scripture*, because, *in Them we Live, and Move, and have our Being*: As likewise by Philosophy, because they are *All in All, and All in every Part*. Besides, said they, separate these two, and you will 10
find the Body to be only a sensless unsavory Carcass. By all which it is manifest, that the outward Dress must needs be the Soul.

TO this System of Religion were tagged several subaltern Doctrines, which were entertained with great Vogue: as particularly, the Faculties of the Mind were deduced by the Learned among them in this manner: *Embroidery*, was *Sheer wit*; *Gold Fringe* was *agreeable Conversation*, *Gold Lace* was *Repartee*, a huge long Periwig was *Humor*, and a *Coat full of Powder* was very good *Raillery*: All which required abundance of *Finesse* and *Delicatesse* to manage with Advantage, as well as a strict Observance after Times and Fashions.

I have with much Pains and Reading, collected out of antient Authors, this 20
short Summary of a Body of Philosophy and Divinity, which seems to have been composed by a Vein and Race of Thinking, very different from any other Systems, either *Antient* or *Modern*. And it was not meerly to entertain or satisfy the Reader's Curiosity, but rather to give him Light into several Circumstances of the following Story: that knowing the State of Dispositions and Opinions in an Age so remote, he may better comprehend those great Events which were the issue of them. I advise therefore the courteous Reader, to peruse with a world of Application, again and again, whatever I have written upon this Matter. And leaving these broken Ends, I carefully gather up the chief Thread of my Story, and proceed. 30

THESE Opinions therefore were so universal, as well as the Practices of them, among the refined Part of Court and Town, that our three Brother-Adventurers, as their Circumstances then stood, were strangely at a loss. For, on the one side, the three Ladies they address'd themselves to (whom we have named already) were ever at the very Top of the Fashion, and abhorred all that were below it, but the breadth of a Hair. On the other side, their Father's

The first part of the Tale *is the History of* Peter; *thereby* Popery *is exposed, every Body knows the* Papists *have made great Additions to Christianity, that indeed is the great Exception which the* Church *of England makes against them, accordingly* Peter *begins his Pranks, with adding a* Shoulder-knot *to his Coat.* W. Wotton.

His Description of the Cloth of which the Coat was made, has a farther meaning than the Words may seem to import, "The Coats their Father had left them, were of very good Cloth and besides so neatly Sown, you would swear it had been all of a Piece, but at the same time very plain with little or no Ornament." *This is the distinguishing Character of the Christian Religion.* Christiana Religio absoluta & simplex, *was Ammianus Marcellinus's Description of it, who was himself a Heathen.* W. Wotton.

---

[79] *Ex traduce:* Hereditary; The view that one's soul like one's body is trans- mitted by his parents is called traducian- ism.

Will was very precise, and it was the main Precept in it, with the greatest Penalties annexed, not to add to, or diminish from their Coats, one Thread, without a positive Command in the Will. Now, the Coats their Father had left them were, 'tis true, of very good Cloth, and besides, so neatly sown, you would swear they were all of a Piece, but at the same time, very plain, and with little or no Ornament; And it happened, that before they were a Month in Town, great *Shoulder-knots came up; Strait, all the World was Shoulder-knots; no approaching the Ladies Ruelles[80] without the Quota of Shoulder-knots? That Fellow, cries one, has no Soul; where is his Shoulder-knot? Our three Brethren soon discovered their Want by sad Experience, meeting in their Walks with   10 forty Mortifications and Indignities. If they went to the Play-house, the Doorkeeper shewed them into the Twelve-peny Gallery. If they called a Boat, says a Water-man, I am first Sculler: If they stept to the Rose to take a Bottle, the Drawer would cry, Friend, we sell no Ale. If they went to visit a Lady, a Footman met them at the Door with, Pray send up your Message. In this unhappy Case, they went immediately to consult their Father's Will, read it over and over, but not a Word of the Shoulder-knot. What should they do? What Temper[81] should they find? Obedience was absolutely necessary, and yet Shoulder-knots appeared extreamly requisite. After much Thought, one of the Brothers who happened to be more Book-learned than the other two, said he had found an   20 Expedient. 'Tis true, said he, there is nothing here in this Will, †totidem verbis,[82] making mention of Shoulder-knots, but I dare conjecture, we may find them inclusive, or totidem syllabis. This Distinction was immediately approved by all; and so they fell again to examine the Will. But their evil Star had so directed the Matter, that the first Syllable was not to be found in the whole Writing. Upon which Disappointment, he, who found the former Evasion, took heart, and said, Brothers, there is yet Hopes; for tho' we cannot find them totidem verbis, nor totidem syllabis, I dare engage we shall make them out tertio modo, or totidem literis.[83] This Discovery was also highly commended, upon which they fell once more to the Scrutiny, and picked out S, H, O, U, L, D, E, R; when the same Planet,   30 Enemy to their Repose, had wonderfully contrived, that a K was not to be found. Here was a weighty Difficulty! But the distinguishing Brother (for whom we shall hereafter find a Name) now his Hand was in, proved by a very good Argument, that K was a modern illegitimate Letter, unknown to the Learned Ages, nor any where to be found in antient Manuscripts. ‡ Quibus-Calendæ hath in ‡Q.V.C. been sometimes writ with a K, but errone-   dam ously, for in the best Copies it is ever spelt with a C. And by conse-   Veteribus quence it was a gross Mistake in our Language to spell Knot with a K,   Codicibus.

---

* By this is understood the first introducing of Pageantry, and unnecessary Ornaments in the Church, such as were neither for Convenience nor Edification, as a Shoulder-knot, in which there is neither Symmetry nor Use.

† When the Papists cannot find any thing which they want in Scripture, they go to Oral Tradition: Thus Peter is introduced satisfy'd with the Tedious way of looking for all the Letters of any Word, which he has occasion for in the Will, when neither the constituent Syllables, nor much much less the whole Word, were there in Terminis. W. Wotton.

‡ Some antient Manuscripts.

---

[80] Ladies Ruelles: Ladies' bedsides.   [82] Totidem verbis: In so many words.
[81] Temper: Compromise.   [83] Totidem literis: In so many letters.

but that from henceforward, he would take care it should be writ with a *C*. Upon this, all farther Difficulty vanished; *Shoulder-Knots* were made clearly out, to be *Jure Paterno*,[84] and our three Gentlemen swaggered with as large and as slanting ones as the best.

BUT, as human Happiness is of a very short Duration, so in those Days were human Fashions, upon which it entirely depends. *Shoulder-Knots* had their Time, and we must now imagine them in their Decline; for a certain Lord came just from *Paris*, with fifty Yards of *Gold Lace* upon his Coat, exactly trimm'd after the Court-Fashion of that *Month*. In two Days, all Mankind appear'd closed up in Bars of **Gold Lace*: whoever durst peep abroad without his Complement of *Gold Lace*, was as scandalous as a ——, and as ill received among the Women. What should our three Knights do in this momentous Affair? They had sufficiently strained a Point already, in the Affair of *Shoulder-Knots*: Upon Recourse to the Will, nothing appeared there but *altum silentium*.[85] That of the *Shoulder-Knots* was a loose, flying, circumstantial Point; but this of *Gold Lace*, seemed too considerable an Alteration without better Warrant; it did *aliquo modo essentiæ adhærere*,[86] and therefore required a positive Precept. But about this time it fell out, that the Learned Brother aforesaid, had read *Aristotelis Dialectica*,[87] and especially that wonderful Piece *de Interpretatione*, which has the Faculty of teaching its Readers to find out a Meaning in every Thing but it self; like Commentators on the *Revelations*, who proceed Prophets without understanding a Syllable of the Text. *Brothers*, said he, †*You are to be informed, that, of Wills*, duo sunt genera,[88] ‡*Nuncupatory*[89] *and scriptory: that to the Scriptory Will here before us, there is no Precept or Mention about Gold Lace,* conceditur: But, si idem affirmetur de nuncupatorio, negatur,[90] *For Brothers, if you remember, we heard a Fellow say when we were Boys, that he heard my Father's Man say, that he heard my Father say, that he would advise his Sons to get* Gold Lace *on their Coats, as soon as ever they could procure Money to buy it. By G—— that is very true*, cries the other; *I remember it perfectly well*, said the third. And so without more ado they got the largest *Gold Lace* in the Parish, and walk'd about as fine as Lords.

---

* *I cannot tell whether the Author means any new Innovation by this Word, or whether it be only to introduce the new Methods of forcing and perverting Scripture.*

† *The next Subject of our Author's Wit, is the Glosses and Interpretations of Scripture, very many absurd ones of which are allow'd in the most Authentick Books of the* Church of Rome. W. Wotton.

‡ *By this is meant* Tradition, *allowed to have equal Authority with the Scripture, or rather greater.*

---

[84] *Jure Paterno:* According to the father's law.

[85] *Altum silentium:* Profound silence.

[86] *Aliquo modo essentiæ adhærere:* In some manner pertain to the essence [of the will].

[87] *Aristotelis Dialectica:* Aristotle's logical treatises (in Latin). *De Interpretatione* is a work on the relationship between language and thought.

[88] *Duo sunt genera:* There are two kinds.

[89] *Nuncupatory:* By word of mouth.

[90] *No . . . Mention about Gold Lace, conceditur: But, si idem affirmetur de nuncupatorio, negatur:* No mention about Gold Lace, it must be granted: But if the same view were asserted about the tradition, by word of mouth, it must be denied.

A while after, there came up *all in Fashion*, a pretty sort of *flame Coloured *Sattin* for Linings, and the *Mercer* brought a Pattern of it immediately to our three Gentlemen, *An please your Worships* (said he) †*My Lord C—, and Sir J. W. had Linings out of this very Piece last Night; it takes wonderfully, and I shall not have a Remnant left, enough to make my Wife a Pin-cushion by to morrow Morning at ten a Clock,* Upon this, they fell again to romage the Will, because the present Case also required a positive Precept, the Lining being held by Orthodox Writers to be of the Essence of the Coat. After long search, they could fix upon nothing to the Matter in hand, except a short Advice of their Fathers in the Will, ‡to take care of *Fire*, and put out their *Candles* before they went to Sleep. 10 This tho' a good deal for the Purpose, and helping very far towards Self-Conviction, yet not seeming wholly of Force to establish a Command; and being resolved to avoid farther Scruple, as well as future Occasion for Scandal, says He that was the Scholar; *I remember to have read in Wills, of a Codicil annexed, which is indeed a Part of the Will, and what it contains hath equal authority with the rest. Now, I have been considering of this same Will here before us, and I cannot reckon it to be compleat for want of such a Codicil. I will therefore fasten one in its proper Place very dexterously; I have have had it by me some Time, it was written by a* §*Dog-keeper of my Grand-father's, and talks a great deal (as good Luck would have it) of this very flame-colour'd Sattin.* The Project was immediately approved 20 by the other two; an old Parchment Scrowl was tagged on according to Art, in the Form of a *Codicil annext,* and the *Sattin* bought and worn.

NEXT Winter, a *Player,* hired for the Purpose by the Corporation of *Fringe-makers,* acted his Part in a new Comedy, all covered with   *Silver Fringe,* and according to the laudable Custom gave Rise to that Fashion. Upon which, the Brothers consulting their Father's Will, to their great Astonishment found these Words; *Item, I charge and command my said three Sons, to wear no sort of* Silver Fringe *upon or about their said Coats,* &c. with a Penalty in case of Disobedience, too long here to insert. However, after some Pause the Brother so often mentioned for his Erudition, who was well skill'd in Criticisms, had 30 found in a certain Author, which he said should be nameless, that the same Word which in the Will is called *Fringe,* does also signifie a *Broom-stick;* and doubtless ought to have the same Interpretation in this Paragraph. This, another of the Brothers disliked, because of that Epithet, *Silver,* which could not, he humbly conceived, in Propriety of Speech be reasonably applied to a *Broom-stick:* but it was replied upon him, that this Epithet was understood in a *Mytho-*

---

* *This is Purgatory, whereof he speaks more particularly hereafter, but here only to shew how Scripture was perverted to prove it, which was done by giving equal Authority with the* Canon *to* Apocrypha, *called here a* Codicil annex'd.

It is likely the Author, in every one of these Changes in the Brother's Dresses, referrs to some particular Error in the Church *of* Rome; *tho' it is not easy I think to apply them all, but by this of* Flame Colour'd Satin *is manifestly intended* Purgatory; *by* Gold Lace *may perhaps be understood, the lofty Ornaments and Plate in the Churches, The* Shoulder-knots *and* Silver Fringe, *are not so obvious, at least to me; but the* Indian *Figures of Men, Women and Children plainly relate to the Pictures in the Romish Churches, of God like an old Man, of the Virgin* Mary *and our Saviour as a Child.*

† *This shews the Time the Author writ, it being about fourteen Years since those two Persons were reckoned the fine Gentlemen of the Town.*

‡ *That is, to take care of Hell, and, in order to do that, to subdue and extinguish their Lusts.*

§ *I believe this refers to that part of the* Apocrypha *where mention is made of* Tobit *and his* Dog.

‖ *This is certainly the farther introducing the Pomps of Habit and Ornament.*

logical, and *Allegorical* Sense. However, he objected again, why their Father should forbid them to wear a *Broom-stick* on their Coats, a Caution that seemed unnatural and impertinent; upon which he was taken up short, as one that spoke irreverently of a *Mystery*, which doubtless was very useful and significant, but ought not to be over-curiously pryed into, or nicely reasoned upon. And in short, their Father's Authority being now considerably sunk, this Expedient was allowed to serve as a lawful Dispensation, for wearing their full Proportion of *Silver Fringe*.

A while after, was revived an old Fashion, long antiquated, of *Embroidery* with *Indian Figures of Men, Women and Children. Here they remembered but   10 too well, how their Father had always abhorred this Fashion; that he made several Paragraphs on purpose, importing his utter Detestation of it, and bestowing his everlasting Curse to his Sons whenever they should wear it. For all this, in a few Days, they appeared higher in the Fashion than any Body else in the Town. But they solved the Matter by saying, that these Figures were not at all the *same* with those that were formerly worn, and were meant in the Will. Besides, they did not wear them in that Sense, as forbidden by their Father, but as they were a commendable Custom, and of great Use to the Publick. That these rigorous Clauses in the Will did therefore require some *Allowance*, and a favourable Interpretation, and ought to be understood *cum grano Salis*.   20

BUT, Fashions perpetually altering in that Age, the Scholastick Brother grew weary of searching farther Evasions, and solving everlasting Contradictions. Resolved therefore at all Hazards, to comply with the Modes of the World, they concerted Matters together, and agreed unanimously, to †lock up their Father's Will in a *Strong-Box*, brought out of *Greece* or *Italy* (I have forgot which), and trouble themselves no farther to examine it, but only refer to its Authority whenever they thought fit. In consequence whereof, a while after, it grew a general Mode to wear an infinite Number of *Points*, most of them *tagg'd with Silver*: Upon which the Scholar pronounced ‡*ex Cathedra*,[91] that *Points* were absolutely *Jure Paterno*,[92] as they might very well remember. 'Tis true   30 indeed, the Fashion prescribed somewhat more than were directly named in the Will; However, that they, as Heirs general of their Father, had power to make and add certain Clauses for publick Emolument, though not deducible, *totidem verbis*,[93] from the Letter of the Will, or else, *Multa absurda sequerentur*.[94]

---

* *The Images of Saints, the Blessed Virgin, and our Saviour an Infant.*
Ibid. *Images in the* Church of Rome *give him but too fair a Handle*, The Brothers remembred, *&c. The Allegory here is direct.* W. Wotton.
† *The Papists formerly forbad the People the Use of Scripture in a Vulgar Tongue*, Peter *therefore locks up his Father's Will in a* Strong Box, *brought out of* Greece *or* Italy. *Those Countries are named because the* New Testament *is written in Greek; and the* Vulgar Latin, *which is the Authentick Edition of the* Bible *in the Church of* Rome, *is in the Language of old* Italy. W. Wotton.
‡ *The Popes in their Decretals and Bulls, have given their Sanction to very many gainful Doctrines which are now received in the* Church of Rome *that are not mention'd in Scriptures, and are unknown to the Primitive Church*, Peter *accordingly pronounces* ex Cathedra. *That* Points *tagged with Silver were absolutely* Jure Paterno, *and so they wore them in great Numbers.* W. Wotton.

---

[91] *Ex Cathedra:* From the seat of authority.
[92] *Jure Paterno:* According to the father's law.
[93] *Totidem verbis:* In so many words.
[94] *Multa absurda sequerentur:* Many absurd things would follow.

This was understood for *Canonical,* and therefore on the following *Sunday* they came to Church all covered with *Points.*

THE Learned Brother so often mentioned, was reckon'd the best Scholar in all that or the next Street to it; insomuch, as having run something behind-hand with the World, he obtained the Favour from a *certain Lord, to receive him into his House, and to teach his Children. A while after, the *Lord* died, and he by long Practice of his Father's Will, found the way of contriving a *Deed of Convey-ance* of that House to Himself and his Heirs: Upon which he took Possession, turned the young Squires out, and received his Brothers in their stead.

Sect. III. A Digression concerning Criticks

THO' I have been hitherto as cautious as I could, upon all Occasions, most   10
nicely to follow the Rules and Methods of Writing, laid down by the Example of our illustrious *Moderns*; yet has the unhappy shortness of my Memory led me into an Error, from which I must immediately extricate my self, before I can decently pursue my Principal Subject. I confess with Shame, it was an un-pardonable Omission to proceed so far as I have-already done, before I had performed the due Discourses, Expostulatory, Supplicatory, or Deprecatory with my *good Lords* the *Criticks.* Towards some Atonement for this grievous Neglect, I do here make humbly bold to present them with a short Account of themselves and their *Art*, by looking into the Original and Pedigree of the Word, as it is generally understood among us, and very briefly considering the   20
antient and present State thereof.

BY the Word, *Critick,* at this Day so frequent in all Conversations, there have sometimes been distinguished three very different Species of Mortal Men, according as I have read in *Antient Books and Pamphlets.* For first, by this Term was understood such Persons as invented or drew up Rules for themselves and the World, by observing which, a careful Reader might be able to pronounce upon the productions of the *Learned,* from his Taste to a true Relish of the *Sub-lime* and the *Admirable,* and divide every Beauty of Matter or of Style from the Corruption that Apes it: In their common perusal of Books, singling out the Errors and Defects, the Nauseous, the Fulsome, the Dull, and the Imperti-   30
nent, with the Caution of a Man that walks thro' *Edenborough* Streets in a Morn-ing, who is indeed as careful as he can, to watch diligently, and spy out the Filth in his Way, not that he is curious to observe the Colour and Complexion of the Ordure, or take its Dimensions, much less to be padling in, or tasting it: but only with a Design to come out as cleanly as he may. These men seem, tho' very erroneously, to have understood the Appellation of *Critick* in a literal Sence; That one principal part of his Office was to Praise and Acquit; and, that a *Critick,* who sets up to Read, only for an Occasion of Censure and Reproof, is a Creature as barbarous as a *Judge,* who should take up a Resolution to hang all Men that came before him upon a Tryal.   40

* *This was* Constantine the Great, *from whom the* Popes *pretend a Donation of St.* Peter's *Patrimony, which they have been never able to produce.*
    Ibid *The Bishops of* Rome *enjoyed their Priviledges in* Rome *at first by the favour of Emperors, whom at last they shut out of their own Capital City, and then forged a Donation from* Constantine the Great, *the better to justifie what they did. In Imitation of this,* Peter having run something behind hand in the World, obtained Leave of a certain Lord, *&c.*
    W. Wot on.

AGAIN; by the Word *Critick*, have been meant, the Restorers of Antient Learning from the Worms, and Graves, and Dust of Manuscripts.

NOW, the Races of these two have been for some Ages utterly extinct; and besides, to discourse any farther of them would not be at all to my purpose.

THE Third, and Noblest Sort, is that of the *TRUE CRITICK*, whose Original is the most Antient of all. Every *True Critick* is a Hero born, descending in a direct Line from a Celestial Stem, by *Momus* and *Hybris*, who begat *Zoilus*, who begat *Tigellius*, who begat *Etcætera* the Elder, who begat *B-tly*, and *Rym-r*, and *W-tton*, and *Perrault*, and *Dennis*,[95] who begat *Etcætera* the Younger.

AND these are the *Criticks* from whom the Commonwealth of Learning   10
has in all Ages received such immense benefits, that the Gratitude of their Admirers placed their Origine in Heaven, among those of *Hercules*, *Theseus*, *Perseus*, and other great Deservers of Mankind. But Heroick Virtue it self hath not been exempt from the Obloquy of Evil Tongues. For it hath been objected, that those Antient Heroes, famous for their Combating so many Giants, and Dragons, and Robbers, were in their own Persons a greater Nuisance to Mankind, than any of those Monsters they subdued; and therefore, to render their Obligations more Compleat, when all *other* Vermin were destroy'd, should in Conscience have concluded with the same Justice upon themselves: *Hercules* most generously did,[96] and hath upon that Score, procured to himself more   20
Temples and Votaries than the best of his Fellows. For these Reasons, I suppose, it is why some have conceived, it would be very expedient for the Publick Good of Learning, that every *True Critick*, as soon as he had finished his Task assigned, should immediately deliver himself up to Ratsbane, or Hemp, or from some convenient *Altitude*, and that no Man's Pretensions to so illustrious a Character, should by any means be received, before That Operation were performed.

NOW, from this Heavenly Descent of *Criticism*, and the close Analogy it bears to *Heroick Virtue*, 'tis easie to Assign the proper Employment of a *True Antient Genuine Critick*; which is, to travel thro' this vast World of Writings: to pursue and hunt those Monstrous Faults bred within them: to drag out the   30
lurking Errors like *Cacus* from his Den; to multiply them like *Hydra's* Heads; and rake them together like *Augeas's* Dung. Or else drive away a sort of *Dangerous Fowl*, who have a perverse Inclination to plunder the best Branches of the *Tree of Knowledge*, like those *Stimphalian* Birds that eat up the Fruit.[97]

THESE Reasonings will furnish us with an adequate Definition of a true *Critick*; that, He is *a Discoverer and Collector of Writers Faults*. Which may be farther put beyond Dispute by the following Demonstration: That whoever will examine the Writings in all kinds, wherewith this antient Sect has honour'd the World, shall immediately find, from the whole Thread and Tenour of

---

[95] *Momus . . . Dennis:* Momus, a god of censure, a carping critic; Hybris (Hubris), excessive pride: Zoilus, a malignant critic (known for his attacks on Homer); Tigellius, a critic of Horace; Bentley, editor of Phalaris (see the headnote); Rymer, English critic (see n. 32); W-tton, Temple's antagonist (see n. 7); Perrault, a French modern; Dennis (see n. 32).

[96] *Hercules . . . did:* Suffering painful wounds, Hercules had himself placed on a pyre and burned to death.

[97] *Cacus . . . the Fruit:* These are among the beings central to the labors of Hercules: Cacus, a monster who stole cattle from Hercules and hid them in his cave; Hydra, a poisonous many-headed watersnake who grew back heads as they were cut off; Augeas, a king who had vast herds whose filthy stables Hercules had to clean; Stimphalian Birds, who infested the region near Lake Stymphalus.

them, that the Idea's of the Authors have been altogether conversant, and taken up with the Faults and Blemishes, and Oversights, and Mistakes of other Writers; and let the Subject treated on be whatever it will, their Imaginations are so entirely possess'd and replete with the Defects of other Pens, that the very Quintessence of what is bad, does of necessity distill into their own: by which means the Whole appears to be nothing else but an *Abstract* of the *Criticisms* themselves have made.

HAVING thus briefly consider'd the Original and Office of a *Critick*, as the Word is understood in its most noble and universal Acceptation, I proceed to refute the Objections of those who argue from the Silence and Pretermission of   10 Authors; by which they pretend to prove, that the very Art of *Criticism*, as now exercised, and by me explained, is wholly *Modern*; and consequently, that the *Criticks* of *Great Britain* and *France*, have no Title to an Original so Antient and Illustrious as I have deduced. Now, If I can clearly make out on the contrary, that the most Antient Writers have particularly described, both the Person and the Office of a *True Critick*, agreeable to the Definition laid down by me; their Grand Objection, from the Silence of Authors, will fall to the Ground.

I confess to have for a long time born a part in this general Error; from which I should never have acquitted my self, but thro' the Assistance of our Noble *Moderns*; whose most edifying Volumes I turn indefatigably over Night   20 and Day, for the Improvement of my Mind, and the good of my Country: These have with unwearied Pains made many useful Searches into the weak sides of the *Antients*, and given us a comprehensive List of them. *Be-   * *See* sides, they have proved beyond contradiction, that the very finest   *Wotton* Things delivered of old, have been long since invented, and brought   *of* to Light by much later Pens, and that the noblest Discoveries those   *Antient* *Antients* ever made, of Art or of Nature, have all been produced by   *and* the transcending Genius of the present Age. Which clearly shews,   *Modern* how little Merit those *Ancients* can justly pretend to; and takes off that blind   *Learning* Admiration paid them by Men in a Corner, who have the Unhappiness of con-   30 versing too little with *present Things*. Reflecting maturely upon all this, and taking in the whole Compass of Human Nature, I easily concluded, that these *Antients*, highly sensible of their many Imperfections, must needs have endeav- oured from some Passages in their Works, to obviate, soften, or divert the Censorious Reader, by *Satyr*, or *Panegyrick* upon the *True Criticks*, in Imitation of their *Masters* the *Moderns*. Now, in the *Common-Places* of †both   † *Satyr*, these, I was plentifully instructed, by a long Course of useful Study in   *and* *Prefaces* and *Prologues*;[98] and therefore immediately resolved to try   *Pane-* what I could discover of either, by a diligent Perusal of the most   *gyrick* *upon* Antient Writers, and especially those who treated of the earliest   *Criticks.*   40 Times. Here I found to my great Surprize, that although they all entred, upon Occasion, into particular Descriptions of the *True Critick*, according as they were governed by their Fears or their Hopes: yet whatever they touch'd of that kind, was with abundance of Caution, adventuring no farther than *Mythology* and *Hieroglyphick*. This, I suppose, gave ground to superficial Readers, for urging the Silence of Authors, against the Antiquity of the *True Critick*; tho'

[98] *Prefaces and Prologues:* See n. 66.

the *Types* are so apposite, and the Applications so necessary and natural, that it is not easy to conceive, how any Reader of a *Modern Eye* and *Taste* could overlook them. I shall venture from a great Number to produce a few, which I am very confident, will put this Question beyond Dispute.

IT well deserves considering, that these *Antient Writers* in treating Enigmatically upon the Subject, have generally fixed upon the very *same Hieroglyph,* varying only the Story according to their Affections or their Wit. For first; *Pausanias* is of Opinion, that the Perfection of Writing correct was entirely owing to the Institution of *Criticks*; and, that he can possibly mean no other than the *True Critick,* is, I think, manifest enough from the following Description. 10 He says, *They were a Race of Men, who delighted to nibble at the Superfluities, and Excrescencies of Books; which the Learned at length observing, took Warning of their own Accord, to lop the Luxuriant, the Rotten, the Dead, the Sapless, and the Overgrown Branches from their Works.* But now, all this he cunningly shades under the following Allegory; *that the* *Nauplians *in* Argia, *learned the Art of pruning their Vines, by observing, that when an* ASS *had browsed upon one* * *Lib—of them, it thrived the better, and bore fairer Fruit.* But †Herodotus holding † *Lib.* 4. the very same *Hieroglyph,* speaks much plainer, and almost *in terminis.* He hath been so bold as to tax the *True Criticks,* of Ignorance and Malice; telling us openly, for I think nothing can be plainer, that *in the Western Part of* 20 Libya, *there were* ASSES *with* HORNS: Upon which Relation ‡Ctesias yet refines, mentioning the very same Animal about *India,* adding, *That whereas all other* ASSES *wanted a Gall, these horned ones were so redundant in that Part, that their Flesh was not to be eaten because of its extream* Bitterness.
‡ Vide *excerpta ex eo apud* Phot-ium.[99]

NOW, the Reason why those Antient Writers treated this Subject only by Types and Figures, was, because they durst not make open Attacks against a Party so Potent and so Terrible, as the *Criticks* of those Ages were: whose very Voice was so Dreadful, that a Legion of Authors would tremble, and drop their Pens at the Sound; For so §Herodotus tell[s] us expresly in another Place, how *a vast Army of* Scythians *was to put to flight in a Panick Terror, by the Braying of an* ASS. From hence it is conjectured § *Lib.* 4 30 by certain profound *Philologers,* that the great Awe and Reverence paid to a *True Critick,* by the Writers of *Britain,* have been derived to Us, from those our *Scythian* Ancestors. In short, this Dread was so universal, that in process of Time, those Authors who had a mind to publish their Sentiments more freely, in describing the *True Criticks* of their several Ages, were forced to leave off the use of the former *Hieroglyph,* as too nearly approaching the *Prototype,* and invented other Terms instead thereof that were more cautious and mystical; so ‖Diodorus speaking to the same purpose, ventures no farther than to ‖ *Lib.* 40 say, That *in the Mountains of* Helicon *there grows a certain* Weed, *which bears a Flower of so damned a Scent, as to poison those who offer to smell it.* Lucretius gives exactly the Same Relation,

[99] *Ctesias . . . Photium:* Ctesias was a Greek physician of the fourth century B.C. He wrote a long history of Persia. Photius, to whom Swift's note directs the reader, compiled (ninth century A.D.) a critical account of 280 prose works, including those of Ctesias.

*Est etiam in magnis Heliconis montibus arbos,
Floris odore hominem retro consueta necare. Lib. 6.

BUT *Ctesias*, whom we lately quoted, hath been a great deal bolder; He had been used with much severity by the *True Criticks* of his own Age, and therefore could not forbear to leave behind him, at least one deep Mark of his Vengeance against the whole Tribe. His Meaning is so near the Surface, that I wonder how it possibly came to be overlook'd by those who deny the Antiquity of *True Criticks*. For pretending to make a Description of many strange Animals about *India*, he hath set down these remarkable Words. *Amongst the rest*, says he, *there is a* Serpent *that wants Teeth, and consequently cannot bite, but if its* 10 Vomit *(to which it is much addicted) happens to fall upon any Thing, a certain Rotenness or Corruption ensues: These* Serpents *are generally found among the Mountains where* Jewels *grow, and they frequently emit a* poisonous Juice *whereof, whoever drinks, that Person's Brains flie out of his Nostrils.*

THERE was also among the *Antients* a sort of *Critick*, not distinguisht in *Specie* from the Former, but in Growth or Degree, who seem to have been only the *Tyro's* or *junior* Scholars; yet, because of their differing Employments, they are frequently mentioned as a Sect by themselves. The usual exercise of these younger Students, was to attend constantly at Theatres, and learn to Spy out the *worst Parts* of the Play, whereof they were obliged carefully to take 20 Note, and render a rational Account, to their Tutors. Flesht at these smaller Sports, like young Wolves, they grew up in Time, to be nimble and strong enough for hunting down large Game. For it hath been observed both among Antients and Moderns, that a *True Critick* hath one Quality in common with a *Whore* and an *Alderman*, never to change his Title or his Nature; that a *Grey Critick* has been certainly a *Green* one, the Perfections and Acquirements of his Age being only the improved Talents of his Youth; like *Hemp*, which some Naturalists inform us, is bad for *Suffocations*, tho' taken but in the Seed. I esteem the Invention, or at least the Refinement of *Prologues*, to have been owing to these younger Proficients, of whom *Terence*[100] makes frequent and honourable 30 mention, under the Name of *Malevoli*.

NOW, 'tis certain, the Institution of the *True Criticks*, was of absolute Necessity to the Commonwealth of Learning. For all Human Actions seem to be divided like *Themistocles* and his Company; One Man can *Fiddle*, and another can make a *small Town a great City*, and he that cannot do either one or the other, deserves to be kick'd out of the Creation. The avoiding of which Penalty, has doubtless given the first Birth to the Nation of *Criticks* and withal, an Occasion for their secret Detractors to report; that a *True Critick* is a sort of Mechanick, set up with a Stock and Tools for his Trade, at as little Expence as a *Taylor*; and that there is much Analogy between the Utensils and Abilities of both: 40 That the *Taylor's Hell*[101] is the Type of a Critick's *Common-Place-Book*, and his

---

* *Near Helicon, and round the Learned Hill,*
  Grow Trees, whose Blossoms with their Odour kill.

---

[100] *Terence:* The Roman comedian in his prologue to *Andria* (and elsewhere) observes that he is forced to waste the occasion by answering a malevolent old playwright (Luscius Lavinius).

[101] *Taylor's Hell:* A receptacle into which a tailor throws his scraps.

Wit and Learning held forth by the *Goose*:[102] That it requires at least as many of these, to the making up of one Scholar, as of the others to the Composition of a Man: That the Valour of both is equal, and their *Weapons* near of a Size. Much may be said in answer to those invidious Reflections; and I can positively affirm the first to be a Falshood: For, on the contrary, nothing is more certain, than that it requires greater Layings out, to be free of the *Critick's* Company, than of any other you can name. For, as to be a *true Beggar*, it will cost the richest Candidate every Groat he is worth; so, before one can commence a *True Critick*, it will cost a man all the good Qualities of his Mind; which, perhaps, for a less Purchase, would be thought but an indifferent Bargain. 10

HAVING thus amply proved the Antiquity of *Criticism*, and described the Primitive State of it; I shall now examine the present Condition of this Empire, and shew how well it agrees with its antient self. *A certain Author, whose Works have many Ages since been entirely lost, does in his fifth Book and eighth Chapter, say of *Criticks*, that *their Writings are the Mirrors of Learning*. This I understand in a literal Sense, and suppose our Author must mean, that whoever designs to be a perfect Writer, must inspect into the Books of *Criticks*, and correct his Invention there as in a Mirror. Now, whoever considers, that the *Mirrors* of the Antients were made of *Brass, and sine Mercurio*,[103] may presently apply the two Principal Qualifications of a *True Modern Critick*, and consequently, must needs conclude, that these have always been, and must be for ever the same. For, *Brass* is an Emblem of Duration, and when it is skilfully burnished, will cast *Reflections* from its own *Superficies*, without any Assistance of *Mercury* from behind. All the other Talents of a *Critick* will not require a particular Mention, being included, or easily deducible to these. However, I shall conclude with three Maxims, which may serve both as Characteristicks to distinguish a *True Modern Critick* from a Pretender, and will be also of admirable Use to those worthy Spirits, who engage in so useful and honourable an Art. 30

A Quotation after the manner of a great Author. Vide Bently's Dissertation, &c. 20

THE first is, That *Criticism*, contrary to all other Faculties of the Intellect, is ever held the truest and best, when it is the very *first* Result of the *Critick's* Mind: As Fowlers reckon the first aim for the surest, and seldom fail of missing the Mark, if they stay not for a Second.

SECONDLY; The *True Criticks* are known by their Talent of swarming about the noblest Writers, to which they are carried meerly by Instinct, as a Rat to the best Cheese, or a Wasp to the fairest Fruit. So, when the *King* is a Horse-back, he is sure to be the *dirtiest* Person of the Company, and they that make their Court best, are such as *bespatter* him most.

LASTLY; A *True Critick*, in the Perusal of a Book, is like a *Dog* at a Feast, 40 whose Thoughts and Stomach are wholly set upon what the Guests *fling away*, and consequently, is apt to *Snarl* most, when there are the fewest *Bones*.

THUS much, I think, is sufficient to serve by way of Address to my Patrons, the *True Modern Criticks*, and may very well atone for my past Silence, as well

[102] *Goose*: Goose-quill (a pen) and a tailor's goose (see n. 75).
[103] *Sine Mercurio*: Without mercury.

The mirrors of the ancients were not made of mercury nor were their "reflections" mercurial—erratic, flighty.

as That which I am like to observe for the future. I hope I have deserved so well of their whole *Body*, as to meet with generous and tender Usage at their *Hands*. Supported by which Expectation, I go on boldly to pursue those Adventures already so happily begun.

Sect. IV. A Tale of a Tub

I have now with much Pains and Study, conducted the Reader to a Period, where he must expect to hear of great Revolutions. For no sooner had Our *Learned Brother*, so often mentioned, got a warm House of his own over his Head, than he began to look big, and to take mightily upon him; insomuch, that unless the Gentle Reader out of his great Candour, will please a little to exalt his Idea, I am afraid he will henceforth hardly know the *Hero* of the Play,   10
when he happens to meet Him; his part, his Dress, and his Mien being so much altered.

HE told his Brothers, he would have them to know, that he was their Elder, and consequently his Father's sole Heir; Nay, a while after, he would not allow them to call Him, Brother, but Mr. *PETER*; And then he must be styl'd, *Father PETER*; and sometimes, *My Lord PETER*. To support this Grandeur, which he soon began to consider, could not be maintained without a Better *Fonde*[104] than what he was born to; After much Thought, he cast about at last, to turn *Projector* and *Virtuoso*,[105] wherein he so well succeeded, that many famous Discoveries, Projects and Machines, which bear great Vogue and Practice   20
at present in the World, are owing entirely to *Lord Peter's* Invention. I will deduce the best Account I have been able to collect of the Chief amongst them, without considering much the Order they came out in; because, I think, Authors are not well agreed as to that Point.

I hope, when this Treatise of mine shall be translated into Foreign Languages (as I may without Vanity affirm, That the Labour of collecting, the Faithfulness in recounting, and the great Usefulness of the Matter to the Publick, will amply deserve that Justice), that the worthy Members of the several *Academies* abroad, especially those of *France* and *Italy*, will favourably accept these humble Offers, for the Advancement of Universal Knowledge. I do also   30
advertise the most Reverend Fathers the *Eastern* Missionaries, that I have purely for their Sakes, made use of such Words and Phrases, as will best admit an easie Turn into any of the *Oriental* Languages, especially the *Chinese*. And so I proceed with great Content of Mind, upon reflecting, how much Emolument this whole Globe of Earth is like to reap by my Labours.

THE first Undertaking of Lord *Peter*, was to purchase a *Large Continent, lately said to have been discovered in *Terra Australis incognita*.[106] This Tract of Land he bought at a very great Penny-worth[107] from the Discoverers them-

* *That is Purgatory.*

---

[104] *Fonde:* Foundation.
[105] *Projector and Virtuoso:* A schemer, a former of extravagant plans; a dilettante in antiquities, the fine arts, or science.

[106] *Terra Australis incognita:* The West Indies.
[107] *Penny-worth:* Bargain.

selves (tho' some pretended to doubt whether they had ever been there), and then retailed it into several Cantons to certain Dealers, who carried over Colonies, but were all Shipwreckt in the Voyage. Upon which, *Lord Peter* sold the said Continent to other Customers *again*, and *again*, and *again*, and *again*, with the same Success.

THE second Project I shall mention, was his Sovereign *Remedy for the *Worms*, especially those in the *Spleen*. †The Patient was to eat nothing after Supper for three Nights: as soon as he went to Bed, he was carefully to lye on one Side, and when he grew weary, to turn upon the other: He must also duly confine his two Eyes to the same Object; and by no means break Wind   10 at both Ends together, without manifest Occasion. These Prescriptions diligently observed, the *Worms* would void insensibly by Perspiration, ascending thro' the *Brain*.

A third Invention, was the Erecting of a ‡ *Whispering-Office*, for the Publick Good and Ease of all such as are Hypochondriacal, or troubled with the Cholick; as Midwives, small Politicians, Friends fallen out, Repeating Poets,[108] Lovers Happy or in Despair, Bawds, Privy-Counsellours, Pages, Parasites and Buffoons; In short, of all such as are in Danger of bursting with too much *Wind*. An *Asse's* Head was placed so conveniently, that the Party affected might easily with his Mouth accost either of the Animal's Ears; which he was to apply close   20 for a certain Space, and by a fugitive Faculty, peculiar to the Ears of that Animal, receive immediate Benefit, either by Eructation, or Expiration, or Evomition.

ANOTHER very beneficial Project of *Lord Peter's* was an §*Office of Ensurance*, for Tobacco-Pipes, Martyrs of the Modern Zeal; Volumes of Poetry, Shadows,————————————and Rivers: That these, nor any of these shall receive Damage by *Fire*. From whence our *Friendly Societies*[109] may plainly find themselves, to be only Transcribers from this Original; tho' the one and the other have been of *great* Benefit to the Undertakers, as well as of *equal* to the Publick.   30

LORD Peter was also held the Original Author of ‖*Puppets* and *Raree-Shows*; the great Usefulness whereof being so generally known, I shall not enlarge farther upon this Particular.

BUT, another Discovery for which he was much renowned, was his fam-

---

* Penance *and* Absolution *are* plaid upon under the Notion of a Sovereign Remedy for the Worms, *especially in the* Spleen, *which by observing* Peters Prescription *would void sensibly by* Perspiration ascending thro' the Brain, &c. W. Wotton.

† *Here the Author ridicules the Penances of the Church of Rome, which may be made as easy to the Sinner as he pleases, provided he will pay for them accordingly.*

‡ *By his* Whispering-Office, *for the Relief of Eves-droppers, Physitians, Bawds, and Privy-counsellours, he ridicules Auricular Confession, and the Priest who takes it, is described by the Asses Head.* W. Wotton.

§ *This I take to be the Office of Indulgences, the gross Abuses whereof first gave Occasion for the Reformation.*

‖ *I believe are the Monkeries and ridiculous Processions, &c. among the Papists.*

---

[108] *Repeating Poets:* Poets who like Addison's later Ned Softly (*Tatler* 163) recite their own verses.

[109] *Friendly Societies:* The Friendly Society was a fire-insurance company.

ous Universal *Pickle. For having remark'd how your †Common Pickle in use among Huswives, was of no farther Benefit than to preserve dead Flesh, and certain kinds of Vegetables; Peter, with great Cost as well as Art, had contrived a Pickle proper for Houses, Gardens, Towns, Men, Women, Children, and Cattle; wherein he could preserve them as Sound as Insects in Amber. Now, this Pickle to the Taste, the Smell, and the Sight, appeared exactly the same, with what is in common Service for Beef and Butter, and Herrings (and has been often that way applied with great Success), but for its many Sovereign Virtues was a quite different Thing. For Peter would put in a certain Quantity of his ‡Powder Pimperlim pimp,[110] after which it never failed of Success. The Operation was performed by Spargefaction[111] in a proper Time of the Moon. The Patient who was to be pickled, if it were a House, would infallibly be preserved from all Spiders, Rats and Weazels; If the Party affected were a Dog he should be exempt from Mange, and Madness, and Hunger. It also infallibly took away all Scabs and Lice, and scall'd Heads from Children, never hindring the Patient from any Duty, either at Bed or Board.

BUT of all Peter's Rarieties,[112] he most valued a certain Set of §Bulls, whose Race was by great Fortune preserved in a lineal Descent from those that guarded the Golden Fleece.[113] Tho' some who pretended to observe them curiously, doubted the Breed had not been kept entirely chast; because they had degenerated from their Ancestors in some Qualities and had acquired others very extraordinary, but a Forein Mixture. The Bulls of Colchos are recorded to have brazen Feet; But whether it happen'd by ill Pasture and Running, by an Allay from intervention of other Parents, from stolen Intrigues; Whether a Weakness in their Progenitors had impaired the seminal Virtue; Or by a Decline necessary thro' a long Course of Time, the Originals of Nature being depraved in these latter sinful Ages of the World; Whatever was the Cause, 'tis certain that Lord Peter's Bulls were extreamely vitiated by the Rust of Time in the Mettal of their Feet, which was now sunk into common Lead. However the terrible roaring peculiar to their Lineage, was preserved; as likewise that Faculty of breathing out Fire from their Nostrils; which notwithstanding many of their Detractors took to be a Feat of Art, to be nothing so terrible as it appeared; proceeding only

---

* Holy Water, he calls an Universal Pickle to preserve Houses, Gardens, Towns, Men, Women, Children and Cattle, wherein he could preserve them as sound as Insects in Amber. W. Wotton.

† This is easily understood to be Holy Water, composed of the same Ingredients with many other Pickles.

‡ And because Holy Water differs only in Consecration from common Water, therefore he tells us that his Pickle by the Powder of Pimperlimpimp receives new Virtues though it differs not in Sight nor Smell from the common Pickles, which preserves Beef, and Butter, and Herrings. W. Wotton.

§ The Papal Bulls are ridicul'd by Name, So that here we are at no loss for the Authors Meaning. W. Wotton.

Ibid. Here the Author has kept the Name, and means the Popes Bulls, or rather his Fulminations and Excommunications, of Heretical Princes, all sign'd with Lead and the Seal of the Fisherman.

---

[110] Powder Pimperlim pimp: Some kind of quite imaginary magic powder.
[111] Spargefaction: Correctly spargefication, the action of sprinkling or scattering.

[112] Rarieties: Rarities.
[113] Golden Fleece: In Greek mythology, the prize sought in Colchis by Jason. The fleece was a ram's not a bull's.

from their usual Course of Dyet, which was of *Squibs* and *Crackers*. However, they had two peculiar Marks which extreamly distinguished them from the *Bulls of Jason*, and which I have not met together in the Description of any other Monster, beside that in *Horace*;

> *Varias inducere plumas,*
> and
> *Atrum desinit in piscem,*[114]

For, these had *Fishes Tails*, yet upon Occasion, could *out-fly* any Bird in the Air. *Peter* put these *Bulls* upon several Employs. Sometimes he would set them a *roaring* to fright †*Naughty Boys*, and make them quiet. Sometimes he would   10
send them out upon Errands of great Importance; where it is wonderful to recount, and perhaps the cautious Reader may think much to believe it; An *Appetitus sensibilis*,[115] deriving itself thro' the whole Family, from their Noble Ancestors, Guardians of the *Golden-Fleece*; they continued so extremely fond of *Gold*, that if *Peter* sent them abroad, though it were only upon a Complement; they would *Roar*, and *Spit*, and *Belch*, and *Piss*, and *Fart*, and *Snivel* out *Fire*, and keep a perpetual *Coyl*,[116] till you flung them a Bit of *Gold*; but then, *Pulveris exigui jactu*,[117] they would grow calm and quiet as Lambs. In short, whether by secret Connivance, or Encouragement from their Master, or out of their own Liquorish Affection to Gold, or both; it is certain they were   20
no better than a sort of sturdy, swaggering Beggars; and where they could not prevail to get an Alms, would make Women miscarry, and Children fall into Fits; who, to this very Day, usually call Sprites and Hobgoblins by the Name of *Bull-Beggars*.[118] They grew at last so very troublesome to the Neighbourhood, that some Gentlemen of the *North-West*, got a Parcel of right *English Bull-Dogs*, and baited them so terribly, that they felt it ever after.

I must needs mention one more of *Lord Peter's* Projects, which was very extraordinary, and discovered him to be Master of a high Reach, and profound Invention. Whenever it happened that any Rogue of *Newgate* was condemned to be hang'd, *Peter* would offer him a Pardon for a certain Sum of Money,   30
which when the poor Caitiff had made all Shifts to scrape up and send; *His Lordship* would return a ‡Piece of Paper in this Form.

To all Mayors, Sheriffs, Jaylors, Constables, Bayliffs, Hangmen, &c. Whereas

---

* *These are the Fulminations of the Pope threatning Hell and Damnation to those Princes who offend him.*

† *That is Kings who incurr his Displeasure.*

‡ *This is a Copy of a General Pardons sign'd* Servus Servorum.[119]

Ibid. *Absolution in* Articulo Mortis, *and the Tax* Cameræ Apostolicæ *are jested upon in* Emperor Peter's *Letter.* W. Wotton.

---

[114] *Varias . . . in piscem:* These are two phrases from the opening lines of Horace's *Ars Poetica*, the sentence in which they occur meaning, "If a painter decided to join a human head to the neck of a horse, and to spread feathers variously colored over randomly selected limbs so that what at the top is a beautiful woman ends below in a black and ugly fish, could you . . . keep from laughing?"

[115] *Appetitus sensibilis:* Appetite of the senses (as opposed to one of the mind).

[116] *Coyl:* Fuss.

[117] *Pulveris exigui jactu:* By the tossing of a little dust.

[118] *Bull-Beggars:* Bogies or bugbears.

[119] *Servus Servorum:* Servant of servants (of God), a title adopted by the Pope.

we are informed that A. B. *remains in the Hands of you, or any of you, under the Sentence of Death. We will and command you upon Sight hereof, to let the said Prisoner depart to his own Habitation, whether he stands condemned for Murder, Sodomy, Rape, Sacrilege, Incest, Treason, Blasphemy,* &c. *for which this shall be your sufficient Warrant: And if you fail hereof,* G—— d——mn *You and Yours to all Eternity. And so we bid you heartily Farewel.*

Your most Humble
Man's Man,
EMPEROR PETER.

THE Wretches trusting to this, lost their Lives and Money too.

I desire of those whom the *Learned* among Posterity will appoint for Commentators upon this elaborate Treatise; that they will proceed with great Caution upon certain dark points, wherein all who are not *Vere adepti*,[120] may be in   10
Danger to form rash and hasty Conclusions, especially in some mysterious Paragraphs, where certain *Arcana*[121] are joyned for brevity sake, which in the Operation must be divided. And, I am certain, that future Sons of Art, will return large Thanks to my Memory, for so grateful, so useful an *Innuendo*.

IT will be no difficult Part to persuade the Reader, that so many worthy Discoveries met with great Success in the World; tho' I may justly assure him that I have related much the smallest Number; My Design having been only to single out such, as will be of most Benefit for Publick Imitation, or which best served to give some Idea of the Reach and Wit of the Inventor. And therefore it need not be wondred, if by this Time, *Lord-Peter* was become exceding Rich.   20
But alas, he had kept his Brain so long, and so violently upon the Rack, that at last it *shook* it self, and began to *turn round* for a little Ease. In short, what with Pride, Projects, and Knavery, poor *Peter* was grown distracted, and conceived the strangest Imaginations in the World. In the Height of his Fits (as it is usual with those who run mad out of Pride), He would call Himself *God Almighty, and sometimes *Monarch of the Universe*. I have seen him (says my Author), take three old †*high-crown'd Hats*, and clap them all on his Head, three Story high, with a huge Bunch of ‡*Keys* at his Girdle, and an *Angling Rod* in his Hand. In which Guise, whoever went to take him by the Hand in the way of Salutation, *Peter* with much Grace like a well educated Spaniel, would present them with   30
his §*Foot*, and if they refused his Civility, then he would raise it as high as their Chops, and give them a damn'd Kick on the Mouth, which hath ever since been call'd *Salute*. Whoever walkt by, without paying him their Complements, having a wonderful strong Breath, he would blow their Hats off into the Dirt. Mean time, his Affairs at home went upside down; and his two Brothe[r]s had a

---

* *The Pope is not only allow'd to be the Vicar of* Christ, *but by several Divines is call'd* God upon Earth, *and other blasphemous Titles.*
† *The Triple Crown.*
‡ *The Keys of the Church.*
Ibid. *The Pope's Universal Monarchy, and his Triple Crown, and Fisher's Ring.* W. Wotton.
§ *Neither does his arrogant way of requiring men to kiss his Slipper, escape Reflexion.* Wotton.

---

[120] *Vere adepti:* True initiates.   [121] *Arcana:* Secret learning.

wretched Time; Where his first *Boutade* was, to kick both their †*Wives* one Morning out of Doors, and his own too, and in their stead, gave Orders to pick up the first three Strolers could be met with in the S[t]reets. A while after, he nail'd up the Cellar-Door: and would not allow his Brothers a ‡Drop of *Drink* to their Victuals. Dining one Day at an Alderman's in the Ci[t]y, *Peter* observed him expatiating after the Manner of his Brethren, in the Praises of his Surloyn of Beef. *Beef*, said the Sage Magistrate, *is the King of Meat; Beef comprehends in it the Quintesscence of Partridge, and Quail, and Venison, and Phesants, and Plum-pudding and Custard.* When *Peter* came home, he would needs take the Fancy of cooking up this Doctrine into Use, and apply the Precept in default of a Sur-   10 loyn, to his brown Loaf: *Bread*, says he, *Dear Brothers, is the Staff of Life; in which Bread is contained, inclusivè, the Quintessence of Beef, Mutton, Veal, Venison, Partidge, Plum-pudding, and Custard: And to render all compleat, there is inter-mingled a due Quantity of Water, whose Crudities are also corrected by Yeast or Barm, thro' which means it becomes a wholesome fermented Liquor, diffused thro' the* Mass of the Bread. Upon the Strength of these Conclusions, next Day at Dinner was the brown Loaf served up in all the Formality of a City Feast. *Come Brothers,* said *Peter, fall to, and spare not; here is excellent good* §*Mutton; or hold, now my Hand is in, I'll help you.* At which word, in much Ceremony, with Fork and Knife, he carves out two good Slices of a Loaf, and presents each on a Plate to   20 his Brothers. The Elder of the two not suddenly entring into *Lord Peter's* Conceit, began with very civil Language to examine the Mystery. *My Lord,* said he, *I doubt, with great Submission, there may be some Mistake. What,* says *Peter, you are pleasant; Come then, let us hear this Jest, your Head is so big with. None in the World, my Lord; but unless I am very much deceived, your Lordship was pleased a while ago, to let fall a Word about Mutton, and I would be glad to see it with all my Heart. How,* said *Peter,* appearing in great Surprise, *I do not comprehend this at all—* Upon which, the younger interposing, to set the Business right; *My Lord,* said he, *My Brother, I suppose is hungry, and longs for the Mutton, your Lordship hath promised us to Dinner. Pray,* said Peter, *take me along with you, either*   30 *you are both mad, or disposed to be merrier than I approve of; If* You there, *do not like your Piece, I will carve you another, tho' I should take that to be the choice Bit of the whole Shoulder. What then, my Lord,* replied the first, *it seems this is a shoulder of Mutton all this while. Pray Sir,* says *Peter, eat your Vittles and leave off your Im-pertinence, if you please, for I am not disposed to relish it at present:* But the other could not forbear, being over-provoked at the affected Seriousness of *Peter's* Countenance. *By G—, My Lord,* said he, *I can only say, that to my Eyes, and Fin-gers, and Teeth, and Nose, it seems to be nothing but a Crust of Bread.* Upon which, the second put in his Word: *I never saw a Piece of Mutton in my Life, so nearly resembling a Slice from a Twelve-peny Loaf.* Look ye, Gentlemen, cries *Peter* in a   40 Rage, *to convince you, what a couple of blind, positive, ignorant, wilful Puppies you*

---

* *This Word properly signifies a sudden Jerk, or Lash of an Horse, when you do not expect it.*

† *The* Celibacy of the Romish *Clergy is struck at in* Peter's *beating his own and Brothers Wives out of Doors.* W. Wotton.

‡ *The* Pope's *refusing the Cup to the Laity, persuading them that the Blood is contain'd in the Bread, and that the Bread is the real and entire Body of* Christ.

§ Transubstantiation. Peter *turns his Bread into Mutton, and according to the Popish Doctrine of Concomitants, his Wine too, which in his way he calls,* Pauming [*palming*] *his* damn'd Crusts upon the Brothers for Mutton. *W. Wotton.*

are, I will use but this plain Argument; By G—, it is true, good, natural Mutton as any in Leaden-Hall *Market; and G—, confound you both eternally, if you offer to believe otherwise.* Such a thundring Proof as this, left to farther Room for Objection: The two Unbelievers began to gather and pocket up their Mistake as hastily as they could. *Why truly,* said the first, *upon more mature Consideration* —Ay, says the other, interrupting him, *now I have thought better on the Thing, your Lordship seems to have a great deal of Reason. Very well,* said *Peter, Here Boy, fill me a Beer-Glass of Claret. Here's to you both with all my Heart.* The two Brethren much delighted to see him so readily appeas'd returned their most humble Thanks, and said, they would be glad to pledge His Lordship. *That you shall,* said Peter, *I am not a Person to refuse you any Thing that is reasonable; Wine moderately taken, is a Cordial; Here is a Glass apiece for you; Tis true natural Juice from the Grape; none of your damn'd* Vintners *Brewings.* Having spoke thus, he presented to each of them another large dry Crust, bidding them drink it off, and not be bashful, for it would do them no Hurt. The two Brothers, after having performed the usual Office in such delicate Conjunctures, of staring a sufficient Period at *Lord Peter,* and each other; and finding how Matters were like to go, resolved not to enter on a new Dispute, but let him carry the Point as he pleased; for he was now got into one of his mad Fits, and to Argue or Expostulate further, would only serve to render him a hundred times more untractable.   20

I have chosen to relate this worthy Matter in all its Circumstances, because it gave a principal Occasion to that great and famous **Rupture,* which happened about the same time among these Brethren, and was never afterwards made up. But, of That, I shall treat at large in another Section.[122]

HOWEVER, it is certain, that *Lord Peter,* even in his lucid Intervals, was very lewdly given in his common Conversation, extream wilful and positive, and would at any time rather argue to the Death, than allow himself to be once in an Error. Besides, he had an abominable Faculty of telling huge palpable *Lies* upon all Occasions; and swearing, not only to the Truth, but cursing the whole Company to Hell, if they pretended to make the least Scruple of believing Him. One time, he swore, he had a †*Cow* at home, which gave as much   30
Milk at a Meal, as would fill three thousand Churches; and what was yet more extraordinary, would never turn Sower. Another time, he was telling of an old ‡*Sign-Post* that belonged to his *Father,* with Nails and Timber enough on it, to build sixteen large Men of War. Talking one Day of *Chinese* Waggons, which were made so light as to sail over Mountains: *Z—nds,* said *Peter, where's the Wonder of that? By G——, I saw a §Large House of Lime and Stone travel over*

* *By this* Rupture *is meant the* Reformation.

† *The ridiculous Multiplying of the Virgin* Mary's Milk *among the Papists, under the Allegory of a* Cow, *which gave as much Milk at a Meal, as would fill three thousand Churches.* W. Wotton.

‡ *By this* Sign-Post *is meant the* Cross *of our Blessed Saviour.*

§ *The Chappel of* Loretto. *He falls here only upon the ridiculous Inventions of Popery: The Church of* Rome *intended by these Things, to gull silly, superstitious People, and rook them of their Money; that the World had been too long in Slavery, our Ancestors gloriously redeem'd us from that Yoke. The Church of* Rome *therefore ought to be expos'd, and he deserves well of Mankind that does expose it.* W. Wotton.

Ibid. *The Chappel of* Loretto, *which travell'd from the* Holy Land *to* Italy.

---

[122] *Another Section:* Section VI.

Sea and Land (granting that it stopt sometimes to bait) above two thousand German Leagues. And that which was the good of it, he would swear desperately all the while, that he never told a Lye in his Life; And at every Word; *By G——, Gentlemen, I tell you nothing but the Truth; And the D——l broil them eternally that will not believe me.*

IN short, *Peter* grew so scandalous, that all the Neighbourhood began in plain Words to say, he was no better than a Knave. And his two Brothers long weary of his ill Usage, resolved at last to leave him; but first, they humbly desired a Copy of their Father's *Will*, which had now lain by neglected, time out of Mind. Instead of granting this Request, he called them *damn'd Sons*   10 *of Whores, Rogues, Traytors,* and the rest of the vile Names he could muster up. However, while he was abroad one Day upon his Projects, the two Youngsters watcht their Opportunity, made a Shift to come at the *Will*, *and took a *Copia vera*,[123] by which they presently saw how grosly they had been abused; Their Father having left them equal Heirs, and strictly commanded, that whatever they got, should lye in common among them all. Pursuant to which, their next Enterprise was to break open the Cellar-Door, and get a little good †*Drink* to spirit and comfort their Hearts. In copying the *Will*, they had met another Precept against Whoring, Divorce, and separate Maintenance; Upon which, their next ‡Work was to discard their Concubines, and send for their Wives.   20 Whilst all this was in agitation, there enters a Sollicitor from *Newgate*, desiring *Lord Peter* would please to procure a *Pardon* for a *Thief* that was to be *hanged* to morrow. But the two Brothers told him, he was a Coxcomb to seek Pardons from a Fellow, who deserv'd to be hang'd much better than his Client; and discovered all the Method of that Imposture, in the same Form I delivered it a while ago, advising the Sollicitor to put his Friend upon obtaining §*a Pardon from the King.* In the midst of all this Clutter and Revolution, in comes *Peter* with a File of ‖*Dragoons* at his Heels, and gathering from all Hands what was in the Wind. He and his Gang, after several Millions of Scurrilities and Curses, not very important here to repeat, by main Force, very fairly ¶kicks them   30 both out of Doors, and would never let them come under his Roof from that Day to this.

Sect. V. A Digression in the Modern Kind

WE whom the World is pleased to honor with the Title of *Modern Authors,* should never have been able to compass our great Design of an everlasting Remembrance, and never-dying Fame, if our Endeavours had not been so highly

---

* *Translated the Scriptures into the vulgar Tongues.*
† *Administred the Cup to the Laity at the Communion.*
‡ *Allowed the Marriages of Priests.*
§ *Directed Penitents not to trust to Pardons and Absolutions procur'd for Money, but sent them to implore the Mercy of God, from whence alone Remission is to be obtain'd.*
‖ *By* Peter's *Dragoons, is meant the Civil Power which those Princes, who were bigotted to the Romish Superstition, employ'd against the Reformers.*
¶ *The Pope shuts all who dissent from him out of the Church.*

---

[123] *Copia vera:* A transcript.

serviceable to the general Good of Mankind. This, *O Universe*, is the Adventurous Attempt of me thy Secretary;

> ————*Quemvis perferre laborem*
> *Suadet, & induct noctes vigilare serenas.*[124]

TO this End, I have some Time since, with a World of Pains and Art, dissected the Carcass of *Humane Nature*, and read many useful Lectures upon the several Parts, both *Containing* and *Contained*; till at last it *smelt* so strong, I could preserve it no longer. Upon which, I have been at a great Expence to fit up all the Bones with exact Contexture, and in due Symmetry; so that I am ready to shew a very compleat Anatomy thereof to all curious *Gentlemen and others*. But not to Digress farther in the midst of a Digression, as I have known some Authors inclose Digressions in one another, like a Nest of Boxes; I do affirm, that having carefully cut up *Humane Nature*, I have found a very strange, new, and important Discovery; That the Publick Good of Mankind is performed by two Ways, *Instruction*, and *Diversion*. And I have farther proved in my said several Readings (which, perhaps, the World may one day see, if I can prevail on any Friend to steal a Copy, or on certain Gentlemen of my Admirers, to be very Importunate), that, as Mankind is now disposed, he receives much greater Advantage by being *Diverted* than *Instructed*; His Epidemical Diseases being *Fastidiosity*, *Amorphy*, and *Oscitation*,[125] whereas in the present universal Empire of Wit and Learning, there seems but little Matter left for *Instruction*. However, in Compliance with a Lesson of Great Age and Authority, I have attempted carrying the Point in all its Heights; and accordingly throughout this Divine Treatise, have skilfully kneaded up both together with a *Layer* of *Utile* and a *Layer* of *Dulce*.[126]

WHEN I consider how exceedingly our Illustrious *Moderns* have eclipsed the weak glimmering Lights of the *Antients*, and turned them out of the Road of all fashionable Commerce, to a degree, that our choice *Town-Wits of most refined Accomplishments, are in grave Dispute, whether there have been ever any *Antients* or no: In which Point we are like to receive wonderful Satisfaction from the most useful Labours and Lucubrations of that Worthy *Modern*, Dr. B——*tly*: I say, when I consider all this, I cannot but bewail, that no famous *Modern* hath ever yet attempted an universal System in a small portable Volume, of all Things that are to be Known, or Believed, or Imagined, or Practised in Life. I am, however, forced to acknowledge, that such an enterprise was thought on some Time ago by a great Philosopher of †*O. Brazile*.[127] The

---

* *The Learned Person here meant by our Author, hath been endeavouring to annihilate so many Antient Writers, that until he is pleas'd to stop his hand it will be dangerous to affirm, whether there have been any Antients in the World.*

† *This is an imaginary Island, of Kin to that which is call'd the Painters Wives Island, placed in some unknown part of the Ocean, meerly at the Fancy of the Map-maker.*

---

[124] *Quemvis . . . serenas:* That induces me to spend nights awake gladly.

[125] *Fastidiosity, Amorphy, and Oscitation:* Swift playfully invents the first two of these terms. Amorphy means formlessness. Oscitation is yawning or gaping.

[126] *Utile and . . . Dulce:* Useful and agreeable. These terms represent Horace's prescription for the qualities of art.

[127] *O. Brazile:* An imaginary island supposed to lie west of Ireland, as the note in the text in part suggests.

Method he proposed, was by a certain curious *Receipt*, a *Nostrum*, which after his untimely Death, I found among his Papers; and do here out of my great Affection to the *Modern Learned*, present them with it, not doubting, it may one Day encourage some worthy Undertaker.

YOU take fair correct Copies, well bound in Calfs Skin, and Lettered at the Back, of all Modern Bodies of Arts and Sciences whatsoever, and in what Language you please. These you distil in balneo Mariæ,[128] *infusing* Quintessence of Poppy Q. S.[129] *together with three Pints of* Lethe,[130] *to be had from the Apothecaries. You cleanse away carefully the* Sordes *and* Caput mortuum,[131] *letting all that is volatile evaporate. You preserve only the first Running, which is again to be distilled seventeen times, till what remains will amount to about two Drams. This you keep in a Glass Viol Hermetically sealed, for one and twenty Days. Then you begin your Catholick Treatise, taking every Morning fasting (first shaking the Viol), three Drops of this Elixir, snuffing it strongly up your Nose. It will dilate it self about the Brain (where there is any) in fourteen Minutes, and you immediately perceive in your Head an infinite Number of* Abstracts, Summaries, Compendiums, Extracts, Collections, Medulla's, Excerpta quædam's, Florilegia's *and the like, all disposed into great Order, and reducible upon Paper.*

    I must needs own, it was by the Assistance of this *Arcanum*,[132] that I, tho' otherwise *impar*,[133] have adventured upon so daring an Attempt; never atchieved or undertaken before, but by a certain Author called *Homer*, in whom, tho' otherwise a Person not without some Abilities, and *for an Ancient*, of a tolerable Genius; I have discovered many gross Errors, which are not to be forgiven his very Ashes, if by chance any of them are left. For whereas, we are assured, he design'd his Work for a *compleat Body of all Knowledge Human, Divine, Political, and Mechanick; it is manifest, he hath wholly neglected some, and been very imperfect in the rest. For, first of all, as eminent a *Cabbalist*[135] as his Disciples would represent Him, his Account of the *Opus magnum* is extreamly poor and deficient; he seems to have read but very superficially, either *Sendivogus, Behmen*, or †*Anthroposophia Theomagica*.[136] He is also quite mistaken about the *Sphæra Pyroplastica*,[137] a neglect not to be atton'd for; and (if the Reader will admit so severe a Censure) *Vix crederem Autorem hunc, unquam audivisse ignis*

* *Homerus omnes res humanas Poematis complexus est.* Xenoph. in conviv.[134]

10

20

30

† *A Treatise written about fifty Years ago, by a* Welsh *Gentleman of* Cambridge, *his Name, as I remember, was* Vaughan, *as appears by the Answer to it, writ by the Learned Dr.* Henry Moor, *it is a Piece of the most unintelligible Fustian, that, perhaps, was ever publish'd in any Language.*

---

[128] *Balneo Mariæ:* Water bath.
[129] *Poppy Q. S.:* Poppy *Quantum Sufficit* (Enough Poppy).
[130] *Lethe:* The river of forgetfulness.
[131] *Sordes . . . mortuum:* Filth and the residue after distillation.
[132] *Arcanum:* Secret learning.
[133] *Impar:* Unequal, not a match for.
[134] *Homerus . . . conviv:* In Xenophon's *Convivium*, IV, 6: Homer, in his poems, encompassed all things human.
[135] *Cabbalist:* One versed in the Jewish

mystic oral tradition handed down from Moses to the Rabbis of the Mishnah and the Talmud.
[136] *Sendivogus, Behmen,* or *Anthroposophia Theomagica:* Sendivogius (d. 1636 or 1646), an alchemist; Jacob Boehme (1575–1624), a German mystic: *Anthroposophia Theomagica*, an alchemical work by Thomas Vaughan (1622–1666).
[137] *Sphæra Pyroplastica:* Fire-formed sphere.

vocem.[138] His Failings are not less prominent in several Parts of the *Mechanicks*. For, having read his Writings with the utmost Application usual among *Modern Wits*, I could never yet discover the least Direction about the Structure of that useful Instrument a *Save-all*.[139] For want of which, if the *Moderns* had not lent their Assistance, we might yet have wandred *in the Dark*. But I have still behind, a Fault far more notorious to tax this Author with; I mean, *his gross Ignorance in the *Common Laws of this Realm*, and in the Doctrine as well as Discipline of the Church of *England*. A Defect indeed, for which both he and all the Ancients stand most justly censured by my worthy and ingenious Friend Mr. *W—tt—on*, Batchelor of Divinity, in his incomparable Treatise of *Ancient and Modern Learn-*   10 *ing*; A Book never to be sufficiently valued, whether we consider the happy Turns and Flowings of the Author's Wit, the great Usefulness of his sublime Discoveries upon the Subject of *Flies* and *Spittle*, or the laborious Eloquence of his Stile. And I cannot forbear doing that Author the Justice of my publick Acknowledgments, for the great *Helps* and *Liftings* I had out of his incomparable Piece, while I was penning this Treatise.

BUT, besides these Omissions in *Homer* already mentioned, the curious Reader will also observe several Defects in that Author's Writings, for which he is not altogether so accountable. For whereas every Branch of Knowledge has received such wonderful Acquirements since his Age, especially within these   20 last three Years,[140] or thereabouts; it is almost impossible, he could be so very perfect in Modern Discoveries, as his Advocates pretend. We freely acknowledge Him to be the Inventor of the *Compass*, of *Gun-Powder*, and the *Circulation of the Blood*: But, I challenge any of his Admirers to shew me in all his Writings, a compleat Account of the *Spleen*; Does he not also leave us wholly to seek in the Art of *Political Wagering*? What can be more defective and unsatisfactory than his long Dissertation upon *Tea*? and as to his Method of *Salivation without Mercury*, so much celebrated of late, it is to my own Knowledge and Experience, a Thing very little to be relied on.

IT was to supply such momentous Defects, that I have been prevailed on   30 after long Sollicitation, to take Pen in Hand; and I dare venture to Promise, the Judicious Reader shall find nothing neglected here, that can be of Use upon any Emergency of Life. I am confident to have included and exhausted all that Human Imagination can *Rise* or *Fall* to. Particularly, I recommend to the Perusal of the Learned, certain Discoveries that are wholly untoucht by others; whereof I shall only mention among a great many more; *My New help of Smatterers*, or the *Art of being Deep-learned, and Shallow-read. A curious Invention about Mouse-Traps. An Universal Rule of Reason, or Every Man his own Carver*; Together with a most useful Engine for *catching of Owls*. All

---

* Mr. W–tt–n (*to whom our Author never gives any Quarter*) *in his Comparison of Antient and Modern Learning, Numbers Divinity, Law*, &c. *among those Parts of Knowledge wherein we excel the Antients.*

---

[138] *Vix crederem . . . ignis vocem:* I can hardly believe this author ever to have heard the voice of fire.
[139] *Save-all:* A device for holding candles so that they burn completely.
[140] *Last three Years:* Since Wotton's *Reflections*, 1694.

which the judicious Reader will find largely treated on, in the several Parts of this Discourse.

I hold my self obliged to give as much Light as is possible, into the Beauties and Excellencies of what I am writing, because it is become the Fashion and Humor most applauded among the first Authors of this Polite and Learned Age, when they would correct the ill Nature of Critical, or inform the Ignorance of Courteous Readers. Besides, there have been several famous Pieces lately published both in Verse and Prose; wherein, if the Writers had not been pleas'd, out of their great Humanity and Affection to the Publick, to give us a nice Detail of the *Sublime*, and the *Admirable* they contain; it is a   10 thousand to one, whether we should ever have discovered one Grain of either. For my own particular, I cannot deny, that whatever I have said upon this Occasion, had been more proper in a Preface, and more agreeable to the Mode, which usually directs it there. But I here think fit to lay hold on that great and honourable Privilege of being the *Last Writer*; I claim an absolute Authority in Right, as the *freshest Modern*, which gives me a Despotick Power over all Authors before me. In the Strength of which Title, I do utterly disapprove and declare against that pernicious Custom, of making the Preface a Bill of Fare to the Book. For I have always lookt upon it as a high Point of Indiscretion in *Monster-mongers* and other *Retailers of strange Sights*; to hang out a fair large   20 Picture over the Door, drawn after the Life, with a most eloquent Description underneath: This hath saved me many a Threepence, for my Curiosity was fully satisfied, and I never offered to go in, tho' often invited by the urging and attending Orator, with his last *moving* and *standing* Piece of Rhetorick; *Sir, Upon my Word, we are just going to begin*. Such is exactly the Fate, at this Time, of *Prefaces, Epistles, Advertisements, Introductions, Prolegomena's, Apparatus's, To-the-Reader's*. This Expedient was admirable at first; Our Great *Dryden* has long carried it as far as it would go, and with incredible Success. He has often said to me in Confidence, that the World would have never suspected him to be so great a Poet, if he had not assured them so frequently in his Prefaces, that it   30 was impossible they could either doubt or forget it. Perhaps it may be so; However, I much fear, his instructions have edify'd out of their Place, and taught Men to grow Wiser in certain Points, where he never intended they should; For it is lamentable to behold, with what a lazy Scorn, many of the yawning Readers in our Age, do now a-days twirl over forty or fifty Pages of *Preface* and *Dedication* (which is the usual *Modern* Stint), as if it were so much *Latin*. Tho' it must be also allowed on the other Hand that a very considerable Number is known to proceed *Criticks* and *Wits*, by reading nothing else. Into which two Factions, I think, all present Readers may justly be divided. Now, for my self, I profess to be of the former Sort; and therefore having the *Modern*   40 inclination to expatiate upon the Beauty of my own Productions, and display the bright Parts of my Discourse; I thought best to do it in the Body of the Work, where, as it now lies, it makes a very considerable Addition to the Bulk of the Volume, *a Circumstance by no means to be neglected by a skilful Writer*.

HAVING thus paid my due Deference and Acknowledgment to an establish'd Custom of our newest Authors, by *a long Digression unsought for*, and *an universal Censure unprovoked;* By forcing into the Light, with much Pains and Dexterity, my own Excellencies and other Mens Defaults, with great Justice to my self and Candor to them; I now happily resume my Subject, to the Infinite Satisfaction both of the Reader and the Author.

Sect. VI. A Tale of a Tub

WE left *Lord Peter* in open Rupture with his two Brethren; both for ever discarded from his House, and resigned to the wide World, with little or nothing to trust to. Which are Circumstances that render them proper Subjects for the Charity of a Writer's Pen to work on; Scenes of Misery, ever affording the fairest Harvest for great Adventures. And in this, the World may perceive the Difference between the Integrity of a generous Author, and that of a common   10
Friend. The latter is observed to adhere close in Prosperity, but on the Decline of Fortune, to drop suddenly off. Whereas, the generous Author, just on the contrary, finds his Hero on the Dunghil, from thence by gradual Steps, raises Him to a Throne, and then immediately withdraws, expecting not so much as Thanks for his Pains: In imitation of which Example, I have placed *Lord Peter* in a Noble House, given Him a Title to wear, and Money to spend. There I shall leave Him for some Time; returning where common Charity directs me, to the Assistance of his two Brothers, at their lowest Ebb. However, I shall by no means forget my Character of an Historian, to follow the Truth, step by step, whatever happens, or where-ever it may lead me.   20
THE two Exiles so nearly united in Fortune and Interest, took a Lodging together; Where, at their first Leisure, they began to reflect on the numberless Misfortunes and Vexations of their Life past, and could not tell, on the sudden, to what Failure in their Conduct they ought to impute them; When, after some Recollection, they called to Mind the Copy of their Father's *Will*, which they had so happily recovered. This was immediately produced, and a firm Resolution taken between them, to alter whatever was already amiss, and reduce all their future Measures to the strictest Obedience prescribed therein. The main Body of the *Will* (as the Reader cannot easily have forgot) consisted in certain admirable Rules about the wearing of their Coats; in the Perusal whereof,   30
the two Brothers at every Period duly comparing the Doctrine with the Practice, there was never seen a wider Difference between two Things; horrible down-right Transgressions of every Point. Upon which, they both resolved without further Delay, to fall imediately upon reducing the Whole, exactly after their Father's Model.
BUT, here it is good to stop the hasty Reader, ever impatient to see the End of an Adventure, before We Writers can duly prepare him for it. I am to record, that these two Brothers began to be distinguished at this Time, by certain Names. One of them desired to be called *MARTIN, and the other took the Appellation of † JACK. These two had lived in much Friendship and   40
Agreement under the Tyranny of their Brother *Peter*, as it is the Talent of Fellow-Sufferers to do; Men in Misfortune, being like Men in the Dark, to whom all Colours are the same: But when they came forward into the World, and

---

* *Martin Luther.*   † *John Calvin.*

began to display themselves to each other, and to the Light, their Complexions[141] appear'd extreamly different; which the present Posture of their Affairs gave them sudden Opportunity to discover.

BUT, here the severe Reader may justly tax me as a Writer of short Memory, a Deficiency to which a true *Modern* cannot but of Necessity be a little subject. Because, *Memory* being an Employment of the Mind upon things past, is a Faculty, for which the Learned, in our Illustrious Age, have no manner of Occasion, who deal entirely with *Invention*, and strike all Things out of themselves, or at least, by Collision, from each other: Upon which Account we think it highly Reasonable to produce our great Forgetfulness, as an Argument unanswerable for our great Wit. I ought in Method, to have informed the Reader about fifty Pages ago, of a Fancy *Lord Peter* took, and infused into his Brothers, to wear on their Coats what ever Trimmings came up in Fashion; never pulling off any, as they went out of the Mode, but keeping on all together; which amounted in time to a Medley, the most Antick you can possibly conceive; and this to a Degree, that upon the Time of their falling out there was hardly a Thread of the Original Coat to be seen, but an infinite Quantity of *Lace*, and *Ribbands*, and *Fringe*, and *Embroidery*, and *Points* (I mean, only those *tagg'd with Silver*, for the rest fell off). Now, this material Circumstance, having been forgot in due Place; as good Fortune hath ordered, comes in very properly here, when the two Brothers are just going to reform their Vestures into the Primitive State, prescribed by their Father's *Will*.

THEY both unanimously entred upon this great Work, looking sometimes on their Coats, and sometimes on the *Will*. *Martin* laid the first Hand; at one twitch brought off a large Handful of *Points*,[142] and with a second pull, stript away ten dozen Yards of *Fringe*.[143] But when He had gone thus far, he demurred a while: He knew very well, there yet remained a great deal more to be done; however, the first Heat being over, his Violence began to cool, and he resolved to proceed more moderately in the rest of the Work; having already very narrowly scap'd a swinging Rent in pulling off the *Points*, which being *tagged with Silver* (as we have observed before) the judicious Workman had with much Sagacity, double sown, to preserve them from *falling*. Resolving therefore to rid his Coat of a huge Quantity of *Gold Lace*; he pickt up the Stitches with much Caution, and diligently gleaned out all the loose Threads as he went, which proved to be a Work of Time. Then he fell about the embroidered *Indian* Figures of Men, Women and Children; against which, as you have heard in its due Place, their Father's Testament was extreamly exact and severe: These, with much Dexterity and Application, were after a while, quite eradicated, or utterly defaced. For the rest, where he observed the Embroidery to be workt so close, as not to be got away without damaging the Cloth, or where it served to hide or strengthen any Flaw in the Body of the

---

* *Points tagg'd with Silver, are those Doctrines that promote the Greatness and Wealth of the Church, which have been therefore woven deepest in the Body of Popery.*

---

[141] *Complexions:* Attitudes, temperaments.

[142] *Points:* Dogmas.

[143] *Yards of Fringe:* The first steps of the English Reformation.

Coat, contracted by the perpetual tampering of Workmen upon it; he concluded the wisest Course was to let it remain, resolving in no Case whatsoever, that the Substance of the Stuff should suffer Injury; which he thought the best Method for serving the true Intent and Meaning of his Father's *Will*. And this is the nearest Account I have been able to collect, of *Martin*'s Proceedings upon this great Revolution.

BUT his Brother *Jack*, whose Adventures will be so extraordinary, as to furnish a great Part in the Remainder of this Discourse; entred upon the Matter with other Thoughts, and a quite different Spirit. For, the Memory of *Lord Peter*'s Injuries, produced a Degree of Hatred and Spight, which had a much greater Share of inciting Him, than any Regards after his Father's Commands, since these appeared at best, only Secondary and Subservient to the other. However, for this Meddly of Humor, he made a Shift to find a very plausible Name, honoring it with the Title of *Zeal*; which is, perhaps, the most significant Word that hath been ever yet produced in any Language; As, I think, I have fully proved in my excellent *Analytical* Discourse upon that Subject; wherein I have deduced a *Histori-theo-physi-logical* Account of *Zeal*,[144] shewing how it first proceeded from a *Notion* into a *Word*, and from thence in a hot Summer ripned into a *tangible Substance*. This Work containing three large Volumes in Folio, I design very shortly to publish by the *Modern* way of *Subscription*,[145] not doubting but the Nobility and Gentry of the Land will give me all possible Encouragement, having already had such a Taste of what I am able to perform.

I record therefore, that Brother *Jack*, brimful of this miraculous Compound, reflecting with Indignation upon *PETER*'s Tyranny, and farther provoked by the Despondency of *Martin*; prefaced his Resolutions to this purpose. *What*; said he; *A Rogue that lock'd up his Drink, turned away our Wives, cheated us of our Fortunes; paumed his damned Crusts upon us for Mutton; and at last kickt us out of Doors; must we be in His Fashions with a Pox? a Rascal, besides, that all the Street cries out against.* Having thus kindled and enflamed himself as high as possible, and by Consequence, in a delicate Temper for beginning a Reformation, he set about the Work immediately, and in three Minutes, made more Dispatch than *Martin* had done in as many Hours. For (Courteous Reader), you are given to understand, that *Zeal* is never so highly obliged, as when you set it a *Tearing*: and *Jack*, who doated on that Quality in himself, allowed it at this Time its full Swinge. Thus it happened, that stripping down a Parcel of *Gold Lace*, a little too hastily, he rent the *main Body* of his *Coat* from Top to Bottom; and whereas his Talent was not of the happiest in *taking up a Stitch*, he knew no better way, than to dern it again with *Packthred* and a *Scewer*. But the Matter was yet infinitely worse (I record it with Tears) when he proceeded to the *Embroidery*: For, being Clumsy by Nature, and of Temper, Impatient; withal, beholding Millions of Stitches, that required the nicest Hand, and sedatest Constitution, to extricate; in a great Rage, he tore off the whole Piece, Cloth and all, and flung it into the Kennel,

---

[144] *Account of Zeal:* See *Treatises wrote by the same Author*, above.
[145] *Subscription:* The practice of having purchasers of a proposed book order and pay for it before it is produced.

and furiously thus continuing his Career; *Ah, Good Brother* Martin, said he, *do as I do, for the Love of God; Strip, Tear, Pull, Rent, Flay off all, that we may appear as unlike the Rogue* Peter, *as it is possible: I would not for a hundred Pounds carry the least Mark about me, that might give Occasion to the Neighbours, of suspecting I was related to such a Rascal.* But *Martin* who at this Time happened to be extremely flegmatick and sedate, *begged his Brother of all Love, not to damage his Coat by any Means; for he never would get such another:* Desired him *to consider, that it was not their Business to form their Actions by any Reflection upon* Peter, *but by observing the Rules prescribed in their Father's* Will. That *he should remember,* Peter *was still their Brother: whatever Faults or Injuries he had committed;* 10 *and therefore they should by all means avoid such a Thought, as that of taking Measures for Good and Evil, from no other Rule, than of Opposition to him.* That *it was true, the Testament of their good Father was very exact in what related to the wearing of their* Coats; *yet was it no less penal and strict in prescribing Agreement, and Friendship, and Affection between them. And therefore, if straining a Point were at all dispensable,*[146] *it would certainly be so, rather to the Advance of Unity, than Increase of Contradiction.*

MARTIN had still proceeded as gravely as he began; and doubtless, would have delivered an admirable Lecture of Morality, which might have exceedingly contributed to my Reader's *Repose, both of Body and Mind* (the true 20 ultimate End of *Ethicks*): But *Jack* was already gone a Flight-shot beyond his Patience. And as in Scholastick Disputes, nothing serves to rouze the Spleen of him that *Opposes,* so much as a kind of Pedantick affected Calmness in the *Respondent*; Disputants being for the most part like unequal Scales, where the *Gravity* of one Side advances the *Lightness* of the Other, and causes it to fly up and kick the Beam;[147] So it happened here, that the *Weight* of *Martin*'s Argument exalted *Jack*'s *Levity,* and made him fly out and spurn against his Brother's Moderation. In short, *Martin*'s *Patience* put *Jack* in a *Rage*; but that which most afflicted him was, to observe his Brother's Coat so well reduced into the State of Innocence; while his own was either wholly rent to his Shirt; or 30 those Places which had scaped his cruel Clutches, were still in *Peter*'s Livery. So that he looked like a drunken *Beau,* half rifled by *Bullies*; Or like a fresh Tenant of *Newgate*, when he has refused the Payment of *Garnish*;[148] Or like a discovered *Shoplifter,* left to the Mercy of *Exchange-Women*;[149] Or like a *Bawd* in her old Velvet-Petticoat, resign'd into the secular Hands of the *Mobile*.[150] Like, any, or like all of these, a Meddley of *Rags,* and *Lace,* and *Rents,* and *Fringes,* unfortunate *Jack* did now appear: He would have been extremely glad to see his Coat in the Condition of *Martin*'s, but infinitely gladder to find that of *Martin*'s in the same Predicament with his. However, since neither of these was likely to come to pass, he thought fit to lend the whole Business another 40 Turn, and to dress up Necessity into a Virtue. Therefore, after as many of the *Fox*'s Arguments, as he could muster up, for bringing *Martin* to *Reason,* as he called it; or as he meant it, into his own ragged, bobtail'd Condition; and

---

[146] *Dispensable:* Possible to arrange.
[147] *Beam:* The transverse bar in scales.
[148] *Newgate . . . Garnish:* Newgate, a prison; Garnish, "Money extorted from a new prisoner as a jailor's fee." OED.

[149] *Exchange-Women:* Women who for the most part kept the shops near the Royal Exchange.
[150] *Mobile:* Mob.

observing he said all to little purpose; what, alas, was left for the forlorn *Jack* to do, but after a Million of Scurrilities against his Brother, to run mad with Spleen, and Spight, and Contradiction. To be short, here began a mortal Breach between these two. *Jack* went immediately to *New Lodgings*, and in a few Days it was for certain reported, that he had run out of his Wits. In a short time after, he appeared abroad, and confirmed the Report, by falling into the oddest Whimsies that ever a sick Brain conceived.

AND now the little Boys in the Streets began to salute him with several Names. Sometimes they would call Him, **Jack the Bald*; sometimes, †*Jack with a Lanthorn*; sometimes, ‡*Dutch Jack*; sometimes, §*French Hugh*; sometimes, ||*Tom the Beggar*; and sometimes, ¶*Knocking Jack of the North*. And it was under one or some, or all of these Appelations (which I leave the Learned Reader to determine) that he hath given Rise to the most Illustrious and Epidemick Sect of *Æolists*, who with honourable Commemoration, do still acknowledge the Renowned *JACK* for their Author and Founder. Of whose Original, as well as Principles, I am now advancing to gratify the World with a very particular Account.

———*Mellæo contingens cuncta Lepore.*[151]

Sect. VII. *A Digression in Praise of Digressions*

I have sometimes *heard* of an *Iliad* in a *Nut-shell*; but it hath been my Fortune to have much oftner *seen* a *Nut-shell* in a *Iliad*. There is no doubt, that Human Life has received most wonderful Advantages from both; but to which of the two the World is chiefly indebted, I shall leave among the Curious, as a Problem worthy of their utmost Enquiry, For the Invention of the latter, I think the Commonwealth of Learning is chiefly obliged to the great *Modern* Improvement of *Digressions*: The late Refinements in Knowledge, running parallel to those of Dyet in our Nation, which among Men of a judicious Taste, are drest up in various Compounds, consisting in *Soups* and *Ollio's*, *Fricassées* and *Ragousts*.[152]

'TIS true, there is a sort of morose, detracting, ill-bred People, who pretend utterly to disrelish these polite Innovations: And as to the Similitude from Dyet, they allow the Parallel, but are so bold to pronounce the Example it self, a Corruption and Degeneracy of Taste. They tell us, that the Fashion of jumbling fifty Things together in a Dish, was at first introduced in Compliance to a depraved and *debauched Appetite*, as well as to a *crazy Constitution*; And to see a Man hunting thro' an *Ollio*, after the *Head* and *Brains* of a *Goose*, a

---

* *That is* Calvin, *from* Calvus, *Bald.*
† *All those who pretend to Inward Light.*
‡ Jack *of* Leyden, *who gave Rise to the* Anabaptists.
§ *The* Hugonots.
|| *The* Gueuses, *by which Name some Protestants in* Flanders *were call'd.*
¶ John Knox, *the Reformer of* Scotland.

---

[151] *Mellæo . . . Lepore:* Touching all with sweet wit.
[152] *Ollio's . . . Ragousts:* An olio is a dish of stewed meat; a ragout is a highly spiced dish of stewed meat and vegetables.

Wigeon,[153] or a *Woodcock*, is a Sign, he wants a Stomach and Digestion for more substantial Victuals. Farther, they affirm, that *Digressions* in a Book, are like *Forein Troops* in a *State*, which argue the Nation to want a *Heart* and *Hands* of its own, and often, either *subdue* the *Natives*, or drive them into the most *unfruitful Corners.*

BUT, after all that can be objected by these supercilious Censors; 'tis manifest, the Society of Writers would quickly be reduced to a very inconsiderable Number, if Men were put upon making Books, with the fatal Confinement of delivering nothing beyond what is to the Purpose. 'Tis acknowledged, that were the Case the same among Us, as with the *Greeks* and *Romans*, when   10 Learning was in its *Cradle*, to be reared and fed, and cloathed by *Invention*; it would be an easy Task to fill up Volumes upon particular Occasions, without farther exspatiating from the Subject, than by moderate Excursions, helping to advance or clear the main Design. But with *Knowledge*, it has fared as with a numerous Army, encamped in a fruitful Country; which for a few Days maintains it self by the Product of the Soyl it is on; Till Provisions being spent, they send to forrage many a Mile, among Friends or Enemies it matters not. Mean while, the neighbouring Fields trampled and beaten down, become barren and dry, affording no Sustenance but Clouds of Dust.

THE whole Course of Things, being thus entirely changed between *Us*   20 and the *Antients*; and the *Moderns* wisely sensible of it, we of this Age have discovered a shorter, and more prudent Method, to become *Scholars* and *Wits*, without the Fatigue of *Reading* or of *Thinking*. The most accomplisht Way of using Books at present, is twofold: Either first, to serve them as some Men do *Lords*, learn their *Titles* exactly, and then brag of their Acquaintance. Or Secondly, which is indeed the choicer, the profounder, and politer Method, to get a thorough Insight into the *Index*, by which the whole Book is governed and turned, like *Fishes* by the *Tail*. For, to enter the Palace of Learning at the *great Gate*, requires an Expence of Time and Forms; therefore Men of much Haste and little Ceremony, are content to get in by the *Back-Door*. For, the Arts   30 are all in a *flying* March, and therefore more easily subdued by attacking them in the *Rear*. Thus Physicians discover the State of the whole Body, by consulting only what comes from *Behind*. Thus Men catch Knowledge by throwing their *Wit* on the *Posteriors* of a Book, as Boys do Sparrows with flinging *Salt* upon their *Tails*. Thus Human Life is best understood by the wise man's Rule of *Regarding the End.* Thus are the Sciences found like *Hercules's* Oxen, by *tracing them Backwards.* Thus are *old Sciences* unravelled like *old Stockings*, by beginning at the *Foot*.

BESIDES all this, the Army of the Sciences hath been of late with a world of Martial Discipline, drawn into its *close Order*, so that a View, or a Muster   40 may be taken of it with abundance of Expedition. For this great Blessing we are wholly indebted to *Systems* and *Abstracts*, in which the *Modern* Fathers of Learning, like prudent Usurers, spent their Sweat for the Ease of Us their Children. For *Labor* is the Seed of *Idleness*, and it is the peculiar Happiness of our Noble Age to gather the *Fruit*.

NOW the Method of growing Wise, Learned, and *Sublime*, having become

---

[153] *Wigeon:* Widgeon, a kind of wild duck.

so regular an Affair, and so established in all its Forms; the Numbers of Writers must needs have encreased accordingly, and to a Pitch that has made it of absolute Necessity for them to interfere continually with each other. Besides, it is reckoned, that there is not at this present, a sufficient Quantity of new Matter left in Nature, to furnish and adorn any one particular Subject to the Extent of a Volume. This I am told by a very skillful *Computer*, who hath given a full Demonstration of it from Rules of *Arithmetick*.

THIS, perhaps, may be objected against, by those, who maintain the Infinity of Matter, and therefore, will not allow that any *Species* of it can be exhausted. For Answer to which, let us examine the noblest Branch of *Modern* Wit or Invention, planted and cultivated by the present Age, and, which of all others, hath born the most, and the fairest Fruit. For tho' some Remains of it were left us by the *Antients*, yet have not any of those, as I remember, been translated or compiled into Systems for *Modern* Use. Therefore We may affirm, to our own Honor, that it has in some sort, been both invented, and brought to a Perfection by the same Hands. What I mean, is that highly celebrated Talent among the *Modern* Wits, of deducing Similitudes, Allusions, and Applications, very Surprizing, Agreeable, and Apposite, from the *Pudenda*[154] of either Sex, together with *their proper Uses*. And truly, having observed how little Invention bears any Vogue, besides what is derived into these *Channels*, I have sometimes had a Thought, That the happy Genius of our Age and Country, was prophetically held forth by that antient *typical   * *Ctesiæ* Description of the *Indian* Pygmies; *whose Stature did not exceed above* *fragm.* *two Foot*; *Sed quorum pudenda crassa, & ad talos usque pertingentia.*[156]   *apud Phot-* Now, I have been very curious to inspect the late Productions, *ium.*[155] wherein the Beauties of this kind have most prominently appeared. And altho' this *Vein* hath bled so freely, and all Endeavours have been used in the Power of Human Breath, to dilate, extend, and keep it open: Like the Scythians, †*who had a Custom, and an Instrument, to blow up the Privities of their*   †*Herodot.* *Mares, that they might yield the more Milk;* Yet I am under an Ap-   L. 4. prehension, it is near growing dry, and past all Recovery; And that either some new *Fonde*[157] of Wit should, if possible, be provided, or else that we must e'en be content with Repetition here, as well as upon all other Occasions.

THIS will stand as an uncontestable Argument, that our *Modern* Wits are not to reckon upon the Infinity of Matter, for a constant Supply. What remains therefore, but that our last Recourse must be had to large *Indexes*, and little *Compendiums*; *Quotations* must be plentifully gathered, and bookt in Alphabet; To this End, tho' Authors need be little consulted, yet *Criticks*, and *Commentators*, and *Lexicons* carefully must. But above all, those judicious Collectors of *bright Parts*, and *Flowers*, and *Observanda's*,[158] are to be nicely dwelt on; by some called the *Sieves* and *Boulters* of Learning; tho' it is left undetermined, whether they dealt in *Pearls* or Meal; and consequently, whether we are more to value that which *passed thro'*, or what *staid behind*.

BY these Methods, in a few Weeks, there starts up many a Writer, capable of

---

[154] *Pudenda*: Genitals.
[155] *Photium*: See n. 99.
[156] *Sed . . . pertingentia*: But whose pudenda are thick and extend all the

way to their ankles.
[157] *Fonde*: Source.
[158] *Observanda's*: Observations.

managing the profoundest, and most universal Subjects. For, what tho' his *Head* be empty, provided his *Common place-Book* be full; And if you will bate him but the Circumstances of *Method*, and *Style*, and *Grammar*, and *Invention*; allow him but the common Priviledges of transcribing from others, and digressing from himelf, as often as he shall see Occasion; He will desire no more Ingredients towards fitting up a Treatise, that shall make a very comely Figure on a Bookseller's Shelf, there to be preserved neat and clean, for a long Eternity, adorn'd with the Heraldry of its Title, fairly inscribed on a Label; never to be thumb'd or greas'd by Students, nor bound to everlasting Chains of Darkness in a Library:[159] But when the Fulness of time is come, shall happily   10
undergo the Tryal of Purgatory, in order *to ascend the Sky.*

WITHOUT these Allowances, how is it possible, we *Modern* Wits should ever have an Opportunity to introduce our Collections listed under so many thousand Heads of a different Nature? for want of which, the Learned World would be deprived of infinite Delight, as well as instruction, and we our selves buried beyond Redress in an inglorious and undistinguisht Oblivion.

FROM such Elements as these, I am alive to behold the Day, wherein the Corporation of Authors can out-vie all its Brethren in the *Field.* A Happiness derived to us with a great many others, from our *Scythian* Ancestors; among whom, the Number of *Pens* was so infinite, that the **Grecian*   **Herodot.*   20
Eloquence had no other way of expressing it, than by saying, *That* L. 4.
in the Regions, far to the North, *it was hardly possible for a Man to travel, the very Air was so replete with* Feathers.

THE Necessity of this Digression, will easily excuse the Length; and **I** have chosen for it as proper a Place as I could readily find. If the judicious Reader can assign a fitter, I do here empower him to remove it into any other Corner he pleases. And so I return with great Alacrity to pursue a more important Concern.

Sect. VIII. A Tale of a Tub

THE Learned **Æolists,* maintain the Original Cause of all Things to be *Wind,* from which Principle this whole Universe was at first produced, and into   30
which it must at last be resolved; that the same Breath which had kindled, and blew *up* the Flame of Nature, should one Day blow it *out.*

Quod procul a nobis flectat Fortuna gubernans.[160]

THIS is what the *Adepti* understand by their *Anima Mundi*; that is to say, the *Spirit,* or *Breath,* or *Wind* of the World: for Examine the whole System by the Particulars of Nature, and you will find it not to be disputed. For, whether you please to call the *Forma informans*[161] of Man, by the Name of *Spiritus, Animus, Afflatus,*[162] or *Anima*; What are all these but several Appellations for *Wind?*

* *All Pretenders to Inspiration whatsoever.*

---

[159] *Chains . . . in a Library:* Books used to be chained in Libraries.

[160] *Quod procul a nobis flectat Fortuna gubernans:* Which, may the pilot, Fortune, steer away from us.

[161] *Forma informans:* Shaping principle.

[162] *Afflatus:* The inspiration of supernatural power; an overwhelming poetic impulse.

which is the ruling *Element* in every Compound, and into which they all resolve upon their Corruption. Farther, what is Life itself, but as it is commonly call'd, the *Breath* of our Nostrils? Whence it is very justly observed by Naturalists, that *Wind* still continues of great Emolument in *certain Mysteries* not to be named, giving Occasion for those happy Epithets of *Turgidus*, and *Inflatus*,[163] apply'd either to the *Emittent*, or *Recipient* Organs.

BY what I have gathered out of antient Records, I find the *Compass* of their Doctrine took in two and thirty Points, wherein it would be tedious to be very particular. However, a few of their most important Precepts, deducible from it, are by no means to be omitted; among which the following Maxim was of much Weight; That since *Wind* had the Master-Share, as well as Operation in every Compound, by Consequence, those Beings must be of chief Excellence, wherein that *Primordium*[164] appears most prominently to abound; and therefore, *Man* is in highest Perfection of all created Things, as having by the great Bounty of Philosophers, been endued with three distinct *Anima's* or *Winds*, to which the Sage *Æolists*, with much Liberality, have added a fourth of equal Necessity, as well as Ornament with the other three;[165] by this *quartum Principium*, taking in our four Corners of the World, which gave Occasion to that Renowned *Cabbalist*, *Bumbastus, of placing the Body of Man, in due position to the four *Cardinal* Points.

IN Consequence of this, their next Principle was, that *Man* brings with him into the World a peculiar Portion or Grain of *Wind*, which may be called a *Quinta essentia*, extracted from the other four. This *Quintessence* is of a Catholick Use upon all Emergencies of Life, is improvable into all Arts and Sciences, and may be wonderfully refined, as well as enlarged by certain Methods in Education. This, when *blown* up to its Perfection, ought not to be covetously hoarded up, stifled, or hid under a Bushel, but freely communicated to Mankind. Upon these Reasons, and others of equal Weight, the Wise *Æolists*, affirm the Gift of BELCHING, to be the noblest Act of a Rational Creature. To cultivate which Art, and render it more serviceable to Mankind, they made Use of several Methods. At certain Seasons of the Year, you might behold the Priests amongst them in vast Numbers, with their †*Mouths gaping wide against a Storm*. At other times were to be seen several Hundreds link'd together in a circular Chain, with every Man a Pair of Bellows applied to his Neighbour's Breech, by which they blew up each other to the Shape and Size of a *Tun*;[166] and for that Reason, with great Propriety of Speech, did usually call their Bodies,

---

* *This is one of the Names of* Paracelsus; *He was call'd* Christophorus, Theophrastus, Paracelsus, Bumbastus.[167]

† *This is meant of those Seditious Preachers, who blow up the Seeds of Rebellion,* &c.

---

[163] *Turgidus . . . Inflatus:* Swollen; blown.

[164] *Primordium:* The first beginning.

[165] *Other three:* In a note, the 1720 edition of *Tale* explains, The three *Anima's* bestow'd on Man by Philosophers are the *Vegetativa, Sensitiva,* and *Rationalis,* and the fourth bestow'd by the Aeolists is the *Spiritualis.*

[166] *Tun:* A large cask. The purpose of this inflation, as the remainder of the passage indicates, was to facilitate *disemboguing* (flowing from the mouth) and *eructation* (belching).

[167] *Paracelsus:* Theophrastus Bombastus von Hohenheim (1493–1541), alchemist, mystic, and physician.

their *Vessels.* When, by these and the like Performances, they were grown sufficiently replete, they would immediately depart, and disembogue for the *Publick Good,* a plentiful Share of their Acquirements into their Disciples Chaps. For we must here observe, that all Learning was esteemed among them to be compounded from the same Principle. Because, First, it is generally affirmed, or confess'd that Learning *puffeth Men up*: And Secondly, they proved it by the following Syllogism; *Words are but Wind*; *and Learning is nothing but Words*; Ergo, *Learning is nothing but Wind.* For this Reason, the Philosophers among them, did in their Schools, deliver to their Pupils, all their Doctrines and Opinions by *Eructation,* wherein they had acquired a wonderful Eloquence, and of incredible   10 Variety. But the great Characteristick, by which their chief Sages were best distinguished, was a certain Position of Countenance, which gave undoubted Intelligence to what Degree or Proportion, the Spirit agitated the inward Mass. For, after certain Gripings, the *Wind* and Vapours issuing forth; having first by their Turbulence and Convulsions within, caused an Earthquake in Man's little World; distorted the Mouth, bloated the Cheeks, and gave the Eyes a terrible kind of *Relievo.*[168] At which Junctures, all their *Belches* were received for Sacred, the Sourer the better, and swallowed with infinite Consolation by their meager Devotees. And to render these yet more compleat, because the Breath of Man's Life is in his Nostrils, therefore, the choicest 'most edifying,   20 and most enlivening *Belches,* were very wisely conveyed thro' that Vehicle, to give them a Tincture as they passed.

THEIR Gods were the four *Winds,* whom they worshipped, as the Spirits that pervade and enliven the Universe, and as those from whom alone all *Inspiration* can properly be said to proceed. However, the Chief of these, to whom they performed the Adoration of *Latria,*[169] was the *Almighty-North.* An antient Deity, whom the Inhabitants of *Megalopolis* in *Greece,* had likewise in highest Reverence. *Omnium Deorum Boream maxime celebrant.*[170] This   * Pausan. God, tho' endued with Ubiquity, was yet supposed by the profounder   L. 8. Æolists, to possess one peculiar Habitation, or (to speak in Form) a *Cælum*   30 *Empyræum,*[171] wherein he was more intimately present. This was situated in a certain Region, well known to the Antient *Greeks,* by them called, Σκοτία, or the *Land of Darkness.* And altho' many Controversies have arisen upon that Matter; yet so much is undisputed, that from a Region of the *like Denomination,*[172] the most refined *Æolists* have borrowed their Original, from whence, in every Age, the zealous among their Priesthood, have brought over their choicest *Inspiration,* fetching it with their own Hands, from the Fountain Head, in certain *Bladders,* and disploding[173] it among the Sectaries in all Nations, who did, and do, and ever will, daily Gasp and Pant after it.

NOW, their Mysteries and Rites were performed in this Manner. 'Tis well   40 known among the Learned, that the Virtuoso's of former Ages, had a Contrivance fo[r] carrying and preserving *Winds* in Casks or Barrels, which was

---

[168] *Relievo:* Relief, as in sculpture; i.e., the eyes bulged.

[169] *Latria:* Divine worship.

[170] *Omnium Deorum Boream maxime celebrant:* Of all the gods they honor Boreas [the North Wind] most.

[171] *Cælum Empyræum:* Highest heaven.

[172] *Like Denomination:* English dissenters.

[173] *Disploding:* Discharging with an explosion.

of great Assistance upon long Sea Voyages; and the loss of so useful an Art at present, is very much to be lamented, tho' I know not how, with great Negligence omitted by *Pancirollus*. It was an Invention ascribed to *Æolus* himself, from whom this Sect is denominated, and who in Honour of their Founder's Memory, have to this Day preserved great Numbers of those *Barrels*, whereof they fix one in each of their Temples, first beating out the Top; into this *Barrel*, upon Solemn Days, the Priest enters; where, having before duly prepared himself by the methods already described, a secret Funnel is also convey'd from his Posteriors, to the Bottom of the Barrel, which admits new Supplies of Inspiration from a *Northern* Chink or Crany. Whereupon, you behold him swell immediately to the Shape and Size of his *Vessel*. In this Posture he disembogues whole Tempests upon his Auditory, as the Spirit from beneath gives him Utterance; which issuing *ex adytis*, and *penetralibus*,[174] is not performed without much Pain and Gripings. And the *Wind* in breaking forth, †deals with his Face, as it does with that of the Sea; first *blackning*, then *wrinkling*, and at last, *bursting it into a Foam*. It is in this Guise, the Sacred *Æolist* delivers his oracular *Belches* to his panting Disciples; Of whom, some are greedily gaping after the sanctified Breath; others are all the while hymning out the Praises of the *Winds*; and gently wafted to and fro by their own Humming, do thus represent the soft Breezes of their Deities appeased.

IT is from this Custom of the Priests, that some Authors maintain these *Æolists*, to have been very antient in the World. Because, the Delivery of their Mysteries, which I have just now mention'd, appears exactly the same with that of other antient Oracles, whose Inspirations were owing to certain subter-[r]aneous *Effluviums* of *Wind*, delivered with the same Pain to the Priest, and much about the *same* Influence on the People. It is true indeed, that these were frequently managed and directed by *Female* Officers, whose Organs were understood to be better disposed for the admission of those Oracular *Gusts*, as entring and passing up thro' a Receptacle of greater Capacity, and causing also a Pruriency by the Way, such as with due Management, hath been refined from Carnal, into a Spiritual Extasie. And to strengthen this profound Conjecture, it is farther insisted, that this Custom of ‡*Female* Priests is kept up still in certain refined Colleges of our *Modern Æolists*, who are agreed to receive their Inspiration, derived thro' the Receptacle aforesaid, like their Ancestors, the *Sibyls*.[175]

AND, whereas the mind of Man, when he gives the Spur and Bridle to his Thoughts, doth never stop, but naturally sallies out into both extreams of High and Low, of Good and Evil; His first Flight of Fancy, commonly transports Him to Idea's of what is most Perfect, finished, and exalted; till having soared out of his own Reach and Sight, not well perceiving how near the Frontiers of Height and Depth, border upon each other; With the same Course and Wing, he falls down plum into the lowest Bottom of Things; like one who

* *An Author who writ* De Artibus Perditis, *&c. of Arts lost, and of Arts invented.*
† *This is an exact Description of the Changes made in the Face by Enthusiastick Preachers.*
‡ *Quakers who suffer their Women to preach and pray.*

---

[174] *Ex adytis . . . penetralibus:* From the recesses of the temple.

[175] *Sibyls:* In antiquity, women supposed to have prophetic powers.

travels the *East* into the *West*; or like a strait line drawn by its own Length into a Circle. Whether a Tincture of Malice in our Natures, makes us fond of furnishing every bright Idea with its Reverse; Or, whether Reason reflecting upon the Sum of things, can, like the Sun, serve only to enlighten one half of the Globe, leaving the other half, by Necessity, under Shade and Darkness, Or, whether Fancy, flying up to the imagination of what is Highest and Best, becomes over-short and Spent, and weary, and suddenly falls like a dead Bird of Paradise, to the Ground.[176] Or, whether after all these *Metaphysical* Conjectures, I have not entirely missed the true Reason; The Proposition, however, which hath stood me in so much Circumstance, is altogethe[r] true; That, as the most unciviliz'd Parts of Mankind, have some way or other, climbed up into the Conception of a *God*, or Supream Power, so they have seldom forgot to provide their Fears with certain ghastly Notions, which instead of better, have served them pretty tolerably for a *Devil*. And this Proceeding seems to be natural enough; For it is with Men, whose Imaginations are lifted up very high, after the same Rate, as with those, whose Bodies are so; that, as they are delighted with the Advantage of a nearer Contemplation upwards, so they are equally terrified with the dismal Prospect of the Precipice below. Thus, in the Choice of a *Devil*, it hath been the usual Method of Mankind, to single out some Being, either in Act, or in Vision, which was in most Antipathy to the God they had framed. Thus also the Sect of *Æolists*, possessed themselves with a Dread, and Horror, and Hatred of two Malignant Natures, betwixt whom, and the Deities they adored, perpetual Enmity was established. The first of these, was the *Camelion sworn Foe to *Inspiration*, who in Scorn, devoured large Influences of their God; without refunding the smallest Blast by *Eructation*.[177] The other was a huge terrible Monster, called *Moulinavent*, who with four strong Arms, waged eternal Battel with all their Divinities, dextrously turning to avoid their Blows, and repay them with Interest.

THUS furnish, and set out with *Gods*, as well as *Devils*, was the renowned Sect of *Æolists;* which makes at this Day so illustrious a Figure in the World, and whereof, that Polite Nation of *Laplanders,* are beyond all Doubt, a most Authentick Branch; Of whom, I therefore cannot, without Injustice, here omit to make honourable Mention; since they appear to be so closely allied in Point of Interest, as well as Inclinations, with their Brother *Æolists* among Us, as not only to buy their *Winds* by wholesale from the *same* Merchants, but also to retail them after the *same* Rate and Method, and to Customers much alike.

NOW, whether the System here delivered, was wholly compiled by *Jack*, or, as some Writers believe, rather copied from the Original at *Delphos*,[178] with certain Additions and Emendations suited to Times and Circumstances, I shall not absolutely determine. This I may affirm, that *Jack* gave it at least a new Turn, and formed it into the same Dress and Model, as it lies deduced by me.

* *I do not well understand what the Author aims at here, any more than by the terrible Monster, mention'd in the following Lines, called* Moulinavent, *which is the* French *Word for a Windmill.*

---

[176] *Bird . . . Ground:* Birds of Paradise were thought to have no feet and to fly perpetually until dead.

[177] *Eructation:* Belching.
[178] *Delphos:* Delphi, shrine of Apollo.

I have long sought after this Opportunity, of doing Justice to a Society of Men, for whom I have a peculiar Honour, and whose Opinions, as well as Practices, have been extreamly misrepresented, and traduced by the Malice or Ignorance of their Adversaries. For, I think it one of the greatest, and best of humane Actions, to remove Prejudices, and place Things in their truest and fairest Light; which I therefore boldly undertake without any Regards of my own, beside the Conscience, the Honour, and the Thanks.

Sect. IX. A Digression concerning the Original, the Use and Improvement of Madness in a Commonwealth

NOR shall it any ways detract from the just Reputation of this famous Sect, that its Rise and Institution are owing to such an Author as I have described *Jack* to be; A Person whose Intellectuals were overturned, and his Brain shaken out 10 of its Natural Position; which we commonly suppose to be a Distemper, and call by the Name of *Madness* or *Phrenzy*. For, if we take a Survey of the greatest Actions that have been performed in the World, under the Influence of Single Men; which are, *The Establishment of New Empires by Conquest: The Advance and Progress of New Schemes in Philosophy; and the contriving, as well as the propagating of New Religions:* We shall find the Authors of them all, to have been Persons, whose natural Reason hath admitted great Revolutions from their Dyet, their Education, the Prevalency of some certain Temper, together with the particular Influence of Air and Climate. Besides, there is something Individual in human Minds, that easily kindles at the accidental Approach and Colli- 20 sion of certain Circumstances, which tho' of paltry and mean Appearance, do often flame out into the greatest Emergencies of Life. For great Turns are not always given by strong Hands, but by lucky Adaption, and at proper Seasons; and it is of no import, where the Fire was kindled, if the Vapor has once got up into the Brain. For the *upper Region* of Man, is furnished like the *middle Region* of the Air; The Materials are formed from Causes of the widest Difference, yet produce at last the same Substance and Effect. Mists arise from the Earth, Steams from Dunghils, Exhalations from the Sea, and Smoak from Fire; yet all Clouds are the same in Composition, as well as Consequences: and the Fumes issuing from a Jakes, will furnish as comely and useful a Vapor, as Incense from 30 an Altar. Thus far, I suppose, will easily be granted me; and then it will follow, that as the Face of Nature never produces Rain, but when it is overcast and disturbed, so Human Understanding, seated in the Brain, must be troubled and overspread by Vapours, ascending from the lower Faculties, to water the Invention, and render it fruitful. Now, altho' these Vapours (as it hath been already said) are of as various Original, as those of the Skies, yet the Crop they produce, differ both in Kind and Degree, meerly according to the Soil. I will produce two instances to prove and Explain what I am now advancing.

*A certain Great Prince raised a mighty Army, filled his Coffers with infinite Treasures, provided an invincible Fleet, and all this, without giving the least 40 Part of his Design to his greatest Ministers, or his nearest Favourites. Immediately the whole World was alarmed; the neighbouring Crowns, in trembling Expec-

* *This was* Harry *the Great of* France.

tations, towards what Point the Storm would burst; the small Politicians, every where forming profound Conjectures. Some believed he had laid a Scheme for Universal Monarchy: Others, after much Insight, determined the Matter to be a Project for pulling down the *Pope*, and setting up the *Reformed* Religion, which had once been his own. Some, again, of a deeper Sagacity, sent him into *Asia* to subdue the *Turk*, and recover *Palestine*. In the midst of all these Projects and Preparations; a certain *State-Surgeon, gathering the Nature of the Disease by these Symptoms, attempted the Cure, at one Blow performed the Operation, broke the Bag, and out flew the *Vapour*; nor did any thing want to render it a compleat Remedy, only, that the Prince unfortunately happened to Die in the Performance. Now, is the Reader exceeding curious to learn, from whence this *Vapour* took its Rise, which had so long set the Nations at a Gaze? What secret Wheel, what hidden Spring could put into Motion so wonderful an Engine? It was afterwards discovered, that the Movement of this whole Machine had been directed by an absent *Female*, whose Eyes had raised a Protuberancy, and before Emission, she was removed into an Enemy's Country. What should an unhappy Prince do in such ticklish Circumstances as these? He tried in vain the Poet's never-failing Receipt of *Corpora quæque*,[179] For,

> *Idque petit corpus mens unde est saucia amore;*
> *Unde feritur, eo tendit, gestitq; coire.* Lucr.[180]

HAVING to no purpose used all peaceable Endeavours, the collected part of the *Semen*, raised and enflamed, became adust, converted to Choler, turned head upon the spinal Duct, and ascended to the Brain. The very same Principle that influences a *Bully* to break the Windows of a Whore, who has jilted him, naturally stirs up a Great Prince to raise mighty Armies, and dream of nothing but Sieges, Battles, and Victories.

> ————*Teterrima belli*
> *Causa*————————[181]

THE other †Instance is, what I have read somewhere, in a very antient Author, of a mighty King, who for the space of above thirty Years, amused himself to take and loose Towns; beat Armies, and be beaten; drive Princes out of their Dominions; fright Children from their Bread and Butter; burn, lay waste, plunder, dragoon, massacre Subject and Stranger, Friend and Foe, Male and Female. 'Tis recorded, that the Philosophers of each Country were in grave Dispute, upon Causes Natural, Moral, and Political, to find out where they should assign an original Solution of this *Phænomenon*. At last the *Vapour* or *Spirit*, which animated the Hero's Brain, being in perpetual Circulation, seized

---

* Ravillac, *who stabb'd* Henry *the Great in his Coach.*
† *This is meant of the Present* French *King.*

---

[179] *Corpora quæque:* Part of a line from Lucretius, *De Rerum Natura*, IV, 1065, which translates: and to cast off the collected fluid *upon any other body* (in *corpora quaeque*).
[180] *Idque . . . coire. Lucr: De Rerum Natura*, IV, 1048, 1055: And the body looks for that which has wounded the mind with love; one reaches out to the source of the blow, and longs to unite.
[181] *Teterrima belli Causa:* Horace, *Satires*, I, iii, 107: *Nam fuit ante Helenam cunnus . . . causa:* for before Helen's day a whore was the most hateful cause of war.

upon that Region of Human Body, so renown'd for furnishing the *Zibeta Occidentalis*, and gathering there into a Tumor, left the rest of the World for that Time in Peace. Of such mighty Consequence it is, where those Exhalations fix; and of so little, from whence they proceed. The same Spirits which in their superior Progress would conquer a Kingdom, descending upon the *Anus*, conclude in a *Fistula*.[182]

LET us next examine the great Introducers of new Schemes in Philosophy, and search till we can find, from what Faculty of the Soul the Disposition arises in mortal Man, of taking it into his Head, to advance new Systems with such an eager Zeal, in things agreed on all hands impossible to be known: from what Seeds this Disposition springs, and to what Quality of human Nature these Grand Innovators have been indebted for their Number of Disciples. Because, it is plain, that several of the chief among them, both *Antient* and *Modern*, were usually mistaken by their Adversaries, and indeed, by all, except their own Followers, to have been Persons Crazed, or out of their Wits, having generally proceeded in the common Course of their Words and Actions, by a Method very different from the vulgar Dictates of *unrefined* Reason: agreeing for the most Part in their several Models, with their present undoubted Successors in the *Academy* of *Modern Bedlam* (whose Merits and Principles I shall farther examine in due Place). Of this Kind were *Epicurus, Diogenes, Apollonius, Lucretius, Paracelsus, Des Cartes*,[183] and others; who, if they were now in the World, tied fast, and separate from their Followers, would in this our undistinguishing Age, incur manifest Danger of *Phlebotomy*,[184] and *Whips*, and *Chains*, and *dark Chambers*, and *Straw*. For, what Man in the natural State, or Course of Thinking, did ever conceive it in his Power, to reduce the Notions of all Mankind, exactly to the same Length, and Breadth, and Heighth of his own? Yet this is the first humble and civil Design of all Innovators in the Empire of Reason. *Epicurus*, modestly hoped, that one Time or other, a certain Fortuitous Concourse of all Mens Opinions, after perpetual Justlings, the Sharp with the Smooth, the Light and the Heavy, the Round and the Square, would by certain *Clinamina*,[185] unite in the Notions of *Atoms* and *Void*, as these did in the Originals of all Things. *Cartesius* reckoned to see before he died, the Sentiments of all Philosophers, like so many lesser Stars in his *Romantick* System, rapt and

---

* Paracelsus, *who was so famous for Chymistry, try'd an Experiment upon human Excrement, to make a Perfume of it, which when he had brought to Perfection, he called* Zibeta Occidentalis, *or* Western-Civet, *the back Parts of Man (according to his Division mention'd by the Author, page 160.) being the* West.[186]

---

[182] *Fistula:* A pipe-like ulcer with a narrow opening.

[183] *Epicurus . . . Des Cartes:* Epicurus, a Greek atomist who sought to explain all things as physical in basis: Diogenes, the cynic who repudiated civilized ways and lived in a tub; Apollonius of Tyana, who gained fame as a mystic and wonder-worker; Lucretius, the Roman atomist who followed Epicurus in believing that atoms fortuitously joined account for the forms of matter we know; Paracelsus (see n.

167); Descartes, the French rationalist.

[184] *Phlebotomy:* The drawing of blood as a therapy.

[185] *Clinamina:* In Epicurus' system (and Lucretius'), atoms before they joined moved at equal, constant speeds through parallel courses, not touching. The clinamen (Lucretius' word) is that bias or deviation of atoms accounting for their union.

[186] *. . . Page 160.) being the West:* Page 394 in this edition.

drawn within his own *Vortex*. Now, I would gladly be informed, how it is possible to account for such Imaginations as these in particular Men, without Recourse to my *Phænomenon* of *Vapours*, ascending from the lower Faculties to over-shadow the Brain, and there distilling into Conceptions, for which the Narrowness of our Mother-Tongue has not yet assigned any other Name, besides that of *Madness* or *Phrenzy*. Let us therefore now conjecture how it comes to pass, that none of these great Prescribers, do ever fail providing themselves and their Notions, with a Number of implicite Disciples. And, I think, the Reason is easie to be assigned: For, there is a peculiar *String* in the Harmony of Human Understanding, which in several individuals is exactly of the same   10
Tuning. This, if you can dexterously screw up to its right Key, and then strike gently upon it; Whenever you have the Good Fortune to light among those of the same Pitch, they will by a secret necessary Sympathy, strike exactly at the same time. And in this one Circumstance, lies all the Skill or Luck of the Matter; for if you chance to jar the String among those who are either above or below your own Height, instead of subscribing to your Doctrine, they will tie you fast, call you Mad, and feed you with Bread and Water. It is therefore a Point of the nicest Conduct to distinguish and adapt this noble Talent, with respect to the Differences of Persons and of Times. *Cicero* understood this very well, when writing to a Friend in *England*, with a Caution, among other Mat-   20
ters, to beware of being cheated by our *Hackney-Coachmen* (who, it seems, in those days, were as arrant Rascals as they are now) has these remark-   * *Epist.*
able Words. **Est quod gaudeas te in ista loca venisse, ubi aliquid sapere* ad Fam.
viderere.*[187] For, to speak a bold Truth, it is a fatal Miscarriage, so ill to   Trebatio.
order Affairs, as to pass for a *Fool* in one Company, when in another you might be treated as a *Philosopher*. Which I desire *some certain Gentlemen of my Acquaintance*, to lay up in their Hearts, as a very seasonable *Innuendo*.

THIS, indeed, was the Fatal Mistake of that worthy Gentleman, my most ingenious Friend, Mr. *W-tt-n*: A Person, in appearance ordain'd for great Designs, as well as Performances; whether you will consider his *Notions* or his   30
Looks. Surely, no Man ever advanced into the Publick, with fitter Qualifications of Body and Mind, for the Propagation of a new Religion. Oh, had those happy Talents misapplied to vain Philosophy, been turned into their proper Channels of *Dreams* and *Visions*, where *Distortion* of Mind and Countenance, are of such Sovereign Use; the base detracting World would not then have dared to report, that something is amiss, that his Brain hath undergone an unlucky Shake; which even his Brother *Modernists* themselves, like Ungrates, do whisper so loud, that it reaches up to the very Garret I am now writing in.

LASTLY, Whosoever pleases to look into the Fountains of *Enthusiasm*, from whence, in all Ages, have eternally proceeded such fatning Streams, will   40
find the Spring Head to have been as *troubled* and *muddy* as the Current; Of such great Emolument, is a Tincture of this *Vapour*, which the World calls *Madness*, that without its Help, the World would not only be deprived of those two great Blessings, *Conquests* and *Systems*, but even all Mankind would happily be reduced to the same Belief in Things Invisible. Now, the former *Postulatum*

[187] *Est quod . . . viderere:* You may well   those places where you pass as a man of
congratulate yourself on having reached   some ability.

being held, that it is of no Import from what Originals this *Vapour* proceeds, but either in what *Angles* it strikes and spreads over the Understanding, or upon what *Species* of Brain it ascends; It will be a very delicate Point, to cut the Feather,[188] and divide the several Reasons to a Nice and Curious Reader, how this numerical Difference in the Brain, can produce Effects of so vast a Difference from the same *Vapour*, as to be the sole Point of Individuation[189] between *Alexander the Great, Jack of Leyden,*[190] and Monsieur *Des Cartes.* The present Argument is the most abstracted that ever I engaged in, it strains my Faculties to their highest Stretch; and I desire the Reader to attend with utmost Perpensity; For, I now proceed to unravel this knotty Point.

    *THERE is in Mankind a certain * * * * * * *
* * * * * * * * * * * * *
Hic multa * * * * * * * * * * * *
desider- * * * * * * * * * * * *
antur. * * * * * * * * * * * *
* * * * * * * * * * * * *
* * And this I take to be a clear Solution of the Matter.

HAVING therefore so narrowly past thro' this intricate Difficulty, the Reader will, I am sure, agree with me in the Conclusion; that if the *Moderns* mean by *Madness,* only a Disturbance or Transposition of the Brain, by Force of certain *Vapours* issuing up from the lower Faculties; Then has this *Madness* been the Parent of all those mighty Revolutions, that have happened in *Empire,* in *Philosophy,* and in *Religion.* For, the Brain, in its natural Position and State of Serenity, disposeth its Owner to pass his Life in the common Forms, without any Thought of subduing Multitudes to his own *Power,* his *Reasons* or his *Visions*; and the more he shapes his Understanding by the Pattern of Human Learning, the less he is inclined to form Parties after his particular Notions; because that instructs him in his private Infirmities, as well as in the stubborn Ignorance of the People. But when a Man's Fancy gets *astride* on his Reason, when Imagination is at Cuffs with the Senses, and common Understanding, as well as common Sense, is Kickt out of Doors; the first Proselyte he makes, is Himself, and when that is once compass'd, the Difficulty is not so great in bringing over others; A strong Delusion always operating from *without,* as vigorously as from *within.* For, Cant and Vision are to the Ear and the Eye, the same that Tickling is to the Touch. Those Entertainments and Pleasures we most value in Life, are such as *Dupe* and play the Wag with the Senses. For, if we take an Examination of what is generally understood by *Happiness,* as it has Respect, either to the Understanding or the Senses, we shall find all its Properties and Adjuncts will herd under this short Definition: That, *it is a perpetual Posses-*

---

    * *Here is another Defect in the Manuscript, but I think the Author did wisely, and that the Matter which thus strained his Faculties, was not worth a Solution; and it were well if all Metaphysical Cobweb Problems were no otherwise answered.* [*Hic multa desiderantur:* Here many (lines) are wanting.]

---

[188] *Cut the Feather:* Split hairs.
[189] *Individuation:* "In Scholastic Philosophy, the process leading to individual existence, as distinct from that of the species." *OED.*

[190] *Jack of Leyden:* Johann Bockholdt (1508–1536), a Dutch Anabaptist fanatic. He had been a tailor until he joined the religious movement he later led.

sion of being well Deceived. And first, with Relation to the Mind or Understanding; 'tis manifest, what mighty Advantages Fiction has over Truth; and the Reason is just at our Elbow; because Imagination can build nobler Scenes, and produce more wonderful Revolutions than Fortune or Nature will be at Expence to furnish. Nor is Mankind so much to blame in his Choice, thus determining him, if we consider that the Debate meerly lies between *Things past,* and *Things conceived*; and so the Question is only this; Whether Things that have Place in the *Imagination,* may not as properly be said to *Exist,* as those that are seated in the *Memory*; which may be justly held in the Affirmative, and very much to the Advantage of the former, since This is acknowledged to be   10 the *Womb* of Things, and the other allowed to be no more than the *Grave.* Again, if we take this Definition of Happiness, and examine it with Reference to the Senses, it will be acknowledged wonderfully adapt. How fading and insipid do all Objects accost us that are not convey'd in the Vehicle of *Delusion*? How shrunk is every Thing, as it appears in the Glass of Nature? So, that if it were not for the Assistance of Artificial *Mediums,* false Lights, refracted Angles, Varnish, and Tinsel; there would be a mighty Level in the Felicity and Enjoyments of Mortal Men. If this were seriously considered by the World, as I have a certain Reason to suspect it hardly will; Men would no longer reckon among their high Points of Wisdom, the Art of exposing weak Sides, and   20 publishing Infirmities; an Employment in my Opinion, neither better nor worse than that of *Unmasking,* which I think, has never been allowed fair Usage, either in the *World* or the *Playhouse.*

IN the Proportion that Credulity is a more peaceful Possession of the Mind, than Curiosity, so far preferable is that Wisdom, which converses about the Surface, to that pretended Philosophy which enters into the Depth of Things, and then comes gravely back with Informations and Discoveries, that in the inside they are good for nothing. The two Senses, to which all Objects first address themselves, are the Sight and the Touch; These never examine farther than the Colour, the Shape, the Size, and whatever other Qualities dwell, or   30 are drawn by Art upon the Outward of Bodies; and then comes Reason officiously, with Tools for cutting, and opening, and mangling, and piercing, offering to demonstrate, that they are not of the same consistence quite thro'. Now, I take all this to be the last Degree of perverting Nature; one of whose Eternal Laws it is, to put her best Furniture forward. And therefore, in order to save the Charges of all such expensive Anatomy for the Time to come; I do here think fit to inform the Reader, that in such Conclusions as these, Reason is certainly in the Right; and that in most Corporeal Beings, which have fallen under my Cognizance, the *Outside* hath been infinitely preferable in the *Inn:* Whereof I have been farther convinced from some late Experiments. Last Week I saw a   40 Woman *flay'd,* and you will hardly believe, how much it altered her Person for the worse. Yesterday I ordered the Carcass of a *Beau* to be stript in my Presence; when we were all amazed to find so many unsuspected Faults under one Suit of Cloaths: Then I laid open his *Brain,* his *Heart,* and his *Spleen*; But, I plainly perceived at every Operation, that the farther we proceeded, we found the Defects encrease upon us in Number and Bulk: from all which, I justly formed this Conclusion to my self; That whatever Philosopher or Projector can find out an Art to sodder and patch up the Flaws and Imperfections of Nature, will deserve much better of Mankind, and teach us a more useful Science, than that so much in present Esteem, of widening and exposing them (like him who held *Anatomy* to be the ultimate End of *Physick*). And he, whose Fortunes and Dispositions have placed him in a convenient Station to enjoy the Fruits of this noble Art; He that can with *Epicurus* content his Ideas with the *Films* and *Images* that fly off upon his Senses from the *Superficies* of Things; Such a Man truly wise, creams off Nature, leaving the Sower and the Dregs, for Philosophy and Reason to lap up. This is the sublime and refined Point of Felicity, called, *the Possession of being well deceived*; The Serene Peaceful State of being a Fool among   10 Knaves.

BUT to return to *Madness.* It is certain, that according to the System I have above deduced; every *Species* thereof proceeds from a Redundancy of *Vapours*; therefore, as some Kinds of *Phrenzy* give double Strength to the Sinews, so there are of other *Species*, which add Vigor, and Life, and Spirit to the Brain: Now, it usually happens, that these active Spirits, getting Possession of the Brain, resemble those that haunt other waste and empty Dwellings, which for want of Business, either vanish, and carry away a Piece of the House, or else stay at home and fling it all out of the Windows. By which are mystically display'd the two principal Branches of *Madness*, and which some Philosophers   20 not considering so well as I, have mistook to be different in their Causes, over-hastily assigning the first to Deficiency, and the other to Redundance.

I think it therfore manifest, from what I have here advanced, that the main Point of Skill and Address, is to furnish Employment for this Redundancy of *Vapour*, and prudently to adjust the Season of it; by which means it may certainly become of Cardinal and Catholick Emolument in a Commonwealth. Thus one Man chusing a proper Juncture, leaps into a Gulph,[191] from whence proceeds a Hero, and is called the Saver of his Country; Another atchieves the same Enterprise,[192] but unluckily timing it, has left the Brand of *Madness*, fixt as a Reproach upon his Memory; Upon so nice a Distinction are we taught to   30 repeat the Name of *Curtius* with Reverence and Love; that of *Empedocles*, with Hatred and Contempt. Thus, also it is usually conceived, that the Elder *Brutus*[193] only personated the *Fool* and *Madman*, for the Good of the Publick: but this was nothing else, than a Redundancy of the same *Vapor*, long misapplied, called by the *Latins*, *Ingenium par negotiis:* Or (to translate it as nearly as I can), a sort of *Phrenzy*, never in its right Element, till you take it up   * *Tacit.* in Business of the State.

UPON all which, and many other Reasons of equal Weight, though not equally curious; I do here gladly embrace an Opportunity I have long sought for, of Recommending it as a very noble Undertaking, to Sir E——d S——r,   40

---

[191] *Gulph:* Curtius leaped into an opening in the Forum to fulfill the prophecy that Rome's chief strength (its armed youth) must be sacrificed to the chasm before it would close. He became a hero.

[192] *Same Enterprise:* Empedocles, Sicilian Greek philosopher and scientist of the fifth century B.C., according to one story threw himself into Etna's crater to test his divinity.

[193] *Brutus:* Lucius Junius Brutus, nephew of King Tarquinius Superbus, feigned idiocy to escape execution by his uncle; later he liberated Rome.

Sir *C——r M——ve*, Sir *J——n B——ls*, *J——n H——w*, Esq;[194] and other
Patriots concerned, that they would move for Leave to bring in a Bill, for
appointing Commissioners to Inspect into *Bedlam*,[195] and the Parts adjacent;
who shall be empowered to *send for Persons, Papers, and Records:* to examine into
the Merits and Qualifications of every Student and Professor; to observe
with utmost Exactness their several Dispositions and Behaviour; by which
means, duly distinguishing and adapting their Talents, they might produce
admirable Instruments for the several Offices in a State, * * * * *
* * *Civil* and *Military*; proceeding in such Methods as I shall here humbly
propose. And, I hope the Gentle Reader will give some Allowance to my great
Solicitudes in this important Affair, upon Account of that high Esteem I have
ever born that honourable Society, whereof I had some Time the Happiness to
be an unworthy Member.

   IS any Student tearing his Straw in piece-meal, Swearing and Blaspheming,
biting his Grate, foaming at the Mouth, and emptying his Pispot in the Spectator's Faces? Let the Right Worshipful, the *Commissioners of Inspection*, give
him a Regiment of Dragoons, and send him into *Flanders* among the *Rest*. Is
another eternally talking, sputtering, gaping, bawling, in a Sound without
Period or Article? What wonderful Talents are here mislaid! Let him be
furnished immediately with a green Bag and Papers, and *three Pence *A Lawyer's
in his Pocket, and away with Him to *Westminster-Hall*.[196] You will Coach-hire.
find a Third, gravely taking the Dimensions of his Kennel; A Person
of Foresight and Insight, tho' kept quite in the Dark; for why, like *Moses, Ecce
†cornuta erat ejus facies.* He walks duly in one Pace, intreats your Penny with due
Gravity and Ceremony; talks much of hard Times, and Taxes, and the *Whore
of Babylon*;[197] Bars up the woodden Window of his Cell constantly at eight a
Clock: Dreams of *Fire*, and *Shop-lifters*, and *Court-Customers*, and *Priviledg'd
Places*. Now, what a Figure would all these Acquirements amount to, if the
Owner were sent into the *City* among his Brethren! Behold a Fourth, in much
and deep Conversation with himself, biting his Thumbs at proper Junctures;
His Countenance chequered with Business and Design; sometimes walking
very fast, with his Eyes nailed to a Paper that he holds in his Hands: A great
Saver of Time, somewhat thick of Hearing, very short of Sight, but more of
Memory. A Man ever in Haste, a great Hatcher and Breeder of Business, and
excellent at the Famous Art of *whispering Nothing*. A huge Idolater of Mono-
syllables and Procrastination; so ready to *Give* his Word to every Body, that he
never *keeps* it. One that has forgot the common *Meaning* of Words, but an ad-

   † Cornutus, *is either Horned or Shining, and by this Term, Moses is described in the
vulgar Latin of the Bible.*[198]

   [194] *Sir E——d S——r . . . J——n
H——w:* Four Tory members of Commons identified in the 1720 edition of
Tale: Edward Seymour, Christopher
Musgrave, John Bowls, John How.
   [195] *Bedlam:* This, the oldest insane
asylum in Europe, housed the mentally
ill beginning some time before 1400.

   [196] *Westminster-Hall:* Meeting place of
the highest court of law.
   [197] *Whore of Babylon:* The woman in
Rev. 17:5 on whose brow was written
MYSTERY, BABYLON THE GREAT, THE
MOTHER OF HARLOTS AND ABOMINATIONS
OF THE EARTH.
   [198] *Bible:* Exod. 34:29–30, indicates
the basis of this ambiguity.

mirable Retainer of the *Sound*. Extreamly subject to the *Loosness*, for his *Occasions* are perpetually *calling him away*. If you approach his Grate in his familiar Intervals; *Sir*, says he, *Give me a Penny, and I'll sing you a Song: But give me the Penny first.* (Hence comes the common Saying, and commoner Practice of parting with Money for a *Song*.) What a compleat System of *Court-Skill* is here described in every Branch of it, and all utterly lost with wrong Application? Accost the Hole of another Kennel, first stopping your Nose, you will behold a surley, gloomy, nasty, slovenly Mortal, raking in his own Dung, and dabling in his Urine. The best Part of his Diet, is the Reversion of his own Ordure, which expiring into Steams, whirls perpetually about, and at last reinfunds. His Complexion is of a dirty Yellow, with a thin scattered Beard, exactly agreeable to that of his Dyet upon its first Declination; like other Insects, who having their Birth and Education in an Excrement, from thence borrow their Colour and their Smell. The Student of this Apartment is very sparing of his Words, but somewhat over-liberal of his Breath; He holds his Hand out ready to receive your Penny, and immediately upon Receipt, withdraws to his former Occupations. Now, is it not amazing to think, the Society of *Warwick-Lane*,[199] should have no more Concern, for the Recovery of so useful a Member, who, if one may judge from these Appearances, would become the greatest Ornament to that Illustrious Body? Another Student struts up fiercely to your Teeth, puffing with his Lips, half squeezing out his Eyes; and very graciously holds you out his Hand to kiss. The *Keeper* desires you not to be afraid of this Professor, for he will do you no Hurt: To him alone is allowed the Liberty of the Anti-Chamber, and the *Orator* of the Place gives you to understand, that this solemn Person is a *Taylor* run mad with Pride. This considerable Student is adorned with many other Qualities, upon which, at present, I shall not farther enlarge. – – – – – – – – *Heark in your Ear* – – – – – – – – – I am strangely mistaken, if all his Address, his Motions, and his Airs, would not then be very natural, and in their proper Element.

I shall not descend so minutely, as to insist upon the vast Number of *Beaux*, *Fidlers*, *Poets*, and *Politicians*, that the World might recover by such a Reformation? But what is more material, besides the clear Gain redounding to the Commonwealth, by so large an Acquisition of Person to employ, whose Talents and Acquirements, if I may be so bold to affirm it, are now buried, or at least misapplied: It would be a mighty Advantage accruing to the Publick from this Enquiry, that all these would very much excel, and arrive at great Perfection in their several Kinds; which, I think, is manifest from what I have already shewn; and shall inforce by this one plain Instance; That even, I my self, the Author of these momentous Truths, am a Person, whose Imaginations are hard-mouth'd, and exceedingly disposed to run away with his *Reason*, which I have observed from long Experience, to be a very light Rider, and easily shook off; upon which Account, my Friends will never trust me alone, without a solemn

---

* *I cannot conjecture what the Author means here, or how this Chasm could be fill'd, tho' it is capable of more than one Interpretation.*

---

[199] *Warwick-Lane:* In Swift's day the ocation of the College of Physicians.

Promise, to vent my Speculations in this, or the like manner, for the universal Benefit of Human kind; which, perhaps, the gentle, courteous, and candid Reader, brimful of that *Modern* Charity and Tenderness, usually annexed to his *Office*, will be very hardly persuaded to believe.

Sect. X. A Tale of a Tub[200]

IT is an unanswerable Argument of a very refined Age, the wonderful Civilities that have passed of late Years, between the Nation of *Authors*, and that of *Readers*. There can hardly *pop out a *Play*, a *Pamphlet*, or a *Poem*, without a Preface full of Acknowledgement to the World, for the general Reception and Applause they have given it, which the Lord knows where, or when, or how, or from whom it received. In due Deference to so laudable a Custom, I do here return my humble Thanks to *His Majesty*, and both Houses of *Parliament*; To the *Lords* of the King's most honourable Privy-Council, to the Reverend the *Judges*: To the *Clergy*, and *Gentry*, and *Yeomantry* of this Land: But in a more especial manner, to my worthy Brethren and Friends at *Will's Coffee-House*, and *Gresham-College*, and *Warwick-Lane*, and *Moor-Fields*, and *Scotland-Yard*, and *Westminster-Hall*, and *Guild-Hall*,[201] In short, to all inhabitants and Retainers whatsoever, either in Court, or Church, or Camp, or City, or Country; for their generous and universal Acceptance of this Divine Treatise. I accept their Approbation, and good Opinion with extream Gratitude, and to the utmost of my poor Capacity, shall take hold of all Opportunities to return the Obligation.

I am also happy, that Fate has flung me into so blessed an Age for the mutual Felicity of *Booksellers* and *Authors*, whom I may safely affirm to be at this Day the two only satisfied Parties in *England*. Ask an *Author* how his last Piece hath succeeded; *Why, truly he thanks his Stars, the World has been very favourable, and he has not the least Reason to complain: And yet, By G—, He writ it in a Week at Bits and Starts, when he could steal an Hour from his urgent Affairs*; as it is a hundred to one, you may see farther in the Preface, to which he refers you; and for the rest, to the Bookseller. There you go as a Customer, and make the same Question: *He blesses his God, the* Thing *takes wonderfully, he is just Printing a Second Edition, and has but three left in his Shop. You beat down the* Price: *Sir, we shall not differ*; and in hopes of your Custom another Time, lets you have it as reasonable as you please; *And, pray send as many of your Acquaintance as you will, I shall upon your Account furnish them all at the same Rate.*

NOW, it is not well enough consider'd, to what Accidents and Occasions the World is indebted for the greatest Part of those noble Writings, which hourly start up to entertain it. If it were not for a *rainy Day, a drunken Vigil, a Fit of the Spleen, a Course of Physick, a sleepy Sunday, an ill Run at Dice, a long*

10

20

30

---

* This is litterally true, as we may observe in the Prefaces to most Plays, Poems, &c.

---

[200] *A Tale of a Tub*: In some editions, this section is named "A Further Digression."
[201] *Will's Coffee-House . . . :* See nn. 72, 55, 199; Bedlam was in Moor-Fields; a well-known coffee-house, Well's, was in Scotland-Yard; see n. 196 for Westminster-Hall; Guild-Hall is the hall of the Corporation of the City of London.

Taylor's Bill, a Beggar's Purse, a factious Head, a hot Sun, costive Dyet, Want of Books, and a just Contempt of Learning. But for these Events, I say, and some Others too long to recite (especially *a prudent Neglect of taking Brimstone inwardly*), I doubt, the Number of *Authors,* and of *Writings* would dwindle away to a Degree most woful to behold, To confirm this Opinion, hear the Words of the famous *Troglodyte*[202] Philosopher: *'Tis certain* (said he) *some Grains of Folly are of course annexed, as Part of the Composition of Human Nature, only the Choice is left us, whether we please to wear them* Inlaid *or* Embossed; *And we need not go very far to seek how that is usually determined, when we remember, it is with Human Faculties as with Liquors, the lightest will be ever at the Top.*   10

THERE is in this famous Island of *Britain* a certain paultry *Scribbler,* very voluminous, whose Character the Reader cannot wholly be a Stranger to. He deals in a pernicious Kind of Writings, called *Second Parts,* and usually passes under the Name of *The Author of the First.* I easily foresee, that as soon as I lay down my Pen, this nimble *Operator* will have stole it, and treat me as inhumanly as he hath already done Dr. Bl——re, L——ge,[203] and many others who shall here be nameless, I therefore fly for Justice and Relief, into the Hands of that great *Rectifier of Saddles,* and *Lover of Mankind,* Dr. B—tly, begging he will take this enormous Grievance into his most *Modern* Consideration: And if it should so happen, that the *Furniture of an Ass,*[204] in the Shape of a *Second Part,* must for my   20 Sins be clapt, by a Mistake upon my Back, that he will immediately please, in the Presence of the World, to lighten me of the Burthen, and take it home to *his own House,* till the *true Beast* thinks fit to call for it.

IN the mean time I do here give this publick Notice, that my Resolutions are, to circumscribe within this Discourse the whole Stock of Matter I have been so many Years providing. Since my *Vein* is once opened, I am content to exhaust it all at a Running, for the peculiar Advantage of my dear Country, and for the universal Benefit of Mankind. Therefore hospitably considering the Number of my Guests, they shall have my whole Entertainment at a Meal; And I scorn to set up the *Leavings* in the Cupboard. What the *Guests* cannot eat   30 may be given to the *Poor,* and the *Dogs under the Table may gnaw the *Bones*; This I understand for a more generous Procceding, than to turn the Company's Stomach, by inviting them again to morrow to a scurvy Meal of *Scraps.*

IF the Reader fairly considers the Strength of what I have advanced in the foregoing Section, I am convinced it will produce a wonderful Revolution in his Notions and Opinions; And he will be abundantly better prepared to receive and to relish the concluding Part of this miraculous Treatise. Readers may be divided into three Classes, the *Superficial,* the *Ignorant,* and the *Learned*: And I have with much Felicity fitted my Pen to the Genius and Advantage of each. The *Superficial* Reader will be strangely provoked to *Laughter*; which   40

---

* *By Dogs, the Author means common injudicious Criticks, as he explains it himself before in his* Digression upon Criticks, *(Page 96).* [p. 373 in this edition.]

---

[202] *Troglodyte:* Cave-dweller.
[203] *Dr. Bl——re, L——ge:* Richard Blackmore (d. 1729) and Roger L'Estrange (1616–1704) both wrote much in haste.
[204] *Furniture of an Ass:* The reference is

to Bentley's use of a Greek proverb: "Leucon carries one thing, and his ass quite another." Perhaps this explains "Rectifier of Saddles," above.

clears the Breast and the Lungs, is Soverain against the *Spleen*, and the most innocent of all *Diureticks*. The *Ignorant* Reader (between whom and the former, the Distinction is extreamly nice) will find himself disposed to *Stare*; which is an admirable Remedy for ill Eyes, serves to raise and enliven the Spirits, and wonderfully helps *Perspiration*. But the Reader truly *Learned*, chiefly for whose Benefit I wake, when others sleep, and sleep when others wake, will here find sufficient Matter to employ his Speculations for the rest of his Life. It were much to be wisht, and I do here humbly propose for an Experiment, that every Prince in *Christendom* will take seven of the *deepest Scholars* in his Dominions, and shut them up close for *seven* Years, in *seven* Chambers, with a Command to write *seven* ample Commentaries on this comprehensive Discourse. I shall venture to affirm, that whatever Difference may be found in their several Conjectures, they will be all, without the least Distortion, manifestly deduceable from the Text. Mean time, it is my earnest Request, that so useful an Undertaking may be entered upon (if their Majesties please) with all convenient speed; because I have a strong Inclination, before I leave the World, to taste a Blessing, which we *mysterious* Writers can seldom reach, till we have got into our Graves. Whether it is, that *Fame* being a Fruit grafted on the Body, can hardly grow, and much less ripen, till the *Stock* is in the Earth: Or, whether she be a Bird of Prey, and is lured among the rest, to pursue after the Scent of a *Carcass*: Or, whether she conceives, her Trumpet sounds best and farthest, when she stands on a *Tomb*, by the Advantage of a rising Ground, and the Echo of a hollow Vault.

’TIS true, indeed, the Republick of *dark* Authors, after they once found out this excellent Expedient of *Dying*, have been peculiarly happy in the Variety, as well as Extent of their Reputation. For, *Night* being the universal Mother of Things, wise Philosophers hold all Writings to be *fruitful* in the Proportion they are *dark*; And therefore, the *true illuminated (that is to say, the *Darkest* of all) have met with such numberless Commentators, whose *Scholiastick* Midwifry hath deliver’d them of Meanings, that the Authors themselves, perhaps, never conceived, and yet may very justly be allowed the Lawful Parents of them: †The Words of such Writers being like Seed, which, however scattered at random, when they light upon a fruitful Ground, will multiply far beyond either the Hopes or Imagination of the Sower.

AND therefore in order to promote so useful a Work, I will here take Leave to glance a few *Innuendo’s*, that may be of great Assistance to those sublime Spirits, who shall be appointed to labor in a universal Comment upon this wonderful Discourse. And First, ‡I have couched a very profound Mystery in the Number of O’s multiply’d by *Seven*, and divided by *Nine*. Also, if a devout Brother of the *Rosy Cross* will pray fervently for sixty three Mornings, with a

*A Name of the Rosycrucians.[205]

† *Nothing is more frequent than for Commentators to force Interpretation, which the Author never meant.*

‡ *This is what the* Cabbalists *among the* Jews *have done with the* Bible, *and pretend to find wonderful Mysteries by it.*

[205] *Rosycrucians:* See *Rape of the Lock*, n. 2.

lively Faith, and then transpose certain Letters and Syllables according to Prescription, in the second and fifth Section; they will certainly reveal into a full Receit of the *Opus Magnum*. Lastly, Whoever will be at the Pains to calculate the whole Number of each Letter in this Treatise, and sum up the Difference exactly between the several Numbers, assigning the true natural Cause for every such Difference; the Discoveries in the Product, will plentifully reward his Labour. But then he must beware of *Bythus and Sige, and be sure not to forget the Qualities of Acamoth,[206] *A cujus lacrymis humecta prodit Substantia, a risu lucida, a tristitia solida, & a timore mobilis,*[207] wherein †*Eugenius Philalethes* hath committed an unpardonable Mistake.

† *Vid. Anima magica abscondita.* 10

Sect. XI. A Tale of a Tub

AFTER so wide a Compass as I have wandred, I do now gladly overtake, and close in with my Subject, and shall henceforth hold on with it an even Pace to the End of my Journey, except some beautiful Prospect appears, within sight of my Way; whereof, tho' at present I have neither Warning nor Expectation, yet upon such an Accident, come when it will, I shall beg my Readers Favour and Company, allowing me to conduct him thro' it along with my self. For in *Writing*, it is as in *Travelling*: If a Man is in haste to be at home (which I acknowledge to be none of my Case, having never so little Business, as when I am there), if his *Horse* be tired with long Riding, and ill Ways, or be naturally a Jade, I advise him clearly to make the straitest and the commonest Road, be it ever so dirty; But, then surely, we must own such a Man to be a scurvy Companion at best; He *spatters* himself and his Fellow-Travellors at every Step: All their Thoughts, and Wishes, and Conversation turn entirely upon the Subject of their Journey's End; and at every Splash, and Plunge, and Stumble, they heartily wish one another at the Devil. 20

ON the other side, when a Traveller and his *Horse* are in Heart and Plight, when his Purse is full, and the Day before him; he takes the Road only where it is clean or convenient; entertains his Company there as agreeably as he can; but upon the first Occasion, carries them along with him to every delightful Scene in View, whether of Art, of Nature, or of both; and if they chance to 30

* *I was told by an Eminent Divine, whom I consulted on this Point, that these two Barbarous Words, with that of Acamoth and its Qualities, as here set down, are quoted from* Irenæus. *This he discover'd by searching that Antient Writer for another Quotation of our Author, which he has placed in the Title Page, and refers to the Book and Chapter; the Curious were very Inquisitive, whether those Barbarous Words,* Basima Eacabasa, *&c. are really in* Irenæus, *and upon enquiry 'twas found they were a sort of Cant or Jargon of certain Hereticks, and therefore very properly prefix'd to such a Book as this of our Author.*

† *To the abovementioned Treatise, called* Anthroposophia Theomagica, *there is another annexed, called* Anima Magica Abscondita, *written by the same Author* Vaughan, *under the Name of* Eugenius Philalethes, *but in neither of those Treatises is there any mention of* Acamoth *or its Qualities, so that this is nothing but Amusement, and a Ridicule of dark, unintelligible Writers; only the Words,* A cujus lacrymis, *&c. are as we have said, transcribed from* Irenæus, *tho' I know not from what part. I believe one of the Authors Designs was to set curious Men a hunting thro' Indexes, and enquiring for Books out of the common Road.*

[206] *Acamoth:* Wisdom.
[207] *A cujus . . . mobilis:* From whose tears comes forth a moist substance, from whose laughter a clear one, from whose sorrow a solid one, and from whose fear an unstable one.

refuse out of Stupidity or Weariness; let them jog on by themselves, and be d—n'd; He'll overtake them at the next Town; at which arriving, he Rides furiously thro', the Men, Women, and Children run out to gaze, a hundred *noisy Curs* run *barking* after him, of which, if he honors the boldest with a *Lash of his Whip*, it is rather out of Sport than Revenge: But should some *sourer Mungrel* dare too near an Approach, he receives a *Salute* on the Chaps by an accidental Stroak from the Courser's Heels (nor is any Ground lost by the Blow) which sends him yelping and limping home.

I now proceed to sum up the singular Adventures of my renowned *Jack*; the State of whose Dispositions and Fortunes, the careful Reader does, no   10 doubt, most exactly remember, as I last parted with them in the Conclusion of a former Section. Therefore, his next Care must be from two of the foregoing, to extract a Scheme of Notions, that may best fit his Understanding for a true Relish of what is to ensue.

JACK had not only calculated the first Revolution of his Brain so prudently, as to give Rise to that Epidemick Sect of *Æolists*, but succeeding also into a new and strange Variety of Conceptions, the Fruitfulness of his Imagination led him into certain Notions, which, altho' in Appearance very unaccountable, were not without their Mysteries and their Meanings, nor wanted Followers to countenance and improve them. I shall therefore be extreamly careful and   20 exact in recounting such material Passages of this Nature, as I have been able to collect, either from undoubted Tradition, or indefatigable Reading; and shall describe them as graphically as it is possible, and as far as Notions of that Height and Latitude can be brought within the Compass of a Pen. Nor do I at all question, but they will furnish Plenty of noble Matter for such, whose converting Imaginations dispose them to reduce all Things into *Types*; who can make *Shadows*, no thanks to the Sun; and then mold them into Substances, no thanks to Philosophy; whose peculiar Talent lies in fixing Tropes and Allegories to the *Letter*, and refining what is Literal into Figure and Mystery.

JACK had provided a fair Copy of his Father's *Will*, engrossed in Form   30 upon a large Skin of Parchment; and resolving to act the Part of a most dutiful Son, he became the fondest Creature of it imaginable. For, altho', as I have often told the Reader, it consisted wholly in certain plain, easy Directions about the management and wearing of their Coats, with Legacies and Penalties, in case of Obedience or Neglect; yet he began to entertain a Fancy, that the Matter was *deeper* and *darker*, and therefore must needs have a great deal more of Mystery at the Bottom. *Gentlemen*, said he, *I will prove this very Skin of Parchment to be Meat, Drink, and Cloth, to be the Philosopher's Stone, and the Universal Medicine.* †In consequence of which Raptures, he resolved to make use of it in the most necessary, as well as the most paltry Occasions of Life. He had a Way of   40 working it into any Shape he pleased; so that it served him for a Night-cap

---

* *By these are meant what the Author calls,* The True Criticks, *Page 96.*[208]
† *The Author here lashes those Pretenders to Purity, who place so much Merit in using Scripture Phrase on all Occasions.*

---

[208] *The True Criticks, Page 96:* Page 373 in this edition.

when he went to Bed, and for an Umbrello in rainy Weather. He would lap a Piece of it about a sore Toe, or when he had Fits, burn two Inches under his Nose; or if any Thing lay heavy on his Stomach, scrape off, and swallow as much of the Powder as would lie on a silver Penny, they were all infallible Remedies. With Analogy to these Refinements, his common Talk and Conversation, *ran wholly in the Phrase of his Will, and he circumscribed the utmost of his Eloquence within that Compass, not daring to let slip a Syllable without Authority from thence. Once at a strange House, he was suddenly taken short, upon an urgent Juncture, whereon it may not be allowed too particularly to dilate; and being not able to call to mind, with that Suddenness, the Occasion required, an Authentick Phrase for demanding the Way to the Backside; he chose rather as the more prudent Course, to incur the Penalty in such Cases usually annexed. Neither was it possible for the united Rhetorick of Mankind to prevail with him to make himself clean again: Because having consulted the Will upon this Emergency, he met a with a †Passage near the Bottom[209] (whether foisted in by the Transcriber, is not known) which seemed to to forbid it.

He made it a Part of his Religion, never to say ‡Grace to his Meat, nor could all the World persuade him, as the common Phrase is, to §eat his Victuals like a Christian.

HE bore a strange kind of Appetite to ||Snap Dragon, and to the livid Snuffs of a burning Candle, which he would catch and swallow with an Agility, wonderful to conceive; and by this Procedure, maintained a perpetual Flame in his Belly, which issuing in a glowing Steam from both his Eyes, as well as his Nostrils, and his Mouth; made his Head appear in a dark Night, like the Scull of an Ass, wherein a roguish Boy hath conveyed a Farthing Candle, to the Terror of His Majesty's Liege Subjects. Therefore, he made use of no other Expedient to light himself home, but was wont to say, That a Wise Man was his own Lanthorn.[210]

HE would shut his Eyes as he walked along the Streets, and if he happened to bounce his Head against a Post, or fall into the Kennel (as he seldom missed either to do one or both), he would tell the gibing Prentices, who looked on, that he submitted with entire Resignation, as to a Trip, or a Blow of Fate, with whom he found, by long Experience, how vain it was either to wrestle or to cuff; and whoever durst undertake to do either, would be sure to come off with a swinging Fall, or a

---

* The Protestant Dissenters use Scripture Phrases in their serious Discourses, and Composures more than the Church of England-Men, accordingly Jack is introduced making his common Talk and Conversation to run wholly in the Phrase of his WILL. W. Wotton.

† I cannot guess the Author's meaning here, which I would be very glad to know, because it seems to be of Importance.

‡ The slovenly way of Receiving the Sacrament among the Fanaticks.

§ This is a common Phrase to express Eating cleanlily, and is meant for an Invective against that undecent Manner among some People in Receiving the Sacrament, so in the Lines before, which is to be understood of the Dissenters refusing to kneel at the Sacrament.

|| I can not well find the Author's meaning here, unless it be the hot, untimely, blind Zeal of Enthusiasts.

---

[209] Passage near the Bottom: The last chapter of the New Testament, Rev. 22:11: ". . . he which is filthy, let him be filthy still. . . ."

[210] Lanthorn: Lantern, a transparent case.

bloody Nose. It was ordained, said he, *some few Days before the Creation, that my Nose and this very Post should have a Rencounter; and therefore, Nature thought fit to send us both into the World in the same Age, and to make us Country-men and Fellow-Citizens. Now, had my Eyes been open, it is very likely, the Business might have been a great deal worse; For, how many a confounded Slip is daily got by Man, with all his Foresight about him? Besides, the Eyes of the Understanding see best, when those of the Senses are out of the way; and therefore, blind Men are observed to tread their Steps with much more Caution, and Conduct, and Judgment, than those who rely with too much Confidence, upon the Virtue of the visual Nerve, which every little Accident shakes out of Order, and a Drop, or a Film, can wholly disconcert; like a* 10 *Lanthorn among a Pack of roaring Bullies, when they scower the Streets; exposing its Owner, and it self, to outward Kicks and Buffets, which both might have escaped, if the Vanity of Appearing would have suffered them to walk in the Dark. But, farther; if we examine the* Conduct *of these boasted Lights, it will prove yet a great deal worse than their* Fortune: *'Tis true, I have broke my Nose against this Post, because Fortune either forgot, or did not think it convenient to twitch me by the Elbow, and give me notice to avoid it. But, let not this encourage either the present Age or Posterity, to trust their* Noses *into the keeping of their* Eyes, *which may prove the fairest Way of losing them for good and all. For, O ye Eyes, Ye blind Guides; miserable Guardians are Ye of our frail Noses; Ye, I say, who fasten upon the first Precipice in view, and* 20 *then tow our wretched willing Bodies after You, to the very Brink of Destruction: But, alas, that Brink is rotten, our feet slip, and we tumble down prone into a Gulph, without one hospitable Shrub in the Way to break the Fall; a Fall, to which not any Nose of mortal Make is equal, except that of the Giant* *Laurcalco,[211] *who was* * *Vide* *Lord of the* Silver Bridge, *Most properly, therefore, O Eyes, and* Don *with great Justice, may You be compared to those foolish Lights, which* Quixot. *conduct Men thro' Dirt and Darkness, till they fall into a deep Pit, or a noisom Bog.*

THIS I have produced, as a Scantling of *Jack's* great Eloquence, and the Force of his Reasoning upon such abstruse Matters. 30

HE was besides, a Person of great Design and Improvement in Affairs of *Devotion,* having introduced a new Deity, who hath since met with a vast Number of Worshippers; by some called *Babel,* by other, *Chaos*; who had an antient Temple of *Gothick* Structure[212] upon *Salisbury*-Plain; famous for its Shrine, and Celebration by Pilgrims.

†WHEN he had some Roguish Trick to play, he would down with his Knees, up with his Eyes, and fall to Prayers, tho' in the midst of the Kennel. Then it was that those who understood his Pranks, would be sure to get far enough out of his Way; And whenever Curiosity attracted Strangers to Laugh, or to Listen; he would of a sudden, with one Hand out with his *Gear,* and piss 40 full in their Eyes, and with the other, all to bespatter them with Mud.

† *The Villanies and Cruelties committed by Enthusiasts and Phanaticks among us, were all performed under the Disguise of Religion and long Prayers.*

---

[211] *Laurcalco:* One of the sheep Quixote's overactive imagination transforms into knights in Part I, Ch. 18.

[212] *Gothick Structure:* Stonehenge; here Gothic means rude, barbarous.

*IN Winter he went always loose and unbuttoned, and clad as thin as possible, to let *in* the ambient Heat; and in Summer, lapt himself close and thick to keep it *out*.

†IN all Revolutions of Government, he would make his Court for the Office of *Hangman* General; and in the Exercise of that Dignity, wherein he was very dextrous, would make use of ‡no other *Vizard* than a long *Prayer*.

HE had a Tongue so Musculous and Subtil, that he could twist it up into his Nose, and deliver a strange Kind of Speech from thence. He was also the first in these Kingdoms, who began to improve the *Spanish* Accomplishment of *Braying*;²¹³ and having large Ears, perpetually exposed and arrected,²¹⁴ he carried his Art to such a Perfection, that it was a Point of great Difficulty to distinguish either by the View or the Sound, between the *Original* and the *Copy*.

HE was troubled with a Disease, reverse to that called the Stinging of the *Tarantula*; and would §run Dog-mad, at the Noise of *Musick*, especially a *Pair of Bag-Pipes*. But he would cure himself again, by taking two or three Turns in *Westminster-Hall*, or *Billingsgate*, or in a *Boarding-School*, or the *Royal-Exchange*, or a *State Coffee-House*.

HE was a Person that ‖ *feared* no *Colours*,²¹⁵ but mortally *hated* all, and upon that Account, bore a cruel Aversion to *Painters*, insomuch, that in his Paroxysms, as he walked the Streets, he would have his Pockets loaden with Stones, to pelt at the *Signs*.

HAVING from this manner of Living, frequent Occasion to *wash* himself, he would often leap over Head and Ears into the Water,²¹⁶ tho' it were in the midst of the Winter, but was always observed to come out again much *dirtier*, if possible, than he went in.

HE was the first that ever found out the Secret of contriving a ¶*Soporiferous* Medicine to be convey'd in at the *Ears*; It was a Compound of *Sulphur* and *Balm of Gilead*, with a little *Pilgrim's Salve*.

HE wore a large Plaister of artificial *Causticks* on his Stomach, with the Fervor of which, he could set himself a *groaning*, like the famous *Board*²¹⁷ upon Application of a red-hot Iron.

**HE would stand in the Turning of a Street, and calling to those who

---

* *They affect Differences in Habit and Behaviour.*
† *They are severe Persecutors, and all in a Form of Cant and Devotion.*
‡ *Cromwell and his Confederates went, as they called it, to seek God, when they resolved to murther the King.*
§ *This is to expose our Dissenters Aversion to Instrumental Musick in Churches.* W. Wotton.
‖ *They quarrel at the most Innocent Decency and Ornament, and defaced the Statues and Paintings on all the Churches in* England.
¶ *Fantatick Preaching, composed either of Hell and Damnation, or a fulsome Description of the Joys of Heaven, both in such a dirty, nauseous Style, as to be well resembled to Pilgrims Salve.*
** *The Fanaticks have always had a way of affecting to run into Persecution, and count vast Merit upon every little Hardship they suffer.*

---

²¹³ *Braying: Don Quixote* Part II, Ch. 25, 27, where Sancho and others bray for the return of an ass.
²¹⁴ *Arrected:* Set upright.
²¹⁵ *Feared no Colours:* Feared no foe.

²¹⁶ *Into the Water:* Baptism.
²¹⁷ *Famous Board:* Certain planks of elm, groaning-boards, when touched with a hot iron produced the sound of a person in pain.

passed by, would cry to One; *Worthy Sir, do me the Honour of a good Slap in the Chaps:* To another, *Honest Friend, pray, favour me with a handsom Kick on the Arse: Madam, shall I entreat a small Box on the Ear, from your Ladyship's fair Hands? Noble Captain, Lend a reasonable Thwack, for the Love of God with that Cane of yours, over these poor Shoulders.* And when he had by such earnest Sollicitations, made a shift to procure a Basting sufficient to swell up his Fancy and his Sides, He would return home extremely comforted, and full of terrible Accounts of what he had undergone for the *Publick Good. Observe this Stroak* (said he, shewing his bare Shoulders), *a plaguy* Janisary *gave it me this very Morning at seven a Clock, as, with much ado, I was driving off the* Great Turk. *Neighbours* 10 *mine, this broken Head deserves a Plaister; had poor* Jack *been tender of his Noddle, you would have seen the* Pope, *and the* French King, *long before this time of Day, among your Wives and your Ware-houses. Dear* Christians, *the* Great Mogul *was come as far as* White-Chappel, *and you may thank these poor Sides that he hath not (God bless us) already swallowed up Man, Woman, and Child.*

*IT was highly worth observing, the singular Effects of that Aversion, or Antipathy, which *Jack* and his Brother *Peter* seemed, even to an Affectation, to bear toward each other. *Peter* had lately done *some Rogueries*, that forced him to abscond; and he seldom ventured to stir out before Night, for fear of Bayliffs. Their Lodgings were at the two most distant Parts of the Town, from each 20 other; and whenever their Occasions, or Humors called them abroad, they would make Choice of the oddest unlikely Times, and most uncouth Rounds they could invent; that they might be sure to avoid one another: Yet after all this, it was their perpetual Fortune to meet. The Reason of which, is easy enough to apprehend: For; the Phrenzy and the Spleen of both, having the same Foundation, we may look upon them as two Pair of Compasses, equally extended, and the fixed Foot of each, remaining in the same Center; which, tho' moving contrary Ways at first, will be sure to encounter somewhere or other in the Circumference. Besides, it was among the great Misfortunes of *Jack*, to bear a huge Personal Resemblance with his Brother *Peter*. Their 30 Humour and Dispositions were not only the same, but there was a close Analogy in their Shape, and Size and their Mien. Insomuch, as nothing was more frequent than for a Bayliff to seize *Jack* by the Shoulders, and cry, *Mr.* Peter, *You are the King's Prisoner.* Or, at other Times, for one of *Peter's* nearest Friends, to accost *Jack* with open Arms, *Dear* Peter, *I am glad to see thee, pray send me one of your best Medicines for the Worms.* This we may suppose, was a mortifying Return of those Pains and Proceedings, *Jack* had laboured in so long; And finding, how directly opposite all his Endeavours had answered to the sole End and Intention, which he had proposed to himself; How could it avoid having terrible Effects upon a Head and Heart so furnished as his? However, 40 the poor Remainders of his *Coat* bore all the Punishment; The orient Sun never entred upon his diurnal Progress, without missing a Piece of it. He hired

---

* *The Papists and Fanaticks, tho' they appear the most Averse to each other, yet bear a near Resemblance in many things, as has been observed by Learned Men.*

Ibid. *The Agreement of our Dissenters and the Papists in that which Bishop* Stillingfleet *called, The Fanaticism of the Church of* Rome, *is ludicrously described for several Pages together by* Jack's *Likeness to* Peter, *and their being often mistaken for each other, and their frequent Meeting, when they least intended it.* W. Wotton.

a Taylor to stitch up the Collar so close, that it was ready to choak him, and squeezed out his Eyes at such a Rate, as one could see nothing but the White. What little was left of the main Substance of the Coat, he rubbed every day for two hours, against a rough-cast Wall, in order to grind away the Remnants of *Lace* and *Embroidery*; but at the same time went on with so much Violence, that he proceeded a *Heathen Philosopher*. Yet after all he could do of this kind the Success continued still to disappoint his Expectation. For, as it is the Nature of Rags, to bear a kind of mock Resemblance to Finery; there being a sort of fluttering Appearance in both, which is not to be distinguished at a Distance, in the Dark, or by Short-sighted Eyes: So, in those Junctures, it fared with *Jack* and his Tatters, that they offered to the first View a ridiculous Flanting,[218] which assisting the Resemblance in Person and Air, thwarted all his Projects of Separation, and left so near a Similitude between them, as frequently deceived the very Disciples and Followers of both   *   *   *   *   *   *

*   *   *   *   *   *   *   *   *   *   *   *   *   *

*   *   *   *   *   *   *   *   *   *   *   *   *Desunt*

*   *   *   *   *   *   *   *   *   *   *   *   *non-*

*   *   *   *   *   *   *   *   *   *   *   *   *nulla.*[219]

*   *   *   *   *   *   *   *   *   *   *   *   *   *

THE old *Sclavonian* Proverb said well, That *it is with* Men, *as with* Asses; *whoever would keep them fast, must find a very good Hold at their Ears.* Yet, I think, we may affirm, that it hath been verified by repeated Experience, that,

Effugiet tamen hæc sceleratus vincula Proteus.[220]

IT is good therefore, to read the Maxims of our Ancestors, with great Allowances to Times and Persons: For, if we look into Primitive Records, we shall find, that no Revolutions have been so great, or so frequent, as those of Human *Ears*. In former Days, there was a curious Invention to catch and keep them; which, I think, we may justly reckon among the *Artes perditæ.*[221] And how can it be otherwise, when in these latter Centuries, the very Species is not only diminished to a very lamentable Degree, but the poor Remainder is also degenerated so far, as to mock our skilfullest *Tenure*? For, if the only slitting of one *Ear* in a Stag, hath been found sufficient to propagate the Defect thro' a whole Forest; Why should we wonder at the greatest Consequences, from so many Loppings and Mutilations, to which the *Ears* of our Fathers and our own, have been of late so much exposed: 'Tis true, indeed, that while this *Island* of ours, was under the *Dominion of Grace*, many Endeavours were made to improve the Growth of *Ears* once more among us. The Proportion of Largeness, was not only lookt upon as an Ornament of the *Outward* Man, but as a Type of Grace in the *Inward*. Besides, it is held by Naturalists, that if there be a Protuberancy of Parts in the *Superiour* Region of the Body, as in the *Ears* and *Nose*, there must be a Parity also in the *Inferior*: And therefore in that truly pious Age, the *Males* in every Assembly, according as they were gifted, appeared very forward in exposing their *Ears* to view, and the Regions about them;

[218] *Flanting:* Flaunting.
[219] *Desunt nonnulla:* Several [lines] are missing.
[220] *Effugiet . . . Proteus:* But your wily Proteus will slip out of all these holds.
[221] *Artes perditæ:* Lost arts.

because *Hippocrates tells us, that *when the Vein behind the Ear happens*   * Lib. de
to be cut, a Man becomes a Eunuch: And the *Females* were nothing   *aere locis*
backwarder in beholding and edifying by them: Whereof those   *& aquis.*
who had already *used the Means*, lookt about them with great Concern,
in hopes of conceiving a suitable Offspring by such a Prospect: Others,
who stood Candidates for *Benevolence*, found there a plentiful Choice, and were
sure to fix upon such as discovered the largest *Ears*, that the Breed might not
dwindle between them. Lastly, the devouter Sisters, who lookt upon all extraordinary Dilatations of that Member, as Protrusions of Zeal, or spiritual
Excrescencies, were sure to honor every Head they sat upon, as if they had   10
been *Marks of Grace*; but, especially, that of the Preacher, whose *Ears* were
usually of the prime Magnitude; which upon that Account, he was very
frequent and exact in exposing with all Advantages to the People: in his
Rhetorical *Paroxysms*, turning sometimes to *hold forth* the one, and sometimes
to *hold forth* the other: From which Custom, the whole Operation of
Preaching is to this very Day among their Professors, styled by the Phrase of
Holding forth.

SUCH was the Progress of the *Saints*, for advancing the Size of that
Member; And it is thought, the Success would have been every way answerable, if in Process of time, a †cruel King had not arose, who raised a bloody   20
Persecution against all *Ears*, above a certain Standard: Upon which, some were
glad to hide their flourishing Sprouts in a black Border, others crept wholly
under a Perewig: some were slit, others cropt, and a great Number sliced off to
the Stumps. But of this, more hereafter, in my *general History of Ears*,[222] which
I design very speedily to bestow upon the Publick.

FROM this brief Survey of the falling State of *Ears*, in the last Age, and the
small Care had to advance their antient Growth in the present, it is manifest,
how little Reason we can have to rely upon a Hold so short, so weak, and so
slippery; and that, whoever desires to catch Mankind fast, must have Recourse
to some other Methods. Now, he that will examine Human Nature with   30
Circumspection enough, may discover several *Handles*, whereof the   ‡ *In-*
‡*Six* Senses afford one apiece, beside a great Number that are screw'd *cluding*
to the Passions, and some few riveted to the Intellect. Among these last, *Scal-*
Curiosity is one, and of all others, affords the firmest Grasp: *Curiosity*, *iger's*[223]
that Spur in the side, that Bridle in the Mouth, that Ring in the nose, of
a lazy, an impatient, and a grunting Reader. By this *Handle* it is, that an Author
should seize upon his Readers; which as soon as he hath once compast, all
Resistance and struggling are in vain; and they become his Prisoners as close as
he pleases, till Weariness or Dullness force him to let go his Gripe.

AND therefore, I the Author of this miraculous Treatise, have hitherto,   40
beyond Expectation, maintained by the aforesaid *Handle*, a firm Hold upon my
gentle Readers; It is with great Reluctance, that I am at length compelled to

---

† *This was King* Charles *the Second, who at his Restauration, turned out all the Dissenting*
Teachers that would not conform.

---

[222] *General History of Ears:* See *Treatises*   [223] *Scaliger's:* The sense of titillation.
wrote by the same Author, p. 331.

remit my Grasp; leaving them in the Perusal of what remains, to that natural *Oscitancy*[224] inherent in the Tribe. I can only assure thee, Courteous Reader, for both our Comforts, that my Concern is altogether equal to thine, for my Unhappiness in losing, or mislaying among my Papers the remaining Part of these Memoirs; which consisted of Accidents, Turns, and Adventures, both New, Agreeable, and Surprizing; and therefore, calculated in all due Points, [t]o the delicate Taste of this our noble Age. But, alas, with my utmost Endeavours, I have been able only to retain a few of the Heads. Under which, there was a full Account, how *Peter* got a *Protection* out of the *King's-Bench*;[225] And of a *Reconcilement between *Jack* and Him, upon a Design they had in a certain *rainy Night*, to trepan Brother *Martin* into a *Spunging-house*, and there strip him to the Skin. How *Martin*, with much ado, shew'd them both a fair pair of Heels. How a *new Warrant* came out against *Peter*: upon which, how *Jack* left him in the lurch, *stole his Protection, and made use of it himself*. How *Jack's* Tatters came into Fashion in *Court* and *City*; How he †*got upon a great Horse, and eat ‡Custard*. But the Particulars of all these, with several others, which have now slid out of my Memory, are lost beyond all Hopes of Recovery. For which Misfortune, leaving my Readers to condole with each other, as far as they shall find it to agree with their several Constitutions; but conjuring them by all the Friendship that hath passed between Us, from the Title-Page to this, not to proceed so far as to injure their Healths, for an Accident past Remedy; I now go on to the Ceremonial Part of an accomplish'd Writer, and therefore, by a Courtly *Modern*, least of all others to be omitted.

The Conclusion

GOING *too long* is a Cause of Abortion as effectual, tho' not so frequent, as *Going too short*; and holds true especially in the *Labors* of the Brain. Well fare the Heart of that Noble §*Jesuit*, who first adventur'd to confess in Print,[226] that Books must be suited to their several Seasons, like §*Pere d'Orleans.* Dress, and Dyet, and Diversions: And better fare our noble Nation, for refining upon this, among other *French* Modes. I am living fast, to see the Time, when a *Book* that misses its Tide, shall be neglected, as the *Moon* by

* In the Reign of King James the Second, the Presbyterians by the King's Invitation, joined with the Papists, against the Church of England, and Address him for Repeal of the Penal-Laws and Test; The King by his Dispensing Power, gave Liberty of Conscience, which both Papists and Presbyterians made use of, but upon the Revolution, the Papists being down of Course, the Presbyterians freely continued their Assemblies, by Virtue of King James's Indulgence, before they had a Toleration by Law; this I believe the Author means by Jack's stealing Peter's Protection, and making use of it himself.

† Sir Humphry Edwyn, a Presbyterian, was some Years ago Lord-Mayor of London, and had the Insolence to go in his Formalities to a Conventicle, with the Ensigns of his Office.

‡ Custard is a famous Dish at a Lord-Mayors Feast.

---

224 *Oscitancy:* Drowsiness.
225 *King's-Bench:* In Swift's day, the supreme court of common law.

226 *To confess in Print:* In an advertisement for *Histoire de M. Constance.*

Day, or like *Mackarel* a Week after the Season. No Man hath more nicely observed our Climate, than the Bookseller who bought the Copy of this Work, He knows to a Tittle what Subjects will best go off in a *dry Year*, and which it is proper to expose foremost, when the Weather-glass is fallen to *much Rain*. When he had seen this Treatise, and consulted his *Almanack* upon it; he gave me to understand, that he had manifestly considered the two Principal Things, which were the *Bulk*, and the *Subject*; and found, it would never *take*, but after a long Vacation, and then only, in case it should happen to be a hard Year for Turnips. Upon which I desired to know, *considering my urgent Necessities*, what he thought might be acceptable this Month. He lookt *Westward*, and said,   10 *I doubt we shalt have a Fit of bad Weather; However, if you could prepare some pretty little* Banter (but not in Verse) *or a small Treatise upon the* —— *it would run like Wild-Fire. But*, if it hold up, *I have already hired an Author to write something against Dr.* B—tl—y, *which, I am sure, will turn to Account.*

AT length we agreed upon this Expedient; That when a Customer comes for one of these, and desires in Confidence to know the Author; he will tell him very privately, as a Friend, naming which ever of the Wits shall happen to be that Week in the Vogue; and if *Durfy's* last Play should be in Course, I had as lieve he may be the Person as *Congreve*. This I mention, because, I am wonderfully well acquainted with the present Relish of Courteous Readers;   20 and have often observed, with singular Pleasure, that a *Fly* driven from a *Honeypot*, will immediately, with very good Appetite alight, and finish his Meal on an *Excrement*.

I have one Word to say upon the Subject of *Profound Writers*, who are grown very numerous of late; And, I know very well, the judicious World is resolved to list me in that Number. I conceive therefore, as to the Business of being *Profound*, that it is with *Writers*, as with *Wells*; A Person with good Eyes may see to the Bottom of the deepest, provided any *Water* be there; and, that often, when there is nothing in the World at the Bottom, besides *Dryness* and *Dirt*, tho' it be but a Yard and half under Ground, it shall pass, however, for   30 wondrous *Deep*, upon no wiser a Reason than because it is wondrous *Dark*.

I am now trying an Experiment very frequent among Modern Authors; which is, to *write upon Nothing*; When the Subject is utterly exhausted, to let the Pen still move on; by some called, the Ghost of Wit, delighting to walk after the Death of its Body. And to say the Truth, there seems to be no Part of Knowledge in fewer Hands, than That of Discerning *when to have Done*. By the Time that an Author has writ out a Book, he and his Readers are become old Acquaintants, and grow very loth to part: So that I have sometimes known it to be in Writing, as in Visiting, where the Ceremony of taking Leave, has employ'd more Time than the whole Conversation before. The Conclusion   40 of a Treatise, resembles the Conclusion of Human Life, which hath sometimes been compared to the End of a Feast; where few are satisfied to depart, *ut plenus vita conviva*:[227] For Men will sit down after the fullest Meal, tho' it be only to *doze*, or to *sleep* out the rest of the Day. But, in this latter, I differ extreamly from other Writers; and shall be too proud, if by all my Labors, I

[227] *Ut plenus vita conviva:* Like a feaster fed full of life.

can have any ways contributed to the *Repose* of Mankind in *Times so turbulent and unquiet as these. Neither, do I think such an Employment so very alien from the Office of a *Wit*, as some would suppose. For among †*Trexenii* a very Polite Nation in †*Greece*, there were the *same* Temples built *Pausan.* and consecrated to *Sleep* and the *Muses*, between which two Deities, l. 2. they believed the strictest Friendship was established.

I have one concluding Favour, to request of my Reader; that he will not expect to be equally diverted and informed by every Line, or every Page of this Discourse; but give some Allowance to the Author's Spleen, and short Fits or Intervals of Dullness, as well as his own; And lay it seriously to his Conscience, whether, if he were walking the Streets, in dirty Weather, or a rainy Day; he would allow it fair Dealing in Folks at their Ease from a Window, to Critick his Gate, and ridicule his Dress at such a Juncture.

IN my Disposure of Employments of the Brain, I have thought fit to make *Invention* the *Master*, and give *Method* and *Reason*, the Office of its *Lacquays*. The Cause of this Distribution was, from observing it my peculiar Case, to be often under a Temptation of being *Witty*, upon Occasion, where I could be neither *Wise* nor *Sound*, nor any thing to the Matter in hand. And, I am too much a Servant of the *Modern* Way, to neglect any such Opportunities, whatever Pains or Improprieties I may be at, to introduce them. For, I have observed, that from a laborious Collection of Seven Hundred Thirty-Eight *Flowers*, and *shining Hints* of the best *Modern* Authors, digested with great Reading, into my Book of *Common-places*; I have not been able after five Years to draw, hook, or force into common Conversation, any more than a Dozen. Of which Dozen, the one Moiety failed of success, by being dropt among unsuitable Company; and the other cost me so many Strains, and Traps, and *Ambages*[228] to introduce, that I at length resolved to give it over. Now, this Disappointment (to discover a Secret), I must own, gave me the first Hint of setting up for an *Author*; and, I have since found among some particular Friends, that it is become a very general Complaint, and has produced the same Effects upon many others. For, I have remarked many a *towardly Word*, to be wholly neglected or despised in *Discourse*, which hath passed very smoothly, with some Consideration and Esteem, after its Preferment and Sanction in *Print*. But now, since by the Liberty and Encouragement of the Press, I am grown absolute Master of the Occasions and Opportunities, to expose the Talents I have acquired; I already discover, that the *Issues* of my *Observanda* begin to grow too large for the *Receipts*. Therefore, I shall here pause awhile, till I find, by feeling the World's Pulse, and my own, that it will be of absolute Necessity for us both, to resume my Pen.

(1704)

* *This was writ before the Peace of* Riswick.

---

[228] *Ambages:* Circumlocutions.

A Full and True Account of the Battel Fought Last Friday
Between the Antient and the Modern Books in St. James's Library

The Bookseller to the Reader

THE following Discourse,[1] as it is unquestionably of the same Author, so it seems to have been written about the same time with the former, I mean, the Year 1697. when the famous Dispute was on Foot, about *Antient and Modern Learning*. The controversy took its Rise from an Essay of Sir *William Temple's*, upon that Subject; which was answer'd by *W. Wotton*, B.D. with an Appendix by Dr. *Bently*, endeavouring to destroy the Credit of *Æsop* and *Phalaris*, for Authors, whom Sir *William Temple* had in the Essay before-mentioned, highly commended. In that Appendix, the Doctor falls hard upon a new Edition of *Phalaris*, put out by the Honourable *Charles Boyle* (now *Earl* of *Orrery*) to which, Mr. *Boyle* replyed at large, with great Learning and   10
Wit; and the Doctor, voluminously, rejoyned. In this Dispute, the Town highly resented to see a Person of Sir *William Temple's* Character and Merits, roughly used by the two Reverend Gentlemen aforesaid, and without any manner of Provocation. At length, there appearing no End of the Quarrel, our Author tells us, that the BOOKS in St. *James's* Library, looking upon them-selves as Parties principally concerned, took up the Controversie, and came to a decisive Battel; But, the Manuscript, by the Injury of Fortune, or Weather, being in several Places imperfect, we cannot learn to which side the Victory fell.

I must warn the Reader to beware of applying to Persons what is here   20
meant, only of Books in the most literal Sense. So, when *Virgil* is mentioned, we are not to understand the Person of a famous Poet, call'd by that Name, but only certain Sheets of Paper, bound up in Leather, containing in Print, the Works of the said Poet, and so of the rest.

The Preface of the Author

SATYR is a sort of Glass, *wherein Beholders do generally discover every body's*

---

[1] *Following Discourse:* For an ex-   tion see the headnote to *Tale* and *Battel*.
planation of the references in this sec-

Face but their Own; which is the chief Reason for that kind Reception it meets in the World, and that so very few are offended with it. But if it should happen otherwise, the Danger is not great; and, I have learned from long Experience, never to apprehend Mischief from those Understandings, I have been able to provoke; For, Anger and Fury, though they add Strength to the Sinews *of the* Body, *yet are found to relax those of the* Mind, *and to render all its Efforts feeble and impotent.*

THERE is a Brain *that will endure but one* Scumming: *Let the Owner gather it with Discretion, and manage his little Stock with Husbandry; but of all things, let him beware of bringing it under the* Lash *of his* Betters; *because, That will make it all bubble up into Impertinence, and he will find no new Supply: Wit, without knowledge, being a Sort of* Cream, *which gathers in a* Night *to the* Top, *and by a skilful Hand, may be soon* whipt *into* Froth; *but one scumm'd away, what appears underneath will be fit for nothing, but to be thrown to the* Hogs.

A Full and True Account
of the Battel Fought Last Friday, &c.

WHOEVER examines with due Circumspection into the *Annual Records* of *Time*, will find it remarked, that *War is the Child of Pride*, and *Pride the Daughter of Riches*; The former of which Assertions may be soon granted; but one cannot so easily subscribe to the latter: For *Pride* is nearly related to Beggary and *Want*, either by Father or Mother, and sometimes by both; And, to speak naturally, it very seldom happens among Men to fall out, when all have enough: Invasions usually travelling from *North* to *South*, that is to say, from Poverty upon Plenty. The most antient and natural Grounds of Quarrels, are *Lust* and *Avarice*; which, tho' we may allow to be Brethren or collateral Branches of *Pride*, are certainly the Issues of *Want*. For, to speak in the Phrase of Writers upon the Politicks, we may observe in the Republick of *Dogs* (which in its Original seems to be an Institution of the *Many*) that the whole State is ever in the profoundest Peace, after a full Meal; and, that Civil Broils arise among them, when it happens for one great *Bone* to be seized on by some *leading Dog*, who either divides it among the *Few*, and then it falls to an *Oligarchy*, or keeps it to Himself, and then it runs up to a *Tyranny*. The same Reasoning also, holds Place among them, in those Dissensions we behold upon a Turgescency in any of their Females. For, the Right of Possession lying in common (it being impossible to establish a Property in so delicate a Case) Jealousies and Suspicious do so abound, that the whole Commonwealth of that Street, is reduced to a manifest *State of War*, of every *Citizen* against every *Citizen*; till some One of more Courage, Conduct, or Fortune than the rest, seizes and enjoys the Prize; Upon which, naturally arises Plenty of Heartburning, and Envy, and Snarling against the *Happy Dog*. Again, if we look upon any of these Republicks engaged in a Forein War, either of Invasion or Defence, we shall find, the same Reasoning will serve, as to the Grounds and Occasions of

Marginal notes:
* Riches produceth Pride; Pride is War's Ground, &c. Vid. Ephem. de Mary Clarke; opt. Edit.[2]

[2] *Vid. Ephem. de Mary Clarke; opt. Edit:* That is, See the *Ephemeris* (Journal) of Mary Clarke; *Optima Editio.* (The publication was an almanac.)

each; and, that *Poverty*, or *Want*, in some Degree or other (whether Real, or in Opinion, which makes no Alteration in the Case), has a great Share, as well as *Pride*, on the Part of the Aggressor.

NOW, whoever will please to take this Scheme, and either reduce or adapt it to an Intellectual State, or Commonwealth of Learning, will soon discover the first Ground of Disagreement between the two great Parties at this Time in Arms; and may form just Conclusions upon the Merits of either Cause. But the Issue or Events of this War are not so easie to conjecture at: For, the present Quarrel is so enflamed by the warm Heads of either Faction, and the Pretensions *somewhere or other* so exorbitant, as not   10 to admit the least Overtures of Accommodation: This Quarrel first began (as I have heard it affirmed by an old Dweller in the Neighbourhood) about a small Spot of Ground, *lying* and *being* upon one of the two Tops of the Hill *Parnassus*;[3] the highest and largest of which, had it seems, been time out of Mind, in quiet Possession of certain Tenants, call'd the *Antients*; And the other was held by the *Moderns*. But, these disliking their present Station, sent certain Ambassadors to the *Antients*, complaining of a great Nuisance, how the Height of that Part of *Parnassus*, quite spoiled the prospect of theirs, especially towards the *East*; and therefore, to avoid a War, offered them the Choice of this Alternative; either that the *Antients* would please to remove   20 themselves and their Effects down to the lower Summity,[4] which the *Moderns* would graciously surrender to them, and advance in their Place; or else, that the said *Antients* will give leave to the *Moderns* to come with Shovels and Mattocks, and level the said Hill, as low as they shall think it convenient. To which, the Antients made Answer: How little they expected such a Message as this, from a Colony, whom they had admitted out of their own Free Grace, to so near a Neighbourhood. That, as to their own Seat, they were *Aborigines* of it, and therefore, to talk with them of a Removal or Surrender, was a Language they did not understand. That, if the Height of the Hill, on their side, shortned the Prospect of the *Moderns*, it was a Disadvantage they could   30 not help, but desired them to consider, whether that Injury (if it be any) were not largely recompenced by the *Shade* and *Shelter* it afforded them. That, as to the levelling or digging down, it was either Folly or Ignorance to propose it, if they did, or did not know, how that side of the Hill was an entire Rock, which would break their Tools and Hearts; without any Damage to itself. That they would therefore advise the *Moderns*, rather to raise their own side of the Hill, than dream of pulling down that of the *Antients*, to the former of which, they would not only give Licence, but also largely contribute. All this was rejected by the *Moderns*, with much Indignation, who still insisted upon one of the two Expedients; And so this Difference broke out into a   40 long and obstinate War, maintain'd on the one Part, by Resolution, and by the Courage of certain Leaders and Allies; but, on the other, by the greatness of their Number, upon all Defeats, affording continual Recruits. In this

---

[3] *Parnassus:* The mountain just north of Delphi associated with Apollo and the Muses, whence its connection with literary production and excellence derives. It has often been referred to as having two summits, one sacred to Apollo, the other to Dionysus.

[4] *Summity:* An old form of summit.

Quarrel, whole Rivulets of *Ink* have been exhausted, and the Virulence of both Parties enormously augmented. Now, it must here be understood, that *Ink* is the great missive Weapon, in all Battels of the *Learned*, which, convey'd thro' a sort of Engine, call'd a *Quill*, infinite Numbers of these are darted at the Enemy, by the Valiant on each side, with equal Skill and Violence, as if it were an Engagement of *Porcupines*. This malignant Liquor was compounded by the Engineer, who invented it, of two Ingredients, which are *Gall* and *Copperas*,[5] by its Bitterness and Venom, to *Suit* in some Degree, as well as to *Foment* the Genius of the Combatants. And as the *Grecians*, after an Engagement, when they could not *agree* about the Victory, were wont to set up   10 Trophies on both sides, the beaten Party being content to be at the same Expence, to keep it self in Countenance (A laudable and antient Custom, happily reviv'd of late, in the Art of War), so the *Learned*, after a sharp and bloody Dispute, do on both sides hang out their Trophies too, which-ever comes by the worst. These Trophies have largely inscribed on them the Merits of the Cause; a full impartial Account of such a Battel, and how the Victory fell clearly to the Party that set them up. They are known to the World under several Names; As, *Disputes, Arguments, Rejoynders, Brief Considerations, Answers, Replies, Remarks, Reflexions, Objections, Confutations*. For a very few Days they are fixed up in all Publick Places, either by themselves or their *Representatives, for   20 Passengers to gaze at: From whence the chiefest and largest are * *Their* removed to certain Magazines, they call, *Libraries*, there to remain   *Title-* in a Quarter purposely assign'd them, and from thenceforth, begin *Pages.* to be called, *Books of Controversie*.

IN these Books, is wonderfully instilled and preserved, the Spirit of each Warrier, while he is alive; and after his Death, his Soul transmigrates there, to inform[6] them. This, at least, is the more common Opinion; But, I believe, it is with Libraries, as with other *Coemeteries*, where some Philosophers affirm, that a certain Spirit, which they call *Brutum hominis*,[7] hovers over the Monument, till the Body is corrupted, and turns to *Dust*, or to *Worms*, but then vanishes or   30 dissolves: So, we may say, a restless Spirit haunts over every *Book*, till *Dust* or *Worms* have seized upon it; which to some, may happen in a few Days, but to others, later; And therefore, *Books* of Controversy, being of all others, haunted by the most disorderly Spirits, have always been confined in a separate Lodge from the rest; and for fear of mutual violence against each other, it was thought Prudent by our Ancestors, to bind them to the Peace with strong Iron Chains. Of which Invention, the original Occasion was this: When the Works of *Scotus*[8] first came out, they were carried to a certain great Library, and had Lodgings appointed them; But this Author was no sooner settled, than he went to visit his Master *Aristotle*, and there both concerted together to seize *Plato*   40 by main Force, and turn him out from his antient Station among the *Divines*,

---

[5] *Copperas*: Formerly a name for copper (iron and zinc) sulphates, now for ferrous sulphate only (green vitriol) used in dyeing, tanning, and making ink.

[6] *Inform*: To imbue with spirit.

[7] *Brutum hominis*: Man's stupidity.

[8] *Scotus*: Johannus Duns Scotus (c.

1265–1308), a great Medieval schoolman, is in a way misrepresented here. Actually Aristotle had displaced Plato in Christian theology before the thirteenth century; moreover, Duns Scotus took exception to certain of Aristotle's (and Aquinas') theoretical (anti-pragmatical) positions.

where he had peaceably dwelt near Eight Hundred Years. The Attempt succeeded, and the two Usurpers have reigned ever since in his stead: But to maintain Quiet for the future, it was decreed, that all *Polemicks* of the larger Size, should be held fast with a Chain.

BY this Expedient, the publick Peace of Libraries, might certainly have been preserved, if a new Species of controversial Books had not arose of late Years, instinct with a most malignant Spirit, from the War above-mentioned, between the *Learned*, about the higher Summity of *Parnassus*.

WHEN these Books were first admitted into the Publick Libraries, I remember to have said upon Occasion, to several Persons concerned, how I was sure,   10
they would create Broyls wherever they came, unless a World of Care were taken: And therefore, I advised, that the Champions of each side should be coupled together, or otherwise mixt, that like the blending of contrary Poysons, their Malignity might be employ'd among themselves. And it seems, I was neither an ill Prophet, nor an ill Counsellor; for it was nothing else but the Neglect of this Caution, which gave Occasion to the terrible Fight that happened on *Friday* last between the *Antient* and *Modern Books* in the *King's Library*. Now, because the Talk of this Battel is so fresh in every body's Mouth, and the Expectation of the Town so great to be informed in the Particulars; I, being possessed of all Qualifications requisite in an *Historian*, and retained by neither   20
Party; have resolved to comply with the urgent *Importunity of my Friends*, by writing down a full impartial Account thereof.

THE *Guardian* of the *Regal Library*,[9] a Person of great Valor, but chiefly renowned for his *Humanity, had been a fierce Champion for the *Moderns*, and in an Engagement upon *Parnassus*, had vowed, with his own Hands, to knock down two of the *Antient* Chiefs,[10] who guarded a small Pass on the superior Rock; but endeavouring to climb up, was cruelly obstructed by his own unhappy Weight, and tendency towards his Center; a Quality, to which, those of the *Modern* Party, are extreme subject; For, being lightheaded, they have in Speculation, a wonderful Agility, and conceive nothing too high for them to   30
mount; but in reducing to Practice, discover a mighty Pressure about their Posteriors and their Heels. Having thus failed in his Design, the disappointed Champion bore a cruel Rancour to the *Antients*, which he resolved to gratifie, by showing all Marks of his Favour to the *Books* of their Adversaries, and lodging them in the fairest Apartments; when at the same time, whatever *Book* had the boldness to own it self for an Advocate of the *Antients*, was buried alive in some obscure Corner, and threatned upon the least Displeasure, to be turned out of Doors. Besides, it so happened, that about this time, there was a strange Confusion of Place among all the *Books* in the Library; for which several Reasons were assigned. Some imputed it to a great heap of *learned Dust*, which a per-   40

* *The Honourable Mr.* Boyle, *in the Preface to his Edition of* Phalaris, *says, he was refus'd a Manuscript by the Library-Keeper,* pro solita Humanitate sua.[11]

---

[9] *Guardian of the Regal Library:* Bentley, librarian of the Royal Library in St. James's Palace.
[10] *Antient Chiefs:* Phalaris and Aesop.

See headnote.
[11] *Pro solita Humanitate sua:* With his usual kindness.

verse Wind blew off from a Shelf of *Moderns* into the *Keeper's* Eyes. Others affirmed, He had a Humour to pick the *Worms* out of the *Schoolmen*, and swallow them fresh and fasting; whereof some fell upon his *Spleen*, and some climbed up into his Head, to the great Perturbation of both. And lastly, others maintained, that by walking much in the dark about the Library, he had quite lost the Situation of it out of his Head; And therefore, in replacing his *Books*, he was apt to mistake, and clap *Des-Cartes* next to *Aristotle*; Poor *Plato* had got between *Hobbes* and the *Seven Wise Masters*,[12] and *Virgil* was hemm'd in with *Dryden* on one side, and *Withers*[13] on the other.

MEAN while, those *Books* that were Advocates for the *Moderns*, chose out one from among them, to make a Progress thro' the whole Library, examine the Number and Strength of their Party, and concert their Affairs. This Messenger performed all things very industriously, and brought back with him a List of their Forces, in all Fifty Thousand, consisting chiefly of *light Horse*, *heavy-armed Foot*, and *Mercenaries*; Whereof the *Foot* were in general but sorrily armed, and worse clad; Their *Horses* large, but extremely out of Case and Heart; However, some few by trading among the *Antients*, had furnisht themselves tolerably enough.

WHILE Things were in this Ferment; *Discord* grew extremely high, hot Words passed on both sides, and ill blood was plentifully bred. Here a solitary *Antient*, squeezed up among a whole Shelf of *Moderns*, offered fairly to dispute the Case, and to prove by manifest Reasons, that the Priority was due to them, from long Possession, and in regard of their Prudence, Antiquity, and above all, their great Merits towards the *Moderns*. But these denied the Premises, and seemed very much to wonder, how the *Antients* could pretend to insist upon their Antiquity, when it was so plain (if they went to that) that the *Moderns* were much the more *Antient of the two. As for any Obligations they owed to the *Antients*, they renounced them all. *'Tis true*, said they, *we are informed, some few of our Party have been so mean to borrow their Subsistence from You; But the rest, infinitely the greater Number (and especially, we French and English) were so far from stooping to so base an Example, that there never passed, till this very hour, six Words between us. For, our Horses are of our own breeding, our Arms of our own forging, and our Cloaths of our own cutting out and sowing.* Plato was by chance upon the next Shelf, and observing those that spoke to be in the ragged Plight, mentioned a while ago; their *Jades*[14] lean and foundred, their *Weapons* of rotten Wood, their *Armour* rusty, and nothing but Raggs underneath; he laugh'd loud, and in his pleasant way, swore, *By G——, he believ'd them.*

* *According to the Modern Paradox.*

NOW, the *Moderns* had not proceeded in their late Negotiation, with Secrecy enough to escape the Notice of the Enemy. For, those Advocates, who had begun the Quarrel, by setting first on Foot the Dispute of Precedency, talkt so loud of coming to a Battel, that *Temple* happened to over-hear them, and gave immediate Intelligence to the *Antients*; who thereupon drew up their

---

[12] *Seven Wise Masters:* Apparently Swift's narrator intends this modern title to balance *The Seven Sages of Rome*, a fourteenth-century romance about Dio-cletian, the Roman emperor.

[13] *Withers:* George Wither (1588–1667), generally thought of as a bad poet.

[14] *Jades:* Horses.

scattered Troops together, resolving to act upon the defensive; Upon which, several of the *Moderns* fled over to their Party, and among the rest, *Temple* himself. This *Temple* having been educated and long conversed among the *Antients*, was, of all the *Moderns*, their greatest Favorite, and became their greatest Champion.

THINGS were at this Crisis, when a material Accident fell out. For, upon the highest Corner of a large Window, there dwelt a certain *Spider*, swollen up to the first Magnitude, by the Destruction of infinite Numbers of *Flies*, whose Spoils lay scattered before the Gates of his Palace, like human Bones before the Cave of some Giant. The Avenues to his Castle were guarded with Turk- 10 pikes, and Palissadoes, all after the *Modern* way of Fortification. After you had passed several Courts, you came to the Center, wherein you might behold the *Constable* himself in his own Lodgings, which had Windows fronting to each Avenue, and Ports to sally out upon all Occasions of Prey or Defence. In this Mansion he had for some Time dwelt in Peace and Plenty, without Danger to his *Person* by *Swallows* from above, or to his *Palace* by *Brooms* from below: When it was the Pleasure of Fortune to conduct thither a wandring *Bee*, to whose Curiosity a broken Pane in the Glass had discovered it self; and in he went, where expatiating a while, he at last happened to alight upon one of the outward Walls of the *Spider's* Cittadel; which yielding to the unequal Weight, sunk down to 20 the very Foundation. Thrice he endeavoured to force his Passage, and Thrice the Center shook. The *Spider* within, feeling the terrible Convulsion, supposed at first, that *Nature* was approaching to her final Dissolution; or else, that *Beelze-bub*[15] with all his Legions, was come to revenge the Death of many thousands of his Subjects, whom his Enemy had slain and devoured. However, he at length valiantly resolved to issue forth, and meet his Fate. Mean while, the *Bee* had acquitted himself of his Toils, and posted securely at some Distance, was employed in cleansing his Wings, and disengaging them from the ragged Remnants of the Cobweb. By this Time the *Spider* was adventured out, when beholding the Chasms, and Ruins, and Dilapidations of his Fortress, he was 30 very near at his Wit's end, he stormed and swore like a Mad-man, and swelled till he was ready to burst. At length, casting his Eye upon the *Bee*, and wisely gathering Causes from Events (for they knew each other by Sight), *A Plague split you*, said he, *for a giddy Son of a Whore; Is it you, with a Vengeance, that have made this Litter here? Could not you look before you, and be d——n'd? Do you think I have nothing else to do (in the Devil's Name) but to Mend and Repair after your Arse? Good Words, Friend*, said the *Bee* (having now pruned himself, and being disposed to drole), *I'll give you my Hand and Word to come near your Kennel no more; I was never in such a confounded Pickle since I was born. Sirrah*, replied the *Spider, if it were not for breaking an old Custom in our Family, never* 40 *to stir abroad against an Enemy, I should come and teach you better Manners. I pray, have Patience*, said the *Bee, or you will spend your Substance, and for ought I see, you may stand in need of it all, towards the Repair of your House. Rogue, Rogue*, replied the *Spider, yet methinks, you should have more Respect to a Person, whom all the World allows to be so much your Betters. By my Troth*, said the *Bee, the Comparison*

---

[15] *Beelzebub:* The Devil.

will amount to a very good Jest, and you will do me a Favour, to let me know the Reasons, that all the World is pleased to use in so hopeful a Dispute. At this, the *Spider* having swelled himself into the Size and Posture of a Disputant, began his Argument in the true Spirit of Controversy, with a Resolution to be heartily scurrilous and angry, to urge *on* his own Reasons, without the least Regard to the Answers or Objections of his Opposite; and fully predetermined in his Mind against all Conviction.

NOT to disparage myself, said he, *by the Comparison with such a Rascal; What art thou but a Vagabond without House or Home, without Stock or Inheritance? Born to no Possession of your own, but a Pair of Wings, and a Drone-Pipe. Your Livelihood is an universal Plunder upon Nature; a Freebooter over Fields and Gardens; and for the sake of Stealing, will rob a Nettle as readily as a Violet. Whereas I am a domestick Animal, furnisht with a Native Stock within my self. This large Castle (to shew my Improvements in the Mathematicks) is all built with my own Hands, and the Materials extracted altogether out of my own Person.*

I am glad, answered the *Bee, to hear you grant at least, that I am come honestly by my Wings and my Voice, for then, it seems, I am obliged to Heaven alone for my Flights and my Musick; and Providence would never have bestowed on me two such Gifts, without designing them for the noblest Ends. I visit, indeed, all the Flowers and Blossoms of the Field and the Garden, but whatever I collect from thence, enriches my self, without the least Injury to their Beauty, their Smell, or their Taste. Now, for you and your Skill in Architecture, and other Mathematicks, I have little to say: In that Building of yours, there might, for ought I know, have been Labor and Method enough, but by woful Experience for us both, 'tis too plain, the Materials are nought, and I hope, you will henceforth take Warning, and consider Duration and matter, as well as method and Art. You, boast, indeed, of being obliged to no other Creature, but of drawing, and spinning out all from your self; That is to say, if we may judge of the Liquor in the Vessel by what issues out, You possess a good plentiful Store of Dirt and Poison in your Breast; And, tho' I would by no means, lessen or disparage your genuine Stock of either, yet, I doubt you are somewhat obliged for an Encrease of both, to a little foreign Assistance. Your inherent Portion of Dirt, does not fail of Acquisitions, by Sweepings exhaled from below: and one Insect furnishes you with a share of Poison to destroy another. So that in short, the Question comes all to this; Whether is the nobler Being of the two, That which by a lazy Contemplation of four Inches round; by an over-weening Pride, which feeding and engendering on it self, turns all into Excrement and Venom; producing nothing at all, but Fly-bane and a Cobweb: Or That, which, by an universal Range, with long Search, much Study, true Judgment, and Distinction of Things, brings home Honey and Wax.*

THIS Dispute was managed with such Eagerness, Clamor, and Warmth, that the two Parties of *Books* in Arms below, stood Silent a while, waiting in Suspense what would be the Issue; which was not long undetermined: For the *Bee* grown impatient at so much loss of Time, fled strait away to a bed of Roses, without looking for a Reply; and left the *Spider* like an Orator, *collected* in himself, and just prepared to burst out.

IT happened upon this Emergency, that *Æsop* broke silence first. He had been of late most barbarously treated by a strange Effect of the *Regent's Humanity,* who had tore off his Title-page, sorely defaced one half of his Leaves, and chained him fast among a Shelf of *Moderns*.[16] Where soon discovering how high the Quarrel was like to proceed, He tried all his Arts, and turned himself to a thousand Forms: At length in the borrowed Shape of an *Ass*, the *Regent* mistook Him for a *Modern*; by which means, he had Time and Opportunity to escape to the *Antients*, just when the *Spider* and the *Bee* were entring into their Contest; to which He gave His Attention with a world of Pleasure; and when it was ended, swore in the loudest Key, that in all his Life, he had never known two Cases so parallel and adapt to each other, as That in the Window, and this upon the Shelves. The *Disputants*, said he, *have admirably managed the Dispute between them, have taken in the full Strength of all that is to be said on both sides, and exhausted the Substance of every Argument* pro *and* con. *It is but to adjust the Reasonings of both to the present Quarrel, then to compare and apply the Labors and Fruits of each, as the* Bee *has learnedly deduced them; and we shall find the Conclusion fall plain and close upon the* Moderns *and Us. For, pray Gentlemen, was ever any thing so* Modern *as the* Spider *in his Air, his Turns, and his Paradoxes?* He *argues in the Behalf of* You *his Brethren, and Himself, with many Boastings of his native Stock, and great Genius; that he Spins and Spits wholly from himself, and scorns to own any Obligation or Assistance from without. Then he displays to you his great Skill in Architecture, and Improvement in the Mathematicks. To all this, the* Bee, *as an Advocate, retained by us the* Antients, *thinks fit to Answer; That if one may judge of the great Genius or Inventions of the* Moderns, *by what they have produced, you will hardly have Countenance to bear you out in boasting of either. Erect your Schemes with as much Method and Skill as you please; yet, if the materials be nothing but Dirt, spun out of your own Entrails (the Guts of* Modern *Brains) the Edifice will conclude at last in a* Cobweb: *The Duration of which, like that of other* Spiders *Webs, may be imputed to their being forgotten, or neglected, or hid in a Corner. For any Thing else of Genuine, that the* Moderns *may pretend to, I cannot recollect; unless it be a large Vein of Wrangling and Satyr, much of a Nature and Substance with the* Spider's *Poison; which, however, to pretend to spit wholly out of themselves, is improved by the same Arts, by feeding upon the* Insects *and Vermin of the Age. As for* Us, *the* Antients, *We are content with the* Bee, *to pretend to Nothing of our own, beyond our* Wings *and our* Voice: *that is to say, our* Flights *and our* Language; *For the rest, whatever we have got, has been by infinite Labor, and search, and ranging thro' every Corner of Nature: The Difference is, that instead of* Dirt *and* Poison, *we have rather chose to fill our Hives with* Honey *and* Wax, *thus furnishing Mankind with the two Noblest of Things, which are* Sweetness *and* Light.

'TIS wonderful to conceive the Tumult arisen among the *Books*, upon the Close of this long Descant of *Æsop;* Both Parties took the Hint, and heightened their Animosities so on a sudden, that they resolved it should come to a Battel. Immediately, the two main Bodies withdrew under their several Ensigns, to the farther Parts of the Library, and there entred into Cabals, and Consults upon the present Emergency. The *Moderns* were in very warm Debates upon the Choice of their *Leaders,* and nothing less than the Fear impending from their Enemies, could have kept them from Mutinies upon this Occasion. The Difference was greatest among the *Horse,* where every private *Trooper* pre-

[16] *Among . . . Moderns:* Bentley had   See the headnote.
demonstrated that Aesop was not classical.

tended to the chief Command, from *Tasso*[17] and *Milton*, to *Dryden* and *Withers*. The *Light-Horse* were Commanded by *Cowly*, and *Despreaux*. There, came the *Bowmen* under their valiant Leaders, *Des-Cartes*, *Gassendi*, and *Hobbes*,[18] whose Strength was such, that they could shoot their Arrows beyond the *Atmosphere*, never to fall down again, but turn like that of *Evander*,[19] into *Meteors*, or like the *Canonball* into *Stars*. *Paracelsus*[20] brought a *Squadron* of *Stink-Pot-Flingers* from the snowy Mountains of *Rhœtia*. There, came a vast Body of *Dragoons*, of different Nations, under the leading of *Harvey*,[21] their great *Aga*: Part armed with *Scythes*, the Weapons of Death; Part with *Launces* and long *Knives*, all steept in *Poison*; Part shot *Bullets* of a most malignant Nature, and used *white Powder* which infallibly killed without *Report*. There, came several Bodies of *heavy-armed Foot*, all *Mercenaries*, under the Ensigns of *Guiccardine*, *Davila*, *Polydore Virgil*, *Buchanan*, *Mariana*, *Cambden*, and others. The *Engineers* were commanded by *Regiomontanus* and *Wilkins*. The rest were a confused Multitude, led by *Scotus*, *Aquinas*, and *Bellarmine*,[22] of mighty Bulk and Stature, but without either Arms, Courage, or Discipline. In the last Place, came infinite Swarms of **Calones*, a disorderly Rout led by *Lestrange*;[23] Rogues and Raggamuffins, that follow the Camp for nothing but the Plunder; All without *Coats* to cover them.

THE Army of the *Antients* was much fewer in Number; *Homer* led the Horse, and *Pindar* the *Light-Horse*; *Euclid* was chief *Engineer*: Plato and *Aristotle* commanded the *Bow men*, *Herodotus* and *Livy* the *Foot*, *Hippocrates* the *Dragoons*. The *Allies*, led by *Vossius*[24] and *Temple*, brought up the Rear.

ALL things violently tending to a decisive *Battel*; *Fame*, who much frequented, and had a large Apartment formerly assigned her in the *Regal Library*, fled up strait to *Jupiter*, to whom she delivered a faithful account of all that passed between the two Parties below. (For, among the Gods, she always tells Truth.) *Jove*, in great concern, convokes a Council in the *Milky-Way*. The Senate assembled, he declares the Occasion of convening them; a bloody *Battel* just impendent between two mighty Armies of *Antient* and *Modern*

* *These are Pamphlets, which are not bound or cover'd.*

---

[17] *Tasso*: Torquato Tasso (1544–1595), Italian epic poet; here a modern.

[18] *Cowly . . . Hobbes*: All moderns here. Swift includes in his list of moderns, poets like Milton, Abraham Cowley, and Nicolas Boileau Despréaux, who were sympathetic to the ancients. Moreover, Descartes, Gassendi, and Hobbes—all philosophers with individual points of view—are alike only in representing modern as opposed to classical philosophy.

[19] *Evander*: It is Acestes' arrow, *Aeneid*, V, 159–544, not Evander's.

[20] *Paracelsus*: See *Tale of a Tub*, n. 166.

[21] *Harvey*: William Harvey (1578–1657), who had discovered the circulation of the blood.

[22] *Guiccardine . . . Bellarmine*: Francesco Guicciardini (1483–1540), Italian historian; Enrico Davila 1576–1631), Italian his-torian; Polydore Vergil (1470–1555), Italian, then naturalized English, historian; George Buchanan (1506–1582), Scottish humanist; Juan de Mariana (1537–1624), Spanish historian; William Camden (1551–1623), English historian; Johann Müller (1436–1476) was the name of Regiomantus the Prussian mathematician; John Wilkins (1614–1672), a founder of the Royal Society; Johannes Duns Scotus (c. 1265–1308), British schoolman; Thomas Aquinas (1226–1274), Italian scholastic theologian; Roberto Bellarmino (1542–1621), Italian Catholic apologist.

[23] *Lestrange*: See *Tale of a Tub*, n. 203.

[24] *Vossius*: Probably Isaac Vossius (1618–1688), a Dutch classical scholar who edited the epistles of Ignatius, Justin, Pomponius Mela, and Catullus.

Creatures, call'd *Books*, wherein the Celestial Interest was but too deeply concerned. *Momus*[25] the Patron of the *Moderns*, made an Excellent Speech in their Favor, which was answered by *Pallas*[26] the Protectress of the *Antients*. The Assembly was divided in their affections; when *Jupiter* commanded the Book of Fate to be laid before Him. Immediately were brought by *Mercury*, three large Volumes in Folio, containing Memoirs of all Things past, present, and to come. The Clasps were of Silver, double Gilt; the Covers, of Celestial Turky-leather, and the Paper such as here on Earth might almost pass for Vellum. *Jupiter* having silently read the Decree, would communicate the Import to none, but presently shut up the Book.   10

WITHOUT the Doors of this Assembly, there attended a vast Number of light, nimble Gods, menial Servants to *Jupiter*: These are his ministring Instruments in all Affairs below. They travel in a Caravan, more or less together, and are fastened to each other like a Link of Gally-slaves, by a light Chain, which passes from them to *Jupiter's* great Toe: And yet in receiving or delivering a Message, they may never approach above the lowest Step of his Throne, where he and they whisper to each other thro' a long hollow Trunk. These Deities are call'd by mortal Men, *Accidents*, or *Events*; but the Gods call them, *Second Causes*. *Jupiter* having delivered his Message to a certain Number of these Divinities, they flew immediately down to the Pinnacle of the Regal Library,   20 and consulting a few Minutes, entered unseen, and disposed the Parties according to their Orders.

MEAN while, *Momus* fearing the worst, and calling to mind an antient Prophecy, which bore no very good Face to his Children the *Moderns*; bent his Flight to the Region of a malignant Deity, call'd *Criticism*. She Dwelt on the Top of a snowy Mountain in *Nova Zembla*;[27] there *Momus* found her extended in her Den, upon the Spoils of numberless Volumes half devoured. At her right Hand sat *Ignorance*, her Father and Husband, blind with Age; at her left; *Pride* her Mother, dressing her up in the Scraps of Paper herself had torn. There, was *Opinion* her Sister, light of Foot, hoodwinkt, and headstrong,   30 yet giddy and perpetually turning. About her play'd her Children, *Noise* and *Impudence*, *Dullness* and *Vanity*, *Positiveness*, *Pedantry*, and *Ill-Manners*. The Goddess herself had Claws like a Cat: Her Head, and Ears, and Voice, resembled those of an *Ass*; Her Teeth fallen out before; Her Eyes turned inward, as if she lookt only upon herself: Her Diet was the overflowing of her own *Gall*: Her *Spleen* was so large, as to stand prominent like a Dug of the first Rate, nor wanted Excrescencies in form of Teats, at which a Crew of ugly Monsters were greedily sucking; and, what is wonderful to conceive, the bulk of Spleen encreased faster than the Sucking could diminish it. *Goddess, said Momus, can you sit idly here, while our devout Worshippers, the* Moderns, *are this Minute entring*   30 *into a cruel Battel, and, perhaps, now lying under the Swords of their Enemies; Who then hereafter, will ever sacrifice, or build Altars to our Divinities? Haste therefore to the* British Isle, *and, if possible, prevent their Destruction, while I make Factions among the Gods, and gain them over to our Party.*

[25] *Momus:* The personification of fault-finding and a son of primeval Night.
[26] *Pallas:* Pallas Athena, patron god-dess of Athens.
[27] *Nova Zembla:* Russian islands in the Arctic Ocean, near the Berents Sea.

MOMUS having thus delivered himself, staid not for an answer, but left the Goddess to her own Resentment; Up she rose in a Rage, and as it is the Form upon such Occasions, began a Soliloquy. *'Tis I* (said she) *who give Wisdom to Infants and Idiots; By Me, Children grow wiser than their Parents. By Me,* Beaux *become Politicians; and* School-boys, *Judges of Philosophy. By Me, Sophisters debate, and conclude upon the Depths of Knowledge; and Coffee-house Wits* instinct[28] *by Me, can correct an Author's Style, and display his minutest Errors, without understanding a Syllable of his Matter or his Language. By Me, Striplings spend their Judgment, as they do their Estate, before it comes into their Hands. 'Tis I, who have deposed Wit and Knowledge from their Empire over* Poetry, *and advanced my self in their stead. And shall a few* upstart Antients *dare oppose me?*——*But, come, my aged Parents, and you, my Children dear, and thou my beauteous Sister; let us ascend my Chariot, and hast to assist our devout* Moderns, *who are now sacrificing to us a* Hecatomb, *as I perceive by that grateful Smell, which from thence reaches my Nostrils.*

THE Goddess and her Train having mounted the Chariot, which was drawn by *tame Geese,* flew over infinite Regions, shedding her Influence in due Places, till at length, she arrived at her beloved Island of *Britain;* but in hovering over its *Metropolis,* what Blessings did she not let fall upon her Seminaries of *Gresham* and *Covent-Garden?*[29] And now she reach'd the fatal Plain of St. *James's* Library, at what time the two Armies were upon the Point to engage; where entring with all her Caravan, unseen, and landing upon a Case of Shelves, now desart, but once inhabited by a Colony of *Virtuoso's,*[30] she staid a while to observe the Posture of both Armies.

BUT here, the tender Cares of a Mother began to fill her Thoughts, and move in her Breast. For, at the Head of a Troop of *Modern Bow-men,* she cast her Eyes upon her Son *W--tt--n;* to whom the Fates had assigned a very short Thread. *W--tt--n,* a young Hero, whom an unknown Father of mortal Race, begot by stollen Embraces with this Goddess. He was the Darling of his Mother, above all her Children, and she resolved to go and comfort Him. But first, according to the good old Custom of Deities, the cast about to change her Shape; for fear the Divinity of her Countenance might dazzle his Mortal Sight, and over-charge the rest of his Senses. She therefore gathered up her Person into an *Octavo*[31] Compass: Her Body grew white and arid, and split in pieces with Driness; the thick turned into Pastboard, and the thin into Paper, upon which, her Parents and Children, artfully strowed a Black Juice, or Decoction of Gall and Soot, in Form of Letters; her Head, and Voice, and Spleen, kept their primitive Form, and that which before, was a Cover of Skin, did still continue so. In which Guise, she march'd on towards the *Moderns,* undistinguishable in Shape and Dress from the *Divine B--ntl--y, W--tt--n's* dearest Friend. *Brave W--t-t--n,* said the Goddess, *Why do our Troops stand idle here, to spend their present Vigour and Opportunity of this Day? Away, let us haste to the Generals, and advise to give the Onset immediately.* Having spoke thus, she took the ugliest of her Monsters, full glutted from her Spleen, and flung it invisibly into his Mouth; which flying strait up into his Head, squeez'd out his Eye-balls, gave him a dis-

---

[28] *Instinct:* Impelled.

[29] *Gresham* and *Covent-Garden:* See *Tale of a Tub,* nn. 55 and 36.

[30] *Virtuoso's:* Dilettantes (and here moderns).

[31] *Octavo:* A size of book, about 6″ × 9″.

torted Look, and half over-turned his Brain. Then she privately ordered two of her beloved Children, *Dulness* and *Ill-Manners*, closely to attend his Person in all Encounters. Having thus accoutred him, she vanished in a Mist, and the *Hero* perceived it was the Goddess, his Mother.

THE destined Hour of Fate, being now arrived, the Fight began; whereof, before I dare adventure to make a particular Description, I must, after the Example of other Authors, petition for a hundred Tongues, and Mouths, and Hands, and Pens; which would all be too little to perform so immense a Work. Say, Goddess, that presidest over History; who it was that first advanced in the Field of Battel. *Paracelsus*, at the Head of his *Dragoons*, observing *Galen*[32] in the adverse Wing, darted his Javelin with a mighty Force, which the brave *Antient* received upon his Shield, the Point breaking in the second fold. *

* * * * * * * * * * * *   *Hic pauca*
* * * * * * * * * * *   *desunt.*[33]

They bore the wounded *Aga*, on their Shields to his Chariot *   *   *
* * * * * * * * * * * *   *Desunt*
* * * * * * * * * * * *   *non-*
* * * * * * * * * * * *   *nulla.*[34]

THEN *Aristotle* observing *Bacon* advance with a furious Mien, drew his Bow to the Head, and let fly his Arrow, which mist the valiant *Modern*, and went hizzing over his Head; but *Des-Cartes* it hit; The Steel Point quickly found a *Defect* in his *Head-piece*; it pierced the Leather and the Past-board, and went in at his Right Eye. The Torture of the Pain, whirled the valiant *Bow-man* round, till Death, like a Star of superior Influence, drew him into his own *Vortex.*   *   *   *   *   *   *   *   *   *
* * * * * * * * * * * *   *Ingens*
* * * * * * * * * * * *   *hiatus hic*
* * * * * * * * * * * *   *in MS.*[35]

when *Homer* appeared at the Head of the Cavalry, mounted on a furious Horse, with Difficulty managed by the Rider himself, but which no other Mortal durst approach; He rode among the Enemies Ranks, and bore down all before him. Say, Goddess, whom he slew first, and whom he slew last. First, *Gondibert*[36] advanced against Him, clad in heavy Armour, and mounted on a staid sober Gelding, not so famed for his Speed as his Docility in kneeling, whenever his Rider would mount or alight. He had made a Vow to *Pallas*, that he would never leave the Field, till he had spoiled *Homer of his   * *Vid.*
Armour; Madman, who had never once *seen* the Wearer, nor under-   *Homer.*
stood his Strength. Him *Homer* overthrew, Horse and Man to the Ground, there to be trampled and choak'd in the Dirt. Then, with a long Spear, he slew *Denham*,[37] a stout *Modern*, who from his †Father's side, derived

† Sir John Denham's *Poems are very Unequal, extremely Good, and very Indifferent, so that that his Detractors said, he was not the real Author of* Coopers-Hill.

---

[32] *Galen:* A Greek physician (c. A.D. 130–201).
[33] *Hic pauca desunt:* Here a bit is missing.
[34] *Desunt nonnulla:* Several [lines] are missing.
[35] *Ingens hiatus hic in MS:* Here is a vast gap in the manuscript.

[36] *Gondibert:* A romantic epic by William D'Avenant, published in 1651. Temple denied it the extraordinary praise it received from others.
[37] *Denham:* John Denham (1615–1659), best known for his topographical poem *Cooper's Hill.*

his Lineage from *Apollo*, but his Mother was of Mortal Race. He fell, and bit the Earth. The Celestial Part *Apollo* took, and made it a Star, but the Terrestrial lay wallowing upon the Ground. Then *Homer* slew *W–sl–y*[38] with a kick of his Horse's heel; He took *Perrault*[39] by mighty Force out of his Saddle, then hurl'd him at *Fontenelle*, with the same Blow dashing out both their Brains.

ON the left Wing of the Horse, *Virgil* appeared in shining Armor, compleatly fitted to his Body; He was mounted on a dapple grey Steed, the slowness of whose Pace, was an Effect of the highest Mettle and Vigour. He cast his Eye on the adverse Wing, with a desire to find an Object worthy of his valour, when behold, upon a sorrel Gelding of a monstrous Size, appear'd a Foe, issuing from among the thickest of the Enemy's Squadrons; But his Speed was less than his Noise; for his Horse, old and lean, spent the Dregs of his Strength in a high Trot, which tho' it made slow advances, yet caused a loud Clashing of his Armor, terrible to hear. The two Cavaliers had now approached within the Throw of a Lance, when the Stranger desired a Parley, and lifting up the Vizard of his Helmet, a Face hardly appeared from within, which after a pause, was known for that of the renowned *Dryden*. The brave *Antient* suddenly started, as one possess'd with Surprize and Disappointment together: For, the Helmet was nine times too large for the Head, which appeared Situate far in the hinder Part, even like the Lady in a Lobster, or like a Mouse under a Canopy of State, or like a shrivled Beau from within the Pent-house of a modern Perewig: And the voice was suited to the Visage, sounding weak and remote. *Dryden* in a long Harangue soothed up the good *Antient*, called him *Father*, and by a large deduction of Genealogies, made it plainly appear, that they were nearly related. Then he humbly proposed an Exchange of Armor, as a lasting Mark of Hospitality between them. *Virgil* consented (for the Goddess *Diffidence* came unseen, and cast a Mist before his Eyes) tho' his was of Gold, and cost a hundred Beeves, the others but of rusty Iron. However, this glittering Armor became the *Modern* yet worse than his Own. Then, they agreed to exchange Horses; but when it came to the Trial, *Dryden* was afraid, and utterly unable to mount. *   *

Vid. Homer.

*   *   *   *   *   *   *   *   *   *   *
*   *   *   *   *   *   *   *   *   *   *

Alter hiatus in MS.[40]

*   *   *   *   *   * *Lucan*[41] appeared upon a fiery Horse, of admirable Shape, but head-strong, bearing the Rider where he list, over the Field; he made a mighty Slaughter among the Enemy's Horse; which Destruction to stop, *Bl–ckm–re*,[42] a famous *Modern* (but one of the *Mercenaries*) strenuously opposed himself; and darted a Javelin, with a strong Hand, which falling short of its Mark, struck deep in the Earth. Then *Lucan* threw a Lance; but *Æsculapius*[43] came unseen, and turn'd off the Point. *Brave* Modern, *said* Lucan,

---

[38] *W—sl—y:* Samuel Wesley (1662–1735), a poetaster whose *Life of Christ*, a heroic poem, inspired a good deal of criticism.

[39] *Perrault:* Perrault (and Fontenelle below) were prominent French moderns.

[40] *Alter hiatus in MS:* Another gap in the manuscript.

[41] *Lucan:* Roman author (A.D. 39–65) best known for *Pharsalia*, an epic.

[42] *Bl—ckm—re:* See *Tale of a Tub*, n. 203. Blackmore wrote a terrible epic, *Prince Arthur*.

[43] *Æsculapius:* Asclepius, in Greek myth, the god of medicine.

I perceive some God protects you, for never did my Arm so deceive me before; But, what Mortal can contend with a God? Therefore, let us Fight no longer, but present Gifts to each other. Lucan then bestowed the *Modern* a Pair of Spurs, and *Bl–ckm–re* gave *Lucan* a Bridle.   *   *   *   *   *   *   *   *   *Pauca*
*   *   *   *   *   *   *   *   *   *   *   *desunt.*[44]

Creech;[45] But, the Goddess *Dulness* took a Cloud, formed into the Shape of *Horace*, armed and mounted, and placed it in a flying Posture before Him. Glad was the Cavalier, to begin a Combat with a flying Foe, and pursued the Image, threatning loud; till at last it led him to the peaceful Bower of his Father *Ogleby*,[46] by whom he was disarmed, and assigned to his Repose.

THEN *Pindar* slew——, and ——, and *Oldham*,[47] and —— and *Afra* the *Amazon*[48] light of foot; Never advancing in a direct Line, but wheeling with incredible Agility and Force, he made a terrible Slaughter among the Enemies *Light-Horse.* Him, when *Cowley* observed, his generous Heart burnt within him, and he advanced against the fierce *Antient*, imitating his Address, and Pace, and Career, as well as the Vigour of his Horse, and his own Skill would allow. When the two Cavaliers had approach'd within the Length of three Javelins; first *Cowley* threw a Lance, which miss'd *Pindar*, and passing into the Enemy's Ranks, fell ineffectual to the Ground. Then *Pindar* darted a Javelin, so large and weighty, that scarce a dozen *Cavaliers*, as *Cavaliers* are in our degenerate Days, could raise it from the Ground: yet he threw it with Ease, and it went by an unerring Hand, singing through the Air; Nor could the *Modern* have avoided present Death, if he had not luckily opposed the Shield that had been given Him by *Venus.* And now both Hero's drew their Swords, but the *Modern* was so aghast and disordered, that he knew not where he was; his Shield dropt from his Hands; thrice he fled, and thrice he could not escape; at last he turned, and lifting up his Hands, in the Posture of a Suppliant, *God-like* Pindar, said he, *spare my Life, and possess my Horse with these Arms; besides the Ransom which my Friends will give, when they hear I am alive, and your Prisoner.* Dog, said Pindar, *Let your Ransom stay with your Friends; But your Carcass shall be left for the* Fowls of the Air, *and the* Beasts of the Field. With that, he raised his Sword, and with a mighty Stroak, cleft the wretched *Modern* in twain, the Sword pursuing the Blow; and one half lay panting on the Ground, to be trod in pieces by the Horses Feet, the other half was born by the frighted Steed thro' the Field. This *Venus took, and wash'd it seven times in *Ambrosia*, then struck it thrice with a Sprig of *Amarant*;[49] upon which, the Leather grew round and soft, and the Leaves turned into Feathers, and being gilded before,

10

20

30

---

* *I do not approve the Author's Judgment in this, for I think* Cowley's Pindaricks *are much preferable to his* Mistress.

---

[44] *Pauca desunt:* A little missing.
[45] *Creech:* Thomas Creech (1659–1700), translator of Lucretius and Horace.
[46] *Father Ogleby:* John Ogilby (1600–1676), translator of Homer and Virgil.
[47] *Oldham:* John Oldham (1653–1683), who published several Pindaric odes. See

the headnote to Dryden's "Oldham."
[48] *Afra the Amazon:* Mrs. Afra (Aphra) Behn (1640–1689), who published some Pindaric odes, though she was chiefly a novelist and playwright.
[49] *Amarant:* An imaginary flower that never fades.

continued gilded still; so it became a *Dove*, and She harness'd it to her Chariot.

```
*   *   *   *   *   *   *   *   *   *   *   *
```
Hiatus
```
*   *   *   *   *   *   *   *   *   *   *   *
```
valde
```
*   *   *   *   *   *   *   *   *   *   *   *
```
deflendus
```
*   *   *   *   *   *   *   *   *   *   *   *
```
in MS.[50]

DAY being far spent, and the numerous Forces of the *Moderns* half inclining to a Retreat, there issued forth from a Squadron of their *heavy*   *The*
armed Foot, a Captain, whose Name was *B–nt–ly*; in Person, the most   *Episode of*
deformed of all the *Moderns*; Tall, but without Shape or Comeliness;   *B–ntl–y*
Large, but without Strength or Proportion. His Armour was   *and*
patch'd up of a thousand incoherent Pieces; and the Sound of it, as he   *W–tt–n.*
march'd, was loud and dry, like that made by the Fall of a Sheet of Lead,
which an *Etesian* Wind[51] blows suddenly down from the Roof of some Steeple.
His Helmet was of old rusty Iron, but the Vizard was Brass, which tainted   10
by his Breath, corrupted into Copperas,[52] nor wanted Gall from the same
Fountain; so, that whenever provoked by Anger or Labour, an atramentous[53]
Quality, of most malignant Nature, was seen to distil from his Lips. In his
*right Hand he grasp'd a Flail, and (that he might never be unprovided of
an *offensive* Weapon) a Vessel full of *Ordure* in his Left: Thus, compleatly arm'd,
he advanc'd with a slow and heavy Pace, where the *Modern* Chiefs were
holding a Consult upon the Sum of Things; who, as he came onwards, laugh'd
to behold his crooked Leg, and hump Shoulder, which his Boot and Armour
vainly endeavouring to hide were forced to comply with, and expose.[54]
The Generals made use of him for his Talent of Railing; which kept within   20
Government, proved frequently of great Service to their Cause, but at other
times did more Mischief than Good; For at the least Touch of Offence, and
often without any at all, he would, like a wounded Elephant, convert it
against his Leaders. Such, at this Juncture, was the Disposition of *B–ntl–y*,
grieved to see the Enemy prevail, and dissatisfied with every Body's Conduct
but his own. He humbly gave the *Modern* Generals to understand, that he
conceived, with great Submission, they were all a Pack of *Rogues*, and *Fools*,
and *Sons of Whores*, and *d——nn'd Cowards*, and *confounded Loggerheads*,
and *illiterate Whelps*, and *nonsensical Scoundrels*; That if Himself had been
constituted General, those *presumptuous Dogs*, the *Antients*, would long   30
before this, have been beaten out of the Field. *You*, said he, *sit here*   *Vid.*
idle, but, when I, or any other valiant Modern, *kill an Enemy, you are*   *Homer.*
sure to seize the Spoil. But, I will not march one Foot against the Foe, till   *de*
you all swear to me, that, whomever I take or kill, his Arms I shall quietly   *Thersite.*
possess. B–ntl–y having spoke thus, *Scaliger*[55] bestowing him a sower Look;

---

* *The Person here spoken of, is famous for letting fly at every Body without Distinction, and*
using mean and foul Scurrilities.

---

[50] *Hiatus valde deflendus in MS:* A very
lamentable gap in the manuscript.
[51] *Etesian Wind:* A Mediterranean
wind that blows from the Northwest
for about forty days each summer.
[52] *Copperas:* See n. 5.
[53] *Atramentous:* Inky.

[54] *Hump Shoulder . . . expose:* Thersites,
an ill-shaped Greek who reviled his
leaders, Iliad, II, 212–264.
[55] *Scaliger:* Either Julius Scaliger (1484–
1558) or Joseph Scaliger (1540–1609),
father and son, both classical scholars.

Miscreant Prater, said he, *Eloquent only in thine own Eyes, Thou railest without Wit, or Truth, or Discretion.* The *Malignity of thy Temper perverteth Nature, Thy* Learning *makes thee more* Barbarous, *thy Study of* Humanity, *more* Inhuman; *Thy* Converse *amongst Poets more* groveling, miry, *and* dull. *All Arts of* civilizing *others, render thee* rude *and* untractable; Courts *have taught thee* ill Manners, *and* polite Conversation *has finish'd thee a* Pedant. *Besides, a greater Coward burtheneth not the Army. But never despond, I pass my Word, whatever Spoil thou takest, shall certainly be thy own; though, I hope, that vile Carcass will first become a prey to Kites and Worms.*

B–NTL–Y durst not reply; but half choaked with Spleen and Rage, withdrew, in full Resolution of performing some great Achievement. With him, for his Aid and Companion, he took his beloved *W–tt–n*; resolving by Policy or Surprize, to attempt some neglected Quarter of the *Antients* Army. They began their March over Carcasses of their slaughtered Friends; then to the Right of their own Forces: then wheeled Northward, till they came to *Aldrovandus's* Tomb,[56] which they pass'd on the side of the declining Sun. And now they arrived with Fear towards the Enemy's Out-guards; looking about, if haply, they might spy the Quarters of the Wounded, or some straggling Sleepers, unarm'd and remote from the rest. As when two *Mungrel-Curs,* whom *native Greediness,* and *domestick Want,* provoke, and join in Partnership, though fearful, nightly to invade the Folds of some rich Grazier; They, with Tails depress'd, and lolling Tongues, creep soft and slow; mean while, the conscious *Moon,* now in her *Zenith,* on their guilty Heads, darts perpendicular Rays; Nor dare they bark, though much provok'd at her refulgent Visage, whether seen in Puddle by Reflexion, or in Sphear direct; but one surveys the Region round, while t'other scouts the Plain, if haply, to discover at distance from the Flock, some *Carcass* half devoured, the Refuse of gorged Wolves, or ominous Ravens. So march'd this lovely, loving Pair of Friends, nor with less Fear and Circumspection; when, at distance, they might perceive two shining Suits of Armor, hanging upon an Oak, and the Owners not far off in a profound Sleep. The two Friends drew Lots, and the pursuing of this Adventure, fell to *B–ntl–y*; On he went, and in his Van *Confusion* and *Amaze*; while *Horror* and *Affright* brought up the Rear. As he came near; Behold two Hero's of the *Antients* Army, *Phalaris* and *Æsop,* lay fast asleep: *B–ntl–y* would fain have dispatch'd them both, and stealing close, aimed his Flail at *Phalaris's* Breast. But, then, the Goddess *Affright* interposing, caught the *Modern* in her icy Arms, and dragg'd him from the Danger she foresaw; For both the dormant Hero's happened to turn at the same Instant, tho' soundly Sleeping, and busy in a Dream. *For *Phalaris* was just that Minute dreaming, how a most vile *Poetaster* had lampoon'd him, and how, he had got him roaring in his *Bull.* And *Æsop* dream'd, that as he and the *Antient Chiefs* were lying on the Ground, a *Wild Ass* broke loose, ran about trampling and kicking, and dunging in their Faces, *B–ntl–y*

* *This is according to* Homer, *who tells the Dreams of those who were kill'd in their Sleep.*

[56] *Aldrovandus's Tomb:* Ulisse Aldrovandi (1522–1605), Italian naturalist, imprisoned in Rome as a heretic in 1549.

leaving the two Hero's asleep, seized on both their Armours, and withdrew in quest of his Darling *W–tt–n*.

HE, in the mean time, had wandred long in search of some Enterprize, till at length, he arrived at a small *Rivulet*, that issued from a Fountain hard by, call'd in the Language of mortal Men, *Helicon*.[57] Here he stopt, and, parch'd with thirst, resolved to allay it in this limpid Stream. Thrice, with profane Hands, he essay'd to raise the Water to his Lips, and thrice it slipt all thro' his Fingers. Then he stoop'd prone on his Breast, but e'er his Mouth had kiss'd the liquid Crystal, *Apollo* came, and, in the Channel, held his *Shield* betwixt the *Modern* and the Fountain, so that he drew up nothing but *Mud*. For, altho' no Fountain on Earth can compare with the Clearness of *Helicon*, yet there lies at Bottom, a thick sediment of *Slime* and *Mud*; For, so *Apollo* begg'd of *Jupiter*, as a Punishment to those who durst attempt to taste it with unhallowed Lips, and for a Lesson to all, not to *draw too deep*, or *far from the Spring*.   10

AT the Fountain Head, *W–tt–n* discerned two Hero's; The one he could not distinguish,[58] but the other was soon known for *Temple*, General of the *Allies* to the *Antients*. His Back was turned, and he was employ'd in Drinking large Draughts in his Helmet, from the Fountain, where he had withdrawn himself to rest from the Toils of the War. *W–tt–n*, observing him,   20 with quaking Knees, and trembling Hands, spoke thus to Himself: *Oh, that I could kill this Destroyer of our Army, what Renown should I purchase among the Chiefs! But to issue out against Him, Man for Man, Shield against Shield,* Vid. *and Launce against Launce; what* Modern *of us dare? For, he fights* Homer. *like a God, and* Pallas *or* Apollo *are ever at his Elbow. But, Oh,* Mother!*[59] if what Fame reports, be true, that I am the Son of so great a Goddess, grant me to Hit* Temple *with this Launce, that the Stroak may send Him to Hell, and that I may return in Safety and Triumph, laden with his Spoils.* The first Part of his Prayer, the Gods granted, at the Intercession of His *Mother* and of *Momus*; but the rest, by a perverse Wind sent from *Fate*, was scattered in   30 the Air. Then *W–tt–n* grasp'd his Launce, and brandishing it thrice over his head, darted it with all his Might, the *Goddess*, his *Mother*, at the same time, adding Strength to his Arm. Away the Launce went hizzing, and reach'd even to the Belt of the averted *Antient*, upon which, lightly grazing, it fell to the Ground. *Temple* neither felt the Weapon touch him, nor heard it fall; And *W–tt–n*, might have escaped to his Army with the Honor of having remitted his Launce against so great a Leader, unrevenged; But, *Apollo* enraged, that a Javelin, flung by the Assistance of so foul a *Goddess*, should pollute his Fountain, put on the shape of——, and softly came to young *Boyle*, who   40 then accompanied *Temple*: He pointed, first to the Launce, then to the distant *Modern* that flung it, and commanded the young Hero to take immediate Revenge. *Boyle*, clad in a suit of Armor which had been *given him by all the Gods*, immediately advanced against the trembling Foe, who now fled before him. As a young Lion, in the *Libyan Plains*, or *Araby Desart*, sent by his aged Sire to

---

[57] *Helicon:* A mountain sacred to the arts.

[58] *One he could not distinguish:* Charles

Boyle, Fourth Earl of Orrery (1676–1731), editor of the spurious *Epistles of Phalaris*.

[59] *Mother:* Criticism.

hunt for Prey, or Health, or Exercise; He scours along, wishing to meet some Tiger from the Mountains, or a furious Boar; If Chance, a *Wild Ass*, with Brayings importune, affronts his Ear, the generous Beast, though loathing to distain his Claws with Blood so vile, yet much provok'd at the offensive Noise; which *Echo*, foolish Nymph, like her *ill judging Sex*, repeats much louder, and with more Delight than *Philomela's* Song: He vindicates the Honor of the Forest, and hunts the noisy, long-ear'd Animal. So *W–tt–n* fled, so *Boyle* pursued. But *W–tt–n* heavy-arm'd, and slow of foot, began to slack his Course; when his Lover *B–ntl–y* appeared, returning laden with the Spoils of the two sleeping *Antients*. *Boyle* observed him well, and soon discovering   10 the Helmet and Shield of *Phalaris*, his Friend, both which he had lately with his own Hands, new polish'd and gilded; Rage sparkled in His Eyes, and leaving his Pursuit after *W–tt–n*, he furiously rush'd on against this new Approacher. Fain would he be revenged on both; but both now fled different Ways: *And as a Woman in a little House, that gets a painful Livelihood *Vid.* by Spinning; if chance her *Geese* be scattered o'er the Common, she *Homer.* courses round the Plain from side to side, compelling here and there, the Straglers to the Flock; They cackle loud, and flutter o'er the Champain. So *Boyle* pursued, so fled this Pair of Friends: finding at length, their Flight was vain, they bravely joyn'd, and drew themselves in *Phalanx*. First, *B–ntl–y*   20 threw a Spear with all his Force, hoping to pierce the Enemy's Breast; But *Pallas* came unseen, and in the Air took off the Point, and clap'd on one of *Lead*, which after a dead Bang against the Enemy's Shield, fell blunted to the Ground. Then *Boyle* observing well his Time, took a Launce of wondrous Length and sharpness; and as this Pair of Friends compacted stood close Side to Side, he wheel'd him to the right, and with unusual Force, darted the Weapon. *B–ntl–y* saw his Fate approach, and flanking down his Arms, close to his Ribs, hoping to save his Body; in went the Point, passing through Arm and Side, nor stopt, or spent its Force, till it had also pierc'd the valiant *W–tt–n*, who going to sustain his dying Friend, shared his Fate. As, when   30 a skilful Cook has truss'd a Brace of *Woodcocks*, He, with Iron Skewer, pierces the tender Sides of both, their Legs and Wings close pinion'd to their Ribs; So was this pair of Friends transfix'd, till down they fell, joyn'd in their Lives, joyn'd in their Deaths; so closely joyn'd, that *Charon*[60] would mistake them both for one, and waft them over *Styx* for half his Fare. Farewel, beloved, loving Pair; Few Equals have you left behind: And happy and immortal shall you be, if all my Wit and Eloquence can make you
AND, now   *   *   *   *   *   *   *   *   *   *   *
*   *   *   *   *   *   *   *   *   *   *   *   *   *
*   *   *   *   *   *   *   *   *   *   *   *   *   *
*   *   *   *   *   *   *   *   *   *   *   *   * *   *   *   *   *   * *   *   *   *   *   * *Desunt cætera.*[61]

(1704)

* *This is also, after the manner of* Homer; *the Woman's getting a painful Livelihood by Spinning, has nothing to do with the Similitude, nor would be excusable without such an Authority.*

---

[60] *Charon:* In Greek mythology Charon was the ferryman who boated the dead across the River Styx to Hades.

[61] *Desunt cætera:* The rest is missing.

Headnote to
THE PARTRIDGE–BICKERSTAFF PAPERS

John Partridge was an incredibly insensitive man who turned from his first trade of cobbler to the more lucrative one of astrologer. His activities included numerous attacks on Catholicism, for which he was rewarded with a court post by King William. Evidently, he made a great deal of money from his predictions, which were highly regarded by many Londoners. Others, however, attacked him frequently, particularly Tom Brown, Ned Ward, and certain of his professional rivals. It was probably in response to some of Partridge's abuses of the Church of England clergy that Swift entered the little war. Appropriating the established name of a fictitious astrologer, Bickerstaff, Swift forecast the death of Partridge in *Predictions for the Year 1708*. Within the week, he also had published *An Account of the Death of Mr. Partridge*. Instead of letting the matter rest, Partridge foolishly answered, arguing that he was alive, and providing Swift with an opportunity to return the fire with his *Vindication*. Here with the first two of Swift's papers is one in which he said he had no hand, *Squire Bickerstaff Detected*, though he apparently permitted it to appear among his works, where it is identified as a piece ". . . written by that famous Poet Nicholas Row, Esq; and therefore being upon the Same Subject, although not by the Same Author, we have thought fit to publish it. . . ." (*Works*, 1735, I, p. 167.) Tradition maintains that its mischievous author, whoever he may have been, had it passed along through intermediaries to Partridge, who (incredible as it may sound) published it as a reply to his attackers.

TEXT. *The Works of Jonathan Swift* (Dublin, 1735).

Predictions
for the Year 1708

Wherein the Month, and Day of the Month, are set down, the Persons named, and the great Actions and Events of next Year particularly related as they will come to pass.

Written to prevent the People of England *from being farther imposed on by vulgar Almanack-Makers.*

BY ISAAC BICKERSTAFF, ESQ.

It is said, that the Author, when he had writ the following Paper, and being at a Loss what Name to prefix to it; passing through Long-Acre, *observed a Sign over a House where a Locksmith dwelt, and found the Name* Bickerstaff *written under it: Which being a Name somewhat uncommon, he chose to call himself* Isaac Bickerstaff. *This Name was sometime afterward made Use of by Sir* Richard Steele, *and Mr.* Addison, *in the* TATLERS; *in which Papers, as well as many of the* SPECTATORS,[1] *it is well known, that the Author had a considerable Part.*

HAVING long considered the gross Abuse of Astrology in this Kingdom; upon debating the Matter with my self, I could not possibly lay the Fault upon the Art, but upon those gross Impostors, who set up to be the Artists. I know, several learned Men have contended, that the whole is a Cheat; that it is absurd and ridiculous to imagine, the Stars can have any Influence at all upon human Actions, Thoughts, or Inclinations: And whoever hath not bent his Studies that Way, may be excused for thinking so, when he sees in how wretched a Manner this noble Art is treated, by a few mean illiterate Traders between us and the Stars; who import a yearly Stock of Nonsense, Lies, Folly, and Impertinence, which they offer to the World as genuine from the Planets; although they descend from no greater a Height than their own Brains. 10

I INTEND, in a short Time, to publish a large and rational Defence of this Art; and, therefore, shall say no more in its Justification at present, than that it hath been in all Ages defended by many learned Men; and among the rest, by *Socrates* himself; whom I look upon as undoubtedly the wisest of uninspired Mortals: To which if we add, that those who have condemned this Art, although otherwise learned, having been such as either did not apply their Studies this Way; or at least did not succeed in their Applications; their Testimony will not be of much Weight to its Disadvantage, since they are liable to the common Objection of condemning what they did not understand. 20

[1] *Many of the Spectators:* See the headnote to *The Spectator.*

NOR am I at all offended, or think it an Injury to the Art, when I see the common Dealers in it, the *Students in Astrology*, the *Philomaths*,[2] and the rest of that Tribe, treated by wise Men with the utmost Scorn and Contempt: But I rather wonder, when I observe Gentlemen in the Country, rich enough to serve the Nation in Parliament, poring in *Partrige's* Almanack, to find out the Events of the Year at Home and Abroad; not daring to propose a Hunting-Match, until *Gadbury*, or he, hath fixed the Weather.

I WILL allow either of the Two I have mentioned, or any other of the Fraternity, to be not only Astrologers, but Conjurers too; if I do not produce an Hundred Instances in all their Almanacks, to convince any reasonable Man, that they do not so much as understand Grammar and Syntax; that they are not able to spell any Word out of the usual Road; nor even in their Prefaces to write common Sense, or intelligible *English*. Then, for their Observations and Predictions, they are such as will equally suit any Age, or Country in the World. *This Month a certain great Person will be threatned with Death, or Sickness.* This the News-Paper will tell them; for there we find at the End of the Year, that no Month passes without the Death of some Person of Note; and it would be hard, if it should be otherwise, when there are at least two Thousand Persons of Note in this Kingdom, many of them old; and the Almanack-maker has the Liberty of chusing the sickliest Season of the Year, where he may fix his Prediction. Again, *This Month an eminent Clergyman will be preferred*; of which there may be some Hundreds, Half of them with one Foot in the Grave. Then, *Such a Planet in such a House shews great Machinations, Plots and Conspiracies, that may in Time be brought to Light:* After which, if we hear of any Discovery, the Astrologer gets the Honour; if not, his Prediction still stands good. And at last, *God preserve King* William *from all his open and secret Enemies, Amen.* When if the King should happen to have died, the Astrologer plainly foretold it; otherwise, it passeth but for the pious Ejaculation of a loyal Subject: Although it unluckily happened in some of their Almanacks, that poor King *William* was prayed for many Months after he was dead; because, it unluckily fell out that he died about the Beginning of the Year.

To mention no more of their impertinent Predictions: What have we to do with their Advertisements about *Pills, and Drink for the Venereal Disease*, or their mutual Quarrels in Verse and Prose of *Whig* and *Tory*? wherewith the Stars have little to do.

HAVING long observed and lamented these, and a hundred other Abuses of this Art, too tedious to repeat; I resolved to proceed in a new Way; which I doubt not will be to the general Satisfaction of the Kingdom. I can this Year produce but a Specimen of what I design for the future; having employed most Part of my Time in adjusting and correcting the Calculations I made for some Years past; because I would offer nothing to the World of which I am not as fully satisfied, as that I am now alive. For these two last Years I have not failed in above one or two Particulars, and those of no very great Moment.

[2] *Philomaths:* Lovers of science, specifically astrology.

I exactly foretold the Miscarriage at *Toulon*,[3] with all its Particulars; and the Loss of Admiral *Shovel*; although I was mistaken as to the Day, placing that Accident about thirty six Hours sooner than it happened; but upon reviewing my Schemes, I quickly found the Cause of that Error. I likewise foretold the Battle at *Almanza*[4] to the very Day and Hour, with the Loss on both Sides, and the Consequences thereof. All which I shewed to some Friends many Months before they happened; that is, I gave them Papers sealed up, to open at such a Time, after which they were at liberty to read them; and there they found my Predictions true in every Article, except one or two, very minute.

As for the few following Predictions I now offer the world, I forbore to publish them, till I had perused the several Almanacks for the Year we are now entered upon: I found them all in the usual Strain, and I beg the Reader will compare their Manner with mine: And here I make bold to tell the World, that I lay the whole Credit of my Art upon the Truth of these Predictions; and I will be content that *Partrige*, and the rest of his Clan, may hoot me for a Cheat and Impostor, if I fail in any single Particular of Moment. I believe any Man, who reads this Paper, will look upon me to be at least a Person of as much Honesty and Understanding, as a common Maker of Almanacks. I do not lurk in the Dark; I am not wholly unknown in the World: I have set my Name at length, to be a Mark of Infamy to Mankind, if they shall find I deceive them.

IN one Point I must desire to be forgiven; that I talk more sparingly of Home-Affairs. As it would be Imprudence to discover Secrets of State, so it might be dangerous to my Person: But in smaller Matters, and such as are not of publick Consequence, I shall be very free: And the Truth of my Conjectures will as much appear from these as the other. As for the most signal Events abroad in *France*, *Flanders*, *Italy* and *Spain*, I shall make no Scruple to predict them in plain Terms: Some of them are of Importance, and I hope, I shall seldom mistake the Day they will happen: Therefore, I think good to inform the Reader, that I all along make use of the *Old Stile*[5] observed in *England*; which I desire he will compare with that of the News-Papers, at the Time they relate the Actions I mention.

I MUST add one Word more: I know it hath been the Opinion of several learned Persons, who think well enough of the true Art of Astrology, That the Stars do only *incline*, and not force the Actions or Wills of Men: And therefore, however I may proceed by right Rules, yet I cannot in Prudence so confidently assure that the Events will follow exactly as I predict them.

---

[3] *Toulon:* A Mediterranean port in Southeast France. There, Sir Cloudesley Shovel, rear-admiral of England, failed in an attack during the War of the Spanish Succession, in 1707; and on his way home, his ship and others struck a rock of the Scilly Isles and sank.

[4] *Battle at Almanza:* In 1707, the French defeated the British and their peninsular allies in Almanza, Spain.

[5] *Old Stile:* Old Style. The calendar determined by Julius Caesar fixed the length of a year at 365 days and six hours—slightly too long a time. As a result, Julian dates fell behind the astronomical year. England did not observe the correction of Pope Gregory XIII (1582) until 1752. Before then Englishmen referred to Julian dates as Old Style (O.S.) and Gregorian dates as New Style (N.S.). N.S. years begin January 1; O.S. years began March 25. February 22, 1732 (N.S.) is February 11, 1731 (O.S.).

I HOPE, I have maturely considered this Objection, which in some Cases is of no little Weight. For Example: A Man may, by the Influence of an over-ruling Planet, be disposed or inclined to Lust, Rage, or Avarice; and yet by the Force of Reason overcome that evil Influence. And this was the Case of *Socrates*: But the great Events of the World usually depending upon Numbers of Men, it cannot be expected they should all unite to cross their Inclinations, from pursuing a general Design, wherein they unanimously agree. Besides, the Influence of the Stars reacheth to many Actions and Events, which are not any way in the Power of Reason; as Sickness, Death, and what we commonly call Accidents; with many more needless to repeat.   10

BUT now it is Time to proceed to my Predictions; which I have begun to calculate from the Time that the *Sun* enters into *Aries*.[6] And this I take to be properly the Beginning of the natural Year. I pursue them to the Time that he enters *Libra*,[7] or somewhat more, which is the busy Period of the Year. The Remainder I have not yet adjusted upon Account of several Impediments needless here to mention. Besides, I must remind the Reader again, that this is but a Specimen of what I design in succeeding Years to treat more at large, if I may have Liberty and Encouragement.

MY first Prediction is but a Trifle; yet I will mention it, to shew how ignorant those sottish Pretenders to Astrology are in their own Concerns: 20 It relates to *Partrige* the Almanack-Maker; I have consulted the Star of his Nativity by my own Rules; and find he will infallibly die upon the 29th of *March* next, about eleven at Night, of a raging Fever: Therefore I advise him to consider of it, and settle his Affairs in Time.

THE Month of *APRIL* will be observable for the Death of many great Persons. On the 4th will die the Cardinal *de Noailles*, Archbishop of *Paris*: On the 11th the young Prince of *Asturias*, Son to the Duke of *Anjou*: On the 14th a great Peer of this Realm will die at his Country-House: On the 19th an old *Layman* of Great Fame for Learning: And on the 23rd an eminent Goldsmith in *Lombard Street*. I could mention others, both at home and abroad, if I did   30 not consider such Events of very little Use or Instruction to the Reader, or to the World.

As to publick Affairs: On the 7th of this Month, there will be an Insurrection in *Dauphine*, occasioned by the Oppressions of the People; which will not be quieted some Months.

ON the 15th will be a violent Storm on the South-East Coast of *France*; which will destroy many of their Ships, and some in the very Harbour.

THE 19th will be famous for the Revolt of a whole Province or Kingdom, excepting one City; by which the Affairs of a certain Prince in the Alliance will take a better Face.   40

MAY, Against common Conjectures, will be no very busy Month in *Europe*; but very signal for the Death of the *Dauphine*, which will happen on the 7th, after a short Fit of Sickness, and grievous Torments with the Strangury. He dies less lamented by the Court than the Kingdom.

---

[6] *Aries:* In astrology, the constellation of the ram, which the sun enters about March 21.

[7] *Libra:* The zodiacal constellation represented as a pair of scales.

ON the 9th a *Mareschal* of *France* will break his Leg by a Fall from his Horse.
have not been able to discover whether he will then die or not.

ON the 11th will begin a most important Siege, which the Eyes of all *Europe*
will be upon: I cannot be more particular; for in relating Affairs that so nearly
concern the *Confedarates*, and consequently this Kingdom; I am forced to confine
my self, for several Reasons very obvious to the Reader.

ON the 15th News will arrive of a very *surprizing Event*, than which nothing
could be more unexpected.

ON the 19th, three Noble Ladies of this Kingdom, will, against all Expectation, prove with Child, to the great Joy of their Husbands.   10

ON the 23d, a famous Buffoon of the Play-House will die a ridiculous
Death, suitable to his Vocation.

JUNE. This Month will be distinguished at home, by the utter dispersing
of those ridiculous deluded Enthusiasts, commonly called the *Prophets*; occasioned chiefly by seeing the Time come, when many of their Prophesies were
to be fulfilled; and then finding themselves deceived by contrary Events. It is
indeed to be admired how any Deceiver can be so weak to foretel Things near
at hand; when a very few Months must of Necessity discover the Imposture
to all the World: In this Point less prudent than common Almanack-Makers,
who are so wise to wander in Generals, talk dubiously, and leave to the Reader   20
the Business of interpreting.

ON the 1st of this Month a *French* General will be killed by a random Shot
of a Cannon-Ball.

ON the 6th a Fire will break out in the Suburbs of *Paris*, which will destroy
above a thousand Houses; and seems to be the Foreboding of what will happen,
to the Surprize of all *Europe*, about the End of the following Month.

ON the 10th a great Battle will be fought, which will begin at four of the
Clock in the Afternoon, and last till nine at Night with great Obstinacy, but
no very decisive Event. I shall not name the Place, for the Reasons aforesaid;
but the Commanders on each left Wing will be killed. ——— I see Bonfires   30
and hear the Noise of Guns for a Victory.

ON the 14th there will be a false Report of the *French* King's Death.

ON the 20th Cardinal *Portocarero* will die of a Dissentery, with great Suspicion of Poison; but the Report of his Intention to revolt to King *Charles* will
prove false.

JULY. The 6th of this Month a *certain General* will, by a glorious Action,
recover the Reputation he lost by former Misfortunes.

ON the 12th a *great Commander* will die a Prisoner in the Hands of his
Enemies.

ON the 14th a shameful Discovery will be made of a *French* Jesuit giving   40
Poison to a great Foreign General; and when he is put to the Torture, will make
wonderful Discoveries.

IN short, this will prove a Month of great Action, if I might have Liberty
to relate the Particulars.

AT home, the Death of an old famous Senator will happen on the 15th at
his Country-House, worn with Age and Diseases.

BUT that which will make this Month memorable to all Posterity, is the

Death of the *French* King *Lewis* the Fourteenth, after a Week's Sickness at *Marli*; which will happen on the 29th, about six a-Clock in the Evening. It seems to be an Effect of the Gout in his Stomach, followed by a Flux. And in three Days after Monsieur *Chamillard* will follow his Master, dying suddenly of an Apoplexy.

In this Month likewise an *Ambassador* will die in *London*; but I cannot assign the Day.

AUGUST. The Affairs of *France* will seem to suffer no Change for a while under the Duke of *Burgundy's* Administration. But the Genius that animated the whole Machine being gone, will be the Cause of mighty Turns and Revolutions in the following Year. The new King makes yet little Change either in the Army or the Ministry; but the Libels against his Grandfather, that fly about his very Court, give him Uneasiness.

I see an Express in mighty Haste, with Joy and Wonder in his Looks, arriving by the Break of Day, on the 26th of this Month, having travelled in three Days a prodigious Journey by Land and Sea. In the Evening I hear Bells and Guns, and see the Blazing of a Thousand Bonfires.

A young Admiral, of noble Birth, does likewise this Month gain immortal Honour, by a great Achievement.

The Affairs of *Poland* are this Month entirely settled: *Augustus* resigns his Pretensions, which he had again taken up for some Time: *Stanislaus* is peaceably possessed of the Throne; and the King of *Sweden* declares for the Emperor.

I cannot omit one particular Accident here at home; that near the End of this Month, much Mischief will be done at *Bartholomew* Fair,[8] by the Fall of a Booth.

SEPTEMBER. This Month begins with a very surprizing Fit of frosty Weather, which will last near twelve Days.

The Pope having long languished last Month; the Swellings in his Legs breaking, and the Flesh mortifying, will die on the 11th Instant: And in three Weeks Time, after a might Contest, be succeeded by a Cardinal of the *Imperial* Faction, but Native of *Tuscany*, who is now about Sixty-One Years old.

The *French* Army acts now wholly on the Defensive, strongly fortified in their Trenches; and the young *French* King sends Overtures for a Treaty of Peace, by the Duke of *Mantua*; which, because it is a Matter of State that concerns us here at home, I shall speak no farther of it.

I shall add but one Prediction more, and that in mystical Terms, which shall be included in a Verse out of *Virgil.*

Alter erit jam Tethys, & altera quæ vehat Argo, Delectos Heroas.[9]

Upon the 25th Day of this Month, the fulfiling of this Prediction will be manifest to every Body.

This is the farthest I have proceeded in my Calculations for the present Year. I do not pretend, that these are all the great Events which will happen

---

[8] *Bartholomew Fair:* A fair held annually from 1133 to 1855 in West Smithfield.

[9] *Alter erit . . . Heroas:* Correctly (*Eclogue*, IV, 34), *Alter erit tum Tiphys, et altera quae vehat Argo delectos heroas. . . .*: A second Tiphys shall arise then, and a second Argo to carry chosen heroes.

in this Period; but that those I have set down will infallibly come to pass. It may, perhaps, still be objected, why I have not spoke more particularly of Affairs at home; or of the Success of our Armies abroad, which I might, and could very largely have done. But those in Power have wisely discouraged Men from meddling in publick Concerns; and I was resolved, by no Means, to give the least Offence. This I will venture to say; that it will be a glorious Campaign for the Allies; wherein the *English* Forces, both by Sea and Land, will have their full Share of Honour: That Her Majesty QUEEN ANNE will continue in Health and Prosperity: And that no ill Accident will arrive to any in the chief Ministry.

As to the particular Events I have mentioned, the Readers may judge by   10 the fulfiling of them, whether I am of the Level with common Astrologers; who, with an old paultry Cant, and a few Pot-hooks for Planets to amuse the Vulgar, have, in my Opinion, too long been suffered to abuse the World. But an honest Physician ought not to be despised, because there are such Things as Mountebanks. I hope, I have some Share of Reputation, which I would not willingly forfeit for a Frolick, or Humour: And I believe no Gentleman, who reads this Paper, will look upon it to be of the same Cast, or Mold, with the common Scribbles that are every Day hawked about. My Fortune hath placed me above the little Regard of writing for a few Pence, which I neither value nor want: Therefore, let not wise Men too hastily condemn this Essay, intended for a   20 good Design, to cultivate and improve an antient Art, long in Disgrace by having fallen into mean unskilful Hands. A little Time will determine whether I have deceived others, or my self; and I think it is no very unreasonable Request, that Men would please to suspend their Judgments till then. I was once of the Opinion with those who despise all Predictions from the Stars, till in the Year 1686, a Man of Quality shewed me, written in his *Album*, that the most learned Astronomer Captain *Hally*,[10] assured him, he would never believe any thing of the Stars Influence, if there were not a great Revolution in *England* in the Year 1688. Since that Time I began to have other Thoughts; and after Eighteen Years' diligent Study and Application, I think I have no Reason to repent of my Pains.   30 I shall detain the Reader no longer than to let him know, that the Account I design to give of next Year's Events, shall take in the principal Affairs that happen in *Europe*: And if I be denied the Liberty of offering it to my own Country, I shall appeal to the learned World, by publishing it in *Latin*, and giving Order to have it printed in *Holland*.

(1708)

[10] *Captain   Hally:*   Edmund   Halley   first   to   predict   the   return   of   a   comet.
1656–1742),   English   astronomer,   the

The Accomplishment of the First of Mr. Bickerstaff's Predictions

Being an Account of the Death of Mr. Partrige, the Almanack-Maker, upon the 29th Inst.

IN A LETTER TO A PERSON OF HONOUR

Written in the Year 1708

My LORD,

IN Obedience to your Lordship's Commands, as well as to satisfy my own Curiosity, I have for some Days past enquired constantly after *Partrige* the Almanack-maker; of whom it was foretold in Mr. *Bickerstaff's* Predictions, published about a Month ago, that he should die the 29th Instant, about Eleven at Night, of a raging Fever. I had some Sort of Knowledge of him when I was employed in the Revenue; because he used every Year to present me with his Almanack, as he did other Gentlemen upon the score of some little Gratuity we gave him. I saw him accidentally once or twice about ten Days before he died; and observed he bagan very much to droop and languish, although I hear his Friends did not seem to apprehend him in any Danger. About two or three Days ago he grew ill; was confined first to his Chamber, and in a few Hours after to his Bed; where *Dr. Case and Mrs. Kirleus were sent for to visit, and to prescribe to him. Upon this Intelligence I sent thrice every Day one Servant or other to enquire after his Health; and Yesterday about four in the Afternoon, Word was brought me that he was past Hopes: Upon which I prevailed with my self to go and see him; partly out of Commiseration, and, I confess, partly out of Curiosity. He knew me very well, seemed surprized at my Condescension,[11] and made me Compliments upon it as well as he could in the Condition he was. The People about him said, he had been for some Time delirious; but when I saw him, he had his Understanding as well as ever I knew, and spoke strong and hearty, without any seeming Uneasiness or Constraint. After I had told him I was sorry to see him in those melancholly Circumstances, and said some other Civilities, suitable to the Occasion; I desired him to tell me freely and ingenuously whether the Predictions Mr. *Bickerstaff* had published relating to his Death, had not too much affected and worked on his Imagination. He confessed he often had it in his Head, but never with much Apprehension till about a Fortnight before; since which Time it had the perpetual Possession of his Mind and Thoughts; and he did verily believe was the true natural Cause of his present Distemper: For, said he, I am thoroughly persuaded, and I think I have very good Reasons, that Mr. *Bickerstaff* spoke altogether by guess, and knew no more what will happen this Year than I did my self. I told him his Discourse surprized me; and I would be glad he were in a State of Health to be

10

20

30

---

* *Two famous Quacks at that Time in* London.

11 *Condescension:* Affability.

able to tell me what Reason he had to be convinced of Mr. *Bickerstaff's* Ignorance. He replied, I am a poor ignorant Fellow, bred to a mean Trade; yet I have Sense enough to know, that all Pretences of foretelling by Astrology are Deceits; for this Manifest Reason, because the Wise and Learned, who can only judge whether there be any Truth in this Science, do all unanimously agree to laugh at and dispise it; and none but the poor ignorant Vulgar give it any Credit, and that only upon the Word of such silly Wretches as I and my Fellows, who can hardly write or read. I then asked him, why he had not caluculated his own Nativity, to see whether it agreed with *Bickerstaff's* Predictions? At which he shook his Head, and said, O! Sir, this no Time for jesting, but for repenting 10 those Fooleries, as I do now from the very Bottom of my Heart. By what I can gather from you, said I, the Observations and Predictions you printed with your Almanacks were meer Impositions upon the People. He replied, if it were otherwise, I should have the less to answer for. We have a common Form for all those Things: As to foretelling the Weather, we never meddle with that, but leave it to the Printer, who takes it out of any old Almanack as he thinks fit: The rest was my own Invention to make my Almanack sell; having a Wife to maintain, and no other Way to get my Bread; for mending old Shoes is a poor Livelihood: And (added he, sighing) I wish I may not have done more Mischief by my Physick than my Astrology; although I had some good Receipts from 20 my Grandmother, and my own Compositions were such, as I thought could, at least do no Hurt.

I HAD some other Discourse with him, which now I cannot call to Mind; and I fear I have already tired your Lordship. I shall only add one Circumstance, That on his Death-Bed he declared himself a Nonconformist, and had a fanatick Preacher to be his spiritual Guide. After half an Hour's Conversation, I took my Leave, being almost stifled by the Closeness of the Room. I imagined he could not hold out long; and therefore withdrew to a little Coffee-House hard by, leaving a Servant at the House with Orders to come immediately, and tell me, as near as he could, the Minute when *Partrige* should expire, which was not 30 above two Hours after; when looking upon my Watch, I found it to be above five Minutes after Seven: By which it is clear, that Mr. *Bickerstaff* was mistaken almost four Hours in his Calculation. In the other Circumstances he was exact enough. But whether he hath not been the Cause of this poor Man's Death, as well as the Predictor, may be very reasonably disputed. However, it must be confessed, the Matter is odd enough, whether we should endeavour to account for it by Chance or the Effect of Imagination: For my own Part, although I believe no Man hath less Faith in these Matters; yet I shall wait with some Impatience, and not without Expectation, the fulfilling of Mr. *Bickerstaff's* second Prediction; that the Cardinal *de Noailles* is to die upon the 4th of *April*; and if 40 that should be verified as exactly as this of poor *Partrige*; I must own, I should be wholly surprized, and at a Loss; and infallibly expect the Accomplishment of all the rest.

(1708)

The following Piece, under the Name of John Partrige, was written by that famous Poet Nicholas Row, Esq; and therefore being upon the same Subject, although not by the same Author, we have thought fit to publish it, that the Reader may have the whole Account together.

'Squire Bickerstaff Detected

OR, THE ASTROLOGICAL IMPOSTOR CONVICTED

BY JOHN PARTRIGE, STUDENT IN PHYSICK AND ASTROLOGY

It is hard, my dear Countrymen of these united Nations: It is very hard, that a *Briton* born, a Protestant Astrologer, a Man of Revolution Principles, an Asserter of the Liberty and Property of the People, should cry out, in vain for Justice against a *Frenchman*, a Papist, and an illiterate Pretender to Science; that would blast my Reputation, most inhumanly bury me alive, and defraud my Native Country of those Services, which in my *double Capacity, I daily offer the Publick.

WHAT great Provocations I have received, let the impartial Reader judge, and how unwillingly, even in my own Defence, I now enter the Lists against Falshood, Ignorance, and Envy: But I am exasperated at length, to drag out this 10
Cacus[12] from the Den of Obscurity where he lurks, detect him by the Light of those Stars he has so impudently traduced, and shew there is not a Monster in the Skies so pernicious and malevolent to Mankind, as an ignorant Pretender to Physick and Astrology. I shall not directly fall on the many gross Errors, nor expose the notorious Absurdities of this prostituted Libeller, till I have let the learned World fairly into the Controversy depending, and then leave the unprejudiced to judge of the Merits and Justice of my Cause.

IT was towards the Conclusion of the Year 1707, when an impudent Pamphlet crept into the World, intituled, *Predictions*, &c. *by* Isaac Bickerstaff, *Esq*; Among the many arrogant Assertions laid down by that lying Spirit of Divin- 20
ation, he was pleased to pitch on the Cardinal *de Noailles*, and my self, among many other eminent and illustrious Persons, that were to die within the Compass of the ensuing Year; and peremptorily fixes the Month, Day, and Hour of our Deaths: This, I think, is sporting with great Men, and publick Spirits, to he Scandal of Religion, and Reproach of Power; and if sovereign Princes, and

---

* *Physician and Astrologer.*

---

[12] *Cacus:* A monster or brigand who
lived in a cave.

Astrologers, must make Diversion for the Vulgar; why then, farewel, say I, to all Governments, Ecclesiastical and Civil. But, I thank my better Stars, I am alive to confront this false and audacious Predictor, and to make him rue the Hour he ever affronted a Man of Science and Resentment. The Cardinal may take what Measures he pleases with him; as his Excellency is a Foreigner, and a Papist, he has no Reason to rely on me for his Justification; I shall only assure the World he is alive; but as he was bred to Letters, and is Master of a Pen, let him use it in his own Defence. In the mean Time, I shall present the Publick with a faithful Narrative of the ungenerous Treatment, and hard Usage, I have received from the virulent Papers, and malicious Practices of this pretended   10 Astrologer.

(1708)

A MEDITATION UPON A BROOM-STICK

During one of his visits to England, probably in 1704, Swift stayed with the Berkeleys and served as chaplain to the family. Lady Berkeley was at the time particularly drawn to the very devout *Meditations* of the Hon. Robert Boyle, and she had one read to her each day. Swift, it seems, did not share her relish for these pious utterances. Having composed his own *Meditation Upon A Broom-Stick*, he slipped a copy of it into the volume of Boyle's, and in response to the Lady's request for the next meditation, Swift read his own in solemn tones.

TEXT. *The Works of Jonathan Swift* (Dublin, 1735).

A Meditation upon a Broom-stick

ACCORDING TO THE STYLE AND MANNER OF THE HONOURABLE ROBERT BOYLE'S MEDITATIONS

WRITTEN IN THE YEAR 1703

THIS single Stick, which you now behold ingloriously lying in that neglected Corner, I once knew in a flourishing State in a Forest: It was full of Sap, full of Leaves, and full of Boughs: But now, in vain does the busy Art of Man pretend to vye with Nature, by tying that withered Bundle of Twigs to its sapless Trunk: It is now at best but the Reverse of what it was; a Tree turned upside down, the Branches on the Earth, and the Root in the Air: It is now handled by every dirty Wench, condemned to do her Drugery; and by a capricious Kind of Fate, destined to make other Things clean, and be nasty it self. At length, worn to the Stumps in the Service of the Maids, it is either thrown out of Doors, or condemned to the last Use of kindling a Fire. When I beheld this, I sighed, and said within my self SURELY MORTAL MAN IS A BROOMSTICK; Nature sent him into the World strong and lusty, in a thriving Condition, wearing his own Hair on his Head, the proper Branches of this reasoning Vegetable; till the Axe of Intemperance has lopped off his Green Boughs, and left him a withered Trunk: He then flies to Art, and puts on a *Perriwig*; valuing himself upon an unnatural Bundle of Hairs, all covered with Powder, that never grew on his Head: But now, should this our *Broom-stick* pretend to enter the Scene, proud of those *Birchen* Spoils it never bore, and all covered with Dust, though the sweepings of the finest Lady's Chamber; we should be apt to ridicule and despise its Vanity. Partial Judges that we are of our own Excellencies and other   10 Mens Defaults!

BUT a *Broom-stick*, perhaps you will say, is an Emblem of a Tree standing on its Head; and pray what is Man but a topsy-turvy Creature? His Animal Faculties perpetually mounted on his Rational; his Head where his Heels should be, groveling on the Earth. And yet, with all his Faults, he sets up to be a universal Reformer and Correcter of Abuses; a Remover of Grievances; rakes into every Slut's Corner of Nature, bringing hidden Corruptions to the Light, and raiseth a mighty Dust where there was none before; sharing deeply all the while in the very same Pollutions he pretends to sweep away. His last Days are spent in Slavery to Women, and generally the least deserving; till worn to the Stumps,   20 like his Brother *Bezom*,[1] he is either kicked out of Doors, or made use of to kindle Flames for others to warm themselves by.

(1710)

[1] *Bezom:* Figuratively, any agent that weeps away or cleanses.

AN ARGUMENT AGAINST ABOLISHING CHRISTIANITY

The full title of Swift's ironical essay *An Argument To prove, That the Abolishing of Christianity In England, May, as Things now stand, be attended with some Inconveniencies, and perhaps, not produce those many good Effects proposed thereby* is the strongest possible clue to his method. His narrator is a nominal Christian who urges his fellow skeptics to reconsider their willingness to do away with Christianity. He argues that a religion to which people merely pay lip service can do them no harm; moreover it is valuable as a basis for credit in international trade, as an object of ridicule for the wits, and as a prohibition that makes vice doubly exciting. The piece derives much of the force of its attack upon the self-serving nature of merely public religion from the unfaltering point of view of the agnostic narrator. Swift composed the piece in 1708, while he was still a Whig. It has been suggested that it foreshadows his change of party two years later, a change thought to be largely motivated by his anger over the religious skepticism of Whig politicians.

TEXT. *The Works of Jonathan Swift* (Dublin, 1735).

An Argument to prove, That the Abolishing of Christianity in England

MAY, AS THINGS NOW STAND, BE ATTENDED WITH SOME INCONVENIENCIES, AND PERHAPS, NOT PRODUCE THOSE MANY GOOD EFFECTS PROPOSED THEREBY

WRITTEN IN THE YEAR 1708

I AM very sensible what a Weakness and Presumption it is, to reason against the general Humour and Disposition of the World. I remember it was with great Justice, and a due Regard to the Freedom both of the Publick and the Press, forbidden upon severe Penalties to write or discourse, or lay Wagers against the *Union*,[1] even before it was confirmed by Parliament; Because that was looked upon as a Design to oppose the Current of the People; which besides the Folly of it, is a manifest Breach of the Fundamental Law, that makes this Majority of Opinion the Voice of God. In like Manner, and for the very same Reasons, it may perhaps be neither safe nor prudent to argue against the Abolishing of Christianity, at a Juncture when all Parties appear so unanimously determined upon the Point; as we cannot but allow from their Actions, their Discourses, and their Writings. However, I know not how, whether   10 from the Affectation of Singularity, or the Perverseness of human Nature; but so it unhappily falls out, that I cannot be entirely of this Opinion. Nay, although I were sure an Order were issued out for my immediate Prosecution by the Attorney-General; I should still confess, that in the present Posture of our Affairs at home or abroad, I do not yet see the absolute Necessity of extirpating the Christian Religion from among us.

THIS perhaps may appear too great a Paradox, even for our wise and paradoxical Age to endure: Therefore I shall handle it with all Tenderness, and with the utmost Deference to that great and profound Majority, which is of another Sentiment.   20

AND yet the Curious may please to observe, how much the Genius of a Nation is liable to alter in half an Age: I have heard it affirmed for certain by some very old People, that the contrary Opinion was even in their Memories as much in Vogue as the other is now; and that a Project for the Abolishing Christianity would then have appeared as singular, and been thought as absurd, as it would be at this Time to write or discourse in its Defence.

THEREFORE I freely own, that all Appearances are against me. The System of the Gospel, after the Fate of other Systems is generally antiquated and exploded; and the Mass or Body of the common People, among whom it seems to have had its latest Credit, are now grown as much ashamed of it as their Betters: 30 Opinions, like Fashions always descending from those of Quality to the middle Sort, and thence to the Vulgar, where at length they are dropt and vanish.

BUT here I would not be mistaken; and must therefore be so bold as to borrow a Distinction from the Writers on the other Side, when they make a Difference between nominal and real *Trinitarians*.[2] I hope, no Reader imagines me so weak to stand up in the Defence of *real* Christianity; such as used in primitive Times (if we may believe the Authors of those Ages) to have an Influence upon Mens Belief and Actions: To offer at the Restoring of that, would indeed be a wild Project; it would be to dig up Foundations; to destroy at one Blow *all* the Wit, and *half* the Learning of the Kingdom; to break the entire   40 Frame and Constitution of Things; to ruin Trade, extinguish Arts and Sciences

---

[1] *Against the Union:* The union of England and Scotland, 1707. Swift's entire first paragraph takes into account the occasion to which he addresses himself. The Test Act of 1672, which required those who held public office to take communion in the Church of England, was close to repeal, because the Whigs hoped to win the votes of Dissenters by the action.

Swift, though still friendly to the Whig Party, was a loyal Church of England man, who here offers his ironical censure of politically motivated changes in religion.

[2] *Trinitarians:* Those who hold the Trinity of the Godhead, the belief that Father, Son, and Holy Spirit constitute one God.

with the Professors of them; in short, to turn our Courts, Exchanges and Shops into Desarts: And would be full as absurd as the Proposal of *Horace*, where he advises the *Romans*, all in a Body, to leave their City, and seek a new Seat in some remote Part of the World, by Way of Cure for the Corruption of their Manners.

THEREFORE, I think this Caution was in it self altogether unnecessary (which I have inserted only to prevent all Possibility of cavilling), since every candid Reader will easily understand my Discourse to be intended only in Defence of *nominal* Christianity; the other having been for some Time wholly laid aside by general Consent, as utterly inconsistent with our present Schemes of Wealth and Power.

BUT why we should therefore cast off the Name and Title of Christians, although the general Opinion and Resolution be so violent for it; I confess I cannot (with Submission) apprehend the Consequence necessary. However, since the Undertakers propose such wonderful Advantages to the Nation by this Project; and advance many plausible Objections against the System of Christianity; I shall briefly consider the Strength of both; fairly allow them their greatest Weight, and offer such Answers as I think most reasonable. After which I will beg leave to show what Inconveniencies may possibly happen by such an Innovation, in the present Posture of our Affairs.

First, ONE great Advantage proposed by the Abolishing of Christianity is, That it would very much enlarge and establish Liberty of Conscience, that great Bulwark of our Nation, and of the *Protestant* Religion, which is still too much limited by *Priest-Craft*, notwithstanding all the good Intentions of the Legislature; as we have lately found by a severe Instance. For it is confidently reported, that two young Gentlemen of great Hopes, bright Wit, and profound Judgment, who upon a thorough Examination of Causes and Effects, and by the meer Force of natural Abilities, without the least Tincture of Learning; having made a Discovery, that there was no God, and generously communicating their Thoughts for the Good of the Publick; were some Time ago, by an unparalleled Severity, and upon I know not what *obsolete* Law, broke *only* for *Blasphemy*. And as it hath been wisely observed, if Persecution once begins, no Man alive knows how far it may reach, or where it will end.

IN Answer to all which, with Deference to wiser Judgments; I think this rather shews the Necessity of a *nominal* Religion among us. Great Wits love to be free with the highest Objects; and if they cannot be allowed a *God* to revile or renounce; they will *Speak Evil of Dignities*, abuse the Government, and reflect upon the Ministry; which I am sure, few will deny to be of much more pernicious Consequence; according to the Saying of *Tiberius*, *Deorum offensa Diis curæ*.[3] As to the particular Fact related; I think it is not fair to argue from one Instance; perhaps another cannot be produced; yet (to the Comfort of all those, who may be apprehensive of Persecution) Blasphemy we know is freely spoke a Million of Times in every Coffee-House and Tavern, or whereever else *good Company* meet. It must be allowed indeed, that to break an *English Free-born* Officer only for Blasphemy, was, to speak the gentlest of such

10

20

30

40

---

[3] *Deorum offensa Diis curæ:* Insults to the gods must be their own affair. The source is Tacitus, *Annales*, I, 73, not Tiberius.

an Action, a very high Strain of absolute Power. Little can be said in Excuse for the General; perhaps he was afraid it might give Offence to the Allies, among whom, for ought I know, it may be the Custom of the Country to believe a God. But if he argued, as some have done, upon a mistaken Principle, that an Officer who is guilty of speaking Blasphemy, may, some Time or other, proceed so far as to raise a Mutiny; the Consequence is, by no Means, to be admitted: For, surely the Commander of an *English* Army is like to be but ill obeyed, whose Soldiers fear and reverence him as little as they do a Deity.

It is further objected against the Gospel System, that it obliges Men to the Belief of Things too difficult for Free-Thinkers, and such who have shaken off   10 the Prejudices that usually cling to a confined Education. To which I answer, that Men should be cautious how they raise Objections, which reflect upon the Wisdom of the Nation. Is not every Body freely allowed to believe whatever he pleaseth; and to publish his Belief to the World whenever he thinks fit; especially if it serve to strengthen the Party which is in the Right? Would any indifferent Foreigner, who should read the Trumpery lately written by *Asgill, Tindall, Toland, Coward,*[4] and Forty more, imagine the Gospel to be our Rule of Faith, and confirmed by Parliaments? Does any Man either believe, or say he believes, or desire to have it thought that he says he believes one Syllable of the Matter? And is any Man worse received upon that Score; or does he   20 find his Want of *Nominal* Faith a Disadvantage to him, in the Pursuit of any Civil, or Military Employment? What if there be an old dormant Statute or two against him? Are they not now obsolete, to a Degree, that *Empson* and *Dudley*[5] themselves, if they were now alive, would find it impossible to put them in Execution?

It is likewise urged, that there are, by Computation, in this Kingdom, above ten Thousand Parsons; whose Revenues added to those of my Lords the Bishops, would suffice to maintain, at least, two Hundred young Gentlemen of Wit and Pleasure, and Free-thinking; Enemies to Priest-craft, narrow Principles, Pedantry, and Prejudices; who might be an Ornament to the Court and Town: 30 And then again, so great a Number of able (bodied) Divines might be a Recruit to our Fleet and Armies. This, indeed, appears to be a Consideration of some Weight: But then, on the other Side, several Things deserve to be considered likewise: As, First, Whether it may not be thought necessary, that in certain Tracts of Country, like what we call Parishes, there should be *one* Man at least, of Abilities to read and write. Then, it seems a wrong Computation, that the Revenues of the Church throughout this Island, would be large enough to maintain two Hundred young Gentlemen, or even Half that Number, after the present refined Way of Living; that is, to allow each of them such a Rent, as, in the modern Form of Speech, would make them *easy*. But still, there is in this   40

---

[4] *Asgill, Tindall, Toland, Coward:* John Asgill (1659–1738) wrote a pamphlet to prove that by the rules of English law the redeemed need not die; Matthew Tindal (1656–1733) was an English deistical author best known for *Christianity as old as the Creation*; John Toland (1670–1722) was an Irish deistical writer whose *Christianity not Mysterious* adopted a rationalistic attitude;

William Coward (1657?–1725), whose *Estibius Psychalethes* denies the spirituality and immortality of the human soul.

[5] *Empson and Dudley:* These men, ministers of Henry VII, were known for their ability to exact taxes and penalties due the crown. The people thought them tyrannical.

Project a greater Mischief behind; and we ought to beware of the Woman's Folly, who killed the Hen, that every Morning laid her a Golden Egg. For, pray, what would become of the Race of Men in the next Age, if we had nothing to trust to, besides the scrophulous consumptive Productions furnished by our Men of Wit and Pleasure; when having squandered away their Vigour, Health, and Estates; they are forced, by some disagreeable Marriage, to piece up their broken Fortunes, and entail Rottenness and Politeness on their Posterity? Now, here are ten Thousand Persons[6] reduced by the wise Regulations of *Henry* the Eighth, to the Necessity of a low Diet, and moderate Exercise, who are the only great Restorers of our Breed; without which, the Nation would, in   10 an Age or two, become but one great Hospital.

ANOTHER Advantage proposed by the abolishing of Christianity, is, the clear Gain of one Day in Seven, which is now entirely lost, and consequently the Kingdom one Seventh less considerable in Trade, Business, and Pleasure; beside the Loss to the Publick of so many stately Structures now in the Hands of the Clergy; which might be converted into Theatres, Exchanges, Markethouses, common Dormitories, and other publick Edifices.

I HOPE I shall be forgiven a hard Word, if I call this a perfect Cavil. I readily own there hath been an old Custom, Time out of Mind, for People to assemble in the Churches every *Sunday*, and that Shops are still frequently shut;   20 in order, as it is conceived, to preserve the Memory of that antient Practice; but how this can prove a Hindrance to Business, or Pleasure, is hard to imagine. What if the Men of Pleasure are forced, one Day in the Week, to game at home, instead of the *Chocolate-House*? Are not the *Taverns* and *Coffee-Houses* open? Can there be a more convenient Season for taking a Dose of Physick? Are fewer Claps[7] got upon *Sundays* than other Days? Is not that the chief Day for Traders to sum up the Accounts of the Week; and for Lawyers to prepare their Briefs? But I would fain know how it can be pretended, that the Churches are misapplied. Where are more Appointments and Rendezvouzes of Gallantry? Where more Care to appear in the foremost Box with greater Advantage of Dress?   30 Where more Meetings for Business? Where more Bargains driven of all Sorts? And where so many Conveniences, or Incitements to sleep?

THERE is one Advantage, greater than any of the foregoing, proposed by the abolishing of Christianity; that it will utterly extinguish Parties among us, by removing those factious Distinctions of High and Low Church, of *Whig* and *Tory, Presbyterian* and *Church-of-England*; which are now so many grievous Clogs upon publick Proceedings, and dispose Men to prefer the gratifying themselves, or depressing their Adversaries, before the most important Interest of the State.

I CONFESS, if it were certain that so great an Advantage would redound to the   40 Nation by this Expedient, I would submit and be silent: But, will any Man say, that if the Words *Whoring, Drinking, Cheating, Lying, Stealing*, were, by Act of Parliament, ejected out of the *English* Tongue and Dictionaries; we should all awake next Morning chaste and temperate, honest and just, and Lovers of Truth. Is this a fair Consequence? Or if the Physicians would forbid us to pro-

---

[6] *Ten Thousand Persons:* The clergymen of the Church of England, whose livings were created by Henry's break with Rome.
[7] *Claps:* Gonorrhoea.

nounce the Words *Pox*, *Gout*, *Rheumatism*, and *Stone*; would that Expedient serve like so many *Talismans*[8] to destroy the Diseases themselves? Are Party and Faction rooted in Men's Hearts no deeper than Phrases borrowed from Religion; or founded upon no firmer Principles? And is our Language so poor, that we cannot find other Terms to express them? Are Envy, Pride, Avarice and Ambition, such ill Nomenclators,[9] that they cannot furnish Appellations for their Owners? Will not *Heydukes* and *Mamalukes*, *Mandarins*, and *Potshaws*, or any other Words formed at Pleasure, serve to distinguish those who are in the *Ministry* from others, who *would be in it if they could*? What, for Instance, is easier than to vary the Form of Speech; and instead of the Word *Church*, make 10 it a Question in Politicks, Whether the *Monument* be in Danger? Because Religion was nearest at Hand to furnish a few convenient Phrases; is our Invention so barren, we can find no other? Suppose, for Argument Sake, that the *Tories* favoured *Margarita, the *Whigs* Mrs. *Tofts*, and the *Trimmers*[10] *Valentini*; would not *Margaritians*, *Toftians*, and *Valentinians*, be very tolerable Marks of Distinction? The *Prasini* and *Veneti*, two most virulent Factions in *Italy*, began (if I remember right) by a Distinction of Colours in Ribbons; which we might do, with as good a Grace, about the Dignity of the *Blue* and the *Green*; and would serve as properly to divide the Court, the Parliament, and the Kingdom between them, as any Terms of Art whatsoever, borrowed from Religion. Therefore, 20 I think there is little Force in this Objection against *Christianity*; or Prospect of so great an Advantage as is proposed in the Abolishing of it.

IT is again objected, as a very absurd, ridiculous Custom, that a Set of Men should be suffered, much less employed, and hired to bawl one Day in Seven, against the Lawfulness of those Methods most in Use towards the Pursuit of Greatness, Riches, and Pleasure; which are the constant Practice of all Men alive on the other Six. But this Objection is, I think, a little unworthy so refined an Age as ours. Let us argue this Matter calmly. I appeal to the Breast of any polite Free-Thinker, whether in the Pursuit of gratifying a predominant Passion, he hath not always felt a wonderful Incitement, by reflecting it was a Thing for- 30 bidden: And therefore we see, in order to cultivate this Taste, the Wisdom of the Nation hath taken special Care, that the Ladies should be furnished with prohibited Silks, and the Men with prohibited Wine: And, indeed, it were to be wished, that some other Prohibitions were promoted, in order to improve the Pleasures of the Town; which, for want of such Expedients, begin already, as I am told, to flag and grow languid; giving way daily to cruel Inroads from the Spleen.

IT is likewise proposed, as a great Advantage to the Publick, that if we once discard the System of the Gospel, all Religion will, of Course, be banished for ever; and consequently along with it, those grievous Prejudices of Education; 40 which, under the Names of Virtue, Conscience, Honour, Justice, and the like, are so apt to disturb the Peace of human Minds; and the Notions whereof are

* Italian *Singers then in Vogue.*

---

[8] *Talismans:* Charms warding off evil.
[9] *Nomenclators:* Lists of words, vocabularies.

[10] *Trimmers:* One who inclines to each of two opposite parties, as interest dictates, is a trimmer.

so hard to be eradicated by right Reason, or Free-thinking, sometimes during the whole Course of our Lives.

HERE, first, I observe how difficult it is to get rid of a Phrase, which the World is once grown fond of, although the Occasion that first produced it, be entirely taken away. For several Years past, if a Man had but an ill-favoured Nose, the Deep-Thinkers of the Age would, some way or other, contrive to impute the Cause to the Prejudice of his Education. From this Fountain are said to be derived all our foolish Notions of Justice, Piety, Love of our Country; all our Opinions of God, or a future State, Heaven, Hell, and the like: And there might formerly, perhaps, have been some Pretence for this Charge. But so effectual Care hath been since taken, to remove those Prejudices by an entire Change in the Methods of Education; that (with Honour I mention it to our polite Innovators) the young Gentlemen, who are now on the Scene, seem to have not the least Tincture left of those Infusions, or String of those Weeds; and, by Consequence, the Reason for abolishing *Nominal* Christianity upon that Pretext, is wholly ceased.

FOR the rest, it may perhaps admit a Controversy, whether the Banishing all Notions of Religion whatsoever, would be convenient for the Vulgar. Not that I am, in the least of Opinion with those, who hold Religion to have been the Invention of Politicians, to keep the lower Part of the World in Awe, by the Fear of invisible Powers; unless Mankind were then very different from what it is now: For I look upon the Mass, or Body of our People here in *England*, to be as Free-Thinkers, that is to say, as stanch Unbelievers, as any of the highest Rank. But I conceive some scattered Notions about a superior Power to be of singular Use for the common People, as furnishing excellent Materials to keep Children quiet, when they grow peevish; and providing Topicks of Amusement in a tedious Winter Night.

LASTLY, It is proposed as a singular Advantage, that the Abolishing of Christianity, will very much contribute to the uniting of *Protestants*, by enlarging the Terms of Communion, so as to take in all Sorts of *Dissenters*; who are now shut out of the Pale upon Account of a few Ceremonies, which all Sides confess to be Things indifferent: That this alone will effectually answer the great Ends of a Scheme for Comprehension, by opening a large noble Gate, at which all Bodies may enter; whereas the chaffering with *Dissenters*, and dodging about this or the other Ceremony, is but like opening a few Wickets, and leaving them at jar, by which no more than one can get in at a Time, and that not without stooping and sideling, and squeezing his Body.

To all this I answer, That there is one darling Inclination of Mankind, which usually affects to be a Retainer to Religion, although she be neither its Parent, its Godmother, or its Friend; I mean the Spirit of Opposition, that lived long before Christianity, and can easily subsist without it. Let us, for Instance, examine wherein the Opposition of Sectaries among us consists; we shall find Christianity to have no Share in it at all. Does the Gospel any where prescribe a starched squeezed Countenance, a stiff formal Gait, a Singularity of Manners and Habit, or any affected Modes of Speech, different from the reasonable Part of Mankind? Yet, if Christianity did not lend its Name, to stand in the Gap, and to employ or divert these Humours, they must of Necessity be spent in Contraventions to the Laws of the Land, and Disturbance of the publick Peace. There is a Portion of Enthusiasm assigned to every Nation, which if it hath not proper Objects to work on, will burst out, and set all in a Flame. If the Quiet of a State can be bought by only flinging Men a few Ceremonies to devour, it is a Purchase no wise Man would refuse. Let the Mastiffs amuse themselves about a Sheep-skin stuffed with Hay, provided it will keep them from worrying the Flock. The Institution of Convents abroad, seems in one Point a Strain of great Wisdom; there being few Irregularities in human Passions, that may not have recourse to vent themselves in some of those Orders; which are so many Retreats for the Speculative, the Melancholy, the Proud, the Silent, the Poli-   10 tick and the Morose, to spend themselves, and evaporate the noxious Particles; for each of whom, we in this Island are forced to provide a several Sect of Religion, to keep them quiet. And whenever Christianity shall be abolished, the Legislature must find some other Expedient to employ and entertain them. For what imports it, how large a Gate you open, if there will be always left a Number, who place a Pride and a Merit in refusing to enter?

HAVING thus considered the most important Objections against Christianity, and the chief Advantages proposed by the Abolishing thereof; I shall now with equal Deference and Submission to wiser Judgments as before, proceed to mention a few Inconveniences that may happen, if the Gospel should be repealed;   20 which perhaps the Projectors may not have sufficiently considered.

AND first, I am very sensible how much the Gentlemen of Wit and Pleasure are apt to murmur, and be choqued at the Sight of so many daggled-tail Parsons, who happen to fall in their Way, and offend their Eyes: But at the same Time these wise Reformers do not consider what an Advantage and Felicity it is, for great Wits to be always provided with Objects of Scorn and Contempt, in order to exercise and improve their Talents, and divert their Spleen from falling on each other, or on themselves; especially when all this may be done without the least imaginable *Danger to their Persons*.

AND to urge another Argument of a parallel Nature: If Christianity were   30 once abolished, how could the Free-Thinkers, the strong Reasoners, and the Men of profound Learning be able to find another Subject so calculated in all Points whereon to display their Abilities. What wonderful Productions of Wit should we be deprived of, from those whose Genius, by continual Practice hath been wholly turned upon Raillery and Invectives against Religion; and would therefore never be able to shine or distinguish themselves upon any other Subject. We are daily complaining of the great Decline of Wit among us; and would we take away the greatest, perhaps the only Topick we have left? Who would ever have suspected *Asgill* for a Wit, or *Toland* for a Philosopher, if the inexhaustible Stock of Christianity had not been at hand to provide them   40 with Materials? What other Subject through all Art or Nature could have produced *Tindal* for a profound Author, or furnished him with Readers? It is the wise Choice of the Subject that alone adorns and distinguishes the Writer. For had an hundred such Pens as these been employed on the Side of Religion, they would have immediately sunk into Silence and Oblivion.

NOR do I think it wholly groundless, or my Fears altogether imaginary; that the Abolishing of Christianity may perhaps bring the Church in Danger;

or at least put the Senate to the Trouble of another Securing Vote. I desire, I may not be mistaken; I am far from presuming to affirm or think, that the Church is in Danger at present, or as Things now stand; but we know not how soon it may be so, when the Christian Religion is repealed. As plausible as this Project seems, there may a dangerous Design lurk under it. Nothing can be more notorious, than that the *Atheists, Deists, Socinians, Anti-Trinitarians,* and other Subdivisions of Free-Thinkers, are Persons of little Zeal for the present Ecclesiastical Establishment: Their declared Opinion is for repealing the Sacramental Test;[11] they are very indifferent with regard to Ceremonies; nor do they hold the *Jus Divinum*[12] of Episcopacy.[13] Therefore this may be intended as one politick Step towards altering the Constitution of the Church Established, and setting up *Presbytery* in the stead; which I leave to be further considered by those at the Helm.

In the last Place, I think nothing can be more plain, than that by this Expedient, we shall run into the Evil we chiefly pretend to avoid; and that the Abolishment of the Christian Religion, will be the readiest Course we can take to introduce Popery. And I am the more inclined to this Opinion, because we know it hath been the constant Practice of the *Jesuits* to send over Emissaries, with Instructions to personate themselves Members of the several prevailing Sects amongst us. So it is recorded, that they have at sundry Times appeared in the Guise of *Presbyterians, Anabaptists, Independents,* and *Quakers,* according as any of these were most in Credit: So, since the Fashion hath been taken up of exploding Religion, the *Popish* Missionaries have not been wanting to mix with the Free-Thinkers; among whom, *Toland,* the great Oracle of the *Anti-Christians,* is an *Irish* Priest, the Son of an *Irish* Priest; and the most learned and ingenious Author of a Book, called the *Rights of the Christian Church,* was, in a proper Juncture, reconciled to the *Romish* Faith; whose true Son, as appears by an Hundred Passages in his Treatise, he still continues. Perhaps I could add some others to the Number; but the Fact is beyond Dispute; and the Reasoning they proceed by, is right: For, supposing Christianity to be extinguished, the People will never be at Ease, till they find out some other Method of Worship; which will as infallibly produce Superstition, as this will end in *Popery.*

And therefore, if, notwithstanding all I have said, it shall still be thought necessary to have a Bill brought in for repealing Christianity; I would humbly offer an Amendment, that instead of the Word *Christianity,* may be put *Religion* in general; which I conceive, will much better answer all the good Ends proposed by the Projectors of it. For, as long as we leave in Being a God, and his Providence, with all the necessary Consequences, which curious and inquisitive Men will be apt to draw from such Premises; we do not strike at the Root of the Evil, although we should ever so effectually annihilate the present Scheme of the Gospel. For, of what Use is Freedom of Thought, if it will not produce Freedom of Action; which is the sole End, how remote soever, in Appearance,

[11] *Sacramental Test:* See the Test Act discussed in n. 1.
[12] *Jus Divinum:* Divine right or law.
[13] *Episcopacy:* Government of the church by bishops, as is the case in the Church of England, but not among Dissenters. See n. 1.

of all Objections against Christianity? And therefore, the Free-Thinkers consider it as a Sort of Edifice, wherein all the Parts have such a mutual Dependance on each other, that if you happen to pull out one single Nail, the whole Fabrick must fall to the Ground. This was happily expressed by him, who had heard of a Text brought for Proof of the Trinity, which in an antient Manuscript was differently read; he thereupon immediately took the Hint, and by a sudden Deduction of a long *Sorites*,[14] most logically concluded; Why, if it be as you say, I may safely whore and drink on, and defy the Parson. From which, and many the like Instances easy to be produced, I think noth- ing can be more manifest, than that the Quarrel is not against any particular   10 Points of hard Digestion in the Christian System; but against Religion in general; which, by laying Restraints on human Nature, is supposed the great Enemy to the Freedom of Thought and Action.

UPON the whole; if it shall still be thought for the Benefit of Church and State, that Christianity be abolished; I conceive, however, it may be more convenient to defer the Execution to a Time of Peace; and not venture in this Conjuncture to disoblige our Allies; who, as it falls out, are all Chris- tians; and many of them, by the Prejudices of their Education, so bigotted, as to place a Sort of Pride in the Appellation. If, upon being rejected by them, we are to trust to an Alliance with the *Turk*, we shall find our selves   20 much deceived: For, as he is too remote, and generally engaged in War with the *Persian* Emperor; so his People would be more scandalized at our Infidelity, than our Christian Neighbours. Because, the *Turks* are not only strict Observers of religious Worship; but, what is worse, believe a God; which is more than is required of us, even while we preserve the Name of Christians.

To conclude: Whatever some may think of the great Advantages to Trade, by this favourite Scheme; I do very much apprehend, that in six Months Time, after the Act is past for the Extirpation of the Gospel, the Bank and *East-India* Stock may fall, at least, One *per Cent*. And, since that is   30 Fifty Times more than ever the Wisdom of our Age thought fit to venture for the *Preservation* of Christianity, there is no Reason we should be at so great a Loss, meerly for the Sake of *destroying* it.

(1710)

[14] *Sorites:* A conclusion reached by accumulation of arguments.

Headnote to
A MODEST PROPOSAL

Swift's narrator here is a cool economist of sorts, who never experiences the least flicker of a doubt concerning the rationality of his extraordinary proposal for the relief of the poor people of Ireland. One measure of the power of Swift's irony in this piece is the frequency with which the author himself is scored, by perplexed readers, for its cruelty and bad taste. It seems likely that those who have censured Swift in fact blame him for making them feel too keenly the evil he treats satirically in this essay. Even for the modern reader, the predicament of the downtrodden in eighteenth-century Ireland probably serves as an emblem for any related social evil in his own world, and so he may respond strongly to Swift's satire, which is topical and confined at only the most obvious level of meaning. The fact seems to be that Swift's treatment of the Irish poor may cause one to feel more pain than can be put to immediate productive use. That is, though Swift may move his readers deeply, some of them at first seem unable to give constructive shape to their response; they are inspired neither to social action, nor to meditation, nor to pleasure in his art, but to the desire to be rid of the source of their discomfort.

TEXT. *The Works of Jonathan Swift* (Dublin, 1735).

A Modest Proposal

*FOR PREVENTING THE CHILDREN OF
POOR PEOPLE IN IRELAND, FROM BEING A
BURDEN TO THEIR PARENTS OR
COUNTRY; AND FOR MAKING THEM
BENEFICIAL TO THE PUBLICK*

WRITTEN IN THE YEAR 1729

It is a melancholly Object to those, who walk through this great Town, or travel in the Country; when they see the *Streets*, the *Roads*, and *Cabbins-doors* crowded with *Beggars* of the Female Sex, followed by three,

464

four, or six Children, *all in Rags*, and importuning every Passenger for an Alms. These *Mothers*, instead of being able to work for their honest Livelyhood, are forced to employ all their Time in stroling to beg Sustenance for their *helpless Infants*; who, as they grow up, either turn *Thieves* for want of Work; or leave their *dear Native Country, to fight for the Pretender*[1] *in* Spain; or sell themselves to the *Barbadoes*.

I THINK it is agreed by all Parties, that this prodigious Number of Children in the Arms, or on the Backs, or at the *Heels* of their *Mothers*, and frequently of their *Fathers*, is *in the present deplorable State of the Kingdom*, a very great additional Grievance; and therefore, whoever could find out a fair, cheap, 10 and easy Method of making these Children sound and useful Members of the Commonwealth; would deserve so well of the Publick, as to have his Statue set up for a Preserver of the Nation.

BUT my Intention is very far from being confined to provide only for the Children of *professed Beggars*: It is of a much greater Extent, and shall take in the whole Number of Infants at a certain Age, who are born of Parents, in effect as little able to support them, as those who demand our Charity in the Streets.

As to my own Part, having turned my Thoughts for many Years, upon this important Subject; and maturely weighed the several *Schemes of other* 20 *Projectors*, I have always found them grosly mistaken in their Computation. It is true, a Child *just dropt from its Dam*, may be supported by her Milk, for a Solar Year with little other Nourishment; at most not above the Value of two Shillings; which the Mother may certainly get, or the Value in *Scraps*; by her lawful Occupation of *Begging*: And, it is exactly at one Year old, that I propose to provide for them in such a Manner, as, instead of being a Charge upon their *Parents*, or the *Parish*, or *wanting Food and Raiment* for the rest of their Lives; they shall, on the contrary, contribute to the Feeding, and partly to the Cloathing, of many Thousands.

THERE is likewise another great Advantage in my *Scheme*, that it will prevent 30 those *voluntary Abortions*, and that horrid Practice of *Women murdering their Bastard Children*; alas! too frequent among us; sacrificing the *poor innocent Babes*, I doubt, more to avoid the Expence than the Shame; which would move Tears and Pity in the most Savage and inhuman Breast.

THE Number of Souls in *Ireland* being usually reckoned one Million and a half; of these I calculate there may be about Two Hundred Thousand Couple whose Wives are Breeders; from which Number I substract thirty thousand Couples, who are able to maintain their own Children; although I apprehend there cannot be so many, under *the present Distresses of the Kingdom*; but this being granted, there will remain an Hundred and Seventy Thousand Breeders. 40 I again substract Fifty Thousand, for those Women who miscarry, or whose Children die by Accident, or Disease, within the Year. There only remain an

---

[1] *Pretender:* James Francis Edward Stuart (1688–1766), son of Catholic James II of England and his wife Mary of Modena. For years, between 1708 and 1745 particularly, several pretenders attempted the overthrow of the Hanover kings of England, Protestants; James's grandson, Charles Edward Stuart, is generally styled the Young Pretender. See n. l. 34, *The Vanity of Human Wishes*, by Samuel Johnson.

Hundred and Twenty Thousand Children of poor Parents, annually born: The Question therefore is, How this Number shall be reared, and provided for? Which, as I have already said, under the present Situation of Affairs, is utterly impossible, by all the Methods hitherto proposed: For we can *neither employ them in Handicraft* or *Agriculture*; we neither build Houses (I mean in the Country) nor cultivate Land: They can very seldom pick up a Livelyhood *by Stealing* until they arrive at six Years old; except where they are of towardly Parts; although, I confess, they learn the Rudiments much earlier; during which Time, they can, however, be properly looked upon only as *Probationers*; as I have been informed by a principal Gentleman in the County of *Cavan*, who protested to me, that he never knew above one or two Instances under the Age of six, even in a Part of the Kingdom *so renowned for the quickest Proficiency in that Art.*

I AM assured by our Merchants, that a Boy or a Girl before twelve Years old, is no saleable Commodity; and even when they come to this Age, they will not yield above Three Pounds, or Three Pounds and half a Crown at most, on the Exchange; which cannot turn to Account either to the Parents or Kingdom; the Charge of Nutriment and Rags, having been at least four Times that Value.

I SHALL now therefore humbly propose my own Thoughts; which I hope will not be liable to the least Objection.

I HAVE been assured by a very knowing *American* of my Acquaintance in *London*; that a young healthy Child, well nursed, is, at a Year old, a most delicious, nourishing, and wholesome Food; whether *Stewed, Roasted, Baked*, or *Boiled*; and, I make no doubt, that it will equally serve in a *Fricasie*, or *Ragoust*.[2]

I DO therefore humbly offer it to *publick Consideration*, that of the Hundred and Twenty thousand Children, already computed, Twenty thousand may be reserved for Breed; whereof only one Fourth Part to be Males; which is more than we allow to *Sheep, black Cattle*, or *Swine*; and my Reason is, that these Children are seldom the Fruits of Marriage, *a Circumstance not much regarded by our Savages*; therefore, *one Male* will be sufficient to serve *four Females*. That the remaining Hundred thousand, may, at a Year old, be offered in Sale to the *Persons of Quality* and *Fortune*, through the Kingdom; always advising the Mother to let them suck plentifully in the last Month, so as to render them plump, and fat for a good Table. A Child will make two Dishes at an Entertainment for Friends; and when the Family dines alone, the fore or hind Quarter will make a reasonable Dish; and seasoned with a little Pepper or Salt, will be very good Boiled on the fourth Day, especially in *Winter*.

I HAVE reckoned upon a Medium, that a Child just born will weigh Twelve Pounds; and in a solar Year, if tolerably nursed, encreaseth to twenty eight Pounds.

I GRANT this Food will be somewhat dear, and therefore very *proper for Landlords*; who, as they have already devoured most of the Parents, seem to have the best Title to the Children.

---

² *Ragoust:* Ragout, a stew with highly flavored seasoning.

INFANTS Flesh will be in Season throughout the Year; but more plentiful in *March*, and a little before and after: For we are told by a grave *Author, an eminent *French* Physician, that *Fish being a prolifick Dyet*, there are more Children born in *Roman Catholick Countries* about Nine Months after *Lent*, than at any other Season: Therefore reckoning a Year after *Lent*, the Markets will be more glutted than usual; because the Number of *Popish Infants*, is, at least, three to one in this Kingdom; and therefore it will have one other Collateral Advantage, by lessening the Number of *Papists* among us.

I HAVE already computed the Charge of nursing a Beggar's Child (in which List I reckon all *Cottagers, Labourers*, and Four fifths of the *Farmers*) to be   10
about two Shillings *per Annum*, Rags included; and I believe, no Gentleman would repine to give Ten Shillings for the *Carcase of a good fat Child*; which as I have said, will make four Dishes of excellent nutritive Meat, when he hath only some particular Friend, or his own Family, to dine with him. Thus the Squire will learn to be a good Landlord, and grow popular among his Tenants; the Mother will have Eight Shillings net Profit, and be fit for Work until she produceth another Child.

THOSE who are more thrifty (*as I must confess the Times require*) may flay the Carcase; the Skin of which, artificially dressed, will make admirable *Gloves for Ladies*, and *Summer Boots for fine Gentlemen*.   20

As to our City of *Dublin*; Shambles[3] may be appointed for this Purpose, in the most convenient Parts of it; and Butchers we may be assured will not be wanting; although I rather recommend buying the Children alive, and dressing them hot from the Knife, as we do *roasting-Pigs*.

A VERY worthy Person, *a true Lover of his Country*, and whose Virtues I highly esteem, was lately pleased, in discoursing on this Matter, to offer a Refinement upon my Scheme. He said, that many Gentlemen of this King-dom, having of late destroyed their Deer; he conceived, that the Want of Venison might be well supplied by the Bodies of young Lads and Maidens, not exceeding fourteen Years of Age, nor under twelve; so great a Number   30
of both Sexes in every County being now ready to starve, for Want of Work and Service: And these to be disposed of by their Parents, if alive, or other-wise by their nearest Relations. But with due Deference to so excellent a Friend, and so deserving a Patriot, I cannot be altogether in his Sentiments. For as to the Males, my *American* Acquaintance assured me from frequent Experience, that their Flesh was generally tough and lean, like that of our School-boys, by continual Exercise; and their Taste disagreeable; and to fatten them would not answer the Charge. Then, as to the Females, it would, I think, with humble Submission, *be a Loss to the Publick*, because they soon would become Breeders themselves: And besides it is not improbable, that   40
some scrupulous People might be apt to censure such a Practice (although indeed very unjustly) as a little bordering upon Cruelty; which, I confess, hath always been with me the strongest Objection against any Project, how well soever intended.

* Rabelais.

---

[3] *Shambles:* A table or stall for the sale of meat, a slaughter house.

BUT in order to justify my Friend; he confessed, that this Expedient was put into his Head by the famous *Salmanaazor*,[4] a Native of the Island *Formosa*, who came from thence to *London*, above twenty Years ago, and in Conversation told my Friend, that in his Country, when any young Person happened to be put to Death, the Executioner sold the Carcase to *Persons of Quality*, as a prime Dainty; and that, in his Time, the Body of a plump Girl of fifteen, who was crucified for an Attempt to poison the Emperor, was sold to his Imperial *Majesty's prime Minister of State*, and other great *Mandarines* of the Court, *in Joints from the Gibbet*, at Four hundred Crowns. Neither indeed can I deny, that if the same Use were made of several plump young Girls   10 in this Town, who, without one single Groat to their Fortunes, cannot stir Abroad without a Chair, and appear at a *Play-house*, and *Assemblies* in foreign Fineries, which they never will pay for; the Kingdom would not be the worse.

SOME Persons of a desponding Spirit are in great Concern about that vast Number of poor People, who are Aged, Diseased, or Maimed; and I have been desired to employ my Thoughts what Course may be taken, to ease the Nation of so grievous an Incumbrance. But I am not in the least Pain upon that Matter; because it is very well known, that they are every Day *dying*, and *rotting*, by *Cold* and *Famine*, and *Filth*, and *Vermin*, as fast as can be   20 reasonably expected. And as to the younger Labourers, they are now in almost as hopeful a Condition: They cannot get Work, and consequently pine away for Want of Nourishment, to a Degree, that if at any Time they are accidentally hired to common Labour, they have not Strength to perform it; and thus the Country, and themselves, are in a fair Way of being soon delivered from the Evils to come.

I HAVE too long digressed; and therefore shall return to my Subject. I think the Advantages by the Proposal which I have made, are obvious, and many, as well as of the highest Importance.

FOR, *First*, as I have already observed, it would greatly lessen *the Number of*   3 *Papists*, with whom we are yearly over-run; being the principal Breeders of the Nation, as well as our most dangerous Enemies; and who stay at home on Purpose, with a Design *to deliver the Kingdom to the Pretender*; hoping to take their Advantage by the Absence *of so many good Protestants*, who have chosen rather to leave their Country, than stay at home, and pay Tithes against their Conscience, to an idolatrous *Episcopal Curate*.

SECONDLY, The poorer Tenants will have something valuable of their own, which, by Law, may be made liable to Distress,[5] and help to pay their Landlord's Rent; their Corn and Cattle being already seized, and *Money a Thing unknown*.   4

THIRDLY, Whereas the Maintenance of an Hundred Thousand Children, from two Years old, and upwards, cannot be computed at less than ten Shillings a Piece *per Annum*, the Nation's Stock will be thereby encreased

---

[4] *Salmanaazor*: George Psalmanazar (c. 1679–1763), born probably in Languedoc; he passed himself off as a Formosan. He wrote fictitious geographies (including one of Formosa) by means of which he was accepted as an authority.

[5] *Liable to Distress*: Property of a debtor could be legally appropriated by those to whom the debt was owed.

Fifty Thousand Pounds *per Annum*; besides the Profit of a new Dish, introduced to the Tables of all *Gentlemen of Fortune* in the Kingdom, who have any Refinement in Taste; and the Money will circulate among our selves, the Goods being entirely of our own Growth and Manufacture.

FOURTHLY, The constant Breeders, besides the Gain of Eight Shillings *Sterling per Annum*, by the Sale of their Children, will be rid of the Charge of maintaining them after the first Year.

FIFTHLY, This Food would likewise bring great *Custom to Taverns*, where the Vintners will certainly be so prudent, as to procure the best Receipts for dressing it to Perfection; and consequently, have their Houses frequented 10 by all the *fine Gentlemen*, who justly value themselves upon their Knowledge in good Eating; and a skilful Cook, who understands how to oblige his Guests, will contrive to make it as expensive as they please.

SIXTHLY, This would be a great Inducement to Marriage, which all wise Nations have either encouraged by Rewards, or enforced by Laws and Penalties. It would encrease the Care and Tenderness of Mothers towards their Children, when they were sure of a Settlement for Life, to the poor Babes, provided in some Sort by the Publick, to their annual Profit instead of Expence. We should soon see an honest Emulation among the married Women, *which of them could bring the fattest Child to the Market*. Men would 20 become as *fond* of their Wives, during the Time of their Pregnancy, as they are now of their *Mares* in Foal, their *Cows* in Calf, or *Sows* when they are ready to farrow; nor offer to beat or kick them (as it is too *frequent* a Practice) for fear of a Miscarriage.

MANY other Advantages might be enumerated. For Instance, the Addition of some Thousand Carcasses in our Exportation of barrelled Beef: The Propagation of *Swines Flesh*, and Improvement in the Art of making good *Bacon*; so much wanted among us by the great Destruction of *Pigs*, too frequent at our Tables, and are no way comparable in Taste, or Magnificence, to a well-grown fat yearly Child; which, roasted whole, will make a considerable 30 Figure at a *Lord Mayor's Feast*, or any other publick Entertainment. But this, and many others, I omit; being studious of Brevity.

SUPPOSING that one Thousand Families in this City, would be constant Customers for Infants Flesh; besides others who might have it at *merry Meetings*, particularly at *Weddings* and *Christenings;* I compute that *Dublin* would take off, annually, about Twenty Thousand Carcasses; and the rest of the Kingdom (where probably they will be sold somewhat cheaper) the remaining Eighty Thousand.

I CAN think of no one Objection, that will possibly be raised against this Proposal; unless it should be urged, that the Number of People will be thereby 40 much lessened in the Kingdom. This I freely own; and it was indeed one principal Design in offering it to the World. I desire the Reader will observe, that I calculate my Remedy *for this one individual Kingdom of* IRELAND, *and for no other that ever was, is, or I think ever can be upon Earth*. Therefore, let no Man talk to me of other Expedients: *Of taxing our Absentees at five Shillings a Pound: Of using neither Cloaths, nor Houshold Furniture; except what is of our own Growth and Manufacture: Of utterly rejecting the Materials and Instruments that promote foreign Luxury: Of curing the Expensiveness of Pride, Vanity, Idleness, and Gaming in our Women: Of introducing a Vein of Parsimony, Prudence and Temperance: Of learning to love our Country; wherein we differ even from* LAP-LANDERS, *and the Inhabitants of* TOPINAMBOO: *Of quitting our Animosities, and Factions; nor act any longer like the* Jews, *who were murdering one another at the very Moment their City was taken:*[6] *Of being a little cautious not to sell our Country and Consciences for nothing: Of teaching Landlords to have, at least, one Degree of Mercy towards their Tenants.* Lastly, *Of putting a Spirit of Honesty, Industry, and Skill into our Shop-keepers; who, if a Resolution could now be taken to buy only our native Goods, would immediately unite to cheat and exact upon us in the Price, the Measure, and the Goodness; nor could ever yet be brought to make one fair Proposal of just Dealing, though often and earnestly invited to it.*

THEREFORE I repeat; let no Man talk to me of these and the like Expedients; till he hath, at least, a Glimpse of Hope, that there will ever be some hearty and sincere Attempt to put *them in Practice.*

BUT, as to my self; having been wearied out for many Years with offering vain, idle, visionary Thoughts; and at length utterly despairing of Success, I fortunately fell upon this Proposal; which, as it is wholly new, so it hath something *solid* and *real*, of no Expence, and little Trouble, full in our own Power; and whereby we can incur no Danger in *disobliging* ENGLAND: For, this Kind of Commodity will not bear Exportation; the Flesh being of too tender a Consistence, to admit a long Continuance in Salt; *although, perhaps, I could name a Country, which would be glad to eat up our whole Nation without it.*

AFTER all, I am not so violently bent upon my own Opinion, as to reject any Offer proposed by wise Men, which shall be found equally innocent, cheap, easy, and effectual. But before something of that Kind shall be advanced, in Contradiction to my Scheme, and offering a better; I desire the Author, or Authors, will be pleased maturely to consider two Points. *First,* As Things now stand, how they will be able to find Food and Raiment, for a Hundred Thousand useless Mouths and Backs? And *secondly,* There being a round Million of Creatures in human Figure, throughout this Kingdom; whose whole Subsistence, put into a common Stock, would leave them in Debt two Millions of Pounds *Sterling*; adding those, who are Beggars by Profession, to the Bulk of Farmers, Cottagers, and Labourers, with their Wives and Children, who are Beggars in Effect; I desire those Politicians, who dislike my Overture, and may perhaps be so bold to attempt an Answer, that they will first ask the Parents of these Mortals, Whether they would not, at this Day, think it a great Happiness to have been sold for Food at a Year old, in the Manner I prescribe; and thereby have avoided such a perpetual Scene of Misfortunes, as they have since gone through; by the *Oppression of Landlords*; the Impossibility of paying Rent, without Money or Trade; the Want of common Sustenance, with neither House nor Cloaths, to cover them from the Inclemencies of the Weather; and the most inevitable Prospect of intailing the like, or greater Miseries upon their Breed for ever.

I PROFESS, in the Sincerity of my Heart, that I have not the least personal

---

[6] *Their City was taken:* in A.D. 70, the Roman Emperor Titus took Jerusalem, which was divided from within.

Interest, in endeavouring to promote this necessary Work; having no other Motive than the *publick Good of my Country, by advancing our Trade, providing for Infants, relieving the Poor, and giving some Pleasure to the Rich.* I have no Children, by which I can propose to get a single Penny; the youngest being nine Years old, and my Wife past Child-bearing.

(1729)

Headnote to
SWIFT'S POETRY

Swift's earliest compositions were a group of Pindaric odes, only one of which he published, in 1692—"Ode to the Athenian Society." Like his other odes (but quite unlike his poetry and prose generally) this one is falsely elevated and unclear. It is held to be these turgid pieces that prompted Dryden to say to his kinsman, "Cousin Swift, you will never be a poet." Only a few lines from one of them should persuade even Swift's most devoted follower that Dryden and the world have been justified in rejecting his Pindarics. Here, for example, is the first strophe of the "Ode to Sir William Temple":

> Virtue, the greatest of all Monarchies,
> Till its first Emperor rebellious Man
> Depos'd from off his Seat
> It fell, and broke with its own Weight
> Into small States and Principalities,
> By many a petty Lord possess'd,
> But ne'er since seated in one single Breast.
> 'Tis you who must this Land subdue,
> The mighty Conquest's left for you,
> The Conquest and Discovery too:
> Search out this *Utopian* Ground,
> Virtue's *Terra Incognita*,
> Where none ever led the Way,
> Nor ever since but in Descriptions found,
> Like the Philosopher's Stone,
> With rules to search it, yet obtain'd by none.

Fortunately, Swift abandoned his early efforts at Pindarics, and thereafter when he wrote verse he made use, for the most part, of the fast moving octosyllabic couplet, with witty rhymes. It is possible that he learned something about this kind of peotry from Samuel Butler, best known as the author of *Hudibras*, a mock-epic romance, the three parts of which had appeared in 1663, 1664, and 1678. Certainly it is clear that Swift was not at home in the sort of verse whose narrator fixes on a single point of view, idea, or experience and excludes all other considerations, so that one mood occupies his entire attention— fear of death, desperation over the loss of a loved one, the sense of time's swift passage, delight in springtime, or deep conviction about a religious or political or critical point of view. He much preferred the eye of the satirist who penetrates the unifying surface of things and remarks the broken fragments, often ugly to the ordinary perceiver. Swift's narrators apparently have a double vision. For example, they seem to appreciate the illusion of womanly beauty that results from good grooming (the "unifying power") and at the same time to see in exaggerated isolation and ugliness the features and qualities masked by cosmetic art. To be sure, the appreciation of beauty's mask is never directly expressed. It can be inferred, however, by anyone sensitive to the narrator's urgent need to reveal what lies beneath; he would have no wish to expose the sub-surface obvious to him, unless he also saw the surface he thought was deceiving everyone else.

It might be supposed that Swift's personae express either their own fear of being taken in by the illusion or their anger at having penetrated a gross but satisfying deception, except that humor of tone suggests a comic detachment that marks the speaker's objectivity along with this sensitivity. Instead of trying to explain the satirist's dual perceptions in this way, one probably does better to say that the poet has seen into the "truth" of things, a truth which is not simple, being neither completely agreeable, nor—because it is amenable to satire, after all—completely unbearable either. The reconciliation of his disparate visions is accomplished in the satirist's art—no less a "truth" than the beautiful-ugly thing that inspired it.

TEXTS. "A Description of a City Shower," and "Apollo Outwitted":
          Miscellanies in Prose and Verse (London, 1711).
          "Phyllis," "The Furniture of a Woman's Mind," and "On
          Burning a Dull Poem": *The Works of J.S, D.D, D.S.P.D.*
          (4 Vols., Dublin, 1734–1735).
          The Lady's Dressing Room (London, 1732).
          "Verses on the Death of Dr. Swift," a rescension, *The Poems
          of Jonathan Swift*, ed. Harold Williams (3 vols., Oxford,
          1958).

A Description of a City Shower

CAREFUL Observers may fortel the Hour
(By sure Prognosticks) when to dread a Show'r:
While Rain depends, the pensive Cat gives o'er
Her Frolicks, and pursues her Tail no more.
Returning Home at Night, you'll find the Sink   5
Strike your offended Sense with double Stink.
If you be wise, then go not far to Dine,
You'll spend in Coach-hire more than save in Wine.
A coming Show'r your shooting Corns presage,
Old Aches throb, your hollow Tooth will rage.   10
Sauntring in Coffee-house is *Dulman* seen;
He damns the Climate, and complains of Spleen.

    MEAN while the South rising with dabbled Wings,
A Sable Cloud a-thwart the Welkin flings,
That swill'd more Liquor than it could contain,   15
And like a Drunkard gives it up again.
Brisk *Susan* whips her Linen from the Rope,
While the first drizzling Show'r is born aslope,
Such is that Sprinkling which some careless Quean
Flirts on you from her Mop, but not so clean.   20
You fly, invoke the Gods; then turning, stop
To rail; she singing, still whirls on her Mop.
Not yet, the Dust had shun'd th' unequal Strife,
But aided by the Wind, fought still for Life;
And wafted with its Foe by violent Gust,   25
'Twas doubtful which was Rain, and which was Dust.
Ah! where must needy Poet seek for Aid,
When Dust and Rain at once his Coat invade;
His only Coat, where Dust confus'd with Rain,
Roughen the Nap, and leave a mingled Stain.   30

    NOW in contiguous Drops the Flood comes down,
Threat'ning with Deluge this *Devoted* Town.
To Shops in Crouds the dagged Females fly,
Pretend to cheapen Goods, but nothing buy.

---

3. *Depends:* Hangs down; i.e., threatens.
10. *Aches:* Aches was a disyllabic word pronounced "aitches" in Swift's day.
14. *Welkin:* The sky.

33. *Dagged Females:* Sprinkled females.
34. *Pretend to cheapen:* Pretend to bargain.

474

The Templer spruce, while ev'ry Spout's a-broach,   35
Stays till 'tis fair, yet seems to call a Coach.
The tuck'd-up Sempstress walks with hasty Strides,
While Streams run down her oil'd Umbrella's Sides.
Here various Kinds by various Fortunes led,
Commence Acquaintance underneath a shed.   40
Triumphant Tories, and desponding Whigs,
Forget their Fewds, and join to save their Wigs,
Box'd in a Chair the Beau impatient sits,
While Spouts run clatt'ring o'er the Roof by Fits;
And ever and anon with frightful Din   45
The Leather sounds, he trembles from within.
So when *Troy* Chair-men bore the Wooden Steed,
Pregnant with *Greeks*, impatient to be freed
(Those Bully *Greeks*, who, as the Moderns do,
Instead of paying Chair-men, run them thro'.)   50
Laoco'n struck the Outside with his Spear,
And each imprison'd Hero quak'd for Fear.

NOW from all Parts the swelling Kennels flow,
And bear their Trophies with them as they go:
Filth of all Hues and Odours seem to tell   55
What Street they sail'd from, by their Sight and Smell.
They, as each Torrent drives, with rapid Force
From *Smithfield*, or St. *Pulchre's* shape their Course,
And in huge Confluent join at *Snow-Hill* Ridge,
Fall from the *Conduit* prone to *Holborn-Bridge*.   60
Sweepings from Butchers Stalls, Dung, Guts, and Blood,   ⎤
Drown'd Puppies, stinking Sprats, all drench'd in Mud,   ⎬
Dead Cats and Turnip-Tops come tumbling down the Flood.   ⎦

(1710)

35. *The Templer:* Templar. A member of the middle or inner Temple, a lawyer.
41. *Tories . . . Whigs:* Between 1710 and 1714 the Whigs were out of power, the Tories in.
43. *Box'd in a Chair:* In a sedan chair, the taxi of the day, carried by two porters.
51. *Laoco'n struck:* Laocoön. When the Greeks left the wooden horse (filled with warriors), claiming the Trojans must bring it within their walls if they wished to avoid offending Athena, their priest Laocoön hurled his spear defiantly at the false gift.
53. *Kennels:* Cannels, gutters, the surface drains in streets, through which refuse flowed, particularly when it rained.

Apollo Outwitted

TO THE HONOURABLE MRS. FINCH,*
UNDER HER NAME OF ARDELIA

WRITTEN, 1709

PHŒBUS now shortning every Shade,
  Up to the Northern *Tropick* came,
And thence Beheld a Lovely Maid
  Attending on a Royal Dame.

THE God laid down his Feeble Rays,   5
  Then lighted from his Glitt'ring Coach,
But fenc'd his Head with his own Bays
  Before he durst the Nymph approach.

UNDER those Sacred Leaves, Secure
  From common Lightning of the Skies,   10
He fondly thought he might endure
  The Flashes of *Ardeliah's* Eyes.

THE Nymph who oft had read in Books,
  Of that Bright God whom Bards invoke,
Soon knew *Apollo* by his looks,   15
  And Guest his Business e're he Spoke.

HE in the old Celestial Cant,
  Confest his Flame, and swore by *Styx*,
What e're she would desire, to Grant,
  But Wise *Ardelia* knew his Tricks.   20

OVID had warn'd her to beware,
  Of Stroling God's, whose usual Trade is,
Under pretence of Taking Air,
  To pick up Sublunary Ladies.

HOWE'ER she gave no flat Denial,   25
  As having Malice in her Heart,
And was resolv'd upon a Tryal,
  To Cheat the God in his own Art.

---

* *Mrs. Finch:* Anne Finch (1661–1720), Countess of Winchilsea, wrote occasional verse.
  1. *Phœbus:* Phoebus Apollo, the god of light (as well as of medicine, music, archery and prophecy).
  18. *Styx:* In Greek mythology, the principal river in Hades.

HEAR my Request the Virgin said
   Let which I please of all the Nine   30
Attend when e'er I want their Aid,
   Obey may Call, and only mine.

BY Vow Oblig'd, By Passion led,
   The God could not refuse her Prayer;
He wav'd his Wreath Thrice o'er her Head,   35
   Thrice mutter'd something to the Air.

AND now he thought to Seize his due,
   But she the Charm already try'd,
Thalia heard the Call and Flew
   To wait at Bright *Ardelia*'s Side.   40

ON Sight of this Celestial *Prude*,
   Apollo thought it vain to stay,
Nor in her Presence durst be Rude,
   But made his Leg and went away.

HE hop'd to find some lucky Hour,   45
   When on their Queen the Muses wait;
But *Pallas* owns *Ardelia*'s Power,
   For Vows Divine are kept by Fate.

THEN full of Rage *Apollo* Spoke,
   Deceitful Nymph I see thy Art,   50
And tho' I can't my gift revoke,
   I'll disappoint its Nobler Part.

LET Stubborn Pride Possess thee long,
   And be thou Negligent of Fame,
With ev'ry Muse to Grace thy Song,   55
   May'st thou despise a Poets Name.

OF Modest Poets thou be first,
   To silent Shades repeat thy Verse,
Till *Fame* and *Eccho* almost burst,
   Yet hardly dare one Line Rehearse.   60

AND last, my Vengeance to Compleat,
   May you Descend to take Renown,
Prevail'd on by the Thing you hate,
   A — and one that wears a Gown.

(1711)

---

30. *All the Nine:* The Muses, goddesses
of literature and the arts.
39. *Thalia:* The Muse of comedy.
44. *Made his Leg:* Bowed.
47. *Pallas:* Pallas Athena, who is
patroness of certain of the arts, and so
here assumed to govern the Muses, it
seems.
64. *Wears a Gown:* A clergyman's dress.

Phyllis

Or, The Progress of Love

DESPONDING *Phyllis* was endu'd
With ev'ry Talent of a Prude,
She trembled when a Man drew near;
Salute her, and she turn'd her Ear:
If o'er against her you were plac't   5
She durst not look above your Wast;
She'd rather take you to her Bed
Than let you see her dress her Head;
In Church you heard her thro the Crowd
Repeat the Absolution loud;   10
In Church, secure behind her Fan
She durst behold that Monster, Man:
There practic'd how to place her Head,
And bit her Lips to make them red:
Or on the Matt devoutly kneeling   15
Would lift her Eyes up to the Ceeling,
And heave her Bosom unaware
For neighb'ring Beaux to see it bare.
    At length a lucky Lover came,
And found Admittance from the Dame.   20
Suppose all Partyes now agreed,
The Writings drawn, the Lawyer fee'd,
The Vicar and the Ring bespoke:
Guess how could such a Match be broke.
See then what Mortals place their Bliss in!   25
Next morn betimes the Bride was missing,
The Mother scream'd, the Father chid,
Where can this idle Wench be hid?
No news of *Phyl!* The Bridegroom came,
And thought his Bride had sculk't for shame,   30
Because her Father us'd to say
The Girl had such a Bashfull way.
    Now, John the Butler must be sent
To learn the Way that *Phyllis* went;
The Groom was *wisht* to saddle Crop,   35
For John must neither light nor stop;
But find her where so'er she fled,
And bring her back, alive or dead.

---

4. *Salute her:* Kiss her, or greet her   without personal significance.
with a kiss, a customary social gesture,

See here again the Dev'l to do;
For truly John was missing too: 40
The Horse and Pillion both were gone
Phyllis, it seems, was fled with John.
Old Madam who went up to find
What Papers Phyl had left behind,
A Letter on the Toylet sees   45
To my much honor'd Father; These:
('Tis always done, Romances tell us,
When Daughters run away with Fellows)
Fill'd with the choicest common-places,
By others us'd in the like Cases;   50
That, long ago a Fortune-teller
Exactly said what now befell her,
And in a Glass had made her see
A serving-Man of low Degree:
It was her Fate; must be forgiven;   55
For Marriages are made in Heaven:
His Pardon begg'd, but to be plain,
She'd do't if 'twere to do again.
Thank God, 'twas neither Shame nor Sin,
For John was come of honest Kin: 60
Love never thinks of Rich and Poor,
She'd beg with John from Door to Door:
Forgive her, if it be a Crime,
She'll never do't another Time,
She ne'r before in all her Life   65
Once disobey'd him, Maid nor Wife.
One Argument she summ'd up all in,
The Thing was done and past recalling:
And therefore hop'd she would recover
His Favor, when his Passion's over.   70
She valued not what others thought her;
And was—His most obedient Daughter.
    Fair Maidens all attend the Muse
Who now the wandring Pair pursues:
Away they rode in homely Sort   75
Their Journy long, their Money short;
The loving Couple well bemir'd,
The Horse and both the Riders tir'd:
Their Vittells bad, their Lodging worse,
Phyl cry'd, and John began to curse;   80
Phyl wish't, that she had strained a Limb
When first she ventur'd out with him.
John wish't, that he had broke a Leg
When first for her he quitted Peg.

41. *Pillion:* A woman's light saddle.

But what Adventures more befell 'um   85
The Muse has now not time to tell 'um.
How Jonny wheadled, threatned, fawnd,
Till Phyllis all her Trinkets pawn'd:
How oft she broke her marriage Vows
In kindness to maintain her Spouse;   90
Till Swains unwholsome spoyld the Trade,
For now the Surgeon must be paid;
To whom those Perquisites are gone
In Christian Justice due to John.
    When Food and Rayment now grew scarce   95
Fate put a Period to the Farce;
And with exact Poetick Justice:
For John is Landlord, Phyllis Hostess;
They keep at Staines, the *old blue Boar*,
Are Cat and Dog, and Rogue and Whore.   100

    (1727)

The Lady's Dressing Room

FIVE Hours (and who can do it less in?)
By haughty *Celia* spent in Dressing;
The Goddess from her Chamber issues,
Array'd in Lace, Brocades and Tissues.

    Strephon, who found the Room was void,   5
And *Betty* otherwise employ'd;
Stole in, and took a strict Survey,
Of all the Litter as it lay;
Whereof, to make the Matter clear
An Inventory follows here   10

    And first a dirty Smock appear'd,
Beneath the Arm-pits well besmear'd.
Strephon, the Rogue, display'd it wide,
And turn'd it round on every Side.
On such a Point few Words are best,   15
And *Strephon* bids us guess the rest;
But swears how damnably the Men lie,

In calling *Celia* sweet and cleanly.
Now listen while he next produces,
The various Combs for various Uses,   20
Fill'd up with Dirt so closely fixt,
No Brush could force a way betwixt.
A Paste of Composition rare,
Sweat, Dandriff, Powder, Lead and Hair;
A Forehead Cloth with Oyl upon't   25
To smooth the Wrinkles on her Front;
Here Allum Flower to stop the Steams,
Exhal'd from sour unsavoury Streams,
There Night-gloves made of *Tripsy*'s Hide,
Bequeath'd by *Tripsy* when she dy'd,   30
With Puppy Water, Beauty's Help
Distill'd from *Tripsy*'s darling Whelp;
Here Gallypots and Vials plac'd,
Some fill'd with Washes, some with Paste,
Some with Pomatum, Paints and Slops,   35
And Ointments good for scabby Chops.
Hard by a filthy Bason stands,
Fowl'd with the Scouring of her Hands;
The Bason takes whatever comes
The Scrapings of her Teeth and Gums,   40
A nasty Compound of all Hues,
For here she spits, and here she spues.
But oh! it turn'd poor *Strephon*'s Bowels,
When he beheld and smelt the Towels,
Begumm'd, bematter'd, and beslim'd   45
With Dirt, and Sweat, and Ear-Wax grim'd.
No Object *Strephon*'s Eye escapes,
Here Pettycoats in frowzy Heaps;
Nor be the Handkerchiefs forgot
All varnish'd o'er with Snuff and Snot.   50
The Stockings, why shou'd I expose,
Stain'd with the Marks of stinking Toes;
Or greasy Coifs and Pinners reeking,
Which *Celia* slept at least a Week in?
A Pair of Tweezers next he found   55
To pluck her Brows in Arches round,
Or Hairs that sink the Forehead low,
Or on her Chin like Bristles grow.

The Virtues we must not let pass,
Of *Celia*'s magnifying Glass.   60
When frighted *Strephon* cast his Eye on't
It shew'd the Visage of a Gyant.
A Glass that can to Sight disclose,

The smallest Worm in *Celia's* Nose,
And faithfully direct her Nail   65
To squeeze it out from Head to Tail;
For catch it nicely by the Head,
It must come out alive or dead.

Why *Strephon* will you tell the rest?
And must you needs describe the Chest?   70
That careless Wench! no Creature warn her
To move it out from yonder Corner;
But leave it standing full in Sight
For you to exercise your Spight.
In vain, the Workmen shew'd his Wit   75
With Rings and Hinges counterfeit
To make it seem in this Disguise,
A Cabinet to vulgar Eyes;
For *Strephon* ventur'd to look in,
Resolv'd to go thro' thick and thin;   80
He lifts the Lid, there needs no more,
He smelt it all the Time before.
As from within *Pandora's* Box,
When *Epimetheus* op'd the Locks,
A sudden universal Crew   85
Of humane Evils upwards flew;
He still was comforted to find
That *Hope* at last remain'd behind;
So *Strephon* lifting up the Lid,
To view what in the Chest was hid.   90
The Vapours flew from out the Vent
But *Strephon* cautious never meant
The Bottom of the Pan to grope,
And fowl his Hands in Search of *Hope*.
O never may such vile Machine   95
Be once in *Celia's* Chamber seen!
O may she better learn to keep
"Those Secrets of the hoary deep!"

As Mutton Cutlets, Prime of Meat,
Which tho' with Art you salt and beat,   100
As Laws of Cookery require,
And toast them at the clearest Fire;
If from adown the hopeful Chops
The Fat upon a Cinder drops,
To stinking Smoak it turns the Flame   105

84. *Epimetheus:* Brother of Prometheus, Epimetheus (afterthought) was sent Pandora, who brought with her a box, out of which the evils and distempers of the human race issued.
98. *Secrets of the hoary deep:* Milton, *Paradise Lost,* II, 890–891.

Pois'ning the Flesh from whence it came;
And up exhales a greasy Stench,
For which you curse the careless Wench;
So Things, which must not be exprest,
When plumpt into the reeking Chest;   110
Send up an excremental Smell
To taint the Parts from whence they fell.
The Pettycoats and Gown perfume,
Which waft a Stink round every Room.

    Thus finishing his grand Survey,   115
Disgusted *Strephon* stole away
Repeating in his amorous Fits,
Oh! *Celia, Celia, Celia* shits!

    But Vengeance, Goddess never sleeping
Soon punish'd *Strephon* for his Peeping;   120
His foul Imagination links
Each Dame he sees with all her Stinks:
And, if unsav'ry Odours fly,
Conceives a Lady standing by:
All Women his Description fits,   125
And both Idea's jump like Wits:
By vicious Fancy coupled fast.
And still appearing in Contrast.
I pity wretched *Strephon* blind
To all the Charms of Female Kind;   130
Should I the Queen of Love refuse,
Because she rose from stinking Ooze?
To him that looks behind the Scene,
Satira's but some pocky Quean.
When *Celia* in her Glory shows,   135
If *Strephon* would but stop his Nose
(Who now so impiously blasphemes
Her Ointments, Daubs, and Paints and Creams,
Her Washes, Slops, and every Clout,
With which he makes so foul a Rout);   140
He soon would learn to think like me,
And bless his ravisht Sight to see
Such Order from Confusion sprung,
Such gaudy Tulips rais'd from Dung.

    (1732)

134. *Satira:* Perhaps Swift meant Statira, Alexander's wife, daughter of Darius. On the other hand, Satira (or Satura) is Latin for Satire.

The Furniture of
a Woman's Mind

A SET of Phrases learn't by Rote;
A Passion for a Scarlet-Coat;
When at a Play to laugh, or cry,
Yet cannot tell the Reason why:
Never to hold her Tongue a Minute;   5
While all she prates has nothing in it.
Whole Hours can with a Coxcomb sit,
And take his Nonsense all for Wit:
Her Learning mounts to read a Song,
But, half the Words pronouncing wrong;   10
Has ev'ry Repartee in Store,
She spoke ten Thousand Times before.
Can ready Compliments supply
On all Occasions, cut and dry.
Such Hatred to a Parson's Gown,   15
The Sight will put her in a Swown.
For Conversation well endu'd;
She calls it witty to be rude;
And, placing Raillery in Railing,
Will tell aloud your greatest Failing;   20
Nor makes a Scruple to expose
Your bandy Leg, or crooked Nose.
Can, at her Morning Tea, run o'er
The Scandal of the Day before.
Improving hourly in her Skill,   25
To cheat and wrangle at Quadrille.

    IN chusing Lace a Critick nice,
Knows to a Groat the lowest Price;
Can in her Female Clubs dispute
What Lining best the Silk will suit;   30
What Colours each Complexion match:
And where with Art to place a Patch.

    IF chance a Mouse creeps in her Sight,
Can finely counterfeit a Fright;
So, sweetly screams if it comes near her,   35

---

26. *Quadrille:* A card game.
32. *Patch:* A very small piece of black

silk worn by ladies on the face to show off
the complexion by contrast.

She ravishes all Hearts to hear her.
Can dext'rously her Husband teize,
By taking Fits whene'er she please:
By frequent Practice learns the Trick
At proper Seasons to be sick;   40
Thinks nothing gives one Airs so pretty;
At once creating Love and Pity.
If *Molly* happens to be careless,
And but neglects to warm her Hair-Lace,
She gets a Cold as sure as Death;   45
And vows she scarce can fetch her Breath.
Admires how modest Women can
Be so *robustious* like a Man.

    IN Party, furious to her Power;
A bitter Whig, or Tory sow'r;   50
Her Arguments directly tend
Against the Side she would defend:
Will prove herself a Tory plain,
From Principles the Whigs maintain;
And, to defend the Whiggish Cause,   55
Her Topicks from the Tories draws.

    O YES! If any Man can find
More virtues in a Woman's Mind,
Let them be sent to Mrs. *Harding*;
She'll pay the Charges to a Farthing: 60
Take Notice, she has my Commission
To add them in the next Edition;
They may out-sell a better Thing;
So, Holla Boys; God save the King.

    (1735)

59. *Mrs. Harding:* The widow of one
of Swift's printers.

On Burning
a Dull Poem

WRITTEN IN THE YEAR 1729

An Ass's Hoof alone can hold
That pois'nous Juice which kills by Cold.
Methought, when I this Poem read,
No Vessel but an Ass's Head,
Such frigid Fustian could contain;   5
I mean the Head without the Brain,
The cold Conceits, the chilling Thoughts,
Went down like stupifying Draughts:
I found my Head began to swim,
A Numbness crept through ev'ry Limb: 10
In Haste, with Imprecations dire,
I threw the Volume in the Fire:
When, who could think, tho' cold as Ice,
It burnt to Ashes in a Trice.

   How could I more enhaunce it's Fame?   15
Though born in Snow, it dy'd in Flame.

(1735)

1. *An Ass's Hoof:* The water of the River Styx in Hades was said to dissolve every container except one made from the hoof of a horse or an ass.

Verses on the Death of Dr. Swift, D.S.P.D.

OCCASIONED BY READING A MAXIM
IN ROCHEFOULCAULT

*Dans l'adversité de nos meilleurs amis nous trouvons quelque chose,
qui ne nous deplaist pas.*
*In the Adversity of our best Friends, we find something that doth not dis-
please us.*

As *Rochefoucault* his Maxims drew
From Nature, I believe 'em true:
They argue no corrupted Mind
In him; the Fault is in Mankind.

THIS Maxim more than all the rest   5
Is thought too base for human Breast;
"In all Distresses of our Friends
"We first consult our private Ends,
"While Nature kindly bent to ease us,
"Points out some Circumstance to please us.   10

IF this perhaps your Patience move
Let Reason and Experience prove.

WE all behold with envious Eyes,
Our *Equal* rais'd above our *Size*;
Who wou'd not at a crowded Show,   15
Stand high himself, keep others low?
I love my Friend as well as you,
But would not have him stop my View;
Then let him have the higher Post;
I ask but for an Inch at most.   20

IF in a Battle you should find,
One, whom you love of all Mankind,

---

1. *Rochefoucault:* Francois, Sixth Duc
de La Rochefoucauld (1613–1680), French
writer best known for his *Maximes*, aphorisms which analyze man's character
and discover self-love to be his basic
motive.

Had some heroick Action done,
A Champion kill'd, or Trophy won;
Rather than thus be over-topt,   25
Would you not wish his Lawrels cropt?

DEAR honest *Ned* is in the Gout,
Lies rackt with Pain, and you without:
How patiently you hear him groan!
How glad the Case is not your own!   30

WHAT Poet would not grieve to see,
His Brethren write as well as he?
But rather than they should excel,
He'd wish his Rivals all in Hell.

HER End when Emulation misses,   35
She turns to Envy, Stings and Hisses:
The strongest Friendship yields to Pride,
Unless the Odds be on our Side.

VAIN human Kind! Fantastick Race!
Thy various Follies, who can trace?   40
Self-love, Ambition, Envy, Pride,
Their Empire in our Hearts divide:
Give others Riches, Power, and Station,
'Tis all on me an Usurpation.
I have no Title to aspire;   45
Yet, when you sink, I seem the higher.
In POPE, I cannot read a Line,
But with a Sigh, I wish it mine:
When he can in one Couplet fix
More Sense than I can do in Six: 50
It gives me such a jealous Fit,
I cry, Pox take him, and his Wit.

WHY must I be outdone by GAY,
In my own hum'rous biting Way?

ARBUTHNOT is no more my Friend,   55
Who dares to Irony pretend;

---

53. *Gay:* John Gay (1685–1732), English poet and playwright, whose greatest success was *The Beggar's Opera.* The play ridiculed the Whig government of Sir Robert Walpole, to which the Tory Swift was opposed.
55. *Arbuthnot:* John Arbuthnot (1667–1735) Scottish physician to the English Court and author of the *History of John Bull.* Gay and Arbuthnot (together with Pope, Swift, and Thomas Parnell, 1679–1718) were members of the Scriblerus Club, dedicated to satirizing dullness. Their political views were Tory.

Which I was born to introduce,
Refin'd it first, and shew'd its Use.

St. John, as well as Pultney knows,
That I had some repute for Prose;   60
And till they drove me out of Date,
Could maul a Minister of State:
If they have mortify'd my Pride,
And made me throw my Pen aside;
If with such Talents Heav'n hath blest 'em   65
Have I not Reason to detest 'em?

To all my Foes, dear Fortune, send
Thy Gifts, but never to my Friend:
I tamely can endure the first,
But, this with Envy makes me burst.   70

Thus much may serve by way of Proem,
Proceed we therefore to our Poem.

The Time is not remote, when I
Must by the Course of Nature dye:
When I foresee my special Friends,   75
Will try to find their private Ends:
Tho' it is hardly understood,
Which way my Death can do them good;
Yet, thus methinks, I hear 'em speak;
See, how the Dean begins to break: 80
Poor Gentleman, he droops apace,
You plainly find it in his Face:
That old Vertigo in his Head,
Will never leave him, till he's dead:
Besides, his Memory decays,   85
He recollects not what he says;
He cannot call his Friends to Mind;
Forgets the Place where last he din'd:
Plyes you with Stories o'er and o'er,
He told them fifty Times before.   90
How does he fancy we can sit,
To hear his out-of-fashion'd Wit?
But he takes up with younger Fokes,
Who for his Wine will bear his Jokes:
Faith, he must make his Stories shorter,   95

---

59. *St. John . . . Pultney:* Henry St. John, First Viscount Bolingbroke (1678–1751), Tory statesman, and William Pultney, Earl of Bath (1684–1764), together produced the brilliant political journal *The Craftsman*, which opposed the Whigs and their leader, Sir Robert Walpole, beginning in 1726.

Or change his Comrades once a Quarter:
In half the Time, he talks them round;
There must another Sett be found.

For Poetry, he's past his Prime,
He takes an Hour to find a Rhime: 100
His Fire is out, his Wit decay'd
His Fancy sunk, his Muse a Jade.
I'd have him throw away his Pen;
But there's no talking to some Men.

And, then their Tenderness appears,   105
By adding largely to my Years:
"He's older than he would be reckon'd,
"And well remembers *Charles* the Second.

"He hardly drinks a Pint of Wine;
"And that, I doubt, is no good Sign.   110
"His Stomach too begins to fail:
"Last Year we thought him strong and hale;
"But now, he's quite another Thing;
"I wish he may hold out till Spring.

Then hug themselves, and reason thus;   115
"It is not yet so bad with us."

In such a Case they talk in Tropes,
And, by their Fears express their Hopes:
Some great Misfortune to portend,
No Enemy can match a Friend;   120
With all the Kindness they profess,
The Merit of a lucky Guess,
(When daily Howd'y's come of Course,
And Servants answer; *Worse and Worse*)
Wou'd please 'em better than to tell,   125
That, God be prais'd, the Dean is well.
Then he who prophecy'd the best,
Approves his Foresight to the rest:
"You know, I always fear'd the worst,
"And often told you so at first:"   130
He'd rather chuse that I should dye,
Than his Prediction prove a Lye.
Not one foretels I shall recover;
But, all agree, to give me over.

Yet shou'd some Neighbour feel a Pain,   135
Just in the Parts, where I complain;

How many a Message would he send?
What hearty Prayers that I should mend?
Enquire what Regimen I kept;
What gave me Ease, and how I slept?   140
And more lament, when I was dead,
Than all the Sniv'llers round my Bed.

MY good Companions, never fear,
For though you may mistake a Year;
Though your Prognosticks run too fast,   145
They must be verify'd at last.

"BEHOLD the fatal Day arrive!
"How is the Dean? He's just alive.
"Now the departing Prayer is read:
"He hardly breathes. The Dean is dead.   150
"Before the Passing-Bell begun,
"The News thro' half the Town has run.
"O, may we all for Death prepare!
"What has he left? And who's his Heir?
"I know no more than what the News is,   155
"'Tis all bequeath'd to publick Uses.
"To publick Use! A perfect Whim!
"What had the Publick done for him!
"Meer Envy, Avarice, and Pride!
"He gave it all:—But first he dy'd.   160
"And had the Dean, in all the Nation,
"No worthy Friend, no poor Relation?
"So ready to do Strangers good,
"Forgetting his own Flesh and Blood?

Now Grub-Street Wits are all emply'd;   165
With Elegies, the Town is cloy'd:
Some Paragraph in ev'ry Paper,
¹ To *curse* the *Dean*, or *bless* the *Drapier*.

¹ *The Author imagines, that the Scriblers of the prevailing Party, which he always opposed, will libel him after his Death, but that others will remember him with Gratitude, who consider the Service he had done to Ireland, under the Name of M. B. Drapier, by utterly defeating the destructive Project of* Wood's Halfpence, in five Letters to the People of Ireland, *at that Time read universally, and convincing every Reader.* [The notes to the present edition of the poem are generally acknowledged to be Swift's, added to the text probably no later than May, 1732.]

---

168. *Bless the Drapier:* As Swift's own note indicates, he wrote a series of essays (1724–1725) under the name of M. B. Drapier (the *Drapier's Letters*) to encourage the Irish to oppose a patent, granted by the Crown, to the Englishman William Wood, as a result of which he could manufacture and put into circulation in Ireland £100,000 of copper money over a period of fourteen years.

THE Doctors tender of their Fame,
Wisely on me lay all the Blame: 170
"We must confess his Case was nice;
"But he would never take Advice:
"Had he been rul'd, for ought appears,
"He might have liv'd these Twenty Years:
"For when we open'd him we found,   175
"That all his vital Parts were sound.

FROM *Dublin* soon to *London* spread,
2 'Tis told at Court, the Dean is dead.

3 KIND Lady *Suffolk* in the Spleen,
Runs laughing up to tell the Queen.   180
The Queen, so Gracious, Mild, and Good,
Cries, "Is he gone? 'Tis time he shou'd.
"He's dead you say; why let him rot;
4 "I'm glad the Medals were forgot.
"I promis'd them, I own; but when?   185
"I only was the Princess then;
"But now as Consort of the King,
"You know 'tis quite a different Thing.

5 Now, *Chartres* at Sir *Robert's* Levee,
Tells, with a Sneer, the Tidings heavy: 190
"Why, is he dead without his Shoes?

---

2 *The Dean supposeth himself to dye in* Ireland.

3 *Mrs.* Howard, *afterwards Countess of* Suffolk, *then of the Bed-chamber to the Queen, professed much Friendship for the Dean. The Queen then Princess, sent a dozen times to the Dean (then in* London*) with her Command to attend her; which at last he did, by Advice of all his Friends. She often sent for him afterwards, and always treated him very Graciously. He taxed her with a Present worth Ten Pounds, which she promised before he should return to* Ireland, *but on his taking Leave, the Medals were not ready.*

4 *The Medals were to be sent to the Dean in four Months, but she forgot them, or thought them too dear. The Dean, being in* Ireland, *sent Mrs.* Howard *a Piece of* Indian *Plad made in that Kingdom: which the Queen seeing took from her, and wore it herself, and sent to the Dean for as much as would cloath herself and Children, desiring he would send the Charge of it. He did the former. It cost thirty-five Pounds, but he said he would have nothing except the Medals. He was the Summer following in* England, *was treated as usual, and she being then Queen, the Dean was promised a Settlement in* England, *but returned as he went, and, instead of Favour or Medals, hath been ever since under her Majesty's Displeasure.*

5 Chartres *is a most infamous, vile Scoundrel, grown from a Foot-Boy, or worse, to a prodigious Fortune both in* England *and* Scotland: *He had a Way of insinuating himself into all Ministers under every Change, either as Pimp, Flatterer, or Informer. He was Tryed at Seventy for a Rape, and came off by sacrificing a great Part of his Fortune (he is since dead, but this Poem still preserves the Scene and Time it was writ in.)*

---

189. *Chartres:* Francis Charteris (1675–   cheat who became wealthy.
1732) was a well-known scoundrel and

⁶ (Cries *Bob*) "I'm Sorry for the News;
  Oh, were the Wretch but living still,
⁷ And in his Place my good Friend *Will*;
  Or, had a Mitre on his Head   195
⁸ Provided *Bolingbroke* were dead.

   ⁹ Now *Curl* his Shop from Rubbish drains;
  Three genuine Tomes of *Swift's* Remains.
  And then to make them pass the glibber,
¹⁰ Revis'd by *Tibbalds, Moore, and Cibber.*   200
  He'll treat me as he does my Betters.
¹¹ Publish my Will, my Life, my Letters.
  Revive the Libels born to dye;
  Which Pope must bear, as well as I.

   Here shift the Scene, to represent   205
  How those I love, my Death lament.
  Poor Pope will grieve a Month; and Gay
  A Week; and Arbuthnott a Day.

   St. John himself will scarce forbear,
  To bite his Pen, and drop a Tear.   210
  The rest will give a Shrug and cry,
  I'm sorry; but we all must dye.
  Indifference clad in Wisdom's Guise,
  All Fortitude of Mind supplies:
  For how can stony Bowels melt,   215

⁶ *Sir* Robert Walpole, *Chief Minister of State, treated the* Dean *in* 1726, *with great Distinction, invited him to Dinner at* Chelsea, *with the Dean's Friends chosen on Purpose; appointed an Hour to talk with him of* Ireland, *to which Kingdom and People the Dean found him no great Friend; for he defended* Wood's *Project of Half-pence, &c. The* Dean *would see him no more; and upon his next Year's return to* England, *Sir* Robert *on an accidental Meeting, only made a civil Compliment, and never invited him again.*

⁷ *Mr.* William Pultney, *from being Mr.* Walpole's *intimate Friend, detesting his Administration, opposed his Measures, and joined with my* Lord Bolingbroke, *to represent his Conduct in an excellent Paper, called the* Craftsman, *which is still continued.*

⁸ Henry St. John, *Lord Viscount* Bolingbroke, *Secretary of State to* Queen Anne *of blessed Memory. He is reckoned the most Universal Genius in* Europe; Walpole *dreading his Abilities, treated him most injuriously, working with King* George, *who forgot his Promise of restoring the said Lord, upon the restless Importunity of* Walpole.

⁹ Curl *hath been the most infamous Bookseller of any Age or Country: His Character in Part may be found in Mr.* Pope's *Dunciad. He published three Volumes all charged on the* Dean, *who never writ three Pages of them: He hath used many of the Dean's Friends in almost as vile a Manner.*

¹⁰ *Three stupid Verse Writers in* London, *the last to the Shame of the Court, and the highest Disgrace to Wit and Learning, was made Laureat.* Moore, *commonly called* Jemmy Moore, *Son of* Arthur Moore, *whose Father was Jaylor of* Monaghan *in* Ireland. *See the Character of* Jemmy Moore, *and* Tibbalds, Theobald *in the* Dunciad.

¹¹ Curl *is notoriously infamous for publishing the Lives, Letters, and last Wills and Testaments of the Nobility and Ministers of State, as well as of all the Rogues, who are hanged at* Tyburn. *He hath been in Custody of the House of Lords for publishing or forging the Letters of many Peers; which made the Lords enter a Resolution in their Journal Book, that no life or Writings of any Lord should be published without the Consent of the next Heir at Law, or Licence from their House.*

In those who never Pity felt;
When *We* are lash'd, *They* kiss the Rod;
Resigning to the Will of God.

THE Fools, my Juniors by a Year,
Are tortur'd with Suspence and Fear.   220
Who wisely thought my Age a Screen,
When Death approach'd, to stand between:
The Screen remov'd, their Hearts are trembling,
They mourn for me without dissembling.

MY female Friends, whose tender Hearts   225
Have better learn'd to act their Parts.
Receive the News in *doleful Dumps*,
"The Dean is dead, (*and what is Trumps?*)
"Then Lord have Mercy on his Soul.
"(Ladies I'll venture for the *Vole*.)   230
"Six Deans they say must bear the Pall.
"(I wish I knew what *King* to call.)
"Madam, your Husband will attend
"The Funeral of so good a Friend.
"No Madam, 'tis a shocking Sight,   235
"And he's engag'd To-morrow Night!
"My Lady *Club* wou'd take it ill,
"If he shou'd fail her at *Quadrill*.
"He lov'd the Dean. (*I lead a Heart*.)
"But dearest Friends, they say, must part.   240
"His Time was come, he ran his Race;
"We hope he's in a better Place.

WHY do we grieve that Friends should dye?
No Loss more easy to supply.
One Year is past; a different Scene;   245
No further mention of the Dean;
Who now, alas, no more is mist,
Than if he never did exist.
Where's now this Fav'rite of *Apollo?*
Departed; *and his Works must follow*:   250
Must undergo the common Fate;
His Kind of Wit is out of Date.
Some Country Squire to [12]*Lintot* goes,
Enquires for SWIFT in Verse and Prose:
Says *Lintot*, "I have heard the Name: 255

---

[12] Bernard Lintot, *a Bookseller in* London. *Vide Mr.* Pope's *Dunciad.*

---

230. *Vole:* A term in the card games   all tricks.
quadrille and ombre; it stands for winning

"He dy'd a Year ago." The same.
He searcheth all his Shop in vain;
"Sir you may find them in [13]*Duck-lane:*
"I sent them with a Load of Books,
"Last *Monday* to the Pastry-cooks.   260
"To fancy they cou'd live a Year!
"I find you're but a Stranger here.
"The Dean was famous in his Time;
"And had a Kind of Knack at Rhyme:
"His way of Writing now is past;   265
"The Town hath got a better Taste:
"I keep no antiquated Stuff;
"But, spick and span I have enough.
"Pray, do but give me leave to shew 'em;
"Here's *Colley Cibber's* Birth-day Poem.   270
"This Ode you never yet have seen,
"By *Stephen Duck,* upon the Queen.
"Then, here's a Letter finely penn'd
"Against the *Craftsman* and his Friend;
"It clearly shews that all Reflection   275
"On Ministers, is disaffection.
[14] "Next, here's Sir *Robert's* Vindication,
[15] "And Mr. *Henly's* last Oration:
"The Hawkers have not got 'em yet,
"Your Honour please to buy a Set?   280

[16]"HERE's *Wolston's* Tracts, the twelfth Edition;
"'Tis read by ev'ry Politician:
"The Country Members, when in Town,
"To all their Boroughs send them down:
"You never met a Thing so smart;   285
"The Courtiers have them all by Heart:
"Those Maids of Honour (who can read)

[13] *A Place in* London *where old Books are sold.*
[14] Walpole *hires a Set of Party Scriblers, who do nothing else but write in his Defence.*
[15] Henly *is a Clergyman who wanting both Merit and Luck to get Preferment, or even to keep his Curacy in the Established Church, formed a new Conventicle, which he calls an Oratory. There, at set Times, he delivereth strange Speeches compiled by himself and his Associates, who share the Profit with him: Every Hearer pays a Shilling each Day for Admittance. He is an absolute Dunce, but generally reputed crazy.*
[16] Wolston *was a Clergyman, but for want of Bread, hath in several Treatises, in the most blasphemous Manner, attempted to turn Our Saviour and his Miracles into Ridicule. He is much caressed by many great Courtiers, and by all the Infidels, and his Books read generally by the Court Ladies.*

270. *Colley Cibber:* Cibber (1671–1757), a successful theater manager and playwright, was an incompetent versifier named poet laureate in 1730. See the headnote to Pope's *Dunciad.*
272. *Stephen Duck:* Duck (1705–1756) was a farm laborer turned poet; he won the Court's approval for his verse.
274. *Craftsman:* See n. 1. 59.
277. *Sir Robert's:* Walpole's. See n. l. 59.

"Are taught to use them for their Creed.
"The Rev'rend Author's good Intention,
"Hath been rewarded with a Pension: 290
"He doth an Honour to his Gown,
"By bravely running *Priest-craft* down:
"He shews, as sure as GOD's in *Gloc'ster*,
"That *Jesus* was a Grand Impostor:
"That all his Miracles were Cheats,   295
"Perform'd as Juglers do their Feats:
"The Church had never such a Writer:
"A Shame, he hath not got a Mitre!

    Suppose me dead; and then suppose
A Club assembled at the *Rose*;   300
Where from Discourse of this and that,
I grow the Subject of their Chat:
And, while they toss my Name about,
With Favour some, and some without;
One quite indiff'rent in the Cause,   305
My Character impartial draws:

    "The Dean, if we believe Report,
"Was never ill receiv'd at Court:
"As for his Works in Verse and Prose,
"I own my self no Judge of those: 310
"Nor, can I tell what Criticks thought 'em;
"But, this I know, all People bought 'em;
"As with a moral View design'd
"To cure the Vices of Mankind:
"His Vein, ironically grave,   315
"Expos'd the Fool, and lash'd the Knave:
"To steal a Hint was never known,
"But what he writ was all his own.

    "He never thought an Honour done him,
"Because a Duke was proud to own him: 320
"Would rather slip aside, and chuse
"To talk with Wits in dirty Shoes:
"Despis'd the Fools with Stars and Garters,
"So often seen caressing [17]*Chartres*:
"He never courted Men in Station,   325
"*Nor Persons had in Admiration;*
"Of no Man's Greatness was afraid,

[17] *See the Notes before on* Chartres.

300. *Rose:* A famous tavern.

"Because he sought for no Man's Aid.
"Though trusted long in great Affairs,
"He gave himself no haughty Airs: 330
"Without regarding private Ends,
"Spent all his Credit for his Friends:
"And only chose the Wise and Good;
"No Flatt'rers; no Allies in Blood;
"But succour'd Virtue in Distress,   335
"And seldom fail'd of good Success;
"As Numbers in their Hearts must own,
"Who, but for him, had been unknown.

    "WITH Princes kept a due Decorum,
"But never stood in Awe before 'em: 340
"He follow'd *David's* Lesson just,
"*In Princes never put thy Trust.*
"And, would you make him truly sower;
"Provoke him with *a slave in Power:*
"The *Irish* Senate, if you nam'd,   345
"With what Impatience he declaim'd!
"Fair LIBERTY was all his Cry;
"For her he stood prepar'd to die;
"For her he boldly stood alone;
"For her he oft expos'd his own.   350
18 "Two Kingdoms, just as Faction led,
"Had set a Price upon his Head;
"But, not a Traytor cou'd be found,
"To sell him for Six Hundred Pound.

    "HAD he but spar'd his Tongue and Pen,   355
"He might have rose like other Men:
"But, Power was never in his Thought;
"And, Wealth he valu'd not a Groat:
"Ingratitude he often found,
"And pity'd those who meant the Wound: 360
"But, kept the Tenor of his Mind,
"To merit well of human Kind:
"Nor made a Sacrifice of those
"Who still were true, to please his Foes.

---

18 *In the Year* 1713, *the late Queen was prevailed with by an Address of the House of Lords in* England, *to publish a Proclamation, promising Three Hundred Pounds to whatever Person would discover the Author of a Pamphlet called,* The Publick Spirit of the Whiggs; *and in* Ireland, *in the Year* 1724, *my Lord* Carteret *at his first coming into the Government, was prevailed on to issue a Proclamation for promising the like Reward of Three Hundred Pounds, to any Person who could discover the Author of a Pamphlet called,* The Drapier's Fourth Letter, *&c. writ against that destructive Project of coining Half-pence for* Ireland, *but in neither Kingdoms was the Dean discovered.*

19 "He labour'd many a fruitless Hour   365
"To reconcile his Friends in Power;
"Saw Mischief by a Faction brewing,
"While they pursu'd each others Ruin.
"But, finding vain was all his Care,
"He left the Court in meer Despair.   370

"AND, oh! how short are human Schemes!
"Here ended all our golden Dreams.
"What St. JOHN's Skill in State Affairs,
"What ORMOND's *Valour*, OXFORD's Cares,
"To save their sinking Country lent,   375
"Was all destroy'd by one Event.
20 "Too soon that precious Life was ended,
"On which alone, our Weal depended.
21 "When up a dangerous Faction starts,
"With Wrath and Vengeance in their Hearts: 380
"*By solemn League and Cov'nant bound*,
"To ruin, slaughter, and confound;
"To turn Religion to a Fable,
"And make the Government a *Babel*:
"Pervert the Law, disgrace the Gown,   385
"Corrupt the Senate, rob the Crown;
"To sacrifice old *England's* Glory,
"And make her infamous in Story.
"When such a Tempest shook the Land,
"How could unguarded Virtue stand?   390

"WITH Horror, Grief, Despair the Dean
"Beheld the dire destructive Scene:
"His Friends in Exile, or the Tower,

---

19 *Queen* ANNE's *Ministry fell to Variance from the first Year after their Ministry began:* Harcourt *the Chancellor, and Lord* Bolingbroke *the Secretary, were discontented with the Treasurer* Oxford, *for his too much Mildness to the Whig Party; this Quarrel grew higher every Day till the Queen's Death: The Dean, who was the only Person that endeavoured to reconcile them, found it impossible; and thereupon retired to the Country about ten Weeks before that fatal Event: Upon which he returned to his Deanry in* Dublin, *where for many Years he was worried by the new People in Power, and had Hundreds of Libels writ against him in* England.
20 *In the Height of the Quarrel between the Ministers, the Queen died.*
21 *Upon Queen* ANNE's *Death the Whig Faction was restored to Power, which they exercised with the utmost Rage and Revenge; impeached and banished the Chief Leaders of the Church Party, and stripped all their Adherents of what Employments they had, after which* England *was never known to make so mean a Figure in Europe. The greatest Preferments in the Church in both Kingdoms were given to the most ignorant Men, Fanaticks were publickly caressed,* Ireland *utterly ruined and enslaved, only great Ministers heaping up Millions, and so Affairs continue until this present third Day of May, 1732, and are likely to go on in the same Manner.*

---

374. *Ormond's Valour, Oxford's Cares:* James Butler, Second Duke of Ormonde (1665–1746), was in 1711 appointed English commander-in-chief against France and Spain; Robert Harley, First Earl of Oxford (1661–1724), Tory statesman with Bolingbroke, 1710–1714 (see n. l. 59), fell out of favor and was dismissed from office.

²² "Himself within the Frown of Power;
  "Pursu'd by base envenom'd Pens,   395
²³ "Far to the Land of Slaves and Fens;
  "A servile Race in Folly nurs'd,
  "Who truckle most, when treated worst.

  "By Innocence and Resolution,
  "He bore continual Persecution;   400
  "While Numbers to Preferment rose;
  "Whose Merits were, to be his Foes.
  "When, *ev'n his own familiar Friends*
  "Intent upon their private Ends;
  "Like Renegadoes now he feels,   405
  "Against him lifting up their Heels.

  "The Dean did by his Pen defeat
²⁴ "An infamous destructive Cheat.
  "Taught Fools their Int'rest how to know;
  "And gave them Arms to ward the Blow.   410
  "Envy hath own'd it was his doing,
  "To save that helpless Land from Ruin,
  "While they who at the Steerage stood,
  "And reapt the Profit, sought his Blood,

  "To save them from their evil Fate,   415
  "In him was held a Crime of State.
²⁵ "A wicked Monster on the Bench,
  "Whose Fury Blood could never quench;
  "As vile and profligate a Villain,
  "As modern ²⁶*Scroggs*, or old *Tressilian*;   420
  "Who long all Justice had discarded,
  "Nor fear'd he GOD, nor Man regarded;
  "Vow'd on the Dean his Rage to vent,

---

²² *Upon the Queen's Death, the Dean returned to live in* Dublin, *at his Deanry-House: Numberless Libels were writ against him in* England, *as a Jacobite; he was insulted in the Street, and at Nights was forced to be attended by his Servants armed.*

²³ *The Land of Slaves and Fens, is* Ireland.

²⁴ *One* Wood, *a Hardware-man from* England, *had a Patent for coining Copper Half-pence in* Ireland, *to the Sum of* 108,000 l. *which in the Consequence, must leave that Kingdom without Gold or Silver (See* Drapier's Letters.)

²⁵ *One* Whitshed *was then Chief Justice: He had some Years before prosecuted a Printer for a Pamphlet writ by the Dean, to perswade the People of* Ireland *to wear their own Manufactures.* Whitshed *sent the Jury down eleven Times, and kept them nine Hours, until they were forced to bring in a special Verdict. He sat as Judge afterwards on the Tryal of the Printer of the* Drapier's Fourth Letter; *but the Jury, against all he could say or swear, threw out the Bill: All the Kingdom took the* Drapier's *Part, except the Courtiers, or those who expected Places. The* Drapier *was celebrated in many Poems and Pamphlets: His Sign was set up in most Streets of* Dublin (*where many of them still continue) and in several Country Towns.*

²⁶ Scroggs *was Chief Justice under King* Charles *the Second: His Judgment always varied in State Tryals, according to Directions from Court.* Tressilian *was a wicked Judge, hanged above three hundred Years ago.*

"And make him of his Zeal repent;
"But Heav'n his Innocence defends,   425
"The grateful People stand his Friends:
"Not Strains of Law, nor Judges Frown,
"Nor Topics brought to please the Crown,
"Nor Witness hir'd, nor Jury pick'd,
"Prevail to bring him in convict.   430

27 "IN Exile with a steady Heart,
"He spent his Life's declining Part;
"Where, Folly, Pride, and Faction sway,
28 "Remote from ST. JOHN, POPE, and GAY.

29"HIS Friendship there to few confin'd,   435
"Were always of the midling Kind:
"No Fools of Rank, a mungril Breed,
"Who fain would pass for Lords indeed:
30 "Where Titles give no Right or Power,
"And Peerage is a wither'd Flower,   440
"He would have held it a Disgrace,
"If such a Wretch had known his Face.
"On Rural Squires, that Kingdom's Bane,
"He vented oft his Wrath in vain:
31 "Biennial Squires, to Market brought;   445
"Who sell their Souls and Votes for Naught;
"The Nation stript go joyful back,
"To rob the Church, their Tenants rack,
"Go Snacks with Thieves and 32Rapparees,
"And, keep the Peace, to pick up Fees: 450
"In every Jobb to have a Share,
"A Jayl or 33Barrack to repair;
"And turn the Tax for publick Roads
"Commodious to their own Abodes.

---

27 *In Ireland, which he had Reason to call a Place of Exile; to which Country nothing could have driven him, but the Queen's Death, who had determined to fix him in* England, *in Spight of the Dutchess of* Somerset, &c.

28 Henry St. John, *Lord Viscount* Bolingbroke, *mentioned before.*

29 *In* Ireland *the Dean was not acquainted with one single Lord Spiritual or Temporal. He only conversed with private Gentlemen of the Clergy or Laity, and but a small Number of either.*

30 *The Peers of* Ireland *lost a great Part of their Jurisdiction by one single Act, and tamely submitted to this infamous Mark of Slavery without the least Resentment, or Remonstrance.*

31 *The Parliament (as they call it) in* Ireland *meet but once in two Years; and, after giving five Times more than they can afford, return Home to reimburse themselves by all Country Jobs and Oppressions, of which some few only are here mentioned.*

32 *The Highway-Men in* Ireland *are, since the late Wars there, usually called Rapparees, which was a Name given to those* Irish *Soldiers who in small Parties used, at that Time, to plunder the Protestants.*

33 *The Army in* Ireland *is lodged in Barracks, the building and repairing whereof, and other Charges, have cost a prodigious Sum to that unhappy Kingdom.*

"Perhaps I may allow, the Dean   455
"Had too much Satyr in his Vein;
"And seem'd determin'd not to starve it,
"Because no Age could more deserve it.
"Yet, Malice never was his Aim;
"He lash'd the Vice but spar'd the Name.   460
"No Individual could resent,
"Where Thousands equally were meant.
"His Satyr points at no Defect,
"But what all Mortals may correct;
"For he abhorr'd that senseless Tribe,   465
"Who call it Humour when they jibe:
"He spar'd a Hump or crooked Nose,
"Whose Owners set not up for Beaux.
"True genuine Dulness mov'd his Pity,
"Unless it offer'd to be witty.   470
"Those, who their Ignorance confess'd,
"He ne'er offended with a Jest;
"But laugh'd to hear an Idiot quote,
"A Verse from *Horace*, learn'd by Rote.

"He knew an hundred pleasant Stories,   475
"With all the Turns of *Whigs* and *Tories*:
"Was chearful to his dying Day,
"And Friends would let him have his Way.

"He gave the little Wealth he had,
"To build a House for Fools and Mad: 480
"And shew'd by one satyric Touch,
"No Nation wanted it so much:
[34] "That Kingdom he hath left his Debtor,
"I wish it soon may have a Better.

(1739)

[34] *Meaning* Ireland, *where he now lives, and probably may dye.*

Joseph Addison

1672-1719

Joseph Addison was born May 1, 1672, the son of a clergyman who was later to become Dean of Lichfield (the municipality in Staffordshire, famed as the home of Dr. Johnson). Addison attended the Charterhouse, than a school for boys, where he formed a friendship with Steele, and Magdalen College, Oxford, where his abilities as a Latinist won him a demyship (a kind of scholarship). *An Account of the Greatest English Poets* (1694) and a translation of the fourth book of Virgil's *Georgics* earned him a pension of £300 a year (through the efforts of Charles Montagu, Earl of Halifax) and enabled him to make the grand tour of Europe (1699–1703), whence he wrote *Letter to Lord Halifax* and gathered his impressions for *Remarks on Italy*, published in 1705.

Addison was commissioned to write *The Campaign* to celebrate Marlborough's victory at Blenheim; the poem won him a government post, and his next ten years were spent in various official capacities. During this time (1706) he produced the opera *Rosamond*. In 1708, he was elected to Parliament and retained a seat for the duration of his life.

Addison early began to contribute occasional papers to *The Tatler* (April, 1709, to January, 1711); of the 271 numbers only 42 papers were entirely his, though 36 were written in collaboration with Steele. Addison was responsible for developing the character of Sir Roger de Coverly for the *Spectator*, begun in 1711, as well as the famous Saturday papers on Milton's *Paradise Lost*. His *Cato*, a tragedy written according to the French rules, produced in 1713, was an enormous success, largely for political reasons, however. Two years later, Addison quarreled with Pope, who satirized him as Atticus in the *Epistle to Dr. Arbuthnot*, published after Addison's death.

In 1716, Addison married the Dowager Countess of Warwick. The following year he was appointed a Secretary of State, but ill-health forced him to resign the position in 1718. On June 17, 1719, he died at Holland House, his wife's residence in Kensington.

Richard Steele

1672-1729

Richard Steele was born in Dublin in 1672, the son of an English father and perhaps an Irish mother. He attended the Charterhouse, where he met Addison, and Oxford (Christ's and Merton Colleges) but left before taking a degree to join the army. His uneasy conscience, stimulated by his participation in a duel, prompted Steele to write *A Christian Hero* (1701), a prose treatise clearly enough characterized by its title. Next followed a series of plays: *The Funeral, or Grief-a-la-Mode* (1701); *The Lying Lover; or the Ladies' Friendship* (1703); *The Tender Husband* (1705). Steele's most famous and successful play, *The Conscious Lovers*, was not written until seventeen years later, in 1722. In 1707, Steele was appointed writer of *The London Gazette*, the official government news medium, and in the same year he married Mary Scurlock (his second wife), to whom he wrote a series of delightful notes and letters addressed "Dear Prue."

The famous *Tatler* appeared on April 12, 1709, under the pseudonymous editorship of Isaac Bickerstaff. It was issued on Tuesday, Thursday, and Saturday. Addison joined Steele–Bickerstaff shortly afterward and contributed 42 numbers until the paper's sudden termination in January, 1711. Two months later, however, *The Spectator* appeared, on March 1, and continued until December 6, 1712. This was followed by *The Guardian* in 1713.

In the same year Steele entered Parliament; he was expelled after a short time for his authorship of *The Crisis*, a pamphlet in support of the Hanoverian succession. But when George I reached the throne, Steele was appointed supervisor of Drury Lane Theatre and he was knighted.

Steele was estranged from Addison shortly before the latter's death in 1719. Because of financial difficulties, in 1722, Steele was forced to retire to his wife's estate in Wales, where he died on September 1, 1729.

Addison and Steele—Selective Bibliography

Addison Bibliography: *CBEL*, II, pp. 601 f.

Donald F. Bond, ed., *The Spectator*, 5 vols., Oxford, Clarendon Press, 1965.

Walter Graham, ed., *The Letters of Joseph Addison*, Oxford, Clarendon Press, 1941.

Peter Smithers, *The Life of Joseph Addison*, Oxford, Clarendon Press, 1954.

J. Lannering, *Studies in the Prose Style of Joseph Addison*, Uppsala, Univ. Engelska Seminariet, 1951; Cambridge, Mass., Harvard U. P., 1952.

Steele Bibliography: *CBEL*, II, pp. 608 f.

Rae Blanchard, ed., *Richard Steele's Periodical Journalism, 1714–1716*, London, Oxford U. P., 1959.

———, *The Englishman: A Political Journal*, Oxford, Clarendon Press, 1955.

———, *The Occasional Verse of Richard Steele*, Oxford, Clarendon Press, 1952.

———, *Tracts and Pamphlets*, Baltimore, Johns Hopkins Press, 1944.

———, *The Correspondence of Richard Steele*, London, Oxford U. P., 1941.

———, *The Christian Hero*, London, Oxford U. P., 1932.

George Aitken, ed., *The Tatler*, 4 vols., London, Duckworth, 1898–99.

———, *The Complete Plays of Richard Steele*, London, The Mermaid Series, 1894.

Calhuan Winton, *Captain Steele, The Early Career of Richard Steele*, Baltimore, Johns Hopkins Press, 1964.

John Loftis, *Steele at Drury Lane*, Berkeley, I. of California Press, 1952.

George Aitken, *The Life of Richard Steele*, 2 vols., London, W. Isbister, 1889.

Richmond P. Bond, *Introduction to Studies in the Early English Periodical*, Chapel Hill, U. of North Carolina, 1957.

Melvin R. Watson, *Magazine Serials and the Essay Tradition, 1746–1820*, Baton Rouge, Louisiana State U. P., 1956.

Headnote to
THE SPECTATOR

The Spectator offers the best examples of the periodical essay, a literary form whose direct antecedents gained popularity during the last quarter of the seventeenth century. These late-Restoration periodicals were typically printed in two columns on both sides of a single sheet somewhat larger than today's standard typing paper. The form of writing varied considerably from one to another. For example, Sir Roger L'Estrange's *Observator* (1681–1687) employed the device of dialogue; others, like Richard Willis's *Occasional Paper* (1697–1698), were given the form of letters. Among the many other periodicals were those offering foreign news, often made up of discrete items; and argumentative papers, very often politically directed. Few if any of these various types of periodical literature achieved exactly the structural features of the essays Addison and Steele were to write. But those written in the form of letters fairly well anticipated both *The Tatler* and *The Spectator*.

In such periodical letters, the opportunity was early taken to expose certain idiosyncrasies of the letter-writer, so that the reader would recognize his humanity and grow fond of him. The practice met with such success that friends or relatives of the original correspondent were quickly invented and given the opportunity to characterize themselves, until soon a whole family of letter-writers presided over the periodical enterprise. As they formed this group of epistolary persons, the authors behind the letter-writers drew upon certain handy sources—English imitations of Theophrastan Characters and such treatments of everyday life as were to be found in Ned Ward's *London Spy* (1698–1700) and similar periodicals. On the other hand, they seem not to have derived very much from such well-known nonjournalistic essayists as Bacon or Montaigne. By the time Steele began to produce *The Tatler*, on April 12, 1709, he had a quite well-established tradition to work from. And though the periodical essay was not to reach its high point until a few years later, in *The Spectator*, the earlier *Tatler* generally explored the ground to be covered by their second venture.

Steele began *The Tatler* with no assistance except for advice and encouragement from Swift, to whom he was fairly close at the time. He wrote as Isaac Bickerstaff, the tattler—an astrologer in his mid-sixties. Addison, who was in Ireland serving as secretary to the Lord-

Lieutenant, recognized from an early number that his friend Steele was the author of the sheet, because of an allusion to a matter known to them privately. Thereafter he made occasional contributions to the periodical, which appeared on Tuesday, Thursday, and Saturday until January 2, 1711. Of the 271 numbers, however, it was Steele who produced the most by far, 188; Addison wrote 42; they collaborated on a few, and various other hands accounted for the remainder. Like the periodicals immediately preceding it, this one had the twofold Horatian aim—to please and to instruct. Steele tried to accomplish his purpose by stripping away ". . . the disguises of cunning, vanity, and affectation, and to recommend a general simplicity in our dress, our discourse, and our behavior"; to this sober commitment he wisely added numerous signs of his boundless vitality, expressed for the most part by a wide range of topics, particularly in the first fifty or so numbers. He emphasized this diversity by pretending that Bickerstaff's different departments of news originated from various places about town—usually coffee-houses, at each of which he said he had an agent. Reports of "gallantry, pleasure, and entertainment" were said to come from White's, a stylish establishment near St. James's Park; poetry emanated from Will's, which had been Dryden's literary headquarters; news from abroad originated in St. James's coffee-house, located near the palace; and "learning" was reported from the Grecian. Generally Steele wrote all these news items in addition to a section entitled "From my Own Apartment," which soon became the most popular feature, and in fact began to displace the others. Meanwhile Addison added another dimension to the periodical with his memorable portraits of such notables as Tom Folio, a pedant; the Political Upholsterer, who though he had details of foreign affairs at his fingertips, was out of touch with life in his own family; and Ned Softly, who persisted in reading his bad verse aloud. Finally, Steele wrote warmly on marriage, love, and the home; his sentiments were so well received as to accomplish what fiery clergymen of the Restoration had despaired of doing—making morality acceptable.

Two months after *The Tatler* came to an abrupt end, *The Spectator* began its unprecedented daily run of 555 issues. Of these, Addison wrote over 250, and Steele just under 250 numbers; the remaining fifty or so were produced by several others, including Pope. The constant demand on the two chief authors must have been wearing; nevertheless, essay after essay, particularly Addison's, are so unobtrusively graceful and easy, they have quickened the admiration of readers from their first appearance to the present day. In his life of Addison, Johnson says, "His prose is the model of the middle style; on grave subjects not formal, on light subjects not groveling; pure without scrupulosity, and exact without apparent elaboration; always equable, and always easy, without glowing words or pointed sentences. Addison never deviates from his track to snatch a grace; he seeks no ambitious ornaments, and tries no hazardous innovations. His page is always luminous, but never blazes in unexpected splendour."

It was not Addison's style alone that accounted for the success of *The Spectator*, though it would be difficult to exaggerate the value of his unusual felicity of expression. Also important are "Mr. Spectator" and the many other characters whose varied points of view added richness and variety to the enterprise. The Spectator himself is a well-educated, taciturn man of good family, who spends his life observing the activities of other men. The Templar (a student of the law), the Clergymen, Captain Sentry, Will Honeycomb (man about town), and the merchant Sir Andrew Freeport, all represent different professions and ways of life, and their opinions are shaped accordingly. Most prominent among the Characters, however, is Sir Roger de Coverly, the kindly country squire, whose early years had included some wild days in the Restoration; the reader knows him principally as a benevolent old Tory, whose good intentions do not always save him from political naïveté.

Addison and Steele were both Whigs out of employment between 1710 and 1714, when the Tories were in power. Nevertheless, they avoided political controversy (apart from occasional affectionate ridicule directed against Sir Roger and occasional support of the Whig Sir Andrew), devoting themselves generally to a wide range of subjects, including criticism of plays, commentary on *Paradise Lost*, relationships between the sexes, the imagination as a moral and as an aesthetic instrument, the shift in sensibility from Restoration times to the Age of Queen Anne, the values of country living, proper behavior in church, the idiosyncrasies of women, the sights of London, tranquility of the spirit, immortality of the soul, and the virtues (including the advantages to one's country) of a solid career in business. In treating the subjects in this wide-ranging realm, the authors never lost their pleasant sense of humor, however serious the subject, or the point of view they might be forwarding. It is a tribute to them that their readers accepted *The Spectator's* astute observations and gentle admonitions as both pleasurable and instructive. Obviously Addison and Steele had succeeded in their ambitious purpose, announced by Mr. Spectator in No. 10: "Since I have raised to myself so great an audience, I shall spare no pains to make their instruction agreeable, and their diversion useful, for which reasons I shall endeavour to enliven morality with wit, and to temper wit with morality, that my readers may, if possible, both ways find their account in the speculation of the day."

TEXT. *The Spectator* (2 vols., London, 1711–12).

The Spectator

No. 1 [*Addison*]   *Thursday, March 1, 1711*

> *Non fumum ex fulgore, sed ex fumo dare lucem*
> *Cogitat, ut speciosa dehinc miracula promat.*[1]
> — HOR.

To be Continued every Day

I HAVE observed, that a Reader seldom peruses a Book with Pleasure 'till he knows whether the Writer of it be a black or a fair Man, of a mild or cholerick Disposition, Married or a Batchelor, with other Particulars of the like nature, that conduce very much to the right Understanding of an Author. To gratify this Curiosity, which is so natural to a Reader, I design this Paper, and my next, as Prefatory Discourses to my following Writings, and shall give some Account in them of the several Persons that are engaged in this Work. As the chief Trouble of Compiling, Digesting and Correcting will fall to my Share, I must do my self the Justice to open the Work with my own History.

I was born to a small Hereditary Estate, which I find, by the Writings of the   10
Family, was bounded by the same Hedges and Ditches in *William* the Conqueror's Time that it is at present, and has been delivered down from Father to Son whole and entire, without the Loss or Acquisition of a single Field or Meadow, during the Space of six hundred Years. There goes a Story in the Family, that when my Mother was gone with Child of me about three Months, she dreamt that she was brought to Bed of a Judge: Whether this might proceed

---

[1] *Non fumum . . . promat:* He does not plan to give smoke after flame, but after smoke the light, so that he may then produce striking and wonderful tales. Horace, *Ars Poetica*, ll. 143–144.

from a Law-Suit which was then depending in the Family, or my Father's being a Justice of the Peace, I cannot determine; for I am not so vain as to think it presaged any Dignity that I should arrive at in my future Life, though that was the Interpretation which the Neighbourhood put upon it. The Gravity of my Behaviour at my very first Appearance in the World, and all the Time that I sucked, seemed to favour my Mother's Dream: For, as she has often told me, I threw away my Rattle before I was two Months old, and would not make use of my Coral 'till they had taken away the Bells from it.

As for the rest of my Infancy, there being nothing in it remarkable, I shall pass it over in Silence. I find, that, during my Nonage, I had the Reputation of a very sullen Youth, but was always a Favourite of my School-Master, who used to say, *that my Parts were solid and would wear well.* I had not been long at the University, before I distinguished my self by a most profound Silence: For, during the Space of eight Years, excepting in the public Exercises of the College, I scarce uttered the Quantity of an hundred Words; and indeed do not remember that I ever spoke three Sentences together in my whole Life. Whilst I was in this Learned Body I applied my self with so much Diligence to my Studies, that there are very few celebrated Books, either in the Learned or the Modern Tongues, which I am not acquainted with.

Upon the Death of my Father I was resolved to travel into Foreign Countries, and therefore left the University, with the Character of an odd unaccountable Fellow, that had a great deal of Learning, if I would but show it. An insatiable Thirst after Knowledge carried me into all the Countries of *Europe*, where there was any thing new or strange to be seen; nay, to such a Degree was my Curiosity raised, that having read the Controversies of some great Men concerning the Antiquities of *Egypt*, I made a Voyage to *Grand Cairo*, on purpose to take the Measure of a Pyramid; and as soon as I had set my self right in that Particular, returned to my Native Country with great Satisfaction.

I have passed my latter Years in this City, where I am frequently seen in most publick Places, tho' there are not above half a dozen of my select Friends that know me; of whom my next Paper shall give a more particular Account. There is no Place of publick Resort, wherein I do not often make my Appearance; sometimes I am seen thrusting my Head into a Round of Politicians at *Will's*,[2] and listning with great Attention to the Narratives that are made in those little Circular Audiences. Sometimes I smoak a Pipe at *Child's*;[3] and whilst I seem attentive to nothing but the *Post-Man*,[4] overhear the Conversation of every Table in the Room. I appear on *Sunday* Nights at St. *James's* Coffee-House,[5] and sometimes join the little Committee of Politicks in the Inner-Room, as one who comes there to hear and improve. My Face is likewise very well known at the *Grecian*,[6] the *Cocoa-Tree*,[7] and in the Theaters

10

20

30

40

---

[2] *Will's:* Will's Coffee-house is best known as Dryden's headquarters.

[3] *Child's:* Child's Coffee-house, located in St. Paul's churchyard, was much used by physicians and the clergy.

[4] *Post-Man:* A newspaper with a Whig bias; it had a good range of news material nevertheless.

[5] *St. James's Coffee-House:* A fashionable place favored by Whig patrons.

[6] *Grecian:* A coffee-house frequented by learned men, particularly by members of the Royal Society.

[7] *Cocoa-Tree:* A chocolate-house used almost exclusively by Tories.

both of *Drury-Lane*, and the *Hay-Market*. I have taken for a Merchant upon the *Exchange*[8] for above these ten Years, and sometimes pass for a *Jew* in the Assembly of Stock-Jobbers at *Jonathan's*.[9] In short, where-ever I see a Cluster of People I always mix with them, tho' I never open my Lips but in my own Club.

Thus I live in the World, rather as a Spectator of Mankind, than as one of the Species; by which means I have made my self a Speculative Statesman, Soldier, Merchant and Artizan, without ever medling with any Practical Part in Life. I am very well versed in the Theory of an Husband, or a Father, and can discern the Errors in the Oeconomy, Business, and Diversion of others, better than those who are engaged in them; as Standers-by discover Blots,[10] which are apt to escape those who are in the Game. I never espoused any Party with Violence, and am resolved to observe an exact Neutrality between the Whigs and Tories, unless I shall be forc'd to declare my self by the Hostilities of either side. In short, I have acted in all the parts of my Life as a Looker-on, which is the Character I intend to preserve in this Paper.

I have given the Reader just so much of my History and Character, as to let him see I am not altogether unqualified for the Business I have undertaken. As for other Particulars in my Life and Adventures, I shall insert them in following Papers, as I shall see occasion. In the mean time, when I consider how much I have seen, read and heard, I begin to blame my own Taciturnity; and since I have neither Time nor Inclination to communicate the Fulness of my Heart in Speech, I am resolved to do it in Writing; and to Print my self out, if possible, before I Die. I have been often told by my Friends, that it is Pity so many useful Discoveries which I have made, should be in the Possession of a Silent Man. For this Reason therefore, I shall publish a Sheetfull of Thoughts every Morning, for the Benefit of my Contemporaries; and if I can any way contribute to the Diversion or Improvement of the Country in which I live, I shall leave it, when I am summoned out of it, with the secret Satisfaction of thinking that I have not Lived in vain.

There are three very material Points which I have not spoken to in this Paper, and which, for several important Reasons, I must keep to my self, at least for some Time: I mean, an Account of my Name, my Age, and my Lodgings. I must confess I would gratify my Reader in any thing that is reasonable; but as for these three Particulars, though I am sensible they might tend very much to the Embellishment of my Paper, I cannot yet come to a Resolution of communicating them to the Publick. They would indeed draw me out of that Obscurity which I have enjoy'd for many Years, and expose me in publick Places to several Salutes and Civilities, which have been always very disagreeable to me; for the greatest Pains I can suffer, are the being talked to, and being stared at. It is for this Reason likewise, that I keep my Complexion and Dress, as very great Secrets; tho' it is not impossible, but I may make Discoveries of both in the Progress of the Work I have undertaken.

[8] *Exchange:* Probably the Royal Exchange, where merchants of all nations gathered to buy and sell commodities.
[9] *Jonathan's:* Jonathan's Coffee-house was located near the Royal Exchange.
[10] *Blots:* Exposed pieces in backgammon.

After having been thus particular upon my self, I shall in to-Morrow's Paper give an Account of those Gentlemen who are concerned with me in this Work. For, as I have before intimated, a Plan of it is laid and concerted (as all other Matters of Importance are) in a Club. However, as my Friends have engaged me to stand in the Front, those who have a mind to correspond with me, may direct their Letters *To the Spectator*, at Mr. *Buckley's*[11] in *Little Britain*. For I must further acquaint the Reader, that tho' our Club meets only on *Tuesdays* and *Thursdays*, we have have appointed a Committee to sit every Night, for the Inspection of all such Papers[12] as may contribute to the Advancement of the Publick Weal.   10

No. 2 [Steele]   *Friday, March 2, 1711*

> . . . *Ast Alii sex*
> *Et plures uno conclamant ore.*[1]
> —Juv.

THE first of our Society is a Gentleman of *Worcestershire*, of antient Descent, a Baronet, his Name Sir ROGER DE COVERLY.[2] His great Grandfather was Inventor of that famous Country-Dance which is call'd after him.[3] All who know that Shire, are very well acquainted with the Parts and Merits of Sir ROGER. He is a Gentleman that is very singular in his Behaviour, but his Singularities proceed from his good Sense, and are Contradictions to the Manners of the World, only as he thinks the World is in the wrong. However, this Humour creates him no Enemies, for he does nothing with Sowrness or Obstinacy; and his being unconfined to Modes and Forms, makes him but the readier and more capable to please and oblige   20 all who know him. When he is in Town he lives in *Soho-Square*.[4] It is said he keeps himself a Batchelour by reason he was crossed in Love, by a perverse beautiful Widow of the next County to him. Before this Disappointment, Sir ROGER was what you call a fine Gentleman, had often supped with my Lord *Rochester* and Sir *George Etherege*,[5] fought a Duel upon his first coming to Town, and kick'd Bully *Dawson*[6] in a publick Coffee-house for calling him Youngster. But being ill used by the abovementioned Widow, he was very serious for a Year and a half; and tho' his Temper being naturally jovial,

---

[11] *Buckley's: The Spectator* was originally printed (published) by Samuel Buckley.

[12] *Papers:* Letters to *The Spectator* (genuinely from readers) were often printed.

[1] *. . . Ast Alii . . . ore:* So a half-dozen and more shout together. Juvenal, *Satires,* VII, 167–168.

[2] *Roger de Coverly:* See the headnote for Sir Roger and for the Society or Club mentioned earlier in this first sentence.

[3] *Call'd after him:* There was indeed such a dance, probably derived from the De Coverly family, around 1685.

[4] *Soho-Square:* Built in 1681, Soho-Square was the most fashionable part of town in Queen Anne's day.

[5] *Lord Rochester . . . George Etherege:* John Wilmot, Earl of Rochester (1647–1680), a handsome, lively wit, courtier, and poet; Sir George Etherege (1635?–1692), Restoration dramatist.

[6] *Bully Dawson:* A Restoration rake, sharper, swaggerer, and debauchee.

he at last got over it, he grew careless of himself and never dressed afterwards; he continues to wear a Coat and Doublet of the same Cut that were in
Fashion at the Time of his Repulse, which, in his merry Humours, he tells
us, has been in and out twelve Times since he first wore it. 'Tis said Sir ROGER
grew humble in his Desires after he had forgot this cruel Beauty, insomuch
that it is reported he has frequently offended in Point of Chastity with Beggars
and Gypsies; But this is look'd upon by his Friends rather as Matter of Raillery
than Truth. He is now in his Fifty sixth Year, cheerful, gay, and hearty,
keeps a good House both in Town and Country; a great Lover of Mankind;
but there is such a mirthful Cast in his Benaviour, that he is rather beloved   10
than esteemed: His Tenants grow rich, his Servants look satisfied, all the
young Women profess Love to him, and the young Men are glad of his
Company: When he comes into a House he calls the Servants by their Names,
and talks all the way up Stairs to a Visit. I must not omit that Sir ROGER is
a Justice of the *Quorum*;[7] that he fills the Chair at a Quarter-Session with
great Abilities, and three Months ago gain'd universal Applause by explaining a Passage in the Game-Act.[8]

The Gentleman next in Esteem and Authority among us, is another Batchelour, who is a Member of the *Inner-Temple*;[9] a Man of great Probity, Wit,
and Understanding; but he has chosen his Place of Residence rather to obey   20
the Direction of an old humoursome Father than in Pursuit of his own Inclinations. He was plac'd there to study the Laws of the Land, and is the most learned
of any of the House in those of the Stage. *Aristotle* and *Longinus* are much better
understood by him than *Littleton* or *Cooke*.[10] The Father sends up every
Post Questions relating to Marriage-Articles, Leases, and Tenures, in the
Neighbourhood; all which Questions he agrees with an Attorney to answer
and take care of in the Lump: He is studying the Passions themselves, when
he should be inquiring into the Debates among Men which arise from them.
He knows the Argument of each of the Orations of *Demosthenes* and *Tully*,[11]
but not one Case in the Reports of our own Courts. No one ever took him   30
for a Fool, but none, except his intimate Friends, know he has a great deal
of Wit. This Turn makes him at once both disinterested and agreeable:
As few of his Thoughts are drawn from Business, they are most of them
fit for Conversation. His Taste of Books is a little too just for the Age he
lives in; he has read all, but approves of very few. His Familiarity with the
Customs, Manners, Actions, and Writings of the Antients, makes him a
very delicate Observer of what occurs to him in the present World. He is
an excellent Critick, and the Time of the Play, is his Hour of Business; exactly

---

[7] *Quorum:* A group of justices whose
presence was necessary to constitute a
bench.

[8] *Game-Act:* It was illegal for one who
did not own land producing £100 a year
or more to hunt game.

[9] *Inner-Temple:* One of four legal
societies in London—Gray's, Lincoln's,
Middle, and Inner Temple—controlling
admission to the bar.

[10] *Littleton or Cooke:* Sir Thomas
Lyttleton (1402–1481), English jurist who
wrote on *Tenures*, in law French; Sir
Edward Coke (1552–1634), who wrote
several well-known works on the law,
one now called *Coke upon Littleton*.

[11] *Demosthenes and Tully:* These classical authors, like Aristotle and Longinus,
mentioned above, are well known for their
concern with discourse or rhetoric.

at five he passes through *New-Inn*,[12] crosses through *Russel-Court*, and takes a Turn at *Will's* till the Play begins; he has his Shooes rubb'd and his Perriwig powder'd at the Barber's as you go into the *Rose*.[13] It is for the Good of the Audience when he is at a Play, for the Actors have an Ambition to please him.

The Person of next Consideration is Sir ANDREW FREEPORT,[14] a Merchant of great Eminence in the City of *London*: A Person of indefatigable Industry, strong Reason, and great Experience. His Notions of Trade are noble and generous, and (as every rich Man has usually some sly Way of Jesting, which would make no great Figure were he not a rich Man) he calls the Sea the *British Common*. He is acquainted with Commerce in all its Parts, and will tell you that it is a stupid and barbarous Way to extend Dominion by Arms; for true Power is to be got by Arts and Industry. He will often argue, that if this Part of our Trade were well cultivated, we should gàin from one Nation; and if another, from another. I have heard him prove, that Diligence makes more lasting Acquisitions than Valour, and that Sloth had ruin'd more Nations than the Sword. He abounds in several frugal Maxims, among which the greatest Favourite is, 'A Penny saved is a Penny got.' A General Trader of good Sense, is pleasanter Company than a general Scholar; and Sir ANDREW having a natural unaffected Eloquence, the Perspicuity of his Discourse gives the same Pleasure that Wit would in another Man. He has made his Fortunes himself; and says that *England* may be richer than other Kingdoms, by as plain Methods as he himself is richer than other Men; tho' at the same Time I can say this of him, that there is not a Point in the Compass but blows home a Ship in which he is an Owner.

Next to Sir ANDREW in the Club-room sits Captain SENTRY, a Gentleman of great Courage, good Understanding, but invincible Modesty. He is one of those that deserve very well, but are very awkard at putting their Talents within the Observation of such as should take notice of them. He was some Years a Captain, and behaved himself with great Gallantry in several Engagements and at several Sieges; but having a small Estate of his own, and being next Heir to Sir ROGER, he has quitted a Way of Life in which no Man can rise suitably to his Merit, who is not something of a Courtier as well as a Souldier. I have heard him often lament, that in a Profession where Merit is placed in so conspicuous a View, Impudence should get the Better of Modesty. When he has talked to this Purpose I never heard him make a sower Expression, but frankly confess that he left the World because he was not fit for it. A strict Honesty and an even regular Behaviour, are in themselves Obstacles to him that must press through Crowds who endeavour at the same End with himself, the Favour of a Commander. He will however in this Way of Talk excuse Generals for not disposing according to Mens Desert, or enquiring into it: For, says he, that great Man who has a Mind to help me, has as many to break through to come at me, as I have to come at him: Therefore he will conclude, that the Man who would make a Figure, especially in a military

10

20

30

40

---

[12] *New-Inn:* An inn belonging to the Middle Temple; see n. 9.

[13] *Rose:* The Rose Tavern was located in Russell Street, near the Drury Lane Theatre.

[14] *Sir Andrew Freeport:* See the headnote.

Way, must get over all false Modesty, and assist his Patron against the Importunity of other Pretenders by a proper Assurance in his own Vindication. He says it is a civil Cowardice to be backward in asserting what you ought to expect, as it is a military Fear to be slow in attacking when it is your Duty. With this Candour does the Gentleman speak of himself and others. The same Frankness runs through all his Conversation. The military Part of his Life has furnish'd him with many Adventures, in the Relation of which he is very agreeable to the Company; for he is never over-bearing, tho' accustomed to command Men in the utmost Degree below him; nor ever too obsequious, from an Habit of obeying Men highly above him.   10

But that our Society may not appear a Set of Humourists[15] unacquainted with the Gallantries and Pleasures of the Age, we have among us the gallant WILL. HONEYCOMB, a Gentleman who according to his Years should be in the Decline of his Life, but having ever been very careful of his Person, and always had a very easy Fortune, Time has made but very little Impression, either by Wrinkles on his Forehead, or Traces in his Brain. His Person is well turn'd, of a good Height. He is very ready at that Sort of Discourse with which Men usually entertain Women. He has all his Life dressed very well, and remembers Habits as others do Men. He can smile when one speaks to him, and laughs easily. He knows the History of every Mode, and can inform   20 you from which of the *French* King's Wenches our Wives and Daughters had this Manner of curling their Hair, that Way of placing their Hoods; whose Frailty was covered by such a Sort of Petticoat, and whose Vanity to shew her Foot made that Part of the Dress so short in such a Year. In a Word, all his Conversation and Knowledge has been in the female World: As other Men of his Age will take Notice to you what such a Minister said upon such and such an Occasion, he will tell you when the Duke of *Monmouth*[16] danced at Court such a Woman was then smitten, another was taken with him at the Head of his Troop in the *Park*. In all these important Relations, he has ever about the same Time received a kind Glance or a Blow of a Fan from   30 some celebrated Beauty, Mother of the present Lord such-a-one. If you speak of a young Commoner[17] that said a lively thing in the House, he starts up, 'He has good Blood in his Veins, *Tom Mirabell* begot him, the Rogue cheated me in that Affair; that young Fellow's Mother used me more like a Dog than any Woman I ever made Advances to.' This Way of Talking of his very much enlivens the Conversation among us of a more sedate Turn; and I find there is not one of the Company but my self, who rarely speak at all, but speaks of him as of that Sort of Man who is usually called a wellbred fine Gentleman. To conclude his Character, where Women are not concerned, he is an honest worthy Man.   40

I cannot tell whether I am to account him whom I am next to speak of, as one of our Company; for he visits us but seldom, but when he does it adds to

---

[15] *Humourists:* Those subject to humours (to their peculiar compulsions) and not amenable to reason.

[16] *Monmouth:* James, Duke of Monmouth (1649–1685), natural son of

Charles II and Lucy Walters, the Absalom of Dryden's *Absalom and Achitophel.*

[17] *Commoner:* Member of the House of Commons.

every Man else a new Enjoyment of himself. He is Clergyman, a very philosophick Man, of general Learning, great sanctity of Life, and the most exact
good Breeding. He has the Misfortune to be of a very weak Constitution,
and consequently cannot accept of such Cares and Business as Preferments
in his Function would oblige him to: He is therefore among Divines what a
Chamber-Councellor is among Lawyers. The Probity of his Mind, and the
Integrity of his Life, create him Followers, as being eloquent or loud advances
others. He seldom introduces the Subject he speaks upon; but we are so far
gone in Years, that he observes, when he is among us, an Earnestness to have
him fall on some divine Topick, which he always treats with much Authority,   10
as one who has no Interests in this World, as one who is hastening to the
Object of all his Wishes, and conceives Hope from his Decays and Infirmities.
These are my ordinary Companions.

No. 5 [Addison]   *Tuesday, March 6, 1711*

> *Spectatum admissi risum teneatis?* . . .[1]
>   — HOR.

AN Opera may be allowed to be extravagantly lavish in its Decorations, as its
only Design is to gratify the Senses, and keep up an indolent Attention in
the Audience. Common Sense however requires, that there should be nothing
in the Scenes and Machines which may appear Childish and Absurd.[2] How
would the Wits of King *Charles's* Time have laughed to have seen *Nicolini*[3]
exposed to a Tempest in Robes of Ermin, and sailing in an open Boat upon a
Sea of Paste-Board? What a Field of Raillery would they have been let into,   20
had they been entertain'd with painted Dragons spitting Wild-fire, enchanted
Chariots drawn by *Flanders* Mares, and real Cascades in artificial Land-skips?
A little Skill in Criticism would inform us that Shadows and Realities ought not
to be mix'd together in the same Piece; and that Scenes, which are designed as
the Representations of Nature, should be filled with Resemblances, and
not with the Things themselves. If one would represent a wide Champain
Country filled with Herds and Flocks, it would be ridiculous to draw the
Country upon the Scenes, and to crowd several Parts of the Stage with Sheep
and Oxen. This is joining together Inconsistencies, and making the Decoration
partly Real and partly Imaginary. I would recommend what I have here   30
said, to the Directors, as well as to the Admirers, of our Modern Opera.
    As I was walking the Streets about a Fortnight ago, I saw an ordinary
Fellow carrying a Cage full of little Birds upon his Shoulder; and, as I was
wondering with my self what Use he would put them to, he was met very

---

[1] *Spectatum . . . teneatis?* . . . : Given a
private view, could you keep from
laughing? Horace, *Ars Poetica*, l. 5.
    [2] *Absurd:* Italian opera was criticized
severely by many writers, particularly

during the opening decades of the century.
    [3] *Nicolini:* Nicola Grimaldi (1673–
1732), a Neapolitan actor and singer, began
his operatic career as a soprano and later
became a contralto.

luckily by an Acquaintance, who had the same Curiosity. Upon his asking him what he had upon his Shoulder, he told him, that he had been buying Sparrows for the Opera. Sparrows for the Opera, says his Friend, licking his Lips, what, are they to be roasted? No, no, says the other, they are to enter towards the end of the first Act, and to fly about the Stage.

This strange Dialogue awakened my Curiosity so far that I immediately bought the Opera, by which means I perceived that the Sparrows were to act the part of Singing Birds in a delightful Grove: though upon a nearer Enquiry I found the Sparrows put the same Trick upon the Audience, that Sir *Martin Mar-all*[4] practised upon his Mistress; for, though they flew in   10
Sight, the Musick proceeded from a Consort of Flagellets and Bird-calls which was planted behind the Scenes. At the same time I made this Discovery, I found by the Discourse of the Actors, that there were great Designs on foot for the Improvement of the Opera, that it had been proposed to break down a part of the Wall, and to surprize the Audience with a Party of an hundred Horse, and that there was actually a Project of bringing the *New-River*[5] into the House, to be employed in Jetteaus and Water-works. This Project, as I have since heard, is post-poned 'till the Summer-Season; when it is thought the Coolness that proceeds from Fountains and Cascades will be more acceptable and refreshing to People of Quality. In the mean time, to   20
find out a more agreeable Entertainment for the Winter-Season, the Opera of *Rinaldo*[6] is filled with Thunder and Lightning, Illuminations, and Fire-works; which the Audience may look upon without catching Cold, and indeed without much Danger of being burnt; for there are several Engines filled with Water, and ready to play at a Minute's Warning, in case any such Accident should happen. However, as I have a very great Friendship for the Owner of this Theater, I hope that he has been wise enough to *insure* his House before he would let this Opera be acted in it.

It is no wonder, that those Scenes should be very surprizing, which were contrived by two Poets of different Nations, and raised by two Magicians   30
of different Sexes. *Armida* (as we are told in the Argument) was an *Amazonian* Enchantress, and poor Seignior *Cassani* (as we learn from the *Persons repre-sented*) a Christian Conjurer (*Mago Christiano*). I must confess I am very much puzzled to find how an *Amazon* should be versed in the Black Art, or how a Christian should deal with the Devil.

To consider the Poets after the Conjurers, I shall give you a Taste of the Italian, from the first Lines of his Preface. *Eccoti, benigno Lettore, un Parto di poche Sere, che se ben nato di Notte, non è però aborto di Tenebre, mà si farà conoscere Figlio d'Apollo con qualche Raggio di Parnasso. Behold, gentle Reader, the Birth of a few Evenings, which tho' it be the Offspring of the Night, is not the Abortive*   40
of Darkness, but will make it self known to be the Son of Apollo, *with a certain Ray of* Parnassus. He afterwards proceeds to call Seignior *Hendel* the *Orpheus* of our Age, and to acquaint us, in the same Sublimity of Stile, that he Composed

---

[4] *Sir Martin Mar-all:* Sir Martin Mar-all, a play by Dryden. In the last act a character pretends to sing and play the lute to a lady, while in fact his man supplies the music.

[5] *New-River:* A water main in London.

[6] *Rinaldo:* An opera by Handel.

this Opera in a Fortnight. Such are the Wits, to whose Tastes we so ambitiously conform our selves. The Truth of it is, the finest Writers among the Modern *Italians*, express themselves in such a florid form of Words, and such tedious Circumlocutions, as are used by none but Pedants in our own Country; and at the same time, fill their Writings with such poor Imaginations and Conceits, as our Youths are ashamed of, before they have been Two Years at the University. Some may be apt to think, that it is the difference of Genius which produces this difference in the Works of the two Nations; but to show there is nothing in this, if we look into the Writings of the old *Italians*, such as *Cicero* and *Virgil*, we shall find that the *English* Writers, in their way   10 of thinking and expressing themselves, resemble those Authors much more than the Modern *Italians* pretend to do. And as for the Poet himself, from whom the Dreams of this Opera are taken, I must entirely agree with Monsieur *Boileau*, that one Verse in *Virgil*, is worth all the *Clincant* or Tinsel of *Tasso*.[7]

But to return to the Sparrows; there have been so many Flights of them let loose in this Opera, that it is feared the House will never get rid of them; and that in other Plays, they may make their Entrance is very wrong and improper Scenes, so as to be seen flying in a Lady's Bed-Chamber, or pearching upon a King's Throne; besides the Inconveniencies which the Heads of the Audience may sometimes suffer from them. I am credibly informed, that there was once a   20 Design of casting into an Opera, the Story of *Whittington* and his Cat, and that in order to it, there had been got together a great Quantity of Mice; but Mr. *Rich*,[8] the Proprietor of the Play-House, very prudently considered that it would be impossible for the Cat to kill them all, and that consequently the Princes of his Stage might be as much infested with Mice, as the Prince of the Island was before the Cat's arrival upon it; for which Reason, he would not permit it to be Acted in his House. And indeed I cannot blame him; for, as he said very well upon that Occasion, I do not hear that any of the Performers in our Opera, pretend to equal the famous Pied Piper, who made all the Mice of a great Town in *Germany* follow his Musick, and by that means cleared the   30 Place of those little Noxious Animals.

Before I dismiss this Paper, I must inform my Reader, that I hear there is a Treaty on Foot with *London* and *Wise*,[9] who will be appointed Gardiners of the Play-House, to furnish the Opera of *Rinaldo* and *Armida* with an Orange-Grove; and that the next time it is Acted, the Singing Birds will be Personated by Tom-Tits:[10] The Undertakers being resolved to spare neither Pains nor Mony, for the Gratification of the Audience.

[7] *Boileau . . . Tasso:* Nicolas Boileau (1636–1711), French critic; his first work, *Satires*, IX, contains the comment referred to in the text; Torquato Tasso (1544–1595), Italian poet, whose masterpiece is the epic *La Gerusalemme Liberata*.

[8] *Mr. Rich:* Christopher Rich (d. 1714), manager of Drury Lane Theatre.

[9] *London and Wise:* George London and Henry Wise owned a great nursery.

[10] *Tom-Tits:* Small birds, like wrens.

No. 10 [Addison]   *Monday, March 12, 1711*

> *Non aliter quam qui adverso vix flumine lembum*
> *Remigiis subigit: si brachia forte remisit,*
> *Atque illum in præceps prono rapit alveus amni.*[1]
> —VIRG.

IT is with much Satisfaction that I hear this great City inquiring Day by Day after these my Papers, and receiving my Morning Lectures with a becoming Seriousness and Attention. My Publisher tells me, that there are already Three Thousand of them distributed every Day: So that if I allow Twenty Readers to every Paper, which I look upon as a modest Computation, I may reckon about Threescore thousand Disciples in *London* and *Westminster*, who I hope will take care to distinguish themselves from the thoughtless Herd of their ignorant and unattentive Brethren. Since I have raised to my self so great an Audience, I shall spare no Pains to make their Instruction agreeable, and their Diversion useful. For which Reasons I shall endeavour to enliven Morality   10 with Wit, and to temper Wit with Morality, that my Readers may, if possible, both Ways find their Account in the Speculation of the Day. And to the End that their Virtue and Discretion may not be short transient intermitting Starts of Thought, I have resolved to refresh their Memories from Day to Day, till I have recovered them out of that desperate State of Vice and Folly into which the Age is fallen. The Mind that lies fallow but a single Day, sprouts up in Follies that are only to be killed by a constant and assiduous Culture. It was said of *Socrates*, that he brought Philosophy down from Heaven, to inhabit among Men; and I shall be ambitious to have it said of me, that I have brought Philosophy out of Closets and Libraries, Schools and Colleges, to dwell in   20 Clubs and Assemblies, at Tea-Tables, and in Coffee-Houses.

I would therefore in a very particular Manner recommend these my Speculations to all well regulated Families, that set apart an Hour in every Morning for Tea and Bread and Butter; and would earnestly advise them for their Good to order this Paper to be punctually served up, and to be looked upon as a Part of the Tea Equipage.

Sir *Francis Bacon*[2] observes, that a well-written Book compared with its Rivals and Antagonists, is like *Moses's* Serpent, that immediately swallow'd up and devoured those of the *Ægyptians*.[3] I shall not be so vain as to think, that where the SPECTATOR appears, the other publick Prints will vanish; but shall   30 leave it to my Readers Consideration, whether, Is it not much better to be let into the Knowledge of ones-self, than to hear what passes in *Muscovy* or *Poland*;[4] and to amuse our selves with such Writings as tend to the wearing out of

---

[1] *Non aliter. . . . :* Just as if someone whose oars can barely move his boat against the current should accidentally let up with his arms, and there headlong downstream the channel carries it away. Virgil, *Georgics*, I, 201–203.
[2] *Sir Francis Bacon:* Francis, Viscount St. Albans (1561–1626), English Philosopher and statesman; it is in *Advancement of Learning*, Bk. II, Introd. Sec. 14 that he makes the point referred to.
[3] *Ægyptians:* Exod. 7:12.
[4] *Muscovy or Poland:* See the headnote for a brief comment on the subject matter of many periodicals of the day and for the interests of the Political Upholster.

Ignorance, Passion, and Prejudice, than such as naturally conduce to inflame Hatreds and make Enmities irreconcileable?

In the next Place, I would recommend this Paper to the daily Perusal of those Gentlemen whom I cannot but consider as my good Brothers and Allies, I mean the Fraternity of Spectators who live in the World without having any thing to do in it; and either by the Affluence of their Fortunes, or Laziness of their Dispositions, have no other Business with the rest of Mankind but to look upon them. Under this Class of Men are comprehended all contemplative Tradesmen, titular Physitians, Fellows of the Royal Society, Templers[5] that are not given to be contentious, and Statesmen that are out of Business. In short, every one that considers the World as a Theatre, and desires to form a right Judgment of those who are the Actors on it.

There is another Set of Men that I must likewise lay a Claim to, whom I have lately called the Blanks of Society,[6] as being altogether unfurnish'd with Ideas, till the Business and Conversation of the Day has supplied them. I have often considered these poor Souls with an Eye of great Commiseration, when I have heard them asking the first Man they have met with, whether there was any News stirring? and by that Means gathering together Materials for thinking. These needy Persons do not know what to talk of, till about twelve a Clock in the Morning; for by that Time they are pretty good Judges of the Weather, know which Way the Wind sits, and whether the *Dutch* Mail be come in. As they lie at the Mercy of the first Man they meet, and are grave or impertinent all the Day long, according to the Notions which they have imbibed in the Morning, I would earnesly entreat them not to stir out of their Chambers till they have read this Paper, and do promise them that I will daily instil into them such sound and wholesome Sentiments, as shall have a good Effect on their Conversation for the ensuing twelve Hours.

But there are none to whom this Paper will be more useful, than to the female World. I have often thought there has not been sufficient Pains taken in finding out proper Employments and Diversions for the Fair ones. Their Amusements seem contrived for them rather as they are Women, than as they are reasonable Creatures; and are more adapted to the Sex, than to the Species. The Toilet is their great Scene of Business, and the right adjusting of their Hair the principal Employment of their Lives. The sorting of a Suit of Ribbons, is reckon'd a very good Morning's Work; and if they make an Excursion to a Mercer's or a Toy-shop,[7] so great a Fatigue makes them unfit for any thing else all the Day after. Their more serious Occupations are Sowing and Embroidery, and their greatest Drudgery the Preparation of Jellies and Sweet-meats. This, I say, is the State of ordinary Women; tho' I know there are Multitudes of those of a more elevated Life and Conversation, that move in an exalted Sphere of Knowledge and Virtue, that join all the Beauties of the Mind to the Ornaments of Dress, and inspire a kind of Awe and Respect, as well as Love, into their Male-Beholders. I hope to encrease the Number of these by

10

20

30

40

---

[5] *Fellows . . . Templers:* The Royal Society, founded about 1660, was concerned with science; templars were members of the Middle or Inner Temple, men connected with the practice of law.

[6] *Blanks of Society:* Spectator No. 4 characterizes these Blanks.

[7] *Toy-shop:* A boutique, a shop that sells ornamental articles and fancy items for women.

publishing this daily Paper, which I shall always endeavour to make an innocent if not an improving Entertainment, and by that Means at least divert the Minds of my female Readers from greater Trifles. At the same Time, as I would fain give some finishing Touches to those which are already the most beautiful Pieces in humane Nature, I shall endeavour to point out all those Imperfections that are the Blemishes, as well as those Virtues which are the Embellishments, of the Sex. In the mean while I hope these my gentle Readers, who have so much Time on their Hands, will not grudge throwing away a Quarter of an Hour in a Day on this Paper, since they may do it without any Hindrance to Business.

I know several of my Friends and Well-wishers are in great Pain for me,   10 lest I should not be able to keep up the Spirit of a Paper which I oblige my self to furnish every Day: But to make them easy in this Particular, I will promise them faithfully to give it over as soon as I grow dull. This I know will be Matter of great Raillery to the small Wits; who will frequently put me in mind of my Promise, desire me to keep my Word, assure me that it is high Time to give over, with many other little Pleasantries of the like Nature, which Men of a little smart Genius cannot forbear throwing out against their best Friends, when they have such a Handle given them of being witty. But let them remember, that I do hereby enter my Caveat against this Piece of Raillery.

No. 26 [Addison]   *Friday, March 30, 1711*

> *Pallida mors æquo pulsat pede pauperum tabernas*
>   *Regumque turres. O beate Sesti,*
> *Vitæ summa brevis spem nos vetat incohare longam.*
>   *Jam te premet nox, fabulæque manes,*
> *Et domus exilis Plutonia . . .*[1]
>   —HOR.

WHEN I am in a serious Humour, I very often walk by my self in   20 *Westminster* Abbey; where the Gloominess of the Place, and the Use to which it is applied, with the Solemnity of the Building, and the Condition of the People who lye in it, are apt to fill the Mind with a kind of Melancholy, or rather Thoughtfulness, that is not disagreeable. I Yesterday pass'd a whole Afternoon in the Church-yard, the Cloysters, and the Church, amusing my self with the Tomb-stones and Inscriptions that I met with in those several Regions of the Dead. Most of them recorded nothing else of the buried Person, but that he was born upon one Day and died upon another: The whole History of his Life, being comprehended in those two Circumstances that are common to all Mankind. I could not but lookupon these Registers of Existence, whether of Brass or Marble,   30 as a kind of Satyr upon the departed Persons; who had left no other Memorial

---

[1] *Pallida mors . . . :* Pale death with an impartial foot beats at the pauper's hovel and at the palaces of princes. Happy Sestius, the very brief span of life forbids your hopes for the future. Night will soon hold you and the phantom shadows and Pluto's barren realm. Horace, *Epigrams*, X, xlvii, 13.

of them, but that they were born and that they died. They put me in mind of several Persons mentioned in the Battles of Heroic Poems, who have sounding Names given them, for no other Reason but that they may be killed, and are celebrated for nothing but being knocked on the Head.

Γλαῦκόν τε Μέδοντά τε Θερσίλοχόν τε.—HOM.
Glaucumque, Medontaque, Thersilochumque.—VIRG.[2]

The Life of these Men is finely described in Holy Writ,[3] by *the Path of an Arrow* which is immediately closed up and lost.

Upon my going into the Church, I entertain'd my self with the digging of a Grave; and saw in every Shovel-full of it that was thrown up, the Fragment of a Bone or Skull intermixt with a kind of fresh mouldering Earth that some time or other had a Place in the Composition of an humane Body. Upon this, I   10
began to consider with my self what innumerable Multitudes of People lay confus'd together under the Pavement of that ancient Cathedral; how Men and Women, Friends and Enemies, Priests and Soldiers, Monks and Prebendaries, were crumbled amongst one another, and blended together in the same common Mass; how Beauty, Strength, and Youth, with Old-age, Weakness, and Deformity, lay undistinguish'd in the same promiscuous Heap of Matter.

After having thus surveyed this great Magazine of Mortality, as it were in the Lump, I examined it more particularly by the Accounts which I found on several of the Monuments that are raised in every Quarter of that ancient Fabrick. Some of them were covered with such extravagant Epitaphs, that, if it were   20
possible for the dead Person to be acquainted with them, he would blush at the Praises which his Friends had bestow'd upon him. There are others so excessively modest, that they deliver the Character of the Person departed in *Greek* or *Hebrew*, and by that Means are not understood once in a Twelvemonth. In the poetical Quarter, I found there were Poets that had no Monuments, and Monuments that had no Poets. I observed indeed that the present War had filled the Church with many of these uninhabited Monuments, which had been erected to the Memory of Persons and whose Bodies were perhaps buried in the Plains of *Blenheim*[4] or in the Bosom of the Ocean.

I could not but be very much delighted with several modern Epitaphs, which   30
are written with great Elegance of Expression and Justness of Thought, and therefore do Honour to the Living as well as to the Dead. As a Foreigner is very apt to conceive an Idea of the Ignorance or Politeness of a Nation from the Turn of their publick Monuments and Inscriptions, they should be submitted to the Perusal of Men of Learning and Genius before they are put in Execution. Sir *Cloudesly Shovel's* Monument[5] has very often given me great Offence: Instead of the brave rough *English* Admiral, which was the distinguishing Character of that plain gallant Man, he is represented on his Tomb by

[2] . . . *Thersilochumque:* Iliad, XVII, 216; *Aeneid,* VI, 483: Glaucus and Medon and Thersilochus.

[3] *Holy Writ:* The Apocrypha, Wisd. of Sol. 5:12.

[4] *Blenheim:* The English under Marlborough won a victory at Blenheim in 1704.

[5] *Sir Cloudesly Shovel's Monument:* Sir Cloudesley Shovel (1650–1707), English sailor, made rear-Admiral of England in 1705. He was buried in Westminster Abbey, where the monument was placed, his death occurring when his ship hit a rock and went down.

the Figure of a Beau, dress'd in a long Perriwig and reposing himself upon Velvet Cushions under a Canopy of State. The Inscription is answerable to the Monument; for instead of celebrating the many remarkable Actions he had performed in the Service of his Country, it acquaints us only with the Manner of his Death, in which it was impossible for him to reap any Honour. The *Dutch,* whom we are apt to despise for want of Genius, shew an infinitely greater Taste of Antiquity and Politeness in their Buildings and Works of this Nature, than what we meet with in those of our own Country. The monuments of their Admirals, which have been erected at the publick Expence, represent 'em like themselves; and are adorn'd with rostral Crowns and naval Ornaments, with beautiful Festoons of Shells and Coral.

But to return to our Subject. I have left the Respository of our *English* Kings for the Contemplation of another Day, when I shall find my Mind disposed for so serious an Amusement. I know that Entertainments of this Nature, are apt to raise dark and dismal Thoughts in timorous Minds and gloomy Imaginations; but for my own Part, though I am always serious, I do not know what it is to be melancholy; and can therefore take a View of Nature in her deep and solemn Scenes, with the same Pleasure as in her most gay and delightful ones. By this Means I can improve my self with those Objects, which others consider with Terrour. When I look upon the Tombs of the Great, every Emotion of Envy dies in me; when I read the Epitaphs of the Beautiful, every inordinate Desire goes out; when I meet with the Grief of Parents upon a Tomb-stone, my Heart melts with Compassion; when I see the Tomb of the Parents themselves, I consider the Vanity of grieving for those whom we must quickly follow: When I see Kings lying by those who deposed them, when I consider rival Wits plac'd Side by Side, or the holy Men that divided the World with their Contests and Disputes, I reflect with Sorrow and Astonishment on the little Competitions, Factions, and Debates of Mankind. When I read the several Dates of the Tombs, of some that dy'd Yesterday, and some six hundred Years ago, I consider that great Day when we shall all of us be Contemporaries, and make our Appearance together.

No. 34 [Addison]   *Monday, April 9, 1711*

> . . . *parcit*
> *Cognatis maculis similis fera* . . .[1]
> —JUV.

THE Club of which I am a Member, is very luckily compos'd of such Persons as are engag'd in different Ways of Life, and deputed as it were out of the most conspicuous Classes of Mankind: By this Means I am furnish'd with the greatest Variety of Hints and Materials, and know every thing that passes in the

---

[1] . . . *Similis fera* . . . *:* Beasts show   Juvenal, *Satires,* XV, 159–160.
mercy to animals spotted as they are.

different Quarters and Divisions, not only of this great City, but of the whole Kingdom. My Readers too have the Satisfaction to find, that there is no Rank or Degree among them who have not their Representative in this Club, and that there is always some Body present who will take Care of their respective Interests, that nothing may be written or publish'd to the Prejudice or Infringement of their just Rights and Privileges.

I last Night sat very late in company with this select Body of Friends, who entertain'd me with several Remarks which they and others had made upon these my Speculations, as also with the various Success which they had met with among their several Ranks and Degrees of Readers. WILL. HONEYCOMB told   10 me, in the softest Manner he could, That there were some Ladies (but for your Comfort, says WILL. they are not those of the most Wit) that were offended at the Liberties I had taken with the Opera and the Puppet-Show: That some of them were likewise very much surpriz'd, that I should think such serious Points as the Dress and Equipage of Persons of Quality, proper Subjects for Raillery.

He was going on, when Sir ANDREW FREEPORT took him up short, and told him, That the Papers he hinted at, had done great Good in the City, and that all their Wives and Daughters were the better for them: And further added, That the whole City thought themselves very much obliged to me for declaring my generous Intentions to scourge Vice and Folly as they appear   20 in a Multitude, without condescending to be a Publisher of particular Intrigues and Cuckoldoms. In short, says Sir ANDREW, if you avoid that foolish beaten Road of falling upon Aldermen and Citizens, and employ your Pen upon the Vanity and Luxury of Courts, your Paper must needs be of general Use.

Upon this my Friend the TEMPLAR told Sir ANDREW, That he wonder'd to hear a Man of his Sense talk after that Manner; that the City had always been the Province for Satyr; and that the Wits of King *Charles's* Time jested upon nothing else during his whole Reign. He then shew'd by the Examples of *Horace, Juvenal, Boileau,*[2] and the best Writers of every Age, that the Follies of the Stage and Court had never been accounted too sacred for Ridicule, how   30 great soever the Persons might be that patroniz'd them. But after all, says he, I think your Raillery has made too great an Excursion, in attacking several Persons of the Inns of Court; and I do not believe you can shew me any Precedent for your Behaviour in that Particular.

My good Friend Sir ROGER DE COVERLY, who had said nothing all this while, began his Speech with a Pish! and told us, That he wonder'd to see so many Men of Sense so very serious upon Fooleries. Let our good Friend, says he, attack every one that deserves it: I would only advise you, Mr. SPECTATOR, applying himself to me, to take Care how you meddle with Country Squires: They are the Ornaments of the *English* Nation; Men of good Heads and sound   40 Bodies! and let me tell you, some of them take it ill of you that you mention Fox-hunters with so little Respect.

Captain SENTRY spoke very sparingly on this Occasion. What he said was only to commend my Prudence in not touching upon the Army, and advised me to continue to act discreetly in that Point.

[2] *Horace, Juvenal, Boileau:* Mentioned together here because all wrote satires.

By this Time I found every Subject of my Speculations was taken away from me by one or other of the Club; and began to think my self in the Condition of the good Man[3] that had one Wife who took a Dislike to his grey Hairs, and another to his black, till by their picking out what each of them had an Aversion to, they left his Head altogether bald and naked.

While I was thus musing with my self, my worthy Friend the Clergy-man who, very luckily for me, was at the Club that Night, undertook my Cause. He told us, That he wonder'd any Order of Persons should think themselves too considerable to be advis'd: That it was not Quality, but Innocence which exempted Men from Reproof: That Vice and Folly ought to be attacked   10 wherever they could be met with, and especially when they were placed in high and conspicuous Stations of Life. He further added, That my Paper would only serve to aggravate the Pains of Poverty, if it chiefly expos'd those who are already depress'd, and in some Measure turn'd into Ridicule, by the Meanness of their Conditions and Circumstances. He afterwards proceeded to take Notice of the great Use this Paper might be of to the Publick, by reprehending those Vices which are too trivial for the Chastisement of the Law, and too fantastical for the Cognizance of the Pulpit. He then advis'd me to prosecute my Undertaking with Chearfulness; and assur'd me, that whoever might be displeas'd with me, I should be approv'd by all those whose Praises do   20 Honour to the Persons on whom they are bestow'd.

The whole Club pays a particular Deference to the Discourse of this Gentleman, and are drawn into what he says as much by the candid and ingenuous Manner with which he delivers himself, as by the Strength of Argument and Force of Reason which he makes use of. WILL. HONEYCOMBE immediately agreed, that what he had said was right; and that for his Part, he would not insist upon the Quarter which he had demanded for the Ladies. Sir ANDREW gave up the City with the same Frankness. The TEMPLAR would not stand out; and was followed by Sir ROGER and the CAPTAIN: Who all agreed that I should be at Liberty to carry the War into what Quarter I pleased; provided I con-   30 tinued to combat with Criminals in a Body, and to assault the Vice without hurting the Person.[4]

This Debate, which was held for the Good of Mankind, put me in Mind of that which the *Roman* Triumvirate[5] were formerly engaged in, for their Destruction. Every Man at first stood hard for his Friend, till they found that by this Means they should spoil their Proscription: And at length, making a Sacrifice of all their Acquaintance and Relations, furnished out a very decent Execution.

Having thus taken my Resolutions to march on boldly in the Cause of Virtue and good Sense, and to annoy their Adversaries in whatever Degree or   40 Rank of Men they may be found: I shall be deaf for the future to all the Remonstrances that shall be made to me on this Account. If Punch grow extravagant, I shall reprimand him very freely: If the Stage becomes a Nursery of Folly

---

[3] *Good Man:* In Aesop's *Fable* 162.
[4] *Vice . . . Person:* Later, in *Verses on the Death of Dr. Swift,* l. 460, Swift employs the same idea from Martial, *Satires,* X, xxxiii, 10.
[5] *Roman Triumvirate:* Octavius, Antony, and Lepidus, the Second Triumvirate.

and Impertinence, I shall not be afraid to animadvert upon it. In short, If I meet with any thing in City, Court, or Country, that shocks Modesty or good Manners, I shall use my utmost Endeavours to make an Example of it. I must however intreat every particular Person, who does me the Honour to be a Reader of this Paper, never to think himself, or any one of his Friends or Enemies, aimed at in what is said: For I promise him, never to draw a faulty Character which does not fit at least a Thousand People; or to publish a single Paper, that is not written in the Spirit of Benevolence and with a Love to Mankind.

No. 41 [Steele]   *Tuesday, April 17, 1711*

> . . . *Tu non inventa reperta es.*[1]
> —OVID.

COMPASSION for the Gentleman who writes the following Letter, should not prevail upon me to fall upon the Fair Sex, if it were not that I find   10
they are frequently Fairer than they ought to be. Such Impostures are not to be tolerated in Civil Society; and I think his Misfortune ought to be made publick, as a Warning for other Men always to Examine into what they Admire.

SIR,

'SUPPOSING you to be a Person of General Knowledge, I make my Application to you on a very particular Occasion. I have a great Mind to be rid of my Wife, and hope, when you consider my Case, you will be of Opinion I have very just Pretentions to a Divorce. I am a mere Man of the Town, and have very little Improvement, but what I gave got from Plays. I remember in *The Silent Woman*[2] the Learned Dr. *Cutberd*, or Dr. *Otter* (I forget which)   20
makes one of the Causes of Separation to be *Error Personæ*, when a Man marries a Woman, and finds her not to be the same Woman whom he intended to marry, but another. If that be Law, it is, I presume, exactly my Case. For you are to know, Mr. *Spectator*, that there are Women who do not let their Husbands see their Faces 'till they are married.

'Not to keep you in suspense, I mean plainly, that part of the Sex who paint. They are some of them so Exquisitely skilful this Way, that give them but a Tolerable Pair of Eyes to set up with, and they will make Bosom, Lips, Cheeks, and Eyebrows, by their own Industry. As for my Dear, never Man was so inamour'd as I was of her fair Forehead, Neck and Arms, as well as the   30
bright Jett of her Hair; but to my great Astonishment, I find they were all the Effect of Art: Her Skin is so Tarnished with this Practice, that when she first wakes in a Morning, she scarce seems young enough to be the Mother of her whom I carried to Bed the Night before. I shall take the Liberty to part with her by the first Opportunity, unless her Father will make her Portion suitable to her

---

[1] . . . *Reperta es:* Undiscovered you are discovered.

[2] *The Silent Woman:* Ben Jonson, *Epicoene or The Silent Woman*, V, i.

real, not her assumed, Countenance. This I thought fit to let him and her know by your means.

I am, SIR,
Your most Obedient,
Humble Servant.'

I cannot tell what the Law, or the Parents of the Lady, will do for this Injured Gentleman, but must allow he has very much Justice on his side. I have indeed very long observed this Evil, and distinguished those of our Women who wear their own, from those in borrowed Complexions, by the *Picts*[3] and the *British*. There does not need any great Discernment to judge which are   10 which. The *British* have a lively, animated Aspect; The *Picts*, tho' never so Beautiful, have dead, uninformed Countenances. The Muscles of a real Face sometimes swell with soft Passion, sudden Surprize, and are flushed with agreeable Confusions, according as the Objects before them, or the Ideas presented to them, affect their Imagination. But the *Picts* behold all things with the same Air, whether they are Joyful or Sad; The same fix'd Insensibility appears upon all Occasions. A *Pict*, tho' she takes all that Pains to invite the Approach of Lovers, is obliged to keep them at a certain Distance; a Sigh in a Languishing Lover, if fetched too near her, would dissolve a Feature; and a Kiss snatched by a Forward one, might transfer the Complexion of the Mistress to the Admirer. It is   20 hard to speak of these false Fair Ones, without saying something uncomplaisant,[4] but I would only recommend to them to consider how they like coming into a Room new Painted; they may assure themselves, the near Approach of a Lady who uses this Practice is much more offensive.

WILL. HONEYCOMB told us, one Day, an Adventure he once had with a *Pict*. This Lady had Wit, as well as Beauty, at Will, and made it her Business to gain Hearts, for no other Reason, but to rally the Torments of her Lovers. She would make great Advances to insnare Men, but without any manner of Scruple break off when there was no Provocation. Her Ill-Nature and Vanity made my Friend very easily Proof against the Charms of her Wit and Conver-   30 sation; but her beauteous Form, instead of being blemished by her Falshood and Inconstancy, every Day increased upon him, and she had new Attractions every time he saw her. When she observed WILL. irrevocably her Slave, she began to use him as such, and after many steps towards such a Cruelty, she at last utterly banished him. The unhappy Lover strove in vain, by servile Epistles, to revoke his Doom, till at length he was forced to the last Refuge, a a round Sum of Mony to her Maid. This corrupt Attendant placed him early in the Morning behind the Hangings in her Mistress's Dressing-Room. He stood very conveniently to observe, without being seen. The *Pict* begins the Face she designed to wear that Day, and I have heard him protest she had worked a full   40 half Hour before he knew her to be the same Woman. As soon as he saw the Dawn of that Complexion, for which he had so long languished, he thought fit to break from his Concealment, repeating that of *Cowley*:[5]

---

[3] *Picts:* According to Caesar and others, the Picts, ancient Britons, painted their faces blue.

[4] *Uncomplaisant:* Disagreeable.

[5] *Cowley:* "The Waiting-Maid" in Abraham Cowley's "The Mistress."

> *Th' adorning Thee, with so much Art,*
> *Is but a barbarous Skill;*
> *'Tis like the Pois'ning of a Dart,*
> *Too apt before to kill.*

The *Pict* stood before him in the utmost Confusion, with the prettiest Smirk imaginable on the finish'd side of her Face, pale as Ashes on the other. HONEYCOMB seized all her Gally-Pots[6] and Washes, and carried off his Handkerchief full of Brushes, Scraps of *Spanish* Wool,[7] and Phials of Unguents. The Lady went into the Country, the Lover was cured.

It is certain no Faith ought to be kept with Cheats, and an Oath made to a *Pict* is of it self void. I would therefore exhort all the *British* Ladies to single them out, nor do I know any but *Lindamira*, who should be Exempt from Discovery; for her own Complexion is so delicate, that she ought to be allowed the Covering it with Paint, as a Punishment for chusing to be the worst Piece of   10 Art extant, instead of the Masterpiece of Nature. As for my part, who have no Expectations from Women, and Consider them only as they are part of the Species, I do not half so much fear offending a Beauty, as a Woman of Sense; I shall therefore produce several Faces which have been in Publick this many Years, and never appeared; it will be a very pretty Entertainment in the Play-House (when I have abolished this Custom) to see so many Ladies, when they first lay it down, *incog.* in their own Faces.

In the mean time, as a Pattern for improving their Charms, let the Sex study the agreeable *Statira*. Her Features are enlivened with the Chearfulness of her Mind, and good Humour gives an Alacrity to her Eyes. She is Graceful   20 without Affecting an Air, and Unconcerned without appearing Careless. Her having no manner of Art in her Mind, makes her want none in her Person.

How like is this Lady, and how unlike is a *Pict*, to that Description Dr. *Donne* gives of his Mistress?

> *. . . Her Pure and Eloquent Blood*
> *Spoke in her Cheeks, and so distinctly Wrought,*
> *That one would almost say her Body Thought.*[8]

Advertisement

A young Gentlewoman of about Nineteen Years of Age (bred in the Family of a Person of Quality lately deceased) who Paints the Finest Flesh-colour, wants a Place, and is to be heard of at the House of Minheer Grotesque, *a Dutch Painter in Barbican.*[9]

N.B. *She is also well skilled in the Drapery-part, and puts on Hoods and mixes Ribbands so as to suit the Colours of the Face with great Art and Success.*

---

[6] *Gally-pots:* A gallipot was a glazed pot used for ointments.
[7] *Spanish Wool:* "Wool treated with a dye, used as a cosmetic." OED.
[8] *. . . Body Thought:* Donne's *Second Anniversary,* ll. 244–246.
[9] *Barbican:* A street in London.

No. 81 [Addison]   *Saturday, June 2, 1711*

> *Qualis ubi audito venantum murmure Tigris*
> *Horruit in maculas . . .*[1]
>   —STATIUS.

ABOUT the middle of last Winter I went to see an *Opera* at the Theatre in the *Hay-Market*,[2] where I could not but take notice of two Parties of very Fine Women, that had placed themselves in the opposite Side-Boxes, and seemed drawn up in a kind of Battel Array one against another. After a short Survey of them, I found they were *Patched*[3] differently; their Faces, on one Hand, being Spotted on the Right Side of the Forehead, and that upon the other on the Left. I quickly perceived that they cast Hostile Glances upon one another; and that their Patches were placed in those different Situations, as Party Signals to distinguish Friends from Foes. In the Middle-Boxes, between these two opposite Bodies, were several Ladies who Patched indifferently on both 10 sides of their Faces and seemed to sit there with no other Intention but to see the *Opera*. Upon Enquiry I found that the Body of *Amazons* on my Right Hand were Whigs, and those on my Left, Tories; and that those who had placed themselves in the Middle-Boxes were a Neutral Party, whose Faces had not yet declared themselves. These last however, as I afterwards found, diminished daily, and took their Party with one Side or the other, insomuch that I observed in several of them, the Patches which were before dispersed equally, are now all gone over to the Whig or Tory Side of the Face. The Censorious say, That the Men whose Hearts are aimed at are very often the Occasions that one part of the Face is thus Dishonoured, and lyes under a kind 20 of Disgrace, while the other is so much Set off and Adorned by the Owner; and that the Patches turn to the Right or to the Left, according to the Principles of the Man who is most in Favour. But whatever may be the Motives of a few Fantastical Coquets, who do not Patch for the Publick Good, so much as for their own Private Advantage, it is certain that there are several Women of Honour who Patch out of Principle, and with an Eye to the Interest of their Country. Nay, I am informed, that some of them adhere so stedfastly to their Party, and are so far from Sacrificing their Zeal for the Publick to their Passion for any particular Person, that in a late Draught of Marriage Articles a Lady has stipulated with her Husband, That, whatever his Opinions are, she shall be at 30 Liberty to Patch on which side she pleases.

I must here take notice, that *Rosalinda*, a Famous Whig Partizan, has most unfortunately a very beautiful Mole on the Tory part of her Forehead, which, being very conspicuous, has occasioned many Mistakes, and given an Handle to her Enemies to misrepresent her Face, as though it had Revolted from the Whig Interest. But whatever this natural Patch may seem to intimate, it is well known that her Notions of Government are still the same. Thus unlucky Mole

---

[1] *. . . Horruit in maculas . . . :* When the tigress hears the noise of the hunters, the markings on her skin bristle. Statius, *Thebaid*, II, 128–129.

[2] *Hay-market:* A theater, also called the Opera House.

[3] *Patched:* Patches were small pieces of black silk worn on the face to show off the complexion by contrast.

however has mis-led several Coxcombs, and, like the hanging out of false Colours, made some of them Converse with *Rosalinda* in what they thought the Spirit of her Party, when on a sudden she has given them an unexpected Fire, that has sunk them all at once. If *Rosalinda* is unfortunate in her Mole, *Nigranilla* is as unhappy in a Pimple which forces her, against her Inclinations, to Patch on the Whig side.

I am told that many Virtuous Matrons, who formerly have been taught to believe that this Artificial Spotting of the Face was unlawful, are now reconciled by a Zeal for their Cause, to what they could not be prompted by a Concern for their Beauty. This way of declaring War upon one another, puts me in   10
mind of what is reported of the Tigress, that several Spots rise in her Skin when she is angry; or as Mr. *Cowley* has imitated the Verses that stand as the Motto of this Paper,

—*She Swells with angry Pride,*
And calls forth all her Spots on every side.[4]

When I was in the Theatre the time above-mentioned, I had the Curiosity to count the Patches on both Sides, and found the Tory Patches to be about twenty Stronger than the Whig; but to make amends for this small Inequality, I the next Morning found the whole Puppet-show filled with Faces spotted after the Whiggish manner. Whether or no the Ladies had retreated hither in order to rally their Forces I cannot tell, but the next Night they came in so great a Body to the Opera, that they out-numbered the Enemy.   20

This Account of Party-Patches will, I am afraid, appear improbable to those who live at a distance from the fashionable World, but as it is a Distinction of a very singular Nature, and what perhaps may never meet with a Parallel, I think I should not have discharged the Office of a faithful Spectator had I not recorded it.

I have, in former Papers,[5] endeavoured to expose this Party Rage in Women, as it only serves to aggravate the Hatreds and Animosities that reign among Men, and in a great measure deprive the Fair Sex of those peculiar Charms with which Nature has endowed them.

When the *Romans* and *Sabines*[6] were at War, and just upon the point of   30
giving Battel, the Women, who were allied to both of them, interposed with so many Tears and Intreaties that they prevented the mutual Slaughter which threatned both Parties, and united them together in a firm and lasting Peace.

I would recommend this noble Example to our *British* Ladies, at a time when their Country is torn with so many unnatural Divisions, that if they continue, it will be a Misfortune to be born in it. The *Greeks* thought it so improper for Women to interest themselves in Competitions and Contentions, that for this Reason, among others, they forbad them, under Pain of Death, to be present at the *Olympick* Games, notwithstanding these were the Publick Diversions of all *Greece.*   40

[4] . . . *on every side:* Cowley, *Davideis,* III, 403–404.
[5] *Former Papers: Spectator* No. 57.
[6] *Romans and Sabines:* Originally, the Romans, without women, seized the women of their guests, the Sabines. It was later, when the Sabines and Romans were fighting, that the women interfered, and the two people became one.

As our *English* Women excell those of all Nations in Beauty, they should endeavour to outshine them in all other Accomplishments that are proper to the Sex, and to distinguish themselves as tender Mothers and faithful Wives, rather than as furious Partizans. Female Virtues are of a Domestick turn. The Family is the proper Province for Private Women to Shine in. If they must be showing their Zeal for the Publick, let it not be against those who are perhaps of the same Family, or at least of the same Religion or Nation, but against those who are the open, professed, undoubted Enemies of their Faith, Liberty, and Country. When the *Romans* were pressed with a Foreign Enemy, the Ladies voluntarily contributed all their Rings and Jewels to assist the Government   10 under a publick Exigence, which appeared so laudable an Action in the Eyes of their Countrymen, that from thenceforth it was permitted by a Law to pronounce publick Orations at the Funeral of a Woman in Praise of the deceased Person, which till that time was peculiar to Men. Would our *English* Ladies instead of sticking on a Patch against those of their own Country, show themselves so truly Publick-spirited as to Sacrifice every one her Necklace against the Common Enemy, what Decrees ought not to be made in favour of them?

Since I am recollecting upon this Subject such Passages as occur to my Memory out of ancient Authors, I cannot omit a Sentence in the Celebrated Funeral Oration of *Pericles*,[7] which he made in Honour of those brave *Athenians*,   20 that were Slain in a Fight with the *Lacedemonians*. After having addressed himself to the several Ranks and Orders of his Countrymen, and shewn them how they should behave themselves in the Publick Cause, he turns to the Female part of his Audience; 'And as for you (says he) I shall advise you in very few Words; Aspire only to those Virtues that are peculiar to your Sex; follow your natural Modesty, and think it your greatest Commendation not to be talked of one way or other.'

No. 106 [*Addison*]   *Monday, July 2, 1711*

> . . . *Hinc tibi Copia*
> *Manabit ad plenum, benigno*
> *Ruris honorum opulenta cornu.*[1]
>   —HOR.

HAVING often received an Invitation from my Friend Sir ROGER DE COVERLY to pass away a Month with him in the Country, I last Week accompanied him thither, and am settled with him for some Time at his Country-   30 house, where I intend to form several of my ensuing Speculations. Sir ROGER, who is very well acquainted with my Humour, lets me rise and go to bed when I please, dine at his own Table or in my Chamber as I think fit, sit still and say nothing without bidding me be merry. When the Gentlemen of the Country

---

[7] *Oration of Pericles:* Thucydides, *History of the Peloponnesian War*, II, 45.
[1] . . . *Opulenta cornu:* In this place the rich bounty of glories of the field shall flow abundantly to you from the horn of plenty. Horace, *Odes*, I, xvii, 14–17.

come to see him, he only shews me at a Distance: As I have been walking in his Fields I have observed them stealing a Sight of me over an Hedge, and have heard the Knight desiring them not to let me see them, for that I hated to be stared at.

I am the more at Ease in Sir ROGER's Family, because it consists of sober and and staid Persons; for as the Knight is the best Master in the World, he seldom changes his Servants; and as he is beloved by all about him, his Servants never care for leaving him: By this Means his Domesticks are all in Years, and grown old with their Master. You would take his Valet de Chambre for his Brother, his Butler is grey-headed, his Groom is one of the gravest Men that I have ever seen, and his Coachman has the Looks of a Privy-Counsellor. You see the Goodness of the Master even in the old House-dog, and in a grey Pad that is kept in the Stable with great Care and Tenderness out of regard to his past Services, tho' he has been useless for several Years.

I could not but observe with a great deal of Pleasure the Joy that appeared in the Countenances of these ancient Domesticks upon my Friend's Arrival at his Country-Seat. Some of them could not refrain from Tears at the Sight of their old Master; every one of them press'd forward to do something for him, and seemed discouraged if they were not employed. At the same Time the good old Knight, with a Mixture of the Father and the Master of the Family, tempered the Enquiries after his own Affairs with several kind Questions relating to themselves. This Humanity and good Nature engages every Body to him, so that when he is pleasant upon any of them, all his Family are in good Humour, and none so much as the Person whom he diverts himself with: On the Contrary, if he coughs or betrays any Infirmity of old Age, it is easy for a Standerby to observe a secret Concern in the Looks of all his Servants.

My worthy Friend has put me under the particular Care of his Butler, who is a very prudent Man, and, as well as the rest of his Fellow-Servants, wonderfully desirous of pleasing me, because they have often heard their Master talk of me as of his particular Friend.

My chief Companion when Sir ROGER is diverting himself in the Woods or the Fields, is a very venerable Man, who is ever with Sir ROGER, and has lived at his House in the Nature of a Chaplain above thirty Years. This Gentleman is a Person of good Sense and some Learning, of a very regular Life and obliging Conversation: He heartily loves Sir ROGER, and knows that he is very much in the old Knight's Esteem; so that he lives in the Family rather as a Relation than a Dependant.

I have observed in several of my Papers, that my Friend Sir ROGER amidst all his good Qualities, is something of an Humourist; and that his Virtues, as well as Imperfections, are as it were tinged by a certain Extravagance, which makes them particularly *his*, and distinguishes them from those of other Men. This Cast of Mind, as it is generally very innocent in itself, so it renders his Conversation highly agreeable, and more delightful than the same Degree of Sense and Virtue would appear in their common and ordinary Colours. As I was walking with him last Night, he ask'd me, How I liked the good Man whom I have just now mentioned? and without staying for my Answer, told me, That he was afraid of being insulted with *Latin* and *Greek* at his own

Table; for which Reason, he desired a particular Friend of his at the University to find him out a Clergyman rather of plain Sense than much Learning, of a good Aspect, a clear Voice, a sociable Temper, and, if possible, a Man that understood a little of Back-Gammon. My Friend, says Sir ROGER, found me out this Gentleman, who, besides the Endowments I required of him, is, they tell me, a good Scholar though he does not shew it. I have given him the Parsonage of the Parish; and because I know his Value, have settled upon him a good Annuity during his Life. If he out-lives me, he shall find that he was higher in my Esteem than perhaps he thinks he is. He has now been with me thirty Years; and though he does not know I have taken Notice of it, has never in all that   10
Time asked any thing of me for himself, tho' he is every Day solliciting me for something in Behalf of one or other of my Tenants his Parishioners. There has not been a Law-Suit in the Parish since he has lived among them: If any Dispute arises, they apply themselves to him for the Decision; if they do not acquiesce in his Judgment, which I think never happened above once or twice at most, they appeal to me. At his first settling with me, I made him a Present of all the good Sermons that have been printed in *English*, and only begged of him that every *Sunday* he would pronounce one of them in the Pulpit. Accordingly, he has digested them into such a Series, that they follow one another naturally, and make a continued System of practical Divinity.   20

As Sir ROGER was going on in his Story, the Gentleman we were talking of came up to us; and upon the Knight's asking him who preached to Morrow (for it was *Saturday* Night) told us, the Bishop of St. *Asaph*[2] in the Morning, and Doctor *South*[3] in the Afternoon. He then shewed us his List of Preachers for the whole Year, where I saw with a great deal of Pleasure Archbishop *Tillotson*,[4] Bishop *Saunderson*, Doctor *Barrow*, Doctor *Calamy*,[5] with several living Authors who have published Discourses of practical Divinity. I no sooner saw this venerable Man in the Pulpit, but I very much approved of my Friend's insisting upon the Qualifications of a good Aspect and a clear Voice; for I was so charmed with the Gracefulness of his Figure and Delivery, as well as with the   30
Discourses he pronounced, that I think I never passed any Time more to my Satisfaction. A Sermon repeated after this Manner, is like the Composition of a Poet in the Mouth of a graceful Actor.

I could heartily wish that more of our Country-Clergy would follow this Example; and instead of wasting their Spirits in laborious Compositions of their own, would endeavour, after a handsome Elocution and all those other Talents that are proper to enforce what has been penn'd by greater Masters. This would not only be more easy to themselves, but more edifying to the People.

---

[2] *St. Asaph:* William Fleetwood, a popular preacher, who became Bishop of St. Asaph in 1708. He was well known to be a Whig.

[3] *Doctor South:* Robert South (1633–1716) was a high churchman; his sermons were famous for their wit.

[4] *Archbishop Tillotson:* John Tillotson (1630–1694), always a popular preacher, began his clerical career as a Presbyterian and ended it as the Archbishop of Canterbury.

[5] *Saunderson . . . Barrow . . . Calamy:* Robert Sanderson (1587–1663), greatest of English casuists, became Bishop of Lincoln; Isaac Barrow (1630–1677), mathematician and divine, was known for the length of his sermons; Calamy was one of two Puritan clergymen—Benjamin (1642–1686) or his father Edmund (1600–1666).

No. 108 [*Addison*]   *Wednesday, July 4, 1711*

Gratis anhelans, multa agendo nihil agens.[1]
—Phæd.

AS I was Yesterday Morning walking with Sir ROGER before his House, a Country-Fellow brought him a huge Fish, which, he told him, Mr. *William Wimble* had caught that very Morning; and that he presented it, with his Service, to him, and intended to come and dine with him. At the same Time he delivered a Letter, which my Friend read to me as soon as the Messenger left him.

Sir ROGER,
   'I DESIRE you to accept of a Jack,[2] which is the best I have caught this Season. I intend to come and stay with you a Week, and see how the Perch bite in the *Black River*. I observed, with some Concern, the last Time I saw you upon   1·
the Bowling-Green, that your Whip wanted a Lash to it: I will bring half a Dozen with me that I twisted last Week, which I hope will serve you all the Time you are in the Country. I have not been out of the Saddle for six Days last past, having been at *Eaton* with Sir *John's* eldest Son. He takes to his Learning hugely.

I am,
SIR,
Your humble Servant,
Will. Wimble.'

This extraordinary Letter, and Message that accompanied it, made me very   2·
curious to know the Character and Quality of the Gentleman who sent them; which I found to be a follows: *Will. Wimble* is younger Brother to a Baronet, and descended of the ancient Family of the *Wimbles*. He is now between Forty and Fifty; but being bred to no Business and born to no Estate, he generally lives with his elder Brother as Superintendant of his Game. He hunts a Pack of Dogs better than any Man in the Country, and is very famous for finding out a Hare. He is extremely well versed in all the little Handicrafts of an idle Man: He makes a *May*-fly to a Miracle; and furnishes the whole Country with Angle-Rods. As he is a good-natur'd officious[3] Fellow, and very much esteemed upon Account of his Family, he is a welcome Guest at every House, and keeps up a   3·
good Correspondence among all the Gentlemen about him. He carries a Tulip-Root in his Pocket from one to another, or exchanges a Puppy between a couple of Friends that live perhaps in the opposite Sides of the County. *Will.* is a particular Favourite of all the young Heirs, whom he frequently obliges with a Net that he has weaved, or a Setting-dog that he has *made*[4] himself: He now and then presents a Pair of Garters of his own knitting to their Mothers or Sis-

---

[1] *... Nihil agens:* Panting for no reason, and very busy about nothing. Phaedrus, *Fables,* II, v, 3.
   [2] *Jack:* The name of various fishes,
here probably a pike.
   [3] *Officious:* "Doing or ready to do kind offices. . . ." OED.
   [4] *Made:* Trained.

ters, and raises a great deal of Mirth among them, by enquiring as often as he meets them *how they wear*? These Gentleman-like Manufactures and obliging little Humours, make *Will.* the Darling of the Country.

Sir ROGER was proceeding in the Character of him, when we saw him make up to us, with two or three Hazle-twigs in his Hand that he had cut in Sir ROGER's Woods, as he came through them, in his Way to the House. I was very much pleased to observe on one Side the Hearty and sincere Welcome with which Sir ROGER received him, and on the other the secret Joy which his Guest discovered at Sight of the good old Knight. After the first Salutes were over, *Will.* desired Sir ROGER to lend him one of his Servants to carry a Set of   10 Shuttle-cocks he had with him in a little Box to a Lady that liv'd about a Mile off, to whom it seems he had promised such a Present for above this half Year. Sir ROGER's Back was no sooner turn'd, but honest *Will.* begun to tell me of a large Cock-Pheasant that he had sprung in one of the neighbouring Woods, with two or three other Adventures of the same Nature. Odd and uncommon Characters are the Game that I look for, and most delight in; for which Reason I was as much pleased with the Novelty of the Person that talked to me, as he could be for his Life with the springing of a Pheasant, and therefore listned to him with more than ordinary Attention.

In the Midst of his Discourse the Bell rung to Dinner, where the Gentle-   20 man I have been speaking of had the Pleasure of seeing the huge Jack, he had caught, served up for the first Dish in a most sumptuous Manner. Upon our sitting down to it he gave us a long Account how he had hooked it, played with it, foiled it, and at length drew it out upon the Bank, with several other Particulars that lasted all the first Course. A Dish of Wild-fowl that came afterwards furnished Conversation for the rest of the Dinner, which concluded with a late Invention of *Will's* for improving the Quail Pipe.

Upon withdrawing into my Room after Dinner, I was secretly touched with Compassion towards the honest Gentleman that had dined with us; and could not but consider with a great deal of Concern, how so good an   30 Heart and such busy Hands were wholly employed in Trifles; that so much Humanity should be so little beneficial to others, and so much Industry so little advantageous to himself. The same Temper of Mind and Application to Affairs might have recommended him to the publick Esteem, and have raised his Fortune in another Station of Life. What Good to his Country or himself might not a Trader or Merchant have done with such useful tho' ordinary Qualifications?

Will. Wimble's is the Case of many a younger Brother of a great Family, who had rather see their Children starve like Gentlemen, than thrive in a Trade or Profession that is beneath their Quality. This Humour fills several Parts of *Europe* with Pride and Beggary. It is the Happiness of a trading Nation, like   40 ours, that the younger Sons, tho' uncapable of any liberal Art or Profession, may be placed in such a Way of Life, as may perhaps enable them to vie with the best of their Family: Accordingly we find several Citizens that were launched into the World with narrow Fortunes, rising by an honest Industry to greater Estates than those of their elder Brothers. It is not improbable but *Will.* was formerly tried at Divinity, Law, or Physick; and that finding his Genius did not lie that Way, his Parents gave him up at length to his own

Inventions: But certainly, however improper he might have been for Studies
of a higher Nature, he was perfectly well turned for the Occupations of Trade
and Commerce. As I think this is a Point which cannot be too much inculcated,
I shall desire my Reader to compare what I have here written with what I have
said in my Twenty first Speculation.

No. 122 [*Addison*]   *Friday, July 20, 1711*

Comes jucundus in via pro vehiculo est.[1]
—PUBL. SYR. Frag.

A MAN'S first Care should be to avoid the Reproaches of his own Heart;
his next, to escape the Censures of the World: If the last interferes with the
former, it ought to be entirely neglected; but otherwise, there cannot be a
greater Satisfaction to an honest Mind, than to see those Approbations which
it gives itself seconded by the Applauses of the Publick: A Man is more sure of his   1
Conduct, when the Verdict which he passes upon his own Behaviour is thus
warranted, and confirmed by the Opinion of all that know him.

My worthy Friend Sir ROGER is one of those who is not only at Peace within himself, but beloved and esteemed by all about him. He receives a suitable
Tribute for his universal Benevolence to Mankind, in the Returns of Affection
and Good-will, which are paid him by every one that lives within his Neighbourhood. I lately met with two or three odd Instances of that general Respect
which is shewn to the good old Knight. He would needs carry *Will. Wimble*
and my self with him to the County-Assizes: As we were upon the Road *Will.
Wimble* joyned a couple of plain Men who rid before us, and conversed with   2
them for some Time; during which my Friend Sir ROGER acquainted me with
their Characters.

The first of them, says he, that has a Spaniel by his Side, is a Yeoman of
about an hundred Pounds a Year, an honest Man: He is just within the Game-
Act,[2] and qualified to kill an Hare or a Pheasant: He knocks down a Dinner
with his Gun twice or thrice a Week; and by that Means lives much cheaper
than those who have not so good an Estate as himself. He would be a good
Neighbour if he did not destroy so many Partridges: In short, he is a very
sensible Man; shoots flying; and has been several Times Foreman of the Petty-
Jury.[3]   3

The other that rides along with him is *Tom Touchy*, a Fellow famous for
taking the Law of every Body. There is not one in the Town where he lives
that he has not sued at a Quarter-Sessions.[4] The Rogue had once the Impudence
to go to Law with the *Widow*. His Head is full of Costs, Damages, and Eject-

---

[1] . . . *Pro vehiculo est:* On a journey, an
agreeable companion is as good as a
carriage. Publilius Syrus, *Sententiae*, 116.

[2] *Game-Act:* See *Spectator* No. 2, n. 8.

[3] *Petty-Jury:* Trial jury, which decides

final issues of fact in criminal or civil
cases.

[4] *Quarter-Sessions:* One of the four
sessions into which an eighteenth-century
legal calendar was divided.

ments: He plagued a couple of honest Gentlemen so long for a Trespass in breaking one of his Hedges, till he was forced to sell the Ground it enclosed to defray the Charges of the Prosecution: His Father left him four-score Pounds a Year; but he has *cast*[5] and been cast so often, that he is not now worth thirty. I suppose he is going upon the old Business of the Willow-Tree.

As Sir ROGER was giving me this Account of Tom Touchy, Will. Wimble and his two Companions stopped short till we came up to them. After having paid their Respects to Sir ROGER, *Will.* told him that Mr. *Touchy* and he must appeal to him upon a Dispute that arose between them. *Will.* it seems had been giving his Fellow Travellers an Account of his angling one Day in such a Hole; when *Tom Touchy,* instead of hearing out his Story, told him, that Mr. such an One, if he pleased, might *take the Law of him* for fishing in that Part of the River. My Friend Sir ROGER heard them both, upon a round Trot; and after having paused some Time told them, with the Air of a Man who would not give his Judgment rashly, that *much might be said on both Sides.* They were neither of them dissatisfied with the Knight's Determination, because neither of them found himself in theWrong by it: Upon which we made the best of our Way to the Assizes.

The Court was sat before Sir ROGER came, but notwithstanding all the Justices had taken their Places upon the Bench, they made Room for the old Knight at the Head of them; who for his Reputation in the Country took Occasion to whisper in the Judge's Ear, That *he was glad his Lordship had met with so much good Weather in his Circuit.* I was listening to the Proceedings of the Court with much Attention, and infinitely pleased with that great Appearance and Solemnity which so properly accompanies such a publick Administration of our Laws; when, after about an Hour's Sitting, I observed to my great Surprize, in the Midst of a Trial, that my Friend Sir ROGER was getting up to speak. I was in some Pain for him, till I found he had acquitted himself of two or three Sentences, with a Look of much Business and great Intrepidity.

Upon his first Rising the Court was hushed, and a general Whisper ran among the Country-People that Sir ROGER *was up.* The Speech he made was so little to the Purpose, that I shall not trouble my Readers with an Account of it; and I believe was not so much designed by the Knight himself to inform the Court, as to give him a Figure in my Eye, and keep up his Credit in the Country.

I was highly delighted, when the Court rose, to see the Gentlemen of the Country gathering about my old Friend, and striving who should compliment him most; at the same Time that the ordinary People gazed upon him at a Distance, not a little admiring his Courage, that was not afraid to speak to the Judge.

In our Return home we met with a very odd Accident; which I cannot forbear relating, because it shews how desirous all who know Sir ROGER are of giving him Marks of their Esteem. When we were arrived upon the Verge of his Estate, we stopped at a little Inn to rest our selves and our Horses. The Man of the House had it seems been formerly a Servant in the Knight's Family; and to do Honour to his old Master, had some Time since, unknown to Sir ROGER, put him up in a Sign-post before his Door; so that *the Knight's Head*

---

[5] *Cast:* Condemn, in a legal sense.

had hung out upon the Road about a Week before he himself knew any thing of the Matter. As soon as Sir ROGER was acquainted with it, finding that his Servant's Indiscretion proceeded wholly from Affection and Good-will, he only told him that he had made him too high a Compliment; and when the Fellow seemed to think that could hardly be, added with a more decisive Look, That it was too great an Honour for any Man under a Duke; but told him at the same Time that it might be altered with a very few Touches, and that he himself would be at the Charge of it. Accordingly they got a Painter by the Knight's Directions to add a Pair of Whiskers to the Face, and by a little Aggravation of the Features to change it into the *Saracen's Head.* I should not have known this Story, had not the Inn-keeper upon Sir ROGER's alighting told him in my Hearing, That his Honour's Head was brought back last Night with the Alterations that he had ordered to be made in it. Upon this my Friend with his usual Chearfulness related the Particulars above-mentioned, and ordered the Head to be brought into the Room. I could not forbear discovering greater Expressions of Mirth than ordinary upon the Appearance of this monstrous Face, under which, notwithstanding it was made to frown and stare in a most extraordinary Manner, I could still discover a distant Resemblance of my old Friend. Sir ROGER, upon seeing me laugh, desired me to tell him truly if I thought it possible for People to know him in that Disguise. I at first kept my usual Silence; but upon the Knight's conjuring me to tell him whether it was not still more like himself than a *Saracen,* I composed my Countenance in the best Manner I could, and replied, *That much might be said on both Sides.*

These several Adventures, with the Knight's Behaviour in them, gave me as pleasant a Day as ever I met with in any of my Travels.

No. 151 [*Steele*]   *Thursday, August 23, 1711*

Maximas Virtutes Jacere omnes necesse est Voluptate dominante.[1]
—TULL. *De Fin.*

I KNOW no one Character that gives Reason a greater Shock, at the same Time that it presents a good ridiculous Image to the Imagination, than that of a Man of Wit and Pleasure about the Town. This Decsription of a Man of Fashion, spoken by some with a Mixture of Scorn and Ridicule, by others with great Gravity as a laudable Distinction, is in every Body's Mouth that spends any Time in Conversation. My Friend WILL. HONEYCOMB has this Expression very frequently; and I never could understand by the Story which follows, upon his Mention of such a one, but that his Man of Wit and Pleasure was either a Drunkard too old for Wenching, or a young lewd Fellow with some Liveliness, who would converse with you, receive kind Offices of you, and at the

---

[1] . . . *Voluptate dominante:* Where pleasure is dominant, all of the greatest virtues must fall. Cicero, *De Finibus,* II, xxxv, 117.

the same time debauch your Sister or lye with your Wife. According to his Description, a Man of Wit when he could have Wenches for Crowns a Piece which he liked quite as well, would be so extravagant as to bribe Servants, make false Friendships, fight Relations; I say according to him, plain and simple Vice was too little for a Man of Wit and Pleasure; but he would leave an easy and accessible Wickedness, to come at the same thing with only the Addition of certain Falshood, and possible Murder. WILL. thinks the Town grown very dull, in that we do not hear so much as we used to do of these Coxcombs, whom (without observing it) he describes as the most infamous Rogues in Nature, with Relation to Friendship, Love, or Conversation.   10

When Pleasure is made the chief Pursuit of Life, it will necessarily follow that such Monsters as these will arise from a constant Application to such Blandishments as naturally root out the Force of Reason and Reflexion, and substitute in their Place a general Impatience of Thought, and a constant Pruriency of inordinate Desire.

Pleasure, when it is a Man's chief Purpose, disappoints it self; and the constant Application to it palls the Faculty of enjoying it, tho' it leaves the Sense of our Inability for that we wish, with a Disrelish of every thing else. Thus the intermediate Seasons of the Man of Pleasure, are more heavy than one would impose upon the vilest Criminal. Take him when he is awaked too soon   20 after a Debauch, or disappointed in following a worthless Woman without Truth, and there is no Man living whose Being is such a Weight or Vexation as his is. He is an utter Stranger to the pleasing Reflexions in the Evening of a well-spent Day, or the Gladness of Heart or Quickness of Spirit in the Morning after profound Sleep or indolent Slumbers. He is not to be at Ease any longer than he can keep Reason and good Sense without his Curtains; otherwise he will be haunted with the Reflexion, that he could not believe such a one the Woman that upon Tryal he found her. What has he got by his Conquest, but to think meanly of her for whom a Day or two before he had the highest Honour? and of himself for, perhaps, wronging the Man whom of all Men   30 living he himself would least willingly have injured?

Pleasure seizes the whole Man who addicts himself to it, and will not give him Leisure for any good Office in Life which contradicts the Gayety of the present Hour. You may indeed observe in People of Pleasure a certain Complacency and Absence of all Severity, which the Habit of a loose unconcerned Life gives them; but tell the Man of Pleasure your secret Wants, Cares, or Sorrows, and you will find he has given up the Delicacy of his Passions to the Cravings of his Appetites. He little knows the perfect Joy he loses for the disappointing Gratifications which he pursues. He looks at Pleasure as she approaches, and comes to you with the Recommendation of warm Wishes, gay Looks, and grace-   40 ful Motion; but he does not observe how she leaves his Presence with Disorder, Impotence, downcast Shame, and conscious Imperfection. She makes our Youth inglorious, our Age shameful.

WILL. HONEYCOMB gives us twenty Intimations in an Evening of several Hags whose Bloom was given up to his Arms; and would raise a Value to himself for having had, as the Phrase is, very good Women. WILL's good Women are the Comfort of his Heart, and support him, I warrant, by the

Memory of past Interviews with Persons of their Condition. No, there is not in the World an Occasion wherein Vice makes so phantastical a Figure, as at the Meeting of two old People who have been Partners in unwarrantable Pleasure. To tell a toothless old Lady that she once had a good Set, or a defunct Wencher that he once was the admired thing of the Town, are Satyrs instead of Applauses; but on the other Side, consider the old Age of those who have passed their Days in Labour, Industry, and Virtue, their Decays make them but appear the more venerable, and the Imperfections of their Bodies are beheld as a Misfortune to humane Society that their Make is so little durable.

But to return more directly to my Man of Wit and Pleasure. In all Orders of   10
Men where-ever this is the chief Character, the Person who wears it is a negligent Friend, Father, and Husband, and Intails Poverty on his unhappy Descendants. Mortgages, Diseases, and Settlements are the Legacies a Man of Wit and Pleasure leaves to his Family. All the poor Rogues that make such lamentable Speeches after every Sessions at *Tyburn*,[2] were, in their Way, Men of Wit and Pleasure before they fell into the Adventures which brought them thither.

Irresolution and Procrastination in all a Man's Affairs, are the natural Effects of being addicted to Pleasure: Dishonour to the Gentleman and Bankruptcy to the Trader, are the Portion of either whose chief Purpose of Life is Delight. The chief Cause that this Pursuit has been in all Ages received with so much   20
Quarter from the soberer Part of Mankind, has been that some Men of great Talents have sacrificed themselves to it: The shining Qualities of such People have given a Beauty to whatever they were engaged in, and a Mixture of Wit has recommended Madness. For let any Man who knows what it is to have passed much Time in a Series of Jollity, Mirth, Wit, or humourous Entertainments, look back at what he was all that while a doing, and he will find that he has been at one Instant sharp to some Man he is sorry to have offended, impertinent to some one it was Cruelty to treat with such Freedom, ungracefully noisy at such a Time, unskilfully open at such a Time, unmercifully calumnious at such a Time; and from the whole Course of his applauded Satisfactions, unable in the   30
End to recollect any Circumstance which can add to the Enjoyment of his own Mind alone, or which he would put his Character upon with other Men. Thus it is with those who are best made for becoming Pleasures; but how monstrous is it in the Generality of Mankind who pretend this Way, without Genius or Inclination towards it? The Scene then is wild to an Extravagance; this is as if Fools should mimick Madmen. Pleasure of this Kind is the intemperate Meals and loud Jollities of the common Rate of Country Gentlemen, whose Practice and Way of Enjoyment is to put an End as fast as they can to that little Particle of Reason they have when they are sober: These Men of Wit and Pleasure dispatch their Senses as fast as possible, by drinking till they cannot taste,   40
smoaking till they cannot see, and roaring till they cannot hear.

[2] *Tyburn:* The place where those convicted of capital crimes were executed.

No. 156 [Steele]   *Wednesday, August 29, 1711*

> . . . *Sed tu simul obligasti*
> *Perfidum votis caput, enitescis*
> *Pulchrior multo . . .*[1]
> —HOR.

I DO not think any thing could make a pleasanter Entertainment, than the History of the reigning Favourites among the Women from Time to Time about this Town. In such an Account we ought to have a faithful Confession of each Lady for what she liked such and such a Man, and he ought to tell us by what particular Action or Dress he believed he should be most successful. As for my Part, I have always made as easy a Judgment when a Man dresses for the Ladies, as when he is equipped for Hunting or Coursing. The Woman's Man is a Person in his Air and Behaviour quite different from the rest of our Species: His Garb is more loose and negligent, his Manner more soft and indolent; that is to say, in both these Cases there is an apparent Endeavour to appear un- 10 concerned and careless. In catching Birds the Fowlers have a Method of imitating their Voices to bring them to the Snare; and your Woman's Men have always a Similitude of the Creature they hope to betray, in their own Conversation. A Woman's Man is very knowing in all that passes from one Family to another, has little pretty Officiousnesses,[2] is not at a Loss what is good for a Cold, and it is not amiss if he has a Bottle of Spirits in his Pocket in case of any sudden Indisposition.

Curiosity having been my prevailing Passion, and indeed the sole Entertain-ment of my Life, I have sometimes made it my Business to examine the Course of Intreagues, as well as the Manners and Accomplishments of such as have 20 been most successful that Way. In all my Observation, I never knew a Man of good Understanding a general Favourite; some Singularity in his Behaviour, some Whim in his Way of Life, and what would have made him ridiculous among the Men, has recommended him to the other Sex. I should be very sorry to offend a People so fortunate as these of whom I am speaking; but let any one look over the old Beaux, and he will find the Man of Success was remarkable for quarrelling impertinently for their Sakes, for dressing unlike the rest of the World, or passing his Days in an inspid Assiduity about the fair Sex, to gain the Figure he made amongst them. Add to this that he must have the Reputation of being well with other Women, to please any one Woman of Gallantry; for you 30 are to know, that there is a mighty Ambition among the light Part of the Sex to gain Slaves from the Dominion of others. My Friend WILL. HONEYCOMB says it was a common Bite[3] with him to lay Suspicions that he was favoured by a Lady's Enemy, that is some rival Beauty, to be well with her herself. A little Spite is natural to a great Beauty; and it is ordinary to snap up a disagreeable Fellow least another should have him. That impudent Toad *Bareface* fares well

---

[1] . . . *Pulchrior multo . . .* : But you, as soon as you have risked your treacherous head with promises, you shine more bright and more beautiful when you appear.

Horace, *Odes*, II, viii, 5–7.
[2] *Officiousnesses:* The doing, or readiness to do, kind offices.
[3] *Bite:* Deception.

among all the Ladies he converses with, for no other Reason in the World but that he has the Skill to keep them from Explanation with one another. Did they know there is not one who likes him in her Heart, each would declare her Scorn of him the next Moment; but he is well received by them because it is the Fashion, and Opposition to each other brings them insensibly into an Imitation of each other. What adds to him the greatest Grace is, that the Pleasant Thief, as they call him, is the most inconstant Creature living, has a wonderful deal of Wit and Humour, and never wants something to say; besides all which he has a most spiteful dangerous Tongue if you should provoke him.

To make a Woman's Man, he must not be a Man of Sense or a Fool; the Business is to entertain, and it is much better to have a Faculty of arguing than a Capacity of judging right. But the pleasantest of all the Woman's Equipage are your regular Visitants; these are Volunteers in their Service without Hopes of Pay or Preferment: It is enough that they can lead out from a publick Place, that they are admitted on a publick Day, and can be allowed to pass away Part of that heavy Load, their Time, in the Company of the Fair. But commend me above all others to those who are known for your Ruiners of Ladies; these are the choicest Spirits which our Age produces. We have several of these irresistible Gentlemen among us when the Company is in Town. These Fellows are accomplished with the Knowledge of the ordinary Occurrences about Court and Town, have that sort of good Breeding which is exclusive of all Morality, and consists only in being publickly decent, privately dissolute.

It is wonderful how far a fond Opinion of herself can carry a Woman to make her have the least Regard to a professed known Woman's Man: But as scarce one of all the Women who are in the Tour of Gallantries ever hears any thing of what is the common Sense of sober Minds, but are entertained with a continual Round of Flatteries, they cannot be Mistresses of themselves enough to make Arguments for their own Conduct from the Behaviour of these Men to others. It is so far otherwise, that a general Fame for Falshood in this kind is a Recommendation; and the Coxcomb, loaded with the Favours of many others, is received like a Victor that disdains his Trophies to be a Victim to the present Charmer.

If you see a Man more full of Gesture than ordinary in a publick Assembly, if loud upon no Occasion, if negligent of the Company round him, and yet laying wait for destroying by that Negligence, you may take it for granted that he has ruined many a fair One. The Woman's Man expresses himself wholly in that Motion which we call Strutting: An elevated Chest, a pinched[4] Hat, a measurable[5] Step, and a sly surveying Eye, are the Marks of him. Now and then you see a Gentleman with all these Accomplishments; but alass any one of them is enough to undo thousands: When a Gentleman with such Perfections adds to it suitable Learning, there should be publick Warning of his Residence in Town, that we may remove our Wives and Daughters. It happens sometimes that such a fine Man has read all the Miscellany Poems, a few of our Comedies, and has the Translation of *Ovid's* Epistles by Heart. Oh if it were possible that such a one could be as true as he is charming! but that is too much, the Women will share such a dear false Man: 'A little Gallantry to hear him

---

[4] *Pinched:* Pleated.   [5] *Measurable:* Uniform.

Talk one would indulge one's self in, let him reckon the Sticks of one's Fan, say something of the Cupids in it, and then call one so many soft Names which a Man of his Learning has at his Fingers Ends. There sure is some Excuse for Frailty when attack'd by such Force against a weak Woman.' Such is the Soliloquy of many a Lady one might name, at the Sight of one of these who makes it no Iniquity to go on from Day to Day in the Sin of Woman-slaughter.

It is certain that People are got into a way of Affection[6] with a manner of overlooking the most solid Virtues, and admiring the most trivial Excellencies. The Woman is so far from expecting to be contemned for being a very injudicious silly Animal, that while she can preserve her Features and her Mein   10 she knows she is still the Object of Desire; and there is a sort of secret Ambition, from reading frivolous Books, and keeping as frivolous Company, each-side to be amiable in Imperfection, and arrive at the Characters of the dear Deceiver and the perjured Fair.

Advertisement

Mr. SPECTATOR *gives his most humble Service to Mr. R. M. of* Chippenham *in* Wilts, *and hath received the Patridges.*

No. 159 [*Addison*]   *Saturday, September 1, 1711*

> *. . . Omnem quæ nunc obducta tuenti*
> *Mortales hebetat visus tibi, & humida circum*
> *Caligat, nubem eripiam. . . .*[1]
>   —VIRG.

WHEN I was at *Grand Cairo* I picked up several Oriental Manuscripts, which I have still by me. Among others I met with one entituled, *The Visions of Mirzah*, which I have read over with great Pleasure. I intend to give it to the Publick when I have no other Entertainment for them; and shall begin with the first Vision, which I have translated Word for Word as follows.

'ON the fifth Day of the Moon, which according to the Custom of my Fore-   20 fathers I always keep holy, after having washed my self and offered up my Morning Devotions, I ascended the high Hills of *Bagdat*, in order to pass the rest of the Day in Meditation and Prayer. As I was here airing my self on the Tops of the Mountains, I fell into a profound Contemplation on the Vanity of humane Life; and passing from one Thought to another, Surely, said I, Man is but a Shadow and Life a Dream. Whilst I was thus musing, I cast my Eyes to-wards the Summit of a Rock that was not far from me, where I discovered one in the Habit of a Shepherd, with a little Musical Instrument in his Hand. As I

---

[6] *Affection:* "The action of affecting." OED.

[1] . . . *Caligat, nubem eripiam.* . . . : I will tear away all the cloud, which now covering your mortal eyes, dulls your vision and surrounds you with misty shrouds. Virgil, *Aeneid*, II, 604–606.

looked upon him he applied it to his Lips, and began to play upon it. The Sound of it was exceeding sweet, and wrought into a Variety of Tunes that were inexpressibly melodious, and altogether different from any thing I had ever heard. They put me in mind of those heavenly Airs that are played to the departed Souls of good Men upon their first Arrival in Paradise, to wear out the Impressions of their last Agonies, and qualify them for the Pleasures of that happy Place. My Heart melted away in secret Raptures.

'I had been often told that the Rock before me was the Haunt of a Genius;[2] and that several had been entertained with Musick who had passed by it, but never heard that the Musician had before made himself visible. When he had raised   10 my Thoughts, by those transporting Airs whch he played, to taste the Pleasures of his Conversation, as I looked upon him like one astonished, he beckoned to me, and by the waving of his Hand directed me to approach the Place where he sat. I drew near with that Reverence which is due to a superiour Nature; and as my Heart was entirely subdued by the captivating Strains I had heard, I fell down at his Feet and wept. The Genius smiled upon me with a Look of Compassion and Affability that familiarized him to my Imagination, and at once dispelled all the Fears and Apprehensions with which I approached him. He lifted me from the Ground, and taking me by the Hand, *Mirzah*, said he, I have heard thee in thy Soliloquies, follow me.   20

'He then led me to the highest Pinnacle of the Rock, and placing me on the Top of it, Cast thy Eyes Eastward, said he, and tell me what thou seest. I see, said I, a huge Valley and a prodigious Tide of Water rolling through it. The Valley that thou seest, said he, is the Vale of Misery, and the Tide of Water that thou seest is Part of the great Tide of Eternity. What is the Reason, said I, that the Tide I see rises out of a thick Mist at one End, and again loses it self in a thick Mist at the other? What thou seest, said he, is that Portion of Eternity which is called Time, measured out by the Sun, and reaching from the Beginning of the World to its Consummation. Examine now, said he, this Sea that is thus bounded with Darkness at both Ends, and tell me what thou discoverest in it.   30 I see a Bridge, said I, standing in the Midst of the Tide. The Bridge thou seest, said he, is humane Life; consider it attentively. Upon a more leisurely Survey of it, I found that it consisted of threescore and ten entire Arches, with several broken Arches, which added to those that were entire made up the Number about an hundred. As I was counting the Arches, the Genius told me, that this bridge consisted at first of a thousand Arches; but that a great Flood swept away the rest, and left the Bridge in the ruinous Condition I now beheld it. But tell me further, said he, what thou discoverest on it. I see Multitudes of People passing over it, said I, and a black Cloud hanging on each End of it. As I looked more attentively, I saw several of the Passengers dropping thro' the Bridge,   40 into the great Tide that flowed underneath it; and upon further Examination, perceived there were innumerable Trap-doors that lay concealed in the Bridge, which the Passengers no sooner trod upon, but they fell through them into the Tide and immediately disappeared. These hidden Pit-falls were set very thick at the Entrance of the Bridge, so that Throngs of People no sooner broke hrough the Cloud, but many of them fell into them. They grew thinner

[2] *Genius:* A demon or a spirit; a genie.

towards the Middle, but multiplied and lay closer together towards the End of the Arches that were entire.

'There were indeed some Persons, but their Number was very small, that continued a kind of hobbling March on the broken Arches, but fell through one after another, being quite tired and spent with so long a Walk.

'I passed some Time in the Contemplation of this wonderful Structure, and the great Variety of Objects which it presented. My Heart was filled with a deep Melancholy to see several dropping unexpectedly in the Midst of Mirth and Jollity, and catching at every thing that stood by them to save themselves. Some were looking up towards the Heavens in a thoughtful Posture, and in the Midst of a Speculation stumbled and fell out of Sight. Multitudes were very busy in the Pursuit of Bubbles that glittered in their Eyes and danced before them, but often when they thought themselves within the Reach of them their Footing failed, and down they sunk. In this Confusion of Objects, I observed some with Scymetars in their Hands, and others with Urinals, who ran to and fro upon the Bridge, thrusting several Persons on Trap-doors which did not seem to have been laid for them, and which they might have escaped had they not been thus forced upon them.

'The Genius seeing me indulge my self in this melancholy Prospect, told me I had dwelt long enough upon it: Take thine Eyes off the Bridge, said he, and tell me if thou yet seest any thing thou dost not comprehend. Upon looking up, What mean, said I, those great Flights of Birds that are perpetually hovering about the Bridge, and settling upon it from Time to Time? I see Vultures, Harpyes, Ravens, Cormorants, and among many other feathered Creatures several little winged Boys, that perch in great Numbers upon the middle Arches. These, said the Genius, are Envy, Avarice, Superstition, Despair, Love, with the like Cares and Passions that infest humane Life.

'I here fetched a deep Sigh, Alass, said I, Man was made in vain! How is he given away to Misery and Mortality! tortured in Life, and swallowed up in Death! The Genius being moved with Compassion towards me, bid me quit so uncomfortable a Prospect: Look no more, said he, on Man in the first Stage of his Existence, in his setting out for Eternity; but cast thine Eye on that thick Mist into which the Tide bears the several Generations of Mortals that fall into it. I directed my Sight as I was ordered, and (whether or no the good Genius strengthned it with any supernatural Force, or dissipated Part of the Mist that was before too thick for the Eye to penetrate) I saw the Valley opening at the further End, and spreading forth into an immense Ocean, that had a huge Rock of Adamant running through the Midst of it, and dividing it into two equal Halfs. The Cloud still rested on one Half of it, insomuch that I could discover nothing in it; but the other appeared to me a vast Ocean planted with innumerable Islands, that were covered with Fruits and Flowers, and interwoven with a thousand little shining Seas that ran among them. I could see Persons dressed in glorious Habits, with Garlands upon their Heads, passing among the Trees, lying down by the Sides of Fountains, or resting on Beds of Flowers; and could hear a confused Harmony of singing Birds, falling Waters, humane Voices, and musical Instruments. Gladness grew in me upon the Discovery of so delightful a Scene. I wished for the Wings of an Eagle, that I might fly away to those happy Seats; but the Genius told me there was no Passage to them, except through the Gates of Death that I saw opening every Moment upon the Bridge. The Islands, said he, that lie so fresh and green before thee, and with which the whole Face of the Ocean appears spotted as far as thou canst see, are more in Number than the Sands on the Sea-shore; there are Myriads of Islands behind those which thou here discoverest, reaching further than thine Eye or even thine Imagination can extend it self. These are the Mansions of good Men after Death, who according to the Degree and Kinds of Virtue in which they excelled, are distributed among these several Islands, which abound with Pleasures of different Kinds and Degrees, suitable to the Relishes and Perfections of those   10 who are settled in them; every Island is a Paradise accommodated to its respective Inhabitants. Are not these, O *Mirzah*, Habitations worth contending for? Does Life appear miserable, that gives thee Opportunities of earning such a Reward? Is Death to be feared, that will convey thee to so happy an Existence? Think not Man was made in vain, who has such an Eternity reserved for him. I gazed with inexpressible Pleasure on these happy Islands. At length said I, shew me now, I beseech thee, the Secrets that lie hid under those dark Clouds which cover the Ocean on the other Side of the Rock of Adamant. The Genius making me no Answer, I turned about to address my self to him a second time, but I found that he had left me; I then turned again to the Vision which I had been   20 so long contemplating, but instead of the rolling Tide, the arched Bridge, and the happy Islands, I saw nothing but the long hollow Valley of *Bagdat*, with Oxen, Sheep, and Camels, grazing upon the Sides of it.'

The End of the first Vision of Mirzah.

Alexander Pope

1688-1744

Pope was born in London on May 21, 1688, the son of a successful Roman Catholic merchant. The family soon moved to Binfield, on the edge of Windsor Forest, where he grew up. Pope's Catholicism excluded him from attendance at one of the public schools or a university; he was educated privately at home, where he learned to varying degrees of proficiency French, Italian, Latin, and Greek. In 1705, Pope, something of a prodigy, became known to a few of London's well-regarded literary figures, including the playwrights Congreve and Wycherley, to Thomas Betterton the actor, and to the critic William Walsh, who was to become, in some sense at least, his mentor. It may be that Pope's precocity was aided by his continuous ill-health—probably tuberculosis of the spine—which drove him to books and writing for want of other occupations he could engage in and which kept him from a normal life. He never married; on the other hand, he had a lifelong friend in Martha Blount to whom he dedicated his second *Moral Essay* and to whom he left most of his estate.

In 1709, Jacob Tonson, the bookseller, brought out Pope's *Pastorals*; thereafter followed the *Essay on Criticism*, in 1711, and the first version (without the machinery of the sylphs) of *The Rape of the Lock* in 1712. Later in the same month he published the *Messiah*, in *Spectator* No. 378. In 1713, appeared *Windsor Forest* (Pope contributed the prologue to Addison's *Cato* at about the same time), followed in 1714 by the expanded version of *The Rape of the Lock*. (See the relevant headnotes.)

During this period, Pope began to meet with Swift, the poets John Gay and Thomas Parnell, and Dr. John Arbuthnot, physician to Queen Anne and the author of the satirical "John Bull" pamphlets against the Whigs, who together formed the Scriblerus Club, a literary group whose aim was to satirize dullness and pedantry in letters. Some of the works produced at least indirectly as a result of the Club's meetings were *The Memoirs of Martinus Scriblerus* (published late by Pope, in 1741), Gay's *Trivia: or the Art of Walking the Streets of London*, Swift's *Gulliver's Travels*, Pope's *Dunciad*, and *Peri Bathous: or the Art of Sinking in Poetry*.

Pope's translation of the first four books of the *Iliad* was published with great success in 1715 (the work was completed by 1720); its appearance occasioned Pope's break with Addison, because Thomas Tickell, Addison's protégé, brought out (perhaps with his sponsor's encouragement) his own translation of Book I less than a week after Pope's version began to appear. In 1717, *Eloisa to Abelard* and *Verses to the Memory of an Unfortunate Lady* were published in the first edition of the poet's collected works.

Two years later, Pope bought a villa at Twickenham on the Thames, where he practiced baroque gardening and built his famed grotto. In 1721, the *Epistle to Addison* appeared in Tickell's posthumous edition of Addison's works. Next, Pope's edition of Shakespeare (1725) was brought out in six volumes, in addition to the first three volumes of his translation of the *Odyssey*. The following year, Pope's Shakespeare was severely (and justly) criticized by the scholar Lewis Theobald (in *Shakespeare Restored*), who, as a result, was enthroned as the prince of Dullness in the first version of the *Dunciad*, published in 1728. Then followed, in 1731, *Moral Essay IV* (*Epistle to the Earl of Burlington*) *Of the Use of Riches*.

In 1733 appeared the *Epistle to Bathurst* (*Moral Essay III, Of the Use of Riches*), the first of the Horatian satires (Sat. II, i), and, anonymously, the first three epistles of *An Essay on Man*. In 1734, *Epistle to Cobham* (*Moral Essay I, Of the Knowledge and Characters of Men*); in 1735, *Of the Characters of Women, to a Lady* [Martha Blount] (*Moral Essay II*), and *Epistle to Dr. Arbuthnot*. In 1737, appeared two more Horatian imitations (Ep. II, ii and Ep. II, i, in that order). But the year was notable too for the attack upon Pope by Crousaz, for *An Essay on Man*. (See the headnote.) In 1740, Pope met the Reverend William Warburton, the divine, who having fended off Crousaz, was to become the poet's literary executor. And in 1742 and 1743, appeared the *New Dunciad* (Book IV) and *The Dunciad, in Four Books*, with Cibber enthroned. (See the headnote.) Pope died of asthma and dropsy on May 30, 1744, and he was buried at Twickenham.

Alexander Pope—Selective Bibliography

Reginald H. Griffith, *Alexander Pope: A Bibliography*, 2 vols., Austin, U. of Texas Press, 1922–27.

James E. Tobin, *Alexander Pope: A List of Critical Studies from 1895–1944*, New York, Cosmopolitan Science & Art Service Co., 1945. See also *CBEL*, II, pp. 294 f.

The Twickenham Edition of the Poems of Alexander Pope, 10 vols. (11 parts), ed. John Butt, E. Audra, Geoffrey Tillotson, Maynard Mack, James Sutherland, and others, London, Methuen, New Haven, Yale U. P., 1939–67, is now complete; but no modern edition of the complete works exists, that of Whitwell Elwin and William J. Courthope having appeared in 1871–89. An excellent one-volume edition of the Twickenham text, with selected annotations, is *The Poems of Alexander Pope*, ed. John Butt, London, Methuen, New Haven, Yale U. P., 1963.

James E. Wellington, ed., *Eloisa to Abelard*, with the letters of Héloïse to Abelard in the version of John Hughes, 1713, Coral Gables, Fla., U. of Miami Press, 1965.

George Sherburn, ed., *The Correspondence of Alexander Pope*, 5 vols., Oxford, Clarendon Press, 1956.

Edna L. Steeves, ed., *The Art of Sinking in Poetry*, New York, King's Crown Press, 1952.

Norman Ault, ed., *The Prose Works of Alexander Pope*, Vol. I, Oxford, B. Blackwell for the Shakespeare Head Press, 1936 [all published].

George Sherburn, *The Early Career of Alexander Pope*, Oxford, Clarendon Press, 1934; covers the life to 1729.

Jacob Adler, *The Reach of Art: A Study in the Prosody of Pope*, Gainesville, U. of Florida Press, 1964.

Reuben Brower, *Alexander Pope: The Poetry of Allusion*, Oxford, Clarendon Press, 1959.

Thomas R. Edwards, Jr., *This Dark Estate: A Reading of Pope*, Berkeley, Los Angeles, U. of California Press, 1963.

Thomas E. Maresca, *Pope's Horatian Poems*, Columbus, Ohio State U. P., 1966.

Rebecca Price Parkin, *The Poetic Workmanship of Alexander Pope*, Minneapolis, U. of Minnesota Press, 1955.

R. W. Rogers, *The Major Satires of Pope*, Urbana, U. of Illinois Press, 1955.

R. K. Root, *The Poetical Career of Alexander Pope*, Princeton [N.J.] U. P., London, Oxford U. P., 1938.

Geoffrey Tillotson, *On the Poetry of Pope*, Oxford, Clarendon Press, 1938; second edition, 1950.

——, *Pope and Human Nature*, Oxford, Clarendon Press, 1958.

Aubrey L. Williams, *Pope's "Dunciad": A Study of its Meaning*, London, Methuen; Baton Rouge, Louisiana State U. P., 1955.

Maynard Mack, ed., *Essential Articles for the Study of Pope*, Hamden, Conn., Archon Books, 1964. Several excellent articles on Pope also appear in *From Sensibility to Romanticism*, ed., F. W. Hilles and Harold Bloom, New York, Oxford U. P., 1965.

Headnote to
THE PASTORALS

Pope tells us in several places that his Pastorals were written in 1704, when he was about sixteen. They were not published until 1709, in *Pastoral Miscellanies, The Sixth Part* (also referred to as Tonson's, or as Dryden's, *Miscellany*). The volume containing Pope's Pastorals included those of Ambrose Philips as well; indeed, those by Philips began the *Miscellany* and those by Pope ended it, the work of each representing one of the two major opposing theories of pastoral poetry in the age, this opposition being an extension of the battle between ancients and moderns. One of these, usually called the neoclassic theory, can be traced to Rapin, *Dissertatio de Carmine Pastorali*, and the other, the "rationalistic," to Fontenelle, *Discours sur la nature de l'églogue*. As one might infer from the names given these schools, the first applied to classical sources for its authority—the example of pastoral by Virgil and, less directly, Theocritus—and maintained that the proper subject matter of pastoral is the action of shepherds living in a golden age. The second sought its authority in the actual tranquility of rural existence; and the pastorals written in that tradition attempt to represent shepherds as they are if one looks only at the pleasant side of their lives. Obviously such a wilful elimination of unpleasant things from Fontenelle's pastoral world reconciles it in some ways to the pastoral world of the golden age, as Pope, despite his preference for the neoclassic school, makes clear in his *Discourse on Pastoral Poetry*. The real point is simply that the best exemplars of both traditions never lost sight of the fact that art, however closely it may suggest the mind's response to life, is not literally or directly "true to life."

The pastorals of both Pope and Philips had their strong supporters. Because Philips had extravagantly extended Fontenelle's views for the sake of greater "realism"—his pastorals are set in England and peopled by English rustics making references to English folklore, instead of to classical mythology, in a language far from the simple and pure expression thought appropriate to pastoral—he and Pope were much farther apart than nominal followers of these opposing traditions might have been, particularly with Pope's position as temperate as it was. Accordingly, in *Spectator* No. 523, Addison praises Philips for giving "a new life" to pastoral, and in *Guardian*, Nos. 22, 23, 28, 30, and 32, Thomas Tickell quotes from Philips to provide the theoretical basis for accepting the new kind of pastoral, but never once mentions Pope. On the other hand, Sir William Temple, John Gay, and Swift were among those who favored the neoclassical position; and Pope himself, in an anonymous contribution to the *Guardian*, No. 40, ironically endorses the rationalistic view in order to demolish Philips.

Pope's four pastorals, *Spring, Summer, Autumn,* and *Winter* follow the patterns established (1) in the *Idylls* of Theocritus (fl. c. 270 B.C.), the Sicilian poet who developed the form, using a national type of rustic song about the lives and loves of herdsmen as his model and (2) in Virgil's *Eclogues*, which employ Theocritan setting and matter, but generally reduce the Sicilian poet's use of realistic detail and avoid his sometimes gross language. In addition Pope sometimes drew upon the *Shepherd's Calendar*, as he does, for example, in the opening of *Summer*, though generally he thought of Philips as Spenser's follower. It may be that his debt to Spenser is often unconscious, as it seems to be in the case of the lovelorn Alexis, whose prototypes in the eleventh *Idyll* and in the second *Eclogue* seem to come to terms with love, whereas neither he nor Spenser's Colin Clout do so.

TEXT. *The Works of Alexander Pope, Esq.*, ed. William Warburton (9 vols., London, 1751).

Summer

The Second Pastoral, Or Alexis

TO DR. GARTH[1]

A Shepherd's Boy (he seeks no better name)
Led forth his flocks along the silver Thame,
Where dancing sun-beams on the waters play'd,
And verdant alders form'd a quiv'ring shade.
Soft as he mourn'd, the streams forgot to flow,   5

[1] *To Dr. Garth:* Pope says, "Dr. Samuel Garth, author of 'The Dispensary,' was one of the first friends of the author, whose acquaintance with him began at fourteen or fifteen. Their friendship continued from the year 1703 to 1718, which was that of his death."

The flocks around a dumb compassion show,
The Naiads wept in ev'ry wat'ry bow'r,
And Jove consented in a silent show'r.
    Accept, O GARTH, the Muse's early lays,
That adds this wreath of Ivy to thy Bays;   10
Hear what from Love unpractis'd hearts endure,
From Love, the sole disease thou canst not cure.
    Ye shady beeches, and ye cooling streams,
Defence from Phœbus', not from Cupid's beams,
To you I mourn, nor to the deaf I sing;   15
The woods shall answer, and their echo ring.
The hills and rocks attend my doleful lay,
Why art thou prouder and more hard than they?
The bleating sheep with my complaints agree,
They parch'd with heat, and I inflam'd by thee.   20
The sultry Sirius burns the thirsty plains,
While in thy heart eternal winter reigns.
    Where stray ye Muses, in what lawn or grove,
While your Alexis pines in hopeless love?
In those fair fields where sacred Isis glides,   25
Or else where Cam his winding vales divides?
As in the crystal spring I view my face,
Fresh rising blushes paint the wat'ry glass;
But since those graces please thy eyes no more,
I shun the fountains which I sought before.   30
Once I was skill'd in ev'ry herb that grew,
And ev'ry plant that drinks the morning dew;
Ah wretched shepherd, what avails thy art,
To cure thy lambs, but not to heal thy heart!
    Let other swains attend the rural care,   35
Feed fairer flocks, or richer fleeces sheer:
But nigh yon' mountain let me tune my lays,
Embrace my Love, and bind my brows with bays.
That flute is mine which Colin's tuneful breath
Inspir'd when living, and bequeath'd in death;   40
He said, "Alexis, take this pipe, the same

---

7. *Naiads:* Nymphs of springs, rivers, and lakes.

10. *Adds . . . Ivy to thy Bays:* Bays were garlands of laurel awarded to victors at the Pythian games, but early associated with the poet who made the victors' fame permanent by celebrating it in verse; ivy, in post-classical times, came to refer to the learning of the poet as distinct from his inspiration.

16. *The woods shall answer, and their echo ring:* Pope says this "is a line out of Spenser's Epithalamion"; it is in fact a version of Spenser's much-used refrain in that poem.

21. *Sirius:* The Dog-star, which set with the sun in August and marked the period of greatest heat.

25. *Isis:* This name was applied to the Thames near Oxford.

26. *Cam:* A river in Cambridgeshire, England.

36. *Sheer:* Until the text of 1751, the basis of the present text, this word appeared as share; both forms of the word mean shear.

39. *Colin:* Colin Clout is the rustic name Spenser adopts both in his "Shepheard's Calender" and in his "Colin Clout's come home again."

That taught the groves my Rosalinda's name."
But now the reeds shall hang on yonder tree,
For ever silent since despis'd by thee.
Oh! were I made by some transforming pow'r   45
The captive bird that sings within thy bow'r!
Then might my voice thy list'ning ears employ,
And I those kisses he receives, enjoy.
    And yet my numbers please the rural throng,
Rough Satyrs dance, and Pan applauds the song: 50
The Nymphs, forsaking ev'ry cave and spring,
Their early fruit, and milk-white turtles bring;
Each am'rous nymph prefers her gifts in vain,
On you their gifts are all bestow'd again.
For you the swains the fairest flow'rs design,   55
And in one garland all their beauties join;
Accept the wreath which you deserve alone,
In whom all beauties are compriz'd in one.
    See what delights in sylvan scenes appear!
Descending Gods have found Elysium here.   60
In woods bright Venus with Adonis stray'd,
And chaste Diana haunts the forest-shade.
Come, lovely nymph, and bless the silent hours,
When swains from sheering seek their nightly bow'rs;
When weary reapers quit the sultry field,   65
And crown'd with corn their thanks to Ceres yield.
This harmless grove no lurking viper hides,
But in my breast the serpent Love abides.
Here bees from blossoms sip the rosy dew,
But your Alexis knows no sweets but you.   70
Oh deign to visit our forsaken seats,
The mossy fountains, and the green retreats!
Where'er you walk, cool gales shall fan the glade,
Trees, where you sit, shall croud into a shade:
Where'er you tread, the blushing flow'rs shall rise, 75
And all things flourish where you turn your eyes.
Oh! how I long with you to pass my days,
Invoke the Muses, and resound your praise!
Your praise the birds shall chant in ev'ry grove,
And winds shall waft it to the pow'rs above.   80

---

42. *Rosalinda's name:* Rosalind is celebrated as Colin Clout's love in "Shepheard's Calender" and in "Colin Clout's come home again."

60. *Elysium:* The Islands of the Blest where the favorites of the gods enjoy life after death.

61. *Venus with Adonis stray'd:* Though strangely generated, Adonis was a mortal youth, beloved by Venus, goddess of love.

62. *Chaste Diana:* A Roman goddess associated with Greek Artemis, virgin huntress and goddess of wildlife, childbirth, and all young things.

66. *Ceres:* A Roman, perhaps more properly an Italian, deity representing nature's generative power, particularly in agriculture.

But would you sing, and rival Orpheus' strain,
The wond'ring forests soon should dance again,
The moving mountains hear the pow'rful call,
And headlong streams hang list'ning in their fall!
   But see, the shepherds shun the noon-day heat,   85
The lowing herds to murm'ring brooks retreat,
To closer shades the panting flocks remove;
Ye Gods! and is there no relief for Love?
But soon the sun with milder rays descends
To the cool ocean, where his journey ends;   90
On me love's fiercer flames for ever prey,
By night he scorches, as he burns by day.

(1709)

Winter

The Fourth Pastoral, Or Daphne

TO THE MEMORY OF MRS. TEMPEST[1]

Lycidas. Thyrsis, the music of that murm'ring spring
Is not so mournful as the strains you sing.
Nor rivers winding thro' the vales below,
So sweetly warble, or so smoothly flow.
Now sleeping flocks on their soft fleeces lie,   5
The moon, serene in glory, mounts the sky,
While silent birds forget their tuneful lays,
Oh sing of Daphne's fate, and Daphne's praise!

81. *Orpheus:* A pre-Homeric poet of legend, cited here for his musical ability, so great that wild animals were spellbound by his music.

91–92. Pope goes to Virgil, *Eclogue II,* as Virgil had gone to Theocritus, *Idyll II,* for this analogy between the heat of summer and the fire that preys on the lover.

[1] *Mrs. Tempest:* Pope says, "This Lady was of an ancient family in Yorkshire, and particularly admired by the author's friend Mr. Walsh, who having celebrated her in a pastoral elegy, desired his friend to do the same. . . ." It seems likely that Pope offered this tribute to Walsh, his friend and literary guide, in place of a dedication to him, made impossible by Walsh's death in 1708.

8. *Daphne's fate . . . Daphne's praise:* The antiphonal quality of "Winter" derives from a pastoral tradition, the dialogue or singing contest, employed in *Idylls* 5, 6, 7, 8, 27. Though in the seventh *Idyll* a certain Lycidas is praised for his pastoral masquerade, Pope's Lycidas rather brings Milton's to mind. Indeed "Winter" continues the tradition of pastoral mourning, starting with the first *Idyll* of Theocritus, in which Thyrsis mourns Daphnis, a shepherd punished by Aphrodite with a longing for someone unattainable. Other such laments are Bion's for Adonis, Moschus' for Bion, Milton's for Lycidas. Pope's Daphne here is a female counterpart to these objects of mourning.

Thyrsis. Behold the groves that shine with silver frost,
Their beauty wither'd, and their verdure lost.   10
Here shall I try the sweet Alexis strain,
That call'd the list'ning Dryads to the plain?
Thames heard the numbers as he flow'd along,
And bade his willows learn the moving song.
   Lycidas. So may kind rains their vital moisture yield,   15
And swell the future harvest of the field.
Begin; this charge the dying Daphne gave,
And said, "Ye shepherds, sing around my grave!"
Sing, while beside the shaded tomb I mourn,
And with fresh bays her rural shrine adorn.   20
   Thyrsis. Ye gentle Muses, leave your crystal spring,
Let Nymphs and Sylvans cypress garlands bring;
Ye weeping Loves, the stream with myrtles hide,
And break your bows, as when Adonis dy'd;
And with your golden darts, now useless grown,   25
Inscribe a verse on this relenting stone:
"Let nature change, let heav'n and earth deplore,
Fair Daphne's dead, and love is now no more!"
   'Tis done, and nature's various charms decay;
See gloomy clouds obscure the chearful day!   30
Now hung with pearls the dropping trees appear,
Their faded honours scatter'd on her bier.
See, where on earth the flow'ry glories lie,
With her they flourish'd, and with her they die.
Ah what avail the beauties nature wore?   35
Fair Daphne's dead, and beauty is no more!
   For her the flocks refuse their verdant food,
The thirsty heifers shun the gliding flood.
The silver swans her hapless fate bemoan,
In notes more sad than when they sing their own;   40
In hollow caves sweet Echo silent lies,
Silent, or only to her name replies;
Her name with pleasure once she taught the shore,
Now Daphne's dead, and pleasure is no more!
   No grateful dews descend from ev'ning skies,   45
Nor morning odours from the flow'rs arise;
No rich perfumes refresh the fruitful field,
Nor fragrant herbs their native incense yield.
The balmy Zephyrs, silent since her death,

---

12. *Dryads:* Nymphs, each of whom was associated with a particular tree and each of whom died when her tree died.
14. *Willows:* In England, a symbol of grief.
22. *Sylvans:* Spirits of the woods.
24. *Adonis:* He was killed by a boar while hunting. Bion, *Idyll I*, refers to certain actions of his mourners: "This flung upon him arrows, that a bow, this a feather, that a quiver."
41. *Echo:* A nymph who rejected Pan's advances. He changed her into a voice that could only repeat words just spoken.

Lament the ceasing of a sweeter breath;   50
Th' industrious bees neglect their golden store!
Fair Daphne's dead, and sweetness is no more!
   No more the mounting larks, while Daphne sings,
Shall list'ning in mid air suspend their wings;
No more the birds shall imitate her lays,   55
Or hush'd with wonder, hearken from the sprays:
No more the streams their murmurs shall forbear,
A sweeter music than their own to hear,
But tell the reeds, and tell the vocal shore,
Fair Daphne's dead, and music is no more!   60
   Her fate is whisper'd by the gentle breeze,
And told in sighs to all the trembling trees;
The trembling trees, in ev'ry plain and wood,
Her fate remurmur to the silver flood;
The silver flood, so lately calm, appears   65
Swell'd with new passion, and o'erflows with tears;
The winds and trees and floods her death deplore,
Daphne, our grief! our glory now no more!
   But see! where Daphne wond'ring mounts on high
Above the clouds, above the starry sky!   70
Eternal beauties grace the shining scene,
Fields ever fresh, and groves for ever green!
There while you rest in Amaranthine bow'rs,
Or from those meads select unfading flow'rs,
Behold us kindly, who your name implore,   75
Daphne, our Goddess, and our grief no more!
   Lycidas. How all things listen, while thy Muse complains!
Such silence waits on Philomela's strains,
In some still ev'ning, when the whisp'ring breeze
Pants on the leaves, and dies upon the trees.   80
To thee, bright goddess, oft a lamb shall bleed,
If teeming ewes encrease my fleecy breed.
While plants their shade, or flow'rs their odours give,
Thy name, thy honour, and thy praise shall live!
   Thyrsis. But see, Orion sheds unwholsome dews,   85
Arise, the pines a noxious shade diffuse;
Sharp Boreas blows, and Nature feels decay,
Time conquers all, and we must Time obey.
Adieu, ye vales, ye mountains, streams and groves,
Adieu, ye shepherd's rural lays and loves;   90
Adieu, my flocks, farewell ye sylvan crew,
Daphne, farewell, and all the world adieu!

   (1709)

Headnote to
AN ESSAY ON CRITICISM

An Essay on Criticism, first published in 1711, examines the responsibilities of the poet, and of the critic, in a way representative of English neoclassicism. Its references to Greek, Roman, and French ideas make it clear that Pope works in poetic traditions of other times and places; yet his own critical integrity easily survives these uses of the past. Less willing than some French theorists to be guided very closely by critical rules (only Thomas Rymer among the English was a formalist in these matters), Pope establishes a middle ground between formalism and inspiration. The result is not a compromise, however, nor like Dryden's *Essay of Dramatic Poesy* an explanatory excursion through the critical possibilities of the day, but an integration of deeply considered theory and perceptive common sense.

The *Essay*'s treatment of nature and the ancients provides a good example of this fusing power. For the eighteenth century, the term *nature* did not refer primarily to the world of woods, ocean, and sky, but to psychological characteristics and physical laws one might think of as universal because they obtained in any age. The relationship of a man to his culture, or a prism to white light, or a minister to his king; a father's feelings for his daughter, and hers for him; thoughts inspired by the idea of the seasons rather than by a particular season—all these offered to the acute observer patterns regarded as part of general nature, to which the artist (literary or otherwise) applied for his subject matter. Sometimes the term was so used as to indicate that in a sense nature resides in the artist himself; at others, it suggested the power that endowed man with a sense of order and purpose; and often it referred to the complex laws thought to govern the entire universe, including man. In this scheme of things, Homer was thought of as a great author, because the world of his epics seemed an accurate representation of the largest conception of nature—general nature. Accordingly, though the artist coming after Homer might study the universe itself to gather material for his work, as Virgil (Maro) does at first (*Essay*, II, 130–140), he may go directly to Homer with no loss of accuracy. Despite this apparent approval of vicarious experience, it is important to consider that the ideal poet-critic (like Virgil, again) is made to discover the congruence of Homer and general nature for himself.

Several features of *The Essay on Criticism*, though by no means unique in post-classical times, suggest the work's debt to Horace's *Ars Poetica*—Pope's conversational tone, his stress on the need for unity among the parts of a work of art, and his numerous manipulations of the theme that art should give pleasure while it instructs. The poem also includes some of the ideas in Boileau's *Art Poetique*, Rapin's *Reflexions sur la Poétique*, Longinus's *On the Sublime*, Le Bossu's *Traité du Poëme épique*, and many of the critical observations of Jonson, Dryden, and others. Obviously it was not Pope's aim to be original; instead, he tried to state in a clear, telling manner what men of sense knew and accepted. Nevertheless it is not true that Pope just says old things in new ways. He writes so provocatively that old opinions are transformed into new truths:

> Some beauties yet no Precepts can declare,
> For there's a happiness as well as care.   (II, 141–142)

Among other things, the couplet says (1) some beauties exist apart from the power of rules to generate (or comment on) them; (2) beauty is somehow a function of happiness; (3) the existence of beauty-happiness does not displace the need for Precept-care. Also familiar and at the same time new to the eighteenth-century reader were Pope's uses of the terms *wit* and *judgment*. According to one generally held view, wit (or fancy) was thought to be the mind's associative faculty (a superficial faculty according to Hobbes and Locke), which could produce metaphors, among other things; judgment, on the other hand, was believed to result from the solid power of understanding. Pope rejects this arbitrary division, first by using the term *wit* to stand for both operations, and then by stressing their complementary nature:

> Some, to whom Heav'n in wit has been profuse,
> Want as much more, to turn it to its use;
> For wit and judgment often are at strife,
> Tho' meant each other's aid, like man and wife.   (II, 80–83)

Pope's technique of defining one idea in the terms of another, which is closely related to it in the mind of the reader, helps him to show connections and relationships at the very same time that he makes distinctions. As a result, his admittedly didactic, explanatory, discriminating verse, which might otherwise fragment whatever it considers, actually integrates apparently disparate elements. The superficially analytical mind divides as it distinguishes; the superficially integrative claims connections where none exist. Pope is seldom guilty of either fault. Instead, he uses his power to discriminate between elements in such pairs as poet and critic, ancients and moderns, nature and art, rules and inspiration, familiar things and new ones, wit and judgment in such a way that he gathers together what he himself calls the "joint force and full result of all."

TEXT. *The Works of Alexander Pope, Esq.* (9 vols., London, 1751).

An Essay on Criticism

Part I

'TIS hard to say, if greater want of skill
Appear in writing or in judging ill;
But, of the two, less dang'rous is th' offence
To tire our patience, than mislead our sense.
Some few in that, but numbers err in this,   5
Ten censure wrong for one who writes amiss;
A fool might once himself alone expose,
Now one in verse makes many more in prose.
    'Tis with our judgments as our watches, none
Go just alike, yet each believes his own.   10
In Poets as true genius is but rare,
True Taste as seldom is the Critic's share;
Both must alike from Heav'n derive their light,
These born to judge, as well as those to write.
Let such teach others who themselves excel,   15
And censure freely who have written well.
Authors are partial to their wit, 'tis true,
But are not Critics to their judgment too?
    Yet if we look more closely, we shall find
Most have the seeds of judgment in their mind;   20
Nature affords at least a glimm'ring light;
The lines, tho' touch'd but faintly, are drawn right.
But as the slightest sketch, if justly trac'd,   ⎫
Is by ill-colouring but the more disgrac'd,   ⎬
So by false learning is good sense defac'd;   ⎭   25
Some are bewilder'd in the maze of schools,
And some made coxcombs Nature meant but fools.
In search of wit these lose their common sense,
And then turn Critics in their own defence;

Each burns alike, who can, or cannot write,   30
Or with a Rival's, or an Eunuch's spite.
All fools have still an itching to deride,
And fain would be upon the laughing side.
If Mævius scribble in Apollo's spight,
There are, who judge still worse than he can write.   35
   Some have at first for Wits, then Poets past,
Turn'd Critics next, and prov'd plain fools at last.
Some neither can for Wits nor Critics pass,
As heavy mules are neither horse nor ass.
Those half-learn'd witlings, num'rous in our isle,   40
As half-form'd insects on the banks of Nile;
Unfinish'd things, one knows not what to call,
Their generation's so equivocal:
To tell 'em, would a hundred tongues require,
Or one vain wit's, that might a hundred tire.   45
   But you who seek to give and merit fame,
And justly bear a Critic's noble name,
Be sure yourself and your own reach to know,
How far your genius, taste, and learning go;
Launch not beyond your depth, but be discreet,   50
And mark that point where sense and dullness meet.
   Nature to all things fix'd the limits fit,
And wisely curb'd proud man's pretending wit.
As on the land while here the ocean gains,
In other parts it leaves wide sandy plains;   55
Thus in the soul while memory prevails,
The solid pow'r of understanding fails;
Where beams of warm imagination play,
The memory's soft figures melt away.
One science only will one genius fit;   60
So vast is art, so narrow human wit:
Not only bounded to peculiar arts,
But oft' in those confin'd to single parts.
Like Kings we lose the conquests gain'd before,
By vain ambition still to make them more;   65
Each might his sev'ral province well command,
Would all but stoop to what they understand.
   First follow Nature, and your judgment frame
By her just standard, which is still the same:
Unerring NATURE, still divinely bright,   70
One clear, unchang'd, and universal light,
Life, force, and beauty, must to all impart,
At once the source, and end, and test of Art.
Art from that fund each just supply provides,

34. *Mævius:* A poetaster derided by
Virgil and Horace.

Works without show, and without pomp presides: 75
In some fair body thus th' informing soul
With spirits feeds, with vigour fills the whole,
Each motion guides, an ev'ry nerve sustains;
Itself unseen, but in th' effects, remains.
Some, to whom Heav'n in wit has been profuse,   80
Want as much more, to turn it to its use;
For wit and judgment often are at strife,
Tho' meant each other's aid, like man and wife.
'Tis more to guide, than spur the Muse's steed;
Restrain his fury, than provoke his speed;   85
The winged courser, like a gen'rous horse,
Shows most true mettle when you check his course.
   Those RULES of old discover'd, not devis'd,
Are Nature still, but Nature methodiz'd;
Nature, like Liberty, is but restrained   90
By the same Laws which first herself ordain'd.
   Hear how learn'd Greece her useful rules indites,
When to repress, and when indulge our flights:
High on Parnassus' top her sons she show'd,
And pointed out those arduous paths they trod,   95
Held from afar, aloft, th' immortal prize,
And urg'd the rest by equal steps to rise.
Just precepts thus from great examples giv'n,
She drew from them what they deriv'd from Heav'n.
The gen'rous Critic fann'd the Poet's fire,   100
And taught the world with reason to admire.
Then Criticism the Muses handmaid prov'd,
To dress her charms, and make her more belov'd;
But following wits from that intention stray'd,
Who cou'd not win the mistress, woo'd the maid;   105
Against the Poets their own arms they turn'd,
Sure to hate most the men from whom they learn'd.
So modern 'Pothecaries, taught the art
By Doctor's bills to play the Doctor's part,
Bold in the practice of mistaken rules,   110
Prescribe, apply, and call their masters fools.
Some on the leaves of antient authors prey,
Nor time nor moths e'er spoil'd so much as they.
Some drily plain, without invention's aid,
Write dull receits how poems may be made.   115
These leave the sense, their learning to display,
And those explain the meaning quite away.
   You then whose judgment the right course would steer,
Know well each ANCIENT's proper character,

94. *Parnassus:* A mountain associated   goddesses of literature and the arts.
with the worship of Apollo and the Muses,

His Fable, Subject, scope in ev'ry page,   120
Religion, Country, genius of his Age:
Without all these at once before your eyes,
Cavil you may, but never criticize.
Be Homer's works your study and delight,
Read them by day, and meditate by night;   125
Thence form your judgment, thence your maxims bring,
And trace the Muses upward to their spring.
Still with itself compar'd, his text peruse;
And let your comment be the Mantuan Muse.
     When first young Maro in his boundless mind   130
A work t'outlast immortal Rome design'd,
Perhaps he seem'd above the Critic's law,
And but from Nature's fountains scorn'd to draw:
But when t'examine ev'ry part he came,
Nature and Homer were, he found, the same.   135
Convinc'd, amaz'd, he checks the bold design;   ⎫
And rules as strict his labour'd work confine,   ⎬
As if the Stagirite o'erlook'd each line.   ⎭
Learn hence for ancient rules a just esteem;
To copy nature is to copy them.   140
     Some beauties yet no Precepts can declare,
For there's a happiness as well as care.
Music resembles Poetry, in each   ⎫
Are nameless graces which no methods teach,   ⎬
And which a master-hand alone can reach.   ⎭   145
If, where the rules not far enough extend
(Since rules were made but to promote their end),
Some lucky Licence answer to the full
Th'intent propos'd, that Licence is a rule.
Thus Pegasus, a nearer way to take,   150
May boldly deviate from the common track;
From vulgar bounds with brave disorder part,
And snatch a grace beyond the reach of art,
Which, without passing thro' the judgment, gains
The heart, and all its end at once attains.   155
In prospects thus, some objects please our eyes,   ⎫
Which out of nature's common order rise,   ⎬
The shapeless rock, or hanging precipice.   ⎭
Great Wits sometimes may gloriously offend,
And rise to faults true Critics dare not mend.   160
But tho' the Ancients thus their rules invade
(As Kings dispense with laws themselves have made),
Moderns, beware! or if you must offend

129. *Mantuan Muse:* Virgil, born at   159–160. Before the edition of 1744
Andēs, near Mantua.   and after that of 1751, this couplet follows
   138. *Stagirite:* Aristotle, born at Stagira   l. 151.
in Macedonia.

Against the precept, ne'er transgress its End;
Let it be seldom, and compell'd by need,   165
And have, at least, their precedent to plead.
The Critic else proceeds without remorse,
Seizes your fame, and puts his laws in force.
    I know there are, to whose presumptuous thoughts
Those freer beauties, ev'n in them, seem faults.   170
Some figures monstrous and mis-shap'd appear,
Consider'd singly, or beheld too near,
Which, but proportion'd to their light, or place,
Due distance reconciles to form and grace.
A prudent chief not always must display   175
His pow'rs in equal ranks, and fair array,
But with th'occasion and the place comply,
Conceal his force, nay seem sometimes to fly.
Those oft are stratagems which errors seem,
Nor is it Homer nods, but we that dream.   180
    Still green with bays each ancient Altar stands,
Above the reach of sacrilegious hands,
Secure from Flames, from Envy's fiercer rage,
Destructive War, and all-involving Age.
See, from each clime the learn'd their incense bring!   185
Hear, in all tongues consenting Pæans ring!
In praise so just let ev'ry voice be join'd,
And fill the gen'ral chorus of mankind!
Hail, Bards triumphant! born in happier days;
Immortal heirs of universal praise!   190
Whose honours with increase of ages grow,
As streams roll down, enlarging as they flow;
Nations unborn your mighty names shall sound,
And worlds applaud that must not yet be found!
Oh may some spark of your celestial fire,   195
The last, the meanest of your sons inspire
(That on weak wings, from far, pursues your flights;
Glows while he reads, but trembles as he writes)
To teach vain Wits a science little known,
T'admire superior sense, and doubt their own!   200

Part II

    Of all the Causes which conspire to blind
Man's erring judgment, and misguide the mind,
What the weak head with strongest bias rules,
Is *Pride*, the never-failing vice of fools.
Whatever Nature has in worth deny'd,   205
She gives in large recruits of needful Pride;
For as in bodies, thus in souls, we find

What wants in blood and spirits, swell'd with wind;
Pride, where Wit fails, steps in to our defence,
And fills up all the mighty Void of sense.   210
If once right reason drives that cloud away,
Truth breaks upon us with resistless day.
Trust not yourself; but your defects to know,
Make use of ev'ry friend—and ev'ry foe.
   A *little learning* is a dang'rous thing;   215
Drink deep, or taste not the Pierian spring:
There shallow draughts intoxicate the brain,
And drinking largely sobers us again.
Fir'd at first sight with what the Muse imparts,
In fearless youth we tempt the heights of Arts,   220
While from the bounded level of our mind,
Short views we take, nor see the lengths behind;
But more advanc'd, behold with strange surprize
New distant scenes of endless science rise!
So pleas'd at first the tow'ring Alps we try,   225
Mount o'er the vales, and seem to tread the sky;
Th' eternal snows appear already past,
And the first clouds and mountains seem the last:
But, those attain'd, we tremble to survey
The growing labours of the lengthen'd way,   230
Th' increasing prospect tires our wand'ring eyes,
Hills peep o'er hills, and Alps on Alps arise!
   A perfect Judge will read each work of Wit
With the same spirit that its author writ:
Survey the WHOLE, nor seek slight faults to find,   235
Where nature moves, and rapture warms the mind;
Nor lose, for that malignant dull delight,
The gen'rous pleasure to be charm'd with wit.
But in such lays as neither ebb, nor flow,
Correctly cold, and regularly low,   240
That shunning faults, one quiet tenour keep;
We cannot blame indeed—but we may sleep.
In Wit, as Nature, what affects our hearts
Is not th' exactness of peculiar parts;
'Tis not a lip, or eye, we beauty call,   245
But the joint force and full result of all.
Thus when we view some well-proportion'd dome
(The world's just wonder, and ev'n thine, O Rome!)
No single parts unequally surprize,
All comes united to th' admiring eyes;   250
No monstrous height, or breadth, or length, appear;
The Whole at once is bold, and regular.

216. *Pierian spring:* The Muses were   Olympus.
first worshipped at Piera, near Thessalian

Whoever thinks a faultless piece to see,
Thinks what ne'er was, nor is, nor e'er shall be.
In ev'ry work regard the writer's End,   255
Since none can compass more than they intend;
And if the means be just, the conduct true,
Applause, in spight of trivial faults, is due.
As men of breeding, sometimes men of wit,
T' avoid great errors, must the less commit: 260
Neglect the rules each verbal Critic lays,
For not to know some trifles, is a praise.
Most Critics, fond of some subservient art,
Still make the Whole depend upon a Part;
They talk of principles, but notions prize,   265
And all to one lov'd Folly sacrifice.
    Once on a time, La Mancha's Knight, they say,
A certain Bard encount'ring on the way,
Discours'd in terms as just, with looks as sage,
As e'er could Dennis, of the Grecian stage;   270
Concluding all were desp'rate sots and fools,
Who durst depart from Aristotle's rules.
Our Author, happy in a judge so nice,
Produc'd his Play, and begg'd the Knight's advice;
Made him observe the subject, and the plot,   275
The manners, passions, unities, what not?
All which, exact to rule, were brought about,
Were but a Combat in the lists left out.
"What! leave the Combat out?" exclaims the Knight;
"Yes, or we must renounce the Stagirite."   280
"Not so by Heav'n" (he answers in a rage),
"Knights, squires, and steeds, must enter on the stage."
"So vast a throng the stage can ne'er contain."
"Then build a new, or act it in a plain."
    Thus Critics, of less judgment than caprice,   285
Curious, not knowing, not exact, but nice,
Form short Ideas; and offend in arts
(As most in manners) by a love to parts.
    Some to *Conceit* alone their taste confine,
And glitt'ring thoughts struck out at ev'ry line;   290
Pleas'd with a work where nothing's just or fit;
One glaring Chaos and wild heap of wit.

267. *La Mancha's Knight:* In this
episode, ll. 267–284, Pope draws on a
work claiming to be a continuation of
Don Quixote. There, La Mancha's Knight
(Quixote) meets two scholars, one of
whom has written a play which, he says,
does not lightly disregard Aristotle's rules.
Don Quixote at first deplores all such
transgressions, but upon hearing the plot

of the drama, alters his point of view in
order to admit a battle scene.
    270. *Dennis:* John Dennis (1657–1734),
a critic who thought highly of the Greek
stage, was unfairly regarded by many of
his contemporaries as more inflexible about
the rules than in fact he was.
    286. *Curious:* Painstaking. *Nice:* Finicky.

Poets like painters, thus, unskill'd to trace
The naked nature and the living grace,
With gold and jewels cover ev'ry part,   295
And hide with ornaments their want of art.
True Wit is Nature to advantage dress'd,
What oft was thought, but ne'er so well express'd;
Something, whose truth convinc'd at sight we find,
That gives us back the image of our mind: 300
As shades more sweetly recommend the light,
So modest plainness sets off sprightly wit.
For works may have more wit than does 'em good,
As bodies perish thro' excess of blood.
    Others for *Language* all their care express,   305
And value books, as women men, for Dress:
Their praise is still—*The Style is excellent*:
The Sense, they humbly take upon content.
Words are like leaves; and where they most abound,
Much fruit of sense beneath is rarely found.   310
False Eloquence, like the prismatic glass,
Its gaudy colours spreads on ev'ry place;
The face of Nature we no more survey,
All glares alike, without distinction gay:
But true Expression, like th' unchanging Sun,   ⎤   315
Clears, and improves whate'er it shines upon,   ⎬
It gilds all objects, but it alters none.   ⎦
Expression is the dress of thought, and still
Appears more decent, as more suitable;
A vile conceit in pompous words express'd,   320
Is like a clown in regal purple dress'd;
For diff'rent styles with diff'rent subjects sort,
As several garbs with country, town, and court.
Some by old words to fame have made pretence;
Ancients in phrase, meer moderns in their sense;   325
Such labour'd nothings, in so strange a style,
Amaze th' unlearn'd, and make the learned smile.
Unlucky, as Fungoso in the Play,   ⎤
These sparks with aukward vanity display   ⎬
What the fine gentleman wore yesterday!   ⎦   330
And but so mimic ancient wits at best,
As apes our grandsires, in their doublets drest.
In words, as fashions, the same rule will hold;
Alike fantastic, if too new, or old;
Be not the first by whom the new are try'd,   335
Nor yet the last to lay the old aside.
    But most by Numbers judge a Poet's song;

308. *Take upon content*: To accept   328. *Fungoso*: A student in Jonson's
readily, without pause for thought. The   *Every Man out of his Humour.*
House of Lords used the term to mean aye.

And smooth or rough, with them, is right or wrong:
In the bright Muse tho' thousand charms conspire,
Her Voice is all these tuneful fools admire,   340
Who haunt Parnassus but to please their ear,
Not mend their minds; as some to Church repair,
Not for the doctrine, but the music there.
These equal syllables alone require,
Tho' oft the ear the open vowels tire,   345
While expletives their feeble aid do join,
And ten low words oft creep in one dull line,
While they ring round the same unvary'd chimes,
With sure returns of still expected rhymes.
Where-e'er you find "the cooling western breeze,"   350
In the next line, it "whispers thro' the trees";
If crystal streams "with pleasing murmurs creep,"
The reader's threaten'd (not in vain) with "sleep";
Then, at the last and only couplet fraught
With some unmeaning thing they call a thought,   355
A needless Alexandrine ends the song,
That, like a wounded snake, drags its slow length along.
Leave such to tune their own dull rhymes, and know
What's roundly smooth, or languishingly slow;
And praise the easy vigour of a line,   360
Where Denham's strength, and Waller's sweetness join.
True ease in writing comes from art, not chance,
As those move easiest who have learn'd to dance.
'Tis not enough no harshness gives offence,
The sound must seem an Echo to the sense: 365
Soft is the strain when Zephyr gently blows,
And the smooth stream in smoother numbers flows;
But when loud surges lash the sounding shoar,
The hoarse, rough verse should like the torrent roar:
When Ajax strives some rock's vast weight to throw,   370
The line too labours, and the words move slow;
Not so, when swift Camilla scours the plain,
Flies o'er th' unbending corn, and skims along the main.
Hear how Timotheus' vary'd lays surprize,
And bid alternate passions fall and rise !   375

356. *Alexandrine:* A line of verse with
six feet, illustrated in the following line,
357.

361. *Denham and Waller:* John Denham
(1615–1669) and Edmund Waller (1606–
1687) are praised here for their heroic
couplets. Dryden in his *Essay of Dramatic
Poesy* says the Elizabethans ". . . can
produce nothing . . . so even, sweet, and
flowing as Mr. Waller; nothing so majestic,
so correct as Sir John Denham. . . ."

370. *Ajax:* A huge man, second only to
Achilles among the Greek heroes at Troy.

372. *Camilla:* A Volscian princess
(*Aeneid*, VII) who could run so fast she
did not bend the grain as she passed over a
planted field, nor wet her feet as she
skimmed the sea.

374. *Timotheus:* A well-known poet
and musician of Miletus, whose music in
Dryden's *Alexander's Feast* determines the
moods of King Alexander.

While, at each change, the son of Libyan Jove
Now burns with glory, and then melts with love;
Now his fierce eyes with sparkling fury glow,
Now sighs steal out, and tears begin to flow:
Persians and Greeks like turns of nature found,   380
And the World's victor stood subdu'd by Sound!
The pow'r of Music all our hearts allow,
And what Timotheus was, is DRYDEN now.
        Avoid Extremes; and shun the fault of such
Who still are pleas'd too little or too much.   385
At ev'ry trifle scorn to take offence,
That always shows great pride, or little sense;
Those heads, as stomachs, are not sure the best,
Which nauseate all, and nothing can digest.
Yet let not each gay Turn thy rapture move;   390
For fools admire, but men of sense approve:
As things seem large which we thro' mists descry,
Dulness is ever apt to magnify.
        Some foreign writers, some our own despise;
The Ancients only, or the Moderns prize.   395
Thus Wit, like Faith, by each man is apply'd
To one small sect, and all are damn'd beside.
Meanly they seek the blessing to confine,
And force that sun but on a part to shine,
Which not alone the southern wit sublimes,   400
But ripens spirits in cold northern climes;
Which from the first has shone on ages past,
Enlights the present, and shall warm the last;
Tho' each may feel encreases and decays,
And see now clearer and now darker days.   405
Regard not then if Wit be old or new,
But blame the false, and value still the true.
        Some ne'er advance a Judgment of their own,
But catch the spreading notion of the Town;
They reason and conclude by precedent,   410
And own stale nonsense which they ne'er invent.
Some judge of authors names, not works, and then
Nor praise nor blame the writings, but the men.
Of all this servile herd, the worst is he
That in proud dulness joins with Quality.   415
A constant Critic at the great man's board,
To fetch and carry nonsense for my Lord.
What woful stuff this madrigal would be,
In some starv'd hackney sonneteer, or me?
But let a Lord once own the happy lines,   420

376. *Son of Libyan Jove:* Alexander the
Great.

How the wit brightens! how the style refines!
Before his sacred name flies ev'ry fault,
And each exalted stanza teems with thought!
The Vulgar thus through Imitation err;
As oft the Learn'd by being singular; 425
So much they scorn the croud, that if the throng
By chance go right, they purposely go wrong:
So Schismatics the plain believers quit,
And are but damn'd for having too much wit.
Some praise at morning what they blame at night; 430
But always think the last opinion right.
A Muse by these is like a mistress us'd,
This hour she's idoliz'd, the next abus'd;
While their weak heads like towns unfortify'd,
'Twixt sense and nonsense daily change their side. 435
Ask them the cause; they're wiser still, they say;
And still to-morrow's wiser than to-day.
We think our fathers fools, so wise we grow;
Our wiser sons, no doubt, will think us so.
Once School-divines this zealous isle o'er-spread; 440
Who knew most Sentences, was deepest read;
Faith, Gospel, all, seem'd made to be disputed,
And none had sense enough to be confuted.
Scotists and Thomists, now, in peace remain,
Amidst their kindred cobwebs in Duck-lane. 445
If Faith itself has diff'rent dresses worn,
What wonder modes in Wit should take their turn?
Oft', leaving what is natural and fit,
The current folly proves the ready wit;
And authors think their reputation safe, 450
Which lives as long as fools are pleas'd to laugh.
Some valuing those of their own side or mind,
Still make themselves the measure of mankind;
Fondly we think we honour merit then,
When we but praise ourselves in other men. 455
Parties in Wit attend on those of State,
And public faction doubles private hate.
Pride, Malice, Folly, against Dryden rose,
In various shapes of Parsons, Critics, Beaus;
But sense surviv'd, when merry jests were past; 460
For rising merit will buoy up at last.
Might he return, and bless once more our eyes,

444. *Scotists and Thomists:* Followers of John Duns Scotus (1265?–1308) and St. Thomas Aquinas (1225–1274), the one a Scottish, the other an Italian scholastic theologian, whose parties were in constant dispute.

445. *Duck-lane:* Pope says it was "a place where old and second-hand books were sold formerly, near Smithfield."

New Blackmores and new Milbourns must arise;
Nay should great Homer lift his awful head,
Zoilus again would start up from the dead.   465
Envy will merit, as its shade, pursue.
But like a shadow, proves the substance true;
For envy'd Wit, like Sol eclips'd, makes known
Th' opposing body's grossness, not its own.
When first that sun too pow'rful beams displays,   470
It draws up vapours which obscure its rays;
But ev'n those clouds at last adorn its way,
Reflect new glories, and augment the day.
  Be thou the first true merit to befriend;
His praise is lost, who stays 'till all commend.   475
Short is the date, alas, of modern rhymes,
And 'tis but just to let them live betimes.
No longer now that golden age appears,
When Patriarch-wits surviv'd a thousand years;
Now length of Fame (our second life) is lost,   480
And bare threescore is all ev'n that can boast;
Our sons their fathers failing language see,
And such as Chaucer is, shall Dryden be.
So when the faithful pencil has design'd
Some bright Idea of the master's mind,   485
Where a new world leaps out at his command,
And ready Nature waits upon his hand;
When the ripe colours soften and unite,
And sweetly melt into just shade and light,
When mellowing years their full perfection give,   490
And each bold figure just begins to live,
The treach'rous colours the fair art betray,
And all the bright creation fades away!
  Unhappy Wit, like most mistaken things,
Atones not for that envy which it brings.   495
In youth alone its empty praise we boast,
But soon the short-liv'd vanity is lost!
Like some fair flow'r the early spring supplies,
That gayly blooms, but ev'n in blooming dies.
What is this Wit, which must our cares employ?   500
The owner's wife, that other men enjoy;
Then most our trouble still when most admir'd,
And still the more we give, the more requir'd;
Whose fame with pains we guard, but lose with ease,
Sure some to vex, but never all to please;   505

463. *Blackmores and Milbourns:* Richard
Blackmore (c. 1650–1729) and the Reverend
Luke Milbourn (1649–1720) were among
the critics and the parsons who attacked
Dryden, ll. 458–459.

465. *Zoilus:* A Greek critic and
rhetorician (fourth century B.C.) who
became known for his long and severe
criticisms of Homer.

'Tis what the vicious fear, the virtuous shun;
By fools 'tis hated, and by knaves undone!
If Wit so much from Ign'rance undergo,
Ah let not Learning too commence its foe!
Of old, those met rewards who could excell, 510
And such were prais'd who but endeavour'd well:
Tho' triumphs were to gen'rals only due,
Crowns were reserv'd to grace the soldiers too.
Now, they who reach Parnassus' lofty crown,
Employ their pains to spurn some others down; 515
And while self-love each jealous writer rules,
Contending wits become the sport of fools:
But still the worst with most regret commend,
For each ill Author is as bad a Friend.
To what base ends, and by what abject ways, 520
Are mortals urg'd thro' sacred lust of praise!
Ah ne'er so dire a thirst of glory boast,
Nor in the Critic let the Man be lost.
Good-nature and good-sense must ever join;
To err is human, to forgive, divine. 525
    But if in noble minds some dregs remain,
Not yet purg'd off, of spleen and sour disdain,
Discharge that rage on more provoking crimes,
Nor fear a dearth in these flagitious times.
No pardon vile Obscenity should find, 530
Tho' wit and art conspire to move your mind;
But Dulness with Obscenity must prove
As shameful sure as Impotence in love.
In the fat age of pleasure, wealth, and ease,
Sprung the rank weed, and thriv'd with large increase; 535
When love was all an easy Monarch's care;
Seldom at council, never in a war:
Jilts rul'd the state, and statesmen farces writ;
Nay wits had pensions, and young Lords had wit:
The Fair sate panting at a Courtier's play, 540
And not a Mask went unimprov'd away:
The modest fan was lifted up no more,
And Virgins smil'd at what they blush'd before.
The following licence of a Foregin reign
Did all the dregs of bold Socinus drain; 545
Then unbelieving Priests reform'd the nation,
And taught more pleasant methods of salvation;
Where Heav'n's free subjects might their rights dispute,
Lest God himself should seem too absolute:
Pulpits their sacred satire learn'd to spare, 550

545. *Bold Socinus:* Lelio Sozzini (1525– doctrine of atonement through Christ.
1562) rejected Christ's divinity and the

And Vice admir'd to find a flatt'rer there!
Encourag'd thus, Wit's Titans brav'd the skies,
And the press groan'd with licens'd blasphemies.
These monsters, Critics! with your darts engage,
Here point your thunder, and exhaust your rage!   555
Yet shun their fault, who, scandalously nice,
Will needs mistake an author into vice;
All seems infected that th' infected spy,
As all looks yellow to the jaundic'd eye.

Part III

Learn then what MORALS Critics ought to show,   560
For 'tis but half a Judge's task, to know.
'Tis not enough, taste, judgment, learning, join;
In all you speak, let truth and candour shine:
That not alone what to your sense is due
All may allow; but seek your friendship too.   565
Be silent always when you doubt your sense;
And speak, tho' sure, with seeming diffidence:
Some positive, persisting fops we know,
Who, if once wrong, will needs be always so;
But you, with pleasure own your errors past,   570
And make each day a Critic on the last.
'Tis not enough, your counsel still be true;
Blunt truths more mischief than nice falshoods do;
Men must be taught as if you taught them not,
And things unknown propos'd as things forgot.   575
Without Good Breeding, truth is disapprov'd;
That only makes superior sense belov'd.
Be niggards of advice on no pretence;
For the worst avarice is that of sense.
With mean complacence ne'er betray your trust,   580
Nor be so civil as to prove unjust.
Fear not the anger of the wise to raise;
Those best can bear reproof, who merit praise.
'Twere well might Critics still this freedom take,
But Appius reddens at each word you speak,   585
And stares, tremendous, with a threat'ning eye,
Like some fierce Tyrant in old tapestry.
Fear most to tax on Honourable fool,
Whose right it is, uncensur'd to be dull;
Such, without wit, are Poets when they please,   590
As without learning they can take Degrees.
Leave dang'rous truths to unsuccessful Satires,

585. *Appius:* John Dennis, who wrote   He was known to be fond of the word
Appius and Virginia, a play that failed.   "tremendous," l. 586.

And flattery to fulsome Dedicators,
Whom, when they praise, the world believes no more,
Than when they promise to give scribling o'er.   595
'Tis best sometimes your censure to restrain,
And charitably let the dull be vain:
Your silence there is better than your spite,
For who can rail so long as they can write?
Still humming on, their drouzy course they keep,   600
And lash'd so long, like tops, are lash'd asleep.
False steps but help them to renew the race,
As, after stumbling, Jades will mend their pace.
What crouds of these, impenitently bold,
In sounds and jingling syllables grown old,   605
Still run on Poets, in a raging vein,
Ev'n to the dregs and squeezings of the brain;
Strain out the last dull droppings of their sense,
And rhyme with all the rage of Impotence.
Such shameless Bards we have; and yet 'tis true,   610
There are as mad, abandon'd Critics too.
The bookful blockhead, ignorantly read,
With loads of learned lumber in his head,
With his own tongue still edifies his ears,
And always list'ning to himself appears.   615
All books he reads, and all he reads assails,
From Dryden's Fables down to Durfey's Tales.
With him, most authors steal their works, or buy;
Garth did not write his own Dispensary.
Name a new Play, and he's the Poet's friend,   620
Nay show'd his faults—but when would Poets mend?
No place so sacred from such fops is barr'd,
Nor is Paul's church more safe than Paul's church yard:
Nay, fly to Altars; there they'll talk you dead;
For Fools rush in where Angels fear to tread.   625
Distrustful sense with modest caution speaks;   ⎫
It still looks home, and short excursions makes;   ⎬
But rattling nonsense in full vollies breaks;   ⎭
And never shock'd, and never turn'd aside,
Bursts out, resistless, with a thund'ring tide.   630
But where's the man, who counsel can bestow,
Still pleas'd to teach, and yet not proud to know?
Unbiass'd, or by favour, or by spite;
Not dully prepossess'd, not blindly right;
Tho' learn'd, well-bred; and tho' well-bred, sincere;   635
Modestly bold, and humanly severe?

617. *Durfey's Tales:* Thomas Durfey
(1653–1723), a popular author who
wrote songs, tales, satires, and plays.
619. *Garth:* Samuel Garth (1661–1719),
a physician whose poem "The Dispensary"
scores apothecaries for their unwillingness
to supply medicines to outpatient dis-
pensaries.

Who to a friend his faults can freely show,
And gladly praise the merit of a foe?
Blest with a taste exact, yet unconfin'd;
A knowledge both of books and human kind;   640
Gen'rous converse; a soul exempt from pride;
And love to praise, with reason on his side?
   Such once were Critics; such the happy few,
Athens and Rome in better ages knew.
The mighty Stagirite first left the shore,   645
Spread all his sails, and durst the deeps explore;
He steer'd securely, and discover'd far,
Led by the light of the Mæonian Star.
Poets, a race long unconfin'd, and free,
Still fond and proud of savage liberty,   650
Receiv'd his laws; and stood convinc'd 'twas fit,
Who conquer'd Nature, should preside o'er Wit.
   Horace still charms with graceful negligence,
And without method talks us into sense,
Will, like a friend, familiarly convey   655
The truest notions in the easiest way.
He, who supreme in judgment, as in wit,
Might boldly censure, as he boldly writ,
Yet judg'd with coolness, tho' he sung with fire;
His Precepts teach but what his works inspire.   660
Our Critics take a contrary extreme,
They judge with fury, but they write with fle'me:
Nor suffers Horace more in wrong Translations
By Wits, than Critics in as wrong Quotations.
   See Dionysius Homer's thoughts refine,   665
And call new beauties forth from ev'ry line!
   Fancy and art in gay Petronius please,
The scholar's learning, with the courtier's ease.
   In grave Quintilian's copious work, we find
The justest rules, and clearest method join'd;   670
Thus useful arms in magazines we place,
All rang'd in order, and dispos'd with grace,
But less to please the eye, than arm the hand,
Still fit for use, and ready at command.
   Thee, bold Longinus! all the Nine inspire,   675

648. *Mæonian Star:* Homer, who according to one tradition was born in Maeonia, *Maeonia* being an ancient name for Lydia.

662. *They write with fle'me:* They write with phlegm: that is, phlegmatically.

665. *Dionysius:* Dionysius of Halicarnassus (fl. c. 25 B.C.), a sound literary critic and historian, often cited for his view that the style is the man.

667. *Petronius:* Petronius Arbiter (d. A.D. 65?), probably the author of the *Satyricon,* in which various types of Latin prose and verse are used and (sometimes) commented on.

669. *Quintilian:* Roman teacher of rhetoric and author of *Institutio Oratoria* (c. A.D. 35–c. 95).

675. *Longinus:* Thought to be the author of a treatise (first or second century A.D.) *On the Sublime,* a work also admired by Dryden, Addison, Goldsmith, and Gibbon.

And bless their Critic with a Poet's fire.
An ardent Judge, who zealous in his trust,
With warmth gives sentence, yet is always just;
Whose own example strengthens all his laws,
And is himself that great Sublime he draws.   680
   Thus long succeeding Critics justly reign'd,
Licence repress'd, and useful laws ordain'd.
Learning and Rome alike in empire grew;
And Arts still follow'd where her Eagles flew;
From the same foes, at last, both felt their doom,   685
And the same age saw Learning fall, and Rome.
With Tyranny, then Superstition join'd,
As that the body, this enslav'd the mind;
Much was believ'd, but little understood,
And to be dull was constru'd to be good;   690
A second deluge Learning thus o'er-run,
And the Monks finish'd what the Goths begun.
   At length Erasmus, that great injur'd name
(The glory of the Priesthood, and the shame!)
Stem'd the wild torrent of a barb'rous age,   695
And drove those holy Vandals off the stage.
   But see! each Muse, in LEO's golden days,
Starts from her trance, and trim's her wither'd bays;
Rome's ancient Genius, o'er its ruins spread,
Shakes off the dust, and rears his rev'rend head.   700
Then Sculpture and her sister-arts revive;
Stones leap'd to form, and rocks began to live;
With sweeter notes each rising Temple rung;
A Raphael painted, and a Vida sung.
Immortal Vida: on whose honour'd brow   705
The Poet's bays and Critic's ivy grow:
Cremona now shall ever boast thy name,
As next in place to Mantua, next in fame!
   But soon by impious arms from Latium chas'd,
Their ancient bounds the banish'd Muses pass'd;   710
Thence Arts o'er all the northern world advance,
But Critic-learning flourish'd most in France:
The rules a nation, born to serve, obeys;
And Boileau still in right of Horace sways.
But we, brave Britons, foreign laws despis'd,   715
And kept unconquer'd, and unciviliz'd;
Fierce for the liberties of wit, and bold,
We still defy'd the Romans, as of old.
Yet some there were, among the sounder few

---

697. *Leo:* Pope Leo X [Giovanni de'
Medici] (1475–1521), a great patron of the
arts.
   704. *Vida:* Marco Girolamo Vida
1480?–1566), Italian humanist and poet,
whose works include *De Arte Poetica*.
   714. *Boileau:* Nicolas Boileau (1636–
1711), French critic and poet; see the
headnote.

Of those who less presum'd, and better knew,   720
Who durst assert the juster ancient cause,
And here restor'd Wit's fundamental laws.
Such was the Muse, whose rules and practice tell,
"Nature's chief Master-piece is writing well."
Such was Roscommon, not more learn'd than good,   725
With manners gen'rous as his noble blood;
To him the wit of Greece and Rome was known,
And ev'ry author's merit, but his own.
Such late was Walsh—the Muse's judge and friend,
Who justly knew to blame or to commend;   730
To failings mild, but zealous for desert;
The clearest head, and the sincerest heart.
This humble praise, lamented shade! receive,
This praise at least a grateful Muse may give!
The Muse, whose early voice you taught to sing,   735
Prescrib'd her heights, and prun'd her tender wing
(Her guide now lost) no more attempts to rise,
But in low numbers short excursions tries:
Content, if hence th' unlearn'd their wants may view,
The learn'd reflect on what before they knew: 740
Careless of censure, nor too fond of fame,
Still pleas'd to praise, yet not afraid to blame,
Averse alike to flatter, or offend,
Not free from faults, nor yet too vain to mend.

(1711)

724. Pope quotes this line from *Essay on Poetry* by George Villiers (1628–1687), Second Duke of Buckingham.

725. *Roscommon:* Wentworth Dillon (1633?–1685), Fourth Earl of Roscommon, author of a blank verse translation of Horace's *Ars Poetica.*

729. *Walsh:* William Walsh (1663–1708), Pope's friend and early literary counsellor, who advised the young poet to aim for correctness.

Headnote to
MESSIAH

As his advertisement below declares, Pope's "Messiah" (first published in the *Spectator*, May 23, 1712) is an imitation of Virgil's pastoral, *Eclogue* 4, which since the days of Constantine, or earlier, had been taken by some Christian authors to predict the Messiah's birth. Most historians of classical literature doubt that the poem refers to Jesus; but it seems possible that Virgil's interest in apocalyptic ideas led him to investigate the messianic hopes of the Jews, quite a few of whom lived along the West coast of Italy, south of Rome, in his day.

Pope's poem also takes into account the "remarkable parity" between the *Pollio* (another name for the fourth *Eclogue*) and certain parts of Isaiah that refer to a child whose birth will herald a golden age. Biblical scholars are generally agreed that Isaiah's anticipations of deliverance are particular expressions of a generally felt need among the Hebrews, rather than a flat prediction of Christ's coming. It is likely then that both *Eclogue* 4 and Isaiah's prophecies are informed by the same longing for a new age, though perhaps the relationship between them can be best explained by historical and psychological means rather than by any other order of connection.

Obviously, Pope is conscious of the common ground between his Hebrew and Latin antecedents; but it is clear that while his "Messiah" imitates Virgil, it makes no attempt to emulate the literary force of the prophet; it merely makes use of some of his statements as they appear either in the King James Bible or in the seventeenth-century version of the Douai Bible used by Catholics in Pope's day. For Virgil was in a way no more than a peer, who might appropriately supply a model that Pope could attempt to equal or surpass. On the other hand, Isaiah, beyond rivalry, could be properly applied to for the inspired language of religion, which Pope was willing to modify only slightly as he conveyed it to his reader. While on the face of it, his treatment of Isaiah suggests that Pope was profoundly reverent, critics have charged that his "Messiah" employs an excess of stock diction, a fact (they say) revealing the poet's lack of religious feeling. Perhaps one ought to disregard both of these simple views and to consider concomitant possibilities. It could be argued that Pope merely adopted what to him seemed a suitable public manner in his deferential treatment of the prophet, or that his deference (assume it to have been sincere) was more literary than religious, or that in fact Pope's primary response to the Biblical material was veneration. Probably the truth lies in a mixture of the three. What in fact emerges clearly in the "Messiah" is not Pope's attitude toward religion, but the nature of his regard for the ancients. Like most men of the age, he had a deep respect, even a love, for the classical authors; but it was the healthy respect accorded one man by another, not reverence. Had it been otherwise, Pope could not have made use of his model as he does here; and Steele could not have paid to the "Messiah" the final compliment, however deserved, which he offers his friend in a letter on June 1, 1712: "Your Poem is already better than the *Pollio*."

TEXT. *The Works of Alexander Pope, Esq.*, ed. William Warburton (9 vols., London, 1751).

Messiah

A Sacred Eclogue in Imitation of Virgil's Pollio

Advertisement

IN reading several passages of the Prophet Isaiah, which foretell the coming of Christ and the felicities attending it, I could not but observe a remarkable parity between many of the thoughts, and those in the Pollio of Virgil. This will not seem surprising, when we reflect, that the Eclogue was taken from a Sibylline prophecy on the same subject. One may judge that Virgil did not copy it line by line, but selected such ideas as best agreed with the nature of pastoral poetry, and disposed them in that manner which served most to beautify his piece. I have endeavoured the same in this imitation of him, though without admitting any thing of my own; since it was written with this particular view, that the reader, by comparing the several thoughts, might see how far the images and descriptions of the Prophet are superior to those of the Poet. But as I fear I have prejudiced them by my management, I shall subjoin the passages of Isaiah, and those of Virgil,[1] under the same disadvantage of a literal translation. P.

---

[1] *I shall subjoin . . . Isaiah . . . Virgil. . . .:*   the text. Pope's notes to "Messiah" appear below

YE Nymphs of Solyma! begin the song:
To heav'nly themes sublimer strains belong.
The mossy fountains, and the sylvan shades,
The dreams of Pindus and th'Aonian maids
Delight no more—O thou my voice inspire   5
Who touch'd Isaiah's hallow'd lips with fire!
    Rapt into future times, the Bard begun:
A Virgin shall conceive, a Virgin bear a Son!
From ª Jesse's root behold a branch arise,
Whose sacred flow'r with fragrance fills the skies: 10
Th' Æthereal spirit o'er its leaves shall move,
And on its top descends the mystic Dove.
Ye ᵇ Heav'ns! from high the dewy nectar pour,
And in soft silence shed the kindly show'r!
The ᶜ sick and weak the healing plant shall aid,   15
From storms a shelter, and from heat a shade.
All crimes shall cease, and ancient fraud shall fail;
Returning ᵈ Justice lift aloft her scale;
Peace o'er the world her olive wand extend,
And white-rob'd Innocence from heav'n descend.   20
Swift fly the years, and rise th' expected morn!
Oh spring to light, auspicious Babe, be born!

IMITATIONS

VER. 8. *A Virgin shall conceive— All crimes shall cease, etc.*]
VIRG. E. iv. v 6.
              Jam redit et Virgo, redeunt Saturnia regna;
              Jam nova progenies cælo demittitur alto.
              Te duce, si qua manent sceleris vestigia nostri,
              Irrita perpetua solvent formidine terras—
              Pacatumque reget patriis virtutibus orbem.
    *Now the Virgin returns, now the kingdom of Saturn returns, now a new Progeny is sent
down from high heaven. By means of thee, whatever reliques of our crimes remain, shall be wiped
away, and free the world from perpetual fears. He shall govern the earth in peace, with the virtues
of his Father.*
    ISAIAH. Ch. vii. v 14. *Behold a Virgin shall conceive and bear a Son.*—Ch. ix. v 6, 7.
*Unto us a Child is born, unto us a Son is given; the Prince of Peace: of the increase of his govern-
ment, and of his peace, there shall be no end: Upon the throne of David, and upon his kingdom,
to order and to stablish it, with judgment, and with justice, for ever and ever.* P.

ª Isai. xi. v 1.   ᵇ Ch. xlv. v 8.   ᶜ Ch. xxv. v 4.   ᵈ Ch. ix. v 7.

1. *Solyma:* Part of the Greek name for
Jerusalem.
4–5. *Pindus and th'Aonian maids/Delight
no more:* Both Pindus, a mountain in
Thessaly, and Aonia (Boeotia) were
associated with the muses. Pope here says
he is giving over the pastoral tradition of
the pagan world for a higher order of

inspiration.
    6. *Isaiah's . . . lips with fire:* Isa. 6:6–7:
". . . one of the seraphim . . . having in his
hand a burning coal . . . touched my
mouth."
    9. *Jesse's root:* Jesse is the father of
David, from whose family Christ was
descended. See Isa. 11:1.

See Nature hastes her earliest wreaths to bring,
With all the incense of the breathing spring:
See ᵉlofty Lebanon his head advance,   25
See nodding forests on the mountains dance,
See spicy clouds from lowly Saron rise,
And Carmel's flow'ry top perfumes the skies!
Hark! a glad voice the lonely desart chears;
Prepare the ᶠway! a God, a God appears.   30
A God, a God! the vocal hills reply,
The rocks proclaim th' approaching Deity.
Lo, earth receives him from the bending skies!
Sink down ye mountains, and ye valleys rise,
With heads declin'd, ye cedars homage pay;   35
Be smooth ye rocks, ye rapid floods give way!
The Saviour comes! by ancient bards foretold:
Hear ᵍhim, ye deaf, and all ye blind, behold!
He from thick films shall purge the visual ray,
And on the sightless eye-ball pour the day.   40
'Tis he th' obstructed paths of sound shall clear,

IMITATIONS

Ver. 23. *See Nature hastes, etc*]
Virg. E. iv. v 18.
> At tibi prima, puer, nullo munuscula cultu,
> Errántes hederas passim cum baccare tellus,
> Mixtaque ridenti colocasia fundet acantho—
> Ipsa tibi blandos fundent cunabula flores.

For thee, O Child, shall the earth, without being tilled, produce her early offerings; winding ivy, mixed with Baccar, and Colocasia with smiling Acanthus. Thy cradle shall pour forth pleasing flowers about thee.

Isaiah, Ch. xxxv. v 1. *The wilderness and the solitary place shall be glad, and the desart shall rejoice and blossom as the rose. Ch. lx. v 13. The glory of Lebanon shall come unto thee, the firtree, the pine-tree, and the box together, to beautify the place of thy sanctuary.* P.

Ver. 29. *Hark, a glad Voice, etc.*]
Virg. E. iv. v 46.
> Aggredere ô magnos, aderit jam tempus, honores,
> Cara deûm soboles, magnum Jovis incrementum—
> Ipsi lætitia voces ad sydera jactant
> Intonsi montes, ipsæ jam carmina rupes,
> Ipsa sonant arbusta, Deus, deus ille Menalca!   E. v. v 62.

Oh come and receive the mighty honours: the time draws nigh, O beloved offspring of the Gods, O great encrease of Jove! The uncultivated mountains send shouts of joy to the stars, the very rocks sing in verse, the very shrubs cry out, A God, a God!

Isaiah, Ch. xl. v 3, 4. *The voice of him that crieth in the wilderness, Prepare ye the way of the Lord! make strait in the desart a high way for our God! Every valley shall be exalted, and every mountain and hill shall be made low, and the crooked shall be made strait, and the rough places plain. Ch. iv. ver. 23. Break forth into singing, ye mountains! O forest, and every tree therein! for the Lord hath redeemed Israel.* P.

ᵉCh. xxxv. v 2.   ᶠCh. xl. v 3, 4.   ᵍCh. xlii. v 18. Ch. xxxv. v 5, 6.

---

25. *Lebanon:* A mountain west of Damascus. See Isa. 35:2 for ". . . the glory of Lebanon and the excellency of Carmel and Sharon."
27. *Saron:* Sharon, part of the great western plain of Palestine, known for its fertility.
28. *Carmel:* A mountain southwest of Mt. Lebanon.

And bid new music charm th' unfolding ear;
The dumb shall sing, the lame his crutch forego,
And leap exulting like the bounding roe.
No sigh, no murmur the wide world shall hear,   45
From ev'ry face he wipes off ev'ry tear.
In ʰadamantine chains shall Death be bound,
And Hell's grim Tyrant feel th' eternal wound.
As the good ⁱshepherd tends his fleecy care,   50
Seeks freshest pasture and the purest air,
Explores the lost, the wand'ring sheep directs,
By day o'ersees them, and by night protects;
The tender lambs he raises in his arms,
Feeds from his hand, and in his bosom warms;
Thus shall mankind his guardian care engage,   55
The promis'd ᵏfather of the future age,
No more shall ⁱnation against nation rise,
Nor ardent warriours meet with hateful eyes,
Nor fields with gleaming steel be cover'd o'er,
The brazen trumpets kindle rage no more;   60
But useless lances into scythes shall bend,
And the broad faulchion in a plow-share end.
Then palaces shall rise; the joyful ᵐSon
Shall finish what his short-liv'd Sire begun;
Their vines a shadow to their race shall yield,   65
And the same hand that sow'd, shall reap the field.
The swain in barren ⁿdesarts with surprize
See lillies spring, and sudden verdure rise;
And starts, amidst the thirsty wilds to hear
New falls of water murm'ring in his ear.   70
On rifted rocks, the dragon's late abodes,
The green reed trembles, and the bulrush nods.
Waste sandy ᵒvalleys, once perplex'd with thorn,
The spiry fir and shapely box adorn;

IMITATIONS

Ver. 67. *The swain in barren desarts*] Virg. E. iv. v 28.
          Molli paulatim flavescet campus arista,
          Incultisque rubens pendebit sentibus uva,
          Et duræ quercus sudabunt roscida mella.
   The fields shall grow yellow with ripen'd ears, and the red grape shall hang upon the wild brambles, and the hard oaks shall distill honey like dew.
   ISAIAH, Ch. xxxv. v 7. *The parched ground shall become a pool, and the thirsty land springs of water: In the habitations where dragons lay, shall be grass, and reeds, and rushes. Ch. lv. v 13. Instead of the thorn, shall come up the fir-tree, and instead of the briar shall come up the myrtle tree.* P.

ʰ Ch. xxv. v 8.   ⁱCh. xl. v 11.   ᵏCh. ix. v 6.   ⁱCh. ii. v 4.
ᵐCh. lxv. v 21, 22.   ⁿCh. xxxv. v 1, 7.   ᵒCh. xil. v 19. and Ch. lv. v 13.

62. *Faulchion:* Modern *falchion.* A broad-bladed sword.

To leafless shrubs the flow'ring palms succeed,   75
And od'rous myrtle to the noisom weed.
The ᵖlambs with wolves shall graze the verdant mead,
And boys in flow'ry bands the tyger lead;
The steer and lion at one crib shall meet,
And harmless ᵩserpents lick the pilgrim's feet.   80
The smiling infant in his hand shall take
The crested basilisk and speckled snake,
Pleas'd the green lustre of the scales survey,
And with their forky tongue shall innocently play.
Rise, crown'd with light, imperial ʳSalem, rise!   85
Exalt thy tow'ry head, and lift thy eyes!
See, a long ˢrace thy spacious courts adorn;
See future sons, and daughters yet unborn,
In crouding ranks on ev'ry side arise,
Demanding life, impatient for the skies!   90
See barb'rous ᵗnations at thy gates attend,
Walk in thy light, and in thy temple bend;
See thy bright altars throng'd with prostrate kings
And heap'd with products of ᵛSabæan springs!
For thee Idume's spicy forests blow,   95
And seeds of gold in Ophyr's mountains glow.
See heav'n its sparkling portals wide display,

IMITATIONS

VER. 77. *The lambs with wolves etc*] Virg. E. iv. v 21.
> Ipsæ lacte domum referent distenta capellæ
> Ubera, nec magnos metuent armenta leones—
> Occidet et serpens, et fallax herba veneni
> Occidet.—

The goats shall bear to the fold their udders distended with milk: nor shall the herds be afraid of the greatest lions. The serpent shall die, and the herb that conceals poison shall die.
ISAIAH, Ch. xi. v 16, etc. *The wolf shall dwell with the lamb, and the leopard shall lie down with the kid, and the calf and the young lion and the fatling together: and a little child shall lead them.—And the lion shall eat straw like the ox. And the sucking child shall play on the hole of the asp, and the weaned child shall put his hand on the den of the cockatrice.* P.
VER. 85. *Rise, crown'd with light, imperial Salem, rise!*]: The thoughts of Isaiah, which compose the latter part of the poem, are wonderfully elevated, and much above those general exclamations of Virgil, which make the loftiest parts of his Pollio.
> Magnus ab integro sæclorum nascitur ordo!
> —toto surget gens aurea mundo!
> —incipient magni procedere menses!
> Aspice, venturo lætentur ut omnia sæclo! etc.
The reader needs only to turn to the passages of Isaiah, here cited. P.

ᵖ Ch. xi. v 6, 7, 8.   ᵩ Ch. lxv. v 25.   ʳ Ch. lx. v 1.
ˢ Ch. lx. v 4.   ᵗ Ch. lx. v 3.   ᵛ Ch. lx. v 6.

---

82. *Basilisk:* A fabulous serpent or dragon with a crested head. See Isa. 30:6.
85. *Salem:* A name for Jerusalem.
94. *Sabæan springs:* Sabaeans (Shebans) were known for their wealth in gold and incense.
95. *Idume:* Edom, a tract of land south

of the Dead Sea. Though the land is mountainous, a mistaken classical tradition makes it out to be fertile.
96. *Ophyr:* Ophir, which supplied Solomon with gold, silver, sandalwood, and ivory, is associated with great wealth in the Old Testament.

And break upon thee in a flood of day!
No more the rising *Sun shall gild the morn,
Nor ev'ning Cynthia fill her silver horn;   100
But lost, dissolv'd in thy superior rays,
One tide of glory, one unclouded blaze
O'erflow thy courts: the Light himself shall shine
Reveal'd, and God's eternal day be thine!
The *seas shall waste, the skies in smoke decay,   105
Rocks fall to dust, and mountains melt away;
But fix'd his word, his saving pow'r remains;
Thy realm for ever lasts, thy own MESSIAH reigns!

(1712)

ᵂ Ch. lx. v 19, 20.   ˣ Ch. li. v 6. and Ch. liv. v 10.

---

100. *Cynthia:* The moon, because the   Mt. Cynthus in Delos.
moon goddess Diana is associated with

Headnote to
WINDSOR FOREST

"Windsor Forest" is a work unified by means of the poetic interplay of attitudes and traditions well known to readers of the eighteenth century, but remote to those of the twentieth. Nevertheless anyone may enjoy the poem, if he goes genially through it at a slow pace, with just a few facts at his command. The forest itself is both the setting for the work and its subject; it is also a richly varied emblem with which an educated Englishman of Pope's day could be made to experience many associations. It is the place where royal Windsor Castle was built, and the locus, verging on myth, of King Arthur's court; it is a surrogate for both the Garden of Eden and the orderly universe of created things generally (ll. 11–16); it is a link with the classical past of Virgil's *Georgics*—the poem that imparts a new dignity and serenity to natural processes by elevating the struggles of the farmer—and with the classical world of Augustus, during whose rule Rome enjoyed its first long-lived peace at home in more than a century; finally, it is a little England, idealized pastorally to suggest the conditions of the country under Queen Anne, whose Tory ministers (among them Pope's friends) concluded with the French the favourable Peace of Utrecht in 1713. (The parallel here to the Rome of Augustus is obvious.)

Other works of this kind, topographical poems, were available as models to Pope. Sir John Denham's "Cooper's Hill" (1642), though less complex than "Windsor Forest," shows the way, as it combines the description of scenery with moral and political observations. And in fact Virgil, both in the *Georgics* and in the fourth Eclogue, had responded to a similar pattern of interests.

It is unfortunate that, in 1736, Pope said about "Windsor Forest," "This poem was written at two different times: The first part of it, which relates to the country [up to l. 290], in the year 1704, at the same time with the *Pastorals*; the latter part was not added till the year 1713, in which it was published." Actually all the evidence suggests that Pope's revisions of the poem were many and that they were comprehensive. It seems to be true that in this one of his many efforts to establish his youthful facility as a versifier, he only gave rise to the mistaken view that "Windsor Forest" lacks unity, when in fact it is representative of Pope's unusual ability to draw faithfully upon past and present and at the same time to produce integrated compositions of force and originality.

TEXT. *The Works of Alexander Pope, Esq.*, ed. William Warburton (9 vols., London, 1751).

Windsor-Forest

TO THE RIGHT HONOURABLE
GEORGE LORD LANSDOWN[1]

THY forests, Windsor! and thy green retreats,
At once the Monarch's and the Muse's seats,
Invite my lays. Be present, sylvan maids!
Unlock your springs, and open all your shades.
GRANVILLE commands; your aid, O Muses, bring!   5
What Muse for GRANVILLE can refuse to sing?
   The Groves of Eden, vanish'd now so long,
Live in description, and look green in song:
These, were my breast inspir'd with equal flame,
Like them in beauty, should be like in fame.   10
Here hills and vales, the woodland and the plain,
Here earth and water seem to strive again,
Not Chaos-like together crush'd and bruis'd,
But, as the world, harmoniously confus'd:
Where order in variety we see,   15
And where, tho' all things differ, all agree.
Here waving groves a chequer'd scene display,
And part admit, and part exclude the day;
As some coy nymph her lover's warm address
Nor quite indulges, nor can quite repress.   20
There, interspers'd in lawns and op'ning glades,
Thin trees arise that shun each other's shades.
Here in full light the russet plains extend;
There wrapt in clouds the blueish hills ascend.
Ev'n the wild heath displays her purple dyes,   25
And 'midst the desart fruitful fields arise,
That crown'd with tufted trees and springing corn,
Like verdant isles the sable waste adorn.
Let India boast her plants, nor envy we
The weeping amber or the balmy tree,   30
While by our oaks the precious loads are born,
And realms commanded which those trees adorn.
Not proud Olympus yields a nobler sight,
Tho' Gods assembled grace his tow'ring height,
Than what more humble mountains offer here,   35
Where, in their blessings, all those Gods appear.
See Pan with flocks, with fruits Pomona crown'd,
Here blushing Flora paints th'enamel'd ground,

---

[1] *George Lord Lansdown:* George Granville, Lord Lansdowne (1667–1735), who perhaps as early as 1706 had praised Pope's literary powers, was a member of the Tory ministry that brought about the Peace of Utrecht, 1713, celebrated in "Windsor Forest." He may have urged Pope to finish the poem along its present lines.
37. *Pomona:* Roman goddess of fruit.
38. *Flora:* Italian goddess of fertility and flowers.

Here Ceres' gifts in waving prospect stand,
And nodding tempt the joyful reaper's hand;   40
Rich Industry sits smiling on the plains,
And peace and plenty tell, a STUART reigns.
    Not thus the land appear'd in ages past,
A dreary desart, and a gloomy waste,
To savage beasts and savage laws a prey,   45
And kings more furious and severe than they;
Who claim'd the skies, dispeopled air and floods,
The lonely lords of empty wilds and woods:
Cities laid waste, they storm'd the dens and caves
(For wiser brutes were backward to be slaves).   50
What could be free, when lawless beasts obey'd
And ev'n the elements a Tyrant sway'd?
In vain kind seasons swell'd the teeming grain,
Soft show'rs distill'd, and suns grew warm in vain;
The swain with tears his frustrate labour yields,   55
And famish'd dies amidst his ripen'd fields.
What wonder then, a beast or subject slain
Were equal crimes in a despotic reign?
Both doom'd alike, for sportive Tyrants bled,
But while the subject starv'd, the beast was fed.   60
Proud Nimrod first the bloody chace began,
A mighty hunter, and his prey was man.
Our haughty Norman boasts that barb'rous name,
And makes his trembling slaves the royal game.
The fields are ravish'd from th'industrious swains,   65
From men their cities, and from Gods their fanes:
The levell'd towns with weeds lie cover'd o'er;
The hollow winds thro' naked temples roar;
Round broken columns clasping ivy twin'd;
O'er heaps of ruin stalk'd the stately hind;   70
The fox obscene to gaping tombs retires,
And savage howlings fill the sacred quires.
Aw'd by his Nobles, by his Commons curst,
Th' Oppressor rul'd tyrannic where he durst,
Stretch'd o'er the Poor and Church his iron rod,   75
And serv'd alike his Vassals and his God.
Whom ev'n the Saxon spar'd and bloody Dane,
The wanton victims of his sport remain.
But see, the man who spacious regions gave

39. *Ceres:* Italian goddess associated with generative power and with the production of grain.
61. *Nimrod:* A mighty hunter, Gen. 10:8–9, generally thought of as a despot.
63. *Haughty Norman:* William I (1027 or 1028–1087), King of England, surnamed the Conqueror.
65. *The fields are ravish'd:* Pope says this line alludes not to Windsor but ". . . to the destruction made in New Forest, and the tyrannies exercised there by William I."

A waste for beasts, himself deny'd a grave!   80
Stretch'd on the lawn his second hope survey,
At once the chaser, and at once the prey.
Lo Rufus, tugging at the deadly dart,
Bleeds in the forest like a wounded hart.
Succeeding monarchs heard the subjects cries,   85
Nor saw displeas'd the peaceful cottage rise.
Then gath'ring flocks on unknown mountains fed,
O'er sandy wilds were yellow harvests spread,
The forests wonder'd at th'unusual grain,
And secret transport touch'd the conscious swain.   90
Fair Liberty, Britannia's Goddess, rears
Her chearful head, and leads the golden years.
  Ye vig'rous swains! while youth ferments your blood,
And purer spirits swell the sprightly flood,
Now range the hills, the gameful woods beset,   95
Wind the shrill horn, or spread the waving net.
When milder autumn summer's heat succeeds,
And in the new-shorn field the partridge feeds,
Before his lord the ready spaniel bounds,
Panting with hope, he tries the furrow'd grounds,   100
But when the tainted gales the game betray,
Couch'd close he lies, and meditates the prey;
Secure they trust th' unfaithful field beset,
'Till hov'ring o'er 'em sweeps the swelling net.
Thus (if small things we may with great compare)   105
When Albion sends her eager sons to war,
Some thoughtless Town, with ease and plenty blest,
Near, and more near, the closing lines invest;
Sudden they seize th' amaz'd, defenceless prize,
And high in air Britannia's standard flies.   110
  See! from the brake the whirring pheasant springs,
And mounts exulting on triumphant wings;
Short is his joy; he feels the fiery wound,
Flutters in blood, and panting beats the ground.
Ah! what avail his glossy, varying dyes,   115
His purple crest, and scarlet-circled eyes,
The vivid green his shining plumes unfold,
His painted wings, and breast that flames with gold?
  Nor yet, when moist Arcturus clouds the sky,
The woods and fields their pleasing toils deny.   120

80. *Himself deny'd a grave:* Pope says, "The place of [William's] interment at Caen in Normandy was claimed by [another] gentleman . . . the moment [the King's] servant were going to put him in his tomb. . . ."

83. *Rufus:* William II (c. 1056–1100), King of England, surnamed Rufus, was killed in New Forest, perhaps by one Walter Tirel and a certain Ralph of Aix.

106. *Albion:* Great Britain.

119. *Arcturus:* A bright star in the constellation Boötes. In September, when it rose with the sun, the weather was supposed to be bad.

To plains with well-breath'd beagles we repair,
And trace the mazes of the circling hare.
(Beasts, urg'd by us, their fellow-beasts pursue,
And learn of man each other to undo.)
With slaught'ring guns th' unweary'd fowler roves,   125
When frosts have whiten'd all the naked groves;
Where doves in flocks the leafless trees o'ershade,
And lonely woodcocks haunt the wat'ry glade.
He lifts the tube, and levels with his eye;
Strait a short thunder breaks the frozen sky.   130
Oft, as in airy rings they skim the heath,
The clam'rous Lapwings feel the leaden death:
Oft, as the mounting larks their notes prepare,
They fall, and leave their little lives in air.
In genial spring, beneath the quiv'ring shade,   135
Where cooling vapours breathe along the mead,
The patient fisher takes his silent stand,
Intent, his angle trembling in his hand;
With looks unmov'd, he hopes the scaly breed,
And eyes the dancing cork, and bending reed.   140
Our plenteous streams a various race supply:
The bright-ey'd perch with fins of Tyrian dye,
The silver eel, in shining volumes roll'd,
The yellow carp, in scales bedrop'd with gold,
Swift trouts, diversify'd with crimson stains,   145
And pykes, the tyrants of the watry plains.
Now Cancer glows with Phœbus' fiery car;
The youth rush eager to the sylvan war,
Swarm o'er the lawns, the forest walks surround,
Rouze the fleet hart, and chear the opening hound.   150
Th' impatient courser pants in ev'ry vein,
And pawing, seems to beat the distant plain:
Hills, vales, and floods appear already cross'd,
And e'er he starts, a thousand steps are lost.
See the bold youth strain up the threat'ning steep,   155
Rush thro' the thickets, down the valleys sweep,
Hang o'er their coursers heads with eager speed,
And earth rolls back beneath the flying steed.
Let old Arcadia boast her ample plain,
Th' immortal huntress, and her virgin-train;   160
Nor envy, Windsor! since thy shades have seen
As bright a Goddess, and as chaste a QUEEN;

147. *Cancer, Phœbus:* The sun (Phoebus) enters the constellation of the Crab (Cancer) at the summer solstice, June 21 or 22.
159. *Arcadia:* In the center of the Peloponnesus, with large plains in the southern part.
162. *Queen:* Queen Anne (1665–1714), here being favourably compared with Diana (Greek Artemis), "Th' immortal huntress" of l. 160.

Whose care, like hers, protects the sylvan reign,
The Earth's fair light, and Empress of the Main.
  Here too, 'tis sung, of old Diana stray'd,   165
And Cynthus' top forsook for Windsor shade;
Here was she seen o'er airy wastes to rove,
Seek the clear spring, or haunt the pathless grove;
Here arm'd with silver bows, in early dawn,
Her buskin'd Virgins trac'd the dewy lawn.   170
  Above the rest a rural nymph was fam'd,
Thy offspring, Thames! the fair Lodona nam'd.
(Lodona's fate, in long oblivion cast,
The Muse shall sing, and what she sings shall last.)
Scarce could the Goddess from her nymph be known,   175
But by the crescent and the golden zone.
She scorn'd the praise of beauty, and the care,
A belt her waist, a fillet binds her hair,
A painted quiver on her shoulder sounds,
And with her dart the flying deer she wounds.   180
It chanc'd, as eager of the chace, the maid
Beyond the forest's verdant limits stray'd,
Pan saw and lov'd, and burning with desire
Pursu'd her flight, her flight increas'd his fire.
Not half so swift the trembling doves can fly,   185
When the fierce eagle cleaves the liquid sky;
Not half so swiftly the fierce eagle moves,
When thro' the clouds he drives the trembling doves;
As from the God she flew with furious pace,
Or as the God, more furious, urg'd the chace.   190
Now fainting, sinking, pale, the nymph appears;
Now close behind, his sounding steps she hears;
And now his shadow reach'd her as she run
(His shadow lengthen'd by the setting sun),
And now his shorter breath, with sultry air,   195
Pants on her neck, and fans her parting hair.
In vain on father Thames she calls for aid,
Nor could Diana help her injur'd maid.
Faint, breathless, thus she pray'd, nor pray'd in vain;
"Ah Cynthia! ah—tho' banish'd from thy train,   200
"Let me, O let me, to the shades repair,
"My native shades—there weep, and murmur there."
She said, and melting as in tears she lay,
In a soft, silver stream dissolv'd away.
The silver stream her virgin coldness keeps,   205
For ever murmurs, and for ever weeps;

166. *Cynthus:* A mountain in Delos, one of the places with which Diana (Artemis) is associated.

172. *Lodona:* One of Diana's virgin-train of nymphs, who, pursued by Pan, eludes him by becoming a "silver stream," the River Loddon, ll. 171–206.

200. *Cynthia:* A name for Diana.

Still bears the name the hapless virgin bore,
And bathes the forest where she rang'd before.
In her chaste current oft the Goddess laves,
And with celestial tears augments the waves.   210
Oft in her glass the musing shepherd spies
The headlong mountains and the downward skies,
The watry landskip of the pendant woods,
And absent trees that tremble in the floods;
In the clear azure gleam the flocks are seen,   215
And floating forests paint the waves with green.
Thro' the fair scene roll slow the ling'ring streams,
Then foaming pour along, and rush into the Thames.
    Thou too, great father of the British floods!
With joyful pride survey'st our lofty woods,   220
Where tow'ring oaks their growing honours rear,
And future navies on thy shores appear.
Not Neptune's self from all her streams receives
A wealthier tribute, than to thine he gives.
No seas so rich, so gay no banks appear,   225
No lake so gentle, and no spring so clear.
Nor Po so swells the fabling Poet's lays,
While led along the skies his current strays,
As thine, which visits Windsor's fam'd abodes,
To grace the mansion of our earthly Gods.   230
Nor all his stars above a lustre show,
Like the bright Beauties on thy banks below;
Where Jove, subdu'd by mortal Passion still,
Might change Olympus for a nobler hill.
    Happy the man whom this bright Court approves,   235
His Sov'reign favours, and his Country loves;
Happy next him, who to these shades retires,
Whom Nature charms, and whom the Muse inspires,
Whom humbler joys of home-felt quiet please,
Successive study, exercise, and ease.   240
He gathers health from herbs the forest yields,
And of their frag[r]ant physic spoils the fields:
With chymic art exalts the min'ral pow'rs,
And draws the aromatic souls of flow'rs.
Now marks the course of rolling orbs on high;   245
O'er figur'd worlds now travels with his eye;
Of ancient writ unlocks the learned store,
Consults the dead, and lives past ages o'er.
Or wand'ring thoughtful in the silent wood,
Attends the duties of the wise and good,   250
T'observe a mean, be to himself a friend,
To follow nature, and regard his end;
Or looks on heav'n with more than mortal eyes,

Bids his free soul expatiate in the skies,
Amid her kindred stars familiar roam,   255
Survey the region, and confess her home!
Such was the life great Scipio once admir'd,
Thus Atticus, and TRUMBAL thus retir'd.
   Ye sacred Nine! that all my soul possess,
Whose raptures fire me, and whose visions bless,   260
Bear me, oh bear me to sequester'd scenes,
The bow'ry mazes, and surrounding greens;
To Thames's banks which fragrant breezes fill,
Or where ye Muses sport on COOPER's HILL.
(On COOPER's HILL eternal wreaths shall grow,   265
While lasts the mountain, or while Thames shall flow)
I seem thro' consecrated walks to rove,
I hear soft music die along the grove;
Led by the sound, I roam from shade to shade,
By god-like Poets venerable made: 270
Here his first lays majestic DENHAM sung;
There the last numbers flow'd from COWLEY's tongue.
O early lost! what tears the river shed,
When the sad pomp along his banks was led?
His drooping swans on ev'ry note expire,   275
And on his willows hung each Muse's lyre.
   Since fate relentless stop'd their heav'nly voice,
No more the forests ring, or groves rejoice;
Who now shall charm the shades, where COWLEY strung
His living harp, and lofty DENHAM sung?   280
But hark! the groves rejoice, the forest rings!
Are these reviv'd? or is it GRANVILLE sings?
'Tis yours, my Lord, to bless our soft retreats,
And call the Muses to their ancient seats,
To paint anew the flow'ry sylvan scenes,   285
To crown the forests with immortal greens,
Make Windsor-hills in lofty numbers rise,
And lift her turrets nearer to the skies;
To sing those honours you deserve to wear,
And add new lustre to her silver star.   290

257. *Scipio:* Scipio Africanus Major (236–c. 183 B.C.) was responsible for Rome's victory over Carthage in the Second Punic War. Later, he retired to an estate at Liternum, south of Rome.

258. *Atticus:* Titus Pomponius Atticus (109–32 B.C.), in order to avoid civil war in Rome, retired in 88 B.C. to Athens where he wrote, studied, and "published" Cicero's works.

Trumbal: William Trumbull (1639–1716), to whom Pope dedicated his *Pastoral, Spring,* and to whom credit is generally given for suggesting that Pope write a poem on Windsor Forest, retired to Easthampton Park, about a mile from Pope's boyhood home at Binfield in Windsor Forest, around 1700.

264. *Cooper's Hill:* The title of a topographical poem by John Denham. See headnote.

272. *Cowley:* Abraham Cowley (1618–1667), of whom Pope says, "Mr. Cowley died at Chertsey, on the borders of the Forest, and was from thence convey'd to Westminster."

Here noble SURREY felt the sacred rage,
SURREY, the GRANVILLE of a former age:
Matchless his pen, victorious was his lance,
Bold in the lists, and graceful in the dance:
In the same shades the Cupids tun'd his lyre,   295
To the same notes, of love, and soft desire:
Fair Geraldine, bright object of his vow,
Then fill'd the groves, as heav'nly Mira now.
Oh would'st thou sing what Heroes Windsor bore,
What Kings first breath'd upon her winding shore,   300
Or raise old warriours, whose ador'd remains
In weeping vaults her hallow'd earth contains!
With Edward's acts adorn the shining page,
Stretch his long triumphs down thro' ev'ry age,
Draw Monarchs chain'd, and Cressi's glorious field,   305
The lillies blazing on the regal shield.
Then, from her roofs when Verrio's colours fall,
And leave inanimate the naked wall,
Still in thy song should vanquish'd France appear,
And bleed for ever under Britain's spear.   310
Let softer strains ill-fated Henry mourn,
And palms eternal flourish round his urn.
Here o'er the Martyr-King the marble weeps,
And fast beside him, once-fear'd Edward sleeps:
Whom not th' extended Albion could contain,   315
From old Belerium to the northern main,
The grave unites, where ev'n the Great find rest,
And blended lie th' oppressor and th' opprest!
Make sacred Charles's tomb for ever known
(Obscure the place, and un-inscrib'd the stone)   320
Oh fact accurst! what tears has Albion shed,
Heav'ns, what new wounds! and how her old have bled?
She saw her sons with purple deaths expire,
Her sacred domes involv'd in rolling fire,

291. *Surrey:* Pope says, "Henry Howard, Earl of Surrey, one of the first refiners
of English poetry, who flourish'd in the
time of Henry VIII."
297. *Fair Geraldine:* Surrey's love
poetry is addressed to her.
298. *Mira:* Granville, in his songs, uses
the name presumably to refer to one
or another of his mistresses.
303. *Edward:* Pope says, "Edward III
[1312–1377] born here."
305. *Cressi:* Crécy, a town in Northern
France where the English under Edward
III gained a great victory over the French,
on August 26, 1346.
307. *Verrio:* Antonio Verrio (1639–
1709), an Italian painter employed by

Charles II to decorate Windsor Castle.
311. *Ill-fated Henry:* Henry VI (1421–
1471), a saintly man, killed during the
Wars of the Roses, regarded by his followers as the martyr-king. See l. 313.
314. *Edward:* Edward IV (1442–1483),
who with his kinsmen the Nevilles overthrew Henry VI, in 1461. Henry returned
to his throne before he lost it, with his life,
in 1471.
316. *Belerium:* Shortened form of the
Latin name for Land's End, a promontory
in Cornwall.
319. *Sacred Charles's tomb:* It was not
until 1813 that the coffin of the beheaded
Charles I (1600–1649) was identified; it
had lain in the tomb of Henry VIII.

A dreadful series of intestine wars,   325
Inglorious triumphs and dishonest scars.
At length great ANNA said—"Let Discord cease!"
She said, the world obey'd, and all was Peace!
  In that blest moment from his oozy bed
Old father Thames advanc'd his rev'rend head.   330
His tresses drop'd with dews, and o'er the stream
His shining horns diffus'd a golden gleam:
Grav'd on his urn appear'd the moon, that guides
His swelling waters, and alternate tides;
The figur'd streams in waves of silver roll'd,   335
And on their banks Augusta rose in gold.
Around his throne the sea-born brothers stood,
Who swell with tributary urns his flood;
First the fam'd authors of his ancient name,
The winding Isis and the fruitful Tame: 340
The Kennet swift, for silver eels renown'd;
The Loddon slow, with verdant alders crown'd;
Cole, whose dark streams his flow'ry islands lave;
And chalky Wey, that rolls a milky wave:
The blue, transparent Vandalis appears;   345
The gulphy Lee his sedgy tresses rears;
And sullen Mole, that hides his diving flood;
And silent Darent, stain'd with Danish blood.
  High in the midst, upon his urn reclin'd
(His sea-green mantle waving with the wind)   350
The God appear'd: he turn'd his azure eyes
Where Windsor-domes and pompous turrets rise,
Then bow'd and spoke; the winds forget to roar,
And the hush'd waves glide softly to the shore.
  Hail, sacred Peace! hail long-expected days,   355
That Thames's glory to the stars shall raise!
Tho' Tyber's streams immortal Rome behold,
Tho' foaming Hermus swells with tides of gold,
From heav'n itself tho' sev'n-fold Nilus flows,
And harvests on a hundred realms bestows;   360
These now no more shall be the Muse's themes,
Lost in my fame, as in the sea their streams.
Let Volga's banks with iron squadrons shine,
And groves of lances glitter on the Rhine,
Let barb'rous Ganges arm a servile train;   365
Be mine the blessings of a peaceful reign.
No more my sons shall die with British blood

---

327. *Anna:* Queen Anne.
336. *Augusta:* London.
340. *Isis and Tame:* These rivers were
regarded by poets as parents of the
Thames.

340–362. Not only does the catalogue
of rivers help the reader to move from
Pope's time into the classical past, it also
suggests a flow into future times and far
places.

Red Iber's sands, or Ister's foaming flood;
Safe on my shore each unmolested swain
Shall tend the flocks, or reap the bearded grain;   370
The shady empire shall retain no trace
Of war or blood, but in the sylvan chace;
The trumpet sleep, while chearful horns are blown,
And arms employ'd on birds and beasts alone.
Behold! th' ascending Villa's on my side   375
Project long shadows o'er the crystal tide.
Behold! Augusta's glitt'ring spires increase,
And Temples rise, the beauteous works of Peace.
I see, I see, where two fair cities bend
Their ample bow, a new Whitehall ascend!   380
There mighty Nations shall enquire their doom,
The World's great Oracle in times to come;
There Kings shall sue, and suppliant States be seen
Once more to bend before a BRITISH QUEEN.
   Thy trees, fair Windsor! now shall leave their woods,   385
And half thy forests rush into thy floods,
Bear Britain's thunder, and her Cross display,
To the bright regions of the rising day;
Tempt icy seas, where scarce the waters roll,
Where clearer flames glow round the frozen Pole;   390
Or under southern skies exalt their sails,
Led by new stars, and borne by spicy gales!
For me the balm shall bleed, and amber flow
The coral redden, and the ruby glow,
The pearly shell its lucid globe infold,   395
And Phœbus warm the rip'ning ore to gold.
The time shall come, when free as seas or wind
Unbounded Thames shall flow for all mankind,
Whole nations enter with each swelling tide,
And seas but join the regions they divide;   400
Earth's distant ends our glory shall behold,
And the new world launch forth to seek the old.
Then ships of uncouth form shall stem the tyde,
And feather'd people croud my wealthy side,
And naked youths and painted chiefs admire   405
Our speech, our colour, and our strange attire!
Oh stretch thy reign, fair Peace! from shore to shore,
'Till Conquest cease, and Slav'ry be no more,
'Till the freed Indians in their native groves
Reap their own fruits, and woo their sable loves,   410
Peru once more a race of Kings behold,

368. *Iber; Ister:* The Spanish river
Ebro; the Danube. The English won
victories at both.
   380. *Whitehall:* A palace, sometimes
the home of English rulers; burned down
in 1698, it was to have been rebuilt.
   385–386. *Trees . . . into thy floods:*
Trees made into ships and launched.

And other Mexico's be roof'd with gold.
Exil'd by thee from earth to deepest hell,
In brazen bonds, shall barb'rous Discord dwell;
Gigantic Pride, pale Terror, gloomy Care,   415
And mad Ambition shall attend her there:
There purple Vengeance bath'd in gore retires,
Her weapons blunted, and extinct her fires:
There hateful Envy her own snakes shall feel,
And Persecution mourn her broken wheel: 420
There Faction roar, Rebellion bite her chain,
And gasping Furies thirst for blood in vain.
    Here cease thy flight, nor with unhallow'd lays
Touch the fair fame of Albion's golden days.
The thoughts of Gods let GRANVILLE's verse recite,   425
And bring the scenes of op'ning fate to light.
My humble Muse, in unambitious strains,
Paints the green forests and the flow'ry plains,
Where Peace descending bids her olives spring,
And scatters blessings from her dove-like wing.   430
Ev'n I more sweetly pass my careless days,
Pleas'd in the silent shade with empty praise;
Enough for me, that to the list'ning swains
First in these fields I sung the sylvan strains.

    (1713)

ODE FOR MUSIC
ON ST. CECILIA'S DAY

Probably about ten years before his death in 1744, Pope observed to his friend Joseph Spence, "Many people would like my 'Ode on Music' better, if Dryden had not written on that subject. It was at the request of Mr. Steele that I wrote mine; and not with any thought of rivalling that great man, whose memory I do and always have reverenced." Certainly comparisons are not always valuable; yet the obvious one begs attention here, both because Pope's disavowal of rivalry pricks the curiosity, and because like Dryden's "Song for St. Cecilia's Day" and "Alexander's Feast," Pope's "Ode for Music" relishes onomatopoeia; in fact, both poets accentuate the nature of the occasion for which the odes were composed by echoing sense with sound. (See the headnote to Dryden's "Song for St. Cecilia's Day.")

TEXT. *The Works of Alexander Pope, Esq.*, ed. William Warburton (9 vols., London, 1751).

Ode for Music
on St. Cecilia's Day

I

DESCEND, ye Nine! descend and sing;
The breathing instruments inspire,
Wake into voice each silent string,
And sweep the sounding lyre!
   In a sadly-pleasing strain   5
   Let the warbling lute complain:
      Let the loud trumpet sound,
      'Till the roofs all around
      The shrill echos rebound:

While in more lengthen'd notes and slow,   10
The deep, majestic, solemn organs blow.
    Hark! the number soft and clear,
    Gently steal upon the ear;
    Now louder, and yet louder rise,
    And fill with spreading sounds the skies;   15
Exulting in triumph now swell the bold notes,
In broken air, trembling, the wild music floats;
    'Till, by degrees, remote and small,
      The strains decay,
      And melt away,   20
    In a dying, dying fall.

II

By Music, minds an equal temper know,
    Nor swell too high, nor sink too low.
If in the breast tumultuous joys arise,
Music her soft, assuasive voice applies;   25
    Or when the soul is press'd with cares,
    Exalts her in enlivening airs.
Warriors she fires with animated sounds;
Pours balm into the bleeding lover's wounds:
    Melancholy lifts her head;   30
    Morpheus rouzes from his bed;
    Sloth unfolds her arms and wakes;
    List'ning Envy drops her snakes;
Intestine war no more our Passions wage,
And giddy Factions hear away their rage.   35

III

But when our Country's cause provokes to Arms,
How martial music ev'ry bosom warms!
So when the first bold vessel dar'd the seas,
High on the stern the Thracian rais'd his strain,
    While Argo saw her kindred trees   40
    Descend from Pelion to the main.

21. *Dying fall:* Dying cadence; i.e., a cadence that falls away. See *Twelfth Night*, I, i, 1–4, for an earlier use of this musical term. T. S. Eliot also makes use of it in "The Lovesong of J. Alfred Prufrock," l. 52.

39. *The Thracian:* Orpheus, the legendary poet who could tame wild beasts with his sweet music, was one of the Argonauts, the group of heroes accompanying Jason on his voyage in search of the golden fleece. He was also husband of Eurydice, who died prematurely.

With his music, Orpheus induced Persephone to free Eurydice from Hades. The goddess agreed, but required Orpheus not to look back as his wife followed him out of Hades. He failed to keep the bargain and so lost her to the underworld. See ll. 49–116.

40. *Argo:* The Argonauts' ship—the first ship, or the first war-galley ever built.

41. *Pelion:* A wooded mountain near the coast of Thessaly, the Argonauts' point of departure.

Transported demi-gods stood round,
And men grew heroes at the sound,
    Enflam'd with glory's charms:
Each chief his sev'nfold shield display'd,   45
And half unsheath'd the shining blade;
And seas, and rocks, and skies rebound
To arms, to arms, to arms!

IV

But when thro' all th' infernal bounds,
Which flaming Phlegeton surrounds,   50
        Love, strong as Death, the Poet led
        To the pale nations of the dead,
What sounds were heard,
What scenes appear'd,
    O'er all the dreary coasts!   55
        Dreadful gleams,
        Dismal screams,
        Fires that glow,
        Shrieks of woe,
        Sullen moans,   60
        Hollow groans,
        And cries of tortur'd ghosts!
But hark! he strikes the golden lyre;
And see! the tortur'd ghosts respire,
        See, shady forms advance!   65
    Thy stone, O Sysiphus, stands still;
    Ixion rests upon his wheel,
        And the pale spectres dance!
The Furies sink upon their iron beds,
And snakes uncurl'd hang list'ning round their heads.   70

V

    By the streams that ever flow,
    By the fragrant winds that blow
        O'er th' Elysian flow'rs;
    By those happy souls who dwell
    In yellow meands of Asphodel,   75
        Or Amaranthine bow'rs;
    By the hero's armed shades,
    Glitt'ring thro' the gloomy glades;
    By the youths that dy'd for love,

---

50. *Phlegeton:* Pyriphlegethon (the fiery), one of the rivers of Hades.
66, 67. *Sysiphus* and *Ixion:* Both suffered unending punishments in Hades.
Sisyphus (the usual spelling) was condemned to roll a large stone uphill; Ixion was turned perpetually on a wheel.

Wand'ring in the myrtle grove,   80
Restore, restore Eurydice to life:
Oh take the husband, or return the wife!

He sung, and hell consented
    To hear the Poet's prayer:
Stern Proserpine relented,   85
    And gave him back the fair.
    Thus song could prevail
    O'er death and o'er hell,
A conquest how hard and how glorious?
    Tho' fate had fast bound her   90
    With Styx nine times round her,
Yet music and love were victorious.

VI

But soon, too soon, the lover turns his eyes:
Again she falls, again she dies, she dies!
How wilt thou now the fatal sisters move?   95
No crime was thine, if 'tis no crime to love.
    Now under hanging mountains,
    Beside the falls of fountains,
    Or where Hebrus wanders,
    Rolling in Mæanders,   100
        All alone,
        Unheard, unknown,
        He makes his moan;
        And calls her ghost,
    For ever, ever, ever lost!   105
    Now with Furies surrounded,
    Despairing, confounded,
    He trembles, he glows,
    Amidst Rhodope's snows:
See, wild as the winds, o'er the desart he flies; 110
Hark! Hæmus resounds with the Bacchanals cries—
        Ah see, he dies!
Yet ev'n in death Eurydice he sung,
Eurydice still trembled on his tongue,

91. *Styx:* The chief river of Hades.
95. *Fatal sisters:* The Greek Moirai—Clotho, Lachesis, and Atropos—who decided the course of a person's life.
99. *Hebrus:* River in Thrace, birthplace of Orpheus. After Orpheus was torn to pieces by Thracian maenads for interfering with their worship—he is thought to have hated all women after he lost Eurydice—his head, still singing, floated down the Hebrus to the sea and thence to Lesbos, where it was buried. See ll. 110–116.
100. *Mæander:* A river in Phrygia, known for its windings.
109. *Rhodope:* A mountain range in Thrace.
111. *Hæmus:* Ancient name for the Balkan Mountains.

Eurydice the woods,   115
Eurydice the floods,
Eurydice the rocks, and hollow mountains rung.

VII

Music the fiercest grief can charm,
And fate's severest rage disarm:
Music can soften pain to ease,   120
And make despair and madness please:
Our joys below it can improve,
And antedate the bliss above.
This the divine Cecilia found,
And to her Maker's praise confin'd the sound.   125
When the full organ joins the tuneful quire,
   Th' immortal pow'rs incline their ear;
Borne on the swelling notes our souls aspire,
While solemn airs improve the sacred fire;
   And Angels lean from heav'n to hear.   130
Of Orpheus now no more let Poets tell,
To bright Cecilia greater power is giv'n;
   His numbers rais'd a shade from hell,
   Hers lift the soul to heav'n.

(1713)

Headnote to
THE RAPE OF THE LOCK

At the suggestion of John Caryll, a kind of friendly elder statesman who moved easily among the members of England's prominent Catholic community, Pope wrote *The Rape of the Lock* in an effort to reconcile two of its families who had become estranged—the Petres and the Fermors. They were at odds because Robert, Seventh Lord Petre, had snipped off a lock of Arabella Fermor's hair. The poem did little to overcome the difficulty, however, even though Arabella, probably very flattered to have such attention, at first seems to have received the tribute well. Later on, she and certain members of her family objected to it, possibly for several reasons. It involves Arabella in more than a few verbal indecencies (of a sort, it must be said, quite usual in Pope's day), for example, the one in the last two lines of Canto IV; Sir Plume, recognized by the group as Arabella's uncle Sir George Brown, is made to sputter nonsense; and finally, the poem could not have been much fun to the Fermors, because less than two months before it was first published in May, 1712, Lord Petre married Catherine Warmsley, a woman both younger and wealthier than the victim of his rude barbering. Whether or not Arabella had entertained the hope of marrying Robert, the poem, by then, could only stress what at best was an irrelevant association and at worst a painful one. There could be no happy ending for Belinda (Arabella) and the Baron (Robert). In fact, Miss Fermor married a certain Francis Perkins, in 1714 or 1715; and by that time Robert, Lord Petre, had died of smallpox, in March, 1713.

When it first appeared in 1712, *The Rape of the Lock* comprised only two cantos. Fortunately, Pope decided to enlarge the work, most notably by adding the machinery of the sylphs and the game of ombre. Before proceeding, he asked Addison's opinion in the matter, and he was advised not to attempt the amplification. It seems likely that Addison, who had termed the poem in its original form *merum sal*— the perfection of wit—could not imagine it improved. Pope went ahead despite this lack of the approval he had sought, and according to Dr. Johnson (in his life of Pope) produced ". . . the most exquisite example of ludicrous poetry." Modern critics universally agree with Johnson that the greatest mock epic strokes occur in the additions to the two-canto version. (See Geoffrey Tillotson's introduction to *The Rape of the Lock* in the Twickenham edition.)

Epic poetry (along with tragedy) is thought of traditionally as the most elevated and serious of all the forms of literature. Its structure is characterized by long narrative, unified by a single large action, and dominated by a hero who is at once representative of his people and yet larger than life. Generally the scope of epic action is greater than that of classical tragedy, first because it takes up a considerable span of time and typically ranges over a wide geography, whose dimensions are indicated by the travels of the hero upon land and sea (including a journey to the underworld), by the swift and unhampered movement of the gods across vast reaches of the heavens and the earth, and by the poem's sweeping shifts in setting. The action is also enlarged by the national or cultural importance of the hero's undertaking; one understands that if he fails to accomplish his purpose, the world he represents will perish. Though the hero may be renowned for his nobility, his perseverance, or his sagacity, he is unvariably put to the final test in battle; in short, his honor is ultimately measured in martial terms, though never limited to such measurement. In the course of its action, epic fulfills certain other formal requirements. According to a standard neoclassical view, it teaches by presenting the behavior of noble characters in adversity, and it pleases by engendering a sense of wonder, chiefly through its use of the machinery of the gods. Moreover, in formulaic passages, almost ritual in manner and tone, the poet proposes his subject, invokes the aid of the heavens, comments on the action, offers as history certain traditions about his country and countrymen, sends vital information to his hero by means of supernatural characters, sometimes in a dream, arms his warrior characters (occasionally with special armor and weapons), permits them to boast of their prowess, and then sends them into battle, which he often describes with epic simile. As they triumph and live or fail and die, they are elevated to the realm of permanent things. At one level, at least, epic may be thought of as the sanctified history of one's fathers.

When Pope set about writing *The Rape of the Lock*, the comic epic tradition already had a venerable history. In fact, Aristotle refers to a work presumably by Homer, the *Margites*, which he says bears the same relation to comedy as serious epic does to tragedy. The *Iliad*, the *Odyssey*, and the *Aeneid* themselves contain humorous episodes. Specifically mock heroic poetry also had a long postclassical history. In his own day Pope had available to him among the many models of mock epic poetry the nearly contemporary *Le Lutrin* (1674) by Nicholas Boileau and *The Dispensary* (1699) by Samuel Garth, both of which he consulted as he worked. His aim, like theirs, was to employ the techniques of epic as he treated a subject that was trivial and hence inappropriate to the form. With such an emphasis, the result would be less a satire on epic literature than on the actions of his characters, though doubtless the heroically treated military exploits of a vengeful young woman armed with a snuff box, blazing glances, and a sharp tongue tend to reduce the grandeur of epic battle, even while they show her to be ludicrous. The satire cuts both ways.

Still, mere reduction of epic quantities through distortion—a perpetually frightened god, or a hero at once old, flatfooted, and fat—would leave no room for serious treatment of a subject, whereas Pope's emphasis does so. One understands that his treatment of Belinda at war makes fun of the epic warrior, but such a fact cannot displace the stronger judgment that her extravagant anger is intense out of all proportion to the occasion. Under such treatment, she and not epic is the principal object of satire. Pope goes far beyond maintaining this simple distinction, however. Indeed, he offers such an intricate treatment of his subject that some critics, restless with enjoying the poem's hundreds of incredibly deft turns, have vainly searched for an easily stated meaning.

In contrast to the problems and characters of epic, those in *The Rape of the Lock* are of course made to seem trivial. The poem above all presents a superficial world of rustling textures, bright surfaces, and aimless gestures; it is quite devoid of weight, or profundity, or real action. According to epic tradition, it is this world of surfaces that will perish or survive, depending on the abilities of the hero who represents it. That is, Belinda will save this world, or cause it to be lost. Clothes and cosmetics rather than bodies, objects rather than meanings, verbal sallies rather than conversation, games rather than deeds, flirtation rather than seduction or love are its chief features. These are epitomized by Belinda's supreme unconcern with other-than-surface matters. She is unfixed by a conscious purpose, and in fact she seems not only unengaged but incapable of any profound interests. Yet it would be naïve to conclude that Pope censures superficiality. On the contrary, his virgin-dominated universe of brocade and porcelain is in many ways very attractive. This appeal, generally acknowledged by generations of readers, has led some critics to conclude that Pope champions certain of the ways of life one finds in the poem as necessary to the control of relations between the sexes and hence to the stability of the family and society. To prove the point, they call particular attention to Clarissa's speech to that effect, Canto V, 10–34, a section added to the work in 1717, with the poet's explanation that he wished ". . . to open more clearly the Moral of the poem. . . ." This addition can better be taken as a sign that it is hard to find a simple moral in the rest of the poem than as a revelation of the poem's "meaning." To invoke the passage in order to explain *The Rape of the Lock* is to criticize too simply.

With the exception of Clarissa's speech, the superficiality of the world of the work is stressed with a delicate but remorseless consistency, and it is in this feature of the poem that one finds clues to its essential quality. On the one hand it presents a diminutive world—safe, pretty, independent of any reality outside itself, completely absorbed by its own petty concerns, capable of no greater destruction than can be accomplished by a tempest in a teapot. On the other, the contrast between this and the real world is stressed by so many arresting incongruities (often in the form of zeugma), that the real world is always in view, at least potentially. This balance is preserved throughout the poem (except for Clarissa's literal-minded speech, which upsets the tension); it kindles joy over the perfect object-filled little universe quite insulated from workaday affairs and arouses the expectation (perhaps only a self-righteous longing) that it will be shattered because it violates all notions of reality. But this second view is shown to be in error, for even when a crime of violence is committed in the diminutive world it turns out to be not a rape but a rape of a lock. Superficiality maintains itself in the very midst of an emotional danger that one might expect to shatter its surface, and the poem's essential ambivalence is intensified, not relieved. Appropriately enough, Belinda becomes the emblem of this increased tension as she responds to the outrage committed upon her, though at first glance she seems only to stress her customary preference for the surface of things:

> Oh hadst thou, Cruel! been content to seize
> Hairs less in sight, or any Hairs but these.

The most obvious meaning of her cry is that she would have saved her lock at any cost. But the terms that express this deep conviction lead one precisely away from the world Belinda represents to its opposite— to things of flesh and blood. To be sure her plea is ludicrous, but it is no less serious for that. Of the poem itself one might observe the same conclusion—that it is ". . . a most exquisite example of ludicrous poetry. . ." and yet a serious work.

TEXT. *The Works of Alexander Pope, Esq.*, ed. William Warburton (9 vols., London, 1751).

The Rape of the Lock

An Heroi–Comical Poem

WRITTEN IN THE YEAR MDCCXII

To Mrs. Arabella Fermor[1]

MADAM,

IT will be in vain to deny that I have some regard for this piece, since I dedicate it to You. Yet you may bear me witness, it was intended only to divert a few young Ladies, who have good sense and good humour enough to laugh not only at their sex's little unguarded follies, but at their own. But as it was communicated with the air of a Secret, it soon found its way into the world. An imperfect copy having been offer'd to a Bookseller, you had the good-nature for my sake to consent to the publication of one more correct: This I was forc'd to, before I had executed half my design, for the Machinery was entirely wanting to compleat it.

The Machinery, Madam, is a term invented by the Critics, to signify that 10 part which the Deities, Angels, or Dæmons are made to act in a Poem: For the ancient Poets are in one respect like many modern Ladies: let an action be never so trivial in itself, they always make it appear of the utmost importance. These Machines I determin'd to raise on a very new and odd foundation, the Rosicrucian doctrine of Spirits.

I know how disagreeable it is to make use of hard words before a Lady; but 'tis so much the concern of a Poet to have his works understood, and particularly by your Sex, that you must give me leave to explain two or three difficult terms.

The Rosicrucians[2] are a people I must bring you acquainted with. The best 20 account I know of them is in a French book call'd *Le Comte de Gabalis*, which both in its title and size is so like a Novel, that many of the Fair Sex have read it for one by mistake. According to these Gentlemen, the four Elements are inhabited by Spirits, which they call Sylphs, Gnomes, Nymphs, and Salamanders. The Gnomes or Dæmons of Earth delight in mischief; but the Sylphs, whose habitation is in the Air, are the best-condition'd creatures imaginable. For they say, any mortals may enjoy the most intimate familiarities with these gentle Spirits, upon a condition very easy to all true Adepts, an inviolate preservation of Chastity.

As to the following Cantos, all the passages of them are as fabulous, as the 30

---

[1] *Mrs. Arabella Fermor:* Mrs., the form of *mistress* used as a title, was applied in the eighteenth century to both married and unmarried women.

[2] *The Rosicrucians:* Members of an esoteric society whose claim that it has existed since the days of ancient Egypt seems doubtful. The secret learning of the order deals largely with occult symbols— chiefly the rosy cross, the swastika, and the pyramid—employed, probably, by theological reformers of the seventeenth century to arouse interest in their work.

Vision at the beginning, or the Transformation at the end (except the loss of your Hair, which I always mention with reverence). The Human persons are as fictitious as the Airy ones; and the character of Belinda, as it is now manag'd, resembles you in nothing but in Beauty.

If this Poem had as many Graces as there are in your Person, or in your Mind, yet I could never hope it should pass thro' the world half so Uncensur'd as You have done. But let its fortune be what it will, mine is happy enough, to have given me this occasion of assuring you that I am, with the truest esteem,

MADAM,

Your most obedient, Humble Servant,

A. POPE.

Nolueram, Belinda, tuos violare capillos;
Sed juvat, hoc precibus me tribuisse tuis.
—MART.[3]

Canto I

WHAT dire offence from am'rous causes springs,
What mighty contests rise from trivial things,
I sing—This verse to CARYL, Muse! is due:
This, ev'n Belinda may vouchsafe to view:
Slight is the subject, but not so the praise,   5
If She inspire, and He approve my lays.
  Say what strange motive, Goddess! could compel
A well-bred Lord t'assault a gentle Belle?
Oh say what stranger cause, yet unexplor'd,
Could make a gentle Belle reject a Lord?   10
In tasks so bold, can little men engage,
And in soft bosoms dwells such mighty Rage?
  Sol thro' white curtains shot a tim'rous ray,
And ope'd those eyes that must eclipse the day:
Now lap-dogs give themselves the rousing shake,   15
And sleepless lovers, just at twelve, awake:
Thrice rung the bell, the slipper knock'd the ground,
And the press'd watch return'd a silver sound.
Belinda still her downy pillow prest,
Her guardian SYLPH prolong'd the balmy rest: 20

---

[3] *Nolueram, Belinda . . . :* The quotation is from Bk. XII, epigram 84 of Martial: "I was loth, Belinda, to violate your locks, but I am glad to have granted that much to your prayer."
  17. *The slipper knock'd . . . :* Belinda summons Betty, her maid, by this means.
  18. *Th peress'd watch . . . :* Repeating-watches, when pressed, sounded a chime for each hour, then two, four, or six chimes for the nearest quarter hour.
  20. *Sylph:* Pope explains the origins and operations of his machinery—Salamanders, Nymphs, Gnomes, and Sylphs—in ll. 57–114, below.

'Twas He had summon'd to her silent bed
The morning-dream that hover'd o'er her head.
A Youth more glitt'ring than a Birth-night Beau
(That ev'n in slumber caus'd her cheek to glow)
Seem'd to her ear his winning lips to lay,   25
And thus in whispers said, or seem'd to say.
    Fairest of mortals, thou distinguish'd care
Of thousand bright Inhabitants of Air!
If e'er one Vision touch thy infant thought,
Of all the Nurse and all the Priest have taught;   30
Of airy Elves by moonlight shadows seen,
The silver token, and the circled green,
Or virgins visited by Angel-pow'rs,
With golden crowns and wreaths of heav'nly flow'rs,
Hear and believe! thy own importance know,   35
Nor bound thy narrow views to things below.
Some secret truths, from learned pride conceal'd,
To Maids alone and Children are reveal'd:
What tho' no credit doubting Wits may give?
The Fair and Innocent shall still believe.   40
Know then, unnumber'd Spirits round thee fly,
The light Militia of the lower sky:
These, tho' unseen, are ever on the wing,
Hang o'er the Box, and hover round the Ring.
Think what an equipage thou hast in Air,   45
And view with scorn two Pages and a Chair,
As now your own, our beings were of old,
And once inclos'd in Woman's beauteous mould;
Thence, by a soft transition, we repair
From earthly Vehicles to these of air.   50
Think not, when Woman's transient breath is fled,
That all her vanities at once are dead;
Succeeding vanities she still regards,
And tho' she plays no more, o'erlooks the cards.
Her joy in gilded Chariots, when alive,   55
And love of Ombre, after death survive.
For when the Fair in all their pride expire,
To their first Elements their Souls retire:

32. *Silver token . . . circled green:* Fairies
were believed to skim the cream from
milk left outdoors at night, leaving a
silver token (money) as payment; rings
in the grass, probably the result of some
kind of underground plant life ex-
panding from a common center, were
held to be the work of fairies dancing
in the round.
44. *The Box . . . the Ring:* The box
here referred to is a section of a theater.
The Ring was a circular course in Hyde

Park, around which fashionable carriages
drove to see and to be seen. It was also
known as Hyde-Park Circus. See IV, l.
117.
46. *A Chair:* An enclosed chair—a
sedan chair—made to seat one person and
carried through the city by two bearers.
56. *Ombre:* A card game, which serves
as the basis for mock epic battle between
Belinda and the two knights she encounters, Canto III. See III, n. l. 27.

The Sprites of fiery Termagants in Flame
Mount up, and take a Salamander's name.   60
Soft yielding minds to Water glide away,
And sip, with Nymphs, their elemental Tea.
The graver Prude sinks downward to a Gnome,
In search of mischief still on Earth to roam.
The light Coquettes in Sylphs aloft repair,   65
And sport and flutter in the fields of Air.
   Know farther yet; whoever fair and chaste
Rejects mankind, is by some Sylph embrac'd:
For Spirits, freed from mortal laws, with ease
Assume what sexes and what shapes they please.   70
What guards the purity of melting Maids,
In courtly balls, and midnight masquerades,
Safe from the treach'rous friend, the daring spark,
The glance by day, the whisper in the dark,
When kind occasion prompts their warm desires,   75
When music softens, and when dancing fires?
'Tis but their Sylph, the wise Celestials know,
Tho' Honour is the word with Men below.
   Some nymphs there are, too conscious of their face,
For life predestin'd to the Gnomes' embrace.   80
These swell their prospects and exalt their pride,
When offers are disdain'd, and love deny'd:
Then gay Ideas croud the vacant brain,
While Peers, and Dukes, and all their sweeping train,
And Garters, Stars, and Coronets appear,   85
And in soft sounds, Your Grace salutes their ear.
'Tis these that early taint the female soul,
Instruct the eyes of young Coquettes to roll,
Teach Infant-cheeks a bidden blush to know,
And little hearts to flutter at a Beau.   90
   Oft, when the world imagine women stray,
The Sylphs thro' mystic mazes guide their way,
Thro' all the giddy circle they pursue,
And old impertinence expel by new.
What tender maid but must a victim fall   95
To one man's treat, but for another's ball?
When Florio speaks what virgin could withstand,
If gentle Damon did not squeeze her hand?
With varying vanities, from ev'ry part,
They shift the moving Toyshop of their heart;   100
Where wigs with wigs, with sword-knots sword-knots strive,
Beaux banish beaux, and coaches coaches drive.
This erring mortals Levity may call,

85. *Garters, Stars, and Coronets:* All
badges of high rank.

Oh blind to truth! the Sylphs contrive it all.
　Of these am I, who thy protection claim,　　　　　　105
A watchful sprite, and Ariel is my name.
Late, as I rang'd the crystal wilds of air,
In the clear Mirror of thy ruling Star
I saw, alas! some dread event impend,
Ere to the main this morning sun descend,　　　　　　110
But heav'n reveals not what, or how, or where:
Warn'd by the Sylph, oh pious maid, beware!
This to disclose is all thy guardian can:
Beware of all, but most beware of Man!
　He said; when Shock, who thought she slept too long,　　115
Leap'd up, and wak'd his mistress with his tongue.
'Twas then Belinda, if report say true,
Thy eyes first open'd on a Billet-doux;
Wounds, Charms, and Ardors, were no sooner read,
But all the Vision vanish'd from thy head.　　　　　　120
　And now, unveil'd, the Toilet stands display'd,
Each silver Vase in mystic order laid.
First, rob'd in white, the Nymph intent adores,
With head uncover'd, the Cosmetic pow'rs.
A heav'nly Image in the glass appears,　　　　　　125
To that she bends, to that her eyes she rears;
Th' inferior Priestess, at her altar's side,
Trembling, begins the sacred rites of Pride.
Unnumber'd treasures ope at once, and here
The various off'rings of the world appear;　　　　　　130
From each she nicely culls with curious toil,
And decks the Goddess with the glitt'ring spoil.
This casket India's glowing gems unlocks,
And all Arabia breathes from yonder box.
The Tortoise here and Elephant unite,　　　　　　135
Transform'd to combs, the speckled, and the white.
Here files of pins extend their shining rows,
Puffs, Powders, Patches, Bibles, Billet-doux.
Now awful Beauty puts on all its arms;
The fair each moment rises in her charms,　　　　　　140
Repairs her smiles, awakens ev'ry grace,
And calls forth all the wonders of her face;
Sees by degrees a purer blush arise,
And keener lightnings quicken in her eyes.
The busy Sylphs surround their darling care,　　　　　　145
These set the head, and those divide the hair,
Some fold the sleeve, whilst others plait the gown;
And Betty's prais'd for labours not her own.

127. *Th' inferior Priestess:* Betty,
Belinda's Maid. See l. 148.

Canto II

NOT with more glories, in th' etherial plain,
The Sun first rises o'er the purpled main,
Than, issuing forth, the rival of his beams
Launch'd on the bosom of the silver Thames.
Fair Nymphs, and well-drest Youths around her shone,   5
But ev'ry eye was fix'd on her alone.
On her white breast a sparkling Cross she wore,
Which Jews might kiss, and Infidels adore.
Her lively looks a sprightly mind disclose,
Quick as her eyes, and as unfix'd as those: 10
Favours to none, to all she smiles extends;
Oft she rejects, but never once offends.
Bright as the sun, her eyes the gazers strike,
And, like the sun, they shine on all alike.
Yet graceful ease, and sweetness void of pride   15
Might hide her faults, if Belles had faults to hide:
If to her share some female errors fall,
Look on her face, and you'll forget 'em all.
    This Nymph, to the destruction of mankind,
Nourish'd two Locks, which graceful hung behind   20
In equal curls, and well conspir'd to deck
With shining ringlets the smooth iv'ry neck.
Love in these labyrinths his slaves detains,
And mighty hearts are held in slender chains.
With hairy springes we the birds betray,   25
Slight lines of hair surprize the finny prey,
Fair tresses man's imperial race insnare,
And beauty draws us with a single hair.
    Th' advent'rous Baron the bright locks admir'd;
He saw, he wish'd, and to the prize aspir'd.   30
Resolv'd to win, he meditates the way,
By force to ravish, or by fraud betray;
For when success a Lover's toil attends,
Few ask, if fraud or force attain'd his ends.
    For this, ere Phœbus rose, he had implor'd   35
Propitious heav'n, and ev'ry pow'r ador'd,
But chiefly Love—to Love an Altar built,
Of twelve vast French Romances, neatly gilt.
There lay three garters, half a pair of gloves;
And all the trophies of his former loves;   40
With tender Billet-doux he lights the pyre,
And breathes three am'rous sighs to raise the fire.
Then prostrate falls, and begs with ardent eyes
Soon to obtain, and long possess the prize:
The pow'rs gave ear, and granted half his pray'r,   45

The rest, the winds dispers'd in empty air.
  But now secure the painted vessel glides,
The sun-beams trembling on the floating tides:
While melting music steals upon the sky,
And soften'd sounds along the waters die;   50
Smooth flow the waves, the Zephyrs gently play,
Belinda smil'd, and all the world was gay.
All but the Sylph—with careful thoughts opprest,
Th' impending woe sat heavy on his breast.
He summons strait his Denizens of air;   55
The lucid squadrons round the sails repair;
Soft o'er the shrouds aërial whispers breathe,
That seem'd but Zephyrs to the train beneath.
Some to the sun their insect-wings unfold,
Waft on the breeze, or sink in clouds of gold;   60
Transparent forms, too fine for mortal sight,
Their fluid bodies half dissolv'd in light.
Loose to the wind their airy garments flew,
Thin glitt'ring textures of the filmy dew,
Dipt in the richest tincture of the skies,   65
Where light disports in ever-mingling dyes,
While ev'ry beam new transient colours flings,
Colours that change whene'er they wave their wings.
Amid the circle, on the gilded mast,
Superior by the head, was Ariel plac'd;   70
His purple pinions op'ning to the sun,
He rais'd his azure wand, and thus begun.
  Ye Sylphs and Sylphids, to your chief give ear,
Fays, Fairies, Genii, Elves, and Dæmons hear!
Ye know the spheres and various tasks assign'd   75
By laws eternal to th' aërial kind.
Some in the fields of purest Æther play,
And bask and whiten in the blaze of day.
Some guide the course of wand'ring orbs on high,
Or roll the planets thro' the boundless sky.   80
Some less refin'd, beneath the moon's pale light
Pursue the stars that shoot athwart the night,
Or suck the mists in grosser air below,
Or dip their pinions in the painted bow,
Or brew fierce tempests on the wintry main,   85
Or o'er the glebe distil the kindly rain.
Others on earth o'er human race preside,
Watch all their ways, and all their actions guide:
Of these the chief the care of Nations own,
And guard with Arms divine the British Throne.   90
  Our humbler province is to tend the Fair,
Not a less pleasing, tho' less glorious care;

To save the powder from too rude a gale,
Nor let th' imprison'd essences exhale;
To draw fresh colours from the vernal flow'rs;   95
To steal from rainbows e'er they drop in show'rs
A brighter wash; to curl their waving hairs,
Assist their blushes, and inspire their airs;
Nay oft, in dreams, invention we bestow,
To change a Flounce, or add a Furbelow.   100
    This day, black Omens threat the brightest Fair
That e'er deserv'd a watchful spirit's care;
Some dire disaster, or by force, or flight;
But what, or where, the fates have wrapt in night.
Whether the nymph shall break Diana's law,   105
Or some frail China jar receive a flaw;
Or stain her honour, or her new brocade;
Forget her pray'rs, or miss a masquerade;
Or lose her heart, or necklace, at a ball;
Or whether Heav'n has doom'd that Shock must fall.   110
Haste then, ye spirits! to your charge repair:
The flutt'ring fan be Zephyretta's care;
The drops to thee, Brillante, we consign;
And, Momentilla, let the watch be thine;
Do thou, Crispissa, tend her fav'rite Lock;   115
Ariel himself shall be the guard of Shock.
    To fifty chosen Sylphs, of special note,
We trust th' important charge, the Petticoat:
Oft have we known that seven-fold fence to fail,
Tho' stiff with hoops, and arm'd with ribs of whale;   120
Form a strong line about the silver bound,
And guard the wide circumference around.
    Whatever spirit, careless of his charge,
His post neglects, or leaves the fair at large,
Shall feel sharp vengeance soon o'ertake his sins,   125
Be stop'd in vials, or transfix'd with pins;
Or plung'd in lakes of bitter washes lie,
Or wedg'd whole ages in a bodkin's eye:
Gums and Pomatums shall his flight restrain,
While clog'd he beats his silken wings in vain;   130
Or Alum styptics with contracting pow'r
Shrink his thin essence like a rivel'd flow'r;
Or, as Ixion fix'd, the wretch shall feel
The giddy motion of the whirling Mill,
In fumes of burning Chocolate shall glow,   135
And tremble at the sea that froths below!

105. *Diana's law:* The law of chastity.
128. *Bodkin's eye:* A bodkin is a type
of needle.
133. *Ixion:* For his many crimes,
including an attempt to win the love of
Zeus's wife, Ixion was bound on a wheel
that turned forever.

He spoke; the spirits from the sails descend;
Some, orb in orb, around the nymph extend;
Some thrid the mazy ringlets of her hair;
Some hang upon the pendants of her ear;   140
With beating hearts the dire event they wait,
Anxious, and trembling for the birth of Fate.

Canto III

CLOSE by those meads, for ever crown'd with flow'rs,
Where Thames with pride surveys his rising tow'rs,
There stands a structure of majestic frame,
Which from the neighb'ring Hampton takes its name.
Here Britain's statesmen oft the fall foredoom   5
Of foreign Tyrants, and of Nymphs at home;
Here thou, great ANNA! whom three realms obey,
Dost sometimes counsel take—and sometimes Tea.
  Hither the heroes and the nymphs resort,
To taste awhile the pleasures of a Court;   10
In various talk th' instructive hours they past,
Who gave the ball, or paid the visit last;
One speaks the glory of the British Queen,
And one describes a charming Indian screen;
A third interprets motions, looks, and eyes;   15
At ev'ry word a reputation dies.
Snuff, or the fan, supply each pause of chat,
With singing, laughing, ogling, *and all that.*
  Mean while, declining from the noon of day,
The sun obliquely shoots his burning ray;   20
The hungry Judges soon the sentence sign,
And wrethes hang that jury-men may dine;
The merchant from th' Exchange returns in peace,
And the long labours of the Toilet cease.
Belinda now, whom thirst of fame invites,   25
Burns to encounter two adven'trous Knights,
At Ombre singly to decide their doom;

4. *Hampton:* Hampton Court was little used by Queen Anne, who preferred Windsor or Kensington, though much used as the resort of wits.

7. *Anna! whom three realms obey:* The English crown persisted in the claim that it ruled France as well as Great Britain and Ireland.

27. *At Ombre:* Originally a Spanish card game, *Hombre,* in which three players participated. The deck was the standard one reduced by twelve—the 8's, 9's, and 10's—allowing for a hand of nine cards per player, with the remaining thirteen as the stock. The player who got the bid, the Ombre, named trumps, which always included the black aces. The Ace of Spades (always the highest card) was called *Spadille,* and the Ace of Clubs (always third highest), *Basto.* The second highest card, varying for different trumps, was called *Manille.* These were collectively referred to as *Matadors.* (For a full account of the game see Geoffrey Tillotson, Appendix C, *The Rape of the Lock and Other Poems,* The Twickenham Edition, II, London and New Haven, 1962.)

And swells her breast with conquests yet to come.
Strait the three bands prepare in arms to join.
Each band the number of the sacred nine.   30
Soon as she spreads her hand, th' aërial guard
Descend, and sit on each important card:
First Ariel perch'd upon a Matadore,
Then each, according to the rank they bore;
For Sylphs, yet mindful of their ancient race,   35
Are, as when women, wondrous fond of place.
   Behold, four Kings in majesty rever'd,
With hoary whiskers and a forky beard;
And four fair Queens whose hands sustain a flow'r,
Th' expressive emblem of their softer pow'r;   40
Four Knaves in garbs succinct, a trusty band,
Caps on their heads, and halberts in their hand;
And particolour'd troops, a shining train,
Draw forth to combat on the velvet plain.
   The skilful Nymph reviews her force with care: 45
Let Spades be trumps! she said, and trumps they were.
   Now move to war her sable Matadores,
In show like leaders of the swarthy Moors.
Spadillio first, unconquerable Lord!
Led off two captive trumps, and swept the board.   50
As many more Manillio forc'd to yield,
And march'd a victor from the verdant field.
Him Basto follow'd, but his fate more hard
Gain'd but one trump and one Plebeian card.
With his broad sabre next, a chief in years,   55
The hoary Majesty of Spades appears,
Puts forth one manly leg, to sight reveal'd,
The rest, his many-colour'd robe conceal'd.
The rebel Knave, who dares his prince engage,
Proves the just victim of his royal rage.   60
Ev'n mighty Pam, that Kings and Queens o'erthrew,
And mow'd down armies in the fights of Lu,
Sad chance of war! now destitute of aid,
Falls undistinguish'd by the victor Spade!
   Thus far both armies to Belinda yield;   65
Now to the Baron fate inclines the field.
His warlike Amazon her host invades,
Th' imperial consort of the crown of Spades.
The Club's black Tyrant first her victim dy'd,
Spite of his haughty mien, and barb'rous pride: 70
What boots the regal circle on his head,
His giant limbs, in state unweildy spread;

   61. *Pam:* Strongest card (Jack of Clubs)
in the game of Lu.

That long behind he trails his pompous robe,
And, of all monarchs, only grasps the globe?
    The Baron now his Diamonds pours apace;   75
Th' embroider'd King who shows but half his face,
And his refulgent Queen, with pow'rs combin'd
Of broken troops an easy conquest find.
Clubs, Diamonds, Hearts, in wild disorder seen,
With throngs promiscuous strow the level green.   80
Thus when dispers'd a routed army runs,
Of Asia's troops, and Afric's sable sons,
With like confusion different nations fly,
Of various habit, and of various dye;
The pierc'd battalions dis-united fall,   85
In heaps on heaps; one fate o'erwhelms them all.
    The Knave of Diamonds tries his wily arts,
And wins (oh shameful chance!) the Queen of.Hearts.
At this, the blood the virgin's cheek forsook,
A livid paleness spreads o'er all her look;   90
She sees, and trembles at th' approaching ill,
Just in the jaws of ruin, and Codille.
And now (as oft in some distemper'd State)
On one nice Trick depends the gen'ral fate.
An Ace of Hearts steps forth: The King unseen   95
Lurk'd in her hand, and mourn'd his captive Queen:
He springs to vengeance with an eager pace,
And falls like thunder on the prostrate Ace.
The nymph exulting fills with shouts the sky;
The walls, the woods, and long canals reply.   100
    Oh thoughtless mortals! ever blind to fate,
Too soon dejected, and too soon elate.
Sudden, these honours shall be snatch'd away,
And curs'd for ever this victorious day.
    For lo! the board with cups and spoons is crown'd,   105
The berries crackle, and the mill turns round;
On shining Altars of Japan they raise
The silver lamp; the fiery spirits blaze:
From silver spouts the grateful liquors glide,
While China's earth receives the smoaking tide: 110
At once they gratify their scent and taste,
And frequent cups prolong the rich repaste.
Strait hover round the Fair her airy band;
Some, as she sipp'd, the fuming liquor fann'd,
Some o'er her lap their careful plumes display'd,   115
Trembling, and conscious of the rich brocade.

92. *Codille:* A term signifying the loss of the game by the Ombre, in this case Belinda.

106. *Berries crackle:* The reference is to coffee beans being roasted, then ground.

107. *Shining Altars of Japan:* Lacquered tables.

Coffee (which makes the politician wise,
And see thro' all things with his half-shut eyes)
Sent up in vapours to the Baron's brain
New stratagems, the radiant Lock to gain.   120
Ah cease, rash youth! desist ere 'tis too late,
Fear the just Gods, and think of Scylla's Fate!
Chang'd to a bird, and sent to flit in air,
She dearly pays for Nisus' injur'd hair!
But when to mischief mortals bend their will,   125
How soon they find fit instruments of ill!
Just then, Clarissa drew with tempting grace
A two-edg'd weapon from her shining case:
So Ladies in Romance assist their Knight,
Present the spear, and arm him for the fight.   130
He ta¹·es the gift with rev'rence, and extends
The little engine on his fingers' ends;
This just behind Belinda's neck he spread,
As o'er the fragrant steams she bends her head.
Swift to the Lock a thousand Sprites repair,   135
A thousand wings, by turns, blow back the hair;
And thrice they twitch'd the diamond in her ear;
Thrice she look'd back, and thrice the foe drew near.
Just in that instant, anxious Ariel sought
The close recesses of the Virgin's thought.   140
As on the nosegay in her breast reclin'd,
He watch'd th' Ideas rising in her mind,
Sudden he view'd, in spite of all her art,
An earthly Lover lurking at her heart.
Amaz'd, confus'd, he found his pow'r expir'd,   145
Resign'd to fate, and with a sigh retir'd.
The Peer now spreads the glitt'ring Forfex wide,
T' inclose the Lock; now joins it, to divide.
Ev'n then, before the fatal engine clos'd,
A wretched Sylph too fondly interpos'd;   150
Fate urg'd the sheers, and cut the Sylph in twain
(But airy substance soon unites again),
The meeting points the sacred hair dissever
From the fair head, for ever, and for ever!
Then flash'd the living lightning from her eyes,   155
And screams of horror rend th' affrighted skies.
Not louder shrieks to pitying heav'n are cast,
When husbands, or when lap-dogs breathe their last;
Or when rich China vessels, fall'n from high,
In glitt'ring dust, and painted fragments lie!   160

122. *Scylla's Fate:* Scylla was the daughter of Nisus, king of Megara, whose safety depended upon a purple lock of his hair, which his enemy, Minos of Crete, persuaded her to cut off. When she treacherously did so, her father's city was taken, and she was dragged behind the ship of Minos.

Let wreaths of triumph now my temples twine
(The Victor cry'd) the glorious Prize is mine !
While fish in streams, or birds delight in air,
Or in a coach and six the British Fair,
As long as Atalantis shall be read,   165
Or the small pillow grace a Lady's bed,
While visits shall be paid on solemn days,
When num'rous wax-lights in bright order blaze,
While nymphs take treats, or assignations give,
So long my honour, name, and praise shall live !   170
What Time would spare, from Steel receives its date,
And monuments, like men, submit to fate !
Steel could the labour of the Gods destroy,
And strike to dust th' imperial tow'rs of Troy;
Steel could the works of mortal pride confound,   175
And hew triumphal arches to the ground.
What wonder then, fair nymph ! thy hairs should feel,
The conqu'ring force of unresisted steel?

Canto **IV**

BUT anxious cares the pensive nymph oppress'd,
And secret passions labour'd in her breast.
Not youthful kings in battle seiz'd alive,
Not scornful virgins who their charms survive,
Not ardent lovers robb'd of all their bliss,   5
Not ancient ladies when refus'd a kiss,
Not tyrants fierce that unrepenting die,
Not Cynthia when her manteau's pinn'd awry,
E'er felt such rage, resentment, and despair,
As thou, sad Virgin ! for thy ravish'd Hair.   10
    For, that sad moment, when the Sylphs withdrew,
And Ariel weeping from Belinda flew,
Umbriel, a dusky, melancholy sprite,
As ever sully'd the fair face of light,
Down to the central earth, his proper scene,   15
Repair'd to search the gloomy Cave of Spleen.
    Swift on his sooty pinions flits the Gnome,
And in a vapour reach'd the dismal dome.
No chearful breeze this sullen region knows,
The dreaded East is all the wind that blows.   20
Here in a grotto, shelter'd close from air,
And screen'd in shades from day's detested glare,

---

165. *Atalantis:* A libelous book of gossip, which grew to four volumes, *Secret Memoirs and Manners of several Persons of Quality, of Both Sexes. From the New Atalantis, an Island in the Mediter-* ranean (1709–1710) by Mrs. Mary Manley.
    16. *Cave of Spleen:* The object of the mock epic descent to the underworld. Spleen was associated with temperament and irritability.

She sighs for ever on her pensive bed,
Pain at her side, and Megrim at her head.
   Two handmaids wait the throne: alike in place,   25
But diff'ring far in figure and in face.
Here stood Ill-nature like an ancient maid,
Her wrinkled form in black and white array'd;
With store of pray'rs, for mornings, nights, and noons,
Her hand is fill'd; her bosom with lampoons.   30
   There Affectation with a sickly mien,
Shows in her cheek the roses of eighteen,
Practis'd to lisp, and hang the head aside,
Faints into airs, and languishes with pride,
On the rich quilt sinks with becoming woe,   35
Wrapt in a gown, for sickness, and for show.
The fair-ones feel such maladies as these,
When each new night-dress gives a new disease.
   A constant Vapour o'er the palace flies;
Strange phantoms rising as the mists arise;   40
Dreadful, as hermits' dreams in haunted shades,
Or bright, as visions of expiring maids.
Now glaring fiends, and snakes on rolling spires,
Pale spectres, gaping tombs, and purple fires:
Now lakes of liquid gold, Elysian scenes,   45
And crystal domes, and Angels in machines.
   Unnumber'd throngs on ev'ry side are seen,
Of bodies chang'd to various forms by Spleen.
Here living Tea-pots stand, one arm held out,
One bent; the handle this, and that the spout: 50
A Pipkin there, like Homer's Tripod walks;
Here sighs a Jar, and there a Goose-pye talks;
Men prove with child, as pow'rful fancy works,
And maids, turn'd bottles, call aloud for corks.
   Safe past the Gnome thro' this fantastic band,   55
A branch of healing Spleenwort in his hand.
Then thus address'd the pow'r—Hail wayward Queen!
Who rule the sex to fifty from fifteen:
Parent of vapours and of female wit,
Who give th' hysteric, or poetic fit,   60
On various tempers act by various ways,
Make some take physic, others scribble plays;
Who cause the proud their visits to delay,
And send the godly in a pet to pray.
A nymph there is, that all thy pow'r disdains,   65
And thousands more in equal mirth maintains.
But oh! if e'er thy Gnome could spoil a grace,
Or raise a pimple on a beauteous face,

24. *Megrim:* Migraine.

Like Citron-waters matrons' cheeks inflame,
Or change complexions at a losing game;   70
If e'er with airy horns I planted heads,
Or rumpled petticoats, or tumbled beds,
Or caus'd suspicion when no soul was rude,
Or discompos'd the head-dress of a Prude,
Or e'er to costive lap-dog gave disease,   75
Which not the tears of brightest eyes could ease:
Hear me, and touch Belinda with chagrin;
That single act gives half the world the spleen.
    The Goddess with a discontented air
Seems to reject him, tho' she grants his pray'r.   80
A wond'rous Bag with both her hands she binds,
Like that where once Ulysses held the winds;
There she collects the force of female lungs,
Sighs, sobs, and passions, and the war of tongues.
A Vial next she fills with fainting fears,   85
Soft sorrows, melting griefs, and flowing tears.
The Gnome rejoicing bears her gifts away,
Spreads his black wings, and slowly mounts to day.
    Sunk in Thalestris' arms the nymph he found,
Her eyes dejected and her hair unbound.   90
Full o'er their heads the swelling bag he rent,
And all the Furies issu'd at the vent.
Belinda burns with more than mortal ire,
And fierce Thalestris fans the rising fire.
O wretched maid! she spread her hands, and cry'd   95
(While Hampton's echoes, wretched maid! reply'd),
Was it for this you took such constant care
The bodkin, comb, and essence to prepare?
For this your locks in paper durance bound,
For this with tort'ring irons wreath'd around?   100
For this with fillets strain'd your tender head,
And bravely bore the double loads of lead?
Gods! shall the ravisher display your hair,
While the Fops envy, and the Ladies stare!
Honour forbid! at whose unrival'd shrine   105
Ease, pleasure, virtue, all our sex resign.
Methinks already I your tears survey,
Already hear the horrid things they say,
Already see you a degraded toast,
And all your honour in a whisper lost!   110

69. *Citron-waters:* A kind of brandy distilled from citron rind.

82. *Ulysses held the winds:* In the *Odyssey*, Bk. X, Aeolus gives Odysseus (Ulysses) a leather bag filled with the wind adverse to his safe return to Ithaca.

89. *In Thalestris' arms:* Thalestris, Belinda's champion and goad, is Sir Plume's lady (ll. 121–122). Since he represents Arabella's uncle, Thalestris has been regarded as her aunt, or at least as someone very close to her.

How shall I, then, your helpless fame defend?
'Twill then be infamy to seem your friend!
And shall this prize, th' inestimable prize,
Expos'd thro' crystal to the gazing eyes,
And heighten'd by the diamond's circling rays,   115
On that rapacious hand for ever blaze?
Sooner shall grass in Hyde-park Circus grow,
And wits take lodgings in the sound of Bow;
Sooner let earth, air, sea, to Chaos fall,
Men, monkeys, lap-dogs, parrots, perish all!   120
    She said; then raging to Sir Plume repairs
And bids her Beau demand the precious hairs
(Sir Plume of amber snuff-box justly vain,
And the nice conduct of a clouded cane):
With earnest eyes, and round unthinking face,   125
He first the snuff-box open'd, then the case,
And thus broke out—"My Lord, why, what the devil?
"Z—ds! damn the lock! 'fore Gad, you must be civil!
"Plague on't! 'tis past a jest—nay prithee, pox!
"Give her the hair"—he spoke, and rapp'd his box.   130
    It grieves me much (reply'd the Peer again)
Who speaks so well should ever speak in vain.
But by this Lock, this sacred Lock I swear
(Which never more shall join its parted hair;
Which never more its honours shall renew,   135
Clip'd from the lovely head where late it grew),
That while my nostrils draw the vital air,
This hand, which won it, shall for ever wear.
He spoke, and speaking, in proud triumph spread
The long-contended honours of her head.   140
    But Umbriel, hateful Gnome! forbears not so;
He breaks the Vial whence the sorrows flow.
Then see! the nymph in beauteous grief appears,
Her eyes half-languishing, half-drown'd in tears;
On her heav'd bosom hung her drooping head,   145
Which, with a sigh, she rais'd; and thus she said.
    For ever curs'd be this detested day,
Which snatch'd my best, my fav'rite curl away!
Happy! ah ten times happy had I been,
If Hampton-Court these eyes had never seen!   150
Yet am not I the first mistaken maid,
By love of Courts to num'rous ills betray'd.
Oh had I rather un-admir'd remain'd
In some lone isle, or distant Northern land;

117. *Hyde-park Circus:* See I, n. l. 44.
118. *Sound of Bow:* The sound of the
bells of St. Mary-le-Bow in Cheapside,
where no person of fashion would dream
of living.

Where the gilt Chariot never marks the way,   155
Where none learn Ombre, none e'er taste Bohea!
There kept my charms conceal'd from mortal eye,
Like roses, that in deserts bloom and die.
What mov'd my mind with youthful Lords to roam?
O had I stay'd, and said my pray'rs at home!   160
'Twas this, the morning omens seem'd to tell,
Thrice from my trembling hand the patch-box fell;
The tott'ring China shook without a wind,
Nay Poll sat mute, and Shock was most unkind!
A Sylph too warn'd me of the threats of fate,   165
In mystic visions, now believ'd too late!
See the poor remnants of these slighted hairs!
My hands shall rend what ev'n thy rapine spares:
These in two sable ringlets taught to break,
Once gave new beauties to the snowy neck;   170
The sister-lock now sits uncouth, alone,
And in its fellow's fate foresees its own;
Uncurl'd it hangs, the fatal sheers demands,
And tempts, once more, thy sacrilegious hands.
Oh hadst thou, cruel! been content to seize   175
Hairs less in sight, or any hairs but these!

Canto V

SHE said: the pitying audience melt in tears.
But Fate and Jove had stopp'd the Baron's ears.
In vain Thalestris with reproach assails,
For who can move when fair Belinda fails?
Not half so fix'd the Trojan could remain,   5
While Anna begg'd and Dido rag'd in vain.
Then grave Clarissa graceful wav'd her fan;
Silence ensu'd, and thus the nymph began.
    Say why are Beauties prais'd and honour'd most,
The wise man's passion, and the vain man's toast?   10
Why deck'd with all that land and sea afford,
Why Angels call'd, and Angel-like ador'd?
Why round our coaches croud the white-glov'd Beaux,
Why bows the side-box from its inmost rows?
How vain are all these glories, all our pains,   15
Unless good sense preserve what beauty gains:

156. *Bohea:* Originally the name of the finest black tea, now of the poorest.

6. *Anna begg'd and Dido rag'd:* Dido, Queen of Carthage, and Anna, her sister, figure in the first four books of the *Aeneid.* Dido, encouraged by Anna, gives in to her love for Aeneas, who leaves her to continue his attempt to found a city— Rome.

7. *Clarissa:* Pope says, "A new character introduced in the subsequent Editions, to open more clearly the Moral of the poem, in a parody of the speech of Sarpedon to Glaucus in Homer" [*Iliad,* XII].

That men may say, when we the front-box grace,
Behold the first in virtue as in face!
Oh! if to dance all night, and dress all day,
Charm'd the small-pox, or chas'd old-age away;   20
Who would not scorn what housewife's cares produce,
Or who would learn one earthly thing of use?
To patch, nay ogle, might become a Saint,
Nor could it sure be such a sin to paint.
But since, alas! frail beauty must decay,   25
Curl'd or uncurl'd, since Locks will turn to grey;
Since painted, or not painted, all shall fade,
And she who scorns a man, must die a maid;
What then remains but well our pow'r to use,
And keep good-humour still whate'er we lose?   30
And trust me, dear! good-humour can prevail,
When airs, and flights, and screams, and scolding fail.
Beauties in vain their pretty eyes may roll;
Charms strike the sight, but merit wins the soul.
    So spoke the Dame, but no applause ensu'd;   35
Belinda frown'd, Thalestris call'd her Prude.
To arms, to arms! the fierce Virago cries,
And swift as lightning to the combat flies.
All side in parties, and begin th' attack;
Fans clap, silks russle, and tough whalebones crack;   40
Heroes' and Heroines' shouts confus'dly rise,
And base, and treble voices strike the skies.
No common weapons in their hands are found,
Like Gods they fight, nor dread a mortal wound.
    So when bold Homer makes the Gods engage,   45
And heav'nly breasts with human passions rage;
'Gainst Pallas, Mars; Latona, Hermes arms;
And all Olympus rings with loud alarms:
Jove's thunder roars, heav'n trembles all around,
Blue Neptune storms, the bellowing deeps resound: 50
Earth shakes her nodding towr's, the ground gives way,
And the pale ghosts start at the flash of day!
    Triumphant Umbriel on a sconce's height
Clap'd his glad wings, and sate to view the fight:
Prop'd on their bodkin spears, the Sprites survey   55
The growing combat, or assist the fray.
    While thro' the press enrag'd Thalestris flies,
And scatters death around from both her eyes,
A Beau and Witling perish'd in the throng,
One dy'd in metaphor, and one in song.   60
    "O cruel nymph! a living death I bear,"

47. 'Gainst Pallas, Mars; Latona, Hermes
arms: In the Iliad, Bks. V, XX, and elsewhere, Ares (Mars), a pro-Trojan god,
opposes Pallas Athene, a pro-Greek goddess; Leto (Latona), pro-Trojan, opposes
Hermes.

Cry'd Dapperwit, and sunk beside his chair.
A mournful glance Sir Fopling upwards cast,
"Those eyes are made so killing"—was his last.
Thus on Mæander's flow'ry margin lies   65
Th' expiring Swan, and as he sings he dies.
   When bold Sir Plume had drawn Clarissa down,
Chloe stepp'd in, and kill'd him with a frown;
She smil'd to see the doughty hero slain,
But, at her smile, the Beau reviv'd again.   70
   Now Jove suspends his golden scales in air,
Weighs the Men's wits against the Lady's hair;
The doubtful beam long nods from side to side;
At length the wits mount up, the hairs subside.
   See fierce Belinda on the Baron flies,   75
With more than usual lightning in her eyes:
Nor fear'd the Chief th' unequal fight to try,
Who sought no more than on his foe to die.
But this bold Lord with manly strength endu'd,
She with one finger and a thumb subdu'd: 80
Just where the breath of life his nostrils drew,
A charge of Snuff the wily virgin threw;
The Gnomes direct, to ev'ry atome just,
The pungent grains of titillating dust.
Sudden, with starting tears each eye o'erflows,   85
And the high dome re-echoes to his nose.
   Now meet thy fate, incens'd Belinda cry'd,
And drew a deadly bodkin from her side
(The same, his ancient personage to deck,
Her great great grandsire wore about his neck,   90
In three seal-rings; which after, melted down,
Form'd a vast buckle for his widow's gown:
Her infant grandame's whistle next it grew,
The bells she jingled, and the whistle blew;
Then in a bodkin grac'd her mother's hairs,   95
Which long she wore, and now Belinda wears.)
   Boast not my fall (he cry'd) insulting foe!
Thou by some other shalt be laid as low.
Nor think, to die dejects my lofty mind:
All that I dread is leaving you behind!   100
Rather than so, ah let me still survive,
And burn in Cupid's flames,—but burn alive.
   Restore the Lock! she cries; and all around
Restore the Lock! the vaulted roofs rebound.
Not fierce Othello in so loud a strain   105
Roar'd for the handkerchief that caus'd his pain.

78. *To die:* To die had two meanings,
the second of which was to make love.

But see how oft ambitious aims are cross'd,
And chiefs contend 'till all the prize is lost!
The Lock, obtain'd with guilt, and kept with pain,
In ev'ry place is sought, but sought in vain: 110
With such a prize no mortal must be blest,
So heav'n decrees! with heav'n who can contest?
  Some thought it mounted to the Lunar sphere,
Since all things lost on earth are treasur'd there.
There Heroes' wits are kept in pond'rous vases,   115
And Beaux' in snuff-boxes and tweezer-cases.
There broken vows, and death-bed alms are found,
And lovers hearts with ends of ribband bound,
The courtier's promises, and sick man's pray'rs,
The smiles of harlots, and the tears of heirs,   120
Cages for gnats, and chains to yoak a flea,
Dry'd butterflies, and tomes of casuistry.
  But trust the Muse—she saw it upward rise,
Tho' mark'd by none but quick, poetic eyes
(So Rome's great founder to the heav'ns withdrew,   125
To Proculus alone confess'd in view):
A sudden Star, it shot thro' liquid air,
And drew behind a radiant trail of hair.
Not Berenice's Locks first rose so bright,
The heav'ns bespangling with dishevel'd light.   130
The Sylphs behold it kindling as it flies,
And pleas'd pursue its progress thro' the skies.
  This the Beau monde shall from the Mall survey,
And hail with music its propitious ray.
This the blest Lover shall for Venus take,   135
And send up vows from Rosamonda's lake.
This Partridge soon shall view in cloudless skies,
When next he looks thro' Galilæo's eyes;
And hence th' egregious wizard shall foredoom
The fate of Louis, and the fall of Rome.   140
  Then cease, bright Nymph! to mourn thy ravish'd hair,
Which adds new glory to the shining sphere!

125–126. *Rome's . . . founder/To Proculus:* According to Livy, Bk. I, xvi, Proculus Julius, the leader of his people (who were then distraught over the recent loss of their king), called upon Rome's founder, Romulus. He descended from the heavens, promised that Rome should become capital of the world, then returned whence he had come.
129. *Berenice's Locks:* When Ptolemy III went to war (246 B.C.) to support his nephew's royal claims, the warrior's wife, Berenice, dedicated a lock of her hair for her husband's safe return. A court astronomer pretended to discover it transformed into a constellation.
133. *Mall:* An enclosed walk in St. James's Park.
136. *Rosamonda's lake:* A pond in St. James's Park.
137. *Partridge:* Pope says, "John Partridge was a ridiculous star-gazer who in his Almanacks every year never fail'd to predict the downfall of the Pope, and the King of France, then at war with the English."
138. *Galilæo's eyes:* The telescope.

Not all the tresses that fair head can boast
Shall draw such envy as the Lock you lost.
For, after all the murders of your eye,   145
When, after millions slain, yourself shall die;
When those fair suns shall set, as set they must,
And all those tresses shall be laid in dust,
This Lock, the Muse shall consecrate to fame,
And 'midst the stars inscribe Belinda's name.   150

(Two-canto version, 1712)
(1714)

Headnote to
ELEGY ...
UNFORTUNATE LADY

Though many have tried to identify the unfortunate lady of this poem, no one has ever succeeded in doing so. Pope fostered the impression that some particular woman of his acquaintance was his subject, but he refused to give clear information to those of his contemporaries who inquired about her; and now it seems likely that he did not draw her from life. In either case, Pope might have behaved in precisely the way he did. That is, he might have pretended there was a real woman to increase the interest of readers, who in the eighteenth century probably would have thought less of this somewhat romantically turned poem about a suicide if they had known it to have no basis in fact. And if the woman did exist, he might have withheld information about her to keep his reader from coming to the elegy with a mind too fixed by the literal truth to be engaged by the poetic. In short, it seems that Pope may have controlled the relationship between art and life in order to increase the effect of his poetry.

TEXT. *The Works of Alexander Pope, Esq.*, ed. William Warburton (9 vols., London, 1751).

Elegy to the Memory of an Unfortunate Lady

WHAT beck'ning ghost, along the moonlight shade
Invites my steps, and points to yonder glade?
'Tis she!—but why that bleeding bosom gor'd,
Why dimly gleams the visionary sword?
Oh ever beauteous, ever friendly! tell,   5
Is it, in heav'n, a crime to love too well?
To bear too tender, or too firm a heart,
To act a Lover's or a Roman's part?

8. *A Roman's part:* To act a Roman's part in this context is to commit suicide, which is of course against church law.

Is there no bright reversion in the sky,
For those who greatly think, or bravely die?   10
   Why bade ye else, ye Pow'rs! her soul aspire
Above the vulgar flight of low desire?
Ambition first sprung from your blest abodes;
The glorious fault of Angels and of Gods:
Thence to their images on earth it flows,   15
And in the breasts of Kings and Heroes glows.
Most souls, 'tis true, but peep out once an age,
Dull sullen pris'ners in the body's cage:
Dim lights of life, that burn a length of years,
Useless, unseen, as lamps in sepulchres;   20
Like Eastern Kings a lazy state they keep,
And close confin'd to their own palace, sleep.
   From these perhaps (ere nature bade her die)
Fate snatch'd her early to the pitying sky.
As into air the purer spirits flow,   25
And sep'rate from their kindred dregs below;
So flew the soul to its congenial place,
Nor left one virtue to redeem her Race.
   But thou, false guardian of a charge too good,
Thou, mean deserter of thy brother's blood!   30
See on these ruby lips the trembling breath,
These cheeks, now fading at the blast of death;
Cold is that breast which warm'd the world before,
And those love-darting eyes must roll no more.
Thus, if Eternal justice rules the ball,   35
Thus shall your wives, and thus your children fall:
On all the line a sudden vengeance waits,
And frequent herses shall besiege your gates.
There passengers shall stand, and pointing say
(While the long fun'rals blacken all the way)   40
Lo these were they, whose souls the Furies steel'd,
And curs'd with hearts unknowing how to yield.
Thus unlamented pass the proud away,
The gaze of fools, and pageant of a day!
So perish all, whose breast ne'er learn'd to glow   45
For others good, or melt at others woe.
   What can atone (oh ever-injur'd shade!)
Thy fate unpity'd, and thy rites unpaid?
No friend's complaint, no kind domestic tear
Pleas'd thy pale ghost, or grac'd thy mournful bier.   50
By foreign hands thy dying eyes were clos'd,
By foreign hands thy decent limbs compos'd,
By foreign hands thy humble grave adorn'd,

41. *Furies:* In Greek mythology, the
Furies were avenging female spirits.

By strangers honour'd, and by strangers mourn'd!
What tho' no friends in sable weeds appear,   55
Grieve for an hour, perhaps, then mourn a year,
And bear about the mockery of woe
To midnight dances, and the public show?
What tho' no weeping Loves thy ashes grace,
Nor polish'd marble emulate thy face?   60
What tho' no sacred earth allow thee room,
Nor hallow'd dirge be mutter'd o'er thy tomb?
Yet shall thy grave with rising flow'rs be drest,
And the green turf lie lightly on thy breast:
There shall the morn her earliest tears bestow,   65
There the first roses of the year shall blow;
While Angels with their silver wings o'ershade
The ground, now sacred by thy reliques made.
    So peaceful rests, without a stone, a name,
What once had beauty, titles, wealth, and fame.   70
How lov'd, how honour'd once, avails thee not,
To whom related, or by whom begot;
A heap of dust alone remains of thee,
'Tis all thou art, and all the proud shall be!
    Poets themselves must fall, like those they sung,   75
Deaf the prais'd ear, and mute the tuneful tongue.
Ev'n he, whose soul now melts in mournful lays,
Shall shortly want the gen'rous tear he pays;
Then from his closing eyes thy form shall part,
And the last pang shall tear thee from his heart,   80
Life's idle business at one gasp be o'er,
The Muse forgot, and thou belov'd no more!

(1717)

61. *No sacred earth:* Catholics, Angli-
cans, and other Christians generally cannot
be buried in consecrated ground if they are
suicides.

Headnote to
ELOISA TO ABELARD

Pope's classical model for "Eloisa to Abelard" is Ovid's *Heroides*, a series of love poems written in the form of letters in which heroines like Sappho, Medea, Helen, Oenone, and Dido address their lovers or husbands, who in most cases have deserted them. The tone of these varies enormously. The language of Helen's letter reveals a capricious, vain, and shallow woman; Dido's, a rich and passionate character. But each of them in its own way, no matter the persona Ovid presents, allows the poet to reveal the depth and range of his knowledge of women in love.

By the time Pope wrote "Eloisa to Abelard," probably shortly before its publication in 1717, he had a long-established tradition in heroic epistles on which to draw. John Donne's "Sappho to Philaenis," Michael Drayton's *England's Heroicall Epistles* (1597–99), and John Oldmixon's version of the Drayton letters, *Amores Britannici* (1703) are typical of England's contribution to the form. In France, the prose *Lettres Portugaises* had appeared in 1669; they were translated as *Five Love-Letters from a Nun to a Cavalier* by Roger L'Estrange, in 1678. But the work on which Pope's "Eloisa to Abelard" relied specifically as a source was the translation by John Hughes of the late seventeenth-century French version of the letters of Eloisa and Abelard, by Roger de Robutin, Comte de Bussy. Here, Eloisa is a kind of romantic heroine who minutely explores and clearly enjoys the pulse, heat, and rush of resummoned passion.

The historical Peter Abelard (1079–1142), a French nobleman, was a scholastic philosopher and teacher of great reputation. Before he was forty years old, he was made canon and master of Notre Dame, from which place his abilities drew students from all of Europe. Then he fell in love with the beautiful and highly educated Héloïse (Pope's Eloisa), niece of the powerful Canon Fulbert, and seduced her. A son was born to them, after which they were married, though Héloïse tried to persuade Abelard not to risk his career by continuing their relationship. In fact, after the marriage she returned to the convent where she had been educated. Her uncle, believing the lover had put aside his mistress, engaged two men to break into Abelard's rooms one night, and (perhaps with Fulbert's help) emasculate him. In despair, Abelard became a monk, and Héloïse took the veil.

Pope's decision to employ Eloisa as the narrator makes for a near direct expression of emotion rare in his poetry, which more typically offers not feelings, but their effect (the consequences of the critic's pride in *An Essay on Criticism*), or their emblem (ritual mourning for a lost love in "Winter"), or their distortion (comic anger in *Rape of the Lock*). Eloisa directly reveals her predicament, often in physiological terms,

> What means this tumult in a Vestal's veins? (l. 4)

and then she prays she may be able to control it. The balance between will and desire is not well maintained, however. Her passions dominate the occasion not only because they are strong, but because they blasphemously violate the order of things. One is surprised to learn that in Eloisa's mind, Abelard's memory is "... mix'd with God's" (a recurrent image):

> I waste the matin lamp in sighs for thee,
> Thy image steals between my God and me (ll. 267–268)

> Snatch me, just mounting, from the blest abode;
> Assist the fiends, and tear me from my God. (ll. 287–288)

Of course, she immediately offers recantations (ll. 289–290), but they can hardly cancel her earlier prayer to God–Abelard. And so Pope's images of her extravagantly expressed love are more long-lived than those of her repentance, in the mind of the reader. He may sympathize with her plight; he is also likely to recollect her inordinate passion. Yet in her final comment she somehow neutralizes her lack of control by anticipating with pleasure a poetical (therefore impersonal) treatment of her love.

TEXT. *The Works of Alexander Pope, Esq.*, ed. William Warburton (9 vols., London, 1751).

Eloisa to Abelard

Argument

ABELARD and Eloisa flourished in the twelfth Century; they were two of the most distinguished persons of their age in learning and beauty, but for

nothing more famous than for their unfortunate passion. After a long course
of calamities, they retired each to a several Convent, and consecrated the remainder of their days to religion. It was many years after this separation, that a
letter of Abelard's to a Friend, which contained the history of his misfortune,
fell into the hands of Eloisa. This, awakening all her tenderness, occasioned
those celebrated letters (out of which the following is partly extracted), which
give so lively a picture of the struggles of grace and nature, virtue and
Passson.   P.

IN these deep solitudes and awful cells,
Where heav'nly-pensive contemplation dwells,
And ever-musing melancholy reigns;
What means this tumult in a Vestal's veins?
Why rove my thoughts beyond this last retreat?   5
Why feels my heart its long-forgotten heat?
Yet, yet I love!—From Abelard it came,
And Eloïsa yet must kiss the name.
　　Dear fatal name! rest ever unreveal'd,
Nor pass these lips in holy silence seal'd: 10
Hide it, my heart, within that close disguise,
Where mix'd with God's, his lov'd Idea lies.
O write it not my hand—the name appears
Already written—wash it out, my tears!
In vain lost Eloïsa weeps and prays,   15
Her heart still dictates, and her hand obeys.
　　Relentless walls! whose darksome round contains
Repentant sighs, and voluntary pains:
Ye rugged rocks! which holy knees have worn;
Ye grots and caverns shagg'd with horrid thorn!   20
Shrines! where their vigils pale-ey'd virgins keep,
And pitying saints, whose statues learn to weep!
Tho' cold like you, unmov'd and silent grown,
I have not yet forgot myself to stone.
All is not Heav'n while Abelard has part,   25
Still rebel nature holds out half my heart;
Nor pray'rs nor fasts its stubborn pulse restrain,
Nor tears for ages taught to flow in vain.
　　Soon as thy letters trembling I unclose,
That well-known name awakens all my woes.   30
Oh name for ever sad! for ever dear!
Still breath'd in sighs, still usher'd with a tear.
I tremble too, where'er my own I find,
Some dire misfortune follows close behind.
Line after line my gushing eyes o'erflow,   35
Led thro' a sad variety of woe:
Now warm in love, now with'ring in my bloom,
Lost in a convent's solitary gloom!

There stern Religion quench'd th'unwilling flame,
There dy'd the best of passions, Love and Fame.   40
　　Yet write, oh write me all, that I may join
Griefs to thy griefs, and echo sighs to thine.
Nor foes nor fortune take this pow'r away;
And is my Abelard less kind than they?
Tears still are mine, and those I need not spare,   45
Love but demands what else were shed in pray'r;
No happier task these faded eyes pursue;
To read and weep is all they now can do.
　　Then share thy pain, allow that sad relief;
Ah, more than share it, give me all thy grief.   50
Heav'n first taught letters for some wretch's aid,
Some banish'd lover, or some captive maid;
Thy live, they speak, they breathe what love inspires,
Warm from the soul, and faithful to its fires,
The virgin's wish without her fears impart,   55
Excuse the blush, and pour out all the heart,
Speed the soft intercourse from soul to soul,
And waft a sigh from Indus to the Pole.
　　Thou know'st how guiltless first I met thy flame,
When Love approach'd me under Friendship's name;   60
My fancy form'd thee of angelic kind,
Some emanation of th'all-beauteous Mind.
Those smiling eyes, attemp'ring ev'ry ray,
Shone sweetly lambent with celestial day.
Guiltless I gaz'd; heav'n listen'd while you sung;   65
And truths divine came mended from that tongue.
From lips like those what precept fail'd to move?
Too soon they taught me 'twas no sin to love:
Back thro' the paths of pleasing sense I ran,
Nor wish'd an Angel whom I lov'd a Man.   70
Dim and remote the joys of saints I see;
Nor envy them that heav'n I lose for thee.
　　How oft, when press'd to marriage, have I said,
Curse on all laws but those which love has made?
Love, free as air, at sight of human ties,   75
Spreads his light wings, and in a moment flies.
Let wealth, let honour, wait the wedded dame,
August her deed, and sacred be her fame;
Before true passion all those views remove,
Fame, wealth, and honour! what are you to Love?   80
The jealous God, when we profane his fires,
Those restless passions in revenge inspires,
And bids them make mistaken mortals groan,
Who seek in love for aught but love alone.
Should at my feet the world's great master fall,   85

Himself, his throne, his world, I'd scorn 'em all:
Not Cæsar's empress would I deign to prove;
No, make me mistress to the man I love;
If there be yet another name more free,
More fond than mistress, make me that to thee!   90
Oh! happy state! when souls each other draw,
When love is liberty, and nature, law:
All then is full, possessing, and possess'd,
No craving void left aking in the breast:
Ev'n thought meets thought, ere from the lips it part,   95
And each warm wish springs mutual from the heart.
This sure is bliss (if bliss on earth there be)
And once the lot of Abelard and me.
   Alas how chang'd! what sudden horrors rise!
A naked Lover bound and bleeding lies!   100
Where, where was Eloïse? her voice, her hand,
Her ponyard, had oppos'd the dire command.
Barbarian, stay! that bloody stroke restrain;
The crime was common, common be the pain.
I can no more; by shame, by rage suppress'd,   105
Let tears, and burning blushes speak the rest.
   Canst thou forget that sad, that solemn day,
When victims at yon altar's foot we lay?
Canst thou forget what tears that moment fell,
When, warm in youth, I bade the world farewell?   110
As with cold lips I kiss'd the sacred veil,
The shrines all trembled, and the lamps grew pale:
Heav'n scarce believ'd the Conquest it survey'd,
And Saints with wonder heard the vows I made.
Yet then, to those dread altars as I drew,   115
Not on the Cross my eyes were fix'd, but you;
Not grace, or zeal, love only was my call,
And if I lose thy love, I lose my all.
Come! with thy looks, thy words, relieve my woe;
Those still at least are left thee to bestow.   120
Still on that breast enamour'd let me lie,
Still drink delicious poison from thy eye,
Pant on thy lip, and to thy heart be press'd;
Give all thou canst—and let me dream the rest.
Ah no! instruct me other joys to prize,   125
With other beauties charm my partial eyes,
Full in my view set all the bright abode,
And make my soul quit Abelard for God.
   Ah think at least thy flock deserves thy care,
Plants of thy hand, and children of thy pray'r.   130

102. *Ponyard:* A dagger.

From the false world in early youth they fled,
By thee to mountains, wilds, and deserts led.
You rais'd these hallow'd walls; the desert smil'd,
And Paradise was open'd in the Wild.
No weeping orphan saw his father's stores   135
Our shrines irradiate, or emblaze the floors;
No silver saints, by dying misers giv'n,
Here brib'd the rage of ill-requited heav'n:
But such plain roofs as Piety could raise,
And only vocal with the Maker's praise.   140
In these lone walls (their days eternal bound)
These moss-grown domes with spiry turrets crown'd,
Where awful arches make a noon-day night,
And the dim windows shed a solemn light;
Thy eyes diffus'd a reconciling ray,   145
And gleams of glory brighten'd all the day.
But now no face divine contentment wears,
'Tis all blank sadness, or continual tears.
See how the force of others pray'rs I try
(O pious fraud of am'rous charity!)   150
But why should I on others' pray'rs depend?
Come thou, my father, brother, husband, friend!
Ah let thy handmaid, sister, daughter move,
And all those tender names in one, thy love!
The darksome pines that o'er yon rocks reclin'd   155
Wave high, and murmur to the hollow wind,
The wand'ring streams that shine between the hills,
The grots that echo to the tinkling rills,
The dying gales that pant upon the trees,
The lakes that quiver to the curling breeze;   160
No more these scenes my meditation aid,
Or lull to rest the visionary maid.
But o'er the twilight groves and dusky caves,
Long-sounding isles, and intermingled graves,
Black Melancholy sits, and round her throws   165
A death-like silence, and a dread repose:
Her gloomy presence saddens all the scene,
Shades ev'ry flow'r, and darkens ev'ry green,
Deepens the murmur of the falling floods,
And breathes a browner horror on the woods.   170
    Yet here for ever, ever must I stay;
Sad proof how well a lover can obey!
Death, only death, can break the lasting chain;
And here, ev'n then, shall my cold dust remain,
Here all its frailties, all its flames resign,   175
And wait till 'tis no sin to mix with thine.
    Ah wretch! believ'd the spouse of God in vain,

Confess'd within the slave of love and man.
Assist me, heav'n! but whence arose that pray'r?
Sprung it from piety, or from despair?   180
Ev'n here, where frozen chastity retires,
Love finds an altar for forbidden fires.
I ought to grieve, but cannot what I ought;
I mourn the lover, not lament the fault;
I view my crime, but kindle at the view,   185
Repent old pleasures, and sollicit new;
Now turn'd to heav'n, I weep my past offence,
Now think of thee, and curse my innocence.
Of all affliction taught a lover yet,
'Tis sure the hardest science to forget!   190
How shall I lose the sin, yet keep the sense,
And love th'offender, yet detest th'offence?
How the dear object from the crime remove,
Or how distinguish penitence from love?
Unequal task! a passion to resign,   195
For hearts so touch'd, so pierc'd, so lost as mine.
Ere such a soul regains its peaceful state,
How often must it love, how often hate!
How often hope, despair, resent, regret,
Conceal, disdain—do all things but forget.   200
But let heav'n seize it, all at once 'tis fir'd;
Not touch'd, but rapt; not waken'd, but inspir'd!
Oh come! oh teach me nature to subdue,
Renounce my love, my life, my self—and you.
Fill my fond heart with God alone, for he   205
Alone can rival, can succeed to thee.
    How happy is the blameless Vestal's lot!
The world forgetting, by the world forgot.
Eternal sun-shine of the spotless mind!
Each pray'r accepted, and each wish resign'd;   210
Labour and rest, that equal periods keep;
"Obedient slumbers that can wake and weep";
Desires compos'd, affections ever ev'n,
Tears that delight, and sighs that waft to heav'n.
Grace shines around her with serenest beams,   215
And whisp'ring Angels prompt her golden dreams.
For her th'unfading rose of Eden blooms,
And wings of Seraphs shed divine perfumes;
For her the Spouse prepares the bridal ring,
For her white virgins Hymenæals sing;   220
To sounds of heav'nly harps she dies away,
And melts in visions of eternal day.

212. *Obedient slumbers:* Pope says,   "Description of a Religious House."
"Taken from Crashaw"; it is l. 16 of

Far other dreams my erring soul employ,
Far other raptures, of unholy joy:
When at the close of each sad, sorrowing day,   225
Fancy restores what vengeance snatch'd away,
Then conscience sleeps, and leaving nature free,
All my loose soul unbounded springs to thee.
O curst, dear horrors of all-conscious night!
How glowing guilt exalts the keen delight!   230
Provoking Dæmons all restraint remove,
And stir within me ev'ry source of love.
I hear thee, view thee, gaze o'er all thy charms,
And round thy phantom glue my clasping arms.
I wake—no more I hear, no more I view;   235
The phantom flies me, as unkind as you.
I call aloud; it hears not what I say;
I stretch my empty arms; it glides away.
To dream once more I close my willing eyes;
Ye soft illusions, dear deceits, arise!   240
Alas, no more! methinks we wand'ring go
Thro' dreary wastes, and weep each other's woe,
Where round some mould'ring tow'r pale ivy creeps,
And low-brow'd rocks hang nodding o'er the deeps.
Sudden you mount, you beckon from the skies;   245
Clouds interpose, waves roar, and winds arise.
I shriek, start up, the same sad prospect find,
And wake to all the griefs I left behind.
  For thee the fates, severely kind, ordain
A cool suspense from pleasure and from pain;   250
Thy life a long dead calm of fix'd repose;
No pulse that riots, and no blood that glows.
Still as the sea, ere winds were taught to blow,
Or moving spirit bade the waters flow;
Soft as the slumbers of a saint forgiv'n,   255
And mild as op'ning gleams of promis'd heav'n.
  Come, Abelard! for what hast thou to dread?
The torch of Venus burns not for the dead.
Nature stands check'd; Religion disapproves;
Ev'n thou art cold—yet Eloïsa loves.   260
Ah hopeless, lasting flames! like those that burn
To light the dead, and warm th'unfruitful urn.
  What scenes appear where'er I turn my view?
The dear Ideas, where I fly, pursue,
Rise in the grove, before the altar rise,   265
Stain all my soul, and wanton in my eyes.
I waste the Matin lamp in sighs for thee,
Thy image steals between my God and me,
Thy voice I seem in ev'ry hymn to hear,

With ev'ry bead I drop too soft a tear.   270
When from the censer clouds of fragrance roll,
And swelling organs lift the rising soul;
One thought of thee puts all the pomp to flight,
Priests, tapers, temples, swim before my sight:
In seas of flame my plunging soul is drown'd,   275
While Altars blaze, and Angels tremble round.
    While prostrate here in humble grief I lie,
Kind, virtuous drops just gath'ring in my eye,
While praying, trembling, in the dust I roll,
And dawning grace is op'ning on my soul: 280
Come, if thou dar'st, all charming as thou art!
Oppose thyself to heav'n; dispute my heart;
Come, with one glance of those deluding eyes,
Blot out each bright Idea of the skies;
Take back that grace, those sorrows, and those tears;   285
Take back my fruitless penitence and pray'rs;
Snatch me, just mounting, from the blest abode;
Assist the fiends, and tear me from my God!
    No, fly me, fly me, far as Pole from Pole;
Rise Alps between us! and whole oceans roll!   290
Ah, come not, write not, think not once of me,
Nor share one pang of all I felt for thee.
Thy oaths I quit, thy memory resign;
Forget, renounce me, hate whate'er was mine.
Fair eyes, and tempting looks (which yet I view!)   295
Long lov'd, ador'd ideas, all adieu!
O Grace serene! oh virtue heav'nly fair!
Divine oblivion of low-thoughted care!
Fresh blooming Hope, gay daughter of the sky!
And Faith, our early immortality!   300
Enter, each mild, each amicable guest;
Receive, and wrap me in eternal rest!
    See in her cell sad Eloïsa spread,
Propt on some tomb, a neighbour of the dead.
In each low wind methinks a Spirit calls,   305
And more than Echoes talk along the walls.
Here, as I watch'd the dying lamps around,
From yonder shrine I heard a hollow sound.
"Come, sister, come! (it said, or seem'd to say)
"Thy place is here, sad sister, come away!   310
"Once like thyself, I trembled, wept, and pray'd,
"Love's victim then, tho' now a sainted maid:
"But all is calm in this eternal sleep;
"Here grief forgets to groan, and love to weep,
"Ev'n superstition loses ev'ry fear: 315
"For God, not man, absolves our frailties here."

I come, I come! prepare your roseate bow'rs,
Celestial palms, and ever-blooming flow'rs.
Thither, where sinners may have rest, I go,
Where flames refin'd in breasts seraphic glow.   320
Thou, Abelard! the last sad office pay,
And smooth my passage to the realms of day;
See my lips tremble, and my eye-balls roll,
Suck my last breath, and catch my flying soul!
Ah no—in sacred vestments may'st thou stand,   325
The hallow'd taper trembling in thy hand,
Present the Cross before my lifted eye,
Teach me at once, and learn of me to die.
Ah then, thy once-lov'd Eloïsa see!
It will be then no crime to gaze on me.   330
See from my cheek the transient roses fly!
See the last sparkle languish in my eye!
'Till ev'ry motion, pulse, and breath be o'er;
And ev'n my Abelard be lov'd no more.
O Death all-eloquent! you only prove   335
What dust we doat on, when 'tis man we love.
    Then too, when fate shall thy fair frame destroy
(That cause of all my guilt, and all my joy)
In trance extatic may thy pangs be drown'd,
Bright clouds descend, and Angels watch thee round,   340
From op'ning skies may streaming glories shine,
And Saints embrace thee with a love like mine.
    May one kind grave unite each hapless name,
And graft my love immortal on thy fame!
Then, ages hence, when all my woes are o'er,   345
When this rebellious heart shall beat no more;
If ever chance two wand'ring lovers brings
To Paraclete's white walls and silver springs,
O'er the pale marble shall they join their heads,
And drink the falling tears each other sheds,   350
Then sadly say, with mutual pity mov'd,
"Oh may we never love as these have lov'd!"
From the full choir when loud Hosannas rise,
And swell the pomp of dreadful sacrifice,
Amid that scene if some relenting eye   355
Glance on the stone where our cold relicks lie.
Devotion's self shall steal a thought from heav'n,
One human tear shall drop, and be forgiv'n.
And sure if fate some future bard shall join

348. *Paraclete:* The word, which
means intercessor, was the name of the
oratory built for Abelard by grateful
students. Both Eloisa and Abelard were
buried in the monastery of the Paraclete,
perhaps in the same grave, he in 1142 and
she in 1163.

In sad similitude of griefs to mine,   360
Condemn'd whole years in absence to deplore,
And image charms he must behold no more;
Such if there be, who loves so long, so well,
Let him our sad, our tender story tell;
The well-sung woes will sooth my pensive ghost;   365
He best can paint 'em who shall feel 'em most.

   (1717)

Headnote to
EPISTLE IV:
OF THE USE OF RICHES

The four *Epistles to Several Persons*, essentially a set of Horatian satires, were originally conceived by Pope as sections of a vast ethical work of which *An Essay on Man* was to be a major part. These compositions, often referred to now as the *Moral Essays* because Pope's literary executor Warburton applied the name to them, include Epistle I (1734), "Of the Knowledge and Characters of Men," to Sir Richard Temple, Lord Cobham; Epistle II (1735), "Of the Characters of Women," to a Lady; Epistle III (1733), "Of the Use of Riches," to Allen Lord Bathurst; and Epistle IV (1731), also "Of the Use of Riches," to Richard Boyle, Earl of Burlington. Though they vary considerably in excellence, all of them exhibit a keen and immediate sense for the world of men rather than a concern with theoretical principles. One might expect then that in these works Pope's references to people would be always biographical, but he seems more often to have expressed his knowledge of mankind, and of the age, in composites of human frailty. Unfortunately for him, he was several times mistaken by his readers, who in the midst of so much topicality thought surely to discover real people. Most notable of these erroneous ascriptions occurred in connection with the earliest of the Epistles, that to Burlington, presented here (and ultimately numbered IV). The character of Timon, a proud and wealthy nobleman whose taste is very bad, was thought for various reasons to be the Duke of Chandos, who was erroneously believed to have helped Pope with a gift of £1000. To no avail Pope denied the general conclusion; even Johnson perpetuated the charge of his ingratitude. But evidence fairly recently brought to light confirms the truth of Pope's claims of innocence. The real difficulty of course was artistic. How could Pope shape a satiric statement that on the one hand applied to the foibles of many men rather than to those of a single human being and on the other avoided being so general as to have no bite? He wrestled a good deal with the problem and to a great extent solved it in later epistles by actually using some real characters (whom he identified) and some who were (as he told his readers) invented. His largely justified expectation was that his candour in naming some of his subjects would result in the public's

640

diminished interest in searching to identify actual persons in the satire; and most readers have indeed involved themselves in its chief concern— the morals and taste of sensible men.

The fourth epistle, "Of the Use of Riches," was originally called *An Epistle to the Right Honourable Richard Earl of Burlington, Occasioned by his Publishing Palladio's Designs of the Baths, Arches, and Theaters of Ancient Rome.* In a later edition, it was given the half-title *Of False Taste.* Pope's epistle in some senses treats a subject that falls within the limits of these names, for the poem praises his wealthy friend Burlington, who brought out a volume of designs of ancient Roman buildings by Andrea Palladio (1518–1580), the Italian architect, and who applied many of the Italian's principles of classical construction to his own architectural undertakings. But it treats not only the good taste of the few distinguished and capable persons like Burlington, but the bad taste of the many wealthy men who deform the country-side with ostentatious expressions of their pride and squander riches, instead of building grand and utilitarian estates in the Roman tradition, like Burlington's at Chiswick,

> Whose ample lawns are not afraid to feed
> The milky heifer and deserving steed;
> Whose rising forests, not for pride or show,
> But future buildings, future navies, grow. (ll. 185–188.)

TEXT. *The Works of Alexander Pope, Esq.*, ed. William Warburton (9 vols., London, 1751).

From Epistles to Several Persons

Epistle IV

TO RICHARD BOYLE,
EARL OF BURLINGTON

ARGUMENT

Of the Use of Riches

The Vanity of Expence in People of Wealth and Quality. The abuse of the word Taste. That the first principle and foundation, in this as in every thing else, is Good Sense. The chief proof of it is to follow Nature, even in works of mere Luxury and Elegance. Instanced in Architecture and Gardening, where all must be adapted to the Genius and Use of the Place, and the Beauties not forced into it, but resulting from it. How men are disappointed in their most expensive undertakings, for want of this true Foundation, without which nothing can please long, if at all; and the best Examples and Rules will but be perverted into something burdensome or ridiculous. A description of the false Taste of Magnificence; the first grand Error of which is to imagine that Greatness consists in the Size and Dimension, instead of the Proportion and Harmony of the whole, and the second, either in joining together Parts incoherent, or too minutely resembling, or in the Repetition of the same too frequently. A word or two of false Taste in Books, in Music, in Painting, even in Preaching and Prayer, and lastly in Entertainments. Yet PROVIDENCE *is justified in giving Wealth to be squandered in this manner, since it is dispersed to the Poor and Laborious part of mankind (recurring to what is laid down in the first book [the* Essay on Man*], Ep. II, and in the Epistle [to Bathurst] preceding this). What are the proper Objects of Magnificence, and a proper field for the Expence of Great Men, and finally, the Great and Public Works which become a Prince.*

Epistle IV

'TIS strange, the Miser should his Cares employ
To gain those Riches he can ne'er enjoy:
Is it less strange, the Prodigal should wast[e]
His wealth, to purchase what he ne'er can taste?
Not for himself he sees, or hears, or eats;   5
Artists must chuse his Pictures, Music, Meats:
He buys for Topham, Drawings and Designs,

7. *Topham:* Richard Topham was
known for his collection of drawings.

642

For Pembroke Statues, dirty Gods, and Coins;
Rare monkish Manuscripts for Hearne alone,
And Books for Mead, and Butterflies for Sloane.   10
Think we all these are for himself? no more
Than his fine Wife, alas! or finer Whore.
    For what has Virro painted, built, and planted?
Only to show, how many Tastes he wanted.
What brought Sir Visto's ill got wealth to waste?   15
Some Dæmon whisper'd, "Visto! have a Taste."
Heav'n visits with a Taste the wealthy fool,
And needs no Rod but Ripley with a Rule.
See! sportive fate, to punish aukward pride,
Bids Bubo build, and sends him such a Guide: 20
A standing sermon, at each year's expence,
That never Coxcomb reach'd Magnificence!
    You show us, Rome was glorious, not profuse,
And pompous buildings once were things of Use.
Yet shall (my Lord) your just, your noble rules   25
Fill half the land with Imitating-Fools;
Who random drawings from your sheets shall take,
And of one beauty many blunders make;
Load some vain Church with old Theatric state,
Turn Arcs of triumph to a Garden-gate;   30
Reverse your Ornaments, and hang them all
On some patch'd dog-hole ek'd with ends of wall;
Then clap four slices of Pilaster on't,
That, lac'd with bits of rustic, makes a Front;
Shall call the winds thro' long arcades to roar,   35
Proud to catch cold at a Venetian door;
Conscious they act a true Palladian part,
And if they starve, they starve by rules of art.
    Oft have you hinted to your brother Peer,
A certain truth, which many buy too dear: 40

---

8. *Pembroke:* Thomas Herbert, Eighth Earl of Pembroke, was a collector of ancient coins and statuary.

9. *Hearne:* Thomas Hearne was a collector of medieval manuscripts.

10. *Mead . . . Sloane:* Richard Mead had a library of more than 10,000 volumes; Hans Sloane was a naturalist with a great collection of specimens. Both men were distinguished scholars.

13. *Virro:* This reference has never been explained.

15. *Sir Visto's . . . wealth:* Sir Visto's name seems to derive from "vista," a long view, particularly down an avenue of trees, and is hence associated with the practice of landscape gardening.

18. *Ripley:* Pope says, "This man was a carpenter, employed by the first Minister [Walpole], who raised him to an Architect . . . ; [and] after some wretched proofs of his insufficiency in public Buildings, made him Comptroller of the Board of works."

20. *Bubo:* Latin for owl, the bird only ostensibly wise. Elsewhere Pope applies the name to George Bubb Dodington, a minor Whig politician and art patron.

32. *Dog-hole:* A poor dwelling place.

33. *Pilaster:* An upright architectural member—a pier, often treated as a column, but sometimes hidden in a wall. Pope here refers to a false column.

39. *Brother Peer:* The reference here is almost certainly general.

Something there is more needful than Expence,
And something previous ev'n to Taste—'tis Sense:
Good Sense, which only is the gift of Heav'n,
And tho' no Science, fairly worth the seven:
A Light, which in yourself you must perceive;   45
Jones and Le Nôtre have it not to give.
  To build, to plant, whatever you intend,
To rear the Column, or the Arch to bend,
To swell the Terras, or to sink the Grot;
In all, let Nature never be forgot.   50
But treat the Goddess like a modest fair,
Nor over-dress, nor leave her wholly bare;
Let not each beauty ev'ry where be spy'd,
Where half the skill is decently to hide.
He gains all points, who pleasingly confounds,   55
Surprizes, varies, and conceals the Bounds.
  Consult the Genius of the Place in all;
That tells the Waters or to rise, or fall;
Or helps th'ambitious Hill the heav'ns to scale,
Or scoops in circling theatres the Vale;   60
Calls in the Country, catches op'ning glades,
Joins willing woods, and varies shades from shades;
Now breaks or now directs, th' intending Lines;
Paints as you plant, and, as you work, designs.
  Still follow Sense, of ev'ry Art the Soul,   65
Parts answ'ring parts shall slide into a whole,
Spontaneous beauties all around advance,
Start ev'n from Difficulty, strike from Chance;
Nature shall join you; Time shall make it grow
A Work to wonder at —perhaps a STOW.   70
  Without it, proud Versailles! thy glory falls;
And Nero's Terraces desert their walls:
The vast Parterres a thousand hands shall make,
Lo! COBHAM comes, and floats them with a Lake:
Or cut wide views thro' Mountains to the Plain,   75
You'll wish your hill or shelter'd seat again.
Ev'n in an ornament its place remark,

---

46. *Jones and Le Nôtre:* Inigo Jones (1573–1652) was a great English architect. André Le Nôtre (1613–1700) laid out the great symmetrical gardens at Versailles and Fontainebleau. (Pope's own small garden at Twickenham was designed and executed according to principles opposed to those employed by Le Nôtre: instead of balance and formality, Pope preferred the effect of nature unobtrusively controlled, as it is by a landscape painter.)
70. *Stow:* The estate of Richard

Temple, Lord Cobham, ordered according to the "natural" design favored by Pope.
72. *Nero's Terraces:* The reference is probably to Nero's palace, The Golden House, which embraced all the parts of a large farm.
73. *Vast Parterres:* Parterres are ornately arranged flower plots. Pope calls attention here to those of excessive size, which a man of taste (Cobham, l. 74) would want to eliminate.
74. *Floats:* Floods; i.e. covers over.

Nor in an Hermitage set Dr. Clarke.

Behold Villario's ten-years toil compleat
His Quincunx darkens, his Espaliers meet;   80
The Wood supports the Plain, the parts unite,
And strength of Shade contends with strength of Light;
A waving Glow the bloomy beds display,
Blushing in bright diversities of day,
With silver-quiv'ring rills mæander'd o'er—   85
Enjoy them, you! Villario can no more;
Tir'd of the scene Parterres and Fountains yield,
He finds at last he better likes a Field.

Thro' his young Woods how pleas'd Sabinus stray'd
Or sat delighted in the thick'ning shade,   90
With annual joy the red'ning shoots to greet,
Or see the stretching branches long to meet!
His Son's fine Taste an op'ner Vista loves,
Foe to the Dryads of his Father's groves;
One boundless Green, or flourish'd Carpet views,   95
With all the mournful family of Yews;
The thriving plants ignoble broomsticks made,
Now sweep those Alleys they were born to shade.

At Timon's Villa let us pass a day,
Where all cry out, "What sums are thrown away!"   100
So proud, so grand; of that stupendous air,
Soft and Agreeable come never there.
Greatness, with Timon, dwells in such a draught
As brings all Brobdignag before your thought.
To compass this, his building is a Town,   105
His pond an Ocean, his parterre a Down:
Who but must laugh, the Master when he sees,
A puny insect, shiv'ring at a breeze!
Lo, what huge heaps of littleness around!
The whole, a labour'd Quarry above ground.   110
Two Cupids squirt before: a Lake behind

78. *Dr. Clarke:* Queen Caroline anomalously placed the bust of Dr. Samuel Clarke, a heterodox philosopher, in the Hermitage, her grotto, in Richmond Park.

79. *Villario's . . . toil:* Pope apparently derives Villario from "villa."

80. *Quincunx . . . Espalier:* In gardening, a quincunx is an arrangement of five trees, four in the corners of a square or rectangle, and one in the center; espaliers are plants, or rows of plants, trained to grow flat.

89. *Sabinus:* The reference here seems to be general.

94. *Dryads:* A dryad is a nymph whose life is associated with that of her tree.

95. *One boundless Green . . . :* Pope says, "The two extremes . . . equally faulty: a *boundless Green*, large and naked as a field, or a *flourish'd Carpet,* where the greatness and nobleness of the piece is lessened by being divided into too many parts, with scroll'd works and beds. . . ."

96. *Mournful family of Yews:* Pope says this line "Touches upon the ill taste of those who are so fond of Ever-greens (particularly Yews, which are the most tonsile) as to destroy the nobler Forest-trees, to make way for such little ornaments as Pyramids of dark-green continually repeated, not unlike a Funeral procession."

99. *Timon's Villa:* Pope says, "This description is intended to comprise the principles of a false Taste of Magnificence. . . ."

Improves the keenness of the Northern wind.
His Gardens next your admiration call,
On ev'ry side you look, behold the Wall!
No pleasing Intricacies intervene,   115
No artful wildness to perplex the scene;
Grove nods at grove, each Alley has a brother,
And half the platform just reflects the other.
The suff'ring eye inverted Nature sees,
Trees cut to Statues, Statues thick as trees;   120
With here a Fountain, never to be play'd;
And there a Summer-house, that knows no shade;
Here Amphitrite sails thro' myrtle bow'rs;
There Gladiators fight, or die in flow'rs;
Un-water'd see the drooping sea-horse mourn,   125
And swallows roost in Nilus' dusty Urn.
    My Lord advances with majestic mien,
Smit with the mighty pleasure, to be seen:
But soft—by regular approach—not yet—
First thro' the length of yon hot Terrace sweat;   130
And when up ten steep slopes you've drag'd your thighs,
Just at his Study-door he'll bless your eyes.
    His Study! with what Authors is it stor'd?
In Books, not Authors, curious is my Lord;
To all their dated Backs he turns you round: 135
These Aldus printed, those Du Suëil has bound.
Lo some are Vellom, and the rest as good
For all his Lordship knows, but they are Wood.
For Locke or Milton 'tis in vain to look,
These shelves admit not any modern book.   140
    And now the Chapel's silver bell you hear,
That summons you to all the Pride of Pray'r:
Light quirks of Music, broken and uneven,
Make the soul dance upon a Jig to Heav'n.
On painted Cielings you devoutly stare,   145
Where sprawl the Saints of Verrio or Laguerre,
On gilded clouds in fair expansion lie,
And bring all Paradise before your eye.
To rest, the Cushion and soft Dean invite,

118. *Platform:* Terrace.
123. *Amphitrite:* A sea nymph, wife of Poseidon and goddess of the sea.
126. *Nilus' dusty Urn:* Nilus, god of the Nile, is here assigned to a dusty urn to epitomize the inanity of the garden sculpture of the day.
136. *Aldus . . . Du Suëil:* Aldus Manutius (1450–1515) was an Italian printer and a classical scholar; the Abbé Du Suëil was a famous Parisian bookbinder of the eighteenth century.
138. *They are Wood:* Pope says of men with false taste in books that they "... cause the upper shelves to be filled with painted books of wood."
146. *Verrio or Laguerre:* Pope says, "Verrio (Antonio) painted many cielings [*sic*], etc., at Windsor, Hampton-court, etc., and Laguerre at Blenheim-castle and other places."

Who never mentions Hell to ears polite.   150
   But hark! the chiming Clocks to dinner call;
A hundred footsteps scrape the marble Hall:
The rich Buffet well-colour'd Serpents grace,
And gaping Tritons spew to wash your face.
Is this a dinner? this a Genial room?   155
No, 'tis a Temple, and a Hecatomb.
A solemn Sacrifice, perform'd in state,
You drink by measure, and to minutes eat.
So quick retires each flying course, you'd swear
Sancho's dread Doctor and his Wand were there.   160
Between each Act the trembling salvers ring,
From soup to sweet-wine, and God bless the King.
In plenty starving, tantaliz'd in state,
And complaisantly help'd to all I hate,
Treated, caress'd, and tir'd, I take my leave,   165
Sick of his civil Pride from Morn to Eve;
I curse such lavish cost, and little skill,
And swear no Day was ever past so ill.
   Yet hence the Poor are cloath'd, the Hungry fed;
Health to himself, and to his Infants bread   170
The Lab'rer bears: What his hard Heart denies,
His charitable Vanity supplies.
   Another age shall see the golden Ear
Imbrown the Slope, and nod on the Parterre,
Deep Harvests bury all his pride has plann'd,   175
And laughing Ceres re-assume the land.
   Who then shall grace, or who improve the Soil?
Who plants like BATHURST, or who builds like BOYLE.
'Tis Use alone that sanctifies Expence,
And Splendor borrows all her rays from sense.   180
   His Father's Acres who enjoys in peace,
Or makes his Neighbours glad, if he encrease:
Whose chearful Tenants bless their yearly toil,
Yet to their Lord owe more than to the soil
Whose ample Lawns are not asham'd to feed   185
The milky heifer and deserving steed;

150. *Never mentions Hell:* Pope says, ". . . a reverend Dean . . . threatned [*sic*] the sinner with punishment in 'a place which he thought it not decent to name. . . .' "

153. *Serpents:* Here, incongruous ornaments.

154. *Tritons:* Triton, a sea god, made into a fountain.

156. *Hecatomb:* A sacrifice of a hundred cattle.

160. *Sancho's dread Doctor:* In *Don Quixote*, Part II, Bk. III, Ch. xlvii, the physician responsible for Sancho's health uses his magic wand to make various tempting dishes disappear, just as his charge is about to eat.

176. *Ceres:* Goddess of growing vegetation and the harvest.

178. *Bathurst . . . Boyle:* Allen, Lord Bathurst was Pope's friend, to whom the third of the *Epistles to Several Persons* was dedicated; Richard Boyle, Earl of Burlington, is the man to whom this poem is dedicated.

Whose rising Forests, not for pride or show,
But future Buildings, future Navies, grow:
Let his plantations stretch from down to down,
First shade a Country, and then raise a Town.   190
    You too proceed! make falling Arts your care,
Erect new wonders, and the old repair;
Jones and Palladio to themselves restore,
And be whate'er Vitruvius was before:
Till Kings call forth th' Ideas of your mind   195
(Proud to accomplish what such hands design'd),
Bid Harbors open, public Ways extend,
Bid Temples, worthier of the God, ascend;
Bid the broad Arch the dang'rous Flood contain,
The Mole projected break the roaring Main;   200
Back to his bounds their subject Sea command,
And roll obedient Rivers thro' the Land:
These Honours, Peace to happy Britain brings,
These are Imperial Works, and worthy Kings.

(1731)

194. *Vitruvius:* M. Vitruvius Pollio,
Latin author of *De Architectura.*

Headnote to
AN ESSAY ON MAN

Dr. Johnson says that *An Essay on Man* was not ". . . the happiest of Pope's performances . . . [because] metaphysical morality was to him a new study . . . and he was in haste to teach what he had not learned." One of the meanings of Johnson's statement seems to be that Pope was not a formal philosopher, a view with which the poet himself would no doubt have agreed. And though Johnson also believes the poem falls short of exemplifying ". . . Pope's felicity of composition . . . ," he approves its ". . . blaze of embellishment . . . [and] sweetness of melody . . .; [its] vigorous contraction . . . [and] luxuriant amplification . . ." of thought. While modern critics of the *Essay* may offer more praise or censure than does Johnson, they generally perpetuate his fundamental distinction between the work as a philosophical piece and as a poem, though the ground it covers in the world of ideas (however informally it may do so) must continue to engage the student of literature.

Throughout the composition, Pope tries to account for the existence of evil (or better, what he considers to be apparent evil). To accomplish his purpose he characterizes man, the complex world in which he lives, and his relationship to that world in such a way as to show that the entire creation is a vast integration of forces, only a handful of which men can know about. Perforce limited in their knowledge of the scheme of things, they imagine ubiquitous evil, when in fact only local or temporary difficulties exist, these serving some larger constructive purpose. Moreover, the specifically moral evil that occurs among the various and varying constituent parts of the vast whole—in animal life and in man's life of reason and passion—is accounted for and in part defined by the principle of plenitude: God was unable to leave unexpressed the degrees of his perfection, so he expressed them, with the result that man (one of the partial and of course limited expressions of this perfection) includes among his limitations the possibility that he may sin.

God's expression of his own perfection, which results in the created world, has other implications. Since God is the fullest possible Being, it follows that the physical expression of all his attributes has resulted in the fullest possible creation; that is, everything that can exist does exist. Moreover, all the parts of the creation, having emanated from God himself, are related to each other; and finally, the nature of their relationship is not haphazard, but a function of God's self-expression and therefore in the most significant sense orderly. As Pope refers to this idea of order in the poem, he uses the expression "Great Chain of Being," not only to indicate the range, the relationship between the parts, and the patterns in the created world, but also to suggest the connection between the world and God, its Maker. In addition, he treats the beings in the chain in the terms of a hierarchy, each with its assigned place. According to this view—by no means new with Pope—creatures who violate the limits of their position in the fixed scheme of things endanger not only themselves, they threaten the whole structure of the universe with chaos.

By the time of the *Essay's* publication in 1733, Pope had made a good many enemies, mostly small-minded men who awaited a chance to do him harm. In order to misdirect their ire and draw their praise, he published three works under his own name shortly before the anonymous appearance of the *Essay*. The results of this well-conceived little strategy must have pleased Pope. Several of his opponents, assuming he could not have issued the *Essay* as well as three other books is so short a space, jumped at the chance to displace his reputation by lauding the unknown author to the skies. In a few instances the encomia were so full and so explicit they could not be tempered very plausibly after Pope showed his hand. But he required no such effort to win the approval of English readers at large. From the first they accepted the poem as a full and brilliant statement of the plight of humanity as it considers the nature and power of its creator, the multifarious world in which it finds itself, and its own unsettled range of passion and thought. Little bothered by questions about philosophical consistency or ideas remotely heretical in implication, his countrymen believed the poet expressed on the one hand a sane man's faith in the essential orderliness (despite contrary appearances) of the world and human experience, and on the other, the mature man's sense for the point at which rationally perceivable truth merges with the unfathomable.

Matters were different on the continent, however, where in 1736 the poem was first translated (inaccurately and into prose) by the Frenchman Silhouette, who in his preface raised doubts about the orthodoxy of the piece. Among later French commentators these doubts became charges; but it was not until Silhouette's version of the *Essay* reached the Swiss professor J. P. de Crousaz, a teacher of theology and logic, that real damage was done. He offered ponderous proofs that

Pope was logically inconsistent, and he demonstrated that from the principle of plenitude some sort of fatalism might be derived. The critic's credentials and the sheer weight of his proofs were impressive (however irrelevant to the spirit of the poem). At the same time, while ostensibly distinguishing Pope from the rational naturalists Spinoza and Leibniz, Crousaz in fact involved the poet in a heretical association with these two philosophers, who, using variations on the principle of plenitude, had done a great deal to strip God of his moral qualitities by identifying him with the mathematical order of nature itself. Pope, out of his element, experienced considerable embarrassment, until William Warburton, in a series of six letters, 1738–1739, to which a seventh was added in 1740, offered a cogent defense of the *Essay*, arguing that the principle of plenitude had been accepted by the Church fathers from earliest times. In so doing, he rendered the poet's use of it acceptable. Pope was grateful, and Warburton subsequently became his literary executor and the first editor of his works.

The *Essay* has suffered one other kind of attack over the years. Not only has its originality been questioned, but its principal ideas have been said to derive from certain specific sources in addition to the works of the two philosophers noted above. Generally these include Bolingbroke, one-time Tory minister, and the poet's close friend, who indulged interests in politics, religion, and ethics—which in a way measure Pope's range of subject in *An Essay on Man*; the Third Earl of Shaftesbury, who wrote a series of essays, *Characteristics*, which treats, among other things, the integration of the parts of creation and man's aesthetically based love of the world—the first of these ideas being in a general way important in Pope's composition; and William King, a high-ranking Anglican divine, who produced a much-read theodicy, *De Origine Mali*, which inevitably uses many of the same general arguments Pope uses in explaining evil. But modern studies indicate that although Pope may use a few of the views of Bolingbroke, Shaftesbury, and King, he has no interest in those opinions which one thinks of as epitomizing or as representing these three of his predecessors; it is simply that some of his interests coincided with some of their interests to the extent that some similarity of ideas was almost certain to occur. When one adds to this that many of the attitudes Pope might have drawn from them were available in classical, Medieval, or Renaissance authors, and in the coffee-house conversation of his own day, it becomes all but certain that he owes them no specific debt.

It is difficult for men of the twentieth century to understand the hold

An Essay on Man had on their ancestors of the eighteenth; it was far and away the most popular poem of the day. Probably no full explanation of the fact is possible, nor would it have been by Pope's contemporaries. Nevertheless it seems correct to stress this popularity and to suggest a few reasons that may have accounted for it. When Milton set out in *Paradise Lost* to "justify the ways of God to Men" (I, 26), he sought to *explain*, largely by traditional means, the covenant that bound the two levels of being, earthly and heavenly. The result, however, was less a satisfactory theodicy than an aesthetically rich epic with as vast a scope as the universe itself; and the work was received accordingly. Pope's decision to "*vindicate* the ways of God to man" (I, 16) suggests that the Age of Reason had in some sense indicted the Almighty, Who was therefore in need of a full and aggressive defense. Pope's first triumph, it would seem, resulted from his ability to gauge properly God's predicament—in the eyes of eighteenth-century man at least. His second was to employ the kind of argument that would most appeal to his fellows. One notices again a marked contrast to Milton. Whereas the older poet draws upon traditional materials so heavily that the weight of allusion conveys the sense that centuries of lore have been compacted, Pope's *Essay* contains very few concrete references to the past. Indeed, the much shorter *Windsor Forest* is more allusive. In actual fact the *Essay* reveals countless traces of venerable orthodoxy, but Pope creates the impression of arguing in favor of a religious view in non-religious terms—of arguing by means of common sense and reason, not received opinion. No doubt many of his contemporaries enjoyed poetry rich in allusion, and no doubt many accepted religious arguments based on revelation. But it seems that most were strongly drawn by the guarantee of order and security implicit in a universe formed by God only if that universe could be characterized in the plausible terms growing out of and suggesting man's general experience. It almost inevitably follows that inconsistencies of logic would occur—that paradoxes would be required in such an attempt, because, from the viewpoint of the man who lives it, life is not an abstraction logically limited and directed; it comes much closer to being "a mighty maze, but not without a plan."

TEXT. *The Works of Alexander Pope, Esq.*, ed. William Warburton (9 vols., London, 1751).

An Essay on Man

In Four Epistles

TO H. ST. JOHN, LORD BOLINGBROKE

Argument of Epistle I

Of the Nature and State of Man with respect to the Universe

OF Man *in the abstract.*—I. *That we can judge only with regard to our* own system, *being ignorant of the* relations *of systems and things,* v 17, &c. II. *That Man is not to be deemed* imperfect, *but a Being suited to his* place *and* rank *in the creation, agreeable to the* general Order *of things, and conformable to* Ends *and* Relations *to him unknown,* v 35, &c. III. *That it is partly upon his* ignorance *of* future *events, and partly upon the* hope *of a future* state, *that all his happiness in the present depends,* v 77, &c. IV. *The* pride *of aiming at more knowledge, and pretending to more Perfection, the cause of Man's error and misery. The* impiety *of putting himself in the place of* God, *and judging of the fitness or unfitness, perfection or imperfection, justice or injustice of his dispensations,* v 109, &c. V. *The* absurdity *of conceiting himself the* final *cause of the creation, or expecting that perfection in the* moral *world, which is not in the* natural, v 131, &c. VI. *The* unreasonableness *of his complaints against* Providence, *while on the one hand he demands the Perfections of the Angels, and on the other the bodily qualifications of the Brutes; though, to possess any of the* sensitive *faculties in a higher degree, would render him miserable,* v 173, &c. VII. *That throughout the whole visible world, an* universal *order and* gradation *in the sensual and mental faculties is observed, which causes a* subordination *of creature to creature, and of all creatures to Man. The gradations of* sense, instinct, thought, reflection, reason; *that* Reason *alone countervails all the other faculties,* v 207. VIII. *How much farther this* order *and* subordination *of living creatures may extend, above and below us; were any part of which broken, not that part only, but the whole connected* creation *must be destroyed,* v 233. IX. *The* extravagance, madness, *and* pride *of such a desire,* v 250. X. *The consequence of all, the* absolute submission *due to Providence, both as to our* present *and* future state, v 281, &c. *to the end.*

Epistle I

AWAKE, my ST. JOHN! leave all meaner things
To low ambition, and the pride of Kings.
Let us (since Life can little more supply

653

Than just to look about us and to die)
Expatiate free o'er all this scene of Man;   5
A mighty maze! but not without a plan;
A Wild, where weeds and flow'rs promiscuous shoot;
Or Garden, tempting with forbidden fruit.
Together let us beat this ample field,
Try what the open, what the covert yield;   10
The latent tracts, the giddy heights, explore
Of all who blindly creep, or sightless soar;
Eye Nature's walks, shoot Folly as it flies,
And catch the Manners living as they rise;
Laugh where we must, be candid where we can;   15
But vindicate the ways of God to Man.
    I. Say first, of God above, or Man below,
What can we reason, but from what we know?
Of Man, what see we but his station here,
From which to reason, or to which refer?   20
Thro' worlds unnumber'd tho' the God be known,
'Tis ours to trace him only in our own.
He, who thro' vast immensity can pierce,
See worlds on worlds compose one universe,
Observe how system into system runs,   25
What other planets circle other suns,
What vary'd Being peoples ev'ry star,
May tell why Heav'n has made us as we are.
But of this frame the bearings, and the ties,
The strong connections, nice dependencies,   30
Gradations just, has thy pervading soul
Look'd thro'? or can a part contain the whole?
    Is the great chain, that draws all to agree,
And drawn supports, upheld by God, or thee?
    II. Presumptuous Man! the reason wouldst thou find,   35
Why form'd so weak, so little, and so blind?
First, if thou canst, the harder reason guess,
Why form'd no weaker, blinder, and no less?
Ask of thy mother earth, why oaks are made
Taller or stronger than the weeds they shade?   40
Or ask of yonder argent fields above,
Why Jove's Satellites are less than Jove?
    Of Systems possible, if 'tis confest
That Wisdom infinite must form the best,
Where all must full or not coherent be,   45
And all that rises, rise in due degree;
Then, in the scale of reas'ning life, 'tis plain,
There must be, somewhere, such a rank as Man;
And all the question (wrangle e'er so long)
Is only this, if God has plac'd him wrong?   50

Respecting Man, whatever wrong we call,
May, must be right, as relative to all.
In human works, tho' labour'd on with pain,
A thousand movements scarce one purpose gain;
In God's, one single can its end produce; 55
Yet serves to second too some other use.
So Man, who here seems principal alone,
Perhaps acts second to some sphere unknown,
Touches some wheel, or verges to some goal;
'Tis but a part we see, and not a whole. 60
   When the proud steed shall know why Man restrains
His fiery course, or drives him o'er the plains;
When the dull Ox, why now he breaks the clod,
Is now a victim, and now Ægypt's God:
Then shall Man's pride and dulness comprehend 65
His actions', passions', being's, use and end;
Why doing, suff'ring, check'd, impell'd; and why
This hour a slave, the next a deity.
   Then say not Man's imperfect, Heav'n in fault;
Say rather, Man's as perfect as he ought: 70
His knowledge measur'd to his state and place;
His time a moment, and a point his space.
If to be perfect in a certain sphere,
What matter, soon or late, or here or there?
The blest to day is as completely so, 75
As who began a thousand years ago.
   III. Heav'n from all creatures hides the book of Fate,
All but the page prescrib'd, their present state;
From brutes what men, from men what spirits know:
Or who could suffer Being here below? 80
The lamb thy riot dooms to bleed to-day,
Had he thy Reason, would he skip and play?
Pleas'd to the last, he crops the flow'ry food,
And licks the hand just rais'd to shed his blood.
Oh blindness to the future! kindly giv'n, 85
That each may fill the circle mark'd by Heav'n;
Who sees with equal eye, as God of all,
A hero perish, or a sparrow fall,
Atoms or systems into ruin hurl'd,
And now a bubble burst, and now a world. 90
   Hope humbly then; with trembling pinions soar;
Wait the great teacher Death; and God adore.
What future bliss, he gives not thee to know,
But gives that Hope to be thy blessing now.
Hope springs eternal in the human breast: 95

64. *Ægypt's God:* Apis, the sacred bull,   god Ptah of Memphis.
was thought to be an incarnation of the

Man never Is, but always To be blest:
The soul, uneasy and confin'd from home,
Rests and expatiates in a life to come.
   Lo, the poor Indian! whose untutor'd mind
Sees God in clouds, or hears him in the wind;   100
His soul, proud Science never taught to stray
Far as the solar walk, or milky way;
Yet simple Nature to his hope has giv'n,
Behind the cloud-topt hill, an humbler heav'n;
Some safer world in depth of woods embrac'd,   105
Some happier island in the watry waste,
Where slaves once more their native land behold,
No fiends torment, no Christians thirst for gold.
To Be, contents his natural desire,
He asks no Angel's wing, no Seraph's fire;   110
But thinks, admitted to that equal sky,
His faithful dog shall bear him company.
   IV. Go, wiser thou! and, in thy scale of sense,
Weigh thy Opinion against Providence;
Call imperfection what thou fancy'st such,   115
Say, here he gives too little, there too much;
Destroy all creatures for they sport or gust,
Yet cry, If Man's unhappy, God's unjust;
If Man alone ingross not Heav'n's high care,
Alone made perfect here, immortal there: 120
Snatch from his hand the balance and the rod,
Re-judge his justice, be the GOD of GOD.
In Pride, in reas'ning Pride, our error lies;
All quit their sphere, and rush into the skies.
Pride still is aiming at the blest abodes,   125
Men would be Angels, Angels would be Gods.
Aspiring to be Gods, if Angels fell,
Aspiring to be Angels, Men rebel;
And who but wishes to invert the laws
Of ORDER, sins against th'Eternal Cause.   130
   V. Ask for what end the heav'nly bodies shine,
Earth for whose use? Pride answers, " 'Tis for mine:
For me kind Nature wakes her genial pow'r,
Suckles each herb, and spreads out ev'ry flow'r;
Annual for me, the grape, the rose renew   135
The juice nectareous, and the balmy dew;
For me, the mine a thousand treasures beings;
For me, health gushes from a thousand springs;
Seas roll to waft me, suns to light me rise;
My foot-stool earth, my canopy the skies."   140
    But errs not Nature from this gracious end,
From burning suns when livid deaths descend,

When earthquakes swallow, or when tempests sweep
Towns to one grave, whole nations to the deep?
"No ('tis reply'd) the first Almighty Cause   145
Acts not by partial, but by gen'ral laws;
Th'exceptions few; some change since all began,
And what created perfect?"—Why then Man?
If the great end be human Happiness,
Then Nature deviates; and can Man do less?   150
As much that end a constant course requires
Of show'rs and sun-shine, as of Man's desires;
As much eternal springs and cloudless skies,
As Men for ever temp'rate, calm, and wise.
If plagues or earthquakes break not Heav'n's design,   155
Why then a Borgia, or a Catiline?
Who knows but he, whose hand the light'ning forms,
Who heaves old Ocean, and who wings the storms,
Pours fierce Ambition in a Cæsar's mind,
Or turns young Ammon loose to scourge mankind?   160
From pride, from pride, our very reas'ning springs;
Account for moral, as for nat'ral things:
Why charge we Heav'n in those, in these acquit?
In both, to reason right is to submit.
    Better for Us, perhaps, it might appear,   165
Were there all harmony, all virtue here;
That never air or ocean felt the wind;
That never passion discompos'd the mind.
But ALL subsists by elemental strife;
And Passions are the elements of Life.   170
The gen'ral ORDER, since the whole began,
Is kept in Nature, and is kept in Man.
    VI. What would this Man? Now upward will he soar,
And little less than Angel, would be more;
Now looking downwards, just as griev'd appears   175
To want the strength of bulls, the fur of bears.
Made for his use all creatures if he call,
Say what their use, had he the pow'rs of all?
Nature to these, without profusion, kind,
The proper organs, proper pow'rs assign'd;   180
Each seeming want compensated of course,
Here with degrees of swiftness, there of force;
All in exact proportion to the state;
Nothing to add, and nothing to abate.

156. *Borgia, Catiline:* The Borgias were
a powerful Italian Renaissance family,
known for their unscrupulous behavior in
public and in private life; Catiline was an
impoverished Roman patrician, who led
an unsuccessful revolution, which ended
with his death in 62 B.C.

160. *Young Ammon:* Alexander the
Great, who visited the priest of the
Egyptian god Ammon and was thereafter
recognized as that god's son.

Each beast, each insect, happy in its own;   185
Is Heav'n unkind to Man, and Man alone?
Shall he alone, whom rational we call,
Be pleas'd with nothing, if not bless'd with all?
    The bliss of Man (could Pride that blessing find)
Is not to act or think beyond mankind;   190
No pow'rs of body or of soul to share,
But what his nature and his state can bear.
Why has not a Man a microscopic eye?
For this plain reason, Man is not a Fly.
Say what the use, were finer optics giv'n,   195
T'inspect a mite, not comprehend the heav'n?
Or touch, if tremblingly alive all o'er,
To smart and agonize at ev'ry pore?
Or quick effluvia darting thro' the brain,
Die of a rose in aromatic pain?   200
If nature thunder'd in his op'ning ears,
And stunn'd him with the music of the spheres,
How would he wish that Heav'n had left him still
The whisp'ring Zephyr, and the purling rill?
Who finds not Providence all good and wise,   205
Alike in what it gives, and what it denies?
    VII. Far as Creation's ample range extends,
The scale of sensual, mental pow'rs ascends:
Marks how it mounts, to Man's imperial race,
From the green myriads in the peopled grass: 210
What modes of sight betwixt each wide extreme,
The mole's dim curtain, and the lynx's beam:
Of smell, the headlong lioness between,
And hound sagacious on the tainted green:
Of hearing, from the life that fills the flood,   215
To that which warbles thro' the vernal wood:
The spider's touch, how exquisitely fine!
Feels at each thread, and lives along the line:
In the nice bee, what sense so subtly true
From pois'nous herbs extracts the healing dew?   220
How Instinct varies in the grov'ling swine,
Compar'd, half-reas'ning elephant, with thine!
'Twixt that, and Reason, what a nice barrier;
For ever sep'rate, yet for ever near!
Remembrance and Reflection how ally'd;   225
What thin partitions Sense from Thought divide:
And Middle natures, how they long to join,
Yet never pass th'insuperable line!

202. *Music of the spheres:* The orderly
(predictable) movement of the heavenly
bodies was thought to produce music, which
could be heard by angels, but not by men.
    204. *Zephyr:* The west wind, known
for its soft, gentle quality.

Without this just gradation, could they be
Subjected, these to those, or all to thee?   230
The pow'rs of all subdu'd by thee alone,
Is not thy Reason all these pow'rs in one?
   VIII. See, thro' this air, this ocean, and this earth,
All matter quick, and bursting into birth.
Above, how high, progressive life may go!   235
Around, how wide! how deep extend below!
Vast chain of Being! which from God began,
Natures æthereal, human, angel, man,
Beast, bird, fish, insect, what no eye can see,
No glass can reach; from Infinite to thee,   240
From thee to Nothing.—On superior pow'rs
Were we to press, inferior might on ours:
Or in the full creation leave a void,
Where, one step broken, the great scale's destroy'd:
From Nature's chain whatever link you strike,   245
Tenth or ten thousandth, breaks the chain alike.
   And, if each system in gradation roll,
Alike, essential to th'amazing Whole,
The least confusion but in one, not all
That system only, but the Whole must fall.   250
Let Earth unbalanc'd from her orbit fly,
Planets and Suns run lawless thro' the sky;
Let ruling Angels from their spheres be hurl'd,
Being on Being wreck'd, and world on world;
Heav'n's whole foundations to their centre nod,   255
And Nature trembles to the throne of God.
All this dread ORDER break—for whom? for thee?
Vile worm!—oh Madness! Pride! Impiety!
   IX. What if the foot, ordain'd the dust to tread,
Or hand, to toil, aspir'd to be the head?   260
What if the head, the eye, or ear repin'd
To serve mere engines to the ruling Mind?
Just as absurd for any part to claim
To be another, in this gen'ral frame:
Just as absurd, to mourn the tasks or pains,   265
The great directing MIND of ALL ordains.
   All are but parts of one stupendous whole,
Whose body Nature is, and God the soul;
   That, chang'd thro' all, and yet in all the same,
Great in the earth, as in th'æthereal frame;   270
Warms in the sun, refreshes in the breeze,
Glows in the stars, and blossoms in the trees,

---

259 ff. *What if the foot . . . :* Here begins
an argument used by St. Paul, I Cor.
12:15–21, by Plutarch's Menenius Agrippa
in the life of Caius Martius Coriolanus,
and by Shakespeare, *Coriolanus*, I, i, 99 ff.,
who closely follows Plutarch in this regard.

Lives thro' all life, extends thro' all extent,
Spreads undivided, operates unspent,
Breathes in our soul, informs our mortal part,   275
As full, as perfect, in a hair as heart;
As full, as perfect, in vile Man that mourns,
As the rapt Seraph that adores and burns;
To him no high, no low, no great, no small;
He fills, he bounds, connects, and equals all.   280
    X. Cease then, nor ORDER Imperfection name:
Our proper bliss depends on what we blame.
Know thy own point: This kind, this due degree
Of blindness, weakness, Heav'n bestows on thee.
Submit.—In this, or any other sphere,   285
Secure to be as blest as thou canst bear:
Safe in the hand of one disposing Pow'r,
Or in the natal, or the mortal hour.
All Nature is but Art, unknown to thee;
All Chance, Direction, which thou canst not see;   290
All Discord, Harmony not understood;
All partial Evil, universal Good:
And, spite of Pride, in erring Reason's spite,
One truth is clear, WHATEVER IS, is RIGHT.

Argument of Epistle II

Of the Nature and State of Man with respect to Himself, as an Individual

I. THE business of Man not to pry into God, but to study himself. His Middle
Nature; his Powers and Frailties, v 1 to 18. The Limits of his Capacity, v 19,
&c. II. The two Principles of Man, Self-love and Reason, both necessary, v 53,
&c. Self-love the stronger, and why, v 67, &c. Their end the same, v 81, &c.
III. The PASSIONS, and their use, v 93 to 130. The predominant Passion,
and its force, v 132 to 160. Its Necessity, in directing Men to different purposes,
v 165, &c. Its providential Use, in fixing our Principle, and ascertaining our
Virtue, v 177. IV. Virtue and Vice joined in our mixed Nature; the limits
near, yet things separate and evident: What is the Office of Reason, v 202 to 216.
V. How odious Vice in itself, and how we deceive ourselves into it, v 217. VI.
That, however, the Ends of Providence and general Good are answered in our
Passions and Imperfections, v 238, &c. How usefully these are distributed to
all Orders of Men, v 241. How useful they are to Society, v 251. And to the
Individuals, v 263. In every state, and every age of life, v 273, &c.

278. *Rapt Seraph:* A celestial being thought of as fiery—a purifying minister of Jehovah. Such a being can perceive the ultimate reality of God's order, according to St. Thomas Aquinas.

Epistle II

I. KNOW then thyself, presume not to God to scan;
The proper study of Mankind is Man.
Plac'd on this isthmus of a middle state,
A Being darkly wise, and rudely great:
With too much knowledge for the Sceptic side,   5
With too much weakness for the Stoic's pride,
He hangs between; in doubt to act, or rest;
In doubt to deem himself a God, or Beast;
In doubt his Mind or Body to prefer;
Born but to die, and reas'ning but to err;   10
Alike in ignorance, his reason such,
Whether he thinks too little, or too much:
Chaos of Thought and Passion, all confus'd;
Still by himself abus'd, or disabus'd;
Created half to rise, and half to fall;   15
Great lord of all things, yet a prey to all;
Sole judge of Truth, in endless Error hurl'd:
The glory, jest, and riddle of the world!
    Go, wond'rous creature! mount where Science guides,
Go, measure earth, weigh air, and state the tides,   20
Instruct the planets in what orbs to run,
Correct old Time, and regulate the Sun;
Go, soar with Plato to th'empyreal sphere,
To the first good, first perfect, and first fair;
Or tread the mazy round his follow'rs trod,   25
And quitting sense call imitating God;
As Eastern priests in giddy circles run,
And turn their heads to imitate the Sun.
Go, teach Eternal Wisdom how to rule—
Then drop into thyself, and be a fool!   30
    Superior beings, when of late they saw
A mortal Man unfold all Nature's law,
Admir'd such wisdom in an earthly shape,
And shew'd a NEWTON as we shew an Ape.
    Could he, whose rules the rapid Comet bind,   35
Describe or fix one movement of his Mind?
Who saw its fires here rise, and there descend,
Explain his own beginning, or his end?
Alas what wonder! Man's superior part
Uncheck'd may rise, and climb from art to art;   40

---

22. *Correct old Time:* Scholars do not agree upon the precise meaning here. Generally, however, it is thought that Pope makes a distinction between old views about chronology and the more accurate measurement of seventeenth- and eighteenth-century scientists.

23–26. *Soar with Plato . . . imitating God:* It seems likely that Pope here censures religious-philosophical enthusiasm more than he rejects Platonic and neo-Platonic ideas.

But when his own great work is but begun,
What Reason weaves, by Passion is undone.
   Trace Science then, with Modesty thy guide;
First strip off all her equipage of Pride;
Deduct what is but Vanity, or Dress,   45
Or Learning's Luxury, or Idleness;
Or tricks to shew the stretch of human brain,
Mere curious pleasure, or ingenious pain;
Expunge the whole, or lop th'excrescent parts
Of all our Vices have created Arts;   50
Then see how little the remaining sum,
Which serv'd the past, and must the times to come!
   II. Two Principles in human nature reign;
Self-love, to urge, and Reason, to restrain;
Nor this a good, nor that a bad we call,   55
Each works its end, to move or govern all:
And to their proper operation still,
Ascribe all Good; to their improper, Ill.
   Self-love, the spring of motion, acts the soul;
Reason's comparing balance rules the whole.   60
Man, but for that, no action could attend,
And, but for this, were active to no end;
Fix'd like a plant on his peculiar spot,
To draw nutrition, propagate, and rot;
Or, meteor-like, flame lawless thro' the void,   65
Destroying others, by himself destroy'd.
   Most strength the moving principle requires;
Active its talk, it prompts, impels, inspires.
Sedate and quiet the comparing lies,
Form'd but to check, delib'rate, and advise.   70
Self-love still stronger, as its objects nigh;
Reason's at distance, and in prospect lie:
That sees immediate good by present sense;
Reason, the future and the consequence.
Thicker than arguments, temptations throng,   75
At best more watchful this, but that more strong.
The action of the stronger to suspend
Reason still use, to Reason still attend:
Attention, habit and experience gains;
Each strengthens Reason, and Self-love restrains.   80
   Let subtle schoolmen teach these friends to fight,
More studious to divide than to unite;
And Grace and Virtue, Sense and Reason split,
With all the rash dexterity of wit.
Wits, just like Fools, at war about a name,   85
Have full as oft no meaning, or the same.
Self-love and Reason to one end aspire,
Pain their aversion, Pleasure their desire;

But greedy That, its object would devour,
This taste the honey, and not wound the flow'r: 90
Pleasure, or wrong or rightly understood,
Our greatest evil, or our greatest good.
    III. Modes of Self-love the Passions we may call:
'Tis real good, or seeming, moves them all;
But since not ev'ry good we can divide,   95
And Reason bids us for our own provide;
Passions, tho' selfish, if their means be fair,
List under Reason, and deserve her care;
Those, that imparted, court a nobler aim,
Exalt their kind, and take some Virtue's name.   100
    In lazy Apathy let Stoics boast
Their Virtue fix'd; 'tis fix'd as in a frost,
Contracted all, retiring to the breast;
But strength of mind is Exercise, not Rest:
The rising tempest puts in act the soul,   105
Parts it may ravage, but preserves the whole.
On life's vast ocean diversely we sail,
Reason the card, but Passion is the gale;
Nor God alone in the still calm we find,
He mounts the storm, and walks upon the wind.   110
    Passions, like Elements, tho' born to fight,
Yet, mix'd and soften'd, in his work unite:
These 'tis enough to temper and employ;
But what composes Man, can Man destroy?
Suffice that Reason keep to Nature's road,   115
Subject, compound them, follow her and God.
Love, Hope, and Joy, fair pleasure's smiling train,
Hate, Fear, and Grief, the family of pain;
These mix'd with art, and to due bounds confin'd,
Make and maintain the balance of the mind: 120
The lights and shades, whose well accorded strife
Gives all the strength and colour of our life.
    Pleasures are ever in our hands or eyes;
And when, in act, they cease, in prospect, rise;
Present to grasp, and future still to find,   125
The whole employ of body and of mind.
All spread their charms, but charm not all alike;
On diff'rent senses diff'rent objects strike;
Hence diff'rent Passions more or less inflame,
As strong or weak, the organs of the frame;   130
And hence one MASTER PASSION in the breast,
Like Aaron's serpent, swallows up the rest.

108. *Card:* The face of a compass, with its directional markings, made of stiff paper in the eighteenth century.
132. *Aaron's serpent:* In Exod. 7:10–12, Aaron turns his rod into a serpent, which swallows up the similarly transformed rods of Pharaoh's magicians.

As Man, perhaps, the moment of his breath,
Receives the lurking principle of death;
The young disease, that must subdue at length,   135
Grows with his growth, and strengthens with his strength:
So, cast and mingled with his very frame,
The Mind's disease, its RULING PASSION came;
Each vital humour which should feed the whole,
Soon flows to this, in body and in soul.   140
Whatever warms the heart, or fills the head,
As the mind opens, and its functions spread,
Imagination plies her dang'rous art,
And pours it all upon the peccant part.
    Nature its mother, Habit is its nurse;   145
Wit, Spirit, Faculties, but make it worse;
Reason itself but gives it edge and pow'r;
As Heav'n's blest beam turns vinegar more sowr;
    We, wretched subjects tho' to lawful sway,
In this weak queen, some fav'rite still obey.   150
Ah! if she lend not arms, as well as rules,
What can she more than tell us we are fools?
Teach us to mourn our Nature, not to mend,
A sharp accuser, but a helpless friend!
Or from a judge turn pleader, to persuade   155
The choice we make, or justify it made;
Proud of an easy conquest all along,
She but removes weak passions for the strong:
So, when small humours gather to a gout,
The doctor fancies he has driv'n them out.   160
    Yes, Nature's road must ever be prefer'd;
Reason is here no guide, but still a guard:
'Tis hers to rectify, not overthrow,
And treat this passion more as friend than foe:
A mightier Pow'r the strong direction sends,   165
And sev'ral Men impels to sev'ral ends.
Like varying winds, by other passions tost,
This drives them constant to a certain coast.
Let pow'r or knowledge, gold or glory, please,
Or (oft more strong than all) the love of ease;   170
Thro' life 'tis follow'd, ev'n at life's expence;
The merchant's toil, the sage's indolence,
The monk's humility, the hero's pride,
All, all alike, find Reason on their side.
    Th' Eternal Art educing good from ill,   175
Grafts on this Passion our best principle:
'Tis thus the Mercury of Man is fix'd,
Strong grows the Virtue with his nature mix'd;
The dross cements what else were too refin'd,

And in one interest body acts with mind.   180
   As fruits, ungrateful to the planter's care,
On savage stocks inserted, learn to bear;
The surest Virtues thus from Passions shoot,
Wild Nature's vigor working at the root.
What crops of wit and honesty appear   185
From spleen, from obstinacy, hate, or fear!
See anger, zeal and fortitude supply;
Ev'n av'rice, prudence; sloth, philosophy;
Lust, thro' some certain strainers well refin'd,
Is gentle love, and charms all womankind;   190
Envy, to which th'ignoble mind's a slave,
Is emulation in the learn'd or brave;
Nor Virtue, male or female, can we name,
Bur what will grow on Pride, or grow on Shame.
   Thus Nature gives us (let it check our pride)   195
The virtue nearest to our vice ally'd;
Reason the byas turns to good from ill,
And Nero reigns a Titus, if he will.
The fiery soul abhor'd in Catiline,
In Decius charms, in Curtius is divine.   200
The same ambition can detroy or save,
And makes a patriot as it makes a knave.
   [IV.] This light and darkness in our chaos join'd,
What shall divide? The God within the mind.
   Extremes in Nature equal ends produce,   205
In Man they join to some mysterious use;
Tho' each by turns the other's bound invade,
As, in some well-wrought picture, light and shade,
And oft so mix, the diff'rence is too nice
Where ends the Virtue, or begins the Vice.   210
   Fools! who from hence into the notion fall,
That Vice or Virtue there is none at all.
If white and black blend, soften, and unite
A thousand ways, is there no black or white?
Ask your own heart, and nothing is so plain;   215
'Tis to mistake them, costs the time and pain.
   [V.] Vice is a monster of so frightful mien,
As, to be hated, needs but to be seen;
Yet seen too oft, familiar with her face,

198. *Nero reigns a Titus:* Like Nero, Titus had a strong sensual nature; but unlike him, Titus controlled it admirably when he became emperor.

200. *Decius, Curtius:* Though both these Romans acted precipitously, their deeds were constructive. Decius, while leading his troops, was informed by a vision that the general of one side and the army of the other would be destroyed; so he plunged into the thick of things to his death, and his army triumphed. Curtius learned that a chasm in the forum could be filled only if Rome's greatest treasure were thrown into it; regarding himself as a representative of his country's youth, he leaped into the opening.

We first endure, then pity, then embrace.   220
But where th'Extreme of Vice, was ne'er agreed:
Ask where's the North? at York, 'tis on the Tweed;
In Scotland, at the Orcades; and there,
At Greenland, Zembla, or the Lord knows where.
No creature owns it in the first degree,   225
But thinks his neighbour farther gone than he;
Ev'n those who dwell beneath its very zone,
Or never feel the rage, or never own;
What happier natures shrink at with affright,
The hard inhabitant contends is right.   230
    VI. Virtuous and vicious ev'ry Man must be,
Few in th'extreme, but all in the degree;
The rogue and fool by fits is fair and wise,
And ev'n the best, by fits, what they despise.
'Tis but by parts we follow good or ill,   235
For, Vice or Virtue, Self directs it still;
Each individual seeks a sev'ral goal;
But HEAV'N's great view is One, and that the Whole.
That counter-works each folly and caprice;
That disappoints th'effect of ev'ry vice;   240
That, happy frailties to all ranks apply'd;
Shame to the virgin, to the matron pride,
Fear to the statesman, rashness to the chief,
To kings presumption, and to crowds belief;
That, Virtue's ends from Vanity can raise,   245
Which seeks no int'rest, no reward but praise;
And build on wants, and on defects of mind,
The joy, the peace, the glory of Mankind.
    Heav'n forming each on other to depend,
A master, or a servant, or a friend,   250
Bids each on other for assistance call,
'Till one Man's weakness grows the strength of all.
Wants, frailties, passions, closer still ally
The common int'rest, or endear the tie.
To these we owe true friendship, love sincere,   255
Each home-felt joy that life inherits here;
Yet from the same we learn, in its decline,
Those joys, those loves, those int'rests to resign;
Taught half by Reason, half by mere decay,
To welcome death, and calmly pass away.   260
    Whate'er the Passion, knowledge, fame, or pelf,
Not one will charge his neighbour with himself.
The learn'd is happy nature to explore,
The fool is happy that he knows no more;
The rich is happy in the plenty giv'n,   265
The poor contents him with the care of Heav'n.

See the blind beggar dance, the cripple sing,
The sot a hero, lunatic a king;
The starving chemist in his golden views
Supremely blest, the poet in his Muse.   270
   See some strange comfort ev'ry state attend,
And Pride bestow'd on all, a common friend;
See some fit Passion ev'ry age supply,
Hope travels thro', nor quits us when we die.
   Behold the child, by Nature's kindly law,   275
Pleas'd with a rattle, tickled with a straw:
Some livelier play-thing gives his youth delight,
A little louder, but as empty quite:
Scarfs, garters, gold, amuse his riper stage,
And beads and pray'r-books are the toys of age: 280
Pleas'd with this bauble still, as that before;
'Till tir'd he sleeps, and Life's poor play is o'er.
   Mean-while Opinion gilds with varying rays
Those painted clouds that beautify our days;
Each want of happiness by Hope supply'd,   285
And each vacuity of sense by Pride:
These build as fast as knowledge can destroy;
In Folly's cup still laughs the bubble, joy;
One prospect lost, another still we gain;
And not a vanity is giv'n in vain;   290
Ev'n mean Self-love becomes by force divine,
The scale to measure others wants by thine.
See! and confess, one comfort still must rise,
'Tis this, Tho' Man's a fool, yet GOD IS WISE.

Argument of Epistle III

Of the Nature and State of Man with respect to Society

I. THE whole Universe one system of Society, v 7, &c. Nothing made wholly for itself, nor yet wholly for another, v 27. The happiness of Animals mutual, v 49. II. Reason or Instinct operate alike to the good of each Individual, v 79. Reason or Instinct operate also to Society, in all animals, v 109. III. How far Society carried by Instinct, v 115. How much farther by Reason, v 128. IV. Of that which is called the State of Nature, 144. Reason instructed by Instinct in the invention of Arts, v 166, and in the Forms of Society, v 176. V. Origin of Political Societies, v 196. Origin of Monarchy, v 207. Patriarchal government, v 212. VI. Origin of true Religion and Government, from the same principle, of Love, v 231, &c. Origin of Superstition and Tyranny, from the same principle, of Fear, v 237, &c. The Influence of Self-love operating to the social and public Good, v 266. Restoration of true Religion and Government on their first principle, v 285. Mixt Government, v 288. Various Forms of each, and the true end of all, v 300, &c.

Epistle III

HERE then we rest: "The Universal Cause
Acts to one end, but acts by various laws."
In all the madness of superfluous health,
The trim of pride, the impudence of wealth,
Let this great truth be present night and day;   5
But most be present, if we preach or pray.
 Look round our World; behold the chain of Love
Combining all below and all above.
See plastic Nature working to this end,
The single atoms each to other tend,   10
Attract, attracted to, the next in place
Form'd and impell'd its neighbour to embrace.
See Matter next, with various life endu'd,
Press to one centre still, the gen'ral Good.
See dying vegetables life sustain,   15
See life dissolving vegetate again:
All forms that perish other forms supply
(By turns we catch the vital breath, and die)
Like bubbles on the sea of Matter born,
They rise, they break, and to that sea return.   20
Nothing is foreign: Parts relate to whole;
One all-extending, all-preserving Soul
Connects each being, greatest with the least;
Made Beast in aid of Man, and Man of Beast;
All serv'd, all serving: nothing stands alone;   25
The chain holds on, and where it ends, unknown,
 Has God, thou fool! work'd solely for thy good,
Thy joy, thy pastime, thy attire, thy food?
Who for thy table feeds the wanton fawn,
For him as kindly spread the flow'ry lawn: 30
Is it for thee the lark ascends and sings?
Joy tunes his voice, joy elevates his wings:
Is it for thee the linnet pours his throat?
Loves of his own and raptures swell the note:
The bounding steed you pompously bestride,   35
Shares with his lord the pleasure and the pride:
Is thine alone the seed that strews the plain?
The birds of heav'n shall vindicate their grain:
Thine the full harvest of the golden year?
Part pays, and justly, the deserving steer: 40
The hog, that plows not nor obeys thy call,
Lives on the labours of this lord of all.
 Know, Nature's children all divide her care;
The fur that warms a monarch, warm'd a bear.
While Man exclaims, "See all things for my use!"   45

"See man for mine!" replies a pamper'd goose;
And just as short of reason he must fall,
Who thinks all made for one, not one for all.
    Grant that the pow'rful still the weak controul,
Be Man the Wit and Tyrant of the whole: 50
Nature that Tyrant checks; He only knows,
And helps, another creature's wants and woes.
Say, will the falcon, stooping from above,
Smit with her varying plumage, spare the dove?
Admires the jay the insect's gilded wings?   55
Or hears the hawk when Philomela sings?
Man cares for all: to birds he gives his woods,
To beasts his pastures, and to fish his floods;
For some his Int'rest prompts him to provide,
For more his pleasure, yet for more his pride: 60
All feed on one vain Patron, and enjoy
Th'extensive blessing of his luxury.
That very life his learned hunger craves,
He saves from famine, from the savage saves;
Nay, feasts the animal he dooms his feast,   65
And, 'till he ends the being, makes it blest;
Which sees no more the stroke, or feels the pain,
Than favour'd Man by touch etherial slain.
The creature had his feast of life before;
Thou too must perish, when thy feast is o'er!   70
    To each unthinking being, Heav'n a friend,
Gives not the useless knowledge of its end:
To Man imparts it; but with such a view
As, while he dreads it, makes him hope it too:
The hour conceal'd, and so remote the fear,   75
Death still draws nearer, never seeming near.
Great standing miracle! that Heav'n assign'd
Its only thinking thing this turn of mind.
    II. Whether with Reason, or with Instinct blest,
Know, all enjoy that pow'r which suits them best;   80
To bliss alike by that direction tend,
And find the means proportion'd to their end.
Say, where full Instinct is th'unerring guide,
What Pope or Council can they need beside?
Reason, however able, cool at best,   85
Cares not for service, or but serves when prest,
Stays 'till we call, and then not often near;
But honest Instinct comes a volunteer;
Sure never to o'er-shoot, but just to hit,
While still too wide or short is human Wit;   90
Sure by quick Nature happiness to gain,
Which heavier Reason labours at in vain.

This too serves always, Reason never long;
One must go right, the other may go wrong.
See then the acting and comparing pow'rs   95
One in their nature, which are two in ours;
And Reason raise o'er Instinct as you can,
In this 'tis God directs, in that 'tis Man.
    Who taught the nations of the field and wood
To shun their poison, and to chuse their food?   100
Prescient, the tides or tempests to withstand,
Build on the wave, or arch beneath the sand?
Who made the spider parallels design,
Sure as De-moivre, without rule or line?
Who bid the stork, Columbus-like, explore   105
Heav'ns not his own, and worlds unknown before?
Who calls the council, states the certain day,
Who forms the phalanx, and who points the way?
    III. God, in the nature of each being, founds
Its proper bliss, and sets its proper bounds: 110
But as he fram'd a Whole, the Whole to bless,
On mutual Wants built mutual Happiness:
So from the first, eternal ORDER ran,
And creature link'd to creature, man to man.
Whate'er of life all-quick'ning æther keeps,   115
Or breathes thro' air, or shoots beneath the deeps,
Or pours profuse on earth, one nature feeds
The vital flame, and swells the genial seeds.
Not Man alone, but all that roam the wood,
Or wing the sky, or roll along the flood,   120
Each loves itself, but not itself alone,
Each sex desires alike, 'till two are one.
Nor ends the pleasure with the fierce embrace;
They love themselves, a third time, in their race.
Thus beast and bird their common charge attend,   125
The mothers nurse it, and the sires defend;
The young dismiss'd to wander earth or air,
There stops the Instinct, and there ends the care;
The link dissolves, each seeks a fresh embrace,
Another love succeeds, another race.   130
A longer care Man's helpless kind demands;
That longer care contracts more lasting bands:
Reflection, Reason, still the ties improve,
At once extend the int'rest, and the love;
With choice we fix, with sympathy we burn;   135

---

104. *De-moivre:* Abraham Demoivre (1667–1754), a French mathematician, contributed to the theory of probability and helped to settle the contest between Newton and Leibniz concerning the priority of their inventions of fluxions, i.e., the calculus.

Each Virtue in each Passion takes its turn;
And still new needs, new helps, new habits rise,
That graft benevolence on charities.
Still as one brood, and as another rose,
These nat'ral love maintain'd, habitual those: 140
The last, scarce ripen'd into perfect Man,
Saw helpless him from whom their life began;
Mem'ry and fore-cast just returns engage,
That pointed back to youth, this on to age;
While pleasure, gratitude, and hope, combin'd,   145
Still spread the int'rest, and preserv'd the kind.
    IV. Nor think, in NATURE's STATE they blindly trod;
The state of Nature was the reign of God:
Self-love and Social at her birth began,
Union the bond of all things, and of Man.   150
Pride then was not; nor Arts, that Pride to aid;
Man walk'd with beast, joint tenant of the shade;
The same his table, and the same his bed;
No murder cloath'd him, and no murder fed.
In the same temple, the resounding wood,   155
All vocal beings hymn'd their equal God:
The shrine with gore unstain'd, with gold undrest,
Unbrib'd, unbloody, stood the blameless priest:
Heav'n's attribute was Universal Care,
And Man's prerogative to rule, but spare.   160
Ah! how unlike the man of times to come!
Of half that live the butcher and the tomb;
Who, foe to Nature, hears the gen'ral groan,
Murders their species, and betrays his own.
But just disease to luxury succeeds,   165
And ev'ry death it's own avenger breeds;
The Fury-passions from that blood began,
And turn'd on Man a fiercer savage, Man.
    See him from Nature rising slow to Art!
To copy Instinct then was Reason's part;   170
Thus then to Man the voice of Nature spake—
"Go, from the Creatures thy instructions take:
Learn from the birds what food the thickets yield;
Learn from the beasts the physic of the field;
Thy arts of building from the bee receive;   175
Learn of the mole to plow, the worm to weave;
Learn of the little Nautilus to sail,
Spread the thin oar, and catch the driving gale.

177. *Nautilus:* Pope, quoting Oppian, *Halieutica,* Lib. I, says of the fish: "They swim on the surface of the sea, on the back of their shells, which exactly resemble the hulk of a ship; they raise two feet like masts, and extend a membrane between, which serves as a sail; the other two feet they employ as oars at the side."

Here too all forms of social union find,
And hence let Reason, late, instruct Mankind: 180
Here subterranean works and cities see;
There towns aerial on the waving tree.
Learn each small People's genius, policies,
The Ant's republic, and the realm of Bees;
How those in common all their wealth bestow,   185
And Anarchy without confusion know;
And these for ever, tho' a Monarch reign,
Their sep'rate cells and properties maintain.
Mark what unvary'd laws preserve each state,
Laws wise as Nature, and as fix'd as Fate.   190
In vain thy Reason finer webs shall draw,
Entangle Justice in her net of Law,
And right, too rigid, harden into wrong;
Still for the strong too weak, the weak too strong.
Yet go! and thus o'er all the creatures sway,   195
Thus let the wiser make the rest obey;
And for those Arts mere Instinct could afford,
Be crown'd as Monarchs, or as Gods ador'd."
    V. Great Nature spoke; observant Men obey'd;
Cities were built, Societies were made: 200
Here rose one little state; another near
Grew by like means, and join'd, thro' love or fear.
Did here the trees with ruddier burdens bend,
And there the streams in purer rills descend?
What War could ravish, Commerce could bestow,   205
And he return'd a friend, who came a foe.
Converse and Love mankind might strongly draw,
When Love was Liberty, and Nature Law.
Thus States were form'd; the name of King unknown,
'Till common int'rest plac'd the sway in one.   210
'Twas VIRTUE ONLY (or in arts or arms,
Diffusing blessings, or averting harms)
The same which in a Sire the Sons obey'd,
A Prince the Father of a People made.
    VI. Till then, by Nature crown'd, each Patriarch sate,   215
King, priest, and parent of his growing state;
On him, their second Providence, they hung,
Their law his eye, their oracle his tongue.
He from the wond'ring furrow call'd the food,
Taught to command the fire, controul the flood,   220
Draw forth the monsters of th'abyss profound
Or fetch th'aerial eagle to the ground.
'Till drooping, sick'ning, dying they began
Whom they rever'd as God to mourn as Man:
Then, looking up from fire to fire, explor'd   225

One great first father, and that first ador'd.
Or plain tradition that this All begun,
Convey'd unbroken faith from sire to son;
The worker from the work distinct was known,
And simple Reason never sought but one: 230
E'er Wit oblique had broke that steddy light,
Man, like his Maker, saw that all was right;
To Virtue, in the paths of Pleasure, trod,
And own'd a Father when he own'd a God.
LOVE all the faith, and all th'allegiance then;   235
For Nature knew no right divine in Men,
No ill could fear in God; and understood
A sov'reign being but a sov'reign good.
True faith, true policy, united ran,
That was but love of God, and this of Man.   240
    Who first taught souls enslav'd, and realms undone,
Th'enormous faith of many made for one;
That proud exception to all Nature's laws,
T'invert the world, and counter-work its Cause?
Force first made Conquest, and that conquest, Law,   245
'Till Superstition taught the tyrant awe,
Then shar'd the Tyranny, then lent it aid,
And Gods of Conqu'rors, Slaves of Subjects made:
She 'midst the light'ning's blaze, and thunder's sound,
When rock'd the mountains, and when groan'd the ground,   250
She taught the weak to bend, the proud to pray,
To Pow'r unseen, and mightier far than they:
She, from the rending earth and bursting skies,
Saw Gods descend, and fiends infernal rise:
Here fix'd the dreadful, there the blest abodes;   255
Fear made her Devils, and weak Hope her Gods;
Gods partial, changeful, passionate, unjust,
Whose attributes were Rage, Revenge, or Lust;
Such as the souls of cowards might conceive,
And, form'd like tyrants, tyrants would believe.   260
Zeal then, not charity, became the guide,
And hell was built on spite, and heav'n on pride.
Then sacred seem'd th'etherial vault no more;
Altars grew marble then, and reek'd with gore:
Then first the Flamen tasted living food;   265
Next his grim idol smear'd with human blood;
With Heav'n's own thunders shook the world below,
And play'd the God an engine on his foe.
    So drives Self-love, thro' just and thro' unjust,
To one Man's pow'r, ambition, lucre, lust: 270

265. *Flamen:* A priest of the religion of
classical Rome.

The same Self-love, in all, becomes the cause
Of what restrains him, Government and Laws.
For, what one likes if others like as well,
What serves one will, when many wills rebel?
How shall he keep, what, sleeping or awake,   275
A weaker may surprise, a stronger take?
His safety must his liberty restrain:
All join to guard what each desires to gain.
Forc'd into virtue thus by Self-defence,
Ev'n Kings learn'd justice and benevolence: 280
Self-love forsook the path it first pursu'd,
And found the private in the public good.
    'Twas then, the studious head or gen'rous mind,
Follow'r of God or friend of human-kind,
Poet or Patriot, rose but to restore   285
The Faith and Moral, Nature gave before;
Re-lum'd her ancient light, not kindled new;
If not God's image, yet his shadow drew:
Taught Pow'r's due use to People and to Kings,
Taught nor to slack, nor strain its tender strings,   290
The less, or greater, set so justly true,
That touching one must strike the other too;
'Till jarring int'rests, of themselves create
Th'according music of a well-mix'd State.
Such is the World's great harmony, that springs   295
From Order, Union, full Consent of things:
Where small and great, where weak and mighty, made
To serve, not suffer, strengthen, not invade;
More pow'rful each as needful to the rest,
And, in proportion as it blesses, blest;   300
Draw to one point, and to one centre bring
Beast, Man, or Angel, Servant, Lord, or King.
    For Forms of Government let fools contest;
Whate'er is best administer'd is best:
For Modes of Faith let graceless zealots fight;   305
His can't be wrong whose life is in the right:
In Faith and Hope the world will disagree,
But all Mankind's concern is Charity:
All must be false that thwart this One great End;
And all of God, that bless Mankind or mend.   310
    Man, like the gen'rous vine, supported lives;
The strength he gains is from th'embrace he gives.
On their own Axis as the Planets run,
Yet make at once their circle round the Sun;
So two consistent motions act the Soul;   315
And one regards Itself, and one the Whole.
    Thus God and Nature link'd the gen'ral frame,
And bade Self-love and Social be the same.

Argument of Epistle IV

Of the Nature and State of Man with respect to Happiness

I. *FALSE Notions of Happiness, Philosophical and Popular, answered from* v 19 *to* 77. II. *It is the End of all Men, and attainable by all,* v 30. *God intends Happiness to be* equal; *and to be so, it must be* social, *since all particular Happiness depends on* general, *and since he governs by* general, *not particular Laws,* v 37. *As it is necessary for* Order, *and the peace and welfare of* Society, *that* external goods *should be* unequal, *Happiness is not made to consist in these,* v 51. *But, notwithstanding that inequality, the* balance of Happiness *among Mankind is kept even by Providence, by the two Passions of* Hope *and* Fear, v 70. III. *What the Happiness of* Individuals *is, as far as is consistent with the constitution of this world; and that the* good Man *has here the advantage,* v 77. *The error of imputing to Virtue what are only the calamities of* Nature, *or of* Fortune, v 94. IV. *The folly of expecting that God should alter his general Laws in favour of particulars,* v 121. V. *That we are not judges who are good; but that, whoever they are, they must be happiest,* v 133, &c. VI. *That* external goods *are not the proper rewards, but often inconsistent with, or destructive of Virtue,* v 165. *That even these can make no Man happy without Virtue: Instanced in* Riches, v 183. Honours, v 191. Nobility, v 203. Greatness, v 215. Fame, v 235. Superior Talents, v 257, &c. *With pictures of human Infelicity in Men possessed of them all,* v 267, &c. VII. *That Virtue only constitutes a Happiness, whose object is* universal, *and whose prospect* eternal, v 307, &c. *That the* perfection *of Virtue and Happiness consists in a* conformity *to the* Order *of* Providence *here, and a* Resignation *to it here and hereafter,* v 326, &c.

Epistle IV

OH Happiness! our being's end and aim!
Good, Pleasure, Ease, Content! whate'er thy name:
That something still which prompts th'eternal sigh,
For which we bear to live, or dare to die,
Which still so near us, yet beyond us lies,   5
O'er-look'd, seen double, by the fool, and wise.
Plant of celestial seed! if dropt below,
Say, in what mortal soil thou deign'st to grow?
Fair op'ning to some Court's propitious shine,
Or deep with di'monds in the flaming mine?   10
Twin'd with the wreaths Parnassian lawrels yield,
Or reap'd in iron harvests of the field?
Where grows?—where grows it not? If vain our toil,
We ought to blame the culture, not the soil:
Fix'd to no spot is Happiness sincere,   15
'Tis no where to be found, or ev'ry where;
'Tis never to be bought, but always free,

11. *Parnassian lawrels:* Wreaths of   accomplishment.
Parnassian laurels are tokens of a poet's

And fled from monarchs, St. John! dwells with thee.
  Ask of the Learn'd the way? The Learn'd are blind;
This bids to serve, and that to shun mankind;   20
Some place the bliss in action, some in ease,
Those call it Pleasure, and Contentment these;
Some sunk to Beasts, find pleasure end in pain;
Some swell'd to Gods, confess ev'n Virtue vain;
Or indolent, to each extreme they fall,   25
To trust in ev'ry thing, or doubt of all.
  Who thus define it, say they more or less
Than this, that Happiness is Happiness?
  Take Nature's path, and mad Opinion's leave;
All states can reach it, and all heads conceive;   30
Obvious her goods, in no extreme they dwell;
There needs but thinking right, and meaning well;
And mourn our various portions as we please,
Equal is Common Sense, and Common Ease.
  Remember, Man, "the Universal Cause   35
Acts not by partial, but by gen'ral laws";
And makes what Happiness we justly call
Subsist not in the good of one, but all.
There's not a blessing Individuals find,
But some way leans and hearkens to the kind: 40
No Bandit fierce, no Tyrant mad with pride,
No cavern'd Hermit, rests self-satisfy'd:
Who most to shun or hate Mankind pretend,
Seek an admirer, or would fix a friend:
Abstract what others feel, what others think,   45
All pleasures sicken, and all glories sink:
Each has his share; and who would more obtain,
Shall find, the pleasure pays not half the pain.
  Order is Heav'n's first law; and this confest,
Some are, and must be, greater than the rest,   50
More rich, more wise; but who infers from hence
That such are happier, shocks all common sense.
Heav'n to Mankind impartial we confess,
If all are equal in their Happiness:
But mutual wants this Happiness increase;   55
All Nature's diff'rence keeps all Nature's peace.
Condition, circumstance is not the thing;
Bliss is the same in subject or in king,
In who obtain defence, or who defend,
In him who is, or him who finds a friend: 60

18. *St. John:* Henry St. John, Viscount Bolingbroke, Tory statesman and philosopher, whom Pope much admired and whose friendship he much valued. With the Whigs in power after Anne's death in 1714, Pope thinks of the remnants of political virtue as residing in the retired minister.

Heav'n breaths thro' ev'ry member of the whole
One common blessing, as one common soul.
But Fortune's gifts if each alike possest,
And each were equal, must not all contest?
If then to all Men Happiness was meant,   65
God in Externals could not place Content.
   Fortune her gifts may variously dispose,
And these be happy call'd, unhappy those;
But Heav'n's just balance equal will appear,
While those are plac'd in Hope, and these in Fear: 70
Not present good or ill, the joy or curse,
But future views of better, or of worse.
   Oh sons of earth! attempt ye still to rise,
By mountains pil'd on mountains, to the skies?
Heav'n still with laughter the vain toil surveys,   75
And buries madmen in the heaps they raise.
   Know, all the good that individuals find,
Or God and Nature meant to mere Mankind,
Reason's whole pleasure, all the joys of Sense,
Lie in three words, Health, Peace, and Competence.   80
But Health consists with Temperance alone;
And Peace, oh Virtue! Peace is all thy own.
The good or bad the gifts of Fortune gain;
But these less taste them, as they worse obtain.
Say, in pursuit of profit or delight,   85
Who risk the most, that take wrong means, or right?
Of Vice or Virtue, whether blest or curst,
Which meets contempt, or which compassion first?
Count all th'advantage prosp'rous Vice attains,
'Tis but what Virtue flies from and disdains: 90
And grant the bad what happiness they wou'd,
One they must want, which is, to pass for good.
   Oh blind to truth, and God's whole scheme below,
Who fancy Bliss to Vice, to Virtue Woe!
Who sees and follows that great scheme the best,   95
Best knows the blessing, and will most be blest,
But fools, the Good alone, unhappy call,
For ills or accidents that chance to all.
See FALKLAND dies, the virtuous and the just!
See god-like TURENNE prostrate on the dust!   100
See SIDNEY bleeds amid the martial strife!

99. *Falkland:* Lucius Cary, Viscount Falkland (1610–1643), a sensitive and noble-minded royalist, killed fighting on behalf of Charles I at Newbury.
100. *Turenne:* Henri de la Tour d'Auvergne, Vicomte de Turenne (1611–1675), marshal-general of France from 1660, was killed while reconnoitering at Sasbach.
101. *Sidney:* Sir Philip Sidney (1554–1586). The Fnglish poet received his death-wound on September 22 at Zutphen, the Netherlands, and a few weeks later he died.

Was this their Virtue, or Contempt of Life?
Say, was it Virtue, more tho' Heav'n ne'er gave,
Lamented DIGBY! sunk thee to the grave?
Tell me, if Virtue made the Son expire,   105
Why, full of days and honour, lives the Sire?
Why drew Marseille's good bishop purer breath,
When Nature sicken'd, and each gale was death?
Or why so long (in life if long can be)
Lent Heav'n a parent to the poor and me?   110
    What makes all physical or moral ill?
There deviates Nature, and here wanders Will.
God sends not ill; if rightly understood,
Or partial Ill is universal Good,
Or Change admits, or Nature lets it fall,   115
Short, and but rare, till Man improv'd it all.
We just as wisely might of Heav'n complain
That righteous Abel was destroy'd by Cain,
As that the virtuous son is ill at ease
When his lewd father gave the dire disease.   120
Think we, like some weak Prince, th'Eternal Cause,
Prone for his fav'rites to reverse his laws?
    Shall burning Ætna, if a sage requires,
Forget to thunder, and recall her fires?
On air or sea new motions be imprest,   125
Oh blameless Bethel! to relieve thy breast?
When the loose mountain trembles from on high,
Shall gravitation cease, if you go by?
Or some old temple, nodding to its fall,
For Chartres' head reserve the hanging wall?   130
    But still this world (so fitted for the knave)
Contents us not. A better shall we have?
A kingdom of the Just then let it be:
But first consider how those Just agree.
The good must merit God's peculiar care;   135
But who, but God, can tell us who they are?
One thinks on Calvin Heav'n's own spirit fell;
Another deems him instrument of hell;

104. *Digby:* Robert Digby (1686–
1726), the generally well-regarded son of
William Digby, Baron Digby of Geashill,
was long outlived by his father, who did
not die until 1752, when he was ninety.
107. *Marseille's bishop:* Henri F. de
Belsunce (1671–1755) remained in Mar-
seilles during the great plague 1720–1721,
visiting the sick. He was left untouched by
the disease.
123. *Ætna:* According to one tradition
Empedocles, Greek philosopher of the
fifth century B.C., threw himself into the
volcanic crater of Aetna to prove he had
become a god.
126. *Bethel:* Hugh Bethel, one of
Pope's best friends, who seems to have
complained about certain discomforts he
experienced while traveling in Italy.
130. *Chartres:* Francis Charteris (1675–
1732), of whom Pope says in part in a note,
Moral Essays, III, 20: "Fr. Chartres, a man
infamous for all manner of vices . . . ; he
was drumm'd out of [his] regiment for a
cheat. . . . His house was a perpetual
bawdy-house. . . ."

If Calvin feel Heav'n's blessing, or its rod,
This cries there is, and that, there is no God.   140
What shocks one part will edify the rest,
Nor with one system can they all be blest.
The very best will variously incline,
And what rewards your Virtue, punish mine.
WHATEVER IS, is RIGHT.—This world, 'tis true,   145
Was made for Cæsar—but for Titus too:
And which more blest? who chain'd his country, say,
Or he whose Virtue sigh'd to lose a day?
    "But sometimes Virtue starves, while Vice is fed."
What then? Is the reward of Virtue bread?   150
That, Vice may merit, 'tis the price of toil;
The knave deserves it, when he tills the soil,
The knave deserves it, when he tempts the main,
Where Folly fights for kings, or dives for gain.
The good man may be weak, be indolent;   155
Nor is his claim to plenty, but content.
But grant him Riches, your demand is o'er?
"No—shall the good want Health, the good want Pow'r?"
Add Health, and Pow'r, and ev'ry earthly thing,
"Why bounded Pow'r? why private? why no king?"   160
Nay, why external for internal giv'n?
Why is not Man a God, and Earth a Heav'n?
Who ask and reason thus, will scarce conceive
God gives enough, while he has more to give:
Immense the pow'r, immense were the demand;   165
Say, at what part of nature will they stand?
    What nothing earthly gives, or can destroy,
The soul's calm sun-shine, and the heart-felt joy,
Is Virtue's prize: A better would you fix?
Then give Humility a coach and six,   170
Justice a Conq'ror's sword, or Truth a gown,
Or Public Spirit its great cure, a Crown.
Weak, foolish man! will Heav'n reward us there
With the same trash mad mortals wish for here?
The Boy and Man an individual makes,   175
Yet sigh'st thou now for apples and for cakes?
Go, like the Indian, in another life
Expect thy dog, thy bottle, and thy wife:
As well as dream such trifles are assign'd,
As toys and empires, for a god-like mind.   180
Rewards, that either would to Virtue bring
No joy, or be destructive of the thing:
How oft by these at sixty are undone

146. *Titus:* The Roman emperor (see
II, n. 1. 198 above) is supposed to have
sighed all night after he had failed to make
good use of the day.

The virtues of a saint at twenty-one!
To whom can Riches give Repute, or Trust,   185
Content, or Pleasure, but the Good and Just?
Judges and Senates have been bought for gold,
Esteem and Love were never to be sold.
Oh fool! to think God hates the worthy mind,
The lover and the love of human-kind,   190
Whose life is healthful, and whose conscience clear;
Because he wants a thousand pounds a year.
    Honour and shame from no Condition rise;
Act well your part, there all the honour lies.
Fortune in Men has some small diff'rence made,   195
One flaunts in rags, one flutters in brocade;
The cobler apron'd, and the parson gown'd,
The frier hooded, and the monarch crown'd.
"What differ more (you cry) than crown and cowl?"
I'll tell you, friend! a wise man and a Fool.   200
You'll find, if once the monarch acts the monk,
Or, cobler-like, the parson will be drunk,
Worth makes the man, and want of it, the fellow;
The rest is all but leather or prunella.
    Stuck o'er with titles and hung round with strings,   205
That thou may'st be by kings, or whores of kings.
Boast the pure blood of an illustrious race,
In quiet flow from Lucrece to Lucrece;
But by your father's worth if your's you rate,
Count me those only who were good and great.   210
Go! if your ancient, but ignoble blood
Has crept thro' scroundels ever since the flood,
Go! and pretend your family is young;
Nor own, your fathers have been fools so long.
What can ennoble sots, or slaves, or cowards?   215
Alas! not all the blood of all the HOWARDS.
    Look next on Greatness; say where Greatness lies?
"Where, but among the Heroes and the Wise?"
Heroes are much the same, the point's agreed,
From Macedonia's madman to the Swede;   220
The whole strange purpose of their lives, to find
Or make, an enemy of all mankind!
Not one looks backward, onward still he goes,

---

204. *The rest . . . leather or prunella:*
The rest is leather or cloth—materials for
mere dress.

208. *Lucrece:* A Roman matron, who,
having been violated by a leader of her
country's enemy, called in her husband and
friends, made them promise to drive out
the Tarquin foe, then killed herself.

216. *Howard:* The distinguished family
of the Dukes of Norfolk, founded by Sir
William Howard (d. 1308).

220. *Macedonia's madman . . . Swede:*
Alexander the Great and Charles XII
(1682-1718). The Swedish king led the
army of his small country against Russia
at one point in his turbulent reign.

Yet ne'er looks forward farther than his nose.
No less alike the Politic and Wise,   225
All sly slow things, with circumspective eyes:
Men in their loose unguarded hours they take,
Not that themselves are wise, but others weak.
But grant that those can conquer, these can cheat;
'Tis phrase absurd to call a Villain Great: 230
Who wickedly is wise, or madly brave,
Is but the more a fool, the more a knave.
Who noble ends by noble means obtains,
Or failing, smiles in exile or in chains,
Like good Aurelius let him reign, or bleed   235
Like Socrates, that Man is great indeed.
    What's Fame? a fancy'd life in others breath.
A thing beyond us, ev'n before our death.
Just what you hear, you have, and what's unknown
The same (my Lord) if Tully's, or your own.   240
All that we feel of it begins and ends
In the small circle of our foes or friends;
To all beside as much an empty shade,
An Eugene living, as a Cæsar dead;
Alike or when, or where, they shone, or shine,   245
Or on the Rubicon, or on the Rhine.
A Wit's a feather, and a Chief a rod;
An honest Man's the noblest work of God.
Fame but from death a villain's name can save,
As Justice tears his body from the grave;   250
When what t'oblivion better were resign'd,
Is hung on high, to poison half mankind.
All fame is foreign, but of true desert;
Plays round the head, but comes not to the heart:
One self-approving hour whole years out-weighs   255
Of stupid starers, and of loud huzzas;
And more true joy Marcellus exil'd feels,
Than Cæsar with a senate at his heels.
    In Parts superior what advantage lies?
Tell (for You can) what is it to be wise?   260
'Tis but to know how little can be known;

---

235. *Aurelius:* Marcus Aurelius Anto-
ninus (121–180), Roman emperor, known
for his self-discipline, sense of justice, and
magnanimity.
240. *Tully:* A name for Marcus Tullius
Cicero (106–43 B.C.), the famous Roman
orator, statesman, and man of letters.
244. *Eugene:* Francois Eugène de
Savoie Carignan(o) (1663–1736), Austrian
soldier, who during the Spanish War of
Succession helped Marlborough at Blenheim (1704).
248. *Noblest:* The 1751 edition on
which the present text is based gives
noble instead of noblest.
257. *Marcellus:* Marcus Marcellus (d.
46 B.C.) was a member of Pompey's party
(hence Caesar's enemy), who after
Pharsalus (48 B.C.) retired to the city of
Mytilene, where he enjoyed the study of
rhetoric and philosophy for the last few
years of his life.

To see all others faults, and feel our own:
Condemn'd in bus'ness or in arts to drudge,
Without a second, or without a judge:
Truths would you teach, or save a sinking land?   265
All fear, none aid you, and few understand.
Painful preheminence! yourself to view
Above life's weakness, and its comforts too.
    Bring then these blessings to a strict account;
Make fair deductions; see to what they mount: 270
How much of other each is sure to cost;
How each for other oft is wholly lost;
How inconsistent greater goods with these;
How sometimes life is risqu'd, and always ease:
Think, and if still the things thy envy call,   275
Say, would'st thou be the Man to whom they fall?
To sigh for ribbands if thou art so silly,
Mark how they grace Lord Umbra, or Sir Billy:
Is yellow dirt the passion of thy life?
Look but on Gripus, or on Gripus' wife: 280
If Parts allure thee, think how Bacon shin'd,
The wisest, brightest, meanest of mankind:
Or ravish'd with the whistling of a Name,
See Cromwell, damn'd to everlasting fame!
If all, united, thy ambition call,   285
From ancient story learn to scorn them all.
There, in the rich, the honour'd, fam'd, and great,
See the false scale of Happiness complete!
In hearts of Kings, or arms of Queens who lay,
How happy! those to ruin, these betray.   290
Mark by what wretched steps their glory grows,
From dirt and sea-weed as proud Venice rose;
In each how guilt and greatness equal ran,
And all that rais'd the Hero, sunk the Man.
Now Europe's laurels on their brows behold,   295
But stain'd with blood, or ill exchang'd for gold:
Then see them broke with toils, or sunk in ease,
Or infamous for plunder'd provinces.
Oh wealth ill-fated! which no act of fame
E'er taught to shine, or sanctify'd from shame!   300
What greater bliss attends their close of life?
Some greedy minion, or imperious wife.
The trophy'd arches, story'd halls invade,

---

278. *Lord Umbra, Sir Billy:* Men of no
real worth, *Umbra* probably echoing
empty shade of IV, 243 above.
279. *Yellow dirt:* Gold.
280. *Gripus, Gripus' wife:* In Vanbrugh's *The Confederacy*, Gripus' wife
spends his money.

281. *Bacon:* Francis Bacon (1561–1626),
philosopher and statesman, was the
practical creator of scientific induction. He
was well known for his learning and
intelligence; according to one eighteenth-
century view, he was a "coward in
adversity."

And haunt their slumbers in the pompous shade.
Alas! not dazzled with their noon-tide ray,   305
Compute the morn and ev'ning to the day;
The whole amount of that enormous fame,
A Tale, that blends their glory with their shame!
　Know then this truth (enough for Man to know)
"Virtue alone is Happiness below."   310
The only point where human bliss stands still,
And tastes the good without the fall to ill;
Where only Merit constant pay receives,
Is blest in what it takes, and what it gives;
The joy unequal'd, if its end it gain,   315
And if it lose, attended with no pain:
Without satiety, tho' e'er so bless'd,
And but more relish'd as the more distress'd:
The broadest mirth unfeeling Folly wears,
Less pleasing far than Virtue's very tears.   320
Good, from each object, from each place acquir'd,
For ever exercis'd, yet never tir'd;
Never elated, while one man's oppress'd;
Never dejected, while another's bless'd;
And where no wants, no wishes can remain,   325
Since but to wish more Virtue, is to gain.
　See the sole bliss Heav'n could on all bestow!
Which who but feels can taste, but thinks can know:
Yet poor with fortune, and with learning blind,
The bad must miss; the good untaught, will find;   330
Slave to no sect, who takes no private road,
But looks thro' Nature, up to Nature's God;
Pursues that Chain which links th'immense design,
Joins heav'n and earth, and mortal and divine;
Sees, that no Being any bliss can know,   335
But touches some above, and some below;
Learns, from this union of the rising Whole,
The first, last purpose of the human soul;
And knows where Faith, Law, Morals, all began,
All end, in LOVE OF GOD, and LOVE OF MAN.   340
　For him alone, Hope leads from goal to goal,
And opens still, and opens on his soul;
'Till lengthen'd on to Faith, and unconfin'd,
It pours the bliss that fills up all the mind.
He sees, why Nature plants in Man alone   345
Hope of known bliss, and Faith in bliss unknown
(Nature, whose dictates to no other kind
Are giv'n in vain, but what they seek they find):
Wise is her present; she connects in this
His greatest Virtue with his greatest Bliss;   350
At once his own bright prospect to be blest,

And strongest motive to assist the rest.
   Self-love thus push'd to social, to divine,
Gives thee to make thy neightbour's blessing thine.
Is this too little for the boundless heart? 355
Extend it, let thy enemies have part:
Grasp the whole worlds of Reason, Life, and Sense,
In one close system of Benevolence:
Happier as kinder, in whate'er degree,
And height of Bliss but height of Charity. 360
   God loves from Whole to Parts: But human soul
Must rise from Individual to the Whole.
Self-love but serves the virtuous mind to wake,
As the small pebble stirs the peaceful lake;
The centre mov'd, a circle strait succeeds, 365
Another still, and still another spreads;
Friend, parent, neighbour, first it will embrace;
His country next; and next all human race;
Wide and more wide, th'o'erflowings of the mind
Take ev'ry creature in, of ev'ry kind; 370
Earth smiles around, with boundless bounty blest,
And Heav'n beholds its image in his breast.
   Come then, by Friend! my Genius! come along;
Oh master of the poet, and the song!
And while the Muse now stoops, or now ascends, 375
To Man's low passions, or their glorious ends,
Teach me, like thee, in various nature wise,
To fall with dignity, with temper rise;
Form'd by thy converse, happily to steer
From grave to gay, from lively to severe; 380
Correct with spirit, eloquent with ease,
Intent to reason, or polite to please.
Oh! while along the stream of Time thy name
Expanded flies, and gathers all its fame,
Say, shall my little bark attendant fail, 385
Pursue the triumph, and partake the gale?
When statesmen, heroes, kings, in dust repose,
Whose sons shall blush their fathers were thy foes,
Shall then this verse to future age pretend
Thou wert my guide, philosopher, and friend? 390
That urg'd by thee, I turn'd the tuneful art
From sounds to things, from fancy to the heart;
From Wit's false mirror held up Nature's light;
Shew'd erring Pride, WHATEVER IS, IS RIGHT;
That REASON, PASSION, answer one great aim; 395
That true SELF-LOVE and SOCIAL are the same;
That VIRTUE only makes our Bliss below;
And all our Knowledge is, OURSELVES TO KNOW.

(1733–1734)

Headnote to
EPISTLE TO
DR. ARBUTHNOT

In the summer of 1734, Dr. John Arbuthnot (1667–1735), formerly physician to Queen Anne and longtime friend (and fellow Scriblerian) of Pope, was on his death-bed. Pope, who was at the time traveling about the country, staying at the houses of friends as he moved from place to place, wrote to Arbuthnot, who answered rather more seriously than he might have done otherwise, no doubt because he knew he was dying and, naturally, sought to reach out to an old friend and fellow satirist in a more than casual way. In the correspondence that followed, he urged Pope to continue to employ his writing to express indignation against vice, in one sense at least suggesting that Pope had perhaps too much concerned himself with answering personal attacks in kind. Or it may be that Arbuthnot was afraid his old friend would put himself in danger by directing his pen against persons rather than against their vices alone. It was Pope's view, however, that he must, within certain limits, employ personal satire because general strictures could not produce the desired effect, whereas a few well-chosen examples among men might discourage the transgression of others. But in addition to this opinion of the satirist, Pope offered to Arbuthnot the kindness of a friend, saying that he planned to address an epistle to Arbuthnot, composed in part of pieces he had written over many years, pieces in which he answers the questions ". . . what were, & are my Motives of writing, the objections to them & my answers."[1]

Pope also took the occasion to vindicate himself from a wide range of charges, and particularly, it seems from his Advertisement to the poem, to respond to the authors of *Verses Addressed to the Imitator of Horace* and *An Epistle to a Doctor of Divinity from a Nobleman at Hampton Court*. These were the joint works of Lady Mary Wortley Montagu (1689–1762), for years Pope's friend, with whom he quarreled bitterly shortly after her return to England from Turkey in 1718, and John, Baron Hervey of Ickworth (1696–1743). No one knows just how the quarrel with Lady Mary began, but it seems likely that there is some truth to the tradition that Pope declared his love for her and she laughed quite without control. Whatever the cause, the break

[1] G. A. Aitken, *The Life and Works of John Arbuthnot*, 2 vols., Oxford, 1892, I, p. 159.

between them was irrevocable by 1728, for in the early version of *The Dunciad*, II, 115–116, Pope wrote, cuttingly,

> Whence hapless Monsieur much complains at *Paris*
> Of wrongs from Duchesses and Lady *Marys*.

The Monsieur in question was a certain Rémond to whom Lady Mary had written some indiscreet letters and for whom she invested some money, only to be accused of dishonesty when the venture began to fail. Apparently at some point in her quarrel with Pope, Lady Mary had enlisted the aid of Lord Hervey, and together they produced the two scurrilous pieces Pope refers to in the Advertisement. It is possible that Lady Mary was almost entirely responsible for the first, as Hervey was for the second of these compositions, which together were the immediate stimulus, it seems clear, to several of the sections of *The Epistle to Dr. Arbuthnot* that do not fall within the limits of the plan for the poem as Pope outlined it in the letter to his dying friend.

Warburton, in his edition of 1751, added to the title of the work, without Pope's authority, so that it reads, *Epistle to Dr. Arbuthnot, Being the Prologue to the Satires.* As John Butt points out in his edition of Pope's *Imitations of Horace* (Twickenham, IV, p. 94), "There can be little objection to [Warburton's change], for the poem is the most Horatian of Pope's original works, and its immediate occasion was the *Verses to an Imitator of Horace.*" One other change must also be noted. The 1751 version is arranged so that the poem is in fact a debate, not an epistle, in that some of the lines are given to Arbuthnot, some to Pope. The text that follows eliminates those designations of the speakers (probably Warburton's, possibly Pope's) to restore the poem to its original form—epistle.

TEXT. *The Works of Alexander Pope, Esq.*, ed. William Warburton (9 vols., London, 1751).

Epistle to Dr. Arbuthnot

Being the Prologue to the Satires

Advertisement to the First Publication of This Epistle

This paper is a sort of bill of complaint, begun many years since, and drawn up by snatches, as the several occasions offered. I had no thoughts of publishing it, till it pleased some Persons of Rank and Fortune [the Authors of *Verses to the Imitator of Horace*, and of an *Epistle to a Doctor of Divinity from a Nobleman at Hampton Court*] to attack, in a very extraordinary manner, not only my Writings (of which, being public, the Public is judge) but my *Person*, *Morals*, and *Family*, whereof, to those who know me not, a truer information may be requisite. Being divided between the necessity to say something of *myself*, and my own laziness to undertake so awkward a task, I thought it the shortest way to put the last hand to this Epistle. If it have any thing pleasing,   10
it will be that by which I am most desirous to please, the *Truth* and the *Sentiment*; and if any thing offensive, it will be only to those I am least sorry to offend, *the vicious* or *the ungenerous*.

Many will know their own pictures in it, there being not a circumstance but what is true; but I have, for the most part, spared their *Names*, and they may escape being laughed at, if they please.

I would have some of them know, it was owing to the request of the learned and candid Friend to whom it is inscribed, that I make not as free use of theirs as they have done of mine. However, I shall have this advantage, and honour, on my side, that whereas, by their proceeding, any abuse may be directed at any   20
man, no injury can possibly be done by mine, since a nameless Character can never be found out, but by its *truth* and *likeness*.   P.

> SHUT, shut the door, good John! fatigu'd I said,
> Tye up the knocker, say I'm sick, I'm dead.
> The Dog-star rages! nay 'tis past a doubt,
> All Bedlam, or Parnassus, is let out:

1. *Shut, shut . . . John*] John Searl, his old and faithful servant: whom he has remembered, under that character, in his Will, W. [Notes like this one, marked by a bracket, are Warburton's (W). or Pope's (P.) as given in 1751.]

4. *Bedlam, or Parnassus:* The oldest institution for the mentally ill in England; the mountain in Greece, sacred to the arts (Apollo and the Muses).

Fire in each eye, and papers in each hand,   5
They rave, recite, and madden round the land.
    What walls can guard me, or what shades can hide?
They pierce my thickets, thro' my Grot they glide,
By land, by water, they renew the charge,
They stop the chariot, and they board the barge.   10
No place is sacred, not the Church is free,
Ev'n Sunday shines no Sabbath-day to me:
Then from the Mint walks forth the Man of rhyme,
Happy! to catch me, just at Dinner-time.
    Is there a Parson, much be-mus'd in beer,   15
A maudlin Poetess, a rhyming Peer,
A Clerk, foredoom'd his father's soul to cross,
Who pens a Stanza, when he should *engross*?
Is there, who, lock'd from ink and paper, scrawls
With desp'rate charcoal round his darken'd walls?   20
All fly to TWIT'NAM, and in humble strain
Apply to me, to keep them mad or vain.
Arthur, whose giddy son neglects the Laws,
Imputes to me and my damn'd works the cause:
Poor Cornus sees his frantic wife elope,   25
And curses Wit, and Poetry, and Pope.
    Friend to my Life! (which did not you prolong,
The world had wanted many an idle song)
What *Drop* or *Nostrum* can this plague remove?
Or which must end me, a Fool's wrath or love?   30
A dire dilemma! either way I'm sped,
If foes, they write, if friends, they read me dead.
Seiz'd and ty'd down to judge, how wretched I!
Who can't be silent, and who will not lye:
To laugh, were want of goodness and of grace,   35
And to be grave, exceeds all Pow'r of face.
I sit with sad civility, I read
With honest anguish, and an aching head;
And drop at last, but in unwilling ears,
This saving counsel, "Keep your piece nine years."   40
    Nine years! cries he, who high in Drury-lane,

---

8. *My Grot:* Among Pope's landscaping ventures at his little estate of Twickenham was a much-decorated tunnel, his grotto.

10. *Board the barge:* Pope's home was on the Thames. His literary besiegers could reach him either by water or by road.

13. *From the Mint*] A place to which insolvent debtors retired, to enjoy an illegal protection. . . . W.

21. *Twit'nam:* Twickenham.

23. *Arthur:* Arthur Moore (1666?–1730), a grave member of Parliament, whose son James displeased him.

25. *Cornus:* Cuckold.

29. *Drop:* Joshua Ward (1685–1761) was a quack known as "Spot" Ward, because his drop or pill (nostrums) was supposed to go right to the spot where the patient was ailing.

40. *"Keep . . . nine years":* Horace, *Ars Poetica*, ll. 386 f. gives this advice to young Piso.

41. *Drury-lane:* In Pope's day, the theater was the home of the derelict and disreputable.

Lull'd by soft Zephyrs thro' the broken pane,
Rhymes ere he wakes, and prints before *Term* ends,
Oblig'd by hunger, and request of friends:
"The piece, you think, is incorrect? why take it,   45
I'm all submission, what you'd have it, make it."
　Three things another's modest wishes bound,
My Friendship, and a Prologue, and ten pound.
　Pitholeon sends to me: "You know his Grace,
I want a Patron; ask him for a Place."   50
Pitholeon libell'd me—"but here's a letter
Informs you, Sir, 'twas when he knew no better.
Dare you refuse him? Curl invites to dine,
He'll write a *Journal*, or he'll turn Divine."
　Bless me! a packet.—" 'Tis a stranger sues,   55
A Virgin Tragedy, an Orphan Muse."
If I dislike it, "Furies, death and rage!"
If I approve, "Commend it to the Stage."
There (thank my stars) my whole commission ends,
The Play'rs and I are, luckily, no friends.   60
Fir'd that the house reject him, " 'Sdeath I'll print it,
And shame the fools—Your int'rest, Sir, with Lintot."
Lintot, dull rogue! will think your price too much:
"Not, Sir, if you revise it, and retouch."
All my demurs but double his attacks;   65
At last he whispers, "Do; and we go snacks."
Glad of a quarrel, strait I clap the door,
Sir, let me see your works and you no more.
　'Tis sung, when Midas' Ears began to spring
(Midas, a sacred person and a King)   70
His very Minister who spy'd them first
(Some say his Queen) was forc'd to speak, or burst.
And is not mine, my friend, a sorer case,
When ev'ry coxcomb perks them in my face?
Good friend forbear! you deal in dang'rous things.   75
I'd never name Queens, Ministers, or Kings;
Keep close to Ears, and those let asses prick,
'Tis nothing—Nothing? if they bite and kick?
Out with it, DUNCIAD! let the secret pass,

43 *Term ends:* The terms or quarters were the legal sessions into which the eighteenth-century magistrate's year was divided. Because more people were in town when court was in session, publishers printed books then.

49. *Pitholeon*] The name taken from a foolish poet of Rhodes, who pretended much to *Greek*. Schol. in Horat. l. i. Dr. Bentley pretends that this Pitholeon libelled Cæsar also. . . . P.

53. *Curl:* Edmund Curll (1675–1747), a publisher and bookseller whose speciality was pornography and private manuscripts he had managed to procure.

62. *Lintot:* Bernard Lintot (1675–1736), a publisher, who had brought out many of Pope's works and with whom Pope quarreled while the *Odyssey* was being published.

66. *Go snacks:* To divide profits.

72. *His Queen*] The story is told, by some, of his barber, but by *Chaucer [Wife of Bath's Tale,* ll. 95 f.] of his queen. . . . P.

That secret to each fool, that he's an Ass: 80
The truth once told (and wherefore should we lie?)
The Queen of Midas slept, and so may I.
    You think this cruel? take it for a rule,
No creature smarts so little as a fool.
Let peals of laughter, Codrus! round thee break,   85
Thou unconcern'd canst hear the mighty crack:
Pit, box, and gall'ry in convulsions hurl'd,
Thou stand'st unshook amidst a bursting world.
Who shames a Scribler? break one cobweb thro',
He spins the slight, self-pleasing thread anew: 90
Destroy his fib or sophistry, in vain,
The creature's at his dirty work again,
Thron'd in the centre of his thin designs,
Proud of a vast extent of flimzy lines!
Whom have I hurt? has Poet yet, or Peer,   95
Lost the arch'd eye-brow, or Parnassian sneer?
And has not Colly still his lord, and whore?
His butchers Henley, his free-masons Moor?
Does not one table Bavius still admit?
Still to one Bishop Philips seem a wit?   100
Still Sappho—Hold! for God-sake—you'll offend,
No Names—be calm—learn prudence of a friend:
I too could write, and I am twice as tall;
But foes like these—One Flatt'rer's worse than all.
Of all mad creatures, if the learn'd are right,   105
It is the slaver kills, and not the bite.
A fool quite angry is quite innocent:
Alas! 'tis ten times worse when they *repent*.
    One dedicates in high heroic prose,
And ridicules beyond a hundred foes: 110
One from all Grubstreet will my fame defend,
And more abusive, calls himself my friend.
This prints my *Letters*, that expects a bribe,

---

85. *Codrus:* A poetaster who insists upon reading his verse to those with no desire to hear it.

97. *Colly:* Colley Cibber. See the headnote to *The Dunciad*.

98. *Butchers Henley . . . free-masons Moor:* John Henley (1692–1756), an idiosyncratic preacher, who once delivered a *Butcher's Lecture* to dignify the trade of butcher. James Moore (1702–1734), later James Moore Smythe (in fulfillment of the terms of his grandfather's will), a playwright. Warburton says, "He was of [the Mason's] society, and frequently headed their processions."

99. *Bavius:* A poetaster sarcastically treated in Virgil's Third Ecologue.

100. *Bishop Philips:* Ambrose Philips. See the headnote to the *Pastorals*. The bishop was Hugh Boulter, with whom Philips had traveled to Ireland.

101. *Sappho:* Lady Mary. See the headnote.

106. *Slaver:* Saliva dribbling from the mouth.

111. *Grubstreet:* In London, the place where hack-writing was produced.

113. *Letters:* Curll (see n. l. 53) printed some of Pope's letters without permission. Pope in fact had maneuvered so that a faulty edition of his letters was published without his nominal consent; their appearance, he felt, permitted him to publish a correct copy.

And others roar aloud, "Subscribe, subscribe."
There are, who to my person pay their court: 115
I cough like *Horace*, and, tho' lean, am short,
Ammon's great son one shoulder had too high,
Such *Ovid's* nose, and "Sir! you have an Eye—"
Go on, obliging creatures, make me see
All that disgrac'd my Betters, met in me.   120
Say for my comfort, languishing in bed,
"Just so immortal *Maro* held his head:"
And when I die, be sure you let me know
Great *Homer* dy'd three thousand years ago.
    Why did I write? what sin to me unknown   125
Dipt me in ink, my parents', or my own?
As yet a child, nor yet a fool to fame,
I lisp'd in numbers, for the numbers came.
I left no calling for this idle trade,
No duty broke, no father disobey'd.   130
The Muse but serv'd to ease some friend, not Wife,
To help me thro' this long disease, my Life,
To second, ARBUTHNOT! thy Art and Care,
And teach, the Being you preserv'd, to bear.
    But why then publish? *Granville* the polite,   135
And knowing *Walsh*, would tell me I could write;
Well-natur'd *Garth* inflam'd with early praise,
And *Congreve* lov'd, and *Swift* endur'd my lays;
The courtly *Talbot*, *Somers*, *Sheffield* read,
Ev'n mitred *Rochester* would nod the head,   140
And *St. John's* self (great *Dryden's* friends before)
With open arms receiv'd one Poet more.
Happy my studies, when by these approv'd!
Happier their author, when by these belov'd!
From these the world will judge of men and books,   145
Not from the *Burnets*, *Oldmixons*, and *Cooks*.

114. *Subscribe:* Subscription was a means of financing book publications; in effect, copies were sold and paid for before they were produced.
116. *Like Horace:* Pope was short and slight; Horace short and fat.
117. *Ammon's . . . son:* Alexander the Great.
118. *Have an Eye:* Though Pope's eyes were his finest feature, they gave him trouble.
122. *Maro:* Virgil.
135. *Granville:* George, Baron Lansdowne (1667–1735), poet and statesman.
136. *Walsh:* William Walsh (1663–1708), poet, critic, and one of Pope's first literary friends.
137. *Garth:* Sir Samuel Garth (1661–1719), poet and royal physician to George I.

139. *Talbot, Somers, Sheffield:* Charles, Baron Talbot (1685–1737), England's Lord Chancellor, 1733; John, Baron Somers (1651–1716), Lord Chancellor, 1697; John, First Duke of Buckingham (1648–1721), Lord Justice, 1714.
140. *Rochester:* Francis Atterbury (1662–1732), Bishop of Rochester.
141. *St. John's self:* Henry St. John, Viscount Bolingbroke, Tory statesman and philosopher.
146. *Burnets, Oldmixons, and Cooks:* Thomas Burnet (1694–1753), one of Addison's group, who had attacked Pope; John Oldmixon (1673–1742), a writer who had for profit helped Curll to publish some of Pope's poems surreptitiously; Thomas Cooke (1703–1756), who in his *Battle of the Poets*, 1725, much preferred Philips to Pope.

Soft were my numbers; who could take offence
While pure Description held the place of Sense?
Like gentle *Fanny's* was my flow'ry theme,
A painted mistress, or a purling stream.   150
Yet then did *Gildon* draw his venal quill;
I wish'd the man a dinner, and sate still.
Yet then did *Dennis* rave in furious fret;
I never answer'd, I was not in debt.
If want provok'd, or madness made them print,   155
I wag'd no war with *Bedlam* or the *Mint.*
   Did some more sober Critic come abroad;
If wrong, I smil'd; if right, I kiss'd the rod.
Pains, reading, study, are their just pretence,
And all they want is spirit, taste, and sense.   160
Comma's and points they set exactly right,
And 'twere a sin to rob them of their mite.
Yet ne'er one sprig of laurel grac'd these ribalds,
From slashing *Bentley* down to pidling *Tibalds:*
Each wight, who reads not, and but scans and spells, 165
Each Word-catcher, that lives on syllables,
Ev'n such small Critics some regard may claim,
Preserv'd in *Milton's* or in *Shakespear's* name.
Pretty! in amber to observe the forms
Of hairs, or straws, or dirt, or grubs, or worms! 170
The things, we know, are neither rich nor rare,
But wonder how the devil they got there.
   Were others angry: I excus'd them too;
Well might they rage, I gave them but their due.
A man's true merit 'tis not hard to find;   175
But each man's secret standard in his mind,
That Casting-weight pride adds to emptiness,
This, who can gratify? for who can *guess?*
The Bard whom pilfer'd Pastorals renown,
Who turns a Persian tale for half a Crown,   180
Just writes to make his barrenness appear,
And strains from hard-bound brains, eight lines a year;
He, who still wanting, tho' he lives on theft,
Steals much, spends little, yet has nothing left:

149. *Gentle Fanny's:* Fanny was Lord Hervey. See the headnote.

151. *Gildon:* Charles Gildon (1665–1724) attacked Pope in *A New Rehearsal*, 1714.

153. *Dennis:* John Dennis (1657–1734), critic and playwright. Pope gave him offense in *Essay on Criticism*, and they were thereafter enemies.

156. *Bedlam . . . Mint:* See nn. ll. 4 and 13.

164. *Bentley . . . Tibalds:* Richard Bentley (1662–1742), classical scholar, who is supposed to have said of Pope's Homer, ". . . a pretty poem, Mr. Pope, but you must not call it Homer." Lewis Theobald (1688–1744) had criticized Pope's *Shakespeare.*

180. *Turns a Persian tale*] Amb. Philips translated a Book called the *Persian Tales.* P.

And He, who now to sense, now nonsense leaning,   185
Means not, but blunders round about a meaning:
And He, whose fustian's so sublimely bad,
It is not Poetry, but prose run mad:
All these, my modest Satire bad *translate*,
And own'd that nine such Poets made a *Tate*.   190
How did they fume, and stamp, and roar, and chafe!
And swear, not ADDISON himself was safe.
    Peace to all such! but were there One whose fires
True Genius kindles, and fair Fame inspires;
Blest with each talent and each art to please,   195
And born to write, converse, and live with ease:
Should such a man, too fond to rule alone,
Bear, like the Turk, no brother near the throne,
View him with scornful, yet with jealous eyes,
And hate for arts that caus'd himself to rise;   200
Damn with faint praise, assent with civil leer,
And without sneering, teach the rest to sneer;
Willing to wound, and yet afraid to strike,
Just hint a fault, and hesitate dislike;
Alike reserv'd to blame, or to commend,   205
A tim'rous foe, and a suspicious friend;
Dreading ev'n fools, by Flatterers besieg'd,
And so obliging, that he ne'er oblig'd;
Like *Cato*, give his little Senate laws,
And sit attentive to his own applause;   210
While Wits and Templars ev'ry sentence raise,
And wonder with a foolish face of praise—
Who but must laugh, if such a man there be?
Who would not weep, if ATTICUS were he!
    What tho' my Name stood rubric on the walls,   215
Or plaister'd posts, with claps, in capitals?
Or smoaking forth, a hundred hawkers load,
On wings of winds came flying all abroad?
I sought no homage from the Race that write;
I kept, like *Asian* Monarchs, from their sight: 220
Poems I heeded (now be-rym'd so long)
No more than thou, great GEORGE! a birth-day song.
I ne'er with wits or witlings pass'd my days,

190. *Tate:* Nahum Tate (1652–1715),
a poetaster, who became Poet Laureate in
1692.
    209. *Like Cato:* This line is a hit at
Addison's tragedy *Cato*, which has little to
recommend it dramatically.
    211. *Templars:* A Templar was a
barrister or a student of law, having
chambers in the Temple.
    214. *Atticus*] It was a great falshood,

which some of the Libels reported, that
this Character was written after the
Gentleman's [Addison's] death; which see
refuted in the Testimonies prefixed to the
Dunciad. . . . P.
    216. *Claps:* Posters to be pasted on a
wall or billboard.
    222. *Great George:* George II had no
taste for literature.

To spread about the itch of verse and praise;
Nor like a puppy, daggled thro' the town,   225
To fetch and carry sing-song up and down;
Nor at Rehearsals sweat, and mouth'd, and cry'd,
With handkerchief and orange at my side;
But sick of fops, and poetry, and prate,
To *Bufo* left the whole *Castalian* state.   230
    Proud as *Apollo* on his forked hill,
Sate full-blown *Bufo*, puff'd by ev'ry quill;
Fed with soft Dedication all day long,
Horace and he went hand in hand in song.
His Library (where busts of Poets dead   235
And a true *Pindar* stood without a head)
Receiv'd of wits an undistinguish'd race,
Who first his judgment ask'd, and then a place:
Much they extoll'd his pictures, much his seat,
And flatter'd ev'ry day, and some days eat: 240
Till grown more frugal in his riper days,
He paid some bards with port, and some with praise,
To some a dry rehearsal was assign'd,
And others (harder still) he paid in kind.
Dryden alone (what wonder?) came not nigh,   245
Dryden alone escap'd this judging eye:
But still the *Great* have kindness in reserve,
He help'd to bury whom he help'd to starve.
    May some choice patron bless each gray goose quill!
May ev'ry *Bavius* have his *Bufo* still!   250
So when a Statesman wants a day's defence,
Or Envy holds a whole week's war with Sense,
Or simple pride for flatt'ry makes demands,
May dunce by dunce be whistled off my hands!
Blest be the *Great!* for those they take away,   255
And those they left me; for they left me GAY;
Left me to see neglected Genius bloom,

---

225. *Daggled:* To daggle is to make wet by sprinkling, or to walk through mud in a slovenly way.

230. *Bufo . . . Castalian: Bufo* was a name used to refer to a worthless patron; Pope may be characterizing George Bubb Dodington (1691–1762), who spent tastelessly and who was a bad patron, or Charles Montagu, First Earl of Halifax (1661–1715), who was in fact a fine statesman and an excellent patron. Pope refused one of Halifax's offers of assistance. The Castalian spring, on Parnassus, is sacred to Apollo, whence associated with inspiration in the arts.

231. *Apollo . . . forked hill:* Parnassus was often referred to as having two sum-

mits, one for Apollo, the other for Dionysus.

236. *A true Pindar stood . . .*] Ridicules the affectation of Antiquaries, who frequently exhibit the headless *Trunks* and *Terms* of Statues, for Plato, Homer, Pindar, &c. . . . P.

248. *Help'd to bury*] Mr. *Dryden*, after having liv'd in exigencies, had a magnificent Funeral bestow'd upon him by the contribution of several persons of Quality. P. [Halifax promised a statue in Dryden's honor, but his intention came to nothing.]

256. *Gay:* John Gay (1685–1732), a poet, a member of the Scriblerus Club, and the author of *The Beggar's Opera.* Pope composed Gay's epitaph.

Neglected die, and tell it on his tomb:
Of all thy blameless life the sole return
My Verse, and QUEENSB'RY weeping o'er thy urn!   260
   Oh let me live my own, and die so too!
(To live and die is all I have to do):
Maintain a Poet's dignity and ease,
And see what friends, and read what books I please:
Above a Patron, tho' I condescend   265
Sometimes to call a Minister my friend.
I was not born for Courts or great affairs;
I pay my debts, believe, and say my pray'rs;
Can sleep without a Poem in my head,
Nor know, if *Dennis* be alive or dead.   270
   Why am I ask'd what next shall see the light?
Heav'ns! was I born for nothing but to write?
Has Life no joys for me? or (to be grave)
Have I no friend to serve, no soul to save?
"I found him close with *Swift*"—"Indeed? no doubt"   275
(Cries prating *Balbus*) "something will come out."
'Tis all in vain, deny it as I will.
"No, such a Genius never can lie still";
And then for mine obligingly mistakes
The first Lampoon Sir *Will.* or *Bubo* makes.   280
Poor guiltless I! and can I chuse but smile,
When ev'ry Coxcomb knows me by my *Style*?
   Curst be the verse, how well soe'er it flow,
That tends to make one worthy man my foe,
Give Virtue scandal, Innocence a fear,   285
Or from the soft-ey'd Virgin steal a tear!
But he who hurts a harmless neighbour's peace,
Insults fall'n worth, or Beauty in distress,
Who loves a Lye, lame slander helps about,
Who writes a Libel, or who copies out: 290
That Fop, whose pride affects a patron's name,
Yet absent, wounds an author's honest fame:
Who can *your* merit *selfishly* approve,
And show the *sense* of it without the *love*;
Who has the vanity to call you friend,   295
Yet wants the honour, injur'd, to defend;
Who tells whate'er you think, whate'er you say,
And, if he lye not, must at least betray:

260. *Queensb'ry:* Charles Douglas, Third Duke of Queensbury, who expressed his displeasure to George II when Gay's opera *Polly* was denied a license. Both Queensbury and his wife admired Gay profoundly.

270. *Dennis:* See n. l. 153.

276. *Balbus:* George Hay, Seventh Earl of Kinnoull (d. 1758), known for his bad political and domestic behavior.

280. *Sir Will.* or *Bubo:* Sir William Yonge (d. 1755), a Whig politician whose name had become a byword for corruption. Bubo is Dodington; see n. l. 230, where as Bufo, he shares the satiric character with Halifax.

Who to the *Dean*, and *silver bell* can swear,
And sees at *Cannons* what was never there;   300
Who reads, but with a lust to misapply,
Make Satire a Lampoon, and Fiction Lye.
A lash like mine no honest man shall dread,
But all such babling blockheads in his stead.
   Let *Sporus* tremble—What? that thing of silk,   305
Sporus, that mere white curd of Ass's milk?
Satire or sense, alas! can *Sporus* feel?
Who breaks a butterfly upon a wheel?
Yet let me flap this bug with gilded wings,
This painted child of dirt, that stinks and stings;   310
Whose buzz the witty and the fair annoys,
Yet wit ne'er tastes, and beauty ne'er enjoys:
So well-bred spaniels civilly delight
In mumbling of the game they dare not bite.
Eternal smiles his emptiness betray,   315
As shallow streams run dimpling all the way.
Whether, in florid impotence he speaks,
And, as the prompter breathes, the puppet squeaks;
Or at the ear of *Eve*, familiar Toad,
Half froth, half venom, spits himself abroad,   320
In puns, or politics, or tales, or lies,
Or spite, or smut, or rhymes, or blasphemies.
His wit all see-saw, between *that* and *this*,
Now high, now low, now master up, now miss,
And he himself one vile Antithesis.   325
Amphibious thing! that acting either part,
The trifling head, or the corrupted heart,
Fop at the toilet, flatt'rer at the board,
Now trips a Lady, and now struts a Lord.
Eve's tempter thus the Rabbins have exprest,   330
A Cherub's face, a reptile all the rest,
Beauty that shocks you, parts that none will trust,
Wit that can creep, and pride that licks the dust.
   Not Fortune's worshipper, nor Fashion's fool,
Not Lucre's madman, nor Ambition's tool,   335
Not proud, nor servile; Be one Poet's praise,
That, if he pleas'd, he pleas'd by manly ways:
That Flatt'ry, ev'n to Kings, he held a shame,
And thought a Lye in verse or prose the same.
That not in Fancy's maze he wander'd long,   340
But stoop'd to Truth, and moraliz'd his song:
That not for Fame, but Virtue's better end,

299. *Who to the Dean*] Meaning the
man who would have persuaded the Duke
of Chandos that Mr. P. meant him in those
circumstances ridiculed in the Epistle on
Taste. See Mr. Pope's Letter to the Earl
of Burlington concerning this matter. W.
   305. *Sporus*: Lord Hervey. See the
headnote.
   319. *At the ear of Eve*] See Milton,
Book IV [l. 800]. P.

He stood the furious foe, the timid friend,
The damning critic, half approving wit,
The coxcomb hit, or fearing to be hit;   345
Laugh'd at the loss of friends he never had,
The dull, the proud, the wicked, and the mad;
The distant threats of vengeance on his head,
The blow unfelt, the tear he never shed;
The tale reviv'd, the lye so oft o'erthrown,   350
Th' imputed trash, and dulness not his own;
The morals blacken'd when the writings scape,
The libel'd person, and the pictur'd shape;
Abuse, on all he lov'd, or lov'd him, spread,
A friend in exile, or a father, dead;   355
The whisper, that to greatness still too near,
Perhaps, yet vibrates on his Sov'reign's ear—
Welcome for thee, fair *Virtue!* all the past:
For thee, fair Virtue! welcome ev'n the *last!*
But why insult the poor, affront the great?   360
A knave's a knave, to me, in ev'ry state:
Alike my scorn, if he succeed or fail,
Sporus at court, or *Japhet* in a jail,
A hireling scribler, or a hireling peer,
Knight of the post corrupt, or of the shire;   365
If on a Pillory, or near a Throne,
He gain his Prince's ear, or lose his own.
Yet soft by nature, more a dupe than wit,
Sappho can tell you how this man was bit:
This dreaded Sat'rist *Dennis* will confess   370
Foe to his pride, but friend to his distress:
So humble, he has knock'd at *Tibbald's* door,
Has drunk with *Cibber,* nay has rhym'd for *Moor.*
Full ten years slander'd, did he once reply?
Three thousand suns went down on *Welsted's* lye.   375

351. *Th' imputed trash*] Such as profane *Psalms*, Court-Poems, and other scandalous things, printed in his Name by Curl and others. P.

354. *Abuse, on all he lov'd*] Namely on the Duke of Buckingham, the Earl of Burlington, Lord Bathurst, Lord Bolingbroke, Bishop Atterbury, Dr. Swift, Dr. Arbuthnot, Mr. Gay, his Friends, his Parents, and his very Nurse, aspersed in printed papers by James Moore, G. Ducket, L. Welsted, Tho. Bentley, and other obscure persons. P.

355. *A friend in exile:* Atterbury.

363. *Japhet:* Japhet Crook (1662–1734), a forger, who was mutilated by the authorities and sent to prison for life.

365. *Knight of the post:* "One who got his living by giving false evidence." OED.

374. *Full ten years slander'd*] It was so long after many libels before the Author of the Dunciad published that poem, till when, he never writ a word in answer to the many scurrilities and falsehoods concerning him. P.

375. *Welsted's lye*] This man [Leonard Welsted, a minor poet] had the impudence to tell in print, that Mr. P. had occasioned a *Lady's death*, and to name a person he never heard of. He also publish'd that he libell'd the Duke of Chandos; with whom (it was added) that he had lived in familiarity, and received from him a present of *five hundred pounds*: the falsehood of both which is known to his Grace. Mr. P. never received any present, farther than the subscription for Homer, from him, or from *Any great Man* whatsoever. P.

To please a Mistress one aspers'd his life;
He lash'd him not, but let her be his wife:
Let *Budgel* charge low *Grubstreet* on his quill,
And write whate'er he pleas'd, except his Will;
Let the two *Curls* of Town and Court, abuse   380
His father, mother, body, soul, and muse.
Yet why? that Father held it for a rule,
It was a sin to call our neighbour fool:
That harmless Mother thought no wife a whore:
Hear this, and spare his family, *James Moore!*   385
Unspotted names, and memorable long!
If there be force in Virtue, or in Song.
    Of gentle blood (part shed in Honour's cause,
While yet in *Britain* Honour had applause)
Each parent sprung—What fortune, pray?—Their own,   390
And better got, than *Bestia's* from the throne.
Born to no Pride, inheriting no Strife,
Nor marrying Discord in a noble wife,
Stranger to civil and religious rage,
The good man walk'd innoxious thro' his age.   395
No Courts he saw, no suits would ever try,
Nor dar'd an Oath, nor hazarded a Lye.
Un-learn'd, he knew no schoolman's subtile art,
No language, but the language of the heart.
By Nature honest, by Experience wise,   400
Healthy by temp'rance, and by exercise;
His life, tho' long, to sickness past unknown,
His death was instant, and without a groan.
O grant me, thus to live, and thus to die!
Who sprung from Kings shall know less joy than I.   405
    O Friend! may each domestic bliss be thine!
Be no unpleasing Melancholy mine:
Me, let the tender office long engage,
To rock the cradle of reposing Age,
With lenient arts extend a Mother's breath,   410
Make Langour smile, and smooth the bed of Death,
Explore the thought, explain the asking eye,
And keep a while one parent from the sky!

---

378. *Let Budgel charge*] *Budgel* [Eustace Budgell, a hack writer and Addison's cousin], in a weekly pamphlet called the *Bee*, bestowed much abuse on him, in the imagination that he writ some things about the *Last Will* of Dr. Tindal, in the *Grub-street Journal*; a Paper wherein he never had the least hand, direction, or supervisal, nor the least knowledge of its Author. P.

381. *His father*] In some of Curl's and other pamphlets, Mr. Pope's father was said to be a Mechanic, a Hatter, a Farmer, nay a Bankrupt. . . . Mr. Pope's Father was of a Gentleman's Family in Oxfordshire, the head of which was the Earl of Downe. . . . P. [Pope seems to have been mistaken in claiming this connection.]

385. *James Moore:* See n. l. 98.

391. *Bestia's:* Lucius Calpurnius Bestia, fl. 100 B.C., was long regarded as a traitor for having agreed to poor terms for peace in Rome's war against Numidia (Jugurthine War).

On cares like these if length of days attend,
May Heav'n, to bless those days, preserve my friend,   415
Preserve him social, chearful, and serene,
And just as rich as when he serv'd a QUEEN.
Whether that blessing be deny'd or giv'n,
Thus far was right, the rest belongs to Heav'n.

(1735)

417. *Serv'd a Queen*] An honest compliment to his Friend's real and unaffected disinterestedness, when he was the favourite Physician of Queen Anne. W.

Headnote to
THE DUNCIAD

Pope's *Dunciad*—the successor to *Mac Flecknoe* in that both celebrate the triumph of Dullness—is in many ways his most controversial poem. Those of his enemies whom it skewered and roasted were of course happy to discover its weaknesses—the frequent use of personal satire, the density of topical reference (sometimes lost even on the poet's contemporaries), and the lack of real action. Quite a number of Pope's champions have had similar doubts, however, so that the full praises of a few critics are offset by the highly qualified approval of others. To be sure, neither friend nor foe has dismissed the poem, probably because with Dr. Johnson all have felt its force, intermittently expressed though it may be. Both in his life of Pope and in conversations recorded by Boswell, Johnson particularly commends the concluding verses of Book IV, because, he tells us, ". . . they are noble lines" (Boswell, *Life*, Hill-Powell, II, 84, n. 2). But Johnson elsewhere expresses doubts about the poem. In short, he anticipates the generations of readers who have given *The Dunciad* a mixed reception, much as Pope's contemporaries had done.

The most frequently anthologized section of the poem, Book IV, offers a fulfillment of the prophecies expressed earlier in the work. It is there that Night and Chaos aid the Queen of Darkness as she extinguishes the light of science and art:

> Thus at her felt approach, and secret might,
> Art after art goes out, and all is Night.
> See skulking Truth to her old cavern fled,
> Mountains of casuistry heaped o'er her head!
> Philosophy, that leaned on Heaven before,
> Shrinks to her second cause, and is no more.
> Physic of Metaphysic begs defense,
> And Metaphysic calls for aid on Sense!
> See Mystery to Mathematics fly!
> In vain! they gaze, turn giddy, rave, and die.
> Religion blushing veils her sacred fires,
> And unawares Morality expires.
> Nor public flame, nor private, dares to shine;
> Nor human spark is left, nor glimpse divine!
> Lo! thy dread empire, CHAOS! is restored;
> Light dies before thy uncreating word:
> Thy hand, great Anarch! lets the curtain fall;
> And universal darkness buries All.

Despite the obvious justice of praising this last section of the poem, it seems most readers agree with James Sutherland (Introduction to *The Dunciad* in the Twickenham Edition, VI, xxxii) that the fourth book is sometimes so very obscure that it must ". . . lean too heavily on the explanatory notes to make it intelligible, and more knowledge is often assumed in the reader than could fairly be expected, even in 1742." (For a different view, see George Sherburn, "*The Dunciad*, Book IV," *Studies in English 1944*, Austin, Texas, 1945.) The other three books are occasionally as difficult as the fourth, but they are much less often so. Accordingly, it is Book III that is here offered to represent *The Dunciad*, rather than the usual choice, Book IV.

For fifteen years or more before the first version of *The Dunciad* appeared in 1728, Pope had been part of the informally organized Scriblerus Club, whose purpose was to satirize dull poets and critics. Its membership, which may not in fact have gathered after 1714, included Jonathan Swift, John Gay, John Arbuthnot, and Thomas Parnell. Typical of the kinds of literature its discussions engendered are Book III of *Gulliver's Travels*, *Memoirs of Martinus Scriblerus*, and *Peri Bathous: Or the Art of Sinking in Poetry*, a prose treatise which ironically instructs its readers in the art of very bad (bathetic) writing. Generally these works follow Dryden's tack in *Mac Flecknoe*. That is, they offer mock-encouragement to enterprising stupidity and ineptitude. During this period Pope had of course been busy with other activities as well— the translations of Homer and an edition of Shakespeare. These and other of his works aroused the jealousy of dozens of scribblers, who attacked him spitefully. His dwarfed and misshaped body as well as his supposed religious and political views were the objects of their mean attentions year after year. Though he had provoked almost none of these literary assaults, and so might have been expected to answer angrily, Pope kept his peace until a solid Elizabethan scholar irked him beyond endurance. In 1726, Lewis Theobald, the offending man of letters, offered the world a correction of Pope's edition of Shakespeare (1725), without a word of censure for the editor himself, in a work called *Shakespeare Restored: Or, a Specimen of the Many Errors, As Well Committed as Unamended, by Mr. Pope*. . . . In the same year, Swift— a fellow Scriblerian—came over from Ireland to visit Pope. Some evidence suggests that he prompted his host to write *The Dunciad* to satirize dullards, in whose ranks he placed Theobald, it seems; or if Pope himself began the project, Swift at least encouraged him to continue, making helpful suggestions all the while.

Like Dryden's *Mac Flecknoe*, Pope's subject is the succession to the throne of Dullness. The action of the work takes place on Lord Mayor's Day, and Lewis Theobald is made to succeed Elkanah Settle (actually poet to the City of London, who had died in 1724) as Prince of Dullness. In the process of cutting down his most recent and most formidable enemy, Theobald, Pope took the opportunity to reduce dozens of dunces who had plagued him for so long. In fact he restimulated their anger early in 1728; it was then that he published the *Peri Bathous*, which drew upon their writings in order to illustrate just how bad an author can become, if he will only try. And to further infuriate them, Pope grouped the offenders under such headings as *Parrots*, *Tortoises*, *Eels*, and so on, depending upon the nature of their literary inadequacy; in doing so, however, he identified them not by name, but by initials only, so that two or more men with the same initials (even if the letters were out of order) more than once responded to a single one of Pope's identifications. By the time *The Dunciad* was to appear, many of his old enemies had attacked him anew, and word of the forthcoming poem had made the rounds; when it left the press, the town went wild, and Pope seems to have been in some danger of his life from those he had deftly abused.

Very soon after the poem appeared, readers sought help in understanding its many obscure references. Though various unauthorized keys to the work flowed from the presses, in 1729, Pope himself offered *The Dunciad, In Three Books, with Notes Variorum*. For many years thereafter, this second version of the poem was left essentially unchanged. During that time he worked on other things—particularly the Moral Epistles (or *Epistles to Several Persons*) and the *Imitations of Horace*. Then, in March, 1742, appeared *The New Dunciad: As it was Found in the Year 1741*. In this addition to the earlier three sections, Pope provided a fulfillment of the predictions set forth in Book III; the reign of dullness, only a threat in the first three books, actually begins in Book IV (as *The New Dunciad* was finally to be called). Generally less personal in its satire than the rest of the poem, it concerns itself not with Theobald but with the sorry state of political and social conditions in England after two decades of Whig supremacy. Pope, informed by the same spirit as other Tory satirists—Swift and the older Dryden, for example—here contemplates with dread and muted anger the destruction of the orderly world he has known. But the last step in the development of *The Dunciad* was yet to be taken.

In 1743, Pope brought out a completely new version of the poem,

The Dunciad, In Four Books, in which Theobald, the temperate and learned man, is no longer the Prince of Dunces. In his place is the untutored and insensitive (though energetic and capable) Colley Cibber, who had been a successful comic actor, dramatist, and theater owner. In 1730, after a long career on the stage, he was appointed Poet Laureate (a post for which Pope's religion disqualified him). Perhaps the poet's dislike of the actor can be traced to Cibber's ridicule of *Three Hours After Marriage* (1717), a play on which Gay and Pope had collaborated, though clearly there were many less personal reasons for the antipathy; the men were worlds apart in endowments, training, and temperament. In 1742, matters between them came to a head; maybe Pope precipitated a crisis by letting it be known he planned to unseat Theobald and to enthrone Cibber. This would explain Cibber's cruelly effective pamphlet *A Letter from Mr. Cibber to Mr. Pope* (1742), in which Pope is made to look ridiculous, in part as an ineffectual young man about town. But probably it is futile to attempt to define the steps in Pope's decision. Whatever they were, it results in more advantages than disadvantages to the poem, though both occur. Suffice it to say that where Pope is diligent in revision, as almost invariably he is, the poem is improved by the replacement of Cibber for Theobald, in large measure because one can more readily imagine that an unlearned and intellectually irresponsible buffoon masquerading as a leader of poets is a more dangerous Prince than a kind and circumspect scholar, however dull.

TEXT. *The Works of Alexander Pope, Esq.*, ed. William Warburton (9 vols., London, 1751).

The Dunciad

In Four Books

Book the Third

Argument

After the other persons are disposed in their proper places of rest, the Goddess transports the King to her Temple, and there lays him to slumber with his head on her lap; a position of marvellous virtue, which causes all the Visions of wild enthusiasts, projectors, politicians, inamoratos, castle-builders, chemists, and poets. He is immediately carried on the wings of Fancy, and led by a mad Poetical Sibyl, to the Elysian shade; where, on the banks of Lethe, the souls of the dull are dipped by Bavius, before their entrance into this world. There he is met by the ghost of Settle, and by him made acquainted with the wonders of the place, and with those which he himself is destined to perform. He takes him to a Mount of Vision, from whence he shews him the past triumphs of the Empire of Dulness, then the present, and lastly the future: how small a part of the world was ever conquered by Science, how soon those conquests were stopped, and those very nations again reduced to her dominion. Then distinguishing the Island of Great Britain, shews by what aids, by what persons, and by what degrees it shall be brought to her Empire. Some of the persons he causes to pass in review before his eyes, describing each by his proper figure, character, and qualifications. On a sudden the Scene shifts, and a vast number of miracles and prodigies appear, utterly surprising and unknown to the King himself, 'till they are explained to be the wonders of his own reign now commencing. On this subject Settle breaks into a congratulation, yet not unmixed with concern, that his own times were but the types of these. He prophesies how first the nation shall be over-run with Farces, Operas, and Shows; how the throne of Dulness shall be advanced over the Theatres, and set up even at Court: then how her Sons shall preside in the seats of Arts and Sciences: giving a glimpse, or Pisgah-sight of the future Fulness of her Glory, the accomplishment whereof is the subject of the fourth and last book.

Book III

BUT in her Temple's last recess inclos'd,
On Dulness' lap th'Anointed head repos'd.
Him close the curtains round with Vapours blue,
And soft besprinkles with Cimmerian dew.
Then raptures high the seat of Sense o'erflow,   5
Which only heads refin'd from Reason know.
Hence, from the straw where Bedlam's Prophet nods,

---

2. *Th'Anointed head:* The King's head (Cibber's).

4. *Cimmerian:* The Cimmereii were fabled by the ancients to live in perpetual darkness. The setting for Book III is the underworld, the realm of the dead.

He hears loud Oracles, and talks with Gods:
Hence the Fool's Paradise, the Statesman's Scheme,
The air-built Castle, and the golden Dream,   10
The Maid's romantic wish, the Chemist's flame,
And Poet's vision of eternal Fame.
    And now, on Fancy's easy wing convey'd,
The King descending, views th'Elysian Shade.
A slip-shod Sibyl led his steps along,   15
In lofty madness meditating song;
Her tresses staring from Poetic dreams,
And never wash'd, but in Castalia's streams.
Taylor, their better Charon, lends an oar
(Once swan of Thames, tho' now he sings no more);   20
Benlowes, propitious still to blockheads, bows;
And Shadwell nods the Poppy on his brows.
Here, in a dusky vale where Lethe rolls,
Old Bavius sits, to dip poetic souls,
And blunt the sense, and fit it for a skull   25
Of solid proof, impenetrably dull:
Instant, when dipt, away they wing their flight,
Where Brown and Mears unbar the gates of Light,
Demand new bodies, and in Calf's array,
Rush to the world, impatient for the day.   30
Millions and millions on these banks he views,
Thick as the stars of night, or morning dews,
As thick as bees o'er vernal blossoms fly,
As thick as eggs at Ward in Pillory.
    Wond'ring he gaz'd: When lo! a Sage appears,   35

14. *Elysian:* Pertaining to Elysium, in Greek myth (not the earliest) located in Hades and regarded as the place where favored men go after death.

15. *Sibyl:* A prophetess inspired by a god, most often Apollo.

18. *Castalia:* A nymph who threw herself into a spring when pursued by Apollo. It was thereafter sacred to the god and to the muses.

19. *Taylor:* John Taylor (1580–1653), known as the Water Poet, was a Thames waterman, who after serving in the British Navy kept a public house in Oxford, then in London. There he sold his own bad verse. Charon, to whom Taylor is compared, is also a waterman—the operator of the ferry that carried the dead over the River Styx to Hades.

21. *Benlowes*] A country gentleman, famous for his own bad Poetry, and for patronizing bad Poets. . . . [Notes like this one, preceded by a bracket, are taken from the *Dunciad* text of 1751, edited by Warburton. Unless otherwise attributed, they may be taken as part of Pope's own apparatus.]

22. *Shadwell nods the Poppy*] Shadwell took opium for many years, and died of too large a dose, in the year 1692.

23. *Lethe:* A river in Hades. Those who drank its waters forgot their past.

24. *Bavius*] Bavius was an ancient Poet, celebrated by Virgil for the like cause as Bays by our author, though not in so Christian-like a manner: For heathenishly it is declared by Virgil of Bavius, that he ought to be *hated* and *detested* for his evil works; *Qui Bavium non odit;* whereas we have often had occasion to observe our Poet's great *Good Nature* and *Mercifulness* thro' the whole course of this Poem. SCRIBLERUS.

28. *Brown and Mears*] Booksellers, Printers for any body.

34. *Ward in Pillory*] John Ward of Hackney, Esq. Member of Parliament, being convicted of forgery, was first expelled the House, and then sentenced to the Pillory on the 17th of February 1727. . . .

By his broad shoulders known, and length of ears,
Known by the band and suit which Settle wore
(His only suit) for twice three years before:
All as the vest, appear'd the wearer's frame,
Old in new state, another yet the same.   40
Bland and familiar as in life, begun
Thus the great Father to the greater Son.
   Oh born to see what none can see awake!
Behold the wonders of th'oblivious Lake.
Thou, yet unborn, hast touch'd this sacred shore;   45
The hand of Bavius drench'd thee o'er and o'er.
But blind to former as to future fate,
What mortal knows his pre-existent state?
Who knows how long thy transmigrating soul
Might from Bœotian to Bœotian roll?   50
How many Dutchmen she vouchsaf'd to thrid?
How many stages thro' old Monks she rid;
And all who since, in mild benighted days,
Mix'd the Owl's ivy with the Poet's bays.
As man's Mæanders to the vital spring   55
Roll all their tides, then back their circles bring;
Or whirligigs, twirl'd round by skilful swain,
Suck the thread in, then yield it out again:
All nonsense thus, of old or modern date,
Shall in thee centre, from thee circulate.   60
For this our Queen unfolds to vision true
Thy mental eye, for thou hast much to view:
Old scenes of glory, times long cast behind
Shall, first recall'd, rush forward to thy mind:
Then stretch thy sight o'er all her rising reign,   65
And let the past and future fire thy brain.
   Ascend this hill, whose cloudy point commands
Her boundless empire over seas and lands.
See, round the Poles where keener spangles shine,
Where spices smoke beneath the burning Line   70
(Earth's wide extremes) her sable flag display'd,
And all the nations cover'd in her shade!
   Far eastward cast thine eye, from whence the Sun
And orient Science their bright course begun:

37. *Settle*] Elkannah Settle was once a writer in vogue, as well as Cibber, both for Dramatic Poetry and Politics. Mr. Dennis tells us that "he was a formidable rival to Mr. Dryden, and that in the University of Cambridge there were those who gave him the *preference*. . . ."

42. *Father to the greater Son:* Settle is Cibber's father in the family of the dull.

50. *Bœotian to Bœotian*] Bœotia [a kind of Greek hinterland] lay under the ridicule of the Wits formerly, as Ireland does now; tho' it produced one of the greatest Poets [Pindar, not Hesiod] and one of the greatest Generals [Epaminondas] of Greece. . . .

54. *Owl's ivy:* The owl is a bird of ostensible wisdom only.

57. *Whirligigs:* A toy spun with a string or with the fingers.

One god-like Monarch all that pride confounds,   75
He, whose long wall the wandr'ing Tartar bounds;
Heav'ns! what a pile! whole ages perish there,
And one bright blaze turns Learning into air.
  Thence to the south extend thy gladden'd eyes;
There rival flames with equal glory rise,   80
From shelves to shelves see greedy Vulcan roll,
And lick up all their Physic of the Soul.
  How little, mark! that portion of the ball,
Where, faint at best, the beams of Science fall:
Soon as they dawn, from Hyperborean skies   85
Embody'd dark, what clouds of Vandals rise!
Lo! where Mæotis sleeps, and hardly flows
The freezing Tanais thro' a waste of snows,
The North by myriads pours her mighty sons,
Great nurse of Goths, of Alans, and of Huns!   90
See Alaric's stern port! the martial frame
Of Genseric! and Attila's dread name!
See the bold Ostrogoths on Latium fall;
See the fierce Visigoths on Spain and Gaul!
See, where the morning gilds the palmy shore   95
(The soil that arts and infant letters bore)
His conqu'ring tribes th'Arabian prophet draws,
And saving Ignorance enthrones by Laws.
See Christians, Jews, one heavy sabbath keep,
And all the western world believe and sleep.   100
  Lo! Rome herself, proud mistress now no more
Of arts, but thund'ring against heathen lore;
Her grey-hair'd Synods damning books unread,
And Bacon trembling for his brazen head.
Padua, with sighs, beholds her Livy burn,   105

---

81. *Vulcan:* An early Roman fire-god, only later identified with Hephaestos, the smith-god (and fire-god as well).

82. *Lick up . . . Soul*] The Caliph, Omar I, having conquered Ægypt, caused his General to burn the Ptolemæan library, on the gates of which was this inscription, ΨΥΧΗΣ ΙΑΤΡΕΙΟΝ, the Physic of the Soul. [Modern historians reject this view.]

85. *Hyperborean skies:* Hyperboreans were a legendary people supposed by the Greeks to live beyond the North wind (Boreas).

87. *Mæotis:* The northern arm of the Black Sea.

88. *Tanais:* The River Don, which flows into Maeotis.

91. *Alaric:* Two kings of the Visigoths bore the name; in the fourth and fifth centuries they overran Italy, France, and Spain.

92. *Genseric:* King of the Vandals and Alans.

96–98. *The soil. . . .*] Phœnicia, Syria, Etc. where letters are said to have been invented. In these countries Mahomet began his conquests.

104. *Bacon:* Roger Bacon (c. 1214–1292), English experimental scientist (particularly in optics) and member of the Franciscans, was popularly supposed to have made a brass head that could speak. [Pope's Bacon is afraid—trembling—probably in anticipation of the Church's anger at his presumption.]

105. *Livy burn:* The works of the Roman historian Livy were burned by Pope Gregory, because they stressed heathen rites.

And ev'n th'Antipodes Vigilius mourn.
See, the Cirque falls, th' unpillar'd Temple nods,
Streets pav'd with Heroes, Tyber choak'd with Gods:
'Till Peter's keys some christ'ned Jove adorn,
And Pan to Moses lends his pagan horn;   110
See graceless Venus to a Virgin turn'd,
Or Phidias broken, and Apelles burn'd.
    Behold yon' Isle, by Palmers, Pilgrims trod,
Men bearded, bald, cowl'd, uncowl'd, shod, unshod,
Peel'd, patch'd, and pyebald, linsey-wolsey brothers,   115
Grave Mummers! sleeveless some, and shirtless others.
That once was Britain—Happy! had she seen
No fiercer sons, had Easter never been.
In peace, great Goddess, ever be ador'd;
How keen the war, if Dulness draw the sword!   120
Thus visit not thy own! on this blest age
Oh spread thy Influence, but restrain thy Rage.
    And see, my son! the hour is on its way,
That lifts our Goddess to imperial sway;
This fav'rite Isle, long sever'd from her reign,   125
Dove-like, she gathers to her wings again.
Now look thro' Fate! behold the scene she draws!
What aids, what armies to assert her cause!
See all her progeny, illustrious sight!
Behold, and count them, as they rise to light.   130
As Berecynthia, while her offspring vye
In homage to the Mother of the sky,
Surveys around her, in the blest abode,
An hundred sons, and ev'ry son a God:
Not with less glory mighty Dulness crown'd,   135
Shall take thro' Grub-street her triumphant round;
And her Parnassus glancing o'er at once,
Behold an hundred sons, and each a Dunce.
    Mark first that youth who takes the foremost place,
And thrusts his person full into your face.   140

106. *Antipodes Vigilius mourn:* Virgilius, eighth-century Bishop of Salzburg, was reprimanded publicly for his belief in the existence of the Antipodes—persons or places directly opposite to each other on the globe.
107. *The Cirque:* The Roman Coliseum.
109. *'Till Peter's keys. . . .*] After the government of Rome devolved to the Popes, their zeal was for some time exerted in demolishing the heathen Temples and Statues. . . . At length they spared some of the Temples, by converting them to Churches; and some of the Statues, by modifying them into images of Saints. . . .
115. *Linsey-wolsey:* Originally, a mixture of linen and wool; here, haphazardly assorted.
116. *Mummers:* Those, in England particularly, who play in dumb shows and go about in disguises at Christmas time.
118. *Had Easter never been*] Wars in England anciently, about the right time of celebrating Easter.
131. *Berecynthia:* Cybele, the "Great Mother," a goddess of the powers of nature. Berecyntius, a mountain in Phrygia, was the center of her worship.
136. *Grub-street:* A street in London associated with hack writers.

With all thy Father's virtues blest, be born!
And a new Cibber shall the stage adorn.
    A second see, by meeker manners known,
And modest as the maid that sips alone;
From the strong fate of drams if thou get free,   145
Another Durfey, Ward, shall sing in thee.
Thee shall each alehouse, thee each gill house mourn,
And answ'ring gin-shops sowrer sighs return.
    Jacob, the scourge of Grammar, mark with awe,
Nor less revere him, blunderbuss of Law.   150
Lo P—p—le's brow, tremendous to the town,
Horneck's fierce eye, and Roome's funereal Frown.
Lo sneering Goode, half malice and half whim,
A Fiend in glee, ridiculously grim.
Each Cygnet sweet, of Bath and Tunbridge race,   155
Whose tuneful whistling makes the waters pass:
Each Songster, Riddler, ev'ry nameless name,
All crowd, who foremost shall be damn'd to Fame.
Some strain in rhyme; the Muses, on their racks,
Scream like the winding of ten thousand jacks;   160
Some free from rhyme or reason, rule or check,
Break Priscian's head, and Pegasus's neck;
Down, down they larum, with impetuous whirl,

---

141. *With all thy Father's virtues . . .*] It was very natural to shew to the Hero, before all others, his own Son [Theophilus Cibber], who had already begun to emulate him in his theatrical, poetical, and even political capacities. . . .

146. *Another Durfey, Ward:* Tom Durfey (1653–1723) was a poetaster who enjoyed a vogue among the country squires; he had long been the object of witty literary attack. Edward Ward (1667–1731) was a minor author in verse and prose; he kept an ale house in London, which establishment presumably he had to escape to become "Another Durfey."

149. *Jacob*] "This *Gentleman* is son of a *considerable Malster* of Romsey in Southamptonshire, and bred to the Law under a *very eminent Attorney:* Who, between his *more laborious* studies, has *diverted* himself with Poetry. . . ." GILES JACOB of himself, *Lives of Poets*, vol. I. He very grosly, and unprovok'd, abused in that book the Author's Friend, Mr. Gay. . . .

151. *P—p—le's brow:* William Popple (1701–1764), a solicitor and a dramatist, attacked Pope in a periodical called *The Prompter* in 1735 and 1736.

152. *Horneck's . . . Roome's. . . .*] These two were virulent Party-writers. . . . The first was Philip Horneck, Author of a Billingsgate paper call'd The High German Doctor. Edward Roome... writ some of the papers call'd *Pasquin*, where by malicious Innuendos he endeavoured to represent our Author guilty of malevolent practices with a great man then under prosecution of Parliament. . . .

153. *Goode*] An ill-natur'd Critic, who writ a satire on our Author, call'd *The Mock Æsop*, and many anonymous Libels in News-papers for hire.

155. *Cygnet . . . Bath . . . Tunbridge:* A cygnet is a young swan. Bath and Tunbridge Wells are both watering-places.

156. *Tuneful whistling*] There were several successions of these sort of minor poets, at Tunbridge, Bath, &c. singing the praise of the Annuals flourishing for that season; whose names indeed would be nameless, and therefore the Poet slurs them over with others in general.

160. *Jacks:* A jack is a machine for turning a spit in roasting meat.

162. *Priscian's head . . . Pegasus's neck:* Priscian was a famous grammarian of the sixth century; Pegasus is, in Greek mythology, the winged horse who stamped his hoof and produced the fountain Hippocrene, sacred to the Muses. Hence his connection with poetic inspiration.

163. *Larum:* To sound forth loudly.

    The Pindars, and the Miltons of a Curl.

        Silence, ye Wolves! while Ralph to Cynthia howls,   165
And makes Night hideous—Answer him, ye Owls!

        Sense, speech, and measure, living tongues and dead,
Let all give way—and Morris may be read.
Flow, Welsted, flow! like thine inspirer, Beer;
Tho' stale, not ripe; tho' thin, yet never clear;   170
So sweetly mawkish, and so smoothly dull;
Heady, not strong; o'erflowing, tho' not full.

        Ah Dennis! Gildon ah! what ill-starr'd rage
Divides a friendship long confirm'd by age?
Blockheads with reason wicked wits abhor,   175
But fool with fool is barb'rous civil war.
Embrace, embrace, my sons! be foes no more!
Nor glad vile Poets with true Critics gore.

        Behold yon Pair, in strict embraces join'd;
How like in manners, and how like in mind!   180
Equal in wit, and equally polite,
Shall this a Pasquin, that a Grumbler write;
Like are their merits, like rewards they share,
That shines a Consul, this Commissioner.

        But who is he, in closet close y-pent,   185
Of sober face, with learned dust besprent?
Right well mine eyes arede the myster wight,
On parchment scraps y-fed, and Wormius hight.

164. *Curl:* Edmund Curll (1675–1747) was a piratical publisher whose establishment included a group of hacks ("The Pindars, and the Milton's . . .") who were particularly hostile to Pope.

165. *Ralph to Cynthia howls*] James Ralph, a name inserted after the first editions, not known to our author till he writ a swearing-piece called *Sawney*, very abusive of Dr. Swift, Mr. Gay, and himself. These lines allude to a thing of his, intitled, *Night*, a Poem. . . . [*Cynthia* is a name for the goddess of the moon.]

168. *Morris:* Pope's note on this line directs the reader to Book II of the *Dunciad*. There he says in part, "Besaleel Morris was author of some satires on the translators of Homer, with many other things printed in newspapers." See *Dunciad*, 1751, p. 135, n. 124 and p. 136, n. 126.

169. *Welsted:* Here again Pope directs the reader to an earlier note, where he says in part, "Leonard Welsted, author of *The Triumvirate, or a Letter in verse from Palaemon to Celia at Bath*, which was meant for a satire on Mr. P. and some of his friends about the year 1718. He writ some other things which we cannot remember." See *Dunciad*, 1751, p. 150, n. 207 and p. 196, n. 169.

173. *Dennis . . . Gildon:* John Dennis (1657–1734), critic and dramatist, was Pope's intermittently expressive enemy from 1709, when in *An Essay on Criticism*, ll. 582–587, Pope provoked him, without malice. Charles Gildon (1665–1724), critic and dramatist, attacked Pope in *A New Rehearsal*, 1714, calling him, "an easy Versifyer, Conceited and a Contemner secretly of all others."

179. *Behold yon Pair . . . strict embraces . . . :* Earlier versions of *The Dunciad* identified the two as Sir Thomas Burnet, who in 1715 attacked Pope in *The Grumbler*, a periodical; and George Duckett, who probably wrote the numbers of *Pasquin* in which Pope is abused. Late versions of *The Dunciad* are easier on the pair in the notes as well as in the text itself. Strict embraces are close embraces.

184. *Consul . . . Commissioner*] Such places were given at this time to such sort of Writers.

187. *Myster wight*] Uncouth mortal.

188. *Wormius hight:* Named Wormius. Wormius, the bookworm, was Thomas Hearne (1678–1735), a genuinely learned antiquarian whom Pope derides (in a good-humored way) much as his contemporaries had done. Pope's note begins, "Let not

To future ages may thy dulness last,
As thou preserv'st the dulness of the past!   190
    There, dim in clouds, the poring Scholiasts mark,
Wits, who, like owls, see only in the dark,
A Lumberhouse of books in ev'ry head,
For ever reading, never to be read!
    But, where each Science lifts its modern type,   195
Hist'ry her Pot, Divinity her Pipe,
While proud Philosophy repines to show,
Dishonest sight! his breeches rent below;
Imbrown'd with native bronze, lo! Henley stands,
Tuning his voice, and balancing his hands.   200
How fluent nonsense trickles from his tongue!
How sweet the periods, neither said, nor sung!
Still break the benches, Henley! with thy strain,
While Sherlock, Hare, and Gibson preach in vain.
Oh great Restorer of the good old Stage,   205
Preacher at once, and Zany of thy age!
Oh worthy thou of Ægypt's wise abodes,
A decent priest, where monkeys were the gods!
But fate with butchers plac'd thy priestly stall,
Meek modern faith to murder, hack, and mawl;   210
And bade thee live, to crown Britannia's praise,
In Toland's, Tindal's, and in Woolston's days.
    Yet oh, my sons, a father's words attend
(So may the fates preserve the ears you lend):
'Tis yours, a Bacon, or a Locke to blame,   215
A Newton's genius, or a Milton's flame:
But oh! with One, immortal One dispense,
The source of Newton's Light, of Bacon's Sense.
Content, each Emanation of his fires
That beams on earth, each Virtue he inspires,   220
Each Art he prompts, each Charm he can create,
Whate'er he gives, are giv'n for you to hate.
Persist, by all divine in Man unaw'd,

---

this name, purely fictitious, be conceited
to mean the learned *Olaus Wormius;* much
less . . . our own Antiquary Mr. *Thomas
Hearne,* who had no way aggrieved our
Poet, but on the contrary published many
curious tracts which he hath to his great
contentment perused."
    191. *Scholiasts:* Writers of explanatory
notes on an author, especially an ancient
author.
    199. *Henley stands*] J. Henley the
Orator; he preached on the Sundays upon
Theological matters, and on the Wednes-
days upon all other sciences. . . . He de-
claimed some years against the greatest
persons, and occasionally did our Author

that honour. . . .
    204. *Sherlock, Hare, and Gibson*] Bishops
of Salisbury, Chichester, and London. . . .
    212. *Toland's, Tindal's . . . Woolston's*]
Tho. Woolston was an impious madman,
who wrote in a most insolent style against
the Miracles of the Gospel, in the years
1726, *&c.* [In a note to Bk. II. l. 399, Pope
says of Toland and Tindal, "Two persons,
not so happy as to be obscure, who writ
against the Religion of their Country.
Toland, the Author of the Atheist's liturgy,
Pantheisticon, was a spy. . . . *Tindal* was
author of the *Rights of the Christian Church*
and *Christianity as Old as the Creation."*]

But Learn, ye DUNCES! not to scorn your God.

Thus he, for then a ray of Reason stole   225
Half thro' the solid darkness of his soul;
But soon the cloud return'd—and thus the Sire:
See now, what Dulness and her sons admire?
See what the charms, that smite the simple heart
Not touch'd by Nature, and not reach'd by Art.   230
His never-blushing head he turn'd aside
(Not half so pleas'd when Goodman prophesy'd)
And look'd, and saw a sable Sorc'rer rise,
Swift to whose hand a winged volume flies:
All sudden, Gorgons hiss, and Dragons glare,   235
And ten-horn'd fiends and Giants rush to war.
Hell rises, Heav'n descends, and dance on Earth:
Gods, imps, and monsters, music, rage, and mirth,
A fire, a jigg, a battle, and a ball,
'Till one wide conflagration swallows all.   240
Thence a new world to Nature's laws unknown,
Breaks out refulgent, with a heav'n its own:
Another Cynthia her new journey runs,
And other planets circle other suns.
The forests dance, the rivers upward rise,   245
Whales sport in woods, and dolphins in the skies;
And last, to give the whole creation grace,
Lo! one vast Egg produces human race.
Joy fills his soul, joy innocent of thought;
What pow'r, he cries, what pow'r these wonders wrought?   250
Son, what thou seek'st is in thee! Look, and find
Each Monster meets his likeness in thy mind.
Yet would'st thou more? In yonder cloud behold,
Whose sarsenet skirts are edg'd with flamy gold,
A matchless Youth! his nod these worlds controuls,   255
Wings the red lightning, and the thunder rolls.
Angel of Dulness, sent to scatter round
Her magic charms o'er all unclassic ground:
Yon stars, yon suns, he rears at pleasure higher,
Illumes their light, and sets their flames on fire.   260

232. *Goodman*] Mr. Cibber tells us, in his Life, p. 149, that Goodman being at the rehearsal of a play, in which he had a part, clapped him on the shoulder and cried, "If he does not make a good actor, I'll be d—d.—And (says Mr. Cibber) I make it a question, whether Alexander himself, or Charles the twelfth of Sweden, when at the head of their first victorious armies, could feel a greater transport in their bosoms than I did in mine."
233. *A sable Sorc'rer*] Dr. Faustus, the subject of a set of Farces, which lasted in vogue two or three seasons, in which both Playhouses strove to outdo each other for some years. All the extravagancies in the sixteen lines following were introduced on the Stage. . . .
243. *Cynthia:* The moon.
248. *One vast Egg*] In another of these Farces Harlequin is hatched upon the stage, out of a large Egg.
254. *Sarsenet skirts:* Skirts of fine, soft silk.

Immortal Rich! how calm he sits at ease
'Mid snows of paper, and fierce hail of pease;
And proud his Mistress' orders to perform,
Rides in the whirlwind, and directs the storm.
    But lo! to dark encounter in mid air   265
New wizards rise; I see my Cibber there!
Booth in his cloudy tabernacle shrin'd,
On grinning dragons thou shalt mount the wind.
Dire is the conflict, dismal is the dinn,
Here shouts all Drury, there all Lincoln's-inn;   270
Contending Theatres our empire raise,
Alike their labours, and alike their praise.
    And are these wonders, Son, to thee unknown?
Unknown to thee? These wonders are thy own.
These Fate reserv'd to grace thy reign divine,   275
Foreseen by me, but ah! with-held from mine.
In Lud's old walls tho' long I rul'd, renown'd
Far as loud Bow's stupendous bells resound;
Tho' my own Aldermen confer'd the bays,
To me committing their eternal praise,   280
Their full-fed Heroes, their pacific May'rs,
Their annual trophies, and their monthly wars:
Tho' long my Party built on me their hopes,
For writing Pamphlets, and for roasting Popes;
Yet lo! in me what authors have to brag on!   285
Reduc'd at last to hiss in my own dragon.
Avert it Heav'n! that thou, my Cibber, e'er
Should'st wag a serpent-tail in Smithfield fair!
Like the vile straw that's blown abou the streets,
The needy Poet sticks to all he meets,   290

261. *Immortal Rich*] Mr. John Rich, Master of the Theatre Royal in Covent-garden, was the first that excelled this way. [That is, Rich concerned himself with unusual stage effects.]
266. *Cibber there*] The history of the foregoing absurdities is verified by himself, in these words (Life, Chap. XV.) "Then sprung forth that succession of monstrous medleys that have so long infested the stage. . . . If I am asked why I assented, I have no better excuse for my error than to confess I did it against my conscience, and had not virtue enough to starve. . . ."
267. *Booth*] *Booth* and *Cibber* were joint managers of the Theatre in Drury-lane. [The second of the two major theatres in London of the first half of the eighteenth century was Lincoln's Inn Fields, or after 1732, Covent Garden.]
268. *On grinning dragons . . . mount the wind*] In his Letter to Mr. P. Mr. C. solemnly declares this not to be *literally*
true. We hope therefore the reader will understand it *allegorically* only.
277. *Lud's old walls:* The House of Lords.
278. *Bow's stupendous bells:* The bells at St. Mary-le-Bow in Cheapside.
282. *Annual trophies . . . monthly wars:* Awards were made on the Lord-mayor's day. Military exercises were held each month on the Artillery Ground.
283. *Long my Party*] Settle, like most Party-writers, was very uncertain in his political principles. He was employed to hold the pen in the *Character* of a *popish successor,* but afterwards printed his *Narrative* on the other side. He had managed the ceremony of a famous Pope-burning on Nov. 17, 1680, then became a trooper in [Catholic] King James's army. . . . After the Revolution he kept a booth at Bartholomew-fair, where . . . he acted in his old age in a Dragon of green leather of his own invention. . . .

Coach'd, carted, trod upon, now loose, now fast,
And carry'd off in some Dog's tail at last.
Happier thy fortunes! like a rolling stone,
Thy giddy dulness still shall lumber on,
Safe in its heaviness, shall never stray,   295
But lick up ev'ry blockhead in the way.
Thee shall the Patriot, thee the Courtier taste,
And ev'ry year be duller than the last.
'Till rais'd from booths, to Theatre, to Court,
Her seat imperial Dulness shall transport.   300
Already Opera prepares the way,
The sure fore-runner of her gentle sway;
Let her thy heart, next Drabs and Dice, engage,
The third mad passion of thy doting age.
Teach thou the warb'ling Polypheme to roar,   305
And scream thyself as none e'er scream'd before!
To aid our cause, if Heav'n thou can'st not bend,
Hell thou shalt move; for Faustus is our friend:
Pluto with Cato thou for this shalt join,
And link the Mourning Bride to Proserpine.   310
Grubstreet! thy fall should men and Gods conspire,
Thy stage shall stand, ensure it but from Fire.
Another Æschylus appears! prepare
For new abortions, all ye pregnant fair!
In flames, like Semele's, be brought to bed,   315
While op'ning Hell spouts wild-fire at your head.
    Now Bavius take the poppy from thy brow,
And place it here! here all ye Heroes bow!
This, this is he, foretold by ancient rhymes:
Th' Augustus born to bring Saturnian times.   320
Signs following signs lead on the mighty year!

303. *Drabs:* Prostitutes.

305. *Polypheme*] He [Cibber] translated the Italian Opera of Polifemo; but unfortunately lost the whole jest of the story. The Cyclops asks Ulysses his *name*, who tells him his name is *Noman*: After his eye is put out, he roars and calls the Brother Cyclops to his aid: They enquire *who has hurt him?* he answers *Noman*; whereupon they all go away again. Our ingenious Translator made Ulysses answer, *I take no name*, whereby all that follow'd became unintelligible. . . .

308–309. *Faustus/Pluto*] Names of miserable Farces, which it was the custom to act at the end of the best Tragedies, to spoil the digestion of the audience.

310. *Mourning Bride to Proserpine*] In Tibbald's farce of Prosperpine, a corn-field was set on fire: whereupon the other playhouse had a barn burnt down for the recreation of the spectators. They also rival'd each other in showing the burnings

of hell-fire, in Dr. Faustus.

313. *Another Æschylus appears*] It is reported of Æschylus, that when his tragedy of the Furies was acted, the audience were so terrified that the children fell into fits, and the big-bellied women miscarried.

315. *Flames, like Semele's:* Semele, loved by Zeus, was persuaded by his wife Hera to ask the god to appear to his mistress in all his splendour. When he did so, Semele was consumed by lightning.

317. *Bavius take the poppy:* See nn. 22, 24 above.

320. *Augustus . . . Saturnian:* Augustus was the first Roman emperor, whose reign—though it marked the end of the republic—is generally associated with the restoration of civil peace and stability; he is in short the herald of great days. Pope says, "*Saturnian* here relates to the age of *Lead.* . . ."

See! the dull stars roll round and re-appear.
See, see, our own true Phœbus wears the bays!
Our Midas sits Lord Chancellor of Plays!
On Poets Tombs see Benson's titles writ!   325
Lo! Ambrose Philips is prefer'd for Wit!
See under Ripley rise a new White-hall,
While Jones' and Boyle's united labours fall:
While Wren with sorrow to the grave descends,
Gay dies unpension'd with a hundred friends,   330
Hibernian Politics, O Swift! thy fate;
And Pope's, ten years to comment and translate.
　　　Proceed, great days! 'till Learning fly the shore,
'Till Birch shall blush with noble blood no more,
'Till Thames see Eaton's sons for ever play,   335
'Till Westminster's whole year be holiday,
'Till Isis' Elders reel, their pupils sport,
And Alma mater lie dissolv'd in Port?
　　　Enough! enough! the raptur'd Monarch cries;
And thro' the Iv'ry Gate the Vision flies.   340

(1728, 1729, 1742, 1743)

324. *Our Midas:* The reference is to Cibber as judge of plays. Midas had the poor taste to prefer the flute-playing of Pan to that of Apollo, whereupon Apollo gave him the ears of an ass to indicate his stupidity.

325. *Benson's titles:* William Benson, Surveyor of the Buildings to George I, warned Lords that the House was in danger of falling. Subsequent inspection by other engineers proved Benson wrong, and he was relieved of his duties. Pope's note deplores the favor this incompetent was granted at the expense of ". . . Sir Christopher Wren . . . who built most of the Churches in London . . ." only to be displaced to make room for Benson.

326. *Ambrose Philips:* See the headnote to Pope's *Pastorals,* above.

327. *Ripley:* Thomas Ripley was a carpenter rapidly advanced by the Whig minister Horace Walpole, who defended the builder's skill against Pope's censure.

328. *Jones' and Boyle's . . . labours] . . .* when this poem was written . . . the works of the famous [architect] Inigo Jones had been for many years so neglected, as to be in danger of ruin . . . ; the Earl of Burlington [Richard Boyle] . . . by his publication of the designs of that great Master and Palladio . . . revived the true taste of Architecture in this Kingdom.

329. *Wren:* See n. 325.

330. *Gay dies] . . .* This gentleman was early in the friendship of our author, which continued to his death. He wrote several

works of humour with great success, the Shepherd's Week, Trivia, the What-d'ye-call-it, Fables; and lastly, the celebrated Beggar's Opera; a piece of a satire which hit all tastes and degrees of men, from those of the highest quality to the very rabble. . . . The vast success of it was unprecedented, and almost incredible. . . . It was acted in London sixty-three days, uninterrupted; and renew'd the next season with equal applauses. . . .

331. *Hibernian Politics:* In a note to Bk. I, l. 26, Pope says, "The politics of England and Ireland [Hibernia] were at this time by some thought to be opposite, or interfering with each other: Dr. Swift of course was in the interest of the latter, our Author of the former." See Swift's *A Modest Proposal.*

332. *Pope's . . . to comment . . . translate]* The author . . . began the Iliad in 1713, and finished it in 1719. The Edition of Shakespear . . . took up near two years more. . . .

335. *Eaton's sons:* Students at England's most famous public school, Eton College, located on the left bank of the Thames.

336. *Westminster's . . . year:* Westminster School, another great public school, is located in London.

337 *Isis' Elders:* Isis is the river associated with Oxford University.

340. *The Iv'ry Gate:* In Homer (*Odyssey*, XIX) true dreams pass through the gate of horn; false dreams through the gate of ivory. See also *Aeneid*, VI.

Samuel Johnson

1709-1784

Johnson was born on September 18, 1709, in Lichfield, the son of Michael Johnson, a bookseller, and Sarah Ford Johnson. He is said to have read prodigiously in his father's shop, acquiring knowledge somewhat haphazardly, and retaining it for years by reason of his tenacious memory. He early showed signs of scrofula—lesions appeared on his body when he was only weeks old—which was to impair his senses, particularly his eyes; he was examined by an oculist around 1710 or 1711, and in 1712 was taken to London to be "touched for evil" by the Queen. Despite his difficulties, he grew up to be a large man, whose physical strength was enormous, though because of the diseases contracted in childhood he was often in some senses ill.

Having been prepared at the Lichfield school, and later at Stourbridge, in 1728 he entered Pembroke College, Oxford, but was forced to leave after about a year for lack of funds. During the next few years he held various tutoring positions in the area of Lichfield and Birmingham. In 1735, he married Mrs. Elizabeth Porter (Tetty, as he called her), a widow twenty years his senior, with whom he enjoyed a very good marriage. He was later to observe, "Marriage has many pains, but celibacy has no pleasures."

Johnson's attempt to start a school at Edial, probably in 1736, failed, and he went up to London with David Garrick (his fellow townsman and former student) in 1737 and found employment with Edward Cave, publisher of the *Gentleman's Magazine*. The poem *London*, Johnson's imitation of Juvenal's third satire, appeared in 1738 and won immediate approval. A few years later, in 1744, *An Account of the Life of Mr. Richard Savage* was published anonymously; and in 1749, his *Vanity of Human Wishes*, an imitation of the tenth satire of Juvenal was issued. In the same year Garrick, who had become a famous actor and manager of Drury Lane, produced Johnson's tragedy *Irene* as a favor to his friend, but the work was not a success, running for only nine nights as it did, and disappearing into the pages of literary history.

Johnson's periodical *Rambler* essays appeared twice weekly during 1750–1752; toward the end of this period, in 1752, his beloved Tetty died. The blow was a hard one. Johnson's loss was particularly keen because of his extreme dislike of being alone. But he persevered and he was, in fact, hard-working during this particularly bitter time, producing his dictionary. He was no doubt in part sustained by his deep religious conviction—perhaps the one part of his life he chose to leave unexamined—and by his rigorous sense of social order, both of which convictions seem to have contributed greatly to his sense of stability. It may be that his sensitivity and his intelligence were too constantly active for him to experience much peace of mind without these supports of high church and Tory commitments.

In 1755, Johnson's reputation was at last firmly established with the publication of his *Dictionary of the English Language*, a labor of eight years, which though immediately acclaimed, did little to improve his very modest circumstances. From 1758 to 1760, Johnson composed another series of periodical essays, the *Idler*, less burdened than the sound and well-received, yet sometimes ponderous *Rambler* essays. In 1759, Johnson's mother died. According to his own comment to Reynolds, he wrote *Rasselas* in the evenings of a week to raise money to pay her funeral expenses, and whether or not he took a bit longer to compose the tale, it is certain that he produced it very rapidly.

The circumstances of Johnson's life changed enormously in 1762, when he was awarded a pension of £300 by the Tory government of George III; he was once and for all freed from the uncertainties that attend an unfixed income. During the next year, on May 16, 1763, in Tom Davies' bookshop, he met Boswell, the man who was to become his biographer. In 1764, Johnson helped to form the famous literary *Club;* it included Goldsmith, Reynolds, Burke and others; and a year later, in 1765, he brought out his edition of Shakespeare, which he had been a long time producing. In this same year Johnson began his friendship with Henry and Hester Thrale, a wealthy couple with whom he was to live a good deal of the time until Thrale's death in 1781. Though many factors—particularly his doubtful health—kept Johnson fairly close to home, in 1773 he agreed to travel through Scotland with Boswell, who for years had been trying to persuade his friend to make the trip, partly as a result of one of Johnson's own suggestions. They met in Edinburgh and toured the Hebrides together, and two years later was published Johnson's *A Journey to the Western Islands* (1775). His last major work, *Lives of the Poets*, appeared in 1781. Not too long after Thrale's death, Mrs. Thrale—to whom Johnson was by this time very close—married the Italian music master Gabriel Piozzi, despite her friend's rather strong objections to the match. Shortly before Johnson's death, he and Mrs. Thrale were estranged. But there were many friends to keep him company during his last days. He died on December 13, 1784, and he was buried in Westminster Abbey.

Samuel Johnson—Selective Bibliography

James L. Clifford, *Johnsonian Studies, 1887–1950. A Survey and Bibliography*, Minneapolis, U. of Minnesota Press, 1951.

Clifford and Donald J. Greene compiled a supplement, "Johnsonian Studies, 1950–60," which appears in *Johnsonian Studies*, ed. Magdi Wahba, Cairo, Société Orientale de Publicité, 1962. Clifford and Greene are presently revising both of these lists with a view to publishing the revision in one volume; the plan includes an extension of works listed, from 1887 to Johnson's own lifetime. See also *CBEL*, II, pp. 613 f.

The great Yale edition of Johnson's works, first under the general editorship of Allen T. Hazen (and now under that of John H. Middendorf), Herman W. Liebert, et al., has to date brought out I, *Dairies, Prayers, and Annals*, ed. E. L. McAdam with Donald and Mary Hyde, 1958; II, *The Idler and The Adventurer*, ed. Walter Jackson Bate, John M. Bullit, and L. F. Powell, 1963; VI, *Poems*, ed. E. L. McAdam and George Milne, 1964. Shortly to appear are VII and VIII, *Johnson on Shakespeare*, ed. Arthur Sherbo. Until it is replaced by the Yale edition, the Oxford text of 1825 (9 vols., 11 parts) remains the nearest thing to a standard edition.

Robert W. Chapman, ed., *Rasselas*, Oxford, Clarendon Press, 1927.

———, *The Letters of Samuel Johnson*, 3 vols., Oxford, Clarendon Press, 1952.

Allen T. Hazen, ed., *Prefaces and Dedications*, New Haven, Yale U. P., 1937.

Robert W. Chapman, ed., *A Journey to the Western Islands of Scotland*, with Boswell's *Tour*, London, H. Milford, 1924.

George Birkbeck Hill, ed., *Johnsonian Miscellanies*, 2 vols., Oxford, Clarendon Press, 1897. Kraus Reprint, New York, has announced a reissue, with a new introduction by Walter Jackson Bate.

James L. Clifford, *Young Sam Johnson*, New York, McGraw-Hill, 1955.

Joseph Wood Krutch, *Samuel Johnson*, New York, H. Holt and Co., 1944.

James L. Clifford, *Hester Lynch Piozzi*, Oxford, Clarendon Press, 1941.

James Boswell, *The Life of Samuel Johnson*, 6 vols., ed., George Birkbeck Hill, revised by L. F. Powell, Oxford, Clarendon Press, 1934–1964.

Aleyn Lyell Reade, ed., *Johnsonian Gleanings*, XI Parts, London, privately printed, 1909–1952.

Walter Jackson Bate, *The Achievement of Samuel Johnson*, New York, Oxford U. P., 1955.

Donald J. Greene, *The Politics of Samuel Johnson*, New Haven, Yale U. P., 1960.

Robert Voitle, *Samuel Johnson the Moralist*, Cambridge, Mass., Harvard U. P., 1961.

William K. Wimsatt, *Philosophic Words: A Study of Style and Meaning in the "Rambler" and "Dictionary" of Samuel Johnson*, New Haven, Yale U. P., 1948.

————, *The Prose Style of Samuel Johnson*, New Haven, Yale U. P., 1941.

Donald J. Greene, ed., *Samuel Johnson; A Collection of Critical Essays*, Englewood Cliffs, N.J., Prentice-Hall, 1965.

Frederick W. Hilles, ed., *New Light on Dr. Johnson*, New Haven, Yale U. P., 1959.

Magdi Wahba, ed., *Bicentenary Essays on Rasselas*, Cairo, Société Orientale de Publicité, 1959.

Johnson, Boswell, and Their Circle: Essays Presented to Lawrence Fitzroy Powell in Honour of His Eighty-Fourth Birthday, Oxford, Clarendon Press, 1965.

Gwin J. Kolb, "The Structure of *Rasselas*," *PMLA*, LXVI (1951), 698–717.

Mary Lascelles, "Rasselas Reconsidered," *Essays and Studies 1951* (New Series), London, John Murray, 1951, pp. 37–52.

Headnote to
THE VANITY OF
HUMAN WISHES

By the time Johnson published "The Vanity of Human Wishes," in 1749, he was a fairly well-established writer, whose earliest poetic effort, "London A Poem," 1738, had been favorably compared with Pope's mature work. In both these poems Johnson's ability is characterized by precision and force of statement rather than by his power to suggest a mood or atmosphere that contributes feeling to meaning. In "The Vanity of Human Wishes" the demands on the reader's attention are particularly strong, because Johnson's intellectually acute statements remain essentially unsupported by emotionally productive clues, except for very short, discrete bursts in the form of epithets, like "treach'rous phantoms," "piercing jibe," "stranger's eye," "torpid veins," and "dreaded coast." In large measure the poem works well as a result of individually memorable observations that assert or illustrate the vanity of human wishes.

Johnson's pessimism in this poem (and elsewhere) has been widely remarked. In a general way one must agree that a good deal of evidence supports such a view. Nevertheless it would be well to bear two things in mind. First, "Samuel Johnson was a pessimist with an enormous zest for living," as Joseph Wood Krutch observes in his biography fo the man. Second, Johnson's art is far too complex for a simple statement about its pessimism (and by implication his pessimism) to be very meaningful. Here, for instance, in "The Vanity," Johnson uses Juvenal's Tenth Satire as the basis of his poem, and to the extent that he imitates his model, he must like Juvenal be "pessimistic." Even so, one must recognize that neither Juvenal nor Johnson is overwhelmed with the sense that man is in a predicament that makes satisfaction impossible. Rather, they maintain that what men erroneously desire will inevitably lead to frustration. The subject is not the futility of life, but the inanity of man's desires. Both Juvenal and Johnson point out that men are lost only if they insist upon "going it alone," without the help of some guide.

As might be expected of an accomplished literary craftsman, Johnson integrates this idea of a power beyond the control of man's ordinary consciousness into the poem itself:

> . . . say how hope and fear, desire and hate,
> O'erspread with snares the clouded maze of fate,
> Where wav'ring man, betrayed by ven'trous pride,
> To tread the dreary paths without a guide,
> As treach'rous phantoms in the mist delude,
> Shuns fancied ills, or chases airy good;
> How rarely reason guides the stubborn choice. . . .

That is, the poet urges the view that it is men who fail and not life. And just as he begins the poem with man's false sense of his own strength, so he ends it with the urgent suggestion that men had best hope for certain natural blessings:

> Pour forth thy fervors for a healthful mind,
> Obedient passions, and a will resigned;
> For love, which scarce collective man can fill;
> For patience sov'reign o'er transmuted ill;
> For faith, that panting for a happier seat,
> Counts death kind Nature's signal of retreat. . . .

There is no denying that for Johnson ". . . there was more to be endured than enjoyed, in the general condition of human life . . . ," but such a view expressed by a man of his sensitivity and vitality argues more that life has been in some significant measure understood than that it has been found defeating.*

* For a well-argued contrary view of "The Vanity of Human Wishes," including references to several other scholars who regard the poem as a pessimistic, tragic, or fatalistic work, see Robert Voitle, *Samuel Johnson the Moralist*, Cambridge, Mass., Harvard U. P., 1961, pp. 37–46; but in his Chapter II—"Reason and Freedom"— Voitle presents a more general view of Johnson as a thinker who holds out some hope that men, within limits, have the freedom to act.

The Vanity of
Human Wishes

The Tenth Satire of Juvenal,
Imitated

LET Observation with extensive View,
Survey Mankind, from *China* to *Peru*;
Remark each anxious Toil, each eager Strife,
And watch the busy Scenes of crouded Life;
Then say how Hope and Fear, Desire and Hate,   5
O'erspread with Snares the clouded Maze of Fate,
Where wav'ring Man, betray'd by vent'rous Pride,
To tread the dreary Paths without a Guide;
As treach'rous Phantoms in the Mist delude,
Shuns fancied Ills, or chases airy Good.   10
How rarely Reason guides the stubborn Choice,
Rules the bold Hand, or prompts the suppliant Voice,
How Nations sink, by darling Schemes oppress'd,
When Vengeance listens to the Fool's Request.
Fate wings with ev'ry Wish th' afflictive Dart,   15
Each Gift of Nature, and each Grace of Art,
With fatal Heat impetuous Courage glows,
With fatal Sweetness Elocution flows,
Impeachment stops the Speaker's pow'rful Breath,
And restless Fire precipitates on Death.   20

But scarce observ'd the Knowing and the Bold,
Fall in the gen'ral Massacre of Gold;
Wide-wasting Pest! that rages unconfin'd,
And crouds with Crimes the Records of Mankind,
For Gold his Sword the Hireling Ruffian draws,   25
For Gold the hireling Judge distorts the Laws;
Wealth heap'd on Wealth, nor Truth nor Safety buys,
The Dangers gather as the Treasures rise.

Let Hist'ry tell where rival Kings command,
And dubious Title shakes the madded Land,   30
When Statutes glean the Refuse of the Sword,
How much more safe the Vassal than the Lord,

Low sculks the Hind beneath the Rage of Pow'r,
And leaves the *bonny Traytor* in the *Tow'r*,
Untouch'd his Cottage, and his Slumbers sound,   35
Tho' Confiscation's Vulturs clang around.

   The needy Traveller, serene and gay,
Walks the wild Heath, and sings his Toil away.
Does Envy seize thee? crush th' upbraiding Joy,
Encrease his Riches and his Peace destroy,   40
New Fears in dire Vicissitude invade,
The rustling Brake alarms, and quiv'ring Shade,
Nor Light nor Darkness bring his Pain Relief,
One shews the Plunder, and one hides the Thief.

   Yet still the gen'ral Cry the Skies assails   45
And Gain and Grandeur load the tainted Gales;
Few know the toiling Statesman's Fear or Care,
Th' insidious Rival and the gaping Heir.

   Once more, *Democritus*, arise on Earth,
With chearful Wisdom and instructive Mirth,   50
See motley Life in modern Trappings dress'd,
And feed with varied Fools th' eternal Jest:
Thou who couldst laugh where Want enchain'd Caprice,
Toil crush'd Conceit, and Man was of a Piece;
Where Wealth unlov'd without a Mourner dy'd;   55
And scarce a Sycophant was fed by Pride;
Where ne'er was known the Form of mock Debate,
Or seen a new-made Mayor's unwieldy State;
Where change of Fav'rites made no Change of Laws,
And Senates heard before they judg'd a Cause;   60
How wouldst thou shake at *Britain's* modish Tribe,
Dart the quick Taunt, and edge the piercing Gibe?
Attentive Truth and Nature to descry,
And pierce each Scene with Philosophic Eye.
To thee were solemn Toys or empty Shew,   65
The Robes of Pleasure and the Veils of Woe:
All aid the Farce, and all thy Mirth maintain,
Whose Joys are causeless, or whose Griefs are vain.

   Such was the Scorn that fill'd the Sage's Mind,
Renew'd at ev'ry Glance on Humankind;   70
How just that Scorn ere yet thy Voice declare,

34. *Bonny Traytor:* The Young Pretender, Charles Edward Stuart, grandson of
Catholic James II. In 1745, he and his
followers had attempted to gain the throne.
Later editions give wealthy traitor.

49. *Democritus:* A Greek philosopher,
born at Abdera about 460 B.C. Juvenal
(X. 33) speaks of him as always laughing at
mankind's follies.

Search every State, and canvass ev'ry Pray'r.

Unnumber'd Suppliants croud Preferment's Gate,
Athirst for Wealth, and burning to be great;
Delusive Fortune hears th' incessant Call,   75
They mount, they shine, evaporate, and fall.
On ev'ry Stage the Foes of Peace attend,
Hate dogs their Flight, and Insult mocks their End.
Love ends with Hope, the sinking Statesman's Door
Pours in the Morning Worshiper no more;   80
For growing Names the weekly Scribbler lies,
To growing Wealth the Dedicator flies,
From every Room descends the painted Face,
That hung the bright *Palladium* of the Place,
And smoak'd in Kitchens, or in Auctions sold,   85
To better Features yields the Frame of Gold;
For now no more we trace in ev'ry Line
Heroic Worth, Benevolence Divine:
The Form distorted justifies the Fall,
And Detestation rids th' indignant Wall.   90

But will not *Britain* hear the last Appeal,
Sign her Foes Doom, or guard her Fav'rites Zeal;
Through Freedom's Sons no more Remonstrance rings;
Degrading Nobles and controuling Kings;
Our supple Tribes repress their Patriot Throats,   95
And ask no Questions but the Price of Votes;
With Weekly Libels and Septennial Ale,
Their Wish is full to riot and to rail.

In full-blown Dignity, see *Wolsey* stand,
Law in his Voice, and Fortune in his Hand: 100
To him the Church, the Realm, their Pow'rs consign,
Thro' him the Rays of regal Bounty shine,
Turn'd by his Nod the Stream of Honour flows,
His Smile alone Security bestows:
Still to new Heights his restless Wishes tow'r,   105
Claim leads to Claim, and Pow'r advances Pow'r;
Till Conquest unresisted ceas'd to please,

84. *Palladium:* An image of very great
antiquity (said to be that of Athena, or
Minerva), which Greeks and Romans
thought gave safety to a city. Before Troy
could be destroyed, Diomed and Odysseus
had to carry it off. It is supposed to have
found its way to Rome.
97. *Weekly Libels . . . Septennial Ale:*
Parliament was corrupt, selling its votes to
king and ministers alike: the weekly libels
were politically motivated arguments
appearing in weekly newspapers; Septennial Ale was given by aspiring candidates (Parliament was elected at least every
seven years) to voters.
99. *Wolsey:* Cardinal Wolsey (c. 1475–
1530), whose rise to great secular power
under Henry VIII and his fall (he was
charged with treason) were well known.

And Rights submitted, left him none to seize.
At length his Sov'reign frowns—the Train of State
Mark the keen Glance, and watch the Sign to hate.   110
Where-e'er he turns he mets a Stranger's Eye,
His Suppliants scorn him, and his Followers fly;
Now drops at once the Pride of aweful State,
The golden Canopy, the glitt'ring Plate,
The regal Palace, the luxurious Board,   115
The liv'ried Army, and the menial Lord.
With Age, with Cares, with Maladies oppress'd,
He seeks the Refuge of Monastic Rest.
Grief aids Disease, remember'd Folly stings,
And his last Sighs reproach the Faith of Kings.   120

     Speak thou, whose Thoughts at humble Peace repine,
Shall *Wolsey's* Wealth, with *Wolsey's* End be thine?
Or liv'st thou now, with safer Pride content,
The richest Landlord on the Banks of *Trent*?
For why did *Wolsey* by the Steps of Fate,   125
On weak Foundations raise th' enormous Weight?
Why but to sink beneath Misfortune's Blow,
With louder Ruin to the Gulphs below?

     What gave great *Villiers* to th' Assassin's Knife,
And fix'd Disease on *Harley's* closing Life?   130
What murder'd *Wentworth*, and what exil'd *Hyde*,
By Kings protected and to Kings ally'd?
What but their Wish indulg'd in Courts to shine,
And Pow'r too great to keep or to resign?

     When first the College Rolls receive his Name,   135
The young Enthusiast quits his Ease for Fame;
Resistless burns the Fever of Renown,
Caught from the strong Contagion of the Gown;
O'er *Bodley's* Dome his future Labours spread,
And *Bacon's* Mansion trembles o'er his Head;   140

125. *Steps:* Later texts give Steeps.

129. *Villiers:* George Villiers, First Duke of Buckingham (1592–1628), who was assassinated by a subaltern, John Filton.

130. *Harley's . . . Life:* Robert Harley, First Earl of Oxford (1661–1724), British statesman; Lord Treasurer under Queen Anne, he was imprisoned in 1715, after the Tories lost power, upon Anne's death in 1714.

131. *Wentworth . . . Hyde:* Thomas Wentworth, First Earl of Strafford (1593–1641), advisor of Charles I, was executed as a result of charges brought against him by political enemies; Edward Hyde, First Earl of Clarendon (1608–1674), Lord Chancellor under Charles II from 1658, two years before the Restoration, was impeached. He fled to France, 1667, at Charles's command.

139. *Bodley's Dome:* The Bodleian Library at Oxford.

140. *Bacon's Mansion:* Roger Bacon (c. 1214–1292), an English Franciscan philosopher and enlightened experimental scientist, who spent part of his career at Oxford; tradition had it that his study would collapse when a greater mind than his came to the University.

Are these thy Views? proceed, illustrious Youth,
And Virtue guard thee to the Throne of Truth,
Yet should thy Soul indulge the gen'rous Heat,
Till captive Science yields her last Retreat;
Should Reason guide thee with her brightest Ray,   145
And pour on misty Doubt resistless Day;
Should no false Kindness lure to loose Delight,
Nor Praise relax, nor Difficulty fright;
Should tempting Novelty thy Cell refrain,
And Sloth's bland Opiates shed their Fumes in vain;   150
Should Beauty blunt on Fops her fatal Dart,
Nor claim the Triumph of a letter'd Heart;
Should no Disease thy torpid Veins invade,
Nor Melancholy's Phantoms haunt thy Shade;
Yet hope not Life from Grief or Danger free,   155
Nor think the Doom of Man revers'd for thee:
Deign on the passing World to turn thine Eyes,
And pause awhile from Learning to be wise;
There mark what Ills the Scholar's Life assail;
Toil, Envy, Want, the Garret, and the Jail.   160
See Nations slowly wise, and meanly just,
To buried Merit raise the tardy Bust.
If Dreams yet flatter, once again attend,
Hear *Lydiat's* Life, and *Galileo's* End.

Nor deem, when Learning her lost Prize bestows   165
The glitt'ring Eminence exempt from Foes;
See when the Vulgar 'scap'd, despis'd or aw'd,
Rebellion's vengeful Talons seize on *Laud*.
From meaner Minds, tho' smaller Fines content
The plunder'd Palace or sequester'd Rent;   170
Mark'd out by dangerous Parts he meets the Shock,
And fatal Learning leads him to the Block:
Around his Tomb let Art and Genius weep,
But hear his Death, ye Blockheads, hear and sleep.

The festal Blazes, the triumphal Show,   175

160. *Garret:* In later editions the word patron replaced Garret because of Johnson's bad experience with Philip Stanhope, Fourth Earl of Chesterfield, who agreed to support Johnson's work on the *Dictionary*, but never did so. In a famous letter, February 7, 1755, Johnson expressed his indignation to Chesterfield.
164. *Lydiat's Life . . . Galileo's End:* Thomas Lydiat (1572–1646) was a scholar who died in poverty, because he sided with the Royalists; Galileo Galilei (1564–1642), famous Italian astronomer, was tried and confined by the Inquisition in 1633; his last years were marred by blindness.
168. *Laud:* William Laud (1573–1645), Archbishop of Canterbury, was beheaded in 1645 by the Long Parliament for his very strenuous high-church activities and policies.
170. *Sequester'd Rent:* Here, income from seized or confiscated property. Royalist estates often suffered such loss during the Commonwealth.

The ravish'd Standard, and the captive Foe,
The Senate's Thanks, the Gazette's pompous Tale,
With Force resistless o'er the Brave prevail.
Such Bribes the rapid *Greek* o'er *Asia* whirl'd,
For such the steady *Romans* shook the World;   180
For such in distant Lands the *Britons* shine,
And stain with Blood the *Danube* or the *Rhine*;
This Pow'r has Praise, that Virtue scarce can warm,
Till Fame supplies the universal Charm.
Yet Reason frowns on War's unequal Game,   185
Where wasted Nations raise a single Name,
And mortgag'd States their Grandsires Wreaths regret
From Age to Age in everlasting Debt;
Wreaths which at last the dear-bought Right convey
To rust on Medals, or on Stones decay.   190

On what Foundation stands the Warrior's Pride?
How just his Hopes let *Swedish Charles* decide;
A Frame of Adamant, a Soul of Fire,
No Dangers fright him, and no Labours tire;
O'er Love, o'er Force, extends his wide Domain,   195
Unconquer'd Lord of Pleasure and of Pain;
No Joys to him pacific Scepters yield,
War sounds the Trump, he rushes to the Field;
Behold surrounding Kings their Pow'r combine,
And One capitulate, and One resign;   200
Peace courts his Hand, but spread her Charms in vain;
"Think Nothing gain'd, he cries, till nought remain,
On *Moscow's* Walls till *Gothic* Standards fly,
And all is Mine beneath the Polar Sky."
The March begins in Military State,   205
And Nations on his Eye suspended wait;
Stern Famine guards the solitary Coast,
And Winter barricades the Realms of Frost;
He comes, nor Want nor Cold his Course delay;—
Hide, blushing Glory, hide *Pultowa's* Day: 210
The vanquish'd Hero leaves his broken Bands,
And shews his Miseries in distant Lands;
Condemn'd a needy Supplicant to wait,
While Ladies interpose, and Slaves debate.
But did not Chance at length her Error mend?   215

179. *Greek:* Alexander the Great.
192. *Swedish Charles:* Charles XII of Sweden (1682–1718), crowned at the age of sixteen, was attacked by Denmark, Poland, and Russia. After amazing successes, he was defeated at Pultova by the Russians. After various maneuvers, including an alliance with the Turks, Charles met his death at the siege of Halden in Norway.
200. *One capitulate . . . One resign:* In 1700, Frederick IV of Denmark surrendered to Charles; in 1704, Augustus II of Poland gave over his throne to the young king.

Did no subverted Empire mark his End?
Did rival Monarchs give the fatal Wound?
Or hostile Millions press him to the Ground?
His Fall was destin'd to a barren Strand,
A petty Fortress, and a dubious Hand;   220
He left the Name, at which the World grew pale,
To point a Moral, or adorn a Tale.

    All Times their Scenes of pompous Woes afford,
From *Persia's* Tyrant to *Bavaria's* Lord.
In gay Hostility, and barb'rous Pride,   225
With half Mankind embattled at his Side,
Great *Xerxes* comes to seize the certain Prey,
And starves exhausted Regions in his Way;
Attendant Flatt'ry counts his Myriads o'er,
Till counted Myriads sooth his Pride no more;   230
Fresh Praise is try'd till Madness fires his Mind,
The Waves he lashes, and enchains the Wind;
New Pow'rs are claim'd, new Pow'rs are still bestow'd,
Till rude Resistance lops the spreading God;
The daring *Greeks* deride the Martial Shew,   235
And heap their Vallies with the gaudy Foe;
Th' insulted Sea with humbler Thoughts he gains,
A single Skiff to speed his Flight remains;
Th' incumber'd Oar scarce leaves the dreaded Coast
Through purple Billows and a floating Host.   240

    The bold *Bavarian*, in a luckless Hour,
Tries the dread Summits of *Cesarean* Pow'r,
With unexpected Legions bursts away,
And sees defenceless Realms receive his Sway;
Short Sway! fair *Austria* spreads her mournful Charms,   245
The Queen, the Beauty, sets the World in Arms;
From Hill to Hill the Beacons rousing Blaze
Spreads wide the Hope of Plunder and of Praise;
The fierce *Croatian*, and the wild *Hussar*,
And all the Sons of Ravage croud the War;   250
The baffled Prince in Honour's flatt'ring Bloom
Of hasty Greatness finds the fatal Doom,
His Foes Derision, and his Subjects Blame,
And steals to Death from Anguish and from Shame.

224. *Persia's Tyrant to Bavaria's Lord:* Xerxes was the tyrant; he invaded Greece and after early successes was defeated at Salamis, largely as a result of Athenian naval power. Bavaria's Lord was Charles Albert, who during the War of the Austrian Succession (1740–1748) was crowned (Holy Roman) Emperor Charles VII. Austria's Maria Theresa (see l. 245), however, soon brought about his downfall.

249. *Hussar:* One of a body of light horsemen organized in fifteenth-century Hungary.

Enlarge my Life with Multitude of Days,   255
In Health, in Sickness, thus the Suppliant prays;
Hides from himself his State, and shuns to know,
That Life protracted is protracted Woe.
Time hovers o'er, impatient to destroy,
And shuts up all the Passages of Joy: 260
In vain their Gifts the bounteous Seasons pour,
The Fruit Autumnal, and the Vernal Flow'r,
With listless Eyes the Dotard views the Store,
He views, and wonders that they please no more;
Now pall the tastless Meats, and joyless Wines,   265
And Luxury with Sighs her Slave resigns.
Approach, ye Minstrels, try the soothing Strain,
And yield the tuneful Lenitives of Pain:
No Sounds alas would touch th' impervious Ear,
Though dancing Mountains witness'd *Orpheus* near;   270
Nor Lute nor Lyre his feeble Pow'rs attend,
Nor sweeter Musick of a virtuous Friend,
But everlasting Dictates croud his Tongue,
Perversely grave, or positively wrong.
The still returning Tale, and ling'ring Jest,   275
Perplex the fawning Niece and pamper'd Guest,
While growing Hopes scarce awe the gath'ring Sneer,
And scarce a Legacy can bribe to hear;
The watchful Guests still hint the last Offence,
The Daughter's Petulance, the Son's Expence,   280
Improve his heady Rage with treach'rous Skill,
And mould his Passions till they make his Will.

Unnumber'd Maladies each Joint invade,
Lay Siege to Life and press the dire Blockade;
But unextinguish'd Av'rice still remains,   285
And dreaded Losses aggravate his Pains;
He turns, with anxious Heart and cripled Hands,
His Bonds of Debt, and Mortgages of Lands;
Or views his Coffers with suspicious Eyes,
Unlocks his Gold, and counts it till he dies.   290

But grant, the Virtues of a temp'rate Prime
Bless with an Age exempt from Scorn or Crime;
An Age that melts in unperceiv'd Decay,
And glides in modest Innocence away;
Whose peaceful Day Benevolence endears,   295
Whose Night congratulating Conscience cheers;

270. *Orpheus:* Thracian poet and
musician, who according to Aeschylus and
Euripides could attract trees and stones as
well as wild animals with his music, and
could charm whatever person he wished.

The gen'ral Fav'rite as the gen'ral Friend:
Such Age there is, and who could wish its End?

Yet ev'n on this her Load Misfortune flings,
To press the weary Minutes flagging Wings: 300
New Sorrow rises as the Day returns,
A Sister sickens, or a Daughter mourns.
Now Kindred Merit fills the sable Bier,
Now lacerated Friendship claims a Tear.
Year chases Year, Decay pursues Decay,   305
Still drops some Joy from with'ring Life away;
New Forms arise, and diff'rent Views engage,
Superfluous lags the Vet'ran on the Stage,
Till pitying Nature signs the last Release,
And bids afflicted Worth retire to Peace.   310

But few there are whom Hours like these await,
Who set unclouded in the Gulphs of Fate.
From *Lydia's* Monarch should the Search descend,
By *Solon* caution'd to regard his End,
In Life's last Scene what Prodigies surprise,   315
Fears of the Brave, and Follies of the Wise?
From *Marlb'rough's* Eyes the Streams of Dotage flow,
And *Swift* expires a Driv'ler and a Show.

The teeming Mother, anxious for her Race,
Begs for each Birth the Fortune of a Face: 320
Yet *Vane* could tell what Ills from Beauty spring;
And *Sedley* curs'd the Form that pleas'd a King.
Ye Nymphs of rosy Lips and radiant Eyes,
Whom Pleasure keeps too busy to be wise,
Whom Joys with soft Varieties invite   325
By Day the Frolick, and the Dance by Night,
Who frown with Vanity, who smile with Art,
And ask the latest Fashion of the Heart,
What Care, what Rules your heedless Charms shall save,
Each Nymph your Rival, and each Youth your Slave?   330
An envious Breast with certain Mischief glows,
And Slaves, the Maxim tells, are always Foes.

313. *Lydia's Monarch:* Croesus, cautioned by Solon that, though he was a rich and lucky monarch, he ought not to regard himself happy until he died; Cyrus of Persia later conquered and deposed him.

317. *Marlb'rough's Eyes:* John Churchill, First Duke of Marlborough (1650–1722), English general during most of the War of the Spanish Succession (1702–1713), suffered paralysis by stroke some time before he died.

318. *Swift expires:* Swift was senile for the last four years of a long life (1667–1745).

321. *Vane:* Anne Vane was the mistress of Frederick, Prince of Wales, the son of George II.

322. *Sedley:* Catherine Sedley was the mistress of James, Duke of York, who as James II created her Countess of Dorchester.

Against your Fame with Fondness Hate combines,
The Rival batters, and the Lover mines.
With distant Voice neglected Virtue calls,   335
Less heard, and less the faint Remonstrance falls;
Tir'd with Contempt, she quits the slipp'ry Reign,
And Pride and Prudence take her Seat in vain.
In croud at once, where none the Pass defend,
The harmless Freedom, and the private Friend.   340
The Guardians yield, by Force superior ply'd;
By Int'rest, Prudence; and by Flatt'ry, Pride.
Here Beauty falls betray'd, despis'd, distress'd,
And hissing Infamy proclaims the rest.

    Where then shall Hope and Fear their Objects find?   345
Must dull Suspence corrupt the stagnant Mind?
Must helpless Man, in Ignorance sedate,
Swim darkling down the Current of his Fate?
Must no Dislike alarm, no Wishes rise,
No Cries attempt the Mercies of the Skies?   350
Enquirer, cease, Petitions yet remain,
Which Heav'n may hear, nor deem Religion vain.
Still raise for Good the supplicating Voice,
But leave to Heav'n the Measure and the Choice.
Safe in his Pow'r, whose Eyes discern afar   355
The secret Ambush of a specious Pray'r.
Implore his Aid, in his Decisions rest,
Secure whate'er he gives, he gives the best.
Yet with the Sense of sacred Presence prest,
When strong Devotion fills thy glowing Breast,   360
Pour forth thy Fervours for a healthful Mind,
Obedient Passions, and a Will resign'd;
For Love, which scarce collective Man can fill;
For Patience sov'reign o'er transmuted Ill;
For Faith, that panting for a happier Seat,   365
Thinks Death kind Nature's Signal of Retreat:
These Goods for Man the Laws of Heav'n ordain,
These Goods he grants, who grants the Pow'r to gain;
With these celestial Wisdom calms the Mind,
And makes the Happiness she does not find.   370

    (1749)

Headnote to
THE RAMBLER

On March 20, 1750, was published the first of 208 numbers of *The Rambler*, the collection of periodical essays Johnson was to produce at the rate of two a week for about two years. They were like *The Tatler* and *The Spectator* in general form (see the headnote to *The Spectator*), but it would be difficult to imagine more diverse styles than Johnson's in *The Rambler* and Addison's (or Steele's) in *The Spectator*. Seldom humorous or lively in these papers, usually sober if not somber, typically abstract (on rare occasions his descriptions of people are richly concrete), Johnson commands the reader's attention by force of intellect and by the ultimate clarity and truth of his references to human experience, rather than by his winning ways. Its lack of surface attractiveness notwithstanding, *The Rambler* (and *Dictionary*) made Johnson's reputation among his contemporaries; and he himself said, "My other works are wine and water; but my *Rambler* is pure wine." (Boswell's *Life*, I, p. 210.) It should be added that Boswell reports (IV, p. 5) that years after he wrote the essays, Johnson found at least one of them too wordy. Whatever the reader thinks of Johnson's manner of expression, he is almost certain to acknowledge both that *The Rambler's* moralist anticipates many of the interests and views expressed in *Rasselas* and the later works, and that he argues with great originality and power.

TEXT. *The Rambler* (2 vols., London, 1751 [sic]).

The Rambler

No. 4   *Saturday, March 31, 1750*

Simul et jucunda et idonea dicere Vitæ
—Hor.[1]

THE Works of Fiction, with which the present Generation seems more particularly delighted, are such as exhibit Life in its true State, diversified only by the Accidents that daily happen in the World, and influenced by those Passions and Qualities which are really to be found in conversing with Mankind.

THIS Kind of Writing may be termed not improperly the Comedy of Romance, and is to be conducted nearly by the Rules of Comic Poetry. Its Province is to bring about natural Events by easy Means, and to keep up Curiosity without the Help of Wonder; it is therefore precluded from the Machines and Expedients of the Heroic Romance, and can neither employ Giants to snatch away a Lady from the nuptial Rites, nor Knights to bring her back from Cap- 10 tivity; it can neither bewilder its Personages in Desarts, nor lodge them in imaginary Castles.

I REMEMBER a Remark made by *Scaliger* upon *Pontanus*,[2] that all his Writings are filled with Images, and that if you take from him his Lillies and his Roses, his Satyrs and his Dryads, he will have nothing left that can be called Poetry. In like Manner, almost all the Fictions of the last Age will vanish, if you deprive them of a Hermit and a Wood, a Battle and a Shipwreck.

WHY this wild Strain of Imagination found Reception so long, in polite and learned Ages, it is not easy to conceive; but we cannot wonder, that, while Readers could be procured, the Authors were willing to continue it: For when 20 a Man had, by Practice, gained some Fluency of Language, he had no farther Care than to retire to his Closet, to let loose his Invention, and heat his Mind with Incredibilities; and a Book was produced without Fear of Criticism, without the Toil of Study, without Knowledge of Nature, or Acquaintance with Life.

THE Task of our present Writers is very different; it requires, together with that Learning which is to be gained from Books, that Experience which can never be attained by solitary Diligence, but must arise from general Converse, and accurate Observation of the living World. Their Performances have, as *Horace* expresses it, *plus oneris quantum veniæ minus*,[3] little Indulgence, and there- 30 fore more Difficulty. They are engaged in Portraits of which every one knows the Original, and can therefore detect any Deviation from Exactness of Resemblance. Other Writings are safe, except from the Malice of Learning; but these

---

[1] *Simul . . . dicere Vitæ:* To say things that are at the same time both pleasign and helpful. *Ars Poetica*, l. 334.
[2] *Scaliger upon Pontanus:* J. C. Scaliger (1484–1558), father of the greater J. J. Scaliger, was like his son a classical scholar;

Giovanni Pontano (1426–1503), Italian poet, statesman, and historian.
[3] *Plus . . . minus: Epistles*, II, i, 170. Johnson of course gives the sense of the Latin.

are in danger from every common Reader; as the Slipper ill executed was censured by a Shoemaker who happened to stop in his Way at the *Venus of Apelles*.[4]

But the Danger of not being approved as just Copyers of human Manners, is not the most important Apprehension that an Author of this Sort ought to have before him. These Books are written chiefly to the Young, the Ignorant, and the Idle, to whom they serve as Lectures of Conduct, and Introductions into Life. They are the Entertainment of Minds unfurnished with Ideas, and therefore easily susceptible of Impressions; not fixed by Principles, and therefore easily following the Current of Fancy; not informed by Experience, and consequently open to every false Suggestion and partial Account.   10

That the highest Degree of Reverence should be paid to Youth, and that nothing indecent or unseemly should be suffered to approach their Eyes or Ears, are Precepts extorted by Sense and Virtue from an ancient Writer[5] by no Means eminent for Chastity of Thought. The same Kind, tho' not the same Degree of Caution, is required in every thing which is laid before them, to secure them from unjust Prejudices, perverse Opinions, and improper Combinations of Images.

In the Romances formerly written every Transaction and Sentiment was so remote from all that passes among Men, that the Reader was in very little danger of making any Applications to himself; the Virtues and Crimes were   20 equally beyond his Sphere of Activity; and he amused himself with Heroes and with Traitors, Deliverers and Persecutors, as with Beings of another Species, whose Actions were regulated upon Motives of their own, and who had neither Faults nor Excellencies in common with himself.

But when an Adventurer is levelled with the rest of the World, and acts in such Scenes of the universal Drama, as may be the Lot of any other Man, young Spectators fix their Eyes upon him with closer Attention, and hope by observing his Behaviour and Success to regulate their own Practices, when they shall be engaged in the like Part.

For this Reason these familiar Histories may perhaps be made of greater Use   30 than the Solemnities of professed Morality, and convey the Knowledge of Vice and Virtue with more Efficacy than Axioms and Definitions. But if the Power of Example is so great, as to take Possession of the Memory by a kind of Violence, and produce Effects almost without the Intervention of the Will, Care ought to be taken that, when the Choice is unrestrained, the best Examples only should be exhibited; and that which is likely to operate so strongly, should not be mischievous or uncertain in its Effects.

The chief Advantages which these Fictions have over real Life is, that their Authors are at liberty, tho' not to invent, yet to select Objects, and to cull from the Mass of Mankind, those Individuals upon which the Attention ought most   40 to be employ'd; as a Diamond, though it cannot be made, may be polished by Art, and placed in such a Situation, as to display that Lustre which before was buried among common Stones.

---

[4] *Apelles:* The greatest painter of antiquity, an Ionian of the fourth century B.C., who is supposed to have changed a sandal in one of his paintings, at the suggestion of a cobbler.

[5] *An Ancient Writer:* Juvenal, *Satires*, XIV.

IT is justly considered as the greatest Excellency of Art, to imitate Nature; but it is necessary to distinguish those Parts of Nature, which are most proper for Imitation: Greater Care is still required in representing Life, which is so often discoloured by Passion, or deformed by Wickedness. If the World be promiscuously described, I cannot see of what Use it can be to read the Account; or why it may not be as safe to turn the Eye immediately upon Mankind, as upon a Mirrour which shows all that presents itself without Discrimination.

IT is therefore not a sufficient Vindication of a Character, that it is drawn as it appears; for many Characters ought never to be drawn; nor of a Narrative, that the Train of Events is agreeable to Observation and Experience; for that Observation which is called Knowledge of the World, will be found much more frequently to make Men cunning than good. The Purpose of these Writings is surely not only to show Mankind, but to provide that they may be seen hereafter with less Hazard; to teach the Means of avoiding the Snares which are laid by TREACHERY for INNOCENCE, without infusing any Wish for that Superiority with which the Betrayer flatters his Vanity; to give the Power of counteracting Fraud without the Temptation to practise it; to initiate Youth by mock Encounters in the Art of necessary Defence, and to increase Prudence without impairing Virtue.

MANY Writers for the sake of following Nature, so mingle good and bad Qualities in their principal Personages, that they are both equally conspicuous; and as we accompany them through their Adventures with Delight, and are led by Degrees to interest ourselves in their Favour, we lose the Abhorrence of their Faults, because they do not hinder our Pleasure, or, perhaps, regard them with some Kindness for being united with so much Merit.

THERE have been Men indeed splendidly wicked, whose Endowments throw a Brightness on their Crimes, and whom scarce any Villainy made perfectly detestable, because they never could be wholly diversed of their Excellencies; but such have been in all Ages the great Corrupters of the World, and their Resemblance ought no more to be preserved, than the Art of murdering without Pain.

SOME have advanced, without due Attention to the Consequences of this Notion, that certain Virtues have their correspondent Faults, and therefore to exhibit either apart is to deviate from Probability. Thus Men are observed by *Swift* to be grateful in the same Degree as they are resentful. This Principle, with others of the same Kind, supposes Man to act from a brute Impulse, and pursue a certain Degree of Inclination, without any Choice of the Object; for, otherwise, though it should be allow'd that Gratitude and Resentment arise from the same Constitution of the Passions, it follows not that they will be equally indulged when Reason is consulted; and unless that Consequence be admitted, this sagacious Maxim becomes an empty Sound, without any relation to Practice or to Life.

NOR is it evident, that even the first Motions to these Effects are always in the same Proportion. For Pride, which produces Quickness of Resentment, will frequently obstruct Gratitude, by an Unwillingness to admit that Inferiority which Obligation necessarily implies; and it is surely very unlikely, that he who cannot think he receives a Favour will ever acknowledge it.

It is of the utmost Importance to Mankind, that Positions of this Tendency should be laid open and confuted; for while Men consider Good and Evil as springing from the same Root, they will spare the one for the sake of the other, and in judging, if not of others at least of themselves, will be apt to estimate their Virtues by the Vices. To this fatal Error all those will contribute, who confound the Colours of Right and Wrong, and instead of helping to settle their Boundaries, mix them with so much Art, that no common Mind is able to disunite them.

In Narratives, where historical Veracity has no Place, I cannot discover why there should not be exhibited the most perfect Idea of Virtue; of Virtue   10 not angelical, nor above Probability; for what we cannot credit we shall never imitate; but of the highest and purest Kind that Humanity can reach, which, when exercised in such Trials as the various Revolutions of Things shall bring upon it, may, by conquering some Calamities, and enduring others, teach us what we may hope, and what we can perform. Vice, for Vice is necessary to be shewn, should always disgust; nor should the Graces of Gaiety, or the Dignity of Courage, be so united with it, as to reconcile it to the Mind. Wherever it appears, it should raise Hatred by the Malignity of its Practices; and Contempt, by the Meanness of its Stratagems; for while it is supported by either Parts or Spirit, it will be seldom heartily abhorred. The *Roman* Tyrant was content to be   20 hated, if he was but feared; and there are Thousands of the Readers of Romances willing to be thought wicked, if they may be allowed to be Wits. It is therefore to be always inculcated, that Virtue is the highest Proof of a superior Understanding, and the only solid Basis of Greatness; and that Vice is the natural Consequence of narrow Thoughts; that it begins in Mistake, and ends in Ignominy.

No. 5   *Tuesday, April 3, 1750*

> *Et nunc omnis Ager, nunc omnis parturit Arbos,*
> *Nunc frondent Silvæ, nunc formosissimus Annus.*
> —Virg.[1]

Every Man is sufficiently discontented with some Circumstances of his present State, to suffer his Imagination to range more or less in quest of future Happiness, and to fix upon some Point of Time, in which he shall, by the Removal of the Inconvenience which now perplexes him, or the Acquisition of Advantage which he at present wants, find his Condition of Life very much   30 improved.

When this Time, which is too often expected with great Impatience, at last arrives, it generally comes without the Blessing for which it was desired; but we solace ourselves with some new Prospect, and press forward again with equal Eagerness.

It is some Advantage to a Man, in whom this Temper prevails in any great

---

[1] *Et nunc . . . Annus:* And now every field, every tree is budding; now the woods are green, and the year is at its most beautiful. *Eclogues*, III, 56–57.

Degree, when he turns his Hopes upon Things wholly out of his own Power, since he forbears then to precipitate his Affairs, for the Sake of the great Event that is to complete his Felicity, and waits for the blissful Hour, without neglecting such Measures as are necessary to be taken in the mean Time.

I HAVE long known a Person of this Temper, who indulged his Dream of Happiness with less Hurt to himself than such chimerical Wishes commonly produce, and adjusted his Scheme with such Address, that his Hopes were in full bloom three parts of the Year, and in the other part never wholly blasted. Many, perhaps, would be desirous of learning by what Means he procured to himself such a cheap and lasting Satisfaction. It was gained only by a constant Practice of referring the Removal of all his Uneasiness to the Coming of the next Spring. If his Affairs were disordered, he could regulate them in the Spring; if a Regimen was prescribed him, the Spring was the proper Time of pursuing it; if what he wanted was at a high Price, it would fall its Value in the Spring.

THE Spring, indeed, did often come without any of these Effects; but he was always certain that the next would be more propitious; and was never convinced that the present Spring would fail him until the Middle of Summer; for he always talked of the Spring as coming 'till it was past, and when it was once past, every one agreed with him that it was coming.

BY long Converse with this Man, I am, perhaps, in some Degree brought to feel the same immoderate Pleasure in the Contemplation of this delightful Season; but I have the Satisfaction of finding many, whom it can be no Shame to resemble, infected with the same Enthusiasm; for there is, I believe, scarce any Poet of Eminence, who has not left some Testimony of his Fondness for the Flowers, the Zephyrs, and the Warblers of the Spring. Nor has the most luxuriant Imagination been able to describe the Serenity and Happiness of the golden Age otherwise than by giving a perpetual Spring, as the highest Reward of uncorrupted Innocence.

THERE is, indeed, something inexpressibly pleasing in the annual Renovation of the World, and the new Display of the Treasures of Nature. The Cold and Darkness of Winter, with the naked Deformity of every Object on which we turn our Eyes, makes us necessarily rejoice at the succeeding Season, as well for what we have escaped, as for what we may enjoy; and every budding Flower, which a warm Situation brings early to our View, is considered by us as a Messenger, to inform us of the Approach of more joyous Days.

THE SPRING affords to a Mind, so free from the Disturbance of Cares or Passions as to be vacant to calm Amusements, almost every Thing that our present State makes us capable of enjoying. The variegated Verdure of the Fields and Woods, the Succession of grateful Odours, the Voice of Pleasure pouring out its Notes on every Side, with the Observation of the Gladness apparently conceived by every Animal, from the Growth of his Food, and the Clemency of the Weather, throw over the whole Earth an Air of Gayety, which is very significantly expressed by the Smile of Nature.

THERE are Men to whom these Scenes are able to give no Delight, and who hurry away from all the Varieties of rural Beauty, to lose their Hours, and divert their Thoughts by Cards, or publick Assemblies, a Tavern Dinner, or the Prattle of the Day.

It may be laid down as a Position which will seldom deceive, that when a Man cannot bear his own Company there is something wrong. He must fly from himself, either because he feels a Tediousness in Life from the Equipoise of an empty Mind, which, having no Tendency to one Motion more than another but as it is impelled by some external Power, must always have recourse to foreign Objects; or he must be afraid of the Instusion of some unpleasing Ideas, and, perhaps, is always struggling to escape from the Remembrance of a Loss, the Fear of a Calamity, or some other Thought of greater Horror.

THOSE, who are incapacitated to enjoy the Pleasures of Contemplation, by their Griefs, may, very properly, apply to such Diversions, provided they are innocent, as lay strong hold on the Attention; and those, whom Fear of any future Calamity chains down to Misery, must endeavour to obviate the Danger.

MY Considerations shall, on this Occasion, be turned on such as are burthensome to themselves merely because they want Subjects for Reflection, and to whom the Volume of Nature is thrown open without affording them Pleasure or Instruction, because they never learned to read the Characters.

A FRENCH Author has advanced this seeming Paradox, that *very few Men know how to take a Walk*; and, indeed, it is very true, that few Men know how to take a Walk with a Prospect of any other Pleasure, than the same Company would have afforded them in any other Circumstances.

THERE are Animals that borrow their Colour from the neighbouring Body, and, consequently, vary their Hue as they happen to change their Place. In like manner it ought to be the Endeavour of every Man to derive his Reflexions from the Objects about him; for it is to no purpose that he alters his Position, if his Attention continues fixt to the same Point. The Mind should be kept open to the Access of every new Idea, and so far disengaged from the Predominance of particular Thoughts, as to be able to accommodate itself to emergent Occasions, and remark every Thing that offers itself to present Examination.

A MAN that has formed this Habit of turning every new Object to his Entertainment, finds in the Productions of Nature an inexhaustible Stock of Materials, upon which he can employ himself, without any Temptations to Envy or Malevolence; Faults, perhaps, seldom totally avoided by those, whose Judgment is much exercised upon the Works of Art. He has always a certain Prospect of discovering new Reasons for adoring the Sovereign Author of the Universe, and probable Hopes of making some Discovery of Benefit to others, or of Profit to himself. There is no doubt but many Vegetables and Animals have Qualities that might be of great Use; to the Knowledge of which there is required no great Sagacity of Penetration, or Fatigue of Study, but only frequent Experiments, and close Attention. What is said by the Chymists of their darling Mercury,[2] is, perhaps, true of every Body through the whole Creation, that, if a thousand Lives should be spent upon it, all its Properties would not be found out.

MANKIND must necessarily be diversified by various Tastes, since Life affords and requires such multiplicity of Employments; and a Nation of Naturalists is neither to be hoped, or desired, but it is surely not improper to point out a

---

[2] *Mercury:* In old chemistry, Mercury was regarded as one of the five principles of which all substances were thought to be compounded.

fresh Amusement to those who languish in Health, and repine in Plenty, for want of some Source of Diversion that may be less easily exhausted, and to inform the Multitudes of both Sexes, who are burthened with every new Day, that there are many Shews which they have not seen.

HE that enlarges his Curiosity after the Works of Nature, demonstrably multiplies the Inlets to Happiness, and, therefore, the younger Part of my Readers, to whom I dedicate this vernal Speculation, must excuse me for calling upon them to make use at once of the Spring of the Year, and the Spring of Life; to acquire, while their Minds may be yet impressed with new Images, a Love of innocent Pleasures, and an ardour for useful Knowledge; and to re-   10 member, that a blighted Spring makes a barren Year, and that the vernal Flowers, however beautiful and gay, are only intended by Nature as Preparatives to Autumnal Fruits.

No. 50   *Saturday, September 8, 1750*

> *Credebant hoc grande Nefas, et Morte piandum,*
> *Si Juvenis Vetulo non assurrexerat, atque*
> *Barbato cuicunque Puer, licet ipse videret*
> *Plura Domi Fraga, et majores Glandis Acervos.*
> —Juv.[1]

I HAVE always thought it the Business of those who turn their Speculations upon the living World, to admire and commend the Virtues, as well as to expose and censure the Faults of their Contemporaries, and to confute a false as well as to support a just Accusation; not only because it is peculiarly the Business of a Monitor to keep his own Reputation without Taint, since those who can once charge him with Partiality, will indulge themselves afterwards in disbelieving him at Pleasure; but because he may find real Crimes sufficient to give full Em-   20 ployment to Caution and Repentance, without distracting the Mind by needless Scruples and vain Solicitudes.

THERE are certain fixed and stated Reproaches that one Part of Mankind has in all Ages thrown upon another, which are regularly transmitted through continued Successions, and which he that has once suffered them is certain to use with the same undistinguishing Vehemence, when he has changed his Station, and gained the prescriptive Right of imposing on others, what he had formerly endured himself.

To these hereditary Imputations, of which no Man sees the Justice, till it becomes his Interest to see it, very little Regard is to be shown; since it does   30 not appear that they are produced by Ratiocination or Enquiry, but received implicitly, or caught by a kind of instantaneous Contagion, and supported rather by Willingness to credit, than Ability to prove them.

---

[1] *Credebant . . . Acervos:* When men thought it a terrible sin, suitably punished by death, if a young man did not stand up before his elders, or a boy before any man with a beard, though he might see more strawberries and bigger piles of acorns on his own farm. *Satires,* XIII, 54–57.

It has been, in all Ages of the World, the Practice of those who are desirous to believe themselves made venerable by length of Time, to censure the new Comers into Life, for want of Respect to grey Hairs and sage Experience, for heady Confidence in their own Understandings, for hasty Conclusions upon partial Views, for a contemptuous Disregard of those salutary Counsels, which their Fathers and Grandsires are always ready to afford them, and a rebellious Impatience of that Subordination to which Youth is condemned by Nature, as necessary to its Security from those Evils into which it would be otherwise inevitably precipitated, by the Rashness of Passion, and the Blindness of Ignorance.   10

Every old Man complains of the growing Depravity of the World, of the Petulance and Insolence of the rising Generation. He recounts the Decency and Regularity of former Times, and celebrates the Discipline and Sobriety of the Age in which his Youth was passed; a happy Age! which is now no more to be expected, since Confusion has broke in upon the World, and thrown down all the Boundaries of Civility, Reverence, and Obedience.

It is not always sufficiently considered how much he assumes, who dares to claim the Privilege of complaining: for as every Man has in his own Opinion a full Share of the Miseries of Life, he is inclined to consider all clamorous Uneasiness, as a Proof of Impatience rather than of Affliction, and to ask, What   20
Merit has this Man to show, by which he has acquired a Right to repine at the Distributions of Nature? Or why does he imagine that Exemptions should be granted him from the general Condition of Man? We find ourselves excited rather to Captiousness than Pity, and instead of being in haste to sooth Complaint by Sympathy and Tenderness, we enquire, whether the Pain is proportionate to the Lamentation? And whether, supposing it real, it is not the Effect of Vice and Folly, rather than of Calamity?

The Querulousness and Indignation which is observed so often to disfigure the last Scene of Life, naturally leads us to Enquiries like these. For surely it will be thought at the first View of Things, that if Age be thus contemned and ridi-   30
culed, insulted and neglected, the Crime must at least be equal on both Sides: since they who have had so many Opportunities of establishing their Authority over Minds ductile and unresisting, they who have been the Protectors of Helplessness, and the Instructors of Ig[no]rance, and who yet retain in their own Hands the Power of Wealth, and the Dignity of Command, must defeat their Influence by their own Misconduct, and make use of all these Advantages with very little Skill, if they cannot secure to themselves an Appearance of Respect, and ward off open Mockery, and declared Contempt.

The general Story of Mankind will evince, that lawful and settled Authority is very seldom resisted when it is well employed, and that gross Corruption,   40
or evident Imbecillity is necessary to the Conquest of that Prepossession with which the Majority of Mankind looks upon those Governors, whom they see surrounded by Splendor, and fortified by Power: and though Men are drawn by their Passions into Forgetfulness of invisible Rewards and Punishments, yet they are easily kept obedient to those who have temporal Dominion in their Hands, till their Veneration is dissipated by such Wickedness and Folly as can neither be palliated nor concealed.

IT may, therefore, very reasonably be suspected that the Old draw upon themselves the greatest Part of those Insults, which they so much lament, and that Age is rarely despised but when it is contemptible. If Men imagine that Excess or Debauchery can be made reverend by Time, that Knowledge is the Consequence of long Life however idly and thoughtlessly employed, that Priority of Birth will supply the Want of Steadiness or Honesty, and that the Regard will be paid to Wrinkles, which is due only to Wisdom, can it raise much Wonder that their Hopes are disappointed, and that they see their Posterity rather willing to trust their own Eyes in their Progress into Life, than enlist themselves under Guides who have lost their Way.   10

THERE are, indeed, many Truths which Time necessarily and certainly teaches, and which might, by those who have learned them from Experience, be communicated to their Successors at a cheaper Rate: but Dictates, though liberally enough bestowed, are generally without Effect, because they are not recommended by sufficient Authority, the Teacher gains few Proselytes by Instruction which his own Behaviour contradicts; and young Men miss the Benefit of Counsel, because they want the more powerful Attraction of Example, and are not very ready to believe that those who fall below them in Practice, can much excel them in Theory. Thus the Progress of Mankind in Knowledge is retarded, the World is kept long in the same State, and every new   20 Race is to gain the Prudence of their Predecessors by committing and redressing the same Miscarriages.

To secure to the Old that Influence which they are willing to claim, and which might so much contribute to the Improvement of the Arts of Life, it is absolutely necessary that they give themselves up to the Duties of declining Years; and contentedly resign to Youth its Levity, its Pleasures, its Frolicks, and its Fopperies. It is a useless Endeavour to unite the Contrarieties of Spring and Winter, and unjust to claim the Privileges of Age, and retain the Play-things of Childhood. Young Men always form great Ideas of the Wisdom and Gravity of those, whom they consider as placed at a Distance from them in the Ranks   30 of Existence, and always look on those whom they find trifling with long Beards, and luxurious and vain on the Brink of the Grave, with Contempt and Indignation, like that which Women feel at the Effeminacy of Men. If Dotards will contend with Boys in those Performances in which Boys must always excel them; if they will dress crippled Limbs in Embroidery, and endeavour at Gayety with faltering Voices; if they will drag Infirmity to the Ball, and darken Assemblies of Pleasure with the Ghastliness of Infirmity, they may well expect that those who find their Diversions obstructed will hoot them away; and that if they descend to Competition with Youth, they must bear the Insolence of successful Rivals.   40

Lusisti satis, edisti satis, atque bibisti:
Tempus abire tibi est.[2]

ANOTHER Vice of Age, by which the rising Generation may be alienated

---

[2] *Lusisti . . . tibi est:* You have played enough, eaten enough, and you have drunk enough; it is time to leave. Horace, *Epistles*, II, ii, 214–215.

from it, is Severity and Censoriousness; a Disposition of Mind that gives no Allowance to the Failings of early Life, that expects Artfulness from Childhood, and Constancy from Youth, that is peremptory in every Command, and inexorable to every Failure. There are many who live only to hinder Happiness, and whose Descendants can only tell of long Life, that it produces Suspicion, Malignity, Peevishness and Persecution: and yet such Men can talk of the Ingratitude of the Age, curse their Heirs for Impatience, and wonder that young Men cannot take Pleasure in their Fathers' Company.

HE that would part with Life, with Honour, and Decency, must, when he is young, consider that he shall one Day be old; and lay up Knowledge for his Support, when his Powers of acting shall forsake him; and when he is old he must remember that he has been young, and forbear to animadvert with unnecessary Rigour on Faults, which Experience only can correct.

No. 60   *Saturday, October 13, 1750*

> —*Quid sit pulchrum, quid turpe, quid utile, quid non,*
> *Plenius et melius* Chrysippo *et* Crantore *dicit.*
> —HOR.[1]

ALL Joy or Sorrow for the Happiness or Calamities of others is produced by an Act of the Imagination, that realises the Event however fictitious, or approximates it however remote, by placing us, for a Time, in the Condition of him whose Fortune we contemplate; so that we feel, while the Deception lasts, whatever Motions would be excited by the same Good or Evil happening to ourselves.

OUR Passions are therefore more strongly moved, in proportion as we can more readily adopt the Pains or Pleasures proposed to our Minds, by recognising them as once our own, or considering them as naturally incident to our State of Life. It is not easy for the most artful Writer to give us an Interest in Happiness or Misery, which we think ourselves never likely to feel, and with which we have never yet been made acquainted. Histories of the Downfall of Kingdoms, and Revolutions of Empires are read with great Tranquillity; the imperial Tragedy pleases common Auditors only by its Pomp of Ornament, and Grandeur of Ideas; and the Man whose Faculties have been engrossed by Business, and whose Heart never fluttered but at the Rise or Fall of Stocks, wonders how the Attention can be seized, or the Affections agitated by a Tale of Love.

THOSE parallel Circumstances, and kindred Images to which we readily conform our Minds, are, above all other Writings, to be found in Narratives of the Lives of particular Persons; and there seems therefore no Species of Writing

---

[1] *Quid . . . Crantore dicit:* [Homer tells us] what is beautiful, what is ugly, what is useful, what is not, more plainly and better than Chrysippus or Crantor. Horace, *Epistles*, I, ii, 3–4.

more worthy of Cultivation than Biography, since none can be more delightful, or more useful, none can more certainly enchain the Heart by irresistible Interest, or more widely diffuse Instruction to every Diversity of Condition.

THE general and rapid Narratives of History, which involve a thousand Fortunes in the Business of a Day, and complicate innumerable Incidents in one great Transaction, afford few Lessons applicable to private Life, which derives its Comforts and its Wretchedness from the right or wrong Management of Things, that nothing but their Frequency makes considerable, *Parva si non fiunt quotidie,* says *Pliny,*[2] and which can have no Place in those Relations which never descend below the Consultation of Senates, the Motions of Armies, and   10 the Schemes of Conspirators.

I HAVE often thought that there has rarely passed a Life of which a judicious and faithful Narrative would not be useful. For, not only every Man has in the mighty Mass of the World great Numbers in the same Condition with himself, to whom his Mistakes and Miscarriages, Escapes and Expedients would be of immediate and apparent Use; but there is such an Uniformity in the Life of Man, if it be considered apart from adventitious and separable Decorations and Disguises, that there is scarce any Possibility of Good or Ill, but is common to Humankind. A great Part of the Time of those who are placed at the greatest Distance by Fortune, or by Temper, must unavoidably pass in the same Manner;   20 and though, when the Claims of Nature are satisfied, Caprice, and Vanity, and Accident, begin to produce Discriminations, and Peculiarities, yet the Eye is not very heedful, or quick, which cannot discover the same Causes still terminating their Influence in the same Effects, though sometimes accelerated, sometimes retarded, or perplexed by multiplied Combinations. We are all prompted by the same Motives, all deceived by the same Fallacies, all animated by Hope, obstructed by Danger, entangled by Desire, and seduced by Pleasure.

IT is frequently objected to Relations of particular Lives, that they are not distinguished by any striking or wonderful Vicissitudes. The Scholar who passes his Life among his Books, the Merchant who conducted only his own Affairs, the   30 Priest whose Sphere of Action was not extended beyond that of his Duty, are considered as no proper Objects of publick Regard, however they might have excelled in their several Stations, whatever might have been their Learning, Integrity, and Piety. But this Notion arises from false Measures of Excellence and Dignity, and must be eradicated by considering, that, in the Eye of uncorrupted Reason, what is of most Use is of most Value.

IT is, indeed, not improper to take honest Advantages of Prejudice, and to gain Attention by a great Name; but the Business of the Biographer is often to pass slightly over those Performances and Incidents, which produce vulgar Greatness, to lead the Thoughts into domestick Privacies, and display the   40 minute Details of daily Life, where exterior Appendages are cast aside, and Men excel each other only by Prudence, and by Virtue. The Life of *Thuanus*[3] is, with great Propriety, said by its Author to have been written, that it might lay open to Posterity the private and familiar Character of that Man, *cujus*

---

[2] *Parva . . . quotidie:* Trifles but for their daily occurrence. *Epistles,* III, i, 10.
[3] *Thuanus:* Jacques Auguste de Thou (1553–1617), French historian and statesman.

Ingenium et Candorem ex ipsius Scriptis sunt olim semper miraturi, whose Candour and Genius his Writings will to the End of Time preserve in Admiration.

THERE are many invisible Circumstances, which whether we read as Enquirers after natural or moral Knowledge, whether we intend to enlarge our Science, or encrease our Virtue, are more important than publick Occurrences. Thus *Salust*,[4] the great Master, has not forgot, in his Account of *Catiline*,[5] to remark that *his Walk was now quick, and again slow,* as an Indication of a Mind revolving something with violent Commotion. Thus the Story of *Melancthon*[6] affords a striking Lecture on the Value of Time, by informing us that when he made an Appointment, he expected not only the Hour, but the Minute   10 to be fixed, that Life might not run out in the Idleness of Suspense; and all the Plans and Enterprizes of *De Wit*[7] are now of less Importance to the World, than that Part of his personal Character which represents him as careful of his Health, and negligent of his Life.

BUT Biography has often been allotted to Writers who seem very little acquainted with the Nature of their Task, or very negligent about the Performance. They rarely afford any other Account than might be collected from publick Papers, and imagine themselves writing a Life when they exhibit a chronological Series of Actions or Preferments; and so little regard the Manners or Behaviour of their Heroes, that more Knowledge may be gained of a Man's real Character,   20 by a short Conversation with one of his Servants, than from a formal and studied Narrative, begun with his Pedigree, and ended with his Funeral.

IF now and then they condescend to inform the World of particular Facts, they are not always so happy as to select those which are of most Importance. I know not well what Advantage Posterity can receive from the only Circumstance by which *Tickell* has distinguished *Addison*[8] from the Rest of Mankind, the Irregularity of his Pulse: nor can I think myself overpaid for the Time spent in reading the Life of *Malherb*,[9] by being enabled to relate, after the learned Biographer, that *Malherb* had two predominant Opinions; one, that the Looseness of a single Woman might destroy all the Boast of ancient   30 Descent; the other, that the *French* Beggers made use very improperly and barbarously of the Phrase *noble Gentleman,* because either Word included the Sense of both.

THERE are, indeed, some natural Reasons why these Narratives are often written by such as were not likely to give much Instruction or Delight, and why most Accounts of particular Persons are barren and useless. If a Life be delayed till all Interest and Envy are at an End, and all Motives to Calumny or Flattery are suppressed, we may hope for Impartiality, but must expect little Intelligence;

---

[4] *Salust:* Gaius Sallustius Crispus (86–35 B.C.), Roman politician and historian, whose works include *Bellum Catilinae.*

[5] *Catiline:* The impoverished Roman patrician who attempted (65–63 B.C.) to gain power by revolution.

[6] *Melancthon:* Originally Philip Schwarzerd (black earth, melancthon) (1497–1560), German religious reformer and Luther's fellow-worker.

[7] *De Wit:* Jan De Witt (1625–1672), Dutch statesman and the vehement opponent of Prince William of Orange.

[8] *Tickell . . . Addison:* Thomas Tickell (1686–1740) made contributions to *The Guardian* and *The Spectator* and published a rival translation of the first book of the *Iliad,* just as Pope's appeared. He edited Addison's works in 1721, where he makes the observation to which Johnson refers.

[9] *Malherb:* François de Malherbe (1555–1628), French poet and critic, who established a "correct and refined" poetry.

for the Incidents which give Excellence to Biography are of a volatile and evanescent Kind, such as soon escape the Memory, and are rarely transmitted by Tradition. We know how few can portray a living Acquaintance, except by his most prominent and observable Particularities, and the grosser Features of his Mind; and it may be easily imagined how much of this little Knowledge may lost in imparting it, and how soon a Succession of Copies will lose all Resemlance of the Original.

IF the Biographer writes from personal Knowledge, and makes haste to gratify the publick Curiosity, there is Danger lest his Interest, his Fear, his Gratitude, or his Tenderness, overpower his Fidelity, and tempt him to conceal, if 10 not to invent. There are many who think it an Act of Piety to hide the Faults or Failings of their Friends, even when they can no longer suffer by their Detection; we therefore see whole Ranks of Characters adorned with uniform Panegyrick, and not to be known from one another, but by extrinsick and casual Circumstances. "Let me remember," says *Hale*,[10] "when I find myself inclined to pity a Criminal, that there is likewise a Pity due to the Country." If there is a Regard due to the Memory of the Dead, there is yet more Respect to be paid to Knowledge, to Virtue, and to Truth.

No. 148   *Saturday, August 17, 1751*

> *Me Pater sævis oneret Catenis,*
> *Quod viro clemens misero peperci,*
> *Me vel extremis* Numidarum *in oris*
> *Classe releget.*
>   —Hor.[1]

POLITICIANS remark that no Oppression is so heavy or so lasting as that which is inflicted by the Perversion and Exorbitance of legal Authority. The 20 Robber may be seized, and the Invader may be repelled whenever they are found; they who pretend no Right but that of Force, may by Force be punished or repressed. But when Plunder bears the Name of Impost, and Murder is perpetrated by a judicial Sentence, Fortitude is intimidated and Wisdom confounded, Resistance shrinks from an Alliance with Rebellion, and the Villain is secure in the Robes of the Magistrate.

EQUALLY dangerous and equally detestable are the Cruelties which are often exercised in private Families, under the venerable Sanction of parental Authority, the Power which we are taught to reverence from the first Moments of Reason, which is guarded from Insult and Violation by all that can can im- 30 press Awe upon the Mind of Man, and which therefore may wanton in Cruelty

[10] *Hale:* Sir Matthew Hale (1609–1676), lord chief justice of England, though diligent, non-partisan, and pious in the discharge of his duties, was responsible for the execution of two women for witchcraft in 1664.

[1] *Me Pater . . . releget:* Let my father weigh me down with chains because I spared my unfortunate husband out of mercy. Let him ship me off to the remotest section of Numidia. *Odes,* III, xi, 45–48.

without Controul, and trample the Bounds of Right with innumerable Transgressions, before Duty and Piety will dare to seek Redress, or think themselves at Liberty to recur to any other Means of Deliverance than Tears and Supplications, by which Insolence is elated and Cruelty is gratified.

It was for a long Time imagined by the *Romans*, that no Son could be the Murderer of his Father, and they had therefore no Punishment appropriated to Parricide. They seem likewise to have believed with equal Confidence that no Father could be cruel to his Child, and therefore they allowed every Man the supreme Judicature in his own House, and put the Lives of his Offspring into his Hands; but Experience informed them by Degrees, that they had   10
determined too hastily in Favour of human Nature; they found that Instinct and Habit were not able to counteract Avarice or Malice; that the nearest Relation might be violated, and that Power to whomsoever entrusted, might be ill employed. They were therefore obliged to supply and to change their Institutions, to deter the Parricide by a new Law, and to transfer capital Punishments from the Parent to the Magistrate.

There are indeed many Houses which it is impossible to enter familiarly without discovering that Parents are by no Means exempt from the Intoxications of Dominion, that Impunity seldom fails to produce Guilt, and that he who is in no Danger of hearing Remonstrances but from his own Conscience, will scarcely be long without the Art of controlling his Convictions,   20
and modifying Justice by his own Will.

If, in any Situation, the Heart were inaccessible to Malignity, it might be supposed to be sufficiently secured by parental Relation. To have voluntarily become to any Being the Occasion of its Existence produces an Obligation to make that Existence happy. To see helpless Infancy stretching out her Hands and pouring out her Cries in Testimony of Dependance, without any Powers to alarm Jealousy, or any Guilt to alienate Affection, must surely awaken Tenderness in every human Mind, and Tenderness once excited will be hourly encreased by the natural Contagion of Felicity, by the Repercussion of   30
communicated Pleasure, and the Consciousness of the Dignity of Benefaction. I believe no generous or benevolent Man can see the vilest Animal courting his Regard and shrinking at his Anger, playing his Gambols of Delight before him, calling on him in his Distress, and flying to him in his Danger, without more Kindness than he can persuade himself to feel for the wild and unsocial Inhabitants of the Air and Water. We naturally endear to ourselves those to whom we impart any Kind of Pleasure, because we imagine their Affection and Esteem secured to us by the Benefits which they receive.

There is indeed another Method by which the Pride of Superiority may be   40
likewise gratified. He that has extinguished all the Sensations of Humanity, and has no longer any Satisfaction in the Reflection that he is loved as the Distributer of Happiness, may please himself with exciting Terror as the Inflicter of Misery, he may delight his Solitude with contemplating the Extent of his Power and the Force of his Commands, in imaging the Desires that flutter on the Tongue that is forbidden to utter them, or the Discontent which preys on the Heart in which Fear confines it; he may amuse himself with

new Contrivances of Detection, new Multiplications of Prohibition, and new Varieties of Punishment, and swell with Exultation when he considers how little of the Homage he receives he owes to Choice or to Affection.

THAT Princes of this Character have been known the History of all absolute Kingdoms will inform us; and since, as *Aristotle* observes, ἡ οἰκονομικὴ μοναρχία, *the Government of a Family is naturally monarchical*,[2] it is likewise too often arbitrarily administered. The regal and parental Tyrant differ only in the Extent of their Dominions, and the Number of their Slaves. The same Passions cause the same Miseries, except that seldom any Prince, however despotick, has so far shaken off all Awe of the publick Eye as to venture upon those Freaks of Injustice, which are sometimes indulged under the Secrecy of a private Dwelling. Capricious Injunctions, partial Decisions, unequal Allotments, Distributions of Reward not by Merit but by Fancy, and Punishments regulated not by the Degree of the Offence but by the Humour of the Judge, are seen too frequently where no Power is known but that of a Father.

THAT he delights in the Misery of others no Man will confess, and yet what other Motive will make a Father cruel? The King may be instigated by one Man to the Destruction of another; he may sometimes think himself endangered by the Virtues of a Subject; he may dread the successful General or the popular Orator; his Avarice may point out golden Confiscations, and his Guilt may whisper that he can only be secure, by cutting off all Power of Revenge.

BUT what can a Parent hope from the Oppression of those who were born to his Protection, those who can disturb him with no Competition, who can enrich him with no Spoils? Why Cowards are cruel may be easily discovered; but for what Reason not more infamous than Cowardice can that Man be cruel who has nothing to fear?

THE unjustifiable Severity of a Parent is loaded with this Aggravation, that those whom he injures are always in his Sight. The Injustice of a Prince is often exercised upon those of whom he never had any personal or particular Knowledge, and the Sentence which he pronounces, whether of Banishment, Imprisonment or Death removes from his View the Man whom he condemns. But the domestick Oppressor dooms himself to gaze upon those Faces which he clouds with Terror, and with Sorrow, and behold every Moment the Effects of his own Barbarities. He that can bear to give continual Pain to those who surround him, and can walk with Satisfaction in the Gloom of his own Presence, he that can see submissive Misery without relenting, and meet without Emotion the Eye that implores Mercy, or demands Justice, will scarcely be amended by Remonstrance or Admonition; he has found Means of stopping the Avenues of Tenderness, and steeling his Heart against the Force of Reason.

EVEN though no Consideration should be paid to the great Law of social Beings, by which every Individual is commanded to consult the Happiness of others, the harsh Parent is yet less to be vindicated than any other Criminal, because he less provides for the Happiness of himself. Every Man however little

---

[2] *Government . . . monarchical: Politics,* I, ii.

he loves others would willingly be loved: every Man hopes to live long, and therefore hopes for that Time at which he shall sink back to Imbecillity, and must depend for Ease and Chearfulness upon the Officiousness of others. But how has he obviated the Inconveniences of old Age, who alienates from him the Assistance of his Children, and whose Bed must be surrounded in his last Hours, in the Hours of Languor and Dejection, of Impatience and of Pain, by Strangers to whom his Life is indifferent, or by Enemies to whom his Death is desirable.

It may indeed happen that Piety may overcome Resentment, and that those who have been harrassed by Brutality may forget the Injuries which they have suffered so far as to perform the last Duties with Alacrity and Zeal; but surely no Resentment can be equally painful with Kindness thus undeserved, nor can severer Punishment be imprecated upon a Man not wholly lost in Meanness and Stupidity, than to be pained by every Incident that gives Comfort to others in the Tediousness of Decrepitude, to be reproached by the Kindness of his own Children, to receive the Alms of Attendance, and to owe every Relief of his Miseries not to Gratitude but to Mercy.

No. 154   *Saturday, September 7, 1751*

—Tibi res antiquæ laudis & artis
Aggredior, sanctos ausus recludere fontes.
                    *—*Virg.[1]

The Direction of *Aristotle* to those that study Politicks, is, first to examine and understand what has been written by the Antients upon Government, then to cast their Eyes round upon the World, and consider by what Causes the Prosperity of Communities is visibly influenced, and why some are worse and others better administered.

The same Method must be pursued by him who hopes to become eminent in any other Part of Knowledge. His first Task is to search Books, the next to contemplate Nature. He must first possess himself of the intellectual Treasures which the Diligence of successive Ages has accumulated, and then endeavour to encrease them by his own Collections.

The mental Diseases of the present Generation, are Impatience of Study, Contempt of the great Masters of antient Wisdom, and a Disposition to rely wholly upon unassisted Genius and natural Sagacity. The Wits of these happy Days have discovered a Way to Fame, which the dull Caution of our laborious Ancestors durst never attempt, they cut the Knots of Sophistry which it was formerly the Business of Years to untie, find themselves enabled to solve all Difficulties by sudden Irradiations of Intelligence, and comprehend long processes of Argument by immediate Intuition.

[1] *Tibi . . . fontes:* It is for you [Italy] that I attempt to write about ancient art and what was highly regarded long ago; for you that I unseal the sacred fountains. *Georgics*, II, 174–175.

MEN who have flattered themselves into this Opinion of their own Abilities, look down upon all who waste their Lives in the Perusal of Books, as a Race of inferior Beings whom Nature has condemned to perpetual Pupillage, who are qualified for no higher Employment than that of propagating Opinions implicitly received, who are fruitlesly endevouring to remedy their own Barrenness by incessant Cultivation, and succour their Feebleness by subsidiary Strength. They presume that none would be more industrious than themselves if they were not more sensible of Deficiencies, and readily conclude, that he who places no Confidence in his own Powers, owes his Modesty only to his Weakness.   10

IT is however certain that no Estimate is more in Danger of erroneous Calculations than those by which every Man computes the Force of his own Genius. It generally happens at our Entrance into the World, that by the natural Attraction of Similitude, we are inclined to associate with Men young and sprightly, and ignorant like ourselves; we rate our Accomplishments by a Comparison with theirs, when we have once obtained an acknowledged Superiority over our Acquaintances, a warm Imagination and strong Desire easily extend it over the rest of Mankind, and if no Accident forces us into new Emulations, we grow old and die in Admiration of ourselves.

VANITY, thus confirmed in her Dominion, readily listens to the Voice of Idle-   20
ness, and solaces the Slumber of Life with continual Dreams of Excellence and Greatness. A Man once prejudiced by a Conviction of his own natural Vigour of Fancy and Sagacity of Conjecture, soon concludes that he already possesses whatever Toil and Enquiry can confer; he then listens with Eagerness to all the wild Objections which Folly has raised against the common Means of Improvement, talks of the dark Chaos of indigested Knowledge, describes the mischievous Effects of heterogeneous Sciences fermenting in the Mind, relates the Blunders of lettered Ignorance, expatiates on the heroick Merit of those who deviate from the Tracks of Prescription, and shakes off the Shackles of Authority, and gives Vent to the Inflations of his Heart by declaring   30
that he owes nothing to Pedants and Universities.

ALL these Pretensions, however confident, are very often vain. The Laurels which superficial Acuteness gains by Triumphs over Ignorance unsupported by Vivacity, are observed by *Locke*[2] to be soon lost whenever real Learning and rational Diligence appear against her; the Sallies of Gaiety are soon repressed, the Artifices of Subtilty are soon detected by those who have carefully studied the Question, and are therefore not easily confounded or surprised.

BUT though it should happen that the Contemner of Books, has neither been deceived by others nor by himself, and that he was really born with a   40
Genius surpassing the ordinary Abilities of Mankind; yet surely such Gifts of Providence may be more properly urged as incitements to Labour, than Encouragement to Negligence. He that neglects the Culture of Ground, naturally fertile, is more shamefully culpable than he whose Field would scarcely recompence his Husbandry.

---

[2] *Locke:* John Locke (1632–1704), *Some Thoughts Concerning Education.*
English empiricist; see section 70 of his

CICERO remarks, that not to know what has been transacted in former Times is to continue always a Child. If we make no use of the Labours of our Ancestors the World must remain always in the Infancy of Knowledge. The Discoveries of every Man must terminate in his own Advantage, and the Studies of every Age must be employed on Questions, which the past Generation had determined. We may with as little Reproach to ourselves make use of the Sciences as the Manufactures of our Ancestors, and it is as rational to live in Caves till our own Hands have erected a Palace, as to reject all Knowledge of Architecture, which our own Understandings will not supply.

To the strongest and quickest Mind it is far easier to learn than to invent.   10 The Principles of Arithmetick and Geometry may be comprehended by a close Attention in a few Days, yet who can flatter himself, that the Study of a long Life would have enabled him to discover them, when he sees them yet unknown to so many Nations, whom he cannot suppose less liberally endowed with natural Reason, than the *Grecians* or *Egyptians*?

EVERY Science was thus far advanced towards Perfection, by the emulous Diligence of contemporary Students, and the gradual Discoveries of one Age improving on another, and sometimes unexpected Flashes of Instruction were struck out by the fortuitous Collision of happy Incidents, or an involuntary Concurrence of Ideas, in which the Philosopher to whom they hap-   20 pened had no other Merit than that of knowing their Value, and transmitting unclouded to Posterity that Light which had been kindled by Causes out of his Power. The Happiness of these causal Illuminations no Man can promise to himself, because no Endeavours can procure them; and therefore whatever be his Abilities or Application he must always remain ignorant, unless he will submit to learn from others what perhaps must have lain hid for ever from human Penetration, had not some remote Enquiry brought it to view, as Treasures are thrown up by the Ploughman and the Digger in the rude Exercise of their common Occupations.

THE Man whose Genius qualifies him for great Undertakings must at least   30 be content to learn from Books the present State of human Knowledge, that he may not ascribe to himself the Invention of Arts already known, weary his Attention with Experiments of which the Events has been already registered, and waste, in Attempts which have already succeeded or miscarried in other Hands, that Time, which might have been spent, with Usefulness and Honour, upon new Undertakings.

BUT though the Study of Books is necessary, it is not sufficient to constitute literary Eminence. He that hopes to be counted among the Benefactors of Posterity, must add by his own Toil to the Acquisitions of his Ancestors, and secure his Memory from Neglect by some valuable Improvement. This   40 can only be effected by looking out upon the Wastes of the intellectual World, and extending the Power of Learning over Regions yet undisciplined and barbarous; or by surveying more exactly her antient Dominions, and driving Ignorance from the Fortresses and Retreats where she skulks undetected and undisturbed. Every Science has its Difficulties which yet call for Solution before we attempt new Systems of Knowledge, as every Country has its Forests and Marshes, which perhaps it might be wise to cultivate and drain, before distant Colonies are projected as a necessary Discharge of the Exuberance of Inhabitants.

No Man ever yet became great by Imitation. Whatever can hope for the Veneration of Mankind must have Invention either in the Design or in the Execution, either the Effect must itself be new, or the Means by which it is produced. Either Truths hitherto unknown must be discovered, or those which are already known enforced by stronger Evidence, facilitated by clearer Method, or elucidated by brighter Illustrations.

No Fame can spread wider or endure long that is not rooted in Nature, and manured by Art. That which hopes to resist the Blast of Malignity, and   10 stand firm against the Attacks of Time, must contain in itself some original Principle of Growth. The Reputation which arises from the Detail or Transposition of borrowed Sentiments may spread for a while, like Ivy on the Rind of Antiquity, but will be torn away by Accident or Contempt, and suffered to rot unheeded on the Ground.

Headnote to
RASSELAS

Along with his essays in *The Rambler*, Johnson's *History of Rasselas* is his great work as a moralist. In form, it is related to the Oriental tale, actually a Western genre that grew out of the vogue, popular early in the century, of offering translations and pseudo-translations of Persian, Turkish, Arabic, and Chinese stories, though some competent critics have argued against this classification. Most often these narratives are brief, morally pointed works, like Addison's *The Visions of Mirzah* and Goldsmith's *Asem the Man Hater*. Their Oriental setting provides not atmosphere, generally, but a locus neutralized by its remoteness, so that ideas and attitudes new to the reader may be met out of the context of a known environment, in which strange setting they may receive an objective reception. Admittedly theoretical and abstract, these compositions nevertheless attempt to treat problems with which life typically confronts men.

It is generally held that *Rasselas* was swiftly written because Johnson needed money to help meet his mother's funeral expenses. It has been said that, inevitably, a piece of this length, composed in a single month, January, 1759, must reveal at least a few signs of such speed of execution. *Rasselas*, with its apparently linear, episodic development, seems to be the product of the quick work that produced it. But it would be a naïve error to assume that such a structure conveys less of the complexity of Johnson's vigorous mind than would a more leisurely composition. It is simply that here, in *Rasselas*, the clues are less obvious than they might otherwise be. All the parts of the work, then, ought not to be dismissed as if they had been dealt with the moment they have been understood at the narrative level. And in fact, close study of certain structural patterns, employed by Johnson many times over, will reveal extraordinary richness and complexity of idea, where otherwise rather simple notions might have been thought to control the work.

It has been observed that *Rasselas* is a tale expressing the vanity of human wishes. If it is just that and no more, then it is essentially a skeptical piece, a conclusion open to some question. To be sure the upshot of inquiry and endeavor among the characters in the work seems to be that no philosophy of life is uniformly sustaining and that no practice of life is more than temporarily satisfying. But these demonstrations, which have sometimes been taken to mean that the whole of life is futile, a waste of energy, only suggest that no single way of life will satisfy a person forever. If one considers the obvious evidence against Johnson's apparent pessimism, one may well conclude that *Rasselas* does not deny the value of human experience so much as it reveals it to be complex, yet shaped by man's need to move between conditions of rest after turmoil, and to experiments with new ways of life after one has followed a fixed course for a time. It is usually difficult for men to acknowledge that the decisions they make today may not be uniformly appropriate tomorrow. Johnson requires even more of them than that, however; for his expectation, implicit in Imlac's patient vitality (he willingly joins the Prince who is soon to be on the move, even though he feels his own days of active experience are behind him) is that men will unhesitatingly participate in life, understanding that it is a condition in which absolute philosophies will not serve all occasions, and in which commitments to single courses of action are the effect of rather childish attempts to get bothersome matters settled once and for all. Yet he understands that all men need both stability and motion.

Many elements in the tale serve as clues to this view of life. The most obvious of these are examples of apparently settled lives that require new spheres of action and examples of restless lives that require stability. In the first group are the philosopher, the astronomer, the hermit, and Prince Rasselas; in the second are Imlac after his early travels, Pequah's Arab captor, and the three young people at the end of the work. The most important thing to observe about the two views, however, is that all the characters at various times feel compelled to live according to both.

Other clues reinforcing this double-functioning life of motion and life of rest may be observed in the uses of setting and in the treatment of such matters as the nature of family life and of the production of poetry. Only the first of these will be glanced at here. Briefly, it may be observed that the happy valley so dominates the early book that it stands out in the reader's imagination as a fixed locus whose qualities are predictable; it is the primary emblem of the life of rest. The remainder of the book involves searching action that covers a wide area outside the valley; it is the uncharted realm of the life of motion. Yet the two worlds are joined. For it is in the valley that Rasselas experiences the greatest restlessness; and it is in the midst of an experience charged with potential violence that Pequah, a warrior's captive, discovers unexpected order. Johnson's *Rasselas* offers a simple, pessimistic view only in the sense that it provides no program for the good life. But in its unselfconscious expectation that men will continue to act constructively despite the absence of certainty, it celebrates life.

TEXT. *The Prince of Abbissinia, A Tale* (2 vols., London, 1759).

The History of Rasselas, Prince of Abissinia

Chap. I   Description of a palace in a valley

YE who listen with credulity to the whispers of fancy, and pursue with eagerness the phantoms of hope; who expect that age will perform the promises of youth, and that the deficiencies of the present day will be supplied by the morrow; attend to the history of Rasselas prince of Abissinia.

Rasselas was the fourth son of the mighty emperour, in whose dominions the Father of waters begins his course; whose bounty powers down the streams of plenty, and scatters over half the world the harvests of Egypt.

According to the custom which has descended from age to age among the monarchs of the torrid zone, he was confined in a private palace, with the other sons and daughters of Abissinian royalty, till the order of succession should call   10 him to the throne.

The place, which the wisdom or policy of antiquity had destined for the residence of the Abissinian princes, was a spacious valley in the kingdom of Amhara, surrounded on every side by mountains, of which the summits overhang the middle part. The only passage, by which it could be entered, was a cavern that passed under a rock, of which it has long been disputed whether it was the work of nature or of human industry. The outlet of the cavern was concealed by a thick wood, and the mouth which opened into the valley was closed with gates of iron, forged by the artificers of ancient days, so massy that no man could, without the help of engines, open or shut them.   20

From the mountains on every side, rivulets descended that filled all the valley with verdure and fertility, and formed a lake in the middle inhabited by fish of every species, and frequented by every fowl whom nature has taught to dip the wing in water. This lake discharged its superfluities by a stream which entered a dark cleft of the mountain on the northern side, and fell with dreadful noise from precipice to precipice till it was heard no more.

The sides of the mountains were covered with trees, the banks of the brooks were diversified with flowers; every blast shook spices from the rocks, and every month dropped fruits upon the ground. All animals that bite the grass, or brouse the shrub, whether wild or tame, wandered in this extensive circuit,   30 secured from beasts of prey by the mountains which confined them. On one part were flocks and herds feeding in the pastures, on another all the beasts of chase frisking in the lawns; the spritely kid was bounding on the rocks, the subtle money frolicking in the trees, and the solemn elephant reposing in the shade. All the diversities of the world were brought together, the blessings of nature were collected, and its evils extracted and excluded.

The valley, wide and fruitful, supplied its inhabitants with the necessaries of life, and all delights and superfluities were added at the annual visit which the emperour paid his children, when the iron gate was opened to the sound of musick; and during eight days every one that resided in the valley was required 10 to propose whatever might contribute to make seclusion pleasant, to fill up the vacancies of attention, and lessen the tediousness of time. Every desire was immediately granted. All the artificers of pleasure were called to gladden the festivity; the musicians exerted the power of harmony, and the dancers shewed their activity before the princes, in hope that they should pass their lives in this blisful captivity, to which these only were admitted whose performance was thought able to add novelty to luxury. Such was the appearance of security and delight which this retirement afforded, that they to whom it was new always desired that it might be perpetual; and as those, on whom the iron gate had once closed, were never suffered to return, the effect of longer experience could not be 20 known. Thus every year produced new schemes of delight, and new competitors for imprisonment.

The palace stood on an eminence raised about thirty paces above the surface of the lake. It was divided into many squares or courts, built with greater or less magnificence according to the rank of those for whom they were designed. The roofs were turned into arches of massy stone joined with a cement that grew harder by time, and the building stood from century to century, deriding the solstitial rains and equinoctial hurricanes, without need of reparation.

This house, which was so large as to be fully known to none but some ancient officers who successively inherited the secrets of the place, was built as if 30 suspicion herself had dictated the plan. To every room there was an open and secret passage, every square had a communication with the rest, either from the upper stories by private galleries, or by subterranean passages from the lower apartments. Many of the columns had unsuspected cavities, in which successive monarchs reposited their treasures. They then closed up the opening with marble, which was never to be removed but in the utmost exigencies of the kingdom; and recorded their accumulations in a book which was itself concealed in a tower not entered but by the emperour, attended by the prince who stood next in succession.

Chap. II   The discontent of Rasselas in the happy valley

HERE the sons and daughters of Abissinia lived only to know the soft vicis- 40 situdes of pleasure and repose, attended by all that were skilful to delight, and gratified with whatever the senses can enjoy. They wandered in gardens of fragrance, and slept in the fortresses of security. Every art was practised to make them pleased with their own condition. The sages who instructed them, told them of nothing but the miseries of publick life, and described all beyond the mountains as regions of calamity, where discord was always raging, and where man preyed upon man.

To heighten their opinion of their own felicity, they were daily entertained with songs, the subject of which was the *happy valley*. Their appetites were excited by frequent enumerations of different enjoyments, and revelry and merriment was the business of every hour from the dawn of morning to the close of even.   10

These methods were generally successful; few of the princes had ever wished to enlarge their bounds, but passed their lives in full conviction that they had all within their reach that art or nature could bestow, and pitied those whom fate had excluded from this seat of tranquility, as the sport of chance, and the slaves of misery.

Thus they rose in the morning, and lay down at night, pleased with each other and with themselves, all but Rasselas, who, in the twenty-sixth year of his age, began to withdraw himself from their pastimes and assemblies, and to delight in solitary walks and silent meditation. He often sat before tables covered with luxury, and forgot to taste the dainties that were placed before   20 him: he rose abruptly in the midst of the song, and hastily retired beyond the sound of musick. His attendants observed the change and endeavoured to renew his love of pleasure: he neglected their endeavours, repulsed their invitations, and spent day after day on the banks of rivulets sheltered with trees, where he sometimes listened to the birds in the branches, sometimes observed the fish playing in the stream, and anon cast his eyes upon the pastures and mountains filled with animals, of which some were biting the herbage, and some sleeping among the bushes.

This singularity of his humour made him much observed. One of the Sages, in whose conversation he had formerly delighted, followed him secretly, in   30 hope of discovering the cause of his disquiet. Rasselas, who knew not that any one was near him, having for some time fixed his eyes upon the goats that were brousing among the rocks, began to compare their condition with his own.

"What," said he, "makes the difference between man and all the rest of the animal creation? Every beast that strays beside me has the same corporal necessities with myself; he is hungry and crops the grass, he is thirsty and drinks the stream, his thirst and hunger are appeased, he is satisfied and sleeps; he rises again and is hungry, he is again fed and is at rest. I am hungry and thirsty like him, but when thirst and hunger cease I am not at rest; I am, like him, pained with want, but am not, like him, satisfied with fulness. The intermediate hours   40 are tedious and gloomy; I long again to be hungry that I may again quicken my attention. The birds peck the berries or the corn, and fly away to the groves where they sit in seeming happiness on the branches, and waste their lives in tuning one unvaried series of sounds. I likewise can call the lutanist and the singer, but the sounds that pleased me yesterday weary me to day, and will grow yet more wearisome to morrow. I can discover within me no power of perception which is not glutted with its proper pleasure, yet I do not feel myself delighted.

Man has surely some latent sense for which this place affords no gratification, or he has some desires distinct from sense which must be satisfied before he can be happy."

After this he lifted up his head, and seeing the moon rising, walked towards the palace. As he passed through the fields, and saw the animals around him, "Ye, said he, are happy, and need not envy me that walk thus among you, burthened with myself; nor do I, ye gentle beings, envy your felicity; for it is not the felicity of man. I have many distresses from which ye are free; I fear pain when I do not feel it; I sometimes shrink at evils recollected, and sometimes start at evils anticipated: surely the equity of providence has ballanced peculiar   10 sufferings with peculiar enjoyments."

With observations like these the prince amused himself as he returned, uttering them with a plaintive voice, yet with a look that discovered him to feel some complacence in his own perspicacity, and to receive some solace of the miseries of life, from consciousness of the delicacy with which he felt, and the eloquence with which be bewailed them. He mingled cheerfully in the diversions of the evening, and all rejoiced to find that his heart was lightened.

Chap. III   The wants of him that wants nothing

ON the next day his old instructor, imagining that he had now made himself acquainted with his disease of mind, was in hope of curing it by counsel, and officiously sought an opportunity of conference, which the prince, having   20 long considered him as one whose intellects were exhausted, was not very willing to afford: "Why, said he, does this man thus intrude upon me; shall I be never suffered to forget those lectures which pleased only while they were new, and to become new again must be forgotten?" He then walked into the wood, and composed himself to his usual meditations; when, before his thoughts had taken any settled form, he perceived his persuer at his side, and was at first prompted by his impatience to go hastily away; but, being unwilling to offend a man whom he had once reverenced and still loved, he invited him to sit down with him on the bank.

The old man, thus encouraged, began to lament the change which had been   30 lately observed in the prince, and to enquire why he so often retired from the pleasures of the palace, to loneliness and silence. "I fly from pleasure, said the prince, because pleasure has ceased to please; I am lonely because I am miserable, and am unwilling to cloud with my presence the happiness of others." "You, Sir, said the sage, are the first who has complained of misery in the *happy valley*. I hope to convince you that your complaints have no real cause. You are here in full possession of all that the emperour of Abissinia can bestow; here is neither labour to be endured nor danger to be dreaded, yet here is all that labour or danger can procure. Look round and tell me which of your wants is without supply: if you want nothing, how are you unhappy?"   40

"That I want nothing, said the prince, or that I know not what I want, is the cause of my complaint; if I had any known want, I should have a certain wish; that wish would excite endeavour, and I should not then repine to see the sun move so slowly towards the western mountain, or lament when the day breaks and sleep will no longer hide me from myself. When I see the kids and the lambs chasing one another, I fancy that I should be happy if I had something to pursue. But, possessing all that I can want, I find one day and one hour exactly like another, except that the latter is still more tedious than the former. Let your experience inform me how the day may now seem as short as in my childhood, while nature was yet fresh, and every moment showed me what I never had observed before. I have already enjoyed too much; give me something to desire."

The old man was surprised at this new species of affliction, and knew not   10
what to reply, yet was unwilling to be silent. "Sir, said he, if you had seen the miseries of the world, you would know how to value your present state." "Now, said the prince, you have given me something to desire; I shall long to see the miseries of the world, since the sight of them is necessary to happiness."

Chap. IV   The prince continues to grieve and muse

AT this time the sound of musick proclaimed the hour of repast, and the conversation was concluded. The old man went away sufficiently discontented to find that his reasonings had produced the only conclusion which they were intended to prevent. But in the decline of life shame and grief are of short duration; whether it be that we bear easily what we have born long, or that, finding ourselves in age less regarded, we less regard others; or, that we look   20
with slight regard upon afflictions, to which we know that the hand of death is about to put an end.

The prince, whose views were extended to a wider space, could not speedily quiet his emotions. He had been before terrified at the length of life which nature promised him, because he considered that in a long time much must be endured; he now rejoiced in his youth, because in many years much might be done.

This first beam of hope, that had been ever darted into his mind, rekindled youth in his cheeks, and doubled the lustre of his eyes. He was fired with the desire of doing something, though he knew not yet with distinctness, either   30
end or means.

He was now no longer gloomy and unsocial; but, considering himself as master of a secret stock of happiness, which he could enjoy only by concealing it, he affected to be busy in all schemes of diversion, and endeavoured to make others pleased with the state of which he himself was weary. But pleasures never can be so multiplied or continued, as not to leave much of life unemployed; there were many hours, both of the night and day, which he could spend without suspicion in solitary thought. The load of life was much lightened: he went eagerly into the assemblies, because he supposed the frequency of his presence necessary to the success of his purposes; he retired gladly to privacy, because he   40
had now a subject of thought.

His chief amusement was to picture to himself that world which he had never seen; to place himself in various conditions; to be entangled in imaginary difficulties, and to be engaged in wild adventures: but his benevolence always terminated his projects in the relief of distress, the detection of fraud, the defeat of oppression, and the diffusion of happiness.

Thus passed twenty months of the life of Rasselas. He busied himself so intensely in visionary bustle, that he forgot his real solitude; and, amidst hourly preparations for the various incidents of human affairs, neglected to consider by what means he should mingle with mankind.

One day, as he was sitting on a bank, he feigned to himself an orphan virgin robbed of her little portion by a treacherous lover, and crying after him for restitution and redress. So strongly was the image impressed upon his mind, that he started up in the maid's defence, and run forward to seize the plunderer with all the eagerness of real persuit. Fear naturally quickens the flight of guilt. Rasselas could not catch the fugitive with his utmost efforts; but, resolving to weary, by perseverance, him whom he could not surpass in speed, he pressed on till the foot of the mountain stopped his course.

Here he recollected himself, and smiled at his own useless impetuosity. Then raising his eyes to the mountain, "This, said he, is the fatal obstacle that hinders at once the enjoyment of pleasure, and the exercise of virtue. How long is it that my hopes and wishes have flown beyond this boundary of my life, which yet I never have attempted to surmount!"

Struck with this reflection, he sat down to muse, and remembered, that since he first resolved to escape from his confinement, the sun had passed twice over him in his annual course. He now felt a degree of regret with which he had never been before acquainted. He considered how much might have been done in the time which had passed, and left nothing real behind it. He compared twenty months with the life of man. "In life, said he, is not to be counted the ignorance of infancy, or imbecility of age. We are long before we are able to think, and we soon cease from the power of acting. The true period of human existence may be reasonably estimated as forty years, of which I have mused away the four and twentieth part. What I have lost was certain, for I have certainly possessed it; but of twenty months to come who can assure me?"

The consciousness of his own folly pierced him deeply, and he was long before he could be reconciled to himself. "The rest of my time, said he, has been lost by the crime or folly of my ancestors, and the absurd institutions of my country; I remember it with disgust, but without remorse: but the months that have passed since new light darted into my soul, since I formed a scheme of reasonable felicity, have been squandered by my own fault. I have lost that which can never be restored: I have seen the sun rise and set for twenty months, an idle gazer on the light of heaven: In this time the birds have left the nest of their mother, and committed themselves to the woods and to the skies: the kid has forsaken the teat, and learned by degrees to climb the rocks in quest of independant sustenance. I only have made no advances, but am still helpless and ignorant. The moon, by more than twenty changes, admonished me of the flux of life; the stream that rolled before my feet upbraided my inactivity. I sat feasting on intellectual luxury, regardless alike of the examples of the earth, and the instructions of the planets. Twenty months are past, who shall restore them!"

These sorrowful meditations fastened upon his mind; he past four months in resolving to lose no more time in idle resolves, and was awakened to more vigorous exertion by hearing a maid, who had broken a porcelain cup, remark, that what cannot be repaired is not to be regretted.

This was obvious; and Rasselas reproached himself that he had not discovered it, having not known, or not considered, how many useful hints are obtained by chance, and how often the mind, hurried by her own ardour to distant views, neglects the truths that lie open before her. He, for a few hours, regretted his regret, and from that time bent his whole mind upon the means of escaping from the valley of happiness.   10

Chap. V   The prince meditates his escape

HE now found that it would be very difficult to effect that which it was very easy to suppose effected. When he looked round about him, he saw himself confined by the bars of nature which had never yet been broken, and by the gate, through which none that once had passed it were ever able to return. He was now impatient as an eagle in a grate. He passed week after week in clambering the mountains, to see if there was any aperture which the bushes might conceal, but found all the summits inaccessible by their prominence. The iron gate he despaired to open; for it was not only secured with all the power of art, but was always watched by successive sentinels, and was by its position exposed to the perpetual observation of all the inhabitants.   20

He then examined the cavern through which the waters of the lake were discharged; and, looking down at a time when the sun shone strongly upon its mouth, he discovered it to be full of broken rocks, which, though they permitted the stream to flow through many narrow passages, would stop any body of solid bulk. He returned discouraged and dejected; but, having now known the blessing of hope, resolved never to despair.

In these fruitless searches he spent ten months. The time, however, passed cheerfully away: in the morning he rose with new hope, in the evening applauded his own diligence, and in the night slept sound after his fatigue. He met a thousand amusements which beguiled his labour, and diversified his thoughts.   30 He discerned the various instincts of animals, and properties of plants, and found the place replete with wonders, of which he purposed to solace himself with the contemplation, if he should never be able to accomplish his flight; rejoicing that his endeavours, though yet unsuccessful, had supplied him with a source of inexhaustible enquiry.

But his original curiosity was not yet abated; he resolved to obtain some knowledge of the ways of men. His wish still continued, but his hope grew less. He ceased to survey any longer the walls of his prison, and spared to search by new toils for interstices which he knew could not be found, yet determined to keep his design always in view, and lay hold on any expedient that time should   40 offer.

Chap. VI   A dissertation on the art of flying

AMONG the artists that had been allured into the happy valley, to labour for the accommodation and pleasure of its inhabitants, was a man eminent for his knowledge of the mechanick powers, who had contrived many engines both of use and recreation. By a wheel, which the stream turned, he forced the water into a tower, whence it was distributed to all the apartments of the palace. He erected a pavillion in the garden, around which he kept the air always cool by artificial showers. One of the groves, appropriated to the ladies, was ventilated by fans, to which the rivulet that run through it gave a constant motion; and instruments of soft musick were placed at proper distances, of which some played by the impulse of the wind, and some by the power of the   10
stream.

This artist was sometimes visited by Rasselas, who was pleased with every kind of knowledge, imagining that the time would come when all his acquisitions should be of use to him in the open world. He came one day to amuse himself in his usual manner, and found the master busy in building a sailing chariot: he saw that the design was practicable upon a level surface, and with expressions of great esteem solicited its completion. The workman was pleased to find himself so much regarded by the prince, and resolved to gain yet higher honours. "Sir, said he, you have seen but a small part of what the mechanick sciences can perform. I have been long of opinion, that, instead of   20
the tardy conveyance of ships and chariots, man might use the swifter migration of wings; that the fields of air are open to knowledge, and that only ignorance and idleness need crawl upon the ground."

This hint rekindled the prince's desire of passing the mountains; and having seen what the mechanist had already performed, he was willing to fancy that he could do more; yet resolved to enquire further before he suffered hope to afflict him by disappointment. "I am afraid, said he to the artist, that your imagination prevails over your skill, and that you now tell me rather what you wish than what you know. Every animal has his element assigned him; the birds have the air, and man and beasts the earth." "So, replied the mechanist, fishes have   30
the water, in which yet beasts can swim by nature, and men by art. He that can swim needs not despair to fly: to swim is to fly in a grosser fluid, and to fly is to swim in a subtler. We are only to proportion our power of resistance to the different density of the matter through which we are to pass. You will be necessarily upborn by the air, if you can renew any impulse upon it, faster than the air can recede from the pressure."

"But the exercise of swiming, said the prince, is very laborious; the strongest limbs are soon wearied; I am afraid the act of flying will be yet more violent, and wings will be of no great use, unless we can fly further than we can swim."

"The labour of rising from the ground, said the artist, will be great, as we   40
see it in the heavier domestick fowls; but, as we mount higher, the earth's attraction, and the body's gravity, will be gradually diminished, till we shall arrive at a region where the man will float in the air without any tendency to fall: no care will then be necessary, but to move forwards, which the gentlest impulse will effect. You, Sir, whose curiosity is so extensive, will easily con-

ceive with what pleasure a philosopher, furnished with wings, and hovering in the sky, would see the earth, and all its inhabitants, rolling beneath him, and presenting to him successively, by its diurnal motion, all the countries within the same parallel. How must it amuse the pendent spectator to see the moving scene of land and ocean, cities and desarts! To survey with equal security the marts of trade, and the fields of battle; mountains infested by barbarians, and fruitful regions gladdened by plenty, and lulled by peace! How easily shall we then trace the Nile through all his passage; pass over to distant regions, and examine the face of nature from one extremity of the earth to the other!"

"All this, said the prince, is much to be desired, but I am afraid that no man   10
will be able to breathe in these regions of speculation and tranquility. I have been told, that respiration is difficult upon lofty mountains, yet from these precipices, though so high as to produce great tenuity of the air, it is very easy to fall: and I suspect, that from any height, where life can be supported, there may be danger of too quick descent."

"Nothing, replied the artist, will ever be attempted, if all possible objections must be first overcome. If you will favour my project I will try the first flight at my own hazard. I have considered the structure of all volant[1] animals, and find the folding continuity of the bat's wings most easily accommodated to the human form. Upon this model I shall begin my talk to morrow, and in a year   20
expect to tower into the air beyond the malice or pursuit of man. But I will work only on this condition, that the art shall not be divulged, and that you shall not require me to make wings for any but ourselves."

"Why, said Rasselas, should you envy others so great an advantage? All skill ought to be exerted for universal good; every man has owed much to others, and ought to repay the kindness that he has received."

"If men were all virtuous, returned the artist, I should with great alacrity teach then all to fly. But what would be the security of the good, if the bad could at pleasure invade them from the sky? Against an army sailing through the clouds neither walls, nor mountains, nor seas, could afford any security. A   30
flight of northern savages might hover in the wind, and light at once with irresistible violence upon the capital of a fruitful region that was rolling under them. Even this valley, the retreat of princes, the abode of happiness, might be violated by the sudden descent of some of the naked nations that swarm on the coast of the southern sea."

The prince promised secrecy, and waited for the performance, not wholly hopeless of success. He visited the work from time to time, observed its progress, and remarked the ingenious contrivances to facilitate motion, and unite levity[2] with strength. The artist was every day more certain that he should leave vultures and eagles behind him, and the contagion of his confidence seized upon   40
the prince.

In a year the wings were finished, and, on a morning appointed, the maker appeared furnished for flight on a little promontory: he waved his pinions a while to gather air, then leaped from his stand, and in an instant dropped into the lake. His wings, which were of no use in the air, sustained him in the water, and the prince drew him to land, half dead with terrour and vexation.

[1] *Volant:* Flying.   [2] *Levity:* Lightness.

Chap. VII   The prince finds a man of learning

THE prince was not much afflicted by this disaster, having suffered himself to hope for a happier event, only because he had no other means of escape in view. He still persisted in his design to leave the happy valley by the first opportunity.

His imagination was now at a stand; he had no prospect of entering into the world; and, notwithstanding all his endeavours to support himself, discontent by degrees preyed upon him, and he began again to lose his thoughts in sadness, when the rainy season, which in these countries is periodical, made it inconvenient to wander in the woods.

The rain continued longer and with more violence than had been ever   10
known: the clouds broke on the surrounding mountains, and the torrents streamed into the plain on every side, till the cavern was too narrow to discharge the water. The lake overflowed its banks, and all the level of the valley was covered with the inundation. The eminence, on which the palace was built, and some other spots of rising ground, were all that the eye could now discover. The herds and flocks left the pastures, and both the wild beasts and the tame retreated to the mountains.

This inundation confined all the princes to domestick amusements, and the attention of Rasselas was particularly seized by a poem, which Imlac recited, upon the various conditions of humanity. He commanded the poet to attend   20
him in his apartment, and recite his verses a second time; then entering into familiar talk, he thought himself happy in having found a man who knew the world so well, and could so skilfully paint the scenes of life. He asked a thousand questions about things, to which, though common to all other mortals, his confinement from childhood had kept him a stranger. The poet pitied his ignorance, and loved his curiosity, and entertained him from day to day with novelty and instruction, so that the prince regretted the necessity of sleep, and longed till the morning should renew his pleasure.

As they were sitting together, the prince commanded Imlac to relate his history, and to tell by what accident he was forced, or by what motive induced,   30
to close his life in the happy valley. As he was going to begin his narrative, Rasselas was called to a concert, and obliged to restrain his curiosity till the evening.

Chap. VIII   The history of Imlac

THE close of the day is, in the regions of the torrid zone, the only season of diversion and entertainment, and it was therefore mid-night before the musick ceased, and the princesses retired. Rasselas then called for his companion and required him to begin the story of his life.

"Sir, said Imlac, my history will not be long: the life that is devoted to knowledge passes silently away, and is very little diversified by events. To talk in publick, to think in solitude, to read and to hear, to inquire, and answer inquiries, is the business of a scholar. He wanders about the world without   40
pomp or terrour, and is neither known nor valued but by men like himself.

"I was born in the kingdom of Goiama, at no great distance from the fountain of the Nile. My father was a wealthy merchant, who traded between the inland countries of Africk and the ports of the red sea. He was honest, frugal and diligent, but of mean sentiments, and narrow comprehension: he desired only to be rich, and to conceal his riches, lest he should be spoiled by the governours of the province."

"Surely, said the prince, my father must be negligent of his charge, if any man in his dominions dares take that which belongs to another. Does he not know that kings are accountable for injustice permitted as well as done? If I were emperour, not the meanest of my subjects should be oppressed with impunity. My blood boils when I am told that a merchant durst not enjoy his honest gains for fear of losing by the rapacity of power. Name the governour who robbed the people, that I may declare his crimes to the emperour." 10

"Sir, said Imlac, your ardour is the natural effect of virtue animated by youth: the time will come when you will acquit your father, and perhaps hear with less impatience of the governour. Oppression is, in the Abissinian dominions, neither frequent nor tolerated; but no form of government has been yet discovered, by which cruelty can be wholly prevented. Subordination supposes power on one part and subjection on the other; and if power be in the hands of men, it will sometimes be abused. The vigilance of the supreme magistrate may do much, but much will still remain undone. He can never know all the crimes that are committed, and can seldom punish all that he knows." 20

"This, said the prince, I do not understand, but I had rather hear thee than dispute. Continue thy narration."

"My father, proceeded Imlac, originally intended that I should have no other education, than such as might qualify me for commerce; and discovering in me great strength of memory, and quickness of apprehension, often declared his hope that I should be some time the richest man in Abissinia."

"Why, said the prince, did thy father desire the increase of his wealth, when it was already greater than he durst discover or enjoy? I am unwilling to doubt thy veracity, yet inconsistencies cannot both be true." 30

"Inconsistencies, answered Imlac, cannot both be right, but, imputed to man, they may both be true. Yet diversity is not inconsistency. My father might expect a time of greater security. However, some desire is necessary to keep life in motion, and he, whose real wants are supplied, must admit those of fancy."

"This, said the prince, I can in some measure conceive. I repent that I interrupted thee."

"With this hope, proceeded Imlac, he sent me to school; but when I had once found the delight of knowledge, and felt the pleasure of intelligence and the pride of invention, I began silently to despise riches, and determined to disappoint the purpose of my father, whose grossness of conception raised my pity. I was twenty years old before his tenderness would expose me to the fatigue of travel, in which time I had been instructed, by successive masters, in all the literature of my native country. As every hour taught me something new, I lived in a continual course of gratifications; but, as I advanced towards manhood, I lost much of the reverence with which I had been used to look on my instructors; 40

because, when the lesson was ended, I did not find them wiser or better than common men.

"At length my father resolved to initiate me in commerce, and, opening one of his subterranean treasuries, counted out ten thousand pieces of gold. This, young man, said he, is the stock with which you must negociate. I began with less than the fifth part, and you see how diligence and parsimony have increased it. This is your own to waste or to improve. If you squander it by negligence or caprice, you must wait for my death before you will be rich: if, in four years, you double your stock, we will thenceforward let subordination cease, and live together as friends and partners; for he shall always be equal with me, who is equally skilled in the art of growing rich.   10

"We laid our money upon camels, concealed in bales of cheap goods, and travelled to the shore of the red sea. When I cast my eye on the expanse of waters my heart bounded like that of a prisoner escaped. I felt an unextinguishable curiosity kindle in my mind, and resolved to snatch this opportunity of seeing the manners of other nations, and of learning sciences unknown in Abissinia.

"I remembered that my father had obliged me to the improvement of my stock, not by a promise which I ought not to violate, but by a penalty which I was at liberty to incur, and therefore determined to gratify my predominant desire, and by drinking at the fountains of knowledge, to quench the thirst of   20 curiosity.

"As I was supposed to trade without connexion with my father, it was easy for me to become acquainted with the master of a ship, and procure a passage to some other country. I had no motives of choice to regulate my voyage; it was sufficient for me that, wherever I wandered, I should see a country which I had not seen before. I therefore entered a ship bound for Surat, having left a letter for my father declaring my intention.

Chap. IX   The history of Imlac continued

WHEN I first entered upon the world of waters, and lost sight of land, I looked round about me with pleasing terrour, and thinking my soul enlarged by the boundless prospect, imagined that I could gaze round for ever without   30 satiety; but, in a short time, I grew weary of looking on barren uniformity, where I could only see again what I had already seen. I then descended into the ship, and doubted for a while whether all my future pleasures would not end like this in disgust and disappointment. Yet, surely, said I, the ocean and the land are very different; the only variety of water is rest and motion, but the earth has mountains and vallies, desarts and cities: it is inhabited by men of different customs and contrary opinions; and I may hope to find variety in life, though I should miss it in nature.

"With this hope I quieted my mind, and amused myself during the voyage; sometimes by learning from the sailors the art of navigation, which I have   40 never practised, and sometimes by forming schemes for my conduct in different situations, in not one of which I have been ever placed.

"I was almost weary of my naval amusements when we landed safely at Surat. I secured my money, and purchasing some commodities for show, joined myself to a caravan that was passing into the inland country. My companions, for some reason or other, conjecturing that I was rich, and, by my inquiries and admiration, finding that I was ignorant, considered me as a novice whom they had a right to cheat, and who was to learn at the usual expence the art of fraud. They exposed me to the theft of servants, and the exaction of officers, and saw me plundered upon false pretences, without any advantage to themselves, but that of rejoicing in the superiority of their own knowledge."

"Stop a moment, said the prince, is there such depravity in man, as that he   10
should injure another without benefit to himself? I can easily conceive that all are pleased with superiority; but your ignorance was merely accidental, which, being neither your crime nor your folly, could afford them no reason to applaud themselves; and the knowledge which they had, and which you wanted, they might as effectually have shewn by warning you, as betraying you."

"Pride, said Imlac, is seldom delicate; it will please itself with very mean advantages; and envy feels not its own happiness, but when it may be compared with the misery of others. They were my enemies because they thought me rich, and my oppressors because they delighted to find me weak."

"Proceed, said the prince: I doubt not of the facts which you relate, but   20
imagine that you impute them to mistaken motives."

"In this company, said Imlac, I arrived at Agra, the capital of Indostan, the city in which the great Mogul commonly resides. I applied myself to the language of the country, and in a few months was able to converse with the learned men; some of whom I found morose and reserved, and others easy and communicative; some were unwilling to teach another what they had with difficulty learned themselves; and some shewed that the end of their studies was to gain the dignity of instructing.

"To the tutor of the young princes I recommended myself so much, that I was presented to the emperour as a man of uncommon knowledge. The em-   30
perour asked me many questions concerning my country and my travels; and though I cannot now recollect any thing that he uttered above the power of a common man, he dismissed me astonished at his wisdom, and enamoured of his goodness.

"My credit was now so high, that the merchants, with whom I had travelled, applied to me for recommendations to the ladies of the court. I was surprised at their confidence of solicitation, and gently reproached them with their practices on the road. They heard me with cold indifference, and shewed no tokens of shame or sorrow.

"They then urged their request with the offer of a bribe; but what I would   40
not do for kindness I would not do for money; and refused them, not because they had injured me, but because I would not enable them to injure others; for I knew they would have made use of my credit to cheat those who should buy their wares.

"Having resided at Agra, till there was no more to be learned, I travelled into Persia, where I saw many remains of ancient magnificence, and observed many new accommodations of life. The Persians are a nation eminently social, and their assemblies afforded me daily opportunities of remarking characters and manners, and of tracing human nature through all its variations.

"From Persia I passed into Arabia, where I saw a nation at once pastoral and warlike; who live without any settled habitation; whose only wealth is their flocks and herds; and who have yet carried on, through all ages, an hereditary war with all mankind, though they neither covet nor envy their possessions.

Chap. X   Imlac's history continued.
A dissertation upon poetry

WHEREVER I went, I found that Poetry was considered as the highest learning, and regarded with a veneration somewhat approaching to that which man would pay to the Angelick Nature. And it yet fills me with wonder, that, in almost all countries, the most ancient poets are considered as the best: whether it be that every other kind of knowledge is an acquisition gradually attained, and poetry is a gift conferred at once; or that the first poetry of every nation surprised them as a novelty, and retained the credit by consent which it received by accident at first: or whether the province of poetry is to describe Nature and Passion, which are always the same, and the first writers took possession of the most striking objects for description, and the most probable occurrences for fiction, and left nothing to those that followed them, but transcription of the same events, and new combinations of the same images. Whatever be the reason, it is commonly observed that the early writers are in possession of nature, and their followers of art: that the first excel in strength and invention, and the latter in elegance and refinement.

"I was desirous to add my name to this illustrious fraternity. I read all the poets of Persia and Arabia, and was able to repeat by memory the volumes that are suspended in the mosque of Mecca. But I soon found that no man was ever great by imitation. My desire of excellence impelled me to transfer my attention to nature and to life. Nature was to be my subject, and men to be my auditors: I could never describe what I had not seen: I could not hope to move those with delight or terrour, whose interests and opinions I did not understand.

"Being now resolved to be a poet, I saw every thing with a new purpose; my sphere of attention was suddenly magnified: no kind of knowledge was to be overlooked. I ranged mountains and desarts for images and resemblances, and pictured upon my mind every tree of the forest and flower of the valley. I observed with equal care the crags of the rock and the pinnacles of the palace. Sometimes I wandered along the mazes of the rivulet, and sometimes watched the changes of the summer clouds. To a poet nothing can be useless. Whatever is beautiful, and whatever is dreadful, must be familiar to his imagination: he must be conversant with all that is awfully vast or elegantly little. The plants of the garden, the animals of the wood, the minerals of the earth, and meteors of the sky, must all concur to store his mind with inexhaustible variety: for every idea is useful for the inforcement or decoration of moral or religious truth; and he, who knows most, will have most power of diversifying his scenes, and of gratifying his reader with remote allusions and unexpected instruction.

"All the appearances of nature I was therefore careful to study, and every country which I have surveyed has contributed something to my poetical powers."

"In so wide a survey, said the prince, you must surely have left much unobserved. I have lived, till now, within the circuit of these mountains, and yet cannot walk abroad without the sight of something which I had never beheld   10
before, or never heeded."

"The business of a poet, said Imlac, is to examine, not the individual, but the species; to remark general properties and large appearances: he does not number the streaks of the tulip, or describe the different shades in the verdure of the forest. He is to exhibit in his portraits of nature such prominent and striking features, as recal the original to every mind; and must neglect the minuter discriminations, which one may have remarked, and another have neglected, for those characteristicks which are alike obvious to vigilance and carelesness.

"But the knowledge of nature is only half the task of a poet; he must be acquainted likewise with all the modes of life. His character requires that   20
he estimate the happiness and misery of every condition; observe the power of all the passions in all their combinations, and trace the changes of the human mind as they are modified by various institutions and accidental influences of climate or custom, from the spriteliness of infancy to the despondence of decrepitude. He must divest himself of the prejudices of his age or country; he must consider right and wrong in their abstracted and invariable state; he must disregard present laws and opinions, and rise to general and transcendental truths, which will always be the same: he must therefore content himself with the slow progress of his name; contemn the applause of his own time, and commit his claims to the justice of posterity. He must write as the interpreter of   30
nature, and the legislator of mankind, and consider himself as presiding over the thoughts and manners of successive generations; as a being superiour to time and place. His labour is not yet at an end: he must know many languages and many sciences; and, that his stile may be worthy of his thoughts, must, by incessant practice, familiarize to himself every delicacy of speech and grace of harmony."

Chap. XI   Imlac's narrative continued.
A hint on pilgrimage

IMLAC now felt the enthusiastic fit, and was proceeding to aggrandize his own profession, when the prince cried out, "Enough! Thou hast convinced me, that no human being can ever be a poet. Proceed now with thy narration."

"To be a poet, said Imlac, is indeed very difficult." "So difficult, returned the   40 prince, that I will at present hear no more of his labours. Tell me whither you went when you had seen Persia."

"From Persia, said the poet, I travelled through Syria, and for three years resided in Palestine, where I conversed with great numbers of the northern and western nations of Europe; the nations which are now in possession of all power and all knowledge; whose armies are irresistible, and whose fleets command the remotest parts of the globe. When I compared these men with the natives of our own kingdom, and those that surround us, they appeared almost another order of beings. In their countries it is difficult to wish for any thing that may not be obtained: a thousand arts, of which we never heard, are con-   10
tinually labouring for their convenience and pleasure; and whatever their own climate has denied them is supplied by their commerce."

"By what means, said the prince, are the Europeans thus powerful? or why, since they can so easily visit Asia and Africa for trade or conquest, cannot the Asiaticks and Africans invade their coasts, plant colonies in their ports, and give laws to their natural princes? The same wind that carries them back would bring us thither."

"They are more powerful, Sir, than we, answered Imlac, because they are wiser; knowledge will always predominate over ignorance, as man governs the other animals. But why their knowledge is more than ours, I know not what   20
reason can be given, but the unsearchable will of the Supreme Being."

"When, said the prince with a sigh, shall I be able to visit Palestine, and mingle with this mighty confluence of nations? Till that happy moment shall arrive, let me fill up the time with such representations as thou canst give me. I am not ignorant of the motive that assembles such numbers in that place, and cannot but consider it as the center of wisdom and piety, to which the best and wisest men of every land must be continually resorting."

"There are some nations, said Imlac, that send few visitants to Palestine; for many numerous and learned sects in Europe, concur to censure pilgrimage as superstitious, or deride it as ridiculous."   30

"You know, said the prince, how little my life has made me acquainted with diversity of opinions: it will be too long to hear the arguments on both sides; you, that have considered them, tell me the result."

"Pilgrimage, said Imlac, like many other acts of piety, may be reasonable or superstitious, according to the principles upon which it is performed. Long journies in search of truth are not commanded. Truth, such as is necessary to the regulation of life, is always found where it is honestly sought. Change of place is no natural cause of the increase of piety, for it inevitably produces dissipation of mind. Yet, since men go every day to view the places where great actions have been performed, and return with stronger impressions of the event,   40
curiosity of the same kind may naturally dispose us to view that country whence our religion had its beginning; and I believe no man surveys those awful scenes without some confirmation of holy resolutions. That the Supreme Being may be more easily propitiated in one place than in another, is the dream of idle superstition; but that some places may operate upon our own minds in an uncommon manner, is an opinion which hourly experience will justify. He who supposes that his vices may be more successfully combated in Palestine, will,

perhaps, find himself mistaken, yet he may go thither without folly: he who thinks they will be more freely pardoned, dishonours at once his reason and religion."

"These, said the prince, are European distinctions. I will consider them another time. What have you found to be the effect of knowledge? Are those nations happier than we?"

"There is so much infelicity, said the poet, in the world, that scarce any man has leisure from his own distresses to estimate the comparative happiness of others. Knowledge is certainly one of the means of pleasure, as is confessed by the natural desire which every mind feels of increasing its ideas. Ignorance is mere privation, by which nothing can be produced: it is a vacuity in which the soul sits motionless and torpid for want of attraction; and, without knowing why, we always rejoice when we learn, and grieve when we forget. I am therefore inclined to conclude, that, if nothing counteracts the natural consequence of learning, we grow more happy as our minds take a wider range.

"In enumerating the particular comforts of life we shall find many advantages on the side of the Europeans. They cure wounds and diseases with which we languish and perish. We suffer inclemencies of weather which they can obviate. They have engines for the despatch of many laborious works which we must perform by manual industry. There is such communication between distant places, that one friend can hardly be said to be absent from another. Their policy removes all publick inconveniencies: they have roads cut through their mountains, and bridges laid upon their rivers. And, if we descend to the privacies of life, their habitations are more commodious, and their possessions are more secure."

"They are surely happy, said the prince, who have all these conveniencies, of which I envy none so much as the facility with which separated friends interchange their thoughts."

"The Europeans, answered Imlac, are less unhappy than we, but they are not happy. Human life is every where a state in which much is to be endured, and little to be enjoyed."

Chap. XII   The story of Imlac continued

"I AM not yet willing, said the prince, to suppose that happiness is so parsimoniously distributed to mortals; nor can believe but that, if I had the choice of life, I should be able to fill every day with pleasure. I would injure no man, and should provoke no resentment: I would relieve every distress, and should enjoy the benedictions of gratitude. I would choose my friends among the wise, and my wife among the virtuous; and therefore should be in no danger from treachery, or unkindness. My children should, by my care, be learned and pious, and would repay to my age what their childhood had received. What would dare to molest him who might call on every side to thousands enriched by his bounty, or assisted by his power? And why should not life glide quietly away in the soft reciprocation of protection and reverence? All this may be done without the help of European refinements, which appear by their effects to be rather specious than useful. Let us leave them and persue our journey."

"From Palestine, said Imlac, I passed through many regions of Asia; in the more civilized kingdoms as a trader, and among the Barbarians of the mountains as a pilgrim. At last I began to long for my native country, that I might repose after my travels, and fatigues, in the places where I had spent my earliest years, and gladden my old companions with the recital of my adventures. Often did I figure to myself those, with whom I had sported away the gay hours of dawning life, sitting round me in its evening, wondering at my tales, and listening to my counsels.   10

"When this thought had taken possession of my mind, I considered every moment as wasted which did not bring me nearer to Abissinia. I hastened into Egypt, and, notwithstanding my impatience, was detained ten months in the contemplation of its ancient magnificence, and in enquiries after the remains of its ancient learning. I found in Cairo a mixture of all nations; some brought thither by the love of knowledge, some by the hope of gain, and many by the desire of living after their own manner without observation, and of lying hid in the obscurity of multitudes: for, in a city, populous as Cairo, it is possible to obtain at the same time the gratifications of society, and the secrecy of solitude.   20

"From Cairo I travelled to Suez, and embarked on the red sea, passing along the coast till I arrived at the port from which I had departed twenty years before. Here I joined myself to a caravan and re-entered my native country.

"I now expected the caresses of my kinsmen, and the congratulations of my friends, and was not without hope that my father, whatever value he had set upon riches, would own with gladness and pride a son who was able to add to the felicity and honour of the nation. But I was soon convinced that my thoughts were vain. My father had been dead fourteen years, having divided his wealth among my brothers, who were removed to some other provinces. Of my companions the greater part was in the grave, of the rest some could   30
with difficulty remember me, and some considered me as one corrupted by foreign manners.

"A man used to vicissitudes is not easily dejected. I forgot, after a time, my disappointment, and endeavoured to recommend myself to the nobles of the kingdom; they admitted me to their tables, heard my story, and dismissed me. I opened a school, and was prohibited to teach. I then resolved to sit down in the quiet of domestick life, and addressed a lady that was fond of my conversation, but rejected my suit, because my father was a merchant.

"Wearied at last with solicitation and repulses, I resolved to hide myself for ever from the world, and depend no longer on the opinion or caprice of others.   40
I waited for the time when the gate of the *happy valley* should open, that I might bid farewell to hope and fear: the day came; my performance was distinguished with favour, and I resigned myself with joy to perpetual confinement."

"Hast thou here found happiness at last? said Rasselas. Tell me without reserve; art thou content with thy condition? or, dost thou wish to be again wandering and inquiring? All the inhabitants of this valley celebrate their lot, and, at the annual visit of the emperour, invite others to partake of their felicity."

"Great prince, said Imlac, I shall speak the truth: I know not one of all your attendants who does not lament the hour when he entered this retreat. I am less unhappy than the rest, because I have a mind replete with images, which I can vary and combine at pleasure. I can amuse my solitude by the renovation of the knowledge which begins to fade from my memory, and with the recollection of the accidents of my past life. Yet all this ends in the sorrowful consideration, that my acquirements are now useless, and that none of my pleasures can be again enjoyed. The rest, whose minds have no impression but of the present moment, are either corroded by malignant passions, or sit stupid in the gloom of perpetual vacancy." 10

"What passions can infest those, said the prince, who have no rivals? We are in a place where impotence precludes malice, and where all envy is repressed by community of enjoyments."

"There may be community, said Imlac, of material possessions, but there can never be community of love or of esteem. It must happen that one will please more than another; he that knows himself despised will always be envious; and still more envious and malevolent, if he is condemned to live in the presence of those who despise him. The invitations, by which they allure others to a state which they feel to be wretched, proceed from the natural malignity of hopeless misery. They are weary of themselves, and of each other, and 20 expect to find relief in new companions. They envy the liberty which their folly has forfeited, and would gladly see all mankind imprisoned like themselves.

"From this crime, however, I am wholly free. No man can say that he is wretched by my persuasion. I look with pity on the crowds who are annually soliciting admission to captivity, and wish that it were lawful for me to warn them of their danger."

"My dear Imlac, said the prince, I will open to thee my whole heart, that I have long meditated an escape from the happy valley. I have examined the mountains on every side, but find myself insuperably barred: teach me the way 30 to break my prison; thou shalt be the companion of my flight, the guide of my rambles, the partner of my fortune, and my sole director in the *choice of life*."

"Sir, answered the poet, your escape will be difficult, and, perhaps, you may soon repent your curiosity. The world, which you figure to yourself smooth and quiet as the lake in the valley, you will find a sea foaming with tempests, and boiling with whirlpools: you will be sometimes overwhelmed by the waves of violence, and sometimes dashed against the rocks of treachery. Amidst wrongs and frauds, competitions and anxieties, you will wish a thousand times for these feats of quiet, and willingly quit hope to be free from fear."

"Do not seek to deter me from my purpose, said the prince: I am impatient 40 to see what thou hast seen; and, since thou art thyself weary of the valley, it is evident, that thy former state was better than this. Whatever be the consequence of my experiment, I am resolved to judge with my own eyes of the various conditions of men, and then to make deliberately my *choice of life*."

"I am afraid, said Imlac, you are hindered by stronger restraints than my persuasions; yet, if your determination is fixed, I do not counsel you to despair. Few things are impossible to diligence and skill."

Chap. XIII   Rasselas discovers the means of escape

THE prince now dismissed his favourite to rest, but the narrative of wonders and novelties filled his mind with perturbation. He revolved all that he had heard, and prepared innumerable questions for the morning.

Much of his uneasiness was now removed. He had a friend to whom he could impart his thoughts, and whose experience could assist him in his designs. His heart was no longer condemned to swell with silent vexation. He thought that even the *happy valley* might be endured with such a companion, and that, if they could range the world together, he should have nothing further to desire.

In a few days the water was discharged, and the ground dried. The prince and Imlac then walked out together to converse without the notice of the rest. The   10 prince, whose thoughts were always on the wing, as he passed by the gate, said, with a countenance of sorrow, "Why art thou so strong, and why is man so weak?"

"Man is not weak, answered his companion; knowledge is more than equivalent to force. The master of mechanicks laughs at strength. I can burst the gate, but cannot do it secretly. Some other expedient must be tried."

As they were walking on the side of the mountain, they observed that the conies,[3] which the rain had driven from their burrows, had taken shelter among the bushes, and formed holes behind them, tending upwards in an oblique line. "It has been the opinion of antiquity, said Imlac, that human reason   20 borrowed many arts from the instinct of animals; let us, therefore, not think ourselves degraded by learning from the coney. We may escape by piercing the mountain in the same direction. We will begin where the summit hangs over the middle part, and labour upward till we shall issue out beyond the prominence."

The eyes of the prince, when he heard this proposal, sparkled with joy. The execution was easy, and the success certain.

No time was now lost. They hastened early in the morning to chuse a place proper for their mine. They clambered with great fatigue among crags and brambles, and returned without having discovered any part that favoured   30 their design. The second and the third day were spent in the same manner, and with the same frustration. But, on the fourth, they found a small cavern, concealed by a thicket, where they resolved to make their experiment.

Imlac procured instruments proper to hew stone and remove earth, and they fell to their work on the next day with more eagerness than vigour. They were presently exhausted by their efforts, and sat down to pant upon the grass. The prince, for a moment, appeared to be discouraged. "Sir, said his companion, practice will enable us to continue our labour for a longer time; mark, however, how far we have advanced, and you will find that our toil will some time have an end. Great works are performed, not by strength, but perseverance: yonder   40 palace was raised by single stones, yet you see its height and spaciousness. He that shall walk with vigour three hours a day will pass in seven years a space equal to the circumference of the globe."

They returned to their labour day after day, and, in a short time, found a

[3] *Conies:* Rabbits.

fissure in the rock, which enabled them to pass far with very little obstruction. This Rasselas considered as a good omen. "Do not disturb your mind, said Imlac, with other hopes or fears than reason may suggest: if you are pleased with prognosticks of good, you will be terrified likewise with tokens of evil, and your whole life will be a prey to superstition. Whatever facilitates our work is more than an omen, it is a cause of success. This is one of those pleasing surprises which often happen to active resolution. Many things difficult to design prove easy to performance."

Chap. XIV   Rasselas and Imlac receive an unexpected visit

THEY had now wrought their way to the middle, and solaced their labour with the approach of liberty, when the prince, coming down to refresh himself   10 with air, found his sister Nekayah standing before the mouth of the cavity. He started and stood confused, afraid to tell his design, and yet hopeless to conceal it. A few moments determined him to repose on her fidelity, and secure her secrecy by a declaration without reserve.

"Do not imagine, said the princess, that I came hither as a spy: I had often observed from my window, that you and Imlac directed your walk every day towards the same point, but I did not suppose you had any better reason for the preference than a cooler shade, or more fragrant bank; nor followed you with any other design than to partake of your conversation. Since then not suspicion but fondness has detected you, let me not lose the advantage of my discovery.   20 I am equally weary of confinement with yourself, and not lets desirous of knowing what is done or suffered in the world. Permit me to fly with you from this tasteless tranquility, which will yet grow more loathsome when you have left me. You may deny me to accompany you, but cannot hinder me from following."

The prince, who loved Nekayah above his other sisters, had no inclination to refuse her request, and grieved that he had lost an opportunity of showing his confidence by a voluntary communication. It was therefore agreed that she should leave the valley with them; and that, in the mean time, she should watch, lest any other straggler should, by chance or curiosity, follow them to the mountain.   30

At length their labour was at an end; they saw light beyond the prominence, and, issuing to the top of the mountain, beheld the Nile, yet a narrow current, wandering beneath them.

The prince looked round with rapture, anticipated all the pleasures of travel, and in thought was already transported beyond his father's dominions. Imlac, though very joyful at his escape, had less expectation of pleasure in the world, which he had before tried, and of which he had been weary.

Rasselas was so much delighted with a wider horizon, that he could not soon be persuaded to return into the valley. He informed his sister that the way was open, and that nothing now remained but to prepare for their departure.   40

Chap. XV   The prince and princess leave the valley, and see many wonders

THE prince and princess had jewels sufficient to make them rich whenever they came into a place of commerce, which, by Imlac's direction, they hid in their cloaths, and, on the night of the next full moon, all left the valley. The princess was followed only by a single favourite, who did not know whither she was going.

They clambered through the cavity, and began to go down on the other side. The princess and her maid turned their eyes towards every part, and, seeing nothing to bound their prospect, considered themselves as in danger of being lost in a dreary vacuity. They stopped and trembled. "I am almost afraid, said the princess, to begin a journey of which I cannot perceive an end, and to venture   10
into this immense plain where I may be approached on every side by men whom I never saw." The prince felt nearly the same emotions, though he thought it more manly to conceal them.

Imlac smiled at their terrours, and encouraged them to proceed; but the princess continued irresolute till she had been imperceptibly drawn forward too far to return.

In the morning they found some shepherds in the field, who set milk and fruits before them. The princess wondered that she did not see a palace ready for her reception, and a table spread with delicacies; but, being faint and hungry, she drank the milk and eat the fruits, and thought them of a higher flavour than   20
the products of the valley.

They travelled forward by easy journeys, being all unaccustomed to toil or difficulty, and knowing, that though they might be missed, they could not be persued. In a few days they came into a more populous region, where Imlac was diverted with the admiration which his companions expressed at the diversity of manners, stations and employments.

Their dress was such as might not bring upon them the suspicion of having any thing to conceal, yet the prince, wherever he came, expected to be obeyed, and the princess was frighted, because those that came into her presence did not prostrate themselves before her. Imlac was forced to observe them with great   30
vigilance, lest they should betray their rank by their unusual behaviour, and detained them several weeks in the first village to accustom them to the sight of common mortals.

By degrees the royal wanderers were taught to understand that they had for a time laid aside their dignity, and were to expect only such regard as liberality and courtesy could procure. And Imlac, having, by many admonitions, prepared them to endure the tumults of a port, and the ruggedness of the commercial race, brought them down to the sea-coast.

The prince and his sister, to whom every thing was new, were gratified equally at all places, and therefore remained for some months at the port   40
without any inclination to pass further. Imlac was content with their stay, because he did not think it safe to expose them, unpractised in the world, to the hazards of a foreign country.

At last he began to fear lest they should be discovered, and proposed to fix a day for their departure. They had no pretensions to judge for themselves, and referred the whole scheme to his direction. He therefore took passage in a ship to Suez; and, when the time came, with great difficulty prevailed on the princess to enter the vessel. They had a quick and prosperous voyage, and from Suez travelled by land to Cairo.

Chap. XVI   They enter Cairo, and find every man happy

AS they approached the city, which filled the strangers with astonishment, "This, said Imlac to the prince, is the place where travellers and merchants assemble from all the corners of the earth. You will here find men of every character, and every occupation. Commerce is here honourable: I will act   10
as a merchant, and you shall live as strangers, who have no other end of travel than curiosity; it will soon be observed that we are rich; our reputation will procure us access to all whom we shall desire to know; you will see all the conditions of humanity, and enable yourself at leisure to make your *choice of life.*"

They now entered the town, stunned by the noise, and offended by the crowds. Instruction had not yet so prevailed over habit, but that they wondered to see themselves pass undistinguished along the street, and met by the lowest of the people without reverence or notice. The princess could not at first bear the thought of being levelled with the vulgar, and, for some days, continued in her chamber, where she was served by her favourite as in the palace of the   20
valley.

Imlac, who understood traffick, sold part of the jewels the next day, and hired a house, which he adorned with such magnificence, that he was immediately considered as a merchant of great wealth. His politeness attracted many acquaintance, and his generosity made him courted by many dependants. His table was crowded by men of every nation, who all admired his knowledge, and solicited his favour. His companions, not being able to mix in the conversation, could make no discovery of their ignorance or surprise, and were gradually initiated in the world as they gained knowledge of the language.

The prince had, by frequent lectures, been taught the use and nature of   30
money; but the ladies could not, for a long time, comprehend what the merchants did with small pieces of gold and silver, or why things of so little use should be received as equivalent to the necessaries of life.

They studied the language two years, while Imlac was preparing to set before them the various ranks and conditions of mankind. He grew acquainted with all who had any thing uncommon in their fortune or conduct. He frequented the voluptuous and the frugal, the idle and the busy, the merchants and the men of learning.

The prince, being now able to converse with fluency, and having learned the caution necessary to be observed in his intercourse with strangers, began to   40 accompany Imlac to places of resort, and to enter into all assemblies, that he might make his *choice of life.*

For some time he thought choice needless, because all appeared to him equally happy. Wherever he went he met gayety and kindness, and heard the song of joy, or the laugh of carelesness. He began to believe that the world overflowed with universal plenty, and that nothing was withheld either from want or merit; that every hand showered liberality, and every heart melted with benevolence: "and who then, says he, will be suffered to be wretched?"

Imlac permitted the pleasing delusion, and was unwilling to crush the hope of inexperience, till one day, having sat a while silent, "I know not, said the prince, what can be the reason that I am more unhappy than any of our friends. I see them perpetually and unalterably chearful, but feel my own mind restless and uneasy. I am unsatisfied with those pleasures which I seem most to court; I live in the crowds of jollity, not so much to enjoy company as to shun myself, and am only loud and merry to conceal my sadness."

"Every man, said Imlac, may, by examining his own mind, guess what passes in the minds of others: when you feel that your own gaiety is counterfeit, it may justly lead you to suspect that of your companions not to be sincere. Envy is commonly reciprocal. We are long before we are convinced that happiness is never to be found, and each believes it possessed by others, to keep alive the hope of obtaining it for himself. In the assembly, where you passed the last night, there appeared such spriteliness of air, and volatility of fancy, as might have suited beings of an higher order, formed to inhabit serener regions inaccessible to care or sorrow: yet, believe me, prince, there was not one who did not dread the moment when solitude should deliver him to the tyranny of reflection."

"This, said the prince, may be true of others, since it is true of me; yet, whatever be the general infelicity of man, one condition is more happy than another, and wisdom surely directs us to take the least evil in the *choice of life.*"

"The causes of good and evil, answered Imlac, are so various and uncertain, so often entangled with each other, so diversified by various relations, and so much subject to accidents which cannot be foreseen, that he who would fix his condition upon incontestable reasons of preference, must live and die enquiring and deliberating."

"But surely, said Rasselas, the wise men, to whom we listen with reverence and wonder, chose that mode of life for themselves which they thought most likely to make them happy."

"Very few, said the poet, live by choice. Every man is placed in his present condition by causes which acted without his foresight, and with which he did not always willingly co-operate; and therefore you will rarely meet one who does not think the lot of his neighbour better than his own."

"I am pleased to think, said the prince, that my birth has given me at least one advantage over others, by enabling me to determine for myself. I have here the world before me; I will review it at leisure: surely happiness is somewhere to be found."

Chap. XVII   The prince associates with young men of spirit and gaiety

RASSELAS rose next day, and resolved to begin his experiments upon life. "Youth, cried he, is the time of gladness: I will join myself to the young men, whose only business is to gratify their desires, and whose time is all spent in a succession of enjoyments."

To such societies he was readily admitted, but a few days brought him back weary and disgusted. Their mirth was without images, their laughter without motive; their pleasures were gross and sensual, in which the mind had no part; their conduct was at once wild and mean; they laughed at order and at law, but the frown of power dejected, and the eye of wisdom abashed them.

The prince soon concluded, that he should never be happy in a course of life   10 of which he was ashamed. He thought it unsuitable to a reasonable being to act without a plan, and to be sad or chearful only by chance. "Happiness, said he, must be something solid and permanent, without fear and without uncertainty."

But his young companions had gained so much of his regard by their frankness and courtesy, that he could not leave them without warning and remonstrance. "My friends, said he, I have seriously considered our manners and our prospects, and find that we have mistaken our own interest. The first years of man must make provision for the last. He that never thinks never can be wise. Perpetual levity must end in ignorance; and intemperance, though it may fire the spirits for an hour, will make life short or miserable. Let us consider that   20 youth is of no long duration, and that in maturer age, when the enchantments of fancy shall cease, and phantoms of delight dance no more about us, we shall have no comforts but the esteem of wise men, and the means of doing good. Let us, therefore, stop, while to stop is in our power: let us live as men who are sometime to grow old, and to whom it will be the most dreadful of all evils not to count their past years but by follies, and to be reminded of their former luxuriance of health only by the maladies which riot has produced."

They stared a while in silence one upon another, and, at last, drove him away by a general chorus of continued laughter.

The consciousness that his sentiments were just, and his intentions kind, was   30 scarcely sufficient to support him against the horrour of derision. But he recovered his tranquility, and persued his search.

Chap. XVIII   The prince finds a wise and happy man

AS he was one day walking in the street, he saw a spacious building which all were, by the open doors, invited to enter: he followed the stream of people, and found it a hall or school of declamation, in which professors read lectures to their auditory. He fixed his eye upon a sage raised above the rest, who discoursed with great energy on the government of the passions. His look was venerable, his action graceful, his pronunciation clear, and his diction elegant. He shewed, with great strength of sentiment, and variety of illustration, that human nature is degraded and debased, when the lower faculties predominate over the higher; that when fancy, the parent of passion, usurps the dominion of the mind, nothing ensues but the natural effect of unlawful government, perturbation and confusion; that she betrays the fortresses of the intellect to rebels, and excites her children to sedition against reason their lawful sovereign. He compared reason to the sun, of which the light is constant, uniform, and lasting; and fancy to a meteor, of bright but transitory lustre, irregular in its motion, and delusive in its direction.

He then communicated the various precepts given from time to time for the conquest of passion, and displayed the happiness of those who had obtained the 10 important victory, after which man is no longer the slave of fear, nor the fool of hope; is no more emaciated by envy, inflamed by anger, emasculated by tenderness, or depressed by grief; but walks on calmly through the tumults or the privacies of life, as the sun persues alike his course through the calm or the stormy sky.

He enumerated many examples of heroes immovable by pain or pleasure, who looked with indifference on those modes or accidents to which the vulgar give the names of good and evil. He exhorted his hearers to lay aside their prejudices, and arm themselves against the shafts of malice or misfortune, by invulnerable patience; concluding, that this state only was happiness, and that this 20 happiness was in every one's power.

Rasselas listened to him with the veneration due to the instructions of a superiour being, and, waiting for him at the door, humbly implored the liberty of visiting so great a master of true wisdom. The lecturer hesitated a moment, when Rasselas put a purse of gold into his hand, which he received with a mixture of joy and wonder.

"I have found, said the prince, at his return to Imlac, a man who can teach all that is necessary to be known, who, from the unshaken throne of rational fortitude, looks down on the scenes of life changing beneath him. He speaks, and attention watches his lips. He reasons, and conviction closes his periods. 30 This man shall be my future guide: I will learn his doctrines, and imitate his life."

"Be not too hasty, said Imlac, to trust, or to admire, the teachers of morality: they discourse like angels, but they live like men."

Rasselas, who could not conceive how any man could reason so forcibly without feeling the cogency of his own arguments, paid his visit in a few days, and was denied admission. He had now learned the power of money, and made his way by a piece of gold to the inner apartment, where he found the philosopher in a room half darkened, with his eyes misty, and his face pale. "Sir, said he, you are come at a time when all human friendship is useless; what I suffer cannot be 40 remedied, what I have lost cannot be supplied. My daughter, my only daughter, from whose tenderness I expected all the comforts of my age, died last night of a fever. My views, my purposes, my hopes are at an end: I am now a lonely being disunited from society."

"Sir, said the prince, mortality is an event by which a wise man can never be surprised: we know that death is always near, and it should therefore always be expected." "Young man, answered the philosopher, you speak like one that has never felt the pangs of separation." "Have you then forgot the precepts, said Rasselas, which you so powerfully enforced? Has wisdom no strength to arm the heart against calamity? Consider, that external things are naturally variable, but truth and reason are always the same." "What comfort, said the mourner, can truth and reason afford me? of what effect are they now, but to tell me, that my daughter will not be restored?"

The prince, whose humanity would not suffer him to insult misery with reproof, went away convinced of the emptiness of rhetorical sound, and the inefficacy of polished periods and studied sentences.

Chap. XIX   A Glimpse of pastoral life

HE was still eager upon the same enquiry; and, having heard of a hermit,   10 that lived near the lowest cataract of the Nile, and filled the whole country with the fame of his sanctity, resolved to visit his retreat, and enquire whether that felicity, which publick life could not afford, was to be found in solitude; and whether a man, whose age and virtue made him venerable, could teach any peculiar art of shunning evils, or enduring them.

Imlac and the princess agreed to accompany him, and, after the necessary preparations, they began their journey. Their way lay through fields, where shepherds tended their flocks, and the lambs were playing upon the pasture. "This, said the poet, is the life which has been often celebrated for its innocence and quiet: let us pass the heat of the day among the shepherds tents, and know   20 whether all our searches are not to terminate in pastoral simplicity."

The proposal pleased them, and they induced the shepherds, by small presents and familiar questions, to tell their opinion of their own state: they were so rude and ignorant, so little able to compare the good with the evil of the occupation, and so indistinct in their narratives and descriptions, that very little could be learned from them. But it was evident that their hearts were cankered with discontent; that they considered themselves as condemned to labour for the luxury of the rich, and looked up with stupid malevolence towards those that were placed above them.

The princess pronounced with vehemence, that she would never suffer these   30 envious savages to be her companions, and that she should not soon be desirous of seeing any more specimens of rustick happiness; but could not believe that all the accounts of primeval pleasures were fabulous, and was yet in doubt whether life had any thing that could be justly preferred to the placid gratifications of fields and woods. She hoped that the time would come, when, with a few virtuous and elegant companions, she should gather flowers planted by her own hand, fondle the lambs of her own ewe, and listen, without care, among brooks and breezes, to one of her maidens reading in the shade.

Chap. XX   The danger of prosperity

ON the next day they continued their journey, till the heat compelled them to look round for shelter. At a small distance they saw a thick wood, which   40 they no sooner entered than they perceived that they were approaching the habitations of men. The shrubs were diligently cut away to open walks where the shades were darkest; the boughs of opposite trees were artificially interwoven; seats of flowery turf were raised in vacant spaces, and a rivulet, that wantoned along the side of a winding path, had its banks sometimes opened into small basons, and its stream sometimes obstructed by little mounds of stone heaped together to increase its murmurs.

They passed slowly through the wood, delighted with such unexpected accommodations, and entertained each other with conjecturing what, or who, he could be, that, in those rude and unfrequented regions, had leisure and art for   10
such harmless luxury.

As they advanced, they heard the sound of musick, and saw youths and virgins dancing in the grove; and, going still further, beheld a stately palace built upon a hill surrounded with woods. The laws of eastern hospitality allowed them to enter, and the master welcomed them like a man liberal and wealthy.

He was skilful enough in appearances soon to discern that they were no common guests, and spread his table with magnificence. The eloquence of Imlac caught his attention, and the lofty courtesy of the princess excited his respect. When they offered to depart he entreated their stay, and was the next   20
day still more unwilling to dismiss them than before. They were easily persuaded to stop, and civility grew up in time to freedom and confidence.

The prince now saw all the domesticks chearful, and all the face of nature smiling round the place, and could not forbear to hope that he should find here what he was seeking; but when he was congratulating the master upon his possessions, he answered with a sigh, "My condition has indeed the appearance of happiness, but appearances are delusive. My prosperity puts my life in danger; the Bassa of Egypt is my enemy, incensed only by my wealth and popularity. I have been hitherto protected against him by the princes of the country; but, as the favour of the great is uncertain, I know not how soon my defenders may   30
be persuaded to share the plunder with the Bassa. I have sent my treasures into a distant country, and, upon the first alarm, am prepared to follow them. Then will my enemies riot in my mansion, and enjoy the gardens which I have planted."

They all joined in lamenting his danger, and deprecating his exile; and the princess was so much disturbed with the tumult of grief and indignation, that she retired to her apartment. They continued with their kind inviter a few days longer, and then went forward to find the hermit.

Chap. XXI   The happiness of solitude. The hermit's history

THEY came on the third day, by the direction of the peasants, to the hermit's cell: it was a cavern in the side of a mountain, over-shadowed with palm-   40
trees; at such a distance from the cataract, that nothing more was heard than a

gentle uniform murmur, such as composed the mind to pensive meditation, especially when it was assisted by the wind whistling among the branches. The first rude essay of nature had been so much improved by human labour, that the cave contained several apartments, appropriated to different uses, and often afforded lodging to travellers, whom darkness or tempests happened to overtake.

The hermit sat on a bench at the door, to enjoy the coolness of the evening. On one side lay a book with pens and papers, on the other mechanical instruments of various kinds. As they approached him unregarded, the princess observed that he had not the countenance of a man that had found, or could teach, the way to happiness.

They saluted him with great respect, which he repaid like a man not unaccustomed to the forms of courts. "My children, said he, if you have lost your way, you shall be willingly supplied with such conveniencies for the night as this cavern will afford. I have all that nature requires, and you will not expect delicacies in a hermit's cell."

They thanked him, and, entering, were pleased with the neatness and regularity of the place. The hermit set flesh and wine before them, though he fed only upon fruits and water. His discourse was chearful without levity, and pious without enthusiasm. He soon gained the esteem of his guests, and the princess repented of her hasty censure.

At last Imlac began thus: "I do not now wonder that your reputation is so far extended; we have heard at Cairo of your wisdom, and came hither to implore your direction for this young man and maiden in the *choice of life.*"

"To him that lives well, answered the hermit, every form of life is good; nor can I give any other rule for choice, than to remove from all apparent evil."

"He will remove most certainly from evil, said the prince, who shall devote himself to that solitude which you have recommended by your example."

"I have indeed lived fifteen years in solitude, said the hermit, but have no desire that my example should gain any imitators. In my youth I professed arms, and was raised by degrees to the highest military rank. I have traversed wide countries at the head of my troops, and seen many battles and sieges. At last, being disgusted by the preferment of a younger officer, and finding my vigour beginning to decay, I resolved to close my life in peace, having found the world full of snares, discord, and misery. I had once escaped from the persuit of the enemy by the shelter of this cavern, and therefore chose it for my final residence. I employed artificers to form it into chambers, and stored it with all that I was likely to want.

"For some time after my retreat, I rejoiced like a tempest-beaten sailor at his entrance into the harbour, being delighted with the sudden change of the noise and hurry of war, to stillness and repose. When the pleasure of novelty went away, I employed my hours in examining the plants which grow in the valley, and the minerals which I collected from the rocks. But that enquiry is now grown tasteless and irksome. I have been for some time unsettled and distracted: my mind is disturbed with a thousand perplexities of doubt, and vanities of imagination, which hourly prevail upon me, because I have no opportunities of relaxation or diversion. I am sometimes ashamed to think that I could not secure myself from vice, but by retiring from the practice of virtue, and begin to suspect that I was rather impelled by resentment, than led by devotion, into solitude. My fancy riots in scenes of folly, and I lament that I have lost so much, and have gained so little. In solitude, if I escape the example of bad men, I want likewise the counsel and conversation of the good. I have been long comparing the evils with the advantages of society, and resolve to return into the world to morrow. The life of a solitary man will be certainly miserable, but not certainly devout."

They heard his resolution with surprise, but, after a short pause, offered to conduct him to Cairo. He dug up a considerable treasure which he had hid   10
among the rocks, and accompanied them to the city, on which, as he approached it, he gazed with rapture.

Chap. XXII   The happiness of a life led according to nature

RASSELAS went often to an assembly of learned men, who met at stated times to unbend their minds, and compare their opinions. Their manners were somewhat coarse, but their conversation was instructive, and their disputations acute, though sometimes too violent, and often continued till neither controvertist remembered upon what question they began. Some faults were almost general among them: every one was desirous to dictate to the rest, and every one was pleased to hear the genius or knowledge of another depreciated.

In this assembly Rasselas was relating his interview with the hermit, and   20
the wonder with which he heard him censure a course of life which he had so deliberately chosen, and so laudably followed. The sentiments of the hearers were various. Some were of opinion, that the folly of his choice had been justly punished by condemnation to perpetual perseverance. One of the youngest among them, with great vehemence, pronounced him an hypocrite. Some talked of the right of society to the labour of individuals, and considered retirement as a desertion of duty. Others readily allowed, that there was a time when the claims of the publick were satisfied, and when a man might properly sequester himself, to review his life, and purify his heart.

One, who appeared more affected with the narrative than the rest, thought   30
it likely, that the hermit would, in a few years, go back to his retreat, and, perhaps, if shame did not restrain, or death intercept him, return once more from his retreat into the world: "For the hope of happiness, says he, is so strongly impressed, that the longest experience is not able to efface it. Of the present state, whatever it be, we feel, and are forced to confess, the misery, yet, when the same state is again at a distance, imagination paints it as desirable. But the time will surely come, when desire will be no longer our torment, and no man shall be wretched but by his own fault."

"This, said a philosopher, who had heard him with tokens of great impatience, is the present condition of a wise man. The time is already come,   40
when none are wretched but by their own fault. Nothing is more idle, than to enquire after happiness, which nature has kindly placed within our reach. The

way to be happy is to live according to nature, in obedience to that universal and unalterable law with which every heart is originally impressed; which is not written on it by precept, but engraven by destiny, not instilled by education, but infused at our nativity. He that lives according to nature will suffer nothing from the delusions of hope, or importunities of desire: he will receive and reject with equability of temper; and act or suffer as the reason of things shall alternately prescribe. Other men may amuse themselves with subtle definitions, or intricate raciocination. Let them learn to be wise by easier means: let them observe the hind of the forest, and the linnet of the grove: let them consider the life of animals, whose motions are regulated by instinct; they obey their guide   10 and are happy. Let us therefore, at length, cease to dispute, and learn to live; throw away the incumbrance of precepts, which they who utter them with so much pride and pomp do not understand, and carry with us this simple and intelligible maxim, That deviation from nature is deviation from happiness."

When he had spoken, he looked round him with a placid air, and enjoyed the consciousness of his own beneficence. "Sir, said the prince, with great modesty, as I, like all the rest of mankind, am desirous of felicity, my closest attention has been fixed upon your discourse: I doubt not the truth of a position which a man so learned has so confidently advanced. Let me only know what it is to live according to nature."   20

"When I find young men so humble and so docile, said the philosopher, I can deny them no information which my studies have enabled me to afford. To live according to nature, is to act always with due regard to the fitness arising from the relations and qualities of causes and effects; to concur with the great and unchangeable scheme of universal felicity; to co-operate with the general disposition and tendency of the present system of things."

The prince soon found that this was one of the sages whom he should understand less as he heard him longer. He therefore bowed and was silent, and the philosopher, supposing him satisfied, and the rest vanquished, rose up and departed with the air of a man that had co-operated with the present system.   30

Chap. XXIII   The prince and his sister divide between them the work of observation

RASSELAS returned home full of reflexions, doubtful how to direct his future steps. Of the way to happiness he found the learned and simple equally ignorant; but, as he was yet young, he flattered himself that he had time remaining for more experiments, and further enquiries. He communicated to Imlac his observations and his doubts, but was answered by him with new doubts, and remarks that gave him no comfort. He therefore discoursed more frequently and freely with his sister, who had yet the same hope with himself, and always assisted him to give some reason why, though he had been hitherto frustrated, he might succeed at last.

"We have hitherto, said she, known but little of the world: we have never   40 yet been either great or mean. In our own country, though we had royalty, we had no power, and in this we have not yet seen the private recesses of domestick peace. Imlac favours not our search, lest we should in time find him mistaken. We will divide the task between us: you shall try what is to be found in the splendour of courts, and I will range the shades of humbler life. Perhaps command and authority may be the supreme blessings, as they afford most opportunities of doing good: or, perhaps, what this world can give may be found in the modest habitations of middle fortune; too low for great designs, and too high for penury and distress."

Chap. XXIV   The prince examines the happiness of high stations

RASSELAS applauded the design, and appeared next day with a splendid retinue at the court of the Bassa. He was soon distinguished for his magnificence, and admitted, as a prince whose curiosity had brought him from distant countries, to an intimacy with the great officers, and frequent conversation with the Bassa himself.

He was at first inclined to believe, that the man must be pleased with his own condition, whom all approached with reverence, and heard with obedience, and who had the power to extend his edicts to a whole kingdom. "There can be no pleasure, said he, equal to that of feeling at once the joy of thousands all made happy by wise administration. Yet, since, by the law of subordination, this sublime delight can be in one nation but the lot of one, it is surely reasonable to think there is some satisfaction more popular and accessible, and that millions can hardly be subjected to the will of a single man, only to fill his particular breast with incommunicable content."

These thoughts were often in his mind, and he found no solution of the difficulty. But as presents and civilities gained him more familiarity, he found that almost every man that stood high in employment hated all the rest, and was hated by them, and that their lives were a continual succession of plots and detections, stratagems and escapes, faction and treachery. Many of those, who surrounded the Bassa, were sent only to watch and report his conduct; every tongue was muttering censure, and every eye was searching for a fault.

At last the letters of revocation arrived, the Bassa was carried in chains to Constantinople, and his name was mentioned no more.

"What are we now to think of the prerogatives of power, said Rasselas to his sister; is it without any efficacy to good? or, is the subordinate degree only dangerous, and the supreme safe and glorious? Is the Sultan the only happy man in his dominions? or, is the Sultan himself subject to the torments of suspicion, and the dread of enemies?"

In a short time the second Bassa was deposed. The Sultan, that had advanced him, was murdered by the Janisaries,[4] and his successor had other views and different favourites.

---

[4] *Janisaries:* Turkish soldiers.

Chap. XXV   The princess persues her enquiry with more diligence than success

THE princess, in the mean time, insinuated herself into many families; for there are few doors, through which liberality, joined with good humour, cannot find its way. The daughters of many houses were airy and chearful, but Nekayah had been too long accustomed to the conversation of Imlac and her brother to be much pleased with childish levity and prattle which had no meaning. She found their thoughts narrow, their wishes low, and their merriment often artificial. Their pleasures, poor as they were, could not be preserved pure, but were embittered by petty competitions and worthless emulation. They were always jealous of the beauty of each other; of a quality to which solicitude can add nothing, and from which detraction can take nothing away. Many were   10
in love with triflers like themselves, and many fancied that they were in love when in truth they were only idle. Their affection was seldom fixed on sense or virtue, and therefore seldom ended but in vexation. Their grief, however, like their joy, was transient; every thing floated in their mind unconnected with the past or future, so that one desire easily gave way to another, as a second stone cast into the water effaces and confounds the circles of the first.

With these girls she played as with inoffensive animals, and found them proud of her countenance, and weary of her company.

But her purpose was to examine more deeply, and her affability easily persuaded the hearts that were swelling with sorrow to discharge their secrets in   20
her ear: and those whom hope flattered, or prosperity delighted, often courted her to partake their pleasures.

The princess and her brother commonly met in the evening in a private summer-house on the bank of the Nile, and related to each other the occurrences of the day. As they were sitting together, the princess cast her eyes upon the river that flowed before her. "Answer, said she, great father of waters, thou that rollest thy floods through eighty nations, to the invocations of the daughter of thy native king. Tell me if thou waterest, through all thy course, a single habitation from which thou dost not hear the murmurs of complaint?"

"You are then, said Rasselas, not more successful in private houses than I   30
have been in courts." "I have, since the last partition of our provinces, said the princess, enabled myself to enter familiarly into many families, where there was the fairest show of prosperity and peace, and know not one house that is not haunted by some fiend that destroys its quiet.

"I did not seek ease among the poor, because I concluded that there it could not be found. But I saw many poor whom I had supposed to live in affluence. Poverty has, in large cities, very different appearances: it is often concealed in splendour, and often in extravagance. It is the care of a very great part of mankind to conceal their indigence from the rest: they support themselves by temporary expedients, and every day is lost in contriving for the morrow.   40

"This, however, was an evil, which, though frequent, I saw with less pain, because I could relieve it. Yet some have refused my bounties; more offended with my quickness to detect their wants, than pleased with my readiness to succour them: and others, whose exigencies compelled them to admit my kindness, have never been able to forgive their benefactress. Many, however, have been sincerely grateful without the ostentation of gratitude, or the hope of other favours."

Chap. XXVI   The princess continues her remarks upon private life

NEKAYAH perceiving her brother's attention fixed, proceeded in her narrative.

"In families, where there is or is not poverty, there is commonly discord: if a kingdom be, as Imlac tells us, a great family, a family likewise is a little kingdom, torn with factions and exposed to revolutions. An unpractised observer expects the love of parents and children to be constant and equal; but this kindness seldom continues beyond the years of infancy: in a short time the children become rivals to their parents. Benefits are allayed by reproaches, and gratitude debased by envy.

"Parents and children seldom act in concert: each child endeavours to appropriate the esteem or fondness of the parents, and the parents, with yet less temptation, betray each other to their children; thus some place their confidence in the father, and some in the mother, and, by degrees, the house is filled with artifices and feuds.

"The opinions of children and parents, of the young and the old, are naturally opposite, by the contrary effects of hope and despondence, of expectation and experience, without crime or folly on either side. The colours of life in youth and age appear different, as the face of nature in spring and winter. And how can children credit the assertions of parents, which their own eyes show them to be false?

"Few parents act in such a manner as much to enforce their maxims by the credit of their lives. The old man trusts wholly to slow contrivance and gradual progression: the youth expects to force his way by genius, vigour, and precipitance. The old man pays regard to riches, and the youth reverences virtue. The old man deifies prudence: the youth commits himself to magnanimity and chance. The young man, who intends no ill, believes that none is intended, and therefore acts with openness and candour: but his father, having suffered the injuries of fraud, is impelled to suspect, and too often allured to practice it. Age looks with anger on the temerity of youth, and youth with contempt on the scrupulosity of age. Thus parents and children, for the greatest part, live on to love less and less: and, if those whom nature has thus closely united are the torments of each other, where shall we look for tenderness and consolation?"

"Surely, said the prince, you must have been unfortunate in your choice of acquaintance: I am unwilling to believe, that the most tender of all relations is thus impeded in its effects by natural necessity."

"Domestick discord, answered she, is not inevitably and fatally necessary;

but yet is not easily avoided. We seldom see that a whole family is virtuous: the good and evil cannot well agree; and the evil can yet less agree with one another: even the virtous fall sometimes to variance, when their virtues are of different kinds, and tending to extremes. In general, those parents have most reverence who most deserve it: for he that lives well cannot be despised.

Many other evils infest private life. Some are the slaves of servants whom they have trusted with their affairs. Some are kept in continual anxiety to the caprice of rich relations, whom they cannot please, and dare not offend. Some husbands are imperious, and some wives perverse: and, as it is always more easy to do evil than good, though the wisdom or virtue of one can very rarely make many happy, the folly or vice of one may often make many miserable."   10

"If such be the general effect of marriage, said the prince, I shall, for the future, think it dangerous to connect my interest with that of another, lest I should be unhappy by my partner's fault."

"I have met, said the princess, with many who live single for that reason; but I never found that their prudence ought to raise envy. They dream away their time without friendship, without fondness, and are driven to rid themselves of the day, for which they have no use, by childish amusements, or vicious delights. They act as beings under the constant sense of some known inferiority, that fills their minds with rancour, and their tongues with censure. They are   20 peevish at home, and malevolent abroad; and, as the out-laws of human nature, make it their business and their pleasure to disturb that society which debars them from its privileges. To live without feeling or exciting sympathy, to be fortunate without adding to the felicity of others, or afflicted without tasting the balm of pity, is a state more gloomy than solitude: it is not retreat but exclusion from mankind. Marriage has many pains, but celibacy has no pleasures."

"What then is to be done? said Rasselas; the more we enquire, the less we can resolve. Surely he is most likely to please himself that has no other inclination to regard."

Chap. XXVII   Disquisition upon greatness

THE conversation had a short pause. The prince, having considered his   30 sister's observations, told her, that she had surveyed life with prejudice, and supposed misery where she did not find it. "Your narrative, says he, throws yet a darker gloom upon the prospects of futurity: the predictions of Imlac were but faint sketches of the evils painted by Nekayah. I have been lately convinced that quiet is not the daughter of grandeur, or of power: that her presence is not to be bought by wealth, nor enforced by conquest. It is evident, that as any man acts in a wider compass, he must be more exposed to opposition from enmity or miscarriage from chance; whoever has many to please or to govern, must use the ministry of many agents, some of whom will be wicked, and some ignorant; by some he will be misled, and by others betrayed. If he   40 gratifies one he will offend another: those that are not favoured will think themselves injured; and, since favours can be conferred but upon few, the greater number will be always discontented."

"The discontent, said the princess, which is thus unreasonable, I hope that I shall always have spirit to despise, and you, power to repress."

"Discontent, answered Rasselas, will not always be without reason under the most just or vigilant administration of publick affairs. None, however attentive, can always discover that merit which indigence or faction may happen to obscure; and none, however powerful, can always reward it. Yet, he that sees inferiour desert advanced above him, will naturally impute that preference to partiality or caprice; and, indeed, it can scarcely be hoped that any man, however magnanimous by nature, or exalted by condition, will be able to persist for ever in fixed and inexorable justice of distribution: he will sometimes indulge his own affections, and sometimes those of his favourites; he will permit some to please him who can never serve him; he will discover in those whom he loves qualities which in reality they do not possess; and to those, from whom he receives pleasure, he will in his turn endeavour to give it. Thus will recommendations sometimes prevail which were purchased by money, or by the more destructive bribery of flattery and servility.

"He that has much to do will do something wrong, and of that wrong must suffer the consequences; and, if it were possible that he should always act rightly, yet when such numbers are to judge of his conduct, the bad will censure and obstruct him by malevolence, and the good sometimes by mistake.

"The highest stations cannot therefore hope to be the abodes of happiness, which I would willingly believe to have fled from thrones and palaces to seats of humble privacy and placid obscurity. For what can hinder the satisfaction, or intercept the expectations, of him whose abilities are adequate to his employments, who sees with his own eyes the whole circuit of his influence, who chooses by his own knowledge all whom he trusts, and whom none are tempted to deceive by hope or fear? Surely he has nothing to do but to love and to be loved, to be virtuous and to be happy."

"Whether perfect happiness would be procured by perfect goodness, said Nekayah, this world will never afford an opportunity of deciding. But this, at least, may be maintained, that we do not always find visible happiness in proportion to visible virtue. All natural and almost all political evils, are incident alike to the bad and good: they are confounded in the misery of a famine, and not much distinguished in the fury of a faction; they sink together in a tempest, are driven together from their country by invaders. All that virtue can afford is quietness of conscience, a steady prospect of a happier state; this may enable us to endure calamity with patience; but remember that patience must suppose pain."

Chap. XXVIII   Rasselas and Nekayah continue their conversation

"DEAR princess, said Rasselas, you fall into the common errours of exaggeratory declamation, by producing, in a familiar disquisition, examples of national calamities, and scenes of extensive misery, which are found in books rather than in the world, and which, as they are horrid, are ordained to be rare. Let us not imagine evils which we do not feel, nor injure life by misrepresentations. I cannot bear that querelous eloquence which threatens every city with a siege like that of Jerusalem, that makes famine attend on every flight of locusts, and suspends pestilence on the wing of every blast that issues from the south.

"On necessary and inevitable evils, which overwhelm kingdoms at once, all disputation is vain: when they happen they must be endured. But it is evident, that these bursts of universal distress are more dreaded than felt: thousands and ten thousands flourish in youth, and wither in age, without the knowledge of any other than domestick evils, and share the same pleasures and vexations whether their kings are mild or cruel, whether the armies of their country persue their enemies, or retreat before them. While courts are disturbed with intestine competitions, and ambassadours are negotiating in foreign countries, the smith still plies his anvil, and the husbandman drives his plow forward; the necessaries of life are required and obtained, and the successive business of the seasons continues to make its wonted revolutions.

"Let us cease to consider what, perhaps, may never happen, and what, when it shall happen, will laugh at human speculation. We will not endeavour to modify the motions of the elements, or to fix the destiny of kingdoms. It is our business to consider what beings like us may perform; each labouring for his own happiness, by promoting within his circle, however narrow, the happiness of others.

"Marriage is evidently the dictate of nature; men and women were made to be companions of each other, and therefore I cannot be persuaded but that marriage is one of the means of happiness."

"I know not, said the princess, whether marriage be more than one of the innumerable modes of human misery. When I see and reckon the various forms of connubial infelicity, the unexpected causes of lasting discord, the diversities of temper, the oppositions of opinion, the rude collisions of contrary desire where both are urged by violent impulses, the obstinate contests of disagreeing virtues, where both are supported by consciousness of good intention, I am sometimes disposed to think with the severer casuists of most nations, that marriage is rather permitted than approved, and that none, but by the instigation of a passion too much indulged, entangle themselves with indissoluble compacts."

"You seem to forget, replied Rasselas, that you have, even now, represented celibacy as less happy than marriage. Both conditions may be bad, but they cannot both be worst. Thus it happens when wrong opinions are entertained, that they mutually destroy each other, and leave the mind open to truth."

"I did not expect, answered the princess, to hear that imputed to falshood which is the consequence only of frailty. To the mind, as to the eye, it is difficult to compare with exactness objects vast in their extent, and various in their parts. Where we see or conceive the whole at once we readily note the discriminations and decide the preference: but of two systems, of which neither can be surveyed by any human being in its full compass of magnitude and multiplicity of complication, where is the wonder, that judging of the whole by parts, I am affected by one or the other as either presses on my memory or fancy? We differ from ourselves just as we differ from each other, when we see only part of the question, as in the multifarious relations of politicks and morality: but when we perceive the whole at once, as in numerical computations, all agree in one judgment, and none ever varies his opinion."

"Let us not add, said the prince, to the other evils of life, the bitterness of controversy, nor endeavour to vie with each other in subtilties of argument. We are employed in a search, of which both are equally to enjoy the success, or suffer by the miscarriage. It is therefore fit that we assist each other. You surely conclude too hastily from the infelicity of marriage against its institution. Will not the misery of life prove equally that life cannot be the gift of heaven? The   10
world must be peopled by marriage, or peopled without it."

"How the world is to be peopled, returned Nekayah, is not my care, and needs not be yours. I see no danger that the present generation should omit to leave successors behind them: we are not now enquiring for the world, but for ourselves."

Chap. [XXIX]⁵ The debate on marriage continued

"THE good of the whole, says Rasselas, is the same with the good of all its parts. If marriage be best for mankind it must be evidently best for individuals, or a permanent and necessary duty must be the cause of evil, and some must be inevitably sacrificed to the convenience of others. In the estimate which you have made of the two states, it appears that the incommodities of a single life   20
are, in a great measure, necessary and certain, but those of the conjugal state accidental and avoidable.

"I cannot forbear to flatter myself that prudence and benevolence will make marriage happy. The general folly of mankind is the cause of general complaint. What can be expected but disappointment and repentance from a choice made in the immaturity of youth, in the ardour of desire, without judgment, without foresight, without enquiry after conformity of opinions, similarity of manners, rectitude of judgment, or purity of sentiment.

"Such is the common process of marriage. A youth and maiden meeting by chance, or brought together by artifice, exchange glances, reciprocate civilities,   30
go home, and dream of one another. Having little to divert attention, or diversify thought, they find themselves uneasy when they are apart, and therefore conclude that they shall be happy together, They marry, and discover what nothing but voluntary blindness had before concealed; they wear out life in altercations, and charge nature with cruelty.

"From those early marriages proceeds likewise the rivalry of parents and children: the son is eager to enjoy the world before the father is willing to forsake it, and there is hardly room at once for two generations. The daughter begins to bloom before the mother can be content to fade, and neither can forbear to wish for the absence of the other.   40

"Surely all these evils may be avoided by that deliberation and delay which

⁵ [XXIX]: The copy text mistakenly numbers this chapter XXVIII.

prudence prescribes to irrevocable choice. In the variety and jollity of youthful pleasures life may be well enough supported without the help of a partner. Longer time will increase experience, and wider views will allow better opportunities of enquiry and selection: one advantage, at least, will be certain; the parents will be visibly older than their children."

"What reason cannot collect, said Nekayah, and what experiment has not yet taught, can be known only from the report of others. I have been told that late marriages are not eminently happy. This is a question too important to be neglected, and I have often proposed it to those, whose accuracy of remark, and comprehensiveness of knowledge, made their suffrages worthy of regard. They   10 have generally determined, that it is dangerous for a man and woman to suspend their fate upon each other, at a time when opinions are fixed, and habits are established; when friendships have been contracted on both sides, when life has been planned into method, and the mind has long enjoyed the contemplation of its own prospects.

"It is scarcely possible that two travelling through the world under the conduct of chance, should have been both directed to the same path, and it will not often happen that either will quit the track which custom has made pleasing. When the desultory levity of youth has settled into regularity, it is soon succeeded by pride ashamed to yield, or obtinacy delighting to contend. And   20 even though mutual esteem produces mutual desire to please, time itself, as it modifies unchangeably the external mien, determines likewise the direction of the passions, and gives an inflexible rigidity to the manners. Long customs are not easily broken: he that attempts to change the course of his own life, very often labours in vain; and how shall we do that for others which we are seldom able to do for ourselves?"

"But surely, interposed the prince, you suppose the chief motive of choice forgotten or neglected. Whenever I shall seek a wife, it shall be my first question, whether she be willing to be led by reason?"

"Thus it is, said Nekayah, that philosophers are deceived. There are a thou-   30 sand familiar disputes which reason never can decide; questions that elude investigation, and make logick ridiculous; cases where something must be done, and where little can be said. Consider the state of mankind, and enquire how few can be supposed to act upon any occasions, whether small or great, with all the reasons of action present to their minds. Wretched would be the pair above all names of wretchedness, who should be doomed to adjust by reason every morning all the minute detail of a domestick day.

"Those who marry at an advanced age, will probably escape the encroachments of their children; but, in diminution of this advantage, they will be likely to leave them, ignorant and helpless, to a guardian's mercy: or, if that   40 should not happen, they must at least go out of the world before they see those whom they love best either wise or great.

"From their children, if they have less to fear, they have less also to hope, and they lose, without equivalent, the joys of early love, and the convenience of uniting with manners pliant, and minds susceptible of new impressions, which might wear away their dissimilitudes by long cohabitation, as soft bodies, by continual attrition, conform their surfaces to each other.

"I believe it will be found that those who marry late are best pleased with their children, and those who marry early with their partners."

"The union of these two affections, said Rasselas, would produce all that could be wished. Perhaps there is a time when marriage might unite them, a time neither too early for the father, nor too late for the husband."

"Every hour, answered the princess, confirms my prejudice in favour of the position so often uttered by the mouth of Imlac, 'That nature sets her gifts on the right hand and on the left.' Those conditions, which flatter hope and attract desire, are so constituted, that, as we approach one, we recede from another. There are goods so opposed that we cannot seize both, but, by too much prudence, may pass between them at too great a distance to reach either. This is often the fate of long consideration; he does nothing who endeavours to do more than is allowed to humanity. Flatter not yourself with contrarieties of pleasure. Of the blessings set before you make your choice, and be content. No man can taste the fruits of autumn while he is delighting his scent with the flowers of the spring: no man can, at the same time, fill his cup from the source and from the mouth of the Nile."

Chap. [XXX]   Imlac enters, and changes the conversation

HERE Imlac entered, and interrupted them. His look was clouded with thought; "Imlac, said Rasselas, I have been taking from the princess the dismal history of private life, and am almost discouraged from further search."

"It seems to me, said Imlac that while you are making the choice of life, you neglect to live. You wander about a single city, which, however large and diversified, can now afford few novelties, and forget that you are in a country, famous among the earliest monarchies for the power and wisdom of its inhabitants; a country where the sciences first dawned that illuminate the world, and beyond which the arts cannot be traced of civil society or domestick life.

"The old Egyptians have left behind them monuments of industry and power before which all European magnificence is confessed to fade away. The ruins of their architecture are the schools of modern builders, and from the wonders which time has spared we may conjecture, though uncertainly, what it has destroyed."

"My curiosity, said Rasselas, does not very strongly lead me to survey piles of stone, or mounds of earth; my business is with man. I came hither not to measure fragments of temples, or trace choaked aqueducts, but to look upon the various scenes of the present world."

"The things that are now before us, said the princess, necessarily require attention, and sufficiently deserve it. What have I to do with the heroes or the monuments of ancient times? with times which never can return, and heroes, whose form of life was different from all that the present condition of mankind requires or allows."

"To know any thing, returned the poet, we must know its effects; to see men we must see their works, that we may learn what reason has dictated, or passion has incited, and find what are the most powerful motives of action. To judge rightly of the present we must oppose it to the past; for all judgment is comparative, and of the future nothing can be known. The truth is, that no mind is much employed upon the present: recollection and anticipation fill up almost all our moments. Our passions are joy and grief, love and hatred, hope and fear. Of joy and grief the past is the object, and the future of hope and fear; even love and hatred respect the past, for the cause must have been before the effect.

"The present state of things is the consequence of the former, and it is natural to inquire what were the sources of the good that we enjoy, or of the evil that we suffer. If we act only for ourselves, to neglect the study of history is not prudent: if we are entrusted with the care of others, it is not just. Ignorance, when it is voluntary, is criminal; and he may properly be charged with evil who refused to learn how he might prevent it.

"There is no part of history so generally useful as that which relates the progress of the human mind, the gradual improvement of reason, the successive advances of science, the vicissitudes of learning and ignorance, which are the light and darkness of thinking beings, the extinction and resuscitation of arts, and all the revolutions of the intellectual world. If accounts of battles and invasions are peculiarly the business of princes, the useful or elegant arts are not to be neglected; those who have kingdoms to govern have understandings to cultivate.

"Example is always more efficacious than precept. A soldier is formed in war, and a painter must copy pictures. In this, contemplative life has the advantage: great actions are seldom seen, but the labours of art are always at hand for those who desire to know what art has been able to perform.

"When the eye or the imagination is struck with any uncommon work the next transition of an active mind is to the means by which it was performed. Here begins the true use of such contemplation; we enlarge our comprehension by new ideas, and perhaps recover some art lost to mankind, or learn what is less perfectly known in our own country. At least we compare our own with former times, and either rejoice at our improvements, or, what is the first motion towards good, discover our defects."

"I am willing, said the prince, to see all that can deserve my search." "And I, said the princess, shall rejoice to learn something of the manners of antiquity."

"The most pompous monument of Egyptian greatness, and one of the most bulky works of manual industry, said Imlac, are the pyramids; fabricks raised before the time of history, and of which the earliest narratives afford us only uncertain traditions. Of these the greatest is still standing, very little injured by time."

"Let us visit them to morrow, said Nekayah. I have often heard of the Pyramids, and shall not rest, till I have seen them within and without with my own eyes."

Chap. [XXXI]   They visit the Pyramids

THE resolution being thus taken, they set out the next day. They laid tents upon their camels, being resolved to stay among the pyramids till their curiosity was fully satisfied. They travelled gently, turned aside to every thing remarkable, stopped from time to time and conversed with the inhabitants, and observed the various appearances of towns ruined and inhabited, of wild and cultivated nature.

When they came to the great pyramid they were astonished at the extent of the base, and the height of the top. Imlac explained to them the principles upon which the pyramidal form was chosen for a fabrick intended to co-extend its duration with that of the world: he showed that its gradual diminution gave it such stability, as defeated all the common attacks of the elements, and could scarcely be overthrown by earthquakes themselves, the least resistible of natural 10 violence. A concussion that should shatter the pyramid would threaten the dissolution of the continent.

They measured all its dimensions, and pitched their tents at its foot. Next day they prepared to enter its interiour apartments, and having hired the common guides climbed up to the first passage, when the favourite of the princess, looking into the cavity, stepped back and trembled. "Pekuah, said the princess, of what art thou afraid?" "Of the narrow entrance, answered the lady, and of the dreadful gloom. I dare not enter a place which must surely be inhabited by unquiet souls. The original possessors of these dreadful vaults will start up before us, and, perhaps, shut us up for ever." She spoke, and threw her arms 20 round the neck of her mistress.

"If all your fear be of apparitions, said the prince, I will promise you safety: there is no danger from the dead; he that is once buried will be seen no more."

"That the dead are seen no more, said Imlac, I will not undertake to maintain against the concurrent and unvaried testimony of all ages, and of all nations. There is no people, rude or learned, among whom apparitions of the dead are not related and believed. This opinion, which, perhaps, prevails as far as human nature is diffused, could become universal only by its truth: those, that never heard of one another, would not have agreed in a tale which nothing but experience can make credible. That it is doubted by single cavillers can very 30 little weaken the general evidence, and some who deny it with their tongues confess it by their fears.

"Yet I do not mean to add new terrours to those which have already seized upon Pekuah. There can be no reason why spectres should haunt the pyramid more than other places, or why they should have power or will to hurt innocence and purity. Our entrance is no violation of their privileges; we can take nothing from them, how then can we offend them?"

"My dear Pekuah, said the princess, I will always go before you, and Imlac shall follow you. Remember that you are the companion of the princess of Abissinia."   40

"If the princess is pleased that her servant should die, returned the lady, let her command some death less dreadful than enclosure in this horrid cavern. You know I dare not disobey you: I must go if you command me; but, if I once enter, I never shall come back."

"The princess saw that her fear was too strong for expostulation or reproof, and embracing her, told her that she should stay in the tent till their return. Pekuah was yet not satisfied, but entreated the princess not to persue so dreadful a purpose as that of entering the recesses of the pyramid. "Though I cannot teach courage, said Nekayah, I must not learn cowardi[c]e; nor leave at last undone what I came hither only to do."

Chap. [XXXII]   They enter the Pyramid

PEKUAH descended to the tents, and the rest entered the pyramid: they passed through the galleries, surveyed the vaults of marble, and examined the chest in which the body of the founder is supposed to have been reposited. They then sat down in one of the most spacious chambers to rest a while before they attempted to return.

"We have now, said Imlac, gratified our minds with an exact view of the greatest work of man, except the wall of China.   10

"Of the wall it is very easy to assign the motives. It secured a wealthy and timorous nation from the incursions of Barbarians, whose unskilfulness in arts made it easier for them to supply their wants by rapine than by industry, and who from time to time poured in upon the habitations of peaceful commerce, as vultures descend upon domestick fowl. Their celerity and fierceness made the wall necessary, and their ignorance made it efficacious.

"But for the pyramids no reason has ever been given adequate to the cost and labour of the work. The narrowness of the chambers proves that it could afford no retreat from enemies, and treasures might have been reposited at far less expence with equal security. It seems to have been erected only in compliance   20
with that hunger of imagination which preys incessantly upon life, and must be always appeased by some employment. Those who have already all that they can enjoy, must enlarge their desires. He that has built for use, till use is supplied, must begin to build for vanity, and extend his plan to the utmost power of human performance, that he may not be soon reduced to form another wish.

"I consider this mighty structure as a monument of the insufficiency of human enjoyments. A king, whose power is unlimited, and whose treasures surmount all real and imaginary wants, is compelled to solace, by the erection of a pyramid, the satiety of dominion and tastelesness of pleasures, and to amuse the tediousness of declining life, by seeing thousands labouring without end,   30
and one stone, for no purpose, laid upon another. Whoever thou art, that, not content with a moderate condition, imaginest happiness in royal magnificence, and dreamest that command or riches can feed the appetite of novelty with successive gratifications, survey the pyramids, and confess thy folly!"

Chap. [XXXIII]   The princess meets with an unexpected misfortune

THEY rose up, and returned through the cavity at which they had entered, and the princess prepared for her favourite a long narrative of dark labyrinths, and costly rooms, and of the different impressions which the varieties of the way had made upon her. But, when they came to their train, they found every one silent and dejected: the men discovered shame and fear in their countenances, and the women were weeping in the tents.

What had happened they did not try to conjecture, but immediately enquired. "You had scarcely entered into the pyramid, said one of the attendants, when a troop of Arabs rushed upon us: we were too few to resist them, and too slow to escape. They were about to search the tents, set us on our camels, and drive us along before them, when the approach of some Turkish horsemen put them to flight; but they seized the lady Pekuah with her two maids, and carried them away: the Turks are now persuing them by our instigation, but I fear they will not be able to overtake them."

The princess was overpowered with surprise and grief. Rasselas, in the first heat of his resentment, ordered his servants to follow him, and prepared to persue the robbers with his sabre in his hand. "Sir, said Imlac, what can you hope from violence or valour? the Arabs are mounted on horses trained to battle and retreat; we have only beasts of burthen. By leaving our present station we may lose the princess, but cannot hope to regain Pekuah."

In a short time the Turks returned, having not been able to reach the enemy. The princess burst out into new lamentations, and Rasselas could scarcely forbear to reproach them with cowardice; but Imlac was of opinion, that the escape of the Arabs was no addition to their misfortune, for, perhaps, they would have killed their captives rather than have resigned them.

Chap. [XXXIV] They return to Cairo without Pekuah

THERE was nothing to be hoped from longer stay. They returned to Cairo repenting of their curiosity, censuring the negligence of the government, lamenting their own rashness which had neglected to procure a guard, imagining many expedients by which the loss of Pekuah might have been prevented, and resolving to do something for her recovery, though none could find any thing proper to be done.

Nekayah retired to her chamber, where her women attempted to comfort her, by telling her that all had their troubles, and that lady Pekuah had enjoyed much happiness in the world for a long time, and might reasonably expect a change of fortune. They hoped that some good would befal her wheresoever she was, and that their mistress would find another friend who might supply her place.

The princess made them no answer, and they continued the form of condolence, not much grieved in their hearts that the favourite was lost.

Next day the prince presented to the Bassa a memorial of the wrong which he had suffered, and a petition for redress. The Bassa threatened to punish the robbers, but did not attempt to catch them, nor, indeed, could any account or description be given by which he might direct the persuit.

It soon appeared that nothing would be done by authority. Governors, being accustomed to hear of more crimes than they can punish, and more wrongs than they can redress, set themselves at ease by indiscriminate negligence, and presently forget the request when they lose sight of the petitioner.

Imlac then endeavoured to gain some intelligence by private agents. He found many who pretended to an exact knowledge of all the haunts of the Arabs, and to regular correspondence with their chiefs, and who readily undertook the recovery of Pekuah. Of these, some were furnished with money for their journey, and came back no more; some were liberally paid for accounts which a few days discovered to be false. But the princess would not suffer any means, however improbable, to be left untried. While she was doing something she kept her hope alive. As one expedient failed, another was suggested; when one messenger returned unsuccessful, another was despatched to a different quarter.

Two months had now passed, and of Pekuah nothing had been heard; the hopes which they had endeavoured to raise in each other grew more languid, and the princess, when she saw nothing more to be tried, sunk down inconsolable in hopeless dejection. A thousand times she reproached herself with the easy compliance by which she permitted her favourite to stay behind her. "Had not my fondness, said she, lessened my authority, Pekuah had not dared to talk of her terrours. She ought to have feared me more than spectres. A severe look would have overpowered her; a peremptory command would have compelled obedience. Why did foolish indulgence prevail upon me? Why did I not speak and refuse to hear?"

"Great princess, said Imlac, do not reproach yourself for your virtue, or consider that as blameable by which evil has accidentally been caused. Your tenderness for the timidity of Pekuah was generous and kind. When we act according to our duty, we commit the event to him by whose laws our actions are governed, and who will suffer none to be finally punished for obedience. When, in prospect of some good, whether natural or moral, we break the rules prescribed us, we withdraw from the direction of superiour wisdom, and take all consequences upon ourselves. Man cannot so far know the connexion of causes and events, as that he may venture to do wrong in order to do right. When we persue our end by lawful means, we may always console our miscarriage by the hope of future recompense. When we consult only our own policy, and attempt to find a nearer way to good, by overleaping the settled boundaries of right and wrong, we cannot be happy even by success, because we cannot escape the consciousness of our fault; but, if we miscarry, the disappointment is irremediably embittered. How comfortless is the sorrow of him, who feels at once the pangs of guilt, and the vexation of calamity which guilt has brought upon him?

"Consider, princess, what would have been your condition, if the lady Pekauh had intreated to accompany you, and, being compelled to stay in the tents, had been carried away; or how would you have born the thought, if you had forced her into the pyramid, and she had died before you in agonies of terrour."

"Had either happened, said Nekayah, I could not have endured life till now:

I should have been tortured to madness by the remembrance of such cruelty, or must have pined away in abhorrence of myself."

"This at least, said Imlac, is the present reward of virtuous conduct, that no unlucky consequence can oblige us to repent it."

Chap. [XXXV]   The princess continues to lament Pekuah

NEKAYAH, being thus reconciled to herself, found that no evil is insupportable but that which is accompanied with consciousness of wrong. She was, from that time, delivered from the violence of tempestuous sorrow, and sunk into silent pensiveness and gloomy tranquillity. She sat from morning to evening recollecting all that had been done or said by her Pekuah, treasured up with care every trifle on which Pekuah had set an accidental value, and which   10
might recal to mind any little incident or careless conversation. The sentiments of her, whom she now expected to see no more, were treasured up in her memory as rules of life, and she deliberated to no other end than to conjecture on any occasion what would have been the opinion and counsel of Pekuah.

The women, by whom she was attended, knew nothing of her real condition, and therefore she could not talk to them but with caution and reserve. She began to remit her curiosity, having no great care to collect notions which she had no convenience of uttering. Rasselas endeavoured first to comfort and afterwards to divert her; he hired musicians, to whom she seemed to listen, but did not hear them, and procured masters to instruct her in various arts, whose   20
lectures, when they visited her again, were again to be repeated. She had lost her taste of pleasure and her ambition of excellence. And her mind, though forced into short excursions, always recurred to the image of her friend.

Imlac was every morning earnestly enjoined to renew his enquiries, and was asked every night whether he had yet heard of Pekuah, till not being able to return the princess the answer that she desired, he was less and less willing to come into her presence. She observed his backwardness, and commanded him to attend her. "You are not, said she, to confound impatience with resentment, or to suppose that I charge you with negligence, because I repine at your unsuccessfulness. I do not much wonder at your absence; I know that the unhappy are   30
never pleasing, and that all naturally avoid the contagion of misery. To hear complaints is wearisome alike to the wretched and the happy; for who would cloud by adventitious grief the short gleams of gaiety which life allows us? or who, that is struggling under his own evils, will add to them the miseries of another?

"The time is at hand, when none shall be disturbed any longer by the sighs of Nekayah: my search after happiness is now at an end. I am resolved to retire from the world with all its flatteries and deceits, and will hide myself in solitude, without any other care than to compose my thoughts, and regulate my hours by a constant succession of innocent occupations, till, with a mind purified   40 from all earthly desires, I shall enter into that state, to which all are hastening, and in which I hope again to enjoy the friendship of Pekuah."

"Do not entangle your mind, said Imlac, by irrevocable determinations, nor increase the burthen of life by a voluntary accumulation of misery: the weariness of retirement will continue or increase when the loss of Pekuah is forgotten. That you have been deprived of one pleasure is no very good reason for rejection of the rest."

"Since Pekuah was taken from me, said the princess, I have no pleasure to reject or to retain. She that has no one to love or trust has little to hope. She wants the radical principle of happiness. We may, perhaps, allow that what 10 satisfaction this world can afford, must arise from the conjunction of wealth, knowledge and goodness: wealth is nothing but as it is bestowed, and knowledge nothing but as it is communicated. Goodness affords the only comfort which can be enjoyed without a partner, and goodness may be practised in retirement."

"How far solitude may admit goodness, or advance it, I shall not, replied Imlac, dispute at present. Remember the confession of the pious hermit. You will wish to return into the world, when the image of your companion has left your thoughts." "That time, said Nekayah, will never come. The generous frankness, the modest obsequiousness, and the faithful secrecy of my dear 20 Pekuah, will always be more missed, as I shall live longer to see vice and folly."

"The state of a mind oppressed with a sudden calamity, said Imlac, is like that of the fabulous inhabitants of the new created earth, who, when the first night came upon them, supposed that day never would return. When the clouds of sorrow gather over us, we see nothing beyond them, nor can imagine how they will be dispelled: yet a new day succeeded to the night, and sorrow is never long without a dawn of ease. But they who restrain themselves from receiving comfort, do as the savages would have done, had they put out their eyes when it was dark. Our minds, like our bodies, are in continual flux; some- 30 thing is hourly lost, and something acquired. To lose much at once is inconvenient to either, but while the vital powers remain uninjured, nature will find the means of reparation. Distance has the same effect on the mind as on the eye, and while we glide along the stream of time, whatever we leave behind us is always lessening, and that which we approach increasing in magnitude. Do not suffer life to stagnate; it will grow muddy for want of motion: commit yourself again to the current of the world; Pekuah will vanish by degrees; you will meet in your way some other favourite, or learn to diffuse yourself in general conversation."

"At least, said the prince, do not despair before all remedies have been tried: 40 the enquiry after the unfortunate lady is still continued, and shall be carried on with yet greater diligence, on condition that you will promise to wait a year for the event, without any unalterable resolution."

Nekayah thought this a reasonable demand, and made the promise to her brother, who had been advised by Imlac to require it. Imlac had, indeed, no great hope of regaining Pekuah, but he supposed, that if he could secure the interval of a year, the princess would be then in no danger of a cloister.

Chap. [XXXVI]   Pekuah is still remembered by the princess

NEKAYAH, seeing that nothing was omitted for the recovery of her avourite, and having, by her promise, set her intention of retirement at a distance, began imperceptibly to return to common cares and common pleasures. She rejoiced without her own consent at the suspension of her sorrows, and sometimes caught herself with indignation in the act of turning away her mind from the remembrance of her, whom yet she resolved never to forget.

She then appointed a certain hour of the day for meditation on the merits and fondness of Pekuah, and for some weeks retired constantly at the time fixed, and returned with her eyes swollen and her countenance clouded. By degrees she grew less scrupulous, and suffered any important and pressing avocation to   10 delay the tribute of daily tears. She then yielded to less occasions; sometimes forgot what she was indeed afraid to remember, and, at last, wholly released herself from the duty of periodical affliction.

Her real love of Pekuah was yet not diminished. A thousand occurrences brought her back to memory, and a thousand wants, which nothing but the confidence of friendship can supply, made her frequently regretted. She, therefore, solicited Imlac never to desist from enquiry, and to leave no art of intelligence untried, that, at least, she might have the comfort of knowing that she did not suffer by negligence or sluggishness. "Yet what, said she, is to be expected from our persuit of happiness, when we find the state of life to be such,   20 that happiness itself is the cause of misery? Why should we endeavour to attain that, of which the possession cannot be secured? I shall henceforward fear to yield my heart to excellence, however bright, or to fondness, however tender, lest I should lose again what I have lost in Pekuah."

Chap. [XXXVII]   The princess hears news of Pekuah

IN seven months, one of the messengers, who had been sent away upon the day when the promise was drawn from the princess, returned, after many unsuccessful rambles, from the borders of Nubia, with an account that Pekuah was in the hands of an Arab chief, who possessed a castle or fortress on the extremity of Egypt. The Arab, whose revenue was plunder, was willing to restore her, with her two attendants, for two hundred ounces of gold.   30

The price was no subject of debate. The princess was in extasies when she heard that her favourite was alive, and might so cheaply be ransomed. She could not think of delaying for a moment Pekuah's happiness or her own, but entreated her brother to send back the messenger with the sum required. Imlac, being consulted, was not very confident of the veracity of the relator, and was still more doubtful of the Arab's faith, who might, if he were too liberally trusted, detain at once the money and the captives. He thought it dangerous to put themselves in the power of the Arab, by going into his district, and could not expect that the Arab would so much expose himself as to come into the lower country, where he might be seized by the forces of the Bassa.

It is difficult to negotiate where neither will trust. But Imlac, after some deliberation, directed the messenger to propose that Pekuah should be conducted by ten horsemen to the monast[e]ry of St. Antony, which is situated in the deserts of Upper-Egypt, where she should be met by the same number, and her ransome should be paid.

That no time might be lost, as they expected that the proposal would not be refused, they immediately began their journey to the monast[e]ry; and, when they arrived, Imlac went forward with the former messenger to the Arab's fortress. Rasselas was desirous to go with them, but neither his sister nor Imlac would consent. The Arab, according to the custom of his nation, observed the laws of hospitality with great exactness to those who put themselves into his power, and, in a few days, brought Pekuah with her maids, by easy journeys, to their place appointed, where he received the stipulated price, and, with great respect, restored her to liberty and her friends, and undertook to conduct them back towards Cairo beyond all danger of robbery or violence.

The princess and her favourite embraced each other with transport too violent to be expressed, and went out together to pour the tears of tenderness in secret, and exchange professions of kindness and gratitude. After a few hours they returned into the refectory of the convent, where, in the presence of the prior and his brethren, the prince required of Pekuah the history of her adventures.

Chap. [XXXVIII] The adventures of the lady Pekuah

"AT what time, and in what manner, I was forced away, said Pekuah, your servants have told you. The suddenness of the event struck me with surprise, and I was at first rather stupified than agitated with any passion of either fear or sorrow. My confusion was encreased by the speed and tumult of our flight while we were followed by the Turks, who, as it seemed, soon despaired to overtake us, or were afraid of those whom they made a shew of menacing.

"When the Arabs saw themselves out of danger they slackened their course, and, as I was less harrassed by external violence, I began to feel more uneasiness in my mind. After some time we stopped near a spring shaded with trees in a pleasant meadow, where we were set upon the ground, and offered such refreshments as our masters were partaking. I was suffered to sit with my maids apart from the rest, and none attempted to comfort or insult us. Here I first began to feel the full weight of my misery. The girls sat weeping in silence, and from time to time looked up to me for succour. I knew not to what condition we were doomed, nor could conjecture where would be the place of our captivity, or whence to draw any hope of deliverance. I was in the hands of robbers and savages, and had no reason to suppose that their pity was more than their justice, or that they would forbear the gratification of any ardour of desire, or caprice of cruelty. I, however, kissed my maids, and endeavoured to pacify them by remarking, that we were yet treated with decency, and that, since we were now carried beyond pursuit, there was no danger of violence to our lives.

"When we were to be set again on horseback, my maids clung round me, and refused to be parted, but I commanded them not to irritate those who had us in their power. We travelled the remaining part of the day through an unfrequented and pathless country, and came by moonlight to the side of a hill, where the rest of the troop was stationed. Their tents were pitched, and their fires kindled, and our chief was welcomed as a man much beloved by his dependants.   10

"We were received into a large tent, where we found women who had attended their husbands in the expedition. They set before us the supper which they had provided, and I eat it rather to encourage my maids than to comply with any appetite of my own. When the meat was taken away they spread the carpets for repose. I was weary, and hoped to find in sleep that remission of distress which nature seldom denies. Ordering myself therefore to be undrest, I observed that the women looked very earnestly upon me, not expecting, I supposed, to see me so submissively attended. When my upper vest was taken off, they were apparently struck with the splendour of my cloaths, and one of them timorously laid her hand upon the embroidery. She then went out, and,   20 in a short time, came back with another woman, who seemed to be of higher rank, and greater authority. She did, at her entrance, the usual act of reverence, and, taking me by the hand, placed me in a smaller tent, spread with finer carpets, where I spent the night quietly with my maids.

"In the morning, as I was sitting on the grass, the chief of the troop came towards me: I rose up to receive him, and he bowed with great respect. 'Illustrious lady, said he, my fortune is better than I had presumed to hope; I am told by my women, that I have a princess in my camp.' Sir, answered I, your women have deceived themselves and you; I am not a princess, but an unhappy stranger who intended soon to have left this country, in which I am now to be   30 imprisoned for ever. 'Whoever, or whencesoever, you are, returned the Arab, your dress, and that of your servants, show your rank to be high, and your wealth to be great. Why should you, who can so easily procure your ransome, think yourself in danger of perpetual captivity? The purpose of my incursions is to encrease my riches, or more properly to gather tribute. The sons of Ishmael are the natural and hereditary lords of this part of the continent, which is usurped by late invaders, and low-born tyrants, from whom we are compelled to take by the sword what is denied to justice. The violence of war admits no distinction; the lance that is lifted at guilt and power will sometimes fall on innocence and gentleness.'   40

"How little, said I, did I expect that yesterday it should have fallen upon me."

"Misfortunes, answered the Arab, should always be expected. If the eye of hostility could have learned to spare, excellence like yours had been exempt from injury. But the angels of affliction spread their toils alike for the virtuous and the wicked, for the mighty and the mean. Do not be disconsolate; I am not one of the lawless and cruel rovers of the desart; I know the rules of civil life; I will fix your ransome, give a pasport to your messenger, and perform my stipulation with nice punctuality."

"You will easily believe that I was pleased with his courtesy; and finding that his predominant passion was desire of money, I began now to think my danger less, for I knew that no sum would be thought too great for the release of Pekuah. I told him that he should have no reason to charge me with ingratitude, if I was used with kindness, and that any ransome, which could be expected for a maid of common rank, would be paid, but that he must not persist to rate me as a princess. He said, he would consider what he should demand, and then, smiling, bowed and retired.   10

"Soon after the women came about me, each contending to be more officious than the other, and my maids themselves were served with reverence. We travelled onward by short journeys. On the fourth day the chief told me, that my ransome must be two hundred ounces of gold, which I not only promised him, but told him, that I would add fifty more, if I and my maids were honourably treated.

"I never knew the power of gold before. From that time I was the leader of the troop. The march of every day was longer or shorter as I commanded, and the tents were pitched where I chose to rest. We now had camels and other conveniencies for travel, my own women were always at my side, and I amused   20
myself with observing the manners of the vagrant nations, and with viewing remains of ancient edifices with which these deserted countries appear to have been, in some distant age, lavishly embellished.

"The chief of the band was a man far from illiterate: he was able to travel by the stars or the compass, and had marked in his erratick expeditions such places as are most worthy the notice of a passenger. He observed to me, that buildings are always best preserved in places little frequented, and difficult of access: for, when once a country declines from its primitive splendour, the more inhabitants are left, the quicker ruin will be made. Walls supply stones more easily than quarries, and palaces and temples will be demolished to make   30
stables of granate, and cottages of porphyry.

Chap. [XXXIX]   The adventures of Pekuah continued

"WE wandered about in this manner for some weeks, whether, as our chief pretended, for my gratification, or, as I rather suspected, for some convenience of his own. I endeavoured to appear contented where sullenness and resentment would have been of no use, and that endeavour conduced much to the calmness of my mind; but my heart was always with Nekayah, and the troubles of the night much overbalanced the amusements of the day. My women, who threw all their cares upon their mistress, set their minds at ease from the time when they saw me treated with respect, and gave themselves up to the incidental alleviations of our fatigue without solicitude or sorrow. I was pleased with their   40
pleasure, and animated with their confidence. My condition had lost much of its terrour, since I found that the Arab ranged the country merely to get

riches. Avarice is an uniform and tractable vice: other intellectual distempers are different in different constitutions of mind; that which sooths the pride of one will offend the pride of another; but to the favour of the covetous there is a ready way, bring money and nothing is denied.

"At last we came to the dwelling of our chief, a strong and spacious house built with stone in an island of the Nile, which lies, as I was told, under the tropick. "Lady, said the Arab, you shall rest a few weeks after your journey in this place, where you are to consider yourself as sovereign. My occupation is war: I have therefore chosen this obscure residence, from which I can issue unexpected, and to which I can retire unpersued. You may now repose in security: here are few pleasures, but here is no danger." He then led me into the inner apartments, and seating me in the place of honour, bowed to the ground. His women, who considered me as a rival, looked on me with malignity; but being soon informed that I was a great lady detained only for my ransome, they began to vie with each other in obsequiousness and reverence.

"Being again comforted with new assurances of speedy liberty, I was for some days diverted from impatience by the novelty of the place. The turrets overlooked the country to a great distance, and afforded a view of many windings of the stream. In the day I wandered from one place to another as the course of the sun varied the splendour of the prospect, and saw many things which I had never seen before. The crocodiles and river-horses[6] were common in this unpeopled region, and I often looked upon them with terrour, though I knew that they could not hurt me. For some time I expected to see mermaids and tritons, which, as Imlac has told me, the European travellers have stationed in the Nile, but no such beings ever appeared, and the Arab, when I enquired after them, laughed at my credulity.

"At night the Arab always attended me to a tower set apart for celestial observations, where he endeavoured to teach me the names and courses of the stars. I had no great inclination to this study, but an appearance of attention was necessary to please my instructor, who valued himself for his skill, and, in a little while, I found some employment requisite to beguile the tediousness of time, which was to be passed always amidst the same objects. I was weary of looking in the morning on things from which I had turned away weary in the evening: I therefore was at last willing to observe the stars rather than do nothing, but could not always compose my thoughts, and was very often thinking on Nekayah when others imagined me contemplating the sky. Soon after the Arab went upon another expedition, and then my only pleasure was to talk with my maids about the accident by which we were carried away, and the happiness that we should all enjoy at the end of our captivity."

"There were women in your Arab's fortress, said the princess, why did you not make them your companions, enjoy their conversation, and partake their diversions? In a place where they found business or amusement, why should you alone sit corroded with idle melancholy? or why could not you bear for a few months that condition to which they were condemned for life?"

"The diversions of the women, answered Pekuah, were only childish play, by which the mind accustomed to stronger operations could not be kept busy. I

[6] *River-horses:* Hippopotamuses.

could do all which they delighted in doing by powers merely sensitive, while my intellectual faculties were flown to Cairo. They ran from room to room as a bird hops from wire to wire in his cage. They danced for the sake of motion, as lambs frisk in a meadow. One sometimes pretended to be hurt that the rest might be alarmed, or hid herself that another might seek her. Part of their time passed in watching the progress of light bodies that floated on the river, and part in marking the various forms into which clouds broke in the sky.

"Their business was only needlework, in which I and my maids sometimes helped them; but you know that the mind will easily straggle from the fingers, nor will you suspect that captivity and absence from Nekayah could be much solaced by silken flowers.

"Nor was much satisfaction to be hoped from their conversation: for of what could they be expected to talk? They had seen nothing; for they had lived from eary youth in that narrow spot: of what they had not seen they could have no knowledge, for they could not read. They had no ideas but of the few things that were within their view, and had hardly names for any thing but their cloaths and their food. As I bore a superiour character, I was often called to terminate their quarrels, which I decided as equitably as I could. If it could have amused me to hear the complaints of each against the rest, I might have been often detained by long stories, but the motives of their animosity were so small that I could not listen long without intercepting the tale."

"How, said Rasselas, can the Arab, whom you represented as a man of more than common accomplishments, take any pleasure in his seraglio, when it is filled only with women like these. Are they exquisitely beautiful?"

"They do not, said Pekuah, want that unaffecting and ignoble beauty which may subsist without spriteliness or sublimity, without energy of thought or dignity of virtue. But to a man like the Arab such beauty was only a flower casually plucked and carelesly thrown away. Whatever pleasures he might find among them, they were not those of friendship or society. When they were playing about him he looked on them with inattentive superiority: when they vied for his regard he sometimes turned away disgusted. As they had no knowledge, their talk could take nothing from the tediousness of life: as they had no choice, their fondness, or appearance of fondness, excited in him neither pride nor gratitude; he was not exalted in his own esteem by the smiles of a woman who saw no other man, nor was much obliged by that regard, of which he could never know the sincerity, and which he might often perceive to be exerted not so much to delight him as to pain a rival. That which he gave, and they received, as love, was only a careless distribution of superfluous time, such love as man can bestow upon that which he despises, such as has neither hope nor fear, neither joy nor sorrow."

"You have reason, lady, to think yourself happy, said Imlac, that you have been thus easily dismissed. How could a mind, hungry for knowledge, be willing, in an intellectual famine, to lose such a banquet as Pekuah's conversation?"

"I am inclined to believe, answered Pekuah, that he was for some time in suspense; for, notwithstanding his promise, whenever I proposed to dispatch a messenger to Cairo, he found some excuse for delay. While I was detained in his house he made many incursions into the neighbouring countries, and, perhaps, he would have refused to discharge me, had his plunder been equal to his wishes. He returned always courteous, related his adventures, delighted to hear my observations, and endeavoured to advance my acquaintance with the stars. When I importuned him to send away my letters, he soothed me with professions of honour and sincerity; and, when I could be no longer decently denied, put his troop again in motion, and left me to govern in his absence. I was much afflicted by this studied procrastination, and was sometimes afraid that I should be forgotten; that you would leave Cairo, and I must end my days in an island of the Nile.   10

"I grew at last hopeless and dejected, and cared so little to entertain him, that he for a while more frequently talked with my maids. That he should fall in love with them, or with me, might have been equally fatal, and I was not much pleased with the growing friendship. My anxiety was not long; for, as I recovered some degree of chearfulness, he returned to me, and I could not forbear to despise my former uneasiness.

"He still delayed to send for my ransome, and would, perhaps, never have determined, had not your agent found his way to him. The gold, which he would not fetch, he could not reject when it was offered. He hastened to prepare for our journey hither, like a man delivered from the pain of an intestine   20 conflict. I took leave of my companions in the house, who dismissed me with cold indifference."

Nekayah, having heard her favourite's relation, rose and embraced her, and Rasselas gave her an hundred ounces of gold, which she presented to the Arab for the fifty that were promised.

Chap. [XL]   The history of a man of learning

THEY returned to Cairo, and were so well pleased at finding themselves together, that none of them went much abroad. The prince began to love learning, and one day declared to Imlac, that he intended to devote himself to science, and pass the rest of his days in literary solitude.

"Before you make your final choice, answered Imlac, you ought to examine   30 its hazards, and converse with some of those who are grown old in the company of themselves. I have just left the observatory of one of the most learned astronomers in the world, who has spent forty years in unwearied attention to the motions and appearances of the celestial bodies, and has drawn out his soul in endless calculations. He admits a few friends once a month to hear his deductions and enjoy his discoveries. I was introduced as a man of knowledge worthy of his notice. Men of various ideas and fluent conversation are commonly welcome to those whose thoughts have been long fixed upon a single point, and who find the images of other things stealing away. I delighted him with my remarks, he smiled at the narrative of my travels, and was glad to forget the   40 constellations, and descend for a moment into the lower world.

"On the next day of vacation I renewed my visit, and was so fortunate as to please him again. He relaxed from that time the severity of his rule, and permitted me to enter at my own choice. I found him always busy, and always glad to be relieved. As each knew much which the other was desirous of learning, we exchanged our notions with great delight. I perceived that I had every day more of his confidence, and always found new cause of admiration in the profundity of his mind. His comprehension is vast, his memory capacious and retentive, his discourse is methodical, and his expression clear.

"His integrity and benevolence are equal to his learning. His deepest researches and most favourite studies are willingly interrupted for any opportunity of doing good by his counsel or his riches. To his closest retreat, at his most   10
busy moments, all are admitted that want his assistance: "For though I exclude idleness and pleasure, I will never, says he, bar my doors against charity. To man is permitted the contemplation of the skies, but the practice of virtue is commanded."

"Surely, said the princess, this man is happy."

"I visited him, said Imlac, with more and more frequency, and was every time more enamoured of his conversation: he was sublime without haughtiness, courteous without formality, and communicative without ostentation. I was at first, Madam, of your opinion, thought him the happiest of mankind, and often congratulated him on the blessing that he enjoyed. He seemed to hear   20
nothing with indifference but the praises of his condition, to which he always returned a general answer, and diverted the conversation to some other topick.

"Amidst this willingness to be pleased, and labour to please, I had always reason to imagine that some painful sentiment pressed upon his mind. He often looked up earnestly towards the sun, and let his voice fall in the midst of his discourse. He would sometimes, when we were alone, gaze upon me in silence with the air of a man who longed to speak what he was yet resolved to suppress. He would sometimes send for me with vehement injunctions of haste, though, when I came to him, he had nothing extraordinary to say. And sometimes, when I was leaving him, would call me back, pause a few moments and then dismiss   30
me.

Chap. [XLI]   The astronomer discovers the cause of his uneasiness

AT last the time came when the secret burst his reserve. We were sitting together last night in the turret of his house, watching the emersion of a satellite of Jupiter. A sudden tempest clouded the sky, and disappointed our observation. We sat a while silent in the dark, and then he addressed himself to me in these words: "Imlac, I have long considered thy friendship as the greatest blessing of of my life. Integrity without knowledge is weak and useless, and knowledge without integrity is dangerous and dreadful. I have found in thee all the qualities requisite for trust, benevolence, experience, and fortitude. I have long discharged an office which I must soon quit at the call of nature, and shall   40
rejoice in the hour of imbecility and pain to devolve it upon thee."

"I thought myself honoured by this testimony, and protested that whatever could conduce to his happiness would add likewise to mine."

"Hear, Imlac, what thou wilt not without difficulty credit. I have possessed for five years the regulation of weather, and the distribution of the seasons: the sun has listened to my dictates, and passed from tropick to tropick by my direction; the clouds, at my call, have poured their waters, and the Nile has overflowed at my command; I have restrained the rage of the dogstar, and mitigated the fervours of the crab. The winds alone, of all the elemental powers, have hitherto refused my authority, and multitudes have perished by equinoctial tempests which I found myself unable to prohibit or restrain. I have administered this great office with exact justice, and made to the different nations of the earth an impartial dividend of rain and sunshine. What must have been the misery of half the globe, if I had limited the clouds to particular regions, or confined the sun to either side of the equator?"

Chap. [XLII]   The astronomer justifies his account of himself

"I SUPPOSE he discovered in me, through the obscurity of the room, some tokens of amazement and doubt, for, after a short pause, he proceeded thus":

"Not to be easily credited will neither surprise nor offend me; for I am, probably, the first of human beings to whom this trust has been imparted. Nor do I know whether to deem this distinction a reward or punishment; since I have possessed it I have been far less happy than before, and nothing but the consciousness of good intention could have enabled me to support the weariness of unremitted vigilance."

"How long, Sir, said I, has this great office been in your hands?"

"About ten years ago, said he, my daily observations of the changes of the sky led me to consider, whether, if I had the power of the seasons, I could confer greater plenty upon the inhabitants of the earth. This contemplation fastened on my mind, and I sat days and nights in imaginary dominion, pouring upon this country and that the showers of fertility, and seconding every fall of rain with a due proportion of sunshine. I had yet only the will to do good, and did not imagine that I should ever have the power.

"One day as I was looking on the fields withering with heat, I felt in my mind a sudden wish that I could send rain on the southern mountains, and raise the Nile to an inundation. In the hurry of my imagination I commanded rain to fall, and, by comparing the time of my command, with that of the inundation, I found that the clouds had listned to my lips."

"Might not some other cause, said I, produce this concurrence? the Nile does not always rise on the same day."

"Do not believe, said he with impatience, that such objections could escape me: I reasoned long against my own conviction, and laboured against truth with the utmost obstinacy. I sometimes suspected myself of madness, and should not have dared to impart this secret but to a man like you, capable of distinguishing the wonderful from the impossible, and the incredible from the false."

"Why, Sir, said I, do you call that incredible, which you know, or think you know, to be true."

"Because, said he, I cannot prove it by any external evidence; and I know too well the laws of demonstration to think that my conviction ought to influence another, who cannot, like me, be conscious of its force. I, therefore, shall not attempt to gain credit by disputation. It is sufficient that I feel this power, that I have long possessed, and every day exerted it. But the life of man is short, the infirmities of age increase upon me, and the time will soon come when the regulator of the year must mingle with the dust. The care of appointing a successor has long disturbed me; the night and the day have been spent in comparisons of all the characters which have come to my knowledge, and I have yet found none so worthy as thyself.

Chap. [XLIII] The astronomer leaves Imlac his directions

"HEAR therefore, what I shall impart, with attention, such as the welfare of a world requires. If the task of a king be considered as difficult, who has the care only of a few millions, to whom he cannot do much good or harm, what must be the anxiety of him, on whom depend the action of the elements, and the great gifts of light and heat!—Hear me therefore with attention.

"I have diligently considered the position of the earth and sun, and formed innumerable schemes in which I changed their situation. I have sometimes turned aside the axis of the earth, and sometimes varied the ecliptick of the sun: but I have found it impossible to make a disposition by which the world may be advantaged; what one region gains, another loses by any imaginable alteration, even without considering the distant parts of the solar system with which we are unacquainted. Do not, therefore, in thy administration of the year, indulge thy pride by innovation; do not please thyself with thinking that thou canst make thyself renowned to all future ages, by disordering the seasons. The memory of mischief is no desirable fame. Much less will it become thee to let kindness or interest prevail. Never rob other countries of rain to pour it on thine own. For us the Nile is sufficient."

"I promised that when I possessed the power, I would use it with inflexible integrity, and he dismissed me, pressing my hand." "My heart, said he, will be now at rest, and my benevolence will no more destroy my quiet: I have found a man of wisdom and virtue, to whom I can chearfully bequeath the inheritance of the sun."

The prince heard this narration with very serious regard, but the princess smiled, and Pekuah convulsed herself with laughter. "Ladies, said Imlac, to mock the heaviest of human afflictions is neither charitable nor wise. Few can attain this man's knowledge, and few practise his virtues; but all may suffer his calamity. Of the uncertainties of our present state, the most dreadful and alarming is the uncertain continuance of reason."

The princess was recollected, and the favourite was abashed. Rasselas, more deeply affected, enquired of Imlac, whether he thought such maladies of the mind frequent, and how they were contracted.

Chap. [XLIV]   The dangerous prevalence of imagination

"DISORDERS of intellect, answered Imlac, happen much more often than superficial observers will easily believe. Perhaps, if we speak with rigorous exactness, no human mind is in its right state. There is no man whose imagination does not sometimes predominate over his reason, who can regulate his attention wholly by his will, and whose ideas will come and go at his command. No man will be found in whose mind airy notions do not sometimes tyrannise, and force him to hope or fear beyond the limits of sober probability. All power   10 of fancy over reason is a degree of insanity; but while this power is such as we can controll and repress, it is not visible to others, nor considered as any depravation of the mental faculties: it is not pronounced madness but when it comes ungovernable, and apparently influences speech or action.

"To indulge the power of fiction, and send imagination out upon the wing, is often the sport of those who delight too much in silent speculation. When we are alone we are not always busy; the labour of excogitation is too violent to last long; the ardour of enquiry will sometimes give way to idleness or satiety. He who has nothing external that can divert him, must find pleasure in his own thoughts, and must conceive himself what he is not; for who is pleased with   20 what he is? He then expatiates in boundless futurity, and culls from all imaginable conditions that which for the present moment he should most desire, amuses his desires with impossible enjoyments, and confers upon his pride unattainable dominion. The mind dances from scene to scene, unites all pleasures in all combinations, and riots in delights which nature and fortune, with all their bounty, cannot bestow.

"In time some particular train of ideas fixes the attention, all other intellectual gratifications are rejected, the mind, in weariness or leisure, recurs constantly to the favourite conception, and feasts on the luscious falsehood whenever she is offended with the bitterness of truth. By degrees the reign of fancy is con-   30 firmed; she grows first imperious, and in time despotick. Then fictions begin to operate as realities, false opinions fasten upon the mind, and life passes in dreams of rapture or of anguish.

"This, Sir, is one of the dangers of solitude, which the hermit has confessed not always to promote goodness, and the astronomer's misery has proved to be not always propitious to wisdom."

"I will no more, said the favourite, imagine myself the queen of Abissinia. I have often spent the hours, which the princess gave to my own disposal, in adjusting ceremonies and regulating the court; I have repressed the pride of the powerful, and granted the petitions of the poor; I have built new palaces in   40 more happy situations, planted groves upon the tops of mountains, and have exulted in the beneficence of royalty, till, when the princess entered, I had almost forgotten to bow down before her."

"And I, said the princess, will not allow myself any more to play the shepherdess in my waking dreams. I have often soothed my thoughts with the quiet and innocence of pastoral employments, till I have in my chamber heard the winds whistle, and the sheep bleat; sometimes freed the lamb entangled in the thicket, and sometimes with my crook encountered the wolf. I have a dress like that of the village maids, which I put on to help my imagination, and a pipe on which I play softly, and suppose myself followed by my flocks."

"I will confess, said the prince, an indulgence of fantastick delight more   10
dangerous than yours. I have frequently endeavoured to image the possibility of a perfect government, by which all wrong should be restrained, all vice reformed, and all the subjects preserved in tranquility and innocence. This thought produced innumerable schemes of reformation, and dictated many useful regulations and salutary edicts. This has been the sport and sometimes the labour of my solitude; and I start, when I think with how little anguish I once supposed the death of my father and my brothers."

"Such, says Imlac, are the effects of visionary schemes: when we first form them we know them to be absurd, but familiarise them by degrees, and in time lose sight of their folly."   20

Chap. [XLV]   They discourse with an old man

THE evening was now far past, and they rose to return home. As they walked along the bank of the Nile, delighted with the beams of the moon quivering on the water, they saw at a small distance an old man, whom the prince had often heard in the assembly of the sages. "Yonder, said he, is one whose years have calmed his passions, but not clouded his reason: let us close the disquisitions of the night, by enquiring what are his sentiments of his own state, that we may know whether youth alone is to struggle with vexation, and whether any better hope remains for the latter part of life."

Here the sage approached and saluted them. They invited him to join their walk, and prattled a while as acquaintance that had unexpectedly met one   30
another. The old man was chearful and talkative, and the way seemed short in his company. He was pleased to find himself not disregarded, accompanied them to their house, and, at the prince's request, entered with them. They placed him in the seat of honour, and set wine and conserves before him.

"Sir, said the princess, an evening walk must give to a man of learning, like you, pleasures which ignorance and youth can hardly conceive. You know the qualities and the causes of all that you behold, the laws by which the river flows, the periods in which the planets perform their revolutions. Every thing must supply you with contemplation, and renew the consciousness of your own dignity."   40

"Lady, answered he, let the gay and the vigorous expect pleasure in their excursions, it is enough that age can obtain ease. To me the world has lost its novelty: I look round, and see what I remember to have seen in happier days.

I rest against a tree, and consider, that in the same shade I once disputed upon the annual overflow of the Nile with a friend who is now silent in the grave. I cast my eyes upwards, fix them on the changing moon, and think with pain on the vicissitudes of life. I have ceased to take much delight in physical truth; for what have I to do with those things which I am soon to leave?"

"You may at least recreate yourself, said Imlac, with the recollection of an honourable and useful life, and enjoy the praise which all agree to give you."

"Praise, said the sage, with a sigh, is to an old man an empty sound. I have neither mother to be delighted with the reputation of her son, nor wife to partake the honours of her husband. I have outlived my friends and my rivals. 10 Nothing is now of much importance; for I cannot extend my interest beyond myself. Youth is delighted with applause, because it is considered as the earnest of some future good, and because the prospect of life is far extended: but to me, who am now declining to decrepitude, there is little to be feared from the malevolence of men, and yet less to be hoped from their affection or esteem. Something they may yet take away, but they can give me nothing. Riches would now be useless, and high employment would be pain. My retrospect of life recalls to my view many opportunities of good neglected, much time squandered upon trifles, and more lost in idleness and vacancy. I leave many great designs unattempted, and many great attempts unfinished. My mind is bur- 20 thened with no heavy crime, and therefore I compose myself to tranquility; endeavour to abstract my thoughts from hopes and cares, which, though reason knows them to be vain, still try to keep their old possession of the heart; expect, with serene humility, that hour which nature cannot long delay; and hope to possess in a better state that happiness which here I could not find, and that virtue which here I have not attained."

He rose and went away, leaving his audience not much elated with the hope of long life. The prince consoled himself with remarking, that it was not reasonable to be disappointed by this account; for age had never been considered as the season of felicity, and, if it was possible to be easy in decline and weak- 30 ness, it was likely that the days of vigour and alacrity might be happy; that the noon of life might be bright, if the evening could be calm.

The princess suspected that age was querulous and malignant, and delighted to repress the expectations of those who had newly entered the world. She had seen the possessors of estates look with envy on their heirs, and known many who enjoy pleasure no longer than they can confine it to themselves.

Pekuah conjectured, that the man was older than he appeared, and was willing to impute his complaints to delirious dejection; or else supposed that he had been unfortunate, and was therefore discontented: "For nothing, said she, is more common than to call our own condition, the condition of life." 40

Imlac, who had no desire to see them depressed, smiled at the comforts which they could so readily procure to themselves, and remembered, that at the same age, he was equally confident of unmingled prosperity, and equally fertile of consolatory expedients. He forbore to force upon them unwelcome knowledge, which time itself would too soon impress. The princess and her lady retired; the madness of the astronomer hung upon their minds, and they desired Imlac to enter upon his office, and delay next morning the rising of the sun.

Chap. [XLVI]   The princess and Pekuah visit the astronomer

THE princess and Pekuah having talked in private of Imlac's astronomer, thought his character at once so amiable and so strange, that they could not be satisfied without a nearer knowledge, and Imlac was requested to find the means of bringing them together.

This was somewhat difficult; the philosopher had never received any visits from women, though he lived in a city that had in it many Europeans who followed the manners of their own countries, and many from other parts of the world that lived there with European liberty. The ladies would not be refused, and several schemes were proposed for the accomplishment of their design. It was proposed to introduce them as strangers in distress, to whom the sage was 10 always accessible; but, after some deliberation, it appeared, that by this artifice, no acquaintance could be formed, for their conversation would be short, and they could not decently importune him often. "This, said Rasselas, is true; but I have yet a stronger objection against the misrepresentation of your state. I have always considered it as treason against the great republick of human nature, to make any man's virtues the means of deceiving him, whether on great or little occasions. All imposture weakens confidence and chills benevolence. When the sage finds that you are not what you seemed, he will feel the resentment natural to a man who, conscious of great abilities, discovers that he has been tricked by understandings meaner than his own, and, perhaps, the dis- 20 trust, which he can never afterwards wholly lay aside, may stop the voice of counsel, and close the hand of charity; and where will you find the power of restoring his benefactions to mankind, or his peace to himself?"

To this no reply was attempted, and Imlac began to hope that their curiosity would subside; but, next day, Pekuah told him, she had now found an honest pretence for a visit to the astronomer, for she would solicit permission to continue under him the studies in which she had been initiated by the Arab, and the princess might go with her either as a fellow-student, or because a woman could not decently come alone. "I am afraid, said Imlac, that he will be soon weary of your company: men advanced far in knowledge do not love to repeat the 30 elements of their art, and I am not certain, that even of the elements, as he will deliver them connected with inferences, and mingled with reflections, you are a very capable auditress." "That, said Pekuah, must be my care: I ask of you only to take me thither. My knowledge is, perhaps, more than you imagine it, and by concurring always with his opinions I shall make him think it greater than it is."

The astronomer, in pursuance of this resolution, was told, that a foreign lady, travelling in search of knowledge, had heard of his reputation, and was desirous to become his scholar. The uncommonness of the proposal raised at once his surprise and curiosity, and when, after a short deliberation, he con- 40 sented to admit her, he could not stay without impatience till the next day.

The ladies dressed themselves magnificently, and were attended by Imlac to the astronomer, who was pleased to see himself approached with respect by persons of so splendid an appearance. In the exchange of the first civilities he was timorous and bashful; but, when the talk became regular, he recollected his powers, and justified the character which Imlac had given. Enquiring of Pekuah what could have turned her inclination towards astronomy, he received from her a history of her adventure at the pyramid, and of the time passed in the Arab's island. She told her tale with ease and elegance, and her conversation took possession of his heart. The discourse was then turned to astronomy: Pekuah displayed what she knew: he looked upon her as a prodigy of genius, and intreated her not to desist from a study which she had so happily begun.

They came again and again, and were every time more welcome than be-   10
fore: The sage endeavoured to amuse them, that they might prolong their visits, for he found his thoughts grow brighter in their company; the clouds of solicitude vanished by degrees, as he forced himself to entertain them, and he grieved when he was left at their departure to his old employment of regulating the seasons.

The princess and her favourite had now watched his lips for several months, and could not catch a single word from which they could judge whether he continued, or not, in the opinion of his preternatural commission. They often contrived to bring him to an open declaration, but he easily eluded all their attacks, and on which side soever they pressed him escaped from them to some   20
other topick.

As their familiarity increased they invited him often to the house of Imlac, where they distinguished him by extraordinary respect. He began gradually to delight in sublunary pleasures. He came early and departed late; laboured to recommend himself by assiduity and compliance; excited their curiosity after new arts, that they might still want his assitance; and when they made any excursion of pleasure or enquiry, entreated to attend them.

By long experience of his integrity and wisdom, the prince and his sister were convinced that he might be trusted without danger; and, lest he should draw any false hopes from the civilities which he received, discovered to him   30
their condition, with the motives of their journey, and required his opinion on the choice of life.

"Of the various conditions which the world spreads before you, which you shall prefer, said the sage, I am not able to instruct you. I can only tell that I have chosen wrong. I have passed my time in study without experience: in the attainment of sciences which can, for the most part, be but remotely useful to mankind. I have purchased knowledge at the expence of all the common comforts of life: I have missed the endearing elegance of female friendship, and the happy commerce of domestick tenderness. If I have obtained any prerogatives above other students, they have been accompanied with fear, disquiet,   40
and scrupulosity; but even of these prerogatives, whatever they were, I have, since my thoughts have been diversified by more intercourse with the world, begun to question the reality. When I have been for a few days lost in pleasing dissipation, I am always tempted to think that my enquiries have ended in errour, and that I have suffered much, and suffered it in vain."

Imlac was delighted to find that the sage's understanding was breaking through its mists, and resolved to detain him from the planets till he should forget his talk of ruling them, and reason should recover its original influence.

From this time the astronomer was received into familiar friendship, and partook of all their projects and pleasures: his respect kept him attentive, and the activity of Rasselas did not leave much time unengaged. Something was always to be done; the day was spent in making observations which furnished talk for the evening, and the evening was closed with a scheme for the morrow.

The sage confessed to Imlac, that since he had mingled in the gay tumults of life, and divided his hours by a succession of amusements, he found the conviction of his authority over the skies fade gradually from his mind, and began to trust less to an opinion which he never could prove to others, and which   10
he now found subject to variation from causes in which reason had no part. "If I am accidentally left alone for a few hours, said he, my inveterate persuasion rushes upon my soul, and my thoughts are chained down by some irresistible violence, but they are soon disentangled by the prince's conversation, and instantaneously released at the entrance of Pekuah. I am like a man habitually afraid of spectres, who is set at ease by a lamp, and wonders at the dread which harrassed him in the dark, yet, if his lamp be extinguished, feels again the terrours which he knows that when it is light he shall feel no more. But I am sometimes afraid lest I indulge my quiet by criminal negligence, and voluntarily forget the great charge with which I am intrusted. If I favour myself in a known   20
errour, or am determined by my own ease in a doubtful question of this importance, how dreadful is my crime!"

"No disease of the imagination, answered Imlac, is so difficult of cure, as that which is complicated with the dread of guilt: fancy and conscience then act interchangeably upon us, and so often shift their places, that the illusions of one are not distinguished from the dictates of the other. If fancy presents images not moral or religious, the mind drives them away when they give it pain, but when melancholick notions take the form of duty, they lay hold on the faculties without opposition, because we are afraid to exclude or banish them. For this reason the superstitious are often melancholy, and the melancholy   30
almost always superstitious.

"But do not let the suggestions of timidity overpower your better reason: the danger of neglect can be but as the probability of the obligation, which, when you consider it with freedom, you find very little, and that little growing every day less. Open your heart to the influence of the light, which, from time to time, breaks in upon you: when scruples importune you, which you in your lucid moments know to be vain, do not stand to parley, but fly to business or to Pekuah, and keep this thought always prevalent, that you are only one atom of the mass of humanity, and have neither such virtue nor vice, as that you should be singled out for supernatural favours or afflictions."   40

Chap. [XLVII]   The prince enters and brings a new topick

"ALL this, said the astronomer, I have often thought, but my reason has been so long subjugated by an uncontrolable and overwhelming idea, that it durst not confide in its own decisions. I now see how fatally I betrayed my quiet, by suffering chimeras to prey upon me in secret; but melancholy shrinks from communication, and I never found a man before, to whom I could impart my troubles, though I had been certain of relief. I rejoice to find my own sentiments confirmed by yours, who are not easily deceived, and can have no motive or purpose to deceive. I hope that time and variety will dissipate the gloom that has so long surrounded me, and the latter part of my days will be spent in peace."

"Your learning and virtue, said Imlac, may justly give you hopes."

Rasselas then entered with the princess and Pekuah, and enquired whether they had contrived any new diversion for the next day. "Such, said Nekayah, is the state of life, that none are happy but by the anticipation of change: the change itself is nothing; when we have made it, the next wish is to change again. The world is not yet exhausted; let me see something to morrow which I never saw before."

"Variety, said Rasselas, is so necessary to content, that even the happy valley disgusted me by the recurrence of its luxuries; yet I could not forbear to reproach myself with impatience, when I saw the monks of St. Anthony support without complaint, a life, not of uniform delight, but uniform hardship."

"Those men, answered Imlac, are less wretched in their silent convent than the Abissinian princes in their prison of pleasure. Whatever is done by the monks is incited by an adequate and reasonable motive. Their labour supplies them with necessaries; it therefore cannot be omitted, and is certainly rewarded. Their devotion prepares them for another state, and reminds them of its approach, while it fits them for it. Their time is regularly distributed; one duty succeeds another, so that they are not left open to the distraction of unguided choice, nor lost in the shades of listless inactivity. There is a certain task to be performed at an appropriated hour; and their toils are cheerful, because they consider them as acts of piety, by which they are always advancing towards endless felicity."

"Do you think, said Nekayah, that the monastick rule is a more holy and less imperfect state than any other? May not he equally hope for future happiness who converses openly with mankind, who succours the distressed by his charity, instructs the ignorant by his learning, and contributes by his industry to the general system of life; even though he should omit some of the mortifications which are practised in the cloister, and allow himself such harmless delights as his condition may place within his reach?"

"This, said Imlac, is a question which has long divided the wise, and perplexed the good. I am afraid to decide on either part. He that lives well in the world is better than he that lives well in a monastery. But, perhaps, every one is not able to stem the temptations of publick life; and, if he cannot conquer, he may properly retreat. Some have little power to do good, and have likewise little strength to resist evil. Many are weary of their conflicts with adversity, and are willing to eject those passions which have long busied them in vain. And many are dismissed by age and diseases from the more laborious duties of society. In monasteries the weak and timorous may be happily sheltered, the weary may repose, and the penitent may meditate. Those retreats of prayer and contemplation have something so congenial to the mind of man, that, perhaps, there is scarcely one that does not purpose to close his life in pious abstraction with a few associates serious as himself."

"Such, said Pekuah, has often been my wish, and I have heard the princess declare, that she should not willingly die in a croud."

"The liberty of using harmless pleasures, proceeded Imlac, will not be disputed; but it is still to be examined what pleasures are harmless. The evil of any pleasure that Nekayah can image is not in the act itself, but in its consequences. Pleasure, in itself harmless, may become mischievous, by endearing to us a state which we know to be transient and probatory, and withdrawing our thoughts 10 from that, of which every hour brings us nearer to the beginning, and of which no length of time will bring us to the end. Mortification is not virtuous in itself, nor has any other use, but that it disengages us from the allurements of sense. In the state of future perfection, to which we all aspire, there will be pleasure without danger, and security without restraint."

The princess was silent, and Rasselas, turning to the astronomer, asked him, whether he could not delay her retreat, by shewing her something which she had not seen before.

"Your curiosity, said the sage, has been so general, and your pursuit of knowledge so vigorous, that novelties are not now very easily to be found: but 20 what you can no longer procure from the living may be given by the dead. Among the wonders of this country are the catacombs, or the ancient repositories, in which the bodies of the earliest generations were lodged, and where, by the virtue of the gums which embalmed them, they yet remain without corruption."

"I know not, said Rasselas, what pleasure the sight of the catacombs can afford; but, since nothing else is offered, I am resolved to view them, and shall place this with many other things which I have done, because I would do something."

They hired a guard of horsemen, and the next day visited the catacombs. 30 When they were about to descend into the sepulchral caves, "Pekuah, said the princess, we are now again invading the habitations of the dead; I know that you will stay behind; let me find you safe when I return." "No, I will not be left, answered Pekuah; I will go down between you and the prince."

They then all descended, and roved with wonder through the labyrinth of subterraneous passages, where the bodies were laid in rows on either side.

Chap. [XLVIII] Imlac discourses on the nature of the soul

"WHAT reason, said the prince, can be given, why the Egyptians should thus expensively preserve those carcasses which some nations consume with fire, others lay to mingle with the earth, and all agree to remove from their sight, as soon as decent rites can be performed?" 40

"The original of ancient customs, said Imlac, is commonly unknown; for the practice often continues when the cause has ceased; and concerning super-stitious ceremonies it is vain to conjecture; for what reason did not dictate reason cannot explain. I have long believed that the practice of embalming arose only from tenderness to the remains of relations or friends, and to this opinion I am more inclined, because it seems impossible that this care should have been general: had all the dead been embalmed, their repositories must in time have been more spacious than the dwellings of the living. I suppose only the rich or honourable were secured from corruption, and the rest left to the course of nature.   10

"But it is commonly supposed that the Egyptians believed the soul to live as long as the body continued undissolved, and therefore tried this method of eluding death."

"Could the wise Egyptians, said Nekayah, think so grosly of the soul? If the soul could once survive its separation, what could it afterwards receive or suffer from the body?

"The Egyptians would doubtless think erroneously, said the astronomer, in the darkness of heathenism, and the first dawn of philosophy. The nature of the soul is still disputed amidst all our opportunities of clearer knowledge: some yet say, that it may be material, who, nevertheless, believe it to be   20 immortal."

"Some, answered Imlac, have indeed said that the soul is material, but I can scarcely believe that any man has thought it, who knew how to think; for all the conclusions of reason enforce the immateriality of the mind, and all the notices of sense and investigations of science concur to prove the unconsciousness of matter.

"It was never supposed that cogitation is inherent in matter, or that every particle is a thinking being. Yet, if any part of matter be devoid of thought, what part can we suppose to think? Matter can differ from matter only in form, density, bulk, motion, and direction of motion: to which of these, however   30 varied or combined, can consciousness be annexed? To be round or square, to be solid or fluid, to be great or little, to be moved slowly or swiftly one way or another, are modes of material existence, all equally alien from the nature of cogitation. If matter be once without thought, it can only be made to think by some new modification, but all the modifications which it can admit are equally unconnected with cogitative powers."

"But the materialists, said the astronomer, urge that matter may have quali-ties with which we are unacquainted."

"He who will determine, returned Imlac, against that which he knows, be-cause there may be something which he knows not; he that can set hypotheticaɬ   40 possibility against acknowledged certainty, is not to be admitted among reason-able beings. All that we know of matter is, that matter is inert, senseless and lifeless; and if this conviction cannot be opposed but by referring us to some-thing that we know not, we have all the evidence that human intellect can admit. If that which is known may be over ruled by that which is unknown, no being, not omniscient, can arrive at certainty."

"Yet let us not, said the astronomer, too arrogantly limit the Creator's power."

"It is no limitation of omnipotence, replied the poet, to suppose that one thing is not consistent with another, that the same proposition cannot be at once true and false, that the same number cannot be even and odd, that cogitation cannot be conferred on that which is created incapable of cogitation."

"I know not, said Nekayah, any great use of this question. Does that immateriality, which, in my opinion, you have sufficiently proved, necessarily include eternal duration?"

"Of immateriality, said Imlac, our ideas are negative, and therefore obscure. 10 Immateriality seems to imply a natural power of perpetual duration as a consequence of exemption from all causes of decay: whatever perishes, is destroyed by the solution of its contexture, and separation of its parts; nor can we conceive how that which has no parts, and therefore admits no solution, can be naturally corrupted or impaired."

"I know not, said Rasselas, how to conceive any thing without extension: what is extended must have parts, and you allow, that whatever has parts may be destroyed."

"Consider your own conceptions, replied Imlac, and the difficulty will be less. You will find substance without extension. An ideal form is no less real 20 than material bulk: yet an ideal form has no extension. It is no less certain, when you think on a pyramid, that your mind possesses the idea of a pyramid, than that the pyramid itself is standing. What space does the idea of a pyramid occupy more than the idea of a grain of corn? or how can either idea suffer laceration? As is the effect such is the cause; as thought is, such is the power that thinks; a power impassive and indiscerpible."[7]

"But the Being, said Nekayah, whom I fear to name, the Being which made the soul, can destroy it."

"He, surely, can destroy it, answered Imlac, since, however unperishable in itself, it receives from a higher nature its power of duration. That it will not per- 30 ish by any inherent cause or principle of corruption, may be collected from philosophy; but philosophy can tell no more. That it will not be annihilated by him that made it, we must humbly learn from higher authority."

The whole assembly stood a while silent and collected. "Let us return, said Rasselas, from this scene of mortality. How gloomy would be these mansions of the dead to him who did not know that he shall never die; that what now acts shall continue its agency, and what now thinks shall think on for ever. Those that lie here stretched before us, the wise and the powerful of antient times, warn us to remember the shortness of our present state: they were, perhaps, snatched away while they were busy, like us, in the choice of life." 40

"To me, said the princess, the choice of life is become less important; I hope hereafter to think only on the choice of eternity."

They then hastened out of the caverns, and, under the protection of their guard, returned to Cairo.

[7] *Indiscerpible:* Incapable of being divided into parts.

Chap. [XLIX]   The conclusion, in which nothing is concluded

IT was now the time of the inundation of the Nile: a few days after their visit to the catacombs, the river began to rise.

They were confined to their house. The whole region being under water gave them no invitation to any excursions, and, being well supplied with materials for talk, they diverted themselves with comparisons of the different forms of life which they had observed, and with various schemes of happiness which each of them had formed.

Pekuah was never so much charmed with any place as the convent of St. Anthony, where the Arab restored her to the princess, and wished only to fill it with pious maidens, and to be made prioress of the order: she was weary of   10 expectation and disgust, and would gladly be fixed in some unvariable state.

The princess thought, that of all sublunary things, knowledge was the best: She desired first to learn all sciences, and then purposed to found a college of learned women, in which she would preside, that, by conversing with the old, and educating the young, she might divide her time between the acquisition and communication of wisdom, and raise up for the next age models of prudence, and patterns of piety.

The prince desired a little kingdom, in which he might administer justice in his own person, and see all the parts of government with his own eyes; but he could never fix the limits of his dominion, and was always adding to the number   20 of his subjects.

Imlac and the astronomer were contented to be driven along the stream of life without directing their course to any particular port.

Of these wishes that they had formed they well knew that none could be obtained. They deliberated a while what was to be done, and resolved, when the inundation should cease, to return to Abissinia.

(1759)

Headnote to
Johnson's LIFE OF GRAY

In his final work, *Lives of the English Poets* (1779–1781), Johnson was able to return to the kind of literature he loved most—biography. Earlier, he had written the *Life of Savage* (1744) and numerous lives for *The Gentleman's Magazine*, so that he was already practiced in biography, to which he devoted his literary efforts between his sixty-eighth and his seventy-second years, when he composed the "little Lives and little Prefaces to a little edition of the English Poets" (Boswell, *Life*, Hill-Powell, III, p. 109). The fifty-two "little" lives, which Johnson promised to a group of publishers who were planning an edition of English poetry, grew and grew as he became more and more involved in his task, and in the end (despite several obviously perfunctory biographies) his work filled several volumes.

Johnson did not often undertake a laborious research in order to do his work. Instead, he drew usually on his extraordinarily well-stored mind both for information, often acquired much earlier, and for judgments about the psychology and the poetry of his subject. Occasionally he made errors of fact; and posterity has decided that he was sometimes wrong in his critical views, most notably about Milton and, many believe, in his observations upon Gray's poetry. But it would be difficult to imagine a greater concentration of clear and vigorous, yet balanced, judgments about poetry, or more graphic and penetrating reconstructions of human action than Johnson's in the *Lives of the English Poets*.

TEXT. *The Lives of the Most Eminent English Poets* (4 vols., London, 1781).

The Life of Gray

THOMAS GRAY, the son of Mr. Philip Gray, a scrivener[1] of London, was born in Cornhill, November 26, 1716. His grammatical education he received at Eaton under Mr. Antrobus, his mother's brother; and when he left school, in 1734, entered a pensioner[2] at Peterhouse in Cambridge.

The transition from the school to the college is, to most young scholars, the time from which they date their years of manhood, liberty, and happiness; but Gray seems to have been very little delighted with academical gratifications; he liked at Cambridge neither the mode of life nor the fashion of study, and lived sullenly on to the time when his attendance on lectures was no longer required. As he intended to profess the Common Law, he took no degree.   10

When he had been at Cambridge about five years, Mr. Horace Walpole,[3] whose friendship he had gained at Eaton, invited him to travel with him as his companion. They wandered through France into Italy; and Gray's Letters contain a very pleasing account of many parts of their journey. But unequal friendships are easily dissolved: at Florence they quarrelled, and parted; and Mr. Walpole is now content to have it told that it was by his fault. If we look however without prejudice on the world, we shall find that men, whose consciousness of their own merit sets them above the compliances of servility, are apt enough in their association with superiors to watch their own dignity with troublesome and punctilious jealousy, and in the fervour of independance   20 to exact that attention which they refuse to pay. Part they did, whatever was the quarrel, and the rest of their travels was doubtless more unpleasant to them both. Gray continued his journey in a manner suitable to his own little fortune, with only an occasional servant.

He returned to England in September 1741, and in about two months afterwards buried his father; who had, by an injudicious waste of money upon a new house, so much lessened his fortune, that Gray thought himself too poor to study the law. He therefore retired to Cambridge, where he soon after became Bachelor of Civil Law; and where, without liking the place or its inhabitants, or pretending to like them, he passed, except a short residence at London,   30 the rest of his life.

About this time he was deprived of Mr. West,[4] the son of a chancellor of Ireland, a friend on whom he appears to have set a high value, and who deserved his esteem by the powers which he shews in his Letters, and in the Ode to

---

[1] *Scrivener:* A notary; a manager of private funds for a fee; one empowered to prepare certain legal documents.

[2] *Pensioner:* At Cambridge, an undergraduate who is not on the foundation of a college, but pays for his own provisions.

[3] *Horace Walpole:* Horace, Fourth Earl of Orford (1717–1797), author of the well-known Gothic novel *The Castle of Otranto*, the publisher of some of Gray's poetry at Strawberry-Hill, Walpole's "gothicized" pseudo-castle, and indefatigable letter-writer.

[4] *West:* Richard West (1716–1743), a poet.

May, which Mr. Mason[5] has preserved, as well as by the sincerity with which, when Gray sent him part of *Agrippina*, a tragedy that he had just begun, he gave an opinion which probably intercepted the progress of the work, and which the judgement of every reader will confirm. It was certainly no loss to the English stage that *Agrippina* was never finished.

In this year (1742) Gray seems first to have applied himself seriously to poetry; for in this year were produced the *Ode to Spring*, his *Prospect of Eaton*, and his *Ode to Adversity*. He began likewise a Latin poem, *de Principiis cogitandi*.

It seems to be the opinion of Mr. Mason, that his first ambition was to have excelled in Latin poetry: perhaps it were reasonable to wish that he had prose-   10
cuted his design; for though there is at present some embarrassment in his phrase, and some harshness in his Lyrick numbers, his copiousness of language is such as very few possess; and his lines, even when imperfect, discover a writer whom practice would quickly have made skilful.

He now lived on at Peterhouse, very little solicitous what others did or thought, and cultivated his mind and enlarged his views without any other purpose than of improving and amusing himself; when Mr. Mason, being elected fellow of Pembroke-hall, brought him a companion who was afterwards to be his editor, and whose fondness and fidelity has kindled in him a zeal of admiration, which cannot be reasonably expected from the neutrality of a   20
stranger and the coldness of a critick.

In this retirement he wrote (1747) an ode on the *Death of Mr. Walpole's Cat*; and the year afterwards attempted a poem of more importance, on *Government and Education*, of which the fragments which remain have many excellent lines.

His next production (1750) was his far-famed *Elegy in the Church-yard*, which, finding its way into a Magazine, first, I believe, made him known to the publick.

An invitation from lady Cobham[6] about this time gave occasion to an odd composition called *a Long Story*, which, though perhaps it adds little to Gray's character, was inserted at the end of my preface to the late Collection.   30

Several of his pieces were published (1753), with designs, by Mr. Bentley; and, that they might in some form or other make a book, only one side of each leaf was printed. I believe the poems and the plates recommended each other so well, that the whole impression was soon bought. This year he lost his mother.

Some time afterwards (1756) some young men of the college, whose chambers were near his, diverted themselves with disturbing him by frequent and troublesome noises. This insolence, having endured it a while, he represented to the governors of the society, among whom perhaps he had no friends; and, finding his complaint little regarded, removed himself to Pembroke-hall.   40

In 1757 he published *The Progress of Poetry* and *The Bard*, two compositions at which the readers of poetry were at first content, to gaze in mute amazement. Some that tried them confessed their inability to understand them, though

---

[5] *Mason:* The Reverend William Mason (1724–1797), a minor poet and playwright, and Gray's executor-editor. His *Memoirs of Gray*, from which Johnson derives information, below, appeared in 1775.

[6] *Cobham:* The widowed Lady Cobham was Gray's neighbor at Stoke Poges.

Warburton[7] said that they were understood as well as the works of Milton and Shakspeare, which it is the fashion to praise. Garrick[8] wrote a few lines in their praise. Some hardy champions undertook to rescue them from neglect, and in a short time many were content to be shewn beauties which they could not see.

Gray's reputation was now so high, that, after the death of Cibber,[9] he had the honour of refusing the laurel, which was then bestowed on Mr. Whitehead.[10]

His curiosity, not long after, drew him away from Cambridge to a lodging near the Museum,[11] where he resided near three years, reading and transcribing; and, so far as can be discovered, very little affected by two odes on *Oblivion*   10 and *Obscurity*, in which his Lyrick performances were ridiculed with much contempt and much ingenuity.

When the Professor of Modern Languages at Cambridge died, he was, as he says, *cockered and spirited up*, till he asked it of lord Bute,[12] who sent him a civil refusal; and the place was given to Mr. Brocket, the tutor of Sir James Lowther.[13]

His constitution was weak, and believing that his health was promoted by exercise and change of place, he undertook (1765) a journey into Scotland, of which his account, so far as it extends, is very curious and elegant; for as his comprehension was ample, his curiosity extended to all the works of art, all   20 the appearances of nature, and all the monuments of past events. He naturally contracted a friendship with Dr. Beattie,[14] whom he found a poet, a philosopher, and a good man. The Mareschal College at Aberdeen offered him the degree of Doctor of Laws, which, having omitted to take it at Cambridge, he thought it decent to refuse.

What he had formerly solicited in vain, was at last given him without solicitation. The Professorship of Languages became again vacant, and he received (1768) an offer of it from the duke of Grafton.[15] He accepted, and retained it to his death; always designing lectures, but never reading them; uneasy at his neglect of duty, and appeasing his uneasiness with designs of reformation,   30 and with a resolution which he believed himself to have made of resigning the office, if he found himself unable to discharge it.

Ill health made another journey necessary, and he visited (1769) Westmoreland and Cumberland. He that reads his epistolary narration wishes, that to

[7] *Warburton:* William Warburton (1698–1779), English divine, friend of Pope and the editor of his works, critic.

[8] *Garrick:* David Garrick (1717–1779), English actor and manager (the greatest actor of the age), and once Johnson's student at Edial.

[9] *Cibber:* Colley Cibber (1671–1757), actor, manager, and dramatist. In 1730, he was appointed poet-laureate.

[10] *Whitehead:* William Whitehead (1715–1785), a Cambridge baker's son who was educated there, becoming a fellow in 1742. He was made poet-laureate in 1757, on Cibber's death.

[11] *Museum:* The British Museum in London, opened in 1759; it is the repository of treasures in literature, science, and art.

[12] *Lord Bute:* John Stuart, Third Earl of Bute (1713–1792), during the 1760's, the most influential British minister.

[13] *James Lowther:* James, First Earl of Lonsdale (1736–1802), politically influential, particularly in the North; he is best known in literary history for his arbitrary control of William Wordsworth's inheritance.

[14] *Dr. Beattie:* James Beattie (1735–1803), Scottish poet and essayist.

[15] *Grafton:* Augustus Henry Fitzroy, Third Duke of Grafton (1735–1811), English statesman, a descendant of Charles II and Bute's opponent.

travel, and to tell his travels, had been more of his employment; but it is by studying at home that we must obtain the ability of travelling with intelligence and improvement.

His travels and his studies were now near their end. The gout, of which he had sustained many weak attacks, fell upon his stomach, and, yielding to no medicines, produced strong convulsions, which (July 30, 1771) terminated in death.

His character I am willing to adopt, as Mr. Mason has done, from a nameless writer;[16] and am as willing as his warmest friend to believe it true.

> "Perhaps he was the most learned man in Europe. He was equally   10
> acquainted with the elegant and profound parts of science, and that not superficially but thoroughly. He knew every branch of history, both natural and civil; had read all the original historians of England, France, and Italy; and was a great antiquarian. Criticism, metaphysics, morals, politics, made a principal part of his study; voyages and travels of all sorts were his favourite amusements; and he had a fine taste in painting, prints, architecture, and gardening. With such a fund of knowledge, his conversation must have been equally intructing and entertaining; but he was also a good man, a man of virtue and humanity. There is no character without some speck, some imperfection; and I think the greatest defect in his was an   20
> affectation in delicacy, or rather effeminacy, and a visible fastidiousness, or contempt and disdain of his inferiors in science. He also had, in some degree, that weakness which disgusted Voltaire so much in Mr. Congreve: though he seemed to value others chiefly according to the progress they had made in knowledge, yet he could not bear to be considered himself merely as a man of letters; and though without birth, or fortune, or station, his desire was to be looked upon as a private independent gentleman, who read for his amusement. Perhaps it may be said, What signifies so much knowledge, when it produced so little? Is it worth taking so much pains to leave no memorial but a few poems? But let it be considered that Mr. Gray was,   30
> to others, at least innocently employed; to himself, certainly beneficially. His time passed agreeably; he was every day making some new acquisition in science; his mind was enlarged, his heart softened, his virtue strengthened; the world and mankind were shewn to him without a mask; and he was taught to consider every thing as trifling, and unworthy of the attention of a wise man, except the pursuit of knowledge and practice of virtue, in that state wherein God hath placed us."

To this character Mr. Mason has added a more particular account of Gray's skill in zoology. He has remarked, that Gray's effeminacy was affected most *before those whom he did not wish to please*; and that he is unjustly charged with   40
making knowledge his sole reason of preference, as he paid his esteem to none whom he did not likewise believe to be good.

What has occurred to me, from the slight inspection of his Letters in which my undertaking has engaged me, is, that his mind had a large grasp; that his

---

[16] *Nameless writer:* Later editions say, "as Mr. Mason has done, from a letter written to my friend Mr. Boswell, by the Rev. Mr. Temple, rector of St. Gluvias in Cornwall; and am as willing. . . ."

curiosity was unlimited, and his judgement cultivated; that he was a man likely to love much where he loved at all, but that he was fastidious and hard to please. His contempt however is often employed, where I hope it will be approved, upon scepticism and infidelity. His short account of Shaftesbury[17] I will insert.

"You say you cannot conceive how lord Shaftesbury came to be a philosopher in vogue; I will tell you: first, he was a lord; secondly, he was as vain as any of his readers; thirdly, men are very prone to believe what they do not understand; fourthly, they will believe any thing at all, provided they are under no obligation to believe it; fifthly, they love to take a new road, even when that road leads no where; sixthly, he was reckoned a fine writer, and seems always to mean more than he said. Would you have any more reasons? An interval of above forty years has pretty well destroyed the charm. A dead lord ranks with commoners: vanity is no longer interested in the matter; for a new road is become an old one."[18]

Mr. Mason has added, from his own knowledge, that though Gray was poor, he was not eager of money; and that, out of the little that he had, he was very willing to help the necessitous.

As a writer he had this peculiarity, that he did not write his pieces first rudely, and then correct them, but laboured every line as it arose in the train of composition; and he had a notion not very peculiar, that he could not write but at certain times, or at happy moments; a fantastick foppery, to which my kindness for a man of learning and of virtue wishes him to have been superior.[19]

GRAY's Poetry is now to be considered; and I hope not to be looked on as an enemy to his name, if I confess that I contemplate it with less pleasure than his life.

His ode on *Spring* has something poetical, both in the language and the thought; but the language is too luxuriant, and the thoughts have nothing new. There has of late arisen a practice of giving to adjectives, derived from substantives, the termination of participles; such as the *cultured* plain, the *dasied* bank; but I was sorry to see, in the lines of a scholar like Gray, the *honied* Spring. The morality is natural, but too stale; the conclusion is pretty.

The poem on the *Cat* was doubtless by its author considered as a trifle, but it is not a happy trifle. In the first stanza *the azure flowers* that *blow*, shew resolutely a rhyme is sometimes made when it cannot easily be found. *Selima*, the *Cat*, is called a nymph, with some violence both to language and sense; but there is good use made of it when it is done; for of the two lines,

> What female heart can gold despise?
> What cat's averse to fish?

the first relates merely to the nymph, and the second only to the cat. The sixth

[17] *Shaftesbury:* Anthony Ashley Cooper, Third Earl of Shaftesbury (1671–1713), whose *Characteristics of Men, Manners, Opinions, Times* (1711) had a strong influence in England and on the continent.

[18] . . . *An old one:* The quotation is from Gray's letter to Stonehewer, August 18, 1758.

[19] . . . *Been superior:* Johnson had other views than Gray about the inspiration to composition. Boswell, *Life*, Hill-Powell, III, p. 19: ". . . nothing excites a man to write but necessity."

stanza contains a melancholy truth, that *a favourite has no friend*; but the last ends in a pointed sentence of no relation to the purpose; if *what glistered* had been *gold*, the cat would not have gone into the water; and, if she had, would not less have been drowned.

The *Prospect of Eaton College* suggests nothing to Gray, which every beholder does not equally think and feel. His supplication to father *Thames*, to tell him who drives the hoop or tosses the ball, is useless and puerile. Father *Thames* has no better means of knowing than himself. His epithet *buxom health* is not elegant; he seems not to understand the word. Gray thought his language more poetical as it was more remote from common use: finding in Dryden *honey redolent of Spring*, an expression that reaches the utmost limits of our language, Gray drove it a little more beyond common apprehension, by making *gales* to be *redolent of joy and youth*.

Of the *Ode on Adversity*, the hint was at first taken from *O Diva, gratum quæ regis Antium*;[20] but Gray has excelled his original by the variety of his sentiments, and by their moral application. Of this piece, at once poetical and rational, I will not by slight objections violate the dignity.

My process has now brought me to the *wonderful Wonder of Wonders*, the two Sister Odes; by which, though either vulgar ignorance or common sense at first universally rejected them, many have been since persuaded to think themselves delighted. I am one of those that are willing to be pleased, and therefore would gladly find the meaning of the first stanza of the *Progress of Poetry*.

Gray seems in his rapture to confound the images of *spreading sound* and *running water*. A *stream of musick* may be allowed; but where does *Musick*, however *smooth and strong*, after having visited the *verdant vales, rowl down the the steep amain*, so as that *rocks and nodding groves rebellow to the roar*? If this be said of *Musick*, it is nonsense; if it be said of *Water*, it is nothing to the purpose.

The second stanza, exhibiting Mars's car and Jove's eagle, is unworthy of further notice. Criticism disdains to chase a school-boy to his common places.

To the third it may likewise be objected, that it is drawn from Mythology, though such as may be more easily assimilated to real life. Idalia's *velvet-green* has something of cant. An epithet or metaphor drawn from Nature ennobles Art; an epithet or metaphor drawn from Art degrades Nature. Gray is too fond of words arbitrarily compounded. *Many-twinkling* was formerly censured as not analogical; we may say *many-spotted*, but scarcely *many-spotting*. This stanza, however, has something pleasing.

Of the second ternary of stanzas, the first endeavours to tell something, and would have told it, had it not been crossed by Hyperion:[21] the second describes well enough the universal prevalence of Poetry; but I am afraid that the conclusion will not rise from the premises. The caverns of the North and the plains of Chili are not the residences of *Glory* and *generous Shame*. But that Poetry and Virtue go always together is an opinion so pleasing, that I can forgive him who resolves to think it true.

---

[20] *O Diva . . . Antium:* Horace, *Odes* I, xxxv, 1; the first line, "O goddess that rules pleasing Antium," merely identifies this ode to Fortuna.

[21] *Hyperion:* See *Progress of Poesy*, l. 53, below.

The third stanza sounds big with *Delphi*, and *Egean*, and *Ilissus*, and *Meander*, and *hallowed fountain* and *solemn sound*; but in all Gray's odes there is a kind of cumbrous splendor which we wish away. His position is at last false: in the time of Dante and Petrarch, from whom he derives our first school of Poetry, Italy was over-run by *tyrant power* and *coward vice*; nor was our state much better when we first borrowed the Italian arts.

Of the third ternary, the first gives a mythological birth of Shakspeare. What is said of that mighty genius is true; but it is not said happily: the real effects of this poetical power are put out of sight by the pomp of machinery. Where truth is sufficient to fill the mind, fiction is worse than useless; the counterfeit debases the genuine.

His account of Milton's blindness, if we suppose it caused by study in the formation of his poem, a supposition surely allowable, is poetically true, and happily imagined. But the *car* of Dryden, with his *two coursers*, has nothing in it peculiar; it is a car in which any other rider may be placed.

The Bard appears, at the first view, to be, as Algarotti[22] and others have re-marked, an imitation of the prophecy of Nereus.[23] Algarotti thinks it superior to its original; and, if preference depends only on the imagery and animation of the two poems, his judgement is right. There is in *The Bard* more force, more thought, and more variety. But to copy is less than to invent, and the copy has been unhappily produced at a wrong time. The fiction of Horace was to the Romans credible; but its revival disgusts us with apparent and unconquer-able falsehood. *Incredulus odi.*[24]

To select a singular event, and swell it to a giant's bulk by fabulous append-ages of spectres and predictions, has little difficulty, for he that forsakes the probable may always find the marvellous. And it has little use; we are affected only as we believe; we are improved only as we find something to be imitated or declined. I do not see that *The Bard* promotes any truth, moral or political.

His stanzas are too long, especially his epodes; the ode is finished before the ear has learned its measures, and consequently before it can receive pleasure from their consonance and recurrence.

Of the first stanza the abrupt beginning has been celebrated; but technical beauties can give praise only to the inventor. It is in the power of any man to rush abruptly upon his subject, that has read the ballad of *Johnny Armstrong,*

Is there ever a man in all Scotland—

The initial resemblances, or alliterations, *ruin, ruthless, helm nor hauberk,* are below the grandeur of a poem that endeavours at sublimity.

In the second stanza the *Bard* is well described; but in the third we have the puerilities of obsolete mythology. When we are told that *Cadwallo hush'd the stormy main,* and that *Modred* made *huge Plinlimmon bow his cloud-top'd head,* attention recoils from the repetition of a tale that, even when it was first heard, was heard with scorn.

The *weaving* of the *winding sheet* he borrowed, as he owns, from the nor-

[22] *Algarotti:* Francesco Algarotti (1712–1764), Italian author and critic.
[23] *Nereus:* Horace, *Odes,* I, xv.

[24] *Incredulus odi:* Incredulous, I hate it. Horace, *Ars Poetica,* l. 188.

thern Bards; but their texture, however, was very properly the work of female powers, as the art of spinning the thread of life in another mythology. Theft is always dangerous; Gray has made weavers of his slaughtered bards, by a fiction outrageous and incongruous. They are then called upon to *Weave the warp and weave the woof*, perhaps with no great propriety; for it is by crossing the *woof* with the *warp* that men *weave* the *web* or piece; and the first line was dearly bought by the admission of its wretched correspondent, *Give ample room and verge enough*. He has, however, no other line as bad.

The third stanza of the second ternary is commended, I think, beyond its merit. The personification is indistinct. *Thirst* and *Hunger* are not alike; and their features, to make the imagery perfect, should have been discriminated. We are told, in the same stanza, how *towers* are *fed*. But I will no longer look for particular faults; yet let it be observed that the ode might have been concluded with an action of better example; but suicide is always to be had, without expence of thought.

These odes are marked by glittering accumulations of ungraceful ornaments; they strike, rather than please; the images are magnified by affectation; the language is laboured into harshness. The mind of the writer seems to work with unnatural violence. *Double, double, toil and trouble*. He has a kind of strutting dignity, and is tall by walking on tiptoe. His art and his struggle are too visible, and there is too little appearance of ease or nature.

To say that he has no beauties, would be unjust: a man like him, of great learning and great industry, could not but produce something valuable. When he pleases least, it can only be said that a good design was ill directed.

His translations of Northern and Welsh Poetry deserve praise; the imagery is preserved, perhaps often improved; but the language is unlike the language of other poets.

In the character of his Elegy I rejoice to concur with the common reader; for by the common sense of readers uncorrupted with literary prejudices, after all the refinements of subtilty and the dogmatism of learning, must be finally decided all claim to poetical honours. The *Church-yard* abounds with images which find a mirrour in every mind, and with sentiments to which every bosom returns an echo. The four stanzas beginning *Yet even these bones*, are to me original: I have never seen the notions in any other place; yet he that reads them here, persuades himself that he has always felt them. Had Gray written often thus, it had been vain to blame, and useless to praise him.

(1781)

On the Death of Dr. Robert Levet[*]

CONDEMN'D to hope's delusive mine,
  As on we toil from day to day,
By sudden blasts, or slow decline,
  Our social comforts drop away.

Well tried through many a varying year,   5
  See LEVET to the grave descend;
Officious, innocent, sincere,
  Of ev'ry friendless name the friend.

Yet still he fills affection's eye,
  Obscurely wise, and coarsely kind;   10
Nor, letter'd arrogance, deny
  Thy praise to merit unrefin'd.

When fainting nature call'd for aid,
  And hov'ring death prepar'd the blow,
His vig'rous remedy display'd   15
  The power of art without the show.

In misery's darkest cavern known,
  His useful care was ever nigh,
Where hopeless anguish pour'd his groan,
  And lonely want retir'd to die.   20

No summons mock'd by chill delay,
  No petty gain disdain'd by pride,

* Levet: On January 17, 1782, Robert Levet, for decades Johnson's friend, left this world "by an instantaneous death." In one of his memorandum books, Johnson wrote, in part, "May God have mercy on him. May God have mercy on me." Levet, though less than formally trained as a physician, was apparently a competent (and a conscientious) man of medicine. Boswell, *Life*, Hill-Powell, I, p. 243, records that when "... Levet lived with Johnson, 'much of the day was employed in attendance on his patients, who were chiefly of the lowest rank of tradesman. The remainder of his hours he dedicated to Hunter's lectures, and to as many different opportunities of improvement as he could meet with on the same gratuitous conditions. "All his medical knowledge (said Johnson), and it was not inconsiderable, was obtained through the ear. Though he buys books, he seldom looks into them, or discovers any power by which he can be supposed to judge of an author's merit." ' " On p. 244 of Boswell's *Life*, Mme. D'Arblay is quoted as observing: "Whoever called on Johnson about midday, found him and Levet at breakfast, Johnson in dishabille, as just risen from bed, and Levet filling out tea for himself and his patron alternately, no conversation passing between them."

7. *Officious:* Doing, or ready to do, kind offices; obliging.

The modest wants of ev'ry day
   The toil of ev'ry day supplied.

His virtues walk'd their narrow round,   25
   Nor made a pause, nor left a void;
And sure th' Eternal Master found
   The single talent well employ'd.

The busy day, the peaceful night,
   Unfelt, uncounted, glided by;   30
His frame was firm, his powers were bright,
   Tho' now his eightieth year was nigh.

Then with no throbbing fiery pain,
   No cold gradations of decay,
Death broke at once the vital chain,   35
   And free'd his soul the nearest way.

   (1783)

Thomas Gray

1716-1771

Gray was born December 26, 1716, to Dorothy Antrobus Gray and Philip Gray, a London money-broker. He was sent to Eton at his mother's expense (his parents had been separated); his maternal uncle was a tutor there. It was at Eton that Gray developed friendships with Horace Walpole, Richard West, and Thomas Ashton. In 1734, he entered Peterhouse, Cambridge, but left before taking a degree. In 1739, he began the grand tour of the Continent with Walpole, but the friends quarreled and Gray returned to England alone. The two were reconciled in 1745, after which Walpole published some of Gray's work at his Strawberry Hill press.

After his return to England, Gray resided for some time at Stoke Poges, where his mother had retired with her two sisters. (The place was to become famous as the setting of his *Elegy Written in a Country Churchyard*.) In 1742, he took up residence at Peterhouse and took his LL.B.; later he moved to Pembroke College. In this year he wrote *Ode on the Spring*, *Ode on a Distant Prospect of Eton College*, and *Hymn to Adversity*, but the poems did not appear in print until some years later. Also begun at Stoke Poges was the *Elegy*, which Gray sent to Walpole at Strawberry Hill, where it was printed in 1751. The poem gained immediate fame for its author. In 1757, Walpole published the two pindarics, *The Progress of Poesy* and *The Bard*, which were given an uneven reception.

Gray spent the last years of his life in study and travel. He became a Professor of History and Modern Languages at Cambridge. On July 30, 1771, he died; he was buried at Stoke Poges beside his mother.

Thomas Gray—Selective Bibliography

Clark S. Northrup, *A Bibliography of Thomas Gray*, New Haven, Yale U. P., 1917.

H. W. Starr, *A Bibliography of Thomas Gray, 1917–1951*, Philadelphia, U. of Pennsylvania Press, 1953; supplements Northrup. See also *CBEL*, II, pp. 333 f.

———— and J. R. Hendrickson, eds., *The Complete Poems of Thomas Gray*, Oxford, Clarendon Press, 1966.

Paget Toynbee and Leonard Whibley, eds., *The Correspondence of Thomas Gray*, 3 vols., Oxford, Clarendon Press, 1935.

R. W. Ketton-Cremer, *Thomas Gray, A Biography*, Cambridge U. P., 1955.

Lord David Cecil, *Two Quiet Lives: Dorothy Osborne, Thomas Gray*, Indianapolis, New York, Bobbs-Merrill; London, Constable, 1948.

W. P. Jones, *Thomas Gray, Scholar*, Cambridge, Mass., Harvard U. P., 1937; New York, Russell and Russell, 1966.

H. W. Starr, *Gray as a Literary Critic*, Philadelphia, U. of Pennsylvania, privately printed, 1941.

Patricia M. Spacks, "Statement and Artifice in Thomas Gray," *SEL*, V (1965), 519–532.

Headnote to
GRAY'S POETRY

Gray lived the life of an active scholar, more or less retired from ordinary affairs. He was always an acute and sensitive observer, who regularly recorded his impressions. Only seldom, however, did he feel moved to compose poetry, which for him, perhaps to a greater extent than for poets generally, involved much more than writing down one's ideas and feelings, no matter how compelling they might seem to be. His few poems suggest a knowledge born of a long-lived consideration of his subject, as well as detachment sufficient to make the poems non-personal despite deep feeling. Several fairly obvious characteristics contribute to this general effect. Gray's choice of genres was typically classical, though by no means exhaustive—lesser ode, elegy, Pindaric. Besides, he was such a master of these literary kinds that (with one or two possible exceptions) his poems seem to achieve an independence of their creator impossible in the works of a lesser classicist. Finally, his use of personification and his many universally applicable judgments help to free his works from the bondage of personality. On the few occasions when Gray has been thought to be an obtrusive force in his own poems, the charge has been not that he drew too immediately on personal feeling, but that he faltered in his control of the neoclassical devices of which he usually made such good use. But even under such circumstances one glimpses the artist straining, and not the man on parade.

The subjects of Gray's poems reflect the widening taste regarded by many men of the mid-century as appropriate to neoclassical poetry. In their verse, the new poets treated external nature, various sources of profound or unusual thoughts and feelings, or a particularly noble or a particularly inspired bygone day to which Englishmen might some-how feel themselves related. Some of these poets professed to be departing from current norms of composition they thought moribund. Yet their work was clearly classical in dozens of features apparently beyond the conscious control of the author. Others, like Gray, thought the new subject matter well within the classical range. His "Elegy Written in a Country Churchyard" illustrates the poet's practice in this regard. Though the poem draws upon details of external nature for its setting and makes at least a momentary use of certain personal responses of the narrator—"And leaves the world to darkness and to me"—it remains generally a classical composition, largely because of its diction, its personifications, and its stately commonplaces of human experience, understood but not emotionally exploited in any remarkable degree. The subject of the poem is similarly generalized; it is not about a particular man, but about every average and obscure man.

Gray's earlier "Ode on the Death of a Favourite Cat" and "Ode on a Distant Prospect of Eton College" are more obviously classical. It was the death of Horace Walpole's cat Selima that provided the poet with the occasion for the very successful little mock-heroic piece. The "Eton Ode" is a contemplative poem that makes good use of such representative eighteenth-century devices as apostrophes and personifications, as it ostensibly considers life at Eton. The movement of the composition is actually controlled by the emotions of the narrator, already refined to thought; he elucidates his pessimistic view of the world by regarding Eton's spires and towers, whose beauty almost restores for a moment the illusions of his youth. It also reminds him of the pain of life and its ultimate end, death. The details of his own past are in a sense particularized; and yet they are made suitably impersonal because they are not explicitly presented, only suggested through the lives of Eton's present students.

After Gray finished his great "Elegy," he produced two Pindaric odes, both rigorously correct. (See the headnote to Dryden's odes.) But these poems—"The Progress of Poesy" and "The Bard"—had a force unusual in the century, however truly like Pindar's they might be. The first reflects Gray's study of Pindar and Lysias, the Attic orator of the fifth century B.C.; the second, his exploration of Welsh poetry. Though he thought them his best work, some of his contemporaries found them obscure. In his life of the poet, Johnson refers to them as ". . . . two compositions at which the readers of poetry were at first content to gaze in mute amazement," and later he concludes a fairly detailed criticism by observing:

> These odes are marked by glittering accumulations of ungraceful ornaments: they strike rather than please; the images are magnified by affectation; the language is laboured into harshness. The mind of the writer seems to work with unnatural violence. "Double, double, toil and trouble". He has a kind of strutting dignity, and is tall by walking on tiptoe. His art and his struggle are too visible, and there is too little appearance of ease and nature.

Each reader must decide for himself, of course, whether Johnson's is a just appraisal. It has sometimes been held by later critics that the unusual dramatic force of these poems was misunderstood by many of Gray's contemporaries, who responded not to their sublimity but to what was felt to be their violation of good taste. They clearly attempt to achieve a high order of power, and it is perhaps with this in mind that one should read them.

TEXTS. *Designs by Mr. R. Bentley for six poems by Mr. T. Gray* (London, 1753).
      Odes By Mr. Gray (Strawberry-Hill, 1757).

Ode on the Death of a Favourite Cat, Drowned in a Tub of Gold Fishes

'TWAS on a lofty vase's side,
Where China's gayest art had dy'd
   The azure flowers, that blow;
Demurest of the tabby kind,
The pensive Selima reclin'd,   5
   Gazed on the lake below.

Her conscious tail her joy declar'd;
The fair round face, the snowy beard,
   The velvet of her paws,
Her coat, that with the tortoise vies,   10
Her ears of jet, and emerald eyes,
   She saw; and purr'd applause.

Still had she gaz'd: but 'midst the tide
Two angel forms were seen to glide,
   The Genii of the stream: 15
Their scaly armour's Tyrian hue
Thro' richest purple to the view
   Betray'd a golden gleam.

The hapless Nymph with wonder saw:
A whisker first and then a claw,   20
   With many an ardent wish,
She stretch'd in vain to reach the prize.
What female heart can gold despise?
   What Cat's averse to fish?

7. *Conscious:* "Having guilty knowledge." *OED.*

Presumptuous Maid! with looks intent   25
Again she stretch'd, again she bent,
　　Nor knew the gulf between.
(Malignant Fate sat by, and smil'd)
The slipp'ry verge her feet beguil'd,
　　She tumbled headlong in.   30

Eight times emerging from the flood
She mew'd to ev'ry watry God,
　　Some speedy aid to send.
No Dolphin came, no Nereid stirr'd:
Nor cruel *Tom*, nor *Susan* heard.   35
　　A Fav'rite has no friend!

From hence, ye Beauties, undeceiv'd,
Know, one false step is ne'er retriev'd,
　　And be with caution bold.
Not all that tempts your wand'ring eyes   40
And heedless hearts, is lawful prize;
　　Nor all, that glisters, gold.

(1748)

Ode on a Distant Prospect of
Eton College

YE distant spires, ye antique towers,
That crown the watry glade,
Where grateful Science still adores
Her HENRY's holy Shade;
And ye, that from the stately brow   5
Of WINDSOR's heights th' expanse below
Of grove, of lawn, of mead survey,
Whose turf, whose shade, whose flowers among
Wanders the hoary Thames along
His silver-winding way.   10

　　Ah happy hills, ah pleasing shade,
Ah fields belov'd in vain,
Where once my careless childhood stray'd,
A stranger yet to pain!
I feel the gales, that from ye blow,   15

34. *Dolphin . . . Nereid:* Dolphins, Old Man of the sea, a wise and kind deity.
according to tradition, help drowning 　4. *Henry's holy Shade:* Henry VI
persons; Nereids, children of Nereus, the (1421–1471) founded Eton College in 1440.

A momentary bliss bestow,
As waving fresh their gladsome wing,
My weary soul they seem to sooth,
And, redolent of joy and youth,
To breath a second spring.   20

Say, Father THAMES, for thou hast seen
Full many a sprightly race
Disporting on thy margent green
The paths of pleasure trace,
Who foremost now delight to cleave   25
With pliant arm thy glassy wave?
The captive linnet which enthrall?
What idle progeny succeed
To chase the rolling circle's speed,
Or urge the flying ball?   30

While some on earnest business bent
Their murm'ring labours ply
'Gainst graver hours, that bring constraint
To sweeten liberty:
Some bold adventurers disdain   35
The limits of their little reign,
And unknown regions dare descry:
Still as they run they look behind,
They hear a voice in every wind,
And snatch a fearful joy.   40

Gay hope is theirs by fancy fed,
Less pleasing when possest;
The tear forgot as soon as shed,
The sunshine of the breast:
Theirs buxom health of rosy hue,   45
Wild wit, invention ever-new,
And lively chear of vigour born;
The thoughtless day, the easy night,
The spirits pure, the slumbers light,
That fly th' approach of morn.   50

Alas, regardless of their doom,
The little victims play!
No sense have they of ills to come,
Nor care beyond to-day:
Yet see how all around 'em wait   55
The Ministers of human fate,
And black Misfortune's baleful train!

29. *Rolling circle's speed:* The rolling   the boys at Eton.
circle was a hoop used in a game played by

Ah, shew them where in ambush stand
To seize their prey the murth'rous band!
Ah, tell them, they are men!   60

   These shall the fury Passions tear,
The vulturs of the mind,
Disdainful Anger, pallid Fear,
And Shame that sculks behind;
Or pineing Love shall waste their youth,   65
Or Jealousy with rankling tooth,
That inly gnaws the secret heart,
And Envy wan, and faded Care,
Grim-visag'd comfortless Despair,
And Sorrow's piercing dart.   70

   Ambition this shall tempt to rise,
Then whirl the wretch from high,
To bitter Scorn a sacrifice,
And grinning Infamy.
The stings of Falshood those shall try,   75
And hard Unkindness's alter'd eye,
That mocks the tear it forc'd to flow;
And keen Remorse with blood defil'd,
And moody Madness laughing wild
Amid severest woe.   80

   Lo, in the vale of years beneath
A griesly troop are seen,
The painful family of Death,
More hideous than their Queen:
This racks the joints, this fires the veins,   85
That every labouring sinew strains,
Those in the deeper vitals rage:
Lo, Poverty, to fill the band,
That numbs the soul with icy hand,
And slow-consuming Age.   90

   To each his suff'rings: all are men,
Condemn'd alike to groan,
The tender for another's pain;
Th' unfeeling for his own.
Yet ah! why should they know their fate?   95
Since sorrow never comes too late,
And happiness too swiftly flies.
Thought would destroy their paradise.
No more; where ignorance is bliss,
'Tis folly to be wise.   100

(1747)

Hymn to Adversity

DAUGHTER of JOVE, relentless Power,
Thou Tamer of the human breast,
Whose iron scourge and tort'ring hour
The Bad affright, afflict the Best!
Bound in thy adamantine chain   5
The Proud are taught to taste of pain,
And purple Tyrants vainly groan
With pangs unfelt before, unpitied and alone.

When first thy Sire to send on earth
Virtue, his darling Child, design'd,   10
To thee he gave the heav'nly Birth,
And bad to form her infant mind.
Stern rugged Nurse! thy rigid lore
With patience many a year she bore:
What sorrow was, thou bad'st her know, 15
And from her own she learn'd to melt at other's woe.

Scared at thy frown terrific, fly
Self-pleasing Folly's idle brood,
Wild Laughter, Noise, and thoughtless Joy,
And leave us leisure to be good.   20
Light they disperse, and with them go
The summer Friend, the flatt'ring Foe;
By vain Prosperity received,
To her they vow their truth, and are again believed.

Wisdom in sable garb array'd   25
Immers'd in rapt'rous thought profound,
And Melancholy, silent maid
With leaden eye, that loves the ground,
Still on thy solemn steps attend:
Warm Charity, the gen'ral friend,   30
With Justice to herself severe,
And Pity, dropping soft the sadly-pleasing tear.

Oh, gently on thy Suppliant's head,
Dread Goddess, lay thy chast'ning hand!

---

1. *Daughter of Jove:* Athena, conceived by Metis (wisest of the gods) whom Zeus (most powerful of the gods) devoured, was born out of the head of her father; she is the epitome of wisdom and power.
35. *Gorgon terrors:* Female monsters, represented with hideous faces, glaring eyes, and serpents in their hair—Sthenno, Euryale, and Medusa—of which only Medusa was mortal. The Gorgon's head turned to stone anything that met its gaze.

Not in thy Gorgon terrors clad,   35
Nor circled with the vengeful Band
(As by the Impious thou art seen)
With thund'ring voice, and threat'ning mien,
With screaming Horror's funeral cry,
Despair, and fell Disease, and ghastly Poverty.   40

Thy form benign, oh Goddess, wear,
Thy milder influence impart,
Thy philosophic Train be there
To soften, not to wound my heart,
The gen'rous spark extinct revive,   45
Teach me to love and to forgive,
Exact my own defects to scan,
What others are, to feel, and know myself a Man.

(1753)

Elegy Written in a Country Church Yard

THE Curfew tolls the knell of parting day,
The lowing herd wind slowly o'er the lea,
The plowman homeward plods his weary way,
And leaves the world to darkness and to me.

Now fades the glimmering landscape on the sight,   5
And all the air a solemn stillness holds,
Save where the beetle wheels his droning flight,
And drowsy tinklings lull the distant folds;

Save that from yonder ivy-mantled tow'r
The mopeing owl does to the moon complain   10
Of such, as wand'ring near her secret bow'r,
Molest her ancient solitary reign.

Beneath those rugged elms, that yew-tree's shade,
Where heaves the turf in many a mould'ring heap,
Each in his narrow cell for ever laid,   15
The rude Forefathers of the hamlet sleep.

36. *The Vengeful Band:* The Furies, female avengers, against crimes of kinship particularly. Athena instituted their worship (and their restriction by law) in Athens.
16. *Rude:* "Unlearned or ignorant." *OED.*

The breezy call of incense-breathing Morn,
The swallow twitt'ring from the straw-built shed,
The cock's shrill clarion, or the ecchoing horn,
No more shall rouse them from their lowly bed.   20

For them no more the blazing hearth shall burn,
Or busy houswife ply her evening care:
No children run to lisp their sire's return,
Or climb his knees the envied kiss to share.

Oft did the harvest to their sickle yield,   25
Their furrow oft the stubborn glebe has broke;
How jocund did they drive their team afield!
How bow'd the woods beneath their sturdy stroke!

Let not Ambition mock their useful toil,
Their homely joys, and destiny obscure;   30
Nor Grandeur hear with a disdainful smile,
The short and simple annals of the poor.

The boast of heraldry, the pomp of pow'r,
And all that beauty, all that wealth e'er gave,
Awaits alike th' inevitable hour.   35
The paths of glory lead but to the grave.

Nor you, ye Proud, impute to These the fault,
If Mem'ry o'er their Tomb no Trophies raise,
Where thro' the long-drawn isle and fretted vault
The pealing anthem swells the note of praise.   40

Can storied urn or animated bust
Back to its mansion call the fleeting breath?
Can Honour's voice provoke the silent dust,
Or Flatt'ry sooth the dull cold ear of Death!

Perhaps in this neglected spot is laid   45
Some heart once pregnant with celestial fire,
Hands, that the rod of empire might have sway'd,
Or wak'd to extasy the living lyre.

But Knowledge to their eyes her ample page
Rich with the spoils of time did ne'er unroll;   50
Chill Penury repress'd their noble rage,
And froze the genial current of the soul.

Full many a gem of purest ray serene,
The dark unfathom'd caves of ocean bear:

26. *Glebe:* Land, soil.

Full many a flower is born to blush unseen,   55
And waste its sweetness on the desert air.

Some village-Hampden, that with dauntless breast
The little Tyrant of his fields withstood;
Some mute inglorious Milton here may rest,
Some Cromwell guiltless of his country's blood.   60

Th' applause of list'ning senates to command,
The threats of pain and ruin to despise,
To scatter plenty o'er a smiling land,
And read their hist'ry in a nation's eyes

Their lot forbad: nor circumscrib'd alone   65
Their growing virtues, but their crimes confin'd;
Forbad to wade through slaughter to a throne,
And shut the gates of mercy on mankind,

The struggling pangs of conscious truth to hide.
To quench the blushes of ingenuous shame,   70
Or heap the shrine of Luxury and Pride
With incense kindled at the Muse's flame.

Far from the madding crowd's ignoble strife,
Their sober wishes never learn'd to stray;
Along the cool sequester'd vale of life   75
They kept the noiseless tenor of their way.

Yet ev'n these bones from insult to protect
Some frail memorial still erected nigh,
With uncouth rhimes and shapeless sculpture deck'd,
Implores the passing tribute of a sigh.   80

Their name, their years, spelt by th' unletter'd muse,
The place of fame and elegy supply:
And many a holy text around she strews,
That teach the rustic moralist to dye.

For who to dumb Forgetfulness a prey,   85
This pleasing anxious being e'er resign'd,
Left the warm precincts of the chearful day,
Nor cast one longing ling'ring look behind?

On some fond breast the parting soul relies,
Some pious drops the closing eye requires;   90
Ev'n from the tomb the voice of Nature cries,
Ev'n in our Ashes live their wonted Fires.

57. *Village-Hampden:* John Hampden   patriot.
(1594–1643), English parliamentarian and

For thee, who mindful of th' unhonour'd Dead
Dost in these lines their artless tale relate;
If chance, by lonely contemplation led,   95
Some kindred Spirit shall inquire thy fate,

Haply some hoary-headed Swain may say,
'Oft have we seen him at the peep of dawn
'Brushing with hasty steps the dews away
'To meet the sun upon the upland lawn.   100

'There at the foot of yonder nodding beech
'That wreathes its old fantastic roots so high,
'His listless length at noontide wou'd he stretch,
'And pore upon the brook that babbles by.

'Hard by yon wood, now smiling as in scorn,   105
'Mutt'ring his wayward fancies he wou'd rove,
'Now drooping, woeful wan, like one forlorn,
'Or craz'd with care, or cross'd in hopeless love.

'One morn I miss'd him on the custom'd hill,
'Along the heath and near his fav'rite tree;   110
'Another came; nor yet beside the rill,
'Nor up the lawn, nor at the wood was he,

'The next with dirges due in sad array
'Slow thro' the church-way path we saw him born.
'Approach and read (for thou can'st read) the lay,   115
'Grav'd on the stone beneath yon aged thorn.'

The Epitaph

HERE rests his head upon the lap of Earth
A Youth to Fortune and to Fame unknown,
Fair Science frown'd not on his humble birth,
And Melancholy mark'd him for her own.   120

Large was his bounty, and his soul sincere,
Heav'n did a recompence as largely send:
He gave to Mis'ry all he had, a tear,
He gain'd from Heav'n ('twas all he wish'd) a friend.

No farther seek his merits to disclose,   125
Or draw his frailties from their dread abode
(There they alike in trembling hope repose)
The bosom of his Father and his God.

(1751)

The Progress of Poesy [*]

I.1

AWAKE, Æolian lyre, awake,
And give to rapture all thy trembling strings.
From Helicon's harmonious springs
A thousand rills their mazy progress take:
The laughing flowers, that round them blow,   5
Drink life and fragrance as they flow.
Now the rich stream of music winds along
Deep, majestic, smooth, and strong,
Thro' verdant vales, and Ceres' golden reign:
Now rowling down the steep amain,   10
Headlong, impetuous see it pour:
The rocks, and nodding groves rebellow to the roar.

I.2

Oh! Sovereign of the willing soul,
Parent of sweet and solemn-breathing airs,
Enchanting shell! the sullen Cares,   15
And frantic Passions hear thy soft controul.
On Thracia's hills the Lord of War,
Has curb'd the fury of his car,
And drop'd his thirsty lance at thy command.
Perching on the scept'red hand   20
Of Jove, thy magic lulls the feather'd king
With ruffled plumes, and flagging wing:
Quench'd in dark clouds of slumber lie
The terror of his beak, and light'nings of his eye.

---

* *The Progress of Poesy:* The title given the poem in the first edition, 1757, here presented, was *Ode I.*

1. *Æolian lyre:* Pindar's lyre. In his notes to the edition of the Odes in 1768, *Poems by Mr. Gray*, p. 38, Gray explains the idea of the first strophe: "The subject and simile, as usual with Pindar, are united. The various sources of poetry, which gives life and lustre to all it touches are here described; its quiet majestic progress enriching every subject (otherwise dry and barren) with a pomp of diction and luxuriant harmony of num-bers; and its more rapid and irresistible course, when swoln and hurried away by the conflict of tumultuous passions."

13. *Oh! Sovereign . . .:* Gray, 1768, p. 39, says, "Power of harmony to calm the turbulent sallies of the soul. The thoughts are borrowed from the first Pythian of Pindar."

20. *Perching . . . hand:* Gray, 1768, p. 39, says, "This is a weak imitation of some incomparable lines in the same Ode." The feather'd king on Jove's hand is the eagle, the god's bird.

I.3

Thee the voice, the dance, obey,   25
Temper'd to thy warbled lay.
O'er Idalia's velvet-green
The rosy-crowned Loves are seen
On Cytherea's day
With antic Sports, and blue-eyed Pleasures,   30
Frisking light in frolic measures;
Now pursuing, now retreating,
Now in circling troops they meet:
To brisk notes in cadence beating
Glance their many-twinkling feet.   35
Slow melting strains their Queen's approach declare:
Where'er she turns the Graces homage pay.
With arms sublime, that float upon the air,
In gliding state she wins her easy way:
O'er her warm cheek, and rising bosom, move   40
The bloom of young Desire, and purple light of Love.

II.1

Man's feeble race what Ills await,
Labour, and Penury, the racks of Pain,
Disease, and Sorrow's weeping train,
And Death, sad refuge from the storms of Fate!   45
The fond complaint, my Song, disprove,
And justify the laws of Jove.
Say, has he giv'n in vain the heav'nly Muse?
Night, and all her sickly dews,
Her Spectres wan, and Birds of boding cry,   50
He gives to range the dreary sky:
Till down the eastern cliffs afar
Hyperion's march they spy, and glitt'ring shafts of war.

II.2

In climes beyond the solar road,
Where shaggy forms o'er ice-built mountains roam,   55

25. *Thee the voice:* Gray, 1768, p. 40, says of the first epode, "Power of harmony to produce all the graces of motion in the body."

27. *Idalia's velvet-green:* Idalia or Idaleum (modern Dali) was an ancient town on Cyprus, in which there was located a well-known temple of Aphrodite, one of whose titles was Cytherean, l. 29.

42. *Man's feeble race:* Gray, 1768, p. 42, says of the second strophe, "To compensate the real and imaginary ills of life, the Muse was given to Mankind by the same Providence that sends the Day by its chearful presence to dispel the gloom and terrors of the Night."

53. *Hyperion's march:* March or movement of the sun.

The Muse has broke the twilight-gloom
To chear the shiv'ring Native's dull abode.
And oft, beneath the od'rous shade
Of Chili's boundless forests laid,
She deigns to hear the savage Youth repeat   60
In loose numbers wildly sweet
Their feather-cinctured Chiefs, and dusky Loves.
Her track, where'er the Goddess roves,
Glory pursue, and generous Shame,
Th' unconquerable Mind, and Freedom's holy flame.   65

II.3

Woods, that wave o'er Delphi's steep,
Isles, that crown th' Egæan deep,
Fields, that cool Ilissus laves,
Or where Mæander's amber waves
In lingering Lab'rinths creep,   70
How do your tuneful Echoes languish,
Mute, but to the voice of Anguish?
Where each old poetic Mountain
Inspiration breath'd around:
Ev'ry shade and hallow'd Fountain   75
Murmur'd deep a solemn sound:
Till the sad Nine in Greece's evil hour
Left their Parnassus for the Latian plains.
Alike they scorn the pomp of tyrant-Power,
And coward Vice, that revels in her chains.   80
When Latium had her lofty spirit lost,
They sought, oh Albion! next thy sea-encircled coast.

III.1

Far from the sun and summer-gale,
In thy green lap was Nature's Darling laid,
What time, where lucid Avon stray'd,   85
To Him the mighty Mother did unveil
Her aweful face: The dauntless Child
Stretch'd forth his little arms, and smiled.
This pencil take (she said) whose colours clear

66. *Woods, that wave* . . . : Gray, 1768, p. 44, says of the second epode, "Progress of Poetry from Greece to Italy, and from Italy to England. . . ." At Delphi was a shrine sacred to Apollo, particularly associated with the lyre.

68. *Ilissus:* A river that descends the stony plains of Atticus and runs past Athens.

69. *Mæander:* A river that flows through Phrygia.

77. *The sad Nine:* The Muses, patron goddesses of the arts.

82. *Albion:* England.

84. *Nature's Darling:* Gray, 1786, p. 46, "Shakespeare."

Richly paint the vernal year: 90
Thine too these golden keys, immortal Boy!
This can unlock the gates of Joy;
Of Horrour that, and thrilling Fears,
Or ope the sacred source of sympathetic Tears.

III.2

Nor second He, that rode sublime   95
Upon the seraph-wings of Extasy,
The secrets of th' Abyss to spy.
He pass'd the flaming bounds of Place and Time:
The living Throne, the saphire-blaze,
Where Angels tremble, while they gaze,   100
He saw; but blasted with excess of light,
Closed his eyes in endless night.
Behold, where Dryden's less presumptuous car,
Wide o'er the fields of Glory bear
Two Coursers of ethereal race,   105
With necks in thunder cloath'd, and long-resounding pace.

III.3

Hark, his hands the lyre explore!
Bright-eyed Fancy hovering o'er
Scatters from her pictur'd urn
Thoughts, that breath, and words, that burn.   110
But ah! 'tis heard no more—
Oh! Lyre divine, what daring Spirit
Wakes thee now? tho' he inherit
Nor the pride, nor ample pinion,
That the Theban Eagle bear   115
Sailing with supreme dominion
Thro' the azure deep of air:
Yet oft before his infant eyes would run
Such forms, as glitter, in the Muse's ray
With orient hues, unborrow'd of the Sun: 120
Yet shall he mount, and keep his distant way
Beyond the limits of a vulgar fate,
Beneath the Good how far—but far above the Great.

(1757)

95. *Nor second He:* Gray, 1768, p. 47, "Milton."

99. *The living Throne . . .:* Gray, 1768, p. 48, calls attention to the parallel between these lines and Ezek. 1:20, 26, 28.

111. *But ah! 'tis heard no more:* Gray, 1768, p. 49, says, "We have had in our language no other odes of the sublime kind, than that of Dryden on St. Cecilia's day. . . . That of Pope is not worthy of so great a man. . . ."

115. *The Theban Eagle:* Pindar, who was born very near Thebes.

The Bard*

I.1

'RUIN seize thee, ruthless King!
'Confusion on thy banners wait,
'Tho' fann'd by Conquest's crimson wing
'They mock the air with idle state.
'Helm, nor Hauberk's twisted mail,   5
'Nor even thy virtues, Tyrant, shall avail
'To save thy secret soul from nightly fears,
'From Cambria's curse, from Cambria's tears!'
Such were the sounds, that o'er the crested pride
Of the first Edward scatter'd wild dismay,   10
As down the steep of Snowdon's shaggy side
He wound with toilsome march his long array.
Stout Gloster stood aghast in speechless trance:
To arms! cried Mortimer, and couch'd his quiv'ring lance.

I.2

On a rock, whose haughty brow   15
Frowns o'er old Conway's foaming flood,
Robed in the sable garb of woe,
With haggard eyes the Poet stood
(Loose his beard, and hoary hair
Stream'd, like a meteor, to the troubled air);   20
And with a Master's hand, and Prophet's fire,
Struck the deep sorrows of his lyre.
'Hark, how each giant-oak, and desert cave,
'Sighs to the torrent's aweful voice beneath!
'O'er thee, oh King! their hundred arms they wave,   25
'Revenge on thee in hoarser murmurs breath;

---

* *The Bard:* The title given the poem
in the first edition, 1757, here presented,
was *Ode II.* In an advertisement to the
edition of 1768, Gray explained, "The
following Ode is founded on a Tradition
current in Wales, that Edward the First,
when he compleated the Conquest of that
country, ordered all the Bards, that fell
into his hands, to be put to death."

1. *Ruthless King:* Edward I (1239–1307)
was the elder son of Henry III and Eleanor
of Provence. In 1254, he married Eleanor
of Castile, upon which occasion his father
gave him Gascony, Ireland, and Wales,
where in fighting the violent and brave

Welshmen, he earned the not quite
deserved reputation used by Gray in the
Ode.

8. *Cambria's curse:* Cambria was a name
for Wales.

11. *Snowdon's . . . side:* A mountainous
tract including the highlands of Caernarvonshire and Merionethshire, several
places in which Edward built fortifications.

13. *Gloster:* Son-in-law to Edward.

14. *Mortimer:* A nobleman who was to
be the illicit lover of Isabella, wife of
Edward (son of Edward I). Not only was
she unfaithful, she also was responsible
for her husband's murder. See ll. 54 ff.

'Vocal no more, since Cambria's fatal day,
'To high-born Hoel's harp, or soft Llewellyn's lay.

I.3

'Cold is Cadwallo's tongue,
'That hush'd the stormy main: 30
'Brave Urien sleeps upon his craggy bed:
'Mountains, ye mourn in vain
'Modred, whose magic song
'Made huge Plinlimmon bow his cloud-top'd head.
'On dreary Arvon's shore they lie,   35
'Smear'd with gore, and ghastly pale:
'Far far aloof th' affrighted ravens sail;
'The famish'd Eagle screams, and passes by.
'Dear lost companions of my tuneful art,
'Dear, as the light, that visits these sad eyes,   40
'Dear, as the ruddy drops that warm my heart,
'Ye died amidst your dying country's cries—
'No more I weep. They do not sleep.
'On yonder cliffs, a griesly band,
'I see them sit, they linger yet,   45
'Avengers of their native land:
'With me in dreadful harmony they join,
'And weave with bloody hands the tissue of thy line.'

II.1

"Weave the warp, and weave the woof,
"The winding-sheet of Edward's race.   50
"Give ample room, and verge enough
"The characters of hell to trace.
"Mark the year, and mark the night,
"When Severn shall re-eccho with affright
"The shrieks of death, thro' Berkely's roofs that ring, 55
"Shrieks of an agonizing King!
"She-Wolf of France, with unrelenting fangs,

28. *Hoel's harp:* Hoel was a famous bard, son of a Welsh prince. Llewellyn was characterized as "a tender-hearted prince" in a Welsh poem.

29–33. *Cadwallo's tongue...:* Cadwallo, Urien, Modred are presumably names of Welsh bards.

34. *Plinlimmon:* A mountain in Wales.

35. *Arvon's shore:* The shores of Caernarvonshire. "They" in line 35 presumably refers to the Welsh poets killed by order of Edward I.

49. *Weave the warp:* The second strophe, antistrophe, and epode (as well as the first four lines of strophe III) are the fulfillment of line 47—"With me . . . they join"—the chorus of the bard, who speaks the entire poem, and his lost companions, killed by Edward. They chant a prophesy of destruction among the Norman kings.

54. *When Severn...:* Gray, 1768, p. 60, says, "Edward the Second, cruelly butchered in Berkeley-Castle." See n. l. 14.

57. *She-Wolf of France:* Gray, 1768, p. 61, says, "Isabel of France, Edward the Second's adulterous Queen." See n. l. 14.

"That tear'st the bowels of thy maingled Mate,
"From thee be born, who o'er thy country hangs
"The scourge of Heav'n. What Terrors round him wait !   60
"Amazement in his van, with Flight combined,
"And sorrow's faded form, and solitude behind.

II.2

"Mighty Victor, mighty Lord,
"Low on his funeral couch he lies !
"No pitying heart, no eye, afford   65
"A tear to grace his obsequies.
"Is the sable Warriour fled?
"Thy son is gone. He rests among the Dead.
"The Swarm, that in thy noon-tide beam were born?
"Gone to salute the rising Morn.   70
"Fair laughs the Morn, and soft the Zephyr blows,
"While proudly riding o'er the azure realm
"In gallant trim the gilded Vessel goes;
"Youth on the prow, and Pleasure at the helm;
"Regardless of the sweeping Whirlwind's sway,   75
"That, hush'd in grim repose, expects his evening-prey.

II.3

"Fill high the sparkling bowl,
"The rich repast prepare,
"Reft of a crown, he yet may share the feast:
"Close by the regal chair   80
"Fell Thirst and Famine scowl
"A baleful smile upon their baffled Guest.
"Heard ye the din of battle bray,
"Lance to lance, and horse to horse?
"Long Years of havock urge their destined course,   85
"And thro' the kindred squadrons mow their way.
"Ye Towers of Julius, London's lasting shame,

59. *From thee . . . :* Gray, 1768, p. 61, says, "Triumphs of Edward the Third in France."

64. *Low on his . . . couch:* Gray, 1768, p. 61, says, "Death of that King, abandoned by his Children, and even robbed in his last moments by his Courtiers and his Mistress."

67. *Sable Warriour:* Gray, 1768, p. 62, says, "Edward, the Black Prince [son of Edward III], dead some time [one year] before his father."

71. *Fair laughs . . . :* Gray, 1768, p. 62, says, "Magnificence of Richard the Second's reign. . . ."

77. *Fill high . . . :* Gray, 1768, p. 63, says, "Richard the Second . . . was starved to death. The story of his assassination by Sir Piers of Exon, is of much later date."

83. *Heard ye the din . . . :* Gray, 1768, p. 64, says, "Ruinous civil wars of York and Lancaster."

87. *Ye Towers of Julius:* Gray, 1768, p. 64, says, "Henry the Sixth, George Duke of Clarence, Edward the Fifth, Richard Duke of York, &c. believed to be murdered secretly in the Tower of London. The oldest part of that structure is vulgarly attributed to Julius Caesar."

"With many a foul and midnight murther fed,
"Revere his Consort's faith, his Father's fame,
"And spare the meek Usurper's holy head.   90
"Above, below, the rose of snow,
"Twined with her blushing foe, we spread:
"The bristled Boar in infant-gore
"Wallows beneath the thorny shade.
"Now, Brothers, bending o'er th' accursed loom   95
"Stamp we our vengeance deep, and ratify his doom.

III.1

"Edward, lo! to sudden fate
"(Weave we the woof. The thread is spun)
"Half of thy heart we consecrate.
"(The web is wove. The work is done.)"   100
'Stay, oh stay! nor thus forlorn
'Leave me unbless'd, unpitied, here to mourn:
'In yon bright track, that fires the western skies,
'They melt, they vanish from my eyes.
'But oh! what solemn scenes on Snowdon's height   105
'Descending slow their glitt'ring skirts unroll?
'Visions of glory, spare my aching sight,
'Ye unborn Ages, crowd not on my soul!
'No more our long-lost Arthur we bewail.
'All-hail, ye genuine Kings, Britannia's Issue, hail!   110

III.2

'Girt with many a Baron bold
'Sublime their starry fronts they rear;
'And gorgeous Dames, and Statesmen old
'In bearded majesty, appear.
'In the midst a Form divine!   115
'Her eye proclaims her of the Briton-Line;
'Her lyon-port, her awe commanding face,
'Attemper'd sweet to virgin-grace.
'What strings symphonious tremble in the air,
'What strains of vocal transport round her play!   120

89. *Consort's faith:* Gray, 1768, p. 64, says, "Margaret of Anjou, a woman of heroic spirit, who struggled hard to save her husband [Henry VI] and her crown." "Father's fame" refers to the fame of Henry V.

90. *The meek Usurper:* Gray, 1768, p. 65, says, "Henry the Sixth very near being canonized. The line of Lancaster had no right of inheritance to the Crown."

93. *The bristled Boar:* Richard III.

99. *Half of thy heart . . .:* Eleanor of Castile, who saved her husband, Edward I, by sucking the poison from a wound.

109. *Long-lost Arthur:* In Welsh tradition, Arthur was to return to reign over Britain.

115. *A Form divine:* Queen Elizabeth I.

'Hear from the grave, great Taliessin, hear;
'They breathe a soul to animate thy clay.
'Bright Rapture calls, and soaring, as she sings,
'Waves in the eye of Heav'n her many-colour'd wings.

III.3

'The verse adorn again   125
'Fierce War, and faithful Love,
'And Truth severe, by fairy Fiction drest.
'In buskin'd measures move
'Pale Grief, and pleasing Pain,
'With Horrour, Tyrant of the throbbing breast.   130
'A Voice, as of the Cherub-Choir,
'Gales from blooming Eden bear;
'And distant warblings lessen on my ear,
'That lost in long futurity expire.
'Fond impious Man, think'st thou, yon sanguine cloud,   135
'Rais'd by thy breath, has quench'd the Orb of day?
'To-morrow he repairs the golden flood,
'And warms the nations with redoubled ray.
'Enough for me: With joy I see
'The different doom our Fates assign.   140
'Be thine Despair, and scept'red Care,
'To triumph, and to die, are mine.'
He spoke, and headlong from the mountain's height
Deep in the roaring tide he plung'd to endless night.

(1757)

121. *Great Taliessin:* With Merlin,
Taliessin was a great Welsh prophet, and
a bard.

133. *Distant warblings lessen . . . :* The
poets who follow Shakespeare and Milton.

Oliver Goldsmith

1730?-1774

Goldsmith was born to English parents (his father was a clergyman) either in Roscommon or Longford, Ireland. He attended local schools until 1744, when he entered Trinity College, Dublin. Goldsmith's career at Trinity was mediocre, but he earned a B.A. in 1749.

Shortly thereafter, Goldsmith set out for America, but his journey ended at Cork. In 1752, he began to study medicine at Edinburgh; after two years he proceeded to Leyden, but it remains uncertain whether he earned a medical degree. About this time, he took a walking tour of the Continent; and in 1756, he returned penniless to England.

After attempts at several occupations, Goldsmith turned to hackwriting, contributing to such publications as *The Critical Review*, *The Weekly Magazine*, *The Monthly Review*, and *The British Magazine*. He brought out a series of essays, *The Bee*, in 1759; in the same year appeared his *Enquiry into the Present State of Polite Learning*.

Goldsmith's "Chinese Letters" were first published in *The Public Ledger* in 1760–61; the following year they appeared as *The Citizen of the World*. By this time Goldsmith had made the acquaintance of Samuel Johnson, and eventually he became one of the original members (along with Burke, Joshua Reynolds, and others) of the *Literary Club* (later known as the *Club*) founded in 1764.

The Traveler, a poem in couplets, came out in 1764; in 1766, was published his only novel, *The Vicar of Wakefield*, which achieved immediate success. (It was a work Johnson had hurriedly sold to raise money in order that Goldsmith might pay his overdue rent and avoid arrest.)

Goldsmith's production of such works as *History of Animated*

Nature, History of England, and *Survey of Experimental Philosophy* brought him considerable earnings, but his spendthrift nature and sympathetic generosity kept him in almost perpetual debt. In 1770, *The Deserted Village,* considered by many to be his best poem, was published. In 1773, followed his famous comedy, *She Stoops to Conquer,* an immediate (and enduring) success. Goldsmith died of a fever the following year in his rooms at the Middle Temple. He was buried in the Temple Churchyard and a monument was later erected in Westminster Abbey by his friends in the *Club.*

Oliver Goldsmith—Selective Bibliography

Temple Scott, *Oliver Goldsmith Bibliographically and Biographically Considered;* based on the Collection of Material in the Library of W. M. Elkins, Esq. [Now owned and kept intact by The Free Library, Philadelphia], New York, Bowling Green Press, 1928. See also *CBEL,* II, pp. 636 f.

Arthur Friedman, ed., *Collected Works of Oliver Goldsmith,* 5 vols., Oxford, Clarendon Press, 1966.

Katherine C. Balderston, ed., *The Collected Letters of Oliver Goldsmith,* Cambridge U. Press, 1928.

Ralph M. Wardle, *Oliver Goldsmith,* Lawrence, U. of Kansas Press, 1957; includes a useful bibliography.

Howard J. Bell, "*The Deserted Village* and Goldsmith's Social Doctrines," *PMLA,* LIX (1944), 747–772.

Ricardo Quintana, "*The Deserted Village:* Its Logical and Rhetorical Elements," *College English,* XXVI (1964), 204–214.

Headnote to
ASEM THE MAN HATER

"Asem the Man Hater" is an Eastern tale, related to *Rasselas* in kind, according to some critics, at least. (See the headnote to *Rasselas*.) The narrative involves Asem in a supernatural experience that effects a profound change of heart in him. He learns the folly of unrelieved human benevolence as an ideal, and he learns too that his suicidal misanthropy results from his having theorized about what life ought to be, instead of observing what in fact it is. In these tales the principal's disaffection, his journey to knowledge with the help of a guide, and his return to life with tempered expectations are recurring structural elements.

TEXT. *The Miscellaneous Works of Oliver Goldsmith* (London, 1789).

Asem the Man Hater

An Eastern Tale*

WHERE Tauris lifts its head above the storm, and presents nothing to the sight of the distant traveller, but a prospect of nodding rocks, falling torrents, and all the variety of tremendous nature; on the bleak bosom of this frightful mountain, secluded from society, and detesting the ways of men, lived Asem the Man-hater.

Asem had spent his youth with men; had shared in their amusements; and had been taught to love his fellow-creatures with the most ardent affection: but, from the tenderness of his disposition, he exhausted all his fortune in relieving the wants of the distressed. The petitioner never sued in vain; the weary traveller never passed his door: he only desisted from doing good, when he had   10
no longer the power of relieving.

From a fortune thus spent in benevolence, he expected a grateful return from those he had formerly relieved, and made his application with confidence of redress: the ungrateful world soon grew weary of his importunity; for pity is

---

* *Asem* ...: The title of the work when it first appeared in the *Royal Magazine* for December, 1759, was *The Proceedings of* *Providence Vindicated. An Eastern Tale*. Later it was referred to simply as *Essay XVI*, and finally by the title here given.

but a short-lived passion. He soon, therefore, began to view mankind in a very different light from that in which he had before beheld them. He perceived a thousand vices he had never before expected to exist: wherever he turned, ingratitude, dissimulation, and treachery, contributed to increase his detestation of them. Resolved therefore to continue no longer in a world which he hated, and which repaid his detestation with contempt, he retired to this region of sterility, in order to brood over his resentment in solitude, and converse with the only honest heart he knew, namely, with his own.

A cave was his only shelter from the inclemency of the weather; fruits gathered with difficulty from the mountain's side, his only food; and his drink   10 was fetched with danger and toil from the headlong torrent. In this manner he lived, sequestered from society, passing the hours in meditation, and sometimes exulting that he was able to live independently of his fellow-creatures.

At the foot of the mountain, an extensive lake displayed its glassy bosom, reflecting on its broad surface the impending horrors of the mountain. To this capacious mirror he would sometimes descend, and, reclining on its steep bank, cast an eager look on the smooth expanse that lay before him. "How beautiful," he often cried, "is Nature! how lovely, even in her wildest scenes! How finely contrasted is the level plain that lies beneath me, with yon awful pile that hides its tremendous head in clouds! But the beauty of these scenes is no way com-   20 parable with their utility: from hence an hundred rivers are supplied, which distribute health and verdure to the various countries through which they flow. Every part of the universe is beautiful, just, and wise: but man, vile man, is a solecism in nature, the only monster in the creation. Tempests and whirlwinds have their use; but vicious, ungrateful man, is a blot in the fair page of universal beauty. Why was I born of that detested species, whose vices are almost a reproach to the wisdom of the divine Creator! Were men entirely free from vice, all would be uniformity, harmony, and order. A world of moral rectitude, should be the result of a perfectly moral agent. Why, why then, O Alla! must I be thus confined in darkness, doubt, and despair!"   30

Just as he uttered the word Despair, he was going to plunge into the lake beneath him, at once to satisfy his doubts, and put a period to his anxiety; when he perceived a most majestic being walking on the surface of the water, and approaching the bank on which he stood. So unexpected an object at once checked his purpose: he stopped, contemplated, and fancied he saw something awful and divine in his aspect.

"Son of Adam," cried the genius, "stop thy rash purpose; the father of the faithful has seen thy justice, thy integrity, thy miseries, and hath sent me to afford and adminster relief. Give me thine hand, and follow, without trembling, wherever I shall lead. In me behold the genius of conviction, kept by   40 the great Prophet, to turn from their errors those who go astray, not from curiosity, but a rectitude of intention. Follow me, and be wise."

Asem immediately descended upon the lake, and his guide conducted him along the surface of the water, till, coming near the centre of the lake, they both began to sink; the waters closed over their heads; they descended several hundred fathoms, till Asem, just ready to give up his life as inevitably lost, found himself with his celestial guide in another world, at the bottom of the waters, where human foot had never trod before. His astounishment was beyond description, when he saw a sun like that he had left, a serene sky over his head, and blooming verdure under his feet.

"I plainly perceive your amazement," said the genius; "but suspend it for a while. This world was formed by Alla, at the request, and under the inspection of our great Prophet; who once entertained the same doubts which filled your mind when I found you, and from the consequence of which you were so lately rescued. The rational inhabitants of this world are formed agreeable to your own ideas; they are absolutely without vice. In other respects it resembles your earth, but differs from it in being wholly inhabited by men who never do 10 wrong. If you find this world more agreeable than that you so lately left, you have free permission to spend the remainder of your days in it; but permit me for some time, to attend you, that I may silence your doubts, and make you better acquainted with your company and your new habitation."

"A world without vice! Rational beings without immorality!" cried Asem, in a rapture; "I thank thee, O Alla, who hast at length heard my petitions: this, this indeed will produce happiness, ecstasy and ease. O for an immortality, to spend it among men who are incapable of ingratitude, injustice, fraud, violence, and a thousand other crimes, that render society miserable!"

"Cease thine exclamations," replied the genius. "Look around thee; reflect 20 on every object and action before us, and communicate to me the result of thine observations. Lead wherever you think proper. I shall be your attendant and instructor." Asem and his companion travelled on in silence for some time, the former being entirely lost in astonishment; but, at last, recovering his former serenity, he could not help observing, that the face of the country bore a near resemblance to that he had left, except that this subterranean world still seemed to retain its primeval wildness.

"Here," cried Asem, "I perceive animals of prey, and others that seem only designed for their subsistence: it is the very same in the world over our heads. But had I been permitted to instruct our Prophet, I would have removed this 30 defect, and formed no voracious or destructive animals, which only prey on the other parts of the creation."

"Your tenderness for inferior animals is, I find, remarkable," said the genius, smiling. "But, with regard to meaner creatures, this world exactly resembles the other; and, indeed, for obvious reasons; for the earth can support a more considerable number of animals, by their thus becoming food for each other, than if they had lived entirely on the vegetable productions. So, that animals of different natures thus formed, instead of lessening their multitude, subsist in the greatest number of possible. But let us hasten on to the inhabited country before us, and see what that offers for instruction."   40

They soon gained the utmost verge of the forest, and entered the country inhabited by men without vice; and Asem anticipated in idea the rational delight he hoped to experience in such an innocent society. But they had scarce left the confines of the wood, when they beheld one of the inhabitants flying, with hasty steps, and terror in his countenance, from an army of squirrels that closely pursued him. "Heavens!" cried Asem, "why does he fly? What can he fear from animals so contemptible?" He had scarce spoke, when he perceived two dogs pursuing another of the human species, who, with equal terror and haste attempted to avoid them. "This," cried Asem to his guide, "is truly surprizing; nor can I conceive the reason for so strange an action."

"Every species of animals," replied the genius, "has, of late, grown very powerful in this country; for the inhabitants, at first, thinking it unjust to use either fraud or force in destroying them, they have insensibly increased, and now frequently ravage their harmless frontiers."

"But they should have been destroyed," cried Asem; "you see the consequence of such neglect."

"Where is then that tenderness you so lately expressed for subordinate animals?" replied the genius, smiling: "you seem to have forgot that branch of justice."

"I must acknowledge my mistake," returned Asem: "I am now convinced that we must be guilty of tyranny and injustice to the brute creation if we would enjoy the world ourselves. But let us no longer observe the duty of man to these irrational creatures, but survey their connections with one another."

As they walked farther up the country, the more he was surprized to see no vestiges of handsome houses, no cities, nor any mark of elegant design. His conductor perceiving his surprize, observed, That the inhabitants of this new world were perfectly content with their ancient simplicity; each had an house, which, though homely, was sufficient to lodge his little family; they were too good to build houses, which could only increase their own pride, and the envy of the spectator; what they built was for convenience, and not for show. "At least, then," said Asem, "they have neither architects, painters, or statuaries, in their society; but these are idle arts, and may be spared. However, before I spend much more time here, you should have my thanks for introducing me into the society of some of their wisest men: there is scarce any pleasure to me equal to a refined conversation; there is nothing of which I am so enamoured as wisdom."

"Wisdom!" replied his instructor; "how ridiculous! We have no wisdom here for we have no occasion for it; true wisdom is only a knowledge of our own duty and the duty of others to us: but of what use is such wisdom here? each intuitively performs what is right in himself and expects the same from others. If, by wisdom, you should mean vain curiosity and empty speculation; as such pleasures have their origin in vanity, luxury, or avarice we are too good to pursue them."

"All this may be right," says Asem; "but methinks I observe a solitary disposition prevail among the people; each family keeps separately within their own precincts without society or without intercourse."

"That indeed is true," replied the other; "here is no established society; nor should there be any: all societies are made either through fear or friendship; the people we are among are too good to fear each other; and there are no motives to private friendship, where all are equally meritorious."

"Well then," said the sceptic, "as I am to spend my time here, if I am to have neither the polite arts, nor wisdom, nor friendship in such a world, I should be glad, at least, of an easy companion, who may tell me his thoughts, and to whom I may communicate mine."

"And to what purpose should either do this?" says the genius: "flattery or curiosity are vicious motives, and never allowed of here; and wisdom is out of the question."

"[S]till, however," said Asem, "the inhabitants must be happy; each is contented with his own possessions, nor avariciously endeavours to heap up more than is necessary for his own subsistence: each has therefore leisure to pity those that stand in need of his compassion." He had scarce spoken when his ears were assaulted with the lamentations of a wretch who sat by the way-side, and, in the most deplorable distress, seemed gently to murmur at his own misery. Asem immediately ran to his relief, and found him in the last stage of a consumption. "Strange," cried the son of Adam, "that men who are free from vice should thus suffer so much misery without relief!"

"Be not surprized," said the wretch who was dying: "would it not be the utmost unjustice for beings, who have only just sufficient to support themselves, and are content with a bare subsistence, to take it from their own mouths to put it into mine? They never are possessed of a single meal more than is necessary; and what is barely necessary, cannot be dispensed with."

"They should have been supplied with more than is necessary," cried Asem; "and yet I contradict my own opinion but a moment before: all is doubt, perplexity, and confusion. Even the want of ingratitude is no virtue here, since, they never received a favour. They have, however, another excellency yet behind; the love of their country is still, I hope, one of their darling virtues."

"Peace, Asem," replied the guardian, with a countenance not less severe than beautiful," nor forfeit all thy pretensions to wisdom: the same selfish motives by which we prefer our own interest to that of others, induce us to regard our country preferably to that of another. Nothing less than universal benevolence is free from vice, and that you see is practised here."

"Strange!" cries the disappointed pilgrim, in an agony of distress; "what sort of a world am I now introduced to? There is scarce a single virtue, but that of temperance, which they practise; and, in that, they are no way superior to the very brute creation. There is scarce an amusement which they enjoy: fortitude, liberality, friendship, wisdom, conversation, and love of country, all are virtues entirely unknown here; thus it seems, that to be acquainted with vice is not to know virtue. Take me, O my genius, back to that very world which I have despised: a world which has Alla for its contriver, is much more wise formed than that which has been projected by Mahomet. Ingratitude, contempt, and hatred, I can now suffer; for perhaps I have deserved them. When I arraigned the wisdom of Providence, I only showed my own ignorance: henceforth let me keep from vice myself, and pity it in others."

He had scarce ended, when the genius, assuming an air of terrible complacency, called all his thunders around him, and vanished in a whirlwind. Asem, astonished at the terror of the scene, looked for his imaginary world; when, casting his eyes around, he perceived himself in the very situation, and in the very place where he first began to repine and despair: his right foot had been just advanced to take the fatal plunge, nor had it been yet withdrawn; so instantly did Providence strike the series of truths just imprinted on his soul. He now departed from the water-side in tranquillity, and, leaving his horrid mansion, travelled to Segestan,[1] his native city; where he diligent[ly] applied himself to commerce, and put in practice that wisdom he had learned in solitude. The frugality of a few years soon produced opulence; the number of his domestics increased; his friends came to him from every part of the city; nor did he receive them with disdain: and a youth of misery was concluded with an old age of elegance, affluence, and ease.

(1759)

[1] *Segestan:* Capital of a Persian province of the same name.

Headnote to
THE CITIZEN
OF THE WORLD

Goldsmith's "Chinese Letters" were contributed to *The Public Ledger* during 1760 and 1761; in 1762, they appeared together as *The Citizen of the World*, probably the best of his several groups of essays. They employ the device, originally French, which makes the narrator of the essays a foreigner, usually from the East (and in this case a Chinese philosopher, Lien Chi Altangi). Late in the seventeenth century G. P. Marana initiated the form in *L'Espion Turc*. Better known to English readers were Montesquieu's *Lettres Persanes* (1721), and *Lettres Chinoises* (1739) by the Marquis d'Argens, from whom Goldsmith seems to have derived an interest in the form and a handful of short passages as well.

The device of the foreign narrator (Goldsmith's writes letters to a friend at home) obviously permits the author to criticize established and generally accepted practices with some hope of jarring his reader into a fresh perception of them. One's own countryman cannot easily suggest that local wedding customs or local reasons for growing angry are unreasonable or strange. But someone from China can. The results of such a view of things may be particularly amusing if the foreign philosopher prides himself on the accuracy of his observations, and then fails notably to be accurate from time to time. (See, for example, Letter XII.) Generally, however, Goldsmith's irony is not so subtle as this last variation suggests, though it is often delightful.

TEXT. *The Citizen of The World* (2 vols., London, 1762).

Letters from
A Citizen of the World
To His Friends in the East

Letter I

[Introduction. A character of the Chinese Philosopher.]

[To Mr. **** *Merchant in* London.]

SIR,   Amsterdam
YOURS of the 13th instant, covering two bills, one on Messrs. R. and D.
value 478 1. 10s. and the other on Mr.****, value 285 1. duly came to hand,
the former of which met with honour, but the other has been trifled with, and
I am afraid will be returned protested.

The bearer of this is my friend, therefore let him be yours. He is a native of
of Honan in China, and one who did me signal services when he was a mandarine, and I a factor at Canton. By frequently conversing with [the] English
there, he has learned the language, though intirely a stranger to their manners
and customs. I am told he is a philosopher, I am sure he is an honest man; that   10
to you will be his best recommendation, next to the consideration of his being
the friend of, Sir,   Yours, &c.

Letter II

*[The arrival of the Chinese in London. His motives for the journey.
Some description of the streets and houses.]*

[Lond. *From Lien Chi Altangi to* ****, *Merchant in* Amsterdam.]

Friend of my heart,
*MAY the wings of peace rest upon thy dwelling, and the shield of conscience
preserve thee from vice and misery:* for all thy favours accept my gratitude and
esteem, the only tributes a poor philosophic wanderer can return; sure fortune
is resolved to make me unhappy, when she gives others a power of testifying
their friendship by actions, and leaves me only words to express the sincerity of
mine.

I am perfectly sensible of the delicacy by which you endeavour to lessen   20
your own merit and my obligations. By calling your late instances of friendship
only a return for former favours, you would induce me to impute to your
justice what I owe to your generosity. The services I did you at Canton, justice,

humanity, and my office bade me perform; those you have done me since my arrival at Amsterdam, no laws obliged you to, no justice required, even half your favours would have been greater than my most sanguine expectations.

The sum of money therefore which you privately conveyed into my baggage, when I was leaving Holland, and which I was ignorant of till my arrival in London, I must beg leave to return. You have been bred a merchant, and I a scholar; you consequently love money better than I. You can find pleasure in superfluity, I am perfectly contented with what is sufficient; take therefore what is yours, it may give you some pleasure, even though you have no occasion to use it; my happiness it cannot improve, for I have already all that I want.   10

My passage by sea from Rotterdam to England, was more painful to me than all the journies I ever made on land. I have traversed the immeasurable wilds of Mongul Tartary; felt all the rigours of Siberian skies; I have had my repose an hundred times disturbed by invading savages, and have seen without shrinking the desart sands rise like a troubled ocean all around me; against these calamities I was armed with resolution; but in my passage to England, though nothing occurred that gave the mariners any uneasiness, yet to one who was never at sea before, all was a subject of astonishment and terror. To find the land disappear, to see our ship mount the waves quick as an arrow from the Tartar bow, to hear the wind howling through the cordage, to feel a sickness which   20 depresses even the spirits of the brave; these were unexpected distresses, and consequently assaulted me unprepared to receive them.

You men of Europe think nothing of a voyage by sea. With us of China, a man who has been from sight of land is regarded upon his return with admiration. I have known some provinces where there is not even a name for the ocean. What a strange people therefore am I got amongst, who have founded an empire on this unstable element, who build cities upon billows that rise higher than the mountains of Tipartala,[1] and make the deep more formidable than the wildest tempest.

Such accounts as these, I must confess, were my first motives for seeing   30 England. These induced me to undertake a journey of seven hundred painful days, in order to examine its opulence, buildings, sciences, arts and manufactures on the spot. Judge then how great is my disappointment on entering London, to see no signs of that opulence so much talked of abroad; wherever I turn, I am presented with a gloomy solemnity in the houses, the streets and the inhabitants; none of that beautiful gilding which makes a principal ornament in Chinese architecture. The streets of Nankin are sometimes strewed with gold leaf; very different are those of London: in the midst of their pavements a great lazy puddle moves muddily along;[2] heavy laden machines with wheels of unweildy thickness crowd up every passage; so that a stranger instead of   40 finding time for observation, is often happy if he has time to escape from being crushed to pieces.

The houses borrow very few ornaments from architecture; their chief decoration seems to be a paltry piece of painting, hung out at their doors or

---

[1] *Tipartala:* The present editor has been unable to identify this name.

[2] *Puddle moves . . . along:* Open sewers were the order of the day in Goldsmith's London.

windows, at once a proof of their indigence and vanity.[3] Their vanity in each having one of those pictures exposed to public view; and their indigence in being unable to get them better painted. In this respect, the fancy of their painters is also deplorable. Could you believe it? I have seen five black lions and three blue boars in less than a circuit of half a mile; and yet you know that animals of these colours are no where to be found except in the wild imaginations of Europe.

From these circumstances in their buildings, and from the dismal looks of the inhabitants, I am induced to conclude that the nation is actually poor; and that like the Persians, they make a splendid figure every where but at home. The proverb of Xixofou[4] is, that a man's riches may be seen in his eyes; if we judge of the English by this rule, there is not a poorer nation under the sun.

I have been here but two days, so will not be hasty in my decisions; such letters as I shall write to Fipsihi in Moscow, I beg you'll endeavour to forward with all diligence; I shall send them open, in order that you may take copies or translations, as you are equally versed in the Dutch and Chinese languages. Dear friend, think of my absence with regret, as I sincerely regret yours; even while I write, I lament our separation. Farewell.

Letter III

[*The description of London continued. The luxury of the English. Its benefits. The fine gentleman. The fine lady.*]

[*From Lien Chi Altangi, to the care of Fipsihi, resident in Moscow; to be forwarded by the Russian caravan to Fum Hoam, first president of the ceremonial academy at Pekin in China.*]

THINK not, O thou guide of my youth, that absence can impair my respect, or interposing trackless desarts blot your reverend figure from my memory. The farther I travel I feel the pain of separation with stronger force, those ties that bind me to my native country, and you are still unbroken. By every remove, I only drag a greater length of chain.

Could I find ought worth transmitting from so remote a region as this to which I have wandered, I should gladly send it; but instead of this, you must be contented with a renewal of my former professions, and an imperfect account of a people with whom I am as yet but superficially acquainted. The remarks of a man who has been but three days in the country can only be those obvious circumstances which force themselves upon the imagination: I consider myself here as a newly created Being introduced into a new world, every object strikes with wonder and surprise. The imagination, still unsated, seems the only active principle of the mind. The most trifling occurrences give pleasure, till the gloss of novelty is worn away. When I have ceased to wonder, I may possibly grow

---

[3] *Chief decoration . . . vanity:* Signs, hung outside inns, ale-houses, and shops, identified them at a time when numerical addresses were not used.

[4] *Xixofou:* This and the name *Fipsihi* in the next sentence were derived from Voltaire, as Friedman, I, p. 472, observes.

wise; I may then call the reasoning principle to my aid, and compare those objects with each other which were before examined without reflection.

Behold me then in London, gazing at the strangers, and they at me; it seems they find somewhat absurd in my figure; and had I been never from home it is possible I might find an infinite fund of ridicule in theirs; but by long travelling I am taught to laugh at folly alone, and to find nothing truly ridiculous but villainy and vice.

When I had just quitted my native country, and crossed the Chinese wall, I fancied every deviation from the customs and manners of China was a departing from nature: I smiled at the blue lips and red foreheads of the Tonguese; and could hardly contain when I saw the Daures dress their heads with horns. The Ostiacs powdered with red earth, and the Calmuck beauties tricked out in all the finery of sheep-skin appeared highly ridiculous; but I soon perceived that the ridicule lay not in them but in me; that I falsely condemned others of absurdity, because they happened to differ from a standard originally founded in prejudice or partiality.[5]

I find no pleasure therefore in taxing the English with departing from nature in their external appearance, which is all I yet know of their character; it is possible they only endeavour to improve her simple plan, since every extravagance in dress proceeds from a desire of becoming more beautiful than nature made us; and this is so harmless a vanity that I not only pardon but approve it: A desire to be more excellent than others is what actually makes us so, and as thousands find a livelihood in society by such appetites, none but the ignorant inveigh against them.

You are not insensible, most reverend Fum Hoam, what numberless trades, even among the Chinese, subsist by the harmless pride of each other. Your nose-borers, feet-swathers, tooth-stainers, eye-brow pluckers, would all want bread, should their neighbours want vanity. These vanities, however, employ much fewer hands in China than in England; and a fine gentleman, or a fine lady, here dressed up to the fashion, seems scarcely to have a single limb that does not suffer some distortions from art.

To make a fine gentleman, several trades are required, but chiefly a barber: you have undoubtedly heard of the Jewish champion, whose strength lay in his hair; one would think that the English were for placing all wisdom there: To appear wise, nothing more is requisite here than for a man to borrow hair from the heads of all his neighbours, and clap it like a bush on his own: the distributors of law and physic stick on such quantities, that it is almost impossible, even in idea, to distinguish between the head and the hair.

Those whom I have been now describing, affect the gravity of the lion: those I am going to describe more resemble the pert vivacity of smaller animals. The barber who is still master of the ceremonies cuts their hair close to the crown; and then with a composition of meal and hogs-lard, plaisters the whole in such a manner, as to make it impossible to distinguish whether the patient wears a cap or a plaister; but to make the picture more perfectly striking, conceive the tail of some beast, a greyhound's tail, or a pigs tail for instance, appended to the

[5] . . . *Partiality:* The people whose customs are here observed are treated (though differently) in d'Argens's *Lettres Chinoises.* See the headnote.

back of the head, and reaching down to that place where tails in other animals are generally seen to begin; thus betailed and bepowdered, the man of taste fancies he improves in beauty, dresses up his hard-featured face in smiles, and attempts to look hideously tender. Thus equipped, he is qualified to make love, and hopes for success more from the powder on the outside of his head, than the sentiments within.

Yet when I consider what sort of a creature the fine lady is to whom he is supposed to pay his addresses, it is not strange to find him thus equipped in order to please. She is herself every whit as fond of powder, and tails, and hog's lard as he: to speak my secret sentiments, most reverend Fum, the ladies here are   10 horridly ugly; I can hardly endure the sight of them; they no way resemble the beauties of China; the Europeans have a quite different idea of beauty from us; when I reflect on the small footed perfections of an Eastern beauty, how is it possible I should have eyes for a woman whose feet are ten inches long. I shall never forget the beauties of my native city of Nangfew.[6] How very broad their faces; how very short their noses; how very little their eyes; how very thin their lips; how very black their teeth; the snow on the tops of Bao is not fairer than their cheeks; and their eye-brows are as small as the line by the pencil of Quamsi.[7] Here a lady with such perfections would be frightful; Dutch and Chinese beauties indeed have some resemblance, but English women are en-   20 tirely different; red cheeks, big eyes, and teeth of a most odious whiteness are not only seen here, but wished for, and then they have such masculine feet, as actually serve *some* for walking!

Yet uncivil as nature has been, they seem resolved to outdo her in unkindness; they use white powder, blue powder, and black powder for their hair, and a red powder for the face on some particular occasions.

They like to have the face of various colours, as among the Tartars of Koreki, frequently sticking on with spittle little black patches[8] on every part of it, except on the tip of the nose, which I have never seen with a patch. You'll have a better idea of their manner of placing these spots, when I have finished a map   30 of an English face patch'd up to the fashion, which shall shortly be sent to encrease your curious collection of paintings, medals and monsters.

But what surprizes more than all the rest, is, what I have just now been credibly informed by one of this country; "Most ladies here, says he, have two faces; one face to sleep in, and another to shew in company: the first is generally reserv'd for the husband and family at home, the other put on to please strangers abroad; the family face is often indifferent enough, but the out-door one looks something better; this is always made at the toilet, where the looking-glass, and toad-eater[9] sit in council and settle the complexion of the day."   40

I can't ascertain the truth of this remark, however it is actually certain, that they wear more cloaths within doors than without; and I have seen a lady who seem'd to shudder at a breeze in her own apartment, appear half naked in the streets. Farewell.

[6] *Nangfew:* In the province of Ho-nan, Lien Chi Altangi's home.
[7] *Quamsi:* Presumably a Chinese artist.
[8] *Patches:* A patch is a small piece of black silk worn on the face to show off the complexion by contrast.
[9] *Toad-eater:* An attendant, a fawning flatterer, a parasite.

Letter IX

[*The licentiousness of the English, with regard to women. A character of a woman's man.*]

To the same.

[*From Lien Chi Altangi, to Fum Hoam, first president of the Ceremonial Academy at Pekin, in China.*]

I HAVE been deceived! she whom I fancied a daughter of Paradise has proved to be one of the infamous disciples of Han![10] I have lost a trifle, I have gained the consolation of having discovered a deceiver. I once more, therefore, relax into my former indifference with regard to the English ladies, they once more begin to appear disagreeable in my eyes: Thus is my whole time passed in forming conclusions which the next minute's experience may probably destroy; the present moment becomes a comment on the past, and I improve rather in humility than wisdom.

Their laws and religion forbid the English to keep more than one woman, I therefore concluded that prostitutes were banished from society; I was deceived; every man here keeps as many wives as he can maintain; the laws are cemented with blood, praised and disregarded. The very Chinese, whose religion allows him two wives, takes not half the liberties of the English in this particular. Their laws may be compared to the books of the Sybils, they are held in great veneration, but seldom read, or seldomer understood; even those who pretend to be their guardians dispute about the meaning of many of them, and confess their ignorance of others. The law therefore which commands them to have but one wife, is strictly observed only by those for whom one is more than sufficient, or by such as have not money to buy two. As for the rest they violate it publicly, and some glory in its violation. They seem to think like the Persians, that they give evident marks of manhood by encreasing their seraglio. A mandarine therefore here generally keeps four wives, a gentleman three, and a stage-player two. As for the magistrates, the country justices and squires, they are employed first in debauching young virgins, and then punishing the transgression.

From such a picture you will be apt to conclude, that he who employs four ladies for his amusement, has four times as much constitution to spare as he who is contented with one; that a Mandarin is much cleverer than a gentleman, and a gentleman than a player, and yet it is quite the reverse; a Mandarine is frequently supported on spindle shanks, appears emaciated by luxury, and is obliged to have recourse to variety, merely from the weakness, not the vigour of his constitution, the number of his wives being the most equivocal symptom of his virility.

Beside the country squire there is also another set of men, whose whole employment consists in corrupting beauty; these the silly part of the fair sex call amiable; the more sensible part of them however give them the title of abomi-

---

[10] *Han:* The Han dynasty, relatively short and turbulent (206 B.C.–A.D. 220), grew out of war and led to civil strife. Though it was culturally a very productive period, it seems to have been the emblem for unpredictability. The foregoing may be the basis of Goldsmith's reference.

nable. You will probably demand what are the talents of a man thus caressed by the majority of the opposite sex; what talents, or what beauty is he possessed of superior to the rest of his fellows. To answer you directly, he has neither talents nor beauty, but then he is possessed of impudence and assiduity. With assiduity and impudence men of all ages, and all figures may commence admirers. I have even been told of some who made professions of expiring for love, when all the world could perceive they were going to die of old age: and what is more surprising still, such batter'd beaus are generally most infamously successful.

A fellow of this kind employs three hours every morning in dressing his head, by which is understood only his hair.   10

He is a professed admirer, not of any particular lady, but of the whole sex.

He is to suppose every lady has caught cold every night, which gives him an opportunity of calling to see how she does the next morning.

He is upon all occasions to shew himself in very great pain for the ladies; if a lady drops even a pin, he is to fly in order to present it.

He never speaks to a lady without advancing his mouth to her ear, by which he frequently addresses more senses than one.

Upon proper occasions he looks excessively tender. This is performed by laying his hand upon his heart, shutting his eyes, and shewing his teeth.

He is excessively fond of dancing a minuet with the ladies, by which is only   20
meant walking round the floor eight or ten times with his hat on, affecting great gravity, and sometimes looking tenderly on his partner.

He never affronts any man himself, and never resents an affront from another.

He has an infinite variety of small talk upon all occasions, and laughs when he has nothing more to say.

Such is the killing creature who prostrates himself to the sex till he has undone them; all whose submissions are the effects of design, and who to please the ladies almost becomes himself a lady.

Letter XIII

[An account of Westminster Abbey.]

From the same.

[From Lien Chi Altangi, to Fum Hoam, first president of the Ceremonial Academy at Pekin, in China.]

I AM just returned from Westminster-abbey, the place of sepulture for the   30
philosophers, heroes, and kings of England. What a gloom do monumental inscriptions and all the venerable remains of deceased merit inspire! Imagine a temple marked with the hand of antiquity, solemn as religious awe, adorned with all the magnificence of barbarous profusion, dim windows, fretted pillars, long colonades, and dark cielings. Think then, what were my sensations at being introduced to such a scene. I stood in the midst of the temple, and threw my eyes round on the walls filled with the statues, the inscriptions, and the monuments of the dead.

Alas, I said to myself, how does pride attend the puny child of dust even to the grave! Even humble as I am, I possess more consequence in the present scene than the greatest heroe of them all; they have toiled for an hour to gain a transient immortality, and are at length retired to the grave, where they have no attendant but the worm, none to flatter but the epitaph.

As I was indulging such reflections, a gentleman dressed in black, perceiving me to be a stranger came up, entered into conversation, and politely offered to be my instructor and guide through the temple. If any monument, said he, should particularly excite your curiosity, I shall endeavour to satisfy your demands. I accepted with thanks the gentleman's offer, adding, that "I was come 10 to observe the policy, the wisdom, and the justice of the English, in conferring rewards upon deceased merit. If adulation like this, continued I, be properly conducted, as it can no ways injure those who are flattered, so it may be a glorious incentive to those who are now capable of enjoying it. It is the duty of every good government to turn this monumental pride to its own advantage, to become strong in the aggregate from the weakness of the individual. If none but the truly great have a place in this awful repository, a temple like this will give the finest lessons of morality, and be a strong incentive to true ambition. I am told, that none have a place here but characters of the most distinguished merit." The man in black seemed impatient at my observations, 20 so I discontinued my remarks, and we walked on together to take a view of every particular monument in order as it lay.

As the eye is naturally caught by the finest objects, I could not avoid being particularly curious about one monument which appeared more beautiful than the rest; that, said I to my guide, I take to be the tomb of some very great man. By the peculiar excellence of the workmanship, and the magnificence of the design, this must be a trophy raised to the memory of some king who has saved his country from ruin, or law-giver, who has reduced his fellow-citizens from anarchy into just subjection. It is not requisite, replied my companion smiling, to have such qualifications in order to have a very fine monument here. More 30 humble abilities will suffice. *What, I suppose then, the gaining two or three battles, or the taking half a score towns, is thought a sufficient qualification?* Gaining battles, or taking towns replied the man in black, may be of service; but a gentleman may have a very fine monument here without ever seeing a battle or a siege. *This then is the monument of some poet, I presume, of one whose wit has gained him immortality?* No, sir, replied my guide, the gentleman who lies here never made verses; and as for wit, he despised it in others, because he had none himself. *Pray tell me then in a word, said I peevishly, what is the great man who lies here particularly remarkable for?* Remarkable, sir! said my companion; why, sir, the gentleman that lies here is remarkable, very remarkable—for a tomb in West- 40 minster-abbey. *But, head of my Ancestors! how has he got here; I fancy he could never bribe the guardians of the temple to give him a place? Should he not be ashamed to be seen among company, where even moderate merit would like infamy?* I suppose, replied the man in black, the gentleman was rich, and his friends, as is usual in such a case, told him he was great. He readily believed them; the guardians of the temple, as they got by the self delusion, were ready to believe him too; so he paid his money for a fine monument; and the workman, as you see, has made him one the most beautiful. Think not, however, that this gentleman is singular in his desire of being buried among the great; there are several others in the temple, who, hated and shunned by the great while alive, have come here, fully resolved to keep them company now they are dead.

As we walked along to a particular part of the temple, there, says the gentleman, pointing with his finger, that is the poets corner; there you see the monuments of Shakespear, and Milton, and Prior, and Drayton.[11] Drayton, I replied, I never heard of him before, but I have been told of one Pope, is he there? It is time enough, replied my guide, these hundred years, he is not long dead, people have not done hating him yet. Strange, cried I, can any be found to hate a man, whose life was wholly spent in entertaining and instructing his fellow creatures! Yes, says my guide, they hate him for that very reason. There are a set of men called answerers of books, who take upon them to watch the republic of letters, and distribute reputation by the sheet; they somewhat resemble the eunuchs in a seraglio, who are incapable of giving pleasure themselves, and hinder those that would. These answerers have no other employment but to cry out Dunce, and Scribbler, to praise the dead, and revile the living, to grant a man of confessed abilities some small share of merit, to applaud twenty blockheads in order to gain the reputation of candour, and to revile the moral character of the man whose writings they cannot injure. Such wretches are kept in pay by some mercenary bookseller, or more frequently, the bookseller himself takes this dirty work off their hands, as all that is required is to be very abusive and very dull; every Poet of any genius is sure to find such enemies, he feels, though he seems to despise their malice, they make him miserable here, and in the pursuit of empty fame, at last he gains solid anxiety.

Has this been the case with every poet I see here? cried I—Yes, with every mother's son of them, replied he, except he happen'd to be born a mandarine. If he has much money, he may buy reputation from your book answerers, as well as a monument from the guardians of the temple.

But are there not some men of distinguished taste, as in China, who are willing to patronize men of merit and soften the rancour of malevolent dulness?

I own there are many, replied the man in black, but, alas! Sir, the book answerers croud about them, and call themselves the writers of books; and the patron is too indolent to distinguish; thus poets are kept at a distance, while their enemies eat up all their rewards at the mandarine's table.

Leaving this part of the temple, we made up to an iron gate, thro' which my companion told me we were to pass in order to see the monuments of the kings. Accordingly I marched up without further ceremony, and was going to enter, when a person who held the gate in his hand, told me I must pay first. I was surprised at such a demand; and asked the man whether the people of England kept a *shew*? Whether the paltry sum he demanded was not a national reproach? Whether it was not more to the honour of the country to let their magnificence or their antiquities be openly seen, than thus meanly to tax a curiosity which tended to their own honour? As for your questions, replied the

---

[11] *Prior and Drayton:* Matthew Prior (1664–1721), English diplomatist and poet; Michael Drayton (1563–1631), English poet, best known for his *Polyolbion*, a poem celebrating England.

gate-keeper, to be sure they may be very right, because I don't understand them, but as for that there three-pence, I farm it from one, who rents it from another, who hires it from a third, who leases it from the guardians of the temple, and we all must live. I expected upon paying here to see something extraordinary, since what I had seen for nothing filled me with so much surprize, but in this I was disappointed; there was little more within than black coffins, rusty armour, tatter'd standards, and some few slovenly figures in wax. I was sorry I had paid, but I comforted myself by considering it would be my last payment. A person attended us, who, without once blushing, told an hundred lies, he talked of a lady who died by pricking her finger, of a king with a golden head, and twenty such pieces of absurdity; look ye there, gentlemen, says he, pointing to an old oak chair, there's a curiosity for ye; in that chair the kings of England were crowned, you see also a stone underneath, and that stone is Jacob's pillow.[12] I could see no curiosity either in the oak chair or the stone; could I, indeed, behold one of the old kings of England seated in this, or Jacob's head laid upon the other, there might be something curious in the sight; but in the present case, there was no more reason for my surprize than if I should pick a stone from their streets, and call it a curiosity, merely because one of their kings happened to tread upon it as he passed in a procession.

From hence our conductor led us through several dark walks and winding ways, uttering lies, talking to himself, and flourishing a wand which he held in his hand. He reminded me of the black magicians of Kobi. After we had been almost fatigued with a variety of objects, he, at last desired me to consider attentively a certain suit of armour, which seemed to shew nothing remarkable. This armour, said he, belonged to general Monk.[13] *Very surprising, that a general should wear armour.* And pray, added he, observe this cap, this is general Monk's cap. *Very strange, indeed, very strange, that a general should have a cap also! Pray friend what might this cap have cost originally?* That, Sir, says he, I don't know, but this cap is all the wages I have for my trouble. *A very small recompence, truly,* said I. Not so very small, replied he, for every gentleman puts some money into it, and I spend the money. *What, more money! still more money!* Every gentleman gives something, sir. I'll give thee nothing, returned I; the guardians of the temple should pay you your wages, friend, and not permit you to squeeze thus from every spectator. When we pay our money at the door to see a shew, we never give more as we are going out. Sure the guardians of the temple can never think they get enough. Shew me the gate; if I stay longer, I may probably meet with more of those ecclesiastical beggars.

Thus leaving the temple precipitately, I returned to my lodgings, in order to ruminate over what was great, and to despise what was mean in the occurrences of the day.

10

20

30

40

---

[12] *Jacob's pillow:* The Stone of Scone, or Coronation Stone.
[13] *General Monk:* George Monk, First Duke of Albemarle (1608–1670), an English general instrumental in bringing about the restoration of Charles II.

Letter XIX

[*The English method of treating women caught in adultery. The Russian method.*]

To the same.

[*From Lien Chi Altangi, to Fum Hoam, first president of the Ceremonial Academy at Pekin, in China.*]

THE gentleman dressed in black, who was my companion through Westminster Abbey,[14] came yesterday to pay me a visit; and after drinking tea, we both resolved to take a walk together, in order to enjoy the freshness of the country, which now begins to resume its verdure. Before we got out of the suburbs, however, we were stopped in one of the streets by a crowd of people gathered in a circle round a man and his wife, who seemed too loud and too angry to be understood. The people were highly pleased with the dispute, which upon enquiry we found to be between Dr. Cacafogo, an apothecary, and his wife. The doctor, it seems, coming unexpectedly into his wife's apartment, found a gentleman there in circumstances not in the least equivocal.   10

The doctor, who was a person of nice honour, resolving to revenge the flagrant insult, immediately flew to the chimney-piece, and taking down a rusty blunderbuss, drew the trigger upon the defiler of his bed; the delinquent would certainly have been shot through the head, but that the piece had not been charged for many years. The gallant made a shift to escape through the window, but the lady still remained; and as she well knew her husband's temper, undertook to manage the quarrel without a second. He was furious, and she loud; their noise had gathered all the mob who charitably assembled on the occasion, not to prevent, but to enjoy the quarrel.

Alas, said I to my companion, what will become of this unhappy creature   20 thus caught in adultery! Believe me, I pity her from my heart; her husband, I suppose, will shew her no mercy. Will they burn her as in India, or behead her as in Persia; will they load her with stripes as in Turkey, or keep her in perpetual imprisonment, as with us in China? Prythee what is the wife's punishment in England for such offences? When a lady is thus caught tripping, replied my companion, they never punish her, but the husband. You surely jest, interrupted I; I am a foreigner, and you would abuse my ignorance. I am really serious, returned he; Dr. Cacafogo has caught his wife in the act; but as he had no witnesses, his small testimony goes for nothing; the consequence therefore of his discovery will be, that she may be packed off to live among her relations,   30 and the doctor must be obliged to allow her a separate maintenance. Amazing, cried I! is it not enough that she is permitted to live separate from the object she detests, but must he give her money to keep her in spirits too? That he must, says my guide; and be called a cuckold by all his neighbours into the bargain. The men will laugh at him, the ladies will pity him; and all that his warmest friends can say in his favour, will be, that the *poor good soul has never had any harm in him.* I want patience, interrupted I; what! are there no private chastisements for the wife; no schools of penitence to shew her her folly; no rods for

---

[14] *Westminster Abbey:* See Letter XIII.

such delinquents? Psha man, replied he smiling; if every delinquent among us were to be treated in your manner, one half of the kingdom would flog the other.

I must confess, my dear Fum, that if I were an English husband, of all things I would take care not to be jealous, nor busily pry into those secrets my wife was pleased to keep from me. Should I detect her infidelity, what is the consequence? If I calmly pocket the abuse, I am laugh'd at by her and her gallant; if I talk my griefs aloud like a tragedy heroe, I am laughed at by the whole world. The course then I'd take would be, whenever I went out, to tell my wife where I was going, lest I should unexpectedly meet her abroad in company with some   10
dear deceiver. Whenever I returned, I would use a peculiar rap at the door, and give four loud hems as I walked deliberately up the stair-case. I would never inquisitively peep under her bed, or look behind the curtains. And even though I knew the captain was there, I would calmly take a dish of my wife's cool tea, and talk of the army with reverence.

Of all nations, the Russians seem to me to behave most wisely in such circumstances. The wife promises her husband never to let him see her transgressions of this nature; and he as punctually promises, whenever she is so detected, without the least anger, to beat her without mercy: so they both know what each has to expect; the lady transgresses, is beaten, taken again into favour,   20
and all goes on as before.

When a Russian young lady, therefore, is to be married, her father, with a cudgel in his hand, asks the bridegroom, whether he chuses this virgin for his bride? to which the other replies in the affirmative. Upon this, the father turning the lady three times round, and giving her three strokes with his cudgel on the back; *my dear*, cries he, *these are the last blows you are ever to receive from your tender father, I resign my authority, and my cudgel to your husband; he knows better than me the use of either.* The bridegroom knows decorums too well to accept of the cudgel abruptly, he assures the father that the lady will never want it, and that he would not for the world make any use of it. But the father, who knows   30
what the lady may want better than he, insists upon his acceptance. Upon this, there follows a scene of Russian politeness, while one refuses, and the other offers the cudgel. The whole, however, ends with the bridegroom's taking it, upon which the lady drops a courtesy in token of obedience, and the ceremony proceeds as usual.

There is something excessively fair and open in this method of courtship. By this, both sides are prepared for all the matrimonial adventures that are to follow. Marriage has been compared to a game of skill for life; it is generous thus in both parties to declare they are sharpers in the beginning. In England, I am told both sides use every art to conceal their defects from each other before   40
marriage, and the rest of their lives may be regarded as doing penance for their former dissimulation. Farewell.

Letter XXV*

[*The character of the man in black; with some instances of his inconsistent conduct.*]

To the same.

[*From Lien Chi Altangi, to Fum Hoam, first president of the Ceremonial Academy at Pekin, in China.*]

THO' fond of many acquaintances, I desire an intimacy only with a few. The man in black whom I have often mentioned, is one whose friendship I cou'd wish to acquire, because he possesses my esteem. His manners, it is true, are tinctured with some strange inconsistencies; and he may be justly termed an humourist in a nation of humourists. Tho' he is generous even to profusion, he affects to be thought a prodigy of parsimony and prudence; though his conversation be replete with the most sordid and selfish maxims, his heart is dilated with the most unbounded love. I have known him profess himself a man-hater, while his cheek was glowing with compassion; and while his looks were softened into pity, I have heard him use the language of the most unbounded   10
ill nature. Some affect humanity and tenderness; others boast of having such dispositions from nature; but he is the only man I ever knew who seemed ashamed of his natural benevolence. He takes as much pains to hide his feelings as any hypocrite would to conceal his indifference; but on every unguarded moment the mask drops off, and reveals him to the most superficial observer.

In one of our late excursions into the country, happening to discourse upon the provision that was made for the poor in England, he seemed amazed how any of his countrymen could be so foolishly weak as to relieve occasional objects of charity, when the laws had made such ample provision for their support. In every parish house, says he, the poor are supplied with food, cloaths,   20
fire, and a bed to lie on; they want no more, I desire no more my self; yet still they seem discontented. I'm surprized at the inactivity of our magistrates, in not taking up such vagrants who are only a weight upon the industrious; I'm surprized that the people are found to relieve them, when they must be at the same time sensible that it, in some measure, encourages idleness, extravagance, and imposture. Were I to advise any man for whom I had the least regard, I would caution him by all means not to be imposed upon by their false pretences: let me assure you, Sir, they are impostors, every one of them; and rather merit a prison than relief.

He was proceeding in this strain earnestly, to dissuade me from an impru-   30
dence of which I am seldom guilty; when an old man who still had about him the remnants of tattered finery, implored our compassion. He assured us that he was no common beggar, but forced into the shameful profession, to support a dying wife and five hungry children. Being prepossessed against such falshoods, his story had not the least influence upon me; but it was quite otherwise with the man in black; I could see it visibly operate upon his countenance, and effectually interrupt his harangue. I could easily perceive that his heart burned to relieve the five starving children, but he seemed ashamed to discover

* Friedman numbers this XXVI.

his weakness to me. While he thus hesitated between compassion and pride, I pretended to look another way, and he seized this opportunity of giving the poor petitioner a piece of silver bidding him at the same time, in order that I should hear, go work for his bread, and not teize passengers with such impertinent falsehoods for the future.

As he had fancied himself quite unperceived, he continued, as we proceeded, to rail against beggars with as much animosity as before; he threw in some episodes on his own amazing prudence and œconomy, with his profound skill in discovering impostors; he explained the manner in which he would deal with beggars were he a magistrate, hinted at enlarging some of the prisons for 10 their reception, and told two stories of ladies that were robbed by beggar men. He was beginning a third to the same purpose, when a sailor with a wooden leg once more crossed our walks, desiring our pity, and blessing our limbs. I was for going on without taking any notice, but my friend looking wishfully upon the poor petitioner, bid me stop, and he would shew me with how much ease he could at any time detect an impostor.

He now therefore assumed a look of importance, and in an angry tone began to examine the sailor, demanding in what engagement he was thus disabled and rendered unfit for service. The sailor replied in a tone as angrily as he, that he had been an officer on board a private ship of war, and that he 20 had lost his leg abroad in defence of those who did nothing at home. At this reply, all my friend's importance vanished in a moment; he had not a single question more to ask; he now only studied what method he should take to relieve him unobserved. He had however no easy part to act, as he was obliged to preserve the appearance of ill nature before me, and yet relieve himself by relieving the sailor. Casting therefore a furious look upon some bundles of chips which the fellow carried in a string at his back, my friend demanded how he sold his matches; but not waiting for a reply, desired, in a surly tone, to have a shilling's worth. The sailor seemed at first surprised at his demand, but soon recollecting himself, and presenting his whole bundle, Here, master, 30 says he, take all my cargo, and a blessing into the bargain.

It is impossible to describe with what an air of triumph my friend marched off with his new purchase; he assured me, that he was firmly of opinion that those fellows must have stolen their goods, who could thus afford to sell them for half value; he informed me of several different uses to which those chips might be applied; he expatiated largely upon the savings that would result from lighting candles with a match instead of thrusting them into the fire. He averred, that he would as soon have parted with a tooth as his money to those vagabonds, unless for some valuable consideration. I cannot tell how long this panegyric upon frugality and matches might have continued, had not his 40 attention been called off by another object more distressful than either of the former. A woman in rags, with one child in her arms, and another on her back, was attempting to sing ballads, but with such a mournful voice that it was difficult to determine whether she was singing or crying. A wretch, who, in the deepest distress still aimed at good humour, was an object my friend was by no means capable of withstanding; his vivacity, and his discourse were instantly interrupted; upon this occasion his very dissimulation had forsaken him. Even, in my presence, he immediately applied his hands to his pockets, in order to relieve her, but guess his confusion, when he found he had already given away all the money he carried about him to former objects. The misery painted in the woman's visage, was not half so strongly expressed as the agony in his. He continued to search for some time, but to no purpose, 'till, at length, recollecting himself, with a face of ineffable good nature, as he had no money, he put into her hands his shilling's worth of matches.

Letter XXVI*

[*The history of the man in black.*]

To the same.

[*From Lien Chi Altangi, to Fum Hoam, first president of the Ceremonial Academy at Pekin, in China.*]

AS there appeared something reluctantly good in the character of my companion, I must own it surprized me what could be his motives for thus concealing virtues which others take such pains to display. I was unable to repress my desire of knowing the history of a man who thus seemed to act under continual restraint, and whose benevolence was rather the effect of appetite than reason.

It was not however till after repeated solicitations he thought proper to gratify my curiosity.

"If you are fond, says he, of hearing *hair breadth 'scapes*, my history must certainly please; for I have been for twenty years upon the very verge of starving, without ever being starved. My father, the younger son of a good family, was possessed of a small living in the church. His education was above his fortune, and his generosity greater than his education. Poor as he was, he had his flatterers still poorer than himself; for every dinner he gave them, they returned him an equivalent in praise; and this was all he wanted; the same ambition that actuates a monarch at the head of an army, influenced my father at the head of his table: he told the story of the ivy-tree, and that was laughed at; he repeated the jest of the two scholars and one pair of breeches, and the company laughed at that; but the story of Taffy in the sedan chair was sure to set the table in a roar; thus his pleasure encreased, in proportion to the pleasure he gave; he loved all the world, and he fancied all the world loved him.

"As his fortune was but small, he lived up to the very extent of it; he had no intentions of leaving his children money, for that was dross; he was resolved they should have learning; for learning he used to observe, was better than silver or gold. For this purpose he undertook to instruct us himself; and took as much pains to form our morals, as to improve our understanding, We were told that universal benevolence was what first cemented society; we were taught to consider all the wants of mankind as our own; to regard the *human face divine* with affection and esteem; he wound us up to be mere machines of pity, and rendered us incapable of withstanding the slightest impulse made either by real

---

* Friedman numbers this XXVII.

or fictitious distress; in a word, we were perfectly instructed in the art of *giving away* thousands, before we were taught the more necessary qualifications of *getting* a farthing.

"I cannot avoid imagining, that, thus refined by his lessons out of all my suspicion, and divested of even all the little cunning which nature had given me, I resembled, upon my first entrance into the busy and insidious world, one of those gladiators who were exposed without armour in the amphitheatre at Rome. My father, however, who had only seen the world on one side, seemed to triumph in my superior discernment; though my whole stock of wisdom consisted in being able to talk like himself upon subjects that once were useful, because they were then topics of the busy world; but that now were utterly useless, because connected with the busy world no longer.

"The first opportunity he had of finding his expectations disappointed, was at the very middling figure I made in the university: he had flattered himself that he should soon see me rising into the foremost rank in literary reputation, but was mortified to find me utterly unnoticed and unknown. His disappointment might have been partly ascribed to his having over-rated my talents, and partly to my dislike of mathematical reasonings at a time, when my imagination and memory yet unsatisfied, were more eager after new objects, than desirous of reasoning upon those I knew. This did not, however, please my tutors, who observed, indeed, that I was a little dull; but at the same time allowed, that I seemed to be *very good natured*, and had no harm in me.

"After I had resided at college seven years my father died, and left me— his blessing. Thus shoved from shore without ill nature to protect, or cunning to guide, or proper stores to subsist me in so dangerous a voyage, I was obliged to embark in the wide world at twenty-two. But, in order to settle in life, my friends *advised* (for they always advise when they begin to despise us) they advised me, I say, to go into orders.

"To be obliged to wear a long whig, when I liked a short one, or a black coat, when I generally dressed in brown, I thought was such a restraint upon my liberty, that I absolutely rejected the proposal. A priest in England, is not the same mortified creature with a bonze[15] in China; with us, not he that fasts best, but eats best, is reckoned the best liver; yet I rejected a life of luxury, indolence, and ease, from no other consideration but that boyish one of dress. So that my friends were now perfectly satisfied I was undone, and yet they thought it a pity for one who had not the least harm in him, and was so very good-natured.

"Poverty naturally begets dependance, and I was admitted as flatterer to a great man. At first I was surprised, that the situation of a flatterer at a great man's table could be thought disagreeable; there was no great trouble in listening attentively when his lordship spoke, and laughing when he looked round for applause. This even good manners might have obliged me to perform. I found, however, too soon, that his lordship was a greater dunce than myself; and from that very moment my power of flattery was at an end. I now rather aimed at setting him right, than at receiving his absurdities with submission:

[15] *Bonze:* A term applied by Europeans to the Buddhist clergy of Japan and some-times China.

to flatter those we do not know is an easy task; but to flatter our intimate acquaintances, all whose foibles are strongly in our eye, is drudgery insupportable. Every time I now opened my lips in praise, my falshood went to my conscience; his lordship soon perceived me to be unfit for service; I was therefore discharged; my patron at the same time being graciously pleased to observe, that he believed I was tolerably good natured, and had not the least harm in me.

"Disappointed in ambition I had recourse to love. A young lady who lived with her aunt, and was possessed of a pretty fortune in her own disposal, had given me, as I fancied, some reasons to expect success. The symptoms by which I was guided were striking; she had always laughed with me at her aukward 10 acquaintance, and at her aunt among the number; she always observed, that a man of sense would make a better husband than a fool, and I as constantly applied the observation in my own favour. She continually talked in my company of friendship and the beauties of the mind, and spoke of Mr. Shrimp my rival's high-heel'd shoes with detestation. These were circumstances which I thought strongly in my favour; so after resolving, and re-resolving, I had courage enough to tell her my mind. Miss heard my proposal with serenity, seeming at the same time to study the figures of her fan. Out at last it came. There was but one small objection to complete our happiness, which was no more, than——that she was married three months before to Mr. Shrimp with high- 20 heel'd shoes. By way of consolation however she observed, that tho' I was disappointed in her, my addresses to her aunt would probably kindle her into sensibility, as the old lady always allowed me to be very good-natured, and not to have the least share of harm in me.

"Yet still I had friends, numerous friends, and to them I was resolved to apply. O friendship! thou fond soother of the human breast, to thee we fly in every calamity; to thee the wretched seek for succour; on thee the care-tired son of misery fondly relies; from thy kind assistance the unfortunate always hopes relief, and may be ever sure of——disappointment! My first application was to a city scrivener,[16] who had frequently offered to lend me 30 money when he knew I did not want it. I informed him, that now was the time to put his friendship to the test; that I wanted to borrow a couple of hundreds for a certain occasion, and was resolved to take it up from him. And pray, Sir, cried my friend, do you want all this money? Indeed I never wanted it more, returned I. I am sorry for that, cries the scrivener, with all my heart; for they who want money when they come to borrow, will always want money when they should come to pay.

"From him I flew with indignation to one of the best friends I had in the world, and made the same request. Indeed, Mr. Dry-bone, cries my friend, I always thought it would come to this. You know, sir, I would not advise 40 you but for your own good; but your conduct has hitherto been ridiculous in the highest degree, and some of your acquaintance always thought you a very silly fellow; let me see, you want two hundred pounds; do you want only two hundred, sir, exactly? To confess a truth, returned I, I shall want three hundred; but then I have another friend from whom I can borrow the rest.

---

[16] *Scrivener:* A notary; a manager of private funds for a fee, one empowered   to prepare certain legal documents.

Why then, replied my friend, if you would take my advice, and you know I should not presume to advise you but for your own good, I would recommend it to you to borrow the whole sum from that other friend; and then one note will serve for all, you know.

"Poverty now began to come fast upon me, yet instead of growing more provident or cautious as I grew poor, I became every day more indolent and simple. A friend was arrested for fifty pounds, I was unable to extricate him except by becoming his bail. When at liberty he fled from his creditors, and left me to take his place. In prison I expected greater satisfactions than I had enjoyed at large. I hoped to converse with men in this new world simple and believing like myself, but I found them as cunning and as cautious as those in the world I had left behind. They spunged up my money whilst it lasted, borrowed my coals and never paid them, and cheated me when I play'd at cribbage. All this was done because they believed me to be very good-natured, and knew that I had no harm in me.

"Upon my first entrance into this mansion, which is to some the abode of despair, I felt no sensations different from those I experienced abroad. I was now on one side the door, and those who were unconfined were on the other; this was all the difference between us. At first indeed I felt some uneasiness, in considering how I should be able to provide this week for the wants of the week ensuing; but after some time, if I found myself sure of eating one day, I never troubled my head how I was to be supplied another. I seized every precarious meal with the utmost good humour, indulged no rants of spleen at my situation, never called down heaven and all the stars to behold me dining upon an halfpenny-worth of radishes; my very companions were taught to believe that I liked sallad better than mutton. I contented myself with thinking, that all my life I should either eat white bread or brown; considered that all that happened was best, laughed when I was not in pain, took the world as it went, and read Tacitus[17] often, for want of more books and company.

"How long I might have continued in this torpid state of simplicity I cannot tell, had I not been rouzed by seeing an old acquaintance, whom I knew to be a prudent blockhead preferred to a place in the government. I now found that I had pursued a wrong track, and that the true way of being able to relieve others, was first to aim at independance myself. My immediate care, therefore, was to leave my present habitation, and make an entire reformation in my conduct and behaviour. For a free, open, undesigning deportment, I put on that of closeness, prudence, and œconomy. One of the most heroic actions I ever performed, and for which I shall praise myself as long as I live, was the refusing half a crown to an old acquaintance, at the time when he wanted it, and I had it to spare; for this alone I deserve to be decreed an ovation.[18]

"I now therefore pursued a course of uninterrupted frugality, seldom wanted a dinner, and was consequently invited to twenty. I soon began to get the character of a saving hunks,[19] that had money; and insensibly grew into esteem. Neighbours have asked my advice in the disposal of their daughters,

---

[17] *Tacitus:* Publius (?) Cornelius Tacitus (c. 55–c. 117), Roman historian; also rhetorician.

[18] *Decreed an ovation:* The *ovatio* was a lesser order of celebration than the full *triumphus* (triumph) decreed by the Roman senate for its victorious generals.

[19] *Hunks:* A close-fisted man, a miser.

and I have always taken care not to give any. I have contracted a friendship with an alderman, only by observing, that if we take a farthing from a thousand pound it will be a thousand pound no longer. I have been invited to a pawnbroker's table, by pretending to hate gravy; and am now actually upon treaty of marriage with a rich widow for only having observed that the bread was rising. If ever I am ask'd a question, whether I know it or not, instead of answering, I only smile and look wise. If a charity is proposed, I go about with the hat, but put nothing in myself. If a wretch solicits my pity, I observe that the world is filled with impostors, and take a certain method of not being deceived by never relieving. In short, I now find the truest way of finding esteem   10
even from the indigent, is *to give away nothing, and thus have much in our power to give.*"

Letter XL*

[*The behaviour of the congregation in St. Paul's church at prayers.*]

To the same.

[*From Lien Chi Altangi, to Fum Hoam, first president of the Ceremonial Academy at Pekin, in China.*]

SOME time since I sent thee, oh holy disciple of Confucius, an account of the grand abbey or mausoleum of the kings and heroes of this nation. I have since been introduced to a temple not so ancient, but far superior in beauty and magnificence. In this, which is the most considerable of the empire, there are no pompous inscriptions, no flattery paid the dead; but all is elegant and awfully simple. There are however a few rags hung round the walls, which have at a vast expence been taken from the enemy in the present war. The silk of which they are composed when new, might be valued at half a string   20
of copper money in China; yet this wise people fitted out a fleet and an army in order to seize them; tho' now grown old, and scarce capable of being patched up into a handkerchief. By this conquest the English are said to have gained, and the French to have lost much honour. Is the honour of European nations placed only in tattered silk?

In this temple I was permitted to remain during the whole service; and were you not already acquainted with the religion of the English, you might, from my description, be inclined to believe them as grossly idolatrous as the disciples of Lao. The idol which they seem to address, strides like a colossus over the door of the inner temple, which here, as with the Jews, is esteem'd the   30
most sacred part of the building. It's oracles are delivered in an hundred various tones; which seem to inspire the worshippers with enthusiasm and awe: an old woman who appeared to be the priestess, was employed in various attitudes, as she felt the inspiration. When it began to speak, all the people remained fix'd in silent attention, nodding assent, looking approbation, appearing highly edified by those sounds, which to a stranger might seem inarticulate and unmeaning.

---

* Friedman numbers this letter XLI.

When the idol had done speaking, and the priestess had locked up its lungs with a key; observing almost all the company leaving the temple, I concluded the service was over, and taking my hat, was going to walk away with the crowd, when I was stopt by the man in black, who assur'd me that the ceremony had scarcely yet begun! What, cried I, do I not see almost the whole body of the worshippers leaving the church? Would you persuade me that such numbers who profess religion and morality, would in this shameless manner quit the temple before the service was concluded, you surely mistake; not even the Kalmouks would be guilty of such an indecency, tho' all the object of their worship was but a joint stool! My friend seem'd to blush for his country- men, assuring me that those whom I saw running away, were only a parcel of musical blockheads, whose passion was merely for sounds, and whose heads were as empty as a fiddle case; those who remain behind, says he, are the true Religious; they make use of music to warm their hearts, and to lift them to a proper pitch of rapture; examine their behaviour, and you will confess there are some among us who practise true devotion.

I now looked round me as he directed, but saw nothing of that fervent devotion which he had promised; one of the worshippers appeared to be ogling the company through a glass; another was fervent not in addresses to heaven, but to his mistress; a third whispered, a fourth took snuff; and the priest himself in a drowsy tone, read over the *duties* of the day.

Bless my eyes, cried I, as I happened to look towards the door, what do I see; one of the worshippers fallen fast asleep, and actually sunk down on his cushion: is he now enjoying the benefit of a trance, or does he receive the influence of some mysterious vision! *Alas, alas,* replied my companion, *no such thing; he has only had the misfortune of eating too hearty a dinner, and finds it impossible to keep his eyes open.* Turning to another part of the temple, I perceived a young lady just in the same circumstances and attitude; strange, cried I, can she too have over-eaten herself? *O, fie,* replied my friend, *you now grow censorious. She grow drowsy from eating too much; that would be profanation! She only sleeps now from having sat up all night at a brag party.*[20] Turn me where I will then, says I, I can perceive no single symptom of devotion among the worshippers, except from that old woman in the corner, who sits groaning behind the long sticks of a mourning fan; she indeed seems greatly edified with what she hears. *Aye,* replied my friend, *I knew we should find some to catch you: I know her; that is the deaf lady who lives in the cloysters.*

In short, the remissness of behaviour in almost all the worshippers, and some even of the guardians, struck me with surpize; I had been taught to believe that none were ever promoted to offices in the temple, but men remarkable for their superior sancity, learning, and rectitude; that there was no such thing heard of as persons being introduced into the church merely to oblige a senator, or provide for the younger branch of a noble family: I expected, as their minds were continually set upon heavenly things, to see their eyes directed there also, and hoped from their behaviour to perceive their inclinations corresponding with their duty. But I am since informed, that some are appointed

[20] *Brag party:* A party at which the   played.
card game of brag (similar to poker) was

to preside over temples they never visit; and, while they receive all the money, are contented with letting others do all the good.   Adieu.

Letter LXIX*

[*The marriage act censured.*]

From the same.

[*From Lien Chi Altangi, to Fum Hoam, first president of the Ceremonial Academy at Pekin, in China.*]

NOT far from this city lives a poor tinker, who has educated seven sons, all at this very time in arms and fighting for their country, and what reward do you think has the tinker from the state for such important services? None in the world; his sons, when the war is over, may probably be whipt from parish to parish as vagabonds, and the old man, when past labour, may die a prisoner in some house of correction.

Such a worthy subject in China would be held in universal reverence; his services would be rewarded, if not with dignities, at least with an exemption   10
from labour; he would take the left hand at feasts, and mandarines themselves would be proud to shew their submission. The *English* laws punish vice, the *Chinese* laws do more, they reward virtue!

Considering the little encouragement given to matrimony here, I am not surprized at the discouragements given to propagation. Would you believe it, my dear *Fum Hoam*, there are laws made, which even forbid the peoples marrying each other. By the head of *Confucius* I jest not; there are such laws in being here; and yet their law-givers have neither been instructed among the *Hottentots*, nor imbibed their principles of equity from the natives of *Anamaboo*.

There are laws which ordain, that no man shall marry a woman against her   20
own consent. This, though contrary to what we are taught in *Asia*, and though in some measure a clog upon matrimony, I have no great objection to. There are laws which ordain, that no woman shall marry against her father and mother's consent, unless arrived at an age of maturity; by which is understood those years, when women with us are generally past child-bearing. This must be a clog upon matrimony, as it is more difficult for the lover to please three than one, and much more difficult to please old people than young ones. The laws ordain, that the consenting couple shall take a long time to consider before they marry; this is a very great clog, because people love to have all rash actions done in a hurry. It is ordained, that all marriages shall be proclaimed   30
before celebration; this is a severe clog, as many are ashamed to have their marriage made public, from motives of vicious modesty, and many afraid from views of temporal interest. It is ordained, that there is nothing sacred in the ceremony, but that it may be dissolved to all intents and purposes by the authority of any civil magistrate. And yet opposite to this it is ordained, that the priest shall be paid a large sum of money for granting his sacred permission.

Thus you see, my friend, that matrimony here is hedged round with so

* Friedman numbers this letter LXXII.

many obstructions, that those who are willing to break through or surmount them, must be contented, if at last they find it a bed of thorns. The laws are not to blame, for they have deterred the people from engaging as much as they could. It is indeed become a very serious affair in *England*, and none but serious people are generally found willing to engage. The young, the gay, and the beautiful, who have motives of passion only to induce them, are seldom found to embark, as those inducements are taken away, and none but the old, the ugly, and the mercenary are seen to unite, who, if they have any posterity at all, will probably be an ill-favoured race like themselves.

What gave rise to those laws might have been some such accidents as these. 10
It sometimes happened, that a miser who had spent all his youth, in scraping up money to give his daughter such a fortune as might get her a mandarin husband, found his expectations disappointed at last, by her running away with his footman: this must have been a sad shock to the poor disconsolate parent, to see his poor daughter in a one horse chaise, when he had designed her for a coach and six; what a stroke from providence! to see his dear money, go to enrich a beggar, all nature cried out at the profanation!

It sometimes happened also, that a lady who had inherited all the titles, and all the nervous complaints of nobility, thought fit to impair her dignity and mend her constitution, by marrying a farmer; this must have been a sad shock 20
to her inconsolable relations, to see so fine a flower snatched from a flourishing family and planted in a dunghill; this was an absolute inversion of the first principles of things.

In order therefore to prevent the great from being thus contaminated by vulgar alliances, the obstacles to matrimony have been so contrived, that the rich only can marry among the rich, and the poor, who would leave celibacy, must be content to encrease their poverty with a wife. Thus have their laws fairly inverted the inducements to matrimony; nature tells us, that beauty is the proper allurement to those who are rich, and money of those who are poor; but things here are so contrived, that the rich are invited to marry by that fortune which 30
they do not want, and the poor have no inducement, but that beauty which they do not feel.

An equal diffusion of riches through any country ever constitutes its happiness. Great wealth in the possession of one stagnates, and extreme poverty with another keeps him in unambitious indigence; but the moderately rich are generally active; not too far removed from poverty to fear its calamities, nor too near extreme wealth to slacken the nerve of labour, they remain still between both in a state of continual fluctuation. How impolitic therefore are those laws which promote the accumulation of wealth among the rich, more impolitic still in attempting to increase the depression on poverty. 40

Bacon[21] the English philosopher, compares money to manure; if gathered in heaps, says he, it does no good: on the contrary, it becomes offensive. But being spread, though never so thinly, over the surface of the earth, it enriches the whole country. Thus the wealth a nation possesses must expatiate, or it is of no benefit to the public; it becomes rather a grievance, where matrimonial laws thus confine it to a few.

---

[21] *Bacon:* Sir Francis Bacon (1561–1626), English philosopher and statesman. See his essay "Of Seditions and Troubles," for the point referred to in the text.

But this restraint upon matrimonial community, even considered in a physical light, is injurious. As those who rear up animals take all possible pains to cross the strain in order to improve the breed; so in those countries, where marriage is most free, the inhabitants are found every age to improve in stature and in beauty; on the contrary where it is confined to a *cast*, a *tribe*, or an *hord*, as among the Gaurs, the Jews, or the Tartars, each division soon assumes a family likeness, and every tribe degenerates into peculiar deformity. From hence it may be easily inferred, that if the mandarines here are resolved only to marry among each other, they will soon produce a posterity with mandarine faces; and we shall see the heir of some honourable family scarce equal   10
to the abortion of a country farmer.

These are a few of the obstacles to marriage here, and it is certain they have in some measure answered the end, for celibacy is both frequent and fashionable. Old batchelors appear abroad without a mask, and old maids, my dear *Fum Hoam*, have been absolutely known to ogle. To confess in friendship; if I were an Englishman, I fancy I should be an old batchelor myself; I should never find courage to run through all the adventures prescribed by the law. I could submit to court my mistress herself upon reasonable terms, but to court her father, her mother, and a long tribe of cousins, aunts and relations, and then stand the butt of a whole country church: I would as soon turn tail and make   20
love to her grandmother.

I can conceive no other reason for thus loading matrimony, with so many prohibitions, unless it be that the country was thought already too populous, and this was found to be the most effectual means of thinning it. If this was the motive, I cannot but congratulate the wise projectors on the success of their scheme. Hail, O ye dim-sighted politicians, ye weeders of men! 'Tis yours to clip the wing of industry, and convert Hymen[22] to a broker. 'Tis yours to behold small objects with a microscopic eye, but to be blind to those which require an extent of vision. 'Tis yours, O ye discerners of mankind, to lay the line between society, and weaken that force by dividing, which should bind with   30
united vigour. 'Tis yours, to introduce national real distress, in order to avoid the imaginary distresses of a few. Your actions can be justified by an hundred reasons like truth; they can be opposed by but a few reasons, and those reasons are true.   Farewel.

(1760–1761)

[22] *Hymen:* The god of marriage.

Headnote to
THE DESERTED VILLAGE

The Deserted Village often depends on generalized descriptions, trite sentiments, and a superficial, self-righteous morality. Any close look at the work may expose lapses in verbal sophistication, particularly in diction and in the repetition of rhyme words. It was nevertheless a popular poem in Goldsmith's day, and it still pleases readers of eighteenth-century literature. The reason for this long-lived good reception can hardly be its social or its moral appeal. The explanation is probably to be found in its sentimental attractiveness, and more important, in its art, which moderates the weaknesses noted above. The principle governing the structure of the poem is simple to fix, in its most obvious workings, at least. The narrator begins by characterizing the village of Auburn, fully and lovingly, as his home. Given such a status, it becomes the center of the world of the poem, and more particularly it becomes a place that will always be available, one begins (not logically) to feel. Summer lingers there; everything about the place is humanly warm and welcoming; it is, in short, a realm without tensions—no seasons, no evil, no self-consciousness—to suggest it can be destroyed. Then abruptly, the village is taken away: its ". . . charms are all withdrawn." Goldsmith chose an effective word in "withdrawn." It helps to engender the illusion that one observes a world in which extraordinary things are given, and equally without reference to workaday reality, taken away. Before he completes the fiftieth line, the narrator has formed a permanent little world; and, paradoxically, he has also dissolved it. Goldsmith reinforces this fairly effective tension throughout the poem simply by skipping back and forth between descriptions of the village as it is (desolate), and as it was (full and immutable). It seems fair to conjecture that without this sustained mechanism, the sentimental portraits of the preacher and the master, for example (part of the permanent village of wonder), would become tedious; the description of terrible Georgia to which some of the villagers may migrate (obviously a foil to the wonderful village) would be ludicrous; and the apostrophe to Luxury (the chief power of dissolution) trite.

TEXT. *The Deserted Village, A Poem* (London, 1770).

The Deserted Village[1]

SWEET AUBURN, loveliest village of the plain,
Where health and plenty cheared the labouring swain,
Where smiling spring its earliest visit paid,
And parting summer's lingering blooms delayed,
Dear lovely bowers of innocence and ease,   5
Seats of my youth, when every sport could please,
How often have I loitered o'er thy green,
Where humble happiness endeared each scene;
How often have I paused on every charm,
The sheltered cot, the cultivated farm,   10
The never failing brook, the busy mill,
The decent church that topt the neighbouring hill,
The hawthorn bush, with seats beneath the shade,
For talking age and whispering lovers made.
How often have I blest the coming day,   15
When toil remitting lent its turn to play,
And all the village train from labour free
Led up their sports beneath the spreading tree,
While many a pastime circled in the shade,
The young contending as the old surveyed;   20
And many a gambol frolicked o'er the ground,
And flights of art and feats of strength went round.
And still as each repeated pleasure tired,
Succeeding sports the mirthful band inspired;
The dancing pair that simply sought renown   25
By holding out to tire each other down,
The swain mistrustless of his smutted face,
While secret laughter tittered round the place,
The bashful virgin's side-long looks of love,
The matron's glance that would those looks reprove.   30
These were thy charms, sweet village; sports like these,
With sweet succession, taught even toil to please;
These round thy bowers their chearful influence shed,
These were thy charms—But all these charms are fled.

Sweet smiling village, loveliest of the lawn,   35
Thy sports are fled, and all thy charms withdrawn;

---

[1] *The Deserted Village:* Presumably such villages were deserted because the landowner had decided to enclose (fence in), for his own agricultural use, lands formerly used by his tenants, the villagers; or because a recent purchaser of the village had decided to turn it into an entirely private estate. Such enclosures (and consequent displacements of the rural populations) are recorded in England from the twelfth century, but they seem never to have been as frequent, and therefore as damaging socially, as some of Goldsmith's generalizations in the poem (and elsewhere in his work and correspondence) indicate. See Friedman, IV, pp. 273–277.

Amidst thy bowers the tyrant's hand is seen,
And desolation saddens all thy green:
One only master grasps the whole domain,
And half a tillage stints thy smiling plain;   40
No more thy glassy brook reflects the day,
But choaked with sedges, works its weedy way.
Along thy glades, a solitary guest,
The hollow sounding bittern guards its nest;
Amidst thy desert walks the lapwing flies,   45
And tires their ecchoes with unvaried cries.
Sunk are thy bowers in shapeless ruin all,
And the long grass o'ertops the mouldering wall,
And trembling, shrinking from the spoiler's hand,
Far, far away thy children leave the land.   50

Ill fares the land, to hastening ills a prey,
Where wealth accumulates, and men decay;
Princes and lords may flourish, or may fade;
A breath can make them, as a breath has made.
But a bold peasantry, their country's pride,   55
When once destroyed, can never be supplied.

A time there was, ere England's griefs began,
When every rood of ground maintained its man;
For him light labour spread her wholesome store,
Just gave what life required, but gave no more.   60
His best companions, innocence and health;
And his best riches, ignorance of wealth.

But times are altered; trade's unfeeling train
Usurp the land and dispossess the swain;
Along the lawn, where scattered hamlets rose,   65
Unwieldy wealth, and cumbrous pomp repose;
And every want to luxury allied,
And every pang that folly pays to pride.
These gentle hours that plenty bade to bloom,
Those calm desires that asked but little room,   70
Those healthful sports that graced the peaceful scene,
Lived in each look, and brightened all the green;
These far departing seek a kinder shore,
And rural mirth and manners are no more.

Sweet AUBURN! parent of the blissful hour,   75
Thy glades forlorn confess the tyrant's power.
Here as I take my solitary rounds,
Amidst thy tangling walks, and ruined grounds,
And, many a year elapsed, return to view

Where once the cottage stood, the hawthorn grew,   80
Here, as with doubtful, pensive steps I range,
Trace every scene, and wonder at the change,
Remembrance wakes with all her busy train,
Swells at my breast, and turns the past to pain.

In all my wanderings round this world of care,   85
In all my griefs—and GOD has given my share—
I still had hopes my latest hours to crown,
Amidst these humble bowers to lay me down;
My anxious day to husband near the close,
And keep life's flame from wasting by repose.   90
I still had hopes, for pride attends us still,
Amidst the swains to shew my book-learned skill,
Around my fire an evening groupe to draw,
And tell of all I felt, and all I saw;
And, as an hare whom hounds and horns pursue,   95
Pants to the place from whence at first she flew,
I still had hopes, my long vexations past,
Here to return—and die at home at last.

O blest retirement; friend to life's decline,
Retreats from care that never must be mine,   100
How blest is he who crowns in shades like these,
A youth of labour with an age of ease;
Who quits a world where strong temptations try,
And, since 'tis hard to combat, learns to fly.
For him no wretches, born to work and weep,   105
Explore the mine, or tempt the dangerous deep;
No surly porter stands in guilty state
To spurn imploring famine from his gate,
But on he moves to meet his latter end,
Angels around befriending virtue's friend;   110
Sinks to the grave with unperceived decay,
While resignation gently slopes the way;
And all his prospects brightening to the last,
His Heaven commences ere the world be past!

Sweet was the sound when oft at evening's close,   115
Up yonder hill the village murmur rose;
There as I past with careless steps and slow,
The mingling notes came softened from below;
The swain responsive as the milk-maid sung,
The sober herd that lowed to meet their young;   120
The noisy geese that gabbled o'er the pool,

81–82. Later editions of the poem omit
this couplet.

The playful children just let loose from school;
The watch-dog's voice that bayed the whispering wind,
And the loud laugh that spoke the vacant mind,
These all in soft confusion sought the shade,   125
And filled each pause the nightingale had made.
But now the sounds of population fail,
No chearful murmurs fluctuate in the gale,
No busy steps the grass-grown foot-way tread,
But all the bloomy flush of life is fled.   130
All but yon widowed, solitary thing
That feebly bends beside the plashy spring;
She, wretched matron, forced, in age, for bread,
To strip the brook with mantling cresses spread,
To pick her wintry faggot from the thorn,   135
To seek her nightly shed, and weep till morn;
She only left of all the harmless train,
The sad historian of the pensive plain.

    Near yonder copse, where once the garden smil'd,
And still where many a garden flower grows wild;   140
There, where a few torn shrubs the place disclose,
The village preacher's modest mansion rose.
A man he was, to all the country dear,
And passing rich with forty pounds a year;
Remote from towns he ran his godly race,   145
Nor ere had changed, nor wish'd to change his place;
Unskilful he to fawn, or seek for power,
By doctrines fashioned to the varying hour;
Far other aims his heart had learned to prize,
More bent to raise the wretched than to rise.   150
His house was known to all the vagrant train,
He chid their wanderings, but relieved their pain;
The long remembered beggar was his guest,
Whose beard descending swept his aged breast;
The ruined spendthrift, now no longer proud,   155
Claimed kindred there, and had his claims allowed;
The broken soldier, kindly bade to stay,
Sate by his fire, and talked the night away;
Wept o'er his wounds, or tales of sorrow done,
Shouldered his crutch, and shewed how fields were won.   160
Pleased with his guests, the good man learned to glow,
And quite forgot their vices in their woe;
Careless their merits, or their faults to scan,
His pity gave ere charity began.

    Thus to relieve the wretched was his pride,   165
And even his failings leaned to Virtue's side;

124. *Vacant:* Without occupation.

But in his duty prompt at every call,
He watched and wept, he prayed and felt, for all.
And, as a bird each fond endearment tries,
To tempt its new fledged offspring to the skies;   170
He tried each art, reproved each dull delay,
Allured to brighter worlds, and led the way.

    Beside the bed where parting life was layed,
And sorrow, guilt, and pain, by turns dismayed,
The reverend champion stood. At his control,   175
Despair and anguish fled the struggling soul;
Comfort came down the trembling wretch to raise,
And his last faultering accents whispered praise.

    At church, with meek and unaffected grace,
His looks adorned the venerable place;   180
Truth from his lips prevailed with double sway,
And fools, who came to scoff, remained to pray.
The service past, around the pious man,
With ready zeal each honest rustic ran;
Even children followed with endearing wile,   185
And plucked his gown, to share the good man's smile.
His ready smile a parent's warmth exprest,
Their welfare pleased him, and their cares distrest;
To them his heart, his love, his griefs were given,
But all his serious thoughts had rest in Heaven.   190
As some tall cliff that lifts its awful form
Swells from the vale, and midway leaves the storm,
Tho' round its breast the rolling clouds are spread,
Eternal sunshine settles on its head.

    Beside yon straggling fence that skirts the way,   195
With blossomed furze unprofitably gay,
There, in his noisy mansion, skill'd to rule,
The village master taught his little school;
A man severe he was, and stern to view,
I knew him well, and every truant knew;   200
Well had the boding tremblers learned to trace
The day's disasters in his morning face;
Full well they laugh'd with counterfeited glee,
At all his jokes, for many a joke had he;
Full well the busy whisper circling round,   205
Conveyed the dismal tidings when he frowned;
Yet he was kind, or if severe in aught,
The love he bore to learning was in fault;
The village all declared how much he knew;

208. *Fault:* Fault rhymed with aught;
that is, it was pronounced without an *l*.

'Twas certain he could write, and cypher too;   210
Lands he could measure, terms and tides presage,
And even the story ran that he could gauge.
In arguing too, the parson owned his skill,
For e'en tho' vanquished, he could argue still;
While words of learned length, and thundering sound,   215
Amazed the gazing rustics ranged around,
And still they gazed, and still the wonder grew,
That one small head could carry all he knew.

    But past is all his fame. The very spot
Where many a time he triumphed, is forgot.   220
Near yonder thorn, that lifts its head on high,
Where once the sign-post caught the passing eye,
Low lies that house where nut-brown draughts inspired,
Where grey-beard mirth and smiling toil retired,
Where village statesmen talked with looks profound,   225
And news much older than their ale went round.
Imagination fondly stoops to trace
The parlour splendours of that festive place;
The white-washed wall, the nicely sanded floor,
The varnished clock that clicked behind the door;   230
The chest contrived a double debt to pay,
A bed by night, a chest of drawers by day;
The pictures placed for ornament and use,
The twelve good rules, the royal game of goose;
The hearth, except when winter chill'd the day,   235
With aspen boughs, and flowers, and fennel gay,
While broken tea-cups, wisely kept for shew,
Ranged o'er the chimney, glistened in a row.

    Vain transitory splendours! Could not all
Reprieve the tottering mansion from its fall!   240
Obscure it sinks, nor shall it more impart
An hour's importance to the poor man's heart;
Thither no more the peasant shall repair
To sweet oblivion of his daily care;
No more the farmer's news, the barber's tale,   245
No more the wood-man's ballad shall prevail;
No more the smith his dusky brow shall clear,
Relax his ponderous strength, and lean to hear;
The host himself no longer shall be found

---

211. *Terms and tides:* Both words contribute to the meaning of a definite time at which something is to be done, especially a time for money to be paid; the first term suggests the idea of the condition, the second of the time of payment.

234. *Twelve . . . rules game of . . . goose:* A set of rules supposed to have been enunciated by Charles I; game of goose is ". . . played with counters on a board divided into compartments, in some of which a goose was depicted." *OED.*

Careful to see the mantling bliss go round;   250
Nor the coy maid, half willing to be prest,
Shall kiss the cup to pass it to the rest.

Yes! let the rich deride, the proud disdain,
These simple blessings of the lowly train,
To me more dear, congenial to my heart,   255
One native charm, than all the gloss of art;
Spontaneous joys, where Nature has its play,
The soul adopts, and owns their first born sway,
Lightly they frolic o'er the vacant mind,
Unenvied, unmolested, unconfined.   260
But the long pomp, the midnight masquerade,
With all the freaks of wanton wealth arrayed,
In these, ere trifflers half their wish obtain,
The toiling pleasure sickens into pain;
And, even while fashion's brightest arts decoy,   265
The heart distrusting asks, if this be joy.

Ye friends to truth, ye statesmen who survey
The rich man's joys encrease, the poor's decay,
'Tis yours to judge, how wide the limits stand
Between a splendid and an happy land.   270
Proud swells the tide with loads of freighted ore,
And shouting Folly hails them from her shore;
Hoards, even beyond the miser's wish abound,
And rich men flock from all the world around.
Yet count our gains. This wealth is but a name   275
That leaves our useful products still the same.
Not so the loss. The man of wealth and pride,
Takes up a space that many poor supplied;
Space for his lake, his park's extended bounds,
Space for his horses, equipage, and hounds;   280
The robe that wraps his limbs in silken sloth,
Has robbed the neighbouring fields of half their growth;
His seat, where solitary sports are seen,
Indignant spurns the cottage from the green;
Around the world each needful product flies,   285
For all the luxuries the world supplies.
While thus the land adorned for pleasure all
In barren splendour feebly waits the fall.

As some fair female unadorned and plain,
Secure to please while youth confirms her reign,   290
Slights every borrowed charm that dress supplies,

250. *Mantling:* Coming to a head,
foaming. Mantling bliss is beer or ale.

Nor shares with art the triumph of her eyes.
But when those charms are past, for charms are frail,
When time advances, and when lovers fail,
She then shines forth sollicitous to bless,   295
In all the glaring impotence of dress.
Thus fares the land, by luxury betrayed,
In nature's simplest charms at first arrayed,
But verging to decline, its splendours rise,
Its vistas strike, its palaces surprize;   300
While scourged by famine from the smiling land,
The mournful peasant leads his humble band;
And while he sinks without one arm to save,
The country blooms—a garden, and a grave.

Where then, ah, where shall poverty reside,   305
To scape the pressure of contiguous pride;
If to some common's fenceless limits strayed,
He drives his flock to pick the scanty blade,
Those fenceless fields the sons of wealth divide,
And even the bare-worn common is denied.   310

If to the city sped—What waits him there?
To see profusion that he must not share;
To see ten thousand baneful arts combined
To pamper luxury, and thin mankind;
To see each joy the sons of pleasure know,   315
Extorted from his fellow-creature's woe.
Here, while the courtier glitters in brocade,
There the pale artist plies the sickly trade;
Here, while the proud their long drawn pomps display,
There the black gibbet glooms beside the way.   320
The dome where pleasure holds her midnight reign,
Here richly deckt admits the gorgeous train,
Tumultuous grandeur crowds the blazing square,
The rattling chariots clash, the torches glare;
Sure scenes like these no troubles ere annoy!   325
Sure these denote one universal joy!
Are these thy serious thoughts—Ah, turn thine eyes
Where the poor houseless shivering female lies.
She once, perhaps, in village plenty blest,
Has wept at tales of innocence distrest;   330
Her modest looks the cottage might adorn,
Sweet as the primrose peeps beneath the thorn;
Now lost to all; her friends, her virtue fled,
Near her betrayer's door she lays her head,
And pinch'd with cold, and shrinking from the shower,   335
With heavy heart deplores that luckless hour,

When idly first, ambitious of the town,
She left her wheel and robes of country brown.

Do thine, sweet AUBURN, thine, the loveliest train,
Do thy fair tribes participate her pain?   340
Even now, perhaps, by cold and hunger led,
At proud men's doors they ask a little bread!

Ah, no. To distant climes, a dreary scene,
Where half the convex world intrudes between,
To torrid tracts with fainting steps they go,   345
Where wild Altama murmurs to their woe.
Far different there from all that charm'd before,
The various terrors of that horrid shore.
Those blazing suns that dart a downward ray,
And fiercely shed intolerable day;   350
Those matted woods where birds forget to sing,
But silent bats in drowsy clusters cling,
Those poisonous fields with rank luxuriance crowned
Where the dark scorpion gathers death around;
Where at each step the stranger fears to wake   355
The rattling terrors of the vengeful snake;
Where crouching tigers wait their hapless prey,
And savage men more murderous still than they;
While oft in whirls the mad tornado flies,
Mingling the ravaged landscape with the skies.   360
Far different these from every former scene,
The cooling brook, the grassy vested green,
The breezy covert of the warbling grove,
That only sheltered thefts of harmless love.

Good Heaven! what sorrows gloom'd that parting day,   365
That called them from their native walks away;
When the poor exiles, every pleasure past,
Hung round their bowers, and fondly looked their last,
And took a long farewell, and wished in vain
For seats like these beyond the western main;   370
And shuddering still to face the distant deep,
Returned and wept, and still returned to weep.
The good old sire, the first prepared to go
To new found worlds, and wept for others woe.
But for himself, in conscious virtue brave,   375
He only wished for worlds beyond the grave.
His lovely daughter, lovelier in her tears,

---

346. *Altama:* The Altamaha is a river   several other kinds of cat native to North
in southeast Georgia, U.S.A.   and South America and to Africa.
357. *Tigers:* The name was used for

The fond companion of his helpless years,
Silent went next, neglectful of her charms,
And left a lover's for her father's arms.   380
With louder plaints the mother spoke her woes,
And blest the cot where every pleasure rose;
And kist her thoughtless babes with many a tear,
And claspt them close in sorrow doubly dear;
Whilst her fond husband strove to lend relief   385
In all the decent manliness of grief.

O luxury! Thou curst by heaven's decree,
How ill exchanged are things like these for thee!
How do thy potions with insidious joy,
Diffuse their pleasures only to destroy!   390
Kingdoms by thee, to sickly greatness grown,
Boast of a florid vigour not their own.
At every draught more large and large they grow,
A bloated mass of rank unwieldy woe;
Till sapped their strength, and every part unsound,   395
Down, down they sink, and spread a ruin round.

Even now the devastation is begun,
And half the business of destruction done;
Even now, methinks, as pondering here I stand,
I see the rural virtues leave the land.   400
Down where yon anchoring vessel spreads the sail
That idly waiting flaps with every gale,
Downward they move a melancholy band,
Pass from the shore, and darken all the strand.
Contented toil, and hospitable care,   405
And kind connubial tenderness, are there;
And piety with wishes placed above,
And steady loyalty, and faithful love.
And thou, sweet Poetry, thou loveliest maid,
Still first to fly where sensual joys invade;   410
Unfit in these degenerate times of shame,
To catch the heart, or strike for honest fame;
Dear charming nymph, neglected and decried,
My shame in crowds my solitary pride.
Thou source of all my bliss, and all my woe,   415
That found'st me poor at first, and keep'st me so;
Thou guide by which the nobler arts excell,
Thou nurse of every virtue, fare thee well.
Farewell, and O where'er thy voice be tried,
On Torno's cliffs, or Pambamarca's side,   420

420. *Torno's cliffs . . . Pambamarca's side:*
Cliffs along the river in northern Europe
(Finnish *Tornio,* Swedish *Torne*), flowing
into the Gulf of Bothnia; Pambamarca is
a mountain in Ecuador.

Whether where equinoctial fervours glow,
Or winter wraps the polar world in snow,
Still let thy voice prevailing over time,
Redress the rigours of the inclement clime;
Aid slighted truth, with thy persuasive strain   425
Teach erring man to spurn the rage of gain;
Teach him that states of native strength possest,
Tho' very poor, may still be very blest;
That trade's proud empire hastes to swift decay,
As ocean sweeps the labour'd mole away;   430
While self dependent power can time defy,
As rocks resist the billows and the sky.

(1770)

429–432. Boswell, *Life of Johnson*,   wrote these (and only these) four lines.
Hill-Powell, II, p. 7, records that Johnson   430. *Mole:* A pier or breakwater.

She Stoops to Conquer
Or, The Mistakes of a Night

To Samuel Johnson, L.L.D.

Dear Sir,

BY inscribing this slight performance to you, I do not mean so much to compliment you as myself. It may do me some honour to inform the public, that I have lived many years in intimacy with you. It may serve the interests of mankind also to inform them, that the greatest wit may be found in a character, without impairing the most unaffected piety.

I have, particularly, reason to thank you for your partiality to this perfor- mance. The undertaking a comedy, not merely sentimental, was very danger- ous; and Mr. Colman, who saw this piece in its various stages, always thought it so. However I ventured to trust it to the public; and though it was necessarily   10 delayed till late in the season, I have every reason to be grateful.

I am, Dear Sir,

Your most sincere friend,

And admirer,

OLIVER GOLDSMITH

Dramatis Personae

MEN
Sir *Charles Marlow*
Young *Marlow* (his Son)
Hardcastle
Hastings
Tony Lumpkin
Diggory

WOMEN
Mrs. *Hardcastle*
Miss *Hardcastle*
Miss *Neville*
Maid
Landlord, Servants, Etc.

Prologue

By David Garrick, Esq.[1]

[Enter Mr.Woodward,[2] Dressed in black, and holding a handkerchief to his eyes.

EXCUSE me, sirs, I pray—I can't yet speak—
I'm crying now—and have been all the week!
'Tis not alone this mourning suit, good masters;
I've that within—for which there are no plasters!
Pray would you know the reason why I'm crying!   5
The Comic Muse, long sick, is now a-dying!
And if she goes, my tears will never stop;
For, as a play'r, I can't squeeze out one drop:
I am undone, that's all—shall lose my bread—
I'd rather, but that's nothing—lose my head.   10
When the sweet maid is laid upon the bier,
Shuter and *I* shall be chief mourners here.
To *her* a mawkish drab of spurious breed,
Who deals in *sentimentals,* will succeed!
Poor *Ned*[3] and *I* are dead to all intents,   15
We can as soon speak *Greek* as *sentiments!*
Both nervous grown, to keep our spirits up,
We now and then take down a hearty cup.
What shall we do?—If Comedy forsake us!
They'll turn us out, and no one else will take us,—   20
But why can't I be moral?—Let me try—
My heart thus pressing—fixed my face and eye—
With a sententious look, that nothing means
(Faces are blocks in sentimental scenes)
Thus I begin—*All is not gold that glitters,*   25
Pleasure seems sweet, but proves a glass of bitters.
When ign'rance enters, folly is at hand;
Learning is better far than house and land.
Let not your virtue trip, who trips may stumble,
And virtue is not virtue, if she tumble.   30
    I give it up—morals won't do for me;
To make you laugh, I must play tragedy.
One hope remains—hearing the maid was ill,
A *doctor* comes this night to show his skill.

---

[1] *David Garrick, Esq.:* Earlier, in 1768, Garrick (1717–1779) dramatist and joint-patentee of Drury Lane (and probably the most versatile, and influential, actor in the history of the British stage) had opposed Goldsmith's low comedy *The Good-Natured Man* by running a sentimental comedy, *False Delicacy,* against it. Here Garrick supports Goldsmith's laughing comedy.

[2] *Mr. Woodward:* A member of the Covent Garden Company.

[3] *Ned:* Ned Shuter, another member of the Company. He played Hardcastle in the play.

To cheer her heart, and give your muscles motion,   35
He, in *five draughts* prepared, presents a potion:
A kind of magic charm—for, be assured,
If you will *swallow* it, the maid is cured:
But desp'rate the Doctor, and her case is,
If you reject the dose, and make wry faces!   40
This truth he boasts, will boast it while he lives,
No *pois'nous drugs* are mixed in what he gives.
Should he succeed, you'll give him his degree;
If not, within he will receive no fee!
The college *you*, must his pretensions back,   45
Pronounce him *regular*, or dub him *quack*.

Act I

SCENE, *A chamber in an old-fashioned house.*

[*Enter* Mrs. Hardcastle *and* Mr. Hardcastle.

Mrs. Hard. I vow, Mr. Hardcastle, you're very particular. Is there a creature in the whole country, but ourselves, that does not take a trip to town now and then, to rub off the rust a little? There's the two Miss Hoggs, and our neighbor, Mrs. Grigsby, go to take a month's polishing every winter.

Hard. Ay, and bring back vanity and affectation to last them the whole year. I wonder why London cannot keep its own fools at home. In my time, the follies of the town crept slowly among us, but now they travel faster than a stage-coach. Its fopperies come down, not only as inside passengers, but in the very basket.[1]

Mrs. Hard. Ay, *your* times were fine times, indeed; you have been telling   10
us of *them* for many a long year. Here we live in an old rumbling[2] mansion, that looks for all the world like an inn, but that we never see company. Our best visitors are old Mrs. Oddfish, the curate's wife, and little Cripplegate, the lame dancing-master: And all our entertainment your old stories of Prince Eugene[3] and the Duke of Marlborough. I hate such old-fashioned trumpery.

Hard. And I love it. I love every thing that's old: old friends, old times, old manners, old books, old wine; and, I believe, Dorothy, [*taking her hand*] you'll own I have been pretty fond of an old wife.

Mrs. Hard. Lord, Mr. Hardcastle, you're for ever at your Dorothy's and   20
your old wife's. You may be a Darby, but I'll be no Joan,[4] I promise you. I'm not so old as you'd make me, by more than one good year. Add twenty to twenty, and make money of that.

---

[1] *Basket:* Overhanging compartment at the rear of a stage-coach.

[2] *Rumbling:* Some editors suggest rambling. Rumbling suits both an old house like an inn and Tony's clamorous behavior.

[3] *Prince Eugene:* An Austrian soldier, ally of Marlborough (John Churchill) at the Battle of Blenheim in 1704.

[4] *Joan:* Darby and Joan was a joking term for an attached husband and wife, especially in advanced years and humble life.

Hard. Let me see; twenty added to twenty, makes just fifty and seven.

Mrs. Hard. It's false, Mr. Hardcastle: I was but twenty when I was brought to bed of Tony, that I had by Mr. Lumpkin, my first husband; and he's not come to years of discretion yet.

Hard. Nor ever will, I dare answer for him. Ay, you have taught *him* finely.

Mrs. Hard. No matter, Tony Lumpkin has a good fortune. My son is not to live by his learning. I don't think a boy wants much learning to spend fifteen hundred a year.

Hard. Learning, quotha! A mere composition of tricks and mischief.   10

Mrs. Hard. Humour, my dear: nothing but humour. Come, Mr. Hardcastle, you must allow the boy a little humour.

Hard. I'd sooner allow him an horse-pond. If burning the footmen's shoes, frighting the maids, and worrying the kittens be humour, he has it. It was but yesterday he fastened my wig to the back of my chair, and when I went to make a bow, I popt my bald head in Mrs. Frizzle's face.

Mrs. Hard. And am I to blame? The poor boy was always too sickly to do any good. A school would be his death. When he comes to be a little stronger, who knows what a year or two's Latin may do for him?

Hard. Latin for him! A cat and fiddle. No, no, the ale-house and the   20 stable are the only schools he'll ever go to.

Mrs. Hard. Well, we must not snub the poor boy now, for I believe we shan't have him long among us. Any body that looks in his face may see he's consumptive.

Hard. Ay, if growing too fat be one of the symptoms.

Mrs. Hard. He coughs sometimes.

Hard. Yes, when his liquor goes the wrong way.

Mrs. Hard. I'm actually afraid of his lungs.

Hard. And truly so am I; for he sometimes whoops like a speaking trumpet—[Tony *hallooing behind the Scenes.*]—O there he goes—A very consumptive   30 figure, truly.

[*Enter* Tony, *crossing the Stage.*]

Mrs. Hard. Tony, where are you going, my charmer? Won't you give papa and I a little of your company, lovee?

Tony. I'm in haste, mother, I cannot stay.

Mrs. Hard. You shan't venture out this raw evening, my dear: You look most shockingly.

Tony. I can't stay, I tell you. The Three Pigeons expects me down every moment. There's some fun going forward.

Hard. Ay; the ale-house, the old place: I thought so.   40

Mrs. Hard. A low, paltry set of fellows.

Tony. Not so low neither. There's Dick Muggins the exciseman, Jack Slang the horse doctor, Little Aminadab that grinds the music box, and Tom Twist that spins the pewter platter.

Mrs. Hard. Pray, my dear, disappoint them for one night at least.

Tony. As for disappointing *them,* I should not so much mind; but I can't abide to disappoint *myself.*

Mrs. Hard. [*Detaining him.*] You shan't go.

Tony. I will, I tell you.

Mrs. Hard. I say you shan't.

Tony. We'll see which is strongest, you or I.

[*Exit, hawling her out.*

[Hardcastle, *Solus.*

Hard. Ay, there goes a pair that only spoil each other, But is not the whole age in a combination to drive sense and discretion out of doors? There's my pretty darling Kate; the fashions of the times have almost infected her too. By living a year or two in town, she is as fond of gauze, and French frippery, as the best of them.

[*Enter* Miss Hardcastle.

Hard. Blessings on my pretty innocence! Drest out as usual my Kate.   10 Goodness! What a quantity of superfluous silk has thou got about thee, girl! I could never teach the fools of this age, that the indigent world could be cloathed out of the trimmings of the vain.

Miss Hard. You know our agreement, Sir. You allow me the morning to receive and pay visits, and to dress in my own manner; and in the evening, I put on my housewife's dress to please you.

Hard. Well, remember I insist on the terms of our agreement; and, by the bye, I believe I shall have occasion to try your obedience this very evening.

Miss Hard. I protest, Sir, I don't comprehend your meaning.   20

Hard. Then, to be plain with you, Kate, I expect the young gentleman I have chosen to be your husband from town this very day. I have his father's letter, in which he informs me his son is set out, and that he intends to follow himself shortly after.

Miss Hard. Indeed! I wish I had known something of this before. Bless me, how shall I behave? It's a thousand to one I shan't like him; our meeting will be so formal, and so like a thing of business, that I shall find no room for friendship or esteem.

Hard. Depend upon it, child, I'll never controul your choice; but Mr. Marlow, whom I have pitched upon, is the son of my old friend, Sir Charles   30 Marlow, of whom you have heard me talk so often. The young gentleman has been bred a scholar, and is designed for an employment in the service of his country. I am told he's a man of an excellent understanding.

Miss Hard. Is he?

Hard. Very generous.

Miss Hard. I believe, I shall like him.

Hard. Young and brave.

Miss Hard. I'm sure I shall like him.

Hard. And very handsome.

Miss Hard. My dear Papa, say no more; [*kissing his hand*] he's mine, I'll   40 have him.

Hard. And to crown all, Kate, he's one of the most bashful and reserved young fellows in all the world.

Miss Hard. Eh! you have frozen me to death again. That word reserved has undone all the rest of his accomplishments. A reserved lover, it is said, always makes a suspicious husband.

Hard. On the contrary, modesty seldom resides in a breast that is not enriched with nobler virtues. It was the very feature in his character that first struck me.

Miss Hard. He must have more striking features to catch me, I promise you. However, if he be so young, so handsome, and so every thing, as you mention, I believe he'll do still. I think I'll have him.

Hard. Ay, Kate, but there is still an obstacle. Its more than an even wager, he may not have *you.*

Miss Hard. My dear Papa, why will you mortify one so?—Well, if he refuses,   10
instead of breaking my heart at his indifference, I'll only break my glass for its flattery. Set my cap to some newer fashion, and look out for some less difficult admirer.

Hard. Bravely resolved! In the mean time I'll go prepare the servants for his reception; as we seldom see company, they want as much training as a company of recruits, the first day's muster.   [*Exit.*

[Miss Hardcastle, *Sola.*

Miss Hard. Lud, this news of Papa's, puts me all in a flutter. Young, handsome; these he put last; but I put them foremost. Sensible, good-natured; I like all that. But then reserved, and sheepish, that's much against him. Yet can't he be cured of his timidity, by being taught to be proud of his wife? Yes,   20
and can't I—But I vow I'm disposing of the husband, before I have secured the lover.

[*Enter* Miss Neville.

Miss Hard. I'm glad you're come, Neville, my dear. Tell me, Constance, how do I look this evening? Is there any thing whimsical about me? Is it one of my well looking days, child? Am I in face to day?

Miss Nev. Perfectly, my dear. Yet now I look again—bless me!—sure no accident has happened among the canary birds or the gold fishes. Has your brother or the cat been meddling? Or has the last novel been too moving?

Miss Hard. No; nothing of all this. I have been threatened —I can scarce   30
get it out—I have been threatened with a lover.

Miss Nev. And his name——

Miss Hard. Is Marlow.

Miss Nev. Indeed!

Miss Hard. The son of Sir Charles Marlow.

Miss Nev. As I live, the most intimate friend of Mr. Hastings *my* admirer. They are never asunder. I believe you must have seen him when we lived in town.

Miss Hard. Never.

Miss Nev. He's a very singular character, I assure you. Among women of   40
reputation and virtue, he is the modestest man alive; but his acquaintance give him a very different character among creatures of another stamp: you understand me.

Miss Hard. An odd character, indeed. I shall never be able to manage him. What shall I do? Pshaw, think no more of him, but trust to occurrences for success. But how goes on your own affair, my dear; has my mother been courting you for my brother Tony, as usual?

Miss Nev. I have just come from one of our agreeable tête-a-têtes. She has been saying a hundred tender things, and setting off her pretty monster as the very pink of perfection.

Miss Hard. And her partiality is such, that she actually thinks him so. A fortune like your's is no small temptation. Besides, as she has the sole management of it, I'm not surprized to see her unwilling to let it go out of the family.

Miss Nev. A fortune like mine, which chiefly consists in jewels, is no such mighty temptation. But at any rate if my dear Hastings be but constant, 10 I make no doubt to be too hard for her at last. However, I let her suppose that I am in love with her son, and she never once dreams that my affections are fixed upon another.

Miss Hard. My good brother holds out stoutly. I could almost love him for hating you so.

Miss Nev. It is a good natured creature at bottom, and I'm sure would wish to see me married to any body but himself. But my aunt's bell rings for our afternoon's walk round the improvements. Allons. Courage is necessary as our affairs are critical.

Miss Hard. Would it were bed time and all were well. [*Exeunt.* 20

SCENE, *An alehouse room*

[*Several shabby fellows, with Punch and Tobacco. Tony at the head of the Table, a little higher than the rest: A mallet in his hand.*

Omnes. Hurrea, hurrea, hurrea, bravo.

First Fellow. Now, gentlemen, silence for a song. The 'Squire is going to knock himself down[5] for a song.

Omnes. Ay, a song, a song.

Tony. Then I'll sing you, gentlemen, a song I made upon this ale-house, the Three Pigeons.

SONG

> *Let school-masters puzzle their brain,*
> *With grammar, and nonsense, and learning;*
> *Good liquor, I stoutly maintain,*
> *Gives genus a better discerning.* 30
> *Let them brag of their Heathenish Gods,*
> *Their Lethes, their Styxes, and Stygians;*
> *Their Quis, and their Quas, and their Quods,*
> *They're all but a parcel of Pigeons.[6]*
> > Toroddle, toroddle, toroll.

> *When Methodist preachers come down,*
> *A-preaching that drinking is sinful,*

[5] *Knock himself down:* "Call upon himself [for a song . . .]." OED.   [6] *Pigeons:* Gulls, simpletons.

I'll wager the rascals a crown,
   They always preach best with a skinful.
But when you come down with your pence,
   For a slice of their scurvy religion,
I'll leave it to all men of sense,
   But you my good friend are the pigeon.
                    Toroddle, toroddle, toroll.

Then come, put the jorum[7] about,
   And let us be merry and clever,
Our hearts and our liquors are stout,   10
   Here's the Three Jolly Pigeons for ever.
Let some cry up woodcock or hare,
   Your bustards, your ducks, and your widgeons;
But of all the birds in the air,
   Here's a health to the Three Jolly Pigeons.
                    Toroddle, toroddle, toroll.

Omnes. Bravo, bravo.

First Fellow. The 'Squire has got spunk in him.

Second Fellow. I loves to hear him sing, bekeays he never gives us nothing that's *low.*   20

Third Fellow. O damn any thing that's *low,* I cannot bear it.

Fourth Fellow. The genteel thing is the genteel thing at any time. If so be that a gentleman bees in a concatenation accordingly.

Third Fellow. I like the maxum of it, Master Muggins. What, tho' I am obligated to dance a bear, a man may be a gentleman for all that. May this be my poison if my bear ever dances but to the very genteelest of tunes. Water Parted,[8] or the minuet in Ariadne.[9]

Second Fellow. What a pity it is the 'Squire is not come to his own. It would be well for all the publicans within ten miles round of him.

Tony. Ecod and so it would Master Slang. I'd then shew what it was to   30
keep choice of company.

Second Fellow. O he takes after his own father for that. To be sure old 'Squire Lumpkin was the finest gentleman I ever set my eyes on. For winding the streight horn, or beating a thicket for a hare, or a wench, he never had his fellow. It was a saying in the place, that he kept the best horses, dogs and girls in the whole county.

Tony. Ecod, and when I'm of age I'll be no bastard, I promise you. I have been thinking of Bett Bouncer and the miller's grey mare to begin with. But come, my boys, drink about and be merry, for you pay no reckoning. Well, Stingo, what's the matter?   40

                    [*Enter* Landlord.

Landlord. There be two gentlemen in a post-chaise at the door. They have

---

[7] *Jorum:* A large drinking-bowl.

[8] *Water Parted:* A song from *Artaxerxes,* an opera by the English composer Thomas

Arne (1710–1778).

[9] *Ariadne:* An opera by Handel.

lost their way upo' the forest; and they are talking something about Mr. Hardcastle.

Tony. As sure as can be one of them must be the gentleman that's coming down to court my sister. Do they seem to be Londoners?

Landlord. I believe they may. They look woundily[10] like Frenchmen.

Tony. Then desire them to step this way, and I'll set them right in a twinkling. [*Exit* Landlord.] Gentlemen, as they mayn't be good enough company for you, step down for a moment, and I'll be with you in the squeezing of a lemon. [*Exeunt* ⟨ Fellows ⟩.

Tony. [*solus.*] Father-in-law has been calling me whelp, and hound, this 10 half year. Now, if I pleased, I could be so revenged upon the old grumble-tonian. But then I'm afraid —afraid of what! I shall soon be worth fifteen hundred a year, and let him frighten me out of *that* if he can.

[*Enter* Landlord, *conducting* Marlow *and* Hastings.

Marl. What a tedious, uncomfortable day have we had of it! We were told it was but forty miles across the country, and we have come above three-score!

Hast. And all, Marlow, from that unaccountable reserve of yours, that would not let us enquire more frequently on the way.

Marl. I own, Hastings, I am unwilling to lay myself under an obligation 20 to everyone I meet, and often stand the chance of an unmannerly answer.

Hast. At present, however, we are not likely to receive any answer.

Tony. No offence, gentlemen. But I'm told you have been enquiring for one Mr. Hardcastle, in [these] parts. Do you know what part of the country you are in?

Hast. Not in the least, sir, but should thank you for information.

Tony. Nor the way you came?

Hast. No, sir; but if you can inform us—

Tony. Why, gentlemen, if you know neither the road you are going, nor where you are, nor the road you came, the first thing I have to inform 30 you is, that—you have lost your way.

Marl. We wanted no ghost to tell us that.[11]

Tony. Pray, gentlemen, may I be so bold as to ask the place from whence you came?

Marl. That's not necessary towards directing us where we are to go.

Tony. No offence; but question for question is all fair, you know.— Pray, gentlemen, is not this same Hardcastle a cross-grained, old-fashioned, whimsical fellow, with an ugly face, a daughter, and a pretty son?

Hast. We have not seen the gentleman, but he has the family you mention.

Tony. The daughter, a tall trapesing, trolloping, talkative maypole— 40 The son, a pretty, well-bred, agreeable youth, that every body is fond of.

Marl. Our information differs in this. The daughter is said to be well-

---

[10] *Woundily:* Extremely.

[11] *We wanted no ghost . . . :* A paraphrase of Horatio's lines, *Hamlet*, I, v. Goldsmith's reference may have derived some of its meaning from the earlier public concern with the Cock-lane Ghost, ". . . which, in the year 1762, had gained very general credit in London." Boswell, *Life of Johnson*, Hill-Powell, I, pp. 406 ff.

bred and beautiful; the son, an aukward booby, reared up, and spoiled at his mother's apron-string.

Tony. He-he-hem—Then, gentlemen, all I have to tell you is, that you won't reach Mr. Hardcastle's house this night, I believe.

Hast. Unfortunate!

Tony. It's damn'd long, dark, boggy, dirty, dangerous way. Stingo, tell the gentlemen the way to Mr. Hardcastle's; [*winking upon the* Landlord.] Mr. Hardcastle's, of Quagmire Marsh, you understand me.

Landlord. Master Hardcastle's! Lock-a-daisy, my masters, you're come a deadly deal wrong! When you came to the bottom of the hill, you should   10 have cross'd down Squash-lane.

Marl. Cross down Squash-lane!

Landlord. Then you were to keep streight forward, 'till you came to four roads.

Marl. Come to where four roads meet!

Tony. Ay; but you must be sure to take only one of them.

Marl. O Sir, you're facetious.

Tony. Then keeping to the right, you are to go side-ways till you come upon Crack-skull common: there you must look sharp for the track of the wheel, and go forward, 'till you come to farmer Murrain's barn. Coming to the   20 farmer's barn, you are to turn to the right, and then to the left, and then right about again, till you find out the old mill———

Marl. Zounds, man! we could as soon find out the longitude![12]

Hast. What's to be done, Marlow?

Marl. This house promises but a poor reception; though perhaps the Landlord can accommodate us.

Landlord. Alack, master, we have but one spare bed in the whole house.

Tony. And to my knowledge, that's taken up by three lodgers already. [*After a pause, in which the rest seem disconcerted.*] I have hit it. Don't you think, Stingo, our landlady could accommodate the gentlemen by the fire-side,   30 with———three chairs and a bolster?

Hast. I hate sleeping by the fire-side.

Marl. And I detest your three chairs and a bolster.

Tony. You do, do you?—then let me see—what—if you go on a mile further, to the Buck's Head; the old Buck's Head on the hill, one of the best inns in the whole county?

Hast. O ho! so we have escaped an adventure for this night, however.

Landlord. [*Apart to* Tony.] Sure, you ben't sending them to your father's as an inn, be you?

Tony. Mum, you fool you. Let *them* find that out. [*To them.*] You have   40 only to keep on streight forward, till you come to a large old house by the road side. You'll see a pair of large horns over the door. That's the sign. Drive up the yard, and call stoutly about you.

---

[12] *The longitude:* It was in fact in 1773, when *She Stoops* was first presented, that John Harrison (1693–1776), English inventor, received from Parliament, in accordance with an Act of 1713, the final award (for a total of £20,000) for his chronometer.

Hast. Sir, we are obliged to you. The servants can't miss the way?

Tony. No, no: But I tell you though, the landlord is rich, and going to leave off business; so he wants to be thought a Gentlemen, saving your presence, he! he! he! He'll be for giving you his company, and ecod if you mind him, he'll persuade you that his mother was an alderman, and his aunt a justice of peace.

Landlord. A troublesome old blade to be sure; but a keeps as good wines and beds as any in the whole country.

Marl. Well, if he supplies us with these, we shall want no further con- nexion. We are to turn to the right did you say?   10

Tony. No, no; streight forward. I'll just step myself, and shew you a piece of the way. [*To the* Landlord.] Mum.

Landlord. Ah, bless your heart, for a sweet, pleasant—— damn'd mischie- vous son of a whore.   [*Exeunt.*

Act II

SCENE, *An old-fashioned house*

[*Enter* Hardcastle, *followed by three or four aukward Servants.*

Hard. Well, I hope you're perfect in the table exercise I have been teaching you these three days. You all know your posts and your places, and can shew that you have been used to good company, without ever stirring from home.

Omnes. Ay, ay.

Hard. When company comes, you are not to pop out and stare, and then run in again, like frighted rabbits in a warren.   20

Omnes. No, no.

Hard. You, Diggory, whom I have taken from the barn, are to make a shew at the side-table; and you, Roger, whom I have advanced from the plough, are to place yourself behind *my* chair. But you're not to stand so, with your hands in your pockets. Take your hands from your pockets, Roger; and from your head, you blockhead you. See how Diggory carries his hands. They're a little too stiff, indeed, but that's no great matter.

Digg. Ay, mind how I hold them. I learned to hold my hands this way, when I was upon drill for the militia. And so being upon drill——.

Hard. You must not be so talkative, Diggory. You must be all attention 30 to the guests. You must hear us talk, and not think of talking; you must see us drink, and not think of drinking; you must see us eat, and not think of eating.

Digg. By the laws, your worship, that's parfectly unpossible. Whenever Diggory sees yeating going forward, ecod he's always wishing for a mouthful himself.

Hard. Blockhead! Is not a belly-full in the kitchen as good as a belly-full in the parlour? Stay your stomach with that reflection.

Digg. Ecod I thank your worship, I'll make a shift to stay my stomach with a slice of cold beef in the pantry.   40

Hard. Diggory, you are too talkative. Then if I happen to say a good thing, or tell a good story at table, you must not all burst out a-laughing, as if you made part of the company.

Digg. Then ecod your worship must not tell the story of Ould Grouse in the gun-room: I can't help laughing at that—he! he! he!—for the soul of me. We have laughed at that these twenty years—ha! ha! ha!

Hard. Ha! ha! ha! The story is a good one. Well, honest Diggory, you may laugh at that—but still remember to be attentive. Suppose one of the company should call for a glass of wine, how will you behave? A glass of wine, Sir, if you please. [*to* Diggory.]—Eh, why don't you move?   10

Digg. Ecod, your worship, I never have courage till I see the eatables and drinkables brought upo' the table, and then I'm as bauld as a lion.

Hard. What, will no body move?

First Servant. I'm not to leave this place.

Second Servant. I'm sure it's no pleace of mine.

Third Servant. Nor mine, for sartain.

Digg. Wauns,[1] and I'm sure it canna be mine.

Hard. You numbskulls! and so while, like your betters, you are quarrelling for places, the guests must be starved. O you dunces! I find I must begin all over again,——But don't I hear a coach drive into the yard? To your posts,   20 you blockheads. I'll go in the mean time and give my old friend's son a hearty reception at the gate.   [*Exit* Hardcastle.

Digg. By the elevens,[2] my pleace is gone quite out of my head.

Roger. I know that my pleace is to be every where.

First Servant. Where the devil is mine?

Second Servant. My pleace is to be no where at all; and so Ize go about my business.   [*Exeunt* Servants, *running about as if frighted, different ways.*

[*Enter* Servant *with Candles, shewing in* Marlow *and* Hastings.

Servant. Welcome, gentlemen, very welcome. This way.

Hast. After the disappointments of the day, welcome once more, Charles,   30 to the comforts of a clean room and a good fire. Upon my word, a very well-looking house; antique, but creditable.

Marl. The usual fate of a large mansion. Having first ruined the master by good housekeeping, it at last comes to levy contributions as an inn.

Hast. As you say, we passengers are to be taxed to pay all these fineries. I have often seen a good sideboard, or a marble chimney-piece, tho' not actually put in the bill, enflame a reckoning confoundedly.

Marl. Travellers, George, must pay in all places. The only difference is, that in good inns, you pay dearly for luxuries; in bad inns, you are fleeced and starved.   40

Hast. You have lived pretty much among them. In truth, I have been often surprized, that you who have seen so much of the world, with your natural good sense, and your many opportunities, could never yet acquire a requisite share of assurance.

---

[1] *Wauns:* A corrupt variant of *Swounds,* i.e., God's Wounds.

[2] *By the elevens:* This phrase is ". . . of uncertain origin," *OED.*

Marl. The Englishman's malady. But tell me, George, where could I have learned that assurance you talk of? My life has been chiefly spent in a college, or an inn, in seclusion from that lovely part of the creation that chiefly teach men confidence. I don't know that I was ever familiarly acquainted with a single modest woman—except my mother—But among females of another class you know—

Hast. Ay, among them you are impudent enough of all conscience.

Marl. They are of *us* you know.

Hast. But in the company of women of reputation I never saw such an ideot, such a trembler; you look for all the world as if you wanted an opportunity of stealing out of the room.

Marl. Why man that's because I *do* want to steal out of the room. Faith, I have often formed a resolution to break the ice, and rattle away at any rate. But I don't know how, a single glance from a pair of fine eyes has totally overset my resolution. An impudent fellow may counterfeit modestly, but I'll be hanged if a modest man can ever counterfeit impudence.

Hast. If you could but say half the fine things to them that I have heard you lavish upon the bar-maid of an inn, or even a college bed maker—

Marl. Why, George, I can't say fine things to them, They freeze, they petrify me. They may talk of a comet, or a burning mountain, or some such bagatelle. But to me, a modest woman, drest out in all her finery, is the most tremendous object of the whole creation.

Hast. Ha! ha! ha! At this rate, man, how can you ever expect to marry!

Marl. Never, unless as among kings and princes, my bride were to be courted by proxy. If, indeed, like an Eastern bridegroom, one were to be introduced to a wife he never saw before, it might be endured. But to go through all the terrors of a formal courtship, together with the episode of aunts, grandmothers and cousins, and at last to blurt out the broad staring question, of, *madam, will you marry me?* No, no, that's a strain much above me, I assure you.

Hast. I pity you. But how do you intend behaving to the lady you are come down to visit at the request of your father?

Marl. As I behave to all other ladies. Bow very low. Answer yes, or no, to all her demands—But for the rest, I don't think I shall venture to look in her face, till I see my father's again.

Hast. I'm surprized that one who is so warm a friend can be so cool a lover.

Marl. To be explicit, my dear Hastings, my chief inducement down was to be instrumental in forwarding your happiness, not my own. Miss Neville loves you, the family don't know you, as my friend you are sure of a reception, and let honour do the rest.

Hast. My dear Marlow! But I'll suppress the emotion. Were I a wretch, meanly to carry off a fortune, you should be the last man in the world I would apply to for assistance. But Miss Neville's person is all I ask, and that is mine. both from her deceased father's consent, and her own inclination.

Marl. Happy man! You have talents and art to captivate any woman. I'm doom'd to adore the sex, and yet to converse with the only part of it I despise.

This stammer in my address, and this aukward prepossessing[3] visage of mine, can never permit me to soar above the reach of a milliner's prentice, or one of the dutchesses of Drury-lane.[4] Pshaw! this fellow here to interrupt us.

[*Enter* Hardcastle.

Hard. Gentlemen, once more you are heartily welcome. Which is Mr. Marlow? Sir, you're heartily welcome. It's not my way, you see, to receive my friends with my back to the fire. I like to give them a hearty reception in the old stile at my gate. I like to see their horses and trunks taken care of.

Marl. [*aside.*] He has got our names from the servants already. [*To him.*] We approve your caution and hospitality, sir. [*To* Hastings.] I have been thinking, George, of changing our travelling dresses in the morning. I am   10
grown confoundedly ashamed of mine.

Hard. I beg, Mr. Marlow, you'll use no ceremony in this house.

Hast. I fancy, [Charles], you're right: the first blow is half the battle. I intend opening the campaign with the white and gold.

Hard. Mr. Marlow—Mr. Hastings—gentlemen—pray be under no constraint in this house. This is Liberty-Hall, gentlemen. You may do just as you please here.

Marl. Yet, George, if we open the campaign too fiercely at first, we may want ammunition before it is over. I think to reserve the embroidery to secure a retreat.   20

Hard. Your talking of a retreat, Mr. Marlow, puts me in mind of the Duke of Marlborough, when we went to besiege Denain.[5] He first summoned the garrison—

Marl. Don't you think the *ventre d'or* waistcoat will do with the plain brown?

Hard. He first summoned the garrison, which might consist of about five thousand men—

Hast. I think not: brown and yellow mix but very poorly.

Hard. I say, gentlemen, as I was telling you, he summoned the garrison, which might consist of about five thousand men—   30

Marl. The girls like finery.

Hard. Which might consist of about five thousand men, well appointed with stores, ammunition, and other implements of war. Now, says the Duke of Marlborough, to George Brooks, that stood next to him—You must have heard of George Brooks; I'll pawn my Dukedom, says he, but I take that garrison without spilling a drop of blood. So——

Marl. What, my good friend, if you gave us a glass of punch in the mean time, it would help us to carry on the siege with vigour.

Hard. Punch, Sir! [*Aside.*] This is the most unaccountable kind of modesty I ever met with.   40

Marl. Yes, Sir, Punch. A glass of warm punch, after our journey, will be comfortable. This is Liberty-Hall, you know.

---

[3] *Prepossessing:* Tending to bias or to prejudice.
[4] *Dutchesses of Drury-lane:* Prostitutes.
[5] *Denain:* A place where the French defeated the Allies (1712) in one of the many battles of The War of the Spanish Succession (1701–1714).

Hard. Here's Cup, Sir.

Marl. [*Aside.*] So this fellow, in his Liberty-hall, will only let us have just what he pleases.

Hard. [*Taking the Cup.*] I hope you'll find it to your mind. I have prepared it with my own hands, and I believe you'll own the ingredients are tolerable. Will you, be so good as to pledge me, Sir? Here, Mr. Marlow, here is to our better acquiantance. [*Drinks.*

Marl. [*Aside.*] A very impudent fellow this! but he's a character, and I'll humour him a little. Sir, my service to you. [*Drinks.*

Hast. [*Aside.*] I see this fellow wants to give us his company, and forgets 10 that he's an innkeeper, before he has learned to be a gentleman.

Marl. From the excellence of your cup, my old friend, I suppose you have a good deal of business in this part of the country. Warm work, now and then, at elections, I suppose.

Hard. No, Sir, I have long given that work over. Since our betters have hit upon the expedient of electing each other, there's no business *for us that sell ale.*

Hast. So, then you have no turn for politics I find.

Hard. Not in the least. There was a time, indeed, I fretted myself about the mistakes of government, like other people; but finding myself every day 20 grow more angry, and the government growing no better, I left it to mend itself. Since that, I no more trouble my head about *Heyder Ally*, or *Ally Cawn*,[6] than about *Ally Croaker*.[7] Sir, my service to you.

Hast. So that with eating above stairs, and drinking below, with receiving your friends within, and amusing them without, you lead a good pleasant bustling life of it.

Hard. I do stir about a great deal, that's certain. Half the differences of the parish are adjusted in this very parlour.

Marl. [*After drinking.*] And you have an argument in your cup, old gentle- 30 man, better than any in Westminster-hall.[8]

Hard. Ay, young gentleman, that, and a little philosophy.

Marl. [*Aside.*] Well, this is the first time I ever heard of an innkeeper's philosophy.

Hast. So then, like an experienced general, you attack them on every quarter. If you find their reason manageable, you attack it with your philo- sophy; if you find they have no reason, you attack them with this. Here's your health, my philosopher. [*Drinks.*

Hard. Good, very good, thank you; ha! ha! Your Generalship puts me in mind of Prince Eugene, when he fought the Turks at the battle of Belgrade.[9] You shall hear. 40

Marl. Instead of the battle of Belgrade, I believe it's almost time to talk about supper. What has your philosophy got in the house for supper?

---

[6] *Ally Cawn:* Both Hyder Ali and Ali Khan were Indian rulers of the day.
[7] *Ally Croaker:* A popular Irish song.
[8] *Westminster-hall:* Used as a court of justice in the period.
[9] *Battle of Belgrade:* Where Prince Eugene (see I, n. 3) won a victory (1717).

Hard. For Supper, Sir! [*Aside.*] Was ever such a request to a man in his own house!

Marl. Yes, Sir, supper, Sir; I begin to feel an appetite. I shall make devilish work to-night in the larder, I promise you.

Hard. [*Aside.*] Such a brazen dog sure never my eyes beheld. [*To him.*] Why really, Sir, as for supper I can't well tell. My Dorothy, and the cook maid, settle these things between them. I leave these kind of things entirely to them.

Marl. You do, do you?

Hard. Entirely. By-the-bye, I believe they are in actual consultation upon what's for supper this moment in the kitchen.   10

Marl. Then I beg they'll admit *me* as one of their privy council. It's a way I have got. When I travel, I always chuse to regulate my own supper. Let the cook be called. No offence I hope, Sir.

Hard. O no, Sir, none in the least; yet I don't know how: our Bridget, the cook maid, is not very communicative upon these occasions. Should we send for her, she might scold us all out of the house.

Hast. Let's see your list of the larder then. I ask it as a favour. I always match my appetite to my bill of fare.

Marl. [*To Hardcastle, who looks at them with surprize.*] Sir, he's very right, and it's my way too.   20

Hard. Sir, you have a right to command here. Here, Roger, bring us the bill of fare for to night's supper. I believe it's drawn out. Your manner, Mr. Hastings, puts me in mind of my uncle, Colonel Wallop. It was a saying of his, that no man was sure of his supper till he had eaten it.

Hast. [*Aside.*] All upon the high ropes! His uncle a Colonel! We shall soon hear of his mother being a justice of peace. But let's hear the bill of fare.

Marl. [*Perusing.*] What's here? For the first course; for the second course; for the desert. The devil, Sir, do you think we have brought down the whole Joiners Company, or the Corporation of Bedford, to eat up such a supper? Two or three little things, clean and comfortable, will do.   30

Hast. But, let's hear it.

Marl. [*Reading.*] For the first course at the top, a pig, and pruin sauce.

Hast. Damn your pig, I say.

Marl. And damn your pruin sauce, say I.

Hard. And yet, gentlemen, to men that are hungry, pig, with pruin sauce, is very good eating.

Marl. At the bottom, a calve's tongue and brains.

Hast. Let your brains be knock'd out, my good Sir; I don't like them.

Marl. Or you may clap them on a plate by themselves. I do.

Hard. [*Aside.*] Their impudence confounds me. [*To them.*] Gentlemen,   40 you are my guests, make what alterations you please. Is there any thing else you wish to retrench or alter, gentlemen?

Marl. Item. A pork pie, a boiled rabbet and sausages, a florentine, a shaking pudding, and a dish of tiff—taff—taffety cream!

Hast. Confound your made dishes, I shall be as much at a loss in this house as at a green and yellow dinner at the French ambassador's table. I'm for plain eating.

Hard. I'm sorry, gentlemen, that I have nothing you like, but if there be any thing you have a particular fancy to——

Marl. Why, really, Sir, your bill of fare is so exquisite, that any one part of it is full as good as another. Send us what you please. So much for supper. And now to see that our beds are air'd, and properly taken care of.

Hard. I entreat you'll leave all that to me. You shall not stir a step.

Marl. Leave that to you! I protest, Sir, you must excuse me, I always look to these things myself.

Hard. I must insist, Sir, you'll make yourself easy on that head.

Marl. You see I'm resolved on it. [*Aside.*] A very troublesome fellow   10
this, as ever I met with.

Hard. Well, Sir, I'm resolved at least to attend you. [*Aside.*] This may be modern modesty, but I never saw any thing look so like old-fashioned impudence.   [*Exeunt* Marlow *and* Hardcastle.

Hast. [*solus.*] So I find this fellow's civilities begin to grow troublesome. But who can be angry at those assiduities which are meant to please him? Ha! what do I see? Miss Neville, by all that's happy!
                                                  [*Enter* Miss Neville.

Miss Nev. My dear Hastings! To what unexpected good fortune? to what accident am I to ascribe this happy meeting?

Hast. Rather let me ask the same question, as I could never have hoped to   20
meet my dearest Constance at an inn.

Miss Nev. An inn! sure you mistake! my aunt, my guardian, lives here. What could induce you to think this house an inn?

Hast. My friend Mr. Marlow, with whom I came down, and I, have been sent here as to an inn, I assure you. A young fellow whom we accidentally met at a house hard by directed us hither.

Miss Nev. Certainly it must be one of my hopeful cousin's tricks, of whom you have heard me talk so often, ha! ha! ha! ha!

Hast. He whom your aunt intends for you? He of whom I have such just apprehensions?   30

Miss Nev. You have nothing to fear from him, I assure you. You'd adore him if you knew how heartily he despises me. My aunt knows it too, and has undertaken to court me for him, and actually begins to think she has made a conquest.

Hast. Thou dear dissembler! You must know, my Constance, I have just seized this happy opportunity of my friend's visit here to get admittance into the family. The horses that carried us down are now fatigued with their journey, but they'll soon be refreshed; and then if my dearest girl will trust in her faithful Hastings, we shall soon be landed in France, where even among slaves the laws of marriage are respected.[10]   40

Miss Nev. I have often told you, that though ready to obey you, I yet should leave my little fortune behind with reluctance. The greatest part of it was left

---

[10] *Laws of marriage are respected:* The Royal Marriage Act of 1772 empowered the king to forbid members of his family to marry. Like Goldsmith, who here takes a slap at the Bill, Johnson opposed it. See Boswell, *Life,* Hill-Powell, II, pp. 152–153, for an interesting discussion.

me by my uncle, the India Director, and chiefly consists in jewels. I have been for some time persuading my aunt to let me wear them. I fancy I'm very near succeeding. The instant they are put into my possession you shall find me ready to make them and myself yours.

Hast. Perish the baubles! Your person is all I desire. In the meantime, my friend Marlow must not be let into his mistake. I know the strange reserve of his temper is such, that if abruptly informed of it, he would instantly quit the house before our plan was ripe for execution.

Miss Nev. But how shall we keep him in the deception? Miss Hardcastle is just returned from walking; what if we still continue to deceive him?—— 10 This, this way—— [*They confer.*

[*Enter* Marlow.

Marl. The assiduities of these good people teize me beyond bearing. My host seems to think it ill manners to leave me alone, and so he claps not only himself but his old-fashioned wife on my back. They talk of coming to sup with us too; and then, I suppose, we are to run the gauntlet thro' all the rest of the family.—What have we got here!—

Hast. My dear Charles! Let me congratulate you!— The most fortunate accident!—Who do you think is just alighted?

Marl. Cannot guess.

Hast. Our mistresses, boy, Miss Hardcastle and Miss Neville. Give me leave 20 to introduce Miss Constance Neville to your acquaintance. Happening to dine in the neighbourhood, they called, on their return, to take fresh horses, here. Miss Hardcastle has just stept into the next room, and will be back in an instant. Wasn't it lucky? eh!

Marl. [*Aside.*] I have just been mortified enough of all consience, and here comes something to complete my embarrassment.

Hast. Well! but wasn't it the most fortunate thing in the world?

Marl. Oh! yes. Very fortunate—a most joyful encounter——But our dresses, George, you know, are in disorder——What if we should postpone the happiness 'till to-morrow?——To-morrow at her own house——It 30 will be every bit as convenient—And rather more respectful——To-morrow let it be. [*Offering to go.*

Miss Nev. By no means, Sir. Your ceremony will displease her. The disorder of your dress will shew the ardour of your impatience. Besides, she knows you are in the house, and will permit you to see her.

Marl. O! the devil! how shall I support it? Hem! hem! Hastings, you must not go. You are to assist me, you know. I shall be confoundedly ridiculous. Yet, hang it! I'll take courage. Hem!

Hast. Pshaw man! it's but the first plunge, and all's over. She's but a woman, you know. 40

Marl. And of all women, she that I dread most to encounter!

[*Enter* Miss Hardcastle *as returned from walking, a Bonnet, &c.*

Hast. [*introducing them.*] Miss Hardcastle, Mr. Marlow, I'm proud of bringing two persons of such merit together, that only want to know, to esteem each other.

Miss Hard. [*aside.*] Now, for meeting my modest gentleman with a demure face, and quite in his own manner. [*After a pause, in which he appears very uneasy and disconcerted.*] I'm glad of your safe arrival, Sir——I'm told you had some accidents by the way.

Marl. Only a few madam. Yes, we had some. Yes, Madam, a good many accidents, but should be sorry—Madam—or rather glad of any accidents—that are so agreeably concluded. Hem!

Hast. [*To him.*] You never spoke better in your whole life. Keep it up, and I'll insure you the victory.

Miss Hard. I'm afraid you flatter, Sir. You that have seen so much of the finest company can find little entertainment in an obscure corner of the country.   10

Marl. [*Gathering courage.*] I have lived, indeed, in the world, Madam; but I have kept very little company. I have been but an observer upon life, Madam, while others were enjoying it.

Miss Nev. But that, I am told, is the way to enjoy it at last.

Hast. [*To him.*] Cicero never spoke better. Once more, and you are confirm'd in assurance for ever.

Marl. [*To him.*] Hem! Stand by me then, and when I'm down, throw in a word or two to set me up again.

Miss Hard. An observer, like you, upon life, were, I fear, disagreeably employed, since you must have had much more to censure than to approve.   20

Marl. Pardon me, Madam. I was always willing to be amused. The folly of most people is rather an object of mirth than uneasiness.

Hast. [*To him.*] Bravo, Bravo. Never spoke so well in your whole life. Well! Miss Hardcastle, I see that you and Mr. Marlow are going to be very good company. I believe our being here will but embarrass the interview.

Marl. Not in the least, Mr. Hastings. We like your company of all things. [*To him.*] Zounds! George, sure you won't go? How can you leave us?

Hast. Our presence will but spoil conversation, so we'll retire to the next room. [*To him.*] You don't consider, man, that we are to manage a little   30
tête-à-tête of our own.   [*Exeunt.*

Miss Hard. [*After a pause.*] But you have not been wholly an observer, I presume, Sir: The ladies I should hope have employed some part of your addresses.

Marl. [*Relapsing into timidity.*] Pardon me, Madam, I—I—I—as yet have studied—only—to—deserve them.

Miss Hard. And that some say is the very worst way to obtain them.

Marl. Perhaps so, madam. But I love to converse only with the more grave and sensible part of the sex.——But I'm afraid I grow tiresome.

Miss Hard. Not at all, Sir; there is nothing I like so much as grave con-   40
versation myself; I could hear it for ever. Indeed I have often been surprized how a man of *sentiment* could ever admire those light airy pleasures, where nothing reaches the heart.

Marl. It's——a disease——of the mind, madam. In the variety of tastes there must be some who wanting a relish——for——um—a—um.

Miss Hard. I understand you, Sir. There must be some, who wanting a relish for refined pleasures, pretend to despise what they are incapable of tasting.

Marl. My meaning, madam, but infinitely better expressed. And I can't help observing——a——

Miss Hard. [*Aside.*] Who could ever suppose this fellow impudent upon some occasions. [*To him.*] You were going to observe, Sir——

Marl. I was observing, madam——I protest, madam, I forget what I was going to observe.

Miss Hard. [*Aside.*] I vow and so do I. [*To him.*] You were observing, Sir, that in this age of hypocrisy something about hypocrisy, Sir.

Marl. Yes, madam. In this age of hypocrisy there are few who upon strict enquiry do not—a—a—a——   10

Miss Hard. I understand you perfectly, Sir.

Marl. [*Aside.*] Egad ! and that's more than I do myself.

Miss Hard. You mean that in this hypocritical age there are few that do not condemn in public what they practise in private, and think they pay every debt to virtue when they praise it.

Marl. True, madam; those who have most virtue in their mouths, have least of it in their bosoms. But I'm sure I tire you, madam.

Miss Hard. Not in the least, Sir; there's something so agreeable and spirited in your manner, such life and force—pray, Sir, go on.

Marl. Yes, madam, I was saying——that there are some occasions——   20 when a total want of courage, madam, destroys all the——and puts us—— upon a——a——a——

Miss Hard. I agree with you entirely, a want of courage upon some occasions assumes the appearance of ignorance, and betrays us when we most want to excel. I beg you'll proceed.

Marl. Yes, madam. Morally speaking, madam—But I see Miss Neville expecting us in the next room. I would not intrude for the world.

Miss Hard. I protest, Sir, I never was more agreeably entertained in all my life. Pray go on.

Marl. Yes, madam. I was——But she beckons us to join her. Madam,   30 shall I do myself the honour to attend you?

Miss Hard. Well then, I'll follow.

Marl. [*aside.*] This pretty smooth dialogue has done for me.   [*Exit.*

Miss Hard. [*sola.*] Ha ! ha ! ha ! Was there ever such a sober sentimental interview? I'm certain he scarce look'd in my face the whole time. Yet the fellow, but for his unaccountable bashfulness, is pretty well, too. He has good sense, but then so buried in his fears, that it fatigues one more than ignorance. If I could teach him a little confidence, it would be doing somebody that I know of a piece of service. But who is that somebody?—that, faith, is a question I can scarce answer.   [*Exit.*   40

[*Enter* Tony *and* Miss Neville, *followed by* Mrs. Hardcastle *and* Hastings.

Tony. What do you follow me for, cousin Con? I wonder you're not ashamed to be so very engaging.

Miss Nev. I hope, cousin, one may speak to one's own relations, and not be to blame.

Tony. Ay, but I know what sort of a relation you want to make me though; but it won't do. I tell you, cousin Con, it won't do, so I beg you'll keep your distance, I want no nearer relationship.

[*She follows, coqueting him to the back scene.*

Mrs. Hard. Well! I vow, Mr. Hastings, you are very entertaining. There's nothing in the world I love to talk of so much as London, and the fashions, though I was never there myself.

Hast. Never there! You amaze me! From your air and manner, I concluded you had been bred all your life either at Ranelagh, St. James's, or Tower Wharf.[11]

Mrs. Hard. O! Sir, you're only pleased to say so. We Country persons   10 can have no manner at all. I'm in love with the town, and that serves to raise me above some of our neighbouring rustics; but who can have a manner, that has never seen the Pantheon, the Grotto Gardens, the Borough, and such places where the Nobility chiefly resort? All I can do, is to enjoy London at second-hand. I take care to know every *tête-à-tête* from the *Scandalous Magazine*,[12] and have all the fashions, as they come out, in a letter from the two Miss Rickets of Crooked-lane. Pray how do you like this head, Mr. Hastings?

Hast. Extremely elegant and *degagée*, upon my word, Madam. Your *Friseur*[13] is a Frenchman, I suppose?   20

Mrs. Hard. I protest I dressed it myself from a print in the *Ladies Memorandum-book* for the last year.

Hast. Indeed. Such a head in a side-box, at the Play-house, would draw as many gazers as my Lady May'ress at a City Ball.

Miss. Hard. I vow, since inoculation began,[14] there is no such thing to be seen as a plain woman; so one must dress a little particular or one may escape in the crowd.

Hast. But that can never be your case, Madam, in any dress.   [*Bowing.*

Mrs. Hard. Yet, what signifies *my* dressing when I have such a piece of antiquity by my side as Mr. Hardcastle: all I can say will never argue down   30 a single button from his cloaths. I have often wanted him to throw off his great flaxen wig, and where he was bald, to plaister it over like my Lord Pately, with powder.

Hast. You are right, Madam; for, as among the ladies, there are none ugly, so among the men there are none old.

Mrs. Hard. But what do you think his answer was? Why, with his usual Gothic[15] vivacity, he said I only wanted him to throw off his wig to convert it into a *tête*[16] for my own wearing.

---

[11] . . . *Tower Wharf:* Both Hastings here and Mrs. Hardcastle in the following speech incongruously refer to low and fashionable places of entertainment.

[12] *Scandalous Magazine:* The reference is to *The Town and Country Magazine* (1769–96), which specialized in literary entertainment and the scandals of society.

[13] *Friseur:* Hairdresser.

[14] *Inoculation began:* Lady Mary Wortley Montagu (1689–1762) introduced inoculation against smallpox on her return, in 1718, from Turkey, where she had lived in 1716 with her husband the British Ambassador to Constantinople.

[15] *Gothic:* Barbarous, rude, in bad taste.

[16] *Tête:* A high and elaborately ornamented lady's wig.

Hast. Intolerable! At your age you may wear what you please, and it must become you.

Mrs. Hard. Pray, Mr. Hastings, what do you take to be the most fashionable age about town?

Hast. Some time ago, forty was all the mode; but I'm told the ladies intend to bring up fifty for the ensuing winter.

Mrs. Hard. Seriously. Then I shall be too young for the fashion.

Hast. No lady begins now to put on jewels 'till she's past forty. For instance, Miss there, in a polite circle, would be considered as a child, as a mere maker of samplers.   10

Mrs. Hard. And yet Mrs. Niece[17] thinks herself as much a woman, and is as fond of jewels as the oldest of us all.

Hast. Your niece, is she? And that young gentleman, a brother of yours, I should presume?

Mrs. Hard. My son, Sir. They are contracted to each other. Observe their little sports. They fall in and out ten times a day, as if they were man and wife already. [*To them.*] Well Tony, child, what soft things are you saying to your cousin Constance this evening?

Tony. I have been saying no soft things; but that it's very hard to be followed about so. Ecod! I've not a place in the house now that's left to   20 myself but the stable.

Mrs. Hard. Never mind him, Con, my dear. He's in another story behind your back.

Miss Nev. There's something generous in my cousin's manner. He falls out before faces, to be forgiven in private.

Tony. That's a damned confounded——crack.[18]

Mrs. Hard. Ah! he's a sly one. Don't you think they're like each other about the mouth, Mr. Hastings? The Blenkinsop mouth to a T. They're of a size too. Back to back, my pretties, that Mr. Hastings may see you. Come Tony.   30

Tony. You had as good not make me, I tell you   [*Measuring.*

Miss Nev. O lud! he has almost cracked my head.

Mrs. Hard. O the monster! For shame, Tony. You a man, and behave so!

Tony. If I'm a man, let me have my fortin. Ecod! I'll not be made a fool of no longer.

Mrs. Hard. Is this, ungrateful boy, all that I'm to get for the pains I have taken in your education? I that have rock'd you in your cradle, and fed that pretty mouth with a spoon! Did not I work that waistcoat to make you genteel? Did not I prescribe for you every day, and weep while the receipt was operating?   40

Tony. Ecod! you had reason to weep, for you have been dosing me ever since I was born. I have gone through every receipt in *The Complete Huswife*[19] ten times over; and you have thoughts of coursing me through *Quincy*[20]

[17] *Mrs. Niece:* Miss Neville. The term Mrs. could apply both to married and unmarried women.

[18] *Crack:* Exaggeration, lie.

[19] *The Complete Huswife:* An early eighteenth-century cookbook.

[20] *Through Quincy:* Dr. John Quincy's *Complete English Dispensatory*, a pharmacopoeia, as its title indicates.

next spring. But, Ecod! I tell you, I'll not be made a fool of no longer.

Mrs. Hard. Wasn't it all for your good, viper? Wasn't it all for your good?

Tony. I wish you'd let me and my good alone then. Snubbing[21] this way when I'm in spirits. If I'm to have any good, let it come of itself; not to keep dinging it, dinging it into one so.

Mrs. Hard. That's false; I never see you when you're in spirits. No, Tony, you then go to the alehouse or kennel. I'm never to be delighted with your agreeable, wild notes, unfeeling monster!

Tony. Ecod! Mamma, your own notes are the wildest of the two.   10

Mrs. Hard. Was ever the like? But I see he wants to break my heart, I see he does.

Hast. Dear Madam, permit me to lecture the young gentleman a little. I'm certain I can persuade him to his duty.

Mrs. Hard. Well! I must retire. Come, Constance, my love. You see Mr. Hastings, the wretchedness of my situation: Was ever poor woman so plagued with a dear, sweet, pretty, provoking, undutiful boy.

[*Exeunt* Mrs. Hardcastle *and* Miss Neville.

[Hastings. Tony.

Tony. [*singing.*] *There was a young man riding by, and fain would have his will. Rang do didlo dee.* Don't mind her. Let her cry. It's the comfort of her heart. I have seen her and sister cry over a book for an hour together, and   20 they said, they liked the book the better the more it made them cry.

Hast. Then you're no friend to the ladies, I find, my pretty young gentleman?

Tony. That's as I find 'um.

Hast. Not to her of your mother's chusing, I dare answer? And yet she appears to me a pretty well-tempered girl.

Tony. That's because you don't know her as well as I. Ecod! I know every inch about her; and there's not a more bitter cantanckerous toad in all Christendom.

Hast. [*Aside.*] Pretty encouragement this for a lover!   30

. *Tony.* I have seen her since the height of that. She has as many tricks as a hare in a thicket, or a colt the first day's breaking!

Hast. To me she appears sensible and silent!

Tony. Ay, before company. But when she's with her play-mates she's as loud as a hog in a gate.

Hast. But there is a meek modesty about her that charms me.

Tony. Yes, but curb her never so little, she kicks up, and you're flung in a ditch.

Hast. Well, but you must allow her a little beauty.—Yes, you must allow her some beauty.   40

Tony. Bandbox! She's all a made up thing, mun, Ah! could you but see Bet Bouncer of these parts, you might then talk of beauty. Ecod, she has two eyes as black as sloes, and cheeks as broad and red as a pulpit cushion. She'd make two of she.

---

[21] *Snubbing:* Rebuking sharply.

Hast. Well, what say you to a friend that would take this bitter bargain off your hands?

Tony. Anon.[22]

Hast. Would you thank him that would take Miss Neville and leave you to happiness and your dear Betsy?

Tony. Ay; but where is there such a friend, for who would take *her*?

Hast. I am he. If you but assist me, I'll engage to whip her off to France, and you shall never hear more of her.

Tony. Assist you! Ecod I will, to the last drop of my blood. I'll clap a pair of horses to your chaise that shall trundle you off in a twinkling, and may   10 be get you a part of her fortin beside, in jewels, that you little dream of.

Hast. My dear squire, this looks like a lad of spirit.

Tony. Come along then, and you shall see more of my spirit before you have done with me.   [*Singing.*

> *We are the boys*
> *That fears no noise*
> *Where the thundering cannons roar.*

[*Exeunt.*

Act III

[*Enter* Hardcastle *solus.*

Hard. What could my old friend Sir Charles mean by recommending his son as the modestest young man in town? To me he appears the most impudent piece of brass that ever spoke with a tongue. He has taken possession   20 of the easy chair by the fire-side already. He took off his boots in the parlour, and desired me to see them taken care of. I'm desirous to know how his impudence affects my daughter.—She will certainly be shocked at it.

[*Enter* Miss Hardcastle, *plainly dress'd.*

Hard. Well, my Kate, I see you have changed your dress as I bid you; and yet, I believe, there was no great occasion.

Miss Hard. I find such a pleasure, Sir, in obeying your commands, that I take care to observe them without ever debating their propriety.

Hard. And yet, Kate, I sometimes give you some cause, particularly when I recommended my *modest* gentlemen to you as a lover to-day.

Miss Hard. You taught me to expect something extraordinary, and I   30 find the original exceeds the description.

Hard. I was never so surprised in my life! He has quite confounded all my faculties!

Miss Hard. I never saw any thing like it: And a man of the world too!

Hard. Ay, he learned it all abroad,—what a fool was I, to think a young man could learn modesty by travelling. He might as soon learn wit at a masquerade.

[22] *Anon:* "Beg your pardon! Sir! Eh?" *OED.*

Miss Hard. It seems all natural to him.

Hard. A good deal assisted by bad company and a French dancing-master.

Miss Hard. Sure you mistake, papa! a French dancing-master could never have taught him that timid look,—that aukward address,—that bashful manner——

Hard. Whose look? whose manner? child!

Miss Hard. Mr. Marlow's: his *mauvaise honte*,[1] his timidity struck me at the first sight.

Hard. Then your first sight deceived you; for I think him one of the most brazen first sights that ever astonished my senses.　　10

Miss Hard. Sure, Sir, you rally! I never saw any one so modest.

Hard. And can you be serious! I never saw such a bouncing swaggering puppy since I was born. Bully Dawson[2] was but a fool to him.

Miss Hard. Surprizing! He met me with a respectful bow, a stammering voice, and a look fixed on the ground.

Hard. He met me with a loud voice, a lordly air, and a familiarity that made my blood freeze again.

Miss Hard. He treated me with diffidence and respect; censured the manners of the age; admired the prudence of girls that never laughed; tired me with apologies for being tiresome; then left the room with a bow, and, madam,　20 I would not for the world detain you.

Hard. He spoke to me as if he knew me all his life before. Asked twenty questions, and never waited for an answer. Interrupted my best remarks with some silly pun, and when I was in my best story of the Duke of Marlborough and Prince Eugene, he asked if I had not a good hand at making punch? Yes, Kate, he ask'd your father if he was a maker of punch!

Miss Hard. One of us must certainly be mistaken.

Hard. If he be what he has shewn himself, I'm determined he shall never have my consent.

Miss Hard. And if he be the sullen thing I take him, he shall never have　30 mine.

Hard. In one thing then we are agreed—to reject him.

Miss Hard. Yes. But upon conditions. For if you should find him less impudent, and I more presuming; if you find him more respectful, and I more importunate——I don't know——the fellow is well enough for a man—Certainly we don't meet many such at a horse race in the country.

Hard. If we should find him so——But that's impossible. The first appearance has done my business. I'm seldom deceived in that.

Miss Hard. And yet there may be many good qualities under that first appearance.　　40

Hard. Ay, when a girl finds a fellow's outside to her taste, she then sets about guessing the rest of his furniture. With her, a smooth face stands for good sense, and a genteel figure for every virtue.

Miss Hard. I hope, Sir, a conversation begun with a compliment to my good sense won't end with a sneer at my understanding?

---

[1] *Mauvaise honte:* Bashfulness.

[2] *Bully Dawson:* A ruffian, who figures in the characterization of Sir Roger de Coverly, *Spectator*, No. 2.

Hard. Pardon me, Kate. But if young Mr. Brazen can find the art of reconciling contradictions, he may please us both, perhaps.

Miss Hard. And as one of us must be mistaken, what if we go to make further discoveries

Hard. Agreed. But depend on't I'm in the right.

Miss Hard. And depend on't I'm not much in the wrong.   [*Exeunt.*

[*Enter* Tony *running in with a Casket.*

Tony. Ecod! I have got them. Here they are. My Cousin Con's necklaces, bobs[3] and all. My mother shan't cheat the poor souls out of their fortune neither. O! my genus, is that you?

[*Enter* Hastings.

Hast. My dear friend, how have you managed with your mother? I hope you have amused her with pretending love for your cousin, and that you are willing to be reconciled at last? Our horses will be refreshed in a short time, and we shall soon be ready to set off.   10

Tony. And here's something to bear your charges by the way [*giving the casket.*], Your sweetheart's jewels. Keep them, and hang those, I say, that would rob you of one of them.

Hast. But how have you procured them from your mother?

Tony. Ask me no questions, and I'll tell you no fibs. I procured them by the rule of thumb. If I had not a key to every drawer in mother's bureau, how could I go to the alehouse so often as I do? An honest man may rob himself of his own at any time.   20

Hast. Thousands do it every day. But to be plain with you; Miss Neville is endeavouring to procure them from her aunt this very instant. If she succeeds, it will be the most delicate way at least of obtaining them.

Tony. Well, keep them, till you know how it will be. But I know how it will be well enough, she'd as soon part with the only sound tooth in her head.

Hast. But I dread the effects of her resentment, when she finds she has lost them.

Tony. Never you mind her resentment, leave *me* to manage that. I don't value her resentment the bounce of a cracker. Zounds! here they are. Morrice.[4]   30
Prance.   [*Exit* Hastings.

[Tony, Mrs. Harcdastle, Miss Neville.

Mrs. Hard. Indeed, Constance, you amaze me. Such a girl as you want jewels? It will be time enough for jewels, my dear, twenty years hence, when your beauty begins to want repairs.

Miss Nev. But what will repair beauty at forty, will certainly improve it at twenty, Madam.

Mrs. Hard. Yours, my dear, can admit of none. That natural blush is beyond a thousand ornaments. Besides, child, jewels are quite out at present. Don't you see half the ladies of our acquaintance, my Lady, Kill-day-light, and

---

[3] *Bobs:* Pendants.   [4] *Morrice:* A slang term meaning decamp, i.e., leave.

Mrs. Crump, and the rest of them, carry their jewels to town, and bring nothing but Paste and Marcasites[5] back.

Miss Nev. But who knows, Madam, but somebody that shall be nameless would like me best with all my little finery about me?

Mrs. Hard. Consult your glass, my dear, and then see, if with such a pair of eyes, you want any better sparklers. What do you think, Tony, my dear, does your cousin Con want any jewels, in your eyes, to set off her beauty.

Tony. That's as thereafter may be.

Miss Nev. My dear aunt, if you knew how it would oblige me.

Mrs. Hard. A parcel of old-fashioned rose and table-cut things.[6] They would   10
make you look like the court of king Solomon at a puppet-shew. Besides, I believe I can't readily come at them. They may be missing for aught I know to the contrary.

Tony. [*Apart to* Mrs. Hardcastle.] Then why don't you tell her so at once, as she's so longing for them. Tell her they're lost. It's the only way to quiet her. Say they're lost, and call me to bear witness.

Mrs. Hard. [*Apart to* Tony.] You know, my dear, I'm only keeping them for you. So if I say they're gone, you'll bear me witness, will you? He! he! he!

Tony. Never fear me. Ecod! I'll say I saw them taken out with my own eyes.

Miss Nev. I desire them but for a day, Madam, just to be permitted to   20
show them as relics, and then they may be locked up again.

Mrs. Hard. To be plain with you, my dear Constance, if I could find them you should have them. They're missing, I assure you. Lost, for aught I know; but we must have patience, wherever they are.

Miss Nev. I'll not believe it; this is but a shallow pretence to deny me. I know they're too valuable to be so slightly kept, and as you are to answer for the loss—

Mrs. Hard. Don't be alarmed, Constance. If they be lost, I must restore an equivalent. But my son knows they are missing, and not to be found.

Tony. That I can bear witness to. They are missing, and not to be found,   30
I'll take my oath on't.

Mrs. Hard. You must learn resignation, my dear; for though we lose our fortune, yet we should not lose our patience. See me, how calm I am.

Miss Nev. Ay, people are generally calm at the misfortunes of others.

Mrs. Hard. Now, I wonder a girl of your good sense should waste a thought upon such trumpery. We shall soon find them; and in the meantime you shall make use of my garnets till your jewels be found.

Miss Nev. I detest garnets!

Mrs. Hard. The most becoming things in the world to set off a clear complexion. You have often seen how well they look upon me. You *shall* have   40
them.   [*Exit.*

Miss Nev. I dislike them of all things. You shan't stir.—Was ever any-

---

[5] *Marcasites:* Inexpensive ornaments made of crystallized iron pyrites.

[6] *Rose and table-cut things:* Apparently both kinds of jewelry are undesirable: the first, though large and cut with many facets, is old-fashioned; the second, cut to reveal a full face, is actually very thin.

thing so provoking—to mislay my own jewels, and force me to wear her trumpery?

Tony. Don't be a fool. If she gives you the garnets take what you can get. The jewels are your own already. I have stolen them out of her bureau, and she does not know it. Fly to your spark, he'll tell you more of the matter. Leave me to manage *her.*

Miss Nev. My dear cousin!

Tony. Vanish. She's here, and has missed them already. [*Exit* Miss Neville.] Zounds! how she fidgets and spits about like a Catherine wheel.[7]

[*Enter* Mrs. Hardcastle.

Mrs. Hard. Confusion! thieves! robbers! We are cheated, plundered,   10 broke open, undone!

Tony. What's the matter, what's the matter, mamma? I hope nothing has happened to any of the good family?

Mrs. Hard. We are robbed. My bureau has been broke open, the jewels taken out, and I'm undone!

Tony. Oh! is that all? Ha! ha! ha! By the laws, I never saw it better acted in my life. Ecod, I thought you was ruined in earnest, ha, ha, ha!

Mrs. Hard. Why, boy, I *am* ruined in earnest. My bureau has been broke open, and all taken away.

Tony. Stick to that; ha, ha, ha! stick to that. I'll bear witness, you know, call   10 me to bear witness.

Mrs. Hard. I tell you Tony, by all that's precious, the jewels are gone, and I shall be ruined forever.

Tony. Sure I know they're gone, and I am to say so.

Mrs. Hard. My dearest Tony, but hear me. They're gone, I say.

Tony. By the laws, mamma, you make me for to laugh, ha! ha! I know who took them well enough, ha! ha! ha!

Mrs. Hard. Was there ever such a blockhead, that can't tell the difference between jest and earnest? I can tell you I'm not in jest, booby.

Tony. That's right, that's right! You must be in a bitter passion, and then   30 nobody will suspect either of us. I'll bear witness that they are gone.

Mrs. Hard. Was there ever such a cross-grained brute, that won't hear me? Can you bear witness that you're no better than a fool? Was ever poor woman so beset with fools on one hand, and thieves on the other?

Tony. I can bear witness to that.

Mrs. Hard. Bear witness again, you blockhead you, and I'll turn you out of the room directly. My poor niece, what will become of *her!* Do you laugh, you unfeeling brute, as if you enjoy'd my distress?

Tony. I can bear witness to that.

Mrs. Hard. Do you insult me, monster? I'll teach you to vex your mother,   40 I will.

Tony. I can bear witness to that.   [*He runs off, she follows him.*

[*Enter* Miss Hardcastle *and* Maid.

Miss Hard. What an unaccountable creature is that brother of mine, to

---

[7] *Catherine wheel:* A kind of fireworks, a pin-wheel.

send them to the house as an inn, ha! ha! I don't wonder at his impudence.

Maid. But what is more, madam, the young gentlemen as you passed by in your present dress, ask'd me if you were the bar maid? He mistook you for the bar maid, madam.

Miss Hard. Did he? Then as I live I'm resolved to keep up the delusion. Tell me, Pimple, how do you like my present dress. Don't you think I look something like Cherry in *The Beaux Stratagem*?[8]

Maid. It's the dress, madam, that every lady wears in the country, but when she visits or receives company.

Miss Hard. And are you sure he does not remember my face or person?   10

Maid. Certain of it.

Miss Hard. I vow I thought so; for though we spoke for some time together, yet his fears were such, that he never once looked up during the interview. Indeed, if he had, my bonnet would have kept him from seeing me.

Maid. But what do you hope from keeping him in his mistake?

Miss Hard. In the first place, I shall be *seen*, and that is no small advantage to a girl who brings her face to market. Then I shall perhaps make an acquaintance and that's no small victory gained over one who never addresses any but the wildest of her sex. But my chief aim is to take my gentleman off his guard, and like an invisible champion of romance examine the giant's force before   20
I offer to combat.

Maid. But are you sure you can act your part, and disguise your voice, so that he may mistake that, as he has already mistaken your person?

Miss Hard. Never fear me. I think I have got the true bar cant.—Did your honour call?——Attend the Lion there.——Pipes and tobacco for the Angel.—
The Lamb[9] has been outrageous this half hour.

Maid. It will do, madam. But he's here.   [*Exit* Maid.
                    [*Enter* Marlow.

Marl. What a bawling in every part of the house; I have scarce a moment's repose. If I go to the best room, there I find my host and his story. If I fly to the gallery, there we have my hostess with her curtesy down to the ground.   30
I have at last got a moment to myself, and now for recollection.
                              [*Walks and muses.*

Miss Hard. Did you call, Sir? did your honour call?

Marl. [*Musing.*] As for Miss Hardcastle, she's too grave and sentimental for me.

Miss Hard. Did your honour call?
              [*She still places herself before him, he turning away.*

Marl. No, child. [*musing.*] Besides from the glimpse I had of her, I think she squints.

Miss Hard. I'm sure, Sir, I heard the bell ring.

Marl. No, No. [*Musing.*] I have pleased my father, however, by coming down, and I'll to-morrow please myself by returning.   40
              [*Taking out his tablets, and perusing.*

[8] *Cherry in* The Beaux Stratagem: She is the daughter of Bonniface, the landlord, in Farquhar's play.

[9] *Lion . . . Angel . . . Lamb:* Typical names of inn-rooms.

Miss Hard. Perhaps the other gentleman called, Sir.

Marl. I tell you, no.

Miss Hard. I should be glad to know, Sir. We have such a parcel of servants.

Marl. No, no, I tell you. [*Looks full in her face.*] Yes, child, I think I did call. I wanted——I wanted——I vow, child, you are vastly handsome.

Miss Hard. O la, Sir, you'll make one ashamed.

Marl. Never saw a more sprightly malicious eye. Yes, yes, my dear, I did call. Have you got any of your—a—what d'ye call it in the house?

Miss Hard. No, Sir, we have been out of that these ten days.

Marl. One may call in this house, I find, to very little purpose. Suppose I   10
should call for a taste, just by way of trial, of the nectar of your lips; perhaps I might be disappointed in that too.

Miss Hard. Nectar! nectar! that's a liquor there's no call for in these parts. French, I suppose. We keep no French wines here, Sir.

Marl. Of true English growth, I assure you.

Miss Hard. Then it's odd I should not know it. We brew all sorts of wines in this house, and I have lived here these eighteen years.

Marl. Eighteen years! Why one would think, child, you kept the bar before you were born. How old are you?

Miss Hard. O! Sir, I must not tell my age. They say women and music   20
should never be dated.

Marl. To guess at this distance, you can't be much above forty. [*approaching.*] Yet nearer I don't think so much. [*approaching.*] By coming close to some women they look younger still; but when we come very close indeed [*attempting to kiss her.*

Miss Hard. Pray, Sir, keep your distance. One would think you wanted to know one's age as they do horses, by mark of mouth.

Marl. I protest, child, you use me extremely ill. If you keep me at this distance, how is it possible you and I can be ever acquainted?

Miss Hard. And who wants to be acquainted with you? I want no such   30
acquaintance, not I. I'm sure you did not treat Miss Hardcastle that was here awhile ago in this obstropalous manner. I'll warrant me, before her you look'd dash'd, and kept bowing to the ground, and talk'd for all the world, as if you was before a justice of peace.

Marl. [*Aside.*] Egad! she has hit it, sure enough. [*To her.*] In awe of her, child? Ha! ha! ha! A mere, aukward, squinting thing, no, no. I find you don't know me. I laugh'd, and rallied her a little; but I was unwilling to be too severe. No, I could not be too severe, *curse me!*

Miss Hard. O! then, Sir, you are a favourite, I find, among the ladies?

Marl. Yes, my dear, a great favourite. And yet, hang me, I don't see what   40
they find in me to follow. At the Ladies Club in town,[10] I'm called their agreeable Rattle. Rattle, child, is not my real name, but one I'm known by. My name is Solomons. Mr. Solomons, my dear, at your service. [*Offering to salute her.*

Miss Hard. Hold, Sir; you were introducing me to your club, not to yourself. And you're so great a favourite there you say?

[10] *Ladies Club in town:* The reference is to the Female Coterie, a London club.

Marl. Yes, my dear. There's Mrs. Mantrap, Lady Betty Blackleg, the Countess of Sligo, Mrs. Longhorns, old Miss Biddy Buckskin,[11] and your humble servant, keep up the spirit of the place.

Miss Hard. Then it's a very merry place, I suppose.

Marl. Yes, as merry as cards, suppers, wine, and old women can make us.

Miss Hard. And their agreeable Rattle, ha ! ha ! ha !

Marl. [*Aside.*] Egad ! I don't quite like this chit. She looks knowing, methinks. You laugh, child !

Miss Hard. I can't but laugh to think what time they all have for minding their work or their family. 10

Marl. [*Aside.*] All's well, she don't laugh at me. [*To her.*] Do *you* ever work, child ?

Miss Hard. Ay, sure. There's not a screen or a quilt in the whole house but what can bear witness to that.

Marl. Odso ! Then you must shew me your embroidery. I embroider and draw patterns myself a little. If you want a judge of your work you must apply to me.   [*Seizing her hand.*

Miss Hard. Ay, but the colours don't look well by candle light. You shall see all in the morning.   [*Struggling.*

Marl. And why not now, my angel ? Such beauty fires beyond the power 20 of resistance.———Pshaw ! the father here ! My old luck : I never nick'd seven that I did not throw ames ace three times following.[12] [*Exit* Marlow.

[*Enter* Hardcastle, *who stands in surprize.*

Hard. So, madam ! So I find *this* is your *modest* lover. This is your humble admirer that kept his eyes fixed on the ground, and only ador'd at humble distance. Kate, Kate, art thou not asham'd to deceive your father so ?

Miss Hard. Never trust me, dear papa, but he's still the modest man I first took him for, you'll be convinced of it as well as I.

Hard. By the hand of my body I believe his impudence is infectious ! Didn't I see him seize your hand ? Didn't I see him hawl you about like a milk maid ? and now you talk of his respect and his modesty, forsooth ! 30

Miss Hard. But if I shortly convince you of his modesty, that he has only the faults that will pass off with time, and the virtues that will improve with age, I hope you'll forgive him.

Hard. The girl would actually make one run mad ! I tell you I'll not be convinced. I am convinced. He has scarcely been three hours in the house, and he has already encroached on all my prerogatives. You may like his impudence, and call it modesty. But my son-in-law, madam, must have very different qualifications.

Miss Hard. Sir, I ask but this night to convince you.

Hard. You shall not have half the time, for I have thoughts of turning him 40 out this very hour.

---

[11] *Miss Biddy Buckskin:* Pre-publication MS. of *She Stoops* gives Miss Rachel Buckskin rather than Miss Biddy. The reference is to Miss Rachel Lloyd, a well-known member of the Female Coterie.

[12] *. . . Three times following:* The terms in Marlow's speech are taken from a dice game. He says in effect that whenever he has very good luck, he has very bad luck right after.

Miss Hard. Give me that hour then, and I hope to satisfy you.

Hard. Well, an hour let it be then. But I'll have no trifling with your father. All fair and open do you mind me.

Miss Hard. I hope, Sir, you have ever found that I considered your commands as my pride; for your kindness is such, that my duty as yet has been inclination.　　　　　　　　　　　　　　　　　　　　　　　　*[Exeunt.*

Act IV

[*Enter* Hastings *and* Miss Neville.

Hast. You surprise me! Sir Charles Marlow expected here this night? Where have you had your information?

Miss Nev. You may depend upon it. I just saw his letter to Mr. Hardcastle, in which he tells him he intends setting out a few hours after his son.　10

Hast. Then, my Constance, all must be completed before he arrives. He knows me; and should he find me here, would discover my name, and perhaps my designs, to the rest of the family.

Miss Nev. The jewels, I hope, are safe.

Hast. Yes, yes. I have sent them to Marlow, who keeps the keys of our baggage. In the meantime, I'll go to prepare matters for our elopement. I have had the Squire's promise of a fresh pair of horses; and, if I should not see him again, will write him further directions.　　　　　　*[Exit.*

Miss Nev. Well! success attend you. In the meantime, I'll go amuse my aunt with the old pretence of a violent passion for my cousin.　　　*[Exit.*　20
　　　　　　　　　[*Enter* Marlow, *followed by a* Servant.

Marl. I wonder what Hastings could mean by sending me so valuable a thing as a casket to keep for him, when he knows the only place I have is the seat of a post-coach at an Inn-door. Have you deposited the casket with the landlady, as I ordered you? Have you put it into her own hands?

Servant. Yes, your honour.

Marl. She said she'd keep it safe, did she?

Servant. Yes, she said she'd keep it safe enough; she ask'd me how I came by it? and she said she had a great mind to make me give an account of myself.　　　　　　　　　　　　　　　　　　　　　　　*[Exit* Servant.

Marl. Ha! ha! ha! They're safe however. What an unaccountable set of　30 beings have we got amongst! This little bar-maid though runs in my head most strangely, and drives out the absurdities of all the rest of the family. She's mine, she must be mine, or I'm greatly mistaken.

　　　　　　　　　　　　　　[*Enter* Hastings.

Hast. Bless me! I quite forgot to tell her that I intended to prepare at the bottom of the garden. Marlow here, and in spirits too!

Marl. Give me joy, George! Crown me, shadow me with laurels! Well, George, after all, we modest fellows don't want for success among the women.

Hast. Some women you mean. But what success has your honour's modesty been crowned with now, that it grows so insolent upon us?

Marl. Didn't you see the tempting, brisk, lovely, little thing that runs about the house with a bunch of keys to its girdle?

Hast. Well! and what then?

Marl. She's mine, you rogue you. Such fire, such motion, such eyes, such lips——but, egad! she would not let me kiss them though.

Hast. But are you so sure, so very sure of her?

Marl. Why man, she talk'd of shewing me her work above-stairs, and I am to improve the pattern.

Hast. But how can *you*, Charles, go about to rob a woman of her honour?

Marl. Pshaw! pshaw! we all know the honour of the bar-maid of an inn. 10 I don't intend to *rob* her, take my word for it, there's nothing in this house, I shan't honestly *pay* for.

Hast. I believe the girl has virtue.

Marl. And if she has, I should be the last man in the world that would attempt to corrupt it.

Hast. You have taken care, I hope, of the casket I sent you to lock up? It's in safety?

Marl. Yes, yes. It's safe enough. I have taken care of it. But how could you think the seat of a post-coach at an Inn-door a place of safety? Ah! numb-skull! I have taken better precautions for you than you did for yourself.—— 20 I have——

Hast. What!

Marl. I have sent it to the landlady to keep for you.

Hast. To the landlady!

Marl. The landlady.

Hast. You did.

Marl. I did. She's to be answerable for its forth-coming, you know.

Hast. Yes, she'll bring it forth, with a witness.

Marl. Wasn't I right? I believe you'll allow that I acted prudently upon this ocassion? 30

Hast. [*Aside.*] He must not see my uneasiness.

Marl. You seem a little disconcerted though, methinks. Sure nothing has happened?

Hast. No, nothing. Never was in better spirits in all my life. And so you left it with the landlady, who, no doubt, very readily undertook the charge?

Marl. Rather too readily. For she not only kept the casket; but, thro' her great precaution, was going to keep the messenger too. Ha! ha! ha!

Hast. He! he! he! They're safe however.

Marl. As a guinea in a miser's purse.

Hast. [*Aside.*] So now all hopes of fortune are at an end, and we must set off 40 without it. [*To him.*] Well, Charles, I'll leave you to your meditations on the pretty bar-maid, and, he! he! he! may you be as successful for yourself as you have been for me. [*Exit.*

Marl. Thank ye, George! I ask no more. Ha! ha! ha!

[*Enter* Hardcastle.

Hard. I no longer know my own house. It's turned all topsey-turvey. His servants have got drunk already. I'll bear it no longer, and yet, from

my respect for his father, I'll be calm. [*To him.*] Mr. Marlow, your servant.
I'm your very humble servant.   [*Bowing low.*

Marl. Sir, your humble servant. [*Aside.*] What's to be the wonder now?

Hard. I believe, Sir, you must be sensible, Sir, that no man alive ought to be
more welcome than your father's son, Sir. I hope you think so?

Marl. I do from my soul, Sir. I don't want much intreaty. I generally make
my father's son welcome wherever he goes.

Hard. I believe you do, from my soul, Sir. But tho' I say nothing to your
own conduct, that of your Servants is insufferable. Their manner of drinking
is setting a very bad example in this house, I assure you.   10

Marl. I protest, my very good Sir, that's no fault of mine. If they don't drink
as they ought *they* are to blame. I ordered them not to spare the cellar. I did,
I assure you. [*To the side scene.*] Here, let one of my servants come up. [*To
him.*] My positive directions were, that as I did not drink myself, they should
make up for my deficiencies below.

Hard. Then they had your orders for what they do! I'm satisfied!

Marl. They had, I assure you. You shall hear from one of themselves.

[*Enter* Servant *drunk.*

Marl. You, Jeremy! Come forward, sirrah! What were my orders? Were
you not told to drink freely, and call for what you thought fit, for the good   20
of the house?

Hard. [*Aside.*] I begin to lose my patience.

Jeremy. Please your honour, liberty and Fleet-street[1] for ever! Tho' I'm
but a servant, I'm as good as another man. I'll drink for no man before supper,
Sir, dammy! Good liquor will sit upon a good supper, but a good supper will
not sit upon——hiccup—— upon my conscience, Sir.

Marl. You see, my old friend, the fellow is as drunk as he can possibly be.
I don't know what you'd have more, unless you'd have the poor devil soused
in a beer-barrel.

Hard. Zounds! He'll drive me distracted if I contain myself any longer.   30
Mr. Marlow. Sir; I have submitted to your insolence for more than four
hours, and I see no likelihood of its coming to an end. I'm now resolved to
to be master here, Sir, and I desire that you and your drunken pack may
leave my house directly.

Marl. Leave your house!——Sure you jest, my good friend? What, when
I'm doing what I can to please you.

Hard. I tell you, Sir, you don't please me; so I desire you'll leave my house.

Marl. Sure you cannot be serious? At this time o'night, and such a night.
You only mean to banter me?

Hard. I tell you, Sir, I'm serious; and, now that my passions are rouzed,   40
I say this house is mine, Sir; this house is mine, and I command you to leave
it directly.

Marl. Ha! ha! ha! A puddle in a storm. I shan't stir a step, I assure you.
[*In a serious tone.*] This, your house, fellow! It's my house. This is my house.
Mine, while I chuse to stay. What right have you to bid me leave this house,

---

[1] *Fleet-street:* A London street famous
for its taverns.

Sir? I never met with such impudence, curse me, never in my whole life before.

Hard. Nor I, confound me if ever I did. To come to my house, to call for what he likes, to turn me out of my own chair, to insult the family, to order his servants to get drunk, and then to tell me *This house is mine, Sir.* By all that's impudent it makes me laugh. Ha! ha! ha! Pray, Sir [*bantering.*], as you take the house, what think you of taking the rest of the furniture? There's a pair of silver candlesticks, and there's a fire-screen, and here's a pair of brazen nosed bellows, perhaps you may take a fancy to them?

Marl. Bring me your bill, Sir, bring me your bill, and let's make no more   10
words about it.

Hard. There are a set of prints too. What think you of *The Rake's Progress*[2]
for your own apartment?

Marl. Bring me your bill, I say; and I'll leave you and your infernal house directly.

Hard. Then there's a mahagony table, that you may see your own face in.

Marl. My bill, I say.

Hard. I had forgot the great chair, for your own particular slumbers, after a hearty meal.

Marl. Zounds! bring me my bill, I say, and let's hear no more on't.   20

Hard. Young man, young man, from your father's letter to me, I was taught to expect a well-bred modest man, as a visitor here, but now I find him no better than a coxcomb and a bully; but he will be down here presently, and shall hear more of it.   [*Exit.*

Marl. How's this! Sure I have not mistaken the house! Every thing looks like an inn. The servants cry, coming. The attendance is aukward; the barmaid too to attend us. But she's here, and will further inform me. Whither so fast, child. A word with you.

[*Enter* Miss Hardcastle.

Miss Hard. Let it be short then. I'm in a hurry. [*Aside.*] I believe he begins to find out his mistake, but its too soon quite to undeceive him.   30

Marl. Pray, child, answer me one question. What are you, and what may your business in this house be?

Miss Hard. A relation of the family, Sir.

Marl. What. A poor relation?

Miss Hard. Yes, Sir. A poor relation appointed to keep the keys, and to see that the guests want nothing in my power to give them.

Marl. That is, you act as the bar-maid of this inn.

Miss Hard. Inn! O law!—What brought that into your head? One of the best families in the county keep an inn! Ha! ha! ha! old Mr. Hardcastle's house an inn!   40

Marl. Mr. Hardcastle's house! Is this house Mr. Hardcastle's house, child?

Miss Hard. Ay, sure. Whose else should it be?

Marl. So, then, all's out, and I have been damnably imposed on. O, con-

---

[2] *The Rake's Progress:* A series of engravings by William Hogarth (1697– 1764); they were issued in 1735.

found my stupid head, I shall be laughed at over the whole town. I shall be stuck up in caricatura in all the print-shops—the *Dullissimo Macaroni*.[3] To mistake this house of all others for an inn, and my father's old friend for an innkeeper! What a swaggering puppy must he take me for! What a silly puppy do I find myself! There again, may I be hanged, my dear, but I mistook you for the bar-maid.

Miss Hard. Dear me! dear me! I'm sure there's nothing in my *behavour*[4] to put me upon a level with one of that stamp.

Marl. Nothing, my dear, nothing. But I was in for a list of blunders, and could not help making you a subscriber. My stupidity saw everything   10
the wrong way. I mistook your assiduity for assurance, and your simplicity for allurement. But it's over—this house I no more show *my* face in.

Miss Hard. I hope, sir, I have done nothing to disoblige you. I'm sure I should be sorry to affront any gentleman who has been so polite, and said so many civil things to me. I'm sure I should be sorry [*pretending to cry.*] if he left the family upon my account. I'm sure I should be sorry people said anything amiss, since I have no fortune but my character.

Marl. [*aside.*] By heaven, she weeps! This is the first mark of tenderness I ever had from a modest woman, and it touches me. [*To her.*] Excuse me, my lovely girl, you are the only part of the family I leave with reluctance.   20
But to be plain with you, the difference of our birth, fortune, and education, make an honorable connection impossible; and I can never harbor a thought of seducing simplicity that trusted in my honor, or bringing ruin upon one whose only fault was being too lovely.

Miss Hard. [*aside.*] Generous man! I now begin to admire him. [*To him.*] But I'm sure my family is as good as Miss Hardcastles', and though I'm poor, that's no great misfortune to a contented mind, and, until this moment, I never thought that it was bad to want fortune.

Marl. And why now, my pretty simplicity?

Miss Hard. Because it puts me at a distance from one that, if I had a thousand   30
pound, I would give it all to.

Marl. [*aside.*] This simplicity bewitches me, so that if I stay I'm undone. I must make one bold effort, and leave her. [*To her.*] Your partiality in my favor, my dear, touches me most sensibly, and were I to live for myself alone, I could easily fix my choice. But I owe too much to the opinion of the world, too much to the authority of a father, so that—I can scarcely speak it—it affects me! Farewell.   [*Exit.*

Miss Hard. I never knew half his merit till now. He shall not go, if I have power or art to detain him. I'll still preserve the character in which I stoop'd to conquer, but will undeceive my papa, who, perhaps, may laugh him out of   40
his resolution.   [*Exit.*

[*Enter* Tony, Miss Neville.

---

[3] *The Dullissimo Macaroni:* Many prints of the day caricatured London fops, a practice to which Goldsmith here refers obliquely.

[4] *Behavour:* Miss Hardcastle by degrees permits her true colors to appear as the play proceeds. Here she begins to behave with more circumspection than she before made obvious; she drops the barmaid's cant; but she continues to use a servant's language.

Tony. Ay, you may steal for yourselves the next time. I have done my duty. She has got the jewels again, that's a sure thing; but she believes it was all a mistake of the servants.

Miss Nev. But, my dear cousin, sure you won't forsake us in this distress. If she in the least suspects that I am going off, I shall certainly be locked up, or sent to my aunt Pedigree's, which is ten times worse.

Tony. To be sure, aunts of all kinds are damn'd bad things. But what can I do? I have got you a pair of horses that will fly like Whistlejacket, and I'm sure you can't say but I have courted you nicely before her face. Here she comes, we must court a bit or two more, for fear she should suspect us. 10

[*They retire, and seem to fondle.*

[*Enter* Mrs. Hardcastle.

Mrs. Hard. Well, I was greatly fluttered, to be sure. But my son tells me it was all a mistake of the servants. I shan't be easy, however, till they are fairly married, and then let her keep her own fortune. But what do I see! Fondling together, as I'm alive. I never saw Tony so sprightly before. Ah! have I caught you, my pretty doves! What, billing, exchanging stolen glaces, and broken murmurs. Ah!

Tony. As for murmurs, mother, we grumble a little now and then, to be sure. But there's no love lost between us.

Mrs. Hard. A mere sprinkling, Tony, upon the flame, only to make it burn brighter. 20

Miss Nev. Cousin Tony promises to give us more of his company at home. Indeed, he shan't leave us any more. It won't leave us cousin Tony, will it?

Tony. O! it's a pretty creature. No, I'd sooner leave my horse in a pound, than leave you when you smile upon one so. Your laugh makes you so becoming.

Miss Nev. Agreeable cousin! Who can help admiring that natural humour, that pleasant, broad, red, thoughtless [*patting his cheek.*], ah! it's a bold face.

Mrs. Hard. Pretty innocence.

Tony. I'm sure I always lov'd cousin Con's hazle eyes, and her pretty long fingers, that she twists this way and that, over the haspicholls,[5] like a parcel 30
of bobbins.

Mrs. Hard. Ah, he would charm the bird from the tree. I was never so happy before. My boy takes after his father, poor Mr. Lumpkin, exactly. The jewels, my dear Con, shall be your's incontinently. You shall have them. Isn't he a sweet boy, my dear? You shall be married to-morrow, and we'll put off the rest of his education, like Dr. Drowsy's sermons, to a fitter opportunity.

[*Enter* Diggory.

Digg. Where's the 'Squire? I have got a letter for your worship.

Tony. Give it to my mamma. She reads all my letters first.

Digg. I had orders to deliver it into your own hands. 40

Tony. Who does it come from?

Digg. Your worship mun ask that o' the letter itself.

---

[5] *Haspicholls:* Harpsichord.

Tony. I could wish to know, tho' [*turning the letter, and gazing on it.*

Miss Nev. [*Aside.*] Undone, undone. A letter to him from Hastings. I know the hand. If my aunt sees it, we are ruined for ever. I'll keep her employ'd a little if I can. [*To* Mrs. Hardcastle.] But I have not told you, Madam, of my cousin's smart answer just now to Mr. Marlow. We so laugh'd —You must know, Madam—this way a little, for he must not hear us.   [*They confer.*

Tony. [*Still gazing.*] A damn'd cramp piece of penmanship, as ever I saw in my life. I can read your print-hand very well. But here there are such handles, and shanks, and dashes, that one can scarce tell the head from the tail. *To Anthony Lumpkin, Esquire.* It's very odd, I can read the outside of my letters, where my   10 own name is, well enough. But when I come to open it, it's all—buzz. That's hard, very hard; for the inside of the letter is always the cream of the correspondence.

Mrs. Hard. Ha! ha! ha! Very well, very well. And so my son was too hard for the philosopher.

Miss Nev. Yes, Madam; but you must hear the rest, Madam. A little more this way, or he may hear us. You'll hear how he puzzled him again.

Mrs. Hard. He seems strangely puzzled now himself me-thinks.

Tony. [*Still gazing.*] A damn'd up and down hand, as if it was disguised in liquor. [*Reading.*] *Dear Sir.* Ay, that's that. Then there's an *M,* and *a T,* and   20 an *S,* but whether the next be an *izzard*[6] or an *R,* confound me, I cannot tell.

Mrs. Hard. What's that, my dear. Can I give you any assistance?

Miss Nev. Pray, aunt, let me read it. No body reads a cramp hand better than I. [*Twitching the letter from her.*] Do you know who it is from?

Tony. Can't tell, except from Dick Ginger, the feeder.[7]

Miss Nev. Ay, so it is. [*pretending to read.*] Dear 'Squire, Hoping that you're in health, as I am at this present. The gentlemen of the Shake-bag[8] club has cut the gentlemen of goose-green quite out of feather. The odds—um—odd battle—um—long fighting—um here, here, it's all about cocks, and fighting; it's of no consequence, here, put it up, put it up. [*thrusting the crumpled letter*   30 *upon him.*

Tony. But I tell you, Miss, it's of all the consequence in the world. I would not lose the rest of it for a guinea. Here, mother, do you make it out. Of no consequence! [*giving* Mrs. Hardcastle *the letter.*

Mrs. Hard. How's this! [*Reads.*] Dear 'Squire, I'm now waiting for Miss Neville, with a post-chaise and pair, at the bottom of the garden, but I find my horses yet unable to perform the journey. I expect you'll assist us with a pair of fresh horses, as you promised. Dispatch is necessary, as the *hag* (ay the hag) your mother, will otherwise suspect us. Your's, Hastings. Grant me patience. I shall run distracted. My rage choaks me.   40

Miss Nev. I hope, Madam, you'll suspend your resentment for a few moments, and not impute to me any impertinence, or sinister design that belongs to another.

Mrs. Hard. [*Curtesying very low.*] Fine spoken, Madam, you are most miraculously polite and engaging, and quite the very pink of curtesy and

---

[6] *Izzard:* The letter *Z.*
[7] *The feeder:* A breeder and trainer of fighting cocks.
[8] *Shake-bag:* A large fighting cock.

circumspection, Madam. [*Changing her tone.*] And you, you great ill-fashioned oaf, with scarce sense enough to keep your mouth shut. Were you too join'd against me? But I'll defeat all your plots in a moment. As for you, Madam, since you have got a pair of fresh horses ready, it would be cruel to disappoint them. So, if you please, instead of running away with your spark, prepare, this very moment, to run off with *me*. Your old aunt Pedigree will keep you secure, I'll warrant me. You too, Sir, may mount your horse, and guard us upon the way. Here, Thomas, Roger, Diggory, I'll shew you, that I wish you better than you do yourselves.   [*Exit.*

Miss Nev. So now I'm completely ruined.   10

Tony. Ay, that's a sure thing.

Miss Nev. What better could be expected from being connected with such a stupid fool, and after all the nods and signs I made him.

Tony. By the laws, Miss, it was your own cleverness, and not my stupidity, that did your business. You were so nice and so busy with your Shake-bags and Goose-greens, that I thought you could never be making believe.

[*Enter* Hastings.

Hast. So, Sir, I find by my servant, that you have shewn my letter, and betray'd us. Was this well done, young gentleman.

Tony. Here's another. Ask Miss there who betray'd you. Ecod, it was her doing, not mine.   20

[*Enter* Marlow.

Marl. So I have been finely used here among you. Rendered contemptible, driven into ill manners, despised, insulted, laugh'd at.

Tony. Here's another. We shall have old Bedlam broke loose presently.

Miss Nev. And there, Sir, is the gentleman to whom we all owe every obligation.

Marl. What can I say to him, a mere boy, an ideot, whose ignorance and age are a protection.

Hast. A poor contemptible booby, that would but disgrace correction.

Miss Nev. Yet with cunning and malice enough to make himself merry with all our embarrassments.   30

Hast. An insensible cub.

Marl. Replete with tricks and mischief.

Tony. Baw! damme, but I'll fight you both one after the other,——with baskets.[9]

Marl. As for him, he's below resentment. But your conduct, Mr. Hastings, requires an explanation. You knew of my mistakes, yet would not undeceive me.

Hast. Tortured as I am with my own disappointments, is this a time for explanations. It is not friendly, Mr. Marlow.

Marl. But, Sir—   40

Miss Nev. Mr. Marlow, we never kept on your mistake, till it was too late to undeceive you. Be pacified.

[*Enter* Servant.

[9] *Baskets:* The term referred to the wicker guards for the hilts of a sword-stick and later (as here) to the sticks themselves.

Servant. My mistress desires you'll get ready immediately, Madam. The horses are putting to. Your hat and things are in the next room. We are to go thirty miles before morning.   [*Exit* Servant.

Miss Nev. Well, well; I'll come presently.

Marl. [*To* Hastings.] Was it well done, Sir, to assist in rendering me ridiculous. To hang me out for the scorn of all my acquaintance. Depend upon it, Sir, I shall expect an explanation.

Hast. Was it well done, Sir, if you're upon that subject, to deliver what I entrusted to yourself, to the care of another, Sir.

Miss Nev. Mr. Hastings. Mr. Marlow. Why will you increase my distress   10
by this groundless dispute. I implore, I intreat you——

[*Enter* Servant.

Servant. Your cloak, Madam. My mistress is impatient.

Miss Nev. I come. Pray be pacified. If I leave you thus, I shall die with apprehension.

[*Enter* Servant.

Servant. Your fan, muff, and gloves, Madam. The horses are waiting.

Miss Nev. O, Mr. Marlow! if you knew what a scene of constraint and ill-nature lies before, me I'm sure it would convert your resentment into pity.

Marl. I'm so distracted with a variety of passions, that I don't know what I do. Forgive me, Madam. George, forgive me. You know my hasty temper, and should not exasperate it.   20

Hast. The torture of my situation is my only excuse.

Miss Nev. Well, my dear Hastings, if you have that esteem for me that I think, that I am sure you have, your constancy for three years will but encrease the happiness of our future connexion. If—

Mrs. Hard. [*Within.*] Miss Neville. Constance, why Constance, I say.

Miss Nev. I'm coming. Well, constancy. Remember, constancy is the word.   [*Exit.*

Hast. My heart! How can I support this. To be so near happiness, and such happiness.

Marl. [*To* Tony.] You see now, young gentleman, the effects of your folly.   30
What might be amusement to you, is here disappointment, and even distress.

Tony. [*From a reverie.*] Ecod, I have hit it. Its here. Your hands. Yours and yours, my poor Sulky. My boots there, ho. Meet me two hours hence at the bottom of the garden; and if you don't find Tony Lumpkin a more good-natur'd fellow than you thought for, I'll give you leave to take my best horse, and Bet Bouncer into the bargain. Come along. My boots, ho.   [*Exeunt.*

Act V

SCENE *Continues*

[*Enter* Hastings *and* Servant.

Hast. You saw the Old Lady and Miss Neville drive off, you say.

Servant. Yes, your honour. They went off in a post coach, and the young 'Squire went on horseback. They're thirty miles off by this time.

Hast. Then all my hopes are over.

Servant. Yes, Sir. Old Sir Charles is arrived. He and the Old Gentleman of the house have been laughing at Mr. Marlow's mistake this half hour. They are coming this way.

Hast. Then I must not be seen. So now to my fruitless appointment at the bottom of the garden. This is about the time.   [*Exit.*

[*Enter* Sir Charles *and* Hardcastle.

Hard. Ha! ha! ha! The peremptory tone in which he sent forth his sublime commands.

Sir Charles. And the reserve with which I suppose he treated all your advances.   10

Hard. And yet he might have seen something in me above a common inn-keeper, too.

Sir Charles. Yes, Dick, but he mistook you for an uncommon innkeeper, ha! ha! ha!

Hard. Well, I'm in too good spirits to think of any thing but joy. Yes, my dear friend, this union of our families will make our personal friendships hereditary; and tho' my daughter's fortune is but small——

Sir Charles. Why, Dick, will you talk of fortune to *me*. My son is possessed of more than a competence already, and can want nothing but a good and virtuous girl to share his happiness and encrease it. If they like each other, as you   20 say they do——

Hard. If, man. I tell you they *do* like each other. My daughter as good as told me so.

Sir Charles. But girls are apt to flatter themselves, you know.

Hard. I saw him grasp her hand in the warmest manner myself; and here he comes to put you out of your *ifs*, I warrant him.

[*Enter* Marlow.

Marl. I come, Sir, once more, to ask pardon for my strange conduct. I can scarce reflect on my insolence without confusion.

Hard. Tut, boy, a trifle. You take it too gravely. An hour or two's laughing with my daughter will set all to rights again. She'll never like you the worse   30 for it.

Marl. Sir, I shall be always proud of her approbation.

Hard. Approbation is but a cold word, Mr. Marlow; if I am not deceived, you have something more than approbation thereabouts. You take me.

Marl. Really, Sir, I have not that happiness.

Hard. Come, boy, I'm an old fellow, and know what's what, as well as you that are younger. I know what has past between you; but mum.

Marl. Sure, Sir, nothing has past between us but the most profound respect on my side, and the most distant reserve on her's. You don't think,   40 Sir, that my impudence has been past upon all the rest of the family.

Hard. Impudence! No, I don't say that—Not quite impudence—Though girls like to be play'd with, and rumpled a little too sometimes. But she has told no tales, I assure you.

Marl. I never gave her the slightest cause.

Hard. Well, well, I like modesty in its place well enough. But this is over-acting, young gentleman. You *may* be open. Your father and I will like you the better for it.

Marl. May I die, Sir, if I ever——

Hard. I tell you, she don't dislike you; and as I'm sure you like her——

Marl. Dear Sir—I protest, Sir——

Hard. I see no reason why you should not be joined as fast as the parson can tie you.

Marl. But hear me, Sir——

Hard. Your father approves the match, I admire it, every moment's delay   10
will be doing mischief, so——

Marl. But why won't you hear me? By all that's just and true, I never gave Miss Hardcastle the slightest mark of my attachment, or even the most distant hint to suspect me of affection. We had but one interview, and that was formal, modest and uninteresting.

Hard. [*Aside.*] This fellow's formal modest impudence is beyond bearing.

Sir Charles. And you never grasp'd her hand, or made any protestations!

Marl. As heaven is my witness, I came down in obedience to your commands. I saw the lady without emotion, and parted without reluctance. I hope you'll exact no further proofs of my duty, nor prevent me from leaving   20
a house in which I suffer so many mortifications.   [*Exit.*

Sir Charles. I'm astonish'd at the air of sincerity with which he parted.

Hard. And I'm astonish'd at the deliberate intrepidity of his assurance.

Sir Charles. I dare pledge my life and honour upon his truth.

Hard. Here comes my daughter, and I would stake my happiness upon her veracity.

[Enter Miss Hardcastle.

Hard. Kate, come hither, child. Answer us sincerely. and without reserve; has Mr. Marlow made you any professions of love and affection?

Miss Hard. The question is very abrupt, Sir! But since you require un-reserved sincerity, I think he has.   30

Hard. [*To* Sir Charles.] You see.

Sir Charles. And pray, madam, have you and my son had more than one interview?

Miss Hard. Yes, Sir, several.

Hard. [*To* Sir Charles.] You see.

Sir Charles. But did he profess any attachment?

Miss Hard. A lasting one.

Sir Charles. Did he talk of love?

Miss Hard. Much, Sir.

Sir Charles. Amazing! And all this formally?   40

Miss Hard. Formally.

Hard. Now, my friend, I hope you are satisfied.

Sir Charles. And how did he behave. madam?

Miss Hard. As most profest admirers do. Said some civil things of my face, talked much of his want of merit, and the greatness of mine; mentioned his heart, gave a short tragedy speech, and ended with pretended rapture.

Sir Charles. Now I'm perfectly convinced, indeed. I know his conversation among women to be modest and submissive. This forward canting ranting manner by no means describes him, and I am confident, he never sate for the picture.

Miss Hard. Then what, Sir, if I should convince you to your face of my sincerity? If you and my papa, in about half an hour, will place yourselves behind that screen, you shall hear him declare his passion to me in person.

Sir Charles. Agreed. And if I find him what you describe, all my happiness in him must have an end. [*Exit.*

Miss Hard. And if you don't find him what I describe—I fear my happiness 10 must never have a beginning. [*Exeunt.*

SCENE *changes to the Back of the Garden*
[*Enter* Hastings.

Hast. What an ideot am I, to wait here for a fellow, who probably takes a delight in mortifying me. He never intended to be punctual, and I'll wait no longer. What do I see. It is he, and perhaps with news of my Constance.

[*Enter* Tony, *booted and spattered.*

Hast. My honest 'Squire! I now find you a man of your word. This looks like friendship.

Tony. Ay, I'm your friend, and the best friend you have in the world, if you knew but all. This riding by night, by the bye, is cursedly tiresome. It has shook me worse than the basket of a stagecoach. 20

Hast. But how? Where did you leave your fellow travellers? Are they in safety? Are they housed?

Tony. Five and twenty miles in two hours and a half is no such bad driving. The poor beasts have smoaked for it: Rabbet me, but I'd rather ride forty miles after a fox, than ten with such *varment.*

Hast. Well, but where have you left the ladies? I die with impatience.

Tony. Left them. Why where should I leave them, but where I found them.

Hast. This is a riddle.

Tony. Riddle me this then. What's that goes round the house, and round the house, and never touches the house? 30

Hast. I'm still astray.

Tony. Why that's it, mon. I have led them astray. By jingo, there's not a pond or slough within five miles of the place but they can tell the taste of.

Hast. Ha, ha, ha, I understand; you took them in a round, while they supposed themselves going forward. And so you have at last brought them home again.

Tony. You shall hear. I first took them down Feather-bed-lane, where we stuck fast in the mud. I then rattled them crack over the stones of Up-and-down Hill—I then introduc'd them to the gibbet on Heavy-tree Heath, and from that, with a circumbendibus, I fairly lodged them in the horse-pond at the 40 bottom of the garden.

Hast. But no accident, I hope.

Tony. No, no. Only mother is confoundedly frightened. She thinks herself forty miles off. She's sick of the journey, and the cattle can scarce crawl. So if your own horses be ready, you may whip off with cousin, and I'll be bound that no soul here can budge a foot to follow you.

Hast. My dear friend, how can I be grateful?

Tony. Ay, now its dear friend, noble 'Squire. Just now, it was all ideot, cub, and run me through the guts. Damn *your* way of fighting, I say. After we take a knock in this part of the country, we kiss and be friends. But if you had run me through the guts, then I should be dead, and you might go kiss the hangman.

Hast. The rebuke is just. But I must hasten to relieve miss Neville; if you keep the old lady employed, I promise to take care of the young one.   10

          [*Exit* Hastings.

Tony. Never fear me. Here she comes. Vanish. She's got from the pond, and draggled up to the waist like a mermaid.

       [*Enter* Mrs. Hardcastle.

Mrs. Hard. Oh, Tony, I'm killed. Shook. Battered to death. I shall never survive it. That last jolt that laid us against the quickset hedge has done my business.

Tony. Alack, mama, it was all your own fault. You would be for running away by night, without knowing one inch of the way.

Mrs. Hard. I wish we were at home again. I never met so many accidents in so short a journey. Drench'd in the mud, overturned in a ditch, stuck fast in a slough, jolted to a jelly, and at last to lose our way. Whereabouts do you   20 think we are, Tony?

Tony. By my guess we should be upon Crackskull common, about forty miles from home.

Mrs. Hard. O lud! O lud! the most notorious spot in all the country. We only want a robbery to make a complete night on't.

Tony. Don't be afraid, mama, don't be afraid. Two of the five that kept here[1] are hanged, and the other three may not find us. Don't be afraid. Is that a man that's galloping behind us? No; its only a tree. Don't be afraid.

Mrs. Hard. The fright will certainly kill me.

Tony. Do you see any thing like a black hat moving behind the thicket?   30

Mrs. Hard. O death!

Tony. No, it's only a cow. Don't be afraid, mama; don't be afraid.

Mrs. Hard. As I'm alive, Tony, I see a man coming towards us. Ah! I'm sure on't. If he perceives us we are undone.

Tony. [*Aside.*] Father-in-law, by all that's unlucky, come to take one of his night walks. [*To her.*] Ah, it's a highwayman, with pistils as long as my arm. A damn'd ill-looking fellow.

Mrs. Hard. Good heaven defend us! He approaches.

Tony. Do you hide yourself in that thicket, and leave me to manage him. If there be any danger I'll cough and cry hem. When I cough be sure to keep   40 close.   [Mrs. Hardcastle *hides behind a tree in the back scene.*

       [*Enter* Hardcastle.

Hard. I'm mistaken, or I heard voices of people in want of help. Oh, Tony,

---

[1] *Kept here:* Frequented the place.

is that you? I did not expect you so soon back. Are your mother and her charge in safety?

Tony. Very safe, Sir, at my aunt Pedigree's. Hem.

Mrs. Hard. [*From behind.*] Ah death! I find there's danger.

Hard. Forty miles in three hours; sure, that's too much, my youngster.

Tony. Stout horses and willing minds make short journies, as they say. Hem.

Mrs. Hard. [*From behind.*] Sure he'll do the dear boy no harm.

Hard. But I heard a voice here; I should be glad to know from whence it came? 10

Tony. It was I, Sir, talking to myself, Sir. I was saying that forty miles in four hours was very good going. Hem. As to be sure it was. Hem. I have got a sort of cold by being out in the air. We'll go in, if you please. Hem.

Hard. But if you talk'd to yourself, you did not answer yourself. I am certain I heard two voices, and am resolved [*raising his voice.*] to find the other out.

Mrs. Hard. [*From behind.*] Oh! he's coming to find me out. Oh!

Tony. What need you go, Sir, if I tell you. Hem. I'll lay down my life for the truth—hem—I'll tell you all, Sir. [*Detaining him.*

Hard. I tell you, I will not be detained. I insist on seeing. It's in vain to 20 expect I'll believe you.

Mrs. Hard. [*Running forward from behind.*] O lud, he'll murder my poor boy, my darling. Here, good gentleman, whet your rage upon me. Take my money, my life, but spare that young gentleman, spare my child, if you have any mercy.

Hard. My wife! as I'm a Christian. From whence can she come, or what does she mean!

Mrs. Hard. [*Kneeling.*] Take compassion on us, good Mr. Highwayman. Take our money, our watches, all we have, but spare our lives. We will never bring you to justice, indeed we won't, good Mr. Highwayman. 30

Hard. I believe the woman's out of her senses. What, Dorothy, don't you know *me?*

Mrs. Hard. Mr. Hardcastle, as I'm alive! My fears blinded me. But who, my dear, could have expected to meet you here, in this frightful place, so far from home. What has brought you to follow us?

Hard. Sure, Dorothy, you have not lost your wits. So far from home, when you are within forty yards of your own door. [*To him.*] This is one of your old tricks, you graceless rogue, you. [*To her.*] Don't you know the gate, and the mulberry-tree; and don't you remember the horsepond, my dear?

Mrs. Hard. Yes, I shall remember the horsepond as long as I live; I have caught 40 my death in it. [*To Tony.*] And is it to you, you graceless varlet, I owe all this. I'll teach you to abuse your mother, I will.

Tony. Ecod, mother, all the parish says you have spoil'd me, and so you may take the fruits on't.

Mrs. Hard. I'll spoil you, I will. [*Follows him off the stage. Exit.*

Hard. There's morality, however, in his reply. [*Exit.*

[*Enter* Hastings *and* Miss Neville.

Hast. My dear Constance, why will you deliberate thus? If we delay a moment, all is lost for ever. Pluck up a little resolution, and we shall soon be out of the reach of her malignity.

Miss Nev. I find it impossible. My spirits are so sunk with the agitations I have suffered, that I am unable to face any new danger. Two or three years patience will at last crown us with happiness.

Hast. Such a tedious delay is worse than inconstancy. Let us fly, my charmer. Let us date our happiness from this very moment. Perish fortune. Love and content will encrease what we possess beyond a monarch's revenue. Let me prevail.   10

Miss Nev. No, Mr. Hastings; no. Prudence once more comes to my relief, and I will obey its dictates. In the moment of passion, fortune may be despised, but it ever produces a lasting repentance. I'm resolved to apply to Mr. Hardcastle's compassion and justice for redress.

Hast. But tho' he had the will, he has not the power to relieve you.

Miss Nev. But he has influence, and upon that I am resolved to rely.

Hast. I have no hopes. But since you persist, I must reluctantly obey you.

[*Exeunt.*

SCENE *Changes*

[*Enter* Sir Charles *and* Miss Hardcastle.

Sir Charles. What a situation am I in. If what you say appears, I shall then find a guilty son. If what he says be true, I shall then lose one that, of all others, I most wish'd for a daughter.   20

Miss Hard. I am proud of your approbation, and to shew I merit it, if you place yourselves as I directed, you shall hear his explicit declaration. But he comes.

Sir Charles. I'll to your father, and keep him to the appointment.

[*Exit* Sir Charles.

[*Enter* Marlow.

Marl. Tho' prepar'd for setting out, I come once more to take leave, nor did I, till this moment, know the pain I feel in the separation.

Miss Hard. [*In her own natural manner.*] I believe these sufferings cannot be very great, Sir, which you can so easily remove. A day or two longer, perhaps, might lessen your uneasiness, by shewing the little value of what you now think proper to regret.   30

Marl. [*Aside.*] This girl every moment improves upon me. [*To her.*] It must not be, Madam. I have already trifled too long with my heart. My very pride begins to submit to my passion. The disparity of education and fortune, the anger of a parent, and the contempt of my equals, begin to lose their weight and nothing can restore me to myself, but this painful effort of resolution.

Miss Hard. Then go, Sir. I'll urge nothing more to detain you. Tho' my family be as good as her's you came down to visit, and my education, I hope, not inferior, what are these advantages without equal affluence? I must remain contented with the slight approbation of imputed merit. I must have only the mockery of your addresses, while all your serious aims are fixe'd on fortune.   40

[*Enter* Hardcastle *and* Sir Charles *from behind.*

Sir Charles. Here, behind this screen.

Hard. Ay, Ay, make no noise. I'll engage my Kate covers him with confusion at last.

Marl. By heavens, Madam, fortune was ever my smallest consideration. Your beauty at first caught my eye; for who could see that without emotion. But every moment that I converse with you, steals in some new grace, heightens the picture, and gives it stronger expression. What at first seem'd rustic plainness, now appears refin'd simplicity. What seem'd forward assurance, now strikes me as the result of courageous innocence, and conscious virtue.

Sir Charles. What can it mean! He amazes me!

Hard. I told you how it would be. Hush!   10

Marl. I am now determined to stay, Madam, and I have too good an opinion of my father's discernment, when he sees you, to doubt his approbation.

Miss Hard. No, Mr. Marlow, I will not, cannot detain you. Do you think I could suffer a connexion, in which there is the smallest room for repentance? Do you think I would take the mean advantage of a transient passion, to load you with confusion? Do you think I could ever relish that happiness, which was acquired by lessening your's?

Marl. By all that's good, I can have no happiness but what's in your power to grant me. Nor shall I ever feel repentance, but in not having seen your   20 merits before. I will stay, even contrary to your wishes; and tho' you should persist to shun me, I will make my respectful assiduities atone for the levity of my past conduct.

Miss Hard. Sir, I must entreat you'll desist. As our acquaintance began, so let it end, in indifference. I might have given an hour or two to levity; but seriously, Mr. Marlow, do you think I could ever submit to a connexion, where *I* must appear mercenary, and *you* imprudent? Do you think I could ever catch at the confident addresses of a secure admirer?

Marl. [*Kneeling.*] Does this look like security. Does this look like confidence. No, Madam, every moment that shews me your merit, only serves to encrease   30 my diffidence and confusion. Here let me continue——

Sir Charles. I can hold it no longer. Charles, Charles, how hast thou deceived me! Is this your indifference, your uninteresting conversation!

Hard. Your cold contempt; your formal interview. What have you to say now?

Marl. That I'm all amazement! What can it mean!

Hard. It means that you can say and unsay things at pleasure. That you can address a lady in private, and deny it in public; that you have one story for us, and another for my daughter.

Marl. Daughter!—this lady your daughter!   40

Hard. Yes, Sir, my only daughter. My Kate, whose else should she be?

Marl. Oh, the devil.

Miss Hard. Yes, Sir, that very identical tall squinting lady you were pleased to take me for. [*curtesying.*] She that you addressed as the mild, modest, sentimental man of gravity, and the bold forward agreeable rattle of the ladies club; ha, ha, ha.

Marl. Zounds, there's no bearing this; it's worse than death.

Miss Hard. In which of your characters, Sir, will you give us leave to address you. As the faultering gentleman, with looks on the ground, that speaks just to be heard, and hates hypocrisy; or the loud confident creature, that keeps it up with Mrs. Mantrap, and old Miss Biddy Buckskin,[2] till three in the morning; ha, ha, ha.

Marl. O, curse on my noisy head. I never attempted to be impudent yet, that I was not taken down. I must be gone.

Hard. By the hand of my body, but you shall not. I see it was all a mistake, and I am rejoiced to find it. You shall not, Sir, I tell you. I know she'll forgive you. Won't you forgive him, Kate. We'll all forgive you. Take courage, man.   10

[*They retire, she tormenting him to the back Scene.*
[*Enter* Mrs. Hardcastle, Tony.

Mrs. Hard. So, so, they're gone off. Let them go, I care not.

Hard. Who gone?

Mrs. Hard. My dutiful niece and her gentleman, Mr. Hastings, from Town. He who came down with our modest visitor here.

Sir Charles. Who, my honest George Hastings. As worthy a fellow as lives, and the girl could not have made a more prudent choice.

Hard. Then, by the hand of my body, I'm proud of the connexion.

Mrs. Hard. Well, if he has taken away the lady, he has not taken her fortune; that remains in this family to console us for her loss.

Hard. Sure Dorothy you would not be so mercenary?   20

Mrs. Hard. Ay, that's my affair, not your's.

[*Hard*]. But you know if your son, when of age, refuses to marry his cousin, her whole fortune is then at her own disposal.

[*Mrs.*] *Hard.* Ay, but he's not of age, and she has not thought proper to wait for his refusal.

[*Enter* Hastings *and* Miss Neville.

Mrs. Hard. [*Aside.*] What returned so soon, I begin not to like it.

Hast. [*To* Hardcastle.] For my late attempt to fly off with your niece, let my present confusion be my punishment. We are now come back, to appeal from your justice to your humanity. By her father's consent, I first paid her my addresses, and our passions were first founded in duty.   30

Miss Nev. Since his death, I have been obliged to stoop to dissimulation to avoid oppression. In an hour of levity, I was ready even to give up my fortune to secure my choice. But I'm now recover'd from the delusion, and hope from your tenderness what is denied me from a nearer connexion.

Mrs. Hard. Pshaw, pshaw, this is all but the whining end of a modern novel.

Hard. Be it what it will, I'm glad they're come back to reclaim their due. Come hither, Tony boy. Do you refuse this lady's hand whom I now offer you?

Tony. What signifies my refusing. You know I can't refuse her till I'm of age, father.   40

Hard. While I thought concealing your age boy was likely to conduce to your improvement, I concurred with your mother's desire to keep it secret. But

---

[2] *Miss Biddy Buckskin:* See III, n. 11.

since I find she turns it to a wrong use, I must now declare, you have been of age these three months.

Tony. Of age! Am I of age, father?

Hard. Above three months.

Tony. Then you'll see the first use I'll make of my liberty. [*Taking* Miss Neville's *hand.*] Witness all men by these presents, that I, Anthony Lumpkin, Esquire, of BLANK place, refuse you, Constantia Neville, spinster, of no place at all, for my true and lawful wife. So Constance Neville may marry whom she pleases, and Tony Lumpkin is his own man again.

Sir Charles. O brave 'Squire.   10

Hast. My worthy friend.

Mrs. Hard. My undutiful offspring.

Marl. Joy, my dear George, I give you joy sincerely. And could I prevail upon my little tyrant here to be less arbitrary, I should be the happiest man alive, if you would return me the favour.

Hast. [*To* Miss Hardcastle.] Come, madam, you are now driven to the very last scene of all your contrivances. I know you like him, I'm sure he loves you, and you must and shall have him.

Hard. [*Joining their hands.*] And I say so too. And Mr. Marlow, if she makes as good a wife as she has a daughter, I don't believe you'll ever repent   20 your bargain. So now to supper, to-morrow we shall gather all the poor of the parish about us, and the Mistakes of the Night shall be crowned with a merry morning; so, boy, take her; and as you have been mistaken in the mistress, my wish is, that you may never be mistaken in the wife.

Epilogue

By Dr. Goldsmith

WELL, *having stoop'd to conquer with success,*
And gain'd a husband without aid from dress,
Still as a Bar-maid, I could wish it too,
As I have conquer'd him to conquer you:
And let me say, for all your resolution,   5
That pretty Bar-maids have done execution.
Our life is all a play, compos'd to please,
"We have our exits and our entrances."
The first act shews the simple country maid,
Harmless and young, of ev'ry thing afraid;   10
Blushes when hir'd, and with unmeaning action,
I hopes as how to give you satisfaction.
Her second act displays a livelier scene,—
Th' unblushing Bar-maid of a country inn.
Who whisks about the house, at market caters,   15
Talks loud, coquets the guests, and scolds the waiters.

Next the scene shifts to town, and there she soars,
The chop-house toast of ogling connoissieurs.
On 'Squires and Cits she there displays her arts,
And on the gridiron broils her lover's hearts—   20
And as she smiles, her triumphs to compleat,
Even Common Councilmen forget to eat.
The fourth act shews her wedded to the 'Squire,
And Madam now begins to hold it higher;
Pretends to taste, at Operas cries caro,[1]   25
And quits her Nancy Dawson,[2] *for Che Faro.*[3]
Doats upon dancing, and in all her pride,
Swims round the room, the Heinel[4] *of Cheapside:*
Ogles and leers with artificial skill,
Till having lost in age the power to kill,   30
She sits all night at cards, and ogles at spadille.[5]
Such, thro' our lives, the eventful history—
The fifth and last act still remains for me.
The Bar-maid now for your protection prays,
Turns Female Barrister, and pleads for Bayes.[6]   35

Epilogue*

To be Spoken in the Character of Tony Lumpkin

By J. Craddock,[7] Esq.

WELL—*now all's ended—and my comrades gone,*
Pray what becomes of mother's nonly son?
A hopeful blade!—in town I'll fix my station,
And try to make a bluster in the nation.
As for my cousin Neville, I renounce her,   5
Off—in a crack—I'll carry big Bett Bouncer.
    Why should not I in the great world appear?
I soon shall have a thousand pounds a year;
No matter what a man may here inherit,

*This came too late to be spoken. [See Friedman, V, pp. 87–89.]

[1] *Caro:* Dear. This Italian adjective has a wide range of uses and may be applied properly to actors or their performances.

[2] *Nancy Dawson:* A famous song named after the actress who made it popular in a revival of *The Beggar's Opera*, in 1759.

[3] *Che Faro:* The first words of Orfeo's lament in Gluck's *Orfeo ed Euridice: Che farò senza Euridice:* What shall I do without Eurydice?

[4] *Heinel:* A ballet dancer whose charm had just won London audiences.

[5] *Spadille:* The Ace of Spades, leading trump in Ombre. See III, n. 27, *The Rape of the Lock.*

[6] *Bayes:* The playwright. See the discussion of *The Rehearsal* in the headnote to drama.

[7] *J. Craddock:* Joseph Craddock (1742–1826), man of letters, friend of Goldsmith, and a recorder in his *Memoirs* of many of Dr. Johnson's sallies. Craddock had a tragedy, *Zobeide*, produced in 1771.

In London—'gad, they've some regard to spirit.   10
I see the horses prancing up the streets,
And big Bet Bouncer, bobs to all she meets;
Then hoikes to jiggs and pastimes ev'ry night—
Not to the plays—they say it a'n't polite,
To Sadler's-Wells perhaps, or Operas go,   15
And once by chance, to the roratorio.[8]
Thus here and there, for ever up and down,
We'll set the fashions too, to half the town;
And then at auctions—money ne'er regard,
Buy pictures like the great, ten pounds a yard;   20
Zounds, we shall make these London gentry say,
We know what's damn'd genteel, as well as they.

(1773)

---

[8] *Roratorio:* Presumably a play on the words roar and oratorio. The oratorio is a musical composition, based on the Bible, presented in a theater rather than in a church. It makes use of solo voices, chorus, and orchestra.

General Bibliography

I. Eighteenth-Century Bibliography

The standard bibliography for the student of the eighteenth century is the second volume of *CBEL* (*Cambridge Bibliography of English Literature*), which covers the period 1650–1800 and lists separately the editions of works by the chief writers of the age; it also includes works *about* Restoration and eighteenth-century authors to around 1935. The supplement, *CBEL*, V, covers secondary works to 1955. (*CBEL* is currently being revised.)

The most widely used bibliography of scholarship in the field, covering material from 1926 to 1960, is *English Literature 1660–1800, A Bibliography of Modern Studies Compiled for Philological Quarterly*, eds. Louis A. Landa, R. S. Crane, Louis I. Bredvold, et al., 4 vols., Princeton, N.J., Princeton U. P., 1950–1962. For publications since 1960, the student may consult the July issues of *Philological Quarterly*. Other good lists include the *PMLA Annual Bibliography*, *Annual Bibliography of English Language and Literature*, a publication of The Modern Humanities Research Association, and *Year's Work in English Studies*.

For an excellent check list of works in the field see James L. Clifford *Early Eighteenth-Century English Literature*, New York, Columbia U. P., 1959, revised 1962, and *Later Eighteenth-Century English Literature*, New York, Columbia U. P., revised 1960. A convenient and useful brief bibliography of the period is F. W. Bateson, "An Augustan Reading List, 1650–1800," *A Guide to English Literature*, Garden City, N.Y., Doubleday, 1965. It omits much and can be properly used only as a starting point of investigation.

II. Literary History

George Sherburn, *The Restoration and Eighteenth Century* (*1660–1789*), New York, Appleton-Century-Crofts, 1948. This separately issued work also appears as part III of Albert C. Baugh, ed., *A Literary History of England*; in 1967, Sherburn's work was issued in paper by Appleton-Century-Crofts, with up-to-date bibliographies by Donald F. Bond.

The *Oxford History of English Literature* will include three volumes to cover the eighteenth century. So far only one has appeared, and most students have not found it easily useful: Bonamy Dobrée, *English Literature in the Earlier Eighteenth Century, 1700–1740*, Oxford, Clarendon Press, 1959.

A very useful brief literary history of the period is Alan Dugald McKillop, *English Literature from Dryden to Burns*, New York, Appleton-Century-Crofts, 1948.

The most complete work on Restoration and eighteenth-century plays and theaters is *The London Stage, 1660–1800: A Calendar of Plays, Entertain-*

ments and Afterpieces . . . , 4 parts, 8 vols., eds., W. Van Lennep, E. L. Avery, A. H. Scouten, G. W. Stone, and C. B. Hogan, Carbondale, Southern Illinois U. P., 1960–65.

III. Political History

Herbert Butterfield, *The Whig Interpretation of History*, London, G. Bell and Sons, 1931; a Norton paperback, 1965.

George N. Clark, *The Later Stuarts, 1660–1714*, Oxford, Clarendon Press, 1934; second ed. 1955.

Elizabeth Chapin Furber, ed., *Changing Views on British History: Essays on Historical Writing Since 1939*, Cambridge, Mass., Harvard U. P., 1966.

G. M. Trevelyan, *England under Queen Anne*, 3 vols., London and New York, Longmans, Green and Co., 1930–1934; 3 vols., New York, Humanities (in print, 1966).

———, *England under the Stuarts*, London, Methuen, 1904; twenty-first ed., 1957.

Robert Walcott, Jr., *English Politics in the Early Eighteenth Century*, Cambridge, Mass., Harvard U. P., 1956.

A. F. Basil Williams, *The Whig Supremacy, 1714–1760*, Oxford, Clarendon Press, 1939.

IV. Social History

Robert J. Allen, *The Clubs of Augustan London*, Cambridge, Mass., Harvard U. P., 1933.

Lester Snow King, *The Medical World of the Eighteenth Century*, Chicago, U. of Chicago Press, 1958.

Paul Kirby, *The Grand Tour in Italy (1700–1800)*, New York, S. F. Vanni, 1952.

G. M. Trevelyan, *English Social History*, London and New York, Longmans, Green and Co., 1942; New York, McKay, 1965.

A. S. Turberville, *English Men and Manners in the Eighteenth Century*, Oxford, Clarendon Press, 1926; a Galaxy paperback, 1957.

———, ed., *Johnson's England: An Account of the Life and Manners of His Age*, 2 vols., Oxford, Clarendon Press, 1933.

V. Taste and Aesthetics

B. Sprague Allen, *Tides in English Taste (1619–1800)*, 2 vols., Cambridge, Mass., Harvard U. P., 1937; reprinted, New York, Pageant Books, 1958.

Ralph Dutton, *The English Garden*, London, B. T. Batsford, Ltd., 1937; second ed. revised, London and New York, Batsford, 1950.

Katherine E. Gilbert and Helmut Kuhn, *A History of Esthetics*, Ch. VII, New York, Macmillan, 1939; revised ed., Bloomington, Indiana U. P., 1953.

Marie Luise Gothein, *A History of Garden Art*, 2 vols., ed. W. P. Wright; trans. by Mrs. Archer-Hind, London and Toronto, J. M. Dent; New York, E. P. Dutton, 1928; reprinted, New York, Hacker Art Books, 1966.

Walter J. Hipple, *The Beautiful, the Sublime, & the Picturesque in Eighteenth-Century British Aesthetic Theory*, Carbondale, Southern Illinois U. P., 1957.

Elizabeth W. Manwaring, *Italian Landscape in Eighteenth-Century England*, New York, Oxford U. P., 1925; reprinted, New York, Russell and Russell (in print, 1966).

Henry V. S. and Margaret S. Ogden, *English Taste in Landscape in the Seventeenth Century*, Ann Arbor, U. of Michigan Press, 1955.

VI. History of Criticism

J. W. H. Atkins, *English Literary Criticism: 17th and 18th Centuries*, London, Methuen, 1951; reprinted, New York, Barnes & Noble, 1959.

René Wellek, *A History of Modern Criticism: 1750–1950*, 4 vols., Vol. I, New Haven, Yale U. P., 1955.

W. K. Wimsatt, Jr., and Cleanth Brooks, *Literary Criticism; A Short History*, Part II, New York, Knopf, 1957.

A useful introduction to critical essays by eighteenth-century authors may be found in Scott Elledge, ed., *Eighteenth-Century Critical Essays*, 2 vols., Ithaca, N.Y., Cornell U. P., 1961.

Two collections of seventeenth-century critical essays, with excellent commentary, are Joel Spingarn, ed., *Critical Essays of the Seventeenth Century*, 3 vols., Oxford, Clarendon Press, 1908–1909; Edward W. Tayler, *Literary Criticism of 17th Century England*, New York, Knopf, 1967.

VII. Literary Criticism and History of Ideas

Meyer H. Abrams, *The Mirror and the Lamp*, New York, Oxford U. P., 1953; New York, Norton, 1958.

John Arthos, *The Language of Natural Description in Eighteenth-Century Poetry*, Ann Arbor, U. of Michigan Press, 1949.

Walter Jackson Bate, *From Classic to Romantic*, Cambridge, Mass., Harvard U. P., 1946; Harper Torchbook, 1961.

Carl L. Becker, *The Heavenly City of the Eighteenth-Century Philosophers*, New Haven, Yale U. P., 1932; paperback, 1959.

J. B. Bury, *The Idea of Progress*, London, Macmillan, 1920; reprinted, New York, Peter Smith, 1960.

Ernst Cassirer, *The Philosophy of the Enlightenment*, trans. F. C. A. Koelin and J. P. Pettegrove, Princeton, N.J., Princeton U. P., 1951.

Chester F. Chapin, *Personification in Eighteenth-Century English Poetry*, New York, King's Crown Press, 1955.

J. E. Congleton, *Theories of Pastoral Poetry in England, 1648–1798*, Gainesville, U. of Florida Press, 1952.

Gerald R. Cragg, *Reason and Authority in the Eighteenth Century*, London, Cambridge University Press, 1964.

B. Ifor Evans, *Tradition and Romanticism*, London, Methuen, 1940; Hamden, Conn., Archon Books, 1964.

Hoxie N. Fairchild, *The Noble Savage*, New York, Columbia U. P., 1928; New York, Russell & Russell, 1961.

———, *Religious Trends in English Poetry*, 5 vols., Vols. I, II, III, New York, Columbia U. P., 1939–1962.

Margaret Mary Fitzgerald, *First Follow Nature: Primitivism in English Poetry, 1725–1750*, New York, King's Crown Press, 1947.

Paul Fussell, Jr., *Theory of Prosody in Eighteenth-Century England*, New London, Connecticut College, 1954.

Francis Gallaway, *Reason, Rule, and Revolt in English Classicism*, New York, C. Scribner's Sons, 1940; New York, Octagon, 1965.

Peter Gay, *The Enlightenment*, New York, Knopf, 1966.

F. C. Green, *Minuet: A Critical Survey of French and English Ideas in the Eighteenth Century*, New York, E. P. Dutton, 1935; reissued as *Literary Ideas in 18th Century France and England*, New York, Frederick Ungar, 1966.

Christopher Hussey, *The Picturesque: Studies in a Point of View*, London and New York, G. P. Putnam's Sons, 1927; a reissue is planned by Archon Books, Hamden, Conn.

Ian Jack, *Augustan Satire; Intention and Idiom in English Poetry, 1660–1750*, Oxford, Clarendon Press, 1952.

R. F. Jones, *Ancients and Moderns*, St. Louis, Washington University Studies, 1936; second ed. with new preface and minor revisions, 1961; paperback, Berkeley, U. of California Press, 1961.

William Powell Jones, *The Rhetoric of Science; A Study of Scientific Ideas and Imagery in Eighteenth-Century English Poetry*, Berkeley, U. of California Press, 1966.

Arthur O. Lovejoy, *The Great Chain of Being*, Cambridge, Mass., Harvard U. P., 1936; Harper Torchbook, 1960.

———, *Essays in the History of Ideas*, Baltimore, Johns Hopkins Press, 1948; third printing, 1961; Putnam paperback, 1960.

———, *The Reason, the Understanding, and Time*, Baltimore, Johns Hopkins Press, 1961.

———, G. Chinard, George Boas, and R. S. Crane, eds., *A Documentary History of Primitivism and Related Ideas*, Baltimore, Johns Hopkins Press, 1935; reissued as *Primitivism and Related Ideas in Antiquity*, New York, Octagon, 1965.

Samuel Holt Monk, *The Sublime: A Study of Critical Theories in XVIII-Century England*, New York, Modern Language Association, 1935; with a new preface, Ann Arbor, U. of Michigan Press, 1960.

Marjorie H. Nicolson, *Newton Demands the Muse*, Princeton, N.J., Princeton U. P., 1946; paperback, 1966.

———, *Voyages to the Moon*, New York, Macmillan, 1948; paperback (in print, 1966).

———, *Science and Imagination*, Ithaca, N.Y., Cornell U. P., 1956; paperback (in print, 1966).

———, *Mountain Gloom and Mountain Glory; the Development of the Aesthetics of the Infinite*, Ithaca, N.Y., Cornell U. P., 1959; a Norton paperback, 1963.

George N. Shuster, *The English Ode from Milton to Keats*, New York, Columbia U. P., 1940; reprinted, New York, Peter Smith, 1964.

T. V. Smith and Marjorie Grene, eds., *From Descartes to Kant; Readings in the Philosophy of the Renaissance and Enlightenment*, U. of Chicago Press, 1940; paperback, 2 vols., 1957.

James R. Sutherland, *A Preface to Eighteenth -Century Poetry*, Oxford, Clarendon Press, 1948; paperback (in print, 1966).

———, *English Satire*, London, Cambridge U. P., 1958; paperback (in print, 1966).

Ernest L. Tuveson, *Millennium and Utopia*, Berkeley and Los Angeles, U. of California Press, 1949; a Harper Torchbook, 1964.

———, *The Imagination as a Means of Grace; Locke and the Aesthetics of Romanticism*, Berkeley, U. of California Press, 1960.

Earl R. Wasserman, *The Subtler Language*, Baltimore, Johns Hopkins Press, 1959.

Lois Whitney, *Primitivism and the Idea of Progress*, Baltimore, Johns Hopkins Press, 1934; New York, Octagon, 1965.

Basil Willey, *The Seventeenth-Century Background*, London, Chatto and Windus, 1934; Anchor paperback, 1953.

———, *The Eighteenth-Century Background*, London, Chatto and Windus, 1940; Beacon paperback, 1961.

VIII. Collections of Twentieth-Century Critical Essays

Richard C. Boys, ed., *Studies in the Literature of the Augustan Age: Essays Collected in Honor of Arthur Ellicott Case*, Ann Arbor, distributed for the Augustan Reprint Society by E. Wahr Pub. Co., 1952.

Charles Carroll Camden, ed., *Restoration and Eighteenth-Century Literature: Essays in Honor of Alan Dugald McKillop*, Chicago, published for Rice University by U. of Chicago Press, 1963.

James L. Clifford, ed., *Eighteenth-Century English Literature*, New York, Oxford U. P., 1959.

——— and Louis A. Landa, *Pope and His Contemporaries; Essays Presented to George Sherburn*, Oxford, Clarendon Press, 1949.

Frederick W. Hilles, ed., *The Age of Johnson: Essays Presented to Chauncey Brewster Tinker*, New Haven, Yale U. P., 1949; Yale, paperback, 1964, when Hilles's editorship was first made public.

——— and Harold Bloom, eds., *From Sensibility to Romanticism, Essays Presented to Frederick A. Pottle*, New York, Oxford U. P., 1965.

Earl R. Wasserman, ed., *Aspects of the Eighteenth Century*, Baltimore, Johns Hopkins Press, 1965.

Essays Presented to David Nichol Smith in Honour of His Seventieth Birthday, Oxford, Clarendon Press, 1945.

IX. Anthologies of Eighteenth-Century English Literature

Louis I. Bredvold, A. D. McKillop, Lois Whitney, *Eighteenth-Century Poetry & Prose*, Nelson's English Series, 1939; New York, Ronald Press, 1939; second edition, Ronald, 1956.

———, R. K. Root, and George Sherburn, eds., *Eighteenth-Century Prose*, New York, Ronald Press, 1933.

R. S. Crane, ed., *A Collection of English Poems, 1660–1800*, New York and London, Harper & Brothers, 1932; annotated ed., 1937.

G. H. Nettleton and A. E. Case, eds., *British Dramatists from Dryden to Sheridan*, Boston and New York, Houghton Mifflin, 1939.

Gerald Wester Chapman, ed., *Literary Criticism in England, 1660–1800*, New York, Knopf, 1966.

Jeffrey Hart, ed., *Political Writers of Eighteenth-Century England*, New York, Knopf, 1964.

Ricardo Quintana and Alvin Whitley, eds., *English Poetry of the Mid and Late Eighteenth Century*, New York, Knopf, 1963.

Index of Titles
and First Lines